lonely planet

New Zealand
(Aotearoa)

W9-BXM-873

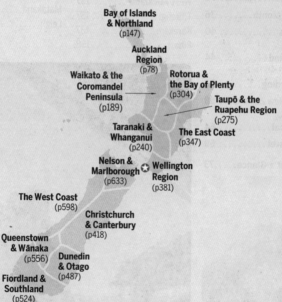

Bay of Islands
& Northland
(p147)

Auckland
Region
(p78)

Waikato & the
Coromandel
Peninsula
(p189)

Rotorua &
the Bay of Plenty
(p304)

Taupō & the
Ruapehu Region
(p275)

Taranaki &
Whanganui
(p240)

The East Coast
(p347)

Nelson &
Marlborough
(p633)

Wellington
Region
(p381)

The West Coast
(p598)

Christchurch
& Canterbury
(p418)

Queenstown
& Wānaka
(p556)

Dunedin
& Otago
(p487)

Fiordland &
Southland
(p524)

Brett Atkinson, Andrew Bain, Peter Dragicevich, Monique Perrin,
Charles Rawlings-Way, Tasmin Waby

Contents

GUIDE ON FRANZ JOSEF GLACIER P606

MATT MAKES PHOTOS/SHUTTERSTOCK ©

CATHEDRAL COVE P232

PARADISE PICTURES/500PX ©

Contents

ON THE ROAD

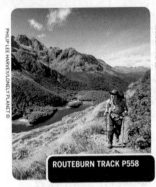

PHILIP LEE HARVEY/LONELY PLANET ©

HANS STRAND/GETTY IMAGES ©

ROUTEBURN TRACK P558

AUCKLAND P84

Contents

Welcome to New Zealand

With epic national parks and stunning landscapes, inspiring Māori culture, and hospitable Kiwi culture, your New Zealand trip will be packed with adventures.

Walk on the Wild Side

There are 4.69 million New Zealanders, scattered across 268,838 sq km: bigger than the UK with one-fourteenth of the population. Filling in the gaps are the sublime forests, mountains, lakes, beaches and fiords that make NZ one of the world's best hiking destinations. Tackle an epic 'Great Walk' – you might've heard of the Heaphy and Milford Tracks – or wander a beach, paddle a canoe, or mountain bike through accessible wilderness. NZ does nature appreciation with gusto.

Māori Culture

The world recognises the chilling *haka* (war cry) of NZ's all-conquering All Blacks, but Māori culture infuses everyday life here, probably more than most Pākehā (white New Zealanders) recognise. Māori tattoo designs and motifs are everywhere; the protection of nature (*kaitiakitanga*: guardianship) is now written into law; and the kindness to visitors (*manaakitanga*: hospitality) makes it a world-class tourism destination. Once relegated to family life and Māori TV and radio, the Māori language can now be heard again, even on bus stop announcements in Auckland. There's a way to go in terms of colonial repatriation, but for cultural significance, NZ is the land of the mighty Māori.

Fresh Flavours

Fish and chips and other British-influenced classics are a mainstay, but chefs across the country are bringing fresh influences from Asia, the South Pacific and Europe to menus of locally sourced ingredients like lamb and seafood (try the abalone, oysters and scallops). Even in rural areas vegetarian and vegan food options are growing more prominent and inventive. Wash those flavours down with Kiwi coffee culture, a happening craft-beer scene and legendary cool-climate wines.

The Real 'Big Easy'

There are few on-the-road frustrations in NZ: buses and trains generally run on time; main roads are good; car parks are fairly easy to find; and places to enjoy nature are everywhere, even in cities. Kiwis have taken to the eco-lifestyle with gusto too, so BYO calico bags and slow down to eat and drink in, not take away with plastic utensils and paper cups – you'll enjoy it more this way. Oh, and did we mention there are no snakes, and only one venomous spider – the endangered katipo? In this decent forward-looking nation, you can relax and enjoy your travels, making more time for the best kind of memories.

Why I Love New Zealand

By Tasmin Waby, Writer

It's hard to know where to start on why I LOVE New Zealand. This is the country my family and *whānau* (extended family) call home, but as a visitor from another land I have to say first: the epic wilderness; the food and the foodie culture; the easy days; and the sense that this bicultural nation is coming closer together in ways the rest of the world looks to with envy. It's also in the talent New Zealand nurtures from Jacinda Ardern to Taika Waititi, and all the honest, open, and hilariously funny people that live here, who – let's be honest – are among the most lovable in the world (plus, that accent!).

For more about our writers, see p736

Above: Taranaki volcano (p252)

New Zealand

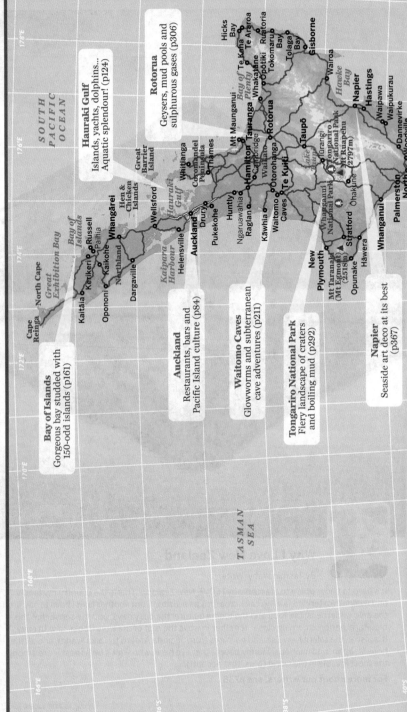

200 km
100 miles

Bay of Islands
Gorgeous bay studded with
150-odd islands (p161)

Hauraki Gulf
Islands, yachts, dolphins...
Aquatic splendour! (p124)

Rotorua
Geysers, mud pools and
sulphurous gases (p306)

Auckland
Restaurants, bars and
Pacific Island culture (p84)

Waitomo Caves
Glowworms and subterranean
cave adventures (p211)

Tongariro National Park
Fiery landscape of craters
and boiling mud (p292)

Napier
Seaside art deco at its best
(p367)

SOUTH
PACIFIC
OCEAN

TASMAN
SEA

Cape
Reinga North Cape
Great
Exhibition Bay
Kaitaia
Kerikeri Russell
Opononi Paihia
Kaikohe
Northland
Dargaville
Bay of
Islands
Whangārei
Hen &
Chicken
Islands
Wellsford
Kaipara
Harbour
Helensville
Auckland
Drury
Pukekohe
Huntly
Ngaruawahia
Raglan
Kāwhia
Waitomo
Caves
Te Kuiti
Great
Barrier
Island
Hauraki
Gulf
Whitianga
Coromandel
Peninsula
Thames
Mt Maunganui
Hamilton Tauranga
Cambridge
Waikato
Otorohanga
Bay of
Plenty
Te Kaha
Whakatāne
Ōpōtiki
Rotorua
Hicks
Bay
Te Araroa
Ruatoria
Tokomaru
Bay
Tolaga
Bay
Gisborne
Wairoa
Hawke
Bay
Napier
Hastings
Waipawa
Waipukurau
Dannevirke
Woodville
New
Plymouth
Mt Taranaki
(Mt Egmont)
(2518m)
Opunake
Hāwera
Stratford
Ōhakune
Whanganui
National Park
Tongariro
National Park
Mt Ruapehu
(2797m)
Taupō
Turangi
Lake
Taupo
Whanganui
Palmerston
North

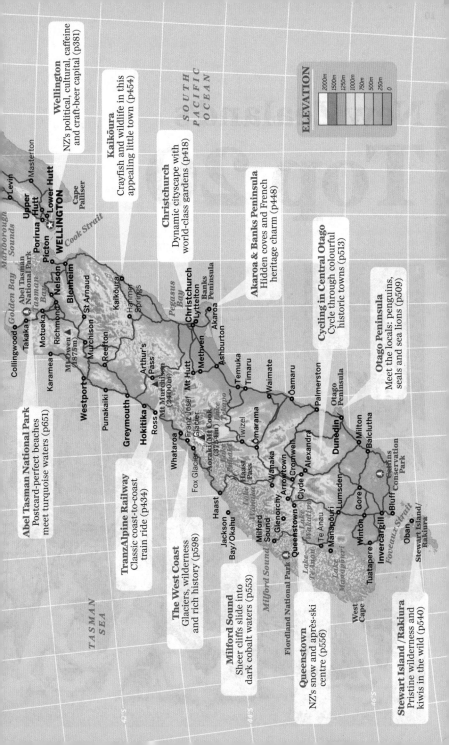

Wellington
NZ's political, cultural, caffeine and craft-beer capital (p381)

Kaikōura
Crayfish and wildlife in this appealing little town (p454)

Christchurch
Dynamic cityscape with world-class gardens (p418)

Akaroa & Banks Peninsula
Hidden coves and French heritage charm (p448)

Cycling in Central Otago
Cycle through colourful historic towns (p513)

Otago Peninsula
Meet the locals: penguins, seals and sea lions (p509)

Abel Tasman National Park
Postcard-perfect beaches meet turquoise waters (p651)

TranzAlpine Railway
Classic coast-to-coast train ride (p434)

The West Coast
Glaciers, wilderness and rich history (p598)

Milford Sound
Sheer cliffs slide into dark cobalt waters (p553)

Queenstown
NZ's snow and après-ski centre (p556)

Stewart Island/Rakiura
Pristine wilderness and kiwis in the wild (p540)

ELEVATION

2000m
1500m
1250m
1000m
750m
500m
250m
0

SOUTH PACIFIC OCEAN

TASMAN SEA

Cook Strait

Marlborough Sounds

Golden Bay

Tasman Bay

Pegasus Bay

Pitt Bay

Foveaux Strait

Milford Sound

Levin
Masterton
Upper Hutt
Lower Hutt
Porirua
Picton
WELLINGTON
Cape Palliser
Collingwood
Takaka
Abel Tasman National Park
Motueka
Nelson
Richmond
Blenheim
St Arnaud
Mt Owen (1875m)
Karamea
Murchison
Kaikōura
Hanmer Springs
Westport
Reefton
Arthur's Pass
Punakaiki
Greymouth
Hokitika
Ross
Methven
Ashburton
Christchurch
Lyttelton
Banks Peninsula
Akaroa
Whataroa
Franz Josef Glacier
Fox Glacier
Aoraki/Mt Cook (3755m)
Mt Murchison (2400m)
Temuka
Timaru
Waimate
Oamaru
Haast
Haast Pass
Twizel
Omarama
Palmerston
Otago Peninsula
Jackson Bay/Okahu
Wanaka
Cromwell
Alexandra
Dunedin
Milton
Balclutha
Milford Sound
Glenorchy
Arrowtown
Clyde
Fiordland National Park
Queenstown
Te Anau
Lumsden
Gore
Manapouri
Winton
Catlins Conservation Park
West Cape
Tuatapere
Invercargill
Bluff
Oban
Stewart Island/Rakiura
Lake Pukaki
Lake Tekapo
Lake Wanaka
Lake Wakatipu
Lake Te Anau
Lake Manapouri

New Zealand's
Top 20

Māori Culture

1 New Zealand's indigenous Māori culture (p690) is accessible and engaging: join in a *haka* (war dance); chow down at a traditional *hāngi* (Māori feast cooked in the ground); carve a pendant from bone or *pounamu* (jade); learn some Māori language; or check out an authentic cultural performance with song, dance, legends, arts and crafts. Big-city and regional museums around NZ are crammed with Māori artefacts and historical items, but this is truly a living culture: vibrant, potent and contemporary. *Kapa haka* performance to commemorate Waitangi Day (p36).

Pacific Auckland

2 Held in the embrace of two harbours and built on the remnants of long-extinct volcanoes, Auckland (p84) isn't your average metropolis. It's regularly rated one of the world's most liveable cities, blessed with good beaches, wine regions, and a thriving dining, drinking and live-music scene, not to mention sub-tropical weather. However, it's the rich culture of this ethnically diverse city that makes Auckland stand out on the global stage. Time your visit for any major cultural event, from Pasifika to Diwali, and you'll see what we mean. *Sky Tower (p85)*

MICHAEL W NZ / SHUTTERSTOCK ©

ARCHITECT GORDON MOLLE / BLAINE HARRINGTON III / GETTY IMAGES ©

KUDL SUARDI / GETTY IMAGES ©

NZ's Great Walks

3 Hiking, or tramping, as the Kiwis call it, is one of NZ's great pastimes (p44). North and South Islands alike offer boundless opportunities to scramble up scree, spot wildlife in the wild, and lose yourself in some outdoors truly deserving of the epithet 'great'. Whether it's the rainforest-shaded shores of Lake Waikaremoana, the newly opened Paparoa Track, or the cloud-nudging uplands of the Crossing, hikers will always find their happy place. Hiker in Aoraki/Mt Cook National Park (p481)

Wilderness on Stewart Island

4 Birdwatching, kayaking, tramping, and cycling are some of the ways you can explore NZ's third island (p540), one where only 400 people live and 85% of the land is protected by Rakiura National Park. It's also your best opportunity to view kiwis in the wild. Seeing these small indigenous birds while walking along the beach in the dark under the dazzling Milky Way is an experience to be savoured. If you're lucky, you might even glimpse the Southern Lights. New Zealand parakeet/Kākāriki

TranzAlpine Railway

5 Among the world's most scenic train journeys, the TranzAlpine (p434) cuts clear across NZ from the Pacific Ocean to the Tasman Sea in less than five hours. Yes, there's a vast mountain range in the way – that's the scenic part. Leaving the Canterbury Plains, a cavalcade of tunnels and viaducts climb up the Southern Alps to Arthur's Pass, where the 8.5km Otira tunnel burrows through the bedrock of NZ's alpine spine. Then it's down the other side to Greymouth...a jumping-off point to adventures aplenty. TranzAlpine crossing through the Southern Alps

The West Coast

6 A remote, end-of-the-road vibe defines the West Coast (p598). Road trips along the SH6, from isolated wildlife haven Haast to hiking outpost Karamea, thread together an alluring combination of sights: Franz Josef and Fox Glaciers, Hokitika's greenstone galleries, and geological wonders like Pancake Rocks (pictured above). There are countless detours to mountain-biking and hiking trails, many of which follow the footsteps of early pioneers. Primeval wilderness is often only a short journey away by foot – or helicopter, or jetboat...

Wellington

7 One of the coolest little capitals in the world, windy Wellington (p383) is also synonymous with cinema, thanks to local boy Peter Jackson. Residents are also proud of its vibrant arts and music scene and special events schedule (from Fringe to WOW), plus dining choices that range from innovative food trucks to high-end gastronomy. But for visitors to the capital, the proximity to mountain-biking and walking trails, not to mention a glistening harbour, scores just as highly. Don't miss it. Wellington Cable Car (p383)

Tongariro National Park

8 At the centre of the North Island, Tongariro National Park (p292) presents an awe-inspiring landscape of alpine desert punctuated by three smouldering volcanoes. Often rated as one of the world's best single-day wilderness walks, the challenging Tongariro Alpine Crossing (p278) skirts the base of two of the mountains and provides views of craters, brightly coloured lakes and the vast Central Plateau. As the crossing's popularity has skyrocketed, DOC has limited visitor numbers per day, so book early. Mt Ngauruhoe (p293)

Waiheke Island & the Hauraki Gulf

9 A yachtie's paradise, the island-studded Hauraki Gulf (p124) is Auckland's aquatic playground, sheltering its harbour and east-coast bays and, despite the busy maritime traffic, its resident whales and dolphins. Rangitoto Island is an icon of the city, its near-perfect volcanic cone providing the backdrop for many a tourist snapshot. Yet it's Waiheke (pictured above), with its beautiful beaches, acclaimed wineries and excellent dining spots, that is Auckland's most popular island escape.

Kaikōura

10 First settled by Maōri, who demonstrated their taste for seafood by naming it Kaikōura (p454; meaning 'to eat crayfish'), this is NZ's best spot for both consuming and communing with marine life. Feast on crayfish, go on a fishing excursion, or take a boat tour or flight to see whales, dolphins, seals and marine birds. Following a severe earthquake in November 2016, Kaikōura has rebounded and is now a fascinating spot to observe the profound impact of seismic activity along the coast. Whale watching off Kaikōura (p457)

Milford Sound

11 Whatever the weather, Milford Sound (p553) will dazzle you with its collage of waterfalls, forbidding cliffs and dark cobalt waters, with the iconic profile of Mitre Peak rising above it all. Fiordland's waterfalls are even more spectacular when fed by rain, but blue-sky days set rainbows sparkling from their mist. Either way, keep your eyes peeled for seals, dolphins and the elusive Fiordland crested penguin, especially if you're exploring NZ's most famous fiord by kayak.

10

Bay of Islands

12 Turquoise waters lapping pretty bays, dolphins frolicking at the bows of boats, pods of orcas gliding gracefully by: chances are, these are the kinds of images that drew you to NZ in the first place, and these are exactly the kinds of experiences that the Bay of Islands (p161) delivers in spades. There are myriad options to tempt you out onto the water to explore the 150-odd islands that dot this beautiful bay. Landlubbers will relish the rich maritime history as successions of visitors arrived on these shores.

Adventure Queenstown

13 Queenstown (p562) may be world renowned as the birthplace of bungy jumping, but there's more to NZ's adventure hub than that. The Remarkables mountain range provides a jagged indigo backdrop to days spent skiing, hiking or mountain biking, before dining in cosmopolitan restaurants or partying in some of NZ's best bars. Keep the adrenaline flowing with hang gliding, kayaking or river rafting, before heading to 'quieter' Wānaka and taking your vertigo into overdrive on the via ferrata. Skyline Luge gondola (p569)

Rotorua

14 The first thing you'll notice about Rotorua (p306) is the sulphurous smell – but volcanic by-products have been one of the main draws since tourism began here in the 1880s: gushing geysers, bubbling mud, steaming cracks in the ground, boiling pools of mineral-rich water... The other key draw: the many cultural experiences, curated and run by local Māori where you can learn about Aotearoa from its First Nations. Expect everything here from *hāngi* and hot springs to mountain biking and luging in this tourism playground. Wai-O-Tapu Thermal Wonderland (p323)

13

BEATRICE SIRINUNTANANON/SHUTTERSTOCK ©

Cycling in Central Otago

15 Here's your chance to balance virtue and vice. Take to two wheels to negotiate the easygoing Otago Central Rail Trail (p514; pictured above), cycling through some of NZ's most beautiful landscapes and the heritage streetscapes of former gold-mining towns. All the while, snack on the summer stone fruit for which the region is famous. Balance the ledger with well-earned beers at one of the numerous historic pubs. Alternatively, taste your way to viticultural ecstasy in the vineyards of one of the country's most acclaimed wine regions.

Art Deco Napier & Hawke's Bay

16 Art deco lovers should add Napier (p367) to their NZ must-do list. Courtesy of a 1931 earthquake that pretty much levelled the place, the town was rebuilt from scratch in one style. Its handsome streets are dotted with splendidly preserved examples of the style – with unique Kiwi motifs – now housing cool new restaurants, hotels, shops and galleries. Hawke's Bay, on which Napier perches, delivers the perfect terroir for winery touring by bicycle or on a driving tour. National Tobacco Company Building (p368)

JFOLTYN / GETTY IMAGES ©

MATTEO COLOMBO / GETTY IMAGES ©

Abel Tasman National Park

17 Here's nature at its most seductive: lush green hills fringed with golden sandy coves, slipping gently into warm shallows before meeting a crystal-clear sea. Abel Tasman National Park (p651) is a postcard-perfect paradise where you can put yourself in the picture, assuming an endless number of poses – hiking, kayaking, swimming, sunbathing – before finally setting up tent at a 'walk-in or boat-in' beachside campground. Book ahead if you want to see it all on the Coast Track, NZ's most popular Great Walk.

Waitomo Caves

18 Waitomo (p211) is an astonishing maze of subterranean caves, canyons and rivers perforating the northern King Country limestone. Black-water rafting is the big lure here (like white-water rafting but through a dark cave), plus glowworm grottoes, underground abseiling and more stalactites and stalagmites than you'll ever see in one place again. Above ground, Waitomo township is a quaint collaboration of businesses: a swish restaurant, craft brewery, pub and some more-than-decent accommodation. But don't linger in the sunlight – it's party time downstairs!

Akaroa & Banks Peninsula

19 Infused with Gallic ambience, Akaroa (p451) bends languidly around one of the prettiest harbours on Banks Peninsula. These cold, clean waters, perfect for kayaking and sailing, are inhabited by the world's rarest dolphin. Elsewhere on the peninsula, the Summit Rd snakes around the rim of an ancient volcano while winding side roads descend to hidden bays and coves. Spend your days discovering the peninsula's many surprises: whimsical gardens, sea-kayaking safaris and the country's largest colonies of Australasian little penguins.

VLADISLAV T. JIROUSEK/SHUTTERSTOCK ©

Otago Peninsula

20 Beyond Dunedin's historic warehouses and Edwardian Baroque buildings housing bars, cafes and boutique hotels, head to the Otago Peninsula (p509) for some of the best wildlife-spotting opportunities in the country. Dozens of little penguins achieve peak cuteness in their nightly beachside waddle, while their much rarer yellow-eyed cousin, the hoiho, can be glimpsed standing sentinel on deserted coves. Sea lions and seals laze around on the rocks while albatrosses from the world's only mainland colony swoop and soar above. Yellow-eyed penguins

20

Need to Know

For more information, see Survival Guide (p703)

Currency
New Zealand dollar ($)

Language
English, Māori, NZ Sign Language

Visas
Visitors need an NZeTA (NZ$12 online). Also, tourists are expected to pay an International Visitor Conservation and Tourism Levy (IVL; $35).

Money
Bank cards are used for most purchases, and are accepted in most hotels and restaurants. ATMs are widely available in cities and larger towns.

Mobile Phones
It's simple to buy a local SIM card and prepaid account at outlets in airports and large towns (provided your mobile is unlocked).

Time
New Zealand time (GMT/UTC plus 12 hours)

When to Go

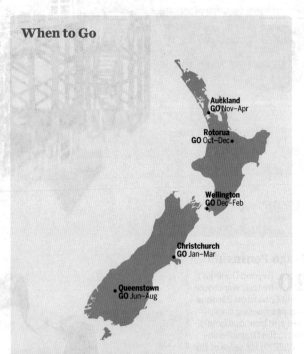

Auckland
GO Nov–Apr

Rotorua
GO Oct–Dec

Wellington
GO Dec–Feb

Christchurch
GO Jan–Mar

Queenstown
GO Jun–Aug

High Season
(Dec–Feb)

➡ Summer brings busy beaches, gorgeous hiking weather, festivals and sporting events.

➡ Accommodation prices rise in most destinations – book ahead.

➡ High season in ski towns is winter (June to August).

Shoulder
(Mar–May)

➡ Fine weather, autumn colours, warmish ocean, long evenings.

➡ Queues are shorter and popular road-trip routes are clear, particularly after Easter.

➡ Spring (September to November) means the end of snow season.

Low Season
(Jun–Aug)

➡ Brilliant skiing and snowboarding from mid-June.

➡ Outside ski resorts, get accommodation deals and a seat in any restaurant.

➡ Warm-weather beach towns may be half asleep, so book accommodation ahead.

Useful Websites

The Spinoff (www.thespinoff.co.nz) Latest culture, arts and politics.

100% Pure New Zealand (www.newzealand.com) Comprehensive government tourism site.

Department of Conservation (www.doc.govt.nz) DOC parks, trail and camping info.

Lonely Planet (www.lonelyplanet.com/new-zealand) Destination information, hotel bookings, traveller forum and more.

Te Ara (www.teara.govt.nz) Online encyclopedia of NZ.

Important Numbers

Regular numbers have a two-digit area code followed by a seven-digit number. When dialling within a region, the area code is required.

NZ's country code	☎64
International access code	☎00
Emergency (Ambulance, Fire, Police)	☎111
Directory Assistance (charges apply)	☎018

Exchange Rates

Australia	A$1	NZ$1.05
Canada	C$1	NZ$1.18
China	¥10	NZ$2.37
Eurozone	€1	NZ$1.82
Japan	¥100	NZ$1.55
Singapore	S$1	NZ$1.17
UK	UK£1	NZ$2.09
US	US$1	NZ$1.68

For current exchange rates, see www.xe.com.

Daily Costs

Budget: Less than $150

➡ Dorm beds or campsites per night: $20–45

➡ Main course in a budget eatery: up to $20

➡ Hop-on hop-off bus pass (12 to 28 days): $699–1779

Midrange: $150–250

➡ Double room in a midrange hotel/motel: $130–200

➡ Main course in a midrange restaurant: $20–35

➡ Car rental per day: from $45

Top End: More than $250

➡ Double room in an upmarket hotel: $200–350

➡ Three-course meal in a classy restaurant: from $80

➡ Domestic flights: from $100

Opening Hours

These vary seasonally depending on where you are. Most places close on Christmas Day and Good Friday.

Banks 9am to 4.30pm Monday to Friday, some also 9am to noon Saturday

Cafes 7am or 8am to 3pm or 4pm

Pubs & bars noon to late

Restaurants noon to 2.30pm and 6pm to 9pm

Shops 9am to 5.30pm Monday to Friday, and 9am to noon or 5pm Saturday

Arriving in New Zealand

Auckland Airport Airbus Express buses (adult/child $17/2) run into the city every 10 to 30 minutes, 24 hours. Prebooked door-to-door shuttle buses run 24 hours (from $25). A taxi into the city costs around $100 (45 minutes).

Wellington Airport Airport Flyer buses ($12) run into the city every 10 to 20 minutes from around 7am to 9pm. Door-to-door shuttles run 24 hours (from $20). A taxi into the city costs around $30 (20 minutes).

Christchurch Airport Christchurch Metro Purple Line runs into the city ($8.50 when paying in cash) regularly from around 7am to 11pm. Door-to-door shut-tles run 24 hours (from $25). A taxi into the city costs around $50 to $75 (20 minutes).

Safe Travel

➡ New Zealand is no more dangerous than other developed countries. Avoid low-level crime by taking normal safety precautions, especially after dark on city streets and in remote areas.

➡ New Zealand does not have any dangerous predators, though shark attacks are not unheard of, so seek local advice when swimming and surfing.

➡ See Safe Travel (p711) for information on a few driving and environmental hazards specific to NZ. Globally, road accidents are one of the biggest dangers when travelling, so take the challenges of NZ driving conditions seriously.

For much more on **getting around**, see p716

First Time New Zealand

For more information, see Survival Guide (p703)

Checklist

➡ Ensure your passport is valid for at least three months past your intended return date from New Zealand (December to February)

➡ Book rental cars, campervans and train tickets well in advance, particularly for travel during summer

➡ Got travel insurance? Does it cover activities like bungy jumping?

➡ Read up on NZ's Māori culture; learn some phrases

What to Pack

➡ Sturdy walking shoes – visiting NZ without doing at least *some* hiking is a crime!

➡ Small day pack

➡ NZ electrical adaptor

➡ Sunglasses for bright southern days

➡ Woolly hat for unexpectedly chilly evenings

➡ Reusable water bottle

➡ Earplugs for hostel dorms

Top Tips for Your Trip

➡ Allow more driving time than you think you need. Outside cities, roads are narrow, winding and slow with mountains and campervans to navigate. Don't try to see the whole country in two weeks.

➡ Booked activities/tours can be cancelled at the last minute due to the weather. Build extra time into your itinerary in case your tour is bumped to the following day.

➡ Don't expect wi-fi to be free (or fast) outside cities. Where they do provide wi-fi, hotels and cafes may sometimes offer vouchers for a limited amount of data.

What to Wear

Given the locals' propensity for the outdoorsy life, dress norms in NZ are generally fairly practical and versatile. Dress up for a night out on the town in major cities (don't expect to get into a classy bar wearing shorts and flip-flops – or 'jandals' as the locals call them) – but elsewhere the key to comfort is to layer up.

The weather here can change in a blink, particularly around Fiordland and the West Coast of the South Island: you'll be best equipped to adapt if you can quickly add or remove clothes to keep pace with the temperature.

Etiquette

New Zealanders are a laid-back, modest bunch as a whole – exercising the usual good manners will help endear you to the locals.

Greetings Shake hands when meeting someone for the first time, and look people in the eye. Always say hello and shout a 'thanks' when getting on and off a bus.

Māori customs Adhere to strict Māori protocols (p693) if visiting *marae* (meeting-house complexes). Otherwise, respectful behaviour goes a long way, as always.

Invitations If you're invited to dinner or a barbecue at someone's house, bring some wine, beer, food or a bunch of flowers.

Language

English, te reo Māori and New Zealand Sign Language are NZ's official languages. These days Māori words cross over into daily parlance: you'll hear *kia ora* (hello) everywhere. Māori place names are now spelled correctly with macrons on most town signs. Online, www.maoridiction ary.co.nz has a handy translator. The app Kupu (www. kupu.co.nz) teaches Māori nouns for everyday objects, and popular language app Duolingo plans to include a te reo Māori course for beginners in 2020.

Bargaining

Haggling and bargaining aren't traditionally part of commercial culture in NZ. The only circumstances where you might have some luck are farmers markets at the end of the day or large private purchases (buying a local's car for a knock-down price). Otherwise, the price is the price.

Tipping

Tipping is completely optional in NZ.

Guides Your kayaking guide or tour-group leader would happily accept tips; $10 is kind.

Restaurants The total on your bill is all you need to pay. If you like, reward good service with 5% to 10%.

Taxis If you round up your fare, don't be surprised if the driver hands back your change.

Māori Language

Here are a few terms to get started on your Māori language understanding:

Aotearoa – Māori name for NZ, most often translated as 'Land of the Long White Cloud'

ariki – chief

aroha – love

awa – river (you'll see it in place names)

haka – any dance, but usually a war dance

hāngi – oven whereby food is steamed in baskets over embers in a hole; a Māori feast

hapū – subtribe or smaller tribal grouping

hei tiki – carved, stylised human figure worn around the neck; also called a tiki

hongi – Māori greeting; the pressing of foreheads and noses, and sharing of life breath

iwi – large tribal grouping with lineage back to the original migration from Hawaiki; people; tribe

ka pai – good; excellent

kai – food

kaitiakitanga – guardianship

kia ora – hello/be safe

koha – donation/gift

mana – spiritual quality of a person or object

manaakitanga – hospitality

mangō – shark

maunga – mountain (you'll see it in place names)

nui – big (you'll see it in place names)

pounamu – jade; greenstone

whakapapa – genealogy

whānau – extended family (aka, your people)

Sleeping

Book beds well in advance in peak tourist seasons.

See Accommodation (p28) for more information.

Expect the Unexpected

Sheep crossing – When you see a sign saying 'Sheep Crossing' there really will be sheep crossing the road.

No snakes – There are no venomous or dangerous animals.

Weather – The day may start with sunshine but it can turn torrential by lunchtime; prepare for all possible weather, especially if out walking.

Safety – People are genuinely friendly, but don't be lulled into thinking NZ is crime-free – normal precautions apply.

Paying the bill – While cafes may have table service it's normal to pay for your bill at the counter when you're ready to leave.

What's New

'Jacindamania' continues to sweep the world, after the PM's compassionate response to the Christchurch mosque attacks and White Island eruption in 2019 fuelled her global popularity. From its greenie consciousness to the decolonising of statues in Gisborne, New Zealand is as progressive today as it was when it first gave women the vote over a century ago.

Adventure Activities

The sheer range of adventure activities in Aotearoa (New Zealand) keeps expanding, with a slew of new options across both islands. The Paparoa Track and Pike29 Memorial Track are newcomers to the Great Walks of New Zealand fold (Hump Ridge Track is to be added next); stand-up paddleboarding (SUP) continues to conquer water sports; and the Nevis Catapult, the world's largest, slings thrill seekers 150m across the Nevis Valley, near Queenstown.

Waitaki Whitestone Geopark

Waitaki is shortlisted to be the first Unesco Global Geopark in Australasia. Reaching from the Southern Alps to the sea, this collection of geological and cultural sites, dating from 60 million years ago to the present, includes the Moeraki Boulders, the spectacular sedimentary Clay Cliffs and the striking limestone Elephant Rocks.

Boutique Distilleries

Small-batch, artisanal distilleries have bloomed like mushrooms after rain in NZ in recent years. The likes of the Reefton Distilling Co (p630) join other South Island newbies such as the Cardrona Distillery (p594) and, in Takaka, Dancing Sands (p656). Expect distinctive whiskies, rums, vodkas and gins made from pure waters and high-quality grains and botanicals.

LOCAL KNOWLEDGE

WHAT'S HAPPENING IN NEW ZEALAND

Tasmin Waby, Lonely Planet writer

New Zealand is going green with gusto. Everyone brings their own bags to the store (that's a given); solar panels are commonplace; e-campervans can be rented, and takeaway meals are delivered in eco-containers (when they're not, there's a heartfelt apology for using plastic).

The buzz concept 'overtourism' is nothing new in NZ, where tourists sometimes outnumber locals, and visitor hotspots (made all the more famous by cinema screens and social media) can suffer from their popular appeal.

To ensure the environment is looked after, visitors are asked to take the Tiaki Promise, a modern day enactment of the Māori *kaitiakitanga* (guardianship). New Zealanders are also been keen to encourage tourism dispersal to less busy (and therefore more innately 'Kiwi') areas.

Dispersal is the hot topic on a local front too, with Aucklanders moving to regional centres where fibre broadband and better road connections are making commuting, or remote work, more manageable. The result? House prices are rising but wages are not... Watch this space.

Cook's Statue Updated

In Gisborne (p355), to mark the 250th anniversary of Cook's landing (1769–2019), the statue of 'The Crook Cook' by the port was given a facelift to incorporate the Māori perspective on his epochal arrival, upon which nine local men were murdered. The $5.3-million upgrade saw the addition of 112 huge steel *tukutuku* (weaving) panels symbolising the meeting of – and differences between – two cultures.

He Ara Kotahi

Meaning 'a pathway that brings people together', this 7.1km track in Palmerston North (p270) links farmland, forests, Māori *pā* (fortified hilltop villages) and the city itself. Open to pedestrians, dogs and cyclists, its centrepiece is the bridge over the Manawatu River.

Hundertwasser Park

The Austrian-born artist Friedensreich Hundertwasser moved to the Bay of Islands in 1975 and designed the world-famous Hundertwasser Toilets in Kawakawa (p167), which officially opened in 1999, two months before his passing. Twenty years later, construction began on Hundertwasser Park: a community arts, culture and environment centre, and homage to the artist.

Tours

New Zealand's already-ample suite of tours just keeps expanding. Of particular note are Waka Tours (p230) in Whitianga, integrating the history and culture of the local Ngāti Hei people; Amiki Local Tours (p434) in Christchurch, combining history, Māori and Pākehā culture and new eating and drinking spots; and zip-line tours at the Driving Creek Conservation Park (p224) and Waitomo Caves (p215).

LISTEN, WATCH & FOLLOW

For inspiration and up-to-date news, visit www.lonelyplanet.com/new-zealand/articles.

Undertheradar (www.undertheradar.co.nz) Music news, gigs and ticket sales.

The Spinoff (www.thespinoff.co.nz) Culture and news.

All Blacks (www.allblacks.com) Follow the nation's unifying obsession.

Noted (www.noted.co.nz) The *Listener*, *Metro* and *North & South* magazines, plus Radio NZ.

FAST FACTS

Food trend Plant-based eating

Language Apps and emotikis in te reo Māori

Pop 4.69 million

Number of venomous snakes Zero

≈ 3 people per sq km

Kiwi Camp

New sites for 'freedom campers' are being developed by a group called Kiwi Camp (www.kiwicamp.nz), which provides basic pay-as-you-use facilities via an app and digital key fob. The group drops in a stand-alone container with showers, toilets and cooking hobs. Other benefits are proper rubbish and recycling facilities and parking. And few little staff or overheads, costs are low, so travellers on a budget can afford to stay while ensuring their visit to New Zealand doesn't negatively impact the natural environment, which has been one of the key concerns with freedom campers in NZ to date.

Accommodation

Find more accommodation reviews throughout the On the Road chapters (from p77)

PRICE RANGES

The following price ranges refer to a double room with bathroom during high season. Price ranges generally increase by 20% to 25% in Auckland, Wellington and Christchurch. Here you can still find budget accommodation at up to $120 per double, but midrange stretches from $120 to $200, with top-end rooms more than $200.

$	less than $120
$$	$120–$200
$$$	more than $200

Accommodation Types

Motels and Pubs Most towns have low-rise, midrange motels. Even small towns usually have a pub with rooms.

B&Bs In NZ B&Bs pop up in the middle of cities, in rural hamlets and on stretches of isolated coastline, with rooms offered in everything from suburban bungalows to stately manors.

Holiday Parks Ideal if you're camping or touring in a campervan. Choose from unpowered tent sites, simple cabins and en-suite units.

Hostels Backpacker hostels include beery, party-prone joints and family-friendly 'flashpackers'.

Pods Small private spaces from airport hotels to glass pods in the forest.

Hotels From small-town pubs to slick global-chain operations – with commensurate prices.

Lodges Luxurious in every sense, from the architecture to the locations, NZ has a stunning array of splash-out-worthy retreats.

Best Places to Stay

Best on a Budget

Sometimes the best places to stay in NZ are in fact the budget options. You won't have your room serviced at these accommodations, and facilities might be shared so expect to do your own dishes. But you will meet other travellers, and the staff – and owners – are that bit friendlier at these and other low-cost, high-value options across NZ.

➡ Ducks & Drakes (p247), New Plymouth

➡ Tasman Bay Backpackers (p640), Nelson

➡ Oamaru Backpackers (p495), Ōamaru

➡ Halfmoon Cottage (p450), Banks Peninsula

➡ Piha Beachstay – Jandal Palace (p138), Piha

➡ Adventure Queenstown (p572), Queenstown

Best for Families

Families are welcome at these top spots, as well as pretty much every holiday park and camping ground across NZ. Kids are happier when they have playgrounds, swimming pools and nature to explore nearby. All that fresh air means bedtime is less likely to be a struggle – but don't expect them (or your neighbours' kids) to stay asleep much past sunrise: you've been warned.

➡ Hot Water Beach Top 10 Holiday Park (p234), Hot Water Beach

➡ Greytown Campground (p413), Greytown

➡ Smiths Farm Holiday Park (p660), Queen Charlotte Track

➡ Fossil Bay Lodge (p128), Waiheke Island

➡ Old Bones Lodge (p495), Ōamaru

➡ Ross Beach Top 10 (p612), Ross

Best for Solo Travellers

Travelling solo has so many advantages: no compromising on spending, no schedules, and even a sleep-in when you want one. The only downside is occasionally talking to yourself after you've been alone for days on end. That's why accommodation where it's easy to meet other travellers with whom to share stories, intel and meals can really make your trip.

➡ Stranded in Paradise (p581), Pacific Coast Hwy

➡ Tombstone Backpackers (p666), Picton

➡ Victoria Railway Hotel (p536), Invercargill

➡ Haka Lodge (p572), Auckland

➡ Jailhouse (p439), Christchurch

➡ Endless Summer (p182), Apihara

Best Luxury Options

New Zealand's luxury lodges and accommodations are blessed not only with astonishing scenery, but also many are in remote locations offering guests privacy and seclusion as well as world-class facilities and unique Kiwi hospitality. If you're going to spoil yourself once in a lifetime, NZ is the place to do it.

➡ Ohtel (p397), Wellington

➡ King & Queen Hotel Suites (p248), New Plymouth

➡ Te Anau Lodge (p50), Te Anau

➡ XSpot (p135), Great Barrier Island

➡ Milford Sound Lodge (p555), Milford Sound

➡ Kiwiesque (p371), Napier

Lake Pearson, Arthur's Pass National Park (p431)

Booking

Local visitor information centres are generally excellent for accommodation in the area; many can also make bookings on your behalf.

Book beds well in advance in peak tourist seasons: November through March (particularly local summer holidays from Christmas to late January), at Easter, and during winter (June to September) in snowy resort towns like Queenstown and Wānaka.

Lonely Planet (www.lonelyplanet.com/hotels) Find independent reviews, as well as recommendations on the best places to stay – and then book them online.

Automobile Association (www.aa.co.nz/travel) Online accommodation bookings (especially good for motels, B&Bs and holiday parks).

Bach Care (www.bachcare.co.nz) Rental listings for apartments of all sizes, including many beachfront options.

Book a Bach (www.bookabach.co.nz) Apartment and holiday-house bookings.

Holiday Houses (www.holidayhouses.co.nz) Holiday-house rentals NZ-wide.

New Zealand Bed & Breakfast (www.bnb.co.nz) Great for all sorts of B&Bs.

Rural Holidays NZ (www.ruralholidays.co.nz) Farm and homestay listings across NZ.

For more information on booking and accommodation types see p704.

Getting Around New Zealand

For more information, see Transport (p715)

Travelling by Car

New Zealand is long and skinny, and most roads are twisty two-lane country byways: getting from A to B will take longer than you may think. However, with your own car (or even better, campervan) you can travel at your own tempo, explore remote areas and visit regions where public transport does not reach.

Car or Campervan Hire

Car hire is available in all major towns; rates from the big international companies are fairly similar. You'll get a better rate from a local NZ firm, but vehicles may be older and service levels less slick. Make sure your contract includes unlimited kilometres.

New Zealand is brilliantly set up for campervans, with a network of excellent holiday parks around the country where people are friendly and there's space for kids to play. Beyond the holiday parks, simple, remote campsites will see you sleeping closer to nature and under the stars.

Top tip: electric campervans can be charged up overnight at holiday parks as well as a at network of charging stations.

RESOURCES

Automobile Associations

New Zealand's **Automobile Association** (AA; ☑0800 500 222; www.aa.co.nz/travel) is a handy resource for maps, insurance and accommodation listings, and provides emergency breakdown assistance for members of many affiliated overseas organisations (bring your membership card).

Road Conditions

New Zealand's weather, particularly in mountainous regions, can change from sunny to stormy in a matter of minutes. Road washouts and closures are common. To check road conditions see www.nzta. govt.nz/traffic or call ☑0800 444 449.

Insurance

New Zealand's no-fault Accident Compensation Corporation (www.acc.co.nz) scheme covers personal injury, but make sure you also have third-party insurance, covering damage to other vehicles if an accident is your fault.

No Car?

Bus

There are reliable, frequent bus services to most major destinations around the country, though services thin out in rural areas. These services aside, you'll be relying on tours to get to key attractions and other destinations.

Plane

Fast-track your holiday with affordable, frequent, fast internal flights. Air New Zealand (p716) is the national carrier, but there are several smaller airlines serving regional hubs beyond the main cities.

Train

Trains in NZ offer reliable, regular and scenic services (if not fast – or cheap) along specific routes on both islands.

Great Journeys of New Zealand (☏04-495 0775, 0800 872 467; www.greatjourneysofnz.co.nz) is the operator, running the *Capital Connection* between Palmerston North and Wellington, the *Coastal Pacific* between Christchurch and Picton, the *Northern Explorer* between Auckland and Wellington, and the *TranzAlpine* over the Southern Alps between Christchurch and Greymouth.

Classic Kiwi Road Trips

Milford Hwy (p552) Gasp at alpine peaks, sigh along thrilling forest-wrapped roads...the drive from Te Anau to Milford Sound is one of the world's finest.

Pacific Coast Hwy (p352) Māori historical sites and bedazzling beaches hem this road

between Ōpōtiki and Gisborne in a long-lost corner of the North Island.

The Great Coast Road (p624) Overhanging cliffs and otherworldly rock formations crop up on this route along the wild, windswept West Coast.

Forgotten World Highway (p254) Be lulled by this lonely forest road, undulating between Stratford and Taumarunui. Don't miss a pit stop at the pub in Whangamomona.

Arthur's Pass (p466) Between Canterbury and the West Coast, the Southern Alps' highest pass is a feat of daredevil engineering. Check the snow report before you hit the road.

Southern Scenic Route (p547) Allow a week to do justice to this meandering route between Queenstown and Dunedin, through a lonesome region known as the Catlins.

DRIVING FAST FACTS
. . . .

➡ Drive on the left; the driver's steering wheel is on the right

➡ Give way to the right at intersections.

➡ Blood alcohol limit 0.05% (0% for drivers under 20).

➡ At single-lane bridges, give way if the smaller red arrow is pointing in your direction of travel.

➡ Speed limit 100km/h; 50km/h in urban areas unless otherwise posted.

ROAD DISTANCES (KM)

	Auckland	Christchurch	Napier	Queenstown
Christchurch	980			
Napier	420	760		
Queenstown	1455	480	1235	
Wellington	640	340	320	815

If You Like...

Māori Culture

Rotorua Catch a cultural performance featuring a *haka* (war dance) and a *hāngi* (Māori feast), with traditional song, dance and storytelling. (p321)

Footprints Waipoua Explore the staggeringly beautiful Waipoua kauri forest on Northland's west coast with a Māori guide. (p185)

Te Ana Māori Rock Art Centre Learn about traditional Māori rock art in Timaru before exploring remote sites around South Canterbury. (p471)

Hokitika The primary source of NZ *pounamu* (greenstone), home to master carvers of stone, bone and paua in traditional Māori designs. (p612)

Toi Hauāuru Studio Visit this Raglan studio for contemporary Māori carving, visual arts and *tā moko* (tattooing). (p202)

Kerikeri Mission Station Set in a tranquil river basin, the museum here tells the early story of Māori ingenuity during early colonial contacts. (p172)

Okains Bay Māori & Colonial Museum This nationally significant collection includes a replica *wharenui* (meeting house), *waka* (canoes) and more. (p449)

Cities

Auckland The City of Sails is infused with vibrant Pacific Islander culture and a world-class foodie scene. (p84)

Wellington Cultural and creative capital, snugly surrounded by hillsides dotted with Victorian architecture. (p383)

Christchurch Despite tragic experiences in recent years, 'ChCh' is a buzzing mix of creative new developments with beautiful historic streetscapes. (p419)

Dunedin Exuding an artsy ambience (so many students!) and close to superb wildlife-viewing opportunities on the Otago Peninsula. (p498)

Napier Art-deco and Spanish Mission architecture, complemented by new restaurants and a modern museum on the waterfront. (p367)

Whangārei This subtropical city surrounded by epic walking tracks is an enclave for artists, sun lovers and escapees from Auckland. (p155)

Beaches

Karekare Spellbinding black-sand beach, an hour's drive west of Auckland, with wild surf. (p137)

Hahei Iconic Kiwi beach experience on the Coromandel Peninsula, with mandatory side trip to Cathedral Cove. (p232)

Wharariki No car park, no ice-cream vans... This isolated stretch near Farewell Spit is for wanderers and ponderers. (p658)

Manu Bay New Zealand's most famous surf break – seen *Endless Summer* (1966)? There's not much sand, but the point break is what you're here for. (p203)

Abel Tasman Coast Track No need to Photoshop this postcard paradise – these golden beaches, blue bays and verdant hills are for real. (p637)

Wainui On the North Island's East Coast: surfing, sandcastles, sunshine... The quintessential beach-bum beach. (p357)

Curio Bay Sure, it gets chilly on the South Island – but punchy waves keep surfers flocking to this arc of golden sand. (p533)

History

Waitangi Treaty Grounds In the Bay of Islands, where Māori chiefs and the British Crown signed the contentious Treaty of Waitangi. (p168)

Arrowtown Gold-rush-era town crammed with heritage buildings and the remains of one of NZ's earliest Chinese settlements. (p582)

Top: Sky Tower (p85), Auckland

Bottom: Vineyard in Blehheim (p667), Marlborough

Ōamaru Victorian Precinct Beautifully restored whitestone buildings and warehouses, now housing eclectic galleries, restaurants and steampunk artisan workshops. (p493)

Te Papa Wellington's vibrant treasure-trove museum, where history – both Māori and Pākehā – speaks, sparkles and shakes. (p383)

Waiuta Explore the rusty relics of a ghost town on the South Island, abandoned to nature in 1951. (p631)

Shantytown Embrace gold-rush nostalgia at this authentic re-creation of an 1860s mining town, south of Greymouth on the West Coast. (p618)

Toitū Otago Settlers Museum Human settlement of the region told through interactive displays and a 100,000-object collection. (p498)

Wine Regions

Marlborough The country's biggest wine region just keeps on turning out superb sauvignon blanc (and other varieties). (p670)

Martinborough A small-but-sweet wine region a day trip from Wellington: easy cycling and easy-drinking pinot noir. (p412)

Waiheke Island Auckland's favourite weekend playground has a hot, dry microclimate: perfect for Bordeaux-style reds and rosés. (p124)

Central Otago Responsible for much of the country's best pinot noir and riesling; drink some. (p523)

Waipara Valley A short hop north of Christchurch are some spectacular vineyards producing equally spectacular riesling. (p429)

Hawke's Bay Warm days shift into chardonnay nights on the sunstroked East Coast. (p373)

Foodie Experiences

Eating in Auckland New restaurants, ethnic culinary enclaves and a strong food-truck scene all make Auckland NZ's eating capital. (p107)

Central Otago vineyard restaurants Autumnal colours combined with the best of NZ food and wine. (p523)

Christchurch's Riverside Market Graze at independent eateries and farmers' market stalls all under one roof. (p440)

Bluff oysters Guzzle silky, salty oysters between March and August; time your visit for May's oyster festival. (p538)

Wellington Night Market Foodie fun after work on Friday, then again after your lazy Saturday. (p404)

West Coast whitebait Whitebait fritters, bound in egg, are a South Island obsession. Try them on pizza, too. (p620)

Coromandel seafood Fresh succulent seafood...make a day of it at September's Whitianga Scallop Festival. (p230)

Extreme Activities

Queenstown Strap yourself into the astonishing Canyon Swing, Catapult or bungy jump, and propel yourself into the void. (p568)

Abel Tasman Canyons Swim, slide, leap and abseil down the granite boulders of the Torrent River. (p651)

Waitomo black-water rafting Don a wet suit, a life vest and a helmet with a headlamp, then float along an underground river. (p213)

Skydive Franz Get an eyeful of the glacier from 20,000ft, NZ's highest jump (you'll see Aoraki/ Mt Cook, too!). (p607)

Extreme Auckland Check out SkyWalk and SkyJump at the Sky Tower, and EcoZip Adventures on Waiheke – thrills with views. (p97)

Canyonz Negotiate cliffs, waterfalls and streams as you climb and abseil through pristine NZ bush on the Coromandel. (p222)

Rafting the Buller River A classic rafting experience served by excellent operators based in Murchison. (p631)

Hiking

Routeburn Track Those with plenty of Great Walk kilometres in their boots rate the Routeburn the best of the bunch. (p558)

Paparoa Track The newest of the Great Walks opened in late 2019, cutting through alpine and limestone landscapes and thriving rainforests. (p600)

Tongariro Alpine Crossing Be dazzled by ultramarine crater lakes and marvel at steamhuffing volcanic vents on this challenging trail. (p278)

Mt Taranaki short walks Hardened hikers can scale the summit, but strolling its photogenic flanks is equally rewarding. (p252)

Lake Angelus Track Yes, the zigzag up Pinchgut Track is a bit of a rude awakening, but the views along Mt Robert Ridge last all day. (p639)

Old Ghost Road Bike it or hike it, this engaging West Coast trail oozes history. (p601)

Queen Charlotte Track The joys of camping (sea breezes, lapping waves, starry nights) or luxurious lodges. Either way, you win. (p638)

Off-the-Beaten-Track Experiences

Stewart Island/Rakiura The end of the line! Catch the ferry to Oban and get lost for a few days in proper Pacific wilderness. (p540)

East Cape Take a few days to detour around this very untouristy corner of the North Island. (p352)

Whanganui River Road Drive alongside the Whanganui River past Māori towns and stands of trees, remnants of failed Pākehā (European New Zealander) farms. (p264)

Forgotten World Highway A lonesome, forested 150km between Taumaranui and Stratford (or the other way around). (p254)

Opononi & Omapere Clear waters, tranquil settlements; the North Island's northwestern coast is seriously understaffed – just how we like it. (p184)

Haast Chat to fishermen and drive to lonely Jackson Bay in the South Island's land of no phone signal. (p602)

Cape Reinga As far as you can go north, head up here at sunrise or sunset to experience this significant Māori site at its most sublime. (p179)

Kayaker in Shag Harbour, Abel Tasman National Park (p651)

Markets

Otago Farmers Market Organic fruit and veg, robust coffee and homemade pies in Dunedin; stock up for life on the road. (p505)

Nelson Market A big, busy weekly market featuring everything from bratwurst to vegan cheese. (p644)

Harbourside Market The ulterior motive for visiting Wellington's weekly fruit-and-veg market is the multi-ethnic food stalls and adjacent artisan City Market. (p404)

Otara Flea Market A taste of the South Pacific in Auckland. (p121)

Rotorua Night Market Thursday night hoedown in downtown Rotorua. Food, drink, buskers... it's all good. (p318)

Hastings Farmers Market One of the original, and still one of the best, farmers markets in NZ. (p379)

Christchurch Farmers Market Local cheeses, organic fruit and craft beer beside historic Riccarton House. (p441)

Month by Month

January

With perfect weather and the cricket season in full swing, it's holiday time for the locals.

☆ Auckland Folk Festival

Kumeū Showgrounds in West Auckland hosts this annual long-weekend festival of traditional, Celtic, Americana and folk music. Camping is available, so you can enjoy the music, dancing, kids' activities and excellent food stalls all night. (p100)

☆ Festival of Lights

New Plymouth's Pukekura Park is regularly plastered with adjectives like 'jewel' and 'gem', but the gardens really sparkle during the seven-week Festival of Lights. Pathways glow and trees shine with thousands of lights and there's live music and family-friendly performances. (p247)

☆ Hamilton Sevens

It's not rugby season, but late January sees the world's seven-a-side rugby teams crack heads in Hamilton as part of the HSBC Sevens World Series. Teams include stalwarts Australia, NZ and South Africa and minnows like Kenya and Canada. (p196)

☆ World Buskers Festival

Christchurch hosts jugglers, musos, tricksters, puppeteers, mime artists and dancers throughout the two-week Bread & Circus World Buskers Festival. Shoulder into the crowd, see who's making a scene at the Spiegeltent and shower the artists with appreciation. (p435)

February

NZ kids are back at school and the 'sauv blanc' is chillin' in the fridge; this is high summer.

☆ Waitangi Day

On 6 February 1840 the Treaty of Waitangi was first signed between Māori and the British Crown. Waitangi Day remains a public holiday across NZ, but in Waitangi itself (the Bay of Islands) there's a lot happening: guided tours, concerts, market stalls and family entertainment. (p170)

☆ Fringe

New Zealand Fringe is where the unusual, emerging, and controversial acts come to play. We're talking cabaret, comedy, spoken word... and pavement chalking. (p394)

☆ Marlborough Wine & Food Festival

New Zealand's biggest and best wine festival features tastings from more than 40 Marlborough wineries, plus fine food and entertainment. The mandatory overindulgence usually happens on a Saturday early in the month. Keep quiet if you don't like sauvignon blanc... (p670)

☆ New Zealand Festival

This month-long spectacular (www.festival.co.nz) in Wellington from February to March on every even-numbered year will spark your imagination. New Zealand's cultural capital exudes artistic enthusiasm with theatre, dance, music, writing and visual arts. International acts aplenty.

★ Art-Deco Festival

Napier, levelled by an earthquake in 1931 and rebuilt during the art-deco era, celebrates its architectural heritage with this high-steppin' fiesta, featuring music, food, wine, vintage cars and costumes over a long weekend in February. (p394)

March

A hint of autumn and harvest time in the vineyards and orchards.

★ Pasifika Festival

With upwards of 140,000 Māori and strong communities of Tongans, Samoans, Cook Islanders, Niueans, Fijians and other South Pacific Islanders, Auckland has the largest Polynesian community in the world. These vibrant cultures come together at this annual fiesta at Western Springs Park. (p100)

★ WOMAD

Local and international music, arts and dance performances fill New Plymouth's Bowl of Brooklands to overflowing at WOMAD. An evolution of the world-music festival dreamed up by rock and art aficionados including Peter Gabriel, who launched the inaugural UK concert in 1982. Perfect for families. (p247)

★ Artists Open Studios & Festival of Glass

Whanganui has earned its artistic stripes as a centre for gorgeous glass, myriad local artists and workshops gearing up for this open-studio festival in March (www.openstudios.co.nz). Expect lots of 'how-to' demonstrations, exhibitions and opportunities to buy gorgeous souvenirs from your trip.

★ Te Matatini National Kapa Haka Festival

This spine-tingling *haka* competition (www.tematatini.co.nz) happens in early March/late February in odd-numbered years, with much gesticulation, eye-bulging and tongue extension. But it's not just the *haka*: expect traditional Māori song, dance, storytelling and other performing arts. Host cities vary.

★ Wildfoods Festival

Eat insects, baby octopi and 'mountain oysters' at Hokitika's comfort-zone-challenging foodie fest. Local classics like whitebait patties are represented too, if you aren't hungry for pork-blood casserole. Tip: NZ brews and wines are available to wash down the worst taste-bud offenders. (p615)

April

The ocean is still swimmable and the weather still mild, with nary a queue in sight.

★ National Jazz Festival

Every Easter, Tauranga hosts the longest-running jazz fest in the southern hemisphere. There's a New Orleans–style village, big band and Māori jazz, and plenty of fine NZ food and wine to accompany the finger-snappin' za-bah-de-dah sonics. (p329)

★ Clyde Wine & Food Festival

Easter is harvest time around Clyde in Central Otago, where the historic main street fills with more than 40 tables and trestles hawking the best regional food and wine (www.promotedunstan.org.nz). This is pinot noir country.

May

Chilly winter beckons, but that doesn't stop the festivals.

★ Bluff Oyster & Food Festival

Truck down to the tip of the South Island for some slippery, salty specimens at this proudly 'unsophisticated' foodie event (www.bluffoysterfest.co.nz). It's chilly in May, but live music and oyster opening (and eating) competitions warm everybody up. Plus there's gourmet burgers, South Island cheese rolls and chowders to keep you warm.

★ New Zealand International Comedy Festival

Local and international acts perform across Auckland, Wellington and various regional centres over three weeks in May. With stand-up, improv, clowning and children's events, you'll find something to tickle your funny bone. (p394)

June

It's ski season! Queenstown and Wānaka come to life in winter.

Matariki

Māori New Year is heralded by the rise of Matariki (aka the Pleiades star cluster) in May. Three days of astronomy, education, ritual, music and community days (www.matarikifestival.org.nz) take place, mainly around Auckland, Wellington and Northland.

☆ New Zealand Gold Guitar Awards

These awards (www.goldguitars.co.nz) in chilly Gore – NZ's country-and-western capital – cap off a week of ever-lovin' country twang and boot-scootin' good times, with plenty of concerts and buskers.

July

Ski season reaches its peak with Queenstown's Winter Festival. If you want to avoid crowds, hit Mt Ruapehu on the North Island.

☆ Queenstown Winter Festival

This southern snow-fest has been running since 1975, and now attracts more than 57,000 visitors. It's a four-day party, with fireworks, live music, comedy, a community carnival, masquerade ball, and wacky ski and snowboard activities on the mountain slopes. (p572)

☆ New Zealand International Film Festival

A touring film festival (www.nzff.co.nz) of local and international gems that hits Wellington, Auckland, Dunedin and Christchurch and then a host of regional towns brimming with film buffs. Check the website for places and dates.

🏃 Russell Birdman

Birdman rallies are so '80s, but that's part of the attraction, no? This one in Russell (www.russellbirdman.co.nz) features a cast of costumed contenders propelling themselves off a jetty in pursuit of weightlessness. Discos, cake-decoration and spaghetti-eating contests for kids round out a satisfying, family-friendly community event.

August

Land a good deal on accommodation pretty much anywhere except ski towns.

🍺 Beervana

Attain beery nirvana at this annual craft-beer guzzle fest (www.beervana.co.nz) in Wellington – it's freezing outside; what else is there to do? Sample the best of NZ's booming beer scene. Not loving beer is heresy, but yes, it also has cider and wine.

☆ Bay of Islands Jazz & Blues Festival

You might think that the Bay of Islands is all about sunning yourself on a yacht while dolphins splash you with saltwater. And you'd be right. But in winter, this jazzy three-day festival (www.jazz-blues.co.nz) provides a toe-tapping alternative, showcasing over 45 acts from around NZ.

September

Spring is sprung. The amazing and surprising World of WearableArt is always a hit.

World of WearableArt

A bizarre (in the best possible way) two-week Wellington event featuring amazing hand-crafted garments. Sometimes spills over into October. (p394)

October

Post-rugby and pre-cricket, sports fans twiddle their thumbs: a trip to Kaikōura, perhaps? Around the rest of NZ, October is 'shoulder season' – reasonable accommodation rates, minimal crowds and no competition for the best campsites.

🎭 Nelson Arts Festival

We know, Nelson is distractingly sunny. But it's worth stepping inside for two weeks of comedy, cabaret, dance and rock opera at this 25-year-old international arts festival (www.nelsonartsfestival.co.nz).

November

Across Northland, the Coromandel Peninsula, the Bay of Plenty and the East Coast, NZ's iconic pohutukawa trees bloom, the weather picks up and tourists start to arrive.

Performers at Queenstown Winter Festival

🎭 NZ Tattoo & Art Festival

Australasia's biggest tattoo culture festival (www.nztattooart.com) attracts artists and fans to New Plymouth every November. Enquire ahead if you're hoping to get inked by one of the many internationally regarded tattooists in attendance.

🍷 Toast Martinborough

Swirl a wine glass, inhale deeply, pretend you can detect hints of berry and oak...it's time to practise your wine-connoisseur face in upmarket Martinborough (www.toastmartinborough.co.nz). The Wairarapa region produces some seriously good pinot noir, and it's perhaps every wine lover's duty to sample some.

🎭 Oamaru Victorian Heritage Celebrations

The good old days... When Queen Vic sat dourly on the throne, when hems were low and collars were high. Old Ōamaru thoroughly enjoys this tongue-in-cheek historic homage (www.vhc.co.nz): expect dress-ups, penny-farthing races, choirs, guided tours and more.

🚴 Lake Taupo Cycle Challenge

Feeling fit? Try cycling 160km around Lake Taupō in NZ's largest cycling event, and then come and talk to us. Held on the last Saturday in November for more than 40 years, Lake Taupō Cycle Challenge (www.cyclechallenge.com) is spectacularly fun to watch too.

December

Summertime! Office workers surge towards the finish line. Everyone gears up for Christmas and shopping centres are packed out.

🎭 Rhythm & Vines

Wine, music and song (all the good things) in sunny east-coast Gisborne over New Year's Eve. DJs, hip-hop acts, bands and singer-songwriters compete for your attention at Rhythm & Vines (www.rhythmandvines.co.nz). Or maybe you'd rather just drink and see the year out under the stars on the beach.

Itineraries

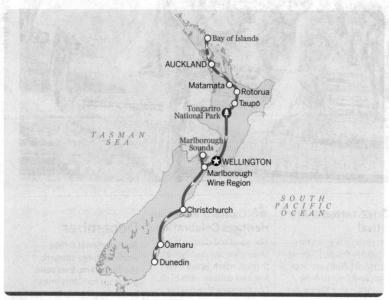

 ## Two Islands, Two Weeks

Here's a quick-fire taste of New Zealand's best for those on a time budget.

Start in **Auckland**: it's NZ's biggest city, with awesome restaurants and bars, galleries and boutiques, beaches and bays. Not an urbanite? Zoom north a few hours to the salt-licked **Bay of Islands** for a day of sailing, kayaking and soaking up history.

Next head south to **Rotorua**, a unique geothermal hotspot: geysers, mud pools, volcanic vents and Māori culture, stopping at **Matamata** for your *Lord of the Rings* fix on the way. Further south, go fishing or boating on stunning **Lake Taupō**, then climb to the ragged craters and Emerald Lakes of **Tongariro National Park** nearby. After some hiking, mountain biking or skydiving, boot down to **Wellington**, a hip little city with an irrepressible arts scene.

Across Cook Strait, for week two: first raise your glass in the world-famous **Marlborough Wine Region**. If you're not a wine fan, the hypnotically hushed inlets, ranges and waterways of the **Marlborough Sounds** are nearby. Swinging further south, cruise into renewed **Christchurch** and on to historic **Dunedin** via steampunk and Victoriana capital **Ōamaru**.

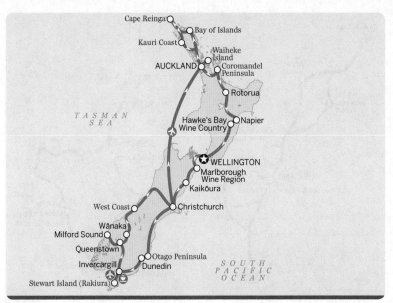

En Zed Classics

Sophisticated Pacific cities, geothermal eruptions, vineyard dining, Māori culture, adrenaline-pumping outdoor activities, empty beaches and lush forests: these are a few of our favourite things.

The 'City of Sails', **Auckland**, is NZ at its most cosmopolitan, with a strong Pacific culture, bars, restaurants, Kiwi designers and artists to check out. Get out onto the harbour on a ferry (or yacht) to spend at least one day exploring the beaches and wineries on nearby **Waiheke Island**. Head north to the **Bay of Islands** for a dose of aquatic adventure (dolphins, sailing). If time allows, add **Cape Reinga** and come back down the **Kauri Coast**, before you lap back down to check out the forests and holiday beaches on the **Coromandel Peninsula**. Further south in **Rotorua**, sample the geothermal bubbles and volcanic mud and learn about Māori culture.

Next? **Napier** on the East Coast, NZ's attractive art deco city. While you're here, don't miss the bottled offerings of the **Hawke's Bay Wine Country** (even better on a cycling tour). Down in **Wellington**, the coffee's hot, the beer's cold and the local blue penguins are adorable. Head to the museums then catch a gig, fashion show or theatre performance.

Switch islands for two weeks to experience the best the south has to offer. Start with a tour of the sauvignon blanc heartland of the **Marlborough Wine Region**, then chill out between the mountains and the whales offshore in laid-back **Kaikōura**. Next stop is the southern capital, **Christchurch**.

Follow the coast road south to the wildlife-rich **Otago Peninsula**, jutting abstractly away from the Victorian facades of Scottish-flavoured and student-filled **Dunedin**.

If time allows, venture down to **Invercargill** then over to **Stewart Island/Rakiura** for some forest wilderness and kiwi spotting. Fly or ferry back to the mainland and head inland to extreme-activity-obsessed **Queenstown** and **Wānaka**. Don't miss a detour over to Fiordland for a jaw-dropping road trip and boat cruise around **Milford Sound**. Return to Christchurch via the indomitable **West Coast** for glaciers and wild weather before you fly back to Auckland.

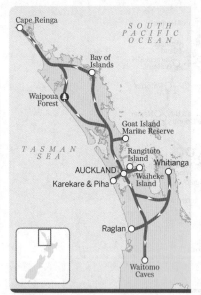

7 DAYS Auckland Taster

Is there another 1.4-million-strong city with access to *two* seas and vibrant Polynesian culture? Immerse yourself in city and seaside, then swing north and south to majestic forests and caves.

Allow at least a couple of days in **Auckland** to hop around its bars and restaurants, museums and beaches. Admire Māori and South Pacific Islander exhibits at Auckland Museum, wander across the Domain to K Rd for lunch. Visit Auckland Art Gallery and the iconic Sky Tower, then Ponsonby or the Viaduct for dinner and drinks.

Ferry over to the hiking trails of **Rangitoto Island** or swim or surf at the dramatic black-sand beaches at **Karekare** and **Piha**. Then plan a day-trip to **Waiheke Island** for wineries, walks and more sedate beaches.

For your next few days, take your pick of activities further out. Driving a northerly loop out of Auckland takes you snorkelling at **Goat Island Marine Reserve**, sailing at the **Bay of Islands**, ocean gazing at **Cape Reinga** and ogling kauri trees at **Waipoua Forest**.

Alternatively, delve south to **Waitomo Caves**, surf at **Raglan** or beach yourself at **Whitianga**.

2 WEEKS Northern Exposure

Three-quarters of New Zealanders live on the North Island – time to find out why!

Begin in **Auckland**, NZ's biggest city. Eat streets abound: try Ponsonby Rd in Ponsonby, K Rd in Newton and New North Rd in Kingsland. Hike up One Tree Hill (Maungakiekie) to burn off resultant calories, and don't miss the Auckland Art Gallery and Auckland Museum.

Venture south through geothermal **Rotorua** – home to some truly amazing volcanic sights – then cruise over to the sunny **East Coast**. By the seaside and encircled by the chardonnay vines of **Hawke's Bay Wine Country**, art deco **Napier** is a hit with architecture buffs. Head south into the farms and vineyards region of **Wairarapa**, before driving over the Remutaka Range into hip, film-obsessed **Wellington**.

Looping back northwest to Auckland, pick and choose your pit stops: the New Zealand Rugby Museum in **Palmerston North**, some crafty glass in **Whanganui** or the epic **Mt Taranaki**, rising like Olympus over New Plymouth. Go underground at **Waitomo Caves** or surf the point breaks near **Raglan**.

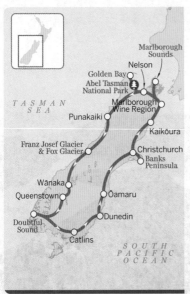

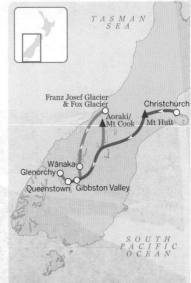

 Southern Circuit
10 DAYS

Winter Wanderer
7 DAYS

Take a long loop through the best of the South Island. Winging into **Christchurch**, you'll find a vibrant city rising up from the serious shakes of the last decade. Grab a coffee, check out the excellent Canterbury Museum and punt into the Botanic Gardens.

City saturated? Visit the geologically/culturally eccentric **Banks Peninsula**, then head north for a wildlife encounter in **Kaikōura**. Continue to the famous **Marlborough Wine Region**, and lose a day on the whisper-still waterways of the **Marlborough Sounds**.

Detour west through artsy **Nelson** to **Abel Tasman National Park** and ecofriendly **Golden Bay**. Dawdle south along the West Coast; stare awestruck at the Pancake Rocks at **Punakaiki** and go on a guided hike or heli-hike at **Franz Josef Glacier** or **Fox Glacier**. Track inland through to Insta-famous **Wānaka** and adventure sports hub **Queenstown**.

Next, venture southwest to Manapōuri for a mesmerising day cruise to **Doubtful Sound** before wending east to the **Catlins**. Back up the east coast, wheel through gothic **Dunedin** to surprisingly creative **Ōamaru**, before rolling back into Christchurch.

We know, a whole bunch of you are here for one thing only: South Island snow!

Fly into **Christchurch** and spend a day acclimatising at its bars and restaurants. Intermediate skier or better? Head to **Mt Hutt** for 365 skiable hectares. As you push south, detour to admire views of snowy **Aoraki/Mt Cook** before continuing to **Queenstown**, offering world-class skiing, great restaurants and a kickin' après-ski scene. Coronet Peak is the area's oldest ski field, with excellent skiing (and snowboarding) for all levels. The visually impressive Remarkables are more family friendly.

Need a break from snow? Drive around Lake Wakatipu to gorgeous **Glenorchy**; or lose an afternoon in the fab wineries of **Gibbston Valley**. Alternatively, Queenstown's extreme activities are still on offer in winter.

Get back on the slopes in **Wānaka**. Nearby ski fields include Treble Cone, Cardrona and Snow Farm New Zealand, NZ's only commercial Nordic (cross-country) ski area. From Wānaka, take an overnight trip to the West Coast to heli-hike **Franz Josef Glacier** and **Fox Glacier**. Backtrack to Queenstown for your flight home.

Hikers at Roy's Peak (p561), Wānaka

Plan Your Trip

Hiking in New Zealand

Hiking (aka trekking, bushwalking, or 'tramping' as Kiwis call it) is the perfect opportunity for a close encounter with New Zealand's natural beauty. There are thousands of kilometres of tracks here – some well marked (including NZ's celebrated 10 'Great Walks'), some barely a line on a map – plus an excellent network of huts enabling hikers to avoid lugging too much gear.

Top NZ Hikes

Top Five Multiday Hikes
Lake Waikaremoana Track, Te Urewera

Abel Tasman Coast Track, Abel Tasman National Park

Heaphy Track, Kahurangi National Park

Routeburn Track, Fiordland/Mt Aspiring National Parks

Milford Track, Fiordland National Park

Top Five Day Hikes
Mt Robert Circuit, Nelson Lakes National Park

Key Summit, Fiordland National Park

Taranaki Falls and Tama Lakes (p298), Tongariro National Park

Ben Lomond Track (p565), Queenstown

Te Paki Coastal Track (p150), Cape Reinga, Northland

Best Hikes for Beginners
Coromandel Coastal Walkway, Coromandel Peninsula

Wainui Falls Track (p651), Golden Bay, Abel Tasman National Park

Rob Roy Track, Mt Aspiring National Park

Mt Manaia Track (p159), Whangārei, Northland

Rangitoto Summit Track, Auckland

Planning
When to Go
Mid-December–late January Good weather, but the Great Walks are as popular as Glastonbury tickets, so book well ahead. Peak season is typically during school summer holidays (a week or two before and after Christmas).

October–April Summer weather lingers into March. Most non-alpine tracks can be walked enjoyably from late October to April, but snow can hang around into summer.

May–September Winter is not the time to be out in the wild, especially on the South Island or at altitude on the North Island – some tracks close in winter because of avalanche danger and have reduced services.

What to Bring
Primary considerations: your feet and your back. Break in your footwear and practise walking with your hiking gear and rucksack before setting out.

Suitable footwear Check that your footwear is suitable for the track you have planned – ask DOC staff or at outdoor stores around NZ.

Backpack and liner You'll be carrying your backpack for most of the trip, so make sure it's a comfy fit and roomy enough for your gear (without being too heavy). Get a waterproof pack liner to keep its contents dry.

All-weather layers Warm clothing, wet-weather gear and sun protection are essential wherever and whenever you hike. Fleece, merino or polypropylene layers are useful, and don't forget sunglasses, sunscreen and a hat (whatever the season). New Zealand's weather is changeable, so expect to remove and add layers throughout the day.

Insect repellent Spray to keep sandflies away (although covering up is best).

Food prep If you're camping or staying in huts without cooking facilities (check with DOC), bring a camping stove. Don't forget your scroggin (trail mix), a mixture of dried fruit and nuts (and sometimes chocolate) for munching en route.

Resources
Before heading into the wilderness, get up-to-date information from an authoritative source – usually the DOC, Mountain Safety Council or regional i-SITE visitor information centres.

Websites
DOC (www.doc.govt.nz) Track descriptions, alerts, and exhaustive flora and fauna information for all parts of the conservation estate. DOC offices supply leaflets (mostly $2 or less) detailing hundreds of NZ walking tracks.

Mountain Safety Council (www.mountainsafety.org.nz) Plenty of info and safety advice, and a handy trip-planning tool that pulls together your route with relevant safety warnings, weather forecasts and a suggested packing list.

Met Service (www.metservice.com) New Zealand's national weather forecaster issues weather warnings and has forecasts specific to outdoor areas.

New Zealand Tramper (www.tramper.co.nz) Articles, photos, lively forums and excellent track and hut information.

Te Araroa (www.teararoa.org.nz) The official website for NZ's 3000km trail from Cape Reinga to Bluff.

Freewalks (www.freewalks.nz) Descriptions, maps and photos of long and short hikes all over NZ.

Tramping New Zealand (www.trampingnz.com) Region-by-region track info with diary-style trip reports.

Maps

The NZ Topo50 topographical map series produced by Land Information New Zealand (LINZ; www.linz.govt.nz) is the most commonly used. Bookshops don't often have a good selection of these maps, but many outdoor stores stock them. The LINZ website has a list of retailers, and DOC offices often sell the latest maps for local tracks. Download free maps in image format from the LINZ website (search for 'Map Chooser'). NZ Topo Map (www.topomap.co.nz) has an interactive topographic map, useful for planning.

Books

DOC publishes detailed books on the flora and fauna, geology and history of NZ's national parks, plus leaflets detailing hundreds of NZ walking tracks.

➡ Lonely Planet's *Hiking & Tramping in New Zealand* (2018) describes around 50 walks of various lengths and degrees of difficulty covering easy wilderness day walks as well as longer Great Walks.

Hiker on Pouakai Circuit (p244), Egmont National Park

➡ Bird's Eye Guides' *Day Walks in New Zealand: 100 Great Tracks* (2016) has amazing topographical maps, as well as inspiring images from one of NZ's most respected hiking authors, Shaun Barnett.

There are countless other books covering hikes, short urban walks and first-hand travelogues around NZ – scan the travel shelf of any local bookshop.

TRACK SAFETY

Thousands of people hike across NZ without incident, but a few folk meet their maker in the mountains, which is entirely avoidable. Many trails are only for fit, well-equipped hikers with plenty of experience – if you don't fit that description, don't attempt them! DOC visitor centres (www.doc.govt.nz) and regional i-SITE visitor information centres offer great advice on walks to suit all levels of experience, so just ask.

New Zealand's constantly changing weather requires hikers to prepare for all conditions. High-altitude walks are subject to snow and ice, even in summer, and rivers can rise rapidly: always check weather and track conditions before setting off, and be prepared to change your plans or sit out bad weather.

Refer to the Mountain Safety Council (www.mountainsafety.org.nz) for safety tips and a trip-planning tool that incorporates weather forecasts and DOC alerts. Log your walk intentions online with Adventure Smart (www.adventuresmart.org.nz), and tell a friend and your local accommodation provider so the alarm is raised in time if you get injured or lost (even if it is 'just' a day walk).

Hiker on Milford Track (p526), Fiordland National Park

Track Classifications

Tracks in NZ are classified according to various features, including level of difficulty. The widely used track classification system is as follows:

Easy Access Short Walk (Easiest) Even track up to an hour long with wheelchair and stroller access. No steps or steep bits.

Short Walk (Easy) Even track up to an hour long, constructed to 'walking shoe' standard (ie walking boots not required). Suitable for all ages and fitness levels.

Walking Track (Easy) Well-formed walks from a few minutes to a full day; walking shoes or boots recommended. Suitable for most ages and fitness levels. Mostly even, possible muddy and steep areas.

Great Walk or Easier Tramping Track (Intermediate) Well formed; major water crossings have bridges and track junctions have signs. Light hiking boots and reasonable fitness required.

Tramping Track (Advanced) Requires skill and experience; hiking boots essential. Suits moderate to high fitness levels. Water crossings may not have bridges, track will be unformed and possibly steep.

Route (Expert) Requires a high degree of skill and experience, plus navigation and outdoor survival skills. Sturdy hiking boots essential. Well-equipped, very fit hikers only.

Guided Walks

If you're new to hiking or just want a more comfortable experience than the DIY alternative, several companies can escort you through the wilds, usually staying in comfortable huts (showers!), with meals cooked and equipment carried for you.

Places on the North Island where you can sign up for a guided walk include Mt Taranaki, Lake Waikaremoana and Tongariro National Park. On the South Island try the Abel Tasman Coast Track, Queen Charlotte Track, Heaphy Track, Old Ghost Road, Routeburn Track, Milford Track or Hollyford Track. Prices for multiday guided walks start at around $1200, and rise to $2000 and beyond for more deluxe experiences.

Trailhead Transport

Getting to and from trailheads isn't always straightforward, except for popular trails serviced by public and dedicated hikers'

...sport. And these (eg Abel Tasman ...st Track) are also the most crowded.

When it comes to one-way trails, having ...vehicle only helps with getting to one end ...f the track (you still have to collect your car afterwards). If you aren't lucky enough to have a local friend to pick you up/drop you off, there are a good number of operators that can bus, boat or fly hikers to/from their desired trailhead (advance booking essential). You can also charter a private vehicle to drop you at one end, then pick you up at the other (unless you're walking back to your vehicle). If you intend to leave a vehicle at a trailhead, don't leave anything valuable inside – theft from cars in isolated areas is a significant problem.

The Great Walks

New Zealand's most popular tracks are its official 'Great Walks', one of which is actually a river canoe trip. A 10th Great Walk, the Paparoa Track, joined the party in 2019. Natural beauty abounds, but at peak times prepare yourself for other people, especially over summer.

New Zealand's Great Walks are described in Lonely Planet's *Hiking & Tramping in New Zealand* (2018), and are detailed in pamphlets provided by DOC visitor centres and online at www.great walks.co.nz.

RESPONSIBLE HIKING

If you went straight from the cradle into a pair of hiking boots, some of these hiking tips will seem ridiculously obvious; others you mightn't have considered. Online, Leave No Trace (www.lnt.org) is a great resource for low-impact hiking and camping, and Freedom Camping (www.freedomcamping.org) has tips on freedom camping etiquette and responsible camping. When in doubt, ask DOC or i-SITE staff.

The obvious:

➡ Time your hike to avoid the height of peak season: less people equals less stress on the environment.

➡ Carry out *all* your rubbish. Burying rubbish disturbs soil and vegetation, encouraging erosion, and animals will dig it up anyway.

➡ Don't use detergents, shampoo or toothpaste in or near lakes and waterways (even if they're biodegradable).

➡ Use lightweight kerosene, alcohol or Shellite (white gas) stoves for cooking; not disposable butane gas canisters.

➡ Where there's a toilet, use it. Where there isn't one, dig a hole and bury your by-product (at least 15cm deep, 100m from any waterway).

You mightn't have considered:

➡ Wash your dishes at hut or campsite facilities, or at least 50m from watercourses; use a scourer, sand or snow instead of detergent.

➡ If you *really* need to scrub your bod, use biodegradable soap and a bucket, at least 50m from any watercourse. Spread the waste water around widely to help the soil filter it.

➡ If open fires are allowed, use only dead, fallen wood in existing fireplaces. Leave any extra wood for the next happy camper.

➡ Keep food-storage bags out of reach of scavengers by stashing them in your pack.

➡ Feeding wildlife (such as inquisitive mountain kea) can lead to unbalanced populations, diseases and animals becoming dependent on handouts. Keep your dried apricots to yourself.

➡ If tracks pass through muddy patches, just plough straight on through – skirting around the outside increases the size of the quagmire.

Top: Hiker at Cascade Saddle pass (p560), near Wānaka

Bottom: Red Crater (p295), Tongariro National Park

MATTEO COLOMBO / GETTY IMAGES ©

Tickets & Bookings

To hike in the Great Walks season (end of October to April), you'll need to book ahead via DOC's Great Walks website. These track-specific passes cover your pre-booked hut accommodation ($130 per person per night; NZ residents pay $65 per adult and Kiwis under 18 are free, but booking is still required) and/or camping ($40 per person per night, or per NZ adult/ child $20/free). You can camp only at designated camping grounds, and probably you wouldn't find a safer spot anyway.

In the off-peak season (May to end of October) fees are substantially lower, but conditions are more challenging; only fit, well-prepared hikers should head out during these months. If you're planning to make more than one trek within a six- or 12-month period, a **Backcountry Hut Pass** will save you money.

Bookings and ticket purchases can be made online (www.doc.govt.nz). Online bookings open in June each year, beginning with the popular Heaphy and Milford Tracks, so get planning early.

Other Tracks

From short and sweet to multiday hikes, there are a lot more walks in NZ than the Great ones!

North Island

A day or less:

Tongariro Alpine Crossing (one day) A tricky 19km hike through surreal Tongariro National Park.

Rangitoto Island Summit (four to five hours) It's a 25-minute ferry ride (or two-hour kayak) from Auckland to the 600-year-old volcano of Rangitoto, best seen from its crater summit after a two-hour loop around the island.

Pinnacles Track (two to four hours) An easyish 4km bushwalk to Aorangi Forest Park's rock stalagmites, which played a starring role in *The Lord of the Rings: The Return of the King* (2003).

Two days or more:

Aotea Track (two to three days) This 25km track follows routes laid down by loggers who came

NEW ZEALAND'S GREAT WALKS

WALK	DISTANCE	TIME (DAYS)	DIFFICULTY	DESCRIPTION
Abel Tasman Coast Track	60km	3-5	Easy to intermediate	NZ's most popular walk (or sea kayak); beaches & bays in Abel Tasman NP (South Island)
Heaphy Track	78km	4-6	Intermediate	Forests, beaches & karst landscapes in Kahurangi NP (South Island)
Kepler Track	60km (loop)	3-4	Intermediate	Lakes, rivers, gorges, glacial valleys & beech forest in Fiordland NP (South Island)
Lake Waikaremoana Track	46km	3-4	Easy to intermediate	Lake views, bush-clad ridges & swimming in Te Urewera (North Island)
Milford Track	54km	4	Easy to intermediate	Rainforest, sheer valleys & peaks, & 580m-high Sutherland Falls in Fiordland NP (South Island)
Paparoa Track & Pike29 Memorial Track	55km	2-4	Intermediate	Limestone cliffs, mining history & majestic sunsets amid the Paparoa Range (South Island)
Rakiura Track	32km (loop)	3	Intermediate	Bird life (kiwi!), beaches & lush bush on remote Stewart Island/Rakiura; off the South Island)
Routeburn Track	32km	2-4	Intermediate	Eye-popping alpine scenery around Mt Aspiring & Fiordland NPs (South Island)
Tongariro Northern Circuit	43km (loop)	3-4	Intermediate to advanced	Through the active volcanic landscape of Tongariro NP (North Island)
Whanganui Journey	87km or 145km	3 or 5	Intermediate	Canoe or kayak down a mysterious river in Whanganui NP (North Island)

Great Walks

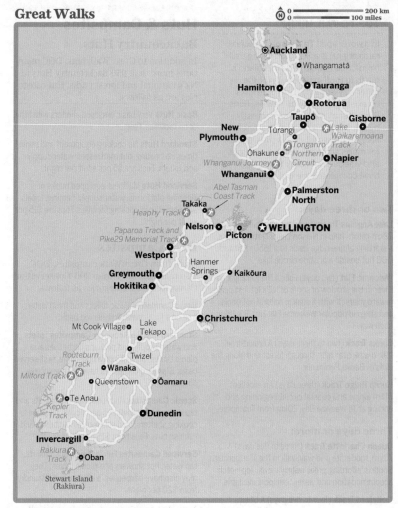

to Great Barrier Island in a quest for kauri trees, leaving historic relics in their wake.

Pouakai Circuit (two to three days) A 25km loop passing lowland rainforest, cliffs and subalpine forest, tussock and swamp at the foot of Mt Taranaki in Egmont National Park.

Mt Holdsworth–Jumbo Circuit (three days) A 24km, medium-to-hard clamber through beech forest to the alpine tops of Tararua Forest Park, close to Masterton.

Te Paki Coastal Track (three to four days) A 48km easy beach hike (camping only) along the rugged Northland coastline.

South Island

A day or less:

Mueller Hut Route (four-hours' ascent) Yes, it involves a hardcore 1040m climb up the Sealy Range near Aoraki/Mt Cook, but the rewards are geological wonders, fascinating plant life and an amazing hut.

Mt Robert Circuit (five hours return) Spy indigo Lake Rotoiti along this special, moderately challenging 9km circuit through ancient rocks and alpine herbs in Nelson Lakes National Park.

TOP-TO-TAIL HIKING

In a word: epic! **Te Araroa** (www.tea raroa.org.nz) is a 3000km hiking trail from Cape Reinga in New Zealand's north to Bluff in the south (or the other way around). The route links up existing tracks with new sections. Built over almost 20 years, mostly by volunteers, it's one of the longest hikes in the world: check the website for maps and track notes, plus blogs and videos from hardy types who have completed the end-to-end epic.

Two or three days:

Lake Angelus Track (two days) On this tough 22km-return hike in Nelson Lakes National Park, a startling alpine ridge leads to a 1650m-altitude DOC hut beside a pristine cirque lake.

Welcome Flat (two days) Follow the Karangarua River in the shadow of some of NZ's loftiest peaks, reward yourself with a soak in natural hot pools, and sleep in popular Welcome Flat Hut. It's 18km each way.

Banks Track (two to three days) A crowd-free 29km walk over hills, through forest and along the cliffs of Banks Peninsula.

Hump Ridge Track (three days) An excellent 61km alpine and coastal circuit beginning and ending at Te Waewae Bay, 20km from Tuatapere.

Three days or more:

Queen Charlotte Track (three to five days) A 70km, moderate one-way walk in the Marlborough Sounds, affording great watery views. Top-notch accommodation and water transport available.

Hollyford Track (four to five days) A 56km low-level hiking track in Fiordland follows in the optimistic footsteps of pioneers. Apple trees mark the site of Jamestown, too isolated to grow into a settlement.

Rees-Dart Track (four to five days) A 70km hard hiking loop in Mt Aspiring National Park, through glacier-fed valleys and over an alpine pass.

St James Walkway (five days) This moderately tough Canterbury hiking track passes through a significant conservation area, home to some 430 species of flora. It's 66km one way.

Huts & Campsites

Backcountry Huts

In addition to Great Walk huts, DOC maintains more than 950 Backcountry Huts in NZ's national and forest parks. Hut categories are as follows:

Basic Huts Very basic enclosed shelters with little or no facilities. Free.

Standard Huts No cooking equipment and sometimes no heating, but mattresses, water supply and toilets. Fees are $5 per adult per night.

Serviced Huts Mattress-equipped bunks or sleeping platforms, water supply, heating, toilets and sometimes cooking facilities. Fees are $15 per adult per night.

DOC Campsites

Aside from Great Walk campsites, DOC also manages more than 200 'Conservation Campsites' with categories as follows:

Basic Campsites Basic toilets and fresh water; free on a first-come, first-served basis.

Standard and Backcountry Campsites Toilets and water supply, and perhaps barbecues and picnic tables; $6 to $8 on a first-come, first-served basis. Standard campsites have boat or vehicle access.

Scenic Campsites High-use sites with toilets and tap water, and sometimes barbecues, fireplaces, cooking shelters, cold showers, picnic tables and rubbish bins. Fees from $15 per night.

Serviced Campsites Full facilities: flush toilets, tap water, hot showers and picnic tables. They may also have barbecues, a kitchen and a laundry; from $20 per night.

Note that bookings are necessary for all Serviced Campsites, plus some Scenic and Standard Campsites in peak season (October to April). Book online (https://booking. doc.govt.nz) or at DOC visitor centres.

DOC publishes free brochures with descriptions, and instructions to find every campsite (even GPS coordinates). Pick up copies from DOC visitor centres before you hit the road, or download them from their website.

Snowboarder on Mt Ruapehu (p293), Tongariro National Park

Plan Your Trip

Skiing & Snowboarding

New Zealand's alpine region is loved by skiers and snowboarders with family-friendly ski areas, cross-country skiing and snowshoeing, daredevil snowboarding terrain and luxe-level heliskiing. The NZ ski season varies between regions, but it's generally mid-June through September, though it can run as late as mid-October on a good year.

Best Skiing & Snowboarding

Best for Beginners or with Kids

Mt Hutt, Central Canterbury

Cardrona, Queenstown

The Remarkables, Queenstown

Mt Dobson, South Canterbury

Roundhill, South Canterbury

Coronet Peak, Queenstown

Best Snowboarding

Mt Hutt, Central Canterbury

Treble Cone, Wānaka

Cardrona, Wānaka

Ohau, South Canterbury

Whakapapa, Tongariro National Park

Best Après-Ski Activities

Bar hopping, Queenstown

Dine at Cardrona Hotel, Cardrona

Soak in an outdoor onsen, Coronet Peak Ski Field

Indoor family climbing, Wānaka

Night luge at Skyline, Queenstown

Planning

Where to Go

The variety of locations and conditions makes it difficult to rate NZ's ski fields in any particular order. Some people like to be near Queenstown's party scene or Mt Ruapehu's volcanic landscapes; others prefer the quality high-altitude runs on Mt Hutt, or uncrowded Tukino. Club areas are publicly accessible and usually less crowded and cheaper than commercial fields, even though nonmembers pay higher fees.

Practicalities

New Zealand's commercial ski areas aren't generally set up as 'resorts' with ski-in chalets or five-star hotels. Rather, visitor accommodation and après-ski carousing is usually in surrounding towns, which are then connected with the slopes via daily bus shuttles. This set-up is a bonus if you want to sample a few different ski areas, as you can base yourself in one town and day trip to a few different resorts. Many smaller 'club' ski fields have lodges where you *can* stay, subject to availability.

Visitor information centres in NZ, and Tourism New Zealand (www.newzealand. com) have information on the various ski areas and can make bookings and organise packages before you go. Lift passes are reasonably priced given the brevity of the ski season (and are usually half price for kids). Lesson-and-lift packages are available at most areas. Ski and snowboard gear and equipment rental is available in ski villages, and discounted for multiday hire.

Websites

www.snow.co.nz Reports, webcams and ski info across the country.

www.nzski.com Reports, employment, passes and webcams for Mt Hutt, Coronet Peak and the Remarkables.

www.skiandride.nz Good all-round online portal for South Island ski areas with road conditions, school holiday dates and other practical info.

www.chillout.co.nz/alpine Portal to info on 13 ski areas and sales of ski passes that access them all. The 'Chill Travel Pass' areas are Awakino, Broken River, Cheeseman, Craigieburn, Fox Peak, Hanmer Springs, Mt Dobson, Mt Lyford, Mt Olympus, Rainbow and Temple Basin (plus a couple of days on Treble Cone and Porters).

www.mtruapehu.com Reports, passes, courses and webcams for Mt Ruapehu's Whakapapa and Turoa ski areas.

North Island

Tongariro National Park

Whakapapa (p296) & Turoa (p296) On either side of Mt Ruapehu, these well-run twin resorts comprise NZ's largest ski area, though it comes at a cost of more exposed terrain (watch those weather reports). Whakapapa has 65 trails spread across 1050 hectares, plus cross-country skiing, a terrain park and NZ's highest dining

Winter Sports Areas

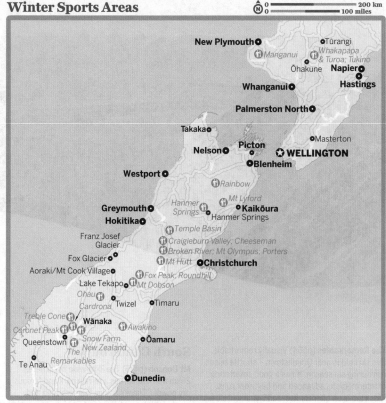

experience at Knoll Ridge Chalet. Drive from Whakapapa Village (6km) or book a shuttle bus from National Park Village, Taupō, Tūrangi or Whakapapa Village (various operators). Smaller Turoa has a beginners lift, snowboarding, downhill and cross-country skiing, and over 722m of vertical descent from the High Noon Express chairlift. There's bookable bus transport from Ōhakune, 17km away, which has the North Island's liveliest après-ski scene.

Tukino (p296) Club-operated Tukino is on Mt Ruapehu's east, 46km south from Tūrangi. It's quite remote, 14km down a gravel road from the sealed Desert Rd (SH1), and you need a 4WD vehicle to get in (unless you book a shuttle to meet you at the 2WD carpark). It's uncrowded, and has runs to suit most levels.

Taranaki

Manganui (p252) Offers volcano-slope, club-run skiing on the eastern slopes of spectacular Mt Taranaki in Egmont National Park, 22km from Stratford, 55km from New Plymouth (and a 25-minute walk from the car park). Taranaki is a surf-mad province, so expect the slopes to be dominated by snowboarders, and most of the terrain is intermediate and advanced. Limited lodge accommodation up the mountain.

South Island

Queenstown & Wānaka

Coronet Peak (p564) At the Queenstown region's oldest commercial ski field, snow-making systems and treeless slopes provide excellent skiing and snowboarding for all levels, with plenty of family-friendly options. There's night skiing on Fridays and Saturdays (and on Wednesdays in July). Shuttles to the slopes run from Queenstown.

Snowboarder at Ohau Ski Field (p480)

The Remarkables (p564) Visually remarkable, this ski field is near Queenstown – shuttle buses run during ski season. It has a good smattering of intermediate, advanced and beginner runs. Kids club is on offer for five- to 15-year-old skiers.

Treble Cone (p587) The highest and largest of the southern lakes ski areas is in a spectacular location 26km from Wānaka, with steep slopes suitable for intermediate to advanced skiers (a rather professional vibe). There are also half-pipes and a terrain park for boarders.

Cardrona (p594) Around 34km from Wānaka, with several high-capacity chairlifts, beginners' tows and the southern hemisphere's biggest park and pipe playground for the freestylers. Buses run from Wānaka and Queenstown during ski season. A friendly scene with good services for skiers with disabilities, plus an on-mountain crèche for juniors if you need it.

Snow Farm New Zealand (p594) New Zealand's only commercial Nordic (cross-country) ski area is 33km from Wānaka on the Pisa Range, high above the Cardrona Valley. There are 55km of groomed trails, huts with facilities and thousands of hectares of open snow.

South Canterbury

Mt Dobson (p476) The 3km-wide basin here, 26km from Fairlie, has a terrain park and famously dry powder. There's a huge learners' area and plenty for intermediates (and up high, dry powder and challenging terrain to suit more experienced skiers). On a clear day you can see Aoraki/Mt Cook and the Pacific Ocean from the summit.

Ohau (p480) This commercial ski area with a secluded feel is on Mt Sutton, 42km from Twizel. There are intermediate and advanced runs, excellent snowboarding, two terrain parks and sociable Lake Ohau Lodge, overlooking glorious views.

Fox Peak (p476) An affordable, uncrowded club ski area 40km from Fairlie in the Two Thumb Range. Expect rope tows, good cross-country skiing and dorm-style accommodation.

Roundhill (p477) A small family-friendly ski area in Canterbury, accessible only by gravel roads, near the town of Lake Tekapo. Best for beginners and snow play.

Central Canterbury

Mt Hutt (p469) One of the highest ski areas in the southern hemisphere, as well as one of NZ's

Chairlift riders at the The Remarkables (p564)

PLAN YOUR TRIP SKIING & SNOWBOARDING

HELISKIING

New Zealand's remote heights are tailor-made for heliskiing, with operators covering a wide off-piste area along the pristine slopes of the Southern Alps, including extreme skiing for the hardcore. Costs range from around $900 to $1450 for three to eight runs. Heliskiing is available at Coronet Peak, Treble Cone, Cardrona, Mt Hutt, Ohau and Hanmer Springs; independent operators include the following:

➡ Alpine Heliski (p565)

➡ Harris Mountains Heli-Ski (p565)

➡ Methven Heliski (p468)

➡ Over The Top (p570)

➡ Southern Lakes Heliski (p565)

best. It's close to Methven; Christchurch is 118km to the east – ski shuttles service both towns. Road access is steep – be extremely cautious in lousy weather. The ski area is exposed to the mercy of the elements, but the snow is usually plentiful. Boasts beginner, intermediate and advanced slopes, with chairlifts, heliskiing and wide-open faces that are good for learning to snowboard.

Porters (p465) The closest commercial ski area to Christchurch (96km away on the Arthur's Pass road). The 'Big Mama' run boasts a 680m drop and gentler slopes, too. It also has a terrain park, good cross-country runs along the ridge, and lodge accommodation.

Temple Basin (p465) A club field with a cult following, 4km from Arthur's Pass. It's a 50-minute walk uphill from the car park to the ski-area lodges. It offers floodlit skiing at night and excellent backcountry runs for snowboarders.

Craigieburn Valley (p465) Centred on Hamilton Peak, Craigieburn Valley is no-frills backcountry heaven, 40km from Arthur's Pass. It's one of NZ's most challenging club areas, with upper intermediate and advanced runs (no beginners). Accommodation in lodges.

Broken River (p565) Not far from Craigieburn Valley, this club field is a 15- to 20-minute walk from the car park and has a real sense of isolation. Reliable snow, a laid-back vibe and sheltered enough to minimise bad-weather closures. Catered or self-catered lodge accommodation available.

Cheeseman (p565) A club area in the Craigieburn Range, this smallish family-friendly operation is around 100km from Christchurch. Based on Mt Cockayne, it's a wide, sheltered basin with drive-to-the-snow road access. Lodge accommodation available.

Mt Olympus (p565) Difficult to find (but worth the search), 2096m Mt Olympus is 58km from Methven and 12km from Lake Ida. This club area has intermediate and advanced runs, and solid cross-country trails to other areas. Access is sometimes 4WD-only, depending on conditions. Lodge accommodation available.

Northern South Island

Hanmer Springs (p460) A friendly commercial field based on Mt St Patrick, 17km from Hanmer Springs township (linked by shuttle buses), with mostly intermediate and advanced runs.

Mt Lyford (p461) Around 60km from Hanmer Springs and Kaikōura, and 4km from Mt Lyford village, this is more of a 'resort' than most NZ ski fields, with accommodation and eating options. It has a good mix of runs and a terrain park.

Sea kayaker at Abel Tasman National Park (p652)

Plan Your Trip

Extreme New Zealand

From mid-air adventures to deep dives, New Zealand is pure
adrenaline. Inspired by NZ's rugged landscape, even the meekest
travellers muster the courage to launch from a hillside, skydive
above mountains or thunder down river rapids. With their unique
ingenuity New Zealanders have pioneered thrills like bungy jumping and jetboating, and their outdoorsy daredevil attitude can be
infectious.

Best Extreme New Zealand

Best Skydive Drop Zones

Queenstown

Taupō

Bay of Islands

Top White-Water Rafting Trips

Tongariro River, Taupō

Kaituna River, Rotorua

Rangitikei River, Taihape

Buller Gorge, Murchison

Top Mountain-Biking Tracks

Redwoods Whakarewarewa Forest, Rotorua

Old Ghost Road, Westport

Queen Charlotte Track, Marlborough

West Coast Wilderness Trail, Hokitika

On the Land

Mountain Biking & Cycle Touring

Rugged mountains interlaced with farm tracks and old railway lines...it would be hard to design better mountain-biking terrain if you planned it. The New Zealand Cycle Trail (www.nzcycletrail.com), some 2500km of tracks, helped mountain biking grow from a weekend sport to a national craze. Its popularity among hardcore outdoors enthusiasts (and a certain level of one-upmanship among certain sectors)

can give the sport an elite air. But there is a variety of trails in NZ providing travellers with a choice of gentle ambles by rural meadows to multiday cycle tours, half-day downhill-thrill rides and challenging week-long MTB adventures.

Mountain-bike parks – most with various trail grades and skills areas (and usually a local bike-hire option) – are great for trying mountain biking while in NZ. The most famous is Rotorua's Redwoods Whakarewarewa Forest, but among legions of others are Wellington's Makara Peak, Auckland's Woodhill Forest and Queenstown's downhill park, fed by the Skyline Gondola.

Classic trails include the 42 Traverse around Tongariro National Park, the Rameka on Takaka Hill and the trails around Christchurch's Port Hills – but this is just the tip of the iceberg. An increasing number of DOC hiking trails have been converted to dual use – such as the tricky but epic Heaphy Track and challenging, history-rich Old Ghost Road – but mountain biking is restricted during peak hiking season.

Your clue that there's some great biking around is the presence of bike-hire outfits across NZ. Most are cycle-obsessed them-

NGĀ HAERENGA (THE JOURNEYS)

The **New Zealand Cycle Trail** (www.nzcycletrail.com) – known in Māori as Ngā Haerenga, 'The Journeys' – is a 22-strong series of off-road trails also known as Great Rides. Spread from north to south, they are of diverse length, terrain and difficulty, with many following history-rich old railway lines and pioneer trails, while others are freshly cut adventures. Almost all penetrate remarkable landscapes.

There are plenty of options for beginner to intermediate cyclists, with several hardcore exceptions including the Old Ghost Road, which is growing to international renown. The majority are also well supported by handy bike hire, shuttles, and dining and accommodation options, making them a desirable way to explore NZ while minding your carbon footprint.

White water rafters on Kaituna River (p324), Rotorua Lakes

selves, and they'll soon direct you to a local ride appropriate to your level. The go-to book is *Classic New Zealand Mountain Bike Rides* (2019; from bookshops, bike shops and www.kennett.co.nz).

If cycle touring is more your pace, check out the *Pedallers' Paradise* booklets by Nigel Rushton (www.paradise-press.co.nz). Changeable weather and occasionally hazardous road conditions in NZ mean that cycle touring is less of a craze, but there are remarkable road journeys, such as the Southern Scenic Route in the South.

Rock Climbing

Time to chalk up your fingers and challenge your physical and mental limits. On the North Island, popular rock-climbing areas include Whanganui Bay, Kinloch, Kawakawa Bay and Motuoapa near Lake Taupō; Mangatepopo Valley and Whakapapa Gorge on the Central Plateau; Humphries Castle and Warwick Castle on Mt Taranaki; and Piarere and popular Wharepapa South in the Waikato.

On the South Island, try the Port Hills area above Christchurch or Castle Hill on the road to Arthur's Pass. West of Nelson,

the marble and limestone mountains of Golden Bay and Takaka Hill provide prime climbing. Other options are Long Beach (north of Dunedin), and Mihiwaka and Lovers Leap on the Otago Peninsula.

Raining? You'll find indoor climbing walls all around the country, including at Rotorua, Whangārei, Auckland, Tauranga, Taupō, Wellington, Christchurch and Hamilton.

Climb New Zealand (www.climbing. nz) has the low-down on the gnarliest overhangs around NZ, plus access and instruction info. Needless to say, instruction is a must for all but the most seasoned climbing pros.

In the Air
Bungy Jumping

Bungy jumping was made famous by Kiwi AJ Hackett's 1987 plunge from the Eiffel Tower, after which he teamed up with champion NZ skier Henry van Asch to turn the endeavour into an accessible pursuit for anyone.

Today their original home base of Queenstown is a spiderweb of bungy cords, including the AJ Hackett's triad: the 134m Nevis Bungy (the highest in NZ); the 43m Kawarau Bungy (the original); and the Ledge Bungy (at the highest altitude – diving off a 400m-high platform). There's another scenic jump at Thrillseekers Canyon near Hanmer Springs. On the North Island, head to Taihape, Rotorua or Auckland, although the most scenic jump is over the Waikato River in Taupō. Huge rope swings offer variation on the theme; head to Queenstown's Shotover Canyon or Nevis Swing for that swooshy buzz.

Paragliding & Hang Gliding

A surprisingly gentle but still thrilling way to take to the skies, paragliding involves setting sail from a hillside or clifftop under a parachute-like wing. Hang gliding is similar but with a smaller, rigid wing. Most flights are conducted in tandem with a master pilot, although it's also possible to get lessons to go it alone. To give it a whirl, try a tandem flight in Queenstown, Wānaka, Nelson, Motueka, Hawke's Bay, Christchurch or Auckland. The New Zealand Hang Gliding and Paragliding Association (www.nzhgpa.org.nz) rules the roost.

Skydiving

With some of the most scenic jump zones in the world, NZ is a fantastic place to take a leap. First-time skydivers can knock off this bucket-list item with a tandem jump, strapped to a qualified instructor, experiencing up to 75 seconds of free fall before the chute opens. The thrill is worth every dollar, from $249 for a 9000ft jump to $559 for NZ's highest free-fall jump (a nerve-jangling 20,000ft, or 85 seconds, on offer over Franz Josef). Extra costs apply for a video recording or photographs capturing your mid-air terror/delight. Check out the New Zealand Parachute Federation (www.nzpf.org) for more info.

On the Water

Jetboating

The jetboat was invented in NZ by an engineer from Fairlie – Bill Hamilton (1899–1978) – who wanted a boat that could navigate shallow, local rivers. He credited his eventual success to Archimedes but, as most jetboat drivers will inevitably tell you, Kiwi Bill is the hero of the jetboat story.

River jetboat tours can be found throughout NZ, and while much is made of the hair-raising 360-degree spins that see passengers drenched and grinning from ear to ear, they are really just a sideshow. Just as Bill would have it, jetboat journeys take you deep into wilderness you could otherwise never see, and as such they offer one of NZ's most rewarding tour experiences. In Haast and Whataroa, jetboat tours plunge visitors into pristine wilderness, aflutter with birds.

Big-ticket trips such as Queenstown's Shotover, Kawarau and Dart all live up to the hype. But the quieter achievers will blow your skirt up just as high. Check out the Buller and Wilkin in Mt Aspiring National Park, and the Whanganui – one of the most magical A-to-B jetboat trips of them all.

Parasailing & Kiteboarding

Parasailing (dangling from a modified parachute over the water, while being pulled along by a speedboat) is perhaps the easiest way for humans to achieve assisted flight. There are operators in the Bay of Islands, Bay of Plenty, Taupō, Wānaka and Queenstown.

Kiteboarding (aka kitesurfing), where a mini parachute drags you across the ocean on a mini surfboard, can be attempted at Paihia, Tauranga, Mt Maunganui, Raglan, Wellington and Nelson. Karikari Peninsula near Cape Reinga on NZ's northern tip is a kiteboarding mecca.

Sea Kayaking

Sea kayaking offers a wonderful perspective of the coastline and gets you close to marine wildlife you may otherwise never see. Meanwhile tandem kayaks (aka 'divorce boats') present a different kind of challenge.

There are ample places to get paddling. Hotspots include Waiheke and Great Barrier Islands, the Bay of Islands and Coromandel Peninsula, Marlborough Sounds (from Picton) and Abel Tasman National Park. Kaikōura is exceptional for wildlife spotting, and Fiordland for jaw-dropping scenery. Wellington and Paihia are noteworthy for offering the chance to paddle a traditional Māori *waka* (canoe). The Kiwi Association of Sea Kayakers (www.kask. org.nz) gives a good primer on paddling techniques, plus resources for kayakers with a disability.

As is the case the world over, stand-up paddleboarding (SUP) is increasingly popular across NZ and another way to get out on the water.

Scuba Diving & Snorkelling

New Zealand is just as enchanting under the waves, with warm waters in the north, interesting sea life all over and some impressive shipwrecks to explore.

The flag-bearer is the Poor Knights Islands, where subtropical currents carry and encourage a vibrant mix of sea life. Also rubbing shoulders with marine life is the wreck of the Greenpeace flagship *Rainbow Warrior,* which slumbers beneath the Cavalli Islands (reached from Matauri Bay).

Other notable sites for scuba and snorkelling beyond the Bay of Islands include Hauraki Gulf, Goat Island and Gisborne's Te Tapuwae o Rongokako Marine Reserve. In the Marlborough Sounds, the MS *Mikhail Lermontov* is one of the world's largest diveable cruise-ship wrecks. In Fiordland, experienced divers can head for Dusky, Milford and Doubtful Sounds, which have clear conditions and the occasional friendly fur seal or dolphin. Snorkellers should check out the reefs of

SURFING IN NEW ZEALAND

North Island

Raglan, Waikato New Zealand's most famous surf break, with a buzzing boarder community and superb surf beaches extending south. Almost a pilgrimage spot for overseas surfers.

Surf Highway, Taranaki Take your pick from consistent Fitzroy Beach, big 'n' busy Stent Rd, experts-only Green Meadows Point (Opunake) and the heavy waves of Ohawe Beach (Hāwera), all along the 'Surf Highway' (Hwy 45).

Whangamata, Coromandel Exceptional surf breaks and gear hire and surf schools aplenty.

Bay of Plenty Mt Maunganui is an all-year all-rounder, suitable for most levels and hugely popular in summer, and Matakana Island has brisk waves that suit intermediate surfers.

Gisborne, East Coast Consistent surf and some of NZ's mildest weather. The town's Midway Beach has waves with clout, while pros are fond of Sponge Bay (be careful, there are hidden rocky hazards).

Wellington Region Head to popular Lyall Bay, exposed but not-too-challenging Castlepoint or (if you're a pro) Tora Point.

South Island

Marlborough & Nelson Wear a thick wet suit in the Kaikōura Peninsula, where you'll share waves with dolphins, or head to the epic surf at Mangamaunu and Hapuku's Meatworks (intermediates and up).

Canterbury Popular Taylors Mistake has some of Christchurch's best surf and North Brighton suits a range of skill levels.

Dunedin, Otago Dunedin is a good base for surfing on the South Island. Head to St Clair Beach for waves worthy of the international surf competitions held here.

West Coast Relatively sheltered Punakaiki Beach is a good mixed-level destination while Tauranga Bay (Westport) is best for experienced surfers.

Southland Colac Bay (near Riverton) is an easy, breezy surf spot while Porridge Point (Pahia) is one for the pros.

Bungy jumpers near Queenstown (p562)

Taputeranga Marine Reserve (Wellington) and wildlife-rich Waiheke Island.

Expect to pay from around $799 for a three/four-day, PADI-approved, ocean-dive course. One-off organised boat-based dives start at around $200. Snorkelling tours are not dissimilar in price, but trips often include food as well as equipment.

New Zealand Underwater Association (www.nzunderwater.org.nz) Clean-seas and diving-safety advocates whose website has safety info, diving tips, gear maintenance advice and more.

Dive New Zealand (www.divenewzealand.com) New Zealand's only dedicated dive magazine, plus safety info and listings of dive clubs and shops.

White-Water Rafting, Kayaking & Canoeing

Epic mountain ranges and associated rainfall mean there's no shortage of great rivers to raft, nor any shortage of operators ready to get you into the rapids. Rivers are graded from I to VI (VI meaning they can't be safely rafted), with operators often running a couple of different trips to suit abil-

ity and age (rougher stretches are usually limited to rafters aged 13 or above).

Queenstown's Shotover and Kawarau Rivers are deservedly popular, but the Rangitata (Geraldine), Buller (Murchison) and the Arnold and Waiho rate just as highly. For a multiday epic, check out the Landsborough. The central North Island dishes up plenty, including the popular Tongariro, Rangitikei, Mohaka and Wairoa. There are also the Kaituna Cascades near Rotorua, the highlight of which is the 7m drop at Okere Falls.

Kayaking and canoeing are rampant, particularly on friendly lake waters, although there are still plenty of places to paddle the rapids, including some relatively easy stuff on the Whanganui 'Great Walk'.

New Zealand Rafting Association (www.nz-rafting.co.nz) River conservation nonprofit; river gradings and listings of rafting operators.

New Zealand Kayak (www.kayaknz.co.nz) Community-based kayaking magazine.

Green-lipped mussels (p66)

Plan Your Trip

Eat & Drink Like a Local

Travellers, bring your appetites! Eating is a highlight of any visit to New Zealand, from fresh seafood and gourmet burgers to farmers market fruit-and-veg and crisp-linen fine dining. Drinking here, too, presents boundless opportunities to have a good time, with coffee, craft beer and wine of world renown.

SRINIL PHOTO / SHUTTERSTOCK ©

The Year in Food

New Zealand's varied topography and bounteous maritime climate translates to great food and drink at any time of the year.

Summer (December to February)

Summer's bounty includes stone fruit, berries, flowering vegetables and even the first apples of the year.

Autumn (March to May)

Citrus and brassicas begin to replace late summer's fruit and vegetables, while Bluff oysters are celebrated in May's annual festival. It's also vintage time for Kiwi wines.

Winter (June to August)

Shellfish are at their best in the coldest months, when fennel, leeks and rhubarb are also in season.

Spring (September to November)

The return of the sun brings asparagus, artichokes and other tasty treats, plus food and wine festivals such as First Light (p358), Toast Martinborough (p411) and Wellington on a Plate (p394).

Food Experiences
Meals of a Lifetime

Pasture (p113) Book months ahead to enjoy some of Auckland's best Modern NZ food.

Mister D (p372) Hip, slick and delicious, D is the pride of Napier's dining scene.

5th Street (p442) Global influences marry perfectly with Kiwi produce at this sparkling Christchurch bistro.

Rātā (p575) Food adventures and genuine hospitality at this uniquely Kiwi restaurant run by Michelin-starred chef Josh Emett.

Three Seven Two (p129) Divine locally sourced ingredients with Waiheke Island ocean views.

Noble Rot (p400) This warmly lit, atmospheric wine bar serves some of Wellington's best food.

Cheap Treats

Fish and Chips The UK may be the spiritual home of this beloved fast-food, but the Kiwis have raised it to an art form. Try Opunake Fish, Chips & More (p257) on the North Island's Surf Highway 45.

Pies Bakeries throughout NZ turn out golden-crusted delights filled with everything from beef to scallops and Thai vegetarian curry. The Fairlie Bakehouse (p476) produces superb examples.

Pineapple Lumps These chewy, tooth-gripping, chocolate-coated sweets have been a Kiwi favourite since the 1950s. Available everywhere.

Dare to Try

Kina New Zealand's native sea urchin, this spiky little echinoderm is harvested on both islands from August to January. It's much prized for its intensely flavoured roe: simply cut open to spoon the creamy, fishy goodness straight from the shell.

Pāua Harvested year-round from the Kaikōura and Southland coasts, and from islands such as Stewart and the Chathams, NZ's abalone are coveted by seafood lovers across the globe. The tough muscle of wild pāua often needs to be tenderised before eating, either raw, braised or flash-fried.

Whitebait fritters In NZ whitebait – the generic name for edible, immature sprats of schooling fish known as galaxids – is often served fried in a crispy, many-eyed fritter. The immature fish resemble translucent worms, posing a sensory challenge to some!

Local Specialities
Auckland

Pacific Island cuisine New Zealand's biggest cosmopolis is home to its largest Pacific Islander community. This is the place to try dishes from Samoa, Fiji and other island nations.

Northland & Bay of Islands

Avocados Subtropical weather makes this home to the prosperous avocado industry, fuelling a thousand weekend brunches across the nation.

Kai, traditional Māori food, usually cooked in *hāngi* (p321)

Coromandel Peninsula & the Waikato

Green-lipped mussels Growing in large, almond-shaped shells with vibrant green edges, these oversized mussels are found only in NZ. Meaty and delicious examples are farmed in Marlborough Sounds, Coromandel, Golden Bay and Stewart Island.

Taranaki & Whanganui

Kumara Otherwise known as sweet potato, this popular, starchy tuber turns up on menus across NZ, as crisp-fried chips, part of a *hāngi* (Māori earth-cooked feast) and in many other guises.

Taupo & the Ruapehu Region

Trout Is there a better place to eat sashimied trout than the trout-fishing capital of NZ?

Rotorua & the Bay of Plenty

Hāngi A full feast of slow-cooked meat and vegetables roasted the traditional Māori way: in the ground over hot stones. Enjoy a genuine geothermal *hāngi* in Rotorua.

East Coast

Fish and chips This beach-fringed, authentically rural slice of the North Island is the ideal place to sample this beloved Kiwi takeaway.

Wellington Region

Coffee The country's capital is also renowned as its cafe capital, with the roasting, grinding and cupping of coffee taken extremely seriously here.

Christchurch & Canterbury

Rock lobster Found in abundance along most of NZ's rocky coastline, these succulent crustaceans are most often associated with Kaikōura on the South Island.

Dunedin & Otago

Hokey Pokey ice cream Certain to rouse childhood nostalgia in Kiwis if you ask where to get the best Hokey Pokey ice cream (vanilla with chunks of honeycomb).

Fiordland & Southland

Bluff oysters Also known by the Māori name *tio paruparu*, these briny bivalves are endemic to NZ's

Pavlova

coast. The eponymous South Island town of Bluff hosts a festival celebrating the catch every May.

Queenstown & Wanaka

Pavlova The queen of Kiwi desserts is a meringue base heaped with cream and berries, kiwifruit or passion fruit. Where else can you indulge guilt-free but in the adventure-sports capital?

Marlborough & Nelson

Sauvignon blanc Such is the world's thirst for NZ 'sav blanc' that the variety accounts for 73% of the nation's wine production, and an even higher proportion of its exports. The best examples, such as those from Marlborough, show characteristics of red pepper, passion fruit and gooseberry. Ideal with seafood, the style also matches tangy and astringent foods.

How to Eat & Drink

When to Eat

Breakfast Kiwi cafes have raised the simple task of getting the day's digestion going to an art form. Good coffee is universally available while breakfast

staples such as eggs, bacon or avocado on toast are steered in imaginative directions, particularly in urban joints aimed at the brunch crowd. And, of course, the simple staples of toast, waffles and granola have never disappeared.

Lunch Lunch, which can be either the day's primary or secondary meal, presents perhaps the widest palette of options. Casual ramen joints and gastropubs are joined by more high-flying restaurants and bistros, most of which open for lunch at least five days a week, in addition to traditional evening hours. With more than 10% of Kiwis adhering to vegetarian and vegan diets, plant-based options are increasingly available even in regional towns.

Dinner The day's concluding meal can be as casual or as fancy as you like (or can afford) in NZ, particularly in its cities. In order to wow the socks

EATING PRICE RANGES

The following price ranges refer to the average price of a main course.

$	less than $15
$$	$15–35
$$$	more than $35

Riverside Market (p440), Christchurch

off increasingly demanding diners, restaurants must now succeed in fusing ingredients and traditions into ever more innovative fare. 'Modern NZ' has been coined to classify this approach: a melange of East and West, a swirl of Atlantic and Pacific Rim, with a dash of classical European technique and Mediterranean sensibility. Late opening is an urban affair; one-pub towns usually offer little after 8pm.

Where to Eat

New Zealand has undergone a dining revolution in the past few decades. The range of places to eat, from fish-and-chip shops to swanky cafes, ethnic restaurants, gastropubs and fine-dining establishments, has never been greater.

Once an occasional treat, eating out is now a commonplace undertaking for a multicultural country that is more food-literate than it has ever been. Principal cities like Auckland, Wellington and Christchurch offer plenty of options at most times of the day; in quieter, rural areas, you'll naturally find narrower options and opening hours. Most eating options are casual walk-ins (pubs, cafes and takeaways), but book top-end restaurants in advance.

Restaurants Open for dinner and lunch. 'Modern NZ' means locally sourced, top-quality fare with international influences.

Cafes Locally roasted beans, expert baristas, savvy breakfast-to-lunch food and usually family-friendly.

Takeaways Thai, Chinese, Indian...the big internationals are here, but the plastic-free revolution is creating a stir when it comes to eco-options.

Pubs and bars You can get a bite to eat at most Kiwi bars and pubs – from standard stodge to delicately wrought tapas and farmer-sized steaks.

Supermarkets In all sizeable towns and offering a huge variety of food, including healthy and gluten-free options. Open until 9pm; later in city centres.

Plan Your Trip
Family Travel

New Zealand's a dream for family travel: kid-centric activities, family-friendly accommodation, a moderate climate and very little danger. Unadventurous palates can always be accommodated and food servers are clued up on dietary requirements. Base yourself in a sizeable town for amenities galore and excursions within a short drive.

Children Will Love...

Beaches

Hahei Beach, Coromandel Peninsula (p232) The classic NZ summer beach.

Ngarunui Beach, Raglan (p204) Learn to surf on gentle Waikato waves in view of lifeguards.

Mt Maunganui (p332) Sand and surf for the kids, cafes and bars for the oldies.

Hot Water Beach, Coromandel Peninsula (p234) Dig your own hot pool in the sand (but check the temperature).

Long Beach, Russell (Oneroa; Long Beach Rd) A short walk or cycle from Russell, calm waters and a couple of trees for shade.

Wildlife Encounters

Kiwi Birdlife Park, Queenstown (p564) Spot a kiwi and myriad squawking birds.

Akaroa Dolphins, Akaroa (p452) Watch dolphins from a catamaran, in the company of a wildlife-spotting dog.

West Coast Wildlife Centre, Franz Josef (p606) Meet the tuatara (pint-sized dinosaurs).

Zealandia, Wellington (p383) Twittering birds in predator-free hills.

Royal Albatross Centre, Otago Peninsula (p510) Watch little penguins waddle ashore at dusk from Pilots Beach.

Aroha Island, Kerikeri (p172) Do a DIY kiwi-spotting walk at this private eco reserve.

Keeping Costs Down

Accommodation

Campsites, holiday parks and kid-friendly motels are all great options for family travel on the cheap with shared kitchens to cook in. Coastal campsites are often located near beaches and may offer other free outdoor activities. Motels sometimes include a kitchenette.

Sightseeing

Most museums, galleries, entertainment parks, wildlife sanctuaries and similar attractions offer kids' concessions and/or family tickets that let the whole tribe in for less.

Eating

Most midrange restaurants and pubs will offer a kids' menu, with choices, portions and prices adapted to the needs of younger diners. When the weather's good, hit farmers markets for an alfresco picnic, where kids don't need to sit still.

Transport

Urban transport networks all offer discounts to children and students; infants usually travel for free. When weather, terrain and your plans allow, consider kitting the family out with rental bikes to take advantage of NZ's fantastic cycling infrastructure, or the flat topography of cities like Christchurch.

Hobbiton movie set (p208), Matamata

Culture with Kids

Te Papa, Wellington (p383) Earthquakes, Māori culture and molten magma.

Auckland Museum (p91) The Auckland volcanic field and a 25m *waka taua* (war canoe).

Hobbiton, Matamata (p208) Tours of hobbit holes and a drink in the Green Dragon Inn.

Canterbury Museum, Christchurch (p424) A mummy, dinosaur bones and a cool Discovery Centre.

Puke Ariki, New Plymouth (p241) A mighty big shark plus Māori exhibits and more.

Shantytown, Greymouth (p618) All aboard a steam train for gold-panning in a recreated gold-rush town.

Active Kids

Queenstown Ice Arena (p562) Skate the rink, watch ice-hockey or hire frisbees for disc golf.

Family Adventures, Queenstown (p569) Kids as young as three can shoot the rapids on the Shotover River.

Coromandel Zipline Tours, Coromandel Peninsula (p224) Eight separate sections traversing the canopy of the Driving Creek Conservation Park.

Paddles & Saddles, Great Barrier Island (p134) Explore the island by bike, kayak or scooter.

Region by Region

Auckland Region

New Zealand's largest city is naturally chock-full of family diversions: beaches (p82), including decent surf on the west coast; the wonderful Auckland Zoo (p94); Kelly Tarlton's Sea Life Aquarium (p93); and entertaining kids' shows at Whoa! Studios (p119).

Bay of Islands & Northland

When you're not out sailing with the family, history is brought to life here at the Waitangi Treaty Ground (p168), Kerikeri Mission Station (p172), and the excellent local museums in Matakohe (p188), Dargaville (p187), Waipu (p153) and Mangawhai (p152).

Waikato & the Coromandel Peninsula

This verdant region offers kayaking around Hahei (p190) and Raglan (p200), the Hobbiton film set (p208), biking on the Hauraki Rail Trail (p224) and the glowworm-lit depths of the Waitomo Caves (p211).

Taranaki & Whanganui

Beaches are the draw here, with no crowds, endless piles of driftwood and good surf for the older kids. Taranaki's Surf Highway 45 (p255), Whanganui's beaches (p259) and New Plymouth's wild Back Beach (p247) spring to mind.

Taupo & the Ruapehu Region

Adventures here don't go to Queenstown extremes but still provide plenty of thrills. Lake Taupō (p277) offers swimming and parasailing, the Spa Park (p284) has free thermal pools, and Middle Earth fans will love Mt Ngauruhoe (p293), aka Mt Doom.

Rotorua & the Bay of Plenty

There's great family accommodation at the likes of Arista (p316), and enough sulphur scents, boiling mud and colourful features to enliven the longest stint at a geothermal field (p307). Kids can also brave Tutea Falls (p325) and splash across to the glowworm caves at Lake Okareka (p310) on stand-up paddle boards (SUPs).

East Coast

Head around East Cape (p352) for an earthy, authentic, no-frills driving tour with the kids. Empty beaches; dune-side holiday parks; fish and chips at the pub; Māori dudes with full-face *tā moko*... It's one of the last really untouristed places on the North Island.

Wellington Region

Wellington itself is small enough to feel like a kids' compact wonderland. Museums and activities here are great for kids – Te Papa (p383), Zealandia (p383) and the Cable Car (p383), especially – and there are plenty of cheap places to eat.

Christchurch & Canterbury

Urban and rural attractions alike lure families to this region, from Christchurch's magical Margaret Mahy Family Playground (p434) to the Orana Wildlife Park (p425), boating on the Avon River (p426) and horse trekking in Mackenzie Country (p477).

Dunedin & Otago

All kids will love the Otago Peninsula (p509) for wildlife, including penguins, fur seals, sea lions, albatrosses and whales. Elsewhere, there's the Otago Central Rail Trail (p514), the steampunk playground that is Ōamaru (p491) and winter sports in Naseby (p517).

Fiordland & Southland

This region is all about outdoor activities, from the all-ages splendour of Milford Sound (p553) to active farm holidays at Slope Point (p533) and the Te Anau Glowworm Caves (p548). Mechanically minded kids will love Invercargill for its two motor museums (p535) and the chance to operate huge diggers at Dig This (p535).

Queenstown & Wanaka

Queenstown (p562), the epicentre of skiing, bungy and general thrill-seeking in New Zealand, may be too extreme for some kids, but at Wānaka the over-nines can test their mettle on the much calmer via ferrata by Wild Wire (p588).

West Coast

While the wild West Coast is less populated and accessible than most parts of NZ, kids will love the re-created gold-rush-era Shantytown (p618), family-friendly rafting (p632) and the chance to net crayfish at the National Kiwi Centre (p613).

Nelson & Marlborough

More than just wineries and wilderness walks, this region offers plenty for families, including Nelson's Tahunanui Beach (p635), kayaking tours in Abel Tasman National Park (p651), and fishing and a petting zoo at the Anatoki Salmon (p654) hatchery.

Good to Know

Look out for the c icon for family-friendly suggestions throughout this guide.

Babies and toddlers Attitudes to public breast-feeding are pretty enlightened throughout New Zealand, while infant formula, nappies and other essentials are readily available in supermarkets, pharmacies and smaller groceries.

Dining out The golden rule is 'be considerate': kids are welcome in most eating establishments, but their behaviour is your responsibility, and fine-dining patrons will expect to enjoy an adults-only environment. Generally, licensed establishments such as pubs welcome well-behaved kids, but not after dinner time.

Prams and pushchairs New Zealand's cities are well paved, well lit and easy to negotiate for parents pushing prams and pushchairs.

Seat belts Everyone must wear seat belts while in moving vehicles, with appropriately anchored chairs and capsules mandated by law for the very youngest.

Public transport Kids' discounts of different kinds exist for all mass-transit systems in New Zealand. Infants travel free.

Hire vehicles If your kids are little, check that your car-hire company can supply the right-sized car seat for your child, and that the seat will be properly fitted. Some companies legally require you to fit car seats yourself. Consider hiring a campervan. These formidable beasts are every-where in NZ, kitted out with beds, kitchens, and even toilets and TVs.

Useful Resources

Lonely Planet Kids (www.lonelyplanetkids.com) Loads of activities and great family-travel blog content.

LetsGoKids (http://letsgokids.co.nz) Download the NZ edition for family travel inspiration and money-saving vouchers.

Kidspot (www.kidspot.co.nz) The 'Family Fun' section has suggestions for child-friendly activi-ties, road trips and more.

Kids' Corner

Say What?

Hello.	Kia ora
Swimsuit.	Togs
Flip-flops/ thongs.	Jandals.
Good.	Sweet as

Did You Know?

- The smallest coin here is the copper 10c coin.

Have You Tried?

Lemon & Paeroa (L&P)
A sweet soft drink

FADHLI ADNAN/SHUTTERSTOCK ©

Regions at a Glance

Auckland Region

Coastline
Eating & Drinking
Volcanoes

Beaches
From the calm, child-friendly bays facing the Hauraki Gulf to the Insta-famous black-sand surf beaches of the west coast, ocean lovers really are spoilt here.

Global Dining
Auckland has some of the nation's best fine dining and ethnically diverse restaurants, a lively cafe and bar scene, and wine regions on three of its flanks.

City of Cones
Auckland is, quite literally, a global hotspot, with more than 50 separate volcanoes forming its unique topography. Take a hike up one of the landscape's dormant cones for a high, wide and handsome city panorama.

p78

Bay of Islands & Northland

Coastline
Wilderness
History

Beaches & Bays
Beaches and beautiful bays line Northland's east coast, making it a favourite spot for families, surfers and fishing enthusiasts. To the west, long windswept beaches stretch for dozens of kilometres, in places forming towering sand dunes.

Giant Forests
Kauri forests once blanketed NZ's north, and in the pockets where the giants remain, particularly in the Waipoua Forest, they're an imposing sight.

Historic Sites
New Zealand was settled top down by both Māori and Europeans, with missionaries erecting the country's oldest surviving buildings in Kerikeri. In nearby Waitangi, the treaty that founded the modern nation was first signed.

p147

Waikato & the Coromandel Peninsula

Coastline
Towns
Caves

Beaches & Surf
Find safe swimming and world-class surf at legendary Manu Bay. Beaches on the Coromandel are extremely popular in summer, but glorious isolation can still be yours.

Small-Town Vibes
Friendly smaller towns in the Waikato such as Te Aroha, Cambridge, Matamata and Raglan have great pubs, cafes and restaurants. On the Coromandel note the Gold Rush roots of Thames and Coromandel Town.

Waitomo Caves
Don't miss Waitomo, NZ's most staggering cave complex. Go black-water rafting along underground rivers or simply float through grottoes speckled with glowworms.

p189

Taranaki & Whanganui

Wilderness
Cities
Coastline

National Parks

Whanganui National Park offers canoeing and kayaking amid the wilderness surrounding the Whanganui River. Near New Plymouth, Mt Taranaki is a picture-perfect peak with fabulous hiking.

Underrated Cities

New Plymouth, Whanganui and Palmerston North are mid-sized cities often overlooked by travellers. Visit for fantastic restaurants and bars, great coffee, wonderful museums and laid-back locals.

Empty Beaches

Hit Surf Highway 45 south of New Plymouth for black-sand beaches and gnarly breaks. Whanganui offers remote, storm-buffeted beaches, while the Horowhenua District has acres of empty brown sand.

p240

Taupō & the Ruapehu Region

Wilderness
Scenery
Outdoor
Activities

Lake & Rivers

New Zealand's mightiest river (the Waikato) is born from NZ's greatest lake (Taupō). Their chilly waters are scenic settings for water sports and activities. And hot springs bubble up on the lakeside and riverbank.

Dramatic Lands

Three steaming, smoking, occasionally erupting volcanoes – Ruapehu, Tongariro and Ngauruhoe – are an imposing sight, and the focus of skiing in winter and hiking the rest of the year.

Extreme Taupō

Skydiving, bungy jumping, white-water rafting, jet-boating, mountain biking, wakeboarding, parasailing, skiing – Taupō has 'em all. Plus the buzz of hiking through a geothermal wonderland.

p275

Rotorua & the Bay of Plenty

Geothermal
Activity
Indigenous
Culture
Activities

Volcanic Hubbub

The Rotorua landscape is littered with geysers, geothermal vents and hot springs. After a day exploring the region, book a soak in a thermal spa.

Māori Culture

Engage with Māori culture in Rotorua. A slew of Māori-owned outfits offer cultural experiences, most involving a traditional dance and musical performance, a *haka* (war dance) and a *hāngi* (Māori earth-cooked feast).

Outdoor Sports

Try mountain biking, paragliding, OGOing, luging, white-water rafting, stand up paddle boarding, kayaking... Or just swim at the beach.

p304

The East Coast

Coastline
Wine
Architecture

Coastal Scenery

Follow in the footsteps (or rather wake) of early Māori and James Cook along this stretch of coastline, home to the East Cape Lighthouse and Cape Kidnappers' gaggling gannet colony.

Wine Regions

Sip your way through Gisborne's bright chardonnays, then head to Hawke's Bay for seriously good Bordeaux-style reds and fine winery dining.

Art-Deco Napier

Napier's art-deco town centre is a magnet for architecture lovers, the keenest of whom time their visit for the annual Art Deco Festival, an extravaganza of music, wine, vintage cars and flapper costumes.

p347

Wellington Region

Arts
Eating & Drinking
Nightlife

Museums & Galleries

Crowbarred into the city centre are quality display spaces including the interactive Te Papa museum and internationally flavoured City Gallery Wellington.

Coffee & Craft Beer

With more than a dozen roasters and scores of cafes, Wellington remains the coffee capital of New Zealand. The city also hosts a happening craft-beer scene and great dining options.

Bar Hopping

Between the boho bars around Cuba St and Courtenay Pl's drinking dens, you should find enough to keep you entertained until sun-up.

p381

Christchurch & Canterbury

History
Outdoor Activities
Scenery

Christchurch Remade

Post-earthquake Christchurch is an architectural mash-up of heritage buildings and creative modern design. Learn about the French and British colonial story in diminutive Akaroa.

Walking & Kayaking

Explore alpine valleys around Arthur's Pass, kayak on Akaroa Harbour, or visit Aoraki/Mt Cook National Park for hiking and kayaking amid majestic glacial lakes.

Banks Peninsula & the Southern Alps

Descend from Banks Peninsula's Summit Rd to explore hidden bays and coves. Experience nature's grand scale in the river valleys, soaring peaks and glaciers of the Southern Alps.

p418

Dunedin & Otago

Wildlife
Wineries
History

Birds, Seals & Sea Lions

Seals, sea lions and penguins patrol the Otago Peninsula, while rocky Taiaroa Head is the planet's only mainland breeding location for the magnificent royal albatross.

Otago Wine Regions

Barrel into the craggy valleys of Bannockburn for excellent vineyard restaurants or delve into the up-and-coming Waitaki Valley wine scene for riesling and pinot gris.

Steam Punk & Victoriana

Explore the artsy and storied streets of Dunedin, or escape by foot or penny-farthing bicycle into the heritage ambience of Ōamaru's Victorian Precinct.

p487

Fiordland & Southland

Scenery
Outdoor Activities
Cruises & Coasts

Panoramic Landscapes

The star of the show is remarkable Milford Sound, but take time to explore the rugged Catlins coast or remote, end-of-the-world Stewart Island/Rakiura.

Mountain Walks

Fiordland National Park comprises much of New Zealand's precious Te Wāhipounamu (Southwest New Zealand) World Heritage Area. Further south, Rakiura National Park showcases Stewart Island's beauty.

Just Get Wet

Cruise or kayak around glorious Doubtful Sound, test the surf in Curio Bay or get sprayed by waterfalls in the Catlins.

p524

Queenstown & Wānaka

Outdoor Activities
Scenery
Wine

Extreme Queenstown

Few places on earth offer so many adventurous activities: bungy jumping, river rafting, skiing and and mountain biking... only scratch Queenstown's adrenaline-fuelled surface.

Mountains & Lakes

Queenstown's combination of Lake Wakatipu and the soaring Remarkables is a real jaw-dropper. Or venture into prime NZ wilderness around Glenorchy and Mt Aspiring National Park.

Southern Wineries

Start with lunch at Amisfield Winery's excellent restaurant, then explore the Gibbston sub-region and finish with a riesling tasting at Rippon, overlooking gorgeous Lake Wānaka.

p556

The West Coast

Natural Wonders
Outdoor Activities
History

Natural Wonders

This region is replete with prehistoric wonders: don't miss Oparara's famous arches, Punakaiki's Pancake Rocks and the sublime Hokitika Gorge.

Hiking Wilderness

Expect dramatic views along hour-long tracks and hardcore epics, like the wind-scoured, wildlife-rich Cape Foulwind Walkway.

Pioneering Heritage

The West Coast's raffish pioneering heritage comes vividly to life in places like Reefton and Shantytown (Greymouth), and in ghost towns like Waiuta.

p598

Nelson & Marlborough

Wine
Wilderness
Wildlife

Marlborough Wine Region

Bobbing in Marlborough's sea of sauvignon blanc, riesling, pinot noir and bubbly are barrel loads of quality cellar-door experiences and regional food.

National Parks

Not satisfied with just one national park, the Nelson region has three: Nelson Lakes, Kahurangi and Abel Tasman. You could hike in all three over a week.

Kaikōura Wildlife

The South Island is home to a menagerie of creatures, both in the water and on the wing. There's myriad wildlife tours on water and wing too.

p633

On the Road

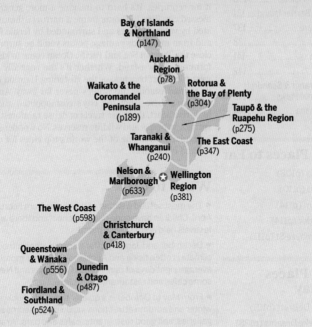

Bay of Islands & Northland (p147)

Auckland Region (p78)

Rotorua & the Bay of Plenty (p304)

Waikato & the Coromandel Peninsula (p189)

Taupō & the Ruapehu Region (p275)

Taranaki & Whanganui (p240)

The East Coast (p347)

Nelson & Marlborough (p633)

Wellington Region (p381)

The West Coast (p598)

Christchurch & Canterbury (p418)

Queenstown & Wānaka (p556)

Dunedin & Otago (p487)

Fiordland & Southland (p524)

Auckland Region

Best Places to Eat

➡ Cassia (p108)

➡ Azabu (p110)

➡ Nanam (p114)

➡ Cazador (p114)

➡ Gemmayze St (p111)

Best Places to Stay

➡ Hotel DeBrett (p101)

➡ Waiheke Dreams (p128)

➡ XSPOT (p135)

➡ Ascot Parnell (p106)

➡ Piha Beachstay –
Jandal Palace (p138)

Why Go?

Paris may be the city of love, but Auckland is the city of many lovers, according to its Māori name, Tāmaki Makaurau. Those lovers so desired this place that they fought over it for centuries. It's hard to imagine a more geographically blessed city. Two harbours frame a narrow isthmus punctuated by volcanic cones and surrounded by fertile farmland, and from numerous vantage points you'll be surprised how close the Tasman Sea and Pacific Ocean come to kissing and forming a new island. Whether it's the ruggedly beautiful west-coast surf beaches, or the glistening Hauraki Gulf with its myriad islands, the water's never far away. And within an hour's drive from the city's cosmopolitan and diverse high-rise heart, there are tracts of dense rainforest, thermal springs, wineries and wildlife reserves. No wonder Auckland is regularly rated one of the world's top cities for quality of life and liveability.

When to Go

➡ The most settled weather of the year is from February to April. Children have gone back to school and there are many festivals held across these months.

➡ December and January offer warm weather, although the climate is often fickle and Auckland's summer months still average eight days of rain. Across Christmas and New Year some cafes and restaurants may close.

➡ From May to October is a quieter time, with Auckland's winter and autumn attractions including museums and galleries, and good restaurants, cafes and bars. Wrap up warmly for boat trips.

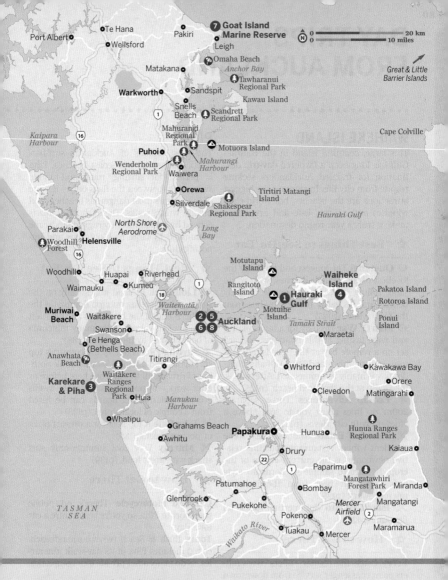

Auckland Highlights

1 **Hauraki Gulf** (p124) Getting out on the water and visiting its island sanctuaries.

2 **Auckland volcanic field** (p123) Going with the flows, exploring Auckland's volcanic mountains, lakes and islands.

3 **West-coast beaches** (p137) Treading the black sands of Karekare and Piha.

4 **Waiheke Island** (p124) Schlepping around world-class wineries and beaches.

5 **Ponsonby** (p116) Buzzing around the cafes, restaurants and bars of the city's hippest inner suburb.

6 **Auckland Museum** (p91) Gaping at the Māori treasures and visiting the eruption

simulation and war memorial galleries.

7 **Goat Island Marine Reserve** (p145) Swimming with the fish a few steps from the beach at this pretty bay.

8 **Pasifika Festival** (p100) Soaking up the Polynesian vibe at this massive March festival at Western Springs Park.

DAY TRIPS FROM AUCKLAND

WAIHEKE ISLAND

This large, beautiful island in the Hauraki Gulf has long been a favoured day-trip destination for frazzled Aucklanders seeking respite from city life. In summer the biggest attractions are the beaches, but world-class wineries and a lively cafe and arts scene make it truly a year-round destination.

☆ Best Things to See/Do/Eat

⊙ **Onetangi** The longest and arguably the loveliest of the island's beaches, with white sand, rolling waves and a couple of lively beach bars. It's easily reached by bus from the ferry wharf. (p125)

⊙ **Man O' War** Drop by for a tapas platter and wine tasting at this boutique vineyard set on a remote bay at the less-visited 'bottom end' of the island; the Valhalla chardonnay is highly recommended. Afterwards, take a dip at the sheltered beach. (p125)

🏄 **EcoZip Adventures** Three separate 200m zip lines allow you to soar above a vineyard with city views. (p127)

✖ **Tantalus Estate** Waiheke has some excellent winery restaurants, but this relative newcomer is the current cream of the crop. Be sure to sample its Bordeaux-style reds and craft beer from the in-house microbrewery. (p129)

✖ **Island Gelato** Summertime seasonal flavours. (p129)

☆ How to Get There

Ferry Catch the regular Fullers (www.full-ers.co.nz) passenger service from downtown Auckland or drive onto a Sealink (www.seal-ink.co.nz) car ferry at either Wynyard Wharf or Half Moon Bay.

PIHA

The most famous of Auckland's surf-battered, black-sand, west-coast beaches, Piha is perfect for surfing, rough-and-tumble swimming (between the flags only – it's one of the region's most dangerous beaches) and moody, wintry walks. The offshore drama is echoed by a magnificently rugged landscape dominated by large rock outcrops and imposing cliffs.

☆ Best Things to See/Do/Eat

⊙ **Lion Rock** Perched majestically on the sands, this imposing outcrop dominates the southern end of the beach. It's all that's left of an ancient volcano after many millennia of being lashed by the ocean. (p138)

🏄 **Surfing** Piha is one of the country's top surf spots, and aficionados will think nothing of driving all the way out here before or after work – or pulling a sickie if the swells are particularly fine. Boards can be hired from a couple of local stores. (p138)

✖ **Piha Cafe** A top spot for a presurf pizza or postsurf beer. (p139)

✖ **Murray** Very cool summer-only surf shack with great food. (p139)

☆ How to Get There

Car and motorcycle There's no public transport to Piha, so you're best to hire a car for a day.

Tours Bush & Beach (www.bushandbeach. co.nz) includes Piha in its day-walk itineraries, as do many other private tour companies.

LEIGH

Nestled at the far northern edge of the Auckland Region, little Leigh is worth visiting for two things: Goat Island Marine Reserve and the Leigh Sawmill Cafe. It can be combined with a day trip to Bohemian Puhoi or the vineyard and craft beer scene of Matakana.

☆ Best Things to See/Do/Eat

◉ Goat Island Marine Reserve In just over 40 years since it was declared a reserve, the marine population in the waters around Goat Island has exploded. Step out from the beach and you'll see plenty of fish; go deeper and put on goggles and you'll see even more. (p145)

Goat Island sits offshore and is surrounded by dive spots with visibility claimed to be 10m or more, 75% of the time. You can also snorkel or dive directly from the beach.

The area was the landing place of a Māori ancestral canoe, and you can browse the interpretive panels to learn about the area's historical significance, as well as the fish species you'll encounter in the reserve.

◉ Goat Island Marine Discovery Centre Children will love the tide pool full of marine creatures, and the interactive marine life exhibits are fascinating. Marine experts and graduate students from the University of Auckland make up the staff. (p145)

⚲ Glass Bottom Boat Tours An easy way to experience Goat Island's marine life without getting wet. (p146)

⚲ Leigh Sawmill Cafe After a day's splashing about, grab a crispy pizza and a beer in the garden bar. However, this place really comes into its own as a live-music venue; check the website to see what's on. (p146)

☆ How to Get There

Car and motorcycle There's no public transport, so consider hiring a car for the day. Head north on SH1 and either continue on the Northern Gateway Toll Road or take the scenic route through Orewa. Leave SH1 at Warkworth and follow the signs.

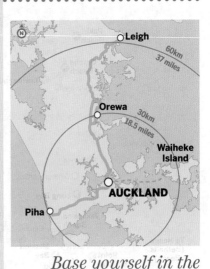

Base yourself in the centre of NZ's biggest city to explore all of the surrounding region, including the Hauraki Gulf islands and beautiful beaches to the west and north.

AUCKLAND'S BEACHES

Pakiri Beach
Goat Island
Leigh
Omaha Beach
Tawharanui
Warkworth
Great Barrier Island
Medlands Beach
Tryphena
SOUTH PACIFIC OCEAN
Hauraki Gulf
Kakanui
Puhoi
Orewa
Whangaparāoa
Helensville
Long Bay
Takapuna Beach
Rangitoto Island
Oneroa
Palm Beach
Onetangi Beach
Te Henga (Bethells Beach)
Devonport
Mission Bay
Waiheke Island
Point Chevalier
Auckland
Tamaki Strait
Firth of Thames
Piha Beach
0   20 km
0   10 miles

HARBOUR BEACHES

Nestled within Auckland's central suburbs is a succession of small, sheltered bays. Other worthwhile contenders include **Orakei**, **Kohimarama**, **St Heliers** and nude-friendly **Ladies Bay**.

☆ Mission Bay

The most famous of the city beaches, Mission Bay offers views to Rangitoto Island, a toddler-splash-friendly art-deco fountain, excellent people-watching, and a bustling strip of cafes, bars and restaurants.

☆ Point Chevalier

It's only good for swimming an hour either side of high tide, but this beach is beloved by locals for its child-friendly waveless waters, swimming pontoons and oodles of shade provided by a sheltering band of spectacular pohutukawa trees.

NORTH SHORE BEACHES

Fine swimming beaches stretch from North Head to Long Bay. The gulf islands shelter them from strong surf, making them safe for supervised children. Aim for high tide unless you fancy a lengthy walk to waist-deep water. **Cheltenham Beach** is a short walk from Devonport. Heading north there's **Narrow Neck**, **St Leonards** (popular with gay men and naturists), **Takapuna**, **Milford** and a succession of suburban beaches known collectively as the **East Coast Bays**.

☆ Takapuna

Takapuna is Auckland's answer to Bondi: it's the city's most popular beach, it's the closest ocean beach to the city centre, and it's backed by a busy town centre. There's a terrific cafe, the **Takapuna Beach Cafe** (p114), down the northern end should you get the hankering for lunch or an ice cream, and further options a couple of streets back.

Proximity to the water is a defining feature of Auckland life, and the city is blessed with a huge diversity of beautiful beaches. Here are some of the best.

☆ Long Bay

The northernmost of Auckland's East Coast Bays, Long Bay is a popular family picnic and swimming spot, attracting more than a million visitors a year. A three-hour-return coastal walk heads north from the sandy beach to the Okura River, taking in secluded Grannys Bay and Pohutukawa Bay (which attracts nude bathers).

WEST COAST BEACHES

The west coast's black sands and wild surf aren't for the fainthearted, but it's here that you'll find some of the most spectacular beaches in the country. They're also incredibly dangerous: swim between the flags. As well as the two listed here, check out **Karekare**, **Anawhata** and **Muriwai**.

☆ Piha

One of NZ's most famous beaches, Piha offers kilometres of black sand, reliable surf breaks and an exceptionally beautiful setting.

☆ Te Henga (Bethells Beach)

Aside from the super-clear waters and black sands of the main beach, there's a small, swimmable lake tucked among the dunes and an excellent little **food-truck cafe** (p139) for postsurf burgers and cake.

ISLAND BEACHES

All of the islands of the Hauraki Gulf have wonderful swimming spots, but the two largest – Waiheke and Great Barrier – have the longest, most spectacular beaches. Waiheke Islanders will argue the case between **Onetangi** and **Palm Beach** as the island's best beach, while others prefer the sheltered coves of **Little Oneroa** or isolated **Man O' War Bay**. You're more likely to get the beach to yourself on distant Great Barrier, especially in places like **Whangapoua**, **Kaitoke**, **Awana Bay** and **Harataonga**. If you've got access to a boat, explore the bays of Motutapu, Motuihe, Rotoroa, Rakino and Kawau Islands.

☆ Onetangi

There's plenty of space for sandcastles, Frisbees, cricket and sun worshipping on the fine white sands of Waiheke's longest beach, with a couple of cafe-bars near at hand.

☆ Medlands

Remote Great Barrier Island has lots of gorgeous beaches and very few people. This spectacular stretch of white sand gazes straight out across the vastness of the Pacific.

NORTH AUCKLAND BEACHES

The beautiful beaches of the increasingly built-up Hibiscus Coast stretch north from the Whangaparāoa Peninsula and include **Manly**, **Stanmore Bay**, **Red Beach**, **Orewa**, **Hatfields Beach** and **Waiwera**. Beyond these are a succession of regional parks: Wenderholm, Mahurangi, Scandrett and Tawharanui, each with unspoilt and often empty stretches of sand. To the north you'll pass the small beach settlements of Omaha and Leigh, before you hit the fish-filled **Goat Island Marine Reserve** (great for snorkelling) and the dazzling Pakiri.

☆ Tawharanui

A partly unsealed road leads to this 588-hectare reserve at the end of a peninsula. This special place is an open sanctuary for native birds, protected by a pest-proof fence, while the northern coast is a marine park. There are plenty of walking tracks, but the main attraction is Anchor Bay, one of the region's finest white-sand beaches. Camping is allowed at two basic sites near the beach.

☆ Pakiri

Blissful, remote Pakiri Beach, 12km past Goat Island, is an unspoilt expanse of white sand and rolling surf – a large chunk of which is a protected regional park. **Pakiri Horse Riding** (☑ 09-422 6275; www.horseride-nz.co.nz; Rahuikiri Rd) has 60 horses available for superb bush-and-beach rides, along with accommodation scattered along the dunes.

ESSENTIAL AUCKLAND

Eat amid the diverse and cosmopolitan scene of Karangahape Rd (p111).

Drink world-class craft beer at the Beer Spot (p140) or the Sawmill Brewery (p145).

Read *Under the Mountain* (1979) – Maurice Gee's teenage tale of slimy things lurking under Auckland's volcanoes.

Listen to *Lightsleeper* (2018), the melodic father-and-son musings from Neil and Liam Finn.

Watch *Outrageous Fortune* (2005–10), the wildly entertaining TV comedy-drama about West Auckland's fictional West family.

Celebrate at Pasifika (p100).

Go online at www.aucklandnz.com; www.lonelyplanet.com/new-zealand/auckland.

🛈 Getting There & Away

Auckland is linked to the rest of the world with direct flights to/from Asia, North America, South America, Australia and the South Pacific. Domestic flights reach all parts of the country, and buses or trains head north and south to the Bay of Islands, Hamilton, Wellington and other provincial centres. Ferries are a vital service to reach Waiheke, Great Barrier and the other islands of the Hauraki Gulf. Auckland Transport (p123) has information on using buses, trains and ferries to get around Auckland and the surrounding region.

AUCKLAND

POP 1.69 MILLION

History

Māori occupation in the Auckland area dates back around 800 years. Initial settlements were concentrated on the Hauraki Gulf islands, but gradually the fertile isthmus beckoned and land was cleared for growing food.

Over hundreds of years Tāmaki's many different tribes wrestled for control of the area, building *pā* (fortified villages) on the numerous volcanic cones. The Ngāti Whatua *iwi* (tribe) from Kaipara Harbour gained the upper hand in 1741, occupying the major *pā* sites. But during the Musket Wars of the 1820s, they were decimated by the northern tribe Ngāpuhi, leaving the land all but abandoned.

When the Treaty of Waitangi was signed in 1840, Governor Hobson had his base in the Bay of Islands. When Ngāti Whatua chief Te Kawau offered 3000 acres (1214 hectares) of land for sale on the northern edge of the Waitematā Harbour, Hobson decided to create a new capital, naming it after one of his patrons, George Eden (Earl of Auckland).

Beginning with just a few tents on a beach, the settlement grew quickly, and soon the port was busy exporting the region's produce, including kauri timber. However, it lost its capital status to centrally located Wellington after just 25 years.

Since the beginning of the 20th century, Auckland has been New Zealand's fastest-growing city and its main industrial centre. Political deals may be done in Wellington, but Auckland is the big smoke in the land of the long white cloud.

In 2010 the municipalities and urban districts that made up the Auckland Region were merged into one 'super-city', and in 2011 the newly minted metropolis was given a buff and shine to prepare it for hosting the Rugby World Cup. The waterfront was redeveloped, the art gallery and zoo were given a makeover, and a swag of new restaurants and bars popped up – leaving a more vibrant city in the Cup's wake.

The years since then have seen Auckland maintain its impetuous growth and increasingly multicultural make-up – it is the preferred destination for new immigrants to NZ – and while housing prices and traffic snarls continue to frustrate residents, it's still thrillingly and energetically the only true international city in the country.

◉ Sights

Auckland is a city of volcanoes, with the ridges of lava flows forming its main thoroughfares and its many cones providing islands of green. As well as being by far the largest, it's also the most multicultural of NZ's cities. A sizeable Asian community rubs shoulders with the biggest Polynesian population of any city in the world.

The traditional Kiwi aspiration for a free-standing house on a quarter-acre section has resulted in a vast, sprawling city. The CBD was long ago abandoned to commerce, and inner-city apartment living has only recently caught on. While geography has been kind, city planning has been less so. Unbridled and ill-conceived development has left the centre of the city with plenty of architectural embarrassments. To get under Auckland's skin you're best to head to the streets of Victorian and Edwardian villas in hip inner-city suburbs such as Ponsonby, Grey Lynn, Kingsland and Mt Eden.

◉ City Centre & Britomart

Stretching for only a small grid of blocks above the train station, Britomart is a compact enclave of historic buildings and new developments that has been transformed into one of the city's best eating, drinking and shopping precincts. Most of Auckland's top fashion designers have recently decamped to the Britomart area from further uptown in High St.

★ Auckland Art Gallery   GALLERY
(Toi o Tāmaki; Map p88; ☑ 09-379 1349; www.aucklandartgallery.com; cnr Kitchener & Wellesley Sts; adult/student/child $20/17/free; ☉ 10am-5pm) Auckland's premier art repository has a striking glass-and-wood atrium grafted onto its 1887 French chateau frame. It showcases the best of NZ art, along with important works by Pieter Bruegel the Younger, Guido Reni, Picasso, Cézanne, Gauguin and Matisse. Highlights include the intimate 19th-century portraits of tattooed Māori subjects by Charles Goldie, and the starkly dramatic text-scrawled canvases of Colin McCahon.

Free 60-minute tours depart from the foyer daily at 11.30am and 1.30pm.

Albert Park   PARK
(Map p88; Princes St) Hugging the hill on the city's eastern flank, Albert Park is a charming Victorian formal garden overrun by students from the neighbouring University of Auckland during term time. The park was once part of the Albert Barracks (1847), a fortification that enclosed 9 hectares during the New Zealand Wars. A portion of the original barracks wall survives at the centre of the university campus.

Sky Tower   TOWER
(Map p88; ☑ 09-363 6000; www.skycityauckland.co.nz; cnr Federal & Victoria Sts; adult/child $32/13; ☉ 8.30am-10.30pm Sun-Thu, to 11.30pm Fri & Sat Nov-Apr, 9am-10pm May-Oct) The impossible-to-miss Sky Tower looks like a giant hypodermic giving a fix to the heavens. Spectacular lighting renders it space age at night and the colours change for special events. At 328m it is the southern hemisphere's tallest structure. A lift takes you up to the observation decks in 40 stomach-lurching seconds; look down through the glass floor panels if you're after an extra kick. Consider visiting at sunset and having a drink in the Sky Lounge Cafe & Bar.

The Sky Tower is also home to the Sky-Walk (p97) and SkyJump (p97).

AUCKLAND REGION AUCKLAND

AUCKLAND IN...

Two Days
Start by acquainting yourself with the inner city. Begin by walking from Karangahape Rd (K Rd; p90) to the Wynyard Quarter (p87), stopping along the way to have at least a quick whizz around the NZ section of the Auckland Art Gallery. Catch a ferry to Devonport (p93), head up North Head (p93) and cool down at Cheltenham Beach (weather and tide permitting), before ferrying back to the city for dinner.

On day two, head up One Tree Hill (p94), wander around Cornwall Park and then visit the Auckland Museum (p91) and Domain (p91). Take a trip along Tamaki Dr (p92), stopping at Bastion (p93) or Achilles Point (p92) to enjoy the harbour views. Spend the evening dining and bar hopping in Ponsonby (p116).

Four Days
On the third day, get out on the Hauraki Gulf (p124). Catch the ferry to Waiheke Island (p124) and divide your time between the beaches and the wineries.

For your final day, head west. Grab breakfast in Titirangi (p137) before exploring the Waitākere Ranges Regional Park (p138), Karekare (p137) and Piha (p138). Freshen up for a night on the town in Britomart.

Auckland

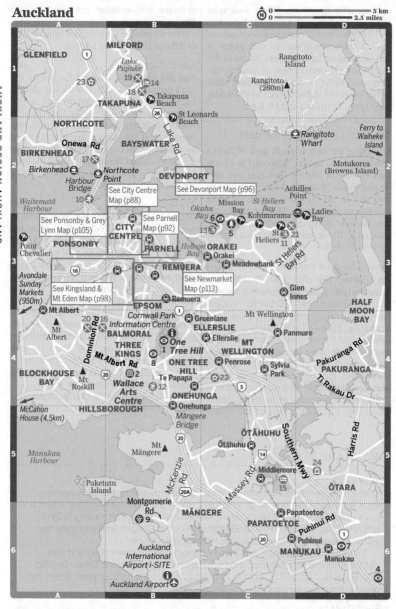

Civic Theatre   THEATRE
(Map p88; ☎ 09-309 2677; www.aucklandlive.co.nz/
venue/the-civic; cnr Queen & Wellesley Sts) The
'mighty Civic' (1929) is one of only seven 'atmospheric theatres' remaining in the world
and a fine survivor from cinema's Golden

Age. The auditorium has lavish Moorish decoration and a starlit southern-hemisphere
night sky in the ceiling, complete with cloud
projections and shooting stars. It's mainly
used for touring musicals, international concerts and film-festival screenings.

Auckland

Old Government House   HISTORIC BUILDING
(Map p88; Waterloo Quadrant; FREE) Built in 1856, this stately building was the colony's seat of power until 1865 when Wellington became the capital. The construction is unusual in that it's actually wooden but made to look like stone. It's now used by the University of Auckland, but feel free to wander through the lush gardens.

University Clock Tower   ARCHITECTURE
(Map p88; 22 Princes St) The University Clock Tower is Auckland's architectural triumph. This stately 'ivory' tower (1926) tips its hat to art nouveau (the incorporation of NZ flora and fauna into the decoration) and the Chicago School (the way it's rooted into the earth). It's usually open, so wander inside.

St Patrick's Cathedral   CHURCH
(Map p88; ☑ 09-303 4509; www.stpatricks.org.nz; 43 Wyndham St; ⊙ 7am-7pm) Auckland's Catholic cathedral (1907) is one of the city's loveliest buildings. Polished wood and Belgian stained glass lend warmth to the interior of the majestic Gothic Revival church. There's a historical display in the old confessional on the left-hand side.

Lighthouse   PUBLIC ART
(Map p88; Queens Wharf) Auckland's most recent installation of public art is this replica 'state house' – a form of public housing popular in NZ in the 1930s and 1940s – erected by artist Michael Parekōwhai at the end of Queens Wharf in early 2017. Maōri-influenced *tukutuku* (woven flax) panels punctuate the exterior, while inside is a neon-lit, stainless-steel representation of British maritime explorer Captain James Cook. The house's idiosyncratic design is a commentary on sovereignty and colonialism. Best visited after dark.

◉ Viaduct Harbour & Wynyard Quarter

Once a busy commercial port, the Viaduct Harbour was given a major makeover for the 1999/2000 and 2003 America's Cup yachting events. It's now a fancy dining and boozing precinct, and guaranteed to have at least a slight buzz any night of the week. Historical plaques, public sculpture and the chance to gawk at millionaires' yachts make it a diverting place for a stroll.

Connected to the Viaduct by a bascule bridge, Wynyard Quarter opened in advance of another sporting tournament, 2011's Rugby World Cup. With its public plazas, waterfront eateries, events centre, fish market and children's playground, it has quickly become Auckland's favourite new place to promenade. At the Silo Park area, down the western end, free outdoor Friday-night movies and weekend markets have become summertime institutions. Most of Wynyard's better restaurants are set back from the water, on Jellicoe St.

New Zealand Maritime Museum   MUSEUM
(Map p88; ☑ 09-373 0800; www.maritimemuseum. co.nz; 149-159 Quay St, Viaduct Harbour; adult/ child $20/10, incl harbour cruise $53/27; ⊙ 10am-5pm, free tours 10.30am & 1pm Mon-Fri) This museum traces NZ's seafaring history, from Māori voyaging canoes to the America's

City Centre

500 m
0.25 miles

See Parnell Map (p92)

Silo Park

Wynyard Wharf

Sealink

Ferry to Great Barrier Island

Wynyard Quarter

Karanga Kiosk

Viaduct Events Centre

Viaduct Harbour

Hobson Wharf

Princes Wharf

DOC Auckland Visitor Centre

Princes Wharf i-SITE

Fullers

Pier 2

Ferry Building

Queens Wharf

Waitematā Harbour

Marsden Wharf

Captain Cook Wharf

Bledisloe Wharf

Bledisloe Terminal

Bledisloe Wharf

Britomart

Queen Elizabeth Sq

Albert Park

Victoria Park

Victoria Park Market

SkyCity i-SITE

SkyCity Coach Terminal

Auckland Bridge Climb & Bungy (1.5km)

Jellicoe St
Daldy St
Madden St
Beaumont St
Halsey St
Gaunt St
Fanshawe St
Customs St W
Nelson St
Market Pl
Sturdee St
Hobson St
Wyndham St
Victoria St
Wellesley St
Sale St
Franklin Rd
Victoria St
Kingston St
Albert St
Durham St
Elliot St
Federal St
Swanson St
Wolfe St
Mills La
Queen St
Customs St
Galway St
Fort La
Commerce St
Fort St
Tyler St
Gore St
Shortland St
Chancery St
Vulcan La
High St
Kitchener St
Bowen Ave
Princes St
Waterloo Qd
Bankside St
Emily Pl
Beach Rd
Quay St
Tangihua St
Māhuhu Cres
Te Taoa Cres
Anzac Ave
Eden Cres
Short St
Parliament St

5
15
16
360
11
6
12
43
14
39
49
45
23
37
26
27
59
63
13
66
31
17
76
52
30
53
24
36
40
22
54
69
61
81
77
80
44
19
9
57
33
38
8
32
72
47
42
28
51

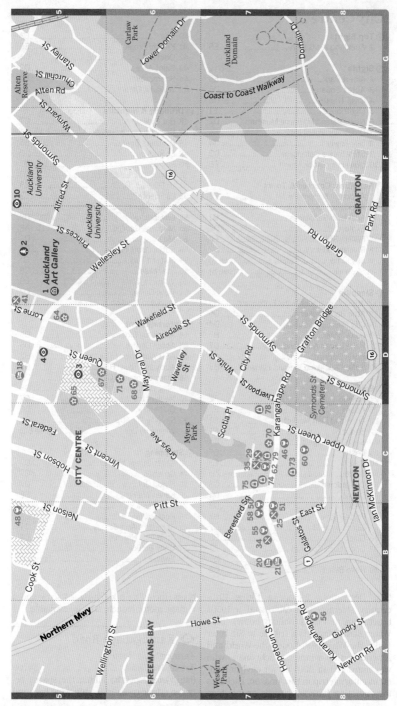

AUCKLAND REGION

89

5

6

7

8

Carlaw Park

Lower Domain Dr

Auckland Domain

Domain Dr

G

Alten Reserve

Churchill St

Stanley St

Alten Rd

Coast to Coast Walkway

Wynyard St

F

Symonds St

16

Auckland University

Alfred St

⊙10

GRAFTON

E

●2

1 Auckland Art Gallery

Princes St

Auckland University

Wellesley St

Grafton Rd

Park Rd

Lorme St

⊗41

64

Wakefield St

Airedale St

Symonds St

City Rd

Grafton Bridge

16

D

18

4

3

Queen St

67

71

68

Mayoral Dr

Waverley St

White St

Liverpool St

Karangahape Rd

Symonds St Cemetery

Symonds St

CITY CENTRE

69

Federal St

Vincent St

Greys Ave

Myers Park

Scotia Pl

78

70

Upper Queen St

Hobson St

35 29

74 62 79

46

73

60

C

Nelson St

Pitt St

75

58 50

55

25 5i

Beresford Sq

NEWTON

B

48

34

20

Galatos St

East St

Ian McKinnon Dr

21

1

Cook St

Northern Mwy

Wellington St

Howe St

FREEMANS BAY

Hopetoun St

Karangahape Rd

56

Gundry St

A

Western Park

Karangahape Rd

Newton Rd

5

6

7

8

City Centre

Cup. Recreations include a tilting 19th-century steerage-class cabin and a 1950s beach store and bach (holiday home). 'Blue Water Black Magic' is a tribute to Sir Peter Blake, the Whitbread-Round-the-World and America's Cup–winning yachtsman who was murdered in 2001 on an environmental monitoring trip in the Amazon. Packages incorporating harbour cruises on heritage boats, including a ketch-rigged scow and a vintage motor launch, are also available.

◉ Karangahape Road

Karangahape Road
Art Gallery Trail   GALLERY
(http://kroad.com/arts) Filling the spaces between ethnic restaurants, hip wine bars and

vintage-clothing shops, Karangahape Rd is home to the highest concentration of studios and art galleries in NZ. Neighbouring Ponsonby also includes public and dealer galleries, artist-run spaces and auction houses. See http://kroad.com/arts to download a map outlining different galleries and studios spaces throughout the Karangahape Rd and Ponsonby areas.

⊙ Mt Eden

★**Mt Eden**   VOLCANO
(Maungawhau; Map p98; 250 Mt Eden Rd) From the top of Auckland's highest volcanic cone (196m), the entire isthmus and both harbours are laid bare. The symmetrical crater (50m deep) is known as Te Ipu Kai a Mataaho (the Food Bowl of Mataaho, the god of things hidden in the ground) and is considered *tapu* (sacred). Do not enter it, but feel free to explore the remainder of the mountain. The remains of *pā* terraces and food-storage pits are clearly visible.

Until recently it was possible to drive right up to the summit, but concerns over erosion have led to vehicle access being restricted to travellers with limited mobility.

Paths lead up the mountain from six different directions and the walk only takes around 15 minutes, depending on your fitness. A network of boardwalks, at the time of writing scheduled to be established in mid-2020, will help protect the historical and cultural significance of the site. Catching bus 27 from Britomart to stop 1870 near Tahaki Reserve is recommended.

Start and finish your exploration of Mt Eden at the nearby **Maungawhau Visitor Experience Centre** (Te Ipu Kōrero o Maungawhau; Map p98; Puhi Huia Rd; ⊙9am-7pm). Opened in late 2019, this excellent visitor centre showcases the geological and Māori cultural history of Maungawhau/Mt Eden. Highlights include an interesting 10-minute video about Auckland's volcanic field, and there's a good cafe with innovative brunch fare and fine views of the city's isthmus location.

Eden Garden   GARDENS
(Map p113; ☑09-638 8395; www.edengarden. co.nz; 24 Omana Ave, Epsom; adult/child $12/free; ⊙9am-4pm) On Mt Eden's rocky eastern slopes, this mature garden is noted for its camellias, rhododendrons and azaleas.

⊙ Parnell & Newmarket

Parnell is one of Auckland's oldest areas, and amid the cafes, restaurants and fancy retailers are several heritage buildings. Neighbouring Newmarket is a busy shopping precinct known for its boutiques.

★**Auckland Museum**   MUSEUM
(Map p92; ☑09-309 0443; www.auckland museum.com; Auckland Domain, Parnell; adult/ child $25/10; ⊙10am-5pm) This imposing neoclassical temple (1929), capped with an impressive copper-and-glass dome (2007), dominates the Auckland Domain and is a prominent part of the Auckland skyline, especially when viewed from the harbour. Admission packages can be purchased, which incorporate a highlights tour and a Māori cultural performance ($40 to $55).

The displays of Pacific Island and Māori artefacts on the museum's ground floor are essential viewing. Highlights include a 25m war canoe and an extant carved meeting house (remove your shoes before entering). There's also a fascinating display on Auckland's volcanic field, including an eruption simulation, and the upper floors showcase military displays, fulfilling the building's dual role as a war memorial. Auckland's main Anzac commemorations take place at dawn on 25 April at the cenotaph in the museum's forecourt.

Check the website for details of interesting, one-off local and international exhibitions.

Auckland Domain   PARK
(Map p92; Domain Dr, Parnell; ⊙24hr) Covering about 80 hectares, this green swath contains the Auckland Museum, sports fields, interesting sculpture, formal gardens, wild corners and the **Wintergarden** (Map p92; Wintergarden Rd, Parnell; ⊙9am-5.30pm Mon-Sat, to 7.30pm Sun Nov-Mar, 9am-4.30pm Apr-Oct) **FREE**, with its fernery, tropical house, cool house, cute cat statue, coffee kiosk and neighbouring cafe. The mound in the centre of the park is all that remains of Pukekaroa, one of Auckland's volcanoes. At its humble peak, a totara tree surrounded by a palisade honours the first Māori king.

St Mary's Church   CHURCH
(Map p92; Parnell Rd, Parnell; ⊙10am-3pm) Next door to the **Holy Trinity Cathedral** (Map p92; ☑09-303 9500; www.holy-trinity. org.nz; cnr St Stephens Ave & Parnell Rd, Parnell;

Parnell

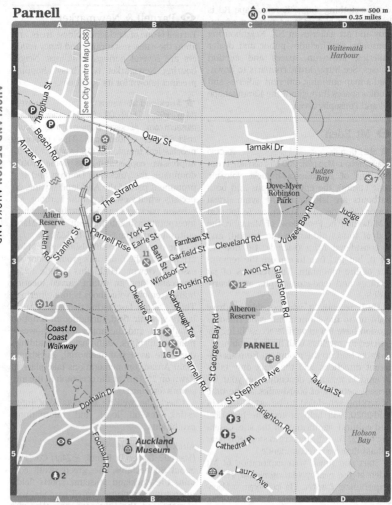

⊙10am-3pm), this wonderful wooden Gothic Revival church (1886) has a burnished interior and interesting stained-glass windows.

Kinder House   HISTORIC BUILDING
(Map p92; ☏09-379 4008; www.kinder.org.nz; 2 Ayr St, Parnell; by donation; ⊙noon-3pm Wed-Sun) Built of volcanic stone, this 1857 home displays the watercolours and memorabilia of the Reverend Dr John Kinder (1819–1903), headmaster of the Church of England Grammar School.

⊙ Tamaki Drive

This scenic, pohutukawa-lined road heads east from the city, hugging the waterfront. In summer it's a jogging, cycling and roller-blading blur.

A succession of child-friendly, peaceful swimming beaches starts at Okahu Bay. Around the headland is Mission Bay, a popular beach with an electric-lit, art-deco fountain, historic mission house, restaurants and bars. Safe swimming beaches Kohimarama and St Heliers follow. Further east along Cliff Rd, the Achilles Point Lookout

Parnell

(Map p86; Cliff Rd, St Heliers) offers panoramic views and Māori carvings. At its base is Ladies Bay, popular with nudists.

The Tamaki Link bus departing from behind Britomart station follows this route.

Kelly Tarlton's
Sea Life Aquarium   AQUARIUM
(Map p86; ✆09-531 5065; www.kellytarltons.co.nz; 23 Tamaki Dr, Orakei; adult/child $39/27; ⊗9.30am-5pm) ✎ In this topsy-turvy aquarium sharks and stingrays swim over and around you in transparent tunnels that were once stormwater tanks. You can also enter the tanks in a shark cage with a snorkel ($89). Other attractions include the Penguin Passport tour (10.30am Tuesday, Thursday and Saturday; $179 per person) where visitors can get up close with Antarctic penguins. For all tickets, there are significant discounts online, especially for midweek visits.

A free shark-shaped shuttle bus departs from the Britomart Transport Centre hourly on the half-hour from 9.30am to 3.30pm. Check the website for the exact location, as construction was taking place around central Auckland at the time of writing.

Bastion Point   PARK
(Map p86; Hapimana St, Orakei) Politics, harbour views and lush lawns combine on this pretty headland with a chequered history. An elaborate clifftop garden mausoleum honours Michael Joseph Savage (1872–1940), the country's first Labour prime minister, whose socialist reforms left him adored by the populace. Follow the lawn to a WWII gun embankment – one of many that line the harbour.

◉ Devonport

With well-preserved Victorian and Edwardian buildings and loads of cafes, Devonport is an extremely pleasant place to visit and only a short ferry trip from the city. There are also two volcanic cones to climb and easy access to the first of the North Shore's beaches.

For self-guided tours of historic buildings, pick up the *Heritage Walks of Devonport* pamphlets from the Devonport Information Centre (p121). Bikes can be hired from the ferry terminal.

Ferries to Devonport (adult/child return $15/7.50, 12 minutes) depart from the Ferry Building at least every 30 minutes from 6.15am to 11.30pm (until 1am Fridays and Saturdays), and from 7.15am to 10pm on Sundays and public holidays. Some Waiheke Island and Rangitoto ferries also stop here.

Mt Victoria (Takarunga; Map p96; Victoria Rd) and North Head (Maungauika; Map p96; Takarunga Rd; ⊗6am-10pm) were Māori pā, and they remain fortresses of sorts, with the navy maintaining a presence. Both have gun embankments and North Head is riddled with tunnels, dug at the end of the 19th century in response to the Russian threat, and extended during WWI and WWII. The gates are locked at night, but that's never stopped teenagers from jumping the fence for scary subterranean explorations.

Between the two, Cambria Reserve stands on the remains of a third volcanic cone that was largely quarried away.

Torpedo Bay Navy Museum   MUSEUM
(Map p96; ✆09-445 5186; www.navymuseum.co.nz; 64 King Edward Pde; ⊗10am-5pm) FREE The navy has been in Devonport since the earliest days of the colony. Its history is on display at this well-presented and often moving museum, focusing on the stories of the sailors themselves.

⊙ Kingsland & Western Springs

Auckland Zoo ZOO
(Map p98; ☑ 09-360 3805; www.aucklandzoo.
co.nz; Motions Rd; adult/child $24/13; ⊙9.30am-
5pm, last entry 4.15pm) 🏄 At this modern, spacious zoo, the big foreigners tend to steal the
attention from the timid natives, but if you
can wrestle the kids away from the tigers
and orangutans, there's a well-presented NZ
section. Called Te Wao Nui, it's divided into
six ecological zones: Coast (seals, penguins),
Islands (mainly lizards, including NZ's
pint-sized dinosaur, the tuatara), Wetlands
(ducks, herons, eels), Night (kiwi, naturally,
along with frogs, native owls and weta), Forest (birds) and High Country (cheekier birds
and lizards).

Check the website for the times of zoo-
keepers' talks, Behind the Scenes experiences and ongoing progress of the zoo's
new South East Asia display (scheduled to
open in late 2020). Catch the number 18 bus
(adult/child $5.50/3) from bus stop 1362
(corner Victoria and Albert Sts) in the city
to bus stop 8124 on Great North Rd, from
where it's a 700m walk to the zoo's entrance.

Western Springs PARK
(Map p98; Great North Rd; 🚻) Parents bring
their children to this picturesque park for
the popular playground. It's a pleasant picnic spot and a good place to get acquainted with pukeko (swamp hens), ducks and
pushy geese. This coastal lake was formed
by a confluence of lava flows, where more
than 4 million litres of spring water bubble
up into the central lake daily. From the city,
catch any bus heading west via Great North
Rd (adult/child $5.50/3). By car, take the
Western Springs exit from the North Western Motorway.

MOTAT MUSEUM
(Museum of Transport & Technology; Map p98;
☑ 09-815 5800; www.motat.org.nz; 805 Great
North Rd, Western Springs; adult/child $19/10;
⊙10am-5pm) This technology boffin's paradise is spread over two sites and 19 hectares. At the Great North Rd site look out
for former Prime Minister Helen Clark's
Honda 50 motorbike and the pioneer village. The Meola Rd site features the Aviation Display Hall with rare military and
commercial planes. The two are linked by
a vintage tram (free with admission, $1 oth-
erwise), which passes Western Springs park
and the zoo. It's a fun kids' ride whether
you visit MOTAT or not.

⊙ Other Areas

★**One Tree Hill** VOLCANO, PARK
(Maungakiekie; Map p86) This volcanic cone
was the isthmus' key *pā* and the greatest fortress in the country. At the top (182m) there
are 360-degree views and the grave of John
Logan Campbell, who gifted the land to the
city in 1901 and requested that a memorial
be built to the Māori people on the summit.
Nearby is the stump of the last 'one tree'. Allow time to explore surrounding **Cornwall
Park** with its mature trees and historic Acacia Cottage (1841).

The Cornwall Park Information Centre
(p121) has fascinating interactive displays
illustrating what the *pā* would have looked
like when 5000 people lived here. Near
the excellent children's playground, the
Stardome (Map p86; ☑ 09-624 1246; www.star-
dome.org.nz; 670 Manukau Rd; shows adult/child
from $12/10; ⊙10am-5pm Mon, to 9.30pm Tue-
Thu, to 11pm Fri-Sun) **FREE** offers regular stargazing and planetarium shows (usually 7pm
and 8pm Wednesday to Sunday, with extra

ONE TREE TO RULE THEM ALL

Looking at One Tree Hill, your first thought will probably be 'Where's the bloody tree?'
Good question. Up until 2000 a Monterey pine stood at the top of the hill. This was a replacement for a sacred totara that was chopped down by British settlers in 1852. Māori
activists first attacked the foreign usurper in 1994, finishing the job in 2000.

After much consultation with local Māori and tree experts, a grove of six pohutukawa
and three totara trees was planted on the summit in mid-2016. In an arboreal version
of the *X-Factor*, the weaker-performing trees will be eliminated, with only one tree left
standing by 2026.

Auckland's most beloved landmark achieved international recognition in 1987 when
U2 released the song 'One Tree Hill' on their acclaimed *The Joshua Tree* album. It was
only released as a single in NZ, where it went to number one for six weeks.

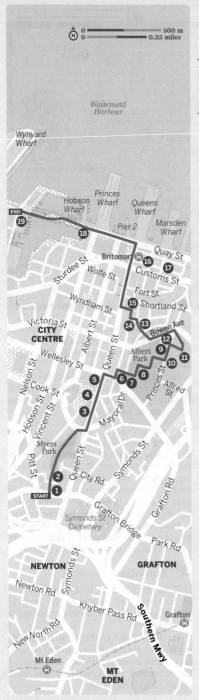

City Walk
City Centre Ramble

START ST KEVIN'S ARCADE, KARANGAHAPE RD
END WYNYARD QUARTER
LENGTH 4.5KM; AROUND 3 HOURS

This walk aims to show you some hidden nooks and architectural treats in Auckland's somewhat scrappy city centre. Start among the restaurants and vintage boutiques of ❶ **St Kevin's Arcade** (p120) and take the stairs down to Myers Park. Look out for the reproduction of Michelangelo's ❷ **Moses** at the bottom of the stairs. Continue through the park, taking the stairs on the right just before the overpass to head up to street level.

Heading down Queen St, you'll pass the ❸ **Auckland Town Hall** (p119) and ❹ **Aotea Sq** (Map p88; Queen St), the civic heart of the city. On the next corner is the wonderful ❺ **Civic Theatre** (p86). Turn right on Wellesley St and then left onto Lorne St. Immediately to your right is ❻ **Khartoum Pl**, with tiling that celebrates NZ women's historic victory, becoming the first in the world to win the vote. Head up the stairs to the ❼ **Auckland Art Gallery** (p85).

Behind the gallery is ❽ **Albert Park** (p85). Cross through it and turn left onto Princes St, where a row of ❾ **Victorian merchants' houses** faces the ❿ **University Clock Tower** (p87). Cut around behind the clock tower to ⓫ **Old Government House** (p87) and then follow the diagonal path back to Princes St. The attractive building on the corner of Princes St and Bowen Ave was once the city's main ⓬ **synagogue**.

Head down Bowen Ave and cut through the park past the ⓭ **Chancery precinct** to the ⓮ **High St** shopping strip. Take a left onto ⓯ **Vulcan Lane**, lined with historic pubs. Turn right onto Queen St and follow it down to the ⓰ **Britomart train station** (p123), housed in the former central post office. You're now standing on reclaimed land – the original shoreline was at Fort St. Detour to the nearby ⓱ **Britomart** precinct for good bars, restaurants and fashion boutiques.

From Britomart train station, turn left on Quay St and head to ⓲ **Viaduct Harbour**, bustling with bars and cafes, and then continue over the bridge to the rejuvenated ⓳ **Wynyard Quarter**.

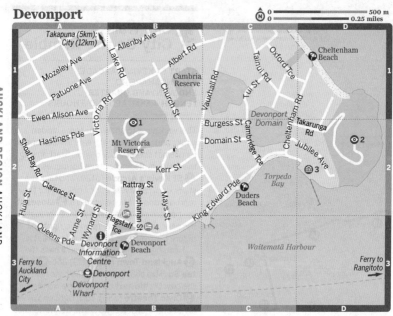

Devonport

© **Sights**

🛏 **Sleeping**

shows on weekends) that aren't dependent on Auckland's fickle weather.

To get to One Tree Hill from the the city, take a train to Greenlane and walk 1km along Green Lane West. By car, take the Greenlane exit off the Southern Motorway and turn right into Green Lane West.

★ **Wallace Arts Centre** GALLERY
(Map p86; 📞09-639 2010; www.wallacearts trust.org.nz; Pah Homestead, 72 Hillsborough Rd, Hillsborough; ⊙10am-3pm Tue-Fri, 8am to 5pm Sat & Sun) **FREE** Housed in a gorgeous 1879 mansion with views to One Tree Hill (p94) and the Manukau Harbour, this arts centre is endowed with contemporary NZ art from an extensive private collection, which is changed every four to six weeks. Have lunch on the veranda at the excellent Homestead Cafe and wander among the magnificent trees in the surrounding park. The art is also very accessible, ranging from a life-size skeletal rugby ruck to a vibrant Ziggy Stardust painted on glass.

Bus 305 or 295 (Lynfield) departs every 15 minutes from Queen St – outside the Civic Theatre (p86) – and heads to Hillsborough Rd ($5.50, 40 minutes).

Auckland Botanic Gardens GARDENS
(Map p86; 📞09-267 1457; www.aucklandbotanic gardens.co.nz; 102 Hill Rd, Manurewa; ⊙8am-6pm Apr-Sep, to 8pm Oct-Mar) **FREE** This 64-hectare park has more than 10,000 plants (including threatened species), dozens of themed gardens and an infestation of wedding parties. By car, take the Southern Motorway, exit at Manurewa and follow the signs. Otherwise take the train to Manurewa ($12.50, 43 minutes) and then walk along Hill Rd (1.5km).

🏃 **Activities**

Nothing gets you closer to the heart and soul of Auckland than sailing on the Hauraki Gulf. If you can't afford a yacht cruise, catch a ferry instead.

Trading on the country's action-packed reputation, Auckland has sprouted its own set of thrill-inducing activities. Look around for backpacker reductions or special offers before booking anything.

Visitor centres and public libraries stock the city council's *Auckland City's Walkways* pamphlet, which has a good selection of urban walks, including information on the Coast to Coast Walkway.

Boating & Kayaking

Explore   BOATING
(Map p88; ✆0800 397 567; www.exploregroup. co.nz; Viaduct Harbour) ⚓ Shoot the breeze for two hours on a genuine America's Cup yacht (adult/child $190/135), take a 90-minute cruise on a glamorous large yacht (adult/child $99/60) or tuck into a 2½-hour Harbour Dinner Cruise (adult/child $145/99).

Auckland Adventure Jet   BOATING
(Map p88; ✆0800 255 538; www.auckland adventurejet.co.nz; Pier 3A, Quay St; adult/child $98/58; ⏱8am-5pm) Exciting 30-minute blasts around Auckland Harbour.

Auckland Sea Kayaks   KAYAKING
(Map p86; ✆0800 999 089; www.auckland seakayaks.co.nz; 384 Tamaki Dr, St Heliers) ⚓ Guided trips (including lunch) to Rangitoto ($195, 6½ hours) and Motukorea (Browns Island; $155, four hours). Multiday excursions and sunset paddles are also available.

Fergs Kayaks   KAYAKING
(Map p86; ✆09-529 2230; www.fergskayaks. co.nz; 12 Tamaki Dr, Orakei; ⏱9am-5pm) Hires kayaks (per hour from $25), paddle boards ($30), bikes ($20) and inline skates ($20). Guided kayak trips head to Devonport ($100, three hours, 8km) or Rangitoto ($160, six hours, 13km).

Extreme Sports

Auckland Bridge
Climb & Bungy   ADVENTURE SPORTS
(Map p86; ✆09-360 7748; www.bungy.co.nz; 105 Curran St, Westhaven; adult/child climb $130/90, bungy $165/135; ⏱9am-3.30pm) ⚓ Climb up or jump off the Auckland Harbour Bridge.

SkyWalk   ADVENTURE SPORTS
(Map p88; ✆0800 759 925; www.skywalk.co.nz; Sky Tower, cnr Federal & Victoria Sts; adult/child $150/120; ⏱10am-4.30pm) The SkyWalk involves circling the 192m-high, 1.2m-wide outside halo of the Sky Tower (p85) without rails or a balcony. Don't worry, it's not completely crazy – there is a safety harness.

SkyJump   ADVENTURE SPORTS
(Map p88; ✆0800 759 586; www.skyjump.co.nz; Sky Tower, cnr Federal & Victoria Sts; adult/child $225/175; ⏱10am-5.15pm) This thrilling 11-second, 85km/h base wire leap from the observation deck of the Sky Tower (p85) is more like a parachute jump than a bungy. Combine it with the SkyWalk in the Look & Leap package ($290).

Other Activities

Auckland Seaplanes   SCENIC FLIGHTS
(Map p88; ✆09-390 1121; www.aucklandsea planes.com; 171 Halsey St, Wynyard Quarter; per person from $225; ⏱8am-7pm) Flights in a cool 1960s floatplane that explore Auckland's harbour and islands. The company's location and departure point may change in the future, so check the website for the latest.

Coast to Coast Walkway   WALKING
(Map p86; www.aucklandcity.govt.nz) Heading right across the country from the Tasman to the Pacific (which is actually only 16km), this walk encompasses One Tree Hill (p94), Mt Eden (p91), the Domain (p91) and the university, keeping mainly to reserves rather than city streets.

Do it in either direction: starting from the Viaduct Basin and heading south, it's marked by yellow markers and milestones; heading north from Onehunga there are blue markers. Our recommendation? Catch the train to Onehunga and finish up at the Viaduct's bars. From Onehunga station, take Onehunga Mall up to Princes St, turn left and pick up the track at the inauspicious park by the motorway.

Rapu NZ Surf'n'Snow Tours   SURFING
(✆09-828 0426; www.rapuadventures.com; 1-/2-/5-/7-/14-day tour $120/199/800/1160/2154) One- or two-day surfing courses include transport, gear and two-hour lessons twice each day, usually at Piha. Tours of five days or longer include accommodation (October to May only). Snow packages include transport to Mt Ruapehu.

Parnell Baths   SWIMMING
(Map p92; ✆09-373 3561; www.parnellbaths. co.nz; Judges Bay Rd, Parnell; adult/child $6.40/free; ⏱6am-8pm Mon-Fri, 8am-8pm Sat & Sun Nov-Easter) Outdoor saltwater pools with an awesome 1950s mural.

👉 Tours

Cultural

Tāmaki Hikoi   CULTURAL
(✆021 146 9593; www.tamakihikoi.co.nz; 1/3hr $55/99) Guides from the Ngāti Whatua *iwi* lead various Māori cultural tours, including

Kingsland & Mt Eden

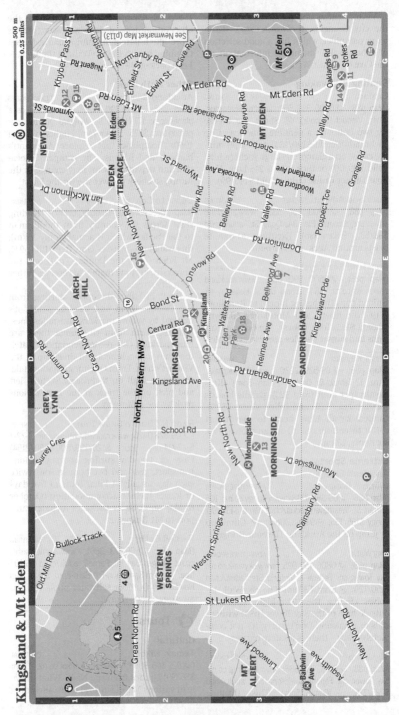

AUCKLAND REGION AUCKLAND

See Newmarket Map (p113)

N
0   500 m
0   0.25 miles

NEWTON

NEWTON

EDEN
TERRACE

ARCH
HILL

GREY
LYNN

KINGSLAND

WESTERN
SPRINGS

MT
ALBERT

MORNINGSIDE

SANDRINGHAM

MT EDEN

Mt Eden

Khyber Pass Rd
Boston Rd
Nugent Rd
Normanby Rd
Enfield St
Edwin St
Clive Rd
Symonds St
Mt Eden Rd
Mt Eden Rd
Mt Eden Rd
Oaklands Rd
Stokes Rd
Bellevue Rd
Esplanade Rd
Sherbourne St
Valley Rd
Grange Rd
Woodford Rd
Pentland Ave
Horoeka Ave
Wynyard St
Bellevue Rd
Valley Rd
View Rd
Dominion Rd
Prospect Tce
Ian McKinnon Dr
New North Rd
Onslow Rd
Bond St
Central Rd
Kingsland
Eden Walters Rd
Bellwood Ave
Reimers Ave
King Edward Pde
North Western Mwy
Kingsland Ave
Great North Rd
Crummer Rd
Surrey Cres
School Rd
Sandringham Rd
New North Rd
Western Springs Rd
Morningside
Morningside Dr
Sainsbury Rd
Old Mill Rd
Bullock Track
Great North Rd
St Lukes Rd
Linwood Ave
Baldwin Ave
Asquith Ave
New North Rd

Kingsland & Mt Eden

walking and interpretation of sites such as Mt Eden (p91) and the Auckland Domain (p91).

TIME Unlimited   CULTURAL

(☑ 09-846 3469; www.newzealandtours.travel; adult/child from $295/147.50) 🌿 Cultural, walking and sightseeing tours from a Māori perspective.

Food & Wine

Big Foody Food Tour   TOURS

(☑ 0800 366 386, 021 481 177; www.thebigfoody.com; per person $85-185) Small-group city tours, including visits to markets and artisan producers, and lots of tastings. Also on offer are hop-fuelled explorations of Auckland's burgeoning craft-beer scene and behind-the-scenes tours of Eden Park (p119), home of rugby and cricket in Auckland.

Auckland Wine Trail Tours   TOURS

(☑ 09-630 1540; www.winetrailtours.co.nz) Small-group tours around West Auckland

wineries and the Waitākere Ranges (half-/full day $135/265); further afield to Matakana ($270); or a 'Coast to Coast' combo of the two ($275).

Fine Wine Tours   TOURS

(☑ 0800 023 111; www.insidertouring.co.nz) Tours of Kumeū and Waiheke wineries, including a four-hour Kumeū tour ($270). Also a five- to six-hour 'Auckland on a Plate' foodie tour ($365).

Walking

Bush & Beach   WALKING

(☑ 09-837 4130; www.bushandbeach.co.nz) 🌿 Tours including guided walks in the Waitākere Ranges and along west-coast beaches ($165 to $255); three-hour city minibus tours ($84); and food and wine tours in either Kumeū or Matakana (half-/full day $255/330).

Bus

Toru Tours   BUS

(☑ 027 457 0011; www.torutours.com; per person $89) The three-hour Express Tour will go with just one booking – ideal for solo travellers.

Auckland Hop On, Hop Off Explorer   BUS

(Map p88; ☑ 0800 439 756; www.explorerbus.co.nz; adult/child per day $45/20) Two services – the red or blue route – take in the best of the waterfront, including attractions along Tamaki Dr (p92), or highlights including Mt Eden (p91) and the Auckland Zoo (p94). Red-route buses depart from near Princes Wharf hourly from 10am to 3pm (more frequently in summer), and it's possible to link to the blue route at the Auckland Museum (p91). Two-day passes (adult/child $55/25) are also available, and both passes include ferry tickets for Devonport.

Boat

Riverhead Ferry   CRUISE

(Map p88; ☑ 09-376 0819; www.riverheadferry.co.nz; Pier 3, Ferry Terminal; per cruise $38) Harbour and gulf cruises, including a 90-minute jaunt up the inner harbour to Riverhead, returning after two hours' pub time. Departure times depend on the tides. Check the website for details.

Fullers 360   CRUISE

(Map p88; ☑ 09-367 9111; www.fullers.co.nz; ⊘ 7am-8pm) Offers ferries to Devonport and Waiheke, harbour cruises, and day trips to other islands in the Hauraki Gulf, including Rangitoto, Motutapu, Tiritiri Matangi and Rotoroa.

DON'T MISS

AUCKLAND VOLCANIC FIELD

Some cities think they're tough just by living in the shadow of a volcano. Auckland's built on 50 of them and, no, they're not all extinct. The last one to erupt was Rangitoto about 600 years ago and no one can predict when the next eruption will occur. Auckland's quite literally a hotspot – with a reservoir of magma 100km below, waiting to bubble to the surface. But relax: this has only happened 19 times in the last 20,000 years.

Some of Auckland's volcanoes are cones, some are filled with water and some have been completely quarried away. Moves are afoot to register the field as a World Heritage site and protect what remains. Most of the surviving cones show evidence of terracing from when they formed a formidable series of Māori *pā* (fortified villages). The most interesting to explore are Mt Eden (p91), One Tree Hill (p94), North Head (p93) and Rangitoto (p124), but Mt Victoria (p93), Mt Wellington (Maungarei), Mt Albert (Owairaka), Mt Roskill (Puketāpapa), Lake Pupuke, Mt Māngere and Mt Hobson (Remuera) are all also worth a visit.

✦ Festivals & Events

Auckland Tourism's website (www.auckland nz.com) has a thorough events calendar.

Laneway Festival   MUSIC
(http://auckland.lanewayfestival.com; Albert Park; ⊘ Jan) International indie bands in a one-day festival on Anniversary Day (the Monday following the last weekend in January).

ASB Classic   SPORTS
(www.asbclassic.co.nz; ⊘ Jan) Watch leading tennis players warm up for the Aussie Open; held early January at the ASB Tennis Centre (Map p92; www.tennisauckland.co.nz; 1 Tennis Lane, Parnell).

Auckland Anniversary
Day Regatta   SPORTS
(www.regatta.org.nz; ⊘ Jan) The 'City of Sails' lives up to its name; held Monday after the last weekend in January.

Auckland Folk Festival   MUSIC
(www.aucklandfolkfestival.co.nz; ⊘ late Jan; ♿) An annual family-friendly long-weekend festival of traditional, Celtic, Americana and folk music held in the Kumeū Showgrounds in West Auckland. Camping is available, so you can enjoy the music, dancing, kids' activities and excellent food stalls all night.

Movies in Parks   FILM
(www.moviesinparks.co.nz; ⊘ Jan-Mar) Free movies on Friday and Saturday nights in various locations.

Music in Parks   MUSIC
(www.musicinparks.co.nz; ⊘ Jan-Mar) Free gigs in various locations.

Lantern Festival   CULTURAL
(www.aucklandnz.com/lantern-festival; Albert Park; ⊘ Feb) Three days of Asian food, culture and elaborately constructed lantern tableaux in Albert Park to welcome the Lunar New Year (usually held in February).

Auckland Pride Festival   LGBTQI+
(www.aucklandpride.org.nz; ⊘ Feb) Two-week festival of music, arts, sport and culture celebrating the LGBTQI+ community. Highlights include the Our March parade, Our Party and the Big Gay Out.

Big Gay Out   LGBTQI+
(www.aucklandpride.org.nz; ⊘ early to mid-Feb) Thousands pack out Coyle Park, Point Chevalier, on a Sunday in mid-February for a giant LGBTQI+ fair day with entertainment, food stalls and bars.

Pasifika Festival   CULTURAL
(www.aucklandnz.com/pasifika; ⊘ Mar) Western Springs (p94) park hosts this giant Polynesian party with cultural performances, and food and craft stalls; held over a weekend in early to mid-March.

Auckland Arts Festival   PERFORMING ARTS
(www.aucklandfestival.co.nz; ⊘ Mar) Held over three weeks in March, this is Auckland's biggest celebration of the arts.

Auckland Cup Week   SPORTS
(www.ellerslie.co.nz; Ellerslie Racecourse; ⊘ early Mar) The year's biggest horse races.

Polyfest   CULTURAL
(www.facebook.com/asbpolyfestnz; Sports Bowl, Manukau; ⊘ mid-Mar) Massive Auckland secondary schools' Māori and Pacific Islands cultural festival.

Royal Easter Show
FAIR

(www.eastershow.co.nz; ASB Showgrounds, 217 Green Lane West; ☉Mar/Apr) It's supposedly agricultural, but most people attend for the funfair rides.

Auckland International Cultural Festival
CULTURAL

(www.facebook.com/culturalfestival; Mt Roskill War Memorial Park; ☉late Mar/early Apr) One-day festival with ethnic food stalls, cultural displays and performances.

NZ International Comedy Festival
COMEDY

(www.comedyfestival.co.nz; ☉Apr-May) Three-week laugh-fest with local and international comedians.

GABS
BEER

(Great Australasian Beer Spectapular; www.gabs festival.com; ASB Showgrounds; ☉late Jun) A dazzling array of craft beer, cider and street food combine at Auckland's brilliant version of one of the world's best beer festivals.

NZ International Film Festival
FILM

(www.nzff.co.nz; ☉Jul) Art-house films for two weeks from mid-July, many in the beautiful Civic Theatre (p86).

NZ Fashion Week
CULTURAL

(www.nzfashionweek.com; ☉Aug) Held at the Viaduct Events Centre.

Auckland Heritage Festival
CULTURAL

(www.heritagefestival.co.nz; ☉Sep) Two weeks of (mainly free) tours of Auckland's neighbourhoods and historic buildings; from late September.

Diwali Festival of Lights
CULTURAL

(www.aucklandnz.com/diwali; Aotea Sq; ☉mid-Oct) Music, dance and food from Auckland's Indian community in Aotea Sq.

Grey Lynn Park Festival
FAIR

(www.greylynnparkfestival.org; ☉Nov) Free festival of arts and crafts, food stalls and live music in one of Auckland's more interesting inner suburbs; third Saturday in late November.

Santa Parade
CHRISTMAS

(www.santaparade.co.nz; ☉late Nov) The big guy in red parades along Queen St before partying in Aotea Sq (p95); last Sunday of November.

Silo Cinema & Markets
FILM

(www.silopark.co.nz; Silo Park, Wynyard Quarter; ☉Dec-Easter) Classic movies screened outdoors on Friday nights, and markets with food trucks, DJs and craft stalls on Friday nights and Saturday and Sunday afternoons.

🛏 Sleeping

Auckland's city centre has a smattering of luxury hotels including international chains. For B&B accommodation, Ponsonby, Mt Eden and Parnell are all recommended, and Devonport has heritage B&Bs a relaxing ferry ride from the city. The city's best backpacker hostels are largely in inner suburbs including Mt Eden and Ponsonby.

Booking two to three months ahead is recommended from December to April. Accommodation routinely books out when there is a major concert or sporting event in the city. Check dates carefully.

🛏 City Centre & Britomart

Attic Backpackers
HOSTEL $

(Map p88; ☏09-973 5887; www.atticbackpackers. co.nz; 31 Wellesley St; dm $30-38, s/tw without bathroom $70/110; @🛜) Centrally located Attic Backpackers features good facilities and an even better vibe. White walls and plenty of windows keep everything bright and fresh, and there's a rooftop area conducive to meeting other travellers.

★ Hotel DeBrett
BOUTIQUE HOTEL $$$

(Map p88; ☏09-925 9000; www.hoteldebrett.com; 2 High St; r from $420; 🛜) This hip historic hotel has been zhooshed up with stripy carpets and clever designer touches in every nook of the 25 extremely comfortable rooms. Prices include a continental breakfast, free unlimited wi-fi and a predinner drink.

Adina Apartment Hotel Britomart
APARTMENT $$$

(Map p88; ☏09-393 8200; www.adinahotels. com; 2 Tapora St; d/apt from $199/2215; P🛜) Handily located for concerts and events at Spark Arena (p118), eating and drinking in the Britomart precinct, and for harbour transport from the Ferry Building (p123), the Adina Britomart has colourful and modern suites and apartments with a touch of Scandi natural-wood style. It has a decent in-house bar and restaurant also.

CityLife
HOTEL $$$

(Map p88; ☏09-379 9222; www.heritagehotels. co.nz/citylife-auckland; 171 Queen St; apt from $270; P🛜❄) 🏊 A worthy tower-block hotel offering numerous apartments over dozens

Where to Stay in Auckland

Takapuna

A good base to explore areas further north like Matakana and Leigh. Nearby Hurstmere Rd has good restaurants and pubs.

Best for Beaches; eating; motels; apartments

Transport Bus to centre in less than 40 minutes

Price Mostly midrange

City Centre

Good shopping, eating and drinking, and also easy access to catch ferries to Waiheke and other Hauraki Gulf islands.

Best for Convenience; eating and drinking

Transport Short walk to Wynyard Quarter

Price Suits all budgets

Ponsonby

Stylish, interesting neighbourhood with good cafes and restaurants. East to get to Karangahape Rd. Features the city's best hostels.

Best for Eating and drinking; luxury B&Bs; hostels

Transport Walk or bus to central city and harbour

Price Top end; budget

Mt Eden

Convenient for visiting Mt Eden, One Tree Hill and sport at Eden Park. Good eating and drinking in Mt Eden and up-and-coming Kingsland.

Best for B&Bs; restaurants

Transport Short bus ride to city centre

Price Midrange; top end

Takapuna

 City Centre

 Ponsonby

Mt Eden

N
0 — 2 km
0 — 1 miles

Waiheke Island
(15km) →

Devonport

Heritage neighboorhood, reached by ferry from the central city. Can be slow to reach by car along busy Lake Rd.

Best for Historic architecture; quiet; seafront

Transport 15-minute ferry to city centre

Price Midrange

 Devonport

Waiheke Island

Auckland's most popular and easily reached Hauraki Gulf island. Summer weekends and around Christmas, New Year and Easter get very busy.

Best for Vineyards; walking; beaches; houses

Transport 45-minute ferry to city centre; bring a car to explore the island

Price Midrange; top end

Parnell & Newmarket

Well-established and leafy central suburbs with excellent shopping, cafes and restaurants.

Best for Eating; museums; B&Bs; apartments

Transport Short bus ride to city centre

Price Midrange; top end

 Parnell & Newmarket

of floors, ranging from studios to three-bedroom suites. Facilities include a heated lap pool, gym and valet parking. The location couldn't be more central.

🛏 Viaduct Harbour & Wynyard Quarter

Sofitel Auckland
Viaduct Harbour   HOTEL $$$

(Map p88; ☏09-909 9000; www.sofitel-auckland.com; 21 Viaduct Harbour Ave; d from $449; P🅿🛜❄) Auckland is one of the world's great harbour cities, so it makes perfect sense to stay beside the water. In close proximity to the restaurants and bars of Viaduct Harbour and the Wynyard Quarter, the Sofitel has classy rooms and suites arrayed around a central ornamental pool. Moored yachts bob nearby, and Auckland's 'City of Sails' moniker definitely rings true.

🛏 Ponsonby & Grey Lynn

Haka Lodge Ponsonby   HOSTEL $

(Map p105; ☏09-973 5577; www.hakalodges.com; 2 Franklin Rd, Ponsonby; dm $34-39, d/apt $99/190; 🛜) Occupying a two-storey villa just metres from Ponsonby Rd, Auckland's second Haka Lodge has spotless double rooms, mixed and female-only dorms with charging stations aplenty, and a media room where guests can fire up their own YouTube and Netflix accounts. Other shared spaces include a modern kitchen and sunny garden, and there's also an apartment accommodating up to four guests.

Verandahs   HOSTEL $

(Map p105; ☏09-360 4180; www.verandahs.co.nz; 6 Hopetoun St; dm $34-38, s $64, d with/without bathroom $106/88; P@🛜) Ponsonby Rd, Karangahape Rd (K Rd) and the city are an easy walk from this grand hostel, housed in two neighbouring villas overlooking the mature trees of Western Park. It's definitely one of Auckland's best backpackers.

Brown Kiwi   HOSTEL $

(Map p105; ☏09-378 0191; www.brownkiwi.co.nz; 7 Prosford St, Ponsonby; dm $32-35, s/d without bathroom $70/84; @🛜) This low-key hostel is tucked away in a busy-by-day commercial strip, a stone's throw from Ponsonby's shopping and grazing opportunities. The garden courtyard is made for mooching.

Abaco on Jervois   MOTEL $$

(Map p105; ☏09-360 6850; www.abaco.co.nz; 57 Jervois Rd, Ponsonby; r/ste from $165/228; P🛜) Well positioned for cafes and buses, this contemporary, neutral-toned motel has stainless-steel kitchens with dishwashers in the fancier units, and fridges and microwaves in the studios. The darker rooms downstairs are cheaper.

Ponsonby Manor   B&B $$

(Map p105; ☏09-360 7977; www.ponsonbymanor.co.nz; 229 Ponsonby Rd, Ponsonby; d from $180; 🛜) A good-value option to experience Ponsonby's combination of heritage ambience and cosmopolitan city style, Ponsonby Manor features accommodation options from standard rooms through to a penthouse suite, a family room and a cottage. Plenty of private garden areas and sunny verandas are a relaxing option after exploring the city. If you're travelling alone, ask about its compact garden single room.

⭐Franklin 38   B&B $$$

(Map p105; ☏021 383 651; www.franklin38.co.nz; 38 Franklin Rd, Ponsonby; ste $450-590; 🛜) Four gloriously sophisticated suites fill this spacious and sunny two-storey villa that was undoubtedly one of Ponsonby's finest homes in earlier times. Now the focus is a seamless blend of heritage and contemporary with stylish bathrooms, wraparound wooden verandas with city views, and a lovely shared guest lounge. Look forward to combining freshly baked croissants and Sky Tower views for breakfast.

Great Ponsonby Arthotel   B&B $$$

(Map p105; ☏09-376 5989; www.greatpons.co.nz; 30 Ponsonby Tce, Ponsonby; r $280-420; P🛜) 🖋 In a quiet cul-de-sac near Ponsonby Rd, this deceptively spacious Victorian villa has gregarious hosts, impressive sustainability practices and great breakfasts. Studio apartments open onto an attractive rear courtyard. Rates include breakfast.

🛏 Karangahape Road & Newton

Haka Lodge Auckland   HOSTEL $

(Map p88; ☏09-379 4556; www.hakalodges.com; 373 Karangahape Rd; dm $31-44, r with/without bathroom $159/109; 🛜) 🖋 The transformation of one of Auckland's dodgiest old pubs into a bright and shiny hostel is a modern miracle. Dorms have custom-made wooden bunks with privacy curtains, lockers and

Ponsonby & Grey Lynn

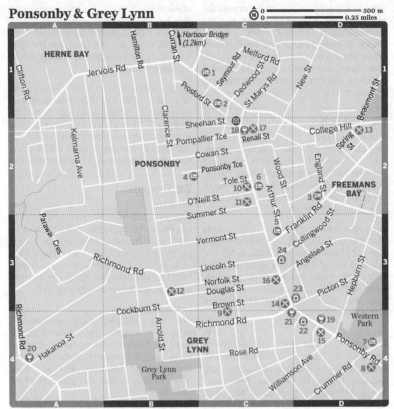

Ponsonby & Grey Lynn

their own power points – making them perhaps the most comfortable bunkrooms in Auckland. Wi-fi is free and unlimited. And it couldn't be better located for accessing the bustling Karangahape Rd scene.

Haka Hotel   HOTEL **$$**
(Map p88; ☑09-281 3097; https://hakahotels. co.nz; 2 Day St, Newton; d from $159; P🐾) Part of the burgeoning Haka empire – also including excellent hostels and tours – this

hotel in a quiet lane just off bohemian Karangahape Rd features chic and modern accommodation ranging from compact studios through to one- and two-bedroom suites. Many rooms have balconies and harbour views, and mod cons include coffee machines and Chromecast functionality on flat-screen TVs.

🛏 Mt Eden

Oaklands Lodge HOSTEL $
(Map p98; ☑09-638 6545; www.oaklandslodge. co.nz; 5a Oaklands Rd; dm $30-38, s/d without bathroom $60/85; P@☎) In a leafy cul-de-sac, this bright, well-kept hostel is close to the cafes, bars and restaurants of Mt Eden village and to city buses.

Eden Park B&B B&B $$
(Map p98; ☑09-630 5721; www.bedandbreakfast nz.com; 20 Bellwood Ave; r $165-180; P☎) The hallowed turf of Auckland's legendary Eden Park (p119) rugby ground is only a block away, and while the rooms aren't overly large, they mirror the Edwardian elegance of this fine wooden villa.

Bavaria B&B $$
(Map p98; ☑09-638 9641; www.bavariabandb hotel.co.nz; 83 Valley Rd; s/d from $165/180; P@☎) This spacious villa offers large, airy, well-kept rooms, all of which have bathrooms, although some of them are closet sized. The communal TV lounge, dining room and deck all encourage mixing and mingling. A hot and cold buffet breakfast is included in the rates.

Eden Villa B&B $$$
(Map p98; ☑09-630 1165; www.edenvilla.co.nz; 16 Poronui St; r $295; P) Accommodation in pretty wooden villas is what Auckland's leafy inner suburbs are all about. This one has three comfortable en-suite bedrooms, a pleasantly old-fashioned ambience and charming hosts who prepare a good cooked breakfast. We prefer the room at the rear, which has the original bath tub and views straight over the garden to Mt Eden (p91) itself.

🛏 Parnell & Newmarket

★ Ascot Parnell B&B $$$
(Map p92; ☑09-309 9012; www.ascotparnell. com; 32 St Stephens Ave, Parnell; r $295-385; P@☎⛵) The Ascot's three luxurious bedrooms share a spacious apartment in a modern mid-rise block. You're in no danger of stumbling into the owners' private space; they have a completely separate apartment next door. The largest room grabs all of the harbour views, but you can enjoy the same vista from the large terrace leading off the communal living area.

Quest Carlaw Park APARTMENT $$$
(Map p92; ☑09-304 0521; www.questcarlaw park.co.nz; 15 Nicholls Lane; apt from $219; P@☎) 🍴 It's in an odd spot, but this set of smart, modern apartments is handy for Parnell, the city and the Domain, and if you've got a car, you're practically on the motorway.

🛏 Devonport

Parituhu B&B $$
(Map p96; ☑09-445 6559; www.parituhu.co.nz; 3 King Edward Pde; r $140-160; P☎) There's only one double bedroom (with its own adjoining bathroom) available in this relaxing and welcoming Edwardian waterfront bungalow. The well-travelled hosts are excellent company and know the city very well.

Peace & Plenty Inn B&B $$$
(Map p96; ☑09-445 2925; www.peaceand plenty.co.nz; 6 Flagstaff Tce; s/d from $195/265; P☎) 🍴 Stocked with antiques, this perfectly located, five-star Victorian house has romantic and luxurious en-suite rooms with TVs, flowers, free sherry/port and local chocolates.

🛏 Other Areas

Grange Lodge MOTEL $$
(Map p86; ☑09-277 8280; www.grangelodge. co.nz; cnr Grange & Great South Rds, Papatoetoe; apt from $189; P☎) If you've driven up from the south, consider staying at this friendly little suburban motel, which is handy for the airport. From the Southern Motorway, take the East Tamaki Rd exit, turn right and right again onto Great South Rd.

Emerald Inn MOTEL $$
(Map p86; ☑09-488 3500; www.emerald -inn.co.nz; 16 The Promenade, Takapuna; d/ste $235/300; P☎⛵) Across the harbour bridge in Takapuna, the Emerald Inn is arrayed around a leafy courtyard and pool. It's just metres from Takapuna Beach, and there are plenty of good eating and drinking opportunities in the immediate area. Options range from studio units to one- and two-bedroom suites, and the friendly owners have plenty of ideas about things to see and do.

✕ Eating

The city's hippest foodie enclaves are Britomart (the blocks above the train station) and Federal St (under the Sky Tower), and new openings reinforce the culinary reputation of Karangahape Rd (p111) and Ponsonby (p109). The Wynyard Quarter (p108) and the former City Works Depot on the corner of Wellesley and Nelson Sts are excellent dining areas. Easily reached by train from the central city, the Morningside Precinct (p112) is another emerging dining destination.

Aucklanders demand good coffee, so you never have to walk too far to find a decent cafe, especially in suburbs like Ponsonby, Mt Eden and Kingsland. Some double as wine bars or have gourmet aspirations, while others are content to fill their counters with fresh, reasonably priced snacks.

You'll find large supermarkets in most neighbourhoods: a particularly handy **Countdown** (Map p88; ☑ 09-275 2567; www.countdown.co.nz; 76 Quay St; ⊙24hr) is at the bottom of town and a **New World** (Map p105; ☑ 09-307 8400; www.newworld.co.nz; 2 College Hill, Freemans Bay; ⊙7am-midnight) is by Victoria Park. Self-caterers should consider the Otara Flea Market (p121) and **Avondale Sunday Markets** (www.avondalesundaymarkets.co.nz; Avondale Racecourse, Ash St; ⊙5am-noon Sun) for cheap, fresh vegetables, and La Cigale (p112) for fancier fare and local artisan produce.

✕ City Centre & Britomart

Best Ugly Bagels   BAKERY **$**

(Map p88; ☑ 09-366 3926; www.bestugly.co.nz; City Works Depot, 90 Wellesley St; filled bagels $7-16; ⊙7am-3pm; ☑) Hand-rolled, boiled and wood-fired, Best Ugly's bagels are a thing of beauty. Call into its super-hip bakery in a converted heavy-vehicle workshop and order one stuffed with pastrami, bacon, smoked salmon or a variety of vegetarian fillings. Or just ask for a cinnamon bagel slathered with cream cheese and jam. The coffee is killer, too.

★ Giapo   ICE CREAM **$$**

(Map p88; ☑ 09-550 3677; www.giapo.com; 12 Gore St; ice cream $12-24; ⊙1-10pm Mon-Fri, noon to 11pm Sat & Sun; ☑) ⦿ That there are queues outside this boutique ice-cream shop even in the middle of winter says a lot about the magical confections that it conjures up. Expect elaborate constructions of ice-cream art topped with all manner of goodies, as Giapo's extreme culinary creativity and experimentation combines with the science of gastronomy to produce quite possibly the planet's best ice-cream extravaganzas.

Depot   MODERN NZ **$$**

(Map p88; ☑ 09-363 7048; www.eatatdepot.co.nz; 86 Federal St; dishes $18-39; ⊙7am-late) TV chef Al Brown's popular eatery offers first-rate comfort food in informal surrounds (communal tables, butcher tiles and a constant buzz). Dishes are designed to be shared, and a pair of clever shuckers serve the city's freshest clams and oysters. It doesn't take bookings, so get there early or expect to wait.

Amano   ITALIAN **$$**

(Map p88; ☑ 09-394 1416; www.amano.nz; 66-68 Tyler St; mains $22-35; ⊙restaurant 7am-late, bakery 6.30am-6pm Mon-Sat, to 4pm Sun) ⦿ Rustic Italian influences underpin this bistro-bakery in a repurposed warehouse in Auckland's Britomart precinct, but there's real culinary savvy evident in the open kitchen. Many dishes harness seasonal produce and ingredients from the owners' farm in West Auckland, and Amano effortlessly transitions from a buzzy caffeine-fuelled daytime cafe to a sophisticated evening bistro featuring NZ wines and craft beers.

The attached bakery has superb sourdough and wood-fired ciabatta sandwiches. Order an Italian meatball sandwich, grab a takeaway espresso and adjourn to a comfy beanbag in nearby Takutai Sq.

MĀORI NZ: AUCKLAND

Evidence of Māori occupation is literally carved into Auckland's volcanic cones. The dominant *iwi* of the isthmus was Ngāti Whatua, but these days there are Māori from almost all of NZ's *iwi* living here.

For an initial taste of Māori culture, start at Auckland Museum (p91), where there's a wonderful Māori collection and a culture show. For a more personalised experience, take a tour with TIME Unlimited (p99), Potiki Adventures (p128) or Ngāti Whatua's Tāmaki Hikoi (p97), or visit the *marae* (meeting house) and recreated village at Te Hana (p144).

Odette's
MODERN NZ $$

(Map p88; 09-309 0304; www.odettes.co.nz; Shed 5, City Works Depot, 90 Wellesley St; dishes $19-40; 8am-3pm Sun & Mon, 7am-11pm Tue-Sat) Nothing about Odette's is run of the mill. Not the bubbly light fixtures or the quirky photography, and certainly not the menu. How about lamb meatballs with saffron mustard for brunch? Or wild mushrooms served with a truffle pancake and cashew cream? In the evening the more cafe-ish items are replaced with dishes for sharing. It gets hectic on weekends.

Ima
MIDDLE EASTERN $$

(Map p88; 09-377 5252; www.imacuisine.co.nz; 53 Fort St; breakfast & lunch $12-26, dinner shared dishes $15-30; 7am-10pm Mon-Fri, from 8.30am Sat) Named after the Hebrew word for mother, Ima's menu features an array of Israeli, Palestinian, Yemeni and Lebanese comfort food, along with meat pies and sandwiches at lunchtime. Rustle up a group for Ima's excellent shared dinners and feast on whole fish, chicken *mesachan* (a whole bird slow-cooked with herbs and spices and then grilled) or slow-cooked lamb shoulder.

Federal & Wolfe
CAFE $$

(Map p88; 09-359 9113; www.facebook.com/FederalandWolfeCafe; 10 Federal St; mains $15-22; 7am-3pm Mon-Fri, 8am-2pm Sat) Packing crates and mismatched chairs lend an air of recycled chic to this corner cafe. Look forward to first-rate coffee and delicious food, much of it organic and free-range.

Scarecrow
CAFE $$

(Map p88; 09-377 1333; www.scarecrow.co.nz; 33 Victoria St East; mains $16-28; 7am-5pm Mon-Fri, 8am-5pm Sat & Sun, kitchen closes 3pm;) Organic and vegan ingredients shine at this bustling cafe near Albert Park. Bentwood chairs add a Gallic ambience, and the menu veers towards European and Middle Eastern flavours. Try the *shakshuka* baked eggs or house-smoked fish cakes for brunch. A compact deli section sells local artisan food products, and there's also an on-site florist.

Kimchi Project
KOREAN $$

(Map p88; 09-302 4002; www.facebook.com/pg/thekimchiprojectnz; 20 Lorne St; snacks $12-18, mains $18-39; 7am-11pm Sun-Thu, 8am-midnight Fri & Sat) Begin with a brunch of matcha latte and yuzu muesli, or escape to the palm-fringed courtyard for Asian-inspired street food, including spicy pulled-pork tacos, and bao (steamed buns) crammed with prawns. Packed with pork belly and topped with an egg, the kimchi fried rice is simple but brilliant.

★ Cassia
INDIAN $$$

(Map p88; 09-379 9702; www.cassiarestaurant.co.nz; 5 Fort Lane; mains $30-39; noon-3pm Wed-Fri, 5.30pm-late Tue-Sat) Occupying a moodily lit basement, Cassia serves modern Indian food with punch and panache. Start with a *pani puri,* a bite-sized crispy shell bursting with flavour, before devouring a decadently rich curry. The Delhi duck is excellent, as is the Goan-style snapper. Artisan gins and NZ craft beer are other highlights. Cassia is often judged Auckland's best restaurant.

Grove
MODERN NZ $$$

(Map p88; 09-368 4129; www.thegroverestaurant.co.nz; St Patrick's Sq, Wyndham St; 4/7-course degustation $119/165; noon-3pm Thu & Fri, 6pm-late Mon-Sat) Romantic fine dining: the room is moodily lit, the menu encourages sensual experimentation and the service is effortless. If you can't find anything to break the ice from the extensive wine list, then give it up – it's never going to happen.

✖ Viaduct Harbour & Wynyard Quarter

Williams Eatery
CAFE $$

(Map p88; 09-373 3906; www.williamseatery.co.nz; 85 Daldy St, Wynyard Quarter; mains $15-33; 7am-3pm Mon-Wed, to late Thu & Fri, 8am-late Sat, 8am-4pm Sun) Serving the residential precinct emerging around the Wynyard Quarter, Williams Eatery's always-excellent coffee partners with hotcakes and mandarin curd for brunch, while the dinner menu includes brilliant pasta and lamb and seafood specials. On-trend organic and natural wines, classic Mimosa and Negroni cocktails, and regional Auckland craft beers all help to pleasantly blur the line between lunch and dinner.

Hello Beasty
ASIAN $$

(Map p88; 021 554 496; https://hellobeasty.nz; 95-97 Customs St W, Viaduct Harbour; shared plates $12-38; 11am-11pm;) Japanese, Korean and Chinese flavours are all filtered through a fun contemporary vibe near Auckland's Viaduct Harbour. Secure a spot with ocean views, and fill your table with shared plates, including steamed bao buns, smoky Japanese-style *tsukune* sausage and barbecued eggplant. The concise drinks list includes sake cocktails and spritzes, and NZ lamb and seafood is regularly featured.

Baduzzi   ITALIAN $$
(Map p88; ☑09-309 9339; www.baduzzi.co.nz; cnr Jellicoe St & Fish Lane, Wynyard Quarter; mains $23-38; ⏱11.30am-late; ✈) This smart and sassy eatery does sophisticated spins on meatballs – try the crayfish ones – and other robust but elegant Italian dishes. Cosy up in the intimate booths, grab a seat at the bar or soak up some Auckland sunshine outside.

Good Luck Coconut   ASIAN $$
(Map p88; ☑09-303 0440; www.thegoodluck coconut.co.nz; 39 Jellicoe St, Wynyard Quarter; shared plates $14-23; ⏱noon-late Thu-Sun, from 4.30pm Wed) Good Luck Coconut's blending of Pacific and Asian design and flavours really suits the overall vibe of the city, especially when combined with briny harbour views in the Wynyard Quarter. Shared plates include *ika mata* (raw fish cured in coconut and lime), soft-shell-crab sliders and a great pork *katsu* burger with kimchi. Great Pacific-inspired cocktails too.

Saint Alice   BISTRO $$
(Map p88; www.saintalice.co.nz; Level 1, 204 Quay St, Viaduct Harbour; shared plates $14-39; ⏱11.30am-late) Viaduct Harbour views and a subtle maritime design vibe make Saint Alice one of Auckland's best places to soak up the harbour-city ambience. Equal parts bar and bistro, it's an energetic and bustling place, and standouts on the seasonal menu always include wood-roasted lamb and the restaurant's signature dish of oyster McMuffins with black garlic aioli.

Auckland Fish Market   MARKET $$
(Map p88; ☑09-379 1490; www.afm.co.nz; 22-32 Jellicoe St, Wynyard Quarter; mains $15-25; ⏱7am-9pm) A makeover in early 2019 incorporated a seafood-focused upscale food court and a relaxed courtyard bar with a good beer and wine selection. Dining options include sashimi, Thai food, South American barbecue, pizza, and fish and chips. Check the website for details of regular seafood cookery classes including Vietnamese and Mediterranean flavours.

✖ Ponsonby & Grey Lynn

Auckland's busiest restaurant-cafe-bar strip is so damn cool it has its own website (www.iloveponsonby.co.nz).

Ponsonby Village International Food Court   FOOD HALL $
(Map p105; www.ponsonbyfoodcourt.co.nz; 106 Ponsonby Rd, Ponsonby; mains $9-20; ⏱11am-10pm; ✈) Japanese, Malaysian, Chinese, Turkish, Thai, Lao and Indian flavours are all on offer here, and excellent Vietnamese and Indonesian. Beer and wine are well priced for a more expensive part of town.

AUCKLAND'S MULTICULTURAL MENU

Around 30% of New Zealanders live in Auckland, and the country's biggest city is also the most ethnically diverse. With immigration – especially from Asia – has come a cosmopolitan restaurant scene, and savvy local foodies (and a few of the city's top chefs) keenly explore neighbourhoods on the edge of the central city for authentic tastes of Auckland's multicultural present and future.

Head to Dominion Rd in Balmoral to be surrounded by Auckland's best regional Chinese food. A few blocks west in the suburb of Sandringham are some of the city's best Indian and Sri Lankan restaurants. Our favourite is **Paradise** (Map p86; ☑09-845 1144; www.paradiseindianfood.co.nz; 591 Sandringham Rd, Sandringham; mains $15-20; ⏱11.30am-9.30pm; ✈), specialising in the Mughlai cuisine you'd find on the streets of Hyderabad.

At the city's bustling night markets – held in a different suburban car park each night of the week – scores of stalls serve food from a diverse range of countries, from Argentina and Samoa, to Hungary and Turkey. Most convenient for travellers is the Thursday **Henderson Night Market** (www.aucklandnightmarket.co.nz; Waitakere Mega Centre; ⏱5.30-11pm Thu). Catch a western-line train from Britomart to Henderson and walk 650m to underneath the Kmart department store.

If you're in town around late March or early April, the Auckland International Cultural Festival (p101) offers a very tasty peek into the city's ethnically diverse future. Online, Cheap Eats (www.cheapeats.co.nz) scours Auckland for the city's best food for under $20. Also check out *Metro* magazine's Top 50 Cheap Eats at www.metromag.co.nz.

AUCKLAND FOR CHILDREN

All of the east-coast beaches (St Heliers, Kohimarama, Mission Bay, Okahu Bay, Cheltenham, Narrow Neck, Takapuna, Milford, Long Bay) are safe for supervised kids, while sights such as the **Rainbow's End theme park** (Map p86; ☑09-262 2030; www.rainbowsend.co.nz; 2 Clist Cres, Manukau; unlimited rides adult/child $60/50; ☺10am-4pm Mon-Fri, to 5pm Sat & Sun; ⊞), Kelly Tarlton's Sea Life Aquarium (p93), Auckland Museum (p91) and Auckland Zoo (p94) are all firm favourites. Parnell Baths (p97) has a children's pool, but on wintry days head to the thermal pools at Parakai (p141).

For a spot of kid-oriented theatre, and a great family restaurant (p114) and children's playground, check out what's scheduled at Whoa! Studios (p119), an easy train journey west of the city in Henderson.

Baby-changing facilities are widespread, often in shopping malls and integrated within public toilets. City buses, trains and ferries offer convenient access for prams, and pavements are generally in good condition.

Dizengoff
CAFE $

(Map p105; ☑09-360 0108; www.facebook.com/dizengoff.ponsonby; 256 Ponsonby Rd, Ponsonby; mains $10-24; ☺6.30am-4pm) This stylish shoebox crams in a disparate crowd of corporate and fashion types, Ponsonby denizens and travellers. There's a Jewish influence to the food, with tasty Israeli platters, chopped liver, bagels and chicken salads, along with tempting baking, heart-starting coffee and a great stack of reading material.

★ Azabu
JAPANESE $$

(Map p105; ☑09-320 5292; www.azabuponsonby.co.nz; 26 Ponsonby Rd, Grey Lynn; mains & shared plates $16-39; ☺noon-late Wed-Sun, from 5pm Mon & Tue) Nikkei cuisine, an exciting blend of Japanese and Peruvian influences, is the focus at Azabu. Amid a dramatic interior enlivened by striking images of Tokyo, standout dishes include the tuna sashimi tostada, Japanese tacos with wasabi avocado, and king prawns with a jalapeño and ponzu dressing. Arrive early and enjoy a basil- and chilli-infused cachaca cocktail at Azabu's Roji bar.

★ Saan
THAI $$

(Map p105; ☑09-320 4237; www.saan.co.nz; 160 Ponsonby Rd, Ponsonby; dishes $12-38; ☺5pm-late Sat-Thu, noon-3pm & 5pm-late Fri) Hot in both senses of the word, this super-fashionable restaurant focuses on the fiery cuisine of the Isaan and Lanna regions of northern Thailand. The menu is conveniently sorted from least to most spicy and split into smaller and larger dishes for sharing. Be sure to order the soft-shell crab.

Lokanta
MEDITERRANEAN $$

(Map p105; ☑09-360 6355; www.lokanta.nz; 137a Richmond Rd, Grey Lynn; meze $7-19, mains $27-34; ☺5pm-late Tue-Sun) Featuring the cuisine of the eastern Mediterranean, unpretentious Lokanta is a laid-back alternative to the trendier eateries along nearby Ponsonby Rd. Greek and Turkish flavours happily coexist, and robust Greek wines partner well with hearty dishes, including chargrilled octopus and roast goat with a barley risotto. The coconut and almond baklava introduces a tropical influence to the classic dessert.

Little Bird Kitchen
CAFE $$

(Map p105; ☑09-555 3278; www.littlebirdorganics.co.nz; 1a Summer St, Ponsonby; mains $15-23; ☺7.30am-4pm daily & 6-9.30pm Wed-Sat; ☑) 🍃 Everything on the menu is prepared raw and uncooked, but is still tasty and healthy. Tuck into dishes studded with acai berries, chia seeds and organic fruit; there are even bagels, risotto, tacos and delicious cakes. For dinner, highlights include pumpkin-and-lemongrass curry and kimchi burgers. The drinks list includes kombucha, juices and smoothies, and organic beer.

Ponsonby Central
CAFE $$

(Map p105; www.ponsonbycentral.co.nz; 136-138 Ponsonby Rd, Ponsonby; mains $17-38; ☺7am-10.30pm Sun-Wed, to midnight Thu-Sat) Restaurants, cafes, bars and gourmet food shops fill this upmarket former warehouse space offering everything from Auckland's best pizza and Argentinian barbecue to Asian street food partnered with zingy cocktails. It's a prime eating and drinking destination and offers excellent dining options from breakfast right through to dinner. And if you're after the city's best gourmet burgers, look no further.

★ **Sidart** MODERN NZ $$$
(Map p105; ☑09-360 2122; www.sidart.co.nz;
Three Lamps Plaza, 283 Ponsonby Rd, Ponson-
by; mains $32-38, 5-/7-course tasting menus
$120/179; ◷6pm-late Tue-Sun, noon-3pm Fri) No
one in Auckland produces creative degus-
tations quite like Sid Sahrawat. It's food as
both art and science but, more importantly,
food to fire up the taste buds, delight the
brain, satisfy the stomach and put a smile
on the face. The restaurant is a little hard
to find, tucked away at the rear of what was
once the Alhambra cinema.

Expect high-end and innovative combi-
nations of European, Asian and Indian fla-
vours. The Chef's Table dinner experience
(per person $195) is a personalised insight
into some of NZ's finest dining.

Cocoro JAPANESE $$$
(Map p105; ☑09-360 0927; www.cocoro.co.nz;
56a Brown St, Ponsonby; dishes $22-49, degus-
tation menus $150-240; ◷noon-2pm & 5.30-
10pm Tue-Sat) Japanese elegance infuses
everything at this excellent restaurant,
from the soft lighting and chic decor to the
delicate flavours of the artistically arranged
food. At lunchtime it offers an affordable
donburi rice bowl ($24 to $29) and a mul-
tiplate option ($45), while in the evening
multicourse degustation menus showcase
the chefs' skills.

✗ **Karangahape Road & Newton**

Karangahape Rd is known for its late-night
clubs, but cafes and plenty of inexpensive
ethnic restaurants are mixed in with the
vintage-clothing stores, secondhand boutiques, tattooists and adult shops. In recent
years it's also attracted some of the city's
best young chefs.

★ **Gemmayze St** LEBANESE $$
(Map p88; ☑09-600 1545; www.gemmayze
street.co.nz; St Kevin's Arcade, 15/183 Karanga-
hape Rd; meze & mains $10-35; ◷5.30-10pm
Thu-Sat; ✎) Located amid the restored
heritage architecture of St Kevin's Arcade,
Gemmayze St presents a stylish update on
Lebanese cuisine. Mint, orange blossom
and rosewater cocktails are prepared at the
beaten-copper bar, while shared tables en-
courage lots of sociable dining on meze and
expertly grilled meats. The optional 'Jeeb'
menu (per person $65) is a brilliant option
for a leisurely feast.

Apero BISTRO $$
(Map p88; ☑09-373 4778; www.apero.co.nz; 280
Karangahape Rd; shared plates $8-25; ◷4pm-late
Wed, Thu, Sat & Sun, noon-late Fri) Housemade
terrines, sausages and charcuterie are the
culinary stars at Apero, another Karangahape Rd establishment offering the perfect
blend of eating and drinking. Service from
the co-owner is relaxed but authoritative
– expect well-considered wine recommendations. Ease into the brick-lined space
knowing everything from the goats' cheese
croquettes to the 'Something Fish' seafood
special will be damn tasty.

Fort Greene CAFE $$
(Map p88; ☑022 425 7791; www.fortgreene.
co.nz; 322 Karangahape Rd; sandwiches $15-21;
◷7.30am-4pm Mon-Fri, 8.30am-3.30pm Sat,
9am-3pm Sun; ✎) ✿ Baked on-site, Auck-
land's best sourdough bread is used for Fort
Greene's tasty gourmet sandwiches. Pick
some up for a picnic or tuck into the Reuben
sandwich with salt-beef brisket and house-
made sauerkraut. Great coffee and eggy
breakfasts too.

Cotto ITALIAN $$
(Map p88; ☑09-394 1555; www.cotto.co.nz; 375
Karangahape Rd; shared plates $16-22; ◷5pm-late
Mon-Sat) Modern Italian cuisine shines at
Cotto, a perpetually busy eatery along Karangahape Rd. On the shared-plates menu,
highlights include spinach and goats' cheese
dumplings with fried sage leaves, and grilled
eggplant with whipped feta cheese. Enjoy
a cocktail in the ramshackle-chic interior.
Queues are frequent on weekends, so aim to
get there when it opens.

Bestie CAFE $$
(Map p88; www.bestiecafe.co.nz; St Kevin's Arcade,
Karangahape Rd; mains $12-22; ◷7.30am-3.30pm
Mon-Fri, 8.30am-3.30pm Sat & Sun; ✎) ✿ One
of the excellent cafes and restaurants in re-
vitalised St Kevin's Arcade, Bestie is a perfect
refuelling stop after trawling the arty and
vintage shops along Karangahape Rd. Try to
secure a table overlooking leafy Myers Park,
and pair coffee or kombucha with signature
dishes such as Bestie's ricotta doughnuts, or
flatbread with chorizo, labneh and a chilli
fried egg.

★ **French Cafe** FRENCH $$$
(Map p98; ☑09-377 1911; www.sidatthefrench
cafe.co.nz; 210 Symonds St, Newton; mains $36-48,
5-/7-course tasting menus $140/180; ◷noon-3pm

Fri, 6pm-late Tue-Sat) ✐ The French Cafe has been rated one of Auckland's top restaurants for more than 30 years. Now helmed by one of Auckland's finest chefs, Sid Sahrawat, there's a subtle and seamless blending of French, Asian and Pacific cuisine. Foraged ingredients regularly feature, as do excellent vegetarian à-la-carte and tasting-menu options.

✖ Kingsland & Mt Eden

Zool Zool   JAPANESE $
(Map p98; ☎ 09-630 4445; www.zoolzool.co.nz; 405 Mt Eden Rd, Mt Eden; snacks $10-18, ramen $15-19; ◷ 11.30am-2pm & 5.30-10pm Tue-Sun) A coproduction between two of Auckland's most respected Japanese chefs, Zool Zool is a stylish and modern take on a traditional izakaya (Japanese pub). Some of the city's best ramen noodle dishes are underpinned by hearty and complex broths, and dishes made for sharing over frosty mugs of Japanese beer include tempura squid, soft-shell crab and panko-crumbed fried chicken.

Atomic Roastery   CAFE $
(Map p98; ☎ 0800 286 642; www.atomiccoffee. co.nz; 420c New North Rd, Kingsland; snacks & meals $6-17; ◷ 7am-3pm Mon-Fri, from 8am Sat & Sun) Java hounds should follow their noses to this, one of the country's best-known coffee roasters. Tasty accompaniments include pies served in mini frying pans, bagels, salads and cakes.

Morningside Precinct   FOOD HALL $$
(Map p98; www.morningside.nz; 14-18 McDonald St, Morningside; snacks & mains $8-36; ◷ hours vary; ⎆) ✐ An easy 300m stroll from Morningside train station, this former curtain factory is now a versatile eating and drinking destination. Highlights include Kind Eatery, specialising in sustainably sourced and plant-based dishes; Bo's Dumplings, a hole-in-the-wall recreation of downtown Shanghai; and Morningcider's compact bar pouring zingy craft ciders. The Morningside Tavern is popular before and after rugby at nearby Eden Park.

Frasers   CAFE $$
(Map p98; ☎ 09-630 6825; www.frasers.nz; cnr Mt Eden & Stokes Rds, Mt Eden; mains $15-30; ◷ 6am-11pm Mon-Fri, 7am-11pm Sat & Sun) One of Mt Eden's most loved cafes has been reborn after a stylish makeover. The coffee and cakes are still great – especially the baked New

York cheesecake – but now wine and craft beer partner the menu of comfort-food classics. Try the mushrooms on sourdough for breakfast, or go for the veal schnitzel with crispy potato gratin at dinner.

Pasta & Cuore   ITALIAN $$
(Map p98; ☎ 09-630 9130; www.pastaecuore.co.nz; 409 Mt Eden Rd, Mt Eden; mains $23-30; ◷ 11am-9pm; ⎆) ✐ Traditional Italian flavours inspired by the cuisine of Bologna shine at this friendly neighbourhood eatery. Secure a table in the rear garden and feast on plump tortellini pasta, and cheese and charcuterie platters perfect for sharing. Takeaway fresh pasta is available, and there's a good selection of natural and organic wines. Book ahead.

Xoong   ASIAN $$
(Map p98; www.xoong.co.nz; 424 Mt Eden Rd, Mt Eden; shared plates $11-32; ◷ noon-late Wed-Sun, from 5pm Tue; ⎆) Pan-Asian shared plates at the stylish Xoong include smoked salmon in a Vietnamese-style curry, Wagyu beef with Thai basil, and kimchi dumplings with shiitake mushrooms. Kick the evening off with cocktails or craft beers from Auckland's Hallertau and Sawmill breweries in Xoong's adjacent bar.

✖ Parnell & Newmarket

Little & Friday   CAFE $
(Map p113; ☎ 09-524 8742; www.littleandfriday. com; 11 McColl St, Newmarket; snacks & mains $10-22; ◷ 7am-3.30pm Mon-Fri, 8am-4pm Sat & Sun) Renowned for some of Auckland's best homestyle baking, the sleek and modern Little & Friday is worth the 500m stroll from Newmarket's main shopping street. Try the cardamom and coconut vanilla porridge with poached pear. Pro tip: the best doughnuts in town usually arrive in store around 10.30am from the external commercial kitchen.

La Cigale   MARKET $
(Map p92; ☎ 09-366 9361; www.lacigale.co.nz; 69 St Georges Bay Rd, Parnell; cafe $10-21; ◷ market 9am-1.30pm Sat & Sun, cafe to 3pm Wed-Fri, to 1.30pm Sat & Sun) Catering to Francophile foodies, this warehouse stocks French imports and has a patisserie-laden cafe. During the weekend farmers markets, this cigale (cicada) really chirps, offering stalls laden with local artisan produce and a fine array of ethnic treats from recent arrivals to the city.

Newmarket

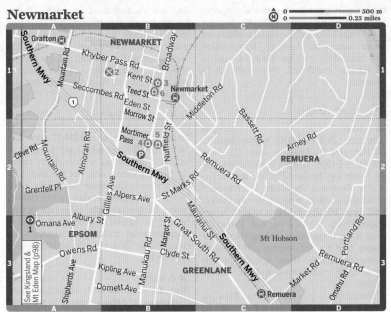

★**Gerome**   GREEK **$$**
(Map p92; ☎09-373 3883; www.gerome.nz;
269 Parnell Rd, Parnell; shared plates $14-34;
⏱11.30am-late) Greek cuisine is rare in Auckland, but Gerome's modern interpretation of traditional Hellenic flavours make it one of Auckland's best restaurants. Highlights include the pork and lamb *manti* (dumplings) with fermented chilli, and the superb slow-roasted lamb *kleftiko* with watermelon jelly and pine nuts. On a warm summer's afternoon or evening, sit in the open-air pavilion out front.

Han   KOREAN **$$**
(Map p92; ☎09-377 0977; www.hanrestaurant.
co.nz; 100 Parnell Rd, Parnell; mains $30-41;
⏱11am-2.30pm Wed-Sat, 5.30-11pm Wed-Sun) 🌿
Korean flavours continue to influence Auckland's dining scene, and Han's evolution from a food truck to a standalone restaurant is testament to the innovation of chef Min Baek. Lunch is a more informal affair – think Korean-style burgers and healthy rice bowls – but the dinner menu really shines with modern dishes, including beef short rib with beetroot and asparagus.

Winona Forever   CAFE **$$**
(Map p92; ☎09-974 2796; www.winonaforever.
co.nz; 100 Parnell Rd, Parnell; mains $20-26;

Newmarket

⏱7am-4pm Mon-Fri, 8am-4pm Sat & Sun) Some of Auckland's best counter food – including stonking cream doughnuts – partners with innovative cafe culture at this always-busy eatery near good shopping and art galleries along Parnell Rd. Locals crowd in with travellers for coffee, craft beer and wine, and one of the cafe's signature dishes: the tempura soft-shell-crab omelette.

★**Pasture**   MODERN NZ **$$$**
(Map p92; ☎09-300 5077; www.pastureakl.com;
3/235 Parnell Rd, Parnell; menu per person $230;
⏱5.45pm-late Wed-Sun; 🗲) 🌿 Pasture is unlike any other dining experience in the city. You'll need to book a few months ahead –

the compact space has just two seatings per night and room for only six diners – to enjoy chef Verner's intensely seasonal multicourse menu harnessing foraging, fermentation and wood-fired cooking. Look forward to an eclectic soundtrack, also of the chef's choosing.

✕ Other Areas

★ Nanam   FILIPINO $$
(Map p86; 📞 09-488 9976; www.nanam.co.nz; 178 Hurstmere Rd, Takapuna; tapas $11, mains $26-33; ⊙ 5-10pm Tue-Wed, 11.30am-10pm Thu-Sat, 5-9pm Sun) Modern Filipino food is the star at Nanam in the North Shore suburb of Takapuna. Dine on innovative updates of traditional Filipino food that made UK chef Marco Pierre White a big fan. Especially good is the *longganisa* sausage combining Wagyu beef and lemongrass and the lamb *adobo* croquettes. Menu options include tapas style, main dishes and set sharing menus.

Bus 82 (30 to 35 minutes) from the Civic Theatre in central Auckland will drop you on Hurstmere Rd right outside the restaurant.

Fortieth & Hurstmere   FOOD HALL $$
(Map p86; www.fortiethandhurstmere.co.nz; 40 Hurstmere Rd, Takapuna; ⊙ hours vary) Easily reached by bus from midtown Auckland, this brick-lined laneway off Takapuna's main shopping street features cool eateries serving up everything from rotisserie chicken to super-healthy Hawaiian poke and Colombian-style barbecue. Check the website for menus and the opening times of the seven distinct operations, including superior wood-fired pizza and Auckland's best burgers.

Takapuna Beach Cafe   CAFE $$
(Map p86; 📞 09-484 0002; www.takapuna beachcafe.co.nz; 22 The Promenade, Takapuna; mains $19-30; ⊙ 6.30am-6pm) Sophisticated cafe fare combined with excellent views of Takapuna Beach ensure that this cafe constantly buzzes. If you can't snaffle a table, grab an award-winning ice cream – our favourite is the salted caramel – and take a lazy stroll along the beach.

Grounds Eatery   CAFE $$
(📞 09-393 8448; www.thegrounds.co.nz; 8-14 Henderson Valley Rd, Henderson; mains $20-33; ⊙ 9am-late Wed-Sun; 🎵) 🌿 Part of the Whoa! Studios (p119) complex in Henderson, the

Grounds has pulled off the trick of being equally attractive to children and their parents. Handmade ice blocks, dumplings and creamy spaghetti bolognese keep the little ones happy, while mum and dad can partner pork-belly steamed buns or the Grounds' Wagyu burger with West Auckland wine and craft beer.

St Heliers Bay Bistro   MODERN NZ $$
(Map p86; www.stheliersbaybistro.co.nz; 387 Tamaki Dr, St Heliers; brunch $16-27, dinner $27-34; ⊙ 7am-11pm) Head along Tamaki Dr to this classy eatery with harbour views. No bookings are taken, but the switched-on crew soon find space for diners. Look forward to upmarket takes on the classics (pasta, burgers, fish and chips), along with cooked breakfasts, tasty salads and lots of Mediterranean influences. Excellent ice cream, too – best enjoyed walking along the beach.

★ Cazador   INTERNATIONAL $$$
(Map p86; 📞 09-620 8730; www.cazador.co.nz; 854 Dominion Rd, Balmoral; tapas $7-10, mains $36; ⊙ 5-10pm Wed-Sat) 🌿 The Persian heritage of the Lolaiy family combines with game meat and foraged ingredients at Cazador. Decor such as stuffed animal heads is largely unchanged since the 1980s, but the food is delicious and includes housemade charcuterie and interesting proteins like venison and wild hare. And don't worry, it's not heavy and stodgy, but rather light and delivered with an innovative touch.

Engine Room   MODERN NZ $$$
(Map p86; 📞 09-480 9502; www.engineroom. net.nz; 115 Queen St, Northcote; mains $36-43; ⊙ noon-3pm Fri, 5.30-11pm Tue-Sat) One of Auckland's best restaurants, this informal eatery serves up lighter-than-air goats'-cheese soufflés, inventive mains and oh-my-God chocolate truffles. It's worth booking ahead and catching the ferry to Northcote Point; the restaurant is a further 1km Uber or walk away.

🍷 Drinking & Nightlife

Auckland's nightlife is quiet during the week – for some vital signs, head to Ponsonby Rd, Britomart or the Viaduct. Karangahape Rd wakes up late on Friday and Saturday; don't even bother staggering this way before 11pm.

LGBTQI+ AUCKLAND

The Queen City (as it's known for completely coincidental reasons) has by far NZ's biggest gay population, with the bright lights attracting gay and lesbian Kiwis from all over the country. However, the even brighter lights of Sydney eventually steal many of the 30- to 40-somethings, leaving a gap in the demographic. There are very few gay venues, and they only really kick off on the weekends. For the latest, see the monthly magazine *Express* (available from gay venues) or visit the website www.gayexpress.co.nz.

The big event on the calendar is February's Auckland Pride Festival (p100). Also worth watching out for are the regular parties held by Urge Events (www.facebook.com/urgebar); the only reliably fun and sexy nights out for the over-30s, they book out quickly.

Venues change with alarming regularity, but these ones were the stayers at the time of writing:

Family (Map p88; 📞 09-309 0213; 270 Karangahape Rd, Newton; ⊙9am-4am) Trashy, brash and extremely young, Family gets crammed on weekends, with drag hosts and dancing into the wee hours, both at the back of the ground-level bar and in the club downstairs.

Staircase (Map p88; 📞 09-303 1661; www.facebook.com/Staircasebar; 25 Cross St; ⊙4.30-11pm Tue-Thu, to 4am Fri & Sat, 5-9pm Sun) Inclusive and welcoming bar with occasional quiz nights and drag shows, and a well-frequented dance floor. Wider age range than other venues. Check Facebook for what's on.

Eagle (Map p88; 📞 09-309 4979; www.facebook.com/the.eagle.bar; 259 Karangahape Rd, Newton; ⊙4pm-1am Mon, Tue & Sun, to 2am Wed & Thu, to 4am Fri & Sat) A cosy place for a quiet drink early in the evening, getting more raucous as the night progresses. Get in quick to put your picks on the video jukebox or prepare for an entire evening of Kylie and Taylor.

🍽 City Centre & Britomart

Little Culprit COCKTAIL BAR
(Map p88; www.littleculprit.co.nz; cnr Wyndham & Queen Sts; ⊙noon-1am Mon-Thu, to 2am Fri & Sat) Some of Auckland's most interesting cocktails feature at this stylish bar, and the owners' background in restaurants also shines through. Graze on a platter of cheese and charcuterie or indulge in a savoury waffle with duck-liver parfait. People-watch at pavement level or adjourn to the more intimate lower lounge downstairs. There's a good selection of natural wines too.

Brothers Beer CRAFT BEER
(Map p88; 📞 09-366 6100; www.brothersbeer.co.nz; City Works Depot, 90 Wellesley St; ⊙noon-10pm) This beer bar combines quirky decor with 18 taps crammed with Brothers' own brews and guest beers from NZ and further afield. Hundreds more bottled beers are chilling in the fridges, and bar food includes pizza. There are occasional movie and comedy nights, and beers are available to take away. The adjacent City Works Depot has other good eating options.

Vultures' Lane PUB
(Map p88; 📞 09-300 7117; www.vultureslane.co.nz; 10 Vulcan Lane; ⊙11.30am-late) With 22 taps, more than 75 bottled beers and sports on the TV, this pleasantly grungy historic pub is popular with Auckland's savviest craft-beer fans. Check the website for what's currently on tap, and also for news of regular tap takeovers from some of NZ's best brewers.

Mo's BAR
(Map p88; 📞 09-366 6066; www.mosbar.co.nz; cnr Wolfe & Federal Sts; ⊙2pm-late Mon-Fri, from 6pm Sat; 🕿) There's something about this tiny corner bar that makes you want to invent problems just so the bartender can solve them with soothing words and an expertly poured martini.

Brewers Co-operative CRAFT BEER
(Map p88; 📞 09-309 4515; 128 Victoria St; ⊙11am-10pm) With 27 craft beers on tap, this corner bar is a good central-city option for an interesting brew and a feed of seafood and chips served the traditional way, in paper. It's popular with the after-work crowd on Fridays.

WORTH A TRIP

WINERY LAYOVER

Clearly the roar of jets doesn't bother grapes, as Villa Maria (Map p86; ☑ 09-255 0666; www.villamaria.co.nz; 118 Montgomerie Rd, Māngere; ☺ 9am-6pm Mon-Fri, to 4pm Sat & Sun), NZ's most awarded winery, is just 4km from the airport. The parklike grounds of Villa Maria are a green oasis in the encircling industrial zone. Short tours ($5) take place at 11am and 2pm. There's a charge for tastings ($10 to $15, refundable on purchase), but lingering over a lunch of wine and antipasto (platters $25 to $55, lunch $29 to $38) on the restaurant's terrace sure beats hanging around the departure lounge.

La Fuente   COCKTAIL BAR

(Map p88; ☑ 09-303 0238; www.lafuente.co.nz; 23 Customs St E, Snickel Lane; ☺ 11am-late) Auckland's only bar specialising in the potent Mexican spirit *mezcal*, La Fuente (The Fountain) is also a fine spot to partner an excellent selection of wine and craft beer with Latin American–inspired snacks, including ceviche and cheese-and-jalapeño croquettes. The knowledgeable bartenders will guide you through more than 20 different *mezcals* from the Mexican region of Oaxaca.

HI SO   COCKTAIL BAR

(Map p88; www.so-auckland.com; cnr Customs St E & Gore St, So/Auckland Hotel; ☺ 4pm-midnight) Every burgeoning international city needs a good rooftop bar, and the stylish HI SO at the So/Auckland ticks all the boxes. Futuristic decor includes a shimmering wall of neon, with the dramatic interior segueing to an outdoor terrace with island and harbour views. Signature cocktails include the chamomile-infused Gulf Spritzer, and bar snacks run from oysters to tiger prawns.

🍷 Viaduct Harbour & Wynyard Quarter

Dr Rudi's   MICROBREWERY

(Map p88; ☑ 021 048 7946; cnr Quay & Hobson Sts, Viaduct Harbour; ☺ 8am-4am Mon-Fri, from 11am Sat & Sun) Viaduct Harbour's best views – usually including a bevy of visiting superyachts – combine with Dr Rudi's very own craft beers and a menu featuring wood-fired pizza and excellent seafood and

barbecue platters designed to defeat even the hungriest group. There are also a couple of tenpin bowling lanes to get active on.

Sixteen Tun   CRAFT BEER

(Map p88; ☑ 09-368 7712; www.16tun.co.nz; 10-26 Jellicoe St, Wynyard Quarter; ☺ 11.30am-late) The glister of burnished copper perfectly complements the liquid amber on offer here in the form of dozens of NZ craft beers by the bottle and a score on tap. If you can't decide, go for a good-value tasting 'crate' of 200mL serves.

Wynyard Pavilion   BAR

(Map p88; ☑ 09-303 1002; www.facebook.com/wynyardpavilion; 17 Jellicoe St, Wynyard Quarter; ☺ 11am-11pm) Formerly a harbourside warehouse, Wynyard Pavilion's high-ceilinged heritage space is now one of the area's most versatile spots to eat, drink and take in maritime views. Oysters and kingfish feature from the raw bar; pizza ingredients include smoked salmon or spicy *'nduja* sausage; and the watermelon and feta salad is perfect for warmer days. Try to snaffle a seat outside.

🍷 Ponsonby & Grey Lynn

Along Ponsonby Rd, the line between cafe, restaurant, bar and club gets blurred. A lot of eateries also have live music or become clubs later on in the evening.

★**Freida Margolis**   BAR

(Map p105; ☑ 09-378 6625; www.facebook.com/freidamargolis; 440 Richmond Rd, Grey Lynn; ☺ 4-11pm Sun-Wed, to 2am Thu-Sat) Formerly a butcher's – look for the Westlynn Organic Meats sign – this corner location is now a great little neighbourhood bar with a backstreets Bogotá ambience. Loyal locals sit outside with their well-behaved dogs, supping on sangria, wine and craft beer, and enjoying eclectic sounds from the owner's big vinyl collection.

Deadshot   COCKTAIL BAR

(Map p105; www.facebook.com/Deadshotnz; 46 Ponsonby Rd, Grey Lynn; ☺ 5pm-2am) Featuring some of Auckland's most experienced bartenders, Deadshot – cowboy parlance for 'strong booze' – is where you can sample the city's cocktail A-game. With bar stools, brick walls, and cosy and intimate booths, there's also a touch of the Wild West in the decor, but it's still a thoroughly cosmopolitan drinking hole. Expect classic cocktails with a twist.

Hoppers Garden Bar BAR
(Map p105; www.hoppersgardenbar.co.nz; 134 Ponsonby Rd, Ponsonby; ⏰4pm-late Mon-Wed, noon-late Thu-Sun) Gin and craft beers from around NZ combine with excellent street-food-inspired bar snacks at the summery and relaxed Hoppers Garden Bar. Ponsonby locals crowd in, often with their canine pals, to enjoy zingy cocktails or seasonal brews from Auckland brewing stars like Behemoth and Hallertau. Flavour-packed menu highlights include salmon ceviche and steamed buns with soft-shell crab.

Annabel's WINE BAR
(Map p105; www.annabelswinebar.com; 277 Ponsonby Rd, Ponsonby; ⏰3-11pm) A self-described 'neighbourhood bar', Annabel's would also be right at home in the backstreets of Bordeaux or Barcelona. Cheese and charcuterie platters combine with a Eurocentric wine list, while Spanish beers and classic Negroni cocktails also help turn the South Pacific into the south of France. A thoroughly unpretentious affair, it's worth a stop before or after dining along Ponsonby Rd.

🍺 Karangahape Road

★**Madame George** BAR
(Map p88; ☎09-308 9039; www.madamegeorge.co.nz; 490 Karangahape Rd; ⏰5pm-late Tue-Sat) Two patron saints of cool – Elvis Presley and Marlon Brando – look down in this compact space. Shoot the breeze with the friendly bar staff over a craft beer or Auckland's best cocktails, or grab a shared table out front and watch the passing theatre of K Rd.

Madame George also offers a classy Peruvian-influenced food menu, either at the bar or in a cosy dining room out back.

Bar Celeste WINE BAR
(Map p88; www.barceleste.com; 146 Karangahape Rd; shared plates $16-32; ⏰3pm-late Tue-Sat) 🍴 Inspired by the 'neo bistro' movement of Paris, Bar Celeste blurs the line between intimate bar and innovative restaurant. Natural wines are regularly featured, there's usually a food-friendly sour beer on the taps, and the menu of seasonal small plates could include sweetbreads, crudo trevally or grilled octopus. Don't miss the superb sourdough bread from K Rd neighbours, Fort Greene.

Lovebucket COCKTAIL BAR
(Map p88; ☎09-869 2469; www.lovebucket.co.nz; K'Road Food Workshop, 309 Karangahape Rd; ⏰4pm-late Tue-Sun) Lovebucket is a more sophisticated alternative to K Rd's often youthful after-dark vibe. Courtesy of shared ownership with the Hallertau Brewery in West Auckland, Lovebucket's craft-beer selection is one of Auckland's best – including barrel-aged and sour beers. Quirky cocktails and a well-informed wine list join interesting bar snacks such as cheeses, charcuterie and gourmet toasted sandwiches.

AUCKLAND REGION AUCKLAND

CRAFT BEER AROUND AUCKLAND

Nelson, as the country's major hop-growing region, and bohemian Wellington both claim to be the 'craft-beer capital of NZ', but while the southern centres have been debating the title over a few brews, Auckland's northern craft-beer scene has been fizzing and fermenting its way to excellence. Driven by the relative size of the market, there are now plenty of opportunities around Auckland for travelling beer fans to explore the diversity of the Kiwi beer scene.

In Auckland's rural hinterland both Hallertau (p140) and Sawmill Brewery (p145) offer award-winning beers with restaurant-worthy food, while across on Waiheke Island there's the stylish, brick-lined Alibi Brewing tasting room at Tantalus Estate (p129).

In the city, Brothers Beer (p115), Brewers Co-operative (p115) and Vultures' Lane (p115) are all good destinations, while June's annual GABS (p101) festival is Auckland's very own version of the world-famous beer festival first launched in Melbourne, Australia. The recently launched Auckland Beer Mile – actually 3.2km – includes Galbraith's Alehouse (p118) and the Garage Project Cellar Door (p118). Check www.facebook.com/aucklandbeermile for events and occasional tap takeovers.

Excellent Auckland-region brewery names to look out for in restaurants and bars include 8 Wired, Behemoth, Liberty and Epic. To join a tour of Auckland's craft-beer scene, contact Big Foody Food Tour (p99) or **Brewbus** (☎027 583 2484; www.brewbus.co.nz; per person $80-220). Brewbus also operates beer-focused tours around other regions of NZ.

Satya Chai Lounge BAR

(Map p88; ✆09-377 0007; www.satya.co.nz/
satya-chai-lounge; 271 Karangahape Rd; ⊙noon-
1.30pm & 6-10pm) Craft beers – many from
Wellington's iconic Garage Project brewery – partner with fiery Indian street food
in this rustic and laid-back space. Cocktails
and a well-considered wine list complete the
picture. There's no signage, so be brave and
push the door open to the cosy interior. Next
door with a great whisky selection is the
equally hip tiki-inspired GGX Flamingo bar.

Wine Cellar WINE BAR

(Map p88; www.facebook.com/winecellarst
kevins; St Kevin's Arcade, 183 Karangahape Rd;
⊙5pm-midnight Mon-Thu, to 1am Fri & Sat) Secreted downstairs in an arcade, the Wine
Cellar is dark, grungy and very cool, with
regular live music in the neighbouring
Whammy Bar.

🍺 Kingsland & Mt Eden

⭐ **Galbraith's Alehouse** BREWERY

(Map p98; ✆09-379 3557; http://alehouse.co.nz;
2 Mt Eden Rd, Mt Eden; ⊙noon-11pm) Brewing
real ales and lagers on-site, this cosy English-style pub in a grand heritage building
offers bliss on tap. There are always more
craft beers from around NZ and the world
on the guest taps, and the food's also very
good. From April to September, Galbraith's
Sunday roast is one of Auckland's best.

Garage Project Cellar Door CRAFT BEER

(Map p98; https://garageproject.co.nz/pages/
kingsland-cellar-door; 357 New North Rd, Kingsland;
⊙noon-8pm Tue, Wed & Sun, to 9pm Thu, 11am-9pm
Fri & Sat) Discover some of NZ's most innovative craft beers at the Auckland outpost of
Wellington's Garage Project. Due to the cellar
door's licence, beers are served in six-beer
tasting trays ($20), and there are always
12 different beers on tap. GP's full range of
beers and wild fermented wines are available
to take away, and bar snacks include cheese
and kimchi toasted sandwiches.

Portland Public House BAR

(Map p98; www.facebook.com/theportlandpublic
house; 463 New North Rd, Kingsland; ⊙4pm-mid-
night Mon-Wed, to 2am Thu & Fri, noon-2am Sat,
noon-midnight Sun) With mismatched furniture, cartoon-themed art and lots of hidden
nooks and crannies, the Portland Public
House is like spending a few lazy hours at
a trendy mate's place. It's also an excellent
location for live music.

⭐ Entertainment

For listings, check the *New Zealand Her-
ald's* *Time Out* magazine on Thursday
and again in its Saturday edition. Tickets
for most major events can be bought from
Ticketek (✆0800 842 538; www.ticketek.co.nz),
which has an outlet at SkyCity Theatre
(Map p88; ✆09-363 6000; www.skycity.co.nz;
cnr Wellesley & Hobson Sts), and Ticketmaster (✆09-970 9700; www.ticketmaster.co.nz) at
Spark Arena and the Aotea Centre (Map
p88; ✆09-309 2677; www.aucklandlive.co.nz; 50
Mayoral Dr). iTicket (✆0508 484 253; www.
iticket.co.nz) handles a lot of smaller gig and
dance-party tickets.

Live Music

Whammy Bar LIVE MUSIC

(Map p88; www.facebook.com/thewhammybar; 183
Karangahape Rd, Newton; ⊙8.30pm-4am Wed-
Sat) Small, but a stalwart on the live indie-
music scene nonetheless.

Neck of the Woods LIVE MUSIC

(Map p88; ✆09-320 5221; www.neckofthe
woods.co.nz; 155 Karangahape Rd, Newton; ⊙varies
by event) New Zealand's best indie bands,
emerging overseas acts, drum-and-bass DJs
and the occasional burlesque show all feature at this versatile upstairs venue keeping
the creative spirit of Karangahape Rd alive.

Ding Dong Lounge LIVE MUSIC

(Map p88; ✆09-377 4712; www.dingdonglounge
nz.com; 26 Wyndham St; ⊙6pm-4am Wed-Fri, from
8pm Sat) Rock, indie and alternative sounds
from live bands and DJs, washed down with
craft beer.

Power Station LIVE MUSIC

(Map p98; www.powerstation.net.nz; 33 Mt Eden Rd,
Mt Eden) Midrange venue popular with up-
and-coming overseas acts and established
Kiwi bands.

Spark Arena STADIUM

(Map p92; ✆09-358 1250; www.sparkarena.co.nz;
Mahuhu Cres, Britomart) Auckland's top indoor
arena for major touring acts.

Cinema

Most cinemas offer cheaper rates on weekdays before 5pm; Tuesday is generally bargain day.

Academy Cinemas CINEMA

(Map p88; ✆09-373 2761; www.academycinemas.
co.nz; 44 Lorne St; tickets adult/child $16/10) For-
eign and art-house films in the basement of
the Central Library. $5 movies on Wednesdays.

Rialto CINEMA
(Map p113; ☑09-369 2417; www.rialto.co.nz; 167 Broadway, Newmarket) Mainly art-house and international films, plus better mainstream fare and regular specialist film festivals.

Theatre, Classical Music & Comedy

Auckland's main arts and entertainment complex is grouped around Aotea Sq. Branded Auckland Live (www.aucklandlive. co.nz), it's composed of the Town Hall, Civic Theatre and Aotea Centre, along with the Bruce Mason Centre in Takapuna. The new ASB Waterfront Theatre in Wynyard Quarter is home to the Auckland Theatre Company.

Whoa! Studios THEATRE
(☑09-838 4553; https://whoastudios.co.nz; 8 Henderson Valley Rd, Henderson; tickets $16-30; ⛵) Exciting and educational kids' shows are performed at this innovative theatre in Henderson – expect extreme fun and irreverence – and the whole shebang also features a brilliant kids' playground and the excellent Grounds Eatery (p114). Check the website for what's scheduled in the theatre – usually across school holidays – but it's worth visiting just for the restaurant and playground.

Whoa! Studios is a short walk from the Henderson train station, reached by a 45-minute journey from Britomart (adult/child $7/4) on the Western line to Swanson.

Q Theatre THEATRE
(Map p88; ☑09-309 9771; www.qtheatre.co.nz; 305 Queen St) Theatre by various companies and intimate live music. Silo Theatre (www. silotheatre.co.nz) often performs here.

ASB Waterfront Theatre THEATRE
(Map p88; ☑box office 0800 282 849; www.asbwaterfronttheatre.co.nz; 138 Halsey St, Wynyard Quarter) The ASB Waterfront Theatre is used by the Auckland Theatre Company and also for occasional one-off shows and concerts. A good selection of bars and restaurants are nearby.

Classic Comedy Club COMEDY
(Map p88; ☑09-373 4321; www.comedy.co.nz; 321 Queen St; ⊙6.30pm-late) Stand-up performances most nights, with legendary late-night shows during the annual Comedy Festival (p101).

Auckland Town Hall CLASSICAL MUSIC
(Map p88; ☑09-309 2677; www.aucklandlive.co.nz; 305 Queen St) This elegant Edwardian venue (1911) hosts the NZ Symphony Orchestra

(www.nzso.co.nz) and Auckland Philharmonia (www.apo.co.nz), among others. Also used for concerts by touring international bands.

Sport

Eden Park SPECTATOR SPORT
(Map p98; ☑09-815 5551; www.edenpark.co.nz; Reimers Ave, Mt Eden) This stadium hosts top rugby (winter) and cricket (summer) tests by the All Blacks (www.allblacks.com) and the Black Caps (www.blackcaps.co.nz), respectively. It's also the home ground of Auckland Rugby (www.aucklandrugby.co.nz), the Blues Super Rugby team (www.theblues.co.nz) and Auckland Cricket (www.aucklandcricket.co.nz). Catch the train from Britomart to Kingsland and follow the crowds.

Behind-the-scenes stadium tours (90 minutes, adult/child $40/20) run at 10am and 2pm Monday to Friday and at 11am on weekends (excluding game days).

Mt Smart Stadium SPECTATOR SPORT
(Map p86; ☑09-366 2048; www.mtsmartstadium.co.nz; 2 Beasley Ave, Penrose) Home ground for the Warriors rugby league team (www.warriors.kiwi), Auckland Football Federation (www.aucklandfootball.org.nz) and Athletics Auckland (www.athleticsauckland.co.nz). Also *really* big concerts.

North Shore Events Centre SPECTATOR SPORT
(Map p86; ☑09-443 8199; www.nseventscentre.co.nz; Argus Pl, Wairau Valley) One of the two

PASIFIKA IN AUCKLAND

There are nearly 195,000 Pacific Islanders (PI) living in Auckland, making it the world's principal Polynesian city. Samoans are by far the largest group, followed by Cook Islanders, Tongans, Niueans, Fijians, Tokelauans and Tuvaluans. The biggest PI communities can be found in South Auckland and pockets of West and central Auckland.

Like the Māori renaissance of recent decades, Pasifika has become a hot commodity for Auckland hipsters. You'll find PI motifs everywhere: in art, architecture, fashion, homewares, movies and especially in music. The annual Pasifika Festival (p100) in March is a wonderful two-day celebration of Pacific culture.

home courts of the NZ Breakers basketball team (www.nzbreakers.co.nz) and an occasional concert venue. The other home court is at Spark Arena (p118).

🛍 Shopping

Followers of fashion should head to the Britomart precinct, Newmarket's Teed and Osborne Sts, and Ponsonby Rd. For vintage clothing and secondhand boutiques, try Karangahape Rd or Ponsonby Rd.

🛍 City Centre & Britomart

★ Real Groovy   MUSIC
(Map p88; ☑ 09-302 3940; www.realgroovy. co.nz; 520 Queen St; ⊗ 9am-7pm) Masses of new, secondhand and rare releases in vinyl and CD format, as well as concert tickets, giant posters, DVDs, books, magazines and clothes.

★ Unity Books   BOOKS
(Map p88; ☑ 09-307 0731; www.unitybooks.co.nz; 19 High St; ⊗ 8.30am-7pm Mon-Fri, 10am-6pm Sat & Sun) The inner-city's best independent bookshop with a fine selection of NZ tomes.

Strangely Normal   CLOTHING
(Map p88; ☑ 09-309 0600; www.strangely normal.com; 19 O'Connell St; ⊗ 10am-6pm Mon-Sat, 11am-4pm Sun) Quality, NZ-made men's tailored shirts straight out of *Blue Hawaii* sit alongside hipster hats, sharp shoes and cufflinks.

Zambesi   CLOTHING
(Map p88; ☑ 09-303 1701; www.zambesi.co.nz; 56 Tyler St; ⊗ 10am-6pm Mon-Fri, 11am-5pm Sat & Sun) Iconic NZ label much sought after by local and international celebs. Also in **Ponsonby** (Map p105; ☑ 09-360 7391; 169 Ponsonby Rd; ⊗ 10am-6pm Mon-Fri, 11am-5pm Sat & Sun) and **Parnell** (Map p92; ☑ 09-308 0363; 287 Parnell Rd; ⊗ 10am-6pm Mon-Fri, 11am-5pm Sat & Sun).

Karen Walker   CLOTHING
(Map p88; ☑ 09-309 6299; www.karenwalker.com; 18 Te Ara Tahuhu Walkway; ⊗ 10am-6pm) Join Madonna and Kirsten Dunst in wearing Walker's cool (but pricey) threads. Also in **Grey Lynn** (Map p105; ☑ 09-361 6723; 128a Ponsonby Rd; ⊗ 10am-5.30pm Mon-Sat, 11am-4pm Sun) and **Newmarket** (Map p113; ☑ 09-522 4286; 6 Balm St; ⊗ 10am-6pm).

Pauanesia   GIFTS & SOUVENIRS
(Map p88; ☑ 09-366 7282; www.pauanesia.co.nz; 35 High St; ⊗ 9.30am-6.30pm Tue-Fri, 10am-5pm Sat-Mon) Homewares and gifts with a Polynesian and Kiwiana influence.

🛍 Ponsonby & Grey Lynn

Women's Bookshop   BOOKS
(Map p105; ☑ 09-376 4399; www.womensbook shop.co.nz; 105 Ponsonby Rd, Ponsonby; ⊗ 10am-6pm Mon-Fri, to 5pm Sat & Sun) Excellent independent bookshop with a great selection of NZ authors and NZ-themed books.

🛍 Karangahape Rd

★ St Kevin's Arcade   SHOPPING CENTRE
(Map p88; www.stkevinsarcade.co.nz; 183 Karangahape Rd) Built in 1924, this historic, renovated shopping arcade has interesting stores selling vintage clothing and organic and sustainable goods. The arcade also has excellent cafes and restaurants.

Crushes   ARTS & CRAFTS
(Map p88; ☑ 09-940 5065; www.crushes.co.nz; 225 Karangahape Rd; ⊗ 10am-6pm Mon-Fri, to 5pm Sat, 11am-5pm Sun) Sells an excellent selection of arts, crafts, foodstuffs and homewares from local NZ designers. Also an interesting array of vintage clothing.

Cross Street Market   MARKET
(Map p88; 4 Cross St; ⊗ 10am-5pm) Vintage apparel, art and design from NZ craftspeople and good coffee make this raffish market a highlight of exploring Karangahape Rd's bohemian scene.

Flying Out MUSIC
(Map p88; ☑ 09-366 1755; www.flyingout.co.nz; 80 Pitt St; ⊙10am-6pm Mon-Thu, to 7pm Fri, to 5pm Sat & Sun) Interesting vinyl aplenty overflows at this compact record shop, which is also a top place to pick up recordings from NZ musicians. Cool T-shirts make it worth a stop even if you're more into streaming.

☐ Kingsland

★ **Royal Jewellery Studio** JEWELLERY
(Map p98; ☑ 09-846 0200; www.royaljewellery studio.com; 486 New North Rd; ⊙10am-4pm Tue-Sun) Work by local artisans, including beautiful Māori designs and authentic *pounamu* (greenstone) jewellery.

☐ Newmarket

Poi Room ART
(Map p113; ☑ 09-520 0399; www.thepoiroom. co.nz; 17 Osborne St; ⊙9.30am-5.30pm Mon-Fri, to 5pm Sat, 10am-4pm Sun) An excellent showcase of work by NZ artists and designers, including prints, paintings, ceramics, jewellery and homewares. Many of the items for sale reference Māori and Pasifika themes.

Huffer CLOTHING
(Map p113; www.huffer.co.nz; 309 Broadway, Westfield Newmarket; ⊙9am-7pm Mon-Wed, Fri & Sat, to 9pm Thu, 10am-7pm Sun) Stylish technical apparel and streetwear from a hip NZ company with its roots in snowboarding and skateboarding.

☐ Other Areas

Otara Flea Market MARKET
(Map p86; ☑ 09-274 0830; www.otarafleamarket. co.nz; Newbury St, Ōtara; ⊙6am-noon Sat) Held in the car park between the Manukau Polytech and the Ōtara town centre, this market has a palpable Polynesian atmosphere and is good for South Pacific food, music and fashion. Catch a train on the southern line to Papatoetoe and then switch to a bus to Ōtara.

ℹ Information

Auckland Council offers free wi-fi in parts of the city centre, Newton, Ponsonby, Kingsland, Mt Eden and Parnell. All public libraries offer free wi-fi.

MEDICAL SERVICES

Auckland City Hospital (☑ 09-367 0000; www.adhb.govt.nz; 2 Park Rd, Grafton; ⊙24hr) The city's main hospital has a dedicated accident and emergency (A&E) service.

Starship Children's Health (☑ 09-307 4949; www.adhb.govt.nz; Park Rd, Grafton; ⊙24hr) Has its own A&E department.

POST

Post Office (Map p88; ☑ 0800 081 190; www.nzpost.co.nz; 151 Queen St; ⊙9am-5pm Mon-Fri)

Post Office (Map p105; ☑ 0800 081 190; www. nzpost.co.nz; 314 Ponsonby Rd, Ponsonby; ⊙9am-5pm Mon-Fri, to 1pm Sat)

TOURIST INFORMATION

Auckland International Airport i-SITE (Map p86; ☑ 09-365 9925; www.aucklandnz.com; International Arrivals Hall; ⊙6.30am-10pm)

Cornwall Park Information Centre (Map p86; ☑ 09-630 8485; www.cornwallpark. co.nz; Huia Lodge, Michael Horton Dr; ⊙10am-4pm)

Devonport Information Centre (Map p96; www.devonport.co.nz; 3 Victoria Rd; ⊙10am-2pm; ☎)

Karanga Kiosk (Map p88; ☑ 09-365 1290; cnr Jellicoe & Halsey Sts, Wynyard Quarter; ⊙9.30am-4.30pm) This volunteer-run centre dispenses information on goings-on around the waterfront.

Princes Wharf i-SITE (Map p88; ☑ 09-365 9914; www.aucklandnz.com; Princes Wharf; ⊙9am-5pm) Auckland's main official information centre, incorporating the **DOC Auckland Visitor Centre** (Map p88; ☑ 09-379 6476; www.doc.govt.nz; Princes Wharf; ⊙9am-5pm).

SkyCity i-SITE (Map p88; ☑ 09-365 9918; www.aucklandnz.com; SkyCity Atrium, cnr Victoria & Federal Sts; ⊙9am-5pm)

ℹ Getting There & Away

AIR
Auckland is the main international gateway to NZ, and a hub for domestic flights. **Auckland Airport** (AKL; Map p86; ☑ 09-275 0789; www. aucklandairport.co.nz; Ray Emery Dr, Māngere) is 21km south of the city centre. It has separate international and domestic terminals a 10-minute walk apart from each other via a signposted footpath; a free shuttle service operates every 15 minutes (5am to 10.30pm). Both terminals have left-luggage facilities, eateries, ATMs and car-rental desks.

The major domestic services flying to/from Auckland:

Air New Zealand (☑ 09-357 3000; www. airnewzealand.co.nz) Flies to Kerikeri,

Whangārei, Tauranga, Rotorua, Taupō, Gisborne, New Plymouth, Napier, Palmerston North, Wellington, Nelson, Blenheim, Christchurch, Queenstown and Dunedin.

Air Chathams (☑ 09-257 0261; www. airchathams.co.nz) Flies from Auckland to Whakatāne, Whanganui, Norfolk Island and the Chatham Islands.

Barrier Air (☑ 09-275 9120, 0800 900 600; www.barrierair.kiwi; adult/child from $99/96) Flies to Great Barrier Island (Claris and Okiwi) and Kaitāia.

FlyMySky (☑ 09-256 7025, 0800 222 123; www.flymysky.co.nz; adult/child one way $109/79) Flies to Claris, Great Barrier Island.

Jetstar (☑ 0800 800 995; www.jetstar.com) Flies to Wellington, Christchurch, Queenstown and Dunedin.

BUS

Coaches depart from 172 Quay St, opposite the Ferry Building, except for InterCity and SKIP services, which depart from **SkyCity Coach Terminal** (Map p88; 102 Hobson St). Many southbound services also stop at the airport.

Go Kiwi (☑ 0800 446 549; www.go-kiwi.co.nz) Offers daily Auckland City–Auckland Airport–Thames–Tairua–Hot Water Beach–Whitianga shuttles.

InterCity (☑ 09-583 5780; www.intercity. co.nz) Has direct services to Kerikeri (from $29, 4½ hours, three daily), Hamilton (from $15, two hours, 16 daily), New Plymouth (from $35, 6¼ hours, daily), Taupō (from $26, five hours, five daily) and Wellington (from $31, 11 hours, four daily).

SKIP (https://skip.travel) Offers direct buses to Whangārei ($22, 2½ hours, two daily) and Hamilton ($13 to $17, two hours, four daily).

CAR & CAMPERVAN

Hire

Auckland's hire agencies are clustered around Beach Rd and Stanley St close to the city centre, and also on the southern end of Victoria Park near Victoria Park Market.

Apex Car Rentals (☑ 0800 737 009, 09-307 1063; www.apexrentals.co.nz; 206 Victoria St; ⊗ 8am-5pm)

Budget (☑ 09-976 2270; www.budget.co.nz; 206 Victoria St; ⊗ 7am-6pm Mon-Fri, 8am-5pm Sat & Sun)

Escape (☑ 09-377 6864; www.escaperentals. co.nz; 61 The Strand, Parnell; ⊗ 9am-4pm Mon-Fri, 9.30am-2pm Sat & Sun) Eccentrically painted campervans.

Go Rentals (☑ 09-257 5142; www.gorentals. co.nz; 3 Joseph Hammond Pl, Māngere; ⊗ 4.30am-2am) Near airport.

Hertz (☑ 09-367 6350; www.hertz.co.nz; 154 Victoria St; ⊗ 7.30am-5.30pm)

Jucy (☑ 0800 399 736; www.jucy.co.nz; 2-16 The Strand, Parnell; ⊗ 8am-5pm)

Kea, Maui & Britz (☑ 09-255 3910; www.maui. co.nz; 36 Richard Pearse Dr, Māngere; ⊗ 8am-4.30pm) Near airport.

NZ Frontiers (☑ 09-299 6705; www. newzealandfrontiers.com; 30 Laurie Ave, Papakura)

Omega (☑ 09-377 5573; www.omegarentals. com; 75 Beach Rd; ⊗ 8am-5.30pm)

Quality (☑ 0800 680 123; www.qualityrental. co.nz; 8 Andrew Baxter Dr, Māngere; ⊗ 8am-4pm) Near airport.

Thrifty (☑ 09-309 0111; www.thrifty.co.nz; 150 Khyber Pass Rd, Grafton; ⊗ 7am-6pm Mon-Fri, 8am-5pm Sat & Sun)

Wilderness Motorhomes (☑ 09-255 5300; www.wilderness.co.nz; 11 Pavilion Dr, Māngere; ⊗ 8am-5pm) Near airport.

Purchase

Mechanical inspection services are on hand at secondhand car fairs, where sellers pay to display their cars.

Auckland Car Fair (☑ 09-529 2233; Ellerslie Racecourse, Greenlane East; display fee $35; ⊗ 9am-noon Sun) Auckland's largest car fair.

Auckland City Car Fair (☑ 09-837 7817; www. aucklandcitycarfair.co.nz; 27 Alten Rd; display fee $30; ⊗ 8am-1pm Sat)

MOTORCYCLE

NZ Motorcycle Rentals (☑ 09-486 2472; www. nzbike.com; 72 Barrys Point Rd, Takapuna; per day $145-290) Guided tours of NZ also available.

TRAIN

Northern Explorer (☑ 0800 872 467; www. greatjourneysofnz.co.nz) trains leave from **Auckland Strand Station** (Ngaoho Pl) at 7.45am on Mondays, Thursdays and Saturdays, and arrive in Wellington at 6.25pm. Stops include Hamilton (at the 2½-hour mark), Ōtorohanga (three hours), Tongariro National Park (5½ hours), Ōhakune (six hours), Palmerston North (8½ hours) and Paraparaumu (9¾ hours). Standard fares to Wellington range from $139 to $219.

⊕ Getting Around

TO/FROM THE AIRPORT

Taxis usually cost $50 to $80 to the city, more if you strike traffic. Uber and local competitors Ola and Zoomy are available from both the domestic and international terminals where there are specific pickup areas for ride-share services.

SkyBus (☑ 09-222 0084; www.skybus.co.nz; one way/return adult $17/32, child $2/4; 🛜)

Runs bright-red buses between the terminals and the city, every 10 to 15 minutes from 5.15am to 7pm and at least half-hourly through the night. Stops include Mt Eden Rd or Dominion Rd, Symonds St, Queen St and Britomart. Reservations are not required; buy a ticket from the driver, the airport kiosk or online. Small discount if you book online.

Super Shuttle (☑ 09-522 5100; www.super shuttle.co.nz) A convenient door-to-door shuttle charging $25 for one person heading between the airport and a city hotel; the price increases for outlying suburbs. Save money by sharing a shuttle. A lengthier alternative is to catch the 380 bus to Onehunga ($3.50, 30 minutes, at least hourly 7am to 7.30pm), where you can catch a train to Britomart in the city centre ($5.50, 27 minutes, half-hourly 6am to 10pm).

BICYCLE

Auckland Transport Publishes free cycle maps, available from public buildings such as stations, libraries and i-SITEs. Bikes can be taken on most ferries and trains for free (dependent on available space), but only folding bikes are allowed on buses.

Adventure Cycles (☑ 09-940 2453; www.adventure-auckland.co.nz; 9 Premier Ave, Western Springs; per day $30-40, per week $120-160, per month $260-350; ☺ 7.30am-7pm Thu-Mon) Hires road, mountain and touring bikes, runs a buy-back scheme and does repairs.

CAR & MOTORCYCLE

Auckland's motorways jam badly at peak times, particularly the Northern and Southern Motorways. It's best to avoid them from 7am to 9am, and from 4pm to 7pm. Things also get tight around 3pm during term time, which is the end of the school day.

Expect to pay for parking in central Auckland from 8am to 10pm. Most parking meters are pay-and-display and take coins and credit cards; display tickets inside your windscreen. City fringe parking is free on Sundays.

Prices can be steep at parking buildings. Better value are the council-run, open-air car parks near the old train station at 126 Beach Rd ($10 per day) and on Ngaoho Pl, off the Strand ($10 per day).

E-SCOOTERS

E-scooters from various companies are available in the city. Unlocking the scooters is done via the companies' smartphone apps.

PUBLIC TRANSPORT

The **Auckland Transport** (☑ 09-366 6400; www.at.govt.nz) information service covers buses, trains and ferries, and has an excellent trip-planning feature.

Auckland's public transport system is run by a hodgepodge of different operators, but there is now an integrated AT HOP smartcard (www.athop.co.nz), which provides discounts of at least 20% on most buses, trains and ferries. AT HOP cards cost $10 (nonrefundable), so are really only worthwhile if you're planning an extended stay in Auckland. An AT HOP day pass costs $18 and provides a day's transport on most trains and buses and on North Shore ferries.

Bus

Bus routes spread their tentacles throughout the city, and you can purchase a ticket from the driver. Some bus stops have electronic displays giving an estimate of waiting times, but be warned, they are often inaccurate.

Single-ride fares in the inner city are $3.50/2 (adult/child). If you're travelling further afield, there are fare stages from $5.50/3 to $11/6.

The most useful services are the environmentally friendly Link Buses that loop in both directions around three routes (taking in many of the major sights) from 7am to 11pm:

City Link (adult/child $1/50c, every seven to 10 minutes) Wynyard Quarter, Britomart, Queen St, Karangahape Rd.

Inner Link (adult/child $3.50/2, every 10 to 15 minutes) Queen St, SkyCity, Victoria Park, Ponsonby Rd, Karangahape Rd, Museum, Newmarket, Parnell, Britomart.

Outer Link (maximum $5.50, every 15 minutes) Art Gallery, Ponsonby, Herne Bay, Westmere, MOTAT 2, Point Chevalier, Mt Albert, St Lukes Mall, Mt Eden, Newmarket, Museum, Parnell, University.

Ferry

Auckland's Edwardian baroque **Ferry Building** (Map p88; 99 Quay St) sits grandly at the end of Queen St. Ferry services are run by **Fullers** (☑ 09-367 9111; www.fullers.co.nz) to Bayswater, Birkenhead, Devonport, Half Moon Bay, Northcote Point, Motutapu, Rangitoto and Waiheke. **Fullers 360** (Map p88; ☑ 09-307 8005; www.fullers.co.nz) runs ferries to Coromandel, Gulf Harbour, Rotoroa and Tiritiri Matangi. Both leave from an adjacent pier.

Sealink (Map p88; ☑ 0800 732 546; www.sealink.co.nz) ferries to Great Barrier Island leave from Wynyard Wharf, along with some car ferries to Waiheke, but most of the Waiheke car ferries leave from Half Moon Bay in East Auckland.

Train

Auckland's train services are limited and infrequent, but the trains are generally clean, cheap and on time – although any hiccup on the lines can bring down the entire network.

Impressive **Britomart train station** (Queen St) has food retailers, foreign-exchange facilities and a ticket office. Downstairs there are left-luggage lockers.

There are just four train routes. One heads west to Swanson, while the other three head south, terminating in Onehunga, Manukau and Pukekohe. Services are at least hourly from around 6am to 10pm (later on the weekends). Buy a ticket from machines or ticket offices at train stations. All trains have wheelchair ramps.

Note that construction of Auckland's massive City Rail Link project is currently taking place and scheduled to continue until late 2024. Be prepared for some disruption to street access and traffic in various parts of the central city as work continues.

TAXI

Auckland's many taxis usually operate from ranks, but they also cruise popular areas. **Auckland Co-op Taxis** (☑ 09-300 3000; www. cooptaxi.co.nz) is one of the biggest companies. Cab companies set their own fares, so there's some variance in rates. There's a surcharge for transport to and from the airport and cruise ships, and for phone orders.

Ride-share services include Uber and local competitors Ola and Zoomy.

HAURAKI GULF ISLANDS

Stretching between Auckland and the Coromandel Peninsula, the Hauraki Gulf is dotted with *motu* (islands), and is as stunning as Northland's Bay of Islands. Some islands are only minutes from the city and make excellent day trips. Wine-soaked Waiheke and volcanic Rangitoto really shouldn't be missed. Great Barrier requires more effort (and cash) to get to, but provides an idyllic escape from modern life.

There are more than 50 islands in the Hauraki Gulf Marine Park, many administered by DOC. Some are good-sized islands, others are no more than rocks jutting out of the sea. They're loosely put into two categories: recreation and conservation. The recreation islands can easily be visited, and their harbours are dotted with yachts in summer. The conservation islands, however, have restricted access. Permits are required to visit some, while others are closed refuges for the preservation of rare plants and animals, especially birds.

❶ Getting There & Away

Frequent passenger ferries depart from the piers by the Ferry Building (p123) on Auckland's Quay St for Waiheke and Rangitoto. Boats to Motutapu, Motuihe, Rotoroa and Tiritiri Matangi are sporadic. Regular car ferries steam out of Wynyard Wharf heading to Waiheke and Great Barrier. Kawau also has good ferry connections, departing from Sandspit, north of Auckland.

Flights head to Great Barrier Island from Auckland Domestic Airport and North Shore Aerodrome.

Rangitoto & Motutapu Islands

POP 75

Sloping elegantly from the Hauraki Gulf, 259m-high Rangitoto (www.rangitoto.org) is the largest and youngest of Auckland's volcanic cones. As recently as 600 years ago it erupted from the sea and was active for several years before settling down. Māori living on Motutapu (Sacred Island; www.motutapu. org.nz), to which Rangitoto is joined by a causeway, certainly witnessed the eruptions, as footprints have been found embedded in ash, and oral history details several generations living here before the eruption.

In contrast to Rangitoto, Motutapu is mainly covered in grassland, which is grazed by sheep and cattle. Archaeologically, this is a very significant island, with the traces of centuries of continuous human habitation etched into its landscape.

In 2011 both islands were officially declared predator-free after an extensive eradication programme. Endangered birds such as takahe and tīeke (saddleback) have been released, and others such as kākāriki and bellbirds have returned of their own volition.

The only accommodation option on the islands is a basic **DOC campsite** (www.doc. govt.nz; sites per adult/child $8/4) at Home Bay, Motutapu. It's a three-hour walk from **Rangitoto Wharf** (Map p86); otherwise Fullers 360 runs direct ferries to Home Bay on weekends and public holidays.

Fullers 360 (☑ 09-367 9111; www.fullers. co.nz; adult/child return $36/18) has ferry services to Rangitoto (25 minutes, three daily on weekdays, four on weekends) from Auckland's Ferry Building (p123) and Devonport (two daily). It also operates the **Volcanic Explorer** (☑ 09-367 9111; www.fullers. co.nz; adult/child incl ferry $70/35; ⊙ departs Auckland 9.15am & 12.15pm), a guided tour around the island in a canopied 'road train'.

Waiheke Island

POP 9650

With a warm, dry microclimate, Waiheke Island is a favourite escape for city dwellers and visitors alike. Emerald waters lap at rocky bays and sandy beaches, while the island's vineyards combine tasting rooms, excellent restaurants and superb views. Art galleries are popular destinations, and for active travellers there's kayaking, zip lining and walking trails – all only a short ferry ride from Auckland.

◉ Sights

Waiheke's two best beaches are Onetangi, a long stretch of white sand at the centre of the island, and Palm Beach, a pretty little horseshoe bay between Oneroa and Onetangi. Both have nudist sections; head west just past some rocks in both cases. Oneroa and neighbouring Little Oneroa are also excellent, but you'll be sharing the waters with moored yachts in summer. Reached by an unsealed road through farmland, Man O' War Bay is a compact sheltered beach that's excellent for swimming.

The *Waiheke Art Map* brochure lists galleries and craft stores.

★ Man O' War   WINERY

(☑ 09-372 9678; www.manowar.co.nz; 725 Man O' War Bay Rd; ⊙ 11am-4pm Thu-Mon) Settle in with a tapas platter and a glass of Man O' War's Valhalla chardonnay at Waiheke's only beachfront tasting room. If the weather is good, go for a swim in beautiful Man O' War Bay. Options to reach the bay include private vehicle, a short but spectacular flight with Auckland Seaplanes (p97), or by prior reservation on Man O' War's summer-only bus from the Matiatia Wharf (p130). See www.manowar.co.nz/book-a-bus.

Wild on Waiheke   WINERY

(bookings for current week ☑ 09-372 3434, future & group bookings ☑ 09-372 4225; www.wildonwaiheke.co.nz; 82 Onetangi Rd; tastings per beer or wine $3; ⊙ 11am-5pm Sat-Thu, to 9pm Fri; ♣) Showcasing its offerings in a modern bar-and-bistro complex, this winery and microbrewery offers tastings and activities including archery and laser clay shooting. Kids can explore the cool wooden-castle playground while parents enjoy a few end-of-week drinks in the garden bar. Good food includes shared plates, mains and platters.

Goldie Estate   WINERY

(☑ 09-372 7493; www.goldieestate.co.nz; 18 Causeway Rd, Surfdale; tastings refundable with purchase $15; ⊙ noon-4pm Wed-Sun) Founded as Goldwater Estate in 1978, this is Waiheke's pioneering vineyard. The attached delicatessen sells well-stocked baskets and platters for a picnic among the vines ($48 to $60 for two people).

WALKING ON RANGITOTO

Rangitoto makes for a great day trip. Its harsh scoria slopes hold a surprising amount of flora (including the world's largest pohutukawa forest) and there are excellent walks, but you'll need sturdy shoes and plenty of water. Although it looks steep, up close it's shaped more like an egg sizzling in a pan. The walk to the summit only takes an hour and is rewarded with sublime views. At the top a loop walk goes around the crater's rim. A walk to lava caves branches off the summit walk and takes 30 minutes return. There's an information board with walk maps at the wharf.

Stonyridge   WINERY

(☑ 09-372 8822; www.stonyridge.com; 80 Onetangi Rd; tastings per wine $10-18; ⊙ 11.30am-5pm) ⊘ Waiheke's most famous vineyard is home to world-famous reds, an atmospheric cafe and the occasional yoga session on the breezy decks. Order a bottle of wine and a gigantic deli platter, and retreat to one of the cabanas in the garden.

Waiheke Island Artworks   ARTS CENTRE

(2 Korora Rd, Oneroa) The Artworks complex houses the Artworks Theatre (☑ 09-372 2941; www.artworkstheatre.org.nz; 2 Korora Rd, Oneroa), the Waiheke Island Community Cinema (☑ 09-372 4240; www.waihekecinema.net; 2 Korora Rd, Oneroa; tickets adult/child $16/9), the attention-grabbing Waiheke Community Art Gallery (☑ 09-372 9907; www.waihekeartgallery.org.nz; 2 Korora Rd, Oneroa; ⊙ 10am-4pm) FREE and Whittaker's Musical Museum (☑ 09-372 5573; www.musical-museum.org; 2 Korora Rd, Oneroa; suggested donation $5; ⊙ 1-4pm), a collection of antique instruments. This is also the place for free internet access, either on a terminal at the Waiheke Library (☑ 09-374 1325; www.aucklandlibraries.govt.nz; 2 Korora Rd, Oneroa; ⊙ 9am-6pm Mon-Fri, 10.30am-4pm Sat; ☎) or on Artworks' wi-fi network.

☆ Activities

The island's beautiful coastal walks (ranging from one to three hours) include the 3km Cross Island Walkway (from Onetangi to Rocky Bay). Other tracks traverse Whakanewha Regional Park, a haven for rare coastal birds and geckos, and the Royal Forest & Bird Protection Society's three reserves: Onetangi (Waiheke Rd),

Waiheke Island

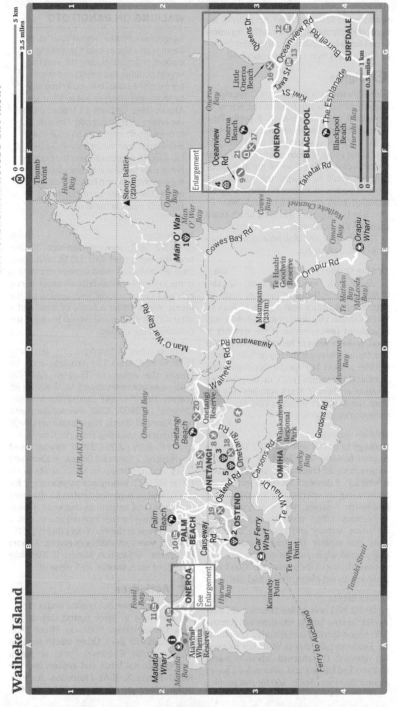

Waiheke Island

Te Haahi-Goodwin (Orapiu Rd) and Atawhai Whenua (Ocean View Rd).

Te Ara Hura is a 100km network of connected trails taking in coastline, forests, vineyard stops and historic places. Route markers indicate the way ahead on the island, and more information and detailed maps are available online at www.auckland council.govt.nz. Search for 'Waiheke Island Walkways'.

iWalkWaiheke   WALKING
(☑ 021 960 690; www.iwalkwaiheke.co.nz; 11 Totara Rd, Onetangi; per person from $249) ✔ Options include the popular three days/three nights Waiheke Walking Holiday option, which includes gourmet meals and accommodation. Shorter walks, overnight stays and food tours are also available. Operator Vicki Angland has been resident on Waiheke for more than 20 years, and walks reflect an eco policy that reinforces the island's environmental, cultural and conservation aspects.

To experience the island in depth, there's the option of a self-guided 85km four-day Te Ara Hura walk.

Hike Bike Ako   WALKING, CYCLING
(☑ 021 465 373; www.hikebikeako.co.nz; from $129; ☺ Nov-Mar) Explore the island with Māori guides on a walking or an e-biking tour, or a combination of both. Tours include pickup from the ferry and a large dose of Māori legend, history and culture.

EcoZip Adventures   ADVENTURE SPORTS
(☑ 09-372 5646; www.ecozipadventures.co.nz; 150 Trig Hill Rd; adult/child/family $129/79/337; ☺ 10.15am, 12.15pm & 2.15pm) With vineyard, native bush and ocean views, EcoZip's three separate 200m zip lines make for an exciting ride, and there's a gentle 1.5km walk back up through the bush after the thrills. Costs include free transfers from Matiatia Wharf (p130) or Oneroa if you don't have your own transport. Booking ahead online is essential.

Waiheke Dive   DIVING
(☑ 09-217 4892; www.waihekedive.com; 110 Ocean View Rd, Oneroa; snorkelling & diving from $70; ☺ 9am-5pm) PADI diving courses, dive trips and snorkelling experiences are all on offer. Guided snorkelling tours including a mask, snorkel and wetsuit leave at 2pm. Book ahead. Snorkelling packages ($30) including a wetsuit, mask, snorkel and fins can also be hired.

Ross Adventures   KAYAKING
(☑ 09-372 5550; www.kayakwaiheke.co.nz; Matiatia Beach; half-/full-day trips $125/195, per 1/2/3/6hr $30/45/50/60) It's the fervently held opinion of Ross that Waiheke offers kayaking every bit as good as the legendary Abel Tasman National Park. He should know – he's been offering guided kayak trips for 20 years. Experienced sea kayakers can comfortably circumnavigate the island in

four days, exploring coves and sand spits inaccessible by land. Paddle boards also available for hire.

☞ Tours

Waiheke Island Wine Tours TOURS
(☑ 09-372 2140; www.waihekeislandwinetours.co.nz) Options include Views, Vines & Wines ($130 per person, six hours with a two-hour break for lunch at a restaurant of your choice), tailor-made Platinum Private Tours ($595 per couple; May to October only) and Indulgence Two-Day Tours ($850 to $1100 per person including accommodation; May to October only).

Potiki Adventures CULTURAL
(☑ 021 422 773; www.potikiadventures.co.nz; adult/child $150/80) Day-long island tours from a Māori cultural perspective, including beaches, a bushwalk, a vineyard visit, and demonstrations of traditional musical instruments and weaving.

Ananda Tours TOURS
(☑ 09-372 7530; www.ananda.co.nz) Wine tours ($185), gourmet wine and food tours ($195), and a wine connoisseurs' tour ($250) are among the options. Small-group, informal tours can be customised, including visits to artists' studios.

Fullers TOURS
(☑ 09-367 9111; www.fullers.co.nz; Matiatia Wharf) Runs a Wine on Waiheke tour (adult $150, 4½ hours, departs Auckland 1pm), visiting three of the island's top wineries, and including a platter of nibbles. There's also the Taste of Waiheke tour (adult $180, six hours, departs Auckland 11am), which includes three wineries plus an olive grove and light lunch.

✸ Festivals & Events

Sculpture on the Gulf ART
(☑ 09-372 9907; www.sotg.nz; adult/child $10/free; ☉ March) A 2.5km clifftop sculpture walk, held for a month in March in odd-numbered years. The next event is in 2021. Check the website for details of special shuttle buses and a dedicated festival information centre adjacent to Matiatia Wharf.

**Waiheke Island
International Jazz Festival** MUSIC
(www.waihekejazzfestival.co.nz; prices vary by event; ☉ Mar/Apr) Local and international acts across the island from Friday to Sunday during Easter.

⬛ Sleeping

Waiheke is so popular in the summer holidays that many locals rent out their houses and go elsewhere. You'll need to book ahead and even then there are few bargains. Prices drop considerably in winter, especially midweek. For midrange accommodation, a good option is to book a holiday home through www.bookabach.co.nz or www.holidayhouses.co.nz.

★ Fossil Bay Lodge CABIN $
(☑ 09-372 8371; www.fossilbaylodge.co.nz; 58 Korora Rd, Oneroa; s $60, d $85-90, tent $100-120, apt $130; ☎) Three cabins face the main building, which houses the communal toilets, kitchen and living area, and a compact self-contained upstairs apartment. 'Glamping' tents each have a proper bed and their own toilet, and one also includes a private outdoor kitchenette. Apart from the occasional squawking duck – or toddler from the adjacent Steiner kindergarten – it's a very peaceful place.

Hekerua Lodge HOSTEL $
(☑ 09-372 8990; www.hekerualodge.co.nz; 11 Hekerua Rd, Oneroa; campsites $30, dm $30-38, s/d/tw $60/100/95; ☎⬛) This secluded hostel is surrounded by native bush and has a barbecue, stone-tiled pool, spa pool, sunny deck and casual lounge area, plus its own walking track. It's far from luxurious, but it has a laid-back and social feel.

Tawa Lodge GUESTHOUSE $$
(☑ 09-372 6675; www.pungalodge.co.nz; 15 Tawa St, Oneroa; r $120-130, apt $175-225; ☎) Between the self-contained two-person cottage at the front (pick of the lot, due to the sublimely romantic views) and the apartment and house at the rear are three reasonably priced loft rooms sharing a small kitchen and bathroom.

★ Waiheke Dreams RENTAL HOUSE $$$
(☑ 09-818 7129; www.waihekedreams.co.nz; 43 Tiri Rd, Oneroa; 1-/2-bedroom house $250/350) Dream a little dream of a luxurious, modern, spacious, open-plan two-bedroom house on the crest of a hill with unsurpassed views over Oneroa Bay and the Hauraki Gulf – then pinch yourself and wake up with a smug smile in View43. Tucked at the rear is the considerably smaller one-bedroom CityLights, which glimpses Auckland's glimmer over the back lawn.

Enclosure Bay
B&B $$$

(☑ 09-372 8882; www.enclosurebay.co.nz; 9 Great Barrier Rd; r/ste $475/650; 🐾) If you're going to shell out for a luxury B&B, you expect it to be special, and that's certainly what's offered here. Each of the three guest rooms have sumptuous views and balconies, and the owners subscribe to the nothing's-too-much-trouble school of hospitality.

✘ Eating

Waiheke has some excellent eateries, and if you're lucky, the views will be enough to distract from the hole being bored into your hip pocket. There's a supermarket in Ostend. Keep an eye out for summertime food trucks from Waiheke's surprisingly global array of residents.

Dragonfired
PIZZA $

(☑ 021 922 289; www.dragonfired.co.nz; Little Oneroa Beach; mains $12-16; ⊙ 10am-8pm daily Nov-Mar, 11am-7pm Fri-Sun Apr-Oct; ☑) Specialising in 'artisan wood-fired food', this caravan by the beach serves the three Ps: pizza, polenta plates and pocket bread. It's one of Waiheke's best places for cheap eats.

Island Gelato
ICE CREAM $

(☑ 021 536 860; www.islandgelato.co.nz; 1 Oceanview Rd; ice cream from $6; ⊙ 8am-7pm) Before school, after school, and on weekdays and weekends, Waiheke locals crowd Island Gelato's shipping-container garden for delicious ice cream, coffee and bagels. Seasonal ice-cream flavours shine, including our favourite, the zingy kaffir-lime-and-coconut sorbet. You'll find all this irresistible goodness at the bottom end of Oneroa village.

Te Matuku Seafood Market
SEAFOOD $

(☑ 09-372 8600; www.tematukuoysters.co.nz; 17 Belgium St; ⊙ 9am-5pm Mon-Sat) ⚓ Head to this combination seafood retailer and deli selling local gourmet produce for the freshest and best-value oysters on the island. Just $26 will get you 12 freshly shucked oysters. Enjoy with lemon juice and Tabasco at the simple stand-up tables for a quintessential Waiheke experience. Mussels and clams are also for sale.

Shed at Te Motu
MODERN NZ $$

(☑ 09-372 6884; www.temotu.co.nz/the-shed; 76 Onetangi Rd; shared plates $20-26; ⊙ 11am-5pm daily, 6pm-late Fri & Sat Nov-Apr, reduced hours May-Oct; ☑) Secure a table shaded by umbrellas in the Shed's rustic courtyard. It serves shared plates imbued with global influences and delivered by the restaurant's savvy and equally international waitstaff. Seasonal highlights could include pan-roasted scallops, slow-cooked beef rib or honey butter pumpkin. Look forward to other good vegetarian options too. Te Motu's standout wines are its stellar Bordeaux-style blends.

Casita Miro
SPANISH $$

(☑ 09-372 7854; www.casitamiro.co.nz; 3 Brown Rd; tapas $9-19, ración $36-38; ⊙ 11.30am-4pm Sun-Thu, to 8pm Fri & Sat) A wrought-iron-and-glass pavilion backed with a Gaudí-esque mosaic garden is the stage for a very entertaining troupe of servers who will guide you through the menu of delectable tapas and *raciones* (larger dishes), designed to be shared. In summer the sides open up, but otherwise, at busy times, it can get noisy. Book ahead.

★ Three Seven Two
BISTRO $$$

(www.threeseventwo.co.nz; 21 The Strand, Onetangi; shared plates $12-22, mains $34-39) ⚓ Referencing the first three digits of Waiheke phone numbers, Three Seven Two's oceanfront location includes an outdoor deck and a shaded rear courtyard. Local ingredients are harnessed for seasonal shared plates including shiitake mushroom dumplings, and bigger main dishes of Wagyu hanger steaks or an eggplant and chermoula pilaf. The drinks list includes local beer and wine.

★ Tantalus Estate
MODERN NZ $$$

(☑ 09-372 2625; www.tantalus.co.nz; 70-72 Onetangi Rd; mains $38-44; ⊙ 11am-5pm) ⚓ Up a winding driveway framed by grapevines, Waiheke's newest vineyard restaurant and tasting room channels an Iberian ambience, but the savvy and diverse menu effortlessly covers the globe. Secure a spot under rustic chandeliers crafted from repurposed tree branches, and enjoy a leisurely lunch imbued with Asian and Mediterranean influences.

Tantalus also crafts its own Rhone- and Bordeaux-style red wines, and makes craft beer on-site under the Alibi Brewing Company label. Check out its seasonal beers in the brick-lined Alibi Brewing tasting room downstairs. A concise menu of bar snacks is also available.

🍷 Drinking & Nightlife

Island Coffee
CAFE

(www.islandcoffeenz.com; 21b Belgium St, Ostend; ⊙ 8.30am-12.30pm Tue-Sat) ⚓ Search out this bohemian spot for Waiheke's best coffee – served with delicious homestyle baking (try

AUCKLAND REGION ROTOROA ISLAND

the cinnamon brioche) – and the chance to spin some retro tunes from the selection of vintage vinyl. It's a compact spot, so be prepared to grab a takeaway coffee.

Charlie's BAR

(☑ 09-372 4106; www.charliefarleys.co.nz; 21 The Strand, Onetangi; ☺ 9am-late) Once you're supping on a Waiheke wine or beer under the pohutukawa on the beach-gazing deck, it's easy to see why Charlie's has been a beloved island institution since 1987. A reappraisal of the menu has seen the addition of tasty bar snacks, including prawns and calamari. Full meals include Wagyu cheeseburgers and seafood risotto.

🛍 Shopping

Waiheke Wine Centre WINE

(☑ 09-372 6139; www.waihekewinecentre.com; 153 Oceanview Rd, Oneroa; ☺ 9.30am-7.30pm Mon-Thu, to 8pm Fri & Sat, from 10am Sun) Located in Oneroa's main street, this well-stocked and authoritative store features wine from all of Waiheke's vineyards, and is a good place to pick up information on wine destinations around the island. A special sampling system allows customers to purchase pours of various wines.

ℹ Information

There is a convenient **tourist information booth** (Matiatia Wharf; ☺ 9am-4pm) open for most arrivals at the ferry terminal at Matiatia Wharf. Online see www.tourismwaiheke.co.nz, www.waiheke.co.nz and www.aucklandnz.com.

There are ATMs in Oneroa.

ℹ Getting There & Away

Fullers 360 (☑ 09-307 8005; www.fullers. co.nz) You can pick up this tourist ferry at Orapiu on its limited voyages between Auckland and Coromandel Town. However, note that Orapiu is quite remote and not served by buses.

Fullers (☑ 09-367 9111; www.fullers.co.nz; return adult/child $42/21; ☺ 5.20am-11.45pm Mon-Fri, 6.15am-11.45pm Sat, 7am-10.30pm Sun) Frequent passenger ferries cross between Auckland's Ferry Building to **Matiatia Wharf** (40 minutes), some via Devonport (adding 10 minutes to the journey).

SeaLink (☑ 0800 732 546; www.sealink. co.nz; return adult/child/car/motorcycle $39/20/175/72; ☺ 6am-6pm) Runs **car ferries** to Kennedy Point, mainly from Half Moon Bay, East Auckland (45 to 60 minutes, at least hourly), but some leave from Wynyard Wharf in the city (60 to 80 minutes, three per day).

ℹ Getting Around

BICYCLE

Various bicycle routes are outlined in the *Bike Waiheke!* brochure, usually available at the Matiatia Wharf. **Waiheke Bike Hire** (☑ 09-372 7937; www.waihekebikehire.co.nz; Matiatia; per day $35) hires mountain bikes from its base in the car park near the wharf.

Parts of Waiheke are quite hilly, so ease the load with a hybrid machine from **eCycles** (☑ 022 050 2233; www.ecyclesnz.com; 108 Oceanview Rd, Oneroa; per day $60), combining pedalling with electric motors.

BUS

Auckland Transport (p123) runs three different island services. Most convenient for visitors are the 50A and 50B services beginning at the passenger ferry terminal at Matiatia Wharf (every 30 minutes, 7am to 7pm, adult/child $3.50/2), and running to various stops including Oneroa village and Onetangi Beach. These routes run along Onetangi Rd, providing access to various vineyard restaurants.

From late October to late April, the 503 summer service is a convenient shuttle (every 30 minutes, 10am to 2pm, adult/child $3.50/2) linking Matiatia with Oneroa.

Another option is the **Waiheke Island Explorer** (www.fullers.co.nz; 1-day adult/child/family incl ferry tickets $68/35/180, 2-day $99/45/270) bus, a hop-on, hop-off service covering 15 different stops around the island. A full circuit takes 90 minutes, and attractions along the route include vineyards, beaches, activities and restaurants.

CAR, MOTORCYCLE & SCOOTER

There are petrol stations in Oneroa and Onetangi.

Island Scoot (☑ 021 062 5997; www. islandscoot.nz; cnr Tui & Mako Sts, Oneroa; per day $79; ☺ 9am-6pm)

Waiheke Auto Rentals (☑ 09-372 8998; www. waihekerentals.co.nz; Matiatia Wharf; per day car/scooter from $89/69)

Waiheke Rental Cars (☑ 09-372 8635; www. waihekerentalcars.co.nz; Matiatia Wharf; per day car/4WD from $89/109)

TAXI

Island Taxis (☑ 09-372 4111; www. islandtaxis.co.nz)

Rotoroa Island

From 1911 to 2005 the only people to have access to this blissful little island on the far side of Waiheke were the alcoholics and drug addicts who came (or were sentenced) here to dry out, and the Salvation Army staff who cared for them. In 2011, 82-hectare Rotoroa (www.rotoroa.org.nz; adult/child $5/3) opened to the public for the first time in a century, giving visitors access to three sandy swimming beaches and the social history and art displays in the restored buildings of the former treatment centre.

There are three well-appointed, wildly retro holiday homes for rent, sleeping four ($395) to eight ($650) people, and excellent hostel accommodation in dorms (per person $40) in the former Superintendent's House.

Departing from near the Ferry Building (p123) in downtown Auckland, the 360 Discovery ferry (☑09-307 8005; www.fullers.co.nz; adult/child from Auckland $55/33, from Orapiu $33/21) takes 75 minutes, stopping at Orapiu on Waiheke Island en route. Services are infrequent and don't run every day. Prices include the island access fee. Recommended guided walks of the island cost $20 extra and can be booked when booking ferry tickets.

Tiritiri Matangi Island

This magical, 220-hectare, predator-free island (www.tiritirimatangi.org.nz) is home to the tuatara (a prehistoric lizard) and lots of endangered native birds, including the very rare and colourful takahe. Other birds that can be seen here include the bellbird, stitchbird, saddleback, whitehead, kākāriki, kokako, little spotted kiwi, brown teal, New Zealand robin, fernbird and penguins; 78 different species have been sighted in total. The saddleback was once close to extinction, with just 150 left, but there are now up to 1000 on Tiritiri alone. To experience the dawn chorus in full flight, stay overnight at the DOC bunkhouse (☑09-425 7812; www.doc.govt.nz; adult/child $30/20); book well ahead and ensure there's room on the ferry.

The island was sold to the Crown in 1841, deforested, and farmed until the 1970s. Since 1984 hundreds of volunteers have planted 250,000 native trees and the forest cover has regenerated. An 1864 lighthouse stands on the eastern end of the island.

It's a good idea to book a guided walk ($5) with your ferry ticket; the guides know where all the really cool birds hang out.

Fullers 360 (☑09-307 8005; www.fullers.co.nz; adult/child return $82/50; ⊙Wed-Sun) ferries depart for the island at 9am from Wednesday to Sunday, leaving the island at 3.30pm. The journey takes 70 minutes from Auckland's ferry terminal.

Kawau Island

POP 300

Kawau Island lies 50km north of Auckland off the Mahurangi Peninsula. There are few proper roads through the island – residents rely mainly on boats.

The main attraction is Mansion House (☑09-422 8882; www.doc.govt.nz; adult/child $4/2; ⊙noon-2pm Mon-Fri, noon-3.30pm Sat & Sun Sep-May), an impressive wooden manor. A set of short walks (10 minutes to two hours) are signposted from Mansion House, leading to beaches, the old copper mine and a lookout; download DOC's *Kawau Island Historic Reserve* map (www.doc.govt.nz).

Online, www.kawauisland.org.nz is also a good source of information, and features a list of self-contained rental accommodation.

Beach House   BOUTIQUE HOTEL $$$
(☑09-422 8850; www.kawaubeachhouse.co.nz; Vivian Bay; r/ste from $450/560) In the north of the island, on Kawau's best sandy beach, this upmarket complex has diverse accommodation options. Choose from beachfront suites, rooms around a courtyard, or rooms surrounded by lush bush and reached by around 100 steps. It's a remote spot, but it has its own restaurant (open to hotel guests only), so there's no need to go anywhere.

Kawau Cruises   FERRY
(☑0800 111 616; https://kawaucruises.co.nz) Departing Sandspit several times daily, the Mansion House Cruise (adult/child $55/39) allows plentiful time on the island before returning via an afternoon departure back to Sandspit. Check the website, as summer and nonsummer departure times vary.

Great Barrier Island

POP 860

Great Barrier has unspoilt beaches, hot springs, old kauri dams, a forest sanctuary and a network of hiking tracks. Because there are no possums on the island, the native bush is lush.

Although only 88km and a 30-minute flight from Auckland, Great Barrier seems a world away. The island has no supermarket, no mains electricity supply (only private solar, wind and diesel generators) and no mains drainage (only septic tanks). Some roads are unsealed and petrol costs are high. Mobile-phone reception is improving but

Great Barrier Island

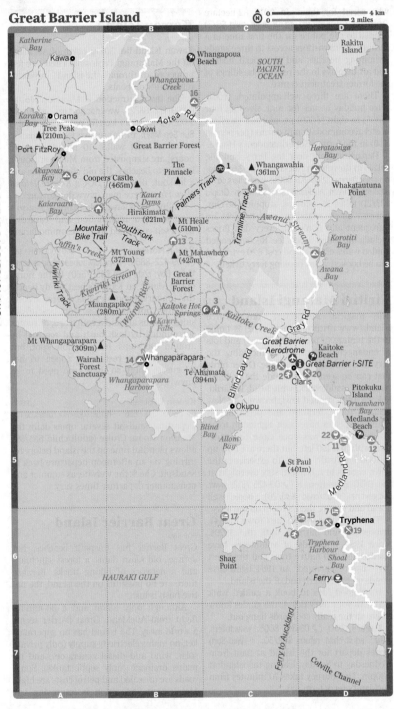

0   4 km
0   2 miles

Katherine Bay

Kawa

Rakitu Island

Whangapoua Beach

SOUTH PACIFIC OCEAN

Whangapoua Creek

16

Aotea Rd

Karaka Bay

Orama

Tree Peak (210m)

Okiwi

Great Barrier Forest

Harataonga Bay

Port FitzRoy

Akapoua Bay

6

Coopers Castle (465m)

The Pinnacle

1

5

Whangawahia (361m)

9

Whakatautuna Point

Kauri Dams

Palmers Track

Tramline Track

Kaiaraara Bay

10

Hirakimata (621m)

Mt Heale (510m)

Awana Stream

Korotiti Bay

Mountain Bike Trail

South Fork Track

13

Mt Matawhero (425m)

8

Awana Bay

Coffin's Creek

Mt Young (372m)

Great Barrier Forest

Kiwiriki Track

Kiwiriki Stream

Wairahi River

Maungapiko (280m)

Kaitoke Hot Springs

3

Kaitoke Creek

Gray Rd

Kauri Falls

Mt Whangaparapara (309m)

14

Whangaparapara

Te Ahumata (394m)

Great Barrier Aerodrome

Kaitoke Beach

18

Great Barrier i-SITE

2

20

Wairahi Forest Sanctuary

Whangaparapara Harbour

Blind Bay Rd

Claris

Pitokuku Island

Oruawharo Bay

Okupu

Blind Bay

Allom Bay

Medlands Beach

22

11

12

St Paul (401m)

Medland Rd

17

15

7

Tryphena

21

19

4

Tryphena Harbour

Shoal Bay

Shag Point

HAURAKI GULF

Ferry

Ferry to Auckland

Colville Channel

Great Barrier Island

still limited, and there are no banks, ATMs or street lights. Two-thirds of the island is publicly owned and managed by DOC.

Peak season is from about mid-December to mid-January, so make sure you book transport, accommodation and activities well in advance.

Named Aotea (Cloud) by the Māori, and Great Barrier (due to its position at the edge of the Hauraki Gulf) by James Cook, this rugged and exceptionally beautiful place falls in behind South, North and Stewart as NZ's fourth-largest island (285 sq km). It closely resembles the Coromandel Peninsula, to which it was once joined, and like the Coromandel it was once a mining, logging and whaling centre (although those industries are long gone).

Tryphena is the main settlement, 4km from the ferry wharf at Shoal Bay. Strung out along several kilometres of coastal road, it consists of a few dozen houses and a handful of shops and accommodation places. From the wharf it's 3km to Mulberry Grove, and then another 1km over the headland to Pah Beach and the Stonewall Store (p135).

The airport is at Claris, 12km north of Tryphena, a small settlement with a general store, bottle shop, laundrette, garage, pharmacy and cafe.

Whangaparapara is an old timber town and the site of the island's 19th-century whaling activities. Port FitzRoy is the other main harbour on the west coast, a one-hour drive from Tryphena. These four main settlements have fuel available.

🏃 Activities

Water Sports

The beaches on the west coast are safe, but care needs to be taken on the surf-pounded eastern beaches. Medlands Beach, with its wide sweep of white sand, is one of the most beautiful and accessible beaches on the island. Remote Whangapoua, in the northeast, requires more effort to get to, while Kaitoke, Awana Bay and Haraitonga on the east coast are also worth a visit.

Okiwi Bar has an excellent right-hand break, while Awana has both left- and right-hand breaks. Pohutukawa trees shelter the pretty bays around Tryphena.

Diving is excellent, with shipwrecks, pinnacles, lots of fish and more than 33m visibility at some times of the year.

Mountain Biking

With rugged scenery and relatively little traffic on the roads, mountain biking is a popular activity on the island. There's a designated 25km ride beginning on Blind Bay Rd, Okupu, winding beneath the Ahumata cliffs before crossing Whangaparapara Rd and beginning the 15km Forest Rd ride through beautiful forest to Port FitzRoy. Cycling on other DOC walking tracks is prohibited.

Walking

The island's very popular walking tracks are outlined in DOC's free *Great Barrier Island (Aotea Island)* booklet. Before setting out, make sure you're properly equipped with water and food, and be prepared for both sunny and wet weather.

The most popular easy walk is the 45-minute **Kaitoke Hot Springs Track**, starting from Whangaparapara Rd and leading to natural hot springs in a bush stream. Check the temperature before getting in and don't put your head under the water.

Windy Canyon, which is only a 15-minute walk from Aotea Rd, has spectacular rock outcrops and affords great views of the island. From Windy Canyon, an excellent trail continues for another two to three hours through scrubby forest to Hirakimata (Mt Hobson; 621m), the highest point on the island, with views across the Hauraki Gulf and Coromandel. Near the top of the mountain are lush forests and a few mature kauri trees that survived the logging days. From Hirakimata it is 40 minutes south to **Mt Heale Hut** (☑ 09-379 6476; www.doc.govt. nz; dm per adult/child $15/7.50).

A more challenging hike is the hilly **Tramline Track** (five hours), which starts on Aotea Rd and follows old logging tramlines to Whangaparapara Harbour. The initial stages of this track are not maintained and in some parts the clay becomes slippery after rain.

Of a similar length, but flatter and easier walking, is the 11km **Harataonga Coastal Walk** (five hours), which heads from Harataonga Bay to Whangapoua.

Many other trails traverse the forest, taking between 30 minutes and five hours. The **Aotea Track** combines bits of other paths into a three-day walk, overnighting in Mt Heale and **Kaiaraara** (☑ 09-379 6476; www. doc.govt.nz; dm per adult/child $15/7.50) huts. Check the DOC website (www.doc.govt.nz) for the latest update and for detailed information on negotiating the Aotea Track.

★ **Star Treks**   WALKING
(☑ 021 865 836; https://startreks.kiwi; 2 people from $395) ✎ Excellent walking experiences combining local history, flora, scenery and dark-sky viewing. Walks are often led by co-operator Benny Bellerby, born and bred on the island, with organic and sustainably sourced snacks and drinks provided for refreshment. Options include a twilight walk combining the Kaitoke Hot Springs Track with stargazing, and an exploration of the former whaling station on Whangaparapara Harbour.

Other Activities

★ **Good Heavens**   OUTDOORS
(☑ 09-429 0876; www.goodheavens.co.nz; group tours per person $120, minimum 2 people private tours $600) ✎ The Milky Way, constellations and other celestial attractions – sometimes including Saturn and Jupiter – are observed through telescopes and the naked eye, and Good Heavens' avid Dark Sky Ambassadors can even set up their sky-watching gear conveniently at your accommodation. Booking ahead is vital, preferably for your first night on the island to allow flexibility for weather conditions.

Paddles & Saddles   ADVENTURE SPORTS
(☑ 027 410 2688; www.paddlesandsaddles.co.nz; 207 Puriri Bay Rd, Tryphena Lodge; scooter/e-bike per day $99/59, single/double/fishing kayak per half-day $50/65/65) ✎ Excellent rental centre run by the friendly Lucy and Pete, with options including e-bikes, scooters, kayaks and paddle boards. Fishing and snorkelling gear is also available, and Pete can advise on local fishing highlights and opportunities. There's also simple but good-value shared bathroom accommodation at their idyllic harbourfront location (double $95 to $120). Don't miss taking a moonlit dip in the outdoor bath tubs.

Crazy Horse Trike Tours   SCENIC DRIVE
(☑ 0800 997 222, 09-429 0222; www.greatbarrier islandtourism.co.nz; per person from $75) Jump on the back of Steve Billingham's custom-built motorised trike and let the friendly GB local drive you around the island. Options include two-hour sightseeing tours, beach visits, kayaking, hot springs and forest walks. Steve's a very entertaining source of information on interesting local stories and island history.

Hooked on Barrier   FISHING
(☑ 09-429 0740; www.hookedonbarrier.co.nz; Claris; casual fishing trip per person $130, half-/full-day boat charter $850/1600) Runs fishing and diving charters and sightseeing tours. Sightseeing cruises including lunch or dinner are $150 to $165 per person.

🛏 Sleeping

Unless you're camping, Great Barrier isn't a cheap place to stay. At pretty much every price point you'll pay more than you would for a similar place elsewhere. In the low season, however, rates drop considerably.

Check accommodation and island information websites for packages including flights and car rental. Note that accommodation rates soar for around two weeks following Christmas, and the island also gets very busy during this time.

Island Accommodation (☑021 138 7293; www.islandaccommodation.co.nz) offers a booking service that's handy for finding self-contained houses for longer stays.

There are **DOC campsites** (☑09-379 6476; www.doc.govt.nz; sites per adult/child $15/7.50) at Harataonga Bay, Medlands Beach, Akapoua Bay, Whangapoua, The Green and Awana Bay. All have basic facilities, including water, cold showers (except for the Green), toilets and a food-preparation shelter. You need to bring your own gas cooking stove as open fires are prohibited. Book in advance online.

Medlands Beach
Backpackers & Villas   HOSTEL $
(☑09-429 0320; www.medlandsbeach.com; 9 Mason Rd; dm/d without bathroom from $40/90, units from $150; ☎) Chill out in the garden of this house on the hill, overlooking beautiful Medlands Beach. The backpackers' area is simple, with a little double chalet for romantic budgeteers at a slight remove from the rest. The self-contained houses sleep up to seven.

Aotea Lodge   APARTMENT $$
(☑09-429 0628; www.aotealodge.com; 41 Medland Rd, Tryphena; apt $130-220; ☎) A well-tended, sunny garden surrounds these reasonably priced units, perched on the hill just above Tryphena. They range from a two-bedroom house to an unusual mezzanine unit loaded with bunks, and each has its own cooking facilities. Look forward to chickens in the surrounding garden. Wi-fi can be patchy.

★XSPOT   APARTMENT $$$
(☑027 429 0877; www.xspot.co.nz; 21 Schooner Bay Rd, Tryphena; d $230; ☎⊠) ✿ Great Barrier's most spectacular accommodation option

is also one of its more remote. A 25-minute drive from Tryphena – rent a 4WD vehicle – XSPOT is a spacious and stylish one-bedroom apartment with expansive windows offering jaw-dropping 270-degree views of the ocean. Equipped with a full kitchen and modern bathroom, it's the kind of place to linger amid spectacular marine vistas.

Trillium Lodge   B&B $$$
(☑09-429 0283; www.trilliumlodge.co.nz; 24 Schooner Bay Rd; r $276-299; ☎) ✿ Uniquely constructed of giant logs milled on the island, Trillium Lodge is one of Great Barrier's more distinctive accommodation options. All of the six luxury rooms enjoy a combination of forest, mountain and sea views, and are enlivened by interesting art from local artists. Excellent breakfasts include locally sourced honey. Check the website for packages including flights and a rental car.

✕ Eating

In summer, most places open daily, but for the rest of the year hours can be sporadic. A monthly guide to opening hours is on www.greatbarrierislandtourism.co.nz, but it pays to call ahead for an evening meal.

Self-caterers will find small stores in Tryphena, Claris, Whangaparapara and Port FitzRoy. Tryphena's **Stonewall Store** (☑09-429 0451; 82 Blackwell Dr; ⊙8.30am-6pm) has a good selection of wine, beer and local produce, and also operates a small market (from 10am Saturday).

Swallow   BURGERS $
(☑09-429 0226; www.facebook.com/BurgerShack GBI; Main Rd, Claris; burgers $15-17; ⊙11am-6pm) Hands down the best burgers on the island, with massive overflowing options including

---

DARK SKY SANCTUARY

Designated a Dark Sky Sanctuary by the International Dark-Sky Association in 2017, Great Barrier has become regarded as one of the southern hemisphere's best places to observe the night sky.

Because there is no mains electricity or street lights on the island – all businesses and residents utilise solar power and batteries – light pollution is extremely minimal, and the Barrier's 88km ocean separation from Auckland means the city's far-reaching 'light dome' has no effect either.

Also, because Great Barrier is almost 60% protected conservation land, future development is legislated to be minimal, and the entire island will be able to maintain this high standard of darkness and Dark Sky Sanctuary status in the future.

Just 30 minutes' flight from the country's international airport and easily accessible for the 1.42 million residents of Auckland, Great Barrier's stellar night sky is a significant tourism asset that the island's residents are keen to enhance and protect.

pork belly or beef, blue cheese and caramelised onions. Also wraps, seafood and Janene's Dreams icy treats handmade on the Barrier.

My Fat Puku
CAFE $$

(☑09-429 0811; www.facebook.com/myfatpuku; 129 Hector Sanderson Rd, Claris; mains $15-23; ☺8am-4pm; ☑) Decent pies, big breakfasts and salads combine with good coffee and locally brewed beer at this spot with lots of outdoor seating and funky Kiwiana decor. We can recommend the Puku burrito with chicken and chilli jam for a Barrier brunch. From late December to Easter, opening hours are extended and it's time for cold beers and My Fat Puku's wood-fired pizza oven.

Warmer months are also the time for cocktails made with Great Barrier's very own Island Gin, crafted entirely off the grid with local honey and triple-filtered Barrier water.

Tipi & Bob's
PUB FOOD $$$

(☑09-429 0550; www.waterfrontlodge.co.nz; 38 Puriri Bay Rd, Tryphena; breakfast $16-20, dinner $39-44; ☺7.30-10am & 5-10pm) Serving simple but satisfying meals in large portions, this popular haunt has an inviting deck overlooking the harbour. The steak and seafood combos are always good. There's also a cheaper menu in the bar.

🍷 Drinking & Nightlife

Currach Irish Pub
IRISH PUB

(☑09-429 0211; www.currachirishpub.co.nz; 78 Blackwell Dr, Tryphena; mains $20-34; ☺4pm-late Boxing Day-Easter, closed Wed Mar-Dec; 🛜🍴) This excellent pub offers island-brewed craft beer, seafood, steak and burgers, and is GB's main social centre. Wood-fired pizzas are another highlight, and there are regular live gigs with a Gaelic and folky bent. Sunday quiz night is loads of fun, and a separate room features rotating exhibitions from local artists, all of it for sale.

Accommodation in renovated heritage rooms ($130 to $160) is available at the attached Innkeepers Lodge, and there's also a compact four-bed dorm ($35) with a full kitchen.

Aotea Brewing
MICROBREWERY

(www.aoteabrewing.co.nz; 50a Mason Rd, Medlands; ☺noon-6pm Fri-Sun) 🍺 Visit Aotea Brewing to purchase craft beers brewed entirely off the grid in the compact on-site microbrewery. Beers including Solar American Pale Ale are available in sustainable and recyclable bottles, both at Aotea's rustic taproom, and at the Rocks bottle shop in Claris. It's hoped that Aotea's licence will be extended to include an on-site bar in the future.

ℹ️ Information

INTERNET ACCESS

There's free wi-fi access at the Great Barrier Aerodrome at Claris and at the **Great Barrier Library** (☑09-377 0209; www. aucklandlibraries.govt.nz; 75 Hector Sanderson Rd, Claris; ☺8.30am-5pm Mon-Fri).

TOURIST INFORMATION

Great Barrier i-SITE (Destination Great Barrier Island; ☑09-420 0033; www.greatbarrier. co.nz; Great Barrier Aerodrome; ☺9am-3pm Mon-Sat; 🛜) At the airport in Claris, this also has a good range of DOC information.

Go Great Barrier Island (☑0800 997 222; www.greatbarrierislandtourism.co.nz) Offers a personal online planning service for island visits, including all transport, rental cars and accommodation. Also runs hiker shuttles to tracks and arranges island tours by van or trike.

🚍 Getting There & Away

AIR

FlyMySky (p122) flies at least three times a day between Claris' **Great Barrier Aerodrome** (Claris Airport) and Auckland. Cheaper flights are available if you travel to the island on a Sunday or leave on a Friday ($89), and there's a special return fare for flying one way and ferrying the other (adult/child $180/148).

Barrier Air (p122) departs from both Auckland Domestic Airport and North Shore Aerodrome 42 times a week for the 30-minute flight to Claris.

BOAT

SeaLink (☑0800 732 546, 09-300 5900; www.sealink.co.nz; adult/child/car one way $90/66/312, return $172/113/511) runs car ferries four days a week from Wynyard Wharf in Auckland to Tryphena's **Shoal Bay** (4½ hours) and once a week to Port FitzRoy (five hours). The last part of the crossing can get rough.

🚗 Getting Around

Most roads are narrow and windy, but even small hire cars can handle the unsealed sections. Many of the accommodation places will pick you up from the airport or wharf if notified in advance.

Aotea Car Rentals (☑0800 426 832; www. aoteacarrentals.co.nz; Mulberry Grove, Shoal Bay) Rents cars (from $60), 4WDs (from $70) and vans (from $99).

Go Great Barrier Island Can arrange rental cars and tramper shuttles to island tracks.

Motubikes (📱022 344 0645; www.motubikes.co.nz; 67 Hector Sanderson Rd, Claris; per hour/day $25/90; ⊙10am-4pm) These sturdy electric motorcycles are equally at home on unsealed roads, and the chatty owner can arrange drop-off and pickup services around the island. Can be rented with a normal driving licence and is located conveniently close to the airport.

WEST AUCKLAND

West Auckland epitomises rugged: wild black-sand beaches, bush-shrouded ranges and mullet-haired, black-T-shirt-wearing 'Westies'. This is just one of several stereotypes of the area's denizens. Others include the back-to-nature hippie, the eccentric bohemian artist and the dope-smoking surfer dude, all attracted to a simple life at the edge of the bush.

Add to the mix Croatian immigrants, earning the fertile fields at the base of the Waitākere Ranges the nickname 'Dallie Valley' after the Dalmatian coast where most hailed from. These pioneering families planted grapes and made wine, founding one of NZ's major industries.

❶ Getting There & Away

There are regular buses as far as Titirangi and Helensville but no services to the west-coast beaches. The best options for the beaches are to rent a car or join a day tour from Auckland.

Titirangi

POP 3468

This little village marks the end of Auckland's suburban sprawl and is a good place to spot all manner of Westie stereotypes over a coffee, wine or cold beer. Once home to NZ's greatest modern painter, Colin McCahon, there remains an artsy feel to the place. Titirangi means 'Fringe of Heaven' – an apt name for the gateway to the Waitākere Ranges. This is the last stop for petrol and ATMs on your way west.

Te Uru Waitakere
Contemporary Gallery GALLERY
(📱09-817 8087; www.teuru.org.nz; 420 Titirangi Rd; ⊙10am-4.30pm) FREE This excellent art gallery is housed in a spectacular modern building on the edge of the village beside the heritage splendour of the former Hotel Titirangi. Rotating exhibitions and installations are sourced both from NZ and internationally, and the curator's remit could stretch from photography and sculpture to mixed media or video. The gallery also features a small shop selling interesting jewellery, pottery and gifts. Check the website for upcoming exhibitions.

McCahon House MUSEUM
(📱09-817 6148; www.facebook.com/McCahon House; 67 Otitori Bay Rd, French Bay; $5; ⊙1-4pm Wed-Sun) It's a mark of the esteem in which Colin McCahon is held that the house he lived and painted in during the 1950s has been opened to the public as a mini museum. The swish pad next door is home to the artist lucky enough to win the McCahon Arts Residency. Look for the signposts pointing down Park Rd, just before you reach Titirangi village. The house is around 2km down the hill.

Deco Eatery MEDITERRANEAN $$
(📱09-817 2664; www.decoeatery.co.nz; Lopdell House, 418 Titirangi Rd; mains $16-38; ⊙7am-late Mon-Fri, 7.30am-late Sat & Sun; 📱) Located amid the heritage vibe of Lopdell House, Deco's decor channels a Turkish ambience, while the menu combines Anatolian classics with a broader Mediterranean focus. The restaurant is spacious and sunny, and a great stop before or after visiting the nearby surf beaches of Piha or Karekare.

❶ Getting There & Away

To get from central Auckland to Titirangi (adult/child $9/5, one hour), catch a train from Britomart on the Western line to New Lynn train station. Transfer to bus 170 or 172 to Titirangi.

Karekare

Few stretches of sand have more personality than Karekare. Those prone to metaphysical musings inevitably settle on descriptions such as 'spiritual' and 'brooding'. Perhaps history has left its imprint: in 1825 it was the site of a ruthless massacre of the local Kawerau *iwi* by Ngāpuhi invaders. Wild and gorgeously undeveloped, this famous beach has been the setting for on-screen moments both high- and low-brow, from Oscar winner *The Piano* to *Xena: Warrior Princess*.

From the car park the quickest route to the black-sand beach involves wading through a stream. Karekare rates as one of the most dangerous beaches in the country, with strong surf and ever-present rips, so don't even think about swimming unless the beach is being patrolled by lifeguards (usually only in summer). Pearl Jam singer Eddie Vedder nearly drowned here while visiting Neil Finn's Karekare pad.

Follow the road over the bridge and up along Lone Kauri Rd for 100m, where a short track leads to the pretty Karekare Falls. This leafy picnic spot is the start of several walking tracks.

There is no public transport to Karekare. To get here, head through Blockhouse Bay and Titirangi from central Auckland, merge onto Scenic Dr, and then continue on Piha Rd until you reach the well-signposted turn-off to Karekare Rd.

Piha

POP 600

If you notice Auckland surfers with a faraway look, chances are they're daydreaming about Piha. This beautifully rugged, iron-sand beach has long been a favourite for Aucklanders escaping from the city's stresses – whether for day trips, weekend teenage parties or family holidays.

Although Piha is popular, it's also incredibly dangerous, with wild surf and strong undercurrents, so much so that it's spawned its own popular reality-TV show, *Piha Rescue*. If you don't want to inadvertently star in it, always swim between the flags, where lifeguards can provide help if you get into trouble.

Piha may be bigger and more populated than neighbouring Karekare, but there's still no supermarket, liquor shop, bank or petrol station, although there is a small general store that doubles as a cafe, takeaway shop and post office.

◉ Sights & Activities

The view of the coast as you drive down Piha Rd is spectacular. Perched on its haunches near the centre of the beach is Lion Rock (101m), whose 'mane' glows golden in the evening light. It's actually the eroded core of an ancient volcano and a Māori *pā* site. A path at the south end of the beach takes you to some great lookouts. At low tide you can walk south along the beach and watch the surf shooting through a ravine in another large rock known as the Camel. A little further along, the waves crash through the Gap and form a safe swimming hole. A small colony of little penguins nests at the beach's north end.

For surfboard hire, try Piha Store (☎09-812 8844; 26 Seaview Rd; snacks $4-10; ☺7.30am-5.30pm) or Piha Surf Shop (☎09-812 8723; www.pihasurf.co.nz; 122 Seaview Rd; ☺8am-5pm).

🛏 Sleeping & Eating

★ Piha Beachstay –
Jandal Palace   HOSTEL $
(☎09-812 8381; www.pihabeachstay.co.nz; 38 Glenesk Rd; dm/s $45/89, d with/without bathroom $159/119; @ 🖙) 🏄 Attractive and ecofriendly, this wood-and-glass lodge has extremely

---

WAITĀKERE RANGES

This 160-sq-km wilderness was covered in kauri until the mid-19th century, when logging claimed most of the giant trees. A few stands of ancient kauri and other mature natives survive amid the dense bush of the regenerating rainforest, which is now protected inside the Waitākere Ranges Regional Park. Bordered to the west by wildly beautiful beaches on the Tasman Sea, the park's rugged terrain makes an excellent day trip from Auckland.

Arataki (☎09-817 0077; www.aucklandcouncil.govt.nz; 300 Scenic Dr; ☺9am-5pm) 🏄 FREE visitor centre is the starting point for the challenging 77km Hillary Trail (www.aucklandcouncil.govt.nz), honouring Everest-conqueror Sir Edmund Hillary. Unfortunately, at the time of writing, most parts of the trail and some other trails in the park were closed because of the kauri dieback disease damaging the park's forests.

Search for 'track closures' on www.aucklandcouncil.govt.nz for the latest information before setting off.

Auckland's Western train line terminates at Swanson, which is within 1km of the north-western edge of the regional park. However, this is a long way away from the main park attractions. There are no bus services through the main part of the park. If you're driving, take the Northwestern Motorway from central Auckland, exit at Te Atatu and continue on SH13.

smart facilities. It's 1km from the beach, but there's a little stream at the bottom of the property and bushwalks nearby. In winter an open fire warms the large communal lounge.

Black Sands Cabins
CABIN $$

(☑021 969 924; www.pihabeach.co.nz; Beach Valley Rd; d $140; 🛜) 🏄 Cosy cabins with bunks and a simple Kiwiana vibe stand amid regenerating native trees at this good-value option. Cabins have a fridge, toaster and kettle, plus all-important mosquito screens on the windows and free wi-fi. Bathroom and cooking facilities are in an adjacent standalone building.

Murray
CAFE $

(www.facebook.com/murray.inc; Marine Pde; snacks from $10; ⊘4-8pm Fri, 11.30am-8pm, 9.30am-8pm Nov-Mar) Cool beats, excellent coffee and top-notch soft-shell-crab tacos are all dispensed from this cool surf shack a short walk from the beach and Lion Rock. Seafood fans should ask if mussel fritters or raw fish salad are available. Chill out on a beanbag in the sun.

Piha Cafe
CAFE $$

(☑09-812 8808; www.facebook.com/thepihacafe; 20 Seaview Rd; mains $14-28; ⊘8am-3pm Mon & Wed, to 8pm Thu-Sat, to 4pm Sun) 🏄 Big-city standards mesh seamlessly with sand-between-toes informality at this attractive ecofriendly cafe. Cooked breakfasts and crispy pizzas provide sustenance for a hard day's surfing. After the waves, head back for a cold beverage on the deck. Black Sands craft beer from nearby West Auckland is usually on tap; the pilsner is especially refreshing.

ℹ️ Getting There & Away

There's no public transport to Piha, but **Rapu** (☑09-828 0426, 021 550 546; www.rapuadventures.com; return from Auckland $50) sometimes shuttles from central Auckland when the surf's up. Piha is also often included in the day-trip itinerary of Bush & Beach (p99).

Te Henga (Bethells Beach)

Breathtaking Bethells Beach is reached by taking Te Henga Rd at the northern end of Scenic Dr in Auckland's western suburbs. It's a raw, black-sand beach with surf, windswept dunes and walks, such as the popular one over giant sand dunes to Lake Wainamu (starting near the bridge on the approach to the beach).

There's no public transport to Te Henga.

Wainamu Luxury Tents
B&B $$$

(☑022 384 0500; www.facebook.com/wainamu; Tasman View Rd; d $250; ⊘Oct-Jun) 🏄 Inspired by safari tents from Botswana and Māori *whare* (houses), these very comfortable tents combine quiet rural locations, recycled timber construction and a luxurious 'glamping' vibe. Cooking is done on barbecues, lighting from gas lamps and candles is practical and romantic, and outdoor baths also enhance the whole experience. Free-range eggs, fresh-baked bread and muesli combine in DIY breakfast packs.

Bethells Cafe
CAFE $

(☑09-810 9381; www.facebook.com/BethellsCafe; Bethells Beach car park; mains $12-20; ⊘5.30-9.30pm Fri, 10am-6pm Sat & Sun Nov-May) Less a cafe and more a food truck with an awning, Bethells Cafe does a roaring trade in burgers (beef and vegetarian), pizza, cakes and coffee. On Friday nights it's pretty much the perfect Kiwi beach scene, with live musicians entertaining the adults while the kids surf the sand dunes.

Kumeū Region

West Auckland's main wine-producing area still has some vineyards owned by the original Croatian families who kick-started NZ's wine industry. The fancy eateries that have mushroomed in recent years haven't changed the region's relaxed farmland feel, but have encouraged an afternoon's indulgence on the way back from the beach or the hot pools. Most cellars offer free tastings. Kumeū itself is a rapidly expanding dormitory suburb of West Auckland, but great wine, food and beer are nearby.

Coopers Creek
WINERY

(☑09-412 8560; www.cooperscreek.co.nz; 601 SH16, Huapai; ⊘10.30am-5.30pm) Buy a bottle, spread out a picnic in the attractive gardens and, from January to Easter, enjoy Sunday-afternoon jazz sessions.

Kumeu River
WINERY

(☑09-412 8415; www.kumeuriver.co.nz; 550 SH16; ⊘9am-4.30pm Mon-Fri, 11am-4.30pm Sat & Sun) Owned by the Brajkovich family, this winery produces one of NZ's best chardonnays, among other varietals.

Tasting Shed
BISTRO $$

(☑09-412 6454; www.thetastingshed.co.nz; 609 SH16, Huapai; dishes $16-32; ⊘4-10pm Wed & Thu, noon-11pm Fri-Sun; ☑) 🏄 Complementing its

THE GREAT GANNET OE

After honing their flying skills, young gannets get the ultimate chance to test them – a 2000km journey to Australia. They usually hang out there for several years before returning home, never to attempt the journey again. Once back in the homeland, they spend a few years waiting for a piece of waterfront property to become available in the colony, before settling down with a regular partner to nest – returning to the same patch of dirt every year. In other words, they're your typical young New Zealander on a rite-of-passage Overseas Experience (OE).

rural aspect with rustic-chic decor, this slick eatery conjures up delicious dishes inspired by the flavours of Asia, the Middle East and Mediterranean Europe. A short menu of proteins – think lamb, fish, salmon and steak – can be partnered with sides, including yams with coconut and cashews, or a salad of white asparagus and burrata cheese.

Hallertau   BREWERY
(☑09-412 5555; www.hallertau.co.nz; 1171 Coatesville-Riverhead Hwy, Riverhead; share plates $11-24, mains $25-35; ☺11am-10pm) Hallertau offers tasting paddles ($12 to $16) of its craft beers served in its spacious and sociable *biergarten*, and inside on cosy tables near the bar. Regular guest beers, good food and occasional weekend DJs and live music make it popular with Auckland's hopheads. Our pick from the food menu are the beef *krokets*. Good wood-fired pizza too.

Beer Spot   CRAFT BEER
(☑09-974 1496; www.thebeerspot.co.nz; 321 Main Rd, Huapai; ☺noon-8pm Mon & Tue, to 9pm Wed, to 10pm Thu-Sun) A hoppy oasis in wine country, the Beer Spot's array of 40 taps of craft beers and ciders is partnered by visiting food trucks on a weekly basis. Check the website page for who's scheduled and what's on tap. There's also a good selection of local wines.

Riverhead   PUB
(☑09-412 8902; www.theriverhead.co.nz; cnr Queen St & York Tce, Riverhead; ☺11am-late) A blissful terrace, shaded by oak trees and overlooking the river, makes this 1857 hotel a memorable drink stop, even if the menu (mains $27 to $36) doesn't quite live up to

its gastropub ambitions. Make a day of it, with a boat cruise (p99) from the city to the pub's own jetty.

❶ Getting There & Away

From central Auckland, Kumeū is 25km up the Northwestern Motorway (SH16). Catch a bus to Westgate and then transfer to bus 122 or 125 to Kumeū.

Muriwai Beach

A rugged black-sand surf beach, Muriwai Beach's main claim to fame is the Takapu Refuge gannet colony, spread over the southern headland and outlying rock stacks. Viewing platforms get you close enough to watch (and smell) these fascinating seabirds. Every August hundreds of adult birds return to this spot to hook up with their regular partners and get busy – expect lots of outrageously cute neck-rubbing, bill-touching and general snuggling. The net result is a single chick per season; December and January are the best times to see the little ones testing their wings before embarking on an impressive odyssey.

Nearby, a couple of short tracks will take you through beautiful native bush to a lookout that offers views along the 60km length of the beach.

Apart from surfing, Muriwai Beach is a popular spot for hang gliding, parapunting, kiteboarding and horse riding. There are also tennis courts, a golf course and a cafe that doubles as a takeaway chippie. Wild surf and treacherous rips mean that swimming is safe only when the beach is patrolled (swim between the flags).

There is no public transport to Muriwai.

Helensville
POP 2643

A smattering of heritage buildings, antique shops and cafes makes village-like Helensville a good whistle-stop for those taking SH16 north.

Tree Adventures   OUTDOORS
(☑0800 827 926; www.treeadventures.co.nz; Restall Rd, Woodhill; ropes courses $20-46; ☺9am-5pm) A set of high-ropes courses within Woodhill Forest, located 14km south of Helensville, consisting of swinging logs, nets, balance beams, Tarzan swings and a flying fox.

Parakai Springs
SWIMMING, SPA

(📞 09-420 8998; www.parakaisprings.co.nz; 150 Parkhurst Rd; adult/child $26/13; ☺10am-8pm Sun-Thu, to 9pm Fri & Sat; 🐾) Aucklanders bring their bored children to Parakai, 2km north-west of Helensville, on wet wintry days. It has large thermally heated swimming pools, private spas (per 30 minutes per person $7) and a couple of hydroslides.

Woodhill Mountain
Bike Park
MOUNTAIN BIKING

(📞 027 278 0969; www.bikeparks.co.nz; Restall Rd, Woodhill; adult/child $15/10, bike hire from $50; ☺8am-5.30pm Thu-Tue, to 10pm Wed) Maintains many challenging tracks (including jumps and beams) within Woodhill Forest, 14km south of Helensville.

Visitor Information
Centre
TOURIST INFORMATION

(📞 09-420 8060; www.helensville.co.nz; 27 Commercial Rd; ☺10am-5pm Mon-Fri, to 2pm Sat) Housed inside the local Citizens Advice Bureau. Pick up free brochures detailing the *Helensville Heritage Trail* and *Helensville Riverside Walkway*.

ⓘ Getting There & Away

From central Auckland to Helensville (adult/child $14.50/8, two hours), catch bus NX1 to the Hibiscus Coast Bus Station and transfer to bus 128 to Helensville.

NORTH AUCKLAND

The Auckland supercity council region continues for 90km north of the CBD to just past the point where SH16 and SH1 converge at Wellsford. The semirural area north of Auckland's suburban sprawl encompasses beautiful beaches, regional parks, tramping trails, quaint villages and wineries. Plus there are excellent opportunities for kayaking, snorkelling and diving. Consider visiting on a day trip from Auckland or as a way to break up your trip on the journey north.

Shakespear Regional Park

Shooting out eastward just before Orewa, the Whangaparāoa Peninsula is a heavily developed spit of land with a sizeable South African expat community. At its tip is this gorgeous 376-hectare regional park, its native wildlife protected by a 1.7km pest-proof fence.

Sheep, cows, peacocks and pukeko ramble over the grassy headland, while pohutukawa-lined Te Haruhi Bay provides great views of the gulf islands and the city. Walking tracks take between 40 minutes and two hours, exploring native forest, WWII gun embankments, Māori sites and lookouts. If you can't bear to leave, there's an idyllic beachfront camping ground (📞 09-366 6400; www.aucklandcouncil.govt.nz; sites per adult/child $16/6.50) with flush toilets and cold showers.

ⓘ Getting There & Away

Driving is the most straightforward way to reach the park, but it is possible to get here via a tortuous two-hour three-bus combination from central Auckland (adult/child $16/9). Another option is to catch the Gulf Harbour ferry from downtown Auckland and link to the 988 bus at Gulf Harbour continuing to the park (adult/child $13/7, 90 minutes).

Orewa
POP 8523

Orewa's main beach is a lovely expanse of sand; however, locals fear that the town is turning into NZ's equivalent of Queensland's Gold Coast. It is, indeed, very built up and high-rise apartment towers have begun to sprout, but unless they start exporting retirees and replacing them with bikini-clad parking wardens, it's unlikely to reach the Gold Coast's extremes. Quieter and more compact Hatfields Beach is just 2km north over the hill.

◉ Sights & Activities

Orewa Beach
BEACH

Orewa's 3km-long stretch of sand is its main drawcard. Being in the Hauraki Gulf, it's sheltered from the surf but still patrolled by lifeguards in peak season.

Te Ara Tahuna Estuary
Cycle & Walkway
CYCLING, WALKING

Starting from South Bridge, this 8km route loops around the estuary and includes explanations of the area's past as a centre for Māori food gathering.

Snowplanet
SNOW SPORTS

(📞 09-427 0044; www.snowplanet.co.nz; 91 Small Rd, Silverdale; day pass adult/child $71/51; ☺10am-10pm Sun-Thu, to midnight Fri, 9am-10pm Sat & Sun) Snowplanet offers indoor skiing, snowboarding and tubing throughout the year. It's just off SH1, 8km south of Orewa.

Sleeping

Orewa Motor Lodge MOTEL $$
(☑09-426 4027; www.orewamotorlodge.co.nz; 290 Hibiscus Coast Hwy; units $160-210; ☞) One of the motels lining Orewa's main road, this refurbished complex has scrupulously clean wooden units prettied up with hanging flower baskets. There's also a spa pool.

Waves MOTEL $$$
(☑09-427 0888; www.waves.co.nz; cnr Hibiscus Coast Hwy & Kohu St; units from $175; ☞) This complex offers spacious, self-contained apartments, and the downstairs units have gardens and spa baths. It's only a few metres from the beach.

Eating & Drinking

Casablanca MEDITERRANEAN $$
(☑09-426 6818; www.casablancacafenz.co.nz; 336 Hibiscus Coast Hwy; mains $16-31; ☉11am-10pm Mon-Fri, 9am-10pm Sat & Sun) Turkish, North African and Mediterranean flavours feature at this buzzy cafe. Try the hearty baked Moorish eggs for brunch and you'll be set for the next chapter of your Kiwi road trip.

Coast CRAFT BEER
(☑09-421 1016; www.coastorewa.co.nz; 342 Hibiscus Coast Hwy; ☉11am-11pm) Craft beer, cocktails and wine combine with good meals and bar snacks – try the barbecued-duck tacos – at this Orewa outpost of Auckland's Deep Creek Brewing. Settle in for ocean views from the upper deck, and look forward to gigs from local musos most Friday and Saturday nights. Deep Creek's hoppy Lupulin Effect brews and hazy beers are always worth trying.

❶ Getting There & Away

To get from central Auckland to Orewa (adult/child $12.50/7, 1¼ hours), catch the NX1 bus from Britomart to the Hibiscus Coast Bus Station, and then transfer to the 981 bus to Orewa.

Puhoi

POP 450

Forget dingy cafes and earnest poets – this quaint village is a slice of the real Bohemia. In 1863 around 200 German-speaking immigrants from the present-day Czech Republic settled here in what was then dense bush.

Church of Sts Peter & Paul CHURCH
(www.holyname.org.nz; Puhoi Rd) The village's pretty Catholic church dates from 1881 and has an interesting tabernacle painting (a copy of one in Bohemia), stained glass and statues.

Puhoi Heritage Museum MUSEUM
(☑09-422 0852; www.puhoiheritagemuseum.co.nz; Puhoi Rd; adult/child $3.50/free; ☉noon-3pm) Tells the story of the hardship and perseverance of the original Bohemian pioneers.

Puhoi River Canoe Hire KAYAKING
(☑09-422 0891; www.puhoirivercanoes.co.nz; 84 Puhoi Rd; ☉mid-Jul–Jun) Hires kayaks and Canadian canoes, either by the hour (single/double kayak $30/60) or for an excellent 8km downstream journey from the village to Wenderholm Regional Park (single/double kayak $55/100, including return transport). Bookings are essential.

Puhoi Valley CAFE $$
(☑09-422 0670; www.puhoivalley.co.nz; 275 Ahuroa Rd; mains $15-25; ☉9.30am-4pm Mon-Fri, 9am-4.30pm Sat & Sun; ☉) Renowned across NZ, Puhoi Valley cheese features heavily on the menu of this upmarket cheese shop and cafe, set blissfully alongside a lake, fountain and children's playground. In the summer there's music on the lawn, perfect with a gourmet ice cream.

★Puhoi Pub PUB
(☑09-422 0812; www.puhoipub.com; 5 Saleyards Rd; ☉10am-10pm Mon-Sat, to 8pm Sun) There's character and then some in this 1879 pub, with walls completely covered in old photos, animal heads and vintage household goods.

❶ Getting There & Away

Puhoi is 1km west of SH1. The turn-off is 2km past the Johnstone Hills tunnel. There's no public transport.

Mahurangi & Scandrett Regional Parks

At the southern and eastern edges of the Mahurangi Peninsula northeast of Auckland, the Mahurangi Regional Park and Scandrett Regional Park are convenient as day trips from the city, or as a relaxing overnight stay in simple accommodation or at basic campsites. Walking tracks, coastal forests, sheltered beaches, and Māori and colonial history all feature.

You'll need your own transport to reach these parks. Some parts can only be reached by boat.

Mahurangi Regional Park   PARK
(☑09-366 2000; http://regionalparks.auckland-council.govt.nz; 190 Ngarewa Dr, Mahurangi West)
Straddling the head of Mahurangi Harbour, Mahurangi Regional Park is a boater's paradise incorporating areas of coastal forest, *pā* sites and a historic homestead and cemetery. Its sheltered beaches offer prime sandy spots for a dip or picnic, and there are loop walks ranging from 1½ to 2½ hours.

Scandrett Regional Park   PARK
(☑09-366 2000; http://regionalparks.auckland-council.govt.nz; 114 Scandrett Rd, Mahurangi East)
On the ocean side of the Mahurangi Peninsula, Scandrett Regional Park has a sandy beach, walking tracks, patches of regenerating forest, a historic homestead, *pā* sites and great views towards Kawau Island. Three baches (sleeping six to eight) are available for rent and there's room for campervans (per adult/child $9/4.50).

Warkworth

POP 5000

River-hugging Warkworth makes a pleasant pit stop, its cutesy main street retaining a village atmosphere. Increases in Auckland's real-estate prices and better motorway access have seen the town grow in popularity in recent years, but it is still a laid-back spot near good beaches and wine country.

Dome Forest   FOREST
(SH1) Two kilometres north of Warkworth, a track leads through this regenerating forest to the Dome summit (336m). On a fine day you can see the Sky Tower from a lookout near the top. The summit walk takes about 1½ hours return, or you can continue for a gruelling seven-hour one-way hike through the Totora Peak Scenic Reserve, exiting on Govan Wilson Rd.

Warkworth District's Museum   MUSEUM
(☑09-425 7093; www.warkworthmuseum.co.nz; Tudor Collins Dr; adult/child $7/3; ⊙10am-4pm) Pioneer-era detritus is displayed at this small local museum. Of more interest is the surrounding Parry Kauri Park, which harbours a couple of giant kauri trees, including the 800-year-old McKinney kauri (girth 7.6m).

Chocolate Brown   CAFE $$
(☑09-422 2677; www.chocolatebrown.co.nz; 6 Mill Lane; mains $10-25; ⊙7am-4pm Mon-Fri, 8am-4pm Sat & Sun) Decked out with quirky

---

❶ WHICH HIGHWAY?

From Auckland, the multilane Northern Motorway (SH1) bypasses Orewa and Waiwera on the Northern Gateway Toll Rd. It will save you about 10 minutes and you need to pay the NZ Transport Agency (☑0800 402 020; www.tollroad. govt.nz; per car & motorbike $2.40) toll online (in advance or within five days of your journey). If you don't pay the toll within the time frame, then you, or your rental-car company, will be charged an additional $5 administration fee. If the toll remains unpaid after 28 days, an additional $40 infringement fee is charged.

Between Christmas and New Year, SH1 can be terribly gridlocked heading north between the toll road and Wellsford; winding SH16 through Kumeū and Helensville is a sensible alternative. The same is true if heading south in the first few days of the new year.

NZ-themed art – mostly for sale – this cafe serves excellent coffee, robust eggy breakfasts and delicious homestyle baking. Definitely leave room for a few cacao-infused goodies from the chocolate shop next door; there are plenty of gift packs for the folks back home.

Tahi Bar   CRAFT BEER
(☑09-422 3674; www.tahibar.com; 1 Neville St; ⊙3pm-late Tue-Thu, noon-late Fri & Sat, noon-8pm Sun) Tucked down a quiet laneway, Tahi features nine taps of NZ craft beer. It's a friendly spot with a rustic and sunny deck. Ask if any beers from award-winning and Warkworth-based 8 Wired Brewing are available. Tahi's new owners have expanded the menu, including seafood empanadas and pulled-pork tacos. Check the website for details of weekend live music.

Honey Centre   FOOD
(☑09-425 8003; www.honeycentre.com; 7 Perry Rd; ⊙8.30am-5pm) About 5km south of Warkworth, the Honey Centre makes a diverting stop-off, with its cafe, free honey tasting and glass-fronted hives. The shop sells all sorts of bee-related products, from candles to mead.

❶ Getting There & Away

InterCity (☑09-583 5780; www.intercity. co.nz) services pass through town, en route between Auckland and the Bay of Islands.

WORTH A TRIP

MĀORI VILLAGE TOUR

You'll see the terraces of a lot of historic *pā* (fortified village) sites etched into hillsides all around NZ, but if you want to get an idea of how these Māori villages actually looked, take a one-hour guided tour of the recreated *pā* at **Te Hana Te Ao Marama** (09-423 8701; www. tehana.co.nz; 307-308 SH1, Te Hana; adult/ child $28.50/18.50; 9am-5pm Wed-Sun). It's best to book ahead.

Matakana
POP 440

Around 15 years ago, Matakana was a nondescript rural village with a handful of heritage buildings and an old-fashioned country pub. Now the locals watch bemused as Auckland's chattering classes idle away the hours in stylish wine bars and cafes.

The reason for this transformation is the area's boutique wineries, which are developing a name for pinot gris, merlot, syrah and a host of obscure varietals. Local vineyards are detailed in the free *Matakana Coast Wine Country* (www.matakanacoast.com) and *Matakana Wine Trail* (www.matakanawine. co.nz) brochures, available from the Matakana Information Centre.

Also available at the centre is information on B&B accommodation, tours exploring the rural and coastal hinterland, and a growing array of local stores specialising in antiques and vintage furniture and homewares.

👁 Sights & Activities

Tawharanui Regional Park   BEACH
(09-366 2000; www.aucklandcouncil.govt.nz; 1181 Takatu Rd) A partly unsealed road leads to this 588-hectare reserve at the end of a peninsula. This special place is an open sanctuary for native birds, protected by a pest-proof fence, while the northern coast is a marine park (bring a snorkel). There are plenty of walking tracks (1½ to four hours), but the main attraction is **Anchor Bay**, one of the region's finest white-sand beaches.

Omaha Beach   BEACH
The nearest swimming beach to Matakana, Omaha has a long stretch of white sand, good surf and ritzy holiday homes. It's the kind of place where you might see a former NZ prime minister on the golf course, which is set a few genteel blocks back from the beach.

Brick Bay Sculpture Trail   GARDENS
(09-425 4690; www.brickbaysculpture.co.nz; Arabella Lane, Snells Beach; adult/child $12/8; 10am-5pm) After taking an hour-long artistic ramble through the beautiful grounds and native bush of Brick Bay Wines, recuperate with a wine tasting at the architecturally impressive cafe. Ask about the annual 'Folly' competition, where an up-and-coming NZ artist is funded to construct their winning design, which is subsequently installed at Brick Bay.

Blue Adventures   WATER SPORTS
(022 630 5705; www.blueadventures.co.nz; 331 Omaha Flats Rd, Omaha; lessons per hour from $59) Offers kitesurfing, paddle-boarding and wakeboarding lessons and rentals from Omaha and Orewa. Two- and three-day retreats including accommodation are also available.

Matakana Bicycle Hire   CYCLING
(09-423 0076; www.matakanabicyclehire.co.nz; Matakana Country Park, 1151 Leigh Rd; half-/full-day hire from $30/40) Hire a bike to explore local vineyards and beaches. Pick up a *Matakana Trails* map from the information centre detailing routes to nearby Omaha and Port Wells. Check Matakana Bicycle Hire's website for details of mountain-bike hire for negotiating tracks in nearby regional parks.

🛏 Sleeping

BeauRegard Accommodation   COTTAGE $$
(021 803 378; www.beauregard.co.nz; 603 Matakana Rd; d incl breakfast $190-250; ❄ 🛜) Sitting in rural surroundings, a 4km drive from Matakana village, these three one-bedroom self-contained cottages are the ideal stylish haven for exploring the beaches and vineyards of the surrounding area. Each of the cottages has a Gallic name – Bel-Air, Voltaire or Bastille – and the French–Kiwi hosts have plenty of ideas for tasty discoveries at local markets and restaurants.

🍴 Eating & Drinking

Charlie's Gelato Garden   ICE CREAM $
(09-422 7942; www.charliesgelato.co.nz; 17 Sharp Rd; ice cream $5-7, pizza slice/whole $6/20; 10am-5pm Mon-Fri, to 6pm Sat & Sun) Superb sorbet and gelato made from fresh fruit and interesting ingredients – try the liquorice or ginger-beer flavours – and excellent wood-fired pizzas during summer from Friday to Sunday.

Matakana PUB FOOD **$$**

(☑ 09-422 7518; www.thematakana.co.nz; 11 Matakana Valley Rd; mains $22-37; ☺ 11.30am-1am) Matakana's heritage pub features stylish decor, local wines and craft beers, and decent bistro food, sometimes including Mahurangi oysters. An American-style smoker turns out good low 'n' slow barbecue – try the pork belly or the spicy ribs – and occasional DJs and live acts enliven the cool outdoor space. Check Facebook for what's on.

★**Sawmill Brewery** MICROBREWERY

(☑ 09-422 6555; www.sawmillbrewery.co.nz; 1004 Leigh Rd; ☺ noon-10pm) Relax with a tasting rack of brews amid the rustic but hip decor, and order widely from the share-plates menu. It's all good, but we're partial to the citrusy Double IPA with goat, hummus and cumin flatbreads. Regular seasonal beers make Sawmill one of NZ's best breweries. Look for the hop bines out front and you're in the right place.

Vintry WINE BAR

(☑ 09-423 0251; www.vintry.co.nz; 2 Matakana Valley Rd; ☺ 3-10pm) In the Matakana Cinemas complex, this wine bar serves as a one-stop cellar door for all the local producers. Beers from local craft breweries are on tap, and the same owners operate a riverside bistro downstairs serving breakfast, lunch and dinner.

☆ **Entertainment**

Matakana Cinemas CINEMA

(☑ 09-422 9833; www.matakanacinemas.co.nz; 2 Matakana Valley Rd) The fantastical Matakana Cinemas complex has a domed roof reminiscent of an Ottoman bathhouse. Titles tend to the art-house end of the spectrum, but major Hollywood blockbusters are also screened.

🛍 **Shopping**

Matakana Village Farmers Market MARKET

(www.matakanavillage.co.nz; Matakana Sq, 2 Matakana Valley Rd; ☺ 8am-1pm Sat) This excellent farmers market lures plenty of Aucklanders up the highway.

ℹ **Information**

Matakana Information Centre (☑ 09-422 7433; www.matakanainfo.org.nz; 2 Matakana Valley Rd; ☺ 10am-late) In the foyer of the Matakana Cinemas complex. It's usually staffed from 10am to 1pm, but is open late daily for maps and brochures.

ℹ **Getting There & Away**

Matakana village is a 10km drive northeast of Warkworth along Matakana Rd; there's no regular public transport. Ferries for Kawau Island leave from Sandspit, 8km east of Warkworth along Sandspit Rd.

Leigh
POP 390

Appealing little Leigh (www.leighbythesea.co.nz) has a picturesque harbour dotted with fishing boats, and a decent swimming beach at Matheson Bay.

Apart from the extraordinary Goat Island Marine Reserve on its doorstep, Leigh's other claim to fame is the legendary live-music venue Leigh Sawmill Cafe (p146), which sometimes sees surprisingly big names drop in to play a set or two.

You'll need your own wheels to get here.

★**Goat Island Marine Reserve** WILDLIFE RESERVE

(www.doc.govt.nz; Cape Rodney to Okakari Point Marine Reserve, Goat Island Rd) Only 3km from Leigh, this 547-hectare aquatic area was established in 1975 as the country's first marine reserve. In less than 40 years the sea has reverted to a giant aquarium, giving an impression of what the NZ coast must have been like before humans arrived. You only need step knee-deep into the water to see snapper (the big fish with blue dots and fins), blue maomao and stripy parore swimming around.

Excellent interpretive panels explain the area's Māori significance (it was the landing place of one of the ancestral canoes) and provide pictures of the species you're likely to encounter.

There are dive areas all around Goat Island, which sits just offshore, or you can snorkel or dive directly from the beach. Colourful sponges, forests of seaweed, boarfish, crayfish and stingrays are common sights, and if you're very lucky, you may see orcas and bottle-nosed dolphins. Visibility is claimed to be at least 10m, 75% of the time.

Goat Island Marine Discovery Centre AQUARIUM

(☑ 09-923 3645; www.goatislandmarine.co.nz; 160 Goat Island Rd; adult/child/family $9/5/20; ☺ 10am-4pm Dec-Apr, Sat, Sun & public & school holidays May-Nov; 🚻) Staffed by marine experts and graduate students from the University of Auckland, this centre is packed with interesting exhibitions on the ecosystem of the marine reserve, and is worth visiting before venturing into Goat Island's waters. The interactive displays and the tide pool full of marine creatures are great for children.

Goat Island Dive & Snorkel
DIVING

(☑ 09-422 6925; www.goatislanddive.co.nz; 142a Pakiri Rd; snorkel set hire adult/child $30/20, incl wetsuit $45/35) This long-standing operator offers guided snorkelling, PADI courses and dive trips in the Goat Island Marine Reserve (p145) and other key sites throughout the year. It also hires snorkelling and diving gear.

Glass Bottom Boat Tours
BOATING

(☑ 09-422 6334; www.glassbottomboat.co.nz; Goat Island Rd; adult/child $40/20; ☺ late Oct-Apr) A glass-bottomed boat provides an opportunity to see the underwater life of Goat Island Marine Reserve (p145) while staying dry. Trips last 45 minutes and run from the beach (weather permitting). Go online or ring to check conditions and to book.

Octopus Hideaway
SNORKELLING

(☑ 021 926 212; www.theoctopushideaway.nz; 2 Seatoun Ave; ☺ 10am-6pm Tue-Sun) This crew hires snorkelling gear (adult/child $25/18, including wetsuit $38/26), and offers guided two-hour ($70/50) snorkel experiences.

Leigh Sawmill Cafe
PUB

(☑ 09-422 6019; www.sawmillcafe.co.nz; 142 Pakiri Rd; ☺ 10am-late late Dec–mid-Feb, Thu-Sun mid-Feb–late Dec) This spunky little venue is a regular stop on the summer rock circuite pizzas ($25) are thin and crunchy like they should be, and best enjoyed in the garden on a lazy summer evening. It sometimes closes for private functions so it's wise to check its Facebook page before setting out.

If you imbibe too much of the good stuff from local wineries and craft breweries, there's accommodation inside the old sawmill shed, including basic backpacker rooms (from $25) and massive doubles with en suites ($125). Alternatively, you can rent the Cosy Sawmill Family Cottage (from $200, sleeps 10) or a stylish apartment ($200).

Bay of Islands & Northland

Best Places to Eat

➜ Plough & Feather (p175)

➜ Charlotte's Kitchen (p171)

➜ Quay (p158)

➜ The Gables (p167)

➜ Ake Ake (p175)

Best Places to Stay

➜ Endless Summer Lodge (p182)

➜ Arcadia Lodge (p166)

➜ Old Oak (p178)

➜ Kahoe Farms Hostel (p177)

➜ Mangawhai Chalets (p153)

Why Go?

For many New Zealanders, the phrase 'up north' evokes sepia-toned images of family holidays with red pohutukawa in bloom and dolphins frolicking in turquoise bays. From school playgrounds to work cafeterias, owning a 'bach' (usually a lo-fi holiday shack) here is a passport to popularity.

Beaches are the main draw, from sheltered inlets to surf spots. Visitors from more crowded countries may be flummoxed to wander onto a sandy strip without a scrap of development or another human in sight. Meanwhile the west coast harbours the most spectacular remnants of the ancient kauri forests that once blanketed the top of the country; the remaining giant trees are awe-inspiring and one of the nation's treasures.

It's not just natural attractions that are on offer in Northland: this is also the birthplace of modern New Zealand with the earliest settlements of both Māori and Europeans and its most significant site, the Waitangi Treaty Grounds.

When to Go

➜ Be warned: Northland's beaches are packed around the New Year period and remain busy throughout January. Prices are higher and accommodation can be in short supply.

➜ The long, lazy days of summer usually continue into February and March, making these the best months to visit.

➜ The 'winterless north' boasts a subtropical climate, most noticeable from Kerikeri northwards. Rainfall is lower, average temperature highs hover around 16°C and the overnight lows around 7°C.

Bay of Islands & Northland Highlights

1 Cape Reinga (p179) Watching oceans collide while souls depart.

2 Waipoua Forest (p185) Paying homage to the ancient kauri giants of this numinous forest.

3 Poor Knights Islands (p160) Diving at one of New Zealand's, if not the world's, top spots.

4 Bay of Islands (p161) Cruising northern waters and claiming your own island paradise among the many in this bay.

5 Ninety Mile Beach (p179) Surfing the giant dunes on this remote and seemingly endless stretch of sand.

6 Waitangi Treaty Grounds (p168) Delving into history and culture, both Māori and colonial.

7 Mangawhai Heads (p152) Soaking up the chilled-out surf-town vibe, honing your body-surfing skills and exploring the rolling dunes across the estuary.

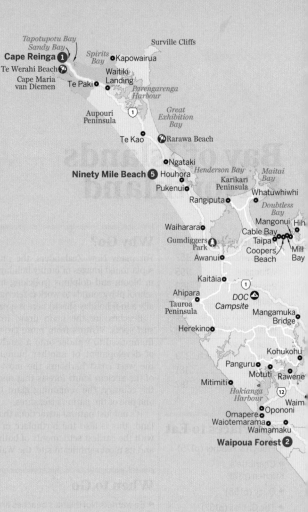

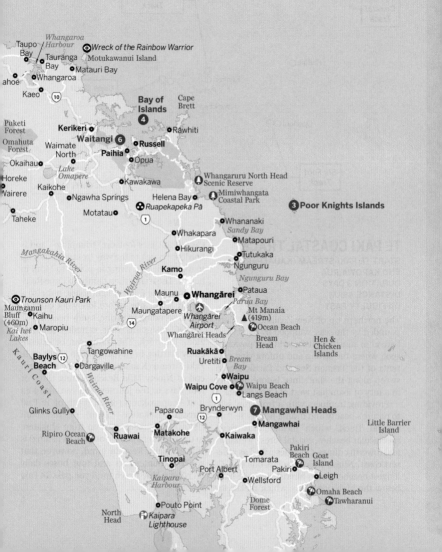

SOUTH PACIFIC OCEAN

0 — 50 km
0 — 25 miles

Taupo Bay

Whangaroa Harbour

Tauranga Bay

Wreck of the Rainbow Warrior

Motukawanui Island

Matauri Bay

ahoe

Whangaroa

Kaeo

10

Bay of Islands 4

Cape Brett

Puketi Forest

Kerikeri

Omahuta Forest

Waimate North

Waitangi 6

Russell

Paihia

Opua

Rāwhiti

Okaihau

Lake Omapere

Horeke

Kawakawa

Kaikohe

Ngawha Springs

Helena Bay

Whangaruru North Head Scenic Reserve

Mimiwhangata Coastal Park

Wairere

Ruapekapeka Pā

1

3 **Poor Knights Islands**

Taheke

Motatau

Whananaki

Sandy Bay

Whakapara

Matapouri

Hikurangi

Tutukaka

Mangakahia River

Ngunguru

Ngunguru Bay

Kamo

Wairua River

Pataua

Maunu

Whangārei

Pataua Bay

Trounson Kauri Park

Maungatapere

Maunganui Bluff (460m)

Kaihu

Whangārei Airport

Mt Manaia ▲ (419m)

Ocean Beach

Maropiu

14

Whangārei Heads

Bream Head

Hen & Chicken Islands

Kai Iwi Lakes

Tangowahine

Ruakākā

Uretiti

Baylys Beach 12

Dargaville

Bream Bay

Waipu

Waipu Cove

Waipu Beach

Langs Beach

Glinks Gully

Paraoa

Brynderwyn

7 **Mangawhai Heads**

12

Ripiro Ocean Beach

Ruawai

Matakohe

Kaiwaka

1

Mangawhai

Little Barrier Island

Tinopai

Tomarata

Pakiri Beach

Goat Island

Port Albert

Pakiri

Wellsford

Leigh

Kaipara Harbour

Pouto Point

Dome Forest

Omaha Beach

7 Tawharanui

North Head

Kaipara Lighthouse

HIKING IN NORTHLAND

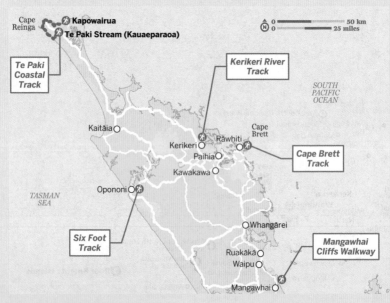

TE PAKI COASTAL TRACK

START TE PAKI STREAM (KAUAEPARAOA)
END KAPOWAIRUA
DURATION 3 DAYS
DISTANCE 48KM
DIFFICULTY EASY

The northern tip of New Zealand is a place pounded by the seas, whipped by winds and bathed in sunshine. It's a wild and powerful spot, where the strong and unforgiving currents of the Tasman Sea and Pacific Ocean sweep along the shorelines before meeting in a fury of foam just west of Cape Reinga.

Providing trampers with a front-row seat to nature's beauty and drama here is Te Paki Coastal Track, which meanders between spectacular beaches, coastal forest, wetlands and towering dunes. Once described as a 'desert coast', Ninety Mile Beach is one of NZ's longest beaches and is almost concrete-hard below the high-tide line – which makes for easy (if at times footsore) tramping – and is bordered much of the way by sand dunes up to 6km wide and rising in places to 143m in height. The tramp then climbs to Cape Reinga, site of the famous lighthouse, but also a sacred Māori site, before following clifftops and descending to idyllic, sandy beaches.

DOC maintains four camping grounds along the track. The tramp can be extended by starting in Ahipara, 83km south of Te Paki Stream (Kauaeparaoa) at the southern end of Ninety Mile Beach, adding three or four days to the journey. You can also join it at Waipapakauri (69km south of Te Paki Stream), Hukatere (51km) or the Bluff (19km) – the 32km portion from Hukatere to the Bluff (a famous spot for surf fishing) is ruler-straight. Keep in mind, however, that you'll encounter cars and tour buses daily on Ninety Mile Beach until you pass Te Paki Stream.

There are excellent tracks scattered all throughout the Northland region, ranging from easy riverside strolls right through to arduous multiday hikes.

CAPE BRETT TRACK

START/END RĀWHITI
DURATION 2 DAYS
DISTANCE 33KM
DIFFICULTY MODERATE

A scenic underscore to the Bay of Islands, Cape Brett is a thin strip of land that famously ends near the Hole in the Rock, the most popular tourist attraction in the area.

But while boats and helicopters hurry to the Hole in the Rock, the Cape Brett Track winds slowly along the tops of the cape, always climbing or descending, and peeling open views of the Bay of Islands before coming to its moment of splendour – as you step through a small saddle just beyond the turn-off to Deep Water Cove, the land plummets away into the Pacific Ocean and the full cliff-lined drama of Cape Brett is revealed. It's a spectacular couple of days on foot, aided by the opportunity to stay a night inside a former lighthouse keepers' cottage, in one of the finest coastal regions in NZ.

Between Rāwhiti and the Deep Water Cove junction, the track crosses private, Māori-owned land. To cover track maintenance along this section, a permit fee of $40 is charged to tramp the track. You'll pay the fee online when you book your stay at the Cape Brett Hut. Bookings and the permit payment can also be made in person at the Bay of Islands i-SITE (p172) in Paihia.

MANGAWHAI CLIFFS WALKWAY

START/END MANGAWHAI HEADS
DURATION 2–3 HOURS RETURN
DISTANCE 10KM RETURN
DIFFICULTY EASY

This short track affords extensive views of sea and land on the beautiful coast heading north from Mangawhai Heads. It can be walked as a loop with a return along the beach at low tide – otherwise you'll come and go via the cliffs. This is part of Te Araroa, the national walking track.

SIX FOOT TRACK

START/END THE END OF MOUNTAIN RD, OPONONI
DURATION 3 HOURS RETURN
DISTANCE 7KM RETURN
DIFFICULTY MODERATE

Leading from the end of a country road to a remote DOC hut, this short hike takes in native bush, waterfalls and views over the Hokianga district. View it as a teaser for the longer, more difficult walks that start from the hut and explore the Waima Forest and Ranges.

KERIKERI RIVER TRACK

START KERIKERI BASIN
END RAINBOW FALLS RD
DURATION 1 HOUR
DISTANCE 4.6KM
DIFFICULTY EASY

This popular walking track meanders through beautiful native bush lining the Kerikeri River. Along the way you'll pass broad Wharepuke Falls, the Fairy Pools swimming holes and the 27m Rainbow Falls.

ⓘ Getting There & Away

AIR

Air New Zealand (☑ 0800 737 000; www.air newzealand.co.nz) Daily flights from Auckland to Whāngārei and Kerikeri.

Barrier Air (p176) Links Kaitāia to Auckland.

BUS

InterCity (www.intercity.co.nz) Bus from Auckland to Kaitāia, Paihia and Whāngārei with additional day tours beyond to Cape Reinga and Hokianga.

Skip (☑ 09-394 9180; https://skip.travel; ☎) Runs a cheap no-frills service to Whāngārei only.

WHANGĀREI DISTRICT

With a mix of dairy farming, wineries and olive groves, combined with surf beaches, underground caves and sheltered river inlets, you can see why this region heaves with Kiwi holidaymakers in summer. Even then, however, it's still possible to find isolated stretches where your footprints are the only ones in the shifting sands.

North of Whāngārei, the Tutukaka Coast is one of the world's best coastlines with stunning forest walks. Offshore are the highly rated dive sites at Poor Knights Islands – accessible from Tutukaka.

Mangawhai

POP 3100

Mangawhai is split between a village nestled at the base of a gorgeous horseshoe estuary, and Mangawhai Heads (5km up the road) with its dramatic surf beach, clifftop walk and increasingly upmarket holiday houses dotted among the traditional fibro beach baches.

Before Europeans settled in in the 1850s, Māori *iwi* (tribes) inhabited the estuary for centuries. In 1807 the Ngāti Whatua defeated the Ngāpuhi in a major battle, letting the survivors escape. One of them was Māori *rangatira* (chief) Hongi Hika, who in 1825 returned to seek justice, and armed with muskets obtained from the Europeans annihilated the Ngāti Whatua in a bloodbath. The district became *tapu* (taboo) so British squatters moved in, rewarded with land titles by the New Zealand government. Ceremonies to lift the *tapu* were eventually performed in the 1990s.

Today Mangawhai is slowly growing, with improved traffic links to the city, new housing subdivisions and fibre broadband, making it an attractive place to move to over Auckland.

New residents bring new money, but this is still a quintessential laid-back NZ beach town.

◉ Sights

★ Mangawhai Heads   BEACH

(Wintle St) Mangawhai's main claim to fame is the surf beach and its large hilltop car park fills up quickly in peak season. To the south a narrow spit of sand stretches for kilometres to form the estuary's southern head, sheltering a seabird sanctuary. Across the estuary the beautiful, seemingly empty expanse of dunes is home to precious wildlife including endangered dotterels and fairy terns who nest in the sand.

★ Mangawhai Museum   MUSEUM

(☑ 09-431 4645; www.mangawhai-museum.org. nz; Molesworth Dr, Mangawhai Heads; adult/child $12/3; ☉ 10am-4pm; ☑) One of regional NZ's best museums, this spectacular building shaped like a stingray is on the main road linking Mangawhai village to Mangawhai Heads. Packed with engaging displays on the area's history and environment with plenty to interest school-aged kids. The gift shop is excellent plus there's a sun-drenched cafe (3pm close), also worthy of a stop.

☆ Activities

Mangawhai Cliffs Walkway   WALKING

Part of Te Araroa, the national walking track, this cliff walkway (p151) takes two to three hours, provided you time it with a return down the beach at low tide.

Aotearoa Surf   SURFING

(☑ 021 442 163; www.aotearoasurf.co.nz; lessons from $53 per person) Book surf lessons (the larger your group the cheaper per person) or hire wetsuits, surfboards or stand-up paddle boards south of Mangawhai at Te Arai beach.

⌨ Sleeping

Mangawhai Heads

Holiday Park   HOLIDAY PARK $

(☑ 09-431 4675; www.mangawhaiheadsholiday park.co.nz; 2 Mangawhai Heads Rd, Mangawhai Heads; sites from $20, units with/without bathroom from $95/70; ☑ ☎ ☑) With an absolute waterfront location on the sandy expanse of Mangawhai's estuary, this laid-back combo of campsites, units and new cabins is a short walk to the surf beach or a longer one to the shops. Visit in summer (note: prices are higher) for a vibrant halo of red pohutukawa trees. It's a family-friendly place, with an expectation of no noise after 10.30pm.

Mangawhai Backpackers: The Coastal Cow HOSTEL $
(☑09-431 5246; www.facebook.com/mangawhai backpackers; 299 Molesworth Dr, Mangawhai Heads; dm/r $35/90; ℗) The rooms at this unassuming house-style hostel are cosy but the vibe is friendly and relaxed. Bathrooms are shared. There's a barbecue area on the deck and it's a short walk to the surf beach, or to shops and cafes.

⭐**Mangawhai Chalets** CHALET $$
(☑09-431 5029; www.mangawhaichalets.co.nz; 252 Molesworth Dr, Mangawhai Heads; units from $140; ℗🛜) There's a Cape Cod feel to the three stylishly decked-out cedar chalets positioned in the lavender-filled garden behind the friendly owners' designer house. There's an open-air communal kitchen with a barbecue, stove and dishwasher, so cook up a storm. The well-stocked supermarket is a very short walk away.

Bach Stay ACCOMMODATION SERVICES $$
(☑09-817 5007; www.bachstay.co.nz; hours vary) Mangawhai is all about the beach bach, from simple fibro affairs to designer hilltop houses, so couples, families and bigger travelling groups have loads of options to live out the Kiwiana dream.

Mangawhai Lodge B&B $$$
(☑09-431 5311; www.seaviewlodge.co.nz; 4 Heather St, Mangawhai Heads; d/apt $210/265; ℗🛜) 🏊 This historic hillside lodge has smartly furnished rooms opening onto a picture-perfect wraparound veranda with expansive sea views. Choose between classic B&B rooms and two apartments with kitchenettes that can take larger groups.

🍴 Eating & Drinking

Dune CAFE $$
(☑09-431 5695; www.dunemangawhai.co.nz; 40 Moir St, Mangawhai village; mains $25-38; ⊙11am-9pm Wed-Fri, 9am-late Sat & Sun) 🏊 Despite the name, Mangawhai's best restaurant is nowhere near the sands. Situated in the heart of the village, Dune is half bar, half cafe, with sunny outdoor tables arrayed around both. The food is excellent, including a deliciously smoky brisket, gourmet pizza and yummy vegetable side dishes. Much of the produce is sourced from the owners' family farms.

Bennetts CAFE $$
(☑09-431 5072; www.bom.co.nz; 52 Moir St, Mangawhai village; mains $13-23; ⊙8am-4pm, kitchen closes at 2pm) Rural Europe comes to

Mangawhai at this atmospheric chocolaterie and its accompanying cafe. Sample handmade chocolates, then fill up on the all-day brunches in a sun-drenched courtyard by the fountain while supping coffee and admiring the olive trees.

Sandbar CAFE, BISTRO $$
(☑09-431 5587; www.sandbarmangawhai.co.nz; Fagan Pl, off Woods St, Mangawhai Heads; mains brunch $11-23, lunch $18-23, dinner $22-30; ⊙9am-3pm daily & 6-9pm Wed-Sat, later in summer; 🚻) Polished concrete floors and a living wall set a quietly stylish scene for a daytime cafe and a night-time bistro. Evening meals are sophisticated and deftly constructed, featuring the likes of fresh fish, Scotch fillet and Asian-inspired dishes like Vietnamese poached chicken salad.

Brewed As Collective COFFEE
(https://brewedintentions.wixsite.com/brewed ascollective; 7 Wood St, Mangawhai village; ⊙8am-3pm Thu-Mon) Originally a pop-up, now a vibrant cafe with wood bars and serious 'third wave' coffee with tasting notes and cold-brew options for summer. Super-healthy breakfasts, and the rustic bakery offerings, are also top quality.

Mangawhai Tavern PUB
(☑09-431 4505; www.mangawhaitavern.co.nz; 2 Moir St, Mangawhai village; ⊙11.30am-late) One of the country's oldest pubs – established in 1865, but twice burnt down since then – the tavern's harbourside location is a top spot for an afternoon beer. There's live music most Saturday nights and Sunday afternoons, and across the Christmas–New Year period some of NZ's top bands rock the outside stage. The meals are also very good.

ℹ️ Getting There & Away

Mangawhai is around 80 minutes by car from Auckland. There is no regular public transport.

Waipu, Langs Beach & Uretiti

POP 1671

Waipu has a proud Gaelic history, and you can learn more on the self-guided walking tour of heritage buildings. There are a couple of excellent swimming beaches nearby at Waipu Cove (as well as a general store, accommodation and a cafe) and at the beautiful sheltered stretch at Langs Beach.

ESSENTIAL BAY OF ISLANDS & NORTHLAND

Eat fresh Orongo Bay oysters.

Drink a glass of syrah with a sea view at Omata Estate (p164) near Russell.

Read *The House of Strife* (1993), Maurice Shadbolt's riveting novel set during the Northland War.

Listen to *Cape Reinga Way* (2011) by The Nukes, ukuleles heading to the afterlife.

Watch *Bellbird* (2019), a modern NZ classic about so much more than a farming family.

Celebrate Waitangi Day (p170).

Go green and sing to the trees with Footprints Waipoua (p184).

Go online at www.northlandnz.com; www.kauricoast.com.

Waipu's original 934 British settlers came from Scotland via Nova Scotia (Canada) between 1853 and 1860. These canny Scots had the good sense to eschew frigid Otago, where so many of their kindred settled, for sunnier northern climes. Waipu celebrates its Scottish heritage with ceilidhs and the annual Highland Games in January. Bream Bay has miles of blissfully deserted beach, blighted only slightly by a giant oil refinery at the north end. At Uretiti, a stretch of beach south of a Department of Conservation (DOC) campsite is unofficially considered 'clothing optional'.

⊙ Sights & Activities

There are excellent walks in the area, including the 3km Waipu Coastal Trail, which heads south from Waipu Cove to Ding Bay via the Pancake Rocks. The 2km Waipu Caves Track starts near the entrance to a large cave containing glowworms and limestone formations; bring a torch and sturdy footwear. The windy drive up there is worth it.

Waipu Museum & Shop   MUSEUM
(☑ 09-432 0746; www.waipumuseum.co.nz; 36 The Centre, Waipu; adult/child $10/5; ⊙ 9.30am-4.30pm) In this fascinating little museum Waipu's Scottish heritage comes to life through holograms, a short film and interactive displays. The shop stocks excellent gifts and souvenirs, and staff have good local intel.

⚜ Festivals & Events

Waipu Highland Games   SPORTS
(www.waipugames.co.nz; ⊙ 1 Jan) Only 10% of current residents are direct descendants of the original Scots, but there's a big get-together every year, when the Highland Games, established in 1871, take place in Caledonian Park.

⛱ Sleeping

Camp Waipu Cove   HOLIDAY PARK $
(☑ 09-432 0410; www.campwaipucove.com; 869 Cove Rd, Waipu Cove; sites/r from $38/45, units with/without bathroom from $120/70; ℗ 🐾) Set beside a blissful stretch of beach with views to craggy islands, this immaculate camping ground has a range of simple cabins, motel-style units, bunk rooms, and tent and campervan sites. Facilities include a colourful and clean toilet block, a communal kitchen, a playground, a giant chess set and a TV room. Native birds flitter around in profusion.

DOC Uretiti Campsite   CAMPGROUND $
(☑ 09-432 1051; www.doc.govt.nz; SH1, Uretiti; sites per adult/child $15/7.50; ℗) At Uretiti, there is a DOC campsite with hot showers ($2) and stellar beach views amid rolling sand dunes.

Waipu Cove Resort   MOTEL $$
(☑ 09-432 0348; www.waipucoveresort.co.nz; 891 Cove Rd, Waipu Cove; units $150-300; ℗ 🐾 🖳) Nestled behind sand dunes at Waipu Cove, this 12-unit complex is more like a motel than a resort as such. The arcing sprawl of the beach is just metres away but there's a pool and a spa here too.

✖ Eating

★ Cove   CAFE $$
(☑ 09-432 0234; www.thecovecafe.co.nz; 910 Cove Rd, Waipu Cove; breakfast $12-19, mains $22-35; ⊙ 8am-late summer, 9am-9pm Thu-Mon winter) This heritage cottage at Waipu Cove covers all the bases, from coffee and breakfast bagels to pizza, gourmet burgers, a small bar *and* healthy smoothies. The wooden deck is a popular spot to dine even in inclement weather, with the beach just across the road.

McLeod's Pizza Barn   PIZZA $$
(☑ 09-432 1011; www.facebook.com/mcleodspizza barn; 2 Cove Rd, Waipu; pizzas $13-29, mains $20-27; ⊙ 11.30am-9pm Wed-Sun Apr-Nov, daily Dec-Feb) The flavour combinations may seem almost as odd as a Scots-named pizzeria, but the crispy-based pizzas are delicious. Try the Gumdigger, with smoked

salmon, asparagus, blue-vein cheese and pesto, and wash it down with a craft beer from Waipu's very own McLeod's Brewery. Other crowd-pleasing menu options include burgers, lamb shanks and pasta dishes.

Waipu Cafe Deli   CAFE **$$**
(☑09-432 0990; www.facebook.com/waipu.cafe.deli; 29 The Centre, Waipu; mains $12-19; ☉8am-3pm) Enticing salads, sandwiches, breakfasts, pasta dishes, muffins and organic fair-trade coffee are served at this pink weatherboard cafe on the main street in Waipu town.

❶ Getting There & Away

InterCity (p152) has three coaches a day to/from Auckland (from $33, 2½ hours), Whangārei (from $23, 25 minutes) and Kerikeri (from $32, 2¼ hours).

Waipu Cove can be reached by a particularly scenic route that heads from Mangawhai Heads through Langs Beach. Otherwise, turn off SH1 38km south of Whangārei.

Whangārei

POP 76,995

Northland's only city is surrounded by tropical natural beauty, and its compact town centre is busy getting gentrified, with developments around the river quayside. It's a city without being a city. There's a thriving artistic community, evidenced by the street art, artisan market and galleries; plus a multitude of nature walks to take, and a global dining scene.

◉ Sights

The attractive riverside marina area is home to museums, galleries, cafes, shops, public sculptures and an information centre. Take a stroll past the moored yachts and follow a marked **Art Walk** and **Heritage Trail** where you'll learn about the fascinating Māori and Pākehā (white–New Zealander) history of the city. An **Artisans Fair** (www.artisansfair.org.nz) is held on Saturday mornings from late October to Easter.

Kiwi North   MUSEUM
(☑09-438 9630; www.kiwinorth.co.nz; 500 SH14, Maunu; adult/child $20/5; ☉10am-4pm) ⌖ Five kilometres west of Whangārei, this park complex includes 19th-century buildings, the Whangārei Museum displaying Māori and colonial artefacts, and a nocturnal kiwi centre offering a rare chance to see the country's feathery fave up close.

AH Reed Memorial Kauri Park   FOREST
(www.wdc.govt.nz; Whareora Rd) ⌖ FREE A grove of immense 500-year-old kauri trees has been preserved in this lush tract of native bush, where a cleverly designed boardwalk leads you effortlessly up into the canopy. To get here, head north on Bank St and turn right into Whareora Rd.

Abbey Caves   CAVE
(Abbey Caves Rd) FREE Abbey Caves is an undeveloped network of three caverns full of glow-worms and limestone formations, 6km east of town. Take a torch, strong shoes, a mate for safety and be prepared to get wet. The surrounding reserve is a forest of crazily shaped rock extrusions. Ask at the i-SITE (p159) about an information sheet for the caves.

Whangārei Quarry Gardens   GARDENS
(☑09-437 7210; www.whangareigardens.org.nz; 37a Russell Rd, Kensington; admission by donation; ☉9am-5pm) ⌖ Green-fingered volunteers have transformed this old quarry into a blissful community park with a lake, waterfalls, pungent floral aromas, wild bits, orderly bits and lots of positive energy. Plus there's a visitor centre and an excellent cafe. To get here, take Rust Ave, turn right into Western Hills Dr and then left into Russell Rd.

Whangārei Falls   WATERFALL
(Otuihau; Ngunguru Rd, Glenbervie) FREE Short walks around these 26m-high falls provide views of the water cascading over the edge of an old basalt lava flow. The falls can be reached on the Tikipunga bus (no service on Sundays), leaving from Rose St in the city.

**Clapham's National
Clock Museum**   MUSEUM
(☑09-438 3993; www.claphamsclocks.com; Lower Dent St, Town Basin; adult/child $10/4; ☉9am-5pm) This charming collection of 1600 ticking, gonging and cuckooing timepieces is housed in a building shaped as a sundial. There are all manner of kooky and kitschy items displayed alongside the more august specimens, such as the venerable 1690 English-built grandfather clock.

Whangārei Art Museum   GALLERY
(☑09-430 4240; www.whangareiartmuseum.co.nz; The Hub, 91 Dent St, Town Basin; ☉10am-4pm) FREE Whangārei's public gallery has an interesting permanent collection, but the two large gallery spaces usually house temporary exhibitions by regional and sometimes international artists in partnership with Wellington's Te Papa.

Whangārei

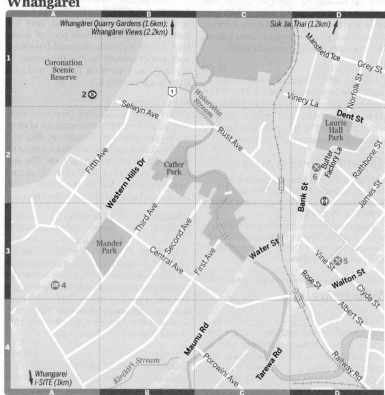

Whangārei

🏃 Activities

The free *Hatea River Walk & Surrounds* brochure, available from the i-SITE (p159), has maps and detailed descriptions of some excellent local tracks. The **Hatea River Walk** follows the river from the Town Basin to Whangārei Falls (90 minutes each way, or return on bus 303A). Longer tracks head through **Parihaka Reserve**, which is just east of the Hatea River and encompasses the remnants of a volcanic cone (241m) and a major *pā* (fortified village) site. The city is spread out for inspection from the lookout at the top, which is accessible by car. Other tracks head through **Coronation Scenic Reserve**, an expanse of bush west of the city centre that includes two *pā* sites and abandoned quarries.

Heads Up Mountain Biking MOUNTAIN BIKING
(📱 09-553 3407; www.headsupadventures.co.nz/mountain-biking-northland; day pass $20, mountain bike hire 1hr/half-day $20/65; ⊙10am-5pm Wed-Sun; 🚲) Just 10km west of the city centre,

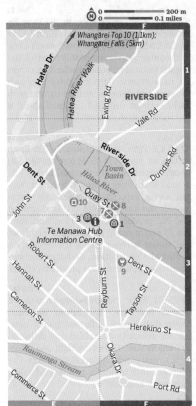

this mountain biking park (through farmland and forest) offers bike hire, track shuttles and monster scooters.

Bream Head Coast Walks
TRAMPING

(☑09-434 0571; www.coastwalks.nz; 395 Ody Rd; 2/3 nights $435/535; ☉Oct-May) Enjoyed across two or three days, this self-guided walking network traverses farmland, public walkways and stunning coastal scenery. Accommodation is in a luxury lodge and excellent food is included. The lodge is used as a base each night after undertaking a variety of walks in the area. Track notes are included and pickups from Whangārei can be arranged.

Pacific Coast Kayaks
KAYAKING

(☑09-436 1947; www.nzseakayaking.co.nz; hire 4/8hr $60/80, tours $120 per person) Hires kayaks and offers guided tours to various locations in the region. Pickups and drop-offs are free from the Whangārei suburb of Onerahi, and charged for paddling locations further afield such as Tutukaka, Matapouri and Whangaroa.

🛏 Sleeping

Whangārei Top 10
HOLIDAY PARK $

(☑09-437 6856; www.whangareitop10.co.nz; 24 Mair St, Kensington; sites from $20, units $96-161; ℗🛜🐕) 🌱 This centrally located riverside holiday park has friendly owners, a better-than-average set of units, and super-shiny stainless-steel surfaces in the shared kitchen area. A great option for families, and a pleasant bushwalk from the park follows the river to town.

Whangārei Falls Holiday Park & Backpackers
HOSTEL, HOLIDAY PARK $

(☑09-437 0609; www.whangareifalls.co.nz; 12 Ngunguru Rd, Glenbervie; sites/dm from $25/34, s/d $60/72; ℗🛜♨) Located 5km from central Whangārei, but a short walk from Whangārei Falls, this holiday park has good-value cabins, some with small kitchenettes but none with private bathrooms. It's also part of the YHA network and has a 10-bed dorm with bunks, along with smaller backpackers rooms.

Kauri Villas
B&B $$

(☑09-436 1797; www.kaurivillas.com; 73 Owhiwa Rd, Parua Bay; studios/apt/ste from $120/195/220; ℗🛜♨) Perched on a hill with views over the harbour to Whangārei, this airy white timber homestead has two massive suites, each with two bedrooms and a sitting room, manicured gardens and a small swimming pool.

Lupton Lodge
B&B $$

(☑09-437 2989; www.luptonlodge.co.nz; 555 Ngunguru Rd, Glenbervie; s/d/ste/apt from $135/170/245/350; ℗🛜♨) The rooms are spacious, luxurious and full of character in this historic homestead (1896), peacefully positioned in farmland 5km past Whangārei Falls in the direction of Tutukaka. Wander the orchard, splash around in the pool or shoot some snooker in the guest lounge. Also available is a stylish apartment in a renovated barn.

Lodge Bordeaux
MOTEL $$

(☑09-438 0404; www.lodgebordeaux.co.nz; 361 Western Hills Dr; apt from $195; ℗❄🛜♨) This upmarket European-styled drive-in motel has tasteful units with stellar kitchens and bathrooms (most with spa baths), private balconies on the upstairs rooms, and access to a barbecue and a small swimming pool.

★ Ara Roa
RENTAL HOUSE $$$

(☑027 320 0770; www.araroa.nz; Harambee Rd, Taiharuru; d $495-1250; ℗🛜♨) This collection of five different architecturally striking properties dotted around a coastal peninsula ranges from the two-bedroom Te Huia – with sunset views and a bush track where kiwi are often heard after dark – to the gorgeous one-bedroom Glasshouse at the very end of the peninsula. Two-bedroom Aria has its own lap pool (worth splashing out on).

Eating

Nectar
CAFE $$

(☑09-438 8084; www.nectarcafe.co.nz; 88 Bank St; mains $10-20; ⊘7am-2.30pm Mon-Fri, 9am-2pm Sat & Sun; ⏥) ⏥ Nectar offers the winning combination of friendly staff, organic milk and coffee, and generous servings from a menu full of Northland produce with paleo, vegetarian and gluten-free options. Check out the urban views from the back windows, and indulge in a healthy restorative smoothie.

Fat Camel
ISRAELI $$

(☑09-438 0831; 12 Quality St; mains $10-25; ⊘9am-9pm) In a pedestrian laneway among a cluster of small restaurants, this little Israeli cafe stands out for its pitta pockets and platters laden with falafels plus fresh salads, hummus and grilled meats, as well as for its friendly service.

★ Quay
CAFE, BISTRO $$

(☑09-430 2628; www.thequaykitchen.co.nz; 31 Quayside, Town Basin; mains brunch $14-18, dinner $29-39, pizza $21-25; ⊘9am-10pm; ⏥) At this beautiful riverside villa turned restaurant, grab a table on the wraparound veranda overlooking yachts bobbing in the neighbouring marina. The menu moves from cooked breakfasts to pizza and bistro-style meals. Kids are catered for as well as vegan diners on separate speciality menus.

Suk Jai Thai
THAI $$

(☑09-437 7287; www.sukjai.co.nz; 93 Kamo Rd, Kensington; mains $19-35; ⊘11.30am-2.30pm Tue-Sat & 5-10pm daily; ⏥) It's well worth a trip to the suburbs to seek out this cheerful and relaxed restaurant, popular with Thai expats for its authentic flavours, gutsy approach to spice, and desserts such as banana with sticky coconut rice. Call or email ahead if you want to secure a table.

TopSail
BISTRO $$$

(☑09-436 2985; www.topsail.co.nz; 206 Beach Rd, Onerahi; mains $34-46; ⊘6pm-late Wed-Sat) Located upstairs in the Onerahi Yacht Club, around 10km from central Whangārei, TopSail serves superlative French-style bistro classics and lots of fresh Northland seafood and NZ produce such as Fiordland venison. If you're ready for a special night out and sunset harbour views, it's definitely a worthwhile destination. Bookings are recommended as it also hosts private functions.

No 8
ASIAN $$$

(☑09-971 8199; www.no8whangarei.co.nz; 8 Quayside, Town Basin; dishes $19-40; ⏥) Asian fusion dishes pack a flavour punch here, but are delicately assembled and delivered by friendly staff. Dishes are light and prices high, so don't arrive desperately hungry. The Express Lunch menu for two is good value. Kids menu available.

Drinking & Nightlife

Parua Bay Tavern
PUB

(☑09-436 5856; www.paruabaytavern.co.nz; 1034 Whangārei Heads Rd; ⊘11.30am-late Wed-Sun; ⏥) A magical spot (10km out of town), especially on a summer's day, this friendly pub

---

MĀORI NZ: BAY OF ISLANDS & NORTHLAND

Known to Māori as Te Tai Tokerau, this region is synonymous with Māori and colonial Pākehā history, and today is one of the most bicultural regions of New Zealand along with Rotorua. In mythology the region is known as the tail of the fish of Māui. In Northland you will often hear Māori being spoken despite many dark decades when it was actively discouraged. Pronouncing place names correctly is important, so don't be embarrassed to simply ask.

Māori sites of particular significance include Cape Reinga (p179), the Waitangi Treaty Grounds (p168), Ruapekapeka Pā (p167) and, in the Waipoua Forest, Tāne Mahuta (p186).

Māori cultural experiences are offered by many local operators, including Footprints Waipoua (p184), Ahikaa Adventures (p180), Sand Safaris (p180) and Rewa's Village (☑09-407 6454; www.rewasvillage.co.nz; 1 Landing Rd; adult/child $10/5; ⊘10am-4pm). Many businesses catering to travellers are owned or run by Māori individuals or *hapū* (subtribal) groups.

overlooks the water with a sole pohutukawa blazing red against the green sea. Grab a seat on the lawn, a cold beverage and a decent pub meal (mains $15 to $28). Kids will love the play equipment.

Old Stone Butter Factory   BAR
(☑09-430 0044; www.thebutterfactory.co.nz; 8 Butter Factory Lane; ⊙10am-late Tue-Sat) This cool basement restaurant-bar hosts lots of live gigs from touring Kiwi bands along with the occasional spoken word night, or gay mixer. As the hours dissolve, DJs kick in. Burgers and pizza are good value, and the sunny courtyard is ideal for a coffee, a craft beer (the range is extensive) or a glass of wine.

Frings   PUB
(☑09-438 4664; www.frings.co.nz; 104 Dent St; ⊙11am-8pm Sun, Tue & Wed, 11am-11.45pm Thu-Sat) This testosterone-fuelled pub brews its own beers, and has a terrace, wood-fired pizzas and live music, including Thursday jam nights. You can't miss the deck shaped like the prow of a ship.

🛍 Shopping

You can often pick up well-priced art, carvings and ceramics at Quarry Arts Centre (☑09-438 1215; www.quarryarts.org; 21 Selwyn Ave; ⊙9.30am-4.30pm) FREE.

Bach   ARTS & CRAFTS
(☑09-438 2787; www.thebach.gallery; Town Basin; ⊙9.30am-4.30pm) Waterfront co-op store and gallery representing over 100 Northland artisans.

ℹ Information

DOC Whangārei Office (☑09-470 3300; www.doc.govt.nz; 2 South End Ave, Raumanga; ⊙8am-4.30pm Mon-Fri) Located just off SH1 around 2km south of central Whangārei.

Te Manawa Hub Information Centre (☑09-430 1188; www.whangareinz.com; 91 Dent St, Town Basin; ⊙9am-5pm; 🛜) Central branch of the i-SITE, in the foyer of the Whangārei Art Museum.

Whangārei i-SITE (☑09-438 1079; www. whangareinz.com; 92 Otaika Rd/SH1; ⊙9am-4.30pm) Information, cafe, toilets and showers.

ℹ Getting There & Away

AIR

Whangārei Airport (WRE; ☑09-436 0047; www.whangareiairport.co.nz; Handforth St, Onerahi; 🛜) is at Onerahi, 6km southeast of the city centre. Air New Zealand (p152) flies to/from Auckland. Taxis into town cost around $25. Bus route 2 ($2) stops at the airport at

WORTH A TRIP

KAIWAKA KAI

If you're feeling peckish on the route between Auckland and Whangārei or the Kauri Coast, stop for *kai* (food) at Kaiwaka.

It's an unusual spot for a Dutch-style delicatessen, but the Kaiwaka Cheese Shop (☑09-431 2195; www.cheese-shop. co.nz; 1957 SH1, Kaiwaka; ⊙9am-5pm, later on weekends) has long been an essential stop for travelling foodies seeking some luxury additions to their holiday provisions. Dutch dominates but you'll also find British and NZ cheeses, and a good selection of wine and other tasty snacks.

least hourly until around 6.30pm on weekdays, but only until 1.30pm on Saturdays; there are no Sunday services.

BUS

Long-distance coaches stop at the Hub in the Town Basin.

InterCity (p152) has three or four buses a day to/from Auckland (from $31, three hours), Waipu (from $18, 25 minutes), Paihia (from $12, 1¼ hours) and Kerikeri (from $12, 1¾ hours).

Skip (p152) runs a low-cost no-frills bus service to Auckland ($22, 2½ hours).

ℹ Getting Around

BUS

City Link Whangarei (www.citylinkwhangarei. co.nz; cash fare per adult/child $2/1) operates buses on seven routes, all departing from Rose St. The most useful are routes 2 (to the airport), 3 (Whangārei Falls) and 6 (Kiwi North). Services are reduced on Saturdays. No buses on Sundays.

TAXI

A1 Cabs (☑0800 228 294; www.whangarei. bluebubbletaxi.co.nz)

Whangārei Heads

Whangārei Heads Rd winds 35km along the northern reaches of the harbour to the heads' entrance, passing mangroves and picturesque pohutukawa-lined bays, Kiwiana-style houses and almost no commercial development at all.

There are epic views from the top of Mt Manaia (419m), a sheer rock outcrop above McLeod Bay, but prepare for a lung- and leg-busting 1½-hour climb on a track recently upgraded to protect the kauri trees.

Bream Head caps off the scraggy isthmus north of Whangārei. A five-hour one-way walking track from Urquharts Bay to Ocean Beach passes through the Bream Head Scenic Reserve and lovely Smugglers Bay and Peach Cove.

Magnificent Ocean Beach stretches for miles on the other side of the headland. There's decent surfing to be had here, and lifeguards patrol the beach in summer. But there's little in the way of shops so come prepared. A detour from Parua Bay takes you to glorious Pataua, a small settlement that lies on a shallow inlet linked to a surf beach by a footbridge.

There's no public transport on this winding ocean-fringed drive.

Tutukaka Coast & the Poor Knights Islands

If you're heading north, this route is an hour or two diversion from the SH1 but worth it for the epic views, and gives easy access to idyllic beaches and coves. Even better, book in some surf lessons to break up your trip.

Offshore at Poor Knights Islands, colourful underwater seascapes combine with two decommissioned navy ships to provide a perfect playground for divers.

Dive boats depart from the bustling marina at Tutukaka, a tiny settlement 28km northeast of Whangārei.

From Tutukaka the road heads slightly inland, before arriving 10km later at the golden sands of Matapouri. A 20-minute coastal walk here leads to Whale Bay, fringed with giant pohutukawa trees. Don't miss it.

Continuing north from Matapouri, the wide expanse of Sandy Bay, one of Northland's premier surf beaches, comes into view. Long-boarding competitions are held here in summer.

The road then loops back to join SH1 at a small town, Hikurangi. A branch leading off from this road doubles back north to the coast at Whananaki, where there are more glorious beaches and the DOC Otamure Bay campsite.

🏃 Activities

Tutukaka's dive crews cater to both first-timers and experienced divers. There are excellent walks along the coast; ask about options and maps at the Whangārei i-SITE (p159) or Bay of Island i-SITE (p172).

Yukon Dive   DIVING
(☑ 09-434 4506; www.yukon.co.nz; Marina Rd; 2 dives incl full gear $310) An owner-operator offering dive trips for a maximum of 12 people at a time. Trips for nondivers incorporating snorkelling and kayaking are also recommended ($200).

Dive! Tutukaka   DIVING
(☑ 0800 288 882; www.diving.co.nz; Marina Rd; 2 dives incl gear $319; 🖪) 🏖 Dive courses include a three-day PADI open-water course ($799). For nondivers, the Perfect Day Ocean Cruise (www.aperfectday.co.nz; $219) includes lunch and snacks, snorkelling in the marine reserve, kayaking through caves and arches, stand-up paddle boarding, and sightings of dolphins (usually) and whales (occasionally).

Tutukaka Surf   SURFING
(☑ 021 227 0072; www.tutukakasurf.co.nz; Marina Rd; 2hr group lesson $75; ⊘ shop 9am-5pm daily Nov-Feb, from 10am Fri-Mon Mar-Oct; 🖪) Runs surf lessons in Sandy Bay, 10km northwest of Tutukaka, most days in summer and on

---

MARINE RICHES AT THE POOR KNIGHTS

Established in 1981, the Poor Knights marine reserve is rated as one of the world's top-10 diving spots. The islands are bathed in a subtropical current from the Coral Sea, so varieties of tropical and subtropical fish not seen in other NZ waters can be observed here. The waters are clear, with no sediment or pollution problems. The 40m to 60m underwater cliffs drop steeply to the sandy bottom and are a labyrinth of archways, caves, tunnels and fissures that attract a wide variety of sponges and colourful underwater vegetation. Schooling fish, eels and rays are common (including manta rays in season).

The two main volcanic islands, Tawhiti Rahi and Aorangi, were home to the Ngāti Wai tribe, but since a raiding-party massacre in 1825 the islands have been *tapu* (forbidden). Even today the public is barred from the islands, in order to protect their pristine environment. Not only do tuatara and Buller's shearwater breed here, but there are unique species of flora, such as the Poor Knights lily.

the weekends otherwise. Private lessons (including family lessons) can be arranged at other times. It also hires surfboards ($50) and wetsuits ($15) for the day from its Tutukaka store if you want to DIY.

🛏 Sleeping & Eating

DOC Otamure Bay Campsite CAMPGROUND $
(☑ 09-433 8402; www.doc.govt.nz; Rockell Rd, Whananaki; sites per adult/child $15/7.50; P 🐾) This scenic campsite is located near a sandy beach with plenty of shade from well-established pohutukawa trees. Expect cold showers, drinking water and little else.

Pacific Rendezvous MOTEL $$
(☑ 09-434 3847; www.pacificrendezvous.co.nz; 73 Motel Rd, Tutukaka; apt from $189; P 🛁 🐾) Perfectly situated for spectacular views on the manicured, lawn-covered southern head of Tutukaka Harbour, this is a great choice for families and small groups. Consistently rated well by guests.

Schnappa Rock CAFE $$
(☑ 09-434 3774; www.schnapparock.co.nz; Marina Rd, Tutukaka; mains brunch $14-23, dinner $26-38; ⊙8am-late Oct-May, closed Sun night Jun-Sep; 🐾) Filled with expectant divers in the morning and those capping off their perfect day on the water in the evening, this cafe-restaurant-bar, with a tropical-island feel, is the place to go. Food is fresh, and as local as possible.

ℹ Getting There & Away

Whangarei Coastal Commuter (☑ 0800 435 355; www.coastalcommuter.co.nz; one way/return per person $30/50) Runs a bookable shuttle for travellers on dive trips, leaving Whangārei in the morning and returning in the evening.

BAY OF ISLANDS

The Bay of Islands ranks as one of New Zealand's top summertime destinations. Lingering shots of its turquoise waters and 150 undeveloped islands feature heavily in the country's tourist promotions. Most of the action here is out on the water, whether you're yachting, fishing, kayaking, paddle boarding, diving or cruising in the company of whales and dolphins.

It's also a place of enormous historical significance. Māori knew it as Pēwhairangi and settled here early in their migrations. As the site of NZ's first permanent British settlement (at Russell), it is the birthplace of European colonisation in the country. It was here that the Treaty of Waitangi was drawn up and first signed in 1840; the treaty remains critical to Māori and Pākehā relations in NZ today.

🏃 Activities

The Bay of Islands offers some fine subtropical diving, made even better by the sinking of the 113m navy frigate HMNZS *Canterbury* in Deep Water Cove near Cape Brett. Local operators also head to the wreck of the *Rainbow Warrior* off the Cavalli Islands (about an hour north of Paihia by boat). Both wrecks offer a colourful feast of pink anemones, yellow sponges and abundant fish life.

On top of the water, there are plenty of opportunities for kayaking, sailing or cruising around the bay, either on a guided tour or by renting a canoe and going it alone. Do note that some boat companies close over the winter months.

Great Escape Yacht Charters BOATING
(☑ 09-402 7143; www.greatescape.co.nz; 4 Richardson St, Opua) Offers introductory sailing lessons (two-day course from $445) and longer options.

Bay of Islands Kayaking KAYAKING
(☑ 021 272 3353; www.bayofislandskayaking.co.nz; tours $80-150) Rents sea kayaks and organises guided expeditions to Haruru Falls (p169) and the outer islands like Urupukapuka.

Paihia Dive DIVING
(☑ 09-402 7551; www.divenz.com; 7 Williams Rd, Paihia; dives from $180; ⊙daily Oct-May, Mon-Sat Jun-Sep) This five-star PADI dive crew offers combined reef and wreck trips to either the *Canterbury* or the *Rainbow Warrior*. It also sells fishing gear and snorkelling sets.

Flying Kiwi Parasail PARASAILING
(☑ 09-402 6068; www.parasailnz.com; solo $129, tandem per adult/child $99/69) Departs from both Paihia and Russell wharves for NZ's highest parasail (1200ft/366m).

👉 Tours

On the Water

Take your pick: sailing boats, jetboats; tall ships and large launches. Boat tours leave from both Paihia or Russell so base yourself at either town.

One of the bay's most striking islands is **Piercy Island (Motukōkako)** off Cape Brett, at the bay's eastern edge. This steep-walled rock fortress features a vast natural

Bay of Islands

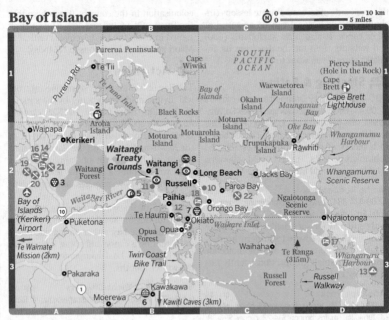

Bay of Islands

arch – the famous **Hole in the Rock**. Provided the conditions are right, most boat tours will pass right through the heart of the island. En route it's likely you'll encounter bottlenose and common dolphins, and you may see orcas, other whales and penguins.

The most luxurious way to explore the bay is under sail. Either help to crew the boat (no experience is required), or just spend the afternoon island-hopping, sunbathing, swimming, snorkelling, kayaking and fishing.

R Tucker Thompson   BOATING
(☎09-402 8430; www.tucker.co.nz; ☺Nov-Mar) Run by a charitable trust with an education focus, the *Tucker* is a majestic tall ship offering day sails (adult/child $159/79.50, including a barbecue lunch) and late-afternoon cruises (adult/child $67/33.75).

Explore NZ
CRUISE

(☑09-359 5987; www.exploregroup.co.nz; cnr Marsden & Williams Rds, Paihia) 🏄 Explore's four-hour Discover the Bay cruise (adult/child $149/90 including barbecue lunch) heads to the Hole in the Rock and stops at Urupukapuka Island.

The Rock
CRUISE

(☑0800 762 527; www.rocktheboat.co.nz; dm/d/f $328/1125/1428) 🏄 A former vehicle ferry that's now a floating hostel, the *Rock* has dorms, private rooms and a bar. Spend the day island-hopping, fishing, kayaking, snorkelling and swimming either on an overnight cruise, including all food and activities (adult $328), or on a six-hour day cruise ($165). YHA members discount is available.

Fullers Great Sights
CRUISE

(☑09-402 7421; www.dolphincruises.co.nz; Maritime Bldg, Marsden Rd, Paihia) 🏄 The four-hour Hole in the Rock Cruise heads out to the famous sea arch and stops at Urupukapuka Island on the way back. Boats stop at Russell wharf for pickups on all trips.

Phantom
BOATING

(☑0800 224 421; www.yachtphantom.com; day sail $125) A fast 15m racing sloop, known for its great platters. It has a licensed cash bar on board for local wines and beers.

She's a Lady
BOATING

(☑0800 724 584; www.sailingbayofislands.com; day sail $100) Day sails include lunch, fishing, snorkelling and paddling a see-through-bottomed kayak.

Ecocruz
CRUISE

(☑0800 432 627; www.ecocruz.co.nz; all-inclusive from $725; ⊘departs 8am Tue & Fri Oct-May) 🏄 Three-day/two-night sailing cruise aboard the 22m ocean-going yacht *Manawanui*. Prices include accommodation, food, kayaking, sustainable fishing and snorkelling.

Gungha II
BOATING

(☑0800 478 900; www.bayofislandssailing.co.nz; day sail $130) A 20m ocean yacht with a friendly crew, departing from both Russell and Paihia; lunch included.

On the Land

It's cheaper and quicker to take trips to Cape Reinga from Ahipara, Kaitāia or Doubtless Bay, *but* if you're short on time, various long day trips (10 to 12 hours) leave from the Bay of Islands. They all take the Ninety Mile Beach route, stopping to sandboard on the dunes.

Fullers Great Sights runs regular bus tours and backpacker-oriented versions, both stopping at Puketi Forest. The standard, child-friendly version (adult/child $150/75) includes an optional lunch at Houhora.

It also runs **Awesome NZ** (☑0800 486 877; www.awesomenz.com; Maritime Bldg, Marsden Rd, Paihia; tour from $140) tours, with louder music, more time sandboarding, and stops for a snack at Taipa and to devour fish and chips at Mangonui.

Explore NZ's Dune Rider tour (adult/child $150/110) gives you the chance to sample Mangonui's feted fish and chips on the waterfront too.

Transport options to the Hokianga and Waipoua Forest are limited, so a day trip makes sense if you don't have your own car or if you're time starved. Fullers' Giants & Glow Worms takes in Tāne Mahuta (p186) and the Kawiti Caves (p167) on an eight-hour tour with local Māori guides.

🛈 Getting There & Away

AIR

Bay of Islands (Kerikeri) Airport (KKE; ☑09-407 6133; www.bayofislandsairport.co.nz; 218 Wiroa Rd) is 8km southwest of Kerikeri. Air New Zealand (p152) flies here from Auckland.

Super Shuttle (☑0800 748 885; www.supershuttle.co.nz; Kerikeri Airport) provides shuttles between Kerikeri Airport and Bay of Islands destinations such as Kerikeri ($15) and Paihia ($30).

ABC Shuttles & Tours (☑022 025 0800; www.abcshuttle.co.nz; tours from $40) also provides airport transfers to Bay of Islands towns.

BUS

InterCity (p152) runs from Auckland to Kawakawa, Paihia and Kerikeri.

Russell

POP 720

Proudly remembered as 'the hellhole of the Pacific', there's little in the way of depravity and debauchery here now. Instead you'll find a historic town made of weatherboard-style colonial buildings dotted with boutiques, souvenir stores and places to eat. The tree-covered hills beyond the harbour overlook fine homes and holiday accommodation – it's hard not to envy the friendly locals who call this slice of paradise home.

Russell

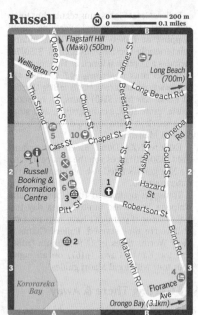

History

Before it was known as a hellhole (you'll read that word a lot before your trip is done), or even as Russell, this was Kororāreka (Sweet Penguin), a fortified Ngāpuhi village. In the early 19th century *iwi* permitted this spot to become Aotearoa's first European settlement, but it quickly became a magnet for fleeing convicts, whalers, enterprising prostitutes and drunken sailors. You can imagine how the Māori must have viewed their new residents!

By the 1830s dozens of whaling ships at a time were anchored in the harbour. In 1839 Charles Darwin described it as full of 'the very refuse of society' in his book *The Voyage of the Beagle* (originally known as *Narrative of the Surveying Voyages of His Majesty's Ships* Adventure *and* Beagle).

In 1830 the settlement was the scene of the so-called Girls' War, when two pairs of Māori women were allegedly vying for the attention of a whaling captain called Brind. A chance meeting between the rivals on the beach led to verbal abuse and fighting. This minor conflict quickly escalated as family members rallied around to avenge the insult and harm done to their respective relatives. Hundreds were killed and injured over a two-week period before missionaries managed to broker a peace agreement.

After the signing of the Treaty of Waitangi in 1840, Okiato (where the car ferry now leaves from) was the residence of the governor and the temporary capital. The capital was officially moved to Auckland in 1841 and Okiato, which was by then known as Russell, was eventually abandoned. The name Russell ultimately replaced Kororāreka.

⊙ Sights

Pompallier Mission   HISTORIC BUILDING
(📞09-403 9015; www.pompallier.co.nz; 5 The Strand; adult/child $15/free; ⊙10am-4pm by guided tour) Built in 1842 to house the Catholic mission's printing press, this rammed-earth building is the mission's last remaining building in the western Pacific, and NZ's oldest industrial building. Over its seven years of operation, a staggering 40,000 books were printed here in Māori. Admission includes extremely interesting hands-on tours that lead you through the entire bookmaking process, from the icky business of tanning animal hides for the covers, to setting the type and stitching together the final books. You can visit the gardens only ($7) if you miss out on the tour.

Omata Estate   WINERY
(📞09-403 8007; www.omata.co.nz; 212 Aucks Rd; ⊙11am-6pm Oct-May, by appointment Jun-Sep) With a growing reputation for red wines – especially its old-growth syrah – Omata Estate is one of Northland's finest wineries. To complement the tastings and sea views, pizzas and shared platters are available. The winery is on the road from Russell to the car ferry at Okiato.

Christt Church CHURCH
(www.oldchurch.org.nz; Church St; admission by donation) English naturalist Charles Darwin made a donation towards the cost of building this, the country's oldest surviving church (1836). The graveyard's biggest memorial commemorates Tamati Waka Nene, a powerful Ngāpuhi chief from the Hokianga who sided against Hōne Heke in the Northland War. The church's wooden exterior has musket and cannonball holes dating from the 1845 battle.

Flagstaff Hill HILL
(Maiki; Flagstaff Rd) Overlooking Russell, this is the hill where Hōne Heke (p170) chopped down the British flagpole four times. You can drive up, but the epic view over Russell and the harbour rewards a good 1.6km climb. Take the track west from the boat ramp along the beach at low tide, or head up Wellington St.

Russell Museum MUSEUM
(☑ 09-403 7701; www.russellmuseum.org.nz; 2 York St; adult/child $10/free; ⊙ 10am-4pm) This small museum has a well-presented Māori section, a large 1:5 scale model of Captain Cook's *Endeavour*, a 10-minute video on the town's history and an interactive digital map of Īpipiri, the Māori name for the region.

Tapeka Point VIEWPOINT, BEACH
North of Russell, on the other side of Maiki hill, Tapeka Rd heads down to a sandy beach in the shadow of a craggy headland. A *pā* once stood at the top of the hill. Follow the pathway for views stretching to the far northern reaches of the Bay of Islands.

Activities

There are some excellent walks in the area, such as a hike up to Maiki (Flagstaff Hill) or the day-long full-circle loop via Opita and Opua to Paihia then back to Russell incorporating two ferry journeys (see www.boiwalkways.co.nz for more information).

On the ocean coast, Rāwhiti is the starting point for the tramp to **Cape Brett lighthouse**, a strenuous eight-hour, 16.3km walk (p151) to the top of the peninsula (slippery when wet) where overnight stays are possible in a former lighthouse keeper's cabin, now the basic 23-bunk **Cape Brett Hut** (☑ 09-407 0300; www.doc.govt.nz; dm adult/child $15/7.50). The hut must be booked in advance through DOC; enquire about access via land or boat – and water supplies.

For those looking for something more sedate, head down to **Oke Bay** (best when the tide is out) for a picture-perfect white-sand swimming beach.

Another good walk near Rāwhiti leads through Māori land and Whangamumu Scenic Reserve to **Whangamumu Harbour**. There are more than 40 ancient Māori sites on the peninsula and the remains of an unusual whaling station.

☞ Tours

Russell Nature Walks ECOTOUR
(☑ 027 908 2334; www.russellnaturewalks.co.nz; 6080 Russell Whakapara Rd; adult/child from $75/40) 🍃 Located in privately owned native forest 2.5km south of Russell, guided day and night tours provide the opportunity to see native birds, including the weka and tui, and insects such as the weta. Glowworms softly illuminate night tours, and after dark there's the opportunity to hear (and very occasionally see) kiwi. The tours help fund conservation projects.

✲✲ Festivals & Events

Tall Ship Regatta SAILING
(www.russellboatingclub.org.nz; ⊙ Jan) Held on the first Saturday after New Year's Day.

CYCLING THE TWIN COAST TRAIL

This inspiring cycle route (Pou Herenga Tai) stretches from the Bay of Islands right across the country to the Hokianga Harbour. It's only 87km, but it definitely gives you boasting rights when you get home. The complete route takes two days and travels from Opua to Kawakawa, Kaikohe, Okaihau and Horeke before finishing at Mangungu Mission Station.

The most popular day ride is the 14km section from **Kaikohe** to **Okaihau**, which passes through an abandoned rail tunnel before skirting Lake Omapere.

If you are cycling to **Horeke**, be aware the pub (p184) there is only open to staying and paying customers; book ahead if you want a meal or a place to sleep.

The trail is well described at www.twincoastcycletrail.kiwi.nz, where you'll find all the information on bike hire (including e-bikes for the less fit among us, we won't tell!) from various towns and shuttle transport to bring you back if you run out of puff.

THE OLD RUSSELL ROAD

The quickest route to Russell takes SH1 to Opua and then crosses by ferry. If you're coming from the south, the old Russell Rd is a snaking alternative but adds about an hour to the trip.

The turn-off is easy to miss, located 6km north of Hikurangi at Whakapara (look for the sign to Oākura). After 13km stop at the **Gallery & Cafe** (☏09-433 9934; www.galleryhelenabay.co.nz; 1392 Russell Rd, Helena Bay; mains $15-20; ⊙9.30am-5pm, kitchen closes 3pm), high above Helena Bay, for fair-trade coffee, scrummy cake, amazing views, and interesting Kiwiana art and craft.

Near Helena Bay an unsealed detour leads 8km to **Mimiwhangata Coastal Park** (www.doc.govt.nz; 453 Mimiwhangata Rd, Helena Bay) FREE, which features sand dunes, pohutukawa trees, jutting headlands and picturesque beaches.

Back on Russell Rd, **The Farm** (☏09-433 6894; www.thefarm.co.nz; 3632 Russell Rd, Whangaruru; sites/dm $15/20, r with/without bathroom $80/60) is a rough-and-ready back-packers that rambles through various buildings, including an old woolshed. The rooms are basic and it's a popular park-up spot for campervans, but off season it's a chilled-out rustic escape. Best of all, you can arrange a horse trek ($50, two hours), dirt biking (from $50), kayaking and fishing.

Next stop, the **Whangaruru North Head Scenic Reserve** has beaches, walking tracks and fine scenery. A loop route from DOC's sheltered **Puriri Bay Campsite** (www.doc.govt.nz; Whangaruru North Rd, Whangaruru; sites per adult/child $15/7.50) leads up to a ridge, offering a remarkable coastal panorama.

If you want to head directly to Russell, continue along Rawhiti Rd for another 7km be-fore veering left onto Manawaora Rd, which skirts a succession of tiny idyllic bays before reconnecting with Russell Rd.

Otherwise take a detour to isolated **Rāwhiti**, a small Ngāpuhi settlement where life still revolves around the *marae* (traditional meeting place). Please be respectful of the communities living in this area and if invited to join people for a meal, offer something of commensurate value in return.

Russell Birdman SPORTS
(www.russellbirdman.co.nz; Russell Wharf; ⊙mid-Jul) Lunatics with various flying contrap-tions jump off Russell wharf into frigid waters.

🛏 Sleeping

Wainui HOSTEL $
(☏09-403 8278; www.wainuilodge-russell-nz.com; 92d Te Wahapu Rd; s/d $54/68; [P][🛜][♨]) Hard to find but worth the effort, this modern bush retreat with direct beach access and kayaks to borrow has two attic rooms, a communal kitchen and super-helpful hosts. It's 5km from Russell on the way to the car ferry so you need your own wheels.

Russell Top 10 HOLIDAY PARK $$
(☏09-403 7826; www.russelltop10.co.nz; 1 James St; sites from $25, unit with/without bathroom from $150/100; [P][@][🛜][♨]) This leafy and extreme-ly well maintained holiday park is close to the town centre, with good facilities, pret-ty hydrangeas, tidy cabins, and excellent self-contained units with decks, coffee ma-chines and views over the bay.

★**Arcadia Lodge** B&B $$$
(☏09-403 7756; www.arcadialodge.co.nz; 10 Flo-rance Ave; r/cabin/ste $220/300/330; ⊙Sep-Jun; [P][🛜]) 🌿 The characterful rooms of this 1890 hillside house are kitted out with interesting antiques and fine linen, while the breakfast is worth staying for alone – complemented by spectacular views over the water from the deck. Grab a book from the library and a bot-tle of local wine from the honesty bar, and find a quiet spot in the garden to relax in.

Duke of Marlborough Hotel HISTORIC HOTEL $$$
(☏09-403 7829; www.theduke.co.nz; 35 The Strand; r $150-280; [🛜]) Holding NZ's oldest pub licence but opulently renovated in recent years, the Duke boasts about 'refreshing ras-cals and reprobates since 1827', although the building has burnt down (twice) since then. The upstairs accommodation ranges from small, bright rooms in a 1930s extension, to snazzy spacious doubles facing the water.

Hananui Lodge & Apartments MOTEL $$$
(☏09-403 7875; www.hananui.co.nz; 4 York St; units $155-250; [P][🛜]) Choose between spark-

ling motel-style units in the trim waterside lodge or apartments in the newer block across the road. The pick of the bunch is the upstairs waterfront units with views straight over the beach.

✕ Eating

★ Hōne's Garden
PIZZA $$

(☏022 466 3710; www.facebook.com/honesgarden; 10 York St; pizza $18-25; ☺noon-10pm Wed-Mon Nov-Apr; ☻) Head out to Hōne's shaded lantern-lit courtyard for wood-fired pizza (gluten-free available), cold craft beer on tap and a thoroughly easy-going vibe. An expanded menu features tasty wraps and healthy salads. Antipasto platters are good for groups and indecisive diners.

Duke of Marlborough Hotel
PUB FOOD $$

(☏09-403 7829; www.theduke.co.nz; 35 The Strand; mains lunch $20-39, dinner $26-42; ☺11.30am-9pm) There's no better spot in Russell to while away a few hours, glass in hand, than the Duke's sunny deck. Thankfully the upmarket bistro food matches the views, plus there's an excellent wine list and a great selection of NZ craft beers.

Sage @ Paroa Bay
BISTRO $$

(www.paroabay.com/sage; 31 Otamarua Rd; ☺noon-5pm Wed & Thu, to 8pm Fri-Sun) With hilltop views over the turquoise waters of the Bay of Islands, this winery restaurant overlooking manicured lawns is worth the drive. A limited mains menu has all the bases covered with quality ingredients and surprising flavours. A side salad comes with *dukkah* spice mix, pickled vegetables and balsamic beetroot, for example. The cheese tasting board is a great afternoon grazing option.

★ The Gables
CONTEMPORARY $$$

(☏09-403 7670; www.thegablesrestaurant.co.nz; 19 The Strand; mains lunch $22-28, dinner $27-35; ☺noon-3pm & 5.30-10pm Wed-Mon) Serving Kiwi classics (lamb, beef, seafood), the Gables occupies an 1847 building (formerly a colonial brothel) on the waterfront built using whale vertebrae for foundations. Book a table by the windows for maritime views, and look forward to excellent service and top-notch local produce, including local cheeses.

☗ Drinking & Nightlife

Duke Tavern
PUB

(☏09-403 7831; www.facebook.com/RussellTav; 19 York St; mains $19-24; ☺noon-11pm Tue-Sat, to 6pm Sun Mar-Nov, noon-late daily Dec-Feb) Not to be confused with the historic hotel of the same name on the waterfront, this cosy locals' tavern dates only from 1976. There are pool tables, a sunny beer garden and pub meals.

ℹ Information

Russell Booking & Information Centre (☏09-403 8020; www.russellinfo.co.nz; Russell Wharf; ☺8am-5pm, extended hours summer)

ℹ Getting There & Away

The quickest way to reach Russell by car is via the Fullers car ferry (car/motorcycle/passenger $13.50/5.5.90/1), which runs every 10 minutes from Opua (5km from Paihia) to Okiato (8km from Russell), between 6am and 9.50pm. Buy your tickets on board. If you're travelling from the south, a detour with walks and other diversions can be taken via the coastal route, Russell Rd.

On foot, the easiest way to reach Russell is on one of several passenger ferry operators from Paihia (adult/child return $12/6). These run from 7am to 9pm (until 10pm in peak season) hourly. Buy your tickets on board, or at the i-SITE (p172) in Paihia.

Kawakawa

☏09 / POP 1580

Hundertwasser architecture put Kawakawa (an otherwise normal regional town) on the tourism map. Not to mention the steam train that runs right down the main street. There is also a pair of important Māori sites nearby, a glowworm cave to tour, and a buzzing gallery in a converted art-deco theatre.

Ruapekapeka Pā
HISTORIC SITE

(www.ruapekapeka.co.nz; Ruapekapeka Rd) FREE For 10 days in January 1846, 1600 British troops bombarded 500 Māori warriors hunkered down in a *pā* composed of trenches, tunnels and wooden palisades on this lonely hillside. Ruapekapeka translates as 'the bat's nest' but by the time the British broke through, the bats had already flown, leaving them (not for the first time) with an empty *pā*. This stalemate was to be the final battle of the Northland War; following this the parties made peace.

Kawiti Caves
CAVE

(☏09-404 0583; www.kawiticaves.co.nz; 49 Waiomio Rd; adult/child $40/20; ☺8.30am-4pm) Explore these glowworm-illuminated limestone caverns on a 30-minute subterranean tour led by direct descendants of Ngāti Hine chief Kawiti, who fought the British at Ruapekapeka Pā during the first of the New Zealand Wars.

King Theatre Creative
GALLERY

(www.facebook.com/KingsTheatreCreative; 80 Gillies St; ☺10am-4pm Wed-Sun) More like a community centre, this art-deco cinema has been repurposed into an art gallery showing works by talented locals, a library and a soon-to-be-added cafe.

Kawakawa Public Toilets
NOTABLE BUILDING

(58 Gillies St) It's rare that public toilets are a town's claim to fame but Kawakawa's were designed by Austrian-born artist and eco-architect Friedensreich Hundertwasser, who lived near Kawakawa in an isolated house without electricity from 1973 until his death in 2000. The most photographed toilets in NZ are typical Hundertwasser – lots of organic, wavy lines decorated with ceramic mosaics and brightly coloured bottles, and with grass and plants on the roof. Other examples of his work can be seen in Vienna and Osaka.

Bay of Islands Vintage Railway
RAIL

(☏09-404 0684; www.bayofislandsvintagerailway.org.nz; Gilies St; adult/child $20/5; ☺10.45am, noon, 1.15pm, 2.30pm Fri-Sun, daily school holidays) Take a 50-minute spin down the main street of Kawakawa to Taumarere and back in a carriage pulled by either Gabriel the steam engine or a vintage diesel engine.

❶ Getting There & Away

InterCity (p152) coaches stop at Kawakawa junction.

ABC Shuttles & Tours (p163) runs tours from Paihia to Kawakawa and the caves.

Cycle the 11km from Opua (p167). You can hire bikes by the half-day near the ferry terminal.

Paihia

POP 3525

Paihia is a gentle tourism-focused town, with an abundance of accommodation and good restaurants, plenty of tours as well as DIY options to get you out on the water, and a strong community spirit that lifts the vibe a few notches. Its name is said to be a mix of Māori and English 'pai' (good); 'hia' (here).

To Paihia's north is the birthplace of New Zealand (as opposed to Aotearoa): Waitangi inhabits a special but somewhat complex place in the national psyche.

◉ Sights

★ **Waitangi Treaty Grounds** HISTORIC SITE

(☏09-402 7437; www.waitangi.org.nz; 1 Tau Henare Dr, Waitangi; adult/child $50/free; ☺9am-5pm)

🖉 Occupying a headland draped in lawns and bush, this is NZ's most significant historic site. Here, on 6 February 1840, after much discussion, the first 43 Māori chiefs signed the Treaty of Waitangi with the British Crown; eventually, over 500 chiefs would sign it. Admission incorporates a guided tour and a spirited cultural performance, and entry to the Museum of Waitangi, the Whare Rūnanga (Carved Meeting House) and the historic Treaty House.

Opened in 2016, **Te Kōngahu Museum of Waitangi** is a modern and comprehensive showcase of the role of the treaty in the past, present and future of Aotearoa New Zealand. It provides a warts-and-all look at the early interactions between Māori and Europeans, the events leading up to the treaty's signing, the long litany of treaty breaches by the Crown, the wars and land confiscations that followed, and the protest movement that led to the current process of redress for historic injustices. Many *taonga* (treasures) associated with Waitangi were previously scattered around NZ, and this excellent museum is now a repository for a number of key historical items. One room is devoted to facsimiles of all the key documents, while another screens a fascinating short film dramatising the events of the initial treaty signing.

The **Treaty House** was shipped over as a kit-set from Australia and erected in 1834 as the four-room home of the official British Resident James Busby. It's now preserved as a memorial and museum containing displays about the house and the people who lived here. Just across the lawn, the magnificently detailed **Whare Rūnanga** was completed in 1940 to mark the centenary of the treaty. The fine carvings represent the major Māori tribes. It's here that the cultural performances take place, starting with a *haka pōwhiri* (challenge and welcome) and then heading inside for *waiata* (songs) and spine-tingling *haka* (war dances).

Near the cove is the 35m, 6-tonne *waka taua* (war canoe) **Ngātokimatawhaorua**, also built for the centenary. A photographic exhibit details how it was fashioned from gigantic kauri logs. There's also an excellent gift shop selling Māori art and design, with a carving studio attached.

Tours leave on the hour from 10am to 3pm. Admission is $25 for NZ residents upon presentation of a passport or driving licence.

St Paul's Anglican Church
CHURCH

(36 Marsden Rd) The characterful St Paul's was constructed of Kawakawa stone in 1925,

Paihia

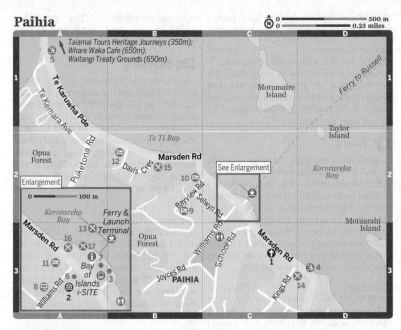

Taiamai Tours Heritage Journeys (350m);
Whare Waka Cafe (650m);
Waitangi Treaty Grounds (650m)

Paihia

⊙ Sights
1 St Paul's Anglican Church	C3
2 Williams House & Gardens	A3

⊕ Activities, Courses & Tours
3 Awesome NZ	B3
4 Bay Beach Hire	D3
5 Coastal Kayakers	A1
6 Explore NZ	A3
7 Fullers Great Sights	A3
8 Paihia Dive	A3

⊜ Sleeping
9 Abri Apartments	B2
10 Breakwater Motel	B2
11 Haka Lodge Backpackers	A3
12 Seabeds	B2

⊗ Eating
13 Charlotte's Kitchen	A3
14 El Cafe	D3
15 Glasshouse Kitchen & Bar	B2
16 Terra	A3
17 Zane Grey's	A3

and stands on the site of the original mission church, a simple raupo (bulrush) hut erected in 1823. Look for the native birds in the stained glass above the altar – the kotare (kingfisher) represents Jesus (the king plus 'fisher of men'), while the tui (parson bird) and kererū (wood pigeon) portray the personalities of the Williams brothers (one scholarly, one forceful), who set up the mission station here.

Williams House & Gardens　HISTORIC BUILDING
(www.williamshousepaihia.com; Williams Rd) `FREE`
The historic buildings and gardens of Paihia's First Mission Station include a restored stone store, and now house a community library and a community secondhand bookshop. Free public wi-fi is available here too.

Haruru Falls　WATERFALL
(Haruru Falls Rd, Haruru) A walking track (one way 1½ hours, 5km) leads from the Treaty Grounds along the Waitangi River to these attractive horseshoe falls. Part of the path follows a boardwalk through the mangroves. Otherwise you can drive here, turning right off Puketona Rd onto Haruru Falls Rd.

🏃 Activities

Bay Beach Hire　KAYAKING, BOATING

(☐ 09-402 6078; www.baybeachhire.co.nz; Marsden Rd; ⊙ 9am-5pm) Hires kayaks (from $20 per hour), sailing catamarans ($50 first hour, $40 per additional hour), mountain bikes ($70 per day) and stand-up paddle boards ($25 per hour). Kayaking tours are also offered, including a twilight paddle ($89), weather and participants provided.

Coastal Kayakers KAYAKING
(✆0800 334 661; www.coastalkayakers.co.nz; Te Karuwha Pde) Runs guided tours (half-/full day from $75 per person, minimum two people) and multiday adventures. Kayaks (half-/full day $50/70) can also be rented for independent exploration.

🖝 Tours

Taiamai Tours Heritage Journeys CULTURAL
(✆09-405 9990; www.taiamaitours.co.nz; 3hr tour $135; ☺departs 9am Tue, Thu, Sat & Sun Oct-Apr) Paddle a traditional 12m carved *waka* (canoe) from the Waitangi bridge to the Haruru Falls. The Ngāpuhi hosts wear traditional garb, and perform the proper *karakia* (incantations) and share stories. The price includes admission to the Waitangi Treaty Grounds (p168) at your leisure (which is otherwise $50).

Total Tours FOOD & DRINK
(✆0800 264 868; www.totaltours.co.nz; tours $90) Departing from Paihia, these bus or van tours head into the countryside around Kerikeri for food and wine tasting or to Kawakawa and Kawiti Caves.

🎇 Festivals & Events

Waitangi Day CULTURAL
(www.waitangi.org.nz/whats-on/waitangi-day; Waitangi Treaty Grounds; ☺6 Feb) Various ceremonial events at Waitangi Treaty Grounds, including speeches, a naval salute and an annual outing for the huge *waka taua*

Ngātokimatawhaorua. The day then continues with food, music and cultural performances.

🛏 Sleeping

Haka Lodge Backpackers HOSTEL $
(✆09-402 5637; www.hakalodge.com; 76 Marsden Rd; dm/r from $36/129; ⓟ⍣) Located directly across the road from the wharf, it's impossible to be more central than Haka Lodge. It also scores points for its modern and colourful decor, and appealing shared spaces with huge flat-screen TVs and unlimited wi-fi access. Accommodation ranges from excellent dorms to private rooms with en suite and TV.

Seabeds HOSTEL $
(✆09-402 5567; www.seabeds.co.nz; 46 Davis Cres; dm/s/d $35/75/120; ⓟ⍣) Offering comfortable, friendly, stylish budget digs in a converted motel, Seabeds is one of Paihia's best hostels. Little design touches give it a stylish ambience, and it's in a quieter location than most of Paihia's more central hostels. Best of all, each room has its own bathroom.

Beachside Holiday Park HOLIDAY PARK $
(✆09-402 7678; www.beachsideholiday.co.nz; 1290 Paihia Rd/SH11; sites from $35, units with/without bathroom from $150/80; ⓟ⍣⍤) Wake up at the water's edge at this small, sheltered camping ground, south of Paihia township (a good 45-minute walk). An on-site food truck serves breakfasts, dinners and, most importantly, coffee, plus there are kayaks for hire.

HŌNE HEKE & THE NORTHLAND WAR

Just five years after he had been the first signatory to the Treaty of Waitangi, Ngāpuhi chief Hōne Heke was so disaffected that he planned to chop down Kororāreka's flagstaff, a symbol of British authority, for the fourth time. Governor FitzRoy was determined not to let that happen and garrisoned the town with soldiers and marines.

On 11 March 1845 the Ngāpuhi staged a diversionary siege of the town. It was a great tactical success, with Chief Kawiti attacking from the south and another party attacking from Long Beach. While the troops rushed off to protect the township, Hōne Heke felled the Union Jack on Maiki (p165) for the fourth and final time. The British were forced to evacuate to ships lying at anchor. The captain of the HMS *Hazard* was wounded severely in the battle and his replacement ordered the ships' cannons to be fired on the town; most of the buildings were razed. The first of the New Zealand Wars had begun.

In the months that followed, British troops (united with Hokianga-based Ngāpuhi) fought Heke and Kawiti in several battles. During this time the modern *pā* was born, effectively the world's first sophisticated system of trench warfare. It's worth stopping at Ruapekapeka Pā (p167), south of Kawakawa, to see how impressive these fortifications were.

Eventually Heke, Kawiti and George Grey (the new governor) made their peace, with no side the clear winner.

Abri Apartments APARTMENT $$

(☑09-402 8003; www.abriapartments.co.nz; 10-12 Bayview Rd; apt $175-225; P🐕) Choose between one of two free-standing pole houses, set within subtropical gardens, or a spacious one-bedroom suite under the owners' home. All three offer wonderful views, updated kitchen facilities and there's a free guest laundry, too.

Breakwater Motel MOTEL $$

(☑09-402 7558; www.breakwatermotel.co.nz; 1 Bayview Rd; unit $180-255; P✳🐕) Located by the little headland that breaks up the Paihia strip, this older motel has been renovated within an inch of its life. The units are tidy and modern, and each has its own kitchen. We recommend the Waterfront Suites, with balconies and patios facing the sea.

🍴 Eating

El Cafe LATIN AMERICAN $

(☑09-402 7637; www.facebook.com/elcafepaihia; 2 Kings Rd; mains $11-14.50; ⊙8am-4pm; 🐕) This excellent Chilean-owned cafe has the best coffee in town and terrific breakfast burritos, tacos and baked-egg dishes, such as spicy *huevos rancheros*. The Cuban pulled-pork sandwich is truly a wonderful thing. The fruit smoothies are also great on a warm Bay of Islands day.

Whare Waka Cafe CAFE $$

(☑09-402 7437; www.waitangi.org.nz; Waitangi Treaty Grounds, 1 Tau Henare Dr, Waitangi; mains $15-19.50; ⊙8am-4pm, shorter hours winter; 👶) Located beside a pond studded with ducks, backed by bush and overlooking the Waitangi Treaty Grounds (p168), the Whare Waka (Boathouse) is a top spot for good cafe fare during the day, and to return to for a *hāngi* (earth-oven-cooked) dinner and concert on Tuesday, Thursday, Friday and Sunday evenings from November to March.

★Charlotte's Kitchen CONTEMPORARY $$

(☑09-402 8296; www.charlotteskitchen.co.nz; Paihia Wharf, 69 Marsden Rd; mains lunch $16-27, dinner $20-35; ⊙11.30am-10pm Mon-Fri, to 11pm Sat & Sun) Named after an escaped Australian convict who was NZ's first white female settler, this hip restaurant-bar occupies a cheeky perch on the main pier. Bits of Kiwiana decorate the walls, while the menu takes a swashbuckling journey around the world, including steamed pork buns, Vietnamese rolls, fresh oysters and pizzas.

DON'T MISS

URUPUKAPUKA ISLAND

The largest of the bay's islands, Urupukapuka is a tranquil spot criss-crossed with walking trails and surrounded by aquamarine waters with safe secluded beaches to swim or join a kayak tour (p163). Native birds are plentiful thanks to a conservation initiative that has rendered this and all of the neighbouring islands predator free. A small licensed cafe serves food and drinks, just don't miss the last ferry back.

Explore NZ (p163) runs ferries to Otehei Bay (return adult/child $50/30) from Paihia and Russell; they can be irregular in winter. Bay of Islands Kayaking (p161) can also arrange overnight kayaking trips with camping gear for the island. Note that it does not rent to solo kayakers, so you'll need to find a friend.

Zane Grey's SEAFOOD $$

(☑09-402 6220; https://zanegreys.co.nz; 69 Marsden Rd; mains $15-38; ⊙8am-10pm) Named after a local fishing legend, and with possibly the biggest deck in all of Northland, Zane Grey's has you covered all day, from traditional breakfasts through to a seafood-focused dinner menu with Asian and Pacific influences. Half of the venue transforms into an enviable bar in the evening with comfy modern lounges ready for conversations fuelled by cocktails or cold beer.

★Terra SEAFOOD $$$

(☑09-945 8376; info@terrarestaurant.co.nz; 76 Marsden Rd; mains $20-38; ⊙5.30pm-late Tue-Sun) Muted colours give way to sea views at this new upstairs seafood restaurant across from Paihia pier. The seasonal menu is largely seafood focused (who can resist Orongo Bay oysters with lemon, seaweed, horopito and sherry mignonette?), but promises to take care of fine-dining vegetarians on request. Be advised to leave room for the cheese-tasting menu with a mix of French and local cheese.

Glasshouse Kitchen & Bar CONTEMPORARY $$$

(☑09-402 0111; www.paihiabeach.co.nz; Paihia Beach Resort, 130 Marsden Rd; mains $30-40; ⊙8-10am & 6pm-late) A concise seasonal menu of main dishes showcasing regional produce and local seafood underpinned by Asian influences and one of Northland's best wine lists. And did we mention the harbour views?

ℹ️ Information

Bay of Islands i-SITE (📞 09-402 7345; www.northlandnz.com; 69 Marsden Rd, Paihia) 🕐 8am-5pm Mar-Dec, to 7pm Jan & Feb) Information and bookings.

ℹ️ Getting There & Around

All **buses** (Maritime Building, Paihia) serving Paihia stop at the Maritime Building by the wharf.

InterCity (p152) has three or four coaches a day to and from Auckland (from $29, four hours), Waipu (from $25, 1¾ hours), Whangārei (from $12, 1¼ hours), Kawakawa (from $15, 20 minutes) and Kerikeri (from $15, 20 minutes).

Ferries (Paihia Wharf) depart regularly for Russell, and there are seasonal services to Urupukapuka Island.

For bike rental, visit Bay Beach Hire (p169).

Kerikeri

POP 7500

Kerikeri is a fairly prosperous inland township surrounded by orchards and vineyards with local farm gate sales of oranges, avocados, kiwifruit, vegetables and, of course, wine. If you're looking for some back-breaking, poorly paid work that the locals aren't keen to do, your working holiday starts here.

A snapshot of early Māori and British interaction is offered by a cluster of historic sites centred on the picturesque river basin. In 1819 the powerful Ngāpuhi chief Hongi Hika allowed Reverend Samuel Marsden to start a mission under the shadow of his

---

WORTH A TRIP

TE WAIMATE MISSION

A pretty little cottage set in verdant farmland 18km (20 minutes) southwest of Kerikeri, Te Waimate Mission (📞 09-405 9734; www.tewaimatemission.co.nz; 344 Te Ahu Ahu Rd, Waimate North; adult/child $10/3.50; 🕐 10am-5pm Fri-Tue Nov-Apr, to 4pm Sat-Mon May-Oct; 🅿️) holds several claims to fame. It's NZ's second-oldest house (built in 1831) and the site of the country's first European-style farm. Many of the exotic trees surrounding it are among the oldest of their kind in the country, and Charles Darwin stayed here in 1835. Inside, the story of the mission station and its inhabitants is outlined in displays in rooms dotted with items of original furniture.

Kororipo Pā. This is a landscape of cultural and historic significance and there's an ongoing campaign to have the area recognised as a Unesco World Heritage site.

◎ Sights

⭐ **Kerikeri Mission Station**   HISTORIC SITE
(📞 09-407 9236; www.historic.org.nz; 246 Kerikeri Rd; museum $8, house tour $12, combined $15, children free; 🕐 10am-5pm Nov-Apr, to 4pm May-Oct; 🅿️) Two of the nation's most significant buildings nestle side by side on the banks of Kerikeri Basin. Start at the **Stone Store**, NZ's oldest stone building (1836). Upstairs there's an interesting little museum, while downstairs the shop sells Kiwiana gifts as well as the type of wood and leather goods that used to be stocked here in the 19th century. Tours of neighbouring **Kemp House** depart from here. Built in 1822 by the missionaries, this humble yet pretty wooden Georgian-style house is NZ's oldest building.

Kororipo Pā   HISTORIC SITE
(Kerikeri Rd; 🅿️) **FREE** Just up the hill from Kerikeri Mission Station is a marked historical walk that leads to the site of Hongi Hika's *pā* and village. Little remains aside from the terracing that once supported wooden palisades. Huge war parties once departed from here, terrorising much of the North Island and slaughtering thousands during the Musket Wars. The role of missionaries in arming Ngāpuhi remains controversial. The walk emerges near the cute wooden St James Anglican Church (1878).

Aroha Island   WILDLIFE RESERVE
(📞 09-407 5243; www.arohaisland.co.nz; 177 Rangitane Rd; 🕐 9.30am-5.30pm; 🅿️) ♿ **FREE** Some 10km from town and reached via a permanent causeway through the mangroves, this 12-hectare island reserve provides a haven for North Island brown kiwi and other native birds. There's an informative visitor centre where you can learn about the kiwi and also arrange after-dark self-guided walks to try to spot these elusive flightless birds in the wild.

🏃 Activities

⭐ **Kerikeri River Track**   WALKING
Starting from Kerikeri Basin, this 4.6km-long track (p151) leads through beautiful native bush past Wharepuke Falls and the Fairy Pools to the **Rainbow Falls**, where even on dim days the 27m drop conjures dancing rainbows. Alternatively, you can reach Rainbow Falls from Rainbow Falls Rd.

Kerikeri

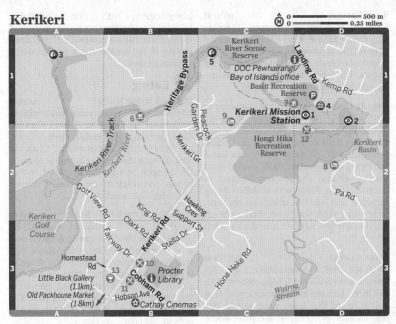

Kerikeri

Northland Paddleboarding   WATER SPORTS
(📞027 777 1035; www.northlandpaddleboarding.
co.nz; beginner lessons per hour $60) Lessons
and guided stand-up paddles departing
from various locations around Kerikeri.
A great way to get out on the water here,
where most of the town is land based.

🛏 Sleeping

★**Aroha Island**   CAMPGROUND $
(📞09-407 5243; www.arohaisland.co.nz; 177 Rangitane Rd; sites/cabins from $16/65, units $150-215;
P🐾) 🌿 Kip among the kiwi on the eco island of love (*aroha*), 12km from town. There's
a wide range of reasonably priced options,

from the peaceful campsites with basic facilities by the shelly beach, to a whole house. The
entire island, indoors and out, is nonsmoking.

**Wharepuke Subtropical
Accommodation**   CABIN $$
(📞09-407 8933; www.accommodation-bay-of
-islands.co.nz; 190 Kerikeri Rd; cabins from $180;
P🐾) 🌿 Best known for its food – Māha
(p175) is located here – and lush gardens,
Wharepuke also rents five self-contained
one-bedroom cottages hidden among the
palms. They have the prefabricated look of
holiday-park cabins, but are a step up in
terms of fixtures and space.

Kauri Park
MOTEL $$

(☑09-407 7629; www.kauripark.co.nz; 512 Kerikeri Rd; units from $130; P ি ⊠) Hidden behind tall trees on the approach to Kerikeri, this well-priced motel has a mixture of units of varying layouts. The rooms are extremely comfortable, spacious and stylishly furnished.

Pagoda Lodge
LODGE, CAMPGROUND $$

(☑09-407 8617; www.pagoda.co.nz; 81 Pa Rd; sites/glamping/units from $40/120/145; ⊙Dec-Mar; P ি) Built in the 1930s by an oddball Scotsman with an Asian fetish, this lodge features pagoda-shaped roofs grafted onto wooden cottages. The property descends to the river and is dotted with Buddhas, gypsy caravans, and safari tents with proper beds, or you can pitch your own. Take Cobham Rd, turn left into Kerikeri Inlet Rd, then left into Pa Rd.

Relax a Lodge
HOMESTAY $$

(☑09-407 6989; www.relaxalodge.co.nz; 1574 Springbank Rd/SH10; s/d $55/70, cottages $130-160; P ি) Located in an orange grove, 4km out of town, this quiet rural retreat has tidy backpacker rooms in the main house (bathrooms are shared) and attractive self-contained cottages, sleeping two to four people, dotted around the property. There's a two-night minimum stay in high season.

Moon Gate Villa
B&B $$$

(☑09-929 5921; www.moongatevilla.com; 462 Kerikeri Rd; ste $339-369, cottage from $279; P ি ⊠) A streamlike water feature flows through the centre of this modern house, set amid tropical foliage on the approach to Kerikeri. The larger of the two suites has a huge spa bath, while the other has an extra single room attached for parties of three. There's also a compact self-contained cottage in the garden and a solar-powered swimming pool.

Eating

Old Packhouse Market
MARKET $

(☑09-401 9588; www.facebook.com/theoldpackhousemarket; 505 Kerikeri Rd; ⊙8am-1.30pm Sat) Local artisans, winemakers and farmers sell their goodies at this market in an old fruit-packing shed on the outskirts of town. It's the spot for a grazing breakfast on Saturdays and check its calendar for themed Thursday-night markets.

Cafe Zest & the Waffle Room
CAFE $$

(☑09-407 7164; 73 Kerikeri Rd; mains $13-22; ⊙7.30am-4pm Mon-Fri, to 2pm Sat & Sun) If sugar is your weakness, the Waffle Room may well be your undoing. You're best to avoid temptation by grabbing a table in the cafe side of Zest and averting your eyes from the heavily laden waffles wafting past. The outside tables are a great city-centre spot to soak up the afternoon sun.

★ Rusty Tractor
CAFE $$

(☑09-407 3322; www.rustytractorcafe.co.nz; 582 Kerikeri Rd; mains breakfast $17-20, lunch $20-26; ⊙8am-3pm; ি ⛶) As decadent breakfasts go, Rusty Tractor's doughnuts with crème fraiche and berries take some beating. There are healthier options, too, and the coffee's up with the best in Kerikeri. Otherwise, treat yourself to a glass of wine while the kids play on the rocket-ship slide on the back lawn.

PRODUCERS OF KERIKERI

You'd be forgiven for thinking that everyone in Kerikeri is involved in some small-scale artisanal enterprise, given the bombardment of craft shops on the way into town. A little further afield, a handful of vineyards are doing their best to stake Northland's claim as a wine region. The little-known red grape chambourcin has proved particularly suited to the region's subtropical humidity, along with pinotage and syrah.

Look out for the *Art & Craft Trail* and *Wine Trail* brochures. Here are our tasty recommendations:

Ake Ake Wine tastings are $8, free with a purchase of wine.

Cottle Hill (☑09-407 5203; www.cottlehill.co.nz; 28 Cottle Hill Dr; tastings $5, free with purchase; ⊙10am-5pm Wed-Sun) Wine, port and grappa tastings, free with a purchase.

Get Fudged & Keriblue Ceramics (☑09-407 1111; www.keribueceramics.co.nz; 1691 SH10; ⊙9am-5pm) An unusual pairing of ceramics and big, decadent slabs of fudge.

Makana Confections Artisan chocolate factory with a cafe attached.

Marsden Estate Wine tastings and lunch on the terrace.

> **WORTH A TRIP**
>
> ## PUKETI & OMAHUTA FORESTS
>
> Inland from Kerikeri, the Puketi and Omahuta Forests form a continuous expanse of native rainforest. Logging in Puketi was stopped in 1951 to protect not only the remaining kauri but also the endangered kokako bird. Keep an eye out for this rare charmer (grey with a blue wattle) on your wanders.
>
> The forests are reached by several entrances and contain a network of walking tracks varying in length from 15 minutes (the wheelchair-accessible Manginangina Kauri Walk) to two days (the challenging Waipapa River Track); see the DOC website (www.doc.govt. nz) for more on these and other walks.
>
> **Adventure Puketi** (☑09-401 9095; www.forestwalks.com; 476 Puketi Rd; tours $80-155) ⬤ leads guided ecowalks through the forest, including night-time tours to seek out the nocturnal wildlife. It also offers very comfortable B&B accommodation on the edge of the forest. Check the website for packages incorporating tours and accommodation.

Cafe Jerusalem ISRAELI $$
(☑09-407 1001; www.cafejerusalem.co.nz; Village Mall, 85 Kerikeri Rd; mains $18.50-22.50; ☺10am-late Mon-Sat) Northland's best falafels, lamb shawarma (kebab) and meze platters, all served with a smile and a social vibe. Most mains come with rice, pitta bread, tabouli and a salad. Try the *shakshuka* (baked eggs in a spicy tomato sauce) for a hearty brunch.

Marsden Estate CONTEMPORARY $$
(☑09-407 9398; www.marsdenestate.co.nz; 56 Wiroa Rd; mains breakfast $18-23, lunch $28-38; ☺cellar door 10am-5pm; 🐾) The interior of this winery restaurant is large and featureless so opt for the covered terrace at the rear, which has wonderful views over the vines and a pretty pond. Cooked breakfasts give way to sophisticated lunches that match prime local produce with flavours from all over the world.

⭐ **Ake Ake** BRITISH, FRENCH $$
(☑09-407 8230; www.akeakevineyard.co.nz; 165 Waimate North Rd; mains $30-36; ☺11.45am-2pm & 5.45-8pm Mon-Sat, lunch only Sun, tastings 10am-4.30pm; 🐾) ⬤ At this upmarket winery restaurant, the rural setting is complemented by hearty but delicious country fare, such as lamb shanks, wild game pie, confit duck and steak. The Sunday roasts are legendary. After lunch, work off some of the calories on the 1km self-guided trail through the vineyard.

⭐ **Plough & Feather** BISTRO $$
(☑09-407 8479; www.ploughandfeather.co.nz; 215 Kerikeri Rd; mains lunch $12-24, dinner $30-32; ☺9am-10pm summer) Kerikeri's best located and most upmarket restaurant occupies an old homestead right on the basin (book ahead for a table on the veranda). Mains run the gamut of bistro favourites like burgers,

steak and fish of the day; plus a good selection of vegan options. There's also an excellent range of NZ craft beers.

Māha THAI, EUROPEAN $$$
(☑09-945 6551; www.maharestaurant.co.nz; 190 Kerikeri Rd; mains $20-40; ☺11am-late Tue-Sat) With one foot in Europe, the other in Japan and its head in the lush vegetation of Wharepuke Subtropical Gardens, this is Kerikeri's most unusual and inspired eatery. Adjacent is the interesting Wharepuke Print Studio.

🍷 Drinking & Nightlife

La Taza Del Diablo BAR
(☑09-407 3912; www.facebook.com/eltazadeldiablo; 3 Homestead Rd; ☺11.30am-late Wed-Sun; 🔊) This Mexican-style bar is about as energetic and raffish as buttoned-down Kerikeri gets, with a decent selection of tequila, Mexican beers and, just maybe, Northland's best margaritas. Tacos, enchiladas and chimichangas all feature on the bar snacks menu, and occasional live gigs sometimes raise the roof in this genteel town.

🛍 Shopping

Makana Confections CHOCOLATE
(☑09-407 6800; www.makana.co.nz; 504 Kerikeri Rd; ☺9am-5.30pm) Sample a chocolate in the shop while watching the artisans at work through the factory window. There's also a cafe attached, selling pastries and gelato.

Little Black Gallery ART
(www.littleblackgallery.co.nz; 394b Kerikeri Rd; ☺10.30am-4pm Tue-Sat, shorter hours winter) Off the beaten track along a bamboo-lined lane, this tiny stylish gallery sells unique jewellery, art and gifts.

❶ Getting There & Away

AIR

Bay of Islands (Kerikeri) Airport (p163) is 8km southwest of town. Air New Zealand flies from Auckland to Kerikeri. Super Shuttle (p163) provides shuttles between Kerikeri Airport and Bay of Islands destinations such as Kerikeri ($15) and Paihia ($30).

BUS

InterCity (p152) buses leave from a stop at 9 Cobham Rd, opposite the library, to Paihia (from $19, 25 minutes), Whangārei (from $14, 1½ hours) and Auckland (from $39, 4¾ hours).

Hokianga Link (☏ 021 405 872; www.buslink. co.nz) offers a weekly minibus service between Kerikeri and regional towns, which expands to twice weekly in summer.

THE FAR NORTH

Here's your chance to get off the beaten track, even if that sometimes means onto unsealed roads. The far-flung Far North always plays second fiddle to the Bay of Islands for attention and funding, yet the subtropical tip of the North Island has more breathtaking coastline per square kilometre than anywhere apart from the offshore islands. While the 'winterless north' may be a popular misnomer, summers here are long and leisurely. Note that parts of the Far North are noticeably economically depressed but every dollar you spend here on petrol, food, accommodation and tours can only be helpful. Just don't leave your valuables sitting on your car dashboard with the windows wound down.

❶ Getting There & Away

Barrier Air (☏ 09-275 9120; www.barrierair. kiwi; Kaitāia Airport) flies between Auckland and Kaitāia.

InterCity (p152) operates a daily coach between Kerikeri and Kaitāia, stopping in all the main Doubtless Bay settlements along the way.

Far North Link (☏ 09-408 1092; www.buslink. co.nz) has limited weekday bus services linking Kaitāia to Mangonui, Ahipara and Pukenui.

If you don't have your own vehicle, tour buses are the best option for reaching Cape Reinga.

Matauri & Tauranga Bays

It's a short detour from SH10, but the exceptionally scenic loop route leading inland to these awesome beaches is a world away from the glitzy face presented for tourists in the Bay of Islands.

Matauri Bay is a long, sandy surf beach, 18km off SH10, with the 17 Cavalli Islands scattered offshore. On top of the headland above the park is a monument to the *Rainbow Warrior;* the Greenpeace ship's underwater resting place among the nearby islands is a popular dive site.

Back on the main road, the route heads west, passing through pleasant Te Ngaere village and a succession of little bays before the turn-off to Tauranga Bay, a smaller beach where the sand is a peachy pink colour.

There is no public transport to these areas.

Northland Sea Kayaking KAYAKING (☏ 09-405 0381; www.northlandseakayaking.co.nz; half-/full-day tours $95/120) Down a private road leading from Tauranga Bay, Northland Sea Kayaking leads kayak explorations of this magical coastline of coves, sea caves and islands.

Matauri Bay Holiday Park HOLIDAY PARK $ (☏ 09-405 0525; www.matauribayholidaypark. co.nz; Matauri Bay Rd; sites/units from $22/65; ℙ 🖶) Taking up the north end of the beach, this beachfront holiday park has only a handful of cabins but plenty of space to pitch a tent or park a campervan. There's also a shop selling groceries and petrol.

Whangaroa Harbour

Just around the headland from Tauranga Bay is the narrow entrance to Whangaroa Harbour. The small fishing village of Whangaroa is 6km from SH10 and calls itself the 'Marlin Capital of NZ'.

There are plenty of charter boats for game-fishing (December to April); prices start at around $1200 a day. If you're planning to hook a monster, insist on it being released once caught – striped marlin and swordfish are among NZ's least-sustainable fishing options.

On the other side of the harbour's north head is Taupo Bay, a surf beach that attracts a loyal Kiwi contingent in summer. On easterly swells, there are quality right-handers to surf at the southern end of the bay, by the river mouth. It's reached by an 11km road signposted from SH10.

An excellent 20-minute hike starts from the car park at the end of Old Hospital Rd and goes up St Paul's Rock (213m), which dominates Whangaroa village. At the top you have to use a wire cable to pull yourself up, but the views make it worth the effort.

The Wairakau Stream Track, heading north to Pekapeka Bay, begins near the church hall on Campbell Rd in Totara North on the other side of the bay. It's an extremely beautiful, undeveloped stretch and you can cool off in swimming holes along the way. The two-hour (5.6km) hike passes through forest, an abandoned farm and around a steep-walled estuary before arriving at DOC's Lane Cove Hut (☑09-407 0300; www.doc.govt.nz; adult/child $15/7.50) 🖉.

★Kahoe Farms Hostel   HOSTEL $
(☑09-405 1804; www.kahoefarms.co.nz; 1266 SH10; dm $32, r with/without bathroom from $116/81; P🐾) On SH10, 10km north of the turn-off to Whangaroa, this hostel has a deservedly great reputation – for its comfortable accommodation, bucolic setting and home-cooked Italian food, but mostly for its welcoming owners. The backpackers' cottage is great, but slightly up the hill there's an even more impressive villa with excellent-value en-suite rooms.

❶ Getting There & Away

There is no public transport to Whangaroa Harbour. Buses usually drop off at SH10 in nearby Kahoe, immediately west of the harbour and 15km from Whangaroa village.

Mangonui & Doubtless Bay
POP 1800

Doubtless Bay gets its unusual name from an entry in Cook's logbook, where he wrote that the body of water was 'doubtless a bay'. No kidding, Cap'n. It's a big bay at that, with a string of pretty swimming beaches heading towards the Karikari Peninsula.

The main centre, Mangonui (meaning 'Big Shark'), retains a fishing-port feel, despite cafes and gift shops now infesting its well-labelled line of historical waterfront buildings. They were constructed in the days when Mangonui was a centre of the whaling industry (1792–1850) and exported flax, kauri wood and gum.

BAY OF ISLANDS & NORTHLAND MANGONUI & DOUBTLESS BAY

THE BOMBING OF THE RAINBOW WARRIOR

On the morning of 10 July 1985, New Zealanders awoke to news reporting that a terrorist attack had killed a man in Auckland Harbour. The Greenpeace flagship *Rainbow Warrior* had been sunk at its anchorage at Marsden Wharf, where it was preparing to sail to Moruroa atoll near Tahiti to protest against French nuclear testing.

A tip-off from a Neighbourhood Watch group eventually led to the arrest of two French foreign intelligence service (DGSE) agents, posing as tourists. The agents had detonated two mines on the boat in staggered explosions – the first designed to cause the crew to evacuate and the second to sink her. However, after the initial evacuation, some of the crew returned to the vessel to investigate and document the attack. Greenpeace photographer Fernando Pereira was drowned below decks following the second explosion.

The arrested agents pleaded guilty to manslaughter and were sentenced to 10 years' imprisonment. In response, the French government threatened to embargo NZ goods from entering the European Economic Community – which would have crippled NZ's economy. A deal was struck whereby France paid $13 million to NZ and apologised, in return for the agents being delivered into French custody on a South Pacific atoll for three years. France eventually paid over $8 million to Greenpeace in reparation – and the bombers were quietly freed before their sentence was served.

Initially French President François Mitterrand denied any government involvement in the attack, but following an inquiry he eventually sacked his Defence Minister and the head of the DGSE, Admiral Pierre Lacoste. On the 20th anniversary of the attack, *Le Monde* newspaper published a report from Lacoste dating from 1986, declaring that the president had personally authorised the operation.

The bombing left a lasting impact on NZ, and French nuclear testing at Moruroa ceased for good in 1996. The wreck of the *Rainbow Warrior* was resunk near Northland's Cavalli Islands, where, today it can be explored by divers. The masts were bought by the North Island's Dargaville Museum (p187) and overlook the town. The memory of Fernando Pereira endures in a peaceful bird hide in Thames, while a memorial to the boat sits atop a Māori *pā* site at Matauri Bay, north of the Bay of Islands.

The popular holiday settlements of **Coopers Beach**, **Cable Bay** and **Taipa** are restful pockets of beachside gentrification.

◉ Sights & Activities

Grab the free *Heritage Trail* brochure from the visitor information centre for a 3km self-guided walk that takes in 22 historic sites. Other walks lead to attractive **Mill Bay**, west of Mangonui, and **Rangikapiti Pā Historic Reserve**, which has ancient Māori terracing and a spectacular view of Doubtless Bay – particularly at sunrise and sunset. A walkway runs from Mill Bay to the *pā*, but you can also drive nearly to the top.

Butler Point Whaling Museum   MUSEUM
(☑ 09-406 0006; www.whalingmuseumbutler point.com; Marchant Rd, Hihi; adult/child $25/5; ☺ by appointment) This small private museum is set in lovely gardens at Hihi, 15km northeast of Mangonui. The centrepiece is a still-lived-in Victorian homestead built by retired whaling captain William Butler, who settled here in 1838, had 13 children and became a trader, farmer, magistrate and Member of Parliament. Visits must be prearranged and start with a guided tour of the house, after which you're welcome to wander around the grounds for as long as you like.

⌂ Sleeping

Mangonui Waterfront Apartments Motel   APARTMENT $$
(☑ 09-406 0347; www.mangonuiwaterfront.co.nz; 88 Waterfront Dr, Mangonui; apt $120-250; P ?) Character radiates from the kauri boards of these apartments, which occupy a set of historic houses on the Mangonui waterfront. Each is different, ranging from a small bedsit to a two-bedroom unit with a full kitchen sleeping up to five people.

★ Old Oak   HISTORIC HOTEL $$$
(☑ 09-406 1250; www.theoldoak.co.nz; 66 Waterfront Dr, Mangonui; s/d/ste from $200/250/275; P ✽ ?) This atmospheric 1861 kauri inn is now an elegant boutique hotel with contemporary design and top-notch furnishings in its six rooms and suites. It oozes personality, not least because the building is reputedly haunted.

Ramada Resort Reia Taipa Beach   RESORT $$$
(☑ 09-406 0656; www.ramadataipa.co.nz; 22 Taipa Point Rd, Taipa; studio from $245; P ✽ ? ⚓) Renovated accommodation and a warm welcome combine at this long-standing resort, which offers a choice between beachfront and poolside studio units and apartments. There's also an on-site restaurant, a tennis court and a spa pool.

✕ Eating

★ The Thai   THAI $$
(☑ 09-406 1220; www.thethaimangonui.co.nz; 80 Waterfront Dr, Mangonui; mains $23-28.50; ☺ 5-11pm Tue-Sun; ✎) Northland's best Thai restaurant serves zingy dishes with intriguing names such as Angry Pig, Kiwi Chick and Mangonui Showtime, and there's also a good range of Isaan (northeastern Thai) dishes to go with a frosty Singha beer. Actually, make that one of New Zealand's best Thai restaurants.

Little Kitchen on the Bay   CAFE $$
(☑ 09-406 1644; www.littlekitchen.co.nz; 118 Waterfront Dr, Mangonui; mains $17-20; ☺ 8am-3pm) With a terrace facing the water and a sun-drenched interior, this cute cafe serves Mangonui's best coffee, excellent counter food and good mains. Menu options include burgers, toasted sandwiches, and a Buddha bowl to keep the vegans content.

ⓘ Information

Doubtless Bay Visitor Information Centre (☑ 09-406 2046; www.doubtlessbay.co.nz; 118 Waterfront Dr, Mangonui; ☺ 10am-5pm Mon-Sat Jan-Apr, to 3pm May-Dec) Excellent source of local information.

ⓘ Getting There & Away

InterCity (p152) stops here daily, en route between Kerikeri ($28, one hour) and Kaitāia ($25, 40 minutes).

Far North Link (p176) has a weekday service to Kaitāia ($5, one hour), timed around office hours.

Both buses stop outside Wilton's Garage in Mangonui, outside the sports store in Coopers Beach, opposite the shop in Cable Bay and outside the Z petrol station in Taipa.

Karikari Peninsula

The oddly shaped Karikari Peninsula bends into a near-perfect right angle. The result is beaches facing north, south, east and west in close proximity, so if the wind's annoying you or you want to catch some surf, a sunrise or a sunset, just swap beaches.

Despite its natural assets, the sun-baked peninsula, with its stands of gum trees reminiscent of neighbouring Australia, has largely escaped development, with farmers well outnumbering tourist operators. There's no public transport and you won't find a lot of shops or eateries either. This is old-school New Zealand, where commercialism has yet to take much of a hold.

Tokerau Beach is the long, sandy stretch forming the western edge of Doubtless Bay. Neighbouring **Whatuwhiwhi** is smaller and more built-up, facing back across the bay. Lovely **Maitai Bay**, with its twin coves, is a great spot for swimming – the water is sheltered enough for the kids, but with enough swell to body surf. It's located at the lonely end of the peninsula down an unsealed road.

Rangiputa faces west at the elbow of the peninsula; the pure white sand and crystal-clear sheltered waters come straight from a Pacific Island daydream. A turn-off on the road to Rangiputa takes you to remote **Puheke Beach**, a long, windswept stretch of snow-white sand dunes forming Karikari's northern edge.

Airzone Kitesurf School   KITESURFING
(📋 021 202 7949; www.kitesurfnz.com; ☉ Nov-Mar) The unique set-up of Karikari Peninsula makes it one of the world's premium spots for kitesurfing. Learners get to hone their skills on flat water before heading to the surf, while the more experienced can chase the wind around the peninsula.

Karikari Lodge   HOSTEL $
(📋 09-406 7378; www.karikarilodge.co.nz; 26 Inland Rd, Whatuwhiwhi; dm/d/cabin $35/85/90; 🅿️🛜) More like a family-run homestay than a backpackers hostel, this super-friendly hostel has only three bedrooms, shared bathrooms, and a separate cabin and caravan in the garden. Perks include free use of kayaks, boogie boards, surfboards and stand-up paddle boards. There's also a full kitchen and barbecue facilities if you get lucky while fishing.

Whatuwhiwhi Top
10 Holiday Park   HOLIDAY PARK $
(📋 09-408 7202; www.whatuwhiwhitop10.co.nz; 17 Whatuwhiwhi Rd; sites from $40, unit with/without bathroom from $100/75; 🅿️🛜🐕) Sheltered by hills and close to the beach, this friendly neat complex has a great location, good facilities, free barbecues and a playground. It also offers dive air fills and kayaks for hire.

DOC Maitai Bay Campsite   CAMPGROUND $
(www.doc.govt.nz; Maitai Bay Rd; sites per adult/child $15/7.50; 🅿️) 🍽 A large first-in, first-served (no bookings) camping ground at the peninsula's most beautiful beach, with flush toilets, drinking water and cold showers.

Cape Reinga
& Ninety Mile Beach

Māori consider Cape Reinga (Te Rerenga Wairua) the jumping-off point for souls as they depart on the journey to their spiritual homeland. That makes the Aupouri Peninsula a giant diving board, and it even resembles one – long and thin, it reaches 108km to form New Zealand's northern extremity. On its west coast Ninety Mile Beach (Ninety Kilometre Beach would be more accurate) is a continuous stretch lined with high sand dunes, flanked by the Aupouri Forest.

⊙ Sights

⭐ **Cape Reinga**   VIEWPOINT
(Far North Rd) State Hwy 1 terminates at this dramatic headland where the waters of the Tasman Sea and Pacific Ocean meet, breaking together into waves up to 10m high in stormy weather. Cape Reinga is the end of the road both literally and figuratively: in Māori tradition the spirits of the dead depart the world from here, making it the most sacred site in all of Aotearoa. Out of respect, you're requested to refrain from eating or drinking in the vicinity.

The actual departure point is believed to be the 800-year-old pohutukawa tree clinging to the rocks on the small promontory of Te Rerenga Wairua (Leaping Place of the Spirits) far below; to those in corporeal form, access is forbidden.

From the car park it's a rolling 1km walk to the lookout, passing the Cape Reinga Lighthouse along the way. Information boards detail the area's ecology, history and cultural significance. Little tufts of cloud sometimes cling to the ridges, giving sudden spooky chills even on hot days.

Contrary to expectation, Cape Reinga isn't actually the northernmost point of the country; that honour belongs to the inaccessible Surville Cliffs, which can be spotted to the right in the distance. In fact, it's much closer to the westernmost point, Cape Maria van Diemen, immediately to the left.

★ **Te Paki Giant Sand Dunes** DUNES
(www.doc.govt.nz; Te Paki Stream Rd) A large chunk of the land around Cape Reinga is part of the Te Paki Recreation Reserves managed by DOC. It's public land with free access; leave the gates as you found them and don't disturb the animals. There are 7 sq km of giant sand dunes on either side of the mouth of Te Paki Stream. For those wishing to clamber up and toboggan back down, you can rent sandboards ($15) from local outfits signposted en route or from a caravan at the car park (during summer only).

Gumdiggers Park MUSEUM
(☑09-406 7166; www.gumdiggerspark.co.nz; 171 Heath Rd, Waiharara; adult/child $12.50/6; ☺10am-4pm, later in summer) Kauri forests covered this area for 100,000 years, leaving ancient logs and the much-prized gum (used for making varnish and linoleum) buried beneath. Digging it out was the region's main industry from the 1870s to the 1920s. In 1900 around 7000 gumdiggers were digging holes all over Northland, including at this site. Start with the 15-minute video, and then walk on the bush tracks, leading past gumdiggers' huts, ancient kauri stumps, huge preserved logs and holes left by the diggers.

🏃 Activities

Te Paki Coastal Track TRAMPING
From Cape Reinga, a walk along **Te Werahi Beach** to **Cape Maria van Diemen** (a five-hour loop) takes you to the westernmost point of NZ. This is one of many sections of the three- to four-day (48km) coastal track (p150) from Kapowairua to Te Paki Stream that can be tackled individually.

Beautiful **Tapotupotu Bay** is a 2½-hour (3km) walk east of Cape Reinga, via Sandy Bay. From Tapotupotu Bay it's a 5½-hour (9km) walk to the Pandora campsite on the western edge of **Spirits Bay**, one of NZ's most spectacular beaches. From here it's a further 3km to the Kapowairua campsite at the eastern end of the beach. Both bays are also accessible by road.

👉 Tours

Bus tours go to Cape Reinga from Kaitāia, Ahipara, Doubtless Bay and the Bay of Islands, but there's no scheduled public transport up here.

Petricevich Cape Reinga Tours ADVENTURE
(☑09-408 2411; www.capereingatours.co.nz; adult/child $70/40) Visit Cape Reinga and the Te Paki dunes and zoom along Ninety Mile Beach in the Dune Rider bus. Sandboarding is included. Pickup points include Mangonui, Kaitāia and Ahipara.

Far North Outback Adventures ADVENTURE
(☑09-409 4586; www.farnorthtours.co.nz; price on application) Flexible, day-long 4WD tours from Kaitāia/Ahipara, including morning tea and lunch. Options include visits to remote areas such as Great Exhibition Bay. Prices depend on the number of participants.

Sand Safaris ADVENTURE
(☑09-408 1778; www.sandsafaris.co.nz; adult/child $70/40) 🚌 Coach trips from Ahipara, Kaitāia and Awanui, including sandboarding and a picnic lunch in Tapotupotu Bay.

Harrisons Cape Runner ADVENTURE
(☑0800 227 373; www.harrisonscapereinga tours.co.nz; adult/child $60/30) Day trips in a 4WD truck-like bus along Ninety Mile Beach to Cape Reinga that include sandboarding and a picnic lunch in Tapotupotu Bay. They depart Kaitāia at 9am daily, returning at 5pm.

Ahikaa Adventures CULTURAL
(☑09-409 8228; www.ahikaa-adventures.co.nz; Te Paki Stream Rd; tours $70-190) Māori culture permeates these tours, which can include sandboarding, kayaking, snorkelling, fishing and pigging out on traditional *kai* (food) cooked in a *hāngi*.

🛏 Sleeping

There are few good accommodation options on the peninsula itself. The DOC has basic but spectacularly positioned **sites** (www.doc. govt.nz; sites per adult/child $8/4) 🚌 at Rarawa Beach, Kapowairua and Tapotupotu Bay. Only water, flush toilets and cold showers are provided. Bring a cooker, as fires are not allowed, and plenty of repellent to ward off mosquitoes and sandflies. 'Freedom/Leave No Trace' camping is allowed along the Te Paki Coastal Track.

North Wind Lodge Backpackers HOSTEL $
(☑09-409 8515; www.northwind.co.nz; 88 Otaipango Rd, Henderson Bay; dm/s/tw/d $30/60/66/80; ☺Sep-May; ℗) Six kilometres down an unsealed road on the Aupouri Peninsula's east side, this unusual turreted house offers a homey environment and plenty of quiet spots on the lawn to sit with a beer and a book. It's within walking distance of a beautiful beach.

❶ Getting There & Away

Apart from numerous tours, there's no public transport past Pukenui – and even this is limited to Thursday-only buses from Kaitāia ($5, 45 minutes) operated by Far North Link (p176).

As well as Far North Rd (SH1), rugged vehicles can travel along Ninety Mile Beach itself. However, cars have been known to hit soft sand and be swallowed by the tides – look out for unfortunate vehicles poking through the sands.

Check tide times before setting out; avoid it 2½ hours either side of high tide. Watch out for 'quicksand' at Te Paki Stream – keep moving! Many car-rental companies prohibit driving on sand; if you get stuck, your insurance won't cover you.

It's best to fill up with petrol before hitting the Aupouri Peninsula.

Kaitāia

POP 4890

This provincial town does not have a strong reputation down south, something local social media page Humans of Kaitāia (www.facebook.com/humansofkaitaianz) is working to dispel, but it's a handy stop if you're after a supermarket, a post office or an ATM. It's also a jumping-off point for tours to Cape Reinga and Ninety Mile Beach. Nearby Ahipara is a better option if you want to stay a few nights in the region.

Te Ahu Centre ARTS CENTRE
(📞 09-401 5200; www.kaitaianz.co.nz; cnr South Rd & Matthews Ave) This civic and community centre features a cinema, a theatre, a tourist information centre, a gallery and the **Te Ahu Heritage** (📞 09-408 9454; www.teahuheritage.co.nz; adult/child $7/free; ⊙10.30am-4.30pm Mon-Fri) exhibits of the Far North Regional Museum. Artefacts include kauri gum, carved *pounamu* (greenstone) weapons and wood carvings dating to the 14th century. There's also a cafe, and free wi-fi at the library. The centre's foyer is circled by a series of *pou* (carved posts) featuring the different cultures – Māori, British, Croatian etc – that have had a major impact in the local area.

Each of the parts of the centre have their own opening hours.

Loredo Motel MOTEL $$
(📞 09-408 3200; www.loredomotel.co.nz; 25 North Rd; units $120-160; 🅿 🗲 🌊) Opting for a breezy Spanish style, this tidy motel has well-kept units set among palm trees and lawns, with a swimming pool.

Gecko Cafe CAFE $
(📞 09-408 1160; 71 Commerce St; mains $9-18; ⊙7am-3pm) Morning queues of locals attest to the Gecko having the best coffee in town (it roasts its own), and the food's pretty good, too. Kick off another day on the road with fresh salads, sandwiches and wraps.

Beachcomber BISTRO $$
(📞 09-408 2010; www.beachcomber.net.nz; 222 Commerce St; mains lunch $19-36, dinner $25-40; ⊙11am-2.30pm Mon-Fri & 5-9pm Mon-Sat; 🖉🖦) This vibrant Pacific-themed family restaurant is the best dinner option in Kaitāia, with a wide range of dishes from paua chowder to grilled meat (or vegetables done three ways), with a well-stocked salad bar.

❶ Information

DOC Kaitāia Area Office (📞 09-408 6014; www.doc.govt.nz; 25 Matthews Ave; ⊙8am-4.30pm Mon-Fri) It's a regional office rather than an information centre, but the staff are happy to provide up-to-date track information and advice.

Far North i-SITE (📞 09-408 9450; www.northlandnz.com; Te Ahu Centre, cnr Matthews Ave & South Rd; ⊙8.30am-5pm) An excellent information centre with advice for all of Northland.

❶ Getting There & Away

AIR

Kaitāia Airport (KAT; 📞 021 818 314; Quarry Rd, Awanui) is 6km north of town. Barrier Air (p176) flies to and from Auckland (one hour).

BUS

Far North Link (p176) has services to Ahipara ($3.50, 15 minutes) and Mangonui ($5, one hour) on weekdays, and to Pukenui ($5, 45 minutes) on Thursdays.

InterCity (p152) buses depart daily from the Te Ahu Centre and head to Kerikeri ($37, 1¾ hours) via Mangonui ($25, 40 minutes).

Ahipara

POP 1060

All good things must come to an end, and Ninety Mile Beach does at this hippie beach town. A few holiday mansions have snuck in, but mostly it's just the locals keeping it real, rubbing shoulders with visiting surfers.

The area is known for its huge sand dunes and massive kauri gumfield, where 2000 people once worked. Sandboarding and quad-bike rides are popular activities on the dunes above Ahipara and further around the Tauroa Peninsula.

⊙ Sights & Activities

Shipwreck Bay BEACH
(Te Kōhanga; Wreck Bay Rd) The best surfing is at this small cove at Ahipara's western edge, so named for shipwrecks still visible at low tide.

Ahipara Treks HORSE RIDING
(✑09-408 2532; www.taitokerauhoney.co.nz/ahipara-horse-treks; 11 Foreshore Rd; 1/2hr $65/85) Offers beach canters, including some farm and ocean riding (when the surf permits).

Ahipara Adventure ADVENTURE SPORTS
(✑09-409 2055; www.ahiparaadventure.co.nz; 15 Takahe Rd) Hires sand toboggans ($15 per half-day), surfboards ($40 per half-day), body boards ($20 per half-day), stand-up paddle boards ($50 per half-day), blokarts for sand yachting ($80 per hour) and quad bikes ($115 per hour).

NZ Surfbros SURFING
(✑021 252 7078; www.nzsurfbros.co.nz; 27 Kaka St; 2hr lesson $60) Rents boards and offers surfing lessons and five-day surf tours (from $599 including accommodation, meals and transport from Auckland).

🛏 Sleeping & Eating

★**Endless Summer Lodge** HOSTEL $
(✑09-409 4181; www.endlesssummer.co.nz; 245 Foreshore Rd; dm/r from $30/86; P🛜) Across from the beach, this superb kauri villa (1880) has been beautifully restored and converted into an exceptional hostel. There's no TV, which encourages bonding around the long table and wood-fired pizza oven on the vine-covered back terrace. Body boards

and sandboards can be borrowed and surfboards can be hired.

Ahipara Holiday Park HOLIDAY PARK $
(✑0800 888 988; www.ahiparaholidaypark.co.nz; 168 Takahe Rd; sites/dm/tw/d from $18/28/75/85, unit with/without bathroom from $105/75; P🛜) There's a large range of accommodation on offer at this holiday park, including cabins, motel units and a worn but perfectly presentable YHA-affiliated backpackers lodge. The communal hall has an open fire and colourful murals.

GEMS Seaside Lodge APARTMENT $$
(✑027 820 9403; www.gemsseasidelodge.co.nz; 14 Kotare St; apt from $150; 🛜) Who cares if it's a bit bourgeois for Ahipara? These two upmarket, self-contained apartments have watery views and there's direct access to the beach. The bottom floor is a spacious studio, while the upper-floor apartment has two bedrooms and two bathrooms.

North Drift Cafe CAFE $
(✑09-409 4093; www.facebook.com/northdriftcafe; 250 Ahipara Rd; mains $9-20; ⊙8am-2.30pm) Start the day with a cooked breakfast and Ahipara's best coffee on the sunny front deck of this relaxed little cafe. Come back at lunch for a burger, fish and chips, or Cajun chicken tacos. In summer, it reopens at 5pm for dinner from Thursday through to Sunday.

ⓘ Getting There & Away

Far North Link (p176) has a weekday bus to Kaitāia ($3.50, 15 minutes), departing Ahipara early in the morning and returning in the evening.

NGĀTI TARARA

As you're travelling around the north you might notice the preponderance of road names ending in '-ich'. Then there's the trilingual signage in the Kaitāia and Dargaville museums. *Haere mai, dobro došli* and welcome to one of the more peculiar ethnic conjunctions in the country.

From the end of the 19th century, men from the Dalmatian coast of what is now Croatia started arriving in New Zealand looking for work. Many ended up in Northland's gumfields. Anglo-NZ society wasn't particularly welcoming to the new immigrants, particularly during WWI, as they were travelling on Austrian passports. Not so the small Māori communities of the north. Here the immigrants found an echo of Dalmatian village life, with its emphasis on extended family and hospitality, not to mention a shared history of injustice at the hands of colonial powers.

The Māori jokingly named them Tarara, as their rapid conversation in their native tongue sounded like 'ta-ra-ra-ra-ra' to Māori ears. Many Croatian men married local *wahine* (women), founding clans that have left several of today's famous Māori with Croatian surnames, such as singer Margaret Urlich and former All Black Frano Botica. You'll find large Tarara communities in the Far North, Dargaville and West Auckland.

HOKIANGA

The Hokianga Harbour stretches out its skinny tentacles to become the fourth-biggest in the country. Its ruggedly beautiful landscape is painted in every shade of green and brown. The water itself is rendered the colour of ginger ale by the bush streams that feed it.

Of all the remote parts of Northland, this is the pocket that feels the most removed from the mainstream. Pretension has no place here. Isolated, predominantly Māori communities nestle around the harbour's many inlets, as they have done for centuries. Discovered by legendary explorer Kupe, it's been settled by Ngāpuhi since the 14th century. Hippies arrived in the late 1960s and their legacy is a thriving little artistic scene.

Many of the roads remain unsealed, and, while tourism dollars are channelled eastward to the Bay of Islands, this truly fascinating corner of the country remains remarkably undeveloped, just as many of the locals like it.

❶ Getting There & Away

The only public transport is a weekly Hokianga Link (p176) minibus service between Kerikeri and Omapere, which expands to twice weekly in summer.

Kohukohu

POP 165

Quick, someone slap a preservation order on Kohukohu before it's too late. There can be few places in New Zealand where a Victorian village full of interesting kauri buildings has been so completely preserved with hardly a modern monstrosity to be seen. During the height of the kauri industry it was a busy town with a sawmill, a shipyard, two newspapers and banks. These days it's a very quiet backwater on the north side of the Hokianga Harbour, 4km from the Rawene car ferry.

Village Arts   GALLERY

(☑ 09-405 5827; www.villagearts.co.nz; 1376 Kohukohu Rd; ◷ 10am-3pm) A sophisticated surprise in such a small place, this volunteer-run gallery fills a restored heritage building with ever-changing exhibitions – mainly from Hokianga artists.

Tree House   HOSTEL $

(☑ 09-405 5855; www.treehouse.co.nz; 168 West Coast Rd; sites/dm/s/d from $20/32/66/82; ℗)

One of the country's best hostels, the Tree House has dorm rooms in the wood-lined main building and brightly painted little cottages set among the surrounding fruit and nut trees. Bathrooms are shared and there's a communal kitchen and dining space. This quiet retreat is 2km from the ferry terminus (turn sharp left as you come off the ferry from Rawene).

Koke Cafe   CAFE $

(☑ 09-405 5808; 1374 Kohukohu Rd; mains $8-16; ◷ 8am-4pm Wed-Sun, extended hours in summer) Set up on the side terrace of the Kohukohu Hotel, this little pavement cafe serves decent coffee and simple food including bagels, pies and cooked breakfasts.

❶ Getting There & Away

There's no public transport, so you'll need your own vehicle. Look forward to the scenic **ferry crossing** (☑ 09-405 2602; www.fndc.govt.nz; car/campervan/motorcycle $20/40/5, passenger $2; ◷ 7.30am-8pm) across the harbour to only slightly less-sleepy Rawene.

Rawene

POP 471

Founded shortly after nearby Horeke, Rawene was New Zealand's third European settlement. A surprising number of historic buildings (including six churches!) remain from a time when the harbour was considerably busier than it is now. Information boards outline a heritage trail of the main sights.

No 1 Parnell   GALLERY

(☑ 09-405 7520; www.no1parnell.weebly.com; 1 Parnell St; ◷ 9am-4.30pm) Occupying a century-old corner building originally built as a grocery store, this upmarket commercial gallery exhibits interesting work by local artists alongside some from further afield. There's a sun-filled cafe and a small book-shop attached.

Rawene Holiday Park   HOLIDAY PARK $$

(☑ 09-405 7720; www.raweneholidaypark.co.nz; 1 Marmon St West; sites from $18, unit with/without bathroom $130/65; ◷ ☀) Tent sites shelter in the bush at this nicely managed hilltop park. The cabins range from basic units where you'll need to bring your own linen (or pay extra to hire a set) to fully made-up units with kitchenettes. The on-site pool enjoys million-dollar views.

BAY OF ISLANDS & NORTHLAND KOHUKOHU

HOREKE & AROUND

Tiny Horeke was New Zealand's second European settlement after Russell. A Wesleyan mission operated here from 1828 to 1855, while in 1840, 3000 Ngāpuhi gathered here for what was the single biggest signing of the Treaty of Waitangi. Nowadays it's an all-but-forgotten hamlet, except that it is the western end point of the Pou Herenga Tai Twin Coast Cycle Trail (p165).

Completed in 1839, the **Māngungu Mission** (🖉 09-405 9734; www.mangungumission. co.nz; Motukiore Rd; adult/child $10/3.50; ⊙10am-3pm Sat-Mon only Dec-Jun) contains relics of the missionaries who once inhabited it, and of Horeke's shipbuilding past. In the grounds there's a large stone cross and a simple wooden church. Māngungu is 1km down the unsealed road leading along the harbour from Horeke village.

The rustic **Horeke Hotel** (🖉 09-401 9133; www.horekehotel.nz; 2118 Horeke Rd; ⊙prebooked meals only, call ahead) is reputedly NZ's oldest pub – the first cold one was poured back in 1826 – and on occasional weekends during summer the garden bar rocks with live music. There's bookable simple, clean accommodation (room $130) with harbour views if you want to stay over. Bikes are available to hire too. However, day-trippers are discouraged as the natural resources are finite here.

There is no public transport to Horeke, so the only way to get here is by bike or car. The main sealed approach to town is Rangiahua Rd, heading south from SH1. Horeke Rd, heading north from SH12, is rough and unsealed.

Boatshed Cafe
CAFE **$**

(🖉 09-405 7728; www.facebook.com/boatshed caferawene; 8 Clendon Esplanade; mains $8.50-15; ⊙8.30am-4pm) You can eat overlooking the water in Hokianga's best cafe, which occupies a historic boat shed near the car ferry. It's a cute place with excellent food and a gift shop that sells local art and crafts.

❶ Getting There & Away

A car ferry (p183) heads to the northern side of the Hokianga, docking 4km south of Kohukohu at least hourly. You can buy your ticket for this 15-minute ride on board. It usually leaves Rawene on the half-hour and the north side on the hour.

You can request a pickup by the Hokianga Link (p176) minivan by calling the Opononi i-SITE. Services head between Opononi (30 minutes) and Kerikeri (one hour) on Thursdays, as well as Tuesdays in summer.

Opononi & Omapere

POP 414

Although they were once separate villages, Opononi and Omapere have now merged into one continuous coastal community spread along a beautiful stretch of coast near the south head of the Hokianga Harbour. The water's much clearer here and good for swimming, and views are dominated by the mountainous sand dunes across the water at North Head. If you're approaching Omapere from the south, the view of the harbour is nothing short of spectacular.

◉ Sights

Arai-te-uru
Recreation Reserve
NATURE RESERVE

(Signal Station Rd, Omapere) Covering the southern headland of the Hokianga Harbour, this reserve offers magnificent views over the harbour and along the wild west coast. A short walk leads to the site of an old signal station built to assist ships making the treacherous passage into the Hokianga. It closed in 1951 due to a decline in ships entering the harbour. A track also heads down to pretty little **Martin's Bay**.

↪ Tours

Footprints Waipoua
CULTURAL

(🖉 09-405 8207; www.footprintswaipoua.co.nz; Copthorne, 334 SH12, Omapere; adult/child $105/45;) 🖉 Led by Māori guides, this four-hour twilight tour into Waipoua Forest is a fantastic introduction to both the culture and the forest giants. Tribal history and stories are shared, and mesmerising *karakia* are recited before the gargantuan trees. Daytime tours ($90) are also available, but the twilight tours amplify the sense of spirituality.

Hokianga Express Charters
ADVENTURE

(🖉 021 405 872; hkexpress@xtra.co.nz; Opononi Jetty; adult/child $27/17; ▣) Take a boat ride across to the north side of the harbour and attack the giant sand dunes armed with a boogie board for a swift descent; at high tide you can skim straight out over the water.

The boat departs daily in summer (weather permitting) and on demand at other times, but bookings are essential regardless.

🛏 Sleeping

Globetrekkers Lodge   HOSTEL $
(☑ 09-405 8183; www.globetrekkerslodge.com; 281 SH12, Omapere; dm/s/d $29/54/70; 🛜) Unwind in casual style at this homey hostel with harbour views and bright dorms. Private rooms don't have their own bathroom but there are plenty of thoughtful touches, such as writing desks, mirrors, art and fluffy towels. There's a stereo but no TV, encouraging plenty of schmoozing in the grapevine-draped barbecue area.

Copthorne Hotel & Resort   HOTEL $$
(☑ 09-405 8737; www.millenniumhotels.com; 336 SH12, Omapere; r/apt from $150/200; 🛜🏊) This ideally positioned beachfront resort consists of a hodgepodge of buildings from different eras. The original Victorian villa at its centre is an attractive spot for a summer's drink or a brasserie-style meal overlooking the lawns and sea.

Kokohuia Lodge   B&B $$$
(☑ 021 779 927; www.kokohuialodge.co.nz; 101 Kokohuia Rd, Omapere; r $320; 🛜) 🌿 Luxury and ecofriendly practices combine at this B&B, nestled in regenerating native bush high above the silvery dune-fringed expanse of the Hokianga Harbour. Solar energy and organic and free-range produce all feature, but there's no trade-off for luxury in the modern and stylish accommodation.

Hokianga Haven   APARTMENT $$$
(☑ 09-405 8285; www.hokiangahaven.co.nz; 226 SH12, Omapere; r $220; 🛜) Fall asleep only steps from the beach in this spacious self-contained studio apartment tucked underneath a modern house. An additional queen room is available for friends or family travelling together. Alternative healing therapies can be arranged.

🍴 Eating & Drinking

Landing Cafe   CAFE $
(☑ 09-405 8169; www.thelandingcafe.co.nz; 29 SH12, Opononi; mains $10-15; ⊙ 9am-3pm; 🛜) Stylish Kiwiana decor combines with good coffee at this appealing place attached to the tourist office. Grab a table on the expansive deck and tuck into scrambled eggs with smoked salmon while gazing over the water. It's head and shoulders above other local eateries.

Opononi Hotel   PUB
(☑ 09-405 8858; www.opononihotel.com; 19 SH12, Opononi) Try to score an outside table at this laid-back local pub (mains $13 to $36) so you can take in the improbable views of Opononi's massive sand dunes just across the harbour. There are regular live gigs in summer and it's a good place to watch a game of rugby with the locals.

ℹ Information

Opononi i-SITE (☑ 09-405 8869; www.hokiangatourism.org.nz; 29 SH12, Opononi; ⊙ 8.30am-5pm) Excellent information office with a good range of local souvenirs.

ℹ Getting There & Away

A Hokianga Link (p176) minivan heads between Omapere and Kerikeri ($15, 1½ hours) on Thursdays. From December to March it also operates on Tuesdays.

KAURI COAST

Apart from the odd bluff and river, this coast is basically unbroken and undeveloped for the 110km between the Hokianga and Kaipara Harbours. The main reason for coming here is to marvel at the kauri forests, one of the great natural highlights of New Zealand. If you're a closet tree hugger, you'll need 8m-long arms to get them around some of the big boys here.

There are few stores or eateries and no ATMs north of Dargaville, so stock up beforehand. Trampers should check DOC's website (www.doc.govt.nz) for walks in the area.

ℹ Getting There & Away

Te Wai Ora Coachlines (p188) has a weekly shuttle between Dargaville and Auckland.

Waipoua Forest

The highlight of Northland's west coast, this superb forest sanctuary – established in 1952 after much public pressure – is the largest remnant of the once-extensive kauri forests of northern New Zealand. The forest road (SH12) stretches for 18km and passes some huge trees – a kauri can reach 60m in height and have a trunk more than 5m in diameter.

Control of the forest has been returned to Te Roroa, the local *iwi,* as part of a settlement for Crown breaches of the Treaty of Waitangi. Te Roroa runs the Waipoua Forest Visitor Centre, cafe and camping ground near the south end of the park.

⭐ **Te Matua Ngahere**   LANDMARK
From the Kauri Walks car park, a 20-minute walk leads past the **Four Sisters**, a graceful stand of four tall trees fused together at the base, to Te Matua Ngahere (The Father of the Forest). At 30m, he has a significant presence. Reinforced by a substantial girth – he's the fattest living kauri (16.4m) – the tree presides over a clearing surrounded by mature trees resembling mere matchsticks in comparison. It's estimated that he could be up to 3000 years old.

A 30-minute (one way) path leads from near the Four Sisters to **Yakas**, the seventh-largest kauri.

⭐ **Tāne Mahuta**   LANDMARK
Near the north end of the park, not far from the road, stands mighty Tāne Mahuta, named for the Māori forest god. At 51.5m, with a 13.8m girth and wood mass of 244.5 cu metres, he's the largest kauri alive, and has been holding court here for somewhere between 1200 and 2000 years. He's easy to find and access, with a well-labelled car park (complete with coffee cart) on the highway.

Waipoua Forest Campground   CAMPGROUND $
(☑ 09-439 6445; www.teroroa.iwi.nz/visit-waipoua; 1 Waipoua River Rd; sites/units from $15/60; ℗) Situated next to the Waipoua River and the visitor centre, this peaceful camping ground offers hot showers, flush toilets and a kitchen. The cabins are extremely spartan, with unmade squab beds (bring your own linen or hire it).

Waipoua Lodge   B&B $$$
(☑ 09-439 0422; www.waipoualodge.co.nz; 4748 SH12; ste $650; ℗ 🛜) 🏊 This fine old villa at the southern edge of the forest has four luxurious, spacious suites, which were originally the stables, the woolshed and the calf-rearing pen.

The business was for sale at the end of 2019, so future plans are unknown.

ℹ **Information**

Waipoua Forest Visitor Centre (☑ 09-439 6445; www.teroroa.iwi.nz/visit-waipoua; 1 Waipoua River Rd; ⊙ 9am-2pm daily Nov-Mar, Wed-Sun Apr-Oct) Te Roroa's information centre has an interesting exhibition on the kauri forests, and a cafe. It can also arrange guided tours ($25) and cultural activities, and there's a swimming hole, picnic area and walking track nearby.

ℹ **Getting There & Away**

There is no public transport to Waipoua Forest. If you don't have a car, consider taking a tour from Omapere with Footprints Waipoua (p184) or from Paihia with Fullers Great Sights (p163).

Trounson Kauri Park

This 586-hectare stand of old-growth forest has been subject to active predator eradication since 1995 and has become an important mainland refuge for threatened native bird species. An easy half-hour (1.8km) loop walk leads from the picnic area by the road, passing through beautiful forest with streams, some fine kauri stands, a couple of fallen trees, and two pairs of trees with conjoined trunks known as the Four Sisters.

The neighbouring holiday park runs guided night walks (adult/child $30/20) or self-guided kiwi-spotting walks (kit hire $25) that explain the flora and nocturnal wildlife that thrives here.

Kauri Coast Top 10 Holiday Park   HOLIDAY PARK $
(☑ 09-439 0621; www.kauricoasttop10.co.nz; 7 Opouteke Rd; sites from $44, units with/without bathroom from $92/118; ℗ 🛜 🐕) Set beside the Kaihu River, 2km from SH12, this excellent holiday park has attractive motel units and a brace of tidy cabins, with or without their own bathroom and kitchen. As well as its famed guided night walks, there's a swimming hole and an adventure playground with a flying fox and a trampoline.

DOC Trounson Kauri Park Campsite   CAMPGROUND $
(www.doc.govt.nz; Trounson Park Rd; sites from $20; ℗) A step up from most DOC campsites, this one has both powered and unpowered sites, and a communal kitchen, flush toilets and hot showers.

ℹ **Getting There & Away**

There is no public transport to Trounson Kauri Park. If you're approaching by car from the north, it's easier to take the second turn-off to the park, near Kaihu, which avoids a rough unsealed road.

KAI IWI LAKES

These three trout-filled freshwater dune lakes nestle together near the coast, 12km off SH12. The largest, Taharoa, has blue water fringed with sandy patches. Lake Waikere (meaning 'Rippling Waters') is popular with waterskiers, while Lake Kai Iwi (Food for the Tribe) is good for kayaking and swimming, as it's off limits to motorised craft. A half-hour walk leads from the lakes to the coast and it's another two hours to reach the base of volcanic Maunganui Bluff (460m); the hike up and down it takes five hours.

At Kai Iwi Lakes Campground (☑ 09-439 0986; www.kaiiwicamp.nz; Domain Rd; adult/child $15/8; P), the largest of the two campsites at the side of Lake Taharoa, Pine Beach has flush toilets and coin-operated hot showers. More sites are available at Promenade Point (cold showers only).

There is no public transport here. From SH12, it is a 12km drive to the coast.

Baylys Beach

Baylys Beach is a village of brightly coloured beach baches and a few new mansions, 12km from Dargaville (where you'll have to return for the food options beyond a solitary diner, Sharkeys Takeaways, in this surf town).

It lies on 100km-long Ripiro Ocean Beach, a surf-pounded stretch of coast that has been the site of many shipwrecks.

Baylys Beach Horse Treks HORSE RIDING (☑ 027 697 9610; www.baylysbeachhorsetreks.webs.com; 1/2hr beach ride $70/125) Offers half-hour riding lessons ($25) and horse treks along the broad expanse of Baylys Beach. The minimum age for beach rides is 14 years, unless the child is experienced. Younger children can take an hour-long paddock ride ($40).

Baylys Beach Holiday Park HOLIDAY PARK $ (☑ 09-439 6349; www.baylysbeach.co.nz; 24 Seaview Rd; sites $20, units $80-130; P🐾) This midsized camping ground has attractive cream-and-green units scattered around a lawn circled by pohutukawa trees. Options range from basic cabins to a self-contained cottage sleeping six. It also rents quad bikes and takes bookings for horse treks.

Sunset View Lodge B&B $$ (☑ 021 231 4114; www.sunsetviewlodge.co.nz; 7 Alcemene Lane; r $175-195; ⊙Jul-May; P🐾) If gin-in-hand sunset gazing is your thing, this large, modern terracotta-coloured B&B will fit the bill. The upstairs rooms have terrific ocean views from the deck, which also overlooks a pool. Children are not permitted.

❶ Getting There & Away

There is no public transport to Baylys Beach. Most travellers visit from Dargaville or en route to/from the Waipoua Forest.

Dargaville

POP 4251

Languid and expansive like the Northern Wairoa River the town is built beside, Dargaville was once a thriving river port exporting felled kauri timber and gum. It's now an unpretentious agricultural centre where heritage weatherboard houses rub shoulders with stockyards. Local diversions include driving along Ripiro Beach and paddling on Kai Iwi Lakes.

The town has basic motels and a hostel, and there are further camping and more luxurious options at nearby (12km) Baylys Beach.

Dargaville Museum MUSEUM (☑ 09-439 7555; www.dargavillemuseum.co.nz; Harding Park; adult/child $15/5; ⊙9am-5pm Nov-Mar, to 4pm Apr-Oct) The hilltop Dargaville Museum is more interesting than most regional museums. There's a large gumdigging display, plus maritime, Māori and musical-instrument sections, and a neat model railway. Outside, the masts of the *Rainbow Warrior* are mounted at a lookout near a *pā* site, and there's a recreation of a gumdiggers' camp.

Ripiro Beach BEACH The beach is a gazetted highway: you can drive along the sand at low tide, although it is primarily for 4WDs. Despite being NZ's longest driveable beach, it's less well known and hence less travelled than Ninety Mile Beach (but no, your car-rental insurance won't cover you if you get stuck). Mobile phone coverage is patchy too.

Blah, Blah, Blah... CAFE $$ (☑ 09-439 6300; 101 Victoria St; breakfast $10-19, lunch $10-20, dinner $22-35; ⊙9am-3.30pm Sun & Mon, to 8pm Tue-Sat; 🐾) The number-one eatery and best bar in central Dargaville has

WORTH A TRIP

POUTO POINT

A narrow spit descends south of Dargaville, bordered by the Tasman Sea and Wairoa River, and comes to an abrupt halt at the entrance of NZ's biggest harbour, the Kaipara. It's an incredibly remote headland, punctuated by dozens of petite dune lakes and the lonely **Kaipara Lighthouse** (built from kauri in 1884). Less than 10km separates Kaipara Harbour's north and south heads, but if you were to drive between the two you'd cover 267km.

A 4WD can be put to its proper use on the ocean-hugging 71km stretch of beach from Glinks Gully near Dargaville. The DOC's *Pouto Hidden Treasures* is a helpful guide for motorists, with tips for protecting both your car and the fragile ecosystem. It can be downloaded at www.doc.govt.nz.

a garden area, hip music, bistro-style food, and beer, wine and cocktails. The global menu includes excellent cooked breakfasts, pizza and steak.

ℹ️ Information

DOC Te Tai Kauri/Kauri Coast Office (☑09-439 3450; www.doc.govt.nz; 150 Colville Rd; ⊙8am-4.30pm Mon-Fri) An area office rather than a visitor centre, but a good source of Northland tramping and camping information.

ℹ️ Getting There & Away

Te Wai Ora Coachlines (☑027 482 2950; www.tewaioracoachlines.com; adult/child $50/40) Runs a prebookable shuttle service between Dargaville and Auckland (2½ hours).

Matakohe

POP 400

Apart from its rural charms, the key reason for visiting Matakohe is the superb Kauri Museum. The museum shop stocks mementos crafted from kauri wood and gum.

Facing the museum is the tiny kauri-built **Matakohe Pioneer Church** (1867), which served both Methodists and Anglicans, and acted as the community's hall and school. Nearby, you can wander through a historic **schoolhouse** (1878) and **post office/telephone exchange** (1909).

⭐**Kauri Museum**   MUSEUM
(☑09-431 7417; www.kau.nz; 5 Church Rd; adult/child $25/8; ⊙9am-5pm) 🌿 The giant cross-sections of trees at this superb museum are astounding in themselves, but the entire industry is animated through life-sized reproductions of a pioneer sawmill, a boarding house, a bushman's hut and a Victorian home – along with photos, artefacts, and fabulous furniture and marquetry. The Gum Room holds a wonderful collection of kauri gum, the jewel-like amber substance that can be carved and sculpted. Working with local *iwi,* a space has opened with Māori artefacts from the region.

Beyond the museum, leave time to visit the school house, post office and gardens.

Matakohe Holiday Park   HOLIDAY PARK $
(☑09-431 6431; www.matakoheholidaypark.co.nz; 66 Church Rd; sites $38, units with/without bathroom from $120/65; P🖰) 🌿 This well-kept little park has modern amenities, plenty of space, a playground and good views of Kaipara Harbour. Accommodation ranges from basic cabins without bathrooms to self-contained two-bedroom motel units.

Matakohe House   B&B $$
(☑09-431 7091; www.matakohehousebnb.com; 24 Church Rd; r from $170; P🛜) This B&B inhabits a pretty villa near the Kauri Museum. The simply furnished rooms open onto a wraparound veranda and offer winning touches, such as complimentary port and chocolates. There's also a small kitchen for making hot beverages and a communal lounge with a piano.

ℹ️ Getting There & Away

Te Wai Ora Coachlines runs a bus to Dargaville leaving Auckland on Friday night and returning on Sunday night. This service stops at Matakohe's Kauri Museum on request.

Waikato & the Coromandel Peninsula

Best Places to Eat

➡ Bistro at the Falls Retreat (p238)

➡ Wharf Road (p226)

➡ Mr Pickles (p197)

➡ Rock-It Kitchen (p201)

➡ Port Road Project (p236)

Best Places to Stay

➡ Earthstead (p206)

➡ Solscape (p200)

➡ Bow Street Studios (p201)

➡ Hush Boutique Accommodation (p225)

➡ Aroha Mountain Lodge (p209)

Why Go?

Visitors here can take in the verdant rolling hills lining New Zealand's mighty Waikato River, and adrenaline junkies can surf at Raglan or undertake extreme underground pursuits in the extraordinary Waitomo Caves.

But this is also Tainui country. In the 1850s this powerful Māori tribal coalition elected a king to resist the loss of land and sovereignty. The fertile Waikato was forcibly taken from them, but they retained control of the rugged King Country to within a whisker of the 20th century.

To the northeast, the Coromandel Peninsula juts into the Pacific, forming the Hauraki Gulf's eastern boundary. The peninsula's east coast has some of the North Island's best white-sand beaches, and the muddy wetlands and picturesque stony bays of the west coast have long been a refuge for alternative lifestylers. Down the middle, the mountains are criss-crossed with walking tracks, allowing hikers to explore large tracts of isolated bush studded with kauri trees.

When to Go

➡ February and March are balmy and much quieter around the Coromandel Peninsula, with settled weather and smaller crowds. Raglan's surf breaks are popular year-round.

➡ Beachy accommodation in Waihi, Whitianga, Whangamatā and Raglan peaks during the summer holidays from Christmas until the end of January. New Year's Eve in particular can be very busy.

Waikato & the Coromandel Peninsula Highlights

1 Far North Coromandel (p227) Travelling remote gravel roads under a crimson canopy of ancient pohutukawa trees.

2 Te Whanganui-A-Hei Marine Reserve (p230) Kayaking around hidden islands, caves and bays.

3 Karangahake Gorge (p238) Penetrating the mystical depths of the dense bush.

4 Hahei Beach (p232) Watching the offshore islands glow in the dying haze of a summer sunset.

5 Waitomo Caves (p211) Seeking subterranean stimulation and trying black-water rafting.

6 Raglan (p200) Hitting the surf (and then the pub) at this unhurried surf town.

7 Sanctuary Mountain Maungatautari (p207) Hiking through an inland island paradise.

8 Hobbiton Movie Set Tours (p208) Channelling your inner Bilbo or Frodo at this fascinating film set.

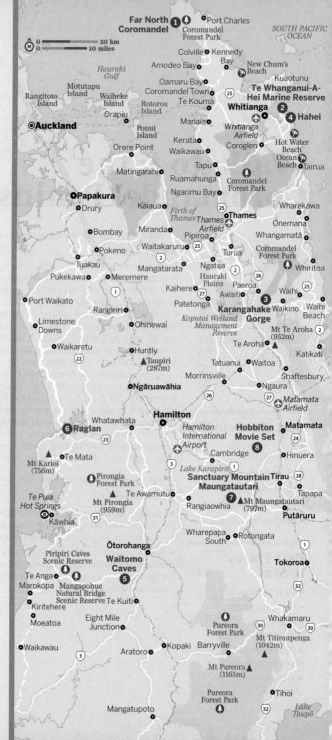

ℹ Getting There & Away

Hamilton is the region's transport hub, with its airport (p199) servicing extensive domestic routes. Buses link the city to everywhere in the North Island. Most inland towns are also well connected by bus routes, but the remote coastal communities (apart from Mōkau on SH3) are less well served.

Transport options on the Coromandel Peninsula are more limited, and the beaches and coastline of the area are most rewarding with independent transport.

WAIKATO

History

By the time Europeans started to arrive, this region – stretching as far north as Auckland's Manukau Harbour – had long been the homeland of the Waikato tribes, descended from the Tainui migration. In settling this land, the Waikato tribes displaced or absorbed tribes from earlier migrations.

Initially European contact was on Māori terms and to the advantage of the local people. Their fertile land, which was already cultivated with kumara (sweet potato) and other crops, was well suited to the introduction of new fruits and vegetables. By the 1840s the Waikato economy was booming, with bulk quantities of produce exported to the settlers in Auckland and beyond.

Relations between the two cultures soured during the 1850s, largely due to the colonists' pressure to purchase Māori land. In response, a confederation of tribes united to elect a king to safeguard their interests, forming what became known as the Kīngitanga (King Movement).

In July 1863 Governor Grey sent a huge force to invade the Waikato and exert colonial control. After almost a year of fighting, known as the Waikato War, the Kingites retreated south to what became branded as King Country.

The war resulted in the confiscation of 3600 sq km of land, much of which was given to colonial soldiers to farm and defend. In 1995 the Waikato tribes received a full Crown apology for the wrongful invasion and confiscation of their lands, as well as a $170 million package, including the return of land that the Crown still held.

Hamilton

POP 170,000

Landlocked cities in an island nation are never going to have the glamorous appeal of their coastal cousins. Rotorua compensates with boiling mud and Taupō has its lake, but Hamilton, despite the majestic Waikato River, is more prosaic.

The city definitely has appeal, with vibrant bars and excellent restaurants and cafes around Hood and Victoria Sts. You'll eat really well after visiting highlights like Hamilton Gardens and Waikato Museum.

The grey-green Waikato River rolls right through town, but the city's layout largely ignores its presence: unless you're driving across a bridge you'll hardly know it's there. Thankfully, a newly completed promenade to the right of Riverbank Lane (p202) now affords excellent views of the river.

Most people blast along SH1 from Auckland to Hamilton in about 1½ hours, but the upper Waikato has some interesting diversions, including **Turangawaewae Marae** (☑ 07-824 5189; 29 River Rd) at Ngāruawāhia.

◉ Sights

★**Waikato Museum**   MUSEUM
(☑ 07-838 6606; www.waikatomuseum.co.nz; 1 Grantham St; by donation; ⊙ 10am-5pm; ☕) **FREE** The excellent Waikato Museum has several main areas: an art gallery; interactive science galleries; a Waikato River exhibition; and Tainui galleries housing Māori treasures, including the magnificently carved *waka taua* (war canoe), *Te Winikawaka*. The museum also runs a rigorous programme of public events. Admission is charged for some displays, and there is a full schedule of one-off and visiting exhibitions.

★**Hamilton Gardens**   GARDENS
(☑ 07-838 6782; www.hamiltongardens.co.nz; Cobham Dr; guided tour adult/child $20/13; ⊙ enclosed gardens 7.30am-7.30pm Oct-Mar, to 5.30pm Apr-Sep, info centre 9am-5pm, guided tours 11am Tue, Thu & Sun; ☕) **FREE** Spread over 50 hectares southeast of the city centre, Hamilton Gardens incorporates a large park, a cafe, a restaurant, and extravagant themed and enclosed gardens. There are separate Italian Renaissance, Chinese, Japanese, English and American gardens, and the Char Bagh Garden is inspired by the gardens near India's famed Taj Mahal. Equally interesting are the

WAIKATO & THE COROMANDEL PENINSULA HAMILTON

HIKING IN THE COROMANDEL

COROMANDEL WALKWAY

START/END STONY BAY
DURATION 6–7 HOURS
DISTANCE 20KM
DIFFICULTY MODERATE

This remote and wild coastal walk near the northern tip of the Coromandel Peninsula combines thick forest, dramatic coastline and views of the Hauraki Gulf islands.

Despite being just 60 straight-line kilometres from Auckland, and 100km by road from Thames, there's a remoteness to the Coromandel Peninsula's northern tip that mere distances can't portray. Forming a boundary between the Pacific Ocean and Hauraki Gulf, there's a real sense of wildness where the sea storms ashore on Poley Bay, and Sugar Loaf and its entourage of rocks stand like petrified waves. With rugged coastline, unruly seas and gorgeous sections of bush, the Coromandel Walkway is a fitting crown for the peninsula, and if the stunning drive up the Coromandel to get here doesn't create expectation, you're not paying attention.

There are DOC campgrounds at both ends of the trail, so you may want to linger for a while either side of your hike, or you can throw on the backpack and turn it into a two-day hike, staying the night at Fletcher Bay.

The walkway can be walked in either direction, but the dramatic surprise of rising to the main lookout point above Shag Bay is enhanced if you walk from Stony Bay, having not yet sighted the coast around Poley Bay and Sugar Loaf.

If you're looking for a shorter hike, the most spectacular section of the walkway is between Stony Bay and Poley Bay.

The postcard-perfect Coromandel Peninsula is criss-crossed with walking tracks, allowing trampers to explore large tracts of untamed bush where kauri trees once towered and are starting to do so again.

KAUAERANGA KAURI TRAIL

START/END KAUAERANGA VALLEY RD
DURATION 2 DAYS
DISTANCE 14KM
DIFFICULTY MODERATE

A hike up the popular Kauaeranga Valley, this trail features historic logging trails and regenerating forests. A side trip to the lofty Pinnacles (p227) gives spectacular views to both coasts.

The 719 sq km of rugged, forested reserves that make up the Coromandel Forest Park are spread across the Coromandel Peninsula. There are more than 30 hikes through the forest park, with the most popular area being the Kauaeranga Valley, which cuts into the Coromandel Range behind Thames.

A logging boom took place in the Coromandel Range during the late 19th century, when stands of massive kauri were extracted. Today, the Kauaeranga Valley is filled with remnants of its lumbering past: packhorse trails, tramway clearings and many old kauri dams. Dancing Camp Dam (close to Pinnacles Hut) has been partly restored, and is one of the few dams which are not now inaccessible and/or unrecognisable.

The DOC Kauaeranga Visitor Centre (p227) has interesting displays about the kauri forest and its history. Maps and conservation resources are available for purchase and staff dispense advice. The centre is 14km off SH25; it's a further 9km along a gravel road to the start of the trails.

Pinnacles Hut ($20 must be booked in advance year-round; DOC hut passes and tickets are not valid. The hut has gas stoves, a solid fuel heater, running water, mattresses, a barbecue and solar-powered lighting. The old hut is now used as a residence for a permanent hut warden.

There are eight self-registration scenic campsites (per person $15) around the valley, all in appealing settings with water supply and toilets. There are also backcountry campsites ($5) near Pinnacles Hut, at Billygoat Basin and Moss Creek.

KARANGAHAKE GORGE

START/END KARANGAHAKE HALL
DURATION 5–6 HOURS
DISTANCE 16.5KM
DIFFICULTY EASY

Combining natural and human history, the Karangahake Gorge hike through a former gold-rich gorge reveals dramatic views and a unique walk through mining remnants.

As SH2 journeys between Auckland and Tauranga it passes through the dramatic Karangahake Gorge, creating one of the most scenic short stretches of road on the North Island. Running along the opposite bank of the gorge, which is cut by the Ohinemuri River, is a network of walking trails that are even more lovely.

This hike follows a shared hiking/cycling trail through the most beautiful stretch of the gorge, branching off onto hiking-only trails that explore the remnants of the gorge's gold-rush days, at one point even burrowing through tunnels carved by miners.

The hike is a NZ rarity – predominantly flat – with a quirky cafe stop at the turnaround point. By hiking standards, this is about as civilised as it gets.

The most spectacular section is the lower gorge and Windows area, so if you only have half a day, walk the Railway Tunnel Loop, which passes through the lower gorge and back through the tunnel, taking in the Windows along the way. Note that the section of the Windows Walk through the lower Waitawheta Gorge can sometimes close due to rockfalls or instability of the cliffs.

Hamilton

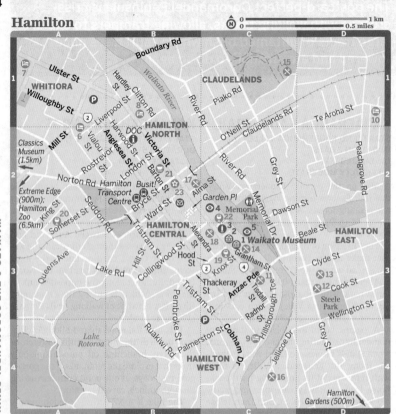

sustainable Productive Garden Collection, fragrant herb garden and precolonisation Māori Te Parapara garden. Look for the impressive *Nga Uri O Hinetuparimaunga* (Earth Blanket) sculpture at the main gates.

Other highlights include a Tudor-style garden and a tropical garden with more than 200 different warm-climate species. A garden inspired by a Katherine Mansfield short story opened in late 2018, and the development of a surrealist garden is also under way. To get to the gardens, catch bus 29 (adult/child $3.30/2.20) from the Hamilton Transport Centre (p199).

Zealong Tea Estate
PLANTATION

(☑ 0800 932 566; www.zealong.com; 495 Gordonton Rd, Gordonton; tea experience adult/child $49/25; ☺ 10am-5pm Nov-Apr, Tue-Sun May-Oct, tours 9.30am & 2pm) Interesting tours learning about the only tea plantation in NZ, located around 10km northeast of Hamilton. Delicious high-tea experiences offering tea-infused treats are

also available (adult/child $49), as is a full cafe menu (mains $28 to $39).

Waikato River
RIVER

Bush-covered walkways run along both sides of the river and provide the city's green belt. Jogging paths continue to the boardwalk circling Lake Rotoroa, west of the centre. Memorial Park is closer to town and has the remains of PS *Rangiriri* – an iron-clad, steam-powered gunboat from the Waikato War – embedded in the riverbank. Near the Riverbank Lane development, there is a terraced area with seating offering a brilliant view of the river.

Riverbank Lane
AREA

(www.theriverbanklane.co.nz; Victoria St) Explore this laneway with good restaurants and cafes and interesting shopping. To the right of the lane, a recently developed outdoor area has good views of, and access to, the Waikato River.

Hamilton

Riff Raff　　MONUMENT
(www.riffraffstatue.org; Victoria St) One of Hamilton's more unusual public artworks is a life-sized statue of *Rocky Horror Picture Show* writer Richard O'Brien, aka Riff Raff, the time-warping alien from the planet Transsexual. It looks over a small park on the site of the former Embassy Theatre where O'Brien worked as a hairdresser, though it's hard to imagine 1960s Hamilton inspired the tale of bisexual alien decadence. Opposite the statue, the bright red 'Frankenfurter's Lab' actually conceals convenient public toilets.

Classics Museum　　MUSEUM
(☑07-957 2230; www.classicsmuseum.co.nz; 11 Railside Pl, Frankton; adult/child $20/8; ☺7am-3pm Mon-Fri, 8am-3pm Sat & Sun; 🚼) Travel back through time amid this collection of more than 100 classic cars from the first half of the 20th century. Even if you're not a motorhead, you'll still be dazzled by the crazy Amphicar and the cool Maserati and Corvette sports cars. The museum is just off SH1, northwest of central Hamilton.

Hamilton Zoo　　ZOO
(☑07-838 6720; www.hamiltonzoo.co.nz; 183 Brymer Rd; adult/child/family $26/12/71, tours extra; ☺9am-4.30pm, last entry 3pm) Hamilton Zoo houses 500-plus species including wily and curious chimpanzees. Guided-tour options include Face2Face opportunities to go behind the scenes to meet various animals, plus daily Meet the Keeper talks (free) from the critters' caregivers. The zoo is 8km northwest of Hamilton city centre.

ArtsPost　　GALLERY
(www.waikatomuseum.co.nz/artspost; 120 Victoria St; ☺10am-5pm) FREE This contemporary gallery and gift shop is housed in a grand former post office. It focuses on the best of local art: paintings, glass, prints, textiles and photography. The Hamilton i-SITE (p199) is also located here.

🏃 Activities

Waikato River Explorer　　CRUISE
(☑0800 139 756; www.waikatoexplorer.co.nz; Hamilton Gardens Jetty; adult/child $35/18; ☺usually Wed-Mon, daily 26 Dec-6 Feb) Scenic one-hour cruises along the Waikato River depart from near the Waikato Museum (p191) or from the Hamilton Gardens (p191) jetty. Days of departure vary, especially outside summer, so check the website for dates and times. Also see the website for other cruises incorporating wine tasting and one-way cruises (adult/child $20/10) linking the museum with the gardens or vice versa.

Extreme Edge　　CLIMBING
(☑07-847 5858; www.extremeedgehamilton.co.nz; 90 Greenwood St; day pass incl harness adult/child $19/15; ☺noon-9.30pm Mon-Fri, 9am-7pm Sat & Sun; 🚼) Near the Frankton train station, west of town, Extreme Edge has hyper-coloured climbing walls, 14m of which are overhanging. It also has a kids' climbing zone and free safety lessons.

Kiwi Balloon Company　　BALLOONING
(☑021 912 679, 07-843 8538; www.kiwiballooncompany.co.nz; adult/child $390/310) Float above lush

Waikato countryside. The whole experience takes about four hours and includes a champagne breakfast and an hour's flying time.

🎉 Festivals & Events

New Zealand Rugby Sevens   SPORTS
(www.sevens.co.nz; 128 Seddon Rd; ⊙late Jan) Held at Hamilton's Stadium Waikato, usually across the last weekend of January, this is the New Zealand leg of the international Rugby Sevens Series. Look forward to lots of running rugby from teams representing many countries. Favourites usually include New Zealand (of course...), Fiji and South Africa, and attending the event in fancy dress is definitely encouraged.

Hamilton Gardens Arts Festival   PERFORMING ARTS
(☑07-859 1317; www.hgaf.co.nz; ⊙Feb) Music, comedy, theatre, dance and movies, all served up alfresco in Hamilton Gardens (p191) during the last two weeks of February.

Balloons over Waikato   SPORTS
(☑07-856 7215; www.balloonsoverwaikato.co.nz; ⊙Mar) A colourful hot-air-balloon fest.

🛏 Sleeping

★City Centre B&B   B&B $
(☑07-838 1671; www.citycentrebnb.co.nz; 3 Anglesea St; r $99-125; @🛜🏊) At the quiet riverside end of a central city street (five minutes' walk from the action on Victoria and Hood Sts), this sparkling self-contained cottage apartment opens onto a swimming pool. There's also a bedroom available in a wing of the main house. Self-catering breakfast is provided. Minimum stay of two nights for the bedroom and a week for the cottage.

Backpackers Central   HOSTEL $
(☑07-839 1928; www.backpackerscentral.co.nz; 846 Victoria St; dm $37, s $59, r $79-94; @🛜) Well-run hostel with dorms and singles on one floor, doubles and family rooms on another – some with en-suite bathrooms and all with access to a shared kitchen and lounge. Worth considering as an alternative to a motel room if you're travelling as a couple or in a group.

Hamilton City Holiday Park   HOLIDAY PARK $
(☑07-855 8255; www.hamiltoncityholidaypark. co.nz; 14 Ruakura Rd; campsites/cabins/units from $40/65/90; @🛜) Simple cabins and leafy sites are the rule at this shady park. It's reasonably close to town (2km east of the centre) and very affordable.

Atrium on Ulster   MOTEL $$
(☑07-839 0839; www.atriumonulster.co.nz; 281 Ulster St; d $159-245; 🛜) Our pick as the best of the motels along Hamilton's Ulster St strip, slightly north of the central city. Studios and one- and two-bedroom apartments all feature stylish decor, facilities include a gym and hot tub, and the sporting attractions at Waikato Stadium are very close.

Anglesea Motel   MOTEL $$
(☑07-834 0010; www.angleseamotel.com; 36 Liverpool St; units from $145; @🛜🎾) Getting great feedback from travellers, the Anglesea has lots of space, friendly managers, a pool, squash and tennis courts, and not unstylish decor.

🍴 Eating

Befitting one of the North Island's biggest cities, Hamilton has a tasty selection of eateries. Around Victoria and Hood Sts you'll find the greatest diversity of eateries, including Vietnamese, Turkish, Mexican and Japanese. For authentic Asian flavours, check out the restaurant strip along Collingwood St, southwest of Victoria St. Across the river, Hamilton East is developing as a dining destination.

Duck Island Ice Cream   ICE CREAM $
(☑07-856 5948; www.duckislandicecream.co.nz; 300 Grey St; ice cream from $5.50; ⊙11am-9pm Sun-Wed, to 10pm Thu-Sat; 🚗🍴) A dazzling array of ever-changing flavours – how does white chocolate, macadamia and pomegranate sound? – makes Duck Island one of NZ's best ice-cream parlours. Try a tasting selection of eight different ice creams for $13 or special ice-cream tacos and sandwiches. There's also a convenient central city location (www.duckislandicecream.co.nz; 298 Victoria Street, Shop 5, Riverbank Lane; ⊙5-9pm Thu-Fri, noon-10pm Sat, noon-6pm Sat) back across the river in Riverbank Lane.

GG's Cafe   CAFE $
(☑07-974 3511; www.facebook.com/GGscafenz; 394 Grey St, Shed 6, Lovegrove Lane; snacks $7-10; ⊙7am-3pm Mon-Fri, 8am-2pm Sat; 🚗) 🌿 Located amid Lovegrove Lane's funky tangle, which includes a florist and a yoga studio, GG's serves up the best coffee across the river in Hamilton East. Take in the retro paraphernalia on the walls and try tasty homestyle baking – including good doughnuts and savoury pies – or regular soup specials and toasties filled with surprising ingredients. Regular vegan offerings too.

Banh Mi Caphe   VIETNAMESE $

(📞 07-839 1141; www.banhmicaphe.co.nz; 298 Victoria St, Riverbank Lane; snacks & mains $10-22; ⊘ noon-9pm Tue-Sat; 🖉) 🖊 Fresh spring rolls, Vietnamese banh mi (sandwiches) and steaming bowls of pho (noodle soup) feature at this hip spot channelling the backstreets of Hanoi. The menu features an OK selection of vegetarian and vegan dishes. Outdoor seating at the new Riverbank Lane location offers excellent views of the Waikato River.

Hamilton Farmers Market   MARKET $

(📞 022 639 1995; www.waikatofarmersmarkets.co.nz; Brooklyn Rd, Claudelands; ⊘ 8am-noon Sun; 🖈) Located northeast across the river in Claudelands, this farmers market is a Sunday-morning feast of local cheeses, baked goods and produce. A piping-hot and flaky Cornish pasty with beef, blue cheese and beer is a good way to start the day. Follow up with a cream-and-jam doughnut from Volare Bread. There's laid-back live music most weekends too.

⭐ Mr Pickles   BISTRO $$

(📞 07-839 7989; www.mrpickles.co.nz; 298 Victoria St, Riverbank Lane; shared plates $18-36; ⊘ noon-late Wed-Sat, noon-4pm & 6-9pm Sun) Mr Pickles is a standout in the Riverbank Lane development. Either sit at the bar near the open kitchen or outside with river views and enjoy shared plates with international influences. Highlights of our visit included lamb kofta and beef cheek croquettes, and platters are packed with cheese and charcuterie. Good cocktails and local Hamilton craft beers seal the deal.

⭐ Hayes Common   CAFE $$

(📞 027 537 1853; www.hayescommon.co.nz; cnr Plunket Tce & Jellicoe Dr, Hamilton East; mains $18-36; ⊘ 7.30am-4pm Sun-Tue, to 10pm Wed-Sat; 🖉) 🖊 Journey across to Hamilton East to this bustling eatery in a former garage. Thoroughly unpretentious, Hayes Common's versatile menu stretches from smoothie bowls for breakfast to chilli-butter-fried eggs or a hoison-spiced duck tortilla for lunch. Dinner options such as spiced Merino lamb are equally cosmopolitan, and the wine list and local craft beers on tap will ensure you linger.

Gothenburg   TAPAS $$

(📞 07-834 3562; www.gothenburg.co.nz; ANZ Centre, 21 Grantham St; shared plates $13-29; ⊘ 9am-11pm Mon-Fri, 11.30am-late Sat) One of our favourite Hamilton restaurants, Gothenburg showcases a scenic riverside spot with high

ceilings and a summer-friendly deck. The menu of shared plates spans the globe – try the pork and kimchi dumplings or the sweet potato gnocchi with a cashew and cumin cream – and the beer list features rotating taps from Scandinavian breweries and local Waikato craft brewers.

River Kitchen   CAFE $$

(📞 07-839 2906; www.theriverkitchen.co.nz; 217 Victoria St; mains $15-22; ⊘ 7am-4pm Mon-Fri, 8am-4pm Sat, to 3pm Sun; 🖉) River Kitchen does things with simple style: great coffee, cakes, gourmet breakfasts and fresh seasonal lunches (angle for the baked eggs with chorizo). It's the kind of place you visit for breakfast, come back to for lunch, then consider for breakfast the next day. We like the more spacious location, just a few doors down from the old digs.

Chim Choo Ree   MODERN NZ $$$

(📞 07-839 4329; www.chimchooree.co.nz; 14 Anzac Pde; mains $25-41; ⊘ 5pm-late Mon-Sat) In a heritage riverside building, Chim Choo Ree focuses on small plates such as confit pork belly, or spiced calamari with pickled cucumber and lemon mayo, plus larger, equally inventive mains using duck, lamb, tofu and snapper. Local foodies wash it all down with a great wine list and flavourful NZ craft beers. Leave room for dessert of coconut panna cotta.

ESSENTIAL WAIKATO & THE COROMANDEL PENINSULA

Eat Coromandel bivalves – mussels, oysters and scallops are local specialities.

Drink local Hamilton craft beer at Brewraucracy (p198).

Read *The Penguin History of New Zealand* (2003) by the late Michael King, a former Opoutere resident.

Listen to the native birdlife at Sanctuary Mountain Maungatautari (p207).

Watch passing schools of fish while snorkelling near Hahei (p232).

Celebrate at the annual Whangamata Beach Hop (p236).

Go green in off-the-grid tepees at Solscape (p200).

Go online at www.thecoromandel.com; www.hamiltonwaikato.com; www.kingcountry.co.nz.

Palate
MODERN NZ $$$

(☑07-834 2921; www.palaterestaurant.co.nz; 20 Alma St; mains $6-41; ⊙11.30am-2pm Tue-Fri, 5.30pm-late Tue-Sat) Simple, sophisticated Palate has a well-deserved reputation for lifting the culinary bar across regional NZ. The innovative menu features hearty highlights such as eye fillet steak with wasabi and sweet potato. The wine selection is one of Hamilton's finest, local craft breweries are well supported with seasonal brews on offer, and a good-value express lunch is $25 for two courses.

Drinking & Nightlife

The blocks around Victoria and Hood Sts make for a boozy bar-hop, with weekend live music and DJs. The city also has a craft-beer scene worth exploring. Friday is the big night of the week.

Craft
CRAFT BEER

(☑07-839 4531; www.crafthamilton.nz; 15 Hood St; ⊙4pm-late Wed-Thu, from 2pm Fri, from 1pm Sat) Fifteen rotating taps of amber goodness flow at Craft, plenty to keep the city's craft-beer buffs coming back. Brews from around NZ make a regular appearance, with occasional surprising additions from international cult breweries. Bar snacks, including braised lamb tacos, are a definite cut above. Pop in for 'Free Beer Thursdays', a popular buy-two, get-one-free deal.

Rocket Coffee Roasters
COFFEE

(☑07-839 6422; www.rocketcoffee.co.nz; 302 Barton St; ⊙8am-4pm Mon-Fri) Worth seeking out in a warehouse tucked behind a central city retail precinct, Rocket lures loyal customers with a winning combo of beans roasted on site and vintage jazz and soul spinning on a turntable. If you're looking for a strong espresso to start the day – a 'short black' in local parlance – this is where to come.

Brewraucracy
MICROBREWERY

(www.brewaucracy.co.nz; 34 Mahana Rd, Te Rapa; ⊙11am-7pm Thu-Sun) In the semi-industrial northern outskirts of Hamilton, Brewraucracy's functional brewhouse space includes a compact and welcoming taproom. Around 16 beers and ciders are usually on tap, and local food trucks often park up on Saturday afternoons. Standout beers are the Anonymous Norman Double IPA and the Manifest Destiny hoppy American stout.

Good George Brewing
BREWERY

(☑07-847 3223; www.goodgeorge.co.nz; 32a Somerset St, Frankton; tours incl beer $22; ⊙11.30am-10pm Mon & Tue, from 11am Wed-Sun) Channelling a cool industrial vibe, the former Church of St George is now a shrine to craft beer. Order a flight of five beers ($16), and partner the hoppy heaven with wood-fired pizzas ($25) or main meals ($26 to $34). Our favourite brews are the citrusy American Pale Ale and the regular seasonal specials. Tours must be booked ahead.

MĀORI NZ: WAIKATO & COROMANDEL PENINSULA

The Waikato and King Country region remains one of the strongest pockets of Māori influence in New Zealand. This is the heartland of the Tainui tribes, descended from those who disembarked from the Tainui *waka* (canoe) in Kāwhia in the 14th century. Split into four main tribal divisions (Waikato, Hauraki, Ngāti Maniapoto and Ngāti Raukawa), Tainui are inextricably linked with the Kīngitanga (King Movement), which has its base in Ngāruawāhia.

The best opportunities to interact with Māori culture is Ngāruawāhia's Regatta Day and Koroneihana celebrations. Interesting *taonga* (treasures) are displayed at museums in Hamilton and Te Awamutu.

Reminders of the Waikato Land War can be found at Rangiriri, Rangiaowhia and Orakau. See www.thewaikatowar.co.nz to download maps, audio files and a smartphone app covering various locations of the fighting from 1863 to 1864.

Dozens of *marae* (meeting house) complexes are dotted around the countryside – including at Awakino, and at Kāwhia, where the Tainui *waka* is buried. You won't be able to visit these without permission, but you can get decent views from the gates. Some regional tours include an element of Māori culture, including Ruakuri Cave (p213) at Waitomo.

Although it has a long and rich Māori history, the nearby Coromandel Peninsula doesn't offer many opportunities to engage with the culture. Historic *pā* (fortified village) sites are dotted around, with the most accessible being Paaku (p234). There are others at Opito Beach, Hahei and Hot Water Beach.

Wonderhorse

BAR

(☑07-839 2281; www.facebook.com/wonderhorse bar; 232 Victoria St; ⊗5pm-3am Wed-Sat) Tucked away around 20m off Victoria St, Wonderhorse regularly features beers from niche local brewers including Brewraucracy. Vintage vinyl is often spinning on the turntable, and sliders and Asian street eats combine with killer cocktails at one of Hamilton's best bars.

☆ Entertainment

Lido Cinema

CINEMA

(☑07-838 9010; www.lidocinema.co.nz; Level 1, Centre Place, 501 Victoria St; tickets adult/child $17/10) Art-house movies with $12 Tuesday tickets.

❶ Information

Anglesea Clinic (☑07-858 0800; www.angleseamedical.co.nz; cnr Anglesea & Thackeray Sts; ⊗24hr) For accidents and urgent medical assistance.

DOC (☑07-858 1000; www.doc.govt.nz; Level 5, 73 Rostrevor St; ⊗8am-4.30pm Mon-Fri) Maps and brochures on walking tracks, campsites and DOC huts. Also sells hut tickets.

Hamilton i-SITE (☑07-958 5960, 0800 242 645; www.visithamilton.co.nz; 120 Victoria St, ArtsPost; ⊗10am-5pm; 🕾) Accommodation, activities and transport bookings.

Post Office (☑07-839 4991; www.nzpost.co.nz; Centre Place; ⊗9am-5.30pm Mon-Sat, 10am-4pm Sun) The most central post office option is located in a Paper Plus store in the Centre Place mall.

Waikato Hospital (☑07-839 8899; www.waikatodhb.govt.nz; Pembroke St; ⊗24hr) Main hospital for the Waikato region; around 3km south of central Hamilton.

❶ Getting There & Away

AIR

Hamilton International Airport (HIA; ☑07-848 9027; www.hamiltonairport.co.nz; Airport Rd) is 12km south of the city. **Air New Zealand** (☑0800 737 000; www.airnewzealand.co.nz) has regular direct flights from Hamilton to Christchurch, Palmerston North and Wellington.

Super Shuttle (☑0800 748 885, 07-843 7778; www.supershuttle.co.nz; one way $32) offers a door-to-door service into the city, while **Raglan Scenic Tours** (☑07-825 0507, 021 0274 7014; www.raglanscenictours.co.nz) links the airport with Raglan. A taxi costs around $65. InterCity runs a direct bus from Hamilton to Auckland Airport.

BUS

All buses arrive at and depart from the **Hamilton Transport Centre** (☑07-834 3457; www.hamilton.co.nz; cnr Anglesea & Bryce Sts; 🕾).

Waikato Regional Council's Busit! coaches serve the region, including Ngāruawāhia, Cambridge, Te Awamutu and Raglan.

InterCity (☑09-583 5780; www.intercity.co.nz) services numerous destinations including the following:

Destination	Price ($)	Duration	Frequency (daily)
Auckland	19-37	2hr	11
Cambridge	10-25	25min	9
Matamata	15	50min	4
Ngāruawāhia	10-15	20min	9
Tauranga	25-30	1½hr	2
Te Awamutu	10-15	35min	3
Wellington	37-65	5hr	3

SKIP (☑09-394 9180; https://skip.travel) services run to the following destinations:

Destination	Price ($)	Duration	Frequency (daily)
Auckland	13-15	2hr	4
Rotorua	20	1hr	3
Tauranga	15	1½hr	2

TRAIN

Hamilton is on the **Northern Explorer** (☑0800 872 467; www.greatjourneysofnz.co.nz) route between Auckland (from $59, 2½ hours) and Wellington (from $119, 9½ hours) via Ōtorohanga (from $59, 45 minutes). Trains depart Auckland on Mondays, Thursdays and Saturdays and stop at Hamilton's **Frankton train station** (Fraser St), 1km west of the city centre; there are no ticket sales here – see the website for ticketing details.

❶ Getting Around

Hamilton's **Busit!** (☑0800 4287 5463; www.busit.co.nz; city routes adult/child $3.30/2.20) network services the city centre and suburbs daily from around 7am to 7.30pm (later on Fridays). All buses pass through Hamilton Transport Centre. Busit! also runs a free CBD shuttle looping around Victoria, Liverpool, Anglesea and Bridge Sts every 10 minutes (7am to 6pm weekdays).

Victoria St is the city's main shopping area and parking can be difficult to secure. You'll have more luck finding parking a few blocks to the west.

For a taxi, try **Hamilton Taxis** (☑0800 477 477, 07-847 7477; www.hamiltontaxis.co.nz). Uber is also available.

Alternatively, you can rent a car from **RaD Car Hire** (☑ 07-839 1049; www.radcarhire.co.nz; 383 Anglesea St; ☺ 7.30am-5pm Mon-Fri, 8am-noon Sat).

Raglan

POP 3310

Laid-back Raglan (Whaingaroa in Māori) may well be New Zealand's perfect surfing town. It's small enough to have escaped mass development, but big enough to exhibit signs of life, including good eateries and a bar that attracts big-name bands in summer. Along with the famous surf spots to the south, the harbour just begs to be kayaked upon. There's also an excellent arts scene, with several galleries and shops worthy of perusal.

◎ Sights & Activities

Old School Arts Centre ARTS CENTRE
(☑ 07-825 0023; www.raglanartscentre.co.nz; Stewart St; ☺ 10am-2pm Mon-Fri) FREE A community hub, the Old School Arts Centre has changing exhibitions and workshops, including weaving, carving, yoga and storytelling. Movies screen here regularly on weekends ($15): grab a snack and a beer to complete the experience. The hippie/artsy Raglan Creative Market happens out the front on the second Sunday (10am to 2pm) of the month. Expect food trucks, organic artisan produce, and interesting arts and crafts.

Raglan Surf School SURFING
(☑ 07-825 7873; www.raglansurfingschool.co.nz; 5a Bankart St; rental per hour surfboards from $20, body boards from $5, wetsuits from $5, 3hr lesson incl transport from Raglan $89) Conveniently located in central Raglan, Raglan Surf School prides itself on getting 95% of first-timers standing during their first lesson.

Raglan Rock CAVING
(☑ 0800 724 7625; www.raglanrock.com; climbing half-day $140, caving & canyoning $129-140) Full instruction and all equipment for climbing on the limestone cliffs of nearby Stone Valley or the exciting and craggy 'Sky Castle'. Caving options include Karamu Cave and the more challenging Rattlesnake. Canyoning is also available – ask about after-dark canyoning trips taking in a glowworm-illuminated waterfall. Minimum two people.

Raglan Kayak & Paddleboard KAYAKING
(☑ 07-825 8862; www.raglaneco.co.nz; Bow St Jetty; single/double kayaks per half-day $45/65, 2/3hr guided paddles per person $79/120; ☺ 9am-5pm Oct-May) Raglan Harbour is great for kayaking. This outfit rents kayaks and runs guided tours. Learn the basics on the gentle Opotoru River, or paddle out to investigate the nooks and crannies of the pancake rocks on the harbour's northern edge. Paddleboard rental, tours and lessons are also available.

Solscape SURFING
(☑ 07-825 8268; www.solscape.co.nz; 611 Wainui Rd; board & wetsuit hire per half-day $35) Super Solscape offers 2½-hour surfing lessons ($85).

⯈ Tours

Wahine Moe Sunset Harbour Cruise CRUISE
(☑ 07-825 7873; www.raglanboatcharters.co.nz; Raglan Wharf; adult/child $49/39; ☺ Thu-Sun late Dec-Mar) Two-hour sunset cruises, including a few drinks, around Raglan Harbour on the *Wahine Moe*. Ninety-minute morning harbour cruises ($30/15 per adult/child) leaving from Raglan's Bow St Jetty are also available on the smaller *Harmony* vessel. Complimentary pickups are included.

Raglan Scenic Tours TOURS
(☑ 07-823 2559; www.raglanscenictours.co.nz; 7a Main Rd; 2½hr Raglan sightseeing tour adult/child $60/20) Sightseeing tours, including the Raglan area and departures (adult/child $48/15) to Bridal Veil Falls or Te Toto Gorge. Mt Karioi treks can be arranged (adult from $60).

⯆ Sleeping

Solscape CABIN $
(☑ 07-825 8268; www.solscape.co.nz; 611 Wainui Rd; campsites per person $22, caboose dm/d $40/92, tepees $92, cottages d $120-245; @☎) ⚲ With a hilltop location fringed by native bush, Solscape's ecofriendly accommodation includes tepees, bell tents, rammed-earth domes, railway carriages and stylish eco-baches. There's room for tents and campervans, and simpler cottages are also available. Environmental impact is minimised with solar energy, and organic produce from the permaculture garden is used for meals in the Conscious Kitchen cafe.

Raglan Backpackers HOSTEL $
(☑ 07-825 0515; www.raglanbackpackers.co.nz; 6 Wi Neera St; vehicle sites per person $20, dm $31-35, s $58, tw & d $80-90; @☎) This laid-back hostel is right on the water, with sea views from some rooms. Other rooms are arranged around a garden courtyard or in a separate building. There are free bikes and kayaks for use, and surfboards for hire, or

Raglan

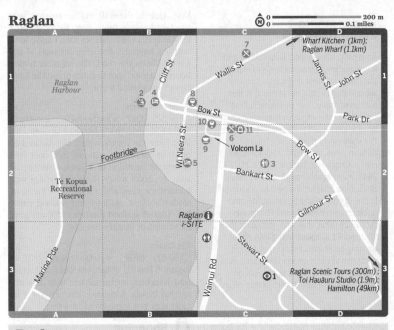

Raglan

◎ Sights
1 Old School Arts Centre C3

◈ Activities, Courses & Tours
2 Raglan Kayak & Paddleboard B1
3 Raglan Surf School C2

▤ Sleeping
4 Bow Street Studios B1
5 Raglan Backpackers B2

✖ Eating
6 Shack C2
7 Ulo's Kitchen C1

◎ Drinking & Nightlife
8 George's Beach Club B1
9 Raglan Roast C2
10 Yot Club C1

⌂ Shopping
11 Jet Collective C2

take a yoga class, strum a guitar or drip in the sauna. One of NZ's best hostels.

★ **Bow Street Studios** APARTMENT **$$**
(☑ 07-825 0551; www.bowstreet.co.nz; 1 Bow St; studios $155-245, cottages $175-195; ☎) With a waterfront location right in town, Bow Street has self-contained studios and a historic cottage. The cool and chic decor is stylish and relaxing. The property is surrounded by a subtropical garden and shaded by well-established pohutukawa trees.

✖ Eating

Ulo's Kitchen JAPANESE **$**
(☑ 022 169 5778; 6 Wallis St; mains $10-16; ⊙5-10pm Tue-Sat; ☑) ✿ Ulo's serves well-priced Japanese and Korean snacks and meals. Highlights include the spicy prawns with

sriracha sauce, the Bang Bang chicken salad and the pork and chive dumplings. Excellent sushi too. Little wonder Ulo's is a popular favourite for Raglan folk. Also open every second Sunday at the Raglan Creative Market.

Raglan Fish FISH & CHIPS **$**
(☑ 07-825 7544; www.facebook.com/raglanfish shop; Raglan Wharf, 92 Wallis St; fish & chips $7-12; ⊙9am-8pm) Super-fresh fish and chips and funky decor at this locals' favourite right on Raglan's wharf about 1km north of town. Fresh oysters, mussels and seafood salads are also available. A classic Kiwi experience.

★ **Rock-It Kitchen** CAFE **$$**
(☑ 07-825 8233; www.rockitraglan.co.nz; 248 Wainui Rd; mains $20-35; ⊙9am-3pm Sun, Mon, Wed & Thu, to late Fri & Sat; ☑) ✿ Around 3km

HORSE RIDING AROUND RAGLAN

Tramping, surfing, paddle boarding and kayaking are all popular ways to explore the blend of forest and ocean scenery around Raglan, but horse riding is also highly regarded. Two well-established operators offer excursions ranging from beach rides – even riding bareback into the shallows of the ocean – through to farm rides and negotiating forested paths. Check out **Surf & Turf** (📞027 435 2648; www.raglanhorseriding.co.nz; 3953B SH23; from $65) for the best opportunities to blend equine and ocean action, and hook up with **Wild Coast Ruapuke** (📞07-825 0059; www.wildcoast.co.nz; 1549 Whaanga Rd, Ruapuke; from $160) 🏄 for exciting combinations of bush, beach and farm scenery around Mt Karioi. Wild Coast also offers rustic but stylish accommodation ($300) with ocean views.

from town adjacent to surf beaches, Rock-It Kitchen combines rustic decor – it's housed in an old woolshed – with the area's best food. New Zealand wines and beer from west Auckland's Hallertau brewery combine with Scotch fillet steak and truffle potato mash for dinner, and the all-day breakfast of kumara hash cakes is popular with hungry surfers.

Shack
INTERNATIONAL $$

(📞07-825 0027; www.theshackraglan.com; 19 Bow St; mains $15-21; ⊗8am-4pm; 🛜🅿) 🏄 Brunch classics – try the chickpea-and-corn fritters – and interesting mains such as kimchi fried rice and slow-roasted lamb shoulder feature at Raglan's best cafe. A longboard strapped to the wall, wobbly old floorboards, up-tempo tunes and international staff serving Kiwi wines and craft beers complete the picture. Service is uniformly excellent, even when busy.

🍷 Drinking & Nightlife

George's Beach Club
PUB

(📞07-825 0565; www.facebook.com/georges beachclubraglan; 2 Bow St; ⊗noon-9pm Wed-Sun) Craft beers courtesy of Hamilton's Good George Brewing combine with tasty burgers and wood-fired pizza at this sunny beer garden in central Raglan.

Raglan Roast
CAFE

(📞07-825 8702; www.raglanroast.co.nz; Volcom Lane; coffee $4-5; ⊗7am-5pm, shorter hours Mar-Nov) Hole-in-the-wall coffee roaster with the best brew in town. Stop by for a cup, a cookie and a conversation. Don't leave town without buying a few fragrant bags of coffee for life on the road. The adjacent noticeboard is a good spot to catch up on the latest goings-on around town.

Wharf Kitchen
CAFE

(📞07-825 0010; www.thewharfkitchenbar.co.nz; 43 Rose St; ⊗10am-late Mon-Fri, from 9am Sat & Sun) Near the town's wharf, this is the best place to combine a wine or cold beer with afternoon sunshine or a Raglan sunset. Inside, the decor mixes Raglan's heritage with a maritime vibe, and a good food menu includes burgers, scallops and seafood chowder. Shared seafood platters ($59) are good for groups or hungry couples.

Yot Club
BAR

(📞07-825 8968; www.facebook.com/YOTClub Raglan; 9 Bow St; ⊗8pm-late Wed-Sat, 4pm-late Sun) Raucous, nocturnal bar with DJs and touring bands. Admission charges apply for most gigs, but some events are free.

🛍 Shopping

★Toi Hauāuru Studio
ART

(📞07-825 0244, 021 174 4629; www.toihauauru. com; 4338 Main Rd; ⊗10am-5pm Wed-Sun) Run by local artist Simon Te Wheoro, this excellent gallery/shop is located 2km from Raglan on the road from Hamilton. Contemporary artwork and sculpture with a Māori influence and *pounamu* (greenstone) carvings are for sale. Simon is also skilled in the Māori art of *tā moko* (tattoo) – if you're keen for one, get in touch via the website. Quirky local surfwear and colourful Māori *hei tiki* (pendants) make affordable and interesting souvenirs.

Tony Sly Pottery
ARTS & CRAFTS

(📞0800 825 037; www.tonyslypottery.com; Raglan Wharf, 90 Wallis St; ⊗9am-5pm) Subtle and natural colours and a mix of rustic and more modern designs feature at this store and workshop at Raglan Wharf.

Soul Shoes
SHOES

(📞07-825 8765; www.soulshoes.co.nz; Raglan Wharf, Wallis St; ⊗10am-5pm) World famous in Raglan since 1973, Soul Shoes' range of handmade leather footwear has been joined by equally cool satchels, backpacks and bags.

Jet Collective
ARTS & CRAFTS

(📞07-825 8566; www.facebook.com/jetcollective; 19a Bow St; ⊗10am-4pm Mon-Fri, to 5pm Sat &

Sun) Gallery-shop showcasing 100% Raglan artists with everything from music CDs and mixed-media pieces through to retro Kiwiana-inspired work. It's also a good spot to drop in and chat with the friendly team about Raglan's growing and diverse arts scene.

ℹ️ Information

Raglan i-SITE (☎ 07-825 0556; www.raglan.org.nz; 13 Wainui Rd; ⏱ 9am-5pm Tue-Thu, to 6.30pm Fri & Sat, to 5.30pm Sun & Mon) DOC brochures, plus information about accommodation and activities, including kitesurfing and paddle boarding. Check out the attached museum, especially the exhibition on the history of Raglan's surfing scene.

Raglan Medical Centre (☎ 07-825 0114; admin@raglanmedicalcentre.co.nz; 9 Wallis St; ⏱ 8am-5pm Mon, Wed & Fri, to 7pm Tue & Thu) General medical assistance.

ℹ️ Getting There & Away

Raglan is 48km west of Hamilton along SH23. Unsealed back roads connect Raglan to Kāwhia, 50km south; they're slow, winding and prone to rockslides, but scenic and certainly off the beaten track. Head back towards Hamilton for 7km and take the Te Mata/Kāwhia turn-off and follow the signs; allow at least an hour.

Waikato District Council's **Busit!** (☎ 0800 4287 5463; www.busit.co.nz; adult/child $9/5.60) heads between Hamilton and Raglan (one hour) four times daily on weekdays and twice daily on weekends.

Raglan Scenic Tours (p200) runs a Raglan–Hamilton shuttle bus (one way $50) and direct transfers to/from Auckland International Airport.

ℹ️ Getting Around

Raglan Shuttle (☎ 027 825 8159) Airport transfers, local tours and local taxi services.

South of Raglan

South of Raglan, the North Island's west coast unfurls with a series of excellent surf beaches. Whale Bay and Manu Bay draw board riders from around the world, and for nonsurfers, there are scenic walking opportunities around Mt Karioi and Mt Pirongia.

◎ Sights

Mt Karioi   MOUNTAIN
In legend, Mt Karioi (756m), the Sleeping Lady (check out that profile), is the sister to Mt Pirongia. At its base (8km south of Whale Bay), Te Toto Gorge is a steep cleft in the mountainside, with a vertigo-inducing lookout perched high over the chasm. Starting from the Te Toto Gorge car park, the strenuous but scenic Te Toto Track goes up the western slope. It takes 2½ hours to reach a lookout point, followed by an easier hour to the summit.

From the eastern side, the Wairake Track is a steeper 2½-hour climb to the summit, where it meets the Te Toto Track.

Waireinga   WATERFALL
(Bridal Veil Falls) Just past Te Mata (a short drive south of the main Raglan–Hamilton road) is the turn-off to the 55m-high Waireinga, 4km from the main road. From the car park, it's an easy 10-minute walk through mossy native bush to the top of the falls (not suitable for swimming). A further 10-minute walk leads down to the bottom. Lock your car: theft is a problem here.

Mt Pirongia   MOUNTAIN
(www.mtpirongia.org.nz) The main attraction of the 170-sq-km Pirongia Forest Park is Mt Pirongia, its 959m summit clearly visible from much of the Waikato. The mountain is usually climbed from Corcoran Rd (three to five hours, one way), with tracks to other lookout points. Interestingly, NZ's tallest known kahikatea tree (66.5m) grows on the mountainside. There's a six-bunk DOC hut near the summit if you need to spend the night: maps and information are available from Hamilton DOC (p199).

🏃 Activities

Surf spots near Raglan – Indicators, Whale Bay and Manu Bay – are internationally famous for their point breaks. Bruce Brown's classic 1964 wave-chaser film *The Endless Summer* features Manu Bay.

Manu Bay   SURFING
A 2.5km journey from Ngarunui Beach (p204) will bring you to Manu Bay, a legendary surf spot said to have the longest left-hand break in the world. The elongated uniform waves are created by the angle at which the Tasman Sea swell meets the coastline (it works best in a southwesterly swell).

Whale Bay   SURFING
Whale Bay is a renowned surf spot 1km west of Manu Bay. It's usually less crowded than Manu Bay, but from the bottom of Calvert Rd you have to clamber 600m over the rocks to get to the break.

Waikato & King Country

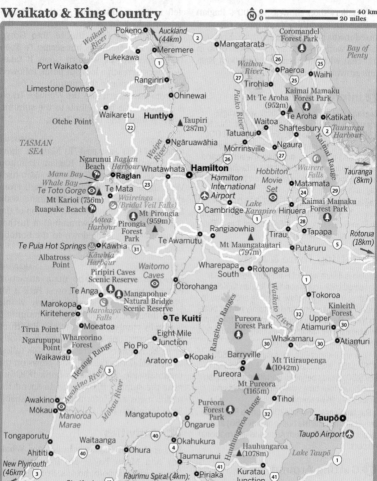

Ngarunui Beach   SURFING

Ngarunui Beach is great for grommets learning to surf. On the clifftop is a clubhouse for the volunteer lifeguards who patrol part of the black-sand beach from late October until April. This is the only beach with lifeguards, and is the best ocean beach for swimming.

🛈 Getting There & Away

There is no public transport. Tours are available with Raglan Scenic Tours (p200).

Te Awamutu

POP 10,035

Deep into dairy-farming country, Te Awamutu (which means 'The River Cut Short'; the Waikato beyond this point was unsuitable for large canoes), with a blossom-tree-lined main street and a good museum, TA (aka Rose Town) makes a decent overnighter.

◉ Sights & Activities

★ **Te Awamutu Museum**   MUSEUM

(☐ 07-872 0085; www.tamuseum.org.nz; 135 Roche St; by donation; ☺ 10am-4pm Mon-Fri, to 2pm

Sat) Te Awamutu Museum has a superb collection of Māori *taonga* (treasures) and an excellent display on the Waikato War. The highlight is the revered *Te Uenuku* (The Rainbow), an ancient Māori carving estimated to be up to 600 years old. If you're a fan of the Finn brothers from Crowded House and Split Enz, videos, memorabilia and a scrapbook are available on request – Te Awamutu is their home town.

Rose Garden GARDENS
(cnr Gorst Ave & Arawata St; ⊙24hr) FREE The Rose Garden has 2500 bushes and 51 varieties with fabulously fruity names such as Lady Gay and Sexy Rexy. The roses usually bloom from November to May.

Bryce's Rockclimbing CLIMBING
(☑07-872 2533; www.rockclimb.co.nz; 1424 Owairaka Valley Rd; ⊙8am-5pm Fri-Mon) Bryce's Rockclimbing is situated in a rural area 25km southeast of Te Awamutu, near hundreds of climbs at various crags (many of which are within walking distance). The surreal landscape provides some of the best rock climbing in the North Island, but it's an area best suited to those with at least basic climbing skills.

Friendly owner Bryce Martin can offer independent advice on accessing the different climbing locations in the region.

On-site is NZ's largest retail climbing store, selling and hiring a full range of gear. Another option is the excellent online store (www.shop.rockclimb.co.nz). There's also comfortable accommodation, and all rooms have private en-suite bathrooms (single and double $84). Breakfast is available to guests by request. Accommodation is also open to hikers, cyclists, anglers and general travellers. Your own transport is required to get here.

Sleeping & Eating

Rosetown Motel MOTEL $$
(☑07-871 5779, 0800 767 386; www.rosetownmotel.co.nz; 844 Kihikihi Rd; d $135-155; ☎❄) The older-style units at Rosetown have kitchens, new linen and TVs, and share a spa. A solid choice if you're hankering for straight-up, small-town sleeps.

Red Kitchen CAFE $$
(☑07-871 8715; www.redkitchen.co.nz; 51 Mahoe St; mains $14-21; ⊙7am-5.30pm Mon-Fri, 7.30am-2.30pm Sat) Excellent coffee, counter food, cosmopolitan brunches and lunches, and a kitchen store all feature at this sunny spot. Try the hearty farmers' breakfast or the home-

made crumpets. Pick up gourmet preprepared meals from Monday to Friday – variations could include chicken and sweet potato curry or beef and pork cannelloni – and fire up the motel microwave for your evening meal.

Fahrenheit Restaurant & Bar MODERN NZ $$
(☑07-871 5429; www.fahrenheitrestaurant.co.nz; 13 Roche St; mains $19-39; ⊙11am-late Tue-Sun) The decor is a tad stark at this spacious upstairs eatery, but a friendly local welcome and plenty of Waikato sunshine easily counter any misgivings about ambience. Shared tapas plates, good pizza, and a decent wine and beer list are all reasons to dine at lunch; for a more high-end experience, order the slow-cooked beef short rib for dinner.

❶ Information

Te Awamutu i-SITE (☑07-871 3259; www.teawamutuinfo.co.nz; 1 Gorst Ave; ⊙9am-5pm Mon-Fri, 10am-3pm Sat & Sun) Has plenty of local information.

❶ Getting There & Away

Te Awamutu is on SH3, halfway between Hamilton and Ōtorohanga (29km either way). The regional bus service **Busit!** (☑0800 4287 5463; www.busit.co.nz) is the cheapest option for Hamilton (adult/child $6.70/4.50, 50 minutes, eight daily weekdays, three daily weekends). Three

TE AWAMUTU'S SACRED SOUND

In the opening lines of Crowded House's first single 'Mean to Me', Neil Finn singlehandedly raised his sleepy home town, Te Awamutu, to international attention. It wasn't the first time it had provided inspiration – Split Enz songs 'Haul Away' and 'Kia Kaha', with big bro Tim, include similar references.

Devotees of New Zealand's brilliant songwriting brothers continue to make the pilgrimage to Te Awamutu, and Neil, especially, remains a versatile and popular artist. Recent albums include the excellent *Lightsleeper* (2018) with son Liam, and in 2018 Neil Finn joined the massively popular Fleetwood Mac.

Ask at the i-SITE about Finn postcards and the interesting scrapbook focused on the brothers' achievements. For Finn completists, there's more to see at the Te Awamutu Museum by request.

daily **InterCity** (09-583 5780; www.intercity. co.nz) services connect Te Awamutu with Auckland (from $18, 2½ hours) and Hamilton ($10, 30 minutes). Buses leave from near the i-SITE.

Cambridge

POP 19,150

The name says it all. Despite the rambunctious Waikato River looking nothing like the Cam, the good people of Cambridge have done all they can to assume an air of English gentility with village greens and tree-lined avenues.

Cambridge is famous for the breeding and training of thoroughbred horses. Equine references are rife in public sculpture, and plaques boast of past Melbourne Cup winners. It's also an emerging dining destination, with some excellent eateries worth the short drive from Hamilton.

◉ Sights

Cambridge Museum   MUSEUM
(07-827 3319; www.cambridgemuseum.org.nz; 24 Victoria St; by donation; ⊙10am-4pm Mon-Fri, to 2pm Sat & Sun) In a former courthouse, the quirky Cambridge Museum has plenty of pioneer relics, a military history room and a range of local history displays.

Jubilee Gardens   GARDENS
(Victoria St) Apart from its Spanish Mission town clock, Jubilee Gardens is a wholehearted tribute to the 'mother country'. A British lion guards the cenotaph, with a plaque that reads 'Tell Britain ye who mark this monument faithful to her we fell and rest content'. Across the road in leafy Victoria Sq, a farmers market is held every Saturday morning.

Lake Karapiro   LAKE
(07-827 4178; www.waipadc.govt.nz; Maungatautari Rd) Eight kilometres southeast of Cambridge, Lake Karapiro is the furthest downstream of a chain of eight hydroelectric power stations on the Waikato River. It's an impressive sight, especially when driving across the top of the 1947 dam. The 21km-long lake is also a world-class rowing venue.

🏃 Activities

Te Awa   CYCLING, WALKING
(The Great New Zealand River Ride; www.te-awa. org.nz) The Te Awa cycling and walking path meanders for 70km along the Waikato River, from Ngāruawāhia north of Hamilton,

to Horahora south of the city. It's a flat and scenic route. Highlights include riding from the Avantidrome in Cambridge – a training hub for NZ's elite cycling athletes – south to the shores of Lake Karapiro. See the website for details.

Boatshed Kayaks   KAYAKING
(07-827 8286; www.theboatshed.net.nz; The Boatshed, 21 Amber Lane; single/double kayak 3hr $25/60, paddle board 2hr $40; ⊙9am-5pm Wed-Sun) Boatshed Kayaks has basic kayaks and paddle boards for hire. You can paddle to a couple of waterfalls in around an hour. There are also guided kayak trips (adult/ child $130/90) at twilight to see a glowworm canyon up the nearby Pokaiwhenua stream; bookings are essential. See the website for other guided kayaking on Lake Karapiro and the Waikato River.

Waikato River Trails   CYCLING
(www.waikatorivertrails.co.nz) The 103km Waikato River Trails track is part of the Nga Haerenga, New Zealand Cycle Trail (www. nzcycletrail.com) project. Winding south and east from near Cambridge – beginning at the Pokaiwhenua Bridge – the trails pass Lake Karapiro and go into the South Waikato area to end at the Atiamuri Dam. Check the website for maps and bike hire locations.

🛏 Sleeping

Cambridge Coach House   B&B $$
(07-823 7922; www.cambridgecoachhouse.co.nz; 3796 Cambridge Rd, Leamington; ste/cottage from $165/185; 🐾⬛) This farmhouse accommodation is a beaut spot to relax amid Waikato's rural splendour. There are two stylish suites and a self-contained cottage. Flat-screen TVs and heat pumps are convenient additions, and guests are welcome to fire up the barbecue in the leafy grounds. It's 2km south of town, en route to Te Awamutu.

★ Earthstead   B&B $$$
(07-827 3771; www.earthstead.co.nz; 3635 Cambridge Rd, Monvale; d $229-449; 🐾) 🌿 In a rural setting a short drive south of Cambridge, Earthstead has two units – Earth House and Cob Cottage – constructed using ecofriendly and sustainable adobe-style architecture, and two other options with an elegant European vibe. Fresh and organic produce from Earthstead's compact farm is used for breakfast, including eggs, honey and freshly baked sourdough bread.

SANCTUARY MOUNTAIN MAUNGATAUTARI

Can a landlocked volcano become an island paradise? Inspired by the success of pest eradication and native species reintroduction in Auckland's Hauraki Gulf, pest-proof fencing has been installed around the three peaks of Maungatautari (797m) to create the impressive Sanctuary Mountain Maungatautari (☑07-870 5180; www. sanctuarymountain.co.nz; 99 Tari Rd, Pukeatua; adult/child $22/10).

Hiking through the mountain's pristine native forest (around six hours) is a popular activity, and shorter guided tours are available from the visitor centre. Fauna-related attractions include two only-in-NZ species: the tuatara and the kiwi. Accommodation and trailhead transport can be provided by Out in the Styx (☑07-872 4505; www.styx. co.nz; 2117 Arapuni Rd, Pukeatua; dm/s/d $125/185/320).

Eating & Drinking

Cambridge Farmers' Market MARKET $
(www.waikatofarmersmarkets.co.nz; ⊙8am-noon Sat) Local flavours abound at this excellent weekly market held in the leafy surroundings of Victoria Sq.

Paddock CAFE $$
(☑07-827 4232; www.paddockcambridge.co.nz; 46a Victoria St; mains $14-24; ⊙8am-4pm) Free-range and organic that punctuate the menu at this cool slice of culinary style that looks like it's dropped in from Auckland or Melbourne. Distressed timber furniture and a vibrant and colourful mural enliven Paddock's corner location, and artisan sodas and healthy smoothies – try the banana, date and cinnamon – partner well with gourmet bagels and burgers.

Alpha Street Kitchen & Bar MODERN NZ $$
(☑07-827 5596; www.alphast.co.nz; 47 Alpha St; mains $24-46; ⊙11am-late; 🐾) Formerly the National Hotel, this heritage space is now one of the Waikato's best restaurants. Sit outside for a leisurely lunch of confit duck leg or sophisticated spins on lamb or venison for dinner. The shared-plates dishes – think pork meatballs, spicy prawns or tempura oysters – also work well as bar snacks. There's an extensive selection of NZ craft beer.

Alpino cucina e vino ITALIAN $$
(☑07-827 5595; www.alpino.co.nz; 43 Victoria St; pizzas $21-26, mains $26-38; ⊙noon-9.30pm Sun-Thu, to midnight Fri & Sat) In a heritage former post office, the stylish and elegant yet informal and approachable Alpino cucina e vino is one of the best restaurants in the Waikato region. The main menu focuses on excellent pasta, hearty Italian-style antipasti and mains – try the braised wild goat with pappardelle or the octopus salad – and top-notch wood-fired pizza is also available for takeaway.

Good Union PUB
(☑07-834 4040; www.goodunion.co.nz; 98 Victoria St; ⊙11am-late Mon-Fri, from 9am Sat & Sun) Hamilton's Good George Brewing (p198) empire has now spread to this Cambridge venue in a colourful and characterful former church. Secure a spot in the interesting heritage interior or grab a place on the huge outdoor deck and partner Good George's excellent beers and ciders with pizza, tacos and hearty main dishes. Visit on a weekend afternoon for occasional live music.

ⓘ Information

Cambridge i-SITE (☑07-823 3456; www. cambridge.co.nz; cnr Victoria & Queen Sts; ⊙9am-5pm Mon-Fri, 10am-4pm Sat & Sun; 🐾) has free Heritage & Tree Trail and town maps, plus internet access.

ⓘ Getting There & Away

Being on SH1, 22km southeast of Hamilton, Cambridge is well connected by bus. Waikato Regional Council's Busit! (☑0800 4287 5463; www.busit.co.nz) heads to Hamilton (adult/child $6.70/4.50, 40 minutes, seven daily weekdays, three daily weekends).

InterCity (☑09-583 5780; www.intercity. co.nz) services numerous destinations including the following:

Destination	Price ($)	Duration	Frequency (daily)
Auckland	15-34	2½hr	12
Hamilton	15	30min	8
Matamata	15	30min	2
Rotorua	15-25	1¼hr	5
Wellington	31-50	8½hr	3

Matamata

POP 7920

Matamata was just one of those pleasant, horsey country towns you drove through until Peter Jackson's epic film trilogy *The Lord of the Rings* put it on the map. During filming, 300 locals got work as extras (hairy feet weren't a prerequisite).

Following the subsequent filming of *The Hobbit,* the town has now ardently embraced its Middle-earth credentials, including a spooky statue of Gollum, and given the local information centre an appropriate makeover.

Most tourists who come to Matamata are dedicated Hobbit-botherers. For everyone else there's good eating and drinking, avenues of mature trees and undulating green hills. From early 2020, the town also became a cycling stop on the Hauraki Rail Trail, with the southern spur now continuing from Te Aroha to Matamata.

⊙ Sights

Hobbiton Movie Set Tours   FILM LOCATION
(☑ 0508 446 224 866, 07-888 1505; www.hobbiton tours.com; 501 Buckland Rd, Hinuera; adult/child tours $84/42, dinner tours $195/153; ⊙ tours 10am-4.30pm) Due to copyright, all the movie sets around NZ were dismantled after the filming of *The Lord of the Rings,* but Hobbiton's owners negotiated to keep their hobbit holes, which were then rebuilt for the filming of *The Hobbit.* Tours include a drink at the wonderful Green Dragon Inn. Free transfers leave from the Matamata i-SITE – check timings on the Hobbiton website. Book ahead. The popular Evening Dinner Tours from Sunday to Wednesday include a banquet dinner.

Wairere Falls   WATERFALL
About 15km northeast of Matamata are these spectacular 153m falls, the highest on the North Island. From the car park it's a 45-minute walk through native bush to the lookout or a steep 1½-hour climb to the summit.

Firth Tower   HISTORIC BUILDING
(☑ 07-888 8369; www.firthtower.co.nz; Tower Rd; grounds free, buildings adult/child $10/5; ⊙ grounds 10am-4pm daily, buildings to 4pm Thu-Mon; 🚻) Firth Tower was built by Auckland businessman Josiah Firth in 1882. The 18m concrete tower was then a fashionable status symbol; now it's filled with Māori and pioneer artefacts. Ten other historic buildings are set around the tower, including a schoolroom, church and jail. It's 3km east of town.

🛏 Sleeping

Matamata Backpackers   HOSTEL $
(☑ 07-880 9745; www.matamatabackpackers. co.nz; 61 Firth St; dm/r $28/74; 🛜) Handily located a short walk from the bus departure point to Hobbiton, this well-run and welcoming 2017 opening offers the best-value beds around town. Colourful bed linen enlivens the simply decorated dorms and private rooms, and hostel facilities include spacious common areas.

**Broadway Motel
& Miro Court Villas**   MOTEL $$
(☑ 07-888 8482; www.broadwaymatamata.co.nz; 128 Broadway; d $110-175, 2-bedroom apt $300; @ 🏊) This sprawling family-run motel complex has spread from a well-maintained older-style block to progressively newer and flasher blocks set back from the street. The nicest are the chic apartment-style Miro Court villas.

🍴 Eating & Drinking

Good Merchant   PUB
(☑ 07-880 9561; www.goodmerchant.co.nz; 44 Broadway; ⊙ 11am-late) Located across the road from the Matamata i-SITE, this spacious and modern shrine to craft beer and cider is also a good place to eat. Sit outside under the market umbrellas and tuck into good wood-fired pizza or superior bar snacks, including pork and fennel arancini or smoked fish Scotch eggs. Wash it down with a seasonal brew or sour beer.

Redoubt Bar & Eatery   PUB
(☑ 07-888 8585; www.redoubtbarandeatery.co.nz; 48 Broadway; ⊙ 11am-1am) Look forward to thin-crust pizzas named after *LOTR* characters, a winning salmon-and-hash stack, movie nights in the adjacent laneway, and live music most weekends. It's also a mini-shrine to all things sporty and Matamata-related, and interesting tap beers definitely hit the spot.

❶ Information

Matamata i-SITE (☑ 07-888 7260; www. matamatanz.co.nz; 45 Broadway; ⊙ 9am-5pm) Housed in a wonderful Hobbit gatehouse. Hobbiton tours leave from here.

❶ Getting There & Away

Matamata is on SH27, 20km north of Tirau.
InterCity (☑ 09-583 5780; www.intercity.co.nz) runs to Cambridge ($15, 40 minutes, two daily), Hamilton ($15, one hour, three daily), Rotorua ($30, one hour, two daily) and Tauranga ($25, one hour, two daily).

Te Aroha

POP 3900

Te Aroha has a great vibe. You could even say that it's got 'the love', which is the literal meaning of its name. Tucked under the elbow of the bush-clad Mt Te Aroha (952m), it's a good base for hiking or 'taking the waters' in the town's therapeutic thermal springs. It's also on the southern section of the Hauraki Rail Trail and in early 2020 this cycling trail was extended from Te Aroha to Matamata. The sleepy main street is good for trawling for quirky antiques, and vintage clothing and accessories. Many of the town's attractions are arrayed around Te Aroha's leafy hillside Domain.

Sights & Activities

Te Aroha Museum
MUSEUM

(☑ 07-884 4427; www.tearoha-museum.com; Te Aroha Domain; adult/child $5/2; ☺ 11am-4pm Nov-Mar, noon-3pm Apr-Oct) In the town's former thermal sanatorium (aka the 'Treasure of Te Aroha'). Displays include quirky ceramics, old spa-water bottles, historical photos and an old printing press.

Mt Te Aroha
HIKING

Trails up Mt Te Aroha start at the top of the Domain. It's a 45-minute climb to Bald Spur/Whakapipi Lookout (350m), then another 2.7km (two hours) to the summit. Ask at the i-SITE about mountain-bike trails.

Te Aroha Mineral Spas
SPA

(☑ 07-884 8717; www.tearohamineralspas.co.nz; Boundary St, Te Aroha Domain; 30min session adult/child $22/11; ☺ 10.30am-9pm Mon-Fri, to 10pm Sat & Sun) In the Edwardian Hot Springs Domain, this spa offers private tubs, massage, beauty therapies and aromatherapy. Also here is the temperamental Mokena Geyser – the world's only known soda geyser – which blows its top around every 40 minutes, shooting water 3m into the air (the most ardent eruptions are between noon and 2pm). Book ahead for spas and treatments.

Sleeping & Eating

Te Aroha Holiday Park
HOLIDAY PARK $

(☑ 07-884 9567; www.tearohaholidaypark.co.nz; 217 Stanley Rd; campsites from $22, on-site vans s/d $30/45, cabins & units $75-110; P @ 🛜 🐕 ♿) Wake up to a bird orchestra among the oaks at this site equipped with a grass tennis court, gym and hot pool, 2km southeast of town.

★ Aroha Mountain Lodge
LODGE, B&B $$

(☑ 07-884 8134; www.arohamountainlodge.co.nz; 5 Boundary St; s/d/cottage $145/145/350) Spread over two lovely Edwardian villas on the hillside above town, the plush Mountain Lodge offers affordable luxury (so much nicer than a regular motel) and optional breakfast ($20 per person). The self-contained Chocolate Box sleeps six to eight.

Domain Cottage Cafe
CAFE $

(☑ 07-884 9222; Whitaker St, Te Aroha Domain; snacks & mains $8-23; ☺ 9am-3pm Tue-Sun) Very pleasant daytime cafe in the heritage surroundings of the Te Aroha Domain. Definitely worth a stop for coffee and cake even if you're only passing through town. The stonking lamb sandwich is perfect after hiking or biking on nearby Mt Te Aroha.

Ironique
CAFE $$

(☑ 07-884 8489; www.ironique.co.nz; 159 Whitaker St; mains $10-35; ☺ 8am-4pm Mon-Wed, to late Thu-Sun) Come for a coffee and a restorative breakfast of eggs Benedict after tackling the Hauraki Rail Trail, or pork belly or pumpkin and ricotta ravioli for dinner. Venture into the quiet courtyard out back for a few drinks.

ⓘ Information

Te Aroha i-SITE (☑ 07-884 8052; www.tearohanz.co.nz; 102 Whitaker St; ☺ 9.30am-5pm Mon-Fri, to 4pm Sat & Sun) Ask about walking trails on Mt Te Aroha and other local sights.

ⓘ Getting There & Away

Te Aroha is on SH26, 21km south of Paeroa and 55km northeast of Hamilton. Waikato Regional Council's **Busit!** (☑ 0800 4287 5463; www.busit.co.nz) runs to/from Hamilton (adult/child $8.40/4.20, one hour, weekdays at 5.15pm).

KING COUNTRY

Holding good claim to the title of New Zealand's rural heartland, this is the kind of no-nonsense place that raises cattle and All Blacks. A bastion of independent Māoridom, it was never conquered in the war against the King Movement. The story goes that King Tawhiao placed his hat on a large map of NZ and declared that all the land it covered would remain under his *mana* (authority), and the region was effectively off-limits to Europeans until 1883.

WAIKATO & THE COROMANDEL PENINSULA TE AROHA

The Waitomo Caves are the area's major drawcard. An incredible natural phenomenon in themselves, they also feature lots of adrenaline-inducing activities.

Kāwhia

POP 670

Along with resisting cultural annihilation, low-key Kāwhia (think mafia with a K) has avoided large-scale development, retaining its sleepy fishing-village vibe. Highlights include an excellent local museum and an interesting local gallery showcasing the work of around 30 local artists. Otherwise there's just the general store, a couple of takeaways and a petrol station. Even Captain Cook blinked and missed the narrow entrance to the large harbour when he sailed past in 1770. Change may be coming, however, with a new Māori trust-owned boutique hotel and restaurant scheduled for completion in late 2020.

◎ Sights

Maketu Marae　　　　　　　　　HISTORIC SITE
(www.kawhia.maori.nz; Kaora St) From Kāwhia Wharf, a track extends along the coast to Maketu Marae, which has an impressively carved meeting house, Auaukiterangi. Two stones here – Hani and Puna – mark the burial place of the Tainui waka (a 14th-century ancestral canoe). You can't see a lot from the road, but the *marae* is private property and shouldn't be entered without permission. Email the Maketu Marae Committee for access.

Ocean Beach　　　　　　　　　　　BEACH
(Te Puia Rd) Four kilometres west of Kāwhia is Ocean Beach and its high, black-sand dunes. Swimming can be dangerous, but one to two hours either side of low tide you can find the Te Puia Hot Springs in the sand – dig a hole for your own natural hot pool. From the car park, walk though the sand dunes for around 300m.

Kawhia Regional Museum & Gallery　　　MUSEUM, GALLERY
(☑07-8710161; www.facebook.com/MuseumKawhia; Omimiti Reserve, Kāwhia Wharf; by gold coin donation; ⊙11am-4pm, reduced hours Mar-Nov) Kāwhia's modest waterside museum has local history, nautical and Māori art and artefacts, as well as regular art exhibitions. Don't miss the huge fossil of an ammonite shell, once thought to have housed a giant squid. The museum doubles as the visitor information centre, and the friendly volunteers staffing it are always up for a good chat.

Post Box Gallery　　　　　　　　GALLERY
(78 Jervois St; ⊙hours vary) This volunteer-run gallery and shop is worth checking out to purchase interesting works and souvenirs from the increasing number of artists and designers who call Kāwhia home. The gallery is housed in a spacious and sunny former post office.

🏃 Activities

Kayaks can be hired from **Kawhia Beachside S-Cape** (☑07-871 0727; www.kawhiabeachsidescape.co.nz; 225 Pouewe St) and Kawhia Motel, and there's also excellent fishing on offer.

Dove Charters　　　　　　　　　FISHING
(☑07-871 5854; www.westcoastfishing.co.nz; full day per person from $120) Full-day fishing trips catching snapper, kingfish, gurnard and kahawai.

🛏 Sleeping & Eating

Kawhia Motel　　　　　　　　MOTEL $$
(☑07-871 0865; www.kawhiamotel.co.nz; cnr Jervois & Tainui Sts; d $129-159; 🐾) These six perkily painted, well-kept, old-school motel units are right next to the shops. Kayaks and bikes are available for hire.

Rusty Snapper　　　　　　　　CAFE $$
(☑07-871 0030; www.facebook.com/rustysnapperkawhia; 64 Jervois St; mains $15-26; ⊙10am-4pm, extended hours Jan & Feb) Freshly baked scones, slices and cakes combine with the best coffee in town, and if you're after fish and chips or fresh, seasonal seafood, the Rusty Snapper's a top spot, too. Local oysters and whitebait fritters often feature.

ℹ Information

For information see www.kawhiaharbour.co.nz.

ℹ Getting There & Away

Kāwhia doesn't have a bus service. Take SH31 from Ōtorohanga (58km) or explore the scenic but rough road to Raglan (50km, 22km unsealed).

Ōtorohanga

POP 2750

Ōtorohanga's main street is festooned with images of cherished Kiwiana icons: sheep, gumboots, jandals, number 8 wire, All Blacks, pavlova and the beloved Buzzy Bee children's toy. The town's Kiwi House is also well worth a visit and the town makes a good base for the nearby Waitomo Caves.

Ed Hillary Walkway   MEMORIAL
As well as the Kiwiana decorating the main street, the Ed Hillary Walkway (running off Maniapoto St) has information panels on the All Blacks, Marmite and, of course, Sir Ed.

Otorohanga Kiwi House & Native Bird Park   ZOO
(☑ 07-873 7391; www.kiwihouse.org.nz; 20 Alex Telfer Dr; adult/child $26/10; ☺ 9am-5pm, kiwi feedings 10.30am, 1.30pm & 3.30pm; ⊞) This bird barn has a nocturnal enclosure where you can see active kiwi energetically digging with their long beaks, searching for food. This is one of the only places where you can see a great spotted kiwi, the biggest of the three kiwi species. Brown kiwi are also on display, and there's a breeding programme for these birds here. Other native birds on show include kākā, kea, morepork and weka, and there's also tuatara, NZ's prehistoric reptiles.

Ō Cafe   CAFE **$$**
(☑ 07-873 8714; www.facebook.com/Cafe.Otorohanga; 35 Maniapoto St; mains $14-24; ☺ 7.30am-3pm) Ōtorohanga's most cosmopolitan cafe is a goodie, with big shared tables, lots of natural light and a versatile menu stretching from breakfast classics and home-style baking through to hearty lunch options. We can personally recommend the lamb burger with zingy beetroot relish. The attached gift shop sells a few eclectic examples of local arts and crafts.

Thirsty Weta   PUB
(☑ 07-873 6699; www.theweta.co.nz; 57 Maniapoto St; ☺ 10am-late; ☎) Hearty meals, including pizza, steak, burgers, pasta and curries (mains $21 to $30). Later on a pub-meets-wine-bar ambience kicks off as the local musos plug in. It's one of just a handful of places you'll find craft beers on tap from the local King Country Brewing Co (p215). Our favourite is the well-balanced pale ale.

ℹ Information

Ōtorohanga i-SITE (☑ 07-873 8951; www.otorohanga.co.nz; 27 Turongo St; ☺ 9am-5pm Mon-Fri year-round, 9am-1pm Sat Oct-Apr; ☎) Free wi-fi and local information.

ℹ Getting There & Away

BUS

InterCity (☑ 09-583 5780; www.intercity.co.nz) buses run from Ōtorohanga to Auckland ($22 to $34, 3¼ hours, three daily), Te Awamutu ($10, 30 minutes, three daily), Te Kuiti ($10, 30 minutes, three daily) and Rotorua ($25, 2½ hours, two daily).

To arrange a shuttle transfer from Ōtorohanga to Waitomo, contact Waitomo Caves Tours & Transfers (p215) or phone ahead to the Ōtorohanga i-SITE to confirm a pickup.

TRAIN

Ōtorohanga is on the **Northern Explorer** (www.greatjourneysofnz.co.nz) train route between Auckland (from $59, 3¼ hours) and Wellington (from $139, nine hours) via Hamilton (from $59, 50 minutes); it also stops at Palmerston North, Ōhakune and National Park. Southbound trains run on Mondays, Thursdays and Saturdays, and northbound trains return from Wellington to Auckland on Tuesdays, Fridays and Sundays.

Waitomo Caves

POP 500
Even if damp, dark tunnels are your idea of hell, head to Waitomo anyway. The limestone caves and glowing bugs here are one of the North Island's premier attractions.

KĪNGITANGA

The concept of a Māori people is a relatively new one. Until the mid-19th century, New Zealand was effectively comprised of many independent tribal nations, operating in tandem with the British from 1840.

In 1856, faced with a flood of Brits, the Kīngitanga King Movement formed to unite the tribes to better resist further loss of land and culture. A gathering of leaders elected Waikato chief Pōtatau Te Wherowhero as the first Māori king, hoping that his increased *mana* (prestige) could achieve the cohesion that the British had under their queen.

Despite the huge losses of the Waikato War and the eventual opening up of the King Country, the Kīngitanga survived – although it has no formal constitutional role. A measure of the strength of the movement was the huge outpouring of grief when Te Arikinui Dame Atairangikaahu, Pōtatau's great-great-great-granddaughter, died in 2006 after 40 years at the helm. Although it's not a hereditary monarchy (leaders of various tribes vote on a successor), Pōtatau's line continues to the present day with King Tūheitia Paki.

Waitomo Caves

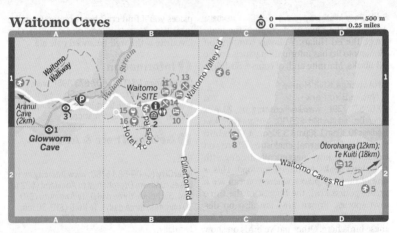

Waitomo Caves

The name Waitomo comes from *wai* (water) and *tomo* (hole or shaft): dotted across this region are numerous shafts dropping into underground cave systems and streams. There are 300-plus mapped caves in the area: the three main caves – Glowworm, Ruakuri and Aranui – have been bewitching visitors for over 100 years.

Your Waitomo experience needn't be claustrophobic: the electrically lit, cathedral-like Glowworm Cave is far from squeezy. But if it's tight, gut-wrenching, soaking-wet, pitch-black excitement you're after, Waitomo can oblige.

There's no petrol in town, but there's an ATM at the Waitomo General Store (☑07-878 8613; www.facebook.com/waitomo generalstore; 15 Waitomo Caves Rd; snacks & mains $10-22; ☺7.30am-8.30pm; ☎). It's best to stock up on cash, groceries and petrol in either Te Kuiti or Ōtorohanga, though.

⊙ Sights

Waitomo Caves Visitor Centre
VISITOR CENTRE
(☑0800 456 922; www.waitomo.com; Waitomo Caves Rd; ☺9am-5pm) The big-three Waitomo Caves are all operated by the same company, based at the spectacular Waitomo Caves Visitor Centre (near the Glowworm Cave). Various combo deals are available, including a Triple Cave Combo (adult/child $97/44), and other deals incorporate exciting underground thrills with the Legendary Black Water Rafting Company. Check the website. For the cave tours, try to avoid the large tour groups, most of which arrive between 10.30am and 2.30pm.

★ Glowworm Cave
CAVE
(☑0800 456 922; www.waitomo.com/experiences/waitomo-glowworm-caves; adult/child $55/25; ☺45min tours half-hourly 9am-5pm; ☎) The guided tour of the Glowworm Cave, which is behind the visitor centre, leads past im-

pressive stalactites and stalagmites into a large cavern known as the Cathedral. The highlight comes at the tour's end when you board a boat and swing off onto the river. As your eyes grow accustomed to the dark you'll see a Milky Way of little lights surrounding you – these are the glowworms. Book your tour at the visitor centre.

Ruakuri Cave CAVE
(☑07-878 6219, 0800 782 587; www.waitomo. com/experiences/ruakuri-cave; adult/child $79/30; ⊙2hr tours half-hourly from 9am-4pm; ♿) Ruakuri Cave has an impressive 15m-high spiral staircase, bypassing a Māori burial site at the cave entrance. Tours lead through 1.6km of the 7.5km system, taking in caverns with glowworms, subterranean streams and waterfalls, and intricate limestone structures. Visitors have described it as spiritual – some claim it's haunted – and it's customary to wash your hands when leaving to remove the *tapu* (taboo). Book tours at the visitor centre, or at the departure point, the Legendary Black Water Rafting Company.

Aranui Cave CAVE
(☑0800 456 922; www.waitomo.com/experiences/ aranui-cave; adult/child $5/25; ⊙1hr tours depart 9am-4pm) Three kilometres west from the Glowworm Cave is Aranui Cave. This cave is dry (hence no glowworms) but compensates with an incredible array of limestone formations. Thousands of tiny 'straw' stalactites hang from the ceiling. Book tours at the visitor centre, from where there is transport to the cave entrance. A 15-minute bushwalk is also included.

Waitomo Caves Discovery Centre MUSEUM
(☑07-878 7640; www.waitomocaves.com; 21 Waitomo Caves Rd; adult/child $5/free; ⊙8.45am-5pm) FREE Adjoining the Waitomo i-SITE, the Waitomo Caves Discovery Centre has excellent exhibits explaining how caves are formed, the flora and fauna that thrive in them, and the history of Waitomo's caves and cave exploration.

🏃 Activities

Underground
Legendary Black Water Rafting Company CAVING
(☑0800 782 5874; www.waitomo.com/experiences; 585 Waitomo Caves Rd) The Black Labyrinth tour ($150, three hours) involves floating in a wetsuit on an inner tube down a river through Ruakuri Cave. The highlight is leaping off a

small waterfall and then floating through a long, glowworm-covered passage. The trip ends with showers, soup and bagels in the cafe. There's also the more adventurous Black Abyss tour ($260, five hours), which includes a 35m abseil into Ruakuri Cave, a zip line and more glowworms and tubing.

Minimum ages apply for all tours, and there are occasional discounts if you prebook online. Check the website for combo deals also incorporating entry to the other Waitomo caves.

Spellbound CAVING
(☑0800 773 552, 07-878 7622; www.glowworm. co.nz; 10 Waitomo Caves Rd; adult/child $75/26; ⊙3hr tours 10am, 11am, 2pm & 3pm) Spellbound is a good option if you don't want to get wet, are more interested in glowworms than an 'action' experience, and want to avoid the big groups in the main caves. Small-group tours access parts of the heavily glowworm-dappled Mangawhitiakau cave system, 12km south of Waitomo (and you still get to ride on a raft!).

Kiwi Cave Rafting CAVING
(☑07-873 9149, 0800 228 372; www.blackwater raftingwaitomo.co.nz; 391 Boddies Road) These small-group expeditions ($290, five hours) start with abseil training, followed by a 27m descent into a natural cave, and then a float along a subterranean river on an inner tube. After some caving, a belayed rock climb up a 20m cliff brings you to the surface. Book directly online with Kiwi Cave Rafting for a significant discount.

Glowing Adventures CAVING
(☑0508 445 694, 07-878 7234; www.glowing.co.nz; 1199 Oparure Rd; per person $159) 🚶 Located on a family farm, these small-group tours (maximum eight people) negotiate more remote and unmodified caves. Tours involve clambering over boulders, up hills and through underground streams, so a moderate level of fitness and adventure is required. Glowworms are aplenty, and you'll spend around two hours of the three-hour tour underground.

Pickups are not available, so you'll need your own transport to rendezvous at the starting point around 25 minutes' drive from Waitomo village.

Waitomo Adventures CAVING
(☑0800 924 866, 07-878 7788; www.waitomo. co.nz; 1227 Waitomo Valley Rd; ♿) Waitomo Adventures offers various cave adventures, with a substantial discount for advance

online bookings at least 12 hours prior. The Lost World trip ($425/595, four/seven hours) combines a 100m abseil with walking, rock climbing, wading and swimming. Haggas Honking Holes ($195, four hours) includes three waterfall abseils, rock climbing and a subterranean river.

TumuTumu Toobing ($160, four hours) is a walking, climbing, swimming and tubing trip. St Benedict's Cavern ($235, three hours) includes abseiling and a subterranean flying fox.

Also on offer at the new Waitomo Valley Rd location is a cafe and spa and massage services, perfect after a bit of active adventure Waitomo-style. For younger travellers, the Troll Cave (adult/child $42/37, one hour) offers exciting subterranean thrills.

CaveWorld
CAVING

(☑07-878 6577, 0800 228 396; www.caveworld.co.nz; cnr Waitomo Caves Rd & Hotel Access Rd) CaveWorld explores the Footwhistle Glowworm Cave ($64, one hour), incorporating a stop in a forest shelter for a mug of restorative kawakawa tea, a natural tonic made with leaves from an indigenous bush plant. Twilight Footwhistle tours exploring the cave at night are $69.

Above Ground
The Waitomo i-SITE has free pamphlets on walks in the area. The walk from Aranui Cave (p213) to Ruakuri Cave (p213) is an excellent short path. From the Waitomo Caves Visitor Centre (p212), the 5km, three-hour-return Waitomo Walkway takes off through farmland, following Waitomo Stream to the Ruakuri Scenic Reserve, where a 30-minute return walk passes by a natural limestone tunnel. There are glowworms here at night – drive to the car park and bring a torch to find your way.

Dundle Hill Walk
HIKING

(☑07-878 7640; www.dundlehill.com; adult/child $80/40) The self-guided privately run Dundle Hill Walk is a 27km, two-day/one-night loop walk through Waitomo's bush and farmland, including overnight bunkhouse accommodation high up in the bush.

Waitomo Caves
Zipline Park
ADVENTURE SPORTS

(☑027 252 2929; www.waitomocavesziplines.co.nz; 24 Te Anga Rd; adult/child/family $55/35/145; ⊙10am, noon, 2pm & 4pm daily Oct-Apr, Wed-Sun May-Sep; ⓓ) Ride 10 zip lines taking in views of the Waitomo region's famed forest landscape. Booking ahead online is recommended. A well-priced introduction to zip lining.

🛏 Sleeping

Waitomo Top 10 Holiday Park
HOLIDAY PARK $

(☑0508 498 666, 07-878 7639; www.waitomopark.co.nz; 12 Waitomo Caves Rd; campsites $54, cabins & units $115-195; 🅿@🕾🕸ⓓ) This lovely holiday park in the heart of the village has spotless facilities, modern cabins and plenty of outdoor distractions to keep the kids busy. The cabins are a good alternative to dorm accommodation for friends travelling together, and renovated communal bathrooms are spotless.

YHA Juno Hall Waitomo
HOSTEL $

(☑07-878 7649; www.junowaitomo.co.nz; 600 Waitomo Caves Rd; campsites from $17, dm $33, d with/without bathroom $90/80; 🅿@🕾🕸) A slick purpose-built hostel 1km from the village with a warm welcome, a warmer wood fire in the woody lounge area, and an outdoor pool and tennis court.

HuHu Chalet
RENTAL HOUSE $$

(www.airbnb.com; 10 Waitomo Caves Rd; d $180) Concealed in a quirky pyramid structure that was once part of an advertising sign, Huhu Chalet has a cosy mezzanine bedroom upstairs, and a vibrant (red!) and modern bathroom and living space downstairs. With its simple wooden walls and a scattering of retro furniture, there's a warm Kiwiana vibe to the chalet, and Waitomo's best restaurant is literally metres away.

Waitomo Caves Guest Lodge
B&B $$

(☑0800 465 762, 07-878 7641; www.waitomocavesguestlodge.co.nz; 7 Waitomo Village Rd; s/d incl breakfast $140/160; 🕾) Bag your own cosy little hillside en-suite cabin at this central operation with a sweet garden setting. The top cabins have valley views. Large continental breakfasts and friendly and helpful owners get big ticks.

Abseil Inn
B&B $$

(☑07-878 7815; www.abseilinn.co.nz; 709 Waitomo Caves Rd; d $150-190; 🕾) Fittingly, a *veeery* steep driveway takes you to this delightful B&B with four themed rooms, great breakfasts and witty hosts. The biggest room has a double bath and valley views.

🍴 Eating & Drinking

★Huhu
MODERN NZ $$

(☑07-878 6674; www.huhucafe.co.nz; 10 Waitomo Caves Rd; mains $25-35; ⊙noon-late; 🕾) Huhu combines expansive terrace views and contemporary NZ food. Sip a Kiwi wine or craft beer – including brews from the local King Country Brewing Co – or graze the menu

GLOWWORM MAGIC

Glowworms are the larvae of the fungus gnat. The larva glowworm has luminescent organs that produce a soft, greenish light. Living in a sort of hammock suspended from an overhang, it weaves sticky threads that trail down and catch unwary insects attracted by its light. When an insect flies towards the light it gets stuck in the threads – the glowworm just has to reel it in for a feed.

The larval stage lasts from six to nine months, depending on how much food the glowworm gets. When it has grown to about the size of a matchstick, it goes into a pupal stage, much like a cocoon. The adult fungus gnat emerges about two weeks later.

The adult insect doesn't live very long because it doesn't have a mouth. It emerges, mates, lays eggs and dies, all within about two or three days. The sticky eggs, laid in groups of 40 or 50, hatch in about three weeks to become larval glowworms.

Glowworms thrive in moist, dark caves but they can survive anywhere if they have the requisites of moisture, an overhang to suspend from and insects to eat. Waitomo is famous for its glowworms but you can see them in many other places around New Zealand, both in caves and outdoors.

When you come upon glowworms, don't touch their hammocks or hanging threads, try not to make loud noises and don't shine a light right on them. All of these things will cause them to dim their lights. It takes them a few hours to become bright again, during which time the grub will go hungry. The glowworms that shine most brightly are the hungriest.

of delights including slow-cooked lamb, smoked salmon and roast duck. The $30 lunch menu is good value.

Tomo PUB
(07-878 8448; www.thetomobar.co.nz; Hotel Access Rd; noon-late) The welcoming Tomo is Waitomo's pub and home turf for the King Country Brewing Co. A frosty pale ale teamed with a fish burger, chowder or the massive pork ribs could be just the thing after a busy day underground. Served on the sunny deck, of course.

King Country Brewing Company BREWERY
(021 498 665; www.kingcountrybrewingco.co.nz; Tomo, Hotel Access Rd; noon-late) This craft brewery based at Tomo pub brews pilsner, IPA, pale ale, wheat beer and cider. Due to contractual issues with bigger breweries, not all the beers are on tap at the pub, but they are all available in Waitomo at Huhu. You'll also find them at Thirsty Weta (p211) in Ōtorohanga.

ℹ Information

Waitomo i-SITE (07-878 7640, 0800 474 839; www.waitomocaves.com; 21 Waitomo Caves Rd; 9am-5.30pm) Internet access, post office and booking agent.

ℹ Getting There & Away

Waitomo Caves Tours & Transfers (07-878 7580; www.waitomocavetours.com; per person $20) links Ōtorohanga and Waitomo on demand.

Book on its website or through local information centres or accommodation providers.

Waitomo Wanderer (03-477 9083, 0800 000 4321; www.travelheadfirst.com) operates a daily return service from Rotorua or Auckland, with optional caving, glowworm and tubing add-ons. It'll even integrate Hobbiton into the mix if you're a JRR Tolkien or Sir Peter Jackson fan.

South from Waitomo to Taranaki

This obscure route heading west of Waitomo on Te Anga Rd is a slow but fascinating alternative to SH3 if Taranaki's your goal. Only 12km of the 111km route remains unsealed, but it's nearly all winding and narrow. Allow around two hours (not including stops) and fill up with petrol. Accommodation is virtually nonexistent.

The **Mangapohue Natural Bridge Scenic Reserve**, 26km west of Waitomo, is a 5.5-hectare reserve with a giant natural limestone arch. It's a five-minute walk to the arch on a wheelchair-accessible pathway.

About 4km further west is **Piripiri Caves Scenic Reserve**, where a five-minute walk leads to a large cave containing fossils of giant oysters. Bring a torch and be prepared to get muddy after heavy rain. Steps wind down into the gloom...

The impressively tiered, 30m **Marokopa Falls** are 32km west of Waitomo. A short track (15 minutes return) from the road leads to the bottom of the falls.

Just past Te Anga you can turn north to Kāwhia, 59km away, or continue southwest to Marokopa (population 1540), a small black-sand village on the coast. The whole Te Anga/Marokopa area is riddled with caves.

The road heads south to Kiritehere, through idyllic farmland to Moeatoa, then turns right (south) into Mangatoa Rd. Now you're in serious backcountry, heading into the dense Whareorino Forest. For hikers, there's the 16-bunk, DOC-run Leitch's Hut (☑07-878 1050; www.doc.govt.nz; per adult $5).

At Waikawau take the 5km detour along the unsealed road to the coast near Ngarupupu Point, where a 100m walk through a dank tunnel opens out onto an exquisitely isolated stretch of black-sand beach. Think twice about swimming here as there are often dangerous rips in the surf.

The road then continues through another twisty 28km, passing lush forest and occasional farms before joining SH3 east of Awakino.

Walks in the Tawarau Forest, 20km west of the Waitomo Caves, are outlined in DOC's *Waitomo & King Country Tracks* booklet ($1, available from DOC in Hamilton or Te Kuiti), including a one-hour track that takes you to the Tawarau Falls from the end of Appletree Rd.

Te Kuiti

POP 4640

Cute Te Kuiti sits in a valley between picturesque hills. Welcome to the shearing capital of the world, especially if you visit for the annual Great New Zealand Muster. It's also the birthplace of the late Sir Colin Meads, one of NZ's most iconic All Blacks.

◉ Sights

Sir Colin Meads Statue   STATUE

(Rora St) This statue commemorates the late Sir Colin Meads, a legendary captain of the All Blacks, and regarded as one of New Zealand's finest rugby players. Nicknamed 'Pinetree', and a lifelong resident of Te Kuiti and the King Country, Sir Colin's laconic and pragmatic demeanour means he's also fond-

ly remembered as the quintessential Kiwi – a 'good bugger' in local parlance.

Big Shearer   LANDMARK

(Rora St) The 7m-high, 7.5-tonne Big Shearer statue is at the southern end of town.

★ Festivals & Events

Great New
Zealand Muster   CULTURAL

(⊘late Mar/early Apr; ◈) The highlight of the Great New Zealand Muster is the legendary Running of the Sheep, when 2000 woolly demons stampede down Te Kuiti's main street. The festival includes sheep-shearing championships, a parade, Māori cultural performances, live music, barbecues, *hāngi* (Māori earth-cooked feast) and market stalls.

🛏 Sleeping & Eating

Waitomo Lodge Motel   MOTEL $$

(☑07-878 0003; www.waitomo-lodge.co.nz; 62 Te Kumi Rd; units $115-160; ℗ 🛜) At the Waitomo end of Te Kuiti, this motel's modern rooms feature contemporary art, flat-screen TVs and decks overlooking Mangaokewa Stream from the units at the back. A couple of resident animals include Willow the friendly terrier.

Bosco Cafe   CAFE $$

(☑07-878 3633; www.boscocafe.me; 57 Te Kumi Rd; mains $14-24; ⊘8am-6pm; 🛜 ◈) This excellent industrial-chic cafe offers great coffee and tempting food – try the bacon-wrapped meatloaf with greens or the tasty chicken wraps. The kids' menu gets two thumbs up from younger travellers.

Stoked Eatery   CAFE $$

(☑07-878 8758; www.facebook.com/stokedeatery; Te Kuiti Railway Station, 2 Rora St; mains $14-32; ⊘10am-8.30pm) This busy restaurant and bar in the former railway station celebrates a great location on the station platform with a relaxed ambience and a menu of hearty fare. Servings are very generous; standouts include lamb shanks or the buttermilk-fried chicken. A decent wine list and local craft beer on tap make Stoked a good option for a drink, too.

❶ Information

Te Kuiti DOC (☑07-878 1050; www.doc.govt.nz; 78 Taupiri St; ⊘8am-4.30pm Mon-Fri) Area office for the surrounding Maniapoto region.

Te Kuiti i-SITE (☑ 07-878 8077; www.waitomo.govt.nz; Rora St; ☉ 9am-5pm Mon-Fri, 10am-2pm Sat & Sun, closed weekends May-Oct; ☎) Internet access and visitor information.

❶ Getting There & Away

InterCity (☑ 09-583 5780; www.intercity.co.nz) buses run daily to the following destinations (among others): Auckland ($24 to $34, 3½ hours, three daily), Ōtorohanga ($10, 20 minutes, three daily) and Taumarunui ($13, 1¼ hours, one daily).

Pio Pio, Awakino & Mōkau

From Te Kuiti, SH3 runs southwest to the coast before following the shoreline to New Plymouth. Detour at Pio Pio (population 400) to Hairy Feet Waitomo, one of New Zealand's newest Middle-earth attractions.

Along this scenic route the sheep stations sprout peculiar limestone formations before giving way to lush native bush as the highway winds along the course of the Awakino River. This river spills into the Tasman at Awakino (population 60), a small settlement where boats shelter in the estuary while locals find refuge at the rustic Awakino Hotel.

Five kilometres further south, as Mt Taranaki starts to emerge on the horizon, is the village of Mōkau (population 400). It offers a fine black-sand beach and good surfing and fishing. From August to November the Mōkau River spawns whitebait and subsequent swarms of territorial whitebaiters.

A little south of Awakino the impressive Maniaroa Marae dominates the cliff above the highway. This important complex houses the anchor stone of the Tainui *waka*, which brought this region's original people from their Polynesian homeland. You can get a good view of the intimidatingly carved meeting house, Te Kohaarua, from outside the fence – don't cross into the *marae* unless someone invites you.

Hairy Feet Waitomo   FILM LOCATION
(☑ 07-877 8003; www.hairyfeetwaitomo.co.nz; 1411 Mangaotaki Rd, Pio Pio; tours adult/child $60/; ☉ tours 10am & 1pm) Detour at Pio Pio northwest to the Mangaotaki Valley and Hairy Feet Waitomo, one of NZ's most interesting Middle-earth–themed attractions. Scenes from *The Hobbit* were filmed here with a background of towering limestone cliffs.

Tainui Historical Society Museum   MUSEUM
(☑ 06-752 9072; www.mokaumuseum.nz; SH3, Mōkau; by donation; ☉ 10am-4pm) Mōkau's in-teresting Tainui Historical Society Museum has old photographs and artefacts from when this once-isolated outpost was a coal and lumber shipping port for settlements along the river. The adjacent art gallery featuring local artists was added in 2016.

Mokau Motel   MOTEL $$
(☑ 06-752 9725; www.mokaumotels.co.nz; SH3, Mōkau; d $125-150; ☎) Above the village, the Mokau Motel offers fishing advice, self-contained units and three luxury suites.

Whitebait Inn   CAFE $$
(☑ 06-752 9713; www.whitebaitinn.co.nz; 55 North St, Mōkau; snacks & mains $12-27; ☉ 7.30am-6.30pm) A great place to try the local speciality of whitebait is this classic Kiwi diner. Look for the quirky statue of the whitebait fisherman on the roof before getting stuck into tasty fritters or an omelette stuffed into a fresh slice of fluffy white bread. Add a squeeze of lemon juice and salt and pepper, and you're good to go.

Awakino Hotel   PUB FOOD $$
(☑ 06-752 9815; www.awakinohotel.com; SH3, Awakino; meals $16-32; ☉ 11am-10pm Sun-Thu, to midnight Fri & Sat) The Awakino River spills into the Tasman at Awakino, where boats shelter in the estuary while locals find refuge at the rustic Awakino Hotel. Look forward to hearty meals, including whitebait fritters, and a pleasant garden bar. There's also decent accommodation (single/double $50/90), including double rooms with private bathrooms.

❶ Getting There & Away

InterCity (www.intercity.co.nz) buses run from Te Kuiti to Mōkau (from $14, one hour, one daily), part of a service linking Auckland to New Plymouth.

Taumarunui

POP 5140

Taumarunui on a cold day can feel a bit miserable, but this town in the heart of the King Country has potential. The main reason to stay here is to kayak on the Whanganui River or as a cheaper base for skiing in Tongariro National Park. There are also some beaut walks and cycling tracks around town.

For details of tours along the Forgotten World Highway between Taumarunui and Stratford, contact Eastern Taranaki Experience (p269). Details on canoeing and kayaking on the Whanganui River can be obtained from Whanganui National Park (p264).

WAIKATO & THE COROMANDEL PENINSULA PIO PIO, AWAKINO & MŌKAU

OFF THE BEATEN TRACK

PUREORA FOREST PARK

Fringing the western edge of Lake Taupō, the 780-sq-km Pureora Forest is home to New Zealand's tallest totara tree. Logging was stopped in the 1980s after a long campaign by conservationists, and the subsequent regeneration is impressive. Hiking routes through the park include tracks to the summits of **Mt Pureora** (1165m) and the rock pinnacle of **Mt Titiraupenga** (1042m). A 12m-high tower, a short walk from the Bismarck Rd car park, provides a canopy-level view of the forest for bird-watchers. Cyclists can ride the spectacular **Timber Trail** from Pureora village in the north of the forest southwest for 85km to Ongarue. Two days is recommended.

For shuttles, bike hire and details of glamping at its Camp Epic location along the trail, contact Epic Cycle Adventures. See www.thetimbertrail.nz for maps, route planning, and shuttle and bike-hire information.

Another recommended accommodation option is **Timber Trail Lodge** (📞0800 885 6343; www.timbertraillodge.co.nz; d $330) in the heart of the park. Rates include all meals, and multiday packages incorporating shuttles are available. There's also the rustic but comfortable **Black Fern Lodge** (📞07-894 7677; www.blackfernlodge.co.nz; Ongarue Stream Rd, Waimiha; per person from $60) at around the halfway point of the Timber Trail. It gets rave reviews for its home cooking.

Awhina Wilderness Experience (www.facebook.com/AwhinaWildernessExperience) offers five-hour walking tours with local Māori guides through virgin bush to the summit of Titiraupenga, their sacred mountain.

Within the park there are also three **DOC campsites** (www.doc.govt.nz; adult/child $8/4), with self-registration boxes. To stay overnight in one of the three standard DOC huts, you'll need to buy hut tickets in advance, unless you have a Backcountry Hut Pass. Hut tickets, maps and information are available from DOC.

There's no scheduled public transport, but Epic Cycle Adventures can arrange shuttles.

⊙ Sights

Te Peka Lookout, across the Ongarue River on the western edge of town, is a good vantage point.

Raurimu Spiral   HISTORIC SITE
The Raurimu Spiral, 30km south of town, is a unique feat of railway engineering that was completed in 1908 after 10 years of work. Rail buffs can experience the spiral by catching the *Northern Explorer* train linking Auckland and Wellington to National Park township. Unfortunately, this train no longer stops in Taumarunui.

🏃 Activities & Tours

The 3km **Riverbank Walk** along the Whanganui River runs from Cherry Grove Domain, 1km south of town, to Taumarunui Holiday Park.

Epic Cycle Adventures   MOUNTAIN BIKING
(📞022 023 7958; www.thetimbertrail.nz; Bennett Rd, Ongarue; bike & shuttle from $120) Arranges bike hire and convenient shuttles if you're keen to tackle the Timber Trail. Check the website for more details on this interesting ride.

Forgotten World Adventures   TOURS
(📞0800 7245 2278; www.forgottenworldadventures.co.nz; 9 Hakiaha St; half-/1-/2-day tours from $169/249/639; ⊘booking office 9am-2pm) Ride the rails on quirky, converted golf carts along the railway line linking Taumarunui to the tiny hamlet of Whangamomona. The most spectacular trip takes in 20 tunnels. Other options include a rail and jetboat combo and a longer two-day excursion covering the full 140km from Taumarunui to Stratford (including an overnight stay in Whangamomona).

Forgotten World Jet   ADVENTURE
(📞0800 7245 2278, 07-895 7181; www.fwj.co.nz; Cherry Grove Domain; 1/2hr from $129/259; ⊘8am-5pm) High-octane jetboat trips on the Whanganui River. Longer eight-hour adventures take in the spectacular Bridge to Nowhere, and trips incorporating rail journeys with Forgotten World Adventures are also available.

🛏 Sleeping & Eating

Taumarunui Holiday Park   HOLIDAY PARK $
(📞07-895 9345; www.taumarunuiholidaypark.co.nz; SH4; campsites from $18, cabins & cottages $55-90;

P @ 🛜 📶) On the banks of the Whanganui River, 4km east of town, this shady camping ground offers safe river swimming and clean facilities. The friendly owners have lots of ideas on what to see and do.

Twin Rivers Motel MOTEL **$$**

(📞 07-895 8063; www.twinrivers.co.nz; 23 Marae St; units $90-215; P 🛜) The 12 units at Twin Rivers are spick and span. Bigger units sleep up to seven.

Buy the Gram BAKERY **$**

(📞 07-896 8804; www.facebook.com/buythegram; 55 Hakiaha St; snacks from $3; ⊙9am-5pm Mon-Fri, 10am-2pm Sat; 📶) 🍴 Artisan muesli, tasty homestyle baking and good coffee all combine at this surprising spot along Taumarunui's main street. Stock up for healthy breakfasts and not-so-healthy treats for life on the road.

❶ Information

Taumarunui i-SITE (📞 07-895 7494; www. visitruapehu.com; 116 Hakiaha St; ⊙8.30am-5.30pm) Visitor information and internet access.

❶ Getting There & Away

Taumarunui is on SH4, 81km south of Te Kuiti and 41km north of National Park township. **InterCity** (📞 0508 353 947; www.intercity. co.nz) buses head to Auckland ($34, 4½ hours) via Te Kuiti and to Palmerston North ($37, 4½ hours) via National Park.

Owhango

POP 210

A pint-sized village where all the street names start with 'O', Owhango makes a cosy base for walkers, mountain bikers – the 42 Traverse (p299) ends here – and skiers who don't want to fork out to stay closer to the slopes in Tongariro National Park. Take Omaki Rd for a two-hour loop walk through virgin forest in Ohinetonga Scenic Reserve.

Blue Duck Station LODGE **$**

(Map p265; 📞 07-895 6276; www.blueduckstation. co.nz; RD2, Whakahoro; dm $45, d $100-195) 🍴 Overlooking the Retaruke River 36km southwest of Owhango (take the Kaitieke turn-off 1km south of town), this ecosavvy place is actually various lodges, offering accommodation from dorms in old shearers' quarters to a self-contained family cottage sleeping eight. The owners are mad-keen conservationists, restoring native-bird habitats and historic buildings. Activities include bush tours, horse riding, kayaking and mountain biking.

❶ Getting There & Away

Owhango is 14km south of Taumarunui on SH4. All the **InterCity** (📞 0508 353 947; www. intercity.co.nz) buses that stop in Taumarunui also stop here.

COROMANDEL PENINSULA

The Coromandel Peninsula juts into the Pacific east of Auckland, forming the eastern boundary of the Hauraki Gulf. Although relatively close to the metropolis, the Coromandel offers easy access to splendid isolation. Its dramatic, mountainous spine bisects it into two very distinct parts.

The east coast has some of the North Island's best white-sand beaches. When Auckland shuts up shop for Christmas and New Year, this is where it heads. The cutesy historic gold-mining towns on the western side escape the worst of the influx, their muddy wetlands and picturesque stony bays holding less appeal for the masses. This coast has long been a refuge for alternative lifestylers. Down the middle, the mountains are crisscrossed with walking tracks.

History

This whole area – including the peninsula, the islands and both sides of the gulf – was known to the Māori as Hauraki. Various *iwi* (tribes) held claim to pockets of it, including the Pare Hauraki branch of the Tainui *iwi* and others descended from Te Arawa and earlier migrations. Polynesian artefacts and evidence of moa-hunting have been found, pointing to around 1000 years of continuous occupation.

The Hauraki *iwi* were some of the first to be exposed to European traders. The region's proximity to Auckland, safe anchorages and ready supply of valuable timber initially led to a booming economy. Kauri logging was big business on the peninsula. Allied to the timber trade was shipbuilding, which took off in 1832 when a mill was established at Mercury Bay. Things got tougher once the kauri around the coast became scarce and the loggers had to penetrate deeper into the bush for timber. Kauri dams, which used water power to propel the huge logs to the coast, were built. By the 1930s virtually no kauri remained and the industry died.

Gold was first discovered in NZ near Coromandel Town in 1852. Although this first rush was short-lived, more gold was discovered

Coromandel Peninsula

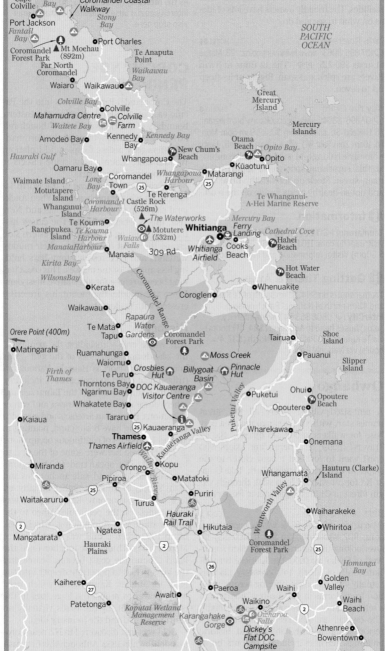

N

0   20 km
0   10 miles

Cape Colville
Fletcher Bay
Coromandel Coastal Walkway
Stony Bay
Port Jackson
Fantail Bay
Coromandel Forest Park
Port Charles
Mt Moehau (892m)
Te Anaputa Point
Far North Coromandel
Waikawau Bay
Waiaro
Waikawau
Colville Bay
Colville
Mahamudra Centre
Colville Farm
Waitete Bay
Kennedy Bay
Kennedy Bay
Amodeo Bay
Whangapoua
New Chum's Beach
Otama Beach
Opito Bay
Opito
Kūaotunu
Oamaru Bay
Hauraki Gulf
Long Bay
Coromandel Town
Whangapoua Harbour
Matarangi
Great Mercury Island
Mercury Islands
Waimate Island
Motutapere Island
Whanganui Island
Te Rerenga
Castle Rock (526m)
The Waterworks
Motutere (532m)
Whitianga
Ferry Landing
Cooks Beach
Te Whanganui-A-Hei Marine Reserve
Rangipukei Island
Te Kouma Harbour
Te Kouma
Coromandel Harbour
Waiau Falls
309 Rd
Whitianga Airfield
Mercury Bay
Cathedral Cove
Hahei Beach
Manaia Harbour
Manaia
Hot Water Beach
Kirita Bay
WilsonsBay
Kerata
Coroglen
Whenuakite
Waikawau
Te Mata
Rapaura Water Gardens
Coromandel Range
Orere Point (400m)
Matingarahi
Tapu
Coromandel Forest Park
Moss Creek
Tairua
Shoe Island
Ruamahunga
Waiomu
Crosbies Hut
Billygoat Basin
Pinnacle Hut
Pauanui
Slipper Island
Firth of Thames
Te Puru
Thorntons Bay
Ngarimu Bay
Whakatete Bay
DOC Kauaeranga Visitor Centre
Puketui Valley
Puketui
Ohui
Opoutere Beach
Opoutere
Kaiaua
Tararu
Kauaeranga
Kauaeranga Valley
Wharekawa
Onemana
Thames
Thames Airfield
Waihou River
Miranda
Orongo
Kopu
Matatoki
Whangamata
Hauturu (Clarke) Island
Pipiroa
Puriri
Wentworth Valley
Waitakaruru
Turua
Hauraki Rail Trail
Hikutaia
Waiharakeke
Ngatea
Whiritoa
Mangatarata
Hauraki Plains
Coromandel Forest Park
Homunga Bay
Kaihere
Awaiti
Paeroa
Waihi
Golden Valley
Patetonga
Koputai Wetland Management Reserve
Karangahake Gorge
Waikino
Owharoa Falls
Waihi Beach
Dickey's Flat DOC Campsite
Athenree
Bowentown

SOUTH PACIFIC OCEAN

around Thames in 1867 and later in other places. The peninsula is also rich in semi-precious gemstones, such as quartz, agate, amethyst and jasper. A fossick on any west-coast beach can be rewarding.

Despite successful interactions with Europeans for decades, the Hauraki *iwi* were some of the hardest hit by colonisation. Unscrupulous dealings by settlers and government to gain access to valuable resources resulted in the Māori losing most of their lands by the 1880s. Even today there is a much lower Māori presence on the peninsula than in neighbouring districts.

ⓘ Getting There & Away

Daily buses on the Auckland–Tauranga Inter-City (www.intercity.co.nz) route pass through Thames and Waihi, while others loop through Coromandel Town, Whitianga and Tairua.

It's definitely worth considering the beautiful **Fullers360** (📞0800 385 5377; www.fullers.co.nz) ferry ride from Auckland via Waiheke Island to Coromandel Town.

Miranda

It's a pretty name for a settlement on the swampy Firth of Thames, just an hour's drive from Auckland. The two reasons to come here are splashing around in the thermal pools and bird-watching.

This is one of the most accessible spots for studying waders or shorebirds all year-round. The vast mudflat is teeming with aquatic worms and crustaceans, which attract thousands of Arctic-nesting shorebirds over the winter – 43 species of wader have been spotted here. The two main species are the bar-tailed godwit and the lesser or red knot, but it isn't unusual to see turnstones, sandpipers and the odd vagrant red-necked stint. One godwit tagged here was tracked making an 11,570km nonstop flight from Alaska. Short-haul travellers include the pied oystercatcher and the threatened wrybill from the South Island, and banded dotterels and pied stilts.

Pukorokoro Miranda Shorebird Centre   WILDLIFE RESERVE
(📞09-232 2781; www.miranda-shorebird.org.nz; 283 East Coast Rd; bird-watching pamphlet $2; ⏰9am-5pm) The Miranda Shorebird Centre has birdlife displays, hires out binoculars and sells useful bird-watching pamphlets. Nearby is a hide and several walks (30 minutes to two hours). The centre offers clean

bunk-style accommodation (dorm beds/rooms $25/95) with a kitchen. Visit the website to check out recent sightings.

Miranda Hot Springs   HOT SPRINGS
(📞07-867 3055; www.mirandahotsprings.co.nz; Front Miranda Rd; adult/child $15/8, private spa extra $15; ⏰9am-9pm) Miranda Hot Springs has a large thermal swimming pool (reputedly the largest in the southern hemisphere), a toasty sauna pool and private spas.

Miranda Holiday Park   HOLIDAY PARK $
(📞07-867 3205; www.mirandaholidaypark.co.nz; 595 Front Miranda Rd; campsites per person $29, units $95-194; ❋＠🛰🏊) 🏌 Next door to the Miranda Hot Springs, Miranda Holiday Park has excellent sparkling-clean units and facilities, its own hot-spring pool and a floodlit tennis court.

ⓘ Getting There & Away

There is no public transport to Miranda. Most travellers visit en route to/from Auckland and Thames.

Thames

POP 7350

Dinky wooden buildings from the 19th-century gold rush still dominate Thames, but grizzly prospectors have long been replaced by alternative lifestylers. It's a good base for hiking or canyoning in the nearby Kauaeranga Valley. There's also good shopping with some interesting stores and galleries along Pollen St.

Captain Cook arrived here in 1769, naming the Waihou River the 'Thames' 'on account of its bearing some resemblance to that river in England'; you may well think otherwise. This area belonged to Ngāti Maru, a tribe of Tainui descent. Their spectacular meeting house, Hotunui (1878), holds pride of place in the Auckland Museum.

After opening Thames to gold miners in 1867, Ngāti Maru were swamped by 10,000 European settlers within a year. When the initial boom turned to bust, a dubious system of government advances resulted in Māori debt and forced land sales.

◉ Sights

★ **Goldmine Experience**   MINE
(📞07-868 8514; www.goldmine-experience.co.nz; cnr Moanataiari Rd & Pollen St; adult/child $15/5; ⏰10am-1pm Apr-Dec, to 4pm Jan-Mar) Walk through a mine tunnel, watch a stamper

Thames

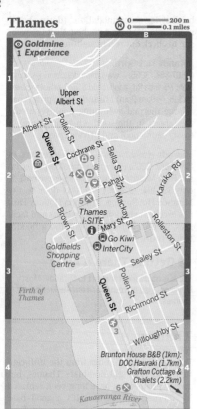

▲ 0 ——— 200 m
Ⓝ 0 ——— 0.1 miles

battery crush rock, learn about the history of the Cornish miners and try your hand at panning for gold. Closed-toe footwear and a waterproof jacket are recommended as the underground tunnel can get damp.

School of Mines & Mineralogical Museum   MUSEUM

(☎ 07-868 6227; www.historicplaces.org.nz; 101 Cochrane St; adult/child $10/free; ☉ 11am-3pm daily Jan-Mar, Wed-Sun Apr-Dec) The Historic Places Trust runs tours of these buildings, which house an extensive collection of NZ rocks, minerals and fossils. The oldest section (1868) was part of a Methodist Sunday School, situated on a Māori burial ground. The Trust has a free self-guided tour pamphlet taking in Thames' significant buildings.

🏃 Activities

Canyonz   OUTDOORS

(☎ 0800 422 696; www.canyonz.co.nz; trips $390) 🏊 All-day canyoning trips to the Sleeping God Canyon in the Kauaeranga Valley. Expect a vertical descent of over 300m, requiring abseiling, water-sliding and jumping. Trips leave from Thames at 8.30am; 7am pickups from Hamilton are also available. Note that Thames is only a 1½-hour drive from central Auckland, so with your own transport a day trip from Auckland is possible.

JollyBikes   CYCLING

(☎ 07-867 9026; www.jollybikes.co.nz; 96 Richmond St; mountain bike/e-bike hire per day from $50/95; ☉ 9.30am-5pm Mon-Fri, to 2pm Sat; 🚲) Rents out mountain bikes and e-bikes, does repairs and has plenty of information on tackling the Hauraki Rail Trail. Check the website for details of one- to four-day tours on the Hauraki Rail Trail.

🛏 Sleeping

Brunton House B&B   B&B $$

(☎ 07-868 5160; www.bruntonhouse.co.nz; 210 Parawai Rd; r from $160; @ 🛜 ⛱) This impressive two-storey kauri villa (1875) has a modern kitchen and bathrooms, while staying true to the building's historic credentials (there are no en suites). Guests can relax in the grounds, by the pool, in the designated lounge or on the upstairs terrace. During summer, lawn tennis is an option on the property's own grass court.

Grafton Cottage & Chalets   CHALET $$

(☎ 07-868 9971; www.graftoncottage.co.nz; 304 Grafton Rd; units $145-220; @ 🛜 ⛱) Most of these attractive wooden chalets perched on a hill have decks with awesome views. The hospitable hosts provide free internet access and breakfast, as well as use of the pool, spa and barbecue areas.

Coastal Motor Lodge MOTEL $$
(☑ 07-868 6843; www.stayatcoastal.co.nz; 608 Tararu Rd; units $161-208; P 🛜) Motel and chalet-style accommodation is provided at this smart, welcoming place, 2km north of Thames. It overlooks the sea, making it a popular choice, especially in the summer months.

✖ Eating & Drinking

Wharf Coffee House & Bar CAFE $
(☑ 07-868 6828; www.facebook.com/thewharf coffeehouseandbar; Shortland Wharf, Queen St; snacks & mains $10-20; ⊙ 9am-3pm Mon & Tue, to 7pm Wed, Sat & Sun, to 8pm Thu & Fri) Perched beside the water, this rustic wood-lined pavilion is a great spot for fish and chips. Order from the nearby kitchen and partner with a beer or a wine to understand why the Wharf is a firm local favourite.

Coco Coffee Bar CAFE $
(☑ 07-868 8616; 661 Pollen St; snacks from $5; ⊙ 7am-2pm Mon-Fri, from 7.30am Sat) Occupying a corner of an old villa, this chic little cafe serves excellent coffee and enticing pastries and cakes.

Cafe Melbourne CAFE $$
(☑ 07-868 3159; www.facebook.com/cafemel bournegrahamstown; 715 Pollen St; mains $15-22; ⊙ 8am-4pm) Stylish and spacious, this cafe definitely channels the cosmopolitan vibe of a certain Australian city. Shared tables promote a convivial ambience, and the menu travels from ricotta pancakes to beef sliders and fish curry for lunch. It's in a repurposed building called the Depot, where you'll also find interesting homeware shops and pop-up art galleries.

Junction Hotel PUB
(☑ 07-868 6008; www.thejunction.net.nz; 700 Pollen St; ⊙ 10am-late) Serving thirsty gold diggers since 1869, the Junction is the archetypal slightly rough-around-the-edges, historic, small-town pub. Live music attracts a younger crowd on the weekends, while families head to the corner-facing Grahamstown Bar & Diner for hearty pub grub of bar snacks, pizza and mains ($20 to $33).

🛍 Shopping

★ Bounty Store ARTS & CRAFTS
(☑ 07-868 8988; www.facebook.com/bountystore; 754 Pollen St; ⊙ 9.30am-4.30pm Tue-Fri, 9.30am-2pm & 5-6pm Sat) Excellent arts-and-crafts shop with loads of local products and a quirky selection of Kiwiana works. Highly recommended for distinctive souvenirs and gifts.

★ ArohArt ART
(www.arohart.co.nz; 724 Pollen St; ⊙ 9am-4pm Wed-Sat) Apparel, jewellery, homewares, prints and carving all come with a Māori design influence at this Māori-owned store. Most of the work is by Māori artists and designers and also craftspeople working and living in Thames and the surrounding Hauraki region.

ℹ Information

DOC Hauraki (☑ 07-867 9180; www.doc.govt. nz; 3/366 SH25; ⊙ 8am-4.30pm Mon-Fri) Offers information on hiking tracks in the area.

Thames i-SITE (☑ 07-868 7284; www.thecoro mandel.com/thames; 200 Mary St; ⊙ 9am-4pm Mon-Fri, to 1pm Sat & Sun) An excellent source of information for the entire Coromandel Peninsula.

ℹ Getting There & Away

InterCity (☑ 09-583 5780; www.intercity. co.nz; Mary St) has bus services to Auckland ($20 to $30, 1½ hours). **Go Kiwi** (☑ 0800 446 549; www.go-kiwi.co.nz; Mary St) services Auckland ($54, 2¼ hours) and Whitianga ($39, 1¾ hours). Buses leave from outside the Thames i-SITE.

Coastal Route from Thames to Coromandel Town

From Thames, narrow SH25 snakes along the coast past pretty little bays and rocky beaches. Seabirds are plentiful, and you can fish, dig for shellfish and fossick for quartz, jasper and even gold-bearing rocks. The landscape turns crimson when the pohutukawa (often referred to as the 'New Zealand Christmas tree') blooms in December.

A handful of stores, motels, B&Bs and camping grounds are scattered around the picturesque bays. At **Tapu** turn inland for a mainly sealed 6km drive to the **Rapaura Water Gardens** (☑ 07-868 4821; www.rapaura watergardens.co.nz; 586 Tapu-Coroglen Rd; adult/

THE HAURAKI RAIL TRAIL

The Hauraki Rail Trail, which runs from Thames south to Paeroa, and then further south to Te Aroha and Matamata, or east to Waihi, is growing in popularity with cyclists, due to its proximity to the bigger cities of Auckland and Hamilton. Two- and three-day itineraries are most popular, but shorter sections of the trail can be very rewarding, too. The spur from Paeroa east through the Karangahake Gorge via Waikino to Waihi is spectacular as it skirts a picturesque river valley. In late 2017, a coastal spur opened linking Kauaia to Thames, and taking in the Pukorokoro Miranda Shorebird Centre (p221). The key centres of Thames, Paeroa, Te Aroha and Waihi have an expanding range of related services, including bike hire, shuttles and accommodation.

See www.haurakirailtrail.co.nz for detailed information including trail maps and recommendations for day rides.

child $15/6; ⊙9am-5pm; ⛫) ⚑, combining water, greenery and sculpture.

From **Wilsons Bay** the road heads away from the coast and negotiates several hills and valleys before dropping down to Coromandel Town, 55km from Thames. The view looking towards the island-studded Coromandel Harbour is exquisite.

Waiomu Beach Cafe   CAFE $$
(⛫07-868 2554; www.facebook.com/waiomubeachcafe; 622 Thames Coast Rd, Waiomu Bay; mains $15-28; ⊙7am-5pm; ⛫) ⚑ Just north of Te Puru, stop at the colourful Waiomu Beach Cafe for hearty breakfasts, gourmet pizza, freshly squeezed juices and healthy salads. Locally brewed craft beer from around the peninsula is also available.

❶ Getting There & Away

Driving your own vehicle is recommended around this spectacular and winding coastal road. InterCity (p223) buses link Whitianga and Coromandel Town.

Coromandel Town

POP 1750

Crammed with heritage buildings, Coromandel Town is a thoroughly quaint little place. Its cafes, art stores, sleeping options and delicious smoked mussels could keep you here longer than you expected.

Gold was discovered nearby at Driving Creek in 1852. Initially the local Patukiriki-ri *iwi* kept control of the land and received money from digging licences. After initial financial success, the same fate befell them as the Ngāti Maru in Thames. By 1871, debt had forced them to sell all but 778 mountainous acres of their land. Today fewer than 100 people remain who identify as part of this *iwi*.

Note that Coromandel Town is just one part of the entire Coromandel Peninsula, and its location on the peninsula's west coast means it is not a good base for visiting Cathedral Cove and Hot Water Beach on the peninsula's east coast.

◉ Sights & Activities

Many historic sites are featured in the Historic Places Trust's *Coromandel Town* pamphlet, available at the Coromandel Town Information Centre (p226).

Coromandel Mining & Historic Museum   MUSEUM
(⛫07-866 8987; 841 Rings Rd; adult/child $5/free; ⊙1-4pm daily Boxing Day-Easter, 1-4pm Sat & Sun Easter-May & late Oct-Boxing Day) Small museum with glimpses of pioneer life.

★**Driving Creek Railway**   RAIL
(⛫07-866 8703; www.dcrail.nz; 380 Driving Creek Rd; adult/child $35/13; ⊙10.15am, 11.30am, 12.45pm, 2pm, 3.15pm & 4.30pm, additional times summer; ⛫) ⚑ A lifelong labour of love for its conservationist owner, the late Barry Brickell, this unique train runs up steep grades, across four trestle bridges, along two spirals and a double switchback, and through two tunnels, finishing at the 'Eye-full Tower'. The one-hour trip passes artworks and regenerating native forest. Booking ahead is recommended in summer. As well as the new zip line launched in late 2019, future plans for Driving Creek Railway include a cafe, pottery workshops and a children's adventure playground.

★**Coromandel Zipline Tours**   ADVENTURE SPORTS
(⛫0800 267 6947; www.dcrail.nz/corozip; 380 Driving Creek Rd, Driving Creek Railway; adult/child/family $127/87/377; ⊙8.15am, 12.15pm & 4.15pm, up to 6 times per day in summer; ⛫) ⚑ Stretching for 705m, Coromandel Town's newest attraction spans eight separate sections amid the forest canopy of the Driving Creek Conservation Park. The experience begins by riding Driving Creek's unique bush railway

to the Kauri Grove starting point amid regenerating kauri forest. Short walks between the zip-line sections include commentary on Driving Creek's native forest conservation programme, and the tour concludes with the thrilling 200m Kōtārē Straight zip line all the way down to Driving Creek village.

👉 Tours

Coromandel Adventures   DRIVING
(📞0800 462 676; www.coromandeladventures. co.nz; 90 Tiki Rd; tours adult/child from $110/70; ⏰8.30am-5pm) Offers various tours around Coromandel Town and the peninsula, including day excursions from Coromandel Town to Cathedral Cove, Hot Water Beach and New Chums Beach. Also shuttles to popular local attractions and to Whitianga. If you're planning on exploring the Coromandel Walkway, Coromandel Adventures provide a convenient one-day transport package (adult/child $145/90) departing from either Coromandel Town or Whitianga.

Coromandel Discovery   WALKING
(📞07-866 8175, 0800 287 432; www.coromandel discovery.co.nz; 105 Wharf Rd, Coromandel Town; Coromandel Walkway adult/child $140/95; ⏰8am-5pm) To skip the return leg of the Coromandel Walkway, Coromandel Discovery will drive you from Coromandel Town (departing 8.30am) up to Fletcher Bay and pick you up from Stony Bay four hours later. Also on offer is the shorter Muriwai Walk (adult/child $99/79), taking in 3km of stunning coastal scenery with an 11.30am departure from Coromandel Town.

Bush e Bikes   CYCLING
(📞027 337 7996, 0800 287 432; https:// bushebikes.co.nz; 105 Wharf Rd, Coromandel Discovery; e-bikes per 2hr/4hr/day $30/50/90; ⏰8am-5pm; 🚲) 🏃 Part of Coromandel Discovery, Bush e Bikes have a full selection of bikes, including electric mountain bikes and tandems. Recommended rides and itineraries include the short beach runs out to Long Bay and Wyuna Bay, ascending the Tokatea lookout for east- and west-coast views, and one- and two-day experiences including accommodation tackling the road north to sleepy Colville. It's also possible to integrate the Coromandel Walkway with an e-bike return south to Coromandel Town.

🛏 Sleeping

Coromandel Town has a good range of accommodation, from hostels to motels and B&Bs. Enquire at **Coromandel Accommodation Solutions** (📞07-866 8803; www. accommodationcoromandel.co.nz; 265 Kapanga Rd; units & apt $129-250; 📶) about renting a house at one of the nearby beaches.

Tui Lodge   HOSTEL $
(📞07-866 8237; www.coromandeltuilodge.co.nz; 60 Whangapoua Rd; campsite per person $20, dm $29-32, r $70-90; 🅿@📶) Pleasantly rural but still just a short walk from town, Coromandel's best backpackers has plenty of trees, free bikes, fruit (in season) and straight-up rooms. The pricier ones have en suites.

Anchor Lodge   MOTEL $
(📞07-866 7992; www.anchorlodgecoromandel. co.nz; 448 Wharf Rd; dm/d $31/75, units $165-370; 🅿@📶🏊) This upmarket backpacker-motel combo has its own gold mine, glowworm cave, small heated swimming pool and spa. The 2nd-floor units have harbour views.

**Coromandel Motel
& Holiday Park**   HOLIDAY PARK $
(📞07-866 8830; www.coromandeltop10.co.nz; 636 Rings Rd; campsites from $46, units $94-217; 🅿@📶🏊🚲) Well kept and welcoming, with nicely painted cabins, attractive units and manicured lawns – it gets busy in summer, so book ahead. Also hires bikes ($20 per day). The spotless cabins with shared bathrooms are good value for backpackers.

**Hush Boutique
Accommodation**   RENTAL HOUSE $$
(📞07-866 7771; www.hushaccommodation.co.nz; 425 Driving Creek Rd; cabins $125-200; 📶) 🏃 Four rustic but stylish private cabins with en-suite bathrooms are scattered throughout native bush at this easygoing spot. Natural wood creates a warm ambience. Located beside a peaceful stream, the alfresco area with a barbecue and full cooking facilities is a top spot to catch up with fellow travellers. The adjacent Hush House accommodates up to six ($355).

Jacaranda Lodge   B&B $$
(📞07-866 8002; www.jacarandalodge.co.nz; 3195 Tiki Rd; s $90, d $155-185; 🅿📶) 🏃 Located among 6 hectares of farmland and rose gardens, this two-storey cottage is a relaxing retreat. Look forward to excellent breakfasts from the friendly owners, Judy and Gerard, often using produce – plums, almonds, macadamia nuts and citrus fruit – from the property's spray-free orchard. Some rooms share bathrooms.

Driving Creek Villas COTTAGE **$$$**
(☑ 07-866 7755; www.drivingcreekvillas.com; 21a Colville Rd; villas $345; P 🛜) This is the posh, grown-up's choice – three spacious, self-contained, modern, wooden villas with plenty of privacy. The Polynesian-influenced interior design is slick and the bush setting, complete with bubbling creek, sublime.

🍴 Eating

Coromandel Oyster Company SEAFOOD **$**
(☑ 07-866 8028; www.freshoysters.co.nz; 1611 SH25/Manaia Rd; snacks & meals $6-20; ⊘ 9am-4.30pm Mon-Thu, to 5.30pm Fri-Sun) Briny-fresh mussels, scallops, oysters and cooked fish and chips and flounder. Coming from Thames, you'll find it around 5km before you reach Coromandel Town. Ask if the excellent seafood chowder is available.

Coromandel Smoking Co SEAFOOD **$**
(☑ 07-866 8757; www.corosmoke.co.nz; 70 Tiki Rd; fish & seafood $10-20; ⊘ 9am-5pm) Smoked fish and seafood for cooking and snacking. Also available is excellent Coromandel artisan cheese and the fiery Uncle Dunkle's chilli sauce made over the hill in Kūaotunu.

★ Wharf Road CAFE, VEGETARIAN **$$**
(☑ 07-866 7538; www.facebook.com/pg/wharfroad; 24 Wharf Rd; mains $13-22; ⊘ 8am-3pm; 🍴) 🌱 Bringing cosmopolitan cool to Coromandel Town, Wharf Road offers the opportunity to ease into another day equipped with excellent coffee, interesting brunch dishes such as avocado bagels or Turkish eggs with chilli butter, and an easy-going soundtrack of loping Kiwi reggae. Lunch amid the wood-lined space is equally popular, with wine and craft beer balancing super-healthy organic and vegetarian bowls.

Weta CAFE **$$**
(☑ 07-866 7535; 46 Kapanga Rd; mains $16-23; ⊘ 8am-3pm Tue-Sun; 🍴) Excellent counter food and creative breakfast and lunch mains make Weta one of the region's standout cafes. Sit outside in the courtyard on a warm day and enjoy dishes like the Beach Bene, with poached eggs and house-smoked salmon atop crunchy rosti made with kumara and karengo (edible seaweed). Innovative and very tasty.

Pepper Tree MODERN NZ **$$**
(☑ 07-866 8211; www.peppertreerestaurant.co.nz; 31 Kapanga Rd; mains lunch $16-28, dinner $25-36; ⊘ 10am-9pm; 🛜🍴) Coromandel Town's most upmarket option dishes up generously proportioned meals with an emphasis on local

seafood. On a summer's evening, the courtyard tables under the shady tree are the place to be. Try the excellent fish and chips with chunky homestyle chips.

Coromandel Mussel Kitchen SEAFOOD **$$**
(☑ 07-866 7245; www.musselkitchen.co.nz; cnr SH25 & 309 Rd; mains $15-26; ⊘ 9am-3pm mid-Oct–Apr) This cool cafe-bar sits among fields 3km south of town. Mussels are served with Thai- and Mediterranean-tinged sauces or grilled on the half-shell. In summer the garden bar is perfect for a mussel-fritter stack and a frosty craft beer from MK Brewing Co, the on-site microbrewery. Smoked and chilli mussels and bottles of the beers are all available for takeaway.

🍷 Drinking & Nightlife

Star & Garter Hotel PUB
(☑ 07-866 8503; www.starandgarter.co.nz; 5 Kapanga Rd; ⊘ 11am-late) Making the most of the simple kauri interior of an 1873 building, this smart pub has pool tables, decent sounds and a roster of live music and DJs on the weekends. The beer garden is smartly clad in corrugated iron.

🛍 Shopping

Source ARTS & CRAFTS
(☑ 07-866 7345; 31 Kapanga Rd; ⊘ 10am-4pm) Creative showcase for more than 30 local artists.

ℹ Information

Coromandel Town Information Centre (☑ 07-866 8598; www.coromandeltown.co.nz; 85 Kapanga Rd; ⊘ 10am-3pm; 🛜) Good maps and local information. Pick up the Historic Places Trust's *Coromandel Town* pamphlet here.

ℹ Getting There & Away

The best way to Coromandel Town from Auckland is on a Fullers360 (p221) ferry. Ferries run to/from Auckland (one way/return $67/103, two hours) via Orapiu on Waiheke Island daily in summer and on Saturday and Sunday during other seasons. The ferry docks at Hannafords Wharf, Te Kouma, from where free buses shuttle passengers the 10km into Coromandel Town. On weekends only, it's also possible to book same-day return packages visiting Coromandel destinations like the Driving Creek Railway.

There's no charge for carrying your bike on a Fullers360 ferry. Touring cyclists can avoid Auckland's traffic fumes and treacherous roads completely by catching the ferry at Gulf Harbour to Auckland's ferry terminal and then leapfrogging directly to Coromandel Town.

COROMANDEL FOREST PARK

More than 30 walks criss-cross the Coromandel Forest Park, spread over several major blocks throughout the centre of the Coromandel Peninsula. The most popular hike is the challenging six- to eight-hour return journey up to the Pinnacles (759m) in the Kauaeranga Valley behind Thames. Other outstanding tramps include the Coromandel Walkway in Far North Coromandel, from Fletcher Bay to Stony Bay, and the Puketui Valley walk to abandoned gold mines. For a guided walking adventure in the Coromandel, contact Walking Legends (☑0800 925 569, 07-312 5297; www.walkinglegends.com; 4-day trip from $1650).

The DOC Pinnacles Hut has 80 beds, gas cookers, heating, toilets and cold showers. The 10-bunk Crosbies Hut is a four- to six-hour tramp from Thames or the Kauaeranga Valley. There are also four backcountry campsites (adult/child $8/4): one near each hut and others at Moss Creek and Billygoat Basin; expect only a toilet. Eight other conservation campsites (adult/child $11/5.50) are accessible from Kauaeranga Valley Rd. Book online at www.doc.govt.nz. Some campsites are only open form late October to Easter.

The DOC Kauaeranga Visitor Centre (☑07-867 9080; www.doc.govt.nz; Kauaeranga Valley Rd; ⊙8.30am-4pm) has interesting displays about the kauri forest and its history. Maps and conservation resources are available for purchase and staff dispense advice. The centre is 14km off SH25; it's a further 9km along a gravel road to the start of the trails.

There is no scheduled public transport, so having a car or arranging a shuttle is necessary. Enquire at the Thames i-SITE (p223) about shuttles.

InterCity (www.intercity.co.nz) has buses linking Coromandel Town to Whitianga ($14, one hour). Buses leave from near the Coromandel Town Information Centre.

Far North Coromandel

Supremely isolated and gobsmackingly beautiful, the rugged tip of the Coromandel Peninsula is well worth the effort required to reach it. The best time to visit is summer, when the gravel roads are dry, the pohutukawa trees are in their crimson glory and camping's an option (there isn't much accommodation up here).

The tiny settlement of Colville is a remote rural community populated by alternative lifestylers. There's not much here except for the quaint Colville General Store (☑07-866 6805; Colville Rd, Colville; ⊙8.30am-5pm; 🅿) 🍴 and the Hereford 'n' a Pickle (☑07-866 6937; www.facebook.com/hereford.n.a.pickle; Colville Rd, Colville; burgers $10-18; ⊙9am-5pm Tue-Sun, reduced hours Apr-Oct; 🛜) cafe. Adjacent to the General Store, the Foragers' Kitchen cafe is open from 9am to 4pm Tuesday to Sunday and also for dinner on Friday and Saturday nights.

Three kilometres north of Colville the sealed road turns to gravel and splits to straddle each side of the peninsula. Following the west coast, ancient pohutukawa shade turquoise waters and stony beaches.

The small DOC-run Fantail Bay Campsite (☑07-866 6685; www.doc.govt.nz; Port Jackson Rd; adult/child $15/7.50) is 23km north of Colville. Another 7km brings you to the beachfront DOC Port Jackson Campsite (☑07-866 6932; www.doc.govt.nz; Port Jackson Rd; adult/child $15/7.50).

There's a spectacular lookout about 4km further on. Great Barrier Island is only 20km away, looking every part the extension of the Coromandel Peninsula that it once was. The road stops at Fletcher Bay – a magical land's end. Although it's only 37km from Colville, allow an hour for the drive. There's another DOC campsite (☑07-866 6685; www.doc.govt. nz; Fletcher Bay; adult/child $15/7.50) here, as well as Fletcher Bay Backpackers (☑07-866 6685; www.doc.govt.nz; Fletcher Bay; dm $26).

At Stony Bay, where the east-coast road terminates, there's another DOC campsite (☑07-866 6822; www.doc.govt.nz; Stony Bay; adult/child $15/7.50, bach $90) and a small DOC-run bach (holiday home) that sleeps five. Heading south there are a couple of nice beaches peppered with baches on the way to the slightly larger settlement of Port Charles, where you'll find Tangiaro Kiwi Retreat (☑07-866 6614; www.kiwiretreat.co.nz; 1299 Port Charles Rd, Port Charles; units $220-350; 🛜).

Another 8km brings you to the turn-off leading back to Colville, or you can continue south to Waikawau Bay, where there's a large DOC campsite (☑07-866 1106; www.doc.

govt.nz; Waikawau Beach Rd, Waikawau Bay; adult/child $15/7.50) that has a summer-only store. The road then winds its way south past **Kennedy Bay** before cutting back to come out near the Driving Creek Railway (p224).

Colville Farm
LODGE $

(☑ 07-866 6820; www.colvillefarmholidays.co.nz; 2140 Colville Rd; campsite/d from $15/80; @ ⓢ) The 1260-hectare Colville Farm has a range of interesting accommodation, including campsites, bare-basics bush lodges and self-contained houses. Guests can try their hands at farm work (including milking) or go on horse treks ($50 to $180, one to five hours).

Mahamudra Centre
RETREAT $

(☑ 07-866 6851; www.mahamudra.org.nz; Colville Rd; campsite/dm/s/tw $18/28/50/80) The Mahamudra Centre is a serene Tibetan Buddhist retreat with a stupa, meditation hall and regular meditation courses. It offers simple accommodation in a parklike setting.

❶ Getting There & Away
There is no public transport. The best time to visit is summer, when the gravel roads are dry.

Coromandel Town to Whitianga

There are two routes from Coromandel Town southeast to Whitianga. The main road is the slightly longer but quicker SH25, which enjoys sea views and has short detours to pristine sandy beaches. The other is the less-travelled but legendary 309 Rd, an unsealed, untamed route through deep bush.

309 Road

Starting 3km south of Coromandel Town, the 309 Rd cuts through the Coromandel Range for 21km (most of which is unsealed but well maintained), rejoining SH25 7km south of Whitianga.

Highlights include a quirky water park, and just 2km further west there's a two-minute walk through bush to the 10m-high **Waiau Falls**. A further 500m east, an easy 10-minute bushwalk leads to an amazing **kauri grove**. This stand of 600-year-old giants escaped the carnage of the 19th century, giving a majestic reminder of what the peninsula once looked like. The biggest tree has a 6m circumference.

Waterworks
PARK

(☑ 07-866 7191; www.thewaterworks.co.nz; 471 309 Rd; adult/child $25/20; ⊙10am-6pm Nov-Mar, to 4pm Apr-Oct;) The Waterworks, 5km east along the 309 Rd from SH25, is a wonderfully bizarre park filled with whimsical water-powered amusements made from old kitchen knives, washing machines, bikes and toilets.

★Wairua Lodge
B&B $$$

(☑ 07-866 0304; www.wairualodge.co.nz; 251 Old Coach Rd; r $225-320) Wairua Lodge is a peaceful B&B with charming hosts, nestled in the bush towards the Whitianga end of the 309 Rd. There's a riverside swimming hole on the property, barbecue, spa and romantic outdoor bath tub.

❶ Getting There & Away
Not all of the 309 Rd is sealed, but it's an easy drive if you take it carefully. No public transport covers this route.

SH25

SH25 starts by climbing sharply to an incredible lookout before heading steeply down. The turn-off at Te Rerenga follows the harbour to **Whangapoua**. There's not much at this beach except for holiday homes and a pleasant holiday park. Walk along the rocky foreshore for 30 minutes to the remote, beautiful and often-deserted and undeveloped **New Chums Beach**, regarded as one of the most beautiful in the country. Be ready to take your shoes off and wade through a lagoon to get there, and consult the map near the beach store in Whangapoua before you start walking.

Continuing east on SH25 you soon reach **Kūaotunu**, a more interesting holiday village on a beautiful stretch of white-sand beach, with a cafe-gallery, a store and an ancient petrol pump.

Heading off the highway at Kūaotunu takes you (via an unsealed road) to one of Coromandel's best-kept secrets. First the long stretch of **Otama Beach** comes into view – deserted but for a few houses and farms. Continuing along the narrowing road, the sealed road finally starts again and you reach **Opito**, a hidden-away enclave of 250 flash properties (too smart to be called baches), of which only 16 have permanent residents. From this magical beach, you can walk to the Ngāti Hei *pā* (fortified village) site at the far end.

Leighton Lodge   B&B $$
(☑ 07-866 0756; www.leightonlodge.co.nz; 17 Stewart Pl, Opito; r $165-230; @) One of the 'real' residences in Opito houses the delightful folks of Leighton Lodge. This smart B&B has chatty owners, an upstairs room with a view-hungry balcony and a self-contained flat downstairs. Say 'hi' to Fern, the owners' very friendly Labrador.

Kuaotunu Bay Lodge   B&B $$$
(☑ 07-866 4396; www.kuaotunubay.co.nz; SH25, Kūaotunu; d $340; P) An elegant B&B set among manicured gardens, offering a small set of spacious sea-gazing rooms.

★ **Luke's Kitchen**   CAFE $$
(☑ 07-866 4420; www.lukeskitchen.co.nz; 20 Blackjack Rd, Kūaotunu; mains & pizza $14-29; ☺ cafe & gallery 8am-3pm daily, restaurant & bar 11am-8pm Fri-Mon; 🖮) Luke's Kitchen has a rustic surf-shack ambience, cold brews including hyper-local craft beer from Kūaotunu's tiny Blue Fridge Brewery and excellent wood-fired pizza. Occasional live music, seafood and creamy fruit smoothies make Luke's an essential stop. Adjacent is Luke's daytime cafe and gallery with excellent coffee, kombucha on tap, home-baked goodies and lots of eclectic local art for sale.

🚌 Getting There & Away

The best way to explore the meandering roads is by car. Kūaotunu is also a stop on Go Kiwi (p232) shuttles linking Matarangi and Auckland.

Whitianga

POP 5100

Whitianga's big attractions are the sandy beaches of Mercury Bay and the diving, boating and kayaking opportunities afforded by the craggy coast and nearby **Te Whanganui-A-Hei Marine Reserve**. The pretty harbour is a renowned base for game-fishing (especially marlin and tuna from January to March).

The legendary Polynesian explorer and seafarer Kupe is believed to have landed near here sometime around AD 950. The name Whitianga is a contraction of Te Whitianga a Kupe (Crossing Place of Kupe).

🄾 Sights

Buffalo Beach stretches along Mercury Bay, north of Whitianga Harbour. A five-minute **passenger ferry** (☑ 07-866 3462; www.whitiangaferry.co.nz; adult/child/bicycle $5/3/1.50; ☺ 7.30am-7.30pm & 8.30-10.30pm) ride will take

Whitianga

you across the harbour to **Ferry Landing**. From here you can walk to local sights like **Whitianga Rock Scenic & Historical Reserve**, a park with great views over the ocean, and the **Shakespeare Cliff Lookout**. Further afield are Hahei Beach (13km), Cathedral Cove (15km) and Hot Water Beach

(18km, one hour by bike). Look forward to rolling terrain if you're keen on riding from Ferry Landing to these other destinations.

Lost Spring
SPRING

(☑ 07-866 0456; www.thelostspring.co.nz; 121a Cook Dr; per 90min/day $45/80; ☺ 9.30am-7pm Sun-Thu, to 9pm Fri & Sat) This expensive but intriguing Disney-meets-Polynesia thermal complex comprises a series of hot pools in a lush jungle-like setting complete with an erupting volcano. It's the ideal spot to relax in tropical tranquillity, with a cocktail in hand. It also has a day spa and cafe. Children under 14 must be accompanied by an adult in the pools.

Mercury Bay Museum
MUSEUM

(☑ 07-866 0730; www.mercurybaymuseum.co.nz; 11a The Esplanade; adult/child $7.50/free; ☺ 10am-4pm Oct-Jun, to 3pm May-Sep) A small but interesting museum focusing on local history – especially Whitianga's most famous visitors, Kupe and Cook.

🏃 Activities

Bike Man
CYCLING

(☑ 07-866 0745; thebikeman@xtra.co.nz; 16 Coghill St; per day $30; ☺ 9am-5pm Mon-Fri, to 1pm Sat; 🚲) Rent a bike to take across on the ferry for the onward journey to Hahei and Hot Water Beach.

Windborne
BOATING

(☑ 027 475 2411; www.windborne.co.nz; day sail $135; ☺ Dec-Apr; 🚲) Day sails in a 19m 1928 schooner from December to April, and also departures to the Mercury Islands ($195) in February and March.

Dive Zone
DIVING

(☑ 07-867 1580; www.divezone.co.nz/whitianga; 10 Campbell St; trips from $170; ☺ 8am-5pm Sun-Thu, to 6pm Fri & Sat) Shore, kayak and boat dives.

☞ Tours

There are a baffling number of tours to Te Whanganui-A-Hei Marine Reserve, where you'll see interesting rock formations and, if you're lucky, dolphins, fur seals, penguins and orcas. Some are straight-out cruises while others offer optional swims and snorkels. Most boat trips depart from Whitianga Wharf. Check when you book.

Waka Tours
TOURS

(☑ 027 231 6789; www.whitiangatours.com; 57b Albert St; 2hr tours per person $110) Tours integrate the history and culture of the local Ngāti Hei people with destinations including Wharekaho where British explorer Captain James Cook was welcomed by local Māori in 1769, and the nearby *pā* site of Wharetaewa. Waka's Supreme Tour (per person $350, three hours) includes storytelling and engagement with local *kaumātua* and *kuia* (Māori elders). Other tours with a Māori focus include visiting Cooks Beach, Hahei and Hot Water Beach.

Visit Waka Tours' Whitianga store for interesting local T-shirts and Māori arts and crafts.

Ocean Leopard
BOATING

(☑ 0800 843 8687; www.oceanleopardtours.co.nz; adult/child $95/60; ☺ 10.30am, 1.30pm & 4pm; 🚲) Two-hour trips taking in coastal scenery, naturally including Cathedral Cove (p232). The boat has a handy canopy for sun protection. A one-hour Whirlwind Tour (adult/child $60/35) is also on offer.

Glass Bottom Boat
BOATING

(☑ 07-867 1962; www.glassbottomboatwhitianga.co.nz; adult/child $105/65; 🚲) Two-hour tours exploring the Te Whanganui-A-Hei Marine Reserve.

Sea Cave Adventures
BOATING

(☑ 0800 806 060; www.seacaveadventures.co.nz; adult/child $95/55; 🚲) A two-hour Sea Cave Adventure in an inflatable.

Cave Cruzer
BOATING

(☑ 0800 427 893; www.cavecruzer.co.nz; adult/child $90/55; 🚲) Two-hour tours on a rigid-hull inflatable.

🎉 Festivals & Events

Scallop Festival
FOOD & DRINK

(☑ 07-867 1510; www.scallopfestival.co.nz; ☺ Sep) One-day showcase of food, entertainment and more than a few people's favourite bivalves.

🛏 Sleeping

Turtle Cove
HOSTEL $

(☑ 07-867 1517; www.turtlecove.co.nz; 14 Bryce St; dm $27-34, d $90-216; @ 🛜) Colourful shared areas and a spacious modern kitchen make Turtle Cove one of the best hostels in the Coromandel Peninsula and Waikato area. The largest dormitories have only six beds, making Turtle Cove more like a friendly homestay than a rip-roaring party palace. The team at reception is unfailingly helpful, with plenty of ideas on how to maximise your time.

Mercury Bay Holiday Park
HOLIDAY PARK $

(☑ 07-866 5579; www.mercurybayholidaypark.co.nz; 121 Albert St; campsites $30, units $100-160;

@ 🛇 🖿 🚽) Strangely planted in a suburban neighbourhood, this small holiday park is comfortable and clean, with playgrounds, trampoline, swimming pool and pool table.

Pipi Dune B&B
B&B $$
(🖉 07-869 5375; www.pipidune.co.nz; 5 Pipi Dune; r $180-200; 🛜) This attractive B&B in a quiet cul-de-sac has guest lounges, kitchenettes, laundries and free wi-fi. To get here, head north on Cook Dr, turn left onto Surf St and then take the first right.

Beachside Resort
MOTEL $$
(🖉 07-867 1356; www.beachsideresort.co.nz; 20 Eyre St; units $195-225; 🛜⛱) Attached to the sprawling Oceans Resort, this modern motel has tidy units with kitchenettes and balconies on the upper level. Despite the name, it's set back from the beach, but it does have a heated pool.

Within the Bays
B&B $$$
(🖉 07-866 2848; www.withinthebays.co.nz; 49 Tarapatiki Dr; r $295-350; @🛜) It's the combination of charming hosts and incredible views that make this B&B set on a hill overlooking Mercury Bay really worth considering. It's extremely well set up for guests with restricted mobility – there's even a wheelchair-accessible bush track on the property. Find it 5km from Whitianga town.

🍴 Eating

Hula
CAFE $$
(🖉 07-866 0323; https://hula.co.nz; 5 Albert St; mains $16-22; ⊙ 7.30am-4pm) Dine at easy-going Hula to fast track to a beachy state of mind. Try the corned beef hash with poached eggs for brekkie, or the fish tacos or coconut fried chicken for lunch. The coffee is among the town's best, and on the last Sunday of each month from 11am to 2pm, DJs add a few vinyl beats to brunch.

Blue Ginger
SOUTHEAST ASIAN $$
(🖉 07-867 1777; www.blueginger.co.nz; 1/10 Blacksmith Lane; shared plates $9-14, mains $22-30; ⊙ 11.30am-2pm Tue-Thu, 5.30pm-late Tue-Sat) Southeast Asian flavours infuse the menu at this relaxed spot with shared tables. Highlights include Indonesian-style beef rendang, pad thai noodles and a great roast-duck red curry. Beer and wine are not served.

Stoked
CAFE, BAR $$
(🖉 07-866 0029; www.getstoked.co.nz; 19 The Esplanade; pizza $20-25, mains $25-34; ⊙ 4-9pm Fri-Mon, 4pm-late Thu) With a charcoal oven as its kitchen hub, Stoked turns out dishes like manuka-smoked salmon, tandoori chicken thigh and good wood-fired pizza. Views of the ocean are mandatory, especially from the deck, and Coromandel wines and craft beer from the tiny Blue Fridge Brewery in Kūaotunu are both proud local touches.

Salt Restaurant & Bar
MODERN NZ $$
(🖉 07-866 5818; www.salt-whitianga.co.nz; 2 Blacksmith Lane; mains $25-39; ⊙ 4pm-late Mon-Thu, from noon Fri-Sun) Views of the Whitianga marina – including the sleepy ferry crossing to Ferry Landing – provide the backdrop for relaxed but stylish dining. In summer the place to be is out on the deck, combining local wines with pan-seared fish with Cloudy Bay clams or Coromandel oysters from the raw bar.

ℹ Information

Whitianga i-SITE (🖉 07-866 5555; www. whitianga.co.nz; 66 Albert St; ⊙ 9am-5pm Mon-Fri, to 4pm Sat & Sun) Information and internet access. Extended hours in summer.

ℹ Getting There & Away

BOAT
A five-minute passenger ferry ride will take you across the harbour to Ferry Landing.

BUS
Buses leave from near the Whitianga i-SITE. **InterCity** (🖉 07-348 0366; www.intercity.co.nz) links Whitianga to Thames ($25, 90 minutes, twice daily) for onward transfer to Auckland and Hamilton. **Go Kiwi** (🖉 07-866 0336; www. go-kiwi.co.nz) links Whitianga to Thames ($39, 90 minutes, one daily) and Auckland ($69, 3½ hours, one daily). This service also loops around Hot Water Beach and Hahei; check the website for timings. **Cathedral Cove Shuttles** (🖉 027 422 5899; www.cathedralcoveshuttles.co.nz; per person depending on destination $15-58; ⊙ 9am-late Dec-Feb, to 10.30pm Mar-Nov) runs a handy service.

Coroglen & Whenuakite

The blink-and-you'll-miss-them villages of Coroglen and Whenuakite are on SH25, south of Whitianga and west of Hot Water Beach. Along this route are a few interesting diversions, including a good craft brewery (p232) and a weekly **farmers market** (🖉 07-866 3315; www.facebook.com/coroglen farmersmarket; SH25, Coroglen; ⊙ 9am-1pm Sun late Oct-early Jun).

WAIKATO & THE COROMANDEL PENINSULA COROGLEN & WHENUAKITE

Seabreeze Holiday Park   HOLIDAY PARK $

(☑ 07-866 3050; www.seabreezeholidaypark.co.nz; 1043 SH25, Whenuakite; campsite $25, dm $30, unit $85-170; 🛜) A friendly and grassy park with the bonus of an on-site craft brewery. What's not to like?

Colenso   CAFE $

(☑ 07-866 3725; www.colensocafe.co.nz; SH25, Whenuakite; mains $10-21; ⊘ 9.30am-3.30pm) Better than your average highway stop, Colenso has excellent fair-trade coffee, scones, cakes and light snacks, as well as a shop selling homewares and gifts. Try the delicious macadamia nut brittle.

Hot Water Brewing Co   CRAFT BEER

(☑ 07-866 3830; www.hotwaterbrewingco.com; Seabreeze Holiday Park, 1043 SH25, Whenuakite; ⊘ noon-8pm Thu-Mon) Hot Water Brewing Co is a modern craft brewery with lots of outdoor seating. Standout brews include the hoppy Kauri Falls Pale Ale and the robust Walker's Porter. OK bar snacks and pizza are available.

Coroglen Tavern   PUB

(☑ 07-866 3809; www.coroglentavern.co.nz; 1937 SH25, Coroglen; ⊘ 10am-late) The legendary Coroglen Tavern is the archetypal middle-of-nowhere country pub that attracts big-name Kiwi bands in summer.

🕕 Getting There & Away

InterCity (p223) buses linking Thames to Whitianga stop at Whenuakite and Coroglen.

Hahei

POP 300

A legendary Kiwi beach town, little Hahei balloons to 7000 people in summer but is nearly abandoned otherwise – apart from the busloads of tourists doing the obligatory stop-off at Cathedral Cove. It's a charming spot and a great place to unwind for a few days, especially in the quieter months. It takes its name from Hei, the eponymous ancestor of the Ngāti Hei people, who arrived in the 14th century on the *Te Arawa* canoe. Online, see www.hahei.co.nz.

In recent years, Cathedral Cove has become increasingly popular, and the local council has introduced a park-and-ride shuttle-bus system to streamline access and transport to the site.

◉ Sights

Cathedral Cove   BEACH

(🚶) Beautiful Cathedral Cove, with its famous gigantic stone arch and natural waterfall shower, is best enjoyed early or late in the day – avoiding the worst of the hordes. From the Cathedral Cove car park, around 2km north of Hahei, it's a rolling walk of around 30 to 40 minutes. On the way there's rocky Gemstone Bay, which has a snorkelling trail where you're likely to see big snapper, crayfish and stingrays, and sandy Stingray Bay.

If you walk from Hahei Beach directly to Cathedral Cove, it will take about 70 minutes. Another option is the 10-minute Cathedral Cove Water Taxi (☑ 027 919 0563; www.cathedralcovewatertaxi.co.nz; adult one way/return $15/30, child $10/20; ⊘ every 30min).

If you're driving, leave your car at the Hahei Visitor Car Park on the right-hand side of the entrance to Hahei village and catch a Go Kiwi shuttle (adult/child/family return $5/3/10, every 20 minutes, 9am to 6pm, October to April) to the beginning of the track to Cathedral Cove.

To reduce traffic congestion in and around Hahei, it's recommended all visitors use this car park located around 900m from the beach.

Note that from October to April the car park at Cathedral Cove is closed. From May to September there's limited parking at Grange Rd near Cathedral Cove ($15 for four hours).

Hahei Beach   BEACH

Long, lovely Hahei Beach is made more magical by the view to the craggy islands in the distance. From the southern end of Hahei Beach, it's a 15-minute walk up to Te Pare, a *pā* site with splendid coastal views.

🏃 Activities & Tours

Cathedral Cove Sea Kayaking   KAYAKING

(☑ 07-866 3877; www.kayaktours.co.nz; 88 Hahei Beach Rd; half-/full day $125/205; ⊘ 8.45am & 1.30pm, additional departures Dec & Jan) This outfit runs guided kayaking trips around the rock arches, caves and islands in the Cathedral Cove and Mercury Bay area. The Remote Coast Tour heads the other way when conditions permit, visiting caves, blowholes and a long tunnel.

Cove Ebike Hire   CYCLING

(☑ 027 245 6095; www.haheiebikes.co.nz) A good option to take the edge off the rolling 8km journey from Hahei to Hot Water Beach, Cove's e-bikes have sturdy and comfortable fat tyres. Other potential destinations from Hahei include Mercury Bay Estate (10km), Cooks Beach (11km) and Cooked cafe at

Ferry Landing (13km). Helmets, hi-visibility vests, a daypack, lock and map are all provided.

Hahei Beach Bikes   CYCLING
(☑ 021 701 093; www.haheibeachbikes.co.nz; bike hire per day $45) Bikes can be picked up from the **Hahei Holiday Resort** (41 Harsant Ave). Friendly owner Jonny provides maps with key points of interest and a spade for digging a spa pool at Hot Water Beach.

Cathedral Cove Dive & Snorkel   DIVING
(☑ 07-866 3955; www.hahei.co.nz/diving; 48 Hahei Beach Rd; dives from $135; 🌐) Offers daily dive trips and rents out scuba gear, snorkelling gear ($25) and body boards ($20). A Discover Scuba half-day beginner course costs $250, including all the gear. Check out its website for recommendations on where to snorkel in the area.

Hahei Explorer   ADVENTURE
(☑ 07-866 3910; www.haheiexplorer.co.nz; adult/child $105/60; 🌐) Hour-long jetboat rides touring the coast.

🛏 Sleeping

Tatahi Lodge   HOSTEL $
(☑ 07-866 3992; www.tatahilodge.co.nz; Grange Rd; dm $38, r $108-146, units from $190; 🅿@🛜) A wonderful place where backpackers are treated with at least as much care and respect as the lush, bromeliad-filled garden. The dorm rooms and excellent communal facilities are just as attractive as the pricier motel units.

The Church   COTTAGE $$
(☑ 07-866 3533; www.thechurchhahei.co.nz; 87 Hahei Beach Rd; cottages $160-240; 🅿🛜) 🍃 Set within a subtropical garden, these beautifully kitted out, rustic timber cottages have plenty of character. The switched-on owners are really welcoming and have loads of ideas on what to do and see around the area.

Purangi Garden
Accommodation   COTTAGE $$
(☑ 07-866 4036; www.purangigarden.co.nz; Lees Rd; d $180-200; 🅿) On a quiet cove at the mouth of the Purangi River, this relaxing spot has accommodation ranging from comfortable chalets through to larger houses and a spacious, self-contained yurt. Well-established gardens and rolling lawns lead to the water – perfect for swimming and kayaking – and don't be surprised if the friendly owners drop off some organic fruit or freshly baked bread.

🍴 Eating & Drinking

Cooked   MEXICAN $$
(☑ 07-777 4058; www.facebook.com/cooked coromandel; 1134 Purangi Rd, Ferry Landing; snacks & mains $14-29; ⊙10am-10pm Thu-Tue; 🌐) Easily reached on the short harbour crossing linking Whitianga to Ferry Landing, Cooked is a colourful homage to Mexican street food. There's an authentic zingy hit of lime in the ceviche, and the tacos go well with robust margarita cocktails and craft brews from around the Coromandel. Leave room for dessert of churro doughnuts with a hit of spiced chocolate.

Mercury Bay Estate   BISTRO $$
(☑ 07-866 4066; www.mercurybayestate.co.nz; 761a Purangi Rd, Cooks Beach; platters $18-48, pizza $20-26, wine tasting $10-19; ⊙11am-4pm Wed-Sun) Repurposed timber and corrugated iron feature at this rustic but chic vineyard en route from Hahei to Ferry Landing. Seafood, cheese and charcuterie platters team well with wines such as the excellent Lonely Bay chardonnay. The Naples-style wood-fired pizzas are also a treat. Local artwork is also for sale. It's 35km from Whitianga, 10km from Hahei, and just under 4km from Ferry Landing.

The Church   MEDITERRANEAN $$$
(☑ 07-866 3797; www.thechurchbistro.co.nz; 87 Hahei Beach Rd; mains $34-39; ⊙5pm-late Tue-Sun Oct-Apr) This charming wooden church is Hahei's swankiest eatery. A concise seasonal menu of European-influenced mains could include slow-roasted beef cheeks with truffle polenta or lamb with eggplant ratatouille. Definitely leave room for excellent desserts and try to book ahead – especially over the peak of summer – as the heritage dining room is relatively compact.

★ Pour House   PUB
(☑ 07-866 3354; www.coromandelbrewingcompany. co.nz; 7 Grange Rd; ⊙noon-late; 🛜) Home base for the Coromandel Brewing Company, this pub and bistro regularly features about five of its own beers in a modern ambience. Hearty meat and seafood mains combine with decent pizzas in the beer garden. Team the Moroccan pizza with the Hahei Doctor American Pale Ale. Keep an eye out for occasional seasonal beers too.

ℹ Getting There & Away

In the absolute height of summer school holidays, the council runs a bus service from the

Cooks Beach side of Ferry Landing to Hot Water Beach, stopping at Hahei. Ask at the Whitianga i-SITE (p231).

Go Kiwi (p232) runs a daily service linking Hahei and Hot Water Beach to Auckland and Whitianga. From early November to Easter, Go Kiwi also offers a five- to six-hour bus tour from Ferry Landing (adult/child/family $69/49/199) incorporating visits to both Cathedral Cove and Hot Water Beach. Morning departure times vary depending on tide times. Check the website.

Cathedral Cove Shuttles (p232) offers a convenient transport service from Ferry Landing to nearby beaches and attractions. Service is by request via phone or text.

From Ferry Landing to Hahei is around 10km. Bikes can be rented from Hahei Beach Bikes (p233), with pickup at Hahei Holiday Resort.

Hot Water Beach

Justifiably famous (and sometimes notoriously crowded), Hot Water Beach is quite extraordinary. For two hours either side of low tide, you can access an area of sand in front of a rocky outcrop at the middle of the beach where hot water oozes up from beneath the surface. Bring a spade, dig a hole and, voila, you've got a personal spa pool. Surfers stop off before the main beach to access some decent breaks. The headland between the two beaches still has traces of a Ngāti Hei *pā*.

Hotties   OUTDOORS
(☑ 07-866 3006; www.hottieseatery.co.nz; Pye Pl; ☺ 9am-5pm; ♿) Spades ($10) can be hired from this combination of cafe and ocean-front general store. Decent global snacks ($26 to $28) include fish tacos and pork-belly steamed buns, and surfboards, paddle boards and body boards can all be hired.

Hot Water Beach
Top 10 Holiday Park   HOLIDAY PARK $
(☑ 07-866 3116; www.hotwaterbeachtop10.co.nz; 790 Hot Water Beach Rd; campsites from $40, dm $32, units $120-200; Ⓟ @ 🛜 ♿) Bordered by tall bamboo and gum trees, this is a very well run holiday park with everything from grassy campsites through to a spacious, spotless backpackers lodge and stylish villas with arched ceilings crafted from NZ timber.

Hot Waves   CAFE $$
(☑ 07-866 3887; 8 Pye Pl; mains $12-27; ☺ 8.30am-4pm Mon-Thu & Sun, to 8.30pm Fri) In summer everyone wants a garden table

at this excellent cafe. For a lazy brunch, try the eggs Benedict with smoked salmon or the legendary Big Breakfast. Ask about occasional Friday-night music sessions. Keep an eye out for the fluffy cat who may well run the place.

❶ Getting There & Away

Cathedral Cove Shuttles (☑ 027 422 5899; www.cathedralcoveshuttles.co.nz; from $15; ♿) and Go Kiwi (p232) both stop here and it's a rolling 8km ride by bicycle from Hahei. There are two paid parking areas (per hour $4) near the main entrance to the beach. Another option is free parking at the Middle Car Park nearer to Hahei, from where it is a 600m walk south along the beach to where the hot springs are.

Tairua & Pauanui

POP 1270

Tairua and its twin town Pauanui sit either side of a river estuary that's perfect for windsurfing or for little kids to splash about in. Both have excellent surf beaches (Pauanui's is probably a shade better) and both are ridiculously popular in the summertime, but that's where the similarity stops. While Tairua is a functioning residential town (with shops, ATMs and a choice of eateries), Pauanui is an upmarket refuge for Aucklanders. Friendly Tairua knows how to keep it real.

Various operators offer fishing charters and sightseeing trips. Enquire at the information centre.

Paaku   MOUNTAIN
Around seven million years ago Paaku was a volcanic island, but now it forms the northern head of Tairua's harbour. Ngāti Hei had a *pā* here before being invaded by Ngāti Maru in the 17th century. It's a steep 15-minute walk to the summit from the top of Paku Dr, with the pay-off being amazing views over Tairua, Pauanui and the Alderman Islands. Plaques along the way detail Tairua's colonial history; only one is devoted to its long Māori occupation.

Tairua Beach
House Backpackers   HOSTEL $
(☑ 07-864 8313; www.facebook.com/tairuabeach housebackpackers; 9 Tairua Palms Pl, Tairua; camping $15, dm $30, r $65-80; 🛜) Rooms are homey and casual at this estuary-edge hostel in a converted house, and the dorm scores great views. Guests can help themselves to fishing rods, kayaks, sailboards and bikes. We like the recent colourful makeover.

Sunlover Retreat
B&B $$$

(📞 07-864 9024; www.sunlover.co.nz; 20 Ridge Rd, Tairua; d $345-380; 🐾) Enjoy stunning views of Paaku and Tairua at this stylish B&B high above the harbour. Two of the three suites have private outdoor balconies, and huge picture windows provide plenty of light and space. Decor is chic, modern and dotted with quirky NZ art, and guests receive a warm welcome from Rover, the Sunlover Retreat labradoodle.

Tairua Beach Club
BISTRO $$

(📞 07-280 0185; www.tairuabeachclub.co.nz; 128 Paku Dr, Tairua; mains $25-34; ⊙ 5-10.30pm Mon-Fri, 9am-3pm & 5-10.30pm Sat & Sun) 🍴 In a historic cottage 2km from central Tairua, the TBC combines a rustic Kiwiana vibe with a focus on sustainable produce and ingredients from the Coromandel. Secure a spot with harbour views under the market umbrellas and enjoy seasonal dishes like sumac-seared scallops or flounder with tarragon and a shellfish mousse. The well-considered wine and beer list is equally interesting.

Manaia Kitchen & Bar
CAFE $$

(📞 07-864 9050; www.manaiakitchenbar.co.nz; 228 Main Rd, Tairua; mains breakfast $12-23, lunch $22-25, dinner $24-42; ⊙ 9am-late Thu-Tue) With courtyard seating for summer brunches and a burnished-copper bar for later in the night, Manaia is the most cosmopolitan spot on the Tairua strip. Interesting menu options include taro croquettes, crispy calamari salad and Tairua's best pizzas. There are occasional live music and DJs on Friday nights. Kick off the morning after with a healthy bliss bowl for breakfast.

ℹ Information

Tairua Information Centre (📞 07-864 7575; www.tairua.co.nz; 2 Manaia Rd, Tairua; ⊙ 9am-5pm Mon-Fri, to noon Sat & Sun) Located in the Tairua library with information, maps, and accommodation and transport bookings.

ℹ Getting There & Away

InterCity (www.intercity.co.nz) and Go Kiwi (www.go-kiwi.co.nz) run bus services to Tairua.

Tairua and Pauanui are connected by a **passenger ferry** (📞 027-497 0316; $5), which departs around every hour from 10am to 4pm across the peak of summer and holiday weekends. In other months the ferry offers a water-taxi service.

Whangamatā
POP 3560

When Auckland's socially ambitious flock to Pauanui, the city's young and free head to Whangamatā to surf, party and hook up. It can be a raucous spot over New Year, when the population swells to more than 40,000. It's a true summer-holiday town, but in the off-season there may as well be tumbleweeds rolling down the main street.

🏃 Activities

Besides fishing (game-fishing runs from January to April), other activities include snorkelling near Hauturu (Clarke) Island, and surfing, orienteering and mountain biking. There are also excellent walks.

The Wentworth Falls walk takes 2½ hours (return); it starts 3km south of the town and 4km down the unsealed Wentworth Valley Rd. A further 3km south of Wentworth Valley Rd is Parakiwai Quarry Rd, at the end of which is the Wharekirauponga walk, a sometimes muddy 10km return track (allow 3½ to four hours) to a mining camp, battery and waterfall that passes unusual hexagonal lava columns and loquacious birdlife.

A popular destination for kayaking and paddle boarding is Whenuakura (Donut Island). Note that in an effort to boost the area's islands' status as wildlife sanctuaries, it's not permitted to land on them. Boating around the islands is allowed.

SurfSup
WATER SPORTS

(📞 021 217 1201; www.surfsup.nz; 101 Winifred Ave; tours/lessons from $40/80) Paddle boarding and surfing lessons are on offer, and kayaking and paddle-boarding tours to Whenuakura are available on a guided and self-guided basis. Also offers leisurely paddles down the nearby Otahu estuary and more challenging coastal kayak adventures.

ℹ BEACH SAFETY

Hot Water Beach has dangerous rips, especially directly in front of the main thermal section. It's one of the four most dangerous beaches in New Zealand in terms of drowning numbers, although this may be skewed by the huge number of tourists that flock here. Regardless, swimming here is *not* safe if the lifeguards aren't on patrol.

WAIKATO & THE COROMANDEL PENINSULA WHANGAMATĀ

OFF THE BEATEN TRACK

OPOUTERE

File this one under Coromandel's best-kept secrets. Apart from a cluster of houses there's nothing for miles around. Swimming can be dangerous, especially near Hikinui Islet, which is close to the beach. On the sand spit is the **Wharekawa Wildlife Refuge**, a breeding ground for the endangered New Zealand dotterel.

On the accommodation front, **Copsefield** (☑07-865 9555; www.copsefield.co.nz; 1055 SH25; r $120-200; ☎) is a peaceful country-style villa set in attractive, lush gardens with a spa and riverside swimming hole. The main house has three attractive B&B rooms, while cheaper accommodation is offered in a separate bach-style cottage.

With a change in Hikuai, it's possible to catch the **Go Kiwi** (☑0800 446 549; www.go-kiwi.co.nz) Auckland–Whitianga shuttle to Opoutere.

Kiwi Dundee Adventures   HIKING
(☑07-865 8809; www.kiwidundee.co.nz; per person from $315) ✎ Originally founded by Doug 'Kiwi Dundee' Johansen, this business has new operators. John Rich and Rosaleen Ward continue to offer informative one- to three-day guided tours focusing on the Coromandel Peninsula.

🎊 Festivals & Events

Whangamata Beach Hop   CULTURAL
(www.beachhop.co.nz; ⊙late Mar-early Apr) This annual celebration of retro American culture – expect hot rods, classic cars, motorbikes and rock and roll – is a great time to be in town. Dust off the classic white T-shirt and leather jacket combo and pile high the beehive hairdo, but definitely book accommodation if you're planning on attending.

🛏 Sleeping

Surf n Stay NZ   HOSTEL $
(☑07-865 8323; http://surfnstaynewzealand.com; 227 Beverly Tce; dm $36-40, s/d $60/120; ☎) In a quiet street a block from the waves, this hostel owned by a friendly Kiwi-Brazilian couple has dorms and private rooms that are clean and comfortable. Cooked breakfast included. It also offers the option of surfing and paddleboarding lessons (from $80), hire of paddle boards, surfboards and kayaks (from $20), and surf camps, some incorporating yoga.

Wentworth Valley Campsite   CAMPGROUND $
(☑07-865 7032; www.doc.govt.nz; 474 Wentworth Valley Rd; adult/child $15/7.50) ✎ More upmarket than most DOC campsites, this spot is accessed from the Wentworth Falls walk and has toilets, showers and gas barbecues.

Breakers   MOTEL $$
(☑07-865 8464; www.breakersmotel.co.nz; 324 Hetherington Rd; units $200-230; ☎▣) Facing the marina on the Tairua approach to Whangamatā, this modern motel features an enticing swimming pool, and spa pools on the decks of the upstairs units.

Southpacific Accommodation   MOTEL $$
(☑07-865 9580; www.thesouthpacific.co.nz; 249 Port Rd; units $170-190; @☎) This hard-to-miss, corner-hogging complex consists of a cafe and warmly decorated, self-contained motel units. Facilities are clean and modern. Bikes and kayaks are available for hire.

🍴 Eating

★**Port Road Project**   CAFE $$
(☑07-865 7288; www.facebook.com/portroadproject; 719 Port Rd; mains $17-23; ⊙8am-2pm Mon-Fri, to 3pm Sat & Sun; ✍) ✎ Sleek Scandi style makes the Port Road Project a standout in sleepy Whangamatā. Join the locals on the sunny, shared tables and partner the all-day menu with fine coffee, Hamilton craft beer and cider, and a good wine list. Check the Facebook page for occasional Saturday-night shared-plate dinners ($65), potentially offering Mexican, vegetarian or barbecue.

Incognito   BISTRO $$
(☑022 477 5441; www.facebook.com/chappy161; 6/701 Port Rd; mains $32-34; ⊙5.30-10pm Fri & Sat) The closest Whangamatā comes to fine dining is this stylish and compact space just off the main street. Mediterranean and Asian starters like salt-and-pepper prawns complement mains such as herb and garlic venison, Moroccan lamb, and a good prawn and fish curry. Incognito's dining room is relatively small, so book ahead.

Sixfortysix   CAFE $$
(☑07-865 6117; www.sixfortysix.co.nz; 646 Port Rd; mains $10-28; ⊙8am-7pm; ✍) ✎ Sixfortysix does tasty counter food like hoisin-pulled-pork baguettes, as well as tasty lunch mains such as fish tacos and a prawn and scallop salad. Shared platters of cheese, meat and seafood kick off around 3pm. Local craft beer, NZ wine and freshly squeezed juices and smoothies join good coffee on the drinks menu.

🍷 Drinking & Nightlife

Smokey Pallet   PUB
(📞 07-865 9050; www.facebook.com/SmokyPallet; 413 Port Rd; ⏱11.30am-late) Craft beers courtesy of Hamilton's Good George Brewing combine with a concise menu of pub snacks amid the Smokey Pallet's spacious white-washed interior. Meet Whanga's chatty locals on the deck and tuck into a platter ($20 to $23) while recounting the afternoon's kayaking adventures.

ℹ️ Information

Whangamata Info Plus (📞 07-865 8340; www.thecoromandel.com/whangamata; 616 Port Rd; ⏱10am-3pm) Friendly and well-informed team.

ℹ️ Getting There & Away

Go Kiwi (📞 0800 446 549; www.go-kiwi.co.nz) has a shuttle service to Auckland ($75, 3½ hours, one daily) and to other parts of the Coromandel region.

Waihi & Waihi Beach

POP 4527 & 1935

Gold and silver have been dragged out of Waihi's Martha Mine, New Zealand's richest, since 1878. The town formed quickly thereafter and blinged itself up with grand buildings and an avenue of impressive phoenix palms.

After closing down in 1952, open-cast mining restarted in 1988, and in late 2019 Australia-based OceanaGold were given approval to continue mining until 2028. Another more low-key bonanza is also taking place, with Waihi an integral part of the excellent cycling path, the Hauraki Rail Trail (p224).

While Waihi is interesting for a brief visit, it's Waihi Beach where you'll want to linger. The two places are as dissimilar as surfing is from mining, separated by 11km of farmland. The long sandy beach stretches 9km to Bowentown, on the northern limits of Tauranga Harbour, where you'll find sheltered beaches such as beautiful Anzac Bay. There's a popular 45-minute walk north through bush to pristine Orokawa Bay.

👁 Sights

Waihi's main drag, Seddon St, has interesting sculptures, information panels about Waihi's golden past and roundabouts that look like squashed daleks. Opposite the visitor centre (p239), the skeleton of a derelict Cornish Pumphouse (1904) is the town's main landmark, atmospherically lit at night. From here the Pit Rim Walkway has fascinating views into the 250m-deep Martha Mine.

The *Historic Hauraki Gold Towns* pamphlet (free from the visitor centre) outlines walking tours of both Waihi and Paeroa.

★ Gold Discovery Centre   MUSEUM
(📞 07-863 9015; www.golddiscoverycentre.co.nz; 126 Seddon St, Waihi; adult/child $25/12; ⏱9am-5pm Dec-Mar, to 4pm Apr-Nov) Waihi's superb Gold Discovery Centre tells of the area's gold-mining past, present and future through interactive displays, focusing on personal and poignant stories. Holograms and short movies both feature, drawing visitors in and informing them through entertainment. Good luck in taking on the grizzled miner at 'virtual' Two-Up (a gambling game using coins).

Athenree Hot Springs   HOT SPRINGS
(📞 07-863 5600; www.athenreehotsprings.co.nz; 1 Athenree Rd, Athenree; adult/child $8/5.50; ⏱10am-7pm) In cooler months, retreat to these two small but blissful outdoor hot pools, hidden within a holiday park (📞 07-863 5600; www.athenreehotsprings.co.nz; 1 Athenree Rd, Athenree; campsite from $28, unit $115-215; @ 🛜 🐕) 🐾 around 8km southeast of Waihi Beach.

🏃 Activities

Waihi Bicycle Hire   CYCLING
(📞 07-863 8418; www.waihibicyclehire.co.nz; 126 Seddon St; bike hire full day from $50; ⏱8am-5pm)

WORTH A TRIP

PUKETUI VALLEY

Located 12km south of Tairua is the turn-off to Puketui Valley and the historic Broken Hills Gold-Mine Workings (www.doc.govt.nz), which are 8km from the main road along a mainly gravel road. There are short walks up to the sites of stamper batteries, but the best hike is through the 500m-long Collins Drive mine tunnel. After the tunnel, keep an eye out for the short 'lookout' side trail, which affords panoramic views. It takes about three hours return. Remember to take a torch and a jacket with you. Look for the DOC brochure in information centres in Tairua and Whangamatā.

Accommodation is limited to a DOC campsite (www.doc.govt.nz; adult/child $15/7.50). There is no public transport to the Puketui Valley. Most travellers visit en route between Tairua and Whangamatā.

WAIKATO & THE COROMANDEL PENINSULA WAIHI & WAIHI BEACH

DON'T MISS

KARANGAHAKE GORGE

The road between Waihi and Paeroa, through the bush-lined ramparts of the Karangahake Gorge, is one of the best short drives in the country. Walking and biking tracks take in old Māori trails, historic mining and rail detritus, and dense bush. In Māori legend the area is said to be protected by a *taniwha* (supernatural creature). The local *iwi* managed to keep this area closed to miners until 1875, aligning themselves with the militant Te Kooti.

The very worthwhile 4.5km **Karangahake Gorge Historic Walkway** (www.doc.govt. nz) takes 1½ hours each way and starts from the car park 14km west of Waihi. The eastern spur of the Hauraki Rail Trail also passes through, and it's possible to combine a ride on the train from Waihi with a spin on the trail through the most spectacular stage of the gorge. Bikes can be rented from the **Waikino Station Cafe** (☑07-863 8640; www.facebook.com/ waikinostationcafe; SH2; mains $10-22; ☺10am-3pm Mon-Fri, 9.30am-4pm Sat & Sun). Across the river from the cafe is the **Victoria Battery Tramway & Museum** (☑027 351 8980; www. vbts.org.nz; Waikino; ☺10am-3pm Sat, Sun & public holidays).

A few kilometres west, Waitawheta Rd leads over the river from SH2 to **Owharoa Falls**. Opposite the falls is the **Bistro at the Falls Retreat** (☑07-863 8770; www.fallsretreat.co.nz; 25 Waitawheta Rd; pizzas $24-26, mains $30-40; ☺11am-10pm Wed-Sun; ♠), while adjacent is the self-contained country-style accommodation of **Falls Retreat** (☑07-212 8087; d $175).

There is a range of shorter walks and loops leading from the main car park at Karangahake Gorge; bring a torch as some pass through tunnels. A two-hour hike will bring you to **Dickey's Flat** (www.doc.govt.nz; Dickey's Flat Rd; adult/child $8/4), where there's a free DOC campsite and a decent swimming hole. You'll find DOC information boards about the walks and the area's history at the main car park. Further up the same road, **Ohinemuri Estate Winery** (☑07-862 8874; www.ohinemuri.co.nz; Moresby St; mains $16-33, shared platters $45; ☺10am-4pm Wed-Sun) has Latvian-influenced architecture and serves excellent lunches.

Goldfields Railway trains link Waihi to Waikino, from where it is an interesting and mainly flat bike ride on a very scenic spur of the Hauraki Rail Trail through the Karangahake Gorge. Otherwise this route is best driven.

Bike hire and loads of information on the Waihi end of the Hauraki Rail Trail. Fun tandems and efficient e-bikes are both available. Located within the same building as the Gold Discovery Centre.

Goldfields Railway RAIL
(☑07-863 8251; www.waihirail.co.nz; 30 Wrigley St, Waihi; adult/child return $20/12, bikes per route extra $2; ☺departs Waihi 10am, 11.45am & 1.45pm Sat, Sun & public holidays) Vintage trains depart Waihi for a 7km, 30-minute scenic journey to Waikino. It's possible to take bikes on the train, so they can be used to further explore the Karangahake Gorge section of the Hauraki Rail Trail. The timetable varies, so check online.

☞ Tours

Waihi Gold Mine Tours TOURS
(☑07-863 9015; www.golddiscoverycentre.co.nz/ tours; Gold Discovery Centre, 126 Seddon St, Waihi; adult/child $39/19; ☺10am & 12.30pm, additional tours Dec-Feb) To get down into the spectacular Martha Mine, join a 1½-hour Waihi Gold Mine Tour departing from the Gold Discovery Centre.

🛌 Sleeping

Bowentown Beach Holiday Park HOLIDAY PARK $
(☑07-863 5381; www.bowentown.co.nz; 510 Seaforth Rd, Waihi Beach; campsites from $50, units $90-200; @♠) Having nabbed a stunning stretch of sand, this impressively maintained holiday park makes the most of it with first-rate motel units and camping facilities.

Beachfront B&B B&B $$
(☑07-863 5393; www.beachfrontbandb.co.nz; 3 Shaw Rd, Waihi Beach; r $150-200) True to its name with spectacular sea views, this comfortable downstairs flat has a TV, fridge and direct access to the surf. It's also just a short stroll to an excellent oceanfront cafe.

Waihi Beach Lodge B&B $$$
(☑07-863 5818; www.waihibeachlodge.co.nz; 170 Seaforth Ave, Waihi Beach; d $295; ♠) A short stroll from the beach, this accommodation features colourful and modern rooms, and a studio apartment with its own kitchenette. Legendary breakfasts are often served on the sunny deck.

Manawa Ridge　　　　　LODGE $$$

(📞07-863 9400; www.manawaridge.co.nz; 267 Ngati-tangata Rd, Waihi; r $950) 🚗 The views from this castle-like eco-retreat, perched on a 310m-high ridge 6km northeast of Waihi, take in the entire Bay of Plenty. Made of recycled railway timber, mudbrick and lime-plastered straw walls, the rooms marry earthiness with sheer luxury.

🍴 Eating

Ti-Tree Cafe & Wine Bar　　　　　CAFE $

(📞07-863 8668; 14 Haszard St, Waihi; mains $12-22; ⊘6.30am-2.30pm Mon-Fri, 8am-2.30pm Sat & Sun; 🛜) Housed in a cute little wooden building with punga-shaded outdoor seating, Ti-Tree serves fair-trade organic coffee, cooked breakfasts and delicious fruit sorbets and ice cream during summer. Occasional live music on Sunday afternoons.

★Surf Shack Eatery　　　　　CAFE $$

(📞07-863 4353; ww.surfshackeatery.co.nz; 123 Emerton Rd, Waihi Beach; mains $12-25; ⊘9am-2.30pm Tue-Sun, 5-9pm Fri & Sat; 🚗) On the outskirts of Waihi Beach, the Surf Shack is definitely worth a detour for its plate-filling salads and quite possibly the best burgers in New Zealand. Other menu highlights include snacks inspired by the street food of Mexico, Greece and Southeast Asia, and the drinks list combining NZ craft beer, kombucha and organic cold-press juices ticks all the boxes.

Flatwhite　　　　　CAFE $$

(📞07-863 1346; www.flatwhite.co.nz; 21 Shaw Rd, Waihi Beach; mains brunch $13-24, dinner $24-40; ⊘8am-10pm; 🛜) Licensed and right by Waihi Beach, Flatwhite has a lively brunch menu, decent pizzas and flash burgers. Our favourite off the dinner menu is the *dukkah*-rubbed salmon with harissa yoghurt. The best place to sit is on the spacious deck or oceanfront lawn as you combine a frosty beer or chilled white wine with brilliant Pacific views.

Down Thyme　　　　　CAFE $$

(📞07-863 8980; www.downthyme.nz; 31 Orchard Rd; mains $20-38; ⊘11am-late Tue-Sat, to 4pm Sun) On the semirural outskirts of Waihi town, Down Thyme successfully combines European and Turkish flavours. Sit on the outdoor deck and enjoy lamb shish kebab for lunch or grilled duck breast for dinner. There's a compact selection of German beers too.

🛈 Information

Waihi i-SITE (📞07-863 9015; www.waihi.org.nz; 126 Seddon St, Waihi; ⊘9am-5pm, to 4pm Apr-Nov) has local info and houses the Gold Discovery Centre. There's also a good **information centre** (www.waihibeachinfo.co.nz; Wilson Rd, Waihi Beach; ⊘11am-2pm) at Waihi Beach. It's volunteer-run, so hours can be flexible.

🛈 Getting There & Away

Waihi is serviced by InterCity (p199) buses, which head to Hamilton ($33, 2½ hours), Tauranga ($19, one hour) and Thames ($15, 50 minutes).

Paeroa

POP 3980

Paeroa is the birthplace of Lemon & Paeroa (L&P), an icon of Kiwiana that markets itself as 'world famous in New Zealand'. The fizzy drink is now owned by Coca-Cola Amatil and produced in Auckland, but generations of Kiwi kids have pestered their parents to take this route just to catch a glimpse of the giant L&P bottles. For fans of yesteryear, Paeroa's main street has a few excellent vintage and antique shops.

★Refinery　　　　　CAFE $

(📞07-862 7678; www.the-refinery.co.nz; 5 Willoughby St; snacks & mains $10-21; ⊘8.30am-4pm Wed-Fri, from 9am Sat & Sun) Get pleasantly lost in the Refinery, a spacious showcase of 1960s and 1970s Kiwiana style including a turntable where customers are encouraged to play the vinyl records that fill overflowing bins. Good coffee and food (especially the grilled sandwiches – try the Cuban) are best enjoyed on the retro collection of old sofas and dining room furniture filling this heritage building.

There's stylish **accommodation** (d from $99; 🛜) here, too. Welcome to a true Kiwi gem and one of the country's best cafes.

🛈 Information

Paeroa Information Centre (📞07-862 6999; www.paeroa.org.nz; Old Post Office Bldg, 101 Normanby Rd; ⊘8.30am-5pm Mon-Fri, 9am-4pm Sat, to 3pm Sun) Information and brochures including how to tackle the Hauraki Rail Trail. Also bike hire.

🛈 Getting There & Away

InterCity (www.intercity.co.nz) runs buses to Paeroa linking to Thames ($15, 30 minutes, three daily) and Hamilton ($25, five hours, one daily).

WAIKATO & THE COROMANDEL PENINSULA PAEROA

Taranaki & Whanganui

Why Go?

Halfway between Auckland and Wellington on the North Island's underrated west coast, Taranaki (aka 'the 'Naki') is New Zealand's Texas, with oil and gas streaming in from offshore rigs. But in New Plymouth, free galleries, a fab provincial museum, bars and dining hotspots are attracting young families from the big smoke, craving affordable real estate without compromising lifestyle. Travellers are following suit.

Behind the city the astonishing Mt Taranaki demands to be explored. The volcanic terrain is responsible for the area's black-sand beaches, lapped up by surfers and holidaymakers during summer.

Further east the history-rich Whanganui River curls its way through Whanganui National Park down to Whanganui city, a 19th-century river port ageing with grace and artistry. Palmerston North, the Manawatu region's main city, is a student town filled with caffeinated Massey University literati. Beyond the city, the region blends rural grace with yesterday's pace.

Best Places to Eat

➜ Ms White (p249)

➜ Viet Nom Nom (p248)

➜ Federal Store (p249)

➜ Citadel (p262)

➜ Lahar (p256)

Best Places to Stay

➜ Ducks & Drakes (p247)

➜ Ahu Ahu Beach Villas (p256)

➜ King & Queen Hotel Suites (p248)

➜ Browns Boutique B&B (p262)

➜ Ngāti Ruanui Stratford Mountain House (p253)

When to Go

➜ In January and February, cruise Taranaki's 105km-long Surf Highway 45 and find your favourite black-sand beach – surf's up in summer! Whanganui has some great beaches, too.

➜ Powder snow and picture-perfect runs on Mt Taranaki make winter (June to August) the ideal time to visit.

➜ In December the crowds arrive to see the lights in New Plymouth's Pukekura Park at the annual Festival of Lights.

ⓘ Getting There & Away

Air New Zealand (p251) is the main regional airline, with direct flights between New Plymouth and Auckland, Wellington and Christchurch, and between Palmerston North and Auckland, Hamilton, Wellington and Christchurch.

InterCity (www.intercity.co.nz) buses service New Plymouth, Whanganui and Palmerston North. Shuttle services run between New Plymouth and Mt Taranaki.

Great Journeys of New Zealand (p273) Northern Explorer trains stop in Palmerston North, travelling between Auckland and Wellington. There's also a weekday commuter service called the Capital Connection running between Palmerston North and Wellington.

New Plymouth

POP 83,100

Dominated (in the best possible way) by Mt Taranaki and surrounded by lush farmland, contemporary New Plymouth was founded in 1841 by Cornish and Devonian settlers, and remains the only international deep-water port in this part of New Zealand. Like in all port towns, the world washes in and out on the tide, leaving the locals buzzing with a global outlook. The city has a bubbling arts scene, some fab cafes and craft-beer joints, and a rootsy, outdoorsy vibe. Surf beaches and Mt Taranaki (Egmont National Park) are just a short hop away.

ⓞ Sights

★**Govett-Brewster Art Gallery/Len Lye Centre**   GALLERY
(✆06-759 6060; www.govettbrewster.com; 42 Queen St; adult/child $16/free, tickets valid 24hr; ⊙10am-5pm) This two-headed artistic beast is arguably NZ's best regional art gallery, presenting contemporary – and often experimental and provocative – local and international shows. 'Great art goes 50-50 with great architecture' – so said NZ artist Len Lye (1901–80), to whom the shimmering Len Lye Centre is dedicated. It's an interlocking facade of tall, mirror-clad concrete flutes, with internal galleries linked by ramps housing Lye's works - kinetic, noisy and surprising. There's also a cinema here, plus regular kids' art sessions. Essential viewing!

★**Pukekura Park**   GARDENS
(✆06-759 6060; buggy tours 06-758 6417; www.pukekura.org.nz; 10 Fillis St; ⊙daylight hours) FREE Lush Pukekura has 49 hectares of gardens, playgrounds, trails, streams, waterfalls, ponds and display houses. In summer, **rowboats** (per half-hour $15) meander across the main lake (full of arm-sized eels), next to which the **Tea House** (✆06-758 7205; www.pukekura.org.nz; Pukekura Park, 10 Fillis St; mains $8-20; ⊙9am-4pm; 🖐) serves light meals. The technicolored Festival of Lights (p247) draws the summer crowds here, as does the impeccably mowed **cricket oval**. For the lethargic, 45-minute motorised **buggy tours** (adult/child $5/free) can whip you around to see the best bits; call for bookings.

★**Puke Ariki**   MUSEUM
(✆06-759 6060; www.pukeariki.com; 1 Ariki St; ⊙9am-6pm Mon-Fri, to 5pm Sat & Sun) FREE Translating as 'Hill of Chiefs', Puke Ariki was once a *pā* (fortified village) site, and is now home to the i-SITE (p250), a fab regional museum, a library, a cafe and **Arborio** (✆06-759 1241; www.arborio.co.nz; Puke Ariki, via 65 St Aubyn St; breakfast & lunch $16-27, dinner $22-39; ⊙9am-late) restaurant. The excellent museum has an extensive collection of Māori artefacts, plus colonial, mountain geology and wildlife exhibits. We hope the shark suspended above the lobby isn't to scale.

Paritutu   HILL
(off Centennial Dr; ⊙daylight hrs) At 156m, this craggy, steep-sided hill is almost as tall as New Plymouth's old power-station chimney down at the port (198m). Paritutu translates as 'rising precipice'. 'Precipice' is right – it's a seriously knee-trembling, 15-minute scramble to the top, the upper reaches over bare rock with a chain to grip on to. If you can ignore your inner screams of common sense, you'll be able to see for miles around from the summit. Save it for another day if the weather ain't pretty.

Sugar Loaf Islands Marine Park   ISLAND
(✆06-759 0350; www.doc.govt.nz; ⊙24hr) About 1km offshore, these rugged islets (Ngā Motu in Māori) are eroded volcanic remnants, offering refuge for 10,000 sea birds and a colony of NZ fur seals. Most seals come here from June to October, but some stay year-round. Visibility can reach up to 20m in summer and autumn, making this a popular diving spot. The i-SITE (p250) can advise on kayak hire, or you can take a tour (p247).

Wind Wand   SCULPTURE
(Puke Ariki Landing, St Aubyn St) The wonderfully eccentric Wind Wand at Puke Ariki Landing was designed by Len Lye – the artist who has put this town on the map in

TARANAKI & WHANGANUI NEW PLYMOUTH

Taranaki & Whanganui Highlights

1 Mt Taranaki
(p252) Hiking up or around this massive volcanic cone.

2 New Zealand Rugby Museum
(p270) Flexing your All Blacks spirit in Palmerston North.

3 Surf Highway 45 (p255) Chasing the breaks along this surf-battered coast.

4 New Plymouth
(p241) Pondering experimental art at the dazzling Len Lye Centre and bouncing from bean to beer in cafes and bars.

5 New Zealand Glassworks
(p259) Watching a glass-blowing demonstration in Whanganui.

6 Whanganui National Park (p264) Redefining serenity on a Whanganui River canoe or kayak trip – or taking on an extreme jetboating adventure.

7 Whanganui River Road (p264) Traversing this scenic riverside road by car or bike – it's all about the journey, not how fast you get there.

North Taranaki Bight

Pukearuhe (10km)

New Plymouth Airport
Waitara
Urenui
Fitzroy Beach
Port Taranaki
Sugar Loaf Islands Marine Park
Bell Block
Paritutu (154m)
4 New Plymouth

Oākura

Egmont Village
Inglewood

Kumara Patch
Stent Road
Okato
Warea

Surf Highway 45 3
Mt Taranaki North Taranaki

Cape Egmont Lighthouse
Cape Egmont
Pungarehu
Parihaka
Manganui
Dawson Falls
North Egmont
East Egmont
Midhurst
Douglas

Egmont National Park
Pembroke
Stratford

Oaonui
Mangatoki
Ngaere

Awatuna
Kaponga
Eltham

Opunake
Te Kiri
Lake Rotokare

Pihama
Auroa

Manaia
Tarere State Forest

Otakeho
Tawhiti Museum

Hāwera

Mokoia

South Taranaki Bight

Kakaramea

Pātea
Waverley

Museum of South Taranaki

Forgotten World Hwy

Tasman Sea

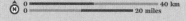

N   0 _____ 40 km
     0 _____ 20 miles

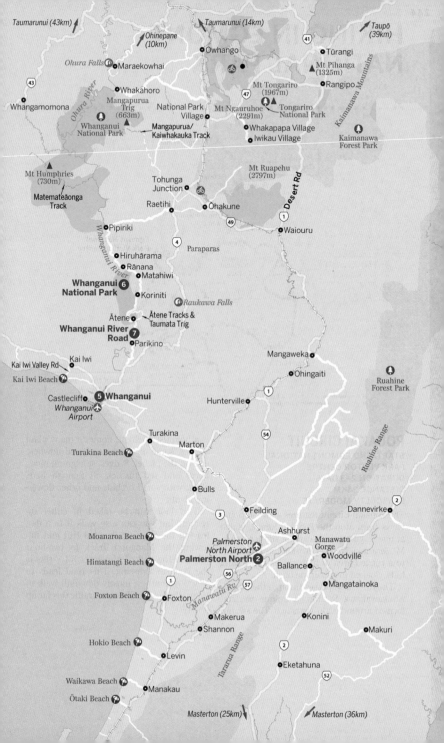

HIKING IN EGMONT NATIONAL PARK

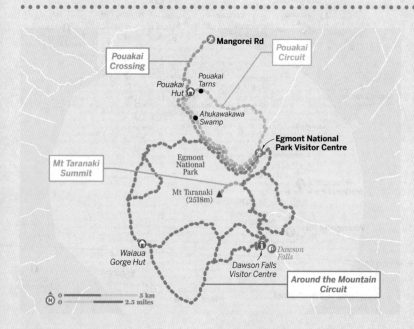

POUAKAI CIRCUIT

START/END EGMONT NATIONAL
PARK VISITOR CENTRE
DURATION 2–3 DAYS
DISTANCE 24KM
DIFFICULTY MODERATE

The Pouakai Circuit features show-stopping views from atop the Pouakai Range, which at one stage was a volcano of similar size to Mt Taranaki. Natural erosion has reduced it to a rugged area of high ridges and rolling hills, cloaked in subalpine bush.

The track also passes through the mighty Ahukawakawa Swamp, a unique wetland formed around 3500 years ago. The swamp is a botanist's delight, home to many plant species, some of which are found nowhere else on the planet. Sedges, sphagnum moss, herbs and red tussock all flourish here, along with small orchids and other flowering plants.

This loop can be hiked in either direction, but you can also walk it in a day, leaving the route at Pouakai Hut and following the Mangorei Track (a two-hour hike) to the end of Mangorei Rd – this is the Pouakai Crossing. This road leads to New Plymouth, a mostly downhill walk of 15km (there's usually scant traffic this far up the hill).

Egmont National Park is dominated by the volcanic, snowy cone of dramatic Mt Taranaki. It's laced with hiking routes, from a contender for NZ's best day hike, to a lap around the peak and a fair-weather summit climb.

POUAKAI CROSSING

START EGMONT NATIONAL PARK VISITOR CENTRE
END MANGOREI RD
DURATION 7½–9½ HOURS
DISTANCE 19KM
DIFFICULTY MODERATE

If the Tongariro Alpine Crossing is widely regarded as the best day walk in New Zealand, the Pouakai Crossing is its heir apparent. This walk is another volcanic highlights reel, taking in amazing cliffs, a waterfall, the primeval Ahukawakawa Wetlands and the (hopefully) mirror-perfect Pouakai Tarns.

It's a walk that packs plenty of panoramic punch without the need to lug a heavy pack filled with overnight gear. It's also a great option for those staying in New Plymouth, allowing you a grand day out with a debrief back among the city lights. Its relatively low altitude means it can also be walked much of the year, though it's worth checking in with Egmont National Park Visitor Centre before you leave to make sure the track's OK.

Starting at the visitor centre, the track follows the first day of the Pouakai Circuit as far as Pouakai Hut before heading down Mangorei Track to the road, where you can be collected by shuttle bus for the return trip to New Plymouth. It's a full-on day, but a hugely satisfying one.

AROUND THE MOUNTAIN CIRCUIT

START/END EGMONT NATIONAL PARK VISITOR CENTRE
DURATION 4–5 DAYS
DISTANCE 52KM
DIFFICULTY MODERATE TO CHALLENGING

The Around the Mountain Circuit (AMC) is exactly what the name on the tin suggests – a spectacular loop around Mt Taranaki on a backcountry track for experienced hikers,

traversing stunted subalpine forest and spectacular volcanic scenery, and with characterful huts en route.

The track can be started at either the Egmont National Park Visitor Centre or Dawson Falls. Hikers starting at Dawson Falls often go directly to Waiaua Gorge Hut via the upper-level tracks on the first day. Note that high- and low-level tracks exist for some sections of the track, giving you the chance to climb high in good weather, or stay low and safe if it's mucky. It's important to remember that there are lots of rivers along the track, and not many bridges – you're going to get wet. Rivers can become dangerous to cross after heavy rain. If in doubt, wait it out.

MT TARANAKI SUMMIT

START/END EGMONT NATIONAL PARK VISITOR CENTRE
DURATION 8–10 HOURS
DISTANCE 14KM
DIFFICULTY MODERATE TO CHALLENGING

Taranaki is the most climbed mountain in New Zealand, and in ideal summer conditions most fit hikers can make it to the summit. But you need to be prepared – the weather conditions here can change in an instant, and a long list of people have met their maker on Taranaki's slopes. It's an ascent of around 1570m – a big day out – so don't take it lightly, whatever the conditions. Don't even think about tackling it without adequate all-season clothing and plenty of supplies. You must check the forecast, and be prepared to turn tail and retreat if the weather deteriorates: check in with the Egmont National Park Visitor Centre for up-to-date information before you set out, and register your hiking intentions. Fear and danger aside, Mt Taranaki is a fabulous ascent, and the clear-day views from the top are utterly worth the endeavour.

New Plymouth

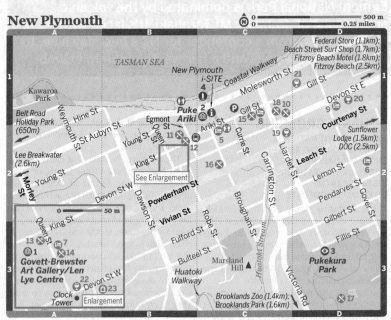

New Plymouth

⊙ Top Sights
1 Govett-Brewster Art Gallery/Len Lye Centre	A3
2 Puke Ariki	C1
3 Pukekura Park	D3

⊙ Sights
4 Wind Wand	C1

🛌 Sleeping
5 Ariki Backpackers	C2
6 Ducks & Drakes	D2
7 King & Queen Hotel Suites	A3
8 Metrotel	C1
9 State Hotel	D1

⊗ Eating
Arborio	(see 2)

10 Arranged Marriage	C1
11 Frederic's	B2
12 Meat & Liquor	B2
13 Monica's Eatery	A3
14 Ms White	A3
15 Portofino	C1
16 Social Kitchen	C2
17 Tea House	D3
18 Viet Nom Nom	C1

⊙ Drinking & Nightlife
19 Hour Glass	C2
20 Mike's	D1
21 Shining Peak Brewing	D1
22 Snug Lounge	A3

⊙ Shopping
23 Kina	B3

modern times. This 45m-high, kooky kinetic sculpture is a truly beloved icon of bendy pole-ness. Look for it all lit up at night – in 2017, it was lit up by lightning.

Brooklands Park PARK
(🖉06-759 6060; www.newplymouthnz.com; Brooklands Park Dr; ☉daylight hrs) Adjoining Pukekura Park (p241), Brooklands Park is home to the Bowl of Brooklands, a world-class natural amphitheatre and sound-shell

that hosts the annual WOMAD festival and old-school rockers like Fleetwood Mac; the talent is separated from the rabid fans by a little lake. Park highlights include a 2000-year-old puriri tree, some colossal Monterrey and Norfolk Island pines, a 300-variety rhododendron dell and the farmy (and free!) **Brooklands Zoo** (🖉06-759 6060; www.newplymouthnz.com; Brooklands Park, Brooklands Park Dr; ☉9am-5pm, last entry 4.30pm; 🖈) FREE.

⚐ Activities

Surfing

New Plymouth's black, volcanic-sand beaches are terrific for surfing. Close to the eastern edge of town are **Fitzroy Beach** (with attendant holiday park if you want to catch the dawn breaks) and **East End Beach** (allegedly the cleanest beach in Oceania). There's also good surf at atmospheric **Back Beach**, near Paritutu (p241), at the western end of the city. Otherwise, head south along Surf Highway 45. For lessons and gear-hire try **Beach Street Surf Shop** (✆06-758 0400; www.facebook.com/beachstreetnz; 39 Beach St; 1hr lessons per person from $100; ⏱10am-5pm Mon-Fri, to 3pm Sat & Sun; ⌂).

Walking

The New Plymouth i-SITE (p250) stocks the *Taranaki: A Walker's Guide* booklet, which includes coastal, local reserve and park walks, including the excellent **Coastal Walkway** (13km) from Bell Block to Port Taranaki, giving you a surf-side perspective on New Plymouth and crossing the much-photographed **Te Rewa Rewa Bridge** (www.visit.taranaki.info; Te Rewa Rewa Bridge). The **Huatoki Walkway** (5km), following Huatoki Stream, is a rambling walk into the city centre. Alternatively, i-SITE also runs guided history walks around the old town ($15 per person, book ahead).

⚐ Tours

Chaddy's Charters　　　BOATING
(✆06-758 9133; www.chaddyscharters.co.nz; Ocean View Pde, Lee Breakwater; trips adult/child $40/15; ⏱8am-4pm Sep-Jun, 9am-4pm Jul & Aug; ⌂) Chug out to visit the Sugar Loaf Islands with Chaddy: expect at least four laughs a minute during a one-hour bob around on the swell. Departs Tuesday to Sunday, tide and weather permitting. You can also hire kayaks (single/double per hour $15/30), bikes ($10 per hour) and stand-up paddle boards ($30 per hour). Reduced winter hours.

City Cycle Tours　　　CYCLING
(✆027 260 6221; www.facebook.com/pg/citycycletoursnp; per person $50) Saddle up for a five-hour bike tour of New Plymouth's must-sees (Pukekura Park, Te Rewa Rewa Bridge, Paritutu, Wind Wand etc), with plenty of time traversing the Coastal Walkway. Free hotel pick-ups.

Canoe & Kayak Taranaki　　　KAYAKING
(✆06-751 2340; www.canoeandkayak.co.nz; per person $95) Book ahead for fair-weather, three-hour kayak tours to see the seals out at Sugar Loaf Islands Marine Park (p241). Tours usually run between January and May; no experience required.

⚐ Festivals & Events

★WOMAD　　　MUSIC
(World of Music, Arts & Dance; www.womad.co.nz; ⏱Mar) A broad sweep of local and international artists perform at the Bowl of Brooklands each March. Hugely popular, with music fans trucking in from across NZ. Camping sites available, too (buy 'em online).

Taranaki Garden Festival　　　CULTURAL
(www.gardenfestnz.co.nz; ⏱Nov) A long-running NZ flower fest in early November (sometimes starting in late October): more rhododendrons than you'll ever see in one place again.

NZ Tattoo & Art Festival　　　CULTURAL
(www.nztattooart.com; ⏱Nov) This saucy skin fest attracts thousands of ink fans over a busy weekend in November. Get yourself a new 'badge', or check out the BMX stunt riders and the burlesque gyrators.

Festival of Lights　　　CULTURAL
(www.festivaloflights.nz; ⏱Dec-Feb) Complete with live music, 1000 light installations and costumed characters roaming the undergrowth, this colourful display illuminates Pukekura Park (p241) from mid-December to early February.

⚐ Sleeping

★Ducks & Drakes　　　HOSTEL $
(✆06-758 0404; www.ducksanddrakes.co.nz; 48 Lemon St; hostel dm/s/d from $32/68/90, hotel r from $130; ❡❅) Brimming with character, D&D occupies a labyrinthine 1920s heritage building with bright feature walls and fancy timberwork. Upstairs rooms are the pick: secluded, quiet and catching the morning sun. Next door is a more private hotel wing with snazzy studios and one-bedroom suites (to which the owners escape when their teenage daughter has friends over). New carpets, new paint. Nice one.

Belt Road Holiday Park　　　HOLIDAY PARK $
(✆06-758 0228; www.beltroad.co.nz; 2 Belt Rd; sites unpowered/powered from $46/50, cabins

ESSENTIAL TARANAKI & WHANGANUI

Eat a big breakfast in one of Palmerston North's good cafes.

Drink a few craft beers at one of new Plymouth's buzzy brew bars.

Read Came a Hot Friday, a 1964 novel by Ronald Hugh Morrieson, born in Hāwera, about two con men who cheat bookmakers throughout the country.

Listen to the rockin' album Back to the Burning Wreck by Whanganui riff monsters The Have.

Watch The Last Samurai (Edward Zwick, 2003), co-starring Tom Cruise (though Mt Taranaki should get top billing).

Go green and paddle a stretch of the Whanganui River, an awe-inspiring slice of NZ wilderness.

Go online at www.visit.taranaki.info; www.visitwhanganui.nz; www.manawatunz.co.nz.

$80-170; P 🛜) Poised on a bluff with grassy lawns and pohutukawa trees, Belt Road has a brilliant outlook over the shimmering (and often tempestuous) Tasman Sea. The half-dozen best cabins have big-dollar views, there's a play area for the kids, and the excellent Coastal Walkway trucks right on by. It's a 15-minute walk into town.

Ariki Backpackers   HOSTEL $
(☑ 06-769 5020; www.arikibackpackers.com; 25 Ariki St; dm from $27, d with/without bathroom $90/75; 🛜) Upstairs at the old Royal Hotel (Queen Liz once stayed here!), welcoming Ariki offers downtown hostelling with retro carpets, a roomy lounge with well-loved couches and an ace roof terrace looking across the park to Puke Ariki (p241). Most rooms have their own shower and toilet. Bikes, surfboards and kayaks for hire.

Sunflower Lodge   HOSTEL $
(☑ 06-759 0050; www.sunflowerlodge.co.nz; 33 Timandra St; dm/s/d from $32/64/80; P 🛜) Down a steep driveway a few minutes' drive south of town (en route to Mt Taranaki), the local YHA does its best to transcend its resthome origins and mostly succeeds. Dorms maxing out at four people, loads of organised activities, quality mattresses and a barbecue pavilion help the cause.

Metrotel   MOTEL $$
(☑ 06-222 0036; www.themetrotel.co.nz; 22 Gill St; d from $135, 2-bedroom ste from $290; P 🛜) Metrotel is just a handful of years old, but there are hints of history in its original 1920s warehouse walls. Rooms are simple and slick – all glass, concrete and steel, with nifty no-fog mirrors and super-comfy beds. The vibe is rather futuristic and institutional (like an astronaut-training facility?), but cheery staff bring some humanity to it.

Fitzroy Beach Motel Apartments   MOTEL $$
(☑ 06-757 2925; www.fitzroybeachmotel.co.nz; 25 Beach St; 1-/2-bedroom units from $180/270, extra person $20; P 🛜) This quiet motel is just 200m from Fitzroy Beach and has been thoroughly redeemed with a major overhaul and extension. Highlights include a calming colour palette, quality carpets, double glazing, lovely bathrooms, big TVs and an absence of poky studio-style units (all are one- or two-bedroom). Free bikes, too.

State Hotel   BOUTIQUE HOTEL $$
(☑ 06-757 5162; www.thestatehotel.co.nz; 162 Devon St E; d from $160; P 🛜) The 15 en-suite rooms upstairs at this former pub are stylishly fitted out with NZ art, patterned cushions and flamingo wallpaper for extra flair (one of the owners is an interior designer). Bathrooms are small but practical; windows in the shared lounge are more generously proportioned. Parking is down the laneway out the back, off Gover St.

★ King & Queen Hotel Suites   BOUTIQUE HOTEL $$$
(☑ 06-757 2999; www.kingandqueen.co.nz; cnr King & Queen Sts; d/ste from $205/235; P 🛜) This regal hotel occupies the corner of King and Queen Sts (get it?) in the cool West End Precinct (great bars and eats). Run by unerringly professional staff, each suite features antique Moroccan and Euro furnishings, lustrous black tiles, hip art, leather couches and touches of industrial chic. A couple of new suites were being constructed when we visited.

✗ Eating

★ Viet Nom Nom   VIETNAMESE $
(☑ 022 040 3994; www.facebook.com/moutain reflection; 21 Liardet St; mains $10-15; ⊙ 11am-2.30pm Tue-Sat, 5-7.30pm Thu & Fri; 🖉) Steaming beef pho (noodle soup), crispy Vietnamese crepes (chicken, pork or tofu) and brilliant banh mi – this fun little Vietnamese joint

is one of several food trucks permanently parked in an alleyway off Liardet St. Imagine blaring soul, old electrical-spool tables, twinkling lights, students, tattoos...it's all good.

★ **Ms White**   PIZZA **$$**
(☑027 406 4314; White Hart Courtyard, 47 Queen St; pizza $14-21; ⊙4pm-late Mon & Tue, 11am-late Wed-Sun; 🍴) Sharing a fairy-light-draped courtyard with Snug Lounge (p250), seductive Ms White serves trad wood-fired Italian pizza and a bedazzling range of 40-plus craft beers from its outdoor kitchen. Choose from pizza *rosse* bases with tomato sauce and mozzarella, or pizza *bianche* with olive oil instead of tomato. Funky communal tables, and rugs for chilly nights.

★ **Federal Store**   CAFE **$$**
(☑06-757 8147; www.thefederalstore.com; 440 Devon St E; mains $15-24; ⊙7am-4.30pm Mon-Fri, 8.30am-4.30pm Sat & Sun; 🍴) Crammed with retro furniture, superpopular Federal conjures up a 1950s corner-store vibe. Switched-on staff in dinky headscarves take your coffee requests, keeping you buoyant until your southern-fried-chicken bagel or eggs Benedict arrives. Sensational counter food includes cakes, tarts and artfully presented rolls overflowing with good fillings. Aim for the back booth, or the footpath tables if it's not blowy.

Arranged Marriage   SOUTH INDIAN **$$**
(☑06-215 4488; www.arrangedmarriage.co.nz; 77 Devon Street E; mains $12-28; ⊙11.30am-2pm & 5pm-late Tue-Sun; 🍴) There's a slightly off-beat humour to proceedings at this stylish option on the main street, the pick of New Plymouth's many Indian eateries. Curries are predictably great (butter chicken, vegetable korma), but the house-special *dosas* (savoury pancakes) are what you're really here for, stuffed with all manner of meats, vegetables and aromatic spices.

Monica's Eatery   MODERN NZ **$$**
(☑06-759 2038; www.monicaseatery.co.nz; cnr King & Queen Sts; mains breakfast $13-20, lunch & dinner $17-39; ⊙6.30am-late; 🍴🍴) Beside the Govett-Brewster Art Gallery/Len Lye Centre (p241), this all-day diner is homey despite its contemporary interior. Perhaps it's seeing handmade pasta lowered into bowls through the open kitchen, or the Bill Withers/Supremes soundtrack, or the

poetry on the walls. It's possibly the staff, who advise using the house focaccia for 'sauce mopping'. Whatever it is, you'll feel right at home.

Bach on Breakwater   CAFE **$$**
(☑06-769 6967; www.bachonbreakwater.co.nz; Ocean View Pde, Lee Breakwater; mains $12-27; ⊙9am-4pm Tue-Sun; 🍴) Constructed from hefty recycled timbers, this cool cafe-bistro in the Lee Breakwater precinct looks like an old sea chest washed up after a storm. The all-day menu ranges from a vegan big breakfast to New Yorker french toast slathered in peanut butter. Also open for dinner on Friday and Saturday from November to February.

Portofino   ITALIAN **$$**
(☑06-757 8686; www.portofino.co.nz; 14 Gill St; mains $20-40; ⊙5pm-late Mon-Sat) Italian-accented staff add authenticity to this discreet family-run restaurant. It's one of a dozen Portofinos across the North Island, but manages to maintain a nonchain vibe with old-fashioned pasta and pizza, just like nonna used to make. Ingredients are a mix of market-fresh and European imports. A consistent performer.

Social Kitchen   LATIN AMERICAN **$$$**
(☑06-757 2711; www.social-kitchen.co.nz; 40 Powderham St; mains $35-60; ⊙noon-late; 🛜) Inside what was once the Salvation Army Citadel, this on-trend restaurant is filled with neon charm and taxidermy...but you can sidestep the hanging pigs' heads in the courtyard, strung with colourful lights. Arrive hungry and share plates of flavour-packed 'firecracker' chicken with organic yoghurt; empanadas; chilli lamb shoulder; and flaming halloumi with lemon, thyme and ouzo.

Meat & Liquor   STEAK **$$$**
(☑06-759 1227; www.meatandliquor.co.nz; 34a Egmont St; mains $19-55; ⊙4pm-late) Push your way through the little red door on King St, around the corner from **Frederic's** (☑06-759 1227; www.frederics.co.nz; 34 Egmont St; mains $10-26; ⊙11am-midnight) gastro-bar, and head upstairs for some hand-picked, dry-aged cuts from the 'meat library' – sustainable beef, lamb, pork and venison. The literal menu also covers 'bird' and 'fish' offerings, or you can bravely select the salted lamb's heart or sweet-and-sour sweetbreads. Utterly fortifying.

MĀORI NZ: TARANAKI & WHANGANUI

Ever since Mt Taranaki fled here to escape romantic difficulties, the Taranaki region has had a turbulent history. Conflicts between local *iwi* (tribes) and invaders from the Waikato were followed by two wars with the government – first in 1860–61, and then again in 1865–69. Then there were massive land confiscations and an extraordinary passive-resistance campaign at Parihaka (p257).

A drive up the Whanganui River Rd takes you into traditional Māori territory, passing the Māori villages of Ātene, Koriniti, Rānana and Hiruhārama along the way. In Whanganui itself, run your eyes over amazing indigenous exhibits at the Whanganui Regional Museum (p259), and check out the superb Māori carvings in Putiki Church (p261).

Over in Palmerston North, Te Manawa (p270) museum has a strong Māori focus, while the New Zealand Rugby Museum (p270) pays homage to Māori All Blacks, without whom the team would never have become three-time Rugby World Cup winners.

Drinking & Nightlife

★ Shining Peak Brewing   CRAFT BEER
(☎06-927 3133; www.shiningpeakbrewing.com; 59 Gill St; ☉11.30am-10pm) Inside an old electronics warehouse on an otherwise dull stretch of Gill St, stouts, IPAs, APAs and a new beer monthly bubble away in 10 huge stainless-steel vats. New-wave '80s tunes wail as craft-beer fans sip and munch on meaty offerings such as tacos, ribs and pork belly (small/large plates from $12/20). Sunny courtyard and kids' food, too.

★ Snug Lounge   COCKTAIL BAR
(☎06-757 9130; www.snuglounge.co.nz; cnr Devon St W & Queen St; ☉4pm-late) Inside what was once the White Hart Hotel, this savvy bar on the downtown fringe is the classiest drinking spot in town (unlike its predecessor). Dress to the nines, order a Tropical Botanical (gin, coconut and mint) and act like you own the town. Japanese share plates ($9 to $20) will ensure you stay vertical.

Hour Glass   BAR
(☎06-758 2299; www.facebook.com/thehourglass49; 49 Liardet St; ☉4pm-late Tue-Sat) On a rise of Liardet St is this late-night tapas and craft-beer bar, with long leather banquettes and a cute little courtyard. Plenty of craft beers, killer cocktails, commendable eats (tapas $5 to $18, mains $28 to $40) and even named lockers for expensive bottles if you're a regular. Check the Facebook page for tastings and jam sessions.

Mike's   CRAFT BEER
(☎027 333 0215; www.mikesbeer.co.nz; 186 Devon St E; ☉noon-10pm Tue-Fri, 10am-10pm Sat, 10am-8pm Sun) Mike's proudly asserts its status as NZ's first craft-beer brewery (founded 1989) and when the beer is this good, why argue? Swing into Mike's new downtown beer bistro (mains $14 to $26) to sample some: its LongLine Lager is king of the regulars, while Led Zeppelin fans will get a kick out of the seasonal Misty Mountain Hops, a New England IPA.

Shopping

★ Kina   JEWELLERY
(☎06-759 1201; www.kina.co.nz; 101 Devon St W; ☉9am-5.30pm Mon-Fri, 9.30am-4pm Sat, 10am-3pm Sun) Fabulous Kiwi crafts, jewellery, and bath and beauty products in a lovely shopfront on the main drag. Art and design gallery exhibitions happen with pleasing regularity. It's the perfect spot to pick up a classy, meaningful NZ souvenir.

ℹ Information

Department of Conservation (DOC; ☎06-759 0350; www.doc.govt.nz; 55a Rimu St; ☉8am-4.30pm Mon-Fri) Info on regional national parks, hiking and camping.

MediCross (☎06-759 8915; www.medicross.co.nz; 8 Egmont St; ☉8am-8pm) Doctors by appointment and urgent medical help. Pharmacy and dentist also on site.

New Plymouth i-SITE (☎06-759 0897; www.taranaki.co.nz; Puke Ariki, 1 Ariki St; ☉9am-6pm Mon-Fri, 9am-5pm Sat & Sun) In the Puke Ariki (p241) building, with an interactive tourist-info database.

Taranaki Base Hospital (☎06-753 6139; www.tdhb.org.nz; 23 David St, Westown; ☉24hr) Accident and emergency.

➊ Getting There & Away

AIR

New Plymouth Airport (☑ 0800 144 129; www.newplymouthairport.com; Airport Dr) is 11km east of the centre off SH3. **Scott's Airport Shuttle** (☑ 06-769 5974; www.npairportshuttle.co.nz; per person from $25) operates a door-to-door shuttle to/from the airport.

Air New Zealand (☑ 0800 737 000; www.airnewzealand.co.nz) runs daily direct flights to/from Auckland, Wellington and Christchurch, with onward connections.

Jetstar (www.jetstar.com) flies the New Plymouth–Auckland route.

Origin Air (www.originair.co.nz) flies between New Plymouth, Nelson and Palmerston North.

BUS

Services run from the **Bus Centre** (☑ 06-765 7127; www.trc.govt.nz; cnr Egmont & Ariki Sts) in central New Plymouth.

InterCity (www.intercity.co.nz) services include the following:

Destination	Cost	Time (hr)	Frequency (daily)
Auckland	from $36	6	3
Hamilton	from $26	3½-4	3
Palmerston North	from $25	4	2
Wellington	from $28	7	2
Whanganui	from $21	2½	2

➊ Getting Around

BICYCLE

Cycle Inn (☑ 06-758 7418; www.cycleinn.co.nz; 133 Devon St E; per 2hr/day $10/20; ☺ 8.30am-5pm Mon-Fri, 9am-4pm Sat, 10am-2pm Sun) rents out bikes, as does Chaddy's Charters (p247) at Lee Breakwater.

BUS

Citylink (☑ 0800 872 287; www.taranakibus.info; tickets adult/child $3.70/2.30) services run Monday to Friday around New Plymouth, as well as north to Waitara and south to Ōakura. Buses depart from the Bus Centre.

CAR

RaD Car Hire (☑ 06-757 5362; www.radcarhire.co.nz; 592 Devon St E; ☺ 8am-5pm Mon-Fri, to noon Sat) For cheap car hire, try RaD.

TAXI

Energy City Cabs (☑ 06-757 5580; www.energycabs.co.nz) Taxis in New Plymouth.

Around New Plymouth

There are some interesting places to check out heading north from New Plymouth along SH3, with various seaward turn-offs to high sand dunes and surf beaches. Mt Taranaki's lower flanks also host a couple of stop-worthy places.

About 35km north of New Plymouth on the SH3 is the turn-off to Pukearuhe and White Cliffs, huge precipices resembling their Dover namesakes. From Pukearuhe boat ramp, you can tackle the **White Cliffs Walkway**, a three-hour loop walk with mesmerising views of the coast and mountains (Taranaki and Ruapehu). The tide can make things dicey along the beach: walk between the two hours either side of low tide.

Continuing north towards Mōkau, stop at the **Three Sisters** rock formation, signposted just south of the Tongaporutu Bridge – you can traverse the shore at low tide. Two sisters stand somewhat forlornly off the coast: their other sister collapsed in a heap last decade, but a new one is emerging from the eroding cliffs. Next to the sisters is **Elephant Rock** – you'll never guess what it looks like.

Pukeiti   GARDENS

(☑ 0800 736 222; www.pukeiti.org.nz; 2290 Carrington Rd, New Plymouth; ☺ 9am-5pm; ⬛) **FREE** This sprawling garden, 23km south of New Plymouth, is home to thriving masses of rhododendrons and azaleas. The blooms are at their bloomin' best between September and November, but it's worth a visit any time. Take a garden walk (45 minutes to two hours), or propel the kids along the self-guided Treehouse Trail adventure. There's a cafe here, too.

Taranaki Aviation, Transport & Technology Museum   MUSEUM

(TATATM; ☑ 06-752 2845; www.tatatm.co.nz; 13 Kent Rd, New Plymouth; adult/child/family $7/2/16; ☺ 10am-4pm Sat & Sun, daily school & public holidays; ⬛) Around 9km south of New Plymouth is this roadside museum, with ramshackle, interactive displays of old planes, trains, automobiles and general household miscellany. Run by volunteer enthusiasts, the collection is always growing, thanks to donations. Play pilot in the cockpit of the Harvard plane.

Mt Taranaki (Egmont National Park) & Around

A near-perfect 2518m volcanic cone dominating the landscape, Mt Taranaki is a magnet to all who catch his eye. Taranaki is the youngest of three large volcanoes – including Kaitake and Pouakai – that stand along the same fault line. With the last eruption more than 350 years ago, experts say that the mountain is overdue for another. That said, it's an absolute beauty and the highlight of any visit to the region, with terrific hiking (and skiing in winter).

Drive yourself up and down Mt Taranaki, or book a shuttle from New Plymouth up the national park's main access roads. InterCity (www.intercity.co.nz) buses run through Stratford and Inglewood on their Whanganui–New Plymouth route.

 Activities

Hiking

Due to its accessibility, Mt Taranaki ranks as the 'most climbed' mountain in NZ. Nevertheless, hiking on this mountain is dangerous and should not be undertaken lightly. Source some solid advice before departing and leave your intentions with a Department of Conservation (DOC) visitors centre, i-SITE or online at www.adventuresmart.nz.

Most walks are accessible from North Egmont, Dawson Falls or East Egmont. Check

> ### ℹ DECEPTIVE MOUNTAIN
>
> Mt Taranaki might look small compared to mountains overseas, but this pretty peak has claimed more than 80 lives. The microclimate changes fast: from summery to white-out conditions almost in an instant. There are also precipitous bluffs and steep icy slopes.
>
> There are plenty of short walks here, safe for much of the year, but for adventurous hikers January to March is the best time to go. Take a detailed topographic map (the Topo50 1:50,000 *Mt Taranaki* or *Mt Egmont* map is good) and consult a DOC officer for current conditions. You must register your hiking intentions with Dawson Falls or North Egmont DOC visitors centres on the mountain, New Plymouth i-SITE (p250) or online via www. adventuresmart.nz.

out DOC's collection of detailed walk pamphlets ($1 to $1.50 each, or free to print off the web) or the free *Taranaki: A Walker's Guide* booklet for more info.

From North Egmont, the main walk is the scenic Pouakai Circuit (p244), a two- to three-day, 24km loop through alpine, swamp and tussock areas with awesome mountain views (a shorter and popular version is the day-long Pouakai Crossing (p245), 19km one-way). Short, easy walks from here include the Ngatoro Loop Track (45 minutes), Veronica Loop (two hours) and Nature Walk (15-minute loop). The Mt Taranaki Summit Climb (p245) also starts from North Egmont. It's a 14km poled route taking five to six hours on the way up and three to four on the way down, and should not be attempted by inexperienced hikers, especially in icy conditions or snow (which can occur in any season).

East Egmont has the Potaema Track (wheelchair accessible; 30 minutes return) and Stratford Plateau Lookout (10 minutes return). A longer walk is the steep Enchanted Track (two to three hours return).

At Dawson Falls you can do several short walks, including Wilkies Pools Loop (1¼ hours return), with great views back up towards the mountain and across the pools, or the excellent but challenging hike to Fanthams Peak (five hours return), which is snowed in during winter. The Kapuni Loop Track (one-hour loop) runs to the impressive 18m Dawson Falls themselves. You can also see the falls from the visitor centre via a 10-minute walk to a viewpoint.

The difficult 52km Around the Mountain Circuit (p245) takes three to five days and is for experienced hikers only. There are a number of huts en route; buy hut tickets in advance.

The York Road Loop Track (up to three hours), accessible from York Rd north of Stratford, follows part of the disused Egmont Branch Railway Line.

You can hike without a guide from January through to April when snowfalls are low, but at other times, inexperienced climbers might want to hire a guide (around $300 per day). Check with DOC for info.

Skiing

Manganui Ski Area　　　　　　　SKIING
(☑ 06-765 8905; www.skitaranaki.co.nz; off Pembroke Rd, East Egmont; daily lift passes adult/child $50/35) From Stratford take Pembroke Rd up to Stratford Plateau, from where it's a 1.5km (20-minute) walk to the small Manganui

Ski Area. The Stratford i-SITE (p255) has daily weather and snow reports; otherwise check the webcam online. There's also shared-facilities ski-lodge accommodation here (adult/child/family \$45/15/100, minimum fee \$250). For up-to-date info, check the Facebook page: www.facebook.com/manganui.

Tours

Taranaki Tours   TOURS
(☑ 06-757 9888; www.taranakitours.com; per person from \$200) Runs an around-the-mountain day tour, strong on Māori culture and natural history. Forgotten World Highway tours, surf tours and mountain shuttle runs also available, to anywhere on the big peak (return \$75).

Top Guides Taranaki   HIKING
(☑ 027 2702 932; www.topguides.co.nz; half-/full-day hikes per person from \$375/450) Guided half- to full-day Mt Taranaki hikes. Shuttles between New Plymouth and the mountain also available.

Beck Helicopters   SCENIC FLIGHTS
(☑ 06-764 7073; www.heli.co.nz; 4512 Mountain Rd, Eltham; flights per person from \$365) Buzz around Taranaki's snowy cone on a scenic helicopter flight (and you thought it looked good from ground level!). Maximum four passengers.

Sleeping

Several DOC huts are scattered through the mountain wilds, accessible via hiking tracks. Most cost \$15 per night (Syme costs \$5); purchase hut tickets in advance (no actual hut bookings, though – first come, first served). BYO cooking, eating and sleeping gear.

Camphouse   HOSTEL \$
(☑ 06-756 0990; www.doc.govt.nz; Egmont Rd, North Egmont; dm adult/child \$25/10, exclusive use \$600; P) Bunkhouse-style accommodation behind the North Egmont Visitor Centre in a historic 1860 corrugated-iron building, complete with gun slots in the walls (through which settlers fired at local Māori during the Taranaki Land Wars). Enjoy endless horizon views from the porch. Sleeps 34 in five rooms, with communal facilities.

★ **Ngāti Ruanui**
Stratford Mountain House   LODGE \$\$
(☑ 06-765 6100; www.stratfordmountainhouse. co.nz; Pembroke Rd, Stratford; d/f from \$160/235; P☎) This efficiently run lodge on the

TARANAKI'S HEARTBREAK

According to Māori legend, Mt Taranaki belonged to a tribe of volcanoes in the middle of the North Island. But after a great battle with Mt Tongariro over Pihanga, the beautiful volcano near Lake Taupō, he was forced to leave. As he fled south (some say in disgrace; others say to keep the peace), Taranaki gouged out a wide scar in the earth – now the Whanganui River – and finally settled in the west in his current position. He remains here in majestic isolation, hiding his face behind a cloud of tears.

Stratford side of the big hill (15km from SH3, 3km to the Manganui Ski Area) has eight motel-style chalets, a twin room and a family room up a short, foresty path. Head for the fireplace in the Euro-style restaurant (breakfast and lunch mains \$12 to \$39, dinner \$31 to \$42). Myriad walks nearby.

Dawson Falls Mountain Lodge   LODGE \$\$
(☑ 06-765 5457; www.dawsonfalls.co.nz; Manaia Rd, Dawson Falls; d incl breakfast from \$190, extra person \$20; P☎) Feel like some (rather amazing) Swiss kitsch with your mountain views? This superfriendly lodge is more than 120 years old, with 12 guest rooms paying homage to all things woody, cosy and carved. Every room is different (views, bed/bathroom configuration and general woodiness). There's an all-day cafe here too (snacks from \$5, mains \$30 to \$42).

ℹ Information

Dawson Falls Visitor Centre (☑ 027 443 0248; www.doc.govt.nz; Manaia Rd, Dawson Falls; ⊙9am-4pm Thu-Sun, daily school holidays) On the southeastern side of the mountain, fronted by an awesome totem pole.

MetService (www.metservice.com) Mountain weather updates.

North Egmont Visitor Centre (☑ 06-756 0990; www.doc.govt.nz; 2879 Egmont Rd, North Egmont; ⊙8am-4pm, reduced winter hours) Current and comprehensive national park info, and definitive details on hiking and huts. There's a basic cafe here too.

ℹ Getting There & Away

There are three main entrance roads to Egmont National Park, all of which are well signposted. The closest to New Plymouth is North Egmont: turn off SH3 at Egmont Village, 12km

TARANAKI & WHANGANUI MT TARANAKI (EGMONT NP) & AROUND

FORGOTTEN WORLD HIGHWAY

The remote 155km road between Stratford and Taumarunui (SH43) has become known as the Forgotten World Highway. The drive winds through hilly bush country, passing Māori *pā*, abandoned coal mines and memorials to those long gone. Just a short section (around 12km) is unsealed road. Allow four hours and plenty of stops, and fill up with petrol at either end (there's no petrol along the route itself). Pick up the *Forgotten World Highway* pamphlet from i-SITEs or DOC visitors centres in the area.

Sights

Founded in 1895, the town of Whangamomona (population 150) is a highlight – a quirky little village that declared itself an independent republic in 1989 after disagreements with local councils. The town celebrates Republic Day in January every odd-numbered year with a themed extravaganza. Don't miss the grand old Whangamomona Hotel (✆06-762 5823; www.whangamomonahotel.co.nz; 6018 Ohura Rd, Whangamomona; tw & d $150, lodge $190), a pub offering simple accommodation and big country meals. Rental-house accommodation options include the heritage Whanga Bridge House (✆06-762 5552; www.whangamomonaaccommodation.co.nz; 6025 Ohura Rd, Whangamomona; s/d incl breakfast $100/150), sleeping eight, and the Whanga Butcher Shop (✆06-762 5552; www.whanga-momonaaccommodation.co.nz; 6024 Ohura Road, Whangamomona; s/d incl breakfast $100/150), sleeping six, both run by the same folks.

Tours

If you're not driving, take a tour along the route with Eastern Taranaki Experience (p269) or Taranaki Tours (p253). See also Forgotten World Adventures (p218) in Taumarunui.

south of New Plymouth, and follow Egmont Rd for 14km. From Stratford, turn off at Pembroke Rd and continue for 15km to East Egmont and the Manganui Ski Area. From the southeast, Manaia Rd leads up to Dawson Falls, 23km from Stratford.

There are no public buses to the national park, but there are a few shuttle/tour operators who will take you there for around $40/60 one way/return (usually cheaper for groups). Advance bookings essential.

Eastern Taranaki Experience (p269) Mountain shuttle services as well as tours and accommodation. Based in Stratford.

Taranaki Mountain Shuttle (✆027 270 2932; www.facebook.com/taranakishuttle; per person return $45) Morning shuttle runs from New Plymouth up to North Egmont, returning at the end of the day. Enough time to go for a hike!

Taranaki Tours (p253) New Plymouth to anywhere on the big peak.

Inglewood

POP 3580

Handy for Mt Taranaki on SH3, unpretentious little main-street Inglewood makes a good stop for supermarket supplies or a casual bite on the run.

Fun Ho! National Toy Museum   MUSEUM
(✆06-756 7030; www.funhotoys.co.nz; 25 Rata St; adult/child $7/3.50; ◷10am-4pm Mon-Fri, to 2pm Sat & Sun; ♿) Inglewood's cute toy museum exhibits (and sells) old-fashioned sand-cast toys. It doubles as the local visitor information centre. Everybody shout, 'Fun Ho!'. Look for the big fire engine on the roof.

Caffe Windsor   CAFE $$
(✆06-756 6665; www.caffewindsor.co.nz; 1 Kelly St; mains breakfast $9-20, lunch & dinner $18-24; ◷8.30am-5pm Sun-Thu, 11am-late Fri & Sat) This fire-engine-red heritage building (1878) was one of Inglewood's first shops. These days, Caffe Windsor sells eggs and waffles in the morning, old-school burgers and grills during the day, and red Thai chicken curry at night (among other things). Try the Naki burger, with sweet pickles and horopito (pepper tree) relish.

Stratford

POP 8990

A gateway town to Mt Taranaki, 40km southeast of New Plymouth on SH3, Stratford plays up its connection to namesake Stratford-upon-Avon, Shakespeare's birthplace, by naming its streets after bardic characters

(Oberon St, Hamlet St...). The town is also home to NZ's first (and last) **glockenspiel clock**, which chimes four times a day (10am, 1pm, 3pm and 7pm): little Romeo and Juliet mannequins give a fairly wooden performance.

Take a stroll along the the 3km **Carrington Walkway**, accessible through the memorial gate at King Edward Park, which hugs the Pātea Stream and takes you across bridges and through farmland and a rhododendron dell. Pick up a map at the i-SITE.

Percy Thomson Gallery   GALLERY
(☑ 06-765 0917; www.percythomsongallery.org.nz; Prospero Pl, 56 Miranda St; ☺10.30am-4pm Mon-Fri, to 3pm Sat & Sun) **FREE** Right next door to Stratford i-SITE, this progressive community gallery (named after a former mayor) displays eclectic local, regional and national art shows. New exhibitions every three to four weeks.

Taranaki Pioneer Village   MUSEUM
(☑ 06-765 5399; www.pioneervillage.co.nz; SH3, Stratford South; adult/child $12/5; ☺10am-4pm; ⓟ) About 1km south of Stratford on SH3, the Taranaki Pioneer Village is a 4-hectare outdoor museum housing 40 historic buildings, many dating back to the early 1850s. It's a safe pastiche of bygone days...but it's actually a little spooky! The Pioneer Express Train is a good way to see it if your feet need a break ($5 or $3 with entry fee). There's a cafe here, too.

Regan House   B&B $$
(☑ 06-765 4189; www.reganhouse.co.nz; 193 Regan St; s/d incl breakfast $100/150; ⓟ⒲) With just one guest suite available, book ahead for a berth in this elegant, early-20th-century house – so much nicer than a motel. An absurdly comfortable bed, bird-filled gardens and a generous cooked breakfast using eggs from the property's farm make Regan feel like home, sweet home. It's right at the start of the Forgotten World Highway.

Amity Court Motel   MOTEL $$
(☑ 06-765 4496; www.amitycourtmotel.co.nz; 35 Broadway N; d from $140, 1-/2-bedroom unit from $160/225; ⓟ⒲) All stone-clad columns, jaunty roof angles, timber louvres and muted cave-colours, Amity Court Motel ups the town's accommodation standings. The two-bedroom apartments are a good set-up for families; couples might angle themselves towards the Mountain View Suite, with its balcony hot tub.

Forgotten 43 Brewing   CRAFT BEER
(☑ 027 533 3024; www.facebook.com/forgotten 43brewing; 279 Broadway; ☺4-9pm Fri, noon-9pm Sat, noon-7pm Sun) As far as contemporary NZ craft-beer bars go, Forgotten 43 Brewing's modest Stratford shopfront is a casual, unsophisticated affair. But, hey, where else can you get a cloudy 'Robo Hop' pale ale on this side of Mt Taranaki?

King's Theatre   CINEMA
(☑ 06-765 8255; www.kingstheatre.co.nz; 213 Broadway; tickets adult/child $12/7; ☺hours vary with screenings) When Stratford's fine old picture house opened on the last day of 1917, movies were still silent, King George V was on the throne back in London and New Zealand had only been an independent country for a decade. Saved from the wrecking ball after it closed in 1986, the restored King's Theatre is now Stratford's cinematic pride and joy.

ⓘ Information

Stratford i-SITE (☑ 06-765 6708; www.stratford.govt.nz; Prospero Pl; ☺8.30am-5pm Mon-Fri, 10am-3pm Sat & Sun) All the local low-down, plus good advice on walks on Mt Taranaki. Down an arcade off the main street.

Surf Highway 45

Sweeping south from New Plymouth around the South Taranaki coastline to Hāwera, the 105km-long SH45 is known as Surf Highway 45. But don't take the name as gospel: there are plenty of black-sand beaches along the way, but the road snakes inland through green paddocks and farmland, too. Pick up the *Surf Highway 45* brochure at visitor centres.

ⓘ Getting There & Away

This part of NZ is refreshingly untouristed and off the main bus routes: you'll need your own wheels to get around (cycling is a good option – the terrain is level most of the way).

Alternatively, once every Friday local **SouthLink** (www.taranakibus.info) buses travel in both directions between New Plymouth and Ōakura ($3,15 minutes), Okato ($4, 25 minutes) and Opunake ($6, one hour), along SH45. On Thursdays, another bus runs between Opunake and Hāwera ($2, 45 minutes) travelling inland via Eltham. This bus continues from Hāwera to New Plymouth once daily Monday to Friday, via Stratford on the inland route.

Citylink (p251) buses from New Plymouth also loop as far south as Ōakura.

TARANAKI & WHANGANUI SURF HIGHWAY 45

Oākura

POP 1640

From New Plymouth, the first cab off the rank is laid-back Oākura, 15km southwest on SH45. For a town with not much more than a souvenir shop, petrol station and family medical centre, Oākura has a disproportionately high number of decent places to eat. Its broad sweep of beach is hailed by waxheads for its right-hander breaks, but it's also great for some family fun.

Oākura Beach is a real beauty (bring sandals – that black sand gets scorching hot!). Drive about 4km down Weld Rd Lower to access its southern reaches, where the rusty, shipwrecked ribs of the SS *Gairlock* (wrecked 1903) arc upwards from the sand.

Sharpen your wave skills with some lessons from **Vertigo Surf** (☑06-752 7363; www.vertigosurf.com; 2 Tasman Pde; lessons from $80; ◷9am-5.30pm Mon-Fri, to 4pm Sat & Sun); check the website for live surf cams.

Oakura Beach Holiday Park HOLIDAY PARK $
(☑06-752 7861; www.oakurabeach.com; 2 Jans Tce; sites unpowered/powered $46/50, cabins $75-150; Ⓟ📶) Wedged between the cliffs and the sea, this better-than-average beachside park caters best to caravans, but some of the self-contained units have uninterrupted ocean views (ask when you book). Absolute beachfront spots for pitching a tent.

★**Ahu Ahu Beach Villas** BOUTIQUE HOTEL $$$
(☑06-752 7370; www.ahu.co.nz; 321 Ahu Ahu Rd; d & f $315, 2-bedroom lodge $650; Ⓟ📶) Set on a knoll overlooking the ocean (pricey on the pocket but with priceless views), these luxury, architecturally designed villas are superbly eccentric, with huge recycled timbers, bottles cast into walls, century-old, lichen-covered French-tile roofs and polished-concrete floors with inlaid paua shell. The lodge sleeps four and is the place for sunset drinks. Fabulous.

High Tide CAFE $
(www.facebook.com/hightideoakura; 1136b SH45; mains $5-15; ◷7am-2pm) Well above the high-tide mark on Oākura's main street, boho little High Tide offers superfresh cabinet fare – maybe a smoked-salmon croissant or some lentil-and-vegie salad – and the coffee is the best in town. Staff are all smiles; music is all reggae.

★**Black Sand Pizzeria & Bistro** PIZZA $$
(☑06-752 7806; www.facebook.com/BlackSandPizzeria; 1 Tasman Pde; mains $18-22; ◷11.30am-2pm Sat & Sun, 5pm-late Thu-Sun; ♿) Right on Oākura's black-sand beach, sharing a building with the surf club, Black Sand plates up surprisingly authentic Napoli-style pizzas – all thin-based and blistered crusts – made in a custom Italian oven and giving the rest of Taranaki a run for its margherita. Sunny terrace, decent wines and Spanish beer on tap.

Okato & Around

Between Oākura and Opunake, Surf Highway 45 veers inland through Okato (population 640), with detours to various surf beaches along the way. There are legendary surf spots at **Stent Rd** (Stent Rd, Warea) just south of Warea (look for the painted-boulder sign – the street sign kept getting stolen!), and **Kumara Patch** (Komene Rd, Okato), west of Okato. Near Pungarehu, Cape Egmont is home to the historic **Cape Egmont Lighthouse** (www.southtaranaki.com; end of Cape Rd, Pungarehu) (which you can ogle from the outside) and the associated **Historic Cape Light & Museum** (☑06-278 0555; www.southtaranaki.com; end of Bayly Rd, Warea; by donation; ◷11am-3pm Sat-Mon), a replica about 12km further north.

Stony River Hotel PUB $$
(☑06-752 4454; www.stonyriverhotel.co.nz; 2502 SH45, Okato; tw/d incl breakfast from $110/150; Ⓟ📶) This lemon-yellow highway hotel dates back to 1875, when horse-riding mailmen would stop here for a rest on their way north. There are three bright, country-style, en-suite rooms upstairs and a restaurant downstairs (mains $21 to $49) serving dinner Wednesday to Sunday. Occasional schnitzel nights with live oom-pah tunes.

★**Lahar** CAFE $$
(☑06-752 4865; www.facebook.com/cafelahar; 64 Carthew St, Okato; mains $12-23; ◷8.30am-4pm Wed & Thu, 8.30am-late Fri-Sun) Chilled-out Lahar occupies an angular, black-trimmed timber box in Okato (hard to miss – there's not much else here). It's a lofty space with a few couches out the front and edibles ranging from big chicken burgers to roast veg and halloumi salad. Sunday-night pizzas, good coffee, beers in the fridge and a garden bar out the back (occasional live tunes).

THE PARIHAKA MOVEMENT
••••••••••••••••••••••••••••

From the mid-1860s Parihaka, a small Māori town 4km east of SH45 near Pungarehu, became the centre of a peaceful resistance movement, one which involved not only other Taranaki tribes, but Māori from around the country. Its leaders, Te Whiti-o-Rongomai and Tohu Kākahi, were of both Taranaki and Te Āti Awa descent.

After the Land Wars, confiscation of tribal lands was the central problem faced by Taranaki Māori, and under Te Whiti's leadership a progressive approach to this issue was developed: resisting European settlement through nonviolent methods.

When the government started surveying confiscated land on the Waimate Plain in 1879, unarmed followers of Te Whiti, wearing the movement's iconic white feather in their hair, obstructed development by ploughing troughs across roads, erecting random fences and pulling survey pegs – all in good humour. Nevertheless, many were arrested and held without trial on the South Island. The protests continued and intensified. Finally, in November 1881, the government sent a force of more than 1600 troops to Parihaka. Its inhabitants were arrested or driven away, and the village was later demolished. Te Whiti and Tohu were arrested and imprisoned until 1883. In their absence Parihaka was rebuilt and the ploughing campaigns continued into the 1890s.

In 2006 the NZ government issued a formal apology and financial compensation to the tribes affected by the invasion and confiscation of Parihaka lands.

Opunake

POP 1400

A sleepy summer town, Opunake is Taranaki's surfie epicentre and there are some sheltered, kid-friendly swim spots here too. There's not much happening on the main strip, but you can't go wrong grabbing some seriously good fish and chips or checking out a film at the restored Everybody's Theatre (p258).

🏃 Activities

Opunake Walkway   WALKING
(www.southtaranaki.com; off Layard St; ⊙ daylight hours) FREE Feel like stretching your pins? The Opunake Walkway is a signposted 7km, three-hour ramble around the Opunake waterfront, starting (or finishing) at the artificial Opunake Lake on Layard St.

Look for *Te Namu Pā*, the site of the famous battle of Te Namu Pā where Wiremu Kingi Matakatea fought off 800 Waikato Māori over a month with a single rifle. You can reach it via Opunake Cemetery and over the Otahi Stream.

Dreamtime Surf Shop   SURFING
(☑ 06-761 7570; www.dreamtimesurf.co.nz; cnr Tasman & Havelock Sts; surfboard/body board/SUP/wet suit per half-day $30/20/50/15; ⊙ 9am-5.30pm Mon-Fri, 9.30am-3pm Sat, also 10am-2pm Sun Nov-Mar) Dreamtime has surf-gear hire, advice on the best local breaks and hot coffee to warm up with afterwards. Hours can be patchy if the surf's up – call in advance.

🛏 Sleeping & Eating

Opunake Beach Holiday Park   HOLIDAY PARK $
(☑ 06-761 7525; www.opunakebeachnz.co.nz; 1 Beach Rd; d campsites/cabins/units from $44/80/120; 🛜 ♿) Opunake Beach Holiday Park is a mellow spot behind Opunake's black-sand surf beach. Sites are grassy, the camp kitchen is big, the amenities block is cavernous and the waves are just a few metres away. The fibreglass dragon slide in the kids' wading pool is a slippery customer.

Headlands   HOTEL $$
(☑ 06-761 8358; www.headlands.co.nz; 4 Havelock St; r $150-250; P 🛜) Just 100m back from the beach, Headlands is an upmarket, three-storey accommodation tower with a Euro-Indian bistro downstairs (mains $12 to $34; the food beats the decor). It's the flashest option in town, and the best rooms snare brilliant sunsets, but they do teeter on the bland side of contemporary.

★ Opunake Fish, Chips & More   FISH & CHIPS $
(☑ 06-761 8478; www.facebook.com/opunakefishchipsandmore; 61 Tasman St; mains $8-30; ⊙ noon-8pm) This is as good as fish and chips gets. With a lengthy history (since the 1960s), hand-cut chips, a range of fish (including fresh catches of the day to take home), smiling staff and big burgers, one meal here and you'll instantly feel part of the Opunake community. A very chipper fish-and-chipper!

GO SNELLY!

Opunake isn't just about surf – it's also the birthplace of iconic middle-distance runner and New Zealand's 'Sports Champion of the 20th Century' Sir Peter Snell (b 1938), who showed his rivals a clean set of heels at the 1960 Rome and 1964 Tokyo Olympics. Old Snelly won the 800m gold in Italy, then followed up with 800m and 1500m golds in Japan, as well as two golds at the 1962 Commonwealth Games in Perth, Australia. Legend! Check out his bronze running statue, with his fab abs, outside the library.

Sugar Juice Café CAFE $$

(☑06-761 7062; 42 Tasman St; mains $9-24; ◷8am-4pm Sun-Thu, to 9pm Fri & Sat, closed Mon Jun-Aug; ⚘) Happy, hippie and wholesome, Sugar Juice Cafe has some of the most reliable food on SH45. It's brimming with delicious and filling cafe edibles: order a homemade sausage roll for lunch, or a 'pulsating' pancake stack after your morning surf. Sip your coffee in the courtyard.

☆ Entertainment

Everybody's Theatre CINEMA

(☑027 383 7926; www.everybodystheatre.co.nz; 72 Tasman St; adult/child $10/8; ◷hours vary) This restored 1920s theatre, run by volunteers, has been redeemed as Opunake's cutural beacon, with couches downstairs and regular movie theatre seats upstairs. Shows new releases as well as classic, foreign and fringe films on 'boutique nights' (tickets $28). Check out the amazing old projector in the lobby.

ⓘ Information

Opunake Library (☑0800 111 323; www.opunakenz.co.nz; 43 Tasman St; ◷8.30am-5pm Mon & Wed-Fri, 9.30am-5pm Tue, 9.30am-1pm Sat; 🛜) Doubles as the local visitor-information centre, with a couple of internet terminals and free 24-hour wi-fi in the forecourt.

Hāwera

POP 12,150

Don't expect much urban virtue from agricultural Hāwera, the largest town in South Taranaki. Still, it's a good pit stop to pick up supplies, grab a coffee, visit the info centre, stretch your legs or bed down for a night.

If you ain't nothin' but a hound dog, don't miss Elvis.

◉ Sights

★ KD's Elvis Presley Museum MUSEUM

(☑027 498 2942; www.elvismuseum.co.nz; 51 Argyle St; admission by donation; ◷by appointment) Elvis lives! At least he does at Kevin D Wasley's astonishing museum, which houses more than 10,000 of the King's records and a mind-blowing collection of Elvis memorabilia collected over many decades. 'Passion is an understatement,' says KD, whose grey hair is slicked back and on theme. Admission by appointment – phone ahead. BYO blue suede shoes.

Hāwera Water Tower VIEWPOINT

(☑06-278 8599; www.southtaranaki.com; 55 High St; adult/child $2.50/1; ◷8.30am-4pm Mon-Fri, 10am-2.30pm Sat & Sun) The austere, 55m-tall Hāwera Water Tower is one of few noteworthy attractions in quiet Hāwera. Grab the key from the neighbouring i-SITE, ascend the 215 steps, then scan the horizon for signs of life (you can see the coast and Mt Taranaki on a clear day).

Museum of South Taranaki MUSEUM

(Aotea Utanganui; ☑0800 111 323; www.museumof southtaranaki.wordpress.com; 127 Egmont St, Pātea; ◷10am-4pm Mon-Sat) FREE In little drive-through Pātea, 27km south of Hāwera, this creative museum does its impressive new timber facade and Māori *maihi* (entrance bargeboards) justice with engaging, community-focused displays on South Taranaki history. Note the 1933 *waka* (canoe) remembrance sculpture across the street.

Tawhiti Museum MUSEUM

(☑06-278 6837; www.tawhitimuseum.co.nz; 401 Ohangai Rd; adult/child $15/5; ◷10am-4pm Fri-Sun Feb-May & Sep-Dec, daily Jan, Sun only Jun-Aug) The quirky Tawhiti Museum houses a collection of exhibits, dioramas and creepily lifelike human figures modelled on people from the region. A large collection of tractors pays homage to the area's rural heritage; there's also a bush railway and a 'Traders & Whalers' boat ride (extra charges for both). It's near the corner of Tawhiti Rd, 4km north of town.

🛏 Sleeping & Eating

Park Motel MOTEL $$

(☑06-278 7275; https://theparkmotel.co.nz; 61 Waihi Rd; d $140, 1-/2-bedroom apt $155/170;

P ⬚) With 18 stylish rooms (black, white, charcoal and a dash of scarlet) across the road from King Edward Park, this place is our pick of Hāwera's motels. Consists of studio units and one- and two-bedroom apartments. Will the new owners maintain the homemade-cookie tradition?

Tairoa Lodge B&B **$$**
(✉06-278 8603; www.tairoa-lodge.co.nz; 3 Puawai St; d from $150, cottage from $220, extra adult/child $50/30, all incl breakfast; P ⬚ ⬚) Set on grassy lawns, gorgeous old Tairoa is a photogenic 1875 Victorian manor house on the eastern outskirts of Hāwera, with three guest rooms and three outlying cottages (two and three bedrooms). Lashings of heritage style, bird-filled gardens (often full of wedding parties, too) and big cooked breakfasts await at the end of the bamboo-lined driveway.

Someday CAFE **$$**
(✉06-278 6097; www.facebook.com/somedaycafe hawera; 90 Princes St; dishes $10-22; ⏰7am-4pm Mon-Fri, 9am-2pm Sat) In a town short on decent places to eat, you can almost hear Someday sigh at its surroundings. Around 20 can fit on the mid-century chairs and at the industrial communal table, where locals chat over cake (killer date-and-orange scones) and the best coffee for many a mile. Just passing through? Don't stop anywhere else.

ℹ Information

South Taranaki i-SITE (✉06-278 8599; www.southtaranaki.com; 55 High St; ⏰8.30am-5pm Mon-Fri, 10am-3pm Sat & Sun; ⬚) Get the South Taranaki low-down, and the keys to the water tower.

Whanganui

POP 47,300

Before Whanganui was Whanganui, it was Petre, a town built at the mouth of the river in 1840. As one of New Zealand's oldest towns (and the fifth-largest until 1936), it's a charmingly raffish amalgamation of Māori culture, heritage buildings and a thriving local arts community.

Despite the occasional flood, the wide Whanganui River is the lifeblood of the town, along with regular markets, scenic walkways and old port buildings being turned into glass-art studios. There are few more appealing places to while away a sunny afternoon than the dog-free zone beneath Victoria Ave's leafy canopy.

⊙ Sights

★ Whanganui Regional Museum MUSEUM
(✉06-349 1110; www.visitwhanganui.nz/whanganui -regional-museum; Queens Park Memorial, Watt St; ⏰10am-4.30pm) FREE Spend an hour or two in one of NZ's better natural history museums. Te Atihaunui-a-Pāpārange Māori exhibits include an amazing *waka*, fire-hardened *here* (bird spears) and some vicious-looking *mere* (greenstone clubs). Colonial and wildlife installations are upstairs, including plenty of fossils and skeletons. Don't miss the amazing old photos of Māori life along the Whanganui River in the early 1900s.

★ New Zealand Glassworks GALLERY
(✉06-927 6803; www.nzglassworks.com; 2 Rutland St; ⏰10am-4.30pm) FREE The pick of Whanganui's many glass studios. Watch glass-blowers working, check out the gallery, take a one-day glass-blowing course ($290, four people max) or a 30-minute 'Make a Paperweight' lesson ($80), or just hang out and warm your bones on a chilly river afternoon.

★ Sarjeant on the Quay GALLERY
(✉06-349 0506; www.sarjeant.org.nz; 38 Taupo Quay; ⏰10.30am-4.30pm) FREE The elegant old neoclassical Sarjeant Gallery building in Queens Park is closed for earthquake-proofing. In the interim, the gallery's estimable art resides on Taupo Quay. There's not as much room here as up on the hill, so exhibits are limited (but revolving); there's more on show above the Whanganui i-SITE (p263) across the road. The gift shop features fab Whanganui glass.

Whanganui Riverboat Centre MUSEUM
(✉06-347 1863; www.waimarie.co.nz; 1a Taupo Quay; museum adult/child $2/free, cruises $45/15; ⏰10am-3pm daily Jan-Apr, 10am-2pm Sat & Sun May-Dec; ⬚) The historical displays here are interesting, but everyone's here for the PS *Waimarie,* the last of the Whanganui River paddle steamers. In 1900 it was shipped out from England and paddled the Whanganui until it sank ingloriously at its mooring in 1952. Submerged for 41 years, it was finally raised, restored, then relaunched on the first day of the 21st century. It now offers two-hour tours up the river, boarding at 10.30am. Book in advance.

Kai Iwi Beach BEACH
(✉0800 926 426; www.visitwhanganui.nz/kai-iwi -beach; Mowhanau Dr, off Rapanui Rd; ⏰24hr; ⬚) Kai Iwi is a wild ocean frontier, strewn with

Whanganui

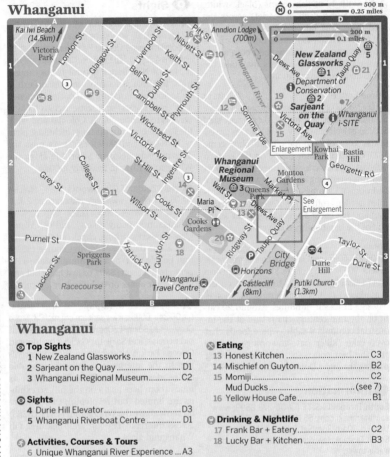

Whanganui

black sand, a ruined WWII gun emplacement and masses of driftwood (you might see locals collecting it for their next 'piece'). There's also a fun playground and paddle-friendly spots for little kids. Follow Great North Rd 4km north of town, turn left onto Rapanui Rd and head seawards for 10km.

Castlecliff Beach BEACH
(☑0800 926 426; www.castlecliff.nz; off Rangiora St, Castlecliff; ⊙24hr; ⊕) Follow the Whanganui River's western riverbank seawards for 8km and you'll arrive in Castlecliff, a wonderfully low-key beach suburb dominated by a huge cat-food factory and the brilliant black-sand-covered Castlecliff Beach. There's patrolled swimming here in summer, plus a playground, skate park and views up the coast all the way to Mt Taranaki. Let the kids roam free.

Putiki Church
CHURCH

(St Paul's Memorial Church; ☎0800 92 64 26; www.visitwhanganui.nz/st-pauls-memorial-church-putiki-whanganui; 20 Anaua St; tours per person $10; ⊙service 9am Sun, tours 2pm Wed-Sun) Across the City Bridge from town and 1km towards the sea is the Putiki Church (aka St Paul's Memorial Church). It's unremarkable externally, but just like the faithful pew-fillers, it's what's inside that counts: the magnificent interior is covered in Māori carvings and *tukutuku* (wall panels). Show up for Sunday service, or book a guided tour via the i-SITE (p263).

Durie Hill Elevator
VIEWPOINT

(☎0800 926 426; www.visitwhanganui.nz/durie-hill-underground-elevator; 42 Anzac Pde; adult/child one way $2/1; ⊙8am-6pm Mon-Fri, 10am-5pm Sat & Sun) Across City Bridge from downtown Whanganui, this elevator was built with grand visions for Durie Hill's residential future. Beyond an entrance lined with Māori carvings, a tunnel burrows 213m into the hillside, from where a 1919 elevator rattles 66m to the top.

At the summit you can climb the 176 steps of the 33.5m War Memorial Tower and scan the horizon for Mt Taranaki and Mt Ruapehu. There's another lookout atop the lift machinery housing (just 41 steps).

☞ Tours

Wanganui City Guided Walking Tours
WALKING

(☎0800 926 426; www.whanganuiwalkingtours.co.nz; 31 Taupo Quay; per person $10; ⊙10am & 2pm Sat & Sun Oct-Apr) Sign up for a 90-minute guided tour through old Whanganui, giving your legs a workout as you pass historic buildings and sights. Tours depart from the i-SITE (p263); book tickets inside. A great intro to the city.

☆ Festivals & Events

Vintage Weekend
CULTURAL

(www.vintageweekend.co.nz; ⊙Jan) Time-travelling cars, clothes, music, markets, architecture and good times over four January days by the Whanganui River.

Artists Open Studios & Festival of Glass
ART

(www.openstudios.co.nz; ⊙Mar) Classy glass fest over two weekends in March. Plenty of open studios, demonstrations and workshops.

Whanganui River Week
CULTURAL

(⊙Nov) The wide Whanganui River gets a bit too wide every now and then – post-flood clean-ups take months. But locals still love their river, and celebrate it over a week in November with all kinds of events. Search for Whanganui River Week on Facebook for updates.

Cemetery Circuit Motorcycle Race
SPORTS

(www.cemeterycircuit.co.nz; ⊙26 Dec) Pandemoniac Boxing Day motorcycle race around Whanganui's city streets, with 300 riders and 10,000 fans. The southern hemisphere's version of the Isle of Man TT?

🛏 Sleeping

★ Anndion Lodge
HOSTEL $

(☎06-343 3593; www.anndionlodge.co.nz; 143 Anzac Pde; s & d with/without bathroom from $115/85, f from $150; P🎧🌐⛱) Formerly run by Ann and Dion (Anndion, get it?), this innovative, black-painted hostel continues to attract travellers with its stereo systems, huge communal kitchen, pool tables, big TVs, spa, sauna, swimming pool, barbecue area and restaurant. It's spread across a couple of converted riverside houses about 3km north of town.

Braemar House YHA
HOSTEL $

(☎06-348 2301; www.braemarhouse.co.nz; 2 Plymouth St; dm/s/tw/d $30/60/75/75, guesthouse incl breakfast s/d $100/130; P🎧) Riverside, calamine-coloured Braemar brings together an 1895 Victorian B&B guesthouse and a reliable YHA backpackers, with separate lounge areas. Centrally heated guesthouse rooms (in a separate wing) are floral and fancy; airy dorms and cabins conjure up a bit more fun out the back. Chooks patrol the lawns.

Tamara Backpackers Lodge
HOSTEL $

(☎06-347 6300; www.tamaralodge.com; 24 Somme Pde; dm from $29; P🎧) Tamara is a photogenic, mazelike, two-storey heritage house (1904) with a wide balcony, lofty ceilings, a TV lounge, a rambling back garden and helpful staff who will tell you what to see and where to be seen. Angle for a bed in one of the rooms overlooking the river.

Whanganui River Top 10 Holiday Park
HOLIDAY PARK $

(☎06-343 8402; www.rivertop10.co.nz; 460 Somme Pde, Aramoho; sites unpowered/powered $40/48, cabins/units from $76/110; P🎧⛱🐾)

This tidy Top 10 park squats on the Whanganui's west bank 6km north of Dublin Bridge. Facilities (pool, games room, jumping pillow) are prodigious. Kayak hire is also available: the owners shuttle you up river then you paddle back. Budget cabins by the river have big-dollar views, or opt for a glamping tent ($100) in summer. Local buses trundle past.

★ **Browns Boutique B&B** B&B $$
(☑ 027 308 2495; www.brownsboutiquebnb.co.nz; 34 College St, College Estate; s/d incl breakfast $185/200; P ☎) Owned by the same family for more than 50 years, this 1910 house was coincidentally built by an unrelated Brown. There are two rooms out the back with private entrances, looking out onto a patio, with tasteful decor and quirky touches (a typewriter for a guestbook, tiles made by a Moroccan–New Zealander...). The gourmet breakfasts with free-range produce are winners.

★ **151 on London** MOTEL $$
(☑ 06-345 8668; www.151onlondon.co.nz; 151 London St; d $130-180, 1-/2-bedroom apt $190/240; ☎) This snappy-looking spaceship of a motel wins plenty of fans with its architectural angles, quality carpets and linen, and natty lime/silver/black colour scheme. At the top of the price tree are some excellent upstairs/downstairs apartment-style units sleeping six: about as ritzy as Whanganui accommodation gets. Cafe across the car park.

Aotea Motor Lodge MOTEL $$
(☑ 06-345 0303; www.aoteamotorlodge.co.nz; 390 Victoria Ave; d from $165, 1-bedroom ste from $285; P ☎) On the upper reaches of Victoria Ave, this flashy, two-storey contemporary motel features roomy suites, lavish linen, leather chairs, dark timbers and plenty of marble and stone. Every room has a spa bath, if you're in need of a soak or want to wash your socks.

✗ Eating

★ **Honest Kitchen** CAFE $
(☑ 06-345 0899; www.honestkitchen.co.nz; 44 Ridgway St; mains $8-15; ☉ 7.30am-3.30pm Mon-Fri; ☞) Inside a downtown heritage timber building (a 1901 saddlery, straight outta Dodge City), Honest Kitchen serves cafe wonders – wraps, sandwiches, bagels, cakes, scones, slices and salads – and has a fridge full of take-home-and-heat-'em-up meals (Italian meatballs, fish pie, vegetarian

lasagne). It's all superfresh and generously sized, with the emphasis squarely on 'local' (eg breads from city baker SourBros). Honestly good!

★ **Mischief on Guyton** CAFE $
(☑ 06-347 1227; www.facebook.com/mischief onguyton; 96 Guyton St; mains $9-19; ☉ 7.30am-3pm Mon-Fri; ☞) With cheeky signage and a flip calendar of witty quotes not suitable to print, Mischief on Guyton is true to its name. Step inside (or through to the courtyard) for a combined brunch and lunch menu featuring interesting dishes like a 'lusty' laksa and the evocatively named 'rockamorocca': oven-baked eggs with *dukkah* (spice mix) on pita bread.

Yellow House Cafe CAFE $
(The Yellow House; ☑ 06-345 0083; www.yellow housecafe.co.nz; cnr Pitt & Dublin Sts; meals $11-19; ☉ 8am-4pm Mon-Fri, 8.30am-4pm Sat & Sun; ☞) Detour away from the fray for funky tunes, buttermilk pancakes, local art and courtyard tables beneath a chunky-trunk cherry blossom tree. Fail to resist a wedge of chocolate-and-blueberry cheesecake with your coffee, or launch into the lamb-and-rosemary burger for lunch on the sunny terrace. Superfriendly staff.

★ **Citadel** BURGERS $$
(☑ 06-344 7076; www.facebook.com/the-citadel. castlecliff; 14a Rangiora St, Castlecliff; mains $14-24; ☉ 9am-9pm Thu-Sat, to 8pm Sun & Mon; ☞) In hot pursuit of the North Island's best burgers? Community-minded Citadel, 10 minutes' drive from downtown Whanganui, is a contender. Alongside the classics, the 'Monster' is a feat of endurance: order one alongside some 'Kevin Bacon' loaded fries and watch heads turn. Breakfast menu, kids' menu and driftwood triceratops sculpture to boot.

Momiji JAPANESE $$
(☑ 06-345 0444; www.facebook.com/pg/Momiji JapaneseRestaurantTakeaway; 26 Victoria Ave; $14-25; ☉ 11am-2.30pm & 5-9pm Tue-Sat, 11am-2.30pm & 5-8.30pm Sun) Understated Momiji is a hit with the locals, especially now it's relocated to a rather less understated former post office on the main drag. The menu is split into entrées, rice bowls, curry, sushi and ramen, but the bento boxes steal the show. Sluice it down with a Japanese beer (Kirin is on tap) or sake.

WHANGANUI OR WANGANUI?

Yes, yes, we know, it's confusing. Is there an 'h' or isn't there? Either way, the pronunciation is identical: 'wong-ga', not 'fong-ga' (as per the rest of the country when a 'w' and 'h' meet).

In the local dialect *whanga* (harbour) is pronounced 'wong-ga', which is how the original 'Wanganui' spelling came about. But in 1991 the New Zealand Geographic Board officially adopted the correct Māori spelling (with an 'h') for the Whanganui River and Whanganui National Park. This was a culturally deferential decision: the Pākehā-dominated town and region retained the old spelling, while the river area – Māori territory – adopted the new.

In 2009 the board assented that the town and region should also adopt the 'h'. This caused much community consternation; opinions on the decision split almost evenly (outspoken Mayor Michael Laws was particularly anti-'h'). Ultimately, NZ Minister for Land Information Maurice Williamson decreed that either spelling was acceptable, and that adopting the querulous 'h' is up to individual businesses or entities. A good old Kiwi compromise!

This middle ground held shakily until 2014, when the Wanganui District Council voted to ask the New Zealand Geographic Board to formalise the change to Whanganui. A public consultation process began, culminating in an announcement in 2015 by Land Information Minister Louise Upston that the district's name would be officially changed to Whanganui. Whanderful!

Drinking & Nightlife

Frank Bar + Eatery
COCKTAIL BAR

(☑ 027 422 2555; www.facebook.com/frank whanganui; 98 Victoria Ave; ☺ 5pm-late) With DJs and gigs lined up every weekend and a rock-solid (rock-liquid?) cocktail list, we'll be Frank when we tell you that this is the place for a night out in Whanganui. The lofty space is split into an industrial-chic dining area with a mezzanine up above. Burgers, pizzas and meaty mains, too ($18 to $38).

Lucky Bar + Kitchen
BAR

(☑ 027 445 5154; www.facebook.com/luckybar whanganui; 53 Wilson St; ☺ 4pm-late Wed-Sat) One of the few places for a late night in Whang, Lucky also serves bar food worth eating (mains $15 to $28: pizzas, pesto spaghetti, polenta chips with aioli). With retro couches, a small stage and dangling bunches of plastic flowers, the vibe here is resolutely 'share house'. Feelin' lucky? Direct yourself to the dance floor.

Entertainment

Embassy 3 Cinemas
CINEMA

(☑ 06-345 7958; www.embassy3.co.nz; 34 Victoria Ave; tickets adult/child from $13.50/10) Nightly new-release blockbusters selling out faster than you can say 'bored Whanganui teenagers'. Arthouse films screen too, plus a new 20-seat boutique cinema called 'The Lounge' with plush seats and superior sound. Cheap tickets on Tuesdays.

Royal Wanganui Opera House
LIVE PERFORMANCE

(☑ 06-349 0511; www.whanganuivenues.co.nz; 69 St Hill St; ☺ box office 10am-4pm Mon-Fri) Whanganui's magnificent white weatherboard opera house (1899) is New Zealand's (and some suggest the southern hemisphere's) last working Victorian-era theatre, with room for 830 bums on seats. The architecture is inspiring; wandering Tina Turner and Bruce Springsteen tribute shows, perhaps less so...

Information

Department of Conservation (DOC; ☑ 06-349 2100; www.doc.govt.nz; 34-36 Taupo Quay; ☺ 8.30am-4.30pm Mon-Fri) For national park and regional camping info.

Whanganui Hospital (☑ 06-348 1234; www.wdhb.org.nz; 100 Heads Rd; ☺ 24hr) Accident and emergency.

Whanganui i-SITE (☑ 06-349 0508; www.whanganuinz.com; 31 Taupo Quay; ☺ 9am-5pm Mon-Fri, to 4pm Sat & Sun; 🛜) Tourist and DOC information (if DOC across the street is closed) in an impressive renovated riverside building (check out the old floorboards!). Sarjeant Gallery (p259) exhibition space upstairs; very decent **Mud Ducks** (☑ 06-348 7626; www.mudducks.co.nz; 31 Taupo Quay; mains $11-22; ☺ 8.30am-5pm Sat-Tue, to 8pm Wed-Fri; 🛜 📶) cafe downstairs.

🛈 Getting There & Away

AIR

Whanganui Airport (☑ 06-348 0536; www.
whanganuiairport.co.nz; Airport Rd; ☻ hours
vary with flights) is 4km south of town, across
the river towards the sea. **Air Chathams**
(☑ 0800 580 127; www.airchathams.co.nz) has
direct flights to/from Auckland.

BUS

InterCity (www.intercity.co.nz) buses operate
from 29 Taupō Quay.

Destination	Cost	Time (hr)	Frequency (daily)
Auckland	from $40	9½	2
Hamilton	from $30	7½	2
New Plymouth	from $20	2½	2
Palmerston North	from $21	1½	3
Wellington	from $28	4	3

🛈 Getting Around

BICYCLE

Velo Ronny's (☑ 06-348 4261; www.veloronnys.
co.nz; 49 Wilson St; bike hire per hour/day
$10/50; ☻ 8am-5pm Mon-Fri, 9.30am-12.30pm
Sat) hires out mountain bikes from $50 per
day, including a helmet and lock. Try **Bike Shed**
(☑ 06-345 5500; www.bikeshed.co.nz; cnr
Ridgway & St Hill Sts; ☻ 8am-5.30pm Mon-Fri,
9am-2pm Sat) for repairs and trail info.

BUS

Horizons (www.horizons.govt.nz; tickets
adult/child $2.50/1.50) Operates several
bus routes departing Trafalgar Sq shopping
centre on Taupo Quay, including orange and
purple routes past the Whanganui River Top 10
Holiday Park in Aramoho, and pink and blue to
Castlecliff.

TAXI

Rivercity Cabs (☑ 06-345 3333; www.
whanganui.bluebubbletaxi.co.nz)

Whanganui National Park

The Whanganui River may not pay taxes
or vote, but it has the same legal rights as
a human being! In 2017 it became the first
river to be legally recognised as a person,
following a 140-year debate on the issue.
The new legislation recognises the spiritual
connection between Māori *iwi* and the river,
considered an ancestor.

Curling 290km from Mt Tongariro to the
Tasman Sea, it's the longest navigable river
in New Zealand, and visitors traverse it by
canoe, kayak, jetboat, and bike.

The native bush here is thick, broad-
leaved podocarp forest interspersed with
ferns. Occasionally you'll see poplars and
other introduced trees along the river, remnants of long-vanished settlements. There
are also traces of Māori settlements, with
old *pā* and *kainga* (village) sites, and Hauhau *niu* (war and peace) poles at the conver-
gence of the Whanganui and Ohura Rivers
at Maraekowhai.

History

In Māori legend the Whanganui River was
formed when Mt Taranaki fled the central
North Island for the sea after fighting with
Mt Tongariro over the lovely Mt Pihanga,
leaving a long gouge behind him. He turned
west at the coast, finally stopping where he
resides today. Mt Tongariro sent cool water
to heal the gouge – and the Whanganui River was born.

Kupe, the great Polynesian explorer, is
believed to have travelled 20km up the
Whanganui around AD 800; Māori lived
here by 1100. By the time Europeans put
down roots in the late 1830s, Māori settlements lined the river valley. Missionaries
sailed upstream and their settlements – at
Hiruhārama, Rānana, Koriniti and Ātene –
have survived to this day.

Steamers first tackled the river in the
mid-1860s. In 1886 a Whanganui company
established the first commercial steamer
transport service. Others soon followed,
utilising the river between Whanganui and
Taumarunui.

New Zealand's contemporary tourism
leviathan was seeded here. Internationally
advertised trips on the 'Rhine of Māoriland'
became so popular that by 1905, 12,000
tourists a year were making the trip upriver
from Whanganui to Pipiriki or downriver
from Taumarunui. The engineering feats
and skippering ability required on the river
became legendary.

From 1918 land upstream of Pipiriki was
granted to returning WWI soldiers. Farming
here was a major challenge, with many families struggling for years to make the rugged
land productive. Only a few endured into
the early 1940s.

The completion of the railway from Auckland to Wellington and improved roads

Whanganui National Park Area

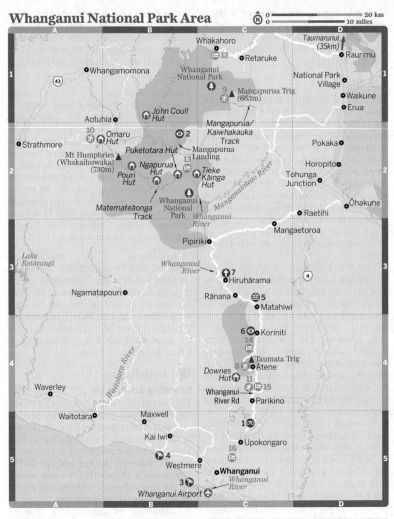

Whanganui National Park Area

Sights

Activities, Courses & Tours

Sleeping

Eating

ultimately signed river transport's death warrant; 1959 saw the last commercial riverboat voyage. Today, just one old-fleet vessel cruises the river – the PS Waimarie (p259), based in Whanganui.

◉ Sights

The scenery along the 64km Whanganui River Rd en route to Pipiriki from Whanganui is camera-conducive stuff – stark, wet mountain slopes plunge into lazy jade stretches of the Whanganui River.

Heading upstream, for a superb introductory view stop at the lookout by the roadside at the top of the first hill you come to, Aramoana Hill. About 4km north of Parikino as the river and road bend into an obvious U-shape, cars slow to eyeball the Oyster Cliffs, where silvery fossilised oysters jut from rock that used to be submerged in the ocean.

The Māori villages of Ātene, Koriniti, Rānana and Hiruhārama crop up as you travel further upstream – ask a local before you go sniffing around. Along the road you'll spot some relics of earlier settlements, such as the 1854 Kawana Flour Mill (☑04-472 4341; www.nzhistory.net.nz/media/photo/kawana-flourmill; 4075 Whanganui River Rd, Matahiwi; ⊙daylight hours) FREE near Matahiwi and *pā* sites. In Ātene, check out the alarmingly high flood-level marker on the roadside barn door, from the big wet of March 1990.

Pipiriki is beside the river at the north end of Whanganui River Rd. It's a rainy river town without much going on – no shops or petrol; just a few shacks, half a 150-year-old old *waka* impaled in the dirt, and the husk of an old hotel, riddled with potential. But it was once a humming holiday hotspot serviced by river steamers and paddle boats. Pipiriki is the end point for canoe trips coming down the river and the launching pad for jetboat rides.

St Joseph's Church   CHURCH
(☑06-342 8190; www.compassion.org.nz; Whanganui River Rd, Hiruhārama; ⊙9am-5pm) FREE Around a corner in the Whanganui River Rd in Jerusalem, the picture-perfect, red-and-mustard spire of St Joseph's Church stands tall on a spur of land above a deep river bend. A French Catholic mission led by Suzanne Aubert established the Daughters of the Sisters of Compassion here in 1892. Slip off your shoes and explore the (slightly creepy) convent and Madeline-like dorms.

The sisters take in bedraggled travellers, offering 20 dorm-style beds (adults $25, children $10, linen $10 extra) and a simple kitchen – book ahead for the privilege. Moutoa Island, site of a historic 1864 battle, is just downriver.

Bridge to Nowhere   BRIDGE
(www.doc.govt.nz; Whanganui River) With no roads on either side, you don't need to be a genius to decipher this bridge's name. Originally built so that horses could cross the river to Mangapurua Valley farmland that was provided to soldiers after WWI, the soldiers deserted the poor soil in 1942, and the forest soon reclaimed its territory. It's on the Mangapurua Track for hikers and mountain bikers, or it's a 40-minute walk from Mangapurua Landing, upstream from Pipiriki, accessible by jetboat or kayak.

Koriniti Marae   CULTURAL CENTRE
(☑06-342 8198; www.wrmtb.co.nz; Koriniti Pa Rd, Koriniti; by donation; ⊙9am-5pm) Unless there's a function happening, you can wander around Koriniti Marae and the little white-painted Koriniti chapel, between the Whanganui River Rd and the river (look for the signs). Gold coin *koha* (donations) welcome. Take off your shoes!

⚹ Activities

Canoeing & Kayaking
The most popular stretch of river for canoeing and kayaking is the 145km downstream run from Taumarunui to Pipiriki – known as the Whanganui Journey, it's one of NZ's 'Great Walks' (for which you must book in advance, between October and April). The Whanganui is a Grade II river – easy enough for the inexperienced, with enough roiling rapids to keep things interesting.

Taumarunui to Pipiriki is a five-day/four-night trip, Ohinepane to Pipiriki is a four-day/three-night trip, and Whakahoro to Pipiriki is a three-day/two-night trip. Taumarunui to Whakahoro is a popular overnight trip, especially for weekenders, or you can do a one-day trip from Taumarunui to Ohinepane or Ohinepane to Whakahoro. From Whakahoro to Pipiriki, 87km downstream, there's no road access so you're wedded to the river for a few days. Most canoeists stop at Pipiriki.

Peak season for canoe trips is from October to April. Up to 5000 people make the river trip each year, mostly between Christmas and the end of January. During winter the river is almost deserted – cold currents run swift and deep as wet weather and short days deter potential paddlers.

To hire a two-person Canadian canoe for one/three/five days costs around $100/200/250 per person not including transport (around $50 per person). A single-person kayak costs about $70 per day. Operators provide you with everything you need, including life jackets and waterproof drums (essential if you go bottom-up).

You can also take guided canoe or kayak trips – prices start at around $350/850 per person for a two-/five-day guided trip. Most operators offer a similar experience: it's more a case of deciding from where you want to start paddling, and where you want to finish up.

Whanganui River Canoes CANOEING
(☑ 06-385 4176; www.whanganuirivercanoes.co.nz; Raetihi Holiday Park, 10 Parapara Rd, Raetihi; hire per person 3/4/5 days from $190/200/210, guided trips per person 3/4/5 days from $705/855/935) Kayak and canoe hire, plus all-inclusive guided trips. A three-hour paddle on the river from Pipiriki downstream to Jerusalem, departing from/returning to Raetihi ($105) is a great introduction to this magnificent river.

Adrift Tongariro CANOEING
(☑ 07-892 2751; www.adriftnz.co.nz; 53 Carroll St, National Park Village; trips 1/3 days $295/950) Paddle downstream with the experts on these guided multiday canoe trips on the wide Whanganui River. Pick-up and drop-off from Adrift's base in National Park Village. One-day trips run from Taumarunui to Ohinepane; three-day from Whakahoro to Pipiriki.

Unique Whanganui River Experience CANOEING
(☑ 027 5544 426; www.uniquewhanganuiriver.co.nz; 71 Carlton Ave, Tawhero, Whanganui; 3-/4-/5-day trips from $690/920/1150) All-inclusive guided three- to five-day river trips with a knowledgeable and experienced 'cultural navigator'. Plenty of good food, history and cultural insights.

Blazing Paddles CANOEING
(Map p294; ☑ 0800 252 946; www.blazing paddles.co.nz; 985 SH4, Manunui; trips 1-8 days per person $100-225) DIY Whanganui River canoe experiences from the Taumarunui end of proceedings, from one hour to one week.

Transport and equipment included; DOC accommodation/camping costs not included. Secure vehicle storage a bonus; *Blazing Saddles* 'bean scene' reenactments optional.

Taumarunui Canoe Hire CANOEING
(☑ 07-895 7483; www.taumarunuicanoehire.co.nz; 292 Hikumutu Rd, Taumarunui; trips per person from $75) Based in Taumarunui, these guys offer unguided canoe-hire river trips with plenty of background support (maps, DOC tickets, jetboats etc). Paddles from two hours to eight days.

Canoe Safaris CANOEING
(☑ 06-385 9237; www.canoesafaris.co.nz; 6 Tay St, Ōhakune; trips 2/3/4/5 days from $525/845/1045/1245) Three- to five-day guided river trips with all the requisite gear, based in Ōhakune. River guides and Rangitikei and Mohaka river trips also available.

Yeti Tours CANOEING
(☑ 06-385 8197; www.yetitours.co.nz; 3 Burns St, Ōhakune; hire 2-8 days $175-250) Canoe and kayak hire, hitting the river near Ōhakune.

Jetboating
Hold onto your hats (and your breakfast!) – jetboat trips give you the chance to see parts of the river that would otherwise take you days to paddle through. Jetboats depart from Pipiriki and Whanganui; four-hour tours start at around $150 per person. Most operators can also provide transport to the river ends of the Matemateāonga and Mangapurua tracks.

Bridge to Nowhere Tours OUTDOORS
(☑ 06-385 4622; www.bridgetonowhere.co.nz; 11 Owairua Rd, Pipiriki; tours from $95) Jetboat tours to see the Bridge to Nowhere, plus canoeing, mountain biking and hiking – the folks at Bridge to Nowhere Lodge (p269) coordinate it all, with accommodation and accommodation-and-meal packages in the middle of nowhere afterwards. Half-day express jetboat/canoe combos ($95) are terrific if you're short on time.

Whanganui Scenic Experience Jet BOATING
(☑ 06-342 5599; www.whanganuiscenicjet.com; 1195 Whanganui River Rd; 2-8hr trips $65-220) Jetboat tours upriver departing Whanganui or the River Rd, plus longer expeditions into the national park with hiking detours. Canoe and canoe/jetboat combo trips also available.

Whanganui River Adventures
BOATING

(📞 06-385 3246; www.whanganuiriveradventures. co.nz; 2522 Pipiriki-Raetihi Rd, Pipiriki; trips from $115) Jetboat rides upriver from Pipiriki, with camping, cabins and a cottage at Pipiriki also available. The one-day jetboat-and-canoe combo ($175) gives you a good taste of the national park if you're in a hurry.

Hiking

Bridge to Nowhere Track
HIKING

(www.doc.govt.nz; Whanganui National Park; ☉daylight hrs) FREE The most popular track in Whanganui National Park is the 40-minute walk from Mangapurua Landing (30km upstream from Pipiriki by jetboat) to the long-lost Bridge to Nowhere (p266). Contact jetboat operators for transport (around $100 per person one way).

Ātene Viewpoint Walk
HIKING

(www.doc.govt.nz; Whanganui River Rd; ☉daylight hrs) At Ātene, on the Whanganui River Rd about 22km north of the SH4 junction, tackle the short Ātene Viewpoint Walk – about a one-hour ascent. The track travels through native bush and farmland along a 1959 roadway built during investigations for a Whanganui River hydroelectric scheme (a dam was proposed at Ātene that would have flooded the river valley almost as far as Taumarunui). The track ends on a black beech ridge – expect great views across the national park.

From the viewpoint walk you can continue along the circular 18km Ātene Skyline Track. The track takes six to eight hours, showcasing native forest, sandstone bluffs and the Taumata Trig (523m), with its broad views as far as Mt Ruapehu, Mt Taranaki and the Tasman Sea. The track ends back on the Whanganui River Rd, 2km downstream from the starting point.

ℹ REMOTE TRACK ACCESS

The Matemateāonga and Mangapurua/ Kaiwhakauka Tracks are brilliant longer hikes (download info from www.doc.govt. nz). Both are one-way tracks beginning (or ending) at remote spots on the river, so you have to organise jetboat transport to or from the river trailheads – ask any jetboat operator. Between Pipiriki and the Matemateāonga Track is around $50 per person; for the Mangapurua Track it's around $100.

Matemateāonga Track
HIKING

(www.doc.govt.nz; Whanganui National Park) FREE The remote, 42km, three- to four-day Matemateāonga Track gets kudos as one of NZ's best walks, but it doesn't attract the hordes of hikers that amass on NZ's more famous tracks. Penetrating deep into wild bush, it follows the crest of the Matemateāonga Range along the route of the Whakaihuwaka Rd. Work on the road began in 1911 to create a more direct link from Stratford to the railway at Raetihi, but WWI stalled the road's progress. Huts en route.

Mangapurua/Kaiwhakauka Track
HIKING

(www.doc.govt.nz; Whanganui National Park) The 40km Mangapurua/Kaiwhakauka Track runs between Whakahoro and the Mangapurua Landing, both on the Whanganui River. The track runs along the Mangapurua and Kaiwhakauka Streams (both Whanganui River tributaries). A side track leads to the 663m Mangapurua Trig, the area's highest point. The route also passes the amazing Bridge to Nowhere (p266). Walking the track takes two to three days (camping en route), or you can mountain-bike it in a day (it's part of the Mountains to Sea cycle trail).

Mountain Biking

The Whanganui River Rd and Mangapurua/Kaiwhakauka Track have been incorporated into the 317km Mountains to Sea Mt Ruapehu–Whanganui bike track (www. mountainstosea.co.nz), itself part of the Ngā Haerenga, New Zealand Cycle Trail project (www.nzcycletrail.com). As part of the experience, from Mangapurua Landing on the Whanganui River near the Bridge to Nowhere, you catch a (prebooked) jetboat downstream to Pipiriki, then continue riding down the Whanganui River Rd. In Whanganui, try Bike Shed (p264) for repairs and info, or Velo Ronny's (p264) for bike hire.

☞ Tours

Whanganui Tours
TOURS

(📞 06-345 3475; www.whanganuitours.co.nz; per person $63) Join the mail carrier on the Whanganui River Rd to Pipiriki (pick-up about 7am), with lots of social and historical commentary. Returns mid-afternoon...but you might have to wait around for an hour or two to pick up canoeists at Pipiriki (there are worse fates in the world).

Eastern Taranaki Experience TOURS
(☏ 06-765 7482; www.eastern-taranaki.co.nz; 5 Verona Pl, Stratford; per person incl lunch $240) Departing Stratford in neighbouring Taranaki (with pick-ups in Whanganui), these full-day trips take you up the Whanganui River Rd to Pipiriki, from where you jetboat upstream to walk to the Bridge to Nowhere, then make the return journey. Minimum six people. Forgotten World Highway tours (in Taranaki) also available (from $60 per person).

🛏 Sleeping

Whanganui National Park has a sprinkling of huts, a lodge and numerous camping grounds (free to $20, depending on the season). Along the Taumarunui–Pipiriki section are two huts classified as Great Walk Huts during summer ($32 per night) and Backcountry Huts in the off-season ($15): John Coull Hut and Tieke Kāinga Hut, which has been revived as a *marae* (you can stay here, but full *marae* protocol must be observed – eg no alcohol). The Whakahoro Bunkroom is also on this stretch of river. On the lower part of the river, Downes Hut is on the west bank, opposite Ātene.

Along the River Rd there are a couple of lodges for travellers to bunk down in. There's also a free (very) informal campsite with a toilet just north of Ātene. Also at Pipiriki are a campsite, some cabins and a cottage run by Whanganui River Adventures. There is also a handful of simple cabins alongside Matahiwi Gallery Cafe; call to book.

Bridge to Nowhere Lodge LODGE $
(☏ 06-385 4622; www.bridgetonowhere.co.nz; Whanganui National Park; tent/dm/lodge per person $15/30/55) This remote lodge lies deep in Whanganui National Park, 21km upriver from Pipiriki near the Matemateāonga Track. The only way to get here is by jetboat from Pipiriki, or on foot. It has a licensed bar, and meals are quality home-cooked affairs. The lodge also runs jetboat, canoe and mountain-bike trips (p267). Transport/accommodation/meals packages available, including DB&B from $160.

Kohu Cottage RENTAL HOUSE $
(☏ 06-342 8178; www.whanganuionline.com/directory/kohu-cottage; 3154 Whanganui River Rd, Koroniti; d from $100; ℗) Over 100 years old, this snug little cream-coloured weatherboard cottage above the road in Koriniti sleeps four people and a fifth for an extra

> ## ℹ CAMPING & HUTS PASSES
>
> Great Walk Tickets are required in Whanganui National Park from 1 October to 30 April for the use of huts (adult/child $32/free) and campsites ($20/free) between Taumarunui and Pipiriki. Outside the main season you'll only need a **Backcountry Hut Pass** (adult/child for one year $122/61, for six months $92/46), or you can pay on a night-by-night basis (adult/child $15/free). Passes and tickets can be purchased online (www.doc.govt.nz) or at DOC offices in Whakapapa, Taumarunui, Ōhakune or Whanganui (p263).

few bucks. It has a basic kitchen and a wood fire for chilly riverside nights. Pay less per night the longer you stay.

Rivertime Lodge LODGE $
(☏ 06-327 6472; www.rivertimelodge.co.nz; 1569 Whanganui River Rd; per person $50-60; ℗) Green-painted Rivertime is a simple riverside cottage with two bedrooms, a laundry, a wood heater and a lovely deck – and no TV! Three additional en-suite cabins sleeping two people each make this a lovely spot for a group, but rooms are hired out exclusively to one group at a time. DB&B packages from $105 per person. Closed May to October.

Flying Fox LODGE $$
(☏ 06-927 6809; www.theflyingfox.co.nz; Whanganui River Rd; campsites $15, glamping from $95, d $90-240, q $345; ☏) 🍃 Accessible only by boat or eponymous flying fox (park on the side of Whanganui River Rd and launch yourself across the river), this eco-attuned getaway is on the riverbank across from Koriniti. You can self-cater in the Riverboat or James K cottages, or in Riru Lodge. Alternatively, opt for a summer glamping set-up or pitch a tent in a bush clearing.

🍴 Eating

There's not much in the way of food on the River Rd: the casual Matahiwi Gallery Cafe (☏ 06-342 8112; www.facebook.com/Matahiwigallery; 3925 Whanganui River Rd, Matahiwi; snacks $4-8, cabins s/d from $45/90; ☺9am-4pm Wed-Sun Oct-May) is really your only option (call ahead to make sure it's open). Otherwise, pack a sandwich.

ℹ️ Information

For national park information, try the affable Whanganui (p263) or Taumarunui (p219) i-SITEs, or check out www.doc.govt.nz and www.whanganuiriver.co.nz. Otherwise, a more tangible resource is the NZ Recreational Canoeing Association's *Guide to the Whanganui River* ($10; see www.rivers.org.nz/whanganui-guide). The i-SITE also stocks the *Whanganui River Road Guide* brochure.

DOC's **Pipiriki** (📞 06-385 5022; www.doc.govt.nz; Owairua Rd, Pipiriki; ⏰ hours vary) and **Taumarunui** (📞 07-895 8201; www.doc.govt.nz; Cherry Grove Rd, Taumarunui; ⏰ hours vary) centres are field bases rather than tourist offices, and aren't always staffed.

Mobile-phone coverage along the River Rd is patchy at best.

ℹ️ Getting There & Away

From the north, there's road access to the Whanganui River at Taumarunui, Ohinepane and Whakahoro, though the last of these is a long, remote drive on mostly unsealed roads. Roads to Whakahoro lead off from Owhango and Raurimu, both on SH4. There isn't any further road access to the river until Pipiriki.

From the south, the Whanganui River Rd veers off SH4 14km north of Whanganui, rejoining it at Raetihi, 91km north of Whanganui. It takes about two hours to drive the 79km between Whanganui and Pipiriki. Alternatively, take a River Rd tour from Whanganui.

At the time of writing, the SH4 route between Whanganui and Raetihi was closed due to a major landslip; check with the Whanganui i-SITE (p263) for updates.

There are no petrol stations or shops along the River Rd.

Palmerston North

POP 88,700

The fertile farming region of Manawatu embraces the districts of Rangitikei to the north and Horowhenua to the south. The hub of it all, on the banks of the Manawatu River, is Palmerston North. Massey University, New Zealand's largest, informs the town's cultural and social structures – 'Palmy' has an open-minded, rurally bookish vibe, with none of the 'town vs gown' angst of old-world university towns.

None of this impressed a visiting John Cleese who reportedly said, 'If you wish to kill yourself but lack the courage to, I think a visit to Palmerston North will do the trick.' The city exacted revenge by naming a rubbish dump after him... We suspect Cleese needs to return (it's been over a decade now) to explore excellent mountain biking trails (can you picture Basil Fawlty on a mountain bike?) and lush walking tracks beyond the city, and great coffee and beer within.

👁️ Sights & Activities

⭐ **New Zealand Rugby Museum** MUSEUM
(📞 06-358 6947; www.rugbymuseum.co.nz; Te Manawa Complex, 326 Main St; adult/child/family $12.50/5/30; ⏰ 10am-5pm) Fans of the oval ball holler about the New Zealand Rugby Museum, an amazing space overflowing with rugby paraphernalia, from a 1905 All Blacks jumper to a scrum machine and the actual whistle used to start the first game of every Rugby World Cup. Of course, NZ won back-to-back Rugby World Cups in 2011 and 2015, but failed ingloriously in 2019: quiz the staff about the All Blacks' 2023 prospects.

⭐ **He Ara Kotahi Bridge** BRIDGE
(www.pncc.govt.nz; off Ruha St; 🚲) Palmerston's North's iconic new landmark is this elegant 194m-long bridge over the Manawatu River – a critical link in a 9km network of cycling and walking trails (of the same name) that now connects Massey University with the city centre. Along the way there's a dairy farm, historic Māori *pā* sites, a tree canopy boardwalk and info plaques on local Ranghitāne lore, with the broad river slowly sliding by. Hire a bike or lace up your boots and go exploring.

Te Manawa MUSEUM
(📞 06-355 5000; www.temanawa.co.nz; 326 Main St; ⏰ 10am-5pm; 🚲) FREE Te Manawa merges a museum and art gallery into one experience, with vast collections joining the dots between art, science and history. The museum has a strong Māori focus and includes plenty of social history, information on native animals and wetlands, and an interactive science display on the Manawatu River. The gallery's exhibits change frequently. Little kids will get a kick out of the interactive play area. The excellent New Zealand Rugby Museum is here too.

The Square PARK
(www.pncc.govt.nz; The Square; ⏰ 24hr) Taking the English village green concept to a whole new level, The Square is Palmy's heart and soul. Its Māori name, Te Marae o Hine, was chosen to symbolise all tribes and races living together peacefully – which

Palmerston North

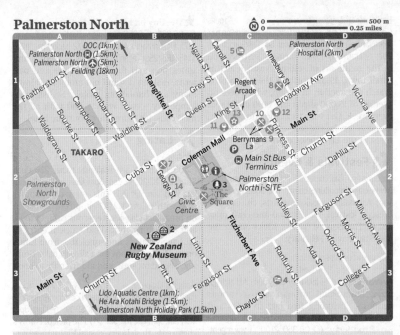

Palmerston North

they certainly do when the sun comes out and everyone sits on the lawn for lunch. The seven spacious hectares feature a clock tower, duck pond, giant chess set, Māori carvings, statues and trees of all seasonal dispositions.

Lido Aquatic Centre   SWIMMING
(☑ 06-357 2684; www.lidoaquaticcentre.co.nz; 50 Park Rd; adult/child/family $5.20/4.20/14.10, hydroslide day passes $12; ⊙ 6am-8pm Mon-Thu, to 9pm Fri, 8am-8pm Sat & Sun) When the summer plains bake, dive into the Lido Aquatic Centre. It's a long way from the Lido Beach in Venice, but it has a 50m pool, water slides, a cafe and a gym.

🌱 Tours

Tui Brewery Tours   TOURS
(☑ 06-376 0815; www.tuihq.co.nz/tours; 5 Mara St, Mangatainoka; tours per person from $20; ⊙ 11am-5pm Sun-Thu, to 6pm Fri & Sat Nov-Apr, closes 1hr later May-Oct) Even if you're more of a craft-beer fan than a drinker of the ubiquitous Tui, this boozy 40-minute brewery tour (11.30am and 2.30pm) 40km east of Palmy is a doldrum-beating outing (book ahead). Check out the interesting old brewery and museum, and taste a Tui or three. Tours aside, order lunch inside (mains $19 to $25) and enjoy the grassy outdoor tables in the sunshine.

Feilding Saleyard Tours
TOURS

(☑ 06-323 3318; www.feildingsaleyards.co.nz/ stockyardtours; 10 Manchester Sq, Feilding; tours $10; ⊙ 11am Fri) Local farmers instruct you in the gentle art of selling livestock at this small town, 19km north of the city centre. Watch the auction in action, which sees an average of 15,000 sheep and 1400 cattle sold every week. Get your tix at the info centre in Manchester Sq; the saleyard is in Manchester St at the Livestock Centre.

✻ Festivals & Events

Festival of Cultures
CULTURAL

(www.festivalofcultures.co.nz; The Square; ⊙ Feb-Mar) A massive week-long arts, culture and lifestyle festival, with a food-and-craft market in The Square (p270). Kicks off on the last Saturday in February.

Manawatu International Jazz & Blues Festival
MUSIC

(www.mjc.org.nz; ⊙ late May-early Jun) All things jazzy, bluesy and swingin' across various venues – including free jazz in cafes and big events at the Globe Theatre and Regent on Broadway (☑ 06-350 2100; www.regent. co.nz; 53 Broadway Ave; ⊙ box office 9am-5.30pm Mon-Fri, 10am-2pm Sat) – as well as plenty of workshops.

🛏 Sleeping

Pepper Tree Hostel
HOSTEL $

(☑ 06-355 4054; www.peppertreehostel.co.nz; 121 Grey St; dm/s/d $31/65/80; ℗ 🛜) Inexplicably strewn with green-painted, succulent-filled boots, this endearing 100-year-old house is the best budget option in town, with room for 35 bods. Mattresses are thick, the kitchen will never run out of spatulas and the piano and wood fire make things feel downright homey. Unisex bathrooms, but there is a gals-only dorm. Primrose Manor (☑ 06-355 4213; www. primrosemanor.co.nz; 123 Grey St; d $145; ℗ 🛜) has two guesthouse rooms next door.

Palmerston North Holiday Park
HOLIDAY PARK $

(☑ 06-358 0349; www.palmerstonnorthholiday park.co.nz; 133 Dittmer Dr; unpowered & powered sites per 2 people from $40, cabins & units with/ without bathroom from $67/43; ℗ 🛜 ♿) About 2km from The Square, off Ruha St, this old-fashioned, shady park with daisy-speckled lawns is quiet, affordable and right beside the He Ara Kotahi Bridge (p270) and walkways. Trees and gardens bring the calm, until the kids consume the playground.

★ Destiny on Fitzherbert
MOTEL $$

(☑ 06-355 0050; www.destinymotel.co.nz; 127 Fitzherbert Ave; d/ste/2-bedroom from $145/165/259; ℗ 🛜) Destiny's 13 studios and suites pop and fizz with colours and patterns, making it stand out amongst Palmy's many safe-but-boring motels. Stylish, contemporary – even witty – and with all the mod cons, it's more like a boutique hotel.

🍴 Eating

★ Café Cuba
CAFE $

(☑ 06-356 5750; www.cafecuba.co.nz; 236 Cuba St; mains $7-20; ⊙ 7am-3pm Mon, to 8pm Tue, to late Wed-Sun; 🍴♿) This eternally popular cafe with a lovely 1917 shopfront zeroes in on breakfast classics, generous cabinet food, and everything from Thai chicken curry to fat bagels, salads and omelettes from lunch onwards. Save room for a slice of cake. Smiling, abundant staff, and kid friendly to boot.

Saigon Corner
VIETNAMESE $

(☑ 06-355 4988; www.facebook.com/saigoncor nernz; 54 Princess St; mains $9-19; ⊙ 11am-3pm Mon-Sat, 5pm-late Tue-Sat; 🍴) The pick of Palmy's cheap eats, this cheery, casual Vietnamese restaurant nails all the classics: pho, banh mi, rice-paper rolls, and noodle and rice dishes. A viscous Vietnamese coffee (hot or iced) will get your motor running. Takeaway, too.

Arranged Marriage
SOUTH INDIAN $$

(☑ 06-351 6300; www.arrangedmarriage.co.nz; 32b The Square; mains $14-28; ⊙ noon-2pm & 5pm-late Tue-Sun; 🍴) Bring your future husband or wife for taste of Kerala right on The Square, with fun, un-Bollywood decor (love the coconut wall) and aromatic food. You'll find butter chicken and vegetable korma here, but order the signature *dosa*. The $14 lunch deals are great bang for your buck.

Yeda
ASIAN $$

(☑ 06-358 3978; www.yeda.co.nz; 78 Broadway Ave; mains $17-22; ⊙ 11am-9pm) Yeda feels like an urban mess hall or uni cafeteria – a long, minimalist room packed with students, with easy-clean concrete floors. It covers all the Asian bases, from Vietnamese pho to Thai chicken and dumplings. Sip sake or an Asahi while you wait (which won't be long). The $15 set lunch menu (entrée, main and miso soup) is a steal.

Nero Restaurant
INTERNATIONAL $$$

(☑ 06-354 0312; www.nerorestaurant.co.nz; 36 Amesbury St; mains $27-46; ⊙ 11am-2pm Tue-Fri, 5pm-late Tue-Sat) Set in a spruced-up 1918

Victorian house with a manicured alfresco dining area, Nero is the peak of fine dining in Palmy. The chef and owner is an ambassador for Beef & Lamb New Zealand, but also serves dishes like sticky pork belly and cauliflower steak with flair. Order the whisky dry-aged beef rib with black garlic butter.

 Drinking & Nightlife

★ Brew Union   CRAFT BEER
(☑ 06-280 3146; www.brewunion.co.nz; 41 Broadway Ave; ⊗ 3-10pm Mon-Wed, 11am-11pm Thu-Sat, 11am-9pm Sun) This impressively converted warehouse is the best spot for a drink in town. Stretching across an entire city block, the bar has 21 beers on tap and 45 gins on the shelf. Come for a drink (try the King Street pilsner), and stay for wood-fired pizza ($13 to $25). Live vinyl-spinners on Fridays and guitar-twangers on Saturdays.

Little Savanna   PUB
(☑ 06-358 7775; www.littlesavanna.co.nz; 45 Princess St; ⊗ 5-10pm Mon, 11am-10pm Tue-Sun) It's not really little and it's a long way from the savanna, but this classy beer barn is one of Palmerston North's best pubs – an L-shaped room lined with concrete and timber panelling, glowing taps and racks of glimmering whisky bottles. An adventurous menu (mains $18 to $39) includes the likes of Mozambique fish stew and ostrich fillet with blue cheese.

 Shopping

Bruce McKenzie Booksellers   BOOKS
(☑ 06-356 9922; www.bmbooks.co.nz; 37 George St; ⊗ 9am-5.30pm Mon-Fri, to 5pm Sat, 10am-4pm Sun) An excellent independent bookshop, with classical music and serene, intelligent vibes. Pick up that guide to NZ craft beer you've been looking for and browse through novels by NZ authors.

ℹ **Information**

Department of Conservation (DOC; ☑ 06-350 9700; www.doc.govt.nz; 28 North St; ⊗ 8am-4.30pm Mon-Fri) DOC information, 2km north of The Square.

Palmerston North Hospital (☑ 06-356 9169; www.midcentraldhb.govt.nz; 50 Ruahine St; ⊗ 24hr) Accident and emergency.

Palmerston North i-SITE (☑ 06-350 1929; www.manawatunz.co.nz; The Square; ⊗ 9am-5pm Mon-Fri, to 2pm Sat & Sun; 📶) A superhelpful source of tourist info, also hiring out electric bikes (one/two hours $20/30) and regular bikes (half-/full day $40/50).

Palms Medical Centre (☑ 06-354 7737; www.palmsmedical.co.nz; 445 Ferguson St; ⊗ 8am-8pm daily) Urgent medical help, plus doctors and dentists by appointment and a pharmacy.

ℹ **Getting There & Away**

AIR

Palmerston North Airport (☑ 06-351 4415; www.pnairport.co.nz; Airport Dr) is 4km north of the town centre.

Air New Zealand (www.airnewzealand.co.nz) runs daily direct flights to Auckland, Christchurch and Wellington. **Jetstar** (www.jetstar.com) also has flights to/from Auckland. **Originair** (www.originair.nz) flies between Palmy and Nelson, down south.

BUS

InterCity (www.intercity.co.nz) buses operate from the **Main St bus terminus** (Main St) on the east side of The Square; destinations include the following:

Destination	Cost	Time (hr)	Frequency (daily)
Auckland	from $33	9¼	3
Napier	from $19	3¼	3
Taupō	from $23	4	4
Wellington	from $25	2¼	8
Whanganui	from $21	1½	2

TRAIN

Great Journeys of New Zealand (☑ 0800 872 467; www.greatjourneysofnz.co.nz) runs long-distance trains between Wellington and Auckland, stopping at the retro-derelict **Palmerston North Train Station** (Matthews Ave), off Tremaine Ave, about 2.5km north of The Square. From Palmy to Wellington, take the Northern Explorer ($69, two hours) departing Monday, Thursday and Saturday; or the weekday Capital Connection commuter service ($35, two hours). To Auckland, the Northern Explorer ($179, nine hours) departs on Wednesday, Friday and Sunday. Buy tickets online (no ticket sales at the station).

ℹ **Getting Around**

TO/FROM THE AIRPORT

A city-to-airport taxi costs around $20, or **Super Shuttle** (☑ 09-522 5100; www.supershuttle.co.nz; tickets from $18) can whizz you into town in a prebooked minivan.

BICYCLE

Crank It Cycles (☑ 06-358 9810; 244 Cuba St; half/full day $35/50; ⊗ 8am-5.30pm Mon-Fri, 9.30am-3pm Sat, 10am-3pm Sun) hires out city bikes, including a helmet and lock (deposit $50). You can also hire bikes (electric and standard) from the i-SITE (p273).

BUS

Horizons (☑06-355 4955; www.horizons.govt. nz; adult/child $2.50/1.50) runs daytime buses departing from the Main St bus stop (p273) on the east side of The Square.

TAXI

Gold & Black Taxis (☑06-351 2345; www. taxisgb.co.nz) Family-run local taxi outfit.

Around Palmerston North

Venture outside Palmerston North for landscapes and beaches in direct contrast with the faster, more corporate pace of the student city. About 12km east of town, SH3 dips into Manawatu Gorge. Māori named the gorge Te Apiti (the Narrow Passage), believing the big reddish rock near the centre of the gorge was its guardian spirit. It's an 11km, uphill slant to get to the viewpoints and takes around four hours one way. On the southwestern edge of the Gorge is the Tararua Wind Farm, allegedly the largest in the southern hemisphere. North of the Gorge is Te Āpiti Wind Farm (☑04-499 5048; www.windenergy.org.nz/te-apiti-wind-farm; off Saddle Rd, Woodville; ☉24hr) **FREE** – more accessible than Tararua – with 55 turbines

creating enough power for around 39,000 New Zealand homes each year. It's on private land just off Saddle Rd, but through the gate there is a public viewing platform with mesmerising views. Alternatively, for equine explorations of these hills, try Timeless Horse Treks (☑06-376 6157; www.timeless horsetreks.co.nz; Gorge Rd, Ballance; 1hr rides from $60; ☙).

Note that at the time of writing, the SH3 road through the Manawatu Gorge remained closed due to landslips, but the walking tracks were open. Check before you go at the Palmerston North i-SITE (p273) or with the Department of Conservation (p273).

South of Palmerston North is Shannon (population 1500) and Foxton (population 3130), quiet country towns en route to Wellington. Foxton Beach is one of a string of broad, shallow Tasman Sea beaches along this stretch of coast – other worthy beaches include Himatangi, Hokio and Waikawa. Levin (population 21,200) is more sizeable, but is too close to both Wellington and Palmerston North to warrant the through-traffic making an extended stop.

Park yourself in Palmy in the evening and treat the rest as day-trip terrain. Take your own car; otherwise InterCity (www.intercity. co.nz) services pass through Levin and Shannon (and sometimes Foxton) en route between Palmerston North and Wellington.

Taupō & the Ruapehu Region

Best Places to Eat

➜ Storehouse (p287)

➜ Replete Cafe & Store (p287)

➜ Knoll Ridge Chalet (p297)

➜ Eat Takeaway Diner (p302)

➜ Blind Finch (p302)

Best Places to Stay

➜ Acacia Cliffs Lodge (p287)

➜ Waitahanui Lodge (p286)

➜ The Lake (p286)

➜ Ruapehu Country Lodge (p302)

➜ Braxmere (p290)

Why Go?

The picturesque landscape of mountains, lakes and native forest at the heart of the North Island owes much of its shape and form to volcanoes – prehistoric, past and modern. The Taupō Volcanic Zone is a line of geothermal activity that stretches via Rotorua to Whakaari (White Island) in the Bay of Plenty. Thermal activity still bubbles and boils beneath the surface, where it's been responsible for creating some of New Zealand's star attractions, including the country's largest lake and the three snowcapped peaks of Tongariro National Park.

Thrill seekers are in for a treat, with this region having the North Island's wildest collection of outdoor escapades. And when the action finally exhausts you (or if you had a relaxing holiday in mind), you can soak the day away in a thermal pool or try some therapeutic fly-fishing.

When to Go

➜ Equally popular in winter and summer, there's not really a bad time to visit the centre of the North Island.

➜ The ski season runs roughly from June to October, but storms and freezing temperatures can occur at any time on the mountains, and above 2500m there is a permanent snowcap; come prepared.

➜ Due to its altitude, the Ruapehu region has a generally cool climate, with average high temperatures ranging from 0°C in winter up to around 24°C in summer.

➜ Lake Taupō is swamped with Kiwi holidaymakers from Christmas to late January, so it pays to book accommodation well in advance during this time.

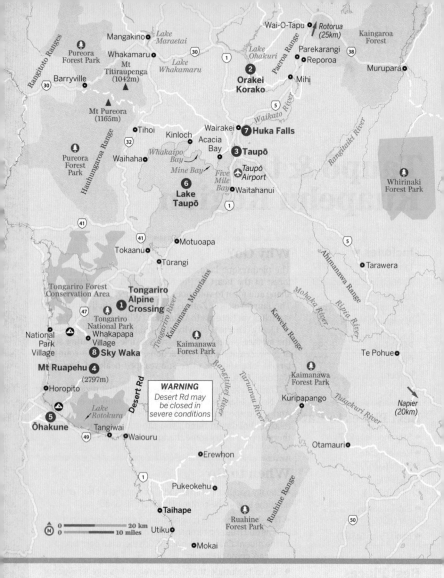

Taupō & the Ruapehu Region Highlights

1 Tongariro Alpine Crossing (p293) Stepping over volcanic scenery on NZ's best day hike.

2 Orakei Korako (p284) Wandering up through a series of colourful geothermal terraces above a lake.

3 Taupo Bungy (p282) Bungy jumping to touch the Waikato River.

4 Mt Ruapehu (p293) Skiing through fresh powder at Turoa or Whakapapa.

5 Ōhakune Old Coach Road (p301) Mountain biking over the curved, 284m-long Hapuawhenua Viaduct.

6 Māori Rock Carvings (p281) Kayaking or cruising across Lake Taupō to this modern cliff masterpiece.

7 Huka Falls (p281) Jetboating up the Waikato River to the base of the powerful falls.

8 Sky Waka (p296) Riding NZ's longest gondola, for stunning views across the spires and upper slopes of Mt Ruapehu.

ℹ Getting There & Away

AIR

Air New Zealand (☏ 0800 737 000, 09-357 3000; www.airnewzealand.co.nz) has daily flights to Taupō from Auckland, and **Sounds Air** (☏ 03-520 3080, 0800 505 005; www.soundsair.com) links Taupō and Wellington 15 times a week.

BUS

Taupō is a hub for **InterCity** (☏ 07-348 0366; www.intercitycoach.co.nz) coach services, with regular services running through on direct routes to Auckland (via Rotorua and Hamilton), Tauranga (via Rotorua), Napier, and Wellington via Tūrangi, Waiouru, Taihape, Palmerston North and Kapiti Coast towns. The Palmerston North–Auckland service passes through Whanganui before skirting the western edge of Tongariro National Park via Ōhakune and National Park Village and heading north via Taumaranui, Te Awamutu and Hamilton.

InterCity's budget bus service, **Skip** (☏ 09-394 9180; https://skip.travel), has routes from Taupō to Wellington (via Tūrangi), Rotorua, Hamilton and Auckland.

TRAIN

KiwiRail Scenic (☏ 0800 872 467, 04-495 0775; www.greatjourneysofnz.co.nz) The *Northern Explorer*, New Zealand's longest-running passenger service, stops at National Park Village and Ōhakune on the Auckland–Hamilton–Palmerston North–Wellington route.

LAKE TAUPŌ REGION

New Zealand's largest lake, Lake Taupō (also known as Taupō Moana), sits in the caldera of a volcano that began erupting about 300,000 years ago. It was formed by a collapse during the Oruanui super-eruption about 26,500 years ago, which spurted 750 cu km of ash and pumice, making Krakatoa (8 cu km) look like a pimple.

The last major cataclysm in AD 180 was the world's most violent eruption of the last 5000 years, shooting enough ash into the atmosphere for ancient Romans and Chinese to record unusual skies. The area is still volcanically active and, like Rotorua, has fascinating thermal hotspots.

Today the lake, which is about the size of Singapore, and its surrounding waterways attract fishing enthusiasts from around the world who visit to snag trophy trout. Positioned by the lake, Taupō and Tūrangi are both popular tourist centres. Taupō, in particular, has plenty of activities and facilities catering to families and independent travellers alike.

Taupō
POP 32,900

Sitting inside a caldera formed by one of the most violent volcanic eruptions on record, Taupō's existence should feel precarious and edgy. But when the lake wakes to a new day as flat as a windowpane, with the snow-capped peaks of Tongariro National Park rising beyond its southern shores, it feels almost paradisiacal.

With an abundance of adrenaline-pumping activities, thermally heated waters, lakeside strolls and some wonderful places to eat, Taupō now rivals Rotorua as the North Island's premier resort town. It's also a magnet for outdoor athletes and one of New Zealand's greatest cycling destinations, both on and off the road.

The Waikato River, NZ's longest, starts at Lake Taupō, running right through town before crashing its way through the Huka Falls and Aratiatia Rapids.

History

Let's start back in AD 180 when the Taupō eruption became the largest and most violent in recorded history. All of New Zealand was covered in ash, in some places up to 10m deep. The column of smoke reached 50km into the sky – about five times the cruising altitude of planes. Everything living was destroyed and

HIKING IN TONGARIRO NATIONAL PARK

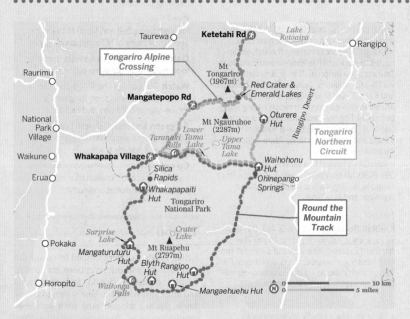

TONGARIRO ALPINE CROSSING

START MANGATEPOPO RD
END KETETAHI RD
DURATION 7–8 HOURS
DISTANCE 19.4KM
DIFFICULTY MODERATE

You don't get to be routinely called the best day walk in New Zealand without being something pretty special. And the Tongariro Alpine Crossing is indeed that. This walk is like a mobile field guide to volcanoes, threading between Mt Tongariro and the conical perfection of Mt Ngauruhoe, passing neon-bright lakes that contrast with the black earth, while vents steam, hiss and fart in sulphurous clouds, and rocks spat shape from the volcanoes take on crazy shapes.

With big reputations come big crowds. In the early 1990s the Crossing would attract around 20,000 hikers a year; today that number is up to around 130,000. On the busiest days there can be more than 2000 people on the track. It's these sorts of numbers that have led to parking restrictions at the trailhead, making it all but compulsory to use the abundant shuttle services. In late 2017 signs marking the side trails to Mts Tongariro and Ngauruhoe were taken down, with hikers requested not to climb the mountains.

The crowds are the price of volcanic excellence, for the Alpine Crossing is truly something to behold. But don't let the big numbers fool you into thinking that it's a casual stroll. It's a long day – and fierce in bad weather – climbing 750m from its start to the top of Red Crater and then descending 700m to Ketetahi Rd. Be prepared for the fact that shuttle services typically don't run if the weather isn't cooperating.

Tongariro is a siren call for hikers, drawing them into the desert-like lands, steam and brilliantly coloured lakes that cover the flanks of New Zealand's most impressive volcanoes.

TONGARIRO NORTHERN CIRCUIT

START/END WHAKAPAPA VILLAGE
DURATION 4 DAYS
DISTANCE 50KM
DIFFICULTY MODERATE

Circumnavigating Mt Ngauruhoe, this track is a Great Walk for a number of good reasons. The route can be easily hiked in four days, and though there is some moderate climbing, the track is well marked and well maintained, putting it within the ability of most people with medium fitness and hiking experience. But most of all, the Northern Circuit includes the sort of spectacular and colourful volcanic areas that have helped earn the park its status as a Unesco World Heritage Site. If the Alpine Crossing is the short story, the Northern Circuit is the novel.

The traditional place to start and finish the hike is Whakapapa Village, the site of the park's visitor centre, though many hikers begin at Mangatepopo Rd to ensure they have good weather for the hike's most dramatic day – the Alpine Crossing section. The Northern Circuit leaves the Alpine Crossing just past the Emerald Lakes, heading out into the moonscape and lava bombs (rocks spat out by the volcanoes) of the so-called Rangipo Desert (which isn't really a desert, despite appearances). It turns back west at Waihohonu Hut, crossing Tama Saddle, which is decorated with the colourful Tama Lakes, and passing 20m-high Taranaki Falls before ending at Whakapapa Village.

ROUND THE MOUNTAIN TRACK

START/END WHAKAPAPA VILLAGE OR ŌHAKUNE MOUNTAIN RD
DURATION 4-6 DAYS
DISTANCE 66.2KM
DIFFICULTY DIFFICULT

While most multiday hikers tramp around Mt Ngauruhoe on the Tongariro Northern Circuit, the Round the Mountain track provides a longer and more challenging loop of the largest of Tongariro National Park's volcanoes, Mt Ruapehu. It's a remote and difficult hike that briefly follows the Northern Circuit but otherwise ventures far from any of the park's popular areas.

The easiest access point for the track, which can be hiked in either direction, is Whakapapa Village. If heading clockwise from here, it begins by funnelling between Mts Ruapehu and Ngauruhoe (along the Northern Circuit), crossing the windswept and lake-covered Tama Saddle. It departs from the Northern Circuit at Waihohonu Hut, passing Ohinepango Springs, where cold water bubbles up from beneath a lava flow, and sets out into a wild and secluded landscape of desert-like valleys, tussock grasslands, mountain beech forest and glacial river valleys.

Above Ōhakune the track passes 39m-high Waitonga Falls (the highest waterfall in the national park) before climbing 300m up the Ōhakune Mountain Rd and setting out again across the slopes to Lake Surprise – on a still morning, expect perfect reflections of Ruapehu in its surface. Returning to Whakapapa, the track descends through the Whakapapa-iti Valley – if you still have energy, consider detouring up the short Silica Rapids Track, where an aerated, cream-coloured stream emerges from the cliffs, shortly before arriving back in the village.

Taupō & Wairakei

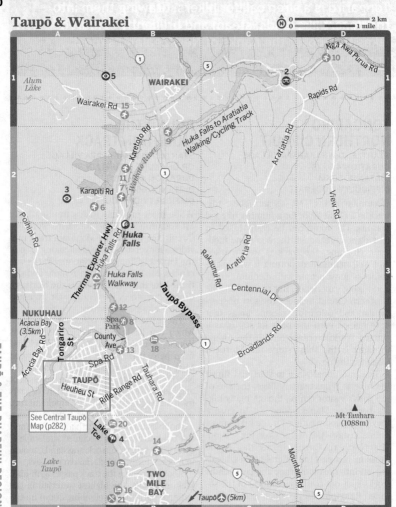

there were reports from ancient Rome and China of unusual red sunsets. In the process, Lake Taupō formed in the volcanic caldera.

Māori legend tells of Ngātoro-i-rangi, a priest who created the lake while searching for a place to settle. Climbing to the top of Mt Tauhara, he saw a vast dust bowl. He hurled a totara tree into it and freshwater swelled to form the lake. One of the early Māori, Tia, was the first to explore the region. After he discovered the lake and slept beside it draped in his cloak, it became known as Taupō Nui a Tia (Great Cloak of Tia). Descendants of the original Ngāti Tūwharetoa inhabitants still live in the area today.

Europeans settled here in force during the East Coast Land War (1868–72), when Taupō was a strategic military base. A redoubt was built in 1869 and a garrison of mounted police remained until the defeat of Te Kooti later that year.

In the 20th century, the proliferation of the motorcar saw Taupō grow from a lakeside village of about 750 people to a large resort town, easily accessible from most points on the North Island. Today the population increases considerably at peak holiday times, when New Zealanders and international visitors alike flock to the 'Great Lake'.

Taupō & Wairakei

⊙ Sights

Many of Taupō's sights are outside the town, with a high concentration around Wairakei, 7km to the north. The main attraction in the centre is the lake – and everything you can do in, on and around it.

★Huka Falls   WATERFALL
(Map p280; Huka Falls Rd) The Waikato, NZ's longest river, squeezes through a narrow chasm at Huka Falls, making a dramatic 11m drop into a surging crystal-blue pool at a rate of 220,000L per second. You can see the full force of this torrent that the Māori called Hukanui (Great Body of Spray) from the footbridge straddling the falls, while walking tracks run along both banks.

★Taupō Museum   MUSEUM
(Map p282; ☑07-376 0414; www.taupodc.govt.nz; 4 Story Pl; adult/child $5/free; ⊙10am-4.30pm) This small but fascinating museum has an excellent Māori gallery and quirky displays, which include a 1960s caravan set up as if the occupants have just popped down to the lake. The centrepiece is an elaborately carved Māori meeting house, Te Aroha o Rongoheikume. Historical displays cover trout fishing, volcanic activity and a scale-model diorama of a sawmill tramway.

Māori Rock Carvings   HISTORIC SITE
Accessible only by boat or kayak, these 14m-high carvings were etched into the cliffs near Mine Bay by master carver Matahi Whakataka-Brightwell in the late 1970s. They depict Ngātoro-i-rangi, the Māori navigator who guided the Tūwharetoa and Te Arawa tribes to the Taupō area 1000 years ago.

You can reach the carvings by boat with Sail Barbary (p285) or Ernest Kemp Cruises (p285), or paddle to them with Taupo Kayaking Adventures (p285) or Canoe & Kayak (p285).

Craters of the Moon   NATURAL FEATURE
(Map p280; ☑027 6564 684; www.cratersof themoon.co.nz; Karapiti Rd; adult/child $8/4; ⊙8.30am-6pm Oct-Mar, to 5pm Apr-Sep) This geothermal area sprang to life when hydro-electric tinkering around the power station in 1958 caused water levels to fall. The pressure shifted, creating new steam vents and bubbling mud pools. The gentle 2.7km walk takes about 45 minutes and loops through a mass of steaming features. A side track constructed in late 2019 adds a five-minute climb to perhaps the most impressive crater, which hisses like a factory boiler.

Aratiatia Rapids   WATERFALL
(Map p280; Aratiatia Rd) Two kilometres off SH5, this gorge was a spectacular part of the Waikato River until a hydroelectric dam was plonked across the waterway, shutting off the flow. But the floodgates still open at 10am, noon and 2pm (plus 4pm from October to March), releasing 80,000L of water a second for 15 minutes. You can see the water surge through the dam from two good vantage points atop the cliffs.

Wairakei Natural
Thermal Valley   NATURAL FEATURE
(Map p280; ☑07-374 8004; www.wairakeitourist park.co.nz; off SH1; adult/child $10/5; ⊙9am-1hr before sunset) This thermal walk (1.8km) on a secluded property explores the steaming banks of the Wairakei Stream and the deep

TAUPŌ & THE RUAPEHU REGION TAUPŌ

Central Taupō

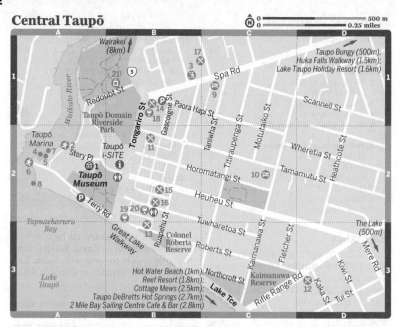

Central Taupō

pit of the Witches Cauldron. Kids will get a kick out of the thermal laser guns for testing the temperature of the ground and steam, which can turn the walk into something of a hot treasure hunt.

The property also has a peaceful campsite (sites $16 to $24, cabins $75 to $95, and cottages from $155), shared with peacocks and a host of farm animals, and a cafe.

🏃 Activities

If you're wanting more than one adrenaline buzz in Taupō, look out for deals that combine several activities for a reduced price. Some operators offer backpacker discounts.

For sizeable discounts on activities, search the deals on www.bookme.co.nz or www.grabone.co.nz/rotorua-taupo.

Adventure & Adrenaline

★ **Taupo Bungy**   BUNGY JUMPING
(Map p280; ☎0800 888 408; www.taupobungy. co.nz; 202 Spa Rd; solo/tandem jump $180/360; ⊙9.30am-5pm Oct-Mar, to 4pm Apr-Sep) On a cliff high above the Waikato River, this picturesque bungy site is the North Island's

most popular. The courageous throw themselves off the edge of a cantilever platform, jutting 34m out over the cliff, for a heart-stopping 47m plunge and NZ's highest water-touch bungy. The 11m Cliffhanger swing is just as terrifying (solo/tandem swing $155/310).

In October 2019, Taupo Bungy was added to the AJ Hackett Bungy stable.

Skydive Taupo ⠀⠀⠀⠀⠀⠀⠀⠀⠀⠀SKYDIVING
(☑07-378 4662, 0800 586 766; www.skydive-taupo.co.nz; 1465 Anzac Memorial Dr; 12,000ft/15,000ft/18,500ft jump from $279/359/499) Head for the skies in the pink plane and then quickly jump out of it, with three altitude options – the 18,500ft (approximately 5600m) skydive includes 75 seconds of free-fall. There's a free limo service from Taupō, and they'll even lay out a 'Will you marry me' sign if you're truly falling for someone.

Hukafalls Jet ⠀⠀⠀⠀⠀⠀⠀ADVENTURE SPORTS
(Map p280; ☑0800 485 253, 07-374 8572; www.hukafallsjet.com; 200 Karetoto Rd; adult/child $139/95; ⊙8.30am-5pm Oct-Nov & Feb-Apr, to 5.30pm Dec & Jan, 9am-4pm May-Sep) This 30-minute thrill ride takes you up the river to the spray-filled foot of the Huka Falls and down to the Aratiatia Dam, all the while dodging daringly and doing acrobatic 360-degree turns. Prices include shuttle transport from Taupō.

Rapids Jet ⠀⠀⠀⠀⠀⠀⠀⠀ADVENTURE SPORTS
(Map p280; ☑0800 727 437, 07-374 8066; www.rapidsjet.com; Nga Awa Purua Rd; adult/child $115/65; ⊙9am-5pm Oct-Mar, 10am-4pm Apr-Sep) This sensational 35-minute jet-boat ride shoots along the lower Aratiatia Rapids (p281) – rivalling trips to Huka Falls for thrills (and price!). The office and departures are 3km past the Aratiatia lookouts. Go down Rapids Rd and turn right into Nga Awa Purua Rd.

Big Sky Parasail ⠀⠀⠀⠀⠀ADVENTURE SPORTS
(Map p282; ☑0800 724 4759; www.bigskyparasail.co.nz; berth 20, Taupō Marina, Redoubt St; tandem/solo $99/119; ⊙10am-5pm mid-Oct–Apr) Lofty 12-minute parasailing flights from the lakefront. Choose from 1000ft or 500ft, with the option of a free-fall descent when the boat stops. Flights depart on the hour. Early-bird (before 11am) solo/tandem special $89/109.

Rock 'n Ropes ⠀⠀⠀⠀⠀⠀⠀⠀⠀OUTDOORS
(Map p280; ☑0800 244 508; www.rocknropes.com; 67 Karetoto Rd; ⊙10am-3pm) With high-wire bridges, trapeze, a high log and a giant swing,

this daredevil aerial course ($100) is all fear and fun in the same basket. Feeling extra brave? Try the Rock Drop ($40), a five-storey free-fall plunge into a giant air bag.

Walking & Cycling

Grab trail maps and hire bikes from **FourB** (Map p280; ☑07-374 8154, 021 0236 3439; www.fourb.nz; 413 Huka Falls Rd; hire hardtail 1hr/full day $25/60, dual suspension 2hr/day $60/105, ebike 2hr/day $65/115; ⊙9am-5pm Oct-Mar, 10am-4pm Apr-Sep), handily located at the base of the Craters MTB Park. The i-SITE (p288) also stocks the *10 Great Rides* map (and a *10 Great Lake Walks* brochure). You'll need to become a temporary member of **Bike Taupō** (www.biketaupo.org.nz; $10 for one week) to ride on local tracks. You can buy the membership at FourB and other bike shops.

The **Huka Trails** (www.lovetaupo.com/en/operators/huka-trails), connecting Taupō to Huka Falls, Aratiatia Rapids and Wairakei, have become a hugely popular bike ride, though note that some sections are a bit more technical than many expect.

Thanks now to Graffiato (p285), Taupō's town centre is now decorated with around 80 murals. The iSITE stocks a dedicated walking map that will lead you into otherwise hidden laneways to view 30 of the murals.

Huka Falls Walkway ⠀⠀⠀⠀⠀⠀⠀WALKING
(Map p280; County Ave) Starting from the Spa Park car park at the end of County Ave (off Spa Rd), this scenic, easy walk is just over 3km one way to reach Huka Falls, following the east bank of the Waikato River. Continuing on from the falls is the 7km **Huka Falls to Aratiatia Rapids walking track** (another two hours).

If walking the latter, you'll need to do so as an out-and-back walk (unless you have two vehicles). We'd recommend beginning at Aratiatia Rapids (p281), so you can time your start to coincide with a water release, turning around at Huka Falls for a 14km return walk.

Craters MTB Park ⠀⠀⠀⠀⠀MOUNTAIN BIKING
(Map p280; www.biketaupo.org.nz; Karapiti Rd; ⊙24hr) FREE With 55km of trails in the Wairakei Forest, Craters has good intermediate riding, a few trails for beginners and three hang-onto-your-handlebars expert runs. A lot of the park's challenges come from the narrowness of the tracks and the sense of exposure, rather than technical wizardry.

ORAKEI KORAKO

Sitting isolated from the other geothermal fields, and thus drawing fewer visitors, Orakei Korako (07-378 3131; www.orakeikorako.co.nz; 494 Orakei Korako Rd; adult/child $39/15; 8am-4.30pm Oct-Mar, to 4pm Apr-Sep) is (since the destruction of the Pink and White Terraces, at least) arguably the most spectacular thermal area left in New Zealand, with active geysers, stunning coloured terraces and one of only two geothermal caves in the world (the other is in Italy). It's also the only one at which you might be looking over waterskiers as you wander, with Lake Ohakuri pooled below the terraces.

A 2.5km walking track (allow 1½ hours) follows stairs and boardwalks around the silica terraces, which ascend like colourful stairs, and passes geysers and Ruatapu Cave. This impressive natural cave has a jade-green pool, thought to have been used as a mirror by Māori women when preparing for rituals (Orakei Korako means 'the Place of Adorning').

Entry includes the boat ride across the lake from the visitor centre. MudCake Cafe, located inside the visitor centre, serves only the likes of sandwiches and pies, but has a lovely terrace overlooking Lake Ohakuri.

There's nowhere to stay in the area, with most travellers visiting en route between Rotorua and Taupō. From Taupō, take SH1 towards Hamilton for 22km, and then travel for 14km from the signposted turn-off. It's around 65km from Rotorua; the turn-off is on SH5 at Mihi Bridge. There's no public transport, but you can arrive with a splash along the Waikato River and beneath the 50m-high cliffs of Tutukau Gorge with New Zealand River Jet (0800 748 375, 07-333 7111; www.riverjet.co.nz; Mihi Bridge, SH5; adult/child $189/99, incl entry to Orakei Korako), which departs from beside Mihi Bridge, 34km north of Taupō on SH5.

Great Lake Trails MOUNTAIN BIKING
(www.lovetaupo.com/en/operators/great-lake-trail) A purpose-built 71km track from Waihaha to Whakaipo Bay along the remote north-western shores of Lake Taupō. It's divided into three distinct stages – the 22km W2K section between Kinloch and Whakaipo has splendid views across the lake to Tongariro National Park – which can all be connected by water-taxi pickups from Bay2Bay Water Taxi (021 333 493; www.bay2bay.nz; per person $50-70).

Hot Springs

★ Spa Thermal
Park Hot Spring HOT SPRINGS
(Map p280; County Ave) FREE The hot thermal waters of the Otumuheke Stream meet the bracing Waikato River at this pleasant spot, redeveloped in 2018, creating a free spa bath with natural nooks. Take care: people have drowned trying to cool off in the fast-moving river. From the car park at the end of County Ave, it's an easy 10-minute walk along the Huka Falls Walkway (p283) to the stream.

Wairakei Terraces
& Thermal Health Spa HOT SPRINGS
(Map p280; 07-378 0913; www.wairakeiterraces. co.nz; Wairakei Rd; pools $25, thermal walk adult/ child $15/7.50, massage from $85; 8.30am-9pm Oct-Mar, to 8.30pm Apr-Sep, pools close 7pm Thu) Three large pools of mineral-laden waters from the Wairakei geothermal steam field are the main drawcard here. The therapeutic pools (open to those 14 years and older) are like extensions to the artificial silica terraces that step down through the valley above. Along the thermal walk, a geyser churns out a thunderstorm of steam, but otherwise it's probably the least interesting of the area's geothermal paths.

Taupo DeBretts Hot Springs HOT SPRINGS
(Map p280; 07-378 8559; www.taupodebretts. co.nz; 76 Napier–Taupō Rd; adult/child $23/12; 8.30am-9.30pm;) A variety of therapeutic mineral-rich indoor and outdoor thermal pools and freshwater chlorinated pools. The kids will love the three slides and the interactive 'Warm Water Playground', while adults can enjoy a great selection of treatments, massages and private pools, but may be happier at quieter springs since these ones can feel like a water park with warmth.

Watersports

Lake Taupō is famously chilly, but in several places – such as Hot Water Beach (Map p280; Lake Tce) FREE, immediately south of the town centre – there are thermal springs just below the surface. You can swim right in front of the town, but grassy Acacia Bay,

5km west, is a particularly pleasant spot. Even better and quieter is Whakaipo Bay, an undeveloped waterfront reserve perfect for a lazy day, another 7km further on.

Canoe & Kayak
CANOEING, KAYAKING

(Map p282; ☑07-378 1003; www.canoeandkayak. co.nz; 54 Spa Rd; ☉9am-5pm Mon-Fri, 10am-2pm Sat) Guided paddles, including a two-hour trip on the Waikato River ($69) and a half-day trip to the Māori rock carvings ($115). Also hires out stand-up paddle boards (half/full day $49/99).

Taupo Kayaking Adventures
KAYAKING

(☑0274 801 231; www.tka.co.nz; 2/876 Acacia Bay Rd, Acacia Bay; tours from adult/child $80/65, 1/2hr hire $20/30) Runs guided kayaking trips from its base in Acacia Bay to the Māori rock carvings, with the return trip taking around four hours ($110, including refreshments). A range of other trips and walk/bike combos also available, as well as a hire service so you can paddle yourself to the carvings ($55).

Lake Fun Taupō
BOATING

(Map p282; ☑07-378 9794, 0800 876 882; www. lakefuntaupo.co.nz; Taupō Marina, Ferry Rd; ☉flexible according to bookings) Located at the tip of the marina, this outfit hires out single/double kayaks ($39/49 per hour), stand-up paddle boards ($35 per hour), a variety of self-drive motor boats (from $125 per hour) and jet skis ($120 per 30 minutes).

Fishing

Taupo Troutcatcher
FISHING

(Map p282; ☑0800 876 882; www.taupotrout catcher.co.nz; Taupō Marina, Ferry Rd; boat per hour from $125) More than two decades of fishing experience on Lake Taupō adds up to a good choice of operator if you're looking to catch your dinner. Three boats, accommodating between five and 10 people, are available. Bookings can be made at Lake Fun Taupō.

🍳 Tours

★ Sail Barbary
BOATING

(Map p282; ☑07-378 5879; www.sailbarbary.com; berths 9 & 10, Taupō Marina, Redoubt St; adult/child day cruises $49/29, evening $54/54; ☉10.30am, 2pm & 5pm) 🛥 Sail to the Māori rock carvings in old-time style with new-time propulsion – a classic 1926 yacht, powered by an emission-free electric motor. The 2½-hour cruises include tea and coffee, and you're welcome to bring your own food and alcohol.

Ernest Kemp Cruises
BOATING

(Map p282; ☑07-378 3444; www.ernestkemp. co.nz; berth 2, Taupō Marina, Redoubt St; adult/child $45/15; ☉10.30am & 2pm; 🖐) Board the *Ernest Kemp* replica steamboat for a two-hour cruise to view the Māori rock carvings, Hot Water Beach, the lakefront and Acacia Bay. There's lively commentary, and a swim stop if conditions allow. From October to April, a 5pm cocktail cruise (adult/child $46/25) includes pizza, wine and beer.

Taupo's Floatplane
SCENIC FLIGHTS

(Map p282; ☑07-378 7500; www.tauposfloat plane.co.nz; Taupō Marina, Ferry Rd; flights $109-870) The floatplane offers a variety of flights, including quick zips over the lake and longer forays over Orakei Korako, Mt Ruapehu or Whakaari (White Island).

Fish Cruise Taupo
CRUISE

(Map p282; ☑07-378 3444; www.fishcruisetaupo. co.nz; Taupō Marina, 65 Redoubt St; ☉9am-5pm Oct-Mar, 9.30am-3pm Apr-Sep) Representing a collective of 11 local tour and fishing boats, this office can book you on a selection of lake cruises right outside its doors, or hook you up with fishing charters.

⭐ Festivals & Events

Graffiato Street Art Festival
ART

(www.taupostreetart.com; ☉Oct) **FREE** Watch local and international street artists create large-scale works in the streets of Taupō over three colourful days.

Lake Taupō Cycle Challenge
SPORTS

(www.cyclechallenge.com; ☉Nov) One of NZ's biggest annual cycling events, the 160km Lake Taupō Cycle Challenge sees around 6000 people pedalling around the lake on the last Saturday in November.

🛏 Sleeping

Taupō has plenty of accommodation, all of which is in hot demand during late December and January and during major sporting events (book ahead). A string of largely interchangeable motels wraps along the lakeshore south of the town centre, while thrifty campers have the option of Hipapatua (Map p280; Huka Falls Rd) **FREE**, a scruffy spot beside the Waikato River that looks like little more than a car park with a fringe of grass and a couple of portaloos. You camp here to save money, and that's it.

Finlay Jacks
HOSTEL $

(Map p282; ✆07-378 9292; www.finlayjacks. co.nz; 20 Taniwha St; dm/s/d/f from $21/ 40/68/109; ⊛) Our pick of Taupō's hostels, homely Finlay Jacks has turned an age-ing motel into a colourful hub. The 12-bed dorms feel spacious, with bunks separated into distinct, connected rooms of eight and four. Private rooms with en suites and Net-flix have supercomfy beds, and hammocks and beanbags are sprinkled around the cen-tral lawn. Two pod-style rooms were added in 2019.

Haka Lodge
HOSTEL $

(Map p282; ✆07-377 0068; www.hakalodges.com; 56 Kaimanawa St; dm $29-37, d with/without bath-room from $93/72, apt $156; ⊛) Haka Lodge has a fantastic community feel from the moment you walk in. We love the custom wooden dorm bunks with privacy curtains and built-in storage, and the 2nd-storey barbecue deck beside the sunny, convivial kitchen. Check out the recipe for pikelets (thin crumpets) on the kitchen wall. There's a comfortable lounge, a volleyball court and a hot tub outside.

★Waitahanui Lodge
MOTEL $$

(✆07-378 7183, 0800 104 321; www.waitahanui lodge.co.nz; 116 SH1, Waitahanui; d $99-209; ⊛) Ten kilometres south of Taupō, these five 1920s-style beach shacks are beautifully modern inside and ideally positioned for swimming, fishing and superb sunsets. Pick of the bunch are the two absolute-lakefront units (rooms 3 and 4), but all have lake ac-cess, sociable communal areas and free use of rowboats, SUPs and kayaks. All units have kitchenettes, or you can fire up the shared barbecues.

★The Lake
MOTEL $$

(Map p280; ✆07-378 4222, 021 951 808; www. thelakemotel.co.nz; 63 Mere Rd; studios/units $135/165; @⊛) Step onto the set of *Mad Men* at this retro-fitted boutique motel crammed with furniture from the era's sig-nature designers. There are four one-bed-room units sleeping between two and four people, and two studios (maximum two peo-ple). Each one is individually styled, but all fit the theme with funky clock radios, shaggy cushions and paintings of well-known mu-sos by the owners' son.

Reef Resort
RESORT $$

(Map p280; ✆0800 733 378, 07-378 5115; www. reefresort.co.nz; 219 Lake Tce; studios/ste from $150/170; ⊛🏊) Reef Resort stands out among Taupō's waterfront complexes for its classy, well-priced studios and one-bedroom suites (plus a two-bedroom and a three-bedroom apartment), bookending an appealing pool patio complete with thermal spa pool. It's worth shelling out a little extra for lake views. Cruiser bikes available to hire for $5 per hour.

Cottage Mews
MOTEL $$

(Map p280; ✆07-378 3004, 0800 555 586; www.cot tagemews.co.nz; 311 Lake Tce, Two Mile Bay; d $145-185, cottages $190; ❄⊛) Charm isn't typically high among the qualities of a motel, but this ranch-like block, festooned with hanging flow-ers, manages to seem almost rustic. It's cute without straying into twee, has direct lake ac-cess, and most units have a spa bath. Grab a Lake End Apartment for the Riviera feel.

Lake Taupo Holiday Resort
HOLIDAY PARK $$

(Map p280; ✆07-378 6860, 0800 332 121; www. laketauporesort.co.nz; 41 Centennial Dr; sites/cab-ins/units from $38/124/182; ❄⊛🏊) This slick 8-hectare park, at the edge of town, has

---

MĀORI NZ: TAUPŌ & THE RUAPEHU REGION

The North Island's central region is home to a group of mountains that feature in several Māori legends of lust and betrayal that end with mountains fleeing to other parts of the island – just like in Mt Taranaki's sad tale (p253).

Long after that was over, the *tohunga* (priest) Ngātoro-i-rangi, fresh off the boat from Hawaiki, explored this region and named the mountains that remained. The most sacred was Tongariro because it had at least 12 volcanic cones and was seen as the leader of all the other mountains.

The major *iwi* (tribe) of the region is Ngāti Tūwharetoa (www.tuwharetoa.co.nz), one of the few *iwi* in New Zealand that has retained an undisputed *ariki* (high chief). The current *ariki* is Sir Tumu Te Heuheu Tukino VIII, whose great-great-grandfather, Horonuku Te Heuheu Tukino IV (a descendant of Ngātoro-i-rangi), gifted the mountains of Tongariro to NZ in 1887.

To discover the stories of local Māori and their ancestors, visit Taupō Museum (p281) or the Māori rock carvings (p281) on the cliff faces at Mine Bay.

---

all mod cons, including a huge thermally heated lagoon swimming pool with a movie screen and swim-up bar, a jumping pillow, pétanque, basketball, volleyball and tennis courts, and an on-site shop. Manicured campsites, swish accommodation options and spotless facilities help make it a contender for camp of the year.

★ **Acacia Cliffs Lodge**   B&B $$$
(☑ 021 821 338, 07-378 1551; www.acaciacliffslodge.co.nz; 133 Mapara Rd, Acacia Bay; d $650-750; ☺ Oct-Apr; @ ☏) ☝ Three of the contemporarily and artfully designed suites at this luxurious B&B, high above Acacia Bay, have the best bed views in Taupō – you'll probably be tempted to sleep with the curtains open – while the fourth has a curvy bath and serene garden view. Gourmet breakfasts are served at a heated table, and predinner drinks, canapés and Taupō Airport transfer are included.

Serenity on Wakeman   B&B $$$
(☑ 027 454 6518; www.tauposerenity.co.nz; 57 Wakeman Rd, Acacia Bay; r $340-450; ✳ ☏) You'd stay at this B&B for the view from the breakfast deck alone, and the upstairs suite, with its private balcony (and king bed and double spa bath), is its equal. There are only two rooms (technically, the third is reserved for groups), so book ahead. Luxurious and peaceful.

✖ Eating

Pauly's Diner   BURGERS $
(Map p282; ☑ 07-378 4315; 3 Paora Hapi St; burgers $10-14; ☺ 11.30am-8.30pm Wed-Sun) Two brothers from Auckland set up this popular burger joint in an old fish and chipper, and it seems they've got the formula just right (selling out isn't uncommon) – good honest burgers (no bun-less options, no gluten-free) of the sort that still believe in mustard and good pickles. Inside it only seats nine, plus a few more at the outside picnic tables.

★ **Storehouse**   CAFE $$
(Map p282; ☑ 07-378 8820; www.storehousetaupo.co.nz; 14 Runanga St; mains $8-26; ☺ 7am-4pm Mon-Fri, 8am-4pm Sat, to 3pm Sun) Taupō's coolest cafe is just outside the town centre, filling an old plumbing store over two warren-like levels. Indoor plants drape over warehouse beams downstairs, and a couple of old Chinese bikes hang from the walls. The fare is mighty fine, and breakfast dishes aren't afraid to mix genres – take the peanut-butter porridge and fried-chicken waffles, for example...

★ **Replete Cafe & Store**   CAFE $$
(Map p282; ☑ 07-377 3011; www.replete.co.nz; 45 Heuheu St; mains $14-20; ☺ 8am-5pm Mon-Fri, to 4pm Sat & Sun; ☏) Under the same ownership since opening in 1993, this fabulous spot is one-half cafe and one-half shop selling designer kitchenware, ceramics and souvenirs. The cafe cabinet is as artistic as the neighbouring galleries, while lunch has an Asian flair (Japanese bolognese or kumara and cashew curry, anyone?).

Cafe Baku   CAFE $$
(Map p282; ☑ 07-378 6715; www.facebook.com/CafeBakuTaupo; 42 Roberts St; breakfast $10-22, lunch $13-25; ☺ 6am-4pm; ☑ ★) You know you're onto a good thing when the cabinet items – ham, cheese and asparagus vol-auvents, keto rolls, corn fritters piled high, bacon scrolls – look even more inviting than the menu. And the view is better still, straight across the lake to the volcanoes. Lunch runs the gamut from harissa squid to chicken schnitzel.

The takeaway packs of dehydrated locusts and scorpions on the counter could be an intriguing post-breakfast nibble.

Bistro   MODERN NZ $$
(Map p282; ☑ 07-377 3111; www.thebistro.co.nz; 17 Tamamutu St; mains $29-39; ☺ 5pm-late) Bistro is in danger of underselling itself with its 'simple but nice' strapline, given its ability to turn local and seasonal produce into creations such as grilled scotch fillet with roasted beets and Parmesan-battered cauliflower. Walnut-brown from ceiling to floor, the restaurant has a dark, wine-bar feel and a small but thoughtful beer-and-wine list.

Southern Meat Kitchen   SOUTH AMERICAN $$
(SMK; Map p282; ☑ 07-378 3582; www.smk.co.nz; 40 Tuwharetoa St; mains $24-32; ☺ 4-11pm) Calling all carnivores! SMK slow-cooks beef brisket, pulled pork and shredded chicken on an American wood-fire smoker. It arrives with mac 'n' cheese, slaw and rice. Save room for jalapeño-and-cheddar cornbread, served with addictive honey butter and coriander. There's even a side dish of 'add more meat' ($8). Beer-tasting paddles for $18.

2 Mile Bay Sailing Centre Cafe & Bar   PIZZA $$
(Map p280; ☑ 021 413 345; www.facebook.com/2miletaupo; 331 Lake Tce; pizza $23-30; ☺ 8.30am-10pm) There's nowhere more lakefront than this Two Mile Bay cafe-pizzeria-bar that's as chilled as the lake (and the Bob

Marley tunes). The main dining room juts over the lake, and there are a few tables on the little beach, but our favourite haunts are the beanbags on the grass. The pizza is good and the location is sunny-day perfection.

Also hires out kayaks (per 30 minutes/hour $20/30), stand-up paddle boards ($20/30) and sailing boats ($45/75), and offers sailing lessons (30 minutes $20).

Brantry   MODERN NZ $$$

(Map p282; ☑ 07-378 0484; www.thebrantry.co.nz; 45 Rifle Range Rd; 3-course set menu $65-75; ☺ from 5.30pm) Run by two local sisters and operating out of an unobtrusive 1950s house, the Brantry reigns as arguably the best in the region for well-executed, brilliant-value fine dining. Dinner centres around a three-course set menu, and there's an impressive wine list. Sit in the covered al fresco dining area (blankets provided) or dine in the cellar.

Drinking & Nightlife

★ **Vine Eatery & Bar**   WINE BAR

(Map p282; ☑ 07-378 5704; www.vineeatery.co.nz; 37 Tuwharetoa St; ☺ 11am-midnight) Wineglass chandeliers hang from the sky-high industrial ceiling at this restaurant-cum-wine bar, where you can sit in comfy booths, on raised stools or in leather chairs by the fire. The wine list is global, if predominantly Kiwi, and tapas ($9 to $17) and meaty mains ($36 to $39) assist with the wine consumption. Stepping back out onto workaday Tuwharetoa St feels strangely surreal afterwards.

Crafty Trout Brewing Co   BREWERY

(Map p282; ☑ 07-929 8570; www.craftytrout.co.nz; 133 Tongariro St; ☺ noon-late Wed-Mon; 🔊) The beer has only had to journey up the stairs at this brewery-bar with 14 beers – Hefe weizen, pale ales, a porter – and ciders on tap amid faux-Alpine decor, complete with five cuckoo clocks. Try to nab one of the three balcony tables overhanging Tongariro St and dig into a wood-fired pizza ($14 to $28). Brewery tours run at 1pm (book ahead).

Lakehouse   CRAFT BEER

(Map p282; ☑ 07-377 1545; www.lakehousetaupo. co.nz; 10 Roberts St; ☺ 8am-late) Craft beers in a craftily chosen spot. Nine taps pour a rotating selection of NZ brews, and there's a fridge filled with other hoppy goodness. You can partner your beer with a pizza, burger or stone-grilled steak (mains $22 to $45) and sit outside for fine views of the Tongariro volcanoes. Check the blackboard wall for the rundown of beers.

Shopping

Taupo Market   FOOD, CRAFTS

(Map p282; ☑ 027 306 6167; www.taupomarket. kiwi.nz; Redoubt St; ☺ 9am-1pm Sat) Plenty of food stalls and trucks, local souvenirs, arts and crafts and a scattering of produce are all good reasons to make your first coffee of the day an al fresco espresso at this popular weekend market.

Kura Gallery   ART

(Map p282; ☑ 07-377 4068; www.kura.co.nz; 47a Heuheu St; ☺ 10am-5pm Mon-Fri, to 4pm Sat & Sun) This skinny gallery represents more than 70 artists from around NZ across a multitude of mediums: carving, painting, ceramics, jewellery... Many items are imbued with a Māori or Pasifika influence.

Information

Taupō i-SITE (Map p282; ☑ 07-376 0027; www.lovetaupo.com; 30 Tongariro St; ☺ 8.30am-5pm) Handles bookings for accommodation, transport and activities; dispenses cheerful advice; and stocks DOC and town maps.

Getting There & Away

Taupō Airport (☑ 07-378 7771; www.taupoairport.co.nz; 1105 Anzac Memorial Dr) is 8km south of town. Expect to pay about $27 to $30 for a taxi to the centre of town. **Great Lake Taxis** (☑ 07-377 8990; www.greatlaketaxis.co.nz) also runs an airport shuttle (one/two people $20/30).

Air New Zealand (p277) flies from Auckland to Taupō two to three times daily (50 minutes), and Sounds Air (p277) flies daily between Wellington and Taupō (one hour).

InterCity (p277) and Skip (p277) services stop outside the Taupō i-SITE, where bookings can be made.

Getting Around

Local buses are run by **BUSIT** (☑ 0800 205 305; www.busit.co.nz), including the Taupō North service running as far as Huka Falls ($2, 35 minutes) and Wairakei ($2, 50 minutes), twice daily Monday to Friday.

Taxi companies include **Blue Bubble Taxis** (☑ 07-378 5100; https://bluebubbletaxi.co.nz) and Great Lake Taxis.

There are plenty of shuttle services operating to Tūrangi and Tongariro National Park, including **Tongariro Expeditions** (☑ 07-377 0435, 0800 828 763; www. tongariroexpeditions.com).

Tūrangi

POP 2950

Tūrangi is a fishing spot with a town built around it. Trout is king here – the town backs onto the Tongariro River, one of the holy grails of world trout fishing and a fantastic white-water rafting destination. The town is also just a short hop, ski and tramp to the ski fields and walking tracks of Tongariro National Park.

Tūrangi blossomed when the Tongariro Hydro Power Development was given the go-ahead in the 1960s. Over two years, the population quadrupled, peaking at 6500 people in 1968. SH1 trucks through the middle of Tūrangi, but it barely disturbs the air of a quiet country town.

◉ Sights

Tongariro National Trout Centre   AQUARIUM

(Map p294; ☏07-386 8085; www.troutcentre. com; 257 SH1; adult/child $15/free; ◷10am-3pm) Around 4km south of Tūrangi, this DOC-managed trout centre has a hatchery, an underwater viewing chamber, a museum with polished educational displays, a collection of rods and reels dating as far back as the 1880s, and freshwater aquariums displaying river life. In summer, it operates a creche for the endangered whio (blue duck), where ducklings are raised for a couple of months before being released.

Volcanic Activity Centre   MUSEUM

(Map p289; www.volcanoes.co.nz; i-SITE, 1 Ngawaka Pl; adult/child $12/7; ◷8.30am-4.30pm Nov-May 8am-4pm Jun-Oct) This interactive science museum inside the i-SITE is a little text-heavy but turns theory to reality with an earthquake simulator, a live seismograph computer and footage of the 1995–96 Ruapehu eruptions.

🏃 Activities

Aside from trout fishing, the Tongariro River Trail offers enjoyable walks and cycles from the centre of town. The i-SITE stocks a handy *Tūrangi Short Walks* brochure detailing 17 walks in the area. Good leg-stretchers include Lake Rotopounamu (2½ hours), departing from the south side of Te Ponanga Saddle, 11km west of Tūrangi on SH47; Tree Trunk Gorge (2½ hours), which sets out from the Urchin campsite, 19km south of Tūrangi, off SH1; and the

Tūrangi

Tauranga–Taupō River walk (30 minutes return), which starts at Te Rangiita, 12km north of Tūrangi on SH1, and follows the river to Lake Taupō.

The Tongariro River has some superb Grade III rapids for river rafting, as well as Grade II stretches suitable for beginners in the lower reaches during summer.

TAUPŌ & THE RUAPEHU REGION TŪRANGI

★ **Tongariro River Trail** WALKING, CYCLING

(Map p289) The Tongariro River Trail is a 15km shared-use walking and cycling track starting from town and taking in the National Trout Centre (p289) as it heads upriver to the Red Hut suspension bridge. Walk the loop (four hours) or cycle it (two hours) on easy terrain. Expect to pass anglers thigh-deep in their waders in the river.

Tongariro River Rafting RAFTING

(Map p289; ☑ 07-386 6409, 0800 101 024; www.trr.co.nz; 95 Atirau Rd; ⊙ 9am-5pm) ✦ Test the Tongariro River's white waters with a Grade II family float (adult/child $99/85) or splash straight into its Grade III rapids ($145/129). There's also a full-day trip fishing from a raft ($700) and a special blue duck tour ($179) with the company owner, learning about the endangered bird as you float – part of your payment goes to the Blue Duck Project.

Rafting New Zealand RAFTING

(Map p289; ☑ 07-386 0352, 0800 865 226; www.raftingnewzealand.com; 41 Ngawaka Pl; ⊙ 8am to 4-7pm, tour dependent) The main trips offered by this slick outfit are a four-hour, Grade III trip through 60 rapids on the Tongariro River with an optional cliff jump (adult/child $179/149), and a family float over more relaxed Grade II rapids ($139/119). Twice a year it runs the Grade IV rapids of the dam-released Tongariro Upper Gorge ($149).

🛏 Sleeping

Motuoapa Bay Holiday Park HOLIDAY PARK $

(☑ 07-386 7162; www.motuoapabayholidaypark.co.nz; 2 Motuoapa Esplanade, Motuoapa; sites $20, cabins & units $70-140; ☎) Around 8km north of Tūrangi, this fun holiday park on Lake Taupō's southern shores boasts assorted accommodation, including colourful, stylised VW Kombi vans and quirky boat-shaped wooden cabins (suitable for two to seven people). There are also self-contained motel units; one sleeps up to eight people.

Riverstone Backpackers HOSTEL $

(Map p289; ☑ 07-386 7004; www.riverstonebackpackers.com; 222 Te Rangitautahanga Rd; dm/tw $45/80, d with/without bathroom $98/92; ☎) This homey hostel resides in a refitted house close to the town centre. Along with an enviable kitchen and a huge lounge with leather sofas, a fire and a guitar, it sports a stylish landscaped yard and a large wooden deck with a hammock and fish smoker.

★ **Braxmere** MOTEL $$

(Map p294; ☑ 07-386 6449; www.braxmere.co.nz; 88 Waihi Rd, Tokaanu; units from $180; ☎) Just 8km from Tūrangi on the southern fringes of Lake Taupō, Braxmere is a line of 10 spacious one-bedroom, self-contained units with only a grassy lawn separating them from the lake. All have decks and barbecues, the decor is maritime-chic and there's the bonus of Lakeland House restaurant on site.

Creel Lodge MOTEL $$

(Map p289; ☑ 0800 273 355, 07-386 8081; www.creel.co.nz; 183 Taupahi Rd; ste $140-155; ✳☎) ✦ Set in lush gardens, this heavenly hideaway backs onto a fine stretch of the Tongariro River and is as peaceful as a trout pool. Nineteen spacious, self-contained one- and two-bedroom suites, sleeping two and four people respectively, are named after fishing flies and local mountains. The Tongariro River Trail runs right beside the lodge's private back gate.

Tongariro Lodge LODGE $$$

(Map p294; ☑ 07-386 7946; www.tongarirolodge.co.nz; 83 Grace Rd; chalets from $175, villas from $269-750; ☎) Famed angler Tony Hayes established Tongariro Lodge in 1982 on the Tongariro River three kilometres north of Tūrangi. Across the 9-hectare property are 10 chalets with sunny decks and en suites, plus a dozen two- to four-bedroom villas. The fantastic restaurant is open daily for dinner (mains $34 to $42). Check out the celebrity wall of fame to see who's used the helipad.

With 15 fishing guides on its books, you've found your spot if you've come to catch trout.

🍴 Eating

Several of Tūrangi's best hotels, including Tongariro Lodge and Braxmere – also have good restaurants open to nonguests.

Lakeland House INTERNATIONAL $$

(Map p294; ☑ 07-386 6442; www.braxmere.co.nz/restaurant; 88 Waihi Rd, Tokaanu; mains lunch $19-33, dinner $26-46; ⊙ 10am-3pm & 6pm-late) Destination dining with a view across Lake Taupō and a menu that stays faithful to its favourites: generous pastas, salads, chowder, pan-fried snapper with hollandaise and Cajun tiger prawns, followed by sticky date pudding with maple-and-walnut ice cream. Craft beer from Tuatara Brewing is on tap. Eight kilometres northwest of Tūrangi, just off SH41. Bookings essential.

Cadillac Cafe CAFE **$$**
(Map p289; ☑ 021 163 0508; www.facebook.com/
cadillaccafeturangi; 35 Town Centre; mains $10-22;
⊗ 8.30am-3pm Wed-Mon) Step back in time at
Cadillac, which is decorated with vintage
chairs, posters and an impressive toy collec-
tion from the 1950s and '60s. Classic board
games are available while you wait, and the
menu is suitably diner-style – burgers, hot
dogs, mac 'n' cheese, milkshakes – with staff
in sock-hop skirts. *Happy Days,* indeed.
Lots of outdoor seating (with blankets).

Rust BURGERS **$$**
(Map p289; ☑ 07-386 5947; https://rust-licensed
-gourmet-burger-bar.business.site; 6/56 Town Centre; burgers $16-19; ⊗ 4pm-late Mon & Tue, noon-late
Wed-Sun) This burger bar, so new it hasn't had
time to gather rust, is furnished with high
stools and one soft cowhide couch. It serves
unusual burgers, such as venison and snapper, as well as beef. The wine list is strong,
and there are plenty of cocktails and shots if
you want to take the night up a notch.

Hydro Eatery CAFE **$$**
(Map p289; ☑ 07-386 6612; www.facebook.com/
Hydroeatery; cnr Ohuanga & Pihanga Rds; breakfast
$9-19, lunch $16-21; ⊗ 8am-3pm) Cavernous and
colourful, with local art for sale on the walls,
Hydro is the town's earliest riser if you're
chasing trout. It commands an elevated po-
sition in the town centre, and serves good
coffee and breakfast classics, with burgers,
mussel spaghetti and beetroot bruschetta
for lunch. The best spot is on the outdoor
deck.

ⓘ Information

Tūrangi i-SITE (Map p289; ☑ 0800 288 726,
07-386 8999; www.lovetaupo.com; 1 Ngawaka
Pl; ⊗ 8.30am-4.30pm Nov-May 8am-4pm Jun-
Oct; ☎) A good source of information on Ton-
gariro National Park, Kaimanawa Forest Park,
trout fishing, and snow and road conditions. It
issues DOC hut tickets, ski passes and fishing
licences, and makes bookings for transport,
accommodation and activities.

ABOUT TROUT

Early European settlers who wanted to improve New Zealand's farming, hunting and
fishing opportunities are responsible for the introduction of such ghastly wreckers as
possums and rabbits. But one of their more benign introductions was that of trout –
brown and rainbow – released into NZ rivers in 1887 and 1898 respectively.

Fishing in the Tongariro River was made famous by US author Zane Grey and the Duke
and Duchess of York in the 1920s. Today the trout are prized by sports anglers, who you'll
find thigh-deep in limpid rivers and on the edge of deep green pools. The Tongariro River
alone has more than 120 trout pools between Lake Taupō and Fence Pool at the edge of
the river's winter fishing limit. More than 28,000 legal trout are bagged annually, by both
domestic and international fishing enthusiasts. More contemporary celebrities have also
tried their luck in these North Island waters, including ex-American president Jimmy
Carter, Michael Keaton, Harrison Ford and Liam Neeson – they've all stayed at the exclu-
sive Tongariro Lodge.

Trout fishing is highly regulated, with plenty of rules regarding where and how they can
be fished. Licences are required and can be bought online at www.doc.govt.nz or www.
fishandgame.org.nz. Our advice is to seek out a guide. Most offer flexible trips, at around
$350 for a half-day.

Creel Tackle House & Cafe (Map p289; ☑ 07-386 7929; www.creeltackle.com; 183 Taupahi
Rd; lunch $10-15; ⊗ 8am-5pm Mon-Fri, 7.30am-3.30pm Sat & Sun) Equipment for hire, fishing
tips and the unusual combination of a cafe and a fishing store.

Flyfishtaupo (☑ 027 445 0223; www.flyfishtaupo.com) Guide Brent Pirie offers a range of
fishing excursions, including seniors-focused trips.

Barry Greig's Sporting World (Map p289; ☑ 07-386 6911; www.greigsports.co.nz; 59 Town
Centre; ⊗ 8.30am-5pm) Sells gear and handles bookings for guides and charters.

Sporting Life (Map p289; ☑ 07-386 8996; www.sportinglife-turangi.co.nz; The Mall, Town
Centre; ⊗ 8.30am-5.30pm Mon-Sat, 9.15am-5pm Sun) Sports store laden with fishing para-
phernalia, available to hire. Its website has the latest fishing reports.

Central Plateau Fishing (☑ 027 681 4134; www.cpf.net.nz) Tūrangi-based guide Brett
Cameron.

ⓘ Getting There & Away

InterCity (p277) and Skip (p277) coaches stop outside the Tūrangi i-SITE (p291). **Active Outdoor Adventures** (☑ 027 228 4831; www.activeoutdooradventures.co.nz) and **Turangi Alpine Shuttles** (☑ 027 232 2135, 0508 427 677; www.alpineshuttles.co.nz) operate shuttles for the Tongariro Alpine Crossing; the former provides Māori cultural interpretation and insight along the way.

ⓘ Getting Around

Call **My Waka Your Waka** (☑ 021 146 7654; www.mywakayourwaka.com) to get to any spots the shuttles don't head to. Hardtail mountain bikes can be hired from **Central Plateau Cycles** (☑ 07-386 0186; www.cpcycles.co.nz; 20 Town Centre; 2hr/day $25/60; ☺ 8.30am-5pm Mon-Fri, 9am-1pm Sat).

RUAPEHU REGION

Few places feel so ominously awesome as the Ruapehu region, which is crowned by a line of three volcanoes and provides the North Island's finest skiing and hiking. The Tongariro Alpine Crossing hike is the area's prize offering, glowing with volcanic lakes and dimpled with steaming craters – it's almost universally lauded as the best day walk in the country. While only hikers and skiers get to play on the slopes of the volcanoes, mountain bikers and kayakers will find plenty to enjoy around National Park Village and Ōhakune.

ⓘ Getting There & Away

InterCity (p277) coaches call into Ōhakune, National Park Village and Waiouri. National Park Village and Ōhakune are also stops on the Northern Explorer (p277) train service linking Auckland and Wellington.

Tongariro National Park

Even before you arrive in Tongariro National Park, its three mighty volcanoes – Ruapehu, Ngauruhoe and Tongariro – will have long dominated your views and thoughts. It's possible to get really close to them on the ski fields and along the other-worldly, day-long Tongariro Alpine Crossing and the three- to four-day Tongariro Northern Circuit (p295), one of NZ's Great Walks, as well as on the new Sky Waka (p296) gondola on the slopes of Ruapehu. The national park covers 796 sq km, but most visitors find themselves so awed by the volcanoes that they don't stray far beyond them.

The national park was gifted to the country by local Tūwharetoa Māori more than a century ago. Long before it was granted dual Unesco World Heritage status for its volcanic landscape and deep cultural importance in 1993, the Māori believed that the mountains were strong warriors who fought each other. In the process, this landscape that attracts more than 200,000 visitors each year was created. Visit once and you'll understand why it was worth fighting for.

History

Established in 1887, Tongariro was New Zealand's first national park. The previous year, during the aftermath of the New Zealand Wars, the Native Land Court met to determine the ownership of the land around Tongariro. Ngāti Tūwharetoa chief Horonuku Te Heuheu Tukino IV pleaded passionately for the area to be left intact, mindful of Pākehā (white people) eyeing it up for grazing. 'If our mountains of Tongariro are included in the blocks passed through the court in the ordinary way,' said the chief, "what will become of them? They will be cut up and sold, a piece going to one Pākehā and a piece to another.'

In 1887 chief Horonuku ensured the land's everlasting preservation when he presented the area to the Crown for the purpose of a national park – only the fourth in the world. With incredible vision for a man of his time, the chief realised that Tongariro's value lay in its priceless beauty and heritage, not as another sheep paddock.

Development of the national park was slow, and it was only after the main trunk railroad reached the region in 1909 that visitors arrived in significant numbers. Development mushroomed in the 1950s and 1960s as roads were sealed, tracks cut and more huts built.

🏃 Activities

Hiking

The DOC and i-SITE visitor centres at Whakapapa (p298), Ōhakune (p303) and Tūrangi (p291) have maps and information on walks in the park, as well as current track and weather conditions. Each January, DOC offers an excellent guided-walks programme in and around the park; ask at DOC centres for information or book online.

THE TONGARIRO TRIO

Tongariro's three mighty volcanoes are among the most active on earth, and despite standing in a huddle they are three very distinct mountains.

At 1967m, the park's namesake **Mt Tongariro** (Map p294) is the lowest of the trio, but it is also the peak with the most recent major volcanic activity. In 2012 a crater called Te Maari erupted twice, spitting ash and rocks kilometres into the sky. One rock smashed through the roof of nearby Ketetahi Hut, crushing a bunk bed. The eruption caused a nine-month partial closure of the Tongariro Alpine Crossing, and the hut has been used only as a day shelter since.

In the middle of the chain stands 2287m **Mt Ngauruhoe** (Map p294), with a classic conical shape like Mt Fuji. It is the national park's youngest volcano, thought to have first erupted 2500 years ago. Until 1975 Ngauruhoe erupted at least every nine years, including a 1954 eruption that lasted 11 months and disgorged 6 million cu metres of lava. Its steam vents have temporarily cooled, suggesting that the main vent has become blocked. These days it's most famously known for its starring role as Mt Doom in *Lord of the Rings*.

Mt Ruapehu (Map p294; www.mtruapehu.com) is the giant of the group, rising to 2797m. It's the North Island's highest mountain and the location of NZ's largest ski area. In modern history, it has been the most active of the three volcanoes. One year-long eruption began in March 1945, spreading lava over Crater Lake and sending clouds of ash as far as Wellington. During the heavy ash falls, hundreds of cases of 'Ruapehu throat' were reported. On Christmas Eve 1953, the rim of Crater Lake ruptured and an enormous lahar (volcanic mudflow) swept away everything in its path, including a railway bridge. A crowded train plunged into the river, killing 151 people in one of NZ's worst tragedies (p302). Ruapehu also rumbled in 1969, 1973 and spectacularly in 1995–96. In 2007 a primary school teacher almost died when a rock was propelled through the roof of a hiking shelter, crushing his leg.

If you want to watch for any bubble and boil on the volcanoes, check out the webcams and monitoring at www.geonet.org.nz/volcano.

The safest and most popular time to hike in the national park is December to March, when the tracks are usually clear of snow and the weather is at its most settled. In winter many of the tracks become full alpine adventures, requiring mountaineering experience, an ice axe and crampons. Guided winter walks across the Tongariro Alpine Crossing are available with Adrift Tongariro (p299) and Adventure Outdoors (p299).

The day-long Alpine Crossing and the three- to four-day Tongariro Northern Circuit (p295) are the park's headline hikes, but there are numerous other tracks to choose from. These range from short ambles to excellent day walks such as the Taranaki Falls (p298) and Tama Lakes (p298) tracks, both of which begin from Whakapapa. There are also a number of challenging routes that should only be attempted by the fit, experienced and well equipped, such as the Round the Mountain Track (p296), a remote 66.2km, four- to six-day hike, circuiting Mt Ruapehu.

Scattered around the park's tracks are 10 huts, most of which are $15 per person. However, as the Tongariro Northern Circuit is one of NZ's listed Great Walks, Mangatepopo, Oturere and Waihohonu huts are designated Great Walk huts ($36) during the Great Walks season (mid-October to April). Each hut has gas cookers, heating, cold running water and long-drop toilets, along with communal bunk rooms with mattresses. Campsites are located next to the huts; the $15 fee allows campers to use the hut facilities.

Great Walk hut tickets must be obtained in advance, either online (www.doc.govt.nz), or from the Tongariro National Park Visitor Centre (p298) or other DOC visitors centres nationwide. It pays to book early during the Great Walks season. Outside of the season, the huts become standard huts ($15), the gas cookers are removed, and fees can be paid with Backcountry Hut Passes and tickets.

See Hiking in Tongariro National Park (p278) for maps and further information.

★**Tongariro Alpine Crossing**   HIKING
(Map p294; www.tongarirocrossing.org.nz) This popular route (p278) is acclaimed as NZ's finest one-day walk, with more than 100,000 hikers crossing yearly. It takes six to eight hours to complete the 19.4km walk amid

Tongariro National Park & Around

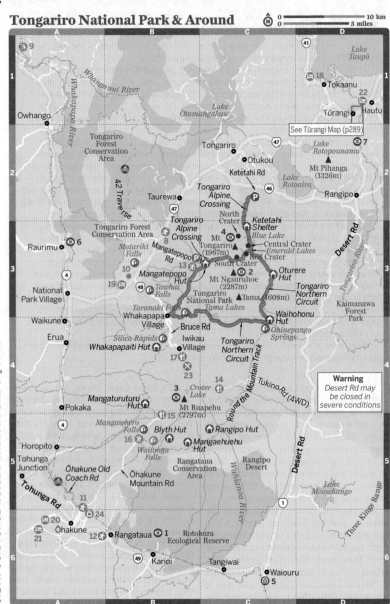

See Tūrangi Map (p289)

Warning
Desert Rd may be closed in severe conditions

steaming vents and springs, stunning rock formations, peculiar moonscape basins, scree slopes and vast views – the photo stop to beat them all is the Emerald Lakes.

This is a fair-weather walk. In poor conditions it is little more than an arduous up-and-down, with only orange-tipped poles to

mark the passing of the day. Strong winds see hikers crawl along the ridge of Red Crater, the high point of the trek, and can blow people off their feet. A sunny day could still be a gusty day, so check in with your nearest information centre or shuttle provider. The most crowded times on the track are the

Tongariro National Park & Around

first nice days after Christmas and Easter, when there can be up to 2000 people strung out between the two road ends.

As the name suggests, this is an alpine crossing, and it needs to be treated with respect. You need a reasonable level of fitness and you should be prepared for all types of weather. Shockingly ill-equipped hikers, wearing ridiculously inappropriate shoes, denim jeans soaked to the skin and no rain jackets, are a legendary sight on this route. As well as proper gear, you'll need to carry enough water and snacks for a whole day. If you prefer to undertake a guided walk, contact Adrift Tongariro (p299) or Adventure Outdoors (p299).The Crossing starts at Mangatepopo Rd car park, off SH47, and finishes at Ketetahi Rd, off SH46. A four-hour parking restriction applies at the Mangatepopo Rd car park, making it pretty much compulsory to organise shuttle transport (p297).

Section	Estimated Walk Time (Summer)
Mangatepopo Rd end to Mangatepopo Hut	15min
Mangatepopo Hut to South Crater	1½-2hr
South Crater to Emerald Lakes	1-1½hr
Emerald Lakes to Ketetahi Shelter	1½hr
Ketetahi Shelter to road end	1½hr

Tongariro Northern Circuit HIKING
(www.doc.govt.nz/tongarironortherncircuit; huts/campsites in Great Walks season $36/15, outside season $15/5) Circumnavigating Mt Ngauruhoe, this 43km Great Walk (p279) typically takes four days from Whakapapa Village or Mangatepopo Rd, both regularly serviced by shuttles. Although there's some moderate climbing, it's well marked and maintained, making it achievable for people of medium fitness. The weather can change suddenly, so be prepared and check in with the visitor centre (p298) before you go.

The Northern Circuit is effectively a parade of volcanic features: craters such as the South Crater, Central Crater and Red Crater; brilliantly colourful lakes, including the Emerald Lakes, Blue Lake and the Upper and Lower Tama Lakes; the cold Soda Springs; and New Zealand's only so-called desert, studded with lava bombs on the eastern side of the volcanoes.

In the Great Walks season (late October through April) huts and campsites must be booked in advance; outside of the season, they're first come, first served.

The usual place to start and finish the hike is Ngauruhoe Pl in Whakapapa Village, just below the site of the park's visitor centre, though many hikers begin at Mangatepopo Rd to ensure they have good weather for the hike's most dramatic day along the Tongariro Alpine Crossing (p293). This reduces it to a three-day hike, with stays at Oturere and Waihohonu Huts, ending at Whakapapa Village.

TAUPŌ & THE RUAPEHU REGION TONGARIRO NATIONAL PARK

Section	Estimated Walk Time (Summer)
Whakapapa Village to Mangatepopo Hut	3–5hr
Mangatepopo Hut to Oturere Hut	5–6hr
Oturere Hut to Waihohonu Hut	3hr
Waihohonu Hut to Whakapapa Village	5½–6hr

Round the Mountain Track   HIKING
(☑ 07-892 3729; www.doc.govt.nz) This off-the-beaten-track hike (p279) is a quieter alternative to the Tongariro Northern Circuit, but it's far tougher, with some potentially tricky river crossings, and isn't recommended for beginners or the unprepared. Looping around Mt Ruapehu, the trail takes in diverse country from glacial rivers to tussocky moors and ominous volcano views. The 66.2km track is usually hiked in four to six days.

You can access Round the Mountain Track from Whakapapa Village, SH1 near Waihohonu Hut, Ōhakune Mountain Rd or near Whakapapaiti Hut. Most hikers start at Whakapapa Village and return there to finish the loop.

The track is safest from December to March when there is little or no snow, and less chance of avalanches. At other times of year, navigation is made difficult by snow covering the track, and full alpine gear (ice axe, crampons and specialised clothing) is a requirement. To attempt the track you should prepare thoroughly. Take sufficiently detailed maps, check on the latest conditions, and carry clothing for all conditions and generous food supplies. Leave your plans and intended return date with a responsible person, and check in when you get back.

This track is served by Waihohonu, Rangipo, Mangaehuehu, Mangaturuturu and Whakapapaiti Huts, and a side trip can be made to Blyth Hut. Note that during the Great Walks season (late October through April), bookings are required for Waihohonu Hut.

Skiing

The linked Whakapapa and Turoa ski fields straddle Mt Ruapehu and are New Zealand's two largest ski areas. Each offers similar skiing at an analogous altitude (highest lift points around 2300m), with areas to suit every level of experience – from beginner slopes to black-diamond runs for the pros. The same lift pass covers both ski areas.

The ski season generally runs from June until near the end of October.

Whakapapa Ski Area   SKIING
(Map p294; ☑ 07-892 4000; www.mtruapehu. com/whakapapa; Bruce Rd; daily lift pass adult/child $149/89) Whakapapa Ski Area, on the northwestern slopes of Mt Ruapehu, is NZ's largest ski area, spread across 550 hectares with a maximum altitude of 2320m. The self-contained Happy Valley learners' area is good for beginners. The only accommodation is in private ski-club lodges, so most visitors stay at Whakapapa or National Park Village.

Whakapapa has night skiing on Fridays and Saturdays and every night through NZ's July school holidays.

Turoa Ski Area   SKIING
(Map p294; ☑ 06-385 8456; www.mtruapehu. com/turoa; Ōhakune Mountain Rd; daily lift pass adult/child $149/89) Turoa Ski Area on the southwestern slopes of Mt Ruapehu has Australasia's longest vertical descent (722m!) and NZ's highest lift, the High Noon Express (2322m). Beginners are well catered for, with gear hire, ski school, two good learner areas and nice easy runs. The town of Ōhakune, around 17km from Turoa, is the most happening hub for après-ski frivolity.

Tukino Ski Area   SNOW SPORTS
(Map p294; ☑ 06-387 6294, 0800 885 466; www. tukino.org; Tukino Access Rd; day pass adult/child $70/35) Club-operated Tukino is on Mt Ruapehu's east side, 46km from Tūrangi and 35km from Waiouru. It's quite remote, 14km down a 4WD-only road from SH1. If you don't have a 4WD, call ahead to book a shuttle from the 2WD car park ($20), 7km off SH1. It offers 170 hectares of uncrowded, backcountry runs, mostly beginner and intermediate, with ski lessons available.

Other Activities

When the conditions are favourable, experienced rock climbers with their own gear can find spots near Mangatepopo Valley and Whakapapa Gorge.

★ **Sky Waka**   CABLE CAR
(☑ 07-892 4000; www.mtruapehu.com/sky-waka; Whakapapa Ski Area, Bruce Rd; adult/child $49/29; ⊙ 9am-4pm) New Zealand's longest gondola ride (1.8km) opened in July 2019. It ascends Mt Ruapehu's slopes from Whakapapa's ski village to Knoll Ridge Chalet (2020m), where a trio of restaurants huddles beneath a striking view of a pinnacle-topped ridge. The

gondola has leather seating and great views of Mt Ngauruhoe on the lower section.

Operating hours are weather dependent, and extended during dinner times at Knoll Ridge Chalet.

Mountain Air SCENIC FLIGHTS
(Map p294; ☑ 0800 922 812; www.mountainair.co.nz; SH47; flights 15/25/35min $125/205/255; ⊙ 8am-7pm) Located by the Whakapapa turn-off on SH47, Mountain Air offers 15-minute flights over the vibrant Emerald Lakes, with longer jaunts taking you over the summits of Mt Ngauruhoe and Mt Ruapehu. Tūrangi and Taupō departures also available.

✖ Eating

Knoll Ridge Chalet INTERNATIONAL $$$
(Map p294; ☑ 07-892 4000; www.mtruapehu.com/sky-waka#knoll-ridge-chalet; Pinnacles breakfast adult/child $25/17.50, lunch $38/27, dinner $59/39; ⊙ 9am-4pm, dinner from 5.30pm) Perched at the top of the Sky Waka gondola is this gathering of three eateries – NZ's highest restaurants – including the food-truck-style **Four Peaks Alley** and the cafeteria-style **Pātaka**. The real treat is **Pinnacles**, which has quality buffet dining with a focus on beef, lamb and vegetables sourced from around the mountains, set against huge windows with an in-your-face view of the eponymous Pinnacle Ridge.

❶ Getting There & Away

InterCity (p277) buses and the *Northern Explorer* train run by KiwiRail Scenic (p277) pass through National Park Village and Ōhakune.

The main gateway into Tongariro National Park is Whakapapa Village, which is also the base for Whakapapa Ski Area on SH48. The park is also bounded by roads: SH1 (called the Desert Rd) to the east, SH4 to the west, SH46 and SH47 to the north and SH49 to the south. Ōhakune Mountain Rd leads up to the Turoa Ski Area from Ōhakune.

The Desert Rd is regularly closed when the weather is bad; detours will be in force. Likewise, Ōhakune Mountain Rd and SH48 are subject to closures, and access beyond certain points may be restricted to 4WDs or cars with snow chains. Ask your hotel or call the national park visitor centre (p298) if you're uncertain.

SHUTTLE TRANSPORT

The following shuttle services operate from the towns around the mountains, predominantly taking hikers to and from the Tongariro Alpine Crossing:

➡ Dempsey Buses (p303) from Ōhakune and Whakapapa Village

➡ Tongariro Crossing Shuttles (p300) from National Park Village

➡ Active Outdoor Adventures (p292) and Tūrangi Alpine Shuttles (p292) from Tūrangi

➡ Tongariro Expeditions (p288) from Taupō

Whakapapa Village

POP 100 (SUMMER), 300 (WINTER)

Located within the bounds of Tongariro National Park on the lower slopes of Mt Ruapehu, Whakapapa Village (pronounced 'fa-ka-pa-pa'; altitude 1140m) is the gateway to the national park, home to its visitor centre and the starting point for numerous walking tracks. It's dominated by one of NZ's most visually striking historic hotels, the Chateau Tongariro.

Whakapapa Village has limited accommodation and during ski season, Christmas/New Year and around Easter, prices skyrocket. Nearby options can be found in National Park Village and Ōhakune. The latter feels more like a town – better eating, shopping, more locals – but if you're hiking the Alpine Crossing or playing around the Whakapapa area, it's an extra 25-minute drive away.

❶ **MOUNTAIN SAFETY**

Many visitors to New Zealand come unstuck in the mountains. Taken at face value, these peaks might seem small compared to some overseas counterparts, but the weather can change dramatically in minutes, and rescues (and fatalities) are not uncommon. When heading out, you must be properly equipped and take safety precautions, including leaving your itinerary with a responsible person. Appropriate clothing is paramount. Think layers of wool and a fleece jacket, topped with a waterproof jacket and even waterproof pants. Gloves and a hat are worth having too, even in summer. And don't even think about wearing anything other than sturdy boots. Take plenty of water, snacks and sunscreen, especially on hot days, and carry a first-aid kit.

The 'Plan My Trip' feature on the New Zealand Mountain Safety Council website (www.mountainsafety.org.nz) is an excellent resource, providing you with relevant local warnings, including weather warnings and DOC track alerts.

Tama Lakes Track   HIKING
(Ngauruhoe Pl) Part of the Tongariro Northern Circuit, and an extension of the Taranaki Falls track, this 17km-return walk leads to the vibrant Tama Lakes (five to six hours return), on the exposed Tama Saddle between Ruapehu and Ngauruhoe. The upper lake affords fine views of Ngauruhoe and Tongariro.

Taranaki Falls Track   HIKING
(Ngauruhoe Pl) A two-hour, 6km loop track heads from the village to Taranaki Falls, which plunge 20m over a 15,000-year-old lava flow into a boulder-ringed pool.

Whakapapa Holiday Park   HOLIDAY PARK $
(📞07-892 3897; www.whakapapa.net.nz; SH48; sites per person $23, dm $28, cabins $76-140, units $130-140; 🛜) This popular park beside Whakapapanui Stream has a wide range of accommodation options, including campervan sites surrounded by beautiful beech forest (site 21 has a mountain view), a five-room, 32-bed backpackers' lodge, cabins sleeping up to six (linen required), and self-contained two-bedroom units with en suites. The store stocks basic groceries. The tidy communal kitchen has 14 hotplates.

Chateau Tongariro Hotel   HOTEL $$$
(📞0800 242 832, 07-892 3809; www.chateau. co.nz; SH48; d $125-255, ste from $500; 🛜❄) Like most old mountain folk, this iconic 1929 hotel has weathered, though its grandeur – in the style of the original US national park hotels – is undeniable. It still creates a beautifully evocative stay, complete with high tea ($45, 11am to 5pm) in the lounge overlooking Mt Ngauruhoe, aperitifs in the foyer bar and formal dining in the elegant Ruapehu Room (www.chateau.co.nz/food-drinks/ruapehu-room; mains $29-48; ⏰6.30-10am, 6pm-late, plus noon-2pm Sun).

Tussock Bar & Restaurant   PUB
(📞0800 242 832, 07-892 3809; www.chateau. co.nz/food-drinks/tussock-bar-restaurant; SH48; ⏰4pm-late; 🛜) Other than the Chateau, Whakapapa's only drinking hole (albeit owned by the Chateau) is this split-personality bar, styled like an Alpine lodge but with a corrugated-iron bar and booths, wagon wheels propped against the wall, and a large pull-down screen cranking out sport. But the welcome and the fireplace are warm, and there's decent pub grub (mains $27 to $34).

ℹ Information

Tongariro National Park Visitor Centre
(Whakapapa Visitor Centre; 📞07-892 3729; www.doc.govt.nz/tongarirovisitorcentre; SH48; ⏰8am-5.30pm Oct-Apr, to 4.30pm May-Sep) has maps and info on all corners of the park, including huts and current skiing, track and weather conditions, plus an entire wall of hiking information. The centre doubles as an i-SITE.

The *Walks in and around Tongariro National Park* brochure ($4) provides a helpful overview of 30 walks and overnight hikes in the park. Exhibits on the geological and human history of the area should keep you busy for a couple of hours on a rainy day, and the Discover Tongariro Theatre shows films about the national park.

ℹ Getting There & Away

In winter, shuttle services travel to Whakapapa Village and its ski field from Taupō and Tūrangi. Many shuttle operators are offshoots or affiliates of accommodation providers, so ask about transport when you book your stay. Turangi Alpine Shuttles (p292) operates a 7.30am bus from Tūrangi to Whakapapa Village ($55), and Tongariro Crossing Shuttles (p300) run four times a day between National Park Village and Whakapapa ($20).

Dempsey Buses (p303) runs a 7am and 8am shuttle service to the Tongariro Alpine Crossing from Whakapapa Village ($40).

National Park Village

POP 200

The small sprawl of National Park Village is the most convenient place to stay when tackling the Tongariro Alpine Crossing (p293) – far closer than Ōhakune and Tūrangi, and with more accommodation, eating and shuttle options than Whakapapa.

There's little to do in the village itself (though it is worth checking out the 3m-high driftwood kiwi sculpture in front of Schnapps), but it is located exceptionally well for the national park's best hikes, as well as mountain-bike trails, canoe trips on the Whanganui River and winter skiing.

The village is busiest during the ski season, but in summer it makes a quieter base than Taupō for travellers who want to make the most of nearby outdoor activities, and it's in good reach of most of the area's offerings. The village is also a hotspot for train enthusiasts, since the *Northern Explorer* stops here.

🏃 Activities

In summer most accommodation providers offer packages including shuttles to the Tongariro Alpine Crossing, while other shuttle operators (p297) head daily from National Park Village to the Tongariro Alpine Crossing and Whakapapa Village in summer, and the ski area in winter.

Ski gear can be hired from the **Alpine Centre** (☑ 07-892 2717; https://thealpinecentre. co.nz; 10 Carroll St; ski-hire day/week $28/89, snowboard-hire day/week $35/116; ⊗ 7.30am-7pm Sat-Thu, to midnight Fri Jun-Oct, 7.30-10.30am & 4-7pm Nov-Apr), sparing you the steeper prices further up the mountain – it's also the only place around the national park to hire out hiking gear in summer.

If you fancy a climb, head to the climbing wall at National Park Backpackers.

My Kiwi Adventure   OUTDOORS
(☑ 0800 784 202, 021 784 202; www.mykiwiadven ture.co.nz; 2 Findlay St; ⊗ 8am-5.30pm) Offers stand-up paddle boarding in sight of volcanoes ($50, 2½ hours) on Lake Otamangakau – trips run Saturday and Sunday, November to April. Also pieces together mountain-biking adventures on standout local tracks. The two-day Tongariro Hike & Bike Adventure Package ($85) combines two of the region's best activities – hiking the Tongariro Alpine Crossing and mountain biking the Fishers Track. Stand-alone bike rental (half/full day $35/70) also available.

Adrift Tongariro   OUTDOORS
(☑ 07-892 2751; www.adriftnz.co.nz; 53 Carroll St) Runs guided Tongariro Alpine Crossing walks (from $255), including winter and sunrise trips, as well as Tongariro Northern Circuit hikes (three days, $1195) and walks to Crater Lake on Mt Ruapehu ($295). Other trips on its roster include canoeing the Whanganui River (one/three days $295/1195) and mountain biking the Ōhakune Old Coach Road ($205).

Adventure Outdoors   OUTDOORS
(☑ 027 242 7209, 0800 386 925; www.adventure outdoors.co.nz; 60 Carroll St) Guided trips on the Tongariro Alpine Crossing (from $249), including in winter and in time for the summer sunrise – its 4am shuttle can have you first on the track, ahead of the crowds. Also runs paddling tours in inflatable two-person kayaks on the Whakapapa River ($235), and family floats on the Whanganui River ($235). Wetsuits and life jackets provided.

42 Traverse   MOUNTAIN BIKING
(Map p294; Kapoors Rd, off SH47) This four- to six-hour, 46km mountain-bike trail through the Tongariro Forest is one of the North Island's best day rides. It follows old logging tracks, and if you start from Kapoors Rd, there's 570m of overall downhill, including a glorious descent to Waione Stream. My Kiwi Adventure runs track shuttles ($35) and combined bike rental/shuttle packages ($95).

🛏 Sleeping

National Park Village is a town of budget and midrange accommodation, since most visitors are here to play in the great outdoors, rather than hang about inside.

Prices are generally more affordable in spring and summer (October to February) than in the winter ski-season and school holidays. To avoid missing out, book in advance. Summer can get busy under the weight of Tongariro Alpine Crossing hikers.

National Park Backpackers   HOSTEL $
(☑ 07-892 2870; www.npbp.co.nz; 4 Findlay St; sites $15, dm $26-30, d $64-90; 🛜) This big, old board-and-batten YHA hostel has a large garden for lounging, a well-equipped kitchen and standard rooms. It's a good one-stop shop for booking activities in the area, and the rooms wrap around a **climbing wall** (☑ 07-892 2870; www.npbp.co.nz; 4 Findlay St; adult/child $15/10, hostel guests $10; ⊗ 9am-8pm) – handy when the weather turns bad. Small shop on-site. Ask about rooms with views of the volcanoes.

Park Hotel   HOTEL $$
(☑ 07-892 2748, 0800 800 491; www.the-park. co.nz; cnr SH4 & Millar St; r from $120; 🛜) Our pick when tackling the Alpine Crossing, the Park has neat, if small, double, king and family mezzanine rooms with photos of Tongariro by a local police officer decorating the walls. The two-night Crossing package ($398 for two people), including breakfast, track transfers and packed lunch, is great value and there are spa pools for a post-hike soak. **Spiral Restaurant & Bar** (mains $20 to $30) is a decent place to eat.

Discovery   LODGE $$
(Map p294; ☑ 0800 122 122, 07-892 2744; www. discoverynz.com; SH47; sites from $18, cabins $60, d & tw from $108, chalets $198-252; ◉) This versatile complex is all things to all people: campsites through to plush, lawn-surrounded wooden chalets with in-your-face volcano views. An on-site summer restaurant has

WORTH A TRIP

LAKE ROTOKURA

For some peaceful moments away from the mountains, consider a walk to this bush-smothered lake (Map p294; www.doc.govt.nz), the centrepiece of the Lake Rotokura Ecological Reserve, 14km southeast of Ōhakune. The track passes the paradoxically named Dry Lake, which is nothing of the sort, and then rises over a low wooded ridge to larger and less-reedy Lake Rotokura, 15 minutes from the car park. Rotokura is *tapu* (sacred) to Māori, so eating, fishing and swimming are prohibited, but there are picnic benches back by Dry Lake.

A more overgrown track loops for another 20 minutes around Lake Rotokura.

To get here, drive 11km southeast along SH49 from Ōhakune, then 3km from the turn-off along Karioi Station Rd. Cross the railway line and continue until you reach the car park at the road's end.

views of the volcanoes from the large deck, plus there's a bar, lounge and Alpine Crossing shuttle transport with 5am departure to help you move ahead of the crowds.

Owner and world-class mountain runner Callum Harland holds the unofficial Crossing record at a mind-boggling 1 hour 25 minutes!

Tongariro Crossing Lodge LODGE $$
(☑ 07-892 2688; www.tongarirocrossinglodge.co.nz; 27 Carroll St; d $189-209; 🐾) This pretty, farmhouse-like cottage is decorated with baby-blue trim and rambling blooms in summer. Suites are large with period furnishings – two studios share a kitchen, two are self-contained and the others are great for families – and there's a licensed bar that's perfect for a sundowner after your own Tongariro Crossing.

Parkview Apartments APARTMENT $$$
(☑ 021 252 4930; www.parkviewnationalpark.com; 24 Waimarino Tokaanu Rd; apt from $220; 🐾) These stylish and thoroughly modern apartments, at the end of a cul-de-sac, both have two bedrooms and sleep up to four people (or two adults and three children). The expansive windows provide such a natural canvas of volcanoes that you might never turn on the big-screen TV. The gas fireplaces will warm chilled mountain bodies. Minimum two-night stay.

✕ Eating & Drinking

Station Cafe CAFE $$
(☑ 07-892 2881; www.stationcafe.co.nz; cnr Findlay St & Station Rd; breakfast $9-22, mains $19-35; ☺ 9am-9pm) This cosy little restored railway station has cakes as timeless as the 1908 station itself – Florentines, spicy apple cakes, crumbles – as well as eggy brunches, sandwiches, coffee and a dinner menu that reads like a neighbourhood gastropub (venison Bourguignon, stuffed portobello mushroom). Sunday is $20 roast night.

Schnapps PUB
(☑ 07-892 2788; www.schnappsbarruapehu.com; cnr SH4 & Findlay St; ☺ noon-late) This popular pub has a menu of hotel standards (meals $20 to $30), potbelly stoves, big-screen TV, pool table and a handy ATM. Things crank up on wintry weekends, and there's a minigolf course (adult/child $11/6) if the alcohol convinces you of your putting skills. Not in the mood to socialise? There's a bottle shop at the entrance.

❶ Information

There's no i-SITE in the village, but the Tongariro National Park Visitor Centre (p298) in Whakapapa Village does double duty as an i-SITE.

❶ Getting There & Away

The Village lies at the junction of SH4 and SH47 at 825m above sea level, 15km from the hub of Whakapapa Village.

InterCity (p277) buses stop at National Park Station at the Station Cafe, where the *Northern Explorer* train run by KiwiRail Scenic (p277) also pulls up.

Tongariro Crossing Shuttles (☑ 07-892 2993; www.tongarirocrossingshuttles.co.nz) offers a shuttle from National Park Village to the Tongariro Alpine Crossing (return $40), and to Whakapapa ($20) for the Tongariro Northern Circuit.

Ōhakune

POP 1000

Ōhakune is a true outdoors town. In winter it pumps with snow enthusiasts, who melt away into hikers and mountain bikers in summer. The vibe is best when snow drifts down on Turoa Ski Area (p296) and people defrost together over a drink back in town. Despite the chill outside, the après-ski culture comes in hot every season.

When the snow clears, the town quietens – and accommodation prices drop. It's the perfect time to mountain bike along the fantastic Old Coach Road, and the town also provides easy access for exploring Whanganui National Park (p256), around 40km to the west.

There are two distinct parts to Ōhakune: the commercial hub is strung along the highway, but in winter the action shuffles up the mountain to Ōhakune Junction, 2km to the north, like a herd moving between its summer and winter pastures. The two areas are linked by the 2km **Mangawhero River Walkway**, a leafy 30-minute amble along the riverbank.

🏃 Activities

There are several scenic walks near the town, and many start from the Ōhakune Mountain Rd, which stretches 17km from Ōhakune to the Turoa Ski Area on Mt Ruapehu. The handy DOC brochure *Walks in and around Tongariro National Park* ($4), available from the Ōhakune i-SITE (p303), includes seven walks around Ōhakune.

★Ōhakune
Old Coach Road   MOUNTAIN BIKING
(Map p294; www.ohakunecoachroad.co.nz) One of NZ's best half-day (three-to-four-hour) bike rides, this gently graded route passes the historic Hapuawhenua and Toanui viaducts – t he only two remaining curved viaducts in the southern hemisphere. It also passes through ancient forests of giant rimu and totara that survived the Taupō blast of AD 180, being in the lee of Ruapehu.

The trailhead is beside the Ōhakune train station in Ōhakune Junction, but it's best to start at the Horopito end, as the trail descends around 150m to Ōhakune.

Mountain Bike Station   MOUNTAIN BIKING
(☑0800 245 464, 06-385 9018; www.mountainbikestation.co.nz; 27 Goldfinch St; ⊙10am-3pm, open later subject to demand) Bike-rental-and-transfer packages for the Old Coach Road (from $50) as well as mountain-bike hire (half/full day from $35/50) and on-demand transfers to various cycling routes – Turoa Ski Field ($25), Horopito ($15) and Whanganui ($180). All prices are for a minimum of two people.

Waitonga Falls Track   HIKING
(Map p294; www.doc.govt.nz; Ōhakune Mountain Rd) The 4km path (1¼ hours return) to Tongariro's highest waterfall (39m) follows a small section of the Round the Mountain Track (p296). It's almost entirely through thick native bush, though halfway along it

pops into an alpine clearing dotted with tarns that gives a fine view of Mt Ruapehu. The track starts from Ōhakune Mountain Rd.

Ruapehu Homestead   HORSE RIDING
(Map p294; ☑027 267 7057; www.ruapehuhomestead.kiwi.nz; cnr Piwari St & SH49, Rangataua; adult $60-150, child $50-120; ⊙treks 10am, noon & 2pm) Four kilometres east of Ōhakune (near Rangataua), Ruapehu Homestead offers one-hour rides along a stream, or into Rangataua, suitable for horse newbies, as well as three-hour outings with Ruapehu views for experienced riders.

🛏 Sleeping

Station Lodge   HOSTEL $
(☑06-385 8797; www.stationlodge.co.nz; 60 Thames St; dm from $30, d $70, apt from $130, chalets from $230; 🖥🚗) 🐾 Housed in a lovely old villa with wooden floors and high ceilings, this excellent YHA hostel has a well-equipped kitchen, two lounges, a spa pool, and a garden with a pizza oven and trampoline. Apartments sleeping between two to six people and separate chalets (some with two bedrooms, gas fireplaces and private spa pools) are available, as are campervan sites.

LKNZ Lodge   HOSTEL $
(☑06-385 9169; www.lknz.co.nz; 1 Rata St; sites from $24, dm $27-32, s from $65, d $85-99, f $159; 🖥) LKNZ is a sprawling village of its own, with rooms spread across four lodges. Tidy doubles with wooden bed-frames are a bargain and there's a drying room, DVDs, bikes for hire, pay-per-use spa pools ($6), a sauna ($10) and the **Storm Shelter Cafe** (open from 7.30am; try the nachos).

SEEING ORANGE

If you're travelling into Ōhakune from Waiouru, the first thing you'll see is a **Big Carrot** (Rangataua Rd; ⓘ) at the Carrot Adventure Park, a cool veg-themed playground. This tribute highlights the fact that Ōhakune is NZ's carrot capital. The local carrot connection goes back to the 1920s, when Chinese settlers cleared the land to grow them. Today the area grows two-thirds of NZ's carrots and has two large packing houses, employing several hundred people. There's even an annual **Carrot Carnival** (www.carrotcarnival.org.nz; ⊙May-Jun).

Snowman Lodge & Spa
MOTEL $
(☑ 028 419 7397, 06-385 8600; https://snowman
lodge.nz; 68 Clyde St; dm from $22, d with/without
bathroom from $80/60, f room from $130; ✵ ☏)
If you've come down from the mountain
with tired limbs, this recent motel makeover
could be just the ticket. Behind the ochre facade is a medley of small and simple dorms,
doubles and family rooms, but also a garden
hot tub, a sauna and Ōhakune's only spa
treatments. The lobby, with pool table, doubles as a dessert cafe and coffee bar.

There's also campervan camping out back
($10 if self-contained, $30 if using Snow-
man's facilities) and mountain-bike hire.

Ohakune Top 10 Holiday Park
HOLIDAY PARK $
(☑ 0800 825 825, 06-385 8561; www.ohakune.net.
nz; 5 Moore St; sites from $52, cabins from $75,
units from $110; ☏ ♨) ✐ A bubbling stream
borders this neat holiday park, which has
a wide range of accommodation, including
small cabins and motel units sleeping up to
six people. Extras include a playground, barbecue area and private spa bath. Help yourself to the herbs hanging from the barbecue
fence. There's a lovely short forest walk
heading across the stream and into town.

★ Ruapehu Country Lodge
B&B $$$
(Map p294; ☑ 021 707 850, 06-385 9594; www.
ruapehucountrylodge.co.nz; 630 Raetihi–Ōhakune
Rd; d $250-320; ☏) Around 5km west of
Ōhakune on the road to Raetihi, this B&B
is the perfect combination of country el-
egance and classy decor. Large bedrooms
have beautiful garden outlooks, and there's
an outdoor hot tub for an après soak. You'll
get a friendly welcome from hosts Heather
and Peter, as well as from the alpacas beside
the driveway that's like a hedge maze.

River Lodge
B&B $$$
(Map p294; ☑ 021 292 2883, 06-385 4771; www.
theriverlodge.co.nz; 206 Mangawhero River Rd; r/
chalets from $270/290; ☏) In a rural setting
8km from town, backing onto the Mangawhero River, this charming property has
three double rooms in the house and two
very cosy chalets. The chalets have private
hot tubs, open fireplaces and rocking chairs
on the porch. If that's not relaxing enough,
grab the hammock.

Powderhorn Chateau
HOTEL $$$
(☑ 06-385 8888; www.powderhorn.co.nz; 194 Man-
gawhero Tce; r from $260; ☏ ▨) At this Swiss-
style chalet, guests stay in rooms where their
favourite *Lord of the Rings* characters set up
during filming. Peter Jackson booked out
the eight-person apartment, but there are
another 33 more affordable options. With
woody interiors, possum-fur blankets and a
spa-temperature indoor pool with an inter-
com to the bar, this is the place for mountain
recovery and revelry.

The Alpine decor of the Powderkeg res-
taurant and bar (mains $24 to $36) might
have you craving schnapps, but it's at the
bar's long table where things usually get in-
teresting – Tolkien fans are regularly found
dancing on it in homage to Hobbits.

✖ Eating & Drinking

★ Eat Takeaway Diner
CAFE $
(☑ 020 4126 5520; www.facebook.com/eattake
awaydiner; 49 Clyde St; mains $11-18; ☺ 8am-3pm;
☏ ✎) ✐ Bagels, innovative salads, and tasty
American and Tex Mex–influenced dishes
combine with the best coffee in town at this
modern, white-as-snow spot on Ōhakune's
main drag. It has a strong focus on organic
ingredients, sustainable practices and a we-
can-make-anything-vegan ethos.

★ Blind Finch
BURGERS $$
(☑ 06-385 8076; www.theblindfinch.co.nz; 29 Gold-
finch St; small/large burgers $12.50/17; ☺ 3pm-late
Mon-Fri, from 11am Sat & Sun; ☏) After a day of
play in the mountains, there's nothing better

TANGIWAI RAIL DISASTER

Mt Ruapehu erupts with random regularity, but never with more consequence
than when the rim of Crater Lake ruptured at 10.21pm on Christmas Eve, 1953.
Almost 2 million cu metres of water and
mud poured down Ruapehu's slopes,
washing away the Tangiwai rail bridge
over the Whangaehu River along its way.
Six minutes after the bridge was toppled,
the Wellington–Auckland express train
arrived, plunging into the river, killing 151
people. Bodies were found up to 24km
downstream, and 20 people were never
found, believed washed out to sea.

The site of the disaster is marked with
a memorial and various monuments
immediately beside SH49, 9km west
of Waiouru and 18km east of Ōhakune.
From the memorial, a walking track
leads 200m to a lookout beside the replacement rail bridge, with Mt Ruapehu
still brooding away in the distance.

than these beast-sized burgers cooked on a custom-made manuka wood-fire grill. A burger's best friend is beer, and there are enough North Island craft beers here to fill a floor-to-ceiling blackboard, plus two shelves of gin.

Industry   GRILL $$
(☑06-385 9006; www.industrybarandgrill.co.nz; 55 Clyde St; mains $28-38; ☺5pm-late Mon-Thu, from 11.30am Fri-Sun) New to town is this grill and bar with hubcap-studded walls. Steak headlines the menu among other meaty mains, with a vegan bake for any non-carnivore who might happen to stray inside.

Kitchen   CRAFT BEER
(Map p294; ☑06-385 8664; www.4thames.co.nz; 4 Thames St; ☺4pm-late) The friendly owner refers to the Kitchen as his 'bach (beach house) with a bar attached'. Serving only NZ craft beer from a range of breweries, it's packed during winter (and for a spring party on the first weekend of September). Local musicians and a simple, tasty menu (mains $16 to $28) that swings between Mexican and Asian fare.

🏠 Shopping

Craft Haus   CLOTHING, ALCOHOL
(Map p294; ☑022 385 8683, 06-385 8683; www.thecrafthaus.co.nz; 31 Thames St; ☺10am-2pm Mon & Wed-Fri, to 5pm Sat & Sun) Ōhakune's heritage-listed 1909 train station is home to the unusual combo of Opus Fresh, a store producing beautiful merino, possum and silk garments, and the Ruapehu Brewing Co, which makes craft IPA, session ale and pale ale. It also serves Volcano Coffee, which is a roaster that began life in this station, but has since moved to Tūrangi.

ℹ Information

Ōhakune i-SITE (☑0800 647 483, 06-385 8427; www.visitruapehu.com; 54 Clyde St; ☺8am-5.30pm), inside Ōhakune's most striking building, can make bookings for activities, transport and accommodation; DOC officers are usually on hand from 9am most days.

Visit Ohakune (www.visitohakune.co.nz) is a useful website for 'The Mountain Town'.

ℹ Getting There & Away

InterCity (p277) has a direct bus service from Auckland (from $37, 7¼ hours), stopping on Clyde St, outside Hello World. Other destinations require transfers. The *Northern Explorer* train, run by KiwiRail Scenic (p277), stops in Ōhakune on its run between Auckland and Wellington.

Dempsey Buses (☑06-385 4022; www.dempseybuses.co.nz) is based locally, offering services around the Ruapehu region, including Tongariro Alpine Crossing shuttles ($50, departing Ōhakune 7am during summer), daily shuttles to the Ōhakune Old Coach Road, shuttles to the Turoa ski-field car park to hit the slopes or take a downhill Ōhakune Mountain Rd ride, and services to and from the Mangapurua Track and Bridge to Nowhere.

Waiouru

POP 740

Waiouru (altitude 792m) is primarily an army base and a refuelling stop for SH1 motorists. With an almost unbroken line of greasy-spoon eateries and petrol stations, the town has the unmistakable feeling of being a highway stop. For visitors, there's not a lot here other than the National Army Museum, but that alone makes it worth a stop.

North of town is a barren landscape of reddish sand with small clumps of tussock. This so-called Rangipo Desert isn't actually a desert. It's a unique landscape that's the result of two million years of volcanic eruptions – especially the AD 180 Taupō eruption that coated the land with thick deposits of pumice and destroyed all vegetation.

Waiouru is located at the junction of SH1 and SH49, 27km east of Ōhakune. InterCity (p277) buses regularly trundle through Waiouru as they run between Auckland (from $28, 6¾ hours) and Wellington (from $25, 4¾ hours). In winter, the highway occasionally closes due to snow.

National Army Museum   MUSEUM
(Map p294; ☑06-387 6911; www.armymuseum.co.nz; cnr SH1 & Hassett Dr; adult/child $15/5; ☺9am-4.30pm) 🚫 At the southern end of the town, in a large, almost Stalinist concrete castle, is the National Army Museum. Proclaimed as 'history without the boring bits', it's actually a serious and fascinating journey through NZ's military history, including the New Zealand Wars. It houses an impressive collection of artillery, tanks, landing craft, uniforms and memorabilia in moving displays.

Waiouru i-SITE   TOURIST INFORMATION
(Map p294; ☑06-387 5279; www.visitruapehu.com; National Army Museum, cnr SH1 & Hassett Dr; ☺9am-4.30pm) Dispensing local knowledge and travel advice on Waiouru and the Ruapehu region from inside the cafe/shop in the National Army Museum. Reservation services available, along with souvenirs.

Rotorua & the Bay of Plenty

Best Places to Eat

➡ Terrace Kitchen (p318)

➡ Abracadabra Cafe & Bar (p318)

➡ Macau (p330)

➡ Alpino (p335)

➡ Moxi (p344)

Best Places to Stay

➡ Prince's Gate Hotel (p317)

➡ Warm Earth Cottage (p338)

➡ Harbour View Motel (p329)

➡ One88 on Commerce (p341)

➡ Ohope Beach Motel (p343)

Why Go?

Captain Cook named the Bay of Plenty when he cruised past in 1769, suggesting he might have been the region's first satisfied tourist. It remains an apt name for this bay, blessed with sunshine and stretches of sand that reach from Waihi Beach in the west to Ōpōtiki in the east, with the holiday hubs of Tauranga, Mt Maunganui and Whakatāne in between.

Smoking away offshore from Whakatāne is one sign of the volcanic activity that defines this region – Whakaari (White Island), New Zealand's most active volcano, which erupted so tragically in December 2019. In Rotorua the daily business of life goes on among steaming hot springs, explosive geysers, bubbling mud pools and the sulphurous scents responsible for the town's trademark eggy smell.

Rotorua and the Bay of Plenty are also strongholds of Māori tradition, presenting numerous opportunities to engage with NZ's rich indigenous culture – check out a power-packed concert performance, chow down at a *hāngi* (Māori feast), or skill up with some Māori arts-and-crafts techniques.

When to Go

➡ The Bay of Plenty is one of NZ's sunniest regions; Whakatāne records a brilliant 2350 average hours of sunshine per year! In summer (December to February) maximums hover in the high 20s (Celsius). Everyone else is here, too, but the holiday vibe is heady and the beaches irresistible.

➡ Visit Rotorua any time: the warming geothermal activity never sleeps, and there are enough beds in any season.

➡ The mercury can slide below 5°C overnight here in winter, making the area's hot pools even more appealing. It's usually warmer on the coast, where you'll have the beaches all to yourself.

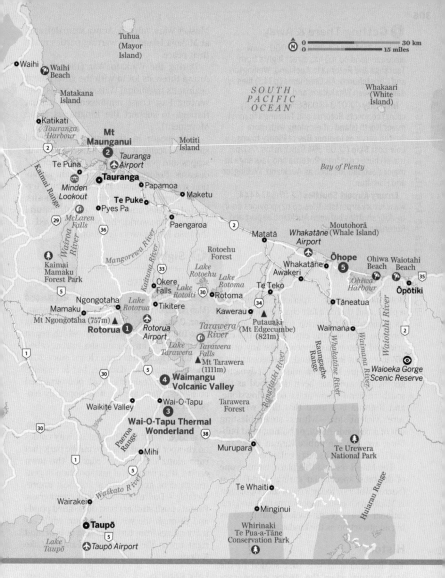

Rotorua & the Bay of Plenty Highlights

1 Rotorua (p306) Peering through the sulphurous steam at a unique town where geothermal activity, Māori culture and world-class mountain biking come together.

2 Mt Maunganui (p332) Lazing at the beach, carving up the surf and hiking up the signature mountain, then relaxing in the hot pools before hitting the region's best restaurants and bars.

3 Wai-O-Tapu Thermal Wonderland (p323) Marvelling at the unearthly hues of the region's most colourful geothermal attraction.

4 Waimangu Volcanic Valley (p323) Walking down through a fizzing, spurting and sizzling valley torn through the country in a 19th-century volcanic eruption.

5 Ōhope (p343) Strolling 11km of picture-perfect beach, then wandering around a headland to discover the even-more-beautiful Otarawairere Bay.

ℹ Getting There & Away

Air New Zealand (📞 0800 737 000; www.airnewzealand.co.nz) has direct flights from Tauranga and Rotorua to Auckland, Wellington and Christchurch. Air Chathams (p343) flies daily between Whakatāne and Auckland.

InterCity (📞 07-348 0366; www.intercity.co.nz) connects Rotorua and Tauranga to most major North Island cities, along with more limited services to other Bay of Plenty towns. Low-cost **Skip** (📞 09-394 9180; https://skip.travel) buses run from Rotorua and Tauranga to major destinations such as Auckland, Wellington and Hamilton.

Luxury Airport Shuttles (📞 07-547 4444; www.luxuryairportshuttles.co.nz) provides door-to-door shuttles between Auckland airport and Rotorua and Tauranga.

ROTORUA

POP 72,500

Rotorua is a sensory experience as much as a place, and there's a fair chance you'll smell its pungent, sulphur-rich (ok, farty) air before you even see the city. Wander the city grid and 'Rotovegas' appears like any other NZ town, but look around its edges and it's utterly unique. New Zealand's most dynamic geothermal area has been described as the southern hemisphere's take on Yellowstone, and Rotorua is a town that flirts with nature's violent side – witness steam blasting out of a roadside drain, or boiling mud bubbling away in the public Kuirau Park, and you'll understand its edgy balance.

The Māori revered this place, naming one of the most spectacular springs Wai-O-Tapu (Sacred Waters). Today 37% of the population is Māori, with cultural performances and traditional *hāngi* (earth-cooked banquets) as big an attraction as the landscape itself.

History

The Rotorua area was first settled in the 14th century when the *Arawa* canoe, captained by Tamatekapua, arrived at Maketu in the central Bay of Plenty. Settlers took the tribal name Te Arawa to commemorate the vessel that brought them here.

In the next few hundred years, subtribes spread and divided through the area (the main subtribe of Te Arawa who live in Rotorua today are known as Ngāti Whakaue). A flashpoint occurred in 1823 when the Arawa lands were attacked by Northland tribe Ngāpuhi, led by Hongi Hika, in the so-called Musket Wars. After Te Arawa were defeated at Mokoia Island, the warring parties made their peace.

During the Waikato War (1863–64), Te Arawa threw its lot in with the government against its traditional Waikato enemies, preventing East Coast reinforcements getting through to support the Kingitanga (King Movement).

With peace in the early 1870s, word spread of scenic wonders, miraculous landscapes and watery cures for all manner of diseases. Rotorua boomed. Its main attraction was the fabulous Pink and White Terraces, formed by volcanic silica deposits. Touted at the time as the eighth natural wonder of the world, they were destroyed in the 1886 Mt Tarawera eruption.

◉ Sights

◉ City Centre

Rotorua Museum NOTABLE BUILDING
(Map p308; 📞 07-350 1814; www.rotoruamuseum.co.nz; Oruawhata Dr) Constructed in a striking faux-Tudor style, this museum, which began life in 1908 as an elegant spa retreat called the Bath House, has been closed since 2016 due to earthquake damage, but it remains one of New Zealand's most photographed buildings. Plans are for it to hopefully reopen in 2021.

Kuirau Park PARK
(Map p308; Ranolf St) Thermal activity comes no cheaper than at this free public park that runs along the western edge of the town centre. It's a wonderful juxtaposition of genteel gardens and nature at its most unpredictable – Dante's *Inferno* with green grass. Parents push strollers past duck-filled ponds and through the wisteria arbour, while activity ranges from tiny bubbling pots of mud right up to the frantically steaming Lake Kuirau.

Lake Rotorua LAKE
(Map p322) Lake Rotorua is the largest of the district's 18 lakes and is – underneath all that water – a spent volcano. Near the centre of the lake is Mokoia Island, a bird sanctuary that was for centuries occupied by various subtribes of the area. The lake can be explored by jetboat, paddle steamer or from the air, with several operators situated at the lakefront.

Katoa Lake Rotorua (p311) can get you onto Mokoia Island.

Government Gardens   GARDENS
(Map p308; Hinemaru St) The manicured Government Gardens surrounding the Rotorua
Museum are a wonderful example of the
blending of English (rose gardens, ponds,
croquet lawns and bowling greens) and
Māori traditions (carvings at the entrance
and subtly blended into the buildings).
Being Rotorua, there are thermal pools
bubbling away, and it's well worth taking a
walk along the active geothermal area at the
lake's edge.

⊙ Whakarewarewa

Rotorua's main drawcard is Whakarewarewa (pronounced 'fah-kah-*reh*-wah-
reh-wah'), a geothermal area 3km south
of the city centre. This area's full name is
Te Whakarewarewa Tanga o te Ope Taua
a Wāhiao, meaning 'The War Dance of the
War Party of Wāhiao'. The area is as famous
for its Māori cultural significance as for its
steam and bubbling mud. There are more
than 500 springs here, including the famed
Pōhutu geyser.

The active area is split between the still-
lived-in Māori village of Whakarewarewa
and the Te Puia complex, which are separated from each other by a fence. Both offer cultural performances and geothermal activity
galore; the village is cheaper to visit but Te
Puia has Pōhutu, a kiwi house and important Māori art institutions.

★ Te Puia   CULTURAL CENTRE
(Map p322; ☑ 07-348 9047; www.tepuia.com;
Hemo Rd, Whakarewarewa; adult/child $60/30, incl
performance $76/38, Te Pō $136/68; ☉ 8am-6pm
Oct-Mar, to 5pm Apr-Sep) Te Puia dials up the
heat on *Māoritanga* (things Māori) with explosive performances from both its cultural
troupe and Pōhutu (Big Splash), its famous
geyser that erupts around 20 times a day,
spurting hot water up to 30m skyward. It
erupts in tandem with the adjoining Prince
of Wales' Feathers geyser. Also here is a
kiwi conservation centre and the New
Zealand Māori Arts and Crafts Institute,
where you can watch students at work.

Daytime visits *(Te Rā)* include an informative guided tour of the entire complex (departing on the hour), which also features a
wharenui (carved meeting house) and a re-created precolonial village (Te Puia is on the site
of a Māori Village that was inhabited for 600
years), the kiwi enclosure and a large chunk

of the Whakarewarewa thermal zone. After
the tour you're welcome to wander around at
your leisure. It's well worth paying extra for
the cultural performance (10.15am, 12.15pm
and 3.15pm), incorporating a traditional
welcome into the *wharenui* and a 45-min-
ute *kapa haka* (traditional song and dance)
concert. The three-hour *Te Pō* (night) experience starts at 6pm and includes a cultural
show and a *hāngi* meal, followed by a tour
through the thermal zone in a people mover.

The Arts and Crafts Institute houses the
national carving and weaving schools, and
you're free to watch the bone and wood carving and the flax weaving.

Whakarewarewa   VILLAGE
(Map p322; ☑ 07-349 3463; www.whakarewarewa.
com; 17 Tryon St; adult/child $45/20, incl hāngi
$70/40; ☉ 8.30am-5pm) Wander the streets
of this living village, where the local Tūhouran-
gi/Ngāti Wāhiao people have resided for
centuries, with its homes, stores, cafes and
lookouts over the Pōhutu geyser in neighbouring Te Puia. Villagers lead the tours (departing hourly from 9am to 4pm) and tell
stories of their way of life amid the steamy
bubbling pools, silica terraces and geysers.

Admission also includes a half-hour cultural performance (daily at 11.15am and
2pm, with an additional show at 12.30pm

Rotorua

ROTORUA & THE BAY OF PLENTY ROTORUA

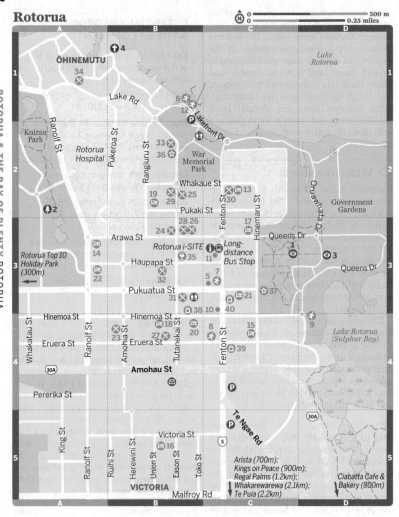

from November to April) and self-guided walks out as far as Lake Kanapanapa/Green Lake (a 40- to 50-minute loop). The village shops sell authentic arts and crafts, and you can learn more about Māori traditions such as flax weaving, carving and *tā moko* (tattooing). Nearby you can eat tasty, buttery sweetcorn ($2) pulled straight out of the hot mineral pool – the only genuine geothermal *hāngi* meal in town.

Redwoods Whakarewarewa Forest FOREST
(Map p322; ☑ 07-350 0110; www.redwoods.co.nz; Long Mile Rd, Whakarewarewa) This magical park of forest giants is 5km southeast of town.

From 1899, 170 tree species were planted here to see which could be grown successfully for timber. Mighty Californian redwoods (up to 72m high) give the park its grandeur today. Walking tracks range from a half-hour wander through the Redwood Memorial Grove to the all-day (34km) Whakarewarewa Track, which loops past the Blue and Green Lakes. Several walks start from the Redwoods i-SITE (Map p322; ☑ 07-350 0110; www.redwoods.co.nz; Long Mile Rd, Whakarewarewa; ☺ 9am-10pm), where you'll also find the spectacular Redwoods Treewalk (p310).

Aside from walking, the forest is great for picnics, and is acclaimed for its

Rotorua

◎ Sights
1 Government Gardens C3
2 Kuirau Park A2
3 Rotorua Museum D3
4 St Faith's Anglican Church B1

◎ Activities, Courses & Tours
5 Happy Ewe Tours C3
6 Katoa Lake Rotorua B1
7 Mountain Bike Rotorua
   Adventure Hub C3
8 O'Keefe's Anglers Depot C4
9 Polynesian Spa D4
10 Rotorua Duck Tours C3
11 Thermal Land Shuttle C3
12 Volcanic Air B1
   Wall .... (see 20)

◎ Sleeping
13 Aura C2
14 Base Rotorua A3
15 Crash Palace C4
16 Funky Green Voyager B5
17 Prince's Gate Hotel C3
18 Quest Rotorua Central B4
19 Regent of Rotorua B2
20 Rock Solid Backpackers B4
21 Rotorua Central Backpackers C3
22 YHA Rotorua A3

◎ Eating
23 Abracadabra Cafe & Bar B4
24 Artisan Cafe B3
25 Atticus Finch B2
26 Blind Finch B3
27 Capers Epicurean B4
28 Fat Dog B3
29 Leonardo's B2
30 Lime Caffeteria C2
31 Rotorua Night Market B3
32 Sabroso B3
33 Terrace Kitchen B2
34 Third Place A1

◎ Drinking & Nightlife
   Brew .... (see 29)
35 Pig & Whistle B3
   Ponsonby Rd .... (see 29)

◎ Entertainment
   Basement Cinema .... (see 20)
36 Matariki B2
37 Tamaki Māori Village C3

◎ Shopping
38 Moko 101 .... B3
39 Mountain Jade C4
40 Rākai Jade C3

mountain biking. There's around 130km of tracks to keep riders of all skill levels happy for days. Note that not all tracks in the forest are designated for bikers, so adhere to the signposts. Pick up a trail map at the i-SITE. Mountain Bike Rotorua (p311) and Planet Bike (p314) offer bike hire across the park, off Waipa State Mill Rd, where there are also toilets and a shower. **Southstar Shuttles** (Map p322; ☑027 654 3038; www.southstaradventures.com; 1/5/16 uplifts $10/40/100) operates bike shuttles from the main car park to the top of the trail network.

◉ Ōhinemutu

Ōhinemutu is a lakeside Māori village that's home to around 260 people. Highlights include the 1905 **Tama-te-Kapua Meeting House** (not open to visitors), many steaming volcanic vents, and the wonderful Māori-British mash-up that is St Faith's. Be respectful if you visit the village: the residents don't appreciate loud, nosy tourists wandering around taking photos of their private property. Village tours can be arranged at the little visitor centre (0800 473 482) two doors up from St Faith's.

St Faith's Anglican Church CHURCH
(Map p308; ☑07-348 2393; Korokai St, Ōhinemutu; admission by donation; ⊙10am-3pm, services 9am Sun) ✱ Consecrated in 1918, Ōhinemutu's historic timber church is intricately decorated with Māori carvings, *tukutuku* (woven panels), painted scrollwork and stained-glass windows. One window features an etched image of Christ wearing a Māori cloak, appearing to walk on the waters of Lake Rotorua, visible through the glass. Behind the church is a military graveyard and memorial – note the above-ground burials due to the geothermal activity.

◉ Surrounds

**Rainbow Springs
Nature Park** NATURE CENTRE
(Map p322; ☑07-350 0440; www.rainbowsprings. co.nz; 192 Fairy Springs Rd, Fairy Springs; adult/child $40/20; ⊙8.30am-5.30pm) ✱ The natural springs here are home to wild trout and eels, which you can peer at through an underwater viewer, and plenty of animals, including tuatara (a native reptile) and native birds. The star feature is the **National Kiwi Hatchery** (tour only $24, with park admission $10), which hatches around 120 chicks a year.

Excellent 30-minute tours, departing on the hour, take you backstage to view the incubator and hatchery areas and three adult kiwi.

Volcanic Hills Winery WINERY
(Map p322; ☑ 07-282 2018; www.volcanichills.co.nz; Skyline Rotorua, 178 Fairy Springs Rd, Fairy Springs; tasting 3/5 wines $11/16; ☺ 11am-6pm) Drink in the view from the top of the Skyline gondola at this winery tasting room. The wine is made at the bottom of the hill from grapes sourced from NZ's main wine regions. It's a personal session, with staff joining you at a window table as you work your way through some of the label's 10 wines. Last tasting at 5.30pm.

Agrodome FARM
(Map p322; ☑ 07-357 1050; www.agrodome. co.nz; 141 Western Rd, Ngongotaha; adult/child shows $36/19, tours $49/25, show & tour $70/37; ☺ 8.30am-5pm) Learn everything you need to know about farming at this 140-hectare model farm. Shows (9.30am, 11am and 2.30pm) include a parade of champion rams, lamb feeding, and shearing, milking and doggy displays. Yes, some of the jokes are corny, but it's still very entertaining. Farm tours on a tractor train depart at 10.40am, 12.10pm, 1.30pm and 3.40pm, giving you a squiz at Agrodome's sheep, deer, alpacas, llamas, cows, ostriches and emus.

Paradise Valley Springs NATURE CENTRE
(☑ 07-348 9667; www.paradisev.co.nz; 467 Paradise Valley Rd; adult/child $30/15; ☺ 8am-dusk, last entry 5pm) 🍂 Tucked in behind Mt Ngongotaha, 10km from Rotorua, this 6-hectare park has trout springs, native longfin eels, native birds and various land-dwelling animals such as deer, alpacas, possums and a pride of lions (fed at 2.30pm). There's also a cafe and an elevated treetop walkway through the tawa trees.

🏃 Activities

Adventure Sports

⭐**Rotorua Canopy Tours** ADVENTURE SPORTS
(Map p322; ☑ 07-343 1001; www.canopytours. co.nz; 147 Fairy Springs Rd, Fairy Springs; Original Tour adult/child $159/129, Ultimate Tour $249/199; ☺ 8am-8pm Oct-Apr, to 6pm May-Sep) Explore a web of bridges, flying foxes, zip lines and platforms high in a lush native forest canopy 10 minutes out of town. The Original Tour is a 1.2km treetop route, while the new 2.1km Ultimate Tour heads higher and includes a cliff walk. All trips depart from its office opposite the gondola.

Paddle Board Rotorua WATER SPORTS
(☑ 027 669 4410; www.paddleboardrotorua.com; glowworm paddle $120) Gentle evening stand-up paddle boarding trips across Lake Okareka to small caves strung with glowworms – you'll see constellations of stars as you paddle on the open lake, and constellations of glowworms inside the caves. Also runs daytime SUP trips on Lake Tarawera ($90). Trips depart from the Rotorua i-SITE.

Redwoods Treewalk WALKING
(Map p322; ☑ 027 536 1010; www.treewalk.co.nz; Long Mile Rd, Whakarewarewa; adult/child $30/20; ☺ 9am-10.30pm, last entry 10pm) 🍂 Billed as 'the world's longest living treewalk', this elevated walkway extends for 700m, crossing 28 bouncy wooden bridges suspended between century-old redwood trees. Most of the pathway is around 6m off the forest floor, but a high-loop option ascends to 20m. It's most impressive at night when it's lit by striking wooden lanterns, hung from the trees.

Velocity Valley ADVENTURE SPORTS
(Map p322; ☑ 0800 949 888, 07-357 4747; https:// velocityvalley.co.nz; 1335 Paradise Valley Rd, Ngongotaha; 1/2/4 rides $55/90/149, bungy $149; ☺ 9am-5pm) Velocity Valley provides a bucolic setting with a buzz, combining a 43m bungy with the 130km/h Swoop swing, the Freefall Xtreme skydiving simulation and the tiny, three-seat Agrojet, one of NZ's fastest jetboats, which reach up to 100km/h around a very tight 1km course.

Alongside is the Shweeb, a monorail velodrome from which you hang in a clear capsule and pedal yourself along at speeds of up to 50km/h, and ramps and the Freestyle Airbag for practising your BMX jumps (two hours $35, BYO bike).

Skyline Rotorua CABLE CAR
(Map p322; ☑ 07-347 0027; www.skyline.co.nz; 178 Fairy Springs Rd, Fairy Springs; adult/child $34/17; ☺ 9am-10pm) The cable-car ride up the slopes of Mt Ngongotaha is only a teaser for the thrills on offer at the top. Most popular is the luge (one/three/five rides $16/32/43), which shoots along three different tracks. For even speedier antics, ride the 150km/h Sky Swing (adult/child $101/84), the Zoom Zipline ($105/94) or the mountain-bike park.

The summit also offers the Stratosfare restaurant (lunch/dinner $41/60), the Volcanic Hills Winery and stargazing sessions (with gondola $97/51). Note the Sky Swing

ROTORUA IN...

One Day

Start with an early stroll along the lakefront into Government Gardens (p307) and admire the exterior of Rotorua Museum (p306), one of NZ's most photographed buildings. For a cultural morning, head to Ōhinemutu and St Faith's Anglican Church (p309) to view the etched figure of Christ walking on Lake Rotorua and the above-ground burials. Grab a bite to eat in the town centre, then head to Te Puia (p307) for a cultural show and to gawk at the dependable Pōhutu geyser. Arguably NZ's best mountain biking through the Redwoods Whakarewarewa Forest (p308) can round out the afternoon. Soak through sunset at the Polynesian Spa (p314), then hit the Eat Streat section of Tutanekai St for a meal and a drink. After dinner, wander high through the trees on the lantern-lit Redwoods Treewalk.

Two Days

Head out of town on the second day to explore the lakes and geothermal fields that surround Rotorua. Spend the morning in Waimangu Volcanic Valley (p323) and/or Wai-O-Tapu Thermal Wonderland (p323). In the afternoon, drive down to Lake Tarawera (p324), stopping to wander the circuit around Tikitapu (Blue Lake) on the way. In the evening, catch a concert and consume a *hāngi* (earth-cooked meal) at Tamaki Māori Village (p320) or Mitai Māori Village (p320).

and Zipline prices include the gondola and five luge rides. A baffling array of combination tickets is available.

Katoa Lake Rotorua BOATING
(Map p308; ☑ 07-343 7600; www.katoalake rotorua.co.nz; 1 Lakefront Dr; 30min adult/child $85/54; ◎9am-6pm) Speed things up by tearing around Lake Rotorua in a jetboat. Katoa also runs jetboat and water-taxi trips to Mokoia Island, with tours led by guides descended from Mokoia islanders. It's the only company allowed to land on Mokoia.

Wall CLIMBING
(Map p308; ☑ 07-350 1400; www.basementcinema. co.nz; 1140 Hinemoa St; adult/child with harness hire $16/13, shoe hire $5; ◎noon-10pm Mon-Fri, 10am-10pm Sat, 10am-9pm Sun) NZ's highest indoor climbing centre – three storeys – has 16 ropes and overhangs aplenty.

Zorb ADVENTURE SPORTS
(Map p322; ☑0800 227 474, 07-343 7676; www. ogo.co.nz; 525 Ngongotaha Rd, Fairy Springs; 1/2/3 rides from $45/85/125; ◎9am-5pm) Careen down a grassy hillside in a big bubble ball, with or without water inside. Zorb has four tracks to choose from, including the world's fastest and steepest such run: the 300m Mega Track. You can fit up to three people inside the ball on most tracks. Look for the grassy hill immediately north of Mitai Maori Village (p320).

Mountain Biking

Between Redwoods Whakarewarewa Forest (p308) and the Skyline Rotorua MTB Gravity Park, Rotorua is well established as one of the world's premier mountain-biking destinations. Additionally, the two-day, 48km Te Ara Ahi (Thermal by Bike) trail starts in Rotorua and heads south via Whakarewarewa, Te Puia, Waimangu Volcanic Valley and Wai-O-Tapu to the Waikite Valley Thermal Pools. This intermediate-level route is designated as one of the New Zealand Cycle Trail's 'Great Rides' (www. nzcycletrail.com). For more cycling information, enquire at the Rotorua i-SITE or get online at www.riderotorua.com.

★**Skyline Rotorua**
MTB Gravity Park MOUNTAIN BIKING
(Map p322; ☑ 07-347 0027; www.skyline.co.nz; 178 Fairy Springs Rd, Fairy Springs; 1/15/40 gondola uplifts with bike $34/67/128; ◎10am-5pm) Rotorua's status as a world-class mountain-biking destination is in part due to the 12km network of tracks coursing down Mt Ngongotaha. Trails here suit intermediate and crack riders, and access to the top of the park is provided by the Skyline gondola. Bike rental is available at the lower chairlift station from Mountain Bike Rotorua.

Mountain Bike Rotorua MOUNTAIN BIKING
(Map p322; ☑ 07-348 4295; www.mtbrotorua.co.nz; Waipa State Mill Rd, Whakarewarewa; hire 2hr/day from $39/60, ebike 2/4hr $99/129, guided rides

1. Mt Maunganui (p332)

From the top of Mauao, you can gaze over the whole of New Zealand's premier surfing town.

2. Māori Rotorua (p314)

Rotorua is a fantastic place to engage with Māori culture, including experiencing authentic *haka* and *hāngi*.

3. Pōhutu geyser (p307)

Whakarewarewa, a geothermal area 3km south of the city centre, is Rotorua's main draw.

4. Inferno Crater Lake (p323)

This powder-blue lake in the Waimangu Volcanic Valley fills and empties every 38 days.

from $150; ⊘9am-5pm) This outfit hires out bikes at the Waipa Mill car park entrance to the Redwoods Whakarewarewa Forest (p308), the hub for the trail network. You can stop by its central Rotorua **adventure hub** (Map p308; ☑07-348 4290; www.mtbrotorua.co.nz; 1213 Fenton St; ⊘9am-5pm) for rentals and trail information, and it can also fit you out with a bike at the Skyline MTB Gravity Park (p311).

Planet Bike   CYCLING
(Map p322; ☑027 280 2817, 07-346 1717; www.planetbike.co.nz; 8 Waipa Bypass Rd, Whakarewarewa; hardtail hire 2hr/day from $35/60, dual suspension $60/130, ebike 2/4hr $70/100; ⊘9am-5pm) Based in an old mill workshop, Planet Bike offers bike hire, repairs and guided mountain-bike rides (from $150) in the Redwoods Whakarewarewa Forest (p308).

Hiking

There are plenty of opportunities to stretch your legs around Rotorua, including the popular lakefront stroll. Begin near the end of Fenton St and head east and you'll pass a couple of small beaches and a host of birdlife before heading along Sulphur Bay, where the lake is fringed with steaming geothermal activity. It should take 30 to 40 minutes to reach the Polynesian Spa. There are also a couple of good walks at Mt Ngongotaha: the easy 1.2km **Ngongotaha Nature Loop** through native forest, and the steep 2.4km return **Jubilee Track** to the (viewless) summit.

There are dozens more challenging tracks in the broader Rotorua Lakes area (p325).

Thermal Pools & Massage

Polynesian Spa   HOT SPRINGS
(Map p308; ☑07-348 1328; www.polynesianspa.co.nz; 1000 Hinemoa St; family pools adult/child $23/10, pavilion/deluxe pools $32/59, private pools per 30min from $23; ⊘8am-11pm) A bathhouse opened at these Government Gardens springs in 1882, and people have been taking to the Poly Pools' waters ever since. The main pavilion and deluxe mineral pools (36°C to 41°C) have lake views, making for a prime sunset soak. The deluxe option offers even more picturesque rock-lined lakeside pools and includes a free locker ($5 otherwise) and towel. Massage, mud and beauty treatments are also available.

Secret Spot   BATHHOUSE
(Map p322; ☑07-348 4442; https://secretspot.nz; 13/33 Waipa State Mill Rd, Whakarewarewa; 45min from $35; ⊘9am-10pm) Is this the perfect marriage? Secret Spot has 12 cedar hot tubs lining the Puarenga Stream at the very base of the Redwoods mountain-bike trails. Even more inviting are the 'shinny dips' – eight minitubs for soaking your feet and shins that are free to use when you purchase a drink.

Fishing

There's always good trout fishing to be had somewhere around Rotorua. Hire a guide or go solo: either way a licence ($34 per day) is essential, and available from **O'Keefe's Anglers Depot** (Map p308; ☑07-346 0178; www.okeefesfishing.co.nz; 1113 Eruera St; ⊘8.30am-5pm Mon-Thu, to 5.30pm Fri, 9am-2pm Sat). Note that not all of the Rotorua Lakes can be fished year-round; check with O'Keefe's or the i-SITE (p321).

MĀORI NZ: ROTORUA & THE BAY OF PLENTY

The Bay of Plenty's Māori name, Te Moana a Toi (The Sea of Toi), recalls an early Polynesian voyager whose descendants first settled in Whakatāne. Most of the Bay's tribes trace their ancestry to a later migration (probably around the 13th or 14th century), when the Mātaatua *waka* (canoe) made landfall in Whakatāne. These tribes include Te Whakatōhea (www.whakatohea.co.nz) of Ōpōtiki, Ngāti Awa (www.ngatiawa.iwi.nz) of Whakatāne, and Ngāi Te Rangi (www.ngaiterangi.org.nz), Ngāti Pūkenga (www.ngatipukenga.com) and Ngāti Ranginui (www.ranginui.co.nz) of the Tauranga area. Te Arawa (www.tearawa.iwi.nz) of Rotorua take their name from a different ancestral *waka*.

Tribes in this region were involved on both sides of the New Zealand Wars in the late 19th century, with those fighting against the government suffering considerable land confiscations that have caused legal problems right up to the present day.

There's a significant Māori population in the region, and many ways for travellers to engage with Māori culture. Whakatāne has a visitor-friendly main-street marae (p338) (traditional meeting place) and Toi's Pā (p340), perhaps New Zealand's oldest *pā* (fortified village) site. Rotorua has Māori villages, *hāngi* (Māori feasts) and cultural performances aplenty.

Trout Man FISHING
(Map p322; ☑021 951 174; www.waiteti.com; 14 Okona Cres, Ngongotaha; 3/5hr trips from $75/150) Learn to fish with experienced angler Harvey Clark.

Other Activities

Volcanic Air SCENIC FLIGHTS
(Map p308; ☑07-348 9984; www.volcanicair.co.nz; Lakefront Dr; trips $115-1095) Offers a variety of float-plane and helicopter flights taking in Mt Tarawera and surrounding geothermal sites.

aMAZEme OUTDOORS
(Map p322; ☑0274 861 700, 07-357 5759; www.amazeme.co.nz; 1335 Paradise Valley Rd, Ngongotaha; adult/child $16/11; ☺10am-5pm; 🐾) This 1.4km maze is constructed from immaculately pruned, head-high escallonia hedge. Lose yourself (or the kids) in the endless spirals. There's also a butterfly house and a few rabbits to pat.

☞ Tours

★Real Rotorua TOURS
(☑027 666 0144; www.realrotorua.co.nz) Runs a selection of trips that go well beyond the obvious sights – its Thermal Path tour (adult/child $80/50), for instance, takes in Kerosene Creek and Rainbow Mountain, as well as Wai-O-Tapu's mud pool and the Waikite Valley Thermal Pools. The night-time glowworm walking tour ($65/40) is highly recommended.

Happy Ewe Tours CYCLING
(Map p308; ☑022 622 9252; www.happyewetours.com; 1115 Pukuatua St; adult/child $69/35; ☺10am & 2pm) Saddle up for a three-hour small-group bike tour of Rotorua, wheeling past 27 sights around the city. It's all flat and slow paced, so you don't need to be at your physical peak (you're on holiday after all).

Elite Adventures TOURS
(☑07-347 8282; www.eliteadventures.co.nz; half/full day from $115/270) Small-group tours covering a selection of Rotorua's major cultural and natural highlights.

Thermal Land Shuttle TOURS
(Map p308; ☑0800 894 287; www.thermalshuttle.co.nz; departs i-SITE, 1167 Fenton St; adult/child from $65/33) Daily scheduled shuttles to Waimangu and Wai-O-Tapu, as well as stops along the Te Ara Ahi cycle trail. Transport-only or entry-inclusive options are available.

Rotorua Duck Tours TOURS
(Map p308; ☑07-345 6522; www.rotoruaducktours.co.nz; 1241 Fenton St; adult/child $75/50; ☺tours 11am & 1pm Oct-Apr, 1pm May-Sep) Ninety-minute trips in a WWII amphibious vehicle take in the major sites around town and head out onto three lakes (Rotorua, Okareka and Tikitapu/Blue). Two-hour Lake Tarawera trips ($95/60) also available.

⌨ Sleeping

Accommodation options in Rotorua are as abundant as bubbling mud pools. Outside of the city centre, motels tend to cluster around Fenton St (the road to Whakarewarewa through Victoria and Fenton Park), with a few B&Bs and a neat little holiday park in Ngongotaha, 7km northwest of the town centre.

★YHA Rotorua HOSTEL $
(Map p308; ☑07-349 4088; www.yha.co.nz; 1278 Haupapa St; dm from $30, with/without bathrooms from $70/45, d from $75/59; @🔊) 🖋 Bright and sparkling, this classy hostel, purpose-built from corrugated iron and wood, is great for those wanting to get outdoors, with bike storage and hire, and staff eager to assist with trip bookings. There's a light-filled common space, a barbecue area and a great deck looking out over Kuirau Park. Off-street parking is a bonus.

Funky Green Voyager HOSTEL $
(Map p308; ☑07-346 1754; www.funkygreenvoyager.co.nz; 4 Union St, Victoria; dm $24-28, with/without bathrooms from $70/45, d $75/59; 🔊🖥) 🖋 Green outside and inside – due to several cans of paint and a dedicated environmental policy – the shoe-free FGV features laid-back tunes and sociable chatter among a spunky bunch of guests and worldly wise owners. The glass sunroom warms winter, and an above-ground pool cools summer. Dorms are roomy – even the 10-bed dorm is actually spread between three rooms.

Crash Palace HOSTEL $
(Map p308; ☑07-348 8842; www.crashpalace.co.nz; 1271 Hinemaru St; dm/s from $26/50, d with/without bathroom $78/70; 🔊) Crash occupies a big, blue 1930s hotel near Government Gardens. The atmosphere strikes a balance between raucous and relaxed – there's a DJ console behind the bar/reception, but also art on the walls and a hidden-from-the-world backyard. It's a two-minute stroll to the Polynesian Spa (though it also has its own thermally heated hot tub).

Waiteti Trout Stream Holiday Park
HOLIDAY PARK $

(Map p322; ☑07-357 5255; www.waiteti.com; 14 Okona Cres, Ngongotaha; sites from $21, backpacker lodge from $35, cabins with/without bathroom $105/60; 🛜🐾) 🏊 This keenly maintained campground is a great option if you don't mind the 10km drive into town. Set in gardens abutting a trout-filled stream, it's a cute classic with characterful motel units, compact cabins, a tidy backpackers' lodge (private rooms only) and beaut campsites by the water. Kayaks and dinghies are free, and there are fishing rods for the kids.

Rotorua Central Backpackers
HOSTEL $

(Map p308; ☑07-349 3285; www.rotoruacentralbackpackers.co.nz; 1076 Pukuatua St; dm $28, d & tw without bathroom $68; 🛜) Built as flats in 1936, this heritage hostel retains original features, including deep bathtubs and geothermally powered radiators. Dorms have no more than six beds (and no bunks), plus there's a spa pool and barbecue. Perfect if you're not looking to party. The front sunroom is the place to curl up at the end of a day spent exploring.

Rock Solid Backpackers
HOSTEL $

(Map p308; ☑07-282 2053; www.rocksolidrotorua.co.nz; 1140 Hinemoa St; dm/s from $27/70, d with/without bathroom $95/75; 🛜) Cavernous Rock Solid occupies a former shopping mall: you might be bunking down in a florist or a delicatessen. Dorms over the street are sunny, and there's a big, bright kitchen. Downstairs is the Wall (p311) rock-climbing facility, and the hostel's spacious lounge/reception looks right out at the big-wall action. Table tennis and pool tables seal the deal.

Base Rotorua
HOSTEL $

(Map p308; ☑07-348 8636; www.stayatbase.com; 1286 Arawa St; dm from $26, r $85-100; @🛜🐾) Things get more active than a geothermal field at this huge hostel that's ever popular with partying backpackers, especially when nights get flowing at the trashy Lava Bar. Dorms can be tight (up to 10 beds) and the lounges are concrete boxes, but extras such as female-only dorms, en suites attached to most rooms and a thermally heated pool compensate.

★Aura
MOTEL $$

(Map p308; ☑07-348 8134; www.aurarotorua.co.nz; 1078 Whakaue St; units from $145; 🛜🐾) 🏊 This eco-minded motel, in a fully renovated older complex near the lake, has two natural mineral-water spas and a heated outdoor swimming pool, composts on site, and donates $5 to charity if you opt not to have your room serviced. There are free Cruiser-style bikes for guests, and a geothermal steam box for your own *hāngi*-style cookout.

Arista
MOTEL $$

(☑0800 114 562, 07-349 0300; www.aristaofrotorua.co.nz; 296 Fenton St; d from $145, f $250-310; 🛜🚿) The best of a clutch of motels on Fenton St, south of the town centre, Arista claims to have Rotorua's largest family rooms. Each room is two-level and huge – somewhere between a standard motel and a house. There's a small playground for kids, the mirrored windows guarantee privacy, and don't be surprised if Boris the cat adopts you. There's bike storage and wash-down facilities for the big kids.

All Seasons Holiday Park
HOLIDAY PARK $$

(Map p322; ☑07-345 6240; www.allseasonsrotorua.co.nz; 50-58 Lee Rd, Hannahs Bay; sites from $25, units with/without bathroom $144/114; ❄️🛜🐾🚿) 🏊 Rotorua's best family camping is at this dinosaur-themed holiday park in lovely Hannahs Bay, 8km northeast of the city centre. Kids will love the 18 concrete dinosaurs, massive playground, covered heated pool and the Kids Cave with foosball, Pac-Man machine and toys. The park is 200m from the lake, and near the airport, but there aren't many flights, and none at night.

B&B @ the Redwoods
B&B $$

(Map p322; ☑07-345 4499; www.theredwoods.co.nz; 3 Awatea St, Lynmore; r $179-239; 🛜) This pleasant place offers three en-suite B&B rooms in a suburban house beside the Redwoods Whakarewarewa Forest (p308). Two have views over the lake, while the third faces the front garden. All guests have access to a large lounge·where you can help yourself to a hot drink or share an evening glass of wine.

Rotorua Top 10 Holiday Park
HOLIDAY PARK $$

(☑07-348 1886; www.rotoruatop10.co.nz; 1495 Pukuatua St; sites from $48, cabins/units from $145/200; ❄️@🛜🐾🚿) Everything's kept spick and span at this small but perfectly formed holiday park. Facilities include a small outdoor pool, hot mineral spas and a super children's playground with bounce pillow and trampolines. Cabins are in good

ROTORUA ON THE CHEAP

In NZ's ever-expanding quest for high-value tourism (ie targeted to the affluent), it can sometimes feel like the urge to fleece has gravitated from the sheep farms to the tourist attractions. Sadly, this is particularly true in Rotorua. However, there are still ways for the budget-conscious traveller to get a good whiff of this geothermal and cultural wonder.

Thermal activity can be seen free of charge in Kuirau Park (p306), Ōhinemutu (p309) and along the lakeshore by Government Gardens (p307). If it's warm water you're after, the main price you pay for a soothing dip at Waitangi Soda Springs (p325) is the drive. Heading south, 29km from Rotorua beside Rainbow Mountain, things are free and natural at **Kerosene Creek** (Map p322; Old Waiotapu Rd) `FREE`, where a warm stream invites a soak beneath a low waterfall.

There are lots of wonderful walks in the area; enquire at the Rotorua i-SITE (p321). If the Redwoods Treewalk (p310) is outside your budget, simply wander into the forest beneath it at night for the magical sight of the lanterns illuminating the canopy.

If you can afford to visit just one of the ticketed geothermal areas, here's a guide to help you choose:

Whakarewarewa (p307) An authentic experience of Māori life amid the steam.

Te Puia (p307) A slick combination of geothermal features, kiwis and traditional Māori culture, but by far the most expensive.

Waimangu Volcanic Valley (p323) The newest volcanic landscape in NZ offers good value, with colourful features and a bus ride back to the visitor centre from the far end.

Wai-O-Tapu Thermal Wonderland (p323) The most impressive and colourful geothermal features and also the cheapest, but usually the most crowded.

Hell's Gate (p324) Pots of mud, a hot waterfall and a mud volcano, with the added bonus of a free muddy foot bath at the end.

---

nick with an adjacent communal kitchen and lounge, or you can opt for a smart self-contained motel unit.

Each campsite comes with its own table and bench.

★ **Prince's Gate Hotel**   BOUTIQUE HOTEL **$$$**
(Map p308; ☑ 07-348 1179, 0800 500 705; www.princesgate.co.nz; 1057 Arawa St; r from $200; ☎ ❄) This grand building constructed from NZ's most cherished wood, kauri, sits directly outside the Government Gardens' main Prince's Gate, and began life in 1897 as a pub in Waihi before being dismantled and moved board-by-board to Rotorua in 1917. Options range from the well-named Snug rooms to the opulent Duchess Suite with balcony overlooking the three pools. Surprisingly good value.

Befitting the period style, it offers high tea every day (11am to 4pm).

★ **Koura Lodge**   B&B **$$$**
(Map p322; ☑ 07-348 5868; www.kouralodge.co.nz; 209 Kawaha Point Rd, Kawaha Point; r from $550; ❄ ☎) Secluded on swanky Kawaha Point, this upmarket lodge features spacious rooms and suites, and a two-bedroom apartment.

Decks and balconies provide lake views, and the hot tub and sauna are right at the lake edge. Gourmet breakfasts around the huge wooden table are perfect for meeting other travellers, while kayaks are on hand for lake exploration.

Jetboats and the floatplane can (in the right conditions) pick you up directly from the lodge's pier.

Kings on Peace   APARTMENT **$$$**
(☑ 07-348 1234, 0800 508 246; www.kingsonpeace.co.nz; 4 Peace St, Fenton Park; apt from $195; ❄ ☎) Rise far above the surrounding motel pack with these five-star apartments, built in 2018. Large studios and one- and two-bedroom apartments feature modern styling, full kitchens, dishwasher, laundry and dryer. The one-bedroom apartments also have a BBQ and spa deck. All rooms have an electric-car charging station, and there's a wash-down station, tools and bike storage for cyclists.

It's the stylish sibling to the neighbouring **Sport of Kings** (☑ 07-348 2135; www.sportofkingsmotel.co.nz; 6 Peace St, Fenton Park; units from $159; ☎ ❄ ☼) motel.

City Lights Boutique Lodge

B&B $$$

(Map p322; ☑ 07-349 1413; www.citylights.nz; 56c Mountain Rd, Western Heights; r/cottages/apt/ ste from $275/275/285/355; ❉@🐾) Looking down on Rotorua from the slopes of Mt Ngongotaha, this upmarket lodge has three en-suite B&B rooms in the main house, a self-contained apartment and a separate garden cottage further down the drive. Not to mention that there's also a spa, sauna and pet alpacas.

Regal Palms Resort

MOTEL $$$

(☑ 07-350 3232; www.regalpalms.co.nz; 350 Fenton St; r from $240; ❉🐾🏊🎲) This resort in the 'burbs was undergoing a massive refurb when we visited, with 26 new apartments and a restaurant being added. Sporting Tuscan colours, it has tree-shaded gardens, swimming pool, gym, sauna, minigolf course, tennis and playground. Rooms and apartments – all with spas – are spacious and modern.

Quest Rotorua Central

APARTMENT $$$

(Map p308; ☑ 07-929 9808; www.questapart ments.co.nz; 1192 Hinemoa St; studios/apt from $210/255; ❉🐾) From the outside, it looks as though you might have to share your room with office workers, but this modern four-storey block provides spacious units and one- and two-bedroom apartments, with full kitchen and laundry facilities, in the heart of the town centre. Double-glazing keeps any street noise at bay.

Regent of Rotorua

BOUTIQUE HOTEL $$$

(Map p308; ☑ 07-348 4079; www.regentrotorua. co.nz; 1191 Pukaki St; r $245-315; ❉🐾🏊) Beauty comes from within at this completely over-hauled 1960s motel. The structure is unmis-takably motel, but inside it delivers glitzy glam in spades, with hip black-and-white decor, and rooms framed around a heated pool with a water feature. If you tire of the well-regarded restaurant, Eat Streat is just a block away.

🍴 Eating

The lake end of Tutanekai St – known as 'Eat Streat' – is a car-free strip of more than a dozen al fresco eateries and bars beneath a canopy roof. There are plenty of restaurants in Rotorua, so bookings aren't typically needed, except at the height of the seasons (Christmas to February, and Easter).

Tea & Happiness

VEGAN $

(Map p322; ☑ 021 0238 1057; www.facebook.com/ teaandhappinessnz; 149 Fairy Springs Rd, Fairy Springs; burgers $10, salad bowls $7-13; ⊙noon-6pm Wed-Sat; 🐾) 🌿 Chiselled into the cor-ner of a supermarket across the highway from Skyline Rotorua, Tea & Happiness has just three tables but 100% devotion to plant-based eating. The Happy Burger is made with seitan, the salad bowls are cre-ative, and the fries are air-fried, so lower in fat.

Ciabatta Cafe & Bakery

CAFE $

(☑ 07-348 3332; www.ciabattabakery.co.nz; 38 White St, Fenton; items $9-12; ⊙8am-3pm Tue-Fri, to 2pm Sat; 🐾) This unexpected and wel-coming find in an industrial complex near Whakarewarewa keeps things simple – ciab-atta sandwiches done well and a well-named 'long dog' hotdog. The coffee is good and the pastries are probably the finest in town – it'll be hard to walk away without one of the decadent cronuts. Jazz sessions every sec-ond Saturday morning.

Rotorua Night Market

MARKET $

(Map p308; www.facebook.com/rotoruanight market; Tutanekai St; ⊙5pm-late Thu) Tutanekai St is closed off on Thursday nights as Roto-rua lays out a world of food. Buskers, coffee vans and clothing and jewellery makers are dotted among a couple of dozen food stalls with global flavours from maple smoked ribs to vegetarian Palestinian.

★Terrace Kitchen

INTERNATIONAL $$

(Map p308; ☑ 07-460 1229; https://terrace. kitchen; 1029 Tutanekai St; mains $21-32; ⊙7.30am-late; 🐾) Overlooking the village green, this bright and breezy restaurant sources herbs and edible flowers from its own yard. Doors peel back to merge the indoor and outdoor areas, and the wide-ranging menu is Asian-influenced (great ramen and bao buns) with fresh forays into brunch, such as mozzarella with salsa verde, shaved fennel and salted lemon.

★Abracadabra Cafe & Bar

INTERNATIONAL $$

(Map p308; ☑ 07-348 3883; www.abracadabra cafe.com; 1263 Amohia St; mains $28-37, tapas $11-17; ⊙7.30am-late Tue-Sat, to 3pm Sun; 🐾🌿) Channelling Mexico and Morocco, sociable Abracadabra is a magical cave of spicy de-lights, from beef-and-apricot tagine to the grande burrito. There's an attractive front deck and a great beer terrace out the back, with a tepee and play area for kids. Vegan menu available.

Artisan Cafe
CAFE $$

(Map p308; ☑07-348 0057; www.artisancafe rotorua.com; 1149 Tutanekai St; mains $11-24; ⊘7am-3.30pm Mon-Fri, from 7.30am Sat & Sun; ⊜⊘) A spinning wheel and a Mary Poppins–style bicycle lend a folksy feel to Rotorua's best cafe. But there's nothing old-fashioned about the town's most creative and tasty breakfast menu, which includes a vegan mushroom ragu, chickpea and kumara (sweet potato) burger, and the Little Miss Bene, an eggs Benedict on rosti.

Atticus Finch
INTERNATIONAL $$

(Map p308; ☑07-460 0400; https://atticusfinch. co.nz; Eat Streat, 1106 Tutanekai St; lunch $16-22, shared plates $6-36; ⊘noon-2.30pm & 5pm-late; ⊘) Named after the righteous lawyer in *To Kill a Mockingbird*, the hippest spot on Eat Streat plays to a theme with the Scout Sangria and Radley Sour cocktails, but it's the extensive menu of around 20 shared plates that makes this place novel in Rotorua. A concise menu of NZ beer and wine imparts a local flavour.

Leonardo's
ITALIAN $$

(Map p308; ☑07-347 7084; www.leonardos. co.nz; Eat Streat, 1099 Tutanekai St; mains $23-38; ⊘11.30am-10pm; ⊘) Italian restaurants bookend Eat Streat, but Leonardo's is our favourite. The wine list is good and while the menu has few surprises – arancini, carbonara, margarita, tiramisu – you can sit out front and pretend the Eat Streat foot traffic is the Italian passeggiata.

Third Place
CAFE $$

(Map p308; ☑07-349 4852; www.thirdplacecafe. co.nz; 35 Lake Rd, Ōhinemutu; breakfast $13-22, lunch $15-24; ⊘7.30am-4pm Mon-Fri, to 3.30pm Sat & Sun; ⊜) This superfriendly cafe is away from the hubbub, with awesome lake views. All-day breakfasts are headlined by a 'mumble jumble' of roast kumara (sweet potato), fried tomatoes and spicy chorizo, topped with a poached egg and hollandaise sauce, while lunchtime brings fish and chips and variations on a BLT theme. Score a window seat overlooking the steaming shores of Ōhinemutu.

Sabroso
LATIN AMERICAN $$

(Map p308; ☑07-349 0591; 1184 Haupapa St; mains $23-29; ⊘5-9pm Wed-Sun) The love child of Venezuelan-born owner Sarah, this Latin American *cantina,* adorned with sombreros, guitars and salt-and-pepper shakers made from Corona bottles, serves a concise but finely honed menu of zingy south-of-the-border fare – the likes of chimichanga, and chorizo and black-bean chilli. Meals come accompanied by Sabroso's house-made hot sauces.

Capers Epicurean
CAFE $$

(Map p308; ☑07-348 8818; www.capers.co.nz; 1181 Eruera St; breakfast $15-25, mains $25-33; ⊘7am-9pm; ⊜⊛) This slick, barn-like delicatessen-cum-cafe is perennially busy, and with good reason. Breakfasts run from potato waffles to slow-cooked chickpeas and the glass cabinets heave with tarts, slices and salads. Dinner ranges from sirloin and risotto to roasted cauliflower wedges. The deli section is stocked with relishes, jams and chocolates.

Lime Caffeteria
CAFE $$

(Map p308; ☑07-350 2033; 1096 Whakaue St; mains $20-26; ⊘7.30am-4.30pm) Occupying a quiet corner near the lake, this zesty cafe offers nostalgic breakfasts with a modern twist, such as mince on toasted ciabatta with a poached egg, and vanilla risotto (rice pudding topped with berries and Black Doris plums). Go alfresco or, if you prefer, get communal around one of the large shared tables.

Fat Dog
CAFE $$

(Map p308; ☑07-347 7586; www.fatdogcafe.co.nz; 1161 Arawa St; breakfast $9-26, mains $18-30; ⊘7am-9pm Sun-Thu, to 9.30pm Fri & Sat; ⊜⊛) With paw prints across the walls and ceiling, this casual and colourful cafe is the most child-friendly cafe in town. During the day it dishes up burgers, nachos and salads; in the evening it's double lamb shanks, ribs and wings. Also a popular post-dinner dessert stop.

Drinking & Nightlife

Quality watering holes aren't abundant in Rotorua, but the Eat Streat dining strip on Tutanekai St might just as easily be named Drink Streat.

Brew
CRAFT BEER

(Map p308; ☑ 07-346 0976; www.brewpub.co.nz; Eat Streat, 1103 Tutanekai St; ⊙ 11.30am-1am) Run by the folks from Croucher Brewing, Rotorua's best microbrewery, Brew sits in a sunny spot on Eat Streat. Thirteen taps showcase the best of Croucher's brews as well as guest beers from NZ and overseas, mopped up by pizzas, burgers and beer snacks such as bratwurst and jalapeño poppers. There's regular live music, and 'Hoppy Hour' every Friday evening.

Ponsonby Rd
COCKTAIL BAR

(Map p308; ☑ 021 151 2036; www.ponsonbyrd. co.nz; Eat Streat, 1109 Tutanekai St; ⊙ 4pm-late Tue-Thu, to 3am Fri & Sat; ☎) What's a lounge bar without chandeliers, a grand piano and red velvet curtains? This place, created by former TV weatherman turned Labour MP Tamati Coffey, is set into a narrow space that seems to remove you from Eat Streat. There's a soulful soundtrack and regular live music (and karaoke). Cocktails are the main focus, and the wine list is mostly faithful to NZ.

Pig & Whistle
PUB

(Map p308; ☑ 07-347 3025; www.pigandwhistle. co.nz; cnr Haupapa & Tutanekai Sts; ⊙ 11.30am-late; ☎) Inside a 1940s former police station (look for the Māori motifs on the facade), this busy pub serves up frosty beer, big-screen TVs, a beer garden, live music and solid pub grub. The brown banquettes retain the building's administrative atmosphere, but the 15 taps are all about craft beer and cider. Weekday happy hours stretch to 2½ hours.

☆ Entertainment

Tamaki Māori Village
TRADITIONAL MUSIC

(Map p308; ☑ 07-349 2999; www.tamakimaorivil lage.co.nz; booking office 1220 Hinemaru St; adult/child $130/75) Modestly proclaiming itself one of the 10 best experiences in the world, Tamaki offers a 3½-hour twilight Māori cultural experience in its recreated precolonial village, 15km south of Rotorua (transfers included). The encounter is very hands-on, taking you on an interactive journey through Māori history, arts, traditions and customs. The concert is followed by a *hāngi*.

Matariki
TRADITIONAL MUSIC

(Map p308; ☑ 0800 444 422, 07-346 3888; 11 Tutanekai St; adult/child $69/35; ⊙ 6.30pm) The Novotel's 2½-hour Māori cultural experience includes a performance of traditional song and dance followed by a *hāngi*. It's held in a separate building adjacent to the hotel, facing the village green.

Mitai Māori Village
TRADITIONAL MUSIC

(Map p322; ☑ 07-343 9132; www.mitai.co.nz; 196 Fairy Springs Rd, Fairy Springs; adult $123, child $25-61; ⊙ 6.30pm) This family-run outfit offers a popular three-hour evening event with a concert, *hāngi* and glowworm bush walk. The experience starts with the arrival of a *waka taua* (war canoe) and can be combined with a night-time tour of Rainbow Springs (p309) next door, including a walk through the kiwi enclosure, or a soak at the Polynesian Spa (p314). Pick-ups included.

Basement Cinema
CINEMA

(Map p308; ☑ 07-350 1400; www.basementcinema. co.nz; 1140 Hinemoa St; adult/child $15/13) Oddly combined with a rock-climbing facility and a hostel, Basement offers offbeat, foreign-language and art-house flicks. Tickets are just $10 on Tuesdays.

🛍 Shopping

Rākai Jade
ARTS & CRAFTS

(Map p308; ☑ 027 443 9295; www.facebook.com/ rakaijade; 1234 Fenton St; ⊙ 9am-5pm Mon-Sat) Purchase off-the-shelf *pounamu* (greenstone/jade) pieces, or work with Rākai's on-site team of local Māori carvers to design and carve your own pendant or jewellery. A day's notice for 'Carve Your Own' experiences (from $150) is preferred – allow a full day and bring your own design.

Moko 101
ART

(Map p308; ☑ 021 165 7624; www.facebook.com/ MOKO101; 1157 Hinemoa St; booking fee $50, tattooing per hour $150; ⊙ 10am-5pm Mon-Fri) Take home a permanent souvenir of traditional *tā moko* (Māori tattooing), albeit done with modern tattooing equipment rather than stone chisels. It doubles as a fine-art gallery with works by local Māori artists.

Mountain Jade
ARTS & CRAFTS

(Map p308; ☑ 07-349 1828; www.mountain jade.co.nz; 1288 Fenton St; ⊙ 9am-6pm) Watch the carvers at work through the streetside window, take a free 15-minute tour of the workshop, or simply peruse the high-end handcrafted greenstone jewellery and other objects.

ℹ Information

Lakes PrimeCare (☑ 07-348 1000; 1165 Tutanekai St; ⊙ 8am-9.30pm) Urgent medical care, with a late-opening pharmacy (8.30am to 9pm) next door.

DON'T MISS

HAKA & HĀNGI

Māori culture is a big-ticket item in Rotorua and, though the experiences are commercialised, they're still a great introduction to authentic Māori traditions. The two big activities are *kapa haka* (traditional performing arts) concerts and *hāngi* (earth-cooked) feasts, usually packaged together in an evening's entertainment featuring a *pōwhiri* (welcoming ceremony), the famous *haka* (war dance), *waiata* (songs) and *poi* dances, where women showcase their dexterity by twirling balls of flax.

Tamaki Māori Village and family-run Mitai Māori Village are established favourites, with the experience heightened due to their re-created precolonial village settings. Te Puia (p307) and Whakarewarewa (p307) offer the added thrill of being situated within an active geothermal zone. Both stage daytime shows; Te Puia also has an evening *hāngi*-and-show package while Whakarewarewa serves *hāngi*-cooked lunches.

Rotorua Hospital (☑07-348 1199; www.lakesdhb.govt.nz; Pukeroa Rd; ◷24hr) Round-the-clock emergency department.

Rotorua i-SITE (Map p308; ☑07-348 5179; www.rotoruanz.com; 1167 Fenton St; ◷7.30am-6pm; ⊜) The hub for travel information and bookings, including Department of Conservation (DOC) huts and Great Walks, and Rotorua's mountain-biking scene. Also has a charging station, currency exchange, showers and lockers.

ⓘ Getting There & Away

AIR

Air New Zealand (p306) flies to/from Auckland, Wellington and Christchurch.

BUS

All of the **long-distance buses** (Map p308; 1167 Fenton St) stop outside the Rotorua i-SITE, where you can arrange bookings.

InterCity (p306) destinations include Auckland (from $26, 3½ hours, six daily), Hamilton (from $15, 1½ hours, five daily), Taupō (from $13, one hour, four daily), Napier (from $18, four hours, daily), Tauranga (from $14, 1½ hours, two daily) and Wellington (from $30, eight hours, two daily).

Skip (p306) has coaches to/from Auckland (from $15, 3½ hours, two daily), Hamilton (from $20, 1½ hours, three daily), Tauranga (from $18, 1¾ hours, daily) and Wellington (from $23, seven hours, daily).

ⓘ Getting Around

TO/FROM THE AIRPORT

Rotorua Airport (ROT; Map p322; ☑07-345 8800; www.rotorua-airport.co.nz; SH30) is located 9km northeast of town. **Super Shuttle** (☑0800 748 885; www.supershuttle.co.nz) offers a door-to-door airport service (first passenger $22, each additional passenger $5).

Baybus (☑0800 422 9287; www.baybus.co.nz) route 10 stops at the airport hourly ($2.80, 8am to 6pm). A taxi to/from the town centre costs about $32.

BUS

Baybus has buses operating on 11 local routes from 6.30am to 6pm (cash fare $2.80, day pass $7). The most useful routes (all leave the CBD half-hourly) are 1 to Ngongotaha (28 minutes) via Rainbow Springs/Skyline Rotorua/Agrodome, 3 to the Redwoods (seven minutes), 10 to the airport (18 minutes) and 11 to Whakarewarewa (13 minutes).

Many local attractions offer free pickup/drop-off shuttle services.

CAR

The big-name car-hire companies vie for your attention at Rotorua Airport. Otherwise, try **RaD Care Hire** (☑07-349 3993; www.radcarhire.co.nz; 39 Fairy Springs Rd, Fairy Springs; ◷8am-5pm Mon-Fri, to 2pm Sat).

TAXI

Rotorua Taxis (☑0800 500 000; www.rotoruataxis.co.nz) Well-established local company.

ROTORUA LAKES

Lake Rotorua is the largest of 18 *roto* (lakes) scattered like splashes from an upturned glass to the north and east of Rotorua. The district's explosive volcanic past and steamy present is on display at various interesting sites. The geothermal areas are strewn around the region – from Hell's Gate in the north, to Wai-O-Tapu Thermal Wonderland, almost halfway to Taupō. White-water activities predominantly focus on the Kaituna River before it flows into Lake Rotoiti in the north.

Rotorua Lakes

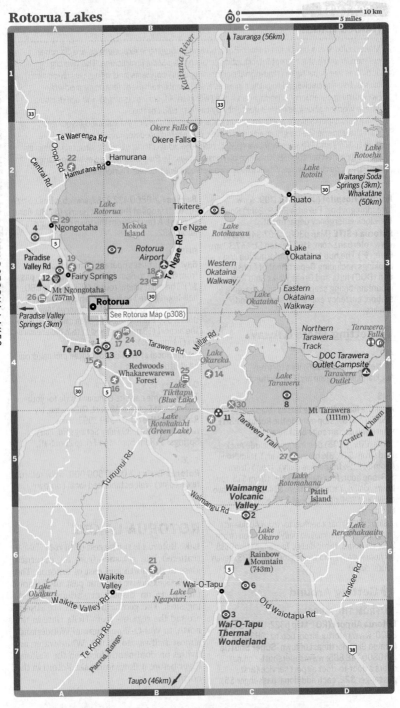

0 ____ 10 km
0 ____ 5 miles

Tauranga (56km)

Kaituna River

33

33

Te Waerenga Rd

Oropi Rd

Central Rd

22
Hamurana Rd
Hamurana

Okere Falls
Okere Falls

Lake Rotoehu

Lake Rotoiti

Waitangi Soda Springs (3km); Whakatāne (50km)

30

Ruato

Lake Rotorua

Tikitere
5

Te Ngae

Lake Rotokawau

Lake Okataina

4
29
Ngongotaha
5

Mokoia Island

Rotorua Airport
7

Western Okataina Walkway

Lake Okataina

Eastern Okataina Walkway

Paradise Valley Rd
9 19
Fairy Springs
28
18
23
12
Te Ngae Rd

Mt Ngongotaha (757m)
26

Paradise Valley Springs (3km)

Rotorua

See Rotorua Map (p308)

30

Lake Okataina

Northern Tarawera Track

Tarawera Falls

Te Puia
1
17 24
13
Tarawera Rd
Millar Rd
Lake Okareka

DOC Tarawera Outlet Campsite
Tarawera Outlet

15
10

Redwoods Whakarewarewa Forest
25
14

Lake Tarawera

30
5
16

Lake Tikitapu (Blue Lake)

8

Mt Tarawera (1111m)

Crater Chasm

Lake Rotokakahi (Green Lake)
11
20
30
Tarawera Trail

27

Lake Rotomahana

Patiti Island

Lake Rereohakauitu

Tumunui Rd

Waimangu Rd

Waimangu Volcanic Valley
2

Lake Okaro

Rainbow Mountain (743m)

Lake Ohakuri

21
Waikite Valley
Waikite Valley Rd

5
Wai-O-Tapu
6

Lake Ngapouri

Old Waiotapu Rd

Yankee Rd

Te Kopia Rd

Paeroa Range

3
Wai-O-Tapu Thermal Wonderland

38

Taupō (46km)

Rotorua Lakes

◎ Sights

★ **Waimangu
Volcanic Valley**   NATURAL FEATURE
(Map p322; ☑07-366 6137; www.waimangu.co.nz;
587 Waimangu Rd; adult/child walk $42/14, cruise
$45/14; ⏰8.30am-5pm, last admission 3.30pm,
to 6pm Jan) The most visible wound from
Mt Tarawera's 1886 eruption, the Waimangu geothermal area spreads down a valley
to Lake Rotomahana (Warm Lake). The
experience is quite different from the other
ticketed thermal areas as it involves a stroll
down the lush, bush-lined valley, with a return by shuttle bus from either the 1.5km,
2.8km or 3.6km point. The 4km trail ends by
the lake, where it's possible to take a 45-min-
ute boat cruise past steaming cliffs.

Highlights include the powder-blue Inferno Crater Lake, which fills and empties
every 38 days; Frying Pan Lake, the world's
largest hot spring; and Warbrick Terrace,
where the valley's colours are at their most
intense. Waimangu (Black Water) refers to
the dark water that once shot out of the
world's mightiest geyser, reaching heights of
up to 400m during its eruptions from 1900
to 1904.

Waimangu is 25 minutes' drive south of
Rotorua, 6km off SH5 (towards Taupō) at a
marked turn-off.

★ **Wai-O-Tapu
Thermal Wonderland**   NATURAL FEATURE
(Map p322; ☑07-366 6333; www.waiotapu.
co.nz; 201 Waiotapu Loop Rd; adult/child $33/11;
⏰8.30am-6pm summer, to 5pm winter) The
most colourful of the region's geothermal
attractions, Wai-O-Tapu (Sacred Waters) has
a variety of features packed into a relatively compact, heavily cratered area, with the
highlights being the orange-rimmed, fizzing
Champagne Pool and the unearthly lemon-
lime-hued Roto Kārikitea. Just down the
road (but included in the entry fee) is the
Lady Knox Geyser, which erupts (with
prompting from an organic soap) punc-
tually at 10.15am and gushes up to 20m –
follow the park exodus just before 10am to
witness it.

All the headline acts are on the shortest
(1.5km) of three interconnecting walking
loops, but you're best to set aside at least a
couple of hours for the full 3km track, which
leads down to a waterfall spilling into Lake
Ngakoro.

Wai-O-Tapu is 27km south of Rotorua along SH5 (towards Taupō), and a further 2km from the marked turn-off.

Lake Tarawera
LAKE

(Map p322; Tarawera Rd) Providing a mirror for the raw slopes of Mt Tarawera (1110m), this pretty lake is a popular destination for swimming, fishing, boating and walks. It may look tranquil now, but it was a very different story on the night of 10 June 1886, when the volcano sprang into life, blanketing the surrounding countryside in ash and mud up to 20m thick. Water taxis and cruises leave from the Landing at the end of Tarawera Rd.

Hell's Gate
NATURAL FEATURE

(Map p322; ☑07-345 3151; www.hellsgate.co.nz; 351 SH30, Tikitere; adult/child $39/20, pools $25/13; ☺8.30am-6.30pm Oct-Mar, to 4pm Apr-Sep, spa to 8.30pm Oct-Mar, to 7.30pm Apr-Sep) Known as Tikitere to the Ngāti Rangiteaorere people, this highly active geothermal reserve lies 16km northeast of Rotorua on the Whakatāne road (SH30). It's not the most colourful of the Rotorua thermal areas but, among all the bubbling pools and steaming vents, there are some unique features, such as a 2.4m-high mud volcano and the largest natural hot waterfall (40°C) in the southern hemisphere. There's also a small but well-priced set of therapeutic outdoor mineral pools attached to the complex.

Walking tracks make a 2.5km figure-eight loop through the reserve, passing all of the geothermal features and providing all the gurgling, burping and boiling you could hope for. Even if you're not hopping in a spa, there's a natural warm mud pool in which you can soak your feet at the end of the loop.

The diabolic name originated from a 1934 visit by Irish playwright George Bernard Shaw, who described it as the gateway to hell. However, Tikitere has long been known to local Māori as a place of healing. Warriors would ritually bathe in the hot waterfall to physically and spiritually cleanse themselves when returning from battle, and sulphur-infused water drawn from the pools was used as an insecticide and to heal septic wounds.

There's a cafe and a workshop where you can try your hand at woodcarving.

Te Wairoa, the Buried Village
ARCHAEOLOGICAL SITE

(Map p322; ☑07-362 8287; www.buriedvillage.co.nz; 1180 Tarawera Rd; adult/child $35/5; ☺9am-5pm Oct-Feb, to 4.30pm Mar-Sep) The village of Te Wairoa was once the main staging post for Victorian-era tourists coming to visit the famous Pink and White Terraces. When Mt Tarawera erupted in 1886, the entire village was covered in mud up to 2m thick. Today, excavations and a museum housing objects dug from the ruins tell its Pompeii-like story. A walking track (40 minutes) loops through the village's excavated area, with a side trail that descends steeply to the base of 30m-high Wairere Falls (p339).

🏃 Activities
Rafting, Kayaking & Sledging

There's plenty of white-water action around Rotorua, with the chance to take on the Grade V Kaituna River, complete with a startling 7m drop at Tutea Falls – the highest commercially rafted waterfall in the world. Some companies head further out to the Rangitaiki River (Grade III–IV) and the truly wild Wairoa River (Grade V), raftable only when the dam is opened every second Sunday between October and April. Sledging is zooming downriver on a body board. Most operators can arrange transfers.

Rotorua Rafting
RAFTING

(☑0800 772 384; www.rotorua-rafting.co.nz; 761 SH33, Okere Falls; rafting $95) The minimum age for rafting the Grade V-rated Kaituna River is 13, but 10-year-olds are allowed on the Grade III 'half trip' on the river. Also rafts the Grade III Okere Awa and the wild churn of the Rangitaiki River ($140). Transfers from central Rotorua included in the price.

River Rats
RAFTING, KAYAKING

(Map p322; ☑07-345 6543; www.riverrats.co.nz; Hangar 14s, Rotorua Airport, 837 Te Ngae Rd) White-water rafting trips on the Kaituna ($109), Wairoa ($149) and Rangitaiki ($149), including a scenic trip on the lower Rangitaiki (Grade II) that's good for youngsters (adult/child $149/100). Kayaking options include hire (two hours from $30) and guided evening paddles to hot pools on Lake Rotoiti ($169). There's also exciting river sledging on the Kaituna ($129), below the waterfall.

Waimarino Kayak Tours
KAYAKING

(☑07-576 4233; www.glowwormkayaking.com; departs Okere Falls Store, 757a SH33, Okere Falls; adult/child $155/100) Take a guided evening paddle on Lake Rotoiti to natural thermal pools and a glowworm cave. Pickup from Rotorua accommodation available for $30.

Wet 'n' Wild   RAFTING
(Map p322; ☑07-348 3191; www.wetnwildrafting.
co.nz; 58a Fryer Rd, Hamurana) Runs trips on the
Kaituna ($105), Wairoa ($120) and Rangitaiki (adult/child $140/120) rivers.

Kaituna Cascades   RAFTING
(☑07-345 4199; www.kaitunacascades.co.nz; 18
Okere Falls Rd, Okere Falls) Rafting on the Kaituna ($95), Rangitaiki ($160) and Wairoa
($140) Rivers, plus combos.

Kaituna Kayaks   KAYAKING
(☑021 277 2855; www.kaitunakayaks.co.nz; departs Kaituna River car park, SH33, Okere Falls, opp
Trout Pool Rd; tandem trip $150; ☺tandem trip
9am, noon & 3pm Oct-Apr) Run the 7m Tutea
Falls in a tandem white-water kayak, even if
you have no experience. White-water lessons
(half/full day from $100/220) also available.

Kaitiaki Adventures   RAFTING, HIKING
(☑07-357 2236; www.kaitiaki.co.nz; 1135 Te Ngae
Rd, Tikitere) Splash into white-water rafting
trips on the Kaituna ($109) and Wairoa
($138) Rivers, or sledge a Grade III section
of the Kaituna ($120). Also leads 4½-hour
guided hikes up Mt Tarawera ($164) – with
encouragement to run down into the crater –
or a helicopter flight to the mountain with a
walk around the red crater rim ($545).

Rotorua Paddle Tours   WATER SPORTS
(☑0800 772 384; www.rotoruapaddletours.co.nz;
Rotorua Rafting, 761 SH33, Okere Falls; trips $85;
☺9am, noon & 3pm) This outfit leads stand-
up paddle boarding trips on Tikitapu (Blue
Lake) and on the channel between Lake Rotorua and Lake Rotoiti. Minimum age: four.
If conditions are right, there's also a trip
paddling over hot-water vents and to a hot
beach on Lake Rotoiti.

Hiking

Numerous walks are outlined in DOC's
Walking and Hiking in Rotorua booklet,
which can be downloaded for free from its
website (www.doc.govt.nz).

A good starting point is the blissfully
beautiful 1½-hour (5.5km) **Blue Lake Track**,
which loops around Lake Tikitapu.

Just north of Wai-O-Tapu on SH5, the
2.5km **Rainbow Mountain Summit Track**
(1½ hours one way) is a strenuous walk up
the peak known to Māori as Maunga Kakaramea (Mountain of Coloured Earth). There
are spectacular views from the top towards
Lake Taupō and the volcanoes of Tongariro
National Park. A shorter walk here climbs

for 15 minutes (1km) to the **Crater Lakes**,
backed by colourful steaming cliffs.

The 10.5km **Eastern Okataina Walkway**
(three hours one way) goes along the eastern
shoreline of Lake Okataina to Lake Tarawera and passes the Soundshell, a natural
amphitheatre that has *pā* (fortified village)
remains and several swimming spots. The
22.5km **Western Okataina Walkway** (sev-
en hours one way) heads through the forest
west of Lake Okataina to Lake Rotoiti.

A 20-minute (700m) walk from Waterfall
Rd into **Tarawera Falls** unveils a 65m-high
waterfall pouring off an old lava flow. From
the falls, you can continue walking another
two hours to **Tarawera Outlet**, where the
Tarawera River squeezes out of Lake Tarawera. There's a **campsite** (Map p322; ☑07-351
7324; www.doc.govt.nz; adult/child $15/7.50) at
the outlet if you want to make an overnight
trip of it.

The **Okere Falls** are about 21km northeast of Rotorua, with an easy 1.2km track (30
minutes each way) passing the falls and, just
downstream, **Tutea Falls**, a 7m-high drop
that's popular with rafters. Stand and watch
for a while and you might see a raft hurtle
over its edge.

Tarawera Trail   HIKING
(Map p322; www.doc.govt.nz) Starting at the
Te Wairoa car park on Tarawera Rd, this
five- to six-hour track meanders 15km along
Lake Tarawera and through the forest to
Hot Water Beach, where there is **camping**
(Map p322; ☑07-349 3463; www.whakarewarewa.
com; adult/child $15/7.50) available. From here,
water taxis (adult/child $28/20) from Totally
Tarawera (p326) can be pre-booked to ferry

you back to the Landing; prices include a vehicle shuttle back to the car park.

Pick up a copy of DOC's *Tarawera Trail* brochure from the Rotorua i-SITE (p321) or download it from the DOC website.

Other Activities

Waikite Valley
Thermal Pools   HOT SPRINGS
(Map p322; ☑07-333 1861; www.hotpools.co.nz; 648 Waikite Valley Rd; adult/child $20/11, private pools 40 min per person $24; ☺10am-9pm) 🏊 Located in a verdant valley around 35km south of Rotorua, these pools provide a low-key (and cheaper) alternative to Rotorua's thermal baths. The outdoor pools range from a large family pool to small tubs, and private spas are available. There's also a cafe and adjoining campsite (sites powered/unpowered $29/25; pools free for campers).

The pools are 6km off SH5; the turn-off is opposite the road to Wai-O-Tapu. The gorgeous valley view as you come over the hill is enough to justify the drive in itself.

Horse Trekking
Lake Okareka   HORSE RIDING
(Map p322; ☑021 292 2233; www.treklakeoka reka.co.nz; 51 Acacia Rd, Lake Okareka; ☺rides 10am & 1.30pm) Farm-based horse riding with views of Rotorua's lakes and Mt Tarawera. Rides range from a 'Nervous Beginners' 30-minute introduction ($50) to a three-hour trek to the highest point on the farm ($150).

🧭 Tours

Totally Tarawera   CRUISE
(Map p322; ☑07-362 8080; www.totallytarawera. com; The Landing, Tarawera Rd) 🏊 Offers guided cruises (adult/child $75/45) on Lake Tarawera, taking in cultural and geothermal sites (including Hot Water Beach and a natural bush hot pool). Also runs a water-taxi service to Hot Water Beach (return $45/30), which is the terminus of the Tarawera Trail (p325). Bookings are essential.

Totally Tarawera also has two glamping sites on the lakeshore, reachable only on foot or by water taxi.

🛏 Sleeping

Blue Lake Top 10
Holiday Park   HOLIDAY PARK $$
(Map p322; ☑0800 808 292, 07-362 8120; www. bluelaketop10.co.nz; 723 Tarawera Rd; sites from $40, units with/without bathroom from $110/70;

📶🚗) 🏊 Encased by bush on the shores of gorgeous Lake Tikitapu (aka Blue Lake), this simple but well-run holiday park has seven types of cabins and motel units, and spotless facilities.

Totally Tarawera
Glamping   TENTED CAMP $$$
(☑07-362 8080; www.totallytarawera.com; Lake Tarawera; tents $325) Absolute seclusion, exclusivity and camping comfort at two hidden-away locations on the shores of Lake Tarawera, named Kanuka and Te Rata. Each site contains a single luxury tent with queen-size bed and Māori-inspired designs, and can only be reached by water taxi or hiking. Te Rata has a natural hot pool. Minimum two-night stay.

🍴 Eating

Okere Falls Store   CAFE $
(☑07-362 4944; www.okerefallsstore.co.nz; 757a SH33, Okere Falls; mains $9-19; ☺7am-7pm Sun-Wed, to 9pm Thu-Sat; ☑) 🏊 Okere Falls, 20km northeast of Rotorua, is a rafting town, so it's not just the fridge full of craft beers that's chilled out here. The food at this store with a beer garden ranges from kimchi-and-cheese toasted sandwiches to vegan kick-start breakfasts. Eat out on the raffish balcony with views over the Kaituna River.

It also hosts regular live music and a beer festival in October.

Landing Cafe   CAFE $$
(Map p322; ☑07-362 8502; The Landing, Tarawera Rd; mains $15-36; ☺9am-8pm, closed for dinner Mon-Wed in winter) Grab a deck table and ponder the power of Mt Tarawera from across the water at this cafe-cum-bar-cum-bistro, serving everything from seafood chowder to *san choi bow* (lettuce wraps) and snapper ceviche.

ℹ Information

The Rotorua i-SITE (p321) has plenty of information about accommodation and sights around the lakes.

ℹ Getting There & Away

Some of the major attractions (such as Hell's Gate) and activity operators provide transfers from Rotorua, but otherwise you'll need your own wheels to explore the area. The InterCity (p306) Hastings–Tauranga bus service runs from Rotorua to Okere Falls, but at inconvenient times (5.15pm and 6.35pm).

> **WORTH A TRIP**
>
> ### WHIRINAKI TE PUA-A-TĀNE CONSERVATION PARK
>
> This lush podocarp (conifer) forest park offers canyons, waterfalls, lookouts and streams, plus the gorgeous Arohaki Lagoon. Walking tracks here vary in length and difficulty: the DOC booklet *Walks and Tracks in Whirinaki Te Pua-a-Tāne Conservation Park* details 10 walking options. It's free online.
>
> The park's most popular walk is the 11km Whirinaki Waterfall Loop Track (three hours), which follows the Whirinaki River to feathery Whirinaki Waterfall. Longer hikes include the Whirinaki Track (two days) and the ultimate, five-day (79km) Te Pua-a-Tāne Circuit. There's also the rampaging 16km Whirinaki Forest Mountain Bike Track.
>
> The conservation park is 90km southeast of Rotorua off SH38, en route to Te Urewera National Park (take the turn-off at Te Whaiti to Minginui). There are several campsites and nine backcountry huts ($5 to $15) in the park. Buy hut tickets at any DOC office or the Rotorua i-SITE (p321) and deposit them in the honesty boxes, or purchase a Backcountry Hut Pass.

BAY OF PLENTY

The Bay of Plenty stretches along the pohutukawa-tree-lined coast from Waihi Beach to Ōpōtiki and inland as far as the Kaimai Range. This is where New Zealanders have been coming on holiday for generations, lapping up salt-tinged activities and lashings of sunshine.

❶ Getting There & Away

Baybus (p321) runs services between towns in the Bay of Plenty region. Tauranga City Airport (p336) has flights to Auckland, Wellington and Christchurch, while Whakatāne Airport (p343) has flights to Auckland. There are no passenger train services.

Tauranga

POP 131,500

Tauranga (pronounced '*toe*-run-gah') has been booming since the 1990s, and in 2017 became NZ's fifth-biggest city. By 2018 its population was said to have increased by 10% in just five years, with the big-city traffic snarls to prove it. It also has NZ's busiest port, with petrol refineries, lumber and loading cranes crowding what was once a lovely view from the city centre to Mt Maunganui.

While it gets overshadowed by its beachside 'burbs of Mt Maunganui and Papamoa, Tauranga's city centre, on a narrow peninsula, has a fine crop of fancy hotels, restaurants and bars enlivening its vampedup waterfront. Even if you're staying in the Mount, it's well worth popping over for a bite and a look around.

◉ Sights

The Elms　　　　　　　　HISTORIC BUILDING

(☎ 07-577 9772; www.theelms.org.nz; 15 Mission St; adult/child $15/7.50; ⊙10am-4pm) Surrounded by mature trees and lovely gardens, Tauranga's original mission station incorporates the Bay of Plenty's earliest buildings, along with one of the country's oldest oaks and first pianos. Fascinating guided tours tell the story of the mission, founded by Anglican priest Alfred Nesbit Brown in 1838, and its relations with local Māori. The property remained in the extended Brown family until 1997, retaining much of its original furniture, books and other chattels.

Tauranga
Art Gallery　　　　　　　　　GALLERY

(☎ 07-578 7933; www.artgallery.org.nz; cnr Wharf & Willow Sts; international visitors $7, NZ residents by donation; ⊙10am-4.30pm) The city's pre-eminent gallery stages challenging exhibitions of thought-provoking contemporary work. The building itself is a former bank, though you'd hardly know it – the atrium can hold massive works, and it's an altogether excellent space with no obvious compromise.

Tauranga

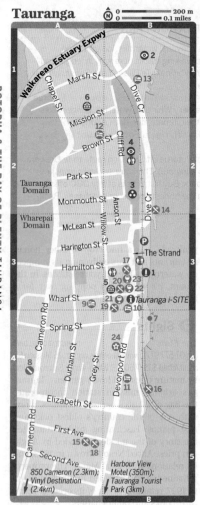

△ 0 ——— 200 m
0 ——— 0.1 miles

Māori and government forces in the 1860s. A prominent red-granite monument honours Rāwiri Puhirake, a Ngāi Te Rangi chief remembered for issuing a code of conduct for dealing mercifully with British civilians and wounded soldiers during the conflict.

Hairy Maclary & Friends SCULPTURE
(Strand Wharf) *Hairy Maclary* author Lynley Dodd lived in Tauranga for years, and NZ's favourite literary animals were immortalised in bronze on Tauranga's wharf in 2015. They're all here – Hairy Maclary, Slinky Malinki, Bottomley Potts et al – customarily harassing Scarface Claw. Just hope the kids aren't too disappointed on discovering that Hercules Morse really isn't as big as a horse.

Mission Cemetery CEMETERY
(Marsh St) This shady little cemetery, overlooking the bridge, has some interesting memorials relating to battles fought between local

Minden Lookout VIEWPOINT
(Minden Rd, Wairoa) On clear days this lofty wooden viewing platform, located about 13km west of the city centre, provides a panorama of nearly the entire Bay of Plenty – see if you can spot Whakaari (White Island) steaming away in the distance. To get here, take SH2 to Te Puna and turn south on Minden Rd; the lookout is about 3km up the road.

Monmouth Redoubt ARCHAEOLOGICAL SITE
(Monmouth St; ⏰24hr) FREE Shaded by huge pohutukawa trees, spooky Monmouth Redoubt was originally a Māori *pā* (fortified

village), then taken over and adapted by British soldiers during the New Zealand Wars.

At the foot of the Redoubt, on the end of the Strand, is Te Awanui, a ceremonial *waka* carved in 1972, on display in an open-sided building.

Robbins Park
GARDENS

(Cliff Rd) At its best in late spring and summer, this verdant pocket of roses sits behind an ivy-covered colonnade on a cliff overlooking the harbour, and is like a formal European garden. The beautifully maintained tropical greenhouse features delicate orchids and giant staghorn ferns.

🏃 Activities

The free, pocket-sized *Tauranga Walkways & Cycleways* pamphlet (from the i-SITE) details trails around Tauranga, Mt Maunganui and Papamoa.

★ Waimarino
Adventure Park
ADVENTURE SPORTS

(☑ 07-576 4233; www.waimarino.com; 36 Taniwha Pl, Bethlehem; day-pass adult/child $46/35; ⊙ 10am-6pm Sep-Apr, to 5pm Mon-Fri May-Aug) On the banks of the Wairoa River, 8km west of town, Waimarino offers kayaking (including a customised kayak slide!), rock climbing, gladiator poles, water trampolines, a rope course and a hydroslide. You can also hire kayaks and stand-up paddle boards (one/three hours $19/28) to paddle on the flat river, or take a guided kayak tour.

Cycle Tauranga
CYCLING

(☑ 07-571 1435; www.cycletauranga.co.nz; Harbour City Motor Inn, 50 Wharf St; 2hr/4hr/day $20/29/49) Has hybrid bikes for hire, including helmets, locks, panniers and maps. Tours also available.

Dive Zone
DIVING

(☑ 07-578 4050; www.divezonetauranga.co.nz; 213 Cameron Rd; trips from $170; ⊙ 8am-6pm Mon-Fri, 7.30am-4pm Sat & Sun) PADI courses and trips to local wrecks and reefs, plus gear rental and live-aboard trips further afield.

☞ Tours

Waimarino Kayak Tours
KAYAKING

(☑ 07-576 4233; www.glowwormkayaking.com; 36 Taniwha Pl, Bethlehem) Kayak tours don't get more magical than an evening paddle across

Lake McLaren to a canyon filled with glow-worms ($135). Daytime tour options include Lake McLaren ($110) and the Wairoa River ($120). Trips include transfers from Waimarino Adventure Park.

Bay Explorer
CRUISE

(☑ 021 605 968; www.bayexplorer.co.nz; Strand Wharf; adult/child $150/90; ⊙ departs 8am) This popular all-day cruise incorporates wildlife spotting – potentially whales, dolphins, orcas and bird life – and opportunities to go paddle boarding, kayaking and swimming. Half-day dolphin-focused trips ($130/75) also run most days.

✦ Festivals & Events

National
Jazz Festival
MUSIC

(☑ 07-577 7460; www.jazz.org.nz; ⊙ Easter) A four-day extravaganza of big blowers and bass, with concerts galore.

Tauranga
Arts Festival
PERFORMING ARTS

(☑ 07-928 6213; www.taurangafestival.co.nz; ⊙ late Oct) Kicking off on Labour Day weekend, this biennial (odd-numbered years) 10-day festival showcases dance, comedy, theatre and other arts.

🛏 Sleeping

Tauranga Tourist Park
HOLIDAY PARK $

(☑ 07-578 3323; www.taurangatouristpark.co.nz; 9 Mayfair St; sites from $28, cabins with/without bathroom $95/65; 🛜) The layout at this harbourside holiday park feels a bit tight (don't expect rolling acres), but it's well maintained, clean and tidy, and offers the closest camping to town, 4km south of the city centre. Aim for a site down by the bay under the pohutukawa trees.

★ Harbour View Motel
MOTEL $$

(☑ 07-578 8621; www.harbourviewmotel.co.nz; 7 Fifth Ave East; units from $165; ❋🛜) This home conversion close to the harbourfront is a haven of soft sounds and soft colours sitting quietly below the main road. Its one-bedroom, self-contained units are a 10- to 15-minute stroll into town, and some of the upstairs rooms have harbour glimpses – you'll likely see rowers zipping past in the morning.

Harbour City Motor Inn MOTEL **$$**
(☑07-571 1435; www.taurangaharbourcity.co.nz; 50 Wharf St; units from $155; ❄ 🛜) With a winning location just 100m from the Wharf St dining precinct, and yet remarkably quiet and neat as a pin, this lemon-yellow motor inn has a spa bath, desk and kitchenette in each room.

Roselands Motel MOTEL **$$**
(☑07-578 2294; www.roselands.co.nz; 21 Brown St; units from $149; 🛜) Spruced up with splashes of lime-green paint, slat-style beds and smart TVs, this sweet, old-style motel is in a central but leafy and quiet location near the Elms (p327). Expect spacious units (all with kitchenettes) and friendly hosts.

850 Cameron MOTEL **$$**
(☑07-577 1774; www.850motel.co.nz; 850 Cameron Rd, South Tauranga; units from $159; 🛜) This slick two-storey motel, 3.5km south of the city centre, has modern, self-contained apartments, ranging from studios to two-bedroom units with spa baths and striking rust-coloured tiling in the bathrooms. All have kitchens and ground-floor rooms have a small rear courtyard.

Hotel on Devonport HOTEL **$$**
(☑07-578 2668; www.hotelondevonport.net.nz; 72 Devonport Rd; r from $185; ❄ 🛜) This hotel is what passes for a futuristic high-rise in Tauranga, meaning every player wins a prize: harbour view or city view. It's slick rather than soulful, appealing to business travellers and upmarket weekenders, but it's also just 200m from the Strand.

Trinity Wharf HOTEL **$$$**
(☑07-577 8700; www.trinitywharf.co.nz; 51 Dive Cres; r from $230; ❄ 🛜 ⓦ) Tauranga's flashiest offering by far, this big white block of a hotel near the bridge has a slick, contemporary lobby decorated with white tiles and spiky pot plants. Amenities include the upmarket in-house Halo Lounge & Dining, an underutilised gym and infinity pool. Harbour King rooms all but overhang the water.

✖ Eating

A one-block section of Wharf St running off the Strand was turned into a dining precinct in 2015; it now contains some of the city's best eating and drinking options.

Grindz Café CAFE **$**
(☑07-579 0017; 50 First Ave; meals $12-20; ⊙7am-4pm Mon-Fri, 8am-3.30pm Sat, 8am-3pm Sun; 🛜 ✐ ⓦ) Side by side with Me & You, Grindz is one half of a well-caffeinated oasis on otherwise scrappy First Ave. It's a roomy, split-level affair – slick and modern at street level; Victorian and venerable upstairs. Cooked breakfasts, smoothies, a fine cake selection and excellent coffee are the order of the day.

Bobby's Fresh Fish Market FISH & CHIPS **$**
(☑07-578 1789; 1 Dive Cres; fish & chips $9.20; ⊙8am-7pm) This local legend sells fresh fish as well as frying up arguably Tauranga's best fish and chips – you can pick a fresh fillet yourself and have it cooked up for an extra $8 per kilogram. If you're feeling fancy, go for the smoked garlic mussels. Grab a seat at the hexagonal outdoor tables on the water's edge, among the expectant seagulls.

Patrick's Pies Gold Star Bakery BAKERY **$**
(☑07-579 2328; www.facebook.com/GoldStarPatricksPies; 19 Bethlehem Rd, Bethlehem; pies $5-6; ⊙8am-4.30pm) Winner of NZ's best pie seven years running. More than 30 types of pie are on offer – mince and cheese is perennially popular but we enjoyed the roast port, caramelised onion, mushroom and cheese pie. Located in a suburban shopping mall, the bakery is simplicity itself, but the walls are covered in more awards than a war veteran's chest.

★ Macau ASIAN **$$**
(☑07-578 8717; www.dinemacau.co.nz; 59 The Strand; small plates $10-21, large plates $19-35; ⊙11.30am-late) Zingy pan-Asian, shared-plate flavours take centre stage at Tauranga's top restaurant. The dark booths are ocean deep, and menu highlights include ginger prawn dumplings and grilled pork belly with mapo tofu and Sichuan pepper. If the chilli chocolate bowl is on the dessert menu, indulge.

★ Me & You CAFE **$$**
(☑07-577 0567; 48 First Ave; mains $13-19; ⊙7am-3.30pm; 🛜 ✐) Our favourite Tauranga cafe pairs an appealing front deck with hip baristas who really know their way around

the coffee machine. A huge array of counter food, including drool-inducing baked goods and vegan raw slices, combines with a menu including eggy and avocado breakfasts and prawn tacos.

Rye Bar & Grill
AMERICAN $$
(☑ 07-571 4138; www.ryekitchen.co.nz; 19 Wharf St; mains $23-40; ⊙ 4.30pm-late Tue-Thu, noon-late Fri-Sun) All your Texan favourites are served up at this rustic and relaxed spot in the Wharf St dining precinct. Grab an outdoor table and combine ribs, a fried-chicken basket or smoked beef brisket with a craft brew or a tasting paddle of bourbon or rye ($18).

Nourished Eatery
VEGAN $$
(☑ 021 0267 0131; www.thenourishingbaker. com; 114 Willow St; mains $15-17; ⊙ 7.30am-3pm Mon-Fri, 8.30am-3pm Sat, 9am-3pm Sun; ☑) Nourished's slow-cooked jackfruit burger and salted caramel French toast add real panache to this vegan menu. The colour scheme is probably a little too like a seven-year-old's bedroom, but who can walk past a harm-free scorched-almond donut? Alongside non-dairy options, cow's milk is available for the coffee, if you prefer.

Harbourside
MODERN NZ $$
(☑ 07-571 0520; www.harboursidetauranga.co.nz; 150 The Strand; mains $28-42; ⊙ 11.30am-2.30pm & 5pm-late) In a wonderfully atmospheric 100-year-old boathouse at the end of the Strand, Harbourside is the place for a romantic dinner, with boats as neighbours and the overhead railway bridge arching over the harbour. The steamed Coromandel mussels with chorizo and coconut cream are hard to beat, or you can just swing by for a moody predinner drink.

Drinking & Nightlife

Barrel Room
BAR
(☑ 07-578 0603; http://barrelroom.co.nz; 26 Wharf St; ⊙ noon-late) Sure, you could wander around town looking for a good wine bar, brewpub or whisky den, but you can also just head to the Barrel Room, which has already done the groundwork for you – top NZ wines, 16 taps of craft beer and a fine selection of Scottish single malts, served up in a barrel-lined bar.

Hop House
CRAFT BEER
(☑ 07-579 4810; www.facebook.com/thehophousenz; 12 Wharf St; ⊙ 3-9pm Tue, noon-10pm Wed, noon-11pm Thu, noon-late Fri & Sat, noon-9pm Sun) With its facade emblazoned with hops, and hops growing out front, the Hop House is single-minded in its passion for craft beer. There are 10 changing NZ brews on tap, or you can grab a tasting rack of four beers for $20. This was also the people's-choice winner for Tauranga's best burgers ($15 to $20) in 2019.

Phoenix
BAR
(☑ 07-578 8741; www.thephoenixtauranga.co.nz; 67 The Strand; ⊙ 10.30am-late Mon-Fri, 8.30am-late Sat & Sun) This big box of a gastropub pours Monteith's beers and serves pizza, burgers and meaty pub meals. This Phoenix rises best on Sunday afternoons and summer Friday nights, when there's live music.

Crown & Badger
PUB
(☑ 07-571 3038; www.crownandbadger.co.nz; 91 The Strand; ⊙ 11am-10pm Mon-Thu, 10.30am-late Fri-Sat, 10.30am-10pm Sun) Convincingly replicating a British boozer, right down to the Sunday roast with Yorkshire puddings and the dogs-welcome policy, this black-painted corner pub gets lively on weekends.

☆ Entertainment

Rialto Cinemas
CINEMA
(☑ 07-577 0445; www.rialtotauranga.co.nz; Goddards Centre, 21 Devonport Rd; adult/child $18/12) The Rialto is the best spot in town to catch a flick – classic, offbeat, art-house or international. And you can sip a coffee or a glass of wine in the darkness. Discounted tickets on Tuesdays.

❶ Information

The Downtown Tauranga website (www. downtowntauranga.co.nz) is a handy resource for all things Tauranga.

Tauranga Hospital (☑ 07-579 8000; www. bopdhb.govt.nz; 829 Cameron Rd, Tauranga South; ⊙ 24hr) Emergency and other services.

Tauranga i-SITE (☑ 07-578 8103; www. bayofplentynz.com; 103 The Strand; ⊙ 8.30am-5pm; ☎) Newly relocated to the Strand, dispensing local tourist information, accommodation bookings, InterCity bus tickets and DOC maps.

ROTORUA & THE BAY OF PLENTY MT MAUNGANUI

ℹ Getting There & Away

AIR

Tauranga City Airport (p336) is across the harbour in Mt Maunganui. Air New Zealand (p306) operates direct daily flights to Auckland, Wellington and Christchurch. If you don't have a rental car, you'll need to catch a taxi into town.

BUS

Coaches stop near the i-SITE on Wharf St. InterCity (p306) destinations include Auckland (from $20, 3¾ hours, three daily), Rotorua ($14, 1½ hours, two daily), Taupō (from $19, three hours, two daily), Napier (from $21, six hours, daily) and Wellington ($36, 9½ hours, daily).

Skip (p306) has buses to/from Auckland (from $12, 4¼ hours), Hamilton (from $15, 1¾ hours) and Rotorua (from $18, 1¼ hours).

Baybus (p321) has services to Mt Maunganui ($3.40, 30 minutes, every 15 minutes), Papamoa ($3.40, 30 minutes, hourly), Whakatāne ($15.20, two hours, daily except Sunday) and Katikati ($8.20, 50 minutes, six daily Monday to Friday).

CAR

If you're heading towards Cambridge on SH29, the Takitimu Dr toll road costs $1.90 per car. Heading east to Whakatāne or south to Rotorua, there's also the option of the Tauranga Eastern Link toll road ($2.10 per car), which begins near Papamoa. In both cases, free but slower alternative routes are possible. Tolls need to be paid online at www.nzta.govt.nz.

ℹ Getting Around

BICYCLE

Cycle Tauranga (p329) has hybrid bikes for hire, including helmets, locks, panniers and maps. Tours also available.

BUS

Tauranga's bright-yellow Baybus (p321) buses run on numerous routes, covering most parts of the city. Bus 81 heads through Bethlehem on its way to Ōmokoroa, while bus 55 passes through South Tauranga.

CAR

Numerous car-rental agencies have offices in Tauranga, including cheapie RaD Car Hire (☑ 07-578 1772; www.radcarhire.co.nz; 19 Fifteenth Ave; ⊙ 8am-5pm Mon-Fri, to noon Sat & Sun).

TAXI

Tauranga Mount Taxis (☑ 0800 829 477; www.taurangataxis.co.nz) A taxi from the centre of Tauranga to the airport or Mt Maunganui costs around $25.

Mt Maunganui

POP 19,100

Occupying a narrow peninsula punctuated with an ancient volcanic cone, the Mount is an uptempo beach town with thermal hot pools, lively cafes and hip bars. Despite being swallowed by Tauranga in 1989, it retains a distinct identity, shaped largely by its sun-soaked surfy vibe.

The town is rather fancifully named, with the so-called 'mount' being a hill just 232m high. But there's a striking allure to that hill, which can be seen for kilometres around – its far more beautiful Māori name, Mauao, means 'caught by the dawn'.

Sunseekers flock to the Mount in summer, served by a cluster of high-rise apartment towers studding the spit, and a great collection of restaurants. On the oceanside, long, lovely Main Beach is popular with surfers and swimmers, or you can cut across to the harbourside for a gentle, more protected dip at Pilot Bay Beach.

◉ Sights

★ Mauao   MOUNTAIN

The steep slopes of 232m-high Mauao swarm with walkers in the morning, when the Mount's early risers perform their ritual climb to the summit. The ascent is signposted to take an hour, though you'll see people striding up it in less than 30 minutes (and often running down). The gentler 3.5km loop around the base should take around 45 minutes.

If you just want a view of Mauao, wander across the causeway to Moturiki (Leisure Island), which peers along Main Beach to the extinct volcanic cone.

Classic Flyers NZ   MUSEUM

(☑ 07-572 4000; www.classicflyersnz.com; 9 Jean Batten Dr; adult/child $15/7.50; ⊙ 9am-4pm; ⊞) This fascinating aviation museum, beside the airport, is filled with predominantly military aircraft. You can scramble through the living quarters of the amphibious aircraft Catalina, or into the cabin of the de Havilland Heron to feel the spartan nature of 1950s commercial flights (note the lack of seatbelts). There's a licensed cafe and an excellent playground incorporating sections of fuselage.

If the nostalgia gets you, scenic flights on a DC3 (from $99) or a short blast in a biplane (from $385) are available.

Mt Maunganui

Mt Maunganui

◉ Top Sights
1 Mauao	A1

✦ Activities, Courses & Tours
2 East Coast Paddler SUP Mauao	B2
3 Hibiscus	C2
4 Mount Hot Pools	B2
5 Mount Surfshop	A4

⌂ Sleeping
6 Beachside Holiday Park	B2
7 Belle Mer	C2
8 Mission Belle Motel	A4
9 Mount Backpackers	A4
10 Pacific Coast Lodge	D4
11 Seagulls Guesthouse	D4
12 Westhaven Motel	B3

✕ Eating
13 Alpino	A4
14 Eddies & Elspeth	D4
15 Eightyeight	A4
16 Fat Cow	A3
17 Fish Face	B4
18 Mount Bistro	B2
19 Pronto	B2
20 The General	A3

⦿ Drinking & Nightlife
21 Astrolabe Brewbar	A4
22 Hide Thirst & Hunger	C3
23 Mount Social Club	C3

⌂ Shopping
24 Little Big Markets	C3

🏃 Activities

The Mount lays claim to being NZ's premier surfing town – they even teach surfing at high school here. You can carve up the waves at **Main Beach**, which has beach breaks. Landlubbers can join the fit folk on the trail to the summit of Mauao.

SNAKES ALIVE

New Zealand is famously free of snakes and other venomous critters, but that claim came momentarily into question in June 2018 when a highly venomous sea snake turned up in Tauranga's marina. The banded sea krait, which is usually docile and unthreatening, is more commonly found in the tropical waters around Southeast Asia, but somehow made its way to Tauranga.

It's not the first time sea snakes have been sighted around New Zealand, nor is it the only tropical ocean visitor to have been seen in the waters around Tauranga. In the same year a venomous lionfish and a sargassum fish were sighted in the area, brought to town by warming ocean currents.

Mount Hot Pools   HOT SPRINGS

(☑07-577 8551; www.mounthotpools.co.nz; 9 Adams Ave; adult/child $15/10; ☺6am-10pm Mon-Sat, 8am-10pm Sun) If you've given your muscles a workout traipsing up and down Mauao, take a relaxing soak at these thermally heated saltwater pools – discovered by a water diviner in the 1950s – looking back up at the hill you just climbed. If the bustling family-friendly environment gets too much, private pools are available ($16 per person, minimum two people).

Hibiscus   SURFING

(☑07-575 3792, 027 279 9687; www.surfschool. co.nz; Main Beach; 2hr/2-day lessons $79/150) Hires boards and offers a range of surfing lessons. Look for its trailer parked at Main Beach in summer.

Mount Surfshop   SURFING

(☑07-575 9133; www.mountsurfshop.co.nz; 98 Maunganui Rd; 4hr board hire $30; ☺9am-5pm Mon-Sat, 10am-5pm Sun) Hires surfboards and sells them alongside beachy threads and skateboards.

Rocktopia   CLIMBING

(☑07-572 4920; www.rocktopia.co.nz; 9 Triton Ave; Rock On $20, Clip 'n Climb $17; ☺9.30am-8pm, to 9pm Thu; ♠) This large climbing centre is split between Rock On, a large climbing wall painted like a bush-lined waterfall, with some serious overhang action, and Clip

'n Climb, featuring child-friendly challenges such as the 'Leap of Faith' and 'Vertical Drop Slide'.

Skydive Tauranga   SKYDIVING

(☑07-574 8533; www.skydivetauranga.com; 2 Kittyhawk Way; 10,000/12,000ft jumps $325/375) Exhilarating jumps with views as far as Whakaari (White Island) and Mt Ruapehu on the way down.

BayStation   ADVENTURE SPORTS

(☑07-570 8599; www.baystation.co.nz; 81 Truman Lane; blokarts 30 min or drift trikes 20 min adult/ child $25/20; ☺10am-6.30pm Sat & Sun, by appointment 2-6.30pm Mon-Fri, 10am-6.30pm daily in school holidays) Want to sail but without the pesky water? This custom-built speedway, 7km south of the town centre, is the place to attempt land-sailing (blokarts are like seated windsurfers on wheels). There's also an indoor track for electric-powered drift trikes, so action is possible whatever the conditions. Both activities are loads of fun, easily mastered and highly recommended.

East Coast
Paddler SUP Mauao   WATER SPORTS

(☑027 451 0579; https://eastcoastpaddler. co.nz; The Mall; board hire 1hr/half-day $25/80; ☺beach station 8am-8pm 26 Dec-9 Feb, 10am-4pm Sat & Sun Oct-Apr) From its beach station on Pilot Bay, this casual operation offers stand-up paddle board hire and tours, as well as running cultural walking trips on Mauao ($79), starting with a *whakatau* (welcome) and filled with stories of Māori legend. Phone to book on days the beach station is closed.

🛏 Sleeping

Seagulls
Guesthouse   HOSTEL $

(☑07-574 2099; www.seagullsguesthouse.co.nz; 12 Hinau St; s without bathroom $79, d with/without bathroom $105/89; ☜) Exuding a hostel vibe – communal kitchen, lounge, travel info – without hostel noise levels, Seagulls is an upmarket backpackers' gem, even if the institutional bathrooms do remind us of a hospital. On a quiet street not far from town, the emphasis is on peace. The best rooms have bathrooms and TVs.

Beachside Holiday Park HOLIDAY PARK $

(☎ 07-575 4471; www.mountbeachside.co.nz; 1 Adams Ave; sites $45-67, on-site vans $70-95, cabins $95-140) Spread across three grassy tiers nooked into the foot of Mauao, this council-run park commands the best position in town. Plus it's right next to the Mount Hot Pools (45% discount for campers) and a strip of eateries. Reception doubles as the local info centre.

Pacific Coast Lodge HOSTEL $

(☎ 07-574 9601; www.pacificcoastlodge.co.nz; 432 Maunganui Rd; dm/r without bathroom from $32/94; @ 🛜) Set on the main road a few blocks from the centre, this efficiently run, sharp-looking hostel is sociable but not party focused, with drinkers gently encouraged to migrate into town after 10pm. Purpose-built bunk rooms are roomy and there's a distinct beach-shack vibe. There are free bikes and surfboards, and a table-tennis table fills much of the lounge.

Mount Backpackers HOSTEL $

(☎ 07-575 0860; www.mountbackpackers.com; 87 Maunganui Rd; dm $32-40, d from $82; 🛜) If location is paramount, this hostel at the epicentre of town – five minutes' walk to the beach, Astrolabe Brewbar right across the road – is prime picking. Who cares about a bit of noise and bustle? The surfboards stacked in the lobby are for hire, as are wetsuits and bikes.

Westhaven Motel MOTEL $$

(☎ 07-575 4753; www.westhavenmotel.co.nz; 27a The Mall; units from $130; 🛜) If you're craving simple sandy times, Westhaven delivers, with its prime position on Pilot Bay. The basic furnishings of the one- and two-bedroom units bring to mind 1970s summer holidays, and rooms 1 and 2 come with elevated harbour views – they're an absolute bargain at $140.

Mission Belle Motel MOTEL $$

(☎ 07-575 2578; www.missionbellemotel.co.nz; 1 Victoria Rd; units from $170, ste from $225; 🛜) This family-run motel sports a Spanish Mission–style exterior resembling something out of an old spaghetti-western movie. The interior is modern, with especially good two-storey family suites - one has electric skylights for indoor stargazing. Some of the studios are tiny, but they all have kitchenettes. Note that the complex backs on to Astrolabe Brewbar (p336), so rear units can be noisy.

Belle Mer APARTMENT $$$

(☎ 07-575 0011; www.bellemer.co.nz; 53 Marine Pde; apt from $250; ❇ 🛜 ♨) With its white, glass-covered facade, this flashy beachside complex looks a bit like a cruise ship coming into dock. Two apartments get the full ocean-extravaganza view, though most of the one-, two- and three-bedroom apartments get partial views or a compensating courtyard. Rooms, with full kitchens and laundries, are huge and tastefully decorated.

✖ Eating

Eating well in the Mount is an easy task, with a host of fine cafes and restaurants that far exceed the usual offerings of a seaside fun town.

★ Eightyeight CAFE $$

(☎ 07-574 0384; www.facebook.com/cafe88mount; 88 Maunganui Rd; mains $16-22; ⊘ 7am-4.30pm) The savoury muffins, scones and cakes bulging across the counter may distract you from the menu at this ever-popular cafe. Seating is limited inside, but the rear courtyard under the flower baskets is the place to be anyway. If you've ever seen larger slices of cake, let us know.

★ Alpino ITALIAN $$

(☎ 07-925 9769; www.alpino.co.nz; 16 Pacific Ave; mains $32-33, pizzas $23-26; ⊘ 5pm-late Wed & Thu, noon-late Fri-Sun) The sea air might easily be Mediterranean at this new restaurant that has brought quality Italian cooking to the Mount. All the accents are Italian, from the staff and the checked tablecloths, to the all-Italian wine list and the buffalo mozzarella balls in the *insalata caprese*. Antipasti and *secondi* are designed to share, or there's a short greatest-hits pizza menu.

Fat Cow GRILL $$

(☎ 07-572 0020; www.thefatcow.co.nz; 70 Maunganui Rd; mains $23-48; ⊘ 2.30pm-late Mon-Thu, 11am-late Fri & Sat, 11am-4pm Sun) Blending South American and Tex-Mex influences, this dark-timbered monument to meat has windows that peel back, and steak that comes straight from the grill – well, the brisket, pork belly and half-chicken come from the smoker (via the grill). Quite simply the best meat in the Bay.

The General CAFE $$

(☎ 07-574 7061; 19b Pacific Ave; mains $12-26; ⊘ 7.30am-2.30pm) Winner of outstanding-cafe-of-the-year awards in 2017 and 2019, this pistachio-green cafe runs an all-day menu that blurs the lines between breakfast and lunch – fabulously fresh macro granola bowls through to dal and a tagine. The space is open, bright and inviting, and we could happily just eat from the side-order menu – potato and leek rosti, lemon-seasoned halloumi – and cake selection.

Fish Face
SEAFOOD **$$**

(☑07-575 2782; www.fish-face.co.nz; 107 Maunganui Rd; mains $26-35; ⊙4-9.30pm Mon-Thu, from noon Fri-Sun; 🖤) A funky fish cartoon sets the scene for this fresh, fun and informal 'seafood and wine bar'. The menu splashes its way through mostly Asian cuisines – Balinese curry, seared tuna on soba noodles – with a medley of the ocean (king prawns, scallops, calamari and hot smoked salmon) in the seafood mornay.

Eddies & Elspeth
CAFE **$$**

(☑07-575 5969; www.elspeth.co.nz; 2a Terrace Ave; mains $14-22; ⊙7am-3pm) A happy marriage of bakery (Elspeth) and brunch parlour (Eddies), this light-filled eatery entices with an inventive menu – Eddie's eggs Benedict comes with pineapple sauerkraut and jalapeños, and the Humble Carrot features the said veggie done five ways. Our coffee art was a Pegasus! Burgers and bao rule the afternoon.

Pronto
BURGERS **$$**

(☑07-572 1109; www.facebook.com/prontogourmetnz; 7/1 Marine Pde; burgers $15-19; ⊙9.30am-8pm Tue-Fri, 9am-8am Sat, 8.30am.3.30pm Sun; 🖤) Pronto's menu of gourmet burgers reads like it belongs in a bistro: chicken parmigiana, herb-grilled chicken salad, scotch and bacon, pulled pork… The peri peri chicken with avocado is pretty hard to beat. Want something sweet enough to kill you? Try one of the 'freak shakes'.

Mount Bistro
BISTRO **$$$**

(☑07-575 3872; www.mountbistro.nz; 6 Adams Ave; mains $36-38; ⊙5.30-late Tue-Sun) Literally in the shadow of Mauao as the sun heads for the horizon, Mount Bistro is one to go to a good thing: quality local meats (lamb, beef, venison, chicken) and fish creatively worked into dishes such as lamb shank tortellini and apple-glazed pork tenderloin. It makes for a classy night out – finish with the macarons to sweeten the deal.

🍷 Drinking & Nightlife

★ Mount Social Club
BAR

(☑07-574 7773; https://social-club.co.nz; 305 Maunganui Rd; ⊙8am-1am; 🛜) 🍷 The quirky Social Club brews its own lager, ale and cider, and if you don't like one part of the venue, simply head to another – each one feels like a different place entirely. The back room evokes Dorothy's Kansas, the front corners Elvis's Hawaii...with a truck and a boat in between.

★ Hide Thirst & Hunger
BAR

(☑07-572 0532; www.hidebar.co.nz; 147b Maunganui Rd; ⊙4pm-late Wed & Thu, noon-late Fri-Sun) Hide by name, hidden by nature. Tucked down a tiny alleyway, Hide has successfully turned a hollow behind the main street into a garden patio. Ten taps of mostly Moa beer pour from a wall, and on cooler nights they stoke up the open fire. There's also a menu of dumplings, pizzas and hearty mains.

Astrolabe Brewbar
PUB

(☑07-574 8155; www.astrolabe.co.nz; 82 Maunganui Rd; ⊙9.30am-late; 🛜🖤) Astrolabe conjures up a funky retro bach (beach-hut) vibe, with floral carpets, forest wallpaper, and pastel-coloured picnic tables (and a caravan) in the beer garden. The taps flow with Mac's beer, Thursday is cocktail night, and there's even a slide for the kids.

🔒 Shopping

Little Big Markets
MARKET

(www.littlebigevents.co.nz; Coronation Park; ⊙9am-2pm 1st Sat of the month Sep-Apr) Rows of arts, crafts, clothing, jewellery and food trucks at this monthly morning market.

ℹ Information

The reception desk at Beachside Holiday Park (p335) doubles as an informal info centre; it's open from 8.30am to 8pm.

ℹ Getting There & Away

AIR

Tauranga City Airport (TRG; ☑07-575 2456; www.taurangacityairport.co.nz; 73 Jean Batten Dr) is actually in Mt Maunganui, about 5km south of the town centre (and 6km from central Tauranga).

BUS

The Mount's main bus stop is at 10 Salisbury Ave, just off Maunganui Rd.

Baybus (p321) has daytime services to Tauranga ($3.40, 30 minutes, every 15 minutes) and Papamoa ($3.40, 40 minutes, hourly).

InterCity (p306) has direct daily services to Hamilton ($20, 2¾ hours), Rotorua (from $11, 1½ hours), Taupō (from $17, three hours) and Napier (from $21, six hours).

CAR

Mt Maunganui is connected to Tauranga by the Tauranga Harbour Bridge, or accessible from the south via SH2. For car hire, try **Rite Price Rentals** (📞07-575 2726; www.ritepricerentals. co.nz; 63 Totara St; ⊙8am-5pm Mon-Fri, to 4pm Sat, to noon Sun).

Papamoa

POP 20,100

Papamoa is Tauranga's second beach suburb, after adjoining Mt Maunganui, but the long beach here suffers nothing for comparisons to its more famous neighbour. Behind the wide, grassy dunes is beach as far as the eye can see, pointing like an arrow north towards Mauao. On its streets are a mix of old-fashioned beach shacks and modern monoliths, though the latter are in the ascendancy – still, you can't blame folks for moving in.

Baybus (p321) has hourly services to Mt Maunganui ($3.40, 40 minutes) and Tauranga ($3.40, 30 minutes), along with a bus to Whakatāne ($13.70, 1½ hours, daily except Sunday).

Beach House Motel MOTEL $$
(📞0800 429 999, 07-572 1424; www.beachhouse motel.co.nz; 224 Papamoa Beach Rd; units from $165; 🖥🐾) With its angular corrugated-iron exterior, this upmarket motel offers an immaculate version of the Kiwi bach (beach house) holiday, relaxed and close to the water. Outside there's a small pool and spa, and the beach is just across the road.

Papamoa Beach Resort HOLIDAY PARK $$
(📞07-572 0816; www.papamoabeach.co.nz; 535 Papamoa Beach Rd; sites from $52, cabins from $96, villas from $200; 🖥🐾) 🏄 Sprawling atop the dunes, this holiday park is a spotless, modern complex, primed and priced beyond its caravan-park origins, with luxurious self-contained villas. Kids will love the playground, the jumping pillow and the beach at your doorstep.

Bluebiyou CAFE $$
(📞07-572 2099; www.bluebiyou.co.nz; 559 Papamoa Beach Rd; mains breakfast $12-21, lunch $20-34, dinner $29-36; ⊙11am-late Tue-Fri, from 9am Sat & Sun; 🖥) Breezy Bluebiyou is a casual, maritime-styled bistro riding high on the dunes and serving big brunches and a mix of meaty and fishy dishes. The beer-battered oysters are excellent. Thursday is $20 fish-and-chips night, and if you come between 9am and 10am, coffee is free with breakfast.

Katikati

POP 4060

'Katikat' to the locals, this busy little stop on the highway, 35km northwest of Tauranga, was the only planned Ulster Scots settlement in the world, and it celebrates this history with a series of colourful murals. There are now more than 70 murals brightening the town centre.

In 2018, Katikat also named itself 'NZ's avocado capital' – the surrounding area contains around 500 orchards, growing two-thirds of the country's avos. You can celebrate everybody's favourite smashed breakfast item at the **Avocado Food & Wine Festival** (www.katikatiavofest.co.nz) each January.

◉ Sights

Haiku Pathway PARK
(Main Rd) Built as a millennium project, this unusual attraction consists of boulders inscribed with haiku verses wending through a pretty park flanking the Uretara River. The entrance is next to Hammer Hardware on SH2.

Katikati Bird Gardens BIRD SANCTUARY
(📞07-549 0912; www.birdgardens.co.nz; 263 Walker Rd East, Aongatete; adult/child $10/6; ⊙10am-4.30pm daily Oct-May, Sat & Sun Jun-Sep; 🐾) About 7km south of town, this gorgeous 4-hectare private garden is all aflap with native and exotic bird life. There's 1.5km of paths, looping out to a bird-filled wetland – check out the moa statue (the one bird you'll never see) – as well as a cafe, gift shop and boutiquey cottage accommodation (doubles $175).

Western Bay Museum MUSEUM
(📞07-549 0651; www.nzmuseum.com; 32 Main Rd; adult/child $5/2; ⊙10am-4pm Mon-Fri, 11am-3pm Sat & Sun) Housed in a former fire station, this little regional museum displays a selection of Māori artefacts from the local tribe, Ngāi Te Rangi, along with temporary exhibitions devoted to aspects of the town's heritage, such as the kauri timber industry – a kauri tree larger than Tāne Mahuta (p186) once grew in this region, but it was felled in 1939.

Leveret Estate WINERY
(📞07-552 0795; www.wineportfolio.co.nz; 2389 SH2, Aongatete; ⊙9.30am-5pm) Transplanting Cape Dutch architecture from South Africa's wine country to SH2, 8km south of Katikati,

this excellent winery is open for tastings and stock-ups. It makes some particularly lovely (and well-priced) sauvignon blanc, chardonnay, pinot noir and late-harvest viognier.

☞ Tours

Katikati Mural Tours CULTURAL
(☑07-549 5250; www.katikatiopenairart.co.nz; per person $10) Guided tours depart on demand from the information centre, taking in some of the 70-plus murals dotting the town.

🛏 Sleeping

Kaimai View Motel MOTEL $$
(☑07-549 0398; www.kaimaiview.co.nz; 84 Main Rd; units from $140; 🛜🏊) This simple motel offers neat rooms with CD players, kitchenettes and a heated pool. The namesake views extend over the back fence.

★**Warm Earth Cottage** COTTAGE $$$
(☑07-549 0962; www.warmearthcottage.co.nz; 2020 Thompsons Track, Aongatete; r $350) The ultimate in rustic romance, this rural idyll has two pretty, electricity-free cottages and a lovely lounge-library for guests. Soak in the wood-heated bathtub, or head across the manicured lawns to clear swimholes in the Waitekohe River, where part of NZ's first *Bachelor* season was filmed. Big breakfast hampers are included. It's 5km south of Katikati, then 2km west of SH2.

🍽 Eating & Drinking

Talisman Hotel PUB
(☑07-549 3218; www.talismanhotel.co.nz; 7 Main Rd; ⊙11.30am-late) The Talisman is better than your average small-town boozer, with a bistro (mains $23 to $41) and an attractive, deck-covered beer garden. Basic accommodation also available.

❶ Information

Katikati Information Centre (☑07-549 5250; www.katikati.org.nz; 36 Main Rd; ⊙9am-4pm Mon-Fri, 10am-2pm Sat & Sun; 🛜) Sells guides to the town's numerous murals (from $5); guided mural tours depart from here. The attached **Carlton Gallery**, featuring mostly local artists, rotates art exhibitions every two weeks.

❶ Getting There & Away

Three InterCity (p306) coaches a day stop here en route to Auckland (from $20, three hours), Thames (from $15, 1¼ hours), Waihi ($15, 25 minutes) and Tauranga ($15, 35 minutes), with one daily to Mt Maunganui ($15, 50 minutes).

Baybus (p321) has buses to Tauranga ($8.20, 50 minutes, six daily Monday to Friday) and a minibus on Tuesday and Thursday to Waihi ($5, 30 minutes) and Waihi Beach ($5, one hour).

Whakatāne

POP 20,230

A true pohutukawa paradise, Whakatāne (pronounced 'fah-kah-*tah*-neh') sits pressed between the mouth of the Whakatāne River and a low bush-covered ridge filled with kiwi. It's the hub of a productive agricultural district and looks longingly out to sea and the twin figures of Moutohorā (Whale Island) and ever-smoking Whakaari (White Island). Typically most visitors came to town to experience the power of Whakaari. With the island's tragic eruption in December 2019, Whakatāne will almost certainly suffer a downturn in tourism, though it also has blissful beaches and is consistently one of the sunniest spots in the country.

◉ Sights

Mataatua HISTORIC BUILDING
(☑07-308 4271; www.mataatua.com; 105 Muriwai Dr; adult/child 2hr tour $125/60, 1hr $49/20; ⊙9am-4pm, tours 10am, noon & 2pm) Mataatua is a large, fantastically carved 1875 *wharenui* (meeting house) that is the centrepiece of Te Mānuka Tūtahi *marae* (traditional meeting place). A visit provides a more intimate experience than the classic tourist cultural show. The two-hour tour is an immersive and personal interaction with the Ngāti Awa, and includes a guided tour, cultural workshops, the 'Hiko: Legend Carved in Light' digital experience and a *hāngi* meal. The one-hour 'express' tour is a bullet-point version.

In 1879 Mataatua was dismantled and sent to Sydney, much to the consternation of the local Ngāti Awa people whose ancestors it embodied. Adding insult to injury, it was re-erected inside out, exposing its precious interior carvings to the harsh Australian elements. After a stint in Melbourne it was sent to London and ended up spending 40 years in the Victoria & Albert Museum cellars. After 71 years in the Otago Museum, where it was cut down to fit the space, it finally came home in 2011.

Whakatāne

Whakatāne

⊙ Sights
1 Mataatua	C1
2 Muriwai's Cave	D1
3 Pōhaturoa	B2
4 Te Kōputu a te whanga a Toi	A2
5 Te Pāpaka & Puketapu	B2
6 Wairere Falls	C2
7 Whakatāne Observatory	B3

Activities, Courses & Tours
8 Diveworks Charters	B2

⊙ Sleeping
9 Tuscany Villas	B2
10 White Island Rendezvous	C2

⊗ Eating
11 L'Epicerie	B2
12 Roquette	B1
13 Soulsa	A2

⊙ Drinking & Nightlife
14 Craic	B2

Wairere Falls   WATERFALL
(Toroa St) Tumbling down the cliffs immediately behind town, tall, skinny Te Wairere occupies a deliciously damp nook. It once powered flax and flour mills, and it supplied Whakatāne's drinking water until 1924. It's a gorgeous spot, and goes almost completely unheralded – in any other country there'd be a ticket booth, interpretive audiovisual displays and an ice-cream van!

Te Kōputu a te whanga a Toi   MUSEUM
(Whakatāne Library & Exhibition Centre; ☏ 07-306 0509; www.whakatanemuseum.org.nz; Esplanade Mall, Kakahoroa Dr; ⊙ 9am-5pm Mon-Fri, 10am-2pm Sat & Sun) FREE Attached to the library, this impressive museum and gallery has artfully presented displays on early Māori and European settlement in the area. A gourd on display travelled from a distant Pacific island on the Mātaatua canoe more than 700 years ago. Other displays focus on Whakaari (White Island) and laud local sporting heroes. The gallery presents a varied series of NZ and international exhibitions.

Te Pāpaka & Puketapu   VIEWPOINT
(Seaview Rd) On the clifftops behind the town are a pair of ancient Ngāti Awa *pā* (fortified village) sites – Te Pāpaka (The Crab) and Puketapu (Sacred Hill) – both of which offer good outlooks over Whakatāne. Puketapu has the better view over the town centre and river mouth. Both tracks start from a small car park at the lower end of Seaview Rd – Puketapu (two-minute walk) heads straight

THE NAMING OF WHAKATĀNE

Whakatāne's name originated some six centuries ago, 200 years after the original Māori settlers arrived here. The warrior Toroa and his family sailed into the estuary in a huge ocean-going *waka* (canoe), the Mātaatua. As the men went ashore to greet local leaders, the tide turned, and the *waka* – with all the women on board – drifted out to sea. Toroa's daughter, Wairaka, cried out *'E! Kia whakatāne au i ahau!'* (Let me act as a man!) and, breaking the traditional *tapu* (taboo) on women steering a *waka*, she took up the paddle and brought the boat safely ashore. A whimsical statue of Wairaka, the **Lady on the Rock**, stands proudly at the mouth of the Whakatāne River in commemoration of her brave deed.

up the hill; Pāpaka (five minutes) begins immediately across Hillcrest Rd.

Pōhaturoa   LANDMARK

(cnr The Strand & Commerce St) Beside a roundabout on The Strand is Pōhaturoa, a large *tapu* (sacred) rock outcrop capped with pohutukawa trees, where birth, death, war and *moko* (tattoo) rites were performed. The Treaty of Waitangi was signed here by Ngāti Awa chiefs in 1840. There's also a monument to respected Ngāti Awa chief Te Hurinui Apanui (1855–1924). The archway through the rock used to be a cave, until road builders arrived in town.

Muriwai's Cave   CAVE

(Te Ana o Muriwai; Muriwai Dr) This shallow, partially collapsed cave once extended 122m into the hillside and was the home of Muriwai, a famous seer and sister of Toroa, captain of the Mātaatua *waka* (canoe). Along with Wairere Falls and a rock in the river mouth, the cave was one of three landmarks Toroa was told to look for by his father Irakewa before setting out from their Polynesian homeland. Carvings of the siblings flank the cave entry.

Whakatāne Observatory   OBSERVATORY

(☏ 07-308 6495; www.whakatane.info/business/whakatane-astronomical-society; 17 Hurinui Ave; adult/child $10/4; ⊙ 7.30pm Tue & Fri) On a hilltop behind town, this observatory offers abundant Bay of Plenty star-spotting when the sky is clear.

🏃 Activities

The *Whakatāne Walkways & Trails* brochure, available from the i-SITE, details some highly scenic walks easily accessible from the town centre. The mother of them all is the **Ngā Tapuwae o Toi (Footsteps of Toi)** trail, a 17.4km loop that takes between four and seven hours to complete. Starting in town it rounds spectacular **Kōhī Point** on a bushy track with panoramic cliff-top views and a genuine 'gasp' moment when you first set eyes on **Otarawairere Bay**. Check the tides because the northern end of the bay (where you approach from Whakatāne) can get cut off at high tide. A short detour along the way rewards you with views from **Toi's Pā** (Kapua-te-rangi), reputedly the oldest *pā* (fortified village) site in NZ. After 7km (about three hours) you'll reach Ōhope (p343), where you can catch the bus back to Whakatāne if there aren't any more kilometres left in your legs.

A good standalone walk that forms part of Ngā Tapuwae o Toi is the **Bird Walk**, a 2.8km forest route running off Gorge Rd that, rather unsurprisingly, has plentiful birdlife. Kiwis wander here at night, and the **Whakatāne Kiwi Trust** (www.whakatanekiwi.org.nz) runs guided night walks from April through June. Kids will enjoy the treasure-hunt challenge of the **Kiwi Wandering** trail, a 1.6km route along the river and into the town centre, with 10 bronze kiwis to be found along the way.

Cyclists should pick up a copy of the *Whakatāne Cycling Guide* from the i-SITE. It details eight rides around the region, including the **Onepū Mountain Bike Park** (SH30, Te Teko) FREE, which has 15km of trails, well suited to novice riders. Bikes can be hired at **Bike Barn** (☏ 07-308 0505; www.bikebarn.co.nz; 13-15 Commerce St; 2hr/day hire $20/80; ⊙ 9am-5pm Mon-Fri, to 3pm Sat, 10am-2pm Sun).

👉 Tours

Kāhu   SCENIC FLIGHTS

(☏ 0800 804 354; www.kahu.nz; Whakatāne Airport; flights from $80) Get the lay of the land and coast from above on one of several short helicopter flights – the pick of the bunch is the Port Pleasure flight (minimum four people), which scoots over Whakatāne, Ōhope and Ohiwa Harbour.

Diveworks Charters   DIVING

(☏ 0800 354 7737, 07-308 2001; www.diveworks-charters.com; 96 The Strand; diving incl gear from $215) 🐟 As well as guided tours to Moutohorā (p342), Diveworks runs afternoon diving trips around it (two dives, $120) and full-day diving trips to Whakaari (two dives $300). Other options include a snorkelling trip among dolphins and seals ($160), and inshore and White Island fishing (from $90).

White Island Flights   SCENIC FLIGHTS
(☑ 07-308 7760; www.whiteislandflights.co.nz; Whakatāne Airport; flights adult/child $249/125) Fixed-wing scenic flights over Whakaari and Moutohorā, with lots of photo opportunities. A Whakaari/Mt Tarawera combo flight costs $339.

🛏 Sleeping

Whakatāne Holiday Park   HOLIDAY PARK $
(☑ 07-308 8694; www.whakataneholidaypark. co.nz; McGarvey Rd; sites from $17, units with/ without bathroom from $85/50; 🛜🌊) This paddock-like riverfront park in a quiet suburban spot has only two large trees to shade campers from the sun, but it's a lovely walk along the river into town, and the flower-filled Whakatāne Gardens are right across the road. The five basic tourist cabins share a kitchen, while other cabins and units have kitchens but remain fairly rudimentary.

★ **One88 on Commerce**   MOTEL $$
(☑ 07-307 0915; www.one88oncommerce.co.nz; 188 Commerce St; units from $149; 🛜) Awarded NZ's best motel in 2018 and 2019, One88 is styled more like a plush hotel than a motel. King beds sit in spacious rooms – the smallest is 50 sq metres – and there's designer styling throughout. Located a 10-minute walk from the town centre, it's pinched between two busy roads but hushed by double glazing.

White Island Rendezvous   MOTEL $$
(☑ 07-308 9500; www.whiteislandrendezvous. co.nz; 15 The Strand E; s/d from $99/159; 🛜) This immaculate complex includes a vaguely Tuscan-looking main block, a 'micro-village' of stylish corrugated-iron cabins, and B&B rooms in a charming villa next door. Some units have spa baths, while micro-village cabins have decks.

Tuscany Villas   MOTEL $$
(☑ 07-308 2244; www.tuscanyvillas.co.nz; 57 The Strand E; units from $159; ❄🛜) This Tuscan outlier offers a few rays of Italian sunshine with wrought-iron balconies, a summertime guest-only, pop-up pizzeria and wine bar, and little swatches of Italiana throughout (check out the Pavarotti mural). Rooms are luxurious and comfy, with superking beds and spa pools. The whole pastiche is beautifully done.

It also hires out bikes (with free pickup when you get to Ōhope) and stand-up paddle boards to guests.

WHAKAARI (WHITE ISLAND)
....

New Zealand's most active volcano lies 49km off the Whakatāne coast, easily identified on clear days by its constant puffs of steam. The island is estimated to be between 150,000 to 200,000 years old and was originally formed from three separate volcanic cones. The two oldest have been eroded, while the younger cone has risen up between them. Mt Gisborne is the highest point on the island, at 321m, but beneath the waterline the mountain descends a further 440m to the seabed. Captain Cook gave it the name White Island, though with the sulphur coating its crater, it might almost be better named Yellow Island.

Despite the harsh conditions, the island is home to a thriving gannet colony and the northern side is covered in a pohutukawa forest. The waters around the island abound with marine life, including whales and dolphins.

The island's steaming vents (temperatures of 600°C to 800°C have been recorded), chimneys of bright-yellow sulphur and the furiously steaming shores of the crater lake had turned Whakaari into the Bay of Plenty's signature tourist experience, with boats and helicopters ferrying visitors to the island for guided walks. That came to a tragic end on the afternoon of 9 December 2019 when the island erupted while a tour group was ashore in the crater. Twenty-one of the 47 people on the island were killed, while around two dozen others suffered severe burns. It wasn't the first tragedy on the island – in 1914, 10 sulphur miners disappeared without a trace following a lahar (volcanic mudflow).

Tours to Whakaari were immediately halted after the December 2019 eruption, and at the time of writing it was unclear when and if they might resume, amid calls for a royal commission and promises of a government inquiry.

WORTH A TRIP

MOUTOHORĀ (WHALE ISLAND)

It's quite unusual for the English version of a Māori place name to be an exact transla-tion, but this volcanic island, 9km off the coast from Whakatāne, really does look like a stylised cartoon whale from certain angles. It's one of the less active members of the Taupō Volcanic Zone, though there are hot springs along its shore. The island's highest point is 353m above sea level, and it contains several historic sites, including an ancient *pā* (fortified village), a quarry and a camp.

Moutohorā was once the site of a Ngāti Awa village, but in 1867 it passed into Europe-an ownership. Since 1965 it has been a DOC-protected wildlife refuge for seabirds and shorebirds, and it's now completely predator free. In 1999, 40 tīeke (the once-endan-gered North Island saddleback) were released; they now number around 1500. Fur seals are also frequently spotted.

The island's protected status means landing is restricted to a handful of licensed operators, departing from Whakatāne.

Diveworks Charters (p340) offers a guided tour of the island (adult/child $120/75), including a climb to its saddle and a swim at the hot-water beach, as well as a dolphin-and-seals encounter ($160) that can have you swimming with seals in an island lagoon.

KG Kayaks heads to the island by catamaran and then unloads the kayaks for a wild-life-spotting paddle around the shoreline, stopping at the hot-water beach at Onepu and entering sea caves when the conditions are right (per person $230).

37 The Landing Motel   MOTEL $$
(☑ 07-307 1297; www.landingmotel.co.nz; 37 Land-ing Rd; r from $160; ❈ 🛜) Away from the town centre, among a small scrum of motels on Landing Road, 37 is the standout and a gen-eral step up in motel comfort. The slate pil-lars on entry set the tone, while the modern spacious rooms feature soft colours, kitch-enettes and large TVs – six units have spas.

Captain's Cabin   APARTMENT $$
(☑ 07-308 5719; www.captainscabin.co.nz; 23 Mu-riwai Dr; d/tr $145/170) On the serene side of town, with sparkling views over the river mouth, this homely self-contained unit is perfect if you're hanging around for a few days (cheaper for two nights or more). A cosy living area cleverly combines bedroom, lounge, kitchen and dining room, with a sec-ond smaller room and bijou bathroom – all sweetly decorated along nautical lines.

✖ Eating

Julian's Berry Farm   CAFE $
(☑ 07-308 4253; www.juliansberryfarm.co.nz; 12 Huna Rd; mains $17-25; ⊙ 8.30am-5.30pm Oct-ear-ly Feb; ﾞ) Join the Kiwi summer tradition of pick-your-own berries, or simply grab a seat on the large sunny cafe terrace at this su-per-popular berry farm, 6km west of the town centre. The ice-cream and smoothie counter is the busiest place of all, and there's also minigolf, beach volleyball and a petting farm.

Soulsa   MODERN NZ $$
(☑ 07-307 8689; www.whakatane.info/website/ 183; 14 Richardson St; mains $30-36; ⊙ 5.30-9pm Mon-Sat) Don't come for the decor – it feels a bit like sitting in a community art gallery – but do come to experience seasonal produce creatively transformed into the likes of lamb with roasted parsnip, or stuffed mushroom sliders with havarti and tomato coulis. Good food, good service, good choice.

L'Epicerie   CAFE $$
(☑ 07-308 5981; www.lepicerie.co.nz; 73 The Strand; crêpes $7-19; ⊙ 7am-2.30pm Mon-Fri, from 8am Sat, from 9am Sun; ﾞ) At this classic French cafe you'll be greeted with a *bonjour,* then a menu of crêpes and a display cabinet of croissants and apple-and-blue-cheese tar-tines. Settle into one of the old salon arm-chairs and enjoy a *très bon* breakfast. The Apteryx coffee is a local roast.

Roquette   MEDITERRANEAN $$
(☑ 07-307 0722; https://roquetterestaurant.co.nz; 29 Quay St; mains lunch $23-37, dinner $30-38; ⊙ 10am-late Mon-Sat) Despite its office-like appearance beneath an apartment block, ritzy waterside Roquette serves up refresh-ing Mediterranean-influenced fare with lots of summery salads, risotto and fish dishes. Try the trio of fresh fish or the twice-cooked duck confit. The $25 dinner-and-wine ear-ly-bird special (arrive between 5pm and 6pm) comes from a simpler menu.

Drinking & Nightlife

Mata
BREWERY

(📞 07-308 9644; www.matabeer.nz; 17 Gateway Cres, Coastlands; ⏰ noon-8pm Sun-Thu, to 9.30pm Fri & Sat) Whakatāne's own craft brewer, in an industrial area at the edge of town, has a welcoming tasting room attached. The flavours are varied and often NZ inspired – think nectarine cider, manuka ale and, um, cola beer. Tasting trays of four beers are $12, and there are pizzas and toasties to help subvert the alcohol.

Craic
IRISH PUB

(📞 07-282 3058; www.whakatanehotel.co.nz; 79 The Strand; ⏰ 11am-late) This bar at the Whakatane Hotel lives up to the promise of its name as the liveliest drinking spot in town. The decor is green (of course) and there are lots of cosy nooks, but when the sun's shining, the street tables are the place to be. You may find live Irish music on weekends.

ℹ Information

Whakatāne i-SITE (📞 07-306 2030; www. whakatane.com; cnr Quay St & Kakahoroa Dr; ⏰ 8.30am-5.30pm Mon-Fri, 9am-4pm Sat & Sun summer, 9am-5pm Mon-Fri, 10am-3pm Sat & Sun winter; 🌐) Tour bookings, accommodation and general DOC enquiries. Check out the new room dedicated to Whakaari (White Island), with a full model of the island and a 20-minute documentary.

ℹ Getting There & Away

AIR

Whakatāne Airport (WHK; 📞 07-308 8397; 216 Aerodrome Rd, Thornton) is 10km northwest of town. **Air Chathams** (📞 0800 580 127; www. airchathams.co.nz) has two to three flights a day between Whakatāne and Auckland. **JNP Airport Shuttle** (📞 0800 872 555; jnptransportservices@yahoo.co.nz) meets all incoming flights and can deliver you into town.

BUS

Baybus (p321) has services to Ōhope ($3.70, 10 minutes, Monday and Wednesday), Ōpōtiki ($9.40, 45 minutes, Monday and Wednesday), Papamoa ($13.70, 1½ hours, daily except Sunday) and Tauranga ($15.20, two hours, daily except Sunday).

InterCity (p306) has daily coaches to Auckland (from $29, 6½ hours), Hamilton (from $26, four hours), Rotorua (from $18, 1¾ hours), Ōpōtiki ($15, 40 minutes) and Gisborne (from $15, 3¼ hours), stopping outside the i-SITE.

Ōhope
POP 2840

Just 6km over the hill from Whakatāne, Ōhope is an extraordinarily gorgeous place, with an 11km beach that's perfect for lazing or surfing. Strung behind the beach is the long, skinny town, backed by sleepy Ohiwa Harbour, a top spot for kayaking and fishing. On 'NZ's most loved beach', West End is definitely the best end, with the beach here set beautifully below the cliffs of Whakatāne Heads.

Activities

The best walk around Ōhope is the short headland wander to Otarawairere Bay (15 minutes from West End beach), which has a castaway, shell-covered beach that may be even finer than Ōhope's main beach. Opened in 2018, the shared-use (walkers and cyclists) Ōhope Harbourside Trail stretches along the Ohiwa Harbour shore for 2.9km between Port Ōhope Wharf and Waterways Dr.

KG Kayaks
KAYAKING

(📞 027 272 4073; www.kgkayaks.co.nz; 93 Kutarere Wharf Rd, Kutarere; tours from $100, 1/2/3hr hire from $30/50/65) Though it's based on the southern shores of Ohiwa Harbour between Ōhope and Ōpōtiki, KG rents out kayaks from Port Ōhope Wharf in summer. Its 2½-hour guided Coastal Adventure paddles around the heads towards Whakatāne via beautiful Otarawairere Bay. It also offers daytime and moonlight excursions on Ohiwa Harbour, and longer trips to Moutohorā.

Salt Spray Surf School
SURFING

(📞 021 149 1972; www.saltspraysurfschool.co.nz; 61 West End Rd; 2hr lessons from $70, board rental 1hr/half-day $20/50; ⏰ Oct-Apr) Rents boards and wetsuits, and offers lessons for beginners, including targeted kids' classes.

🛏 Sleeping

⭐ Ohope Beach Motel
MOTEL $$

(📞 07-312 4159; www.ohopebeachmotel.nz; 52 West End Rd; r from $135; 🌐 ♿) Sitting pretty at the most beautiful end of the beach, this nine-room motel is gingerbread-cute after a fresh paint job and refurb. Rooms range from studios to two-bedroom units, and most have a small patch of garden with deckchairs. Room 1 gets the big-screen ocean view. Boogie boards are available for free.

Moanarua Beach Cottage
B&B $$

(☑ 07-312 5924; www.moanarua.co.nz; 2 Hoterini St; d $180) Well-travelled owners Miria and Taroi combine a warm welcome with information on local Māori heritage, art and culture. Accommodation is in a self-contained garden cottage trimmed with Māori design. Bikes are free to use, as are kayaks if you're staying three or more nights, and you're welcome to use the owners' outdoor spa above the cottage. Two-night minimum stay December to April.

Ohope Beach Top 10 Holiday Park
HOLIDAY PARK $$

(☑ 07-312 4460; www.ohopebeach.co.nz; 367 Harbour Rd; sites from $22, cabins from $80, units from $140, apt from $210; 🛜 🖥 👪) 🍴 This vast complex is the very model of a modern holiday park, with a raft of family-friendly facilities: tennis, volleyball, minigolf, jumping pillow, summer cafe, pool with hydroslides, movie room. There are shady sites, the requisite fine stretch of beach and some great apartments peeking over the dunes. It's busy as a woodpecker in summer (with prices to match).

🍴 Eating

Ohiwa Oyster Farm
FISH & CHIPS $

(☑ 07-312 4565; www.whakatane.info/business/ohiwa-oyster-farm; Wainui Rd; meals $8.50-17; ⊙ 9.30am-6.30pm) Perched over a swampy back-reach of Ohiwa Harbour (serious oyster territory), this classic roadside fish shack is perfect for a fish-and-chip picnic or to slurp down mussels and oysters. When the tide's up, keep an eye out for stingrays hanging around the water's edge hoping for a feed; when the tide's out, it'll be weka birds.

★ Moxi
CAFE $$

(www.moxicafe.co.nz; 23 Pohutukawa Ave; mains $16-25; ⊙ 7am-3pm; 🛜) Cobbled together out of shipping containers, but with a very flash louvred roof, this mainly open-air cafe is Ōhope's best. The coffee is first rate and we recommend the Little Miss Moxi, an eggs Benedict with tomato relish and a potato-hash wedge. Also serves local Mata craft beer and wine, making it a great spot for a post-beach tipple.

Cadera
MEXICAN $$

(☑ 07-312 6122; www.cadera.co.nz; 19 Pohutukawa Ave; mains $11-30; ⊙ 4-10pm Tue-Fri, from 11am Sat & Sun) There's a classic beach vibe on the open back deck of Cadera (despite the intervening car park). It's everything you'd expect of a good Mexican restaurant – quality tacos, burritos, nachos, Coronas, *pueblo* photos on the wall – but with pohutukawa trees and the South Pacific in the view.

Fisherman's Wharf Café
BISTRO $$

(☑ 07-312 4017; www.facebook.com/fisherman-swharfcafe; 340 Harbour Rd; mains $30-36; ⊙ 5.30-8.30pm Wed-Sat) Look forward to stellar harbour views from the spacious deck of this relaxed, beachy restaurant. Meals include excellent steaks and seafood – the shared 'Wharf Plate' starter of jumbo prawns, mussels, calamari and remoulade is the way to begin. Takeaway fish and chips are available from a handy window outside.

❶ Getting There & Away

Baybus (p321) route 122 makes the short haul across the hill from Whakatāne to Ōhope ($3.40, 35 minutes, seven daily Monday to Saturday), while 147 continues on to Ōpōtiki ($9.50, 45 minutes) on Monday and Wednesday.

InterCity (p306) has direct daily coaches to Auckland (from $29, seven hours), Hamilton (from $26, 4¼ hours), Rotorua (from $18, two hours), Ōpōtiki ($15, 30 minutes) and Gisborne (from $15, three hours).

Ōpōtiki
POP 4180

Set out in a tidy grid pattern within the embrace of two rivers, Ōpōtiki is a worn-around-the-edges kind of town with a scattering of historic buildings and a couple of exceptional beaches nearby (Ohiwa and Waiotahi). The Mōtū Trails have helped put the town on the Great Rides cycle map, and it's a good stop between the Bay of Plenty and the crossing to Hawke's Bay. Māori traditions are alive and well here, with more than half of the population claiming Māori descent.

◉ Sights

Pick up the *Historic Ōpōtiki* brochure from the i-SITE (p346) or download it from www.opotikinz.co.nz for the lowdown on the town's heritage buildings.

Hukutaia Domain
FOREST

(501 Woodlands Rd; ⊙ daylight hours) **FREE** Around 8km south of town, this verdant 4.5-hectare patch of forest is home to around 1500 varieties of native plants, which

can be seen on a 20-minute walking circuit. The prize specimen is Taketakerau, a sacred 23m-tall puriri tree, with a huge circumference, estimated to be more than 2000 years old. It was once used as a burial place for the distinguished dead of the Upokorehe *hapū* (subtribe) of Whakatōhea; their remains have since been reinterred elsewhere.

Hiona St Stephen's Church CHURCH
(☑ 07-315 8319; www.hiona.org.nz; 124 Church St) St Stephen's (1862) is a white wooden Anglican church with a timber-lined interior and *tukutuku* (woven flax) panels in the sanctuary. Reverend Carl Völkner, known by the local Whakatōhea tribe to have acted as a government spy during the New Zealand Wars, was executed by Māori here in 1865. In 1992 the governor-general granted Mokomoko, the man the government in turn hanged for his 'murder', a full pardon, which is displayed in the lobby.

The church is usually locked unless a parishioner is present, but the lobby (with the pardon) is kept open most of the day – you can peer through the glass doors into the church.

Ōpōtiki Museum MUSEUM
(☑ 07-315 5193; www.opotikimuseum.org.nz; 123 Church St; adult/child $10/5; ⊙10am-4pm Mon-Fri, to 2pm Sat) Ōpōtiki's museum has heritage displays including Māori artefacts, militaria, recreated shopfronts (barber, carpenter, printer...), and agricultural items including tractors and a horse-drawn wagon. The admission charge includes entry to the locked-in-time, 1950s-era Shalfoon & Francis general store, a few doors down.

Founded in the 1860s, the store closed its doors in 2000 and the shelves are still piled high with old grocery and hardware products. Handbags, sticky-tape dispensers, sets of scales, books – you name it, they had it. An amazing collection.

🏃 Activities

Mōtū Trails CYCLING
(www.motutrails.co.nz) One of the New Zealand Cycle Trail's 'Great Rides', Mōtū Trails comprises three contrasting trails around Ōpōtiki – the easy **Dunes Trail** (10km), the intermediate **Mōtū Road Trail** (67km, with 1600m of climb) and the mountain-bike-only **Pākihi Track** (44km). All those distances are one way, necessitating shuttles, or the trails can be combined to form a 91km loop.

Motu Cycle Trails
(☑ 027 505 2120; www.motucycletrails.com; 148 St John St; bike hire per day hybrid/mountain bike $30/65; ⊙9.30am-3pm) has bike hire and an on-demand shuttle service ($65, minimum four people).

Travel Shop OUTDOORS
(☑ 07-315 8881; www.travelshop.co.nz; 106 Church St; hire half/full day $30/40; ⊙9am-4pm Mon-Thu, to 2pm Fri) This main-street travel agency rents bikes, kayaks and surfboards.

🛏 Sleeping

The Royal HOSTEL $
(☑ 07-315 8840, 027 555 0935; www.theroyalopotiki.co.nz; 102 Church St; dm $35, units with bathroom $120) Dorms are spartan and a bit reminiscent of school camp in this 1814 heritage-listed former pub, but most have only two or three beds and plonk you right in the centre of town. The dimly lit common area has a pool table and dartboard, and there's a great deck overhanging the Church St footpath.

Guests get a 10% discount at the Royal's restaurant (mains $22 to $36) downstairs.

⭐ Island View Holiday Park HOLIDAY PARK $$
(☑ 07-315 7519; www.islandviewholiday.co.nz; 6 Appleton Rd, Waiotahi Beach; dm & sites $25, units with/without bathroom from $130/70; 🛜🛆) Beach life comes no simpler than at this chilled-out holiday park. Cabins open onto shared decks with barbecues and their own toilet blocks, meaning that what you sacrifice in privacy you gain in sociability. There are free kayaks, hammocks slung between trees, a volleyball court, swimming pool and an immaculate kitchen and lounge. The island view? Whakaari (White Island).

Ohiwa Beach Holiday Park HOLIDAY PARK $
(☑ 07-315 4741; www.ohiwaholidays.co.nz; Ohiwa Harbour Rd; sites from $23, units with/without bathroom from $100/70; 🛜🛆🛜) This pocket of peace is squeezed into a remote corner between Ohiwa Harbour and a gorgeous ocean beach, 14km west of Ōpōtiki. Pohutukawa trees, phoenix palms, manicured lawns, rolling waves and endless sands distil the essence of the Kiwi summer. There are only a handful of units, but there's ample space to pitch a tent. Bring coins for the showers.

Ohiwa Beach Apartments Motel MOTEL $$
(☑ 07-315 4649; https://ohiwabeachstay.co.nz; 215 Ohiwa Beach Rd; studios from $140, apt from $160; 🛜) Hide from the world, and wake each morning to the sight of steaming Whakaari, at this glass-fronted collection of cubes

above a no-exit beach road. Paradoxically, the bottom apartments get the larger windows and view, but all have lovely wooden kitchenettes, there's a spa studio, and the beach is straight across the road and dunes. No kids under seven.

Eastland Pacific Motor Lodge MOTEL $$
(07-315 5524; www.eastlandpacific.co.nz; 44 St John St; units from $135;) Bright, clean Eastland is a well-kept motel with units that are simple but pleasantly kitted out. Some have spa baths and, at $175, the two-bedroom units are top value.

Eating & Drinking

Two Fish CAFE $$
(07-315 5448; www.facebook.com/twofishcafe opotiki; 102 Church St; breakfast $16-21; 8am-2.30pm Mon-Sat) This retro-fitted cafe serves up robust homemade burgers, toasties, steak sandwiches and salads, with guest appearances by the likes of pulled-pork pita pockets. The locally roasted Apteryx coffee is excellent, too. Sit inside or in the courtyard for Ōpōtiki's finest and most chilled breakfast.

Crossroads Brew Bar & Restaurant BAR
(07-315 6876; https://crossroads-licensed-bar-restaurantcafe.business.site; 104b Church St; 11am-9pm Wed-Sat, from 4pm Tue & Sun) This unadorned bar looks as rough around the edges as Ōpōtiki itself, but it's also just as welcoming. It brews its own range of beers – from Bohemian pilsner to stout and IPA – and has a lengthy menu of pub-grub staples (mains $15 to $28) and good pizza. Live music Saturday nights in summer.

☆ Entertainment

DeLuxe Theatre CINEMA
(07-315 6110; www.deluxetheatre.co.nz; 127 Church St; adult/child $14/7) Dating from 1926, this beguiling community-run art-deco cinema shows recent movies and hosts the odd concert.

ⓘ Information

The Ōpōtiki i-SITE (07-315 3031; www.opotikinz.co.nz; 70 Bridge St; 9am-4.30pm Mon-Fri, to 1pm Sat & Sun) and **DOC** (07-315 1001; www.doc.govt.nz; 9am-4.30pm Fri) are in the same building. The i-SITE takes bookings for activities and transport, and stocks the indispensable free *Pacific Coast Highway* booklet. Showers are available ($3).

ⓘ Getting There & Away

BUS

Baybus (p321) route 147 heads to Whakatāne ($9.50, 45 minutes) twice daily on Monday and Wednesday (one service each day stops in Ōhope). InterCity (p306) has a coach most days to Auckland ($42, 6¾ hours), Hamilton ($34, 4¼ hours), Rotorua ($23, 2¼ hours), Whakatāne ($15, 44 minutes) and Gisborne ($16, two hours).

CAR

Travelling east from Ōpōtiki there are two routes: SH2 squeezing through the spectacular Waioeka Gorge, or the far-longer SH35 around East Cape. The SH2 route offers a number of day walks in the Waioeka Gorge Scenic Reserve, with the gorge getting steeper and narrower as you travel inland, before the road crosses typically green hills on the descent to Gisborne.

The East Coast

Best Places to Eat

➡ Mister D (p372)

➡ OM Goodness Specialty Breads (p378)

➡ Frank & Albie's (p359)

➡ Maina (p378)

➡ Hunger Monger (p372)

Best Places to Stay

➡ Stranded in Paradise (p354)

➡ Millar Road (p377)

➡ Ahi Kaa Motel (p359)

➡ Kiwiesque (p371)

➡ Seaview Lodge B&B (p371)

Why Go?

New Zealand is known for its wildly diverse landscapes, but on the East Coast it's the sociological contours that are most pronounced. There's a full spectrum of NZ life here, from the earthy little fishing and farming villages around East Cape to Havelock North's moneyed, wine-soaked streets.

Māori culture is never more visible than it is on the East Coast. Exquisitely carved *marae* (meeting house) complexes dot the landscape, and *te reo* and *tikanga* (the language and customs) are alive and well.

Intrepid travellers will have no trouble shaking off the tourist crowds here – along the Pacific Coast Hwy, through rural back roads, on remote beaches or in the mystical wilds of Te Urewera. And when the call of the wild gives way to caffeine/craft beer withdrawal, you can get a quick fix in Gisborne or Napier. You'll also find plenty of wine here: the Hawke's Bay region is striped with vine rows.

When to Go

➡ The East Coast basks in a warm, relatively dry climate (most of the rain dumps on the South Island's West Coast). Summer temperatures (December to March) around balmy Napier and Gisborne nudge 25°C; in winter (June to August) they rarely dip below 8°C.

➡ The Hawke's Bay region enjoys mild, dry, grape-growing conditions year-round, with an average annual rainfall of just 800mm (sublime chardonnay!). Harvest time is autumn (March to May).

➡ In winter, heavy downpours sometimes wash out sections of the Pacific Coast Hwy (SH35) around East Cape: check road conditions at either end (Ōpōtiki or Gisborne) before you hit the highway.

The East Coast Highlights

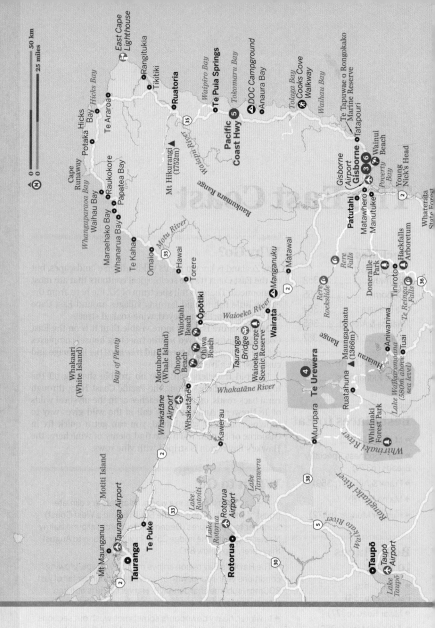

1 Napier (p367)
Time-warping back to the 1930s, surrounded by art-deco design, in this stylish seaside town.

2 Hawke's Bay Wine Region (p373)
Sipping your way around the classy local wineries.

3 Gisborne Wineries (p361)
Nosing your way into yet more fab NZ wine around sunny Gisborne.

4 Te Urewera (p363)
Losing a few days in this area's mighty forests, steeped in Māori lore.

5 Pacific Coast Hwy (p352)
Checking landmarks off your list as you cruise around East Cape: Tolaga Bay, Tokomaru Bay, East Cape Lighthouse...

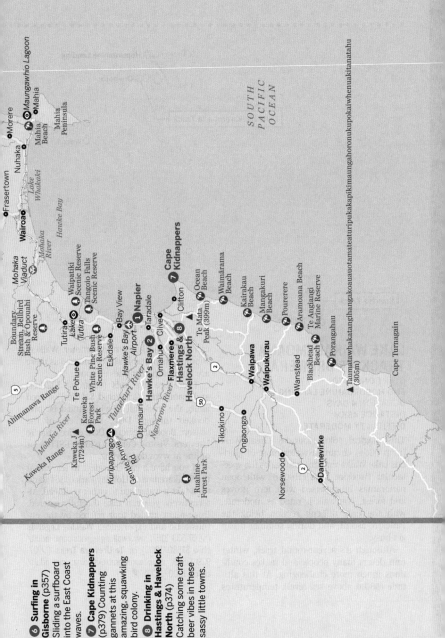

6 Surfing in Gisborne (p357) Sliding a surfboard into the East Coast waves.

7 Cape Kidnappers (p379) Counting gannets at this amazing, squawking bird colony.

8 Drinking in Hastings & Havelock North (p374) Catching some craft-beer vibes in these sassy little towns.

Morere

Frasertown

Nuhaka

Maungawhio Lagoon

Mahia

Mahia Beach

Mahia Peninsula

Lake Whakaki

Wairoa

Hawke Bay

Mohaka River

Mohaka Viaduct

SOUTH PACIFIC OCEAN

Ahimanawa Range

Mohaka River

Kaweka Range

Boundary Stream, Bellbird Bush & Opouahi Reserve

Te Pohue

Kaweka J (1724m)

Kaweka Forest Park

Tutira

Lake Tutira

White Pine Bush Scenic Reserve

Waipatiki Scenic Reserve

Thangoio Falls Scenic Reserve

Eskdale

Bay View

Kuripapango

Gentle Annie Rd

Tutaekuri River

Hawke's Bay Airport

1 Napier

Taradale

Otamauri

Omahu

Olive

Ngaruroro River

Hastings & Havelock North

Flaxmere

Hawke's Bay 2

Te Mata Peak (399m)

Clifton

7 Cape Kidnappers

Ocean Beach

Wainārama Beach

Kairakau Beach

Mangakuri Beach

Pourerere

Aramoana Beach

Te Angiangi Marine Reserve

Porangahau

Ruahine Forest Park

Tikokino

Ongaonga

Waipawa

Waipukurau

Wanstead

Blackhead Beach

Taumatawhakatangihangakoauauotamateaturipukakapikimaungahoronukupokaiwhenuakitanatahu (305m)

Cape Turnagain

Norsewood

Dannevirke

5

50

2

2

HIKING ON THE EAST COAST

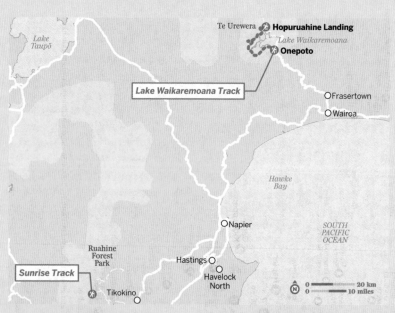

LAKE WAIKAREMOANA TRACK, TE UREWERA

START ONEPOTO
END HOPURUAHINE LANDING
DURATION 4 DAYS
DISTANCE 46KM
DIFFICULTY MODERATE

This magical 46km, four-day Great Walk (map p364) circumnavigates most of glorious Lake Waikaremoana and scales the spectacular Panekire Bluff (1180m), with open panoramas interspersed with fern groves and forest. The walk is rated as moderate, with the only difficult section being the Panekire ascent, and during summer it can get busy.

Although it's a year-round track, winter rain deters many people and makes conditions much more challenging. At this altitude (580m above sea level), temperatures can drop quickly, even in summer. Walkers should take portable stoves and fuel as there are no cooking facilities en route.

There are five **huts** (adult/child $32/free) and **campsites** (adult/child $14/free) spaced along the track, all of which must be pre-booked through DOC, regardless of the season. Book at regional DOC offices, the Te Urewera Visitor Centre (p364), i-SITEs or online at www.doc.govt.nz.

If you have a car, it's safest to leave it at the Waikaremoana Holiday Park (p364), and then take a water taxi to either trailhead. Alternatively, you can take the fully catered, three-night guided tour offered by the enthusiastic and experienced **Walking Legends** (☑07-533 3157; www.walkinglegends.com; adult/child $1530/1000) or **Te Urewera Treks** (☑07-929 9669; www.teureweratreks.co.nz; per adult/child $1500/1100) 🍃.

The beaches along the East Coast are great, but if you're looking for a spectacular hike, head inland to the lush, forest-draped mountains of Te Urewera and the Ruahine Forest Park.

Propel yourself onto the track either clockwise from just outside **Onepoto** in the south, or anticlockwise from **Hopuruahine Landing** in the north.

Estimated walking times:

Route	Time (hr)
Onepoto to Panekire Hut	5
Panekire Hut to Waiopaoa Hut	3-4
Waiopaoa Hut to Marauiti Hut	4-5
Marauiti Hut to Waiharuru Hut	1½
Waiharuru Hut to Whanganui Hut	2
Whanganui Hut to Hopuruahine Landing	2

SUNRISE TRACK, RUAHINE FOREST PARK

START/END **NORTH BLOCK RD**
DURATION **4–5 HOURS RETURN**
DISTANCE **12KM**
DIFFICULTY **EASY TO MODERATE**

This well-graded track is the perfect introduction to mountain hiking in New Zealand, rising slowly through changing forest to offer a glimpse of alpine country: if you're new to life above the treeline it could be love at first sight. The easy gradient and changing scenery also make the Sunrise Track a brilliant family hike.

But this walk is more than just a taster of the mountains: the forest that drapes the slopes of the Ruahine Range is truly beautiful, with the track moving into red beech, rimu and kahikatea forest, rising through mountain beech and *kaikawaka* (mountain cedar) to top out among subalpine herb fields.

If you want to personally discover the reason for the track's name, book a night at Sunrise Hut – if the dawn is clear and fine you'll be rewarded with showstopping views.

From the North Block Rd car park, cross the stile and begin along farm tracks, rising gently through farmland to enter Ruahine Forest Park in just a few minutes. About 100m along, turn left at the second junction, descending at first through a beautiful section of mossy red-beech forest to cross a wooden bridge over a stream. Just beyond the bridge, take the left fork (signed to Sunrise Hut), beginning the climb.

A series of switchbacks ascends through tall kahikatea and rimu, before the track contours across the slopes to a junction with the track to Waipawa Forks Hut (around an hour from the car park). Continue straight ahead. Around the top of the first set of switchbacks past the junction, the forest begins to thin. For the next hour you'll climb through gradually diminishing trees – the final layer of stunted beech, laced with moss, is totally photogenic.

When you step out of the bushline you'll be immediately greeted by **Sunrise Hut** (spoiler alert: you'll actually be greeted first by its toilets). Sitting among tussocks at 1280m, the 20-bunk hut stares east over Hawke's Bay. The mezzanine bunks get the million-dollar views (adult/child $15/8; book in advance via www.doc.govt.nz).

The track to Armstrong Saddle leaves from the right side of the hut and turns immediately right along a narrow ridge. The route follows this ridge north for 1km (20 to 30 minutes) to the saddle. Nearing the saddle – at about the point where the massive landslips fall away to the left – it becomes a poled route to assist when there's low visibility. From **Armstrong Saddle** (1369m), with its beautiful subalpine herb fields, there are clear-day views to Mt Ruapehu. The saddle is named after a pilot, Hamish Armstrong, who crashed his Gypsy Moth plane here in 1935. Armstrong was never found.

Return to Sunrise Hut, then retrace your steps back down the slopes to the North Block Rd car park.

ℹ️ Getting There & Around

The region's only airports are in Gisborne and Napier. **Air New Zealand** (www.airnewzealand.co.nz) flies to both towns from Auckland and Wellington, and also to Napier from Christchurch. **Jetstar** (www.jetstar.com) also flies to Napier from Auckland. Regular **InterCity** (www.intercity.co.nz) bus services ply State Hwy 2 (SH2) connecting Ōpōtiki with Gisborne, Napier, Hastings and the main centres beyond, and State Hwy 5 (SH5), connecting Napier with Taupō.

Transport is limited around East Cape and Te Urewera. On Tuesdays and Thursdays, **Bay Hopper** (www.baybus.co.nz) bus 150 runs once daily in each direction between Ōpōtiki and Potaka on East Cape ($17, two hours). Cooks Couriers (p355) runs between Gisborne and Te Araroa daily Monday to Saturday. Call for prices and departure/arrival times. Otherwise, arrange to have your own wheels.

EAST CAPE

The slow-paced East Cape is a unique and special corner of New Zealand. It's a chilled-out place, where everyone knows everyone, and community ties are built on rural enterprise and a shared connection with the ocean. Horse riding, tractors on the beach, fresh fish for dinner – it's all part of daily life here.

Inland, the wild Raukumara Range forms the Cape's jagged spine. Tracing the fringe of the land, the 327km Pacific Coast Hwy (SH35) runs from Ōpōtiki to Gisborne. Lonely shores lie strewn with driftwood, rusted-out cars collect weeds by the roadside, finches and pheasants dart in and out of hedgerows and picture-postcard bays lure just a handful of visitors.

Pacific Coast Highway

The winding 327km Pacific Coast Hwy (aka SH35), between Ōpōtiki and Gisborne via the North Island's easternmost point, has long been a road-trip rite of passage for New Zealanders. If you like remote scenic drives, this is for you. Drive it in a day if you must, but an overnighter (or longer) is more rewarding.

If you're short on time, head for Gisborne via SH2 from Ōpōtiki – a 147km, 2½-hour alternative via the Waioeka Gorge, where you'll find the two- to three-hour loop walk leading off from the historic Tauranga Bridge.

Both routes are covered in the excellent *Pacific Coast Highway Guide,* available at Gisborne (p361) and Ōpōtiki (p344) i-SITEs.

Set off with plenty of petrol, snacks and groceries – shops and petrol stations are in short supply. Sleeping and eating options are also pretty spread out: do some homework.

◎ Sights

Along the coast east of Ōpōtiki, there are hazy views across to the active volcano Whakaari (White Island; p341), which tragically erupted in 2019 killing 21 tourists who were visiting the island at the time. The desolate beaches at Torere, Hawai and Omaio are steeply shelved and littered with flotsam. Check out the magnificent *whakairo* (carving) on the Torere school gateway. Hawai marks the western boundary of the Whānau-ā-Apanui tribe, whose *rohe* (traditional land) extends to Cape Runaway.

Around 42km east of Ōpōtiki the road crosses the broad pebbly expanse of the Motu River, the first river in New Zealand to be designated as a protected wilderness area.

Some 67km east of Ōpōtiki, the fishing town of Te Kaha once sounded the death knell for passing whales. Here you'll find a shop, holiday park, campground, B&B and resort (of sorts).

Around 24km east of Te Kaha, stop at Papatea Bay to see the gateway of Hinemahuru Marae, intricately carved with images of WWI Māori soldiers. At blink-and-you'll-miss-it Raukokore, the 1894 Anglican Christ Church (📞 07-352 3979; raukokore.church@gmail.com; 9948 SH35, Raukokore; ⊗ 8am-8pm Oct-Apr, 9am-5pm May-Sep) FREE is a sweet beacon of belief on a lonely promontory. The simple white-and-grey interior is suitably demure (look for the mouse on high). There are services at 11am on Sundays.

Some 17km east of Waihau Bay, where there's a petrol pump, pub and accommodation, Whangaparaoa (Cape Runaway) was where kumara (sweet potato) was first introduced to NZ. It can only be reached on foot.

East of Whangaparaoa, the road tracks inland, crossing into hilly Ngāti Porou territory before hitting the coast at Hicks Bay, a real middle-of-nowhere settlement with a grand beach, a store and an old tumble-down jetty at the far end of the bay. Also at the bay's far end is a good swimming hole in the Wharekahika River, 500m upstream from the bridge. You can also swim at Onepoto Bay nearby.

Around 10km east of Hicks Bay is Te Araroa, a lone-dog village with shops, a petrol pump, a takeaway and a beautifully carved *marae.* The geology changes here from igneous outcrops to sandstone cliffs: the dense bush backdrop doesn't seem to mind which it grows on. More than 350 years old, 20m high and 40m wide, Te-Waha-O-Rerekohu, allegedly NZ's largest pohutukawa tree, stands in the Te Araroa schoolyard. You'll get no argument from us: it's impressive.

From Te Araroa, drive out to see the East Cape Lighthouse, the easterly tip of mainland NZ. It's 21km (30 minutes) east of town along a mainly unsealed road, with a 25-minute climb (750 steps!) to the lighthouse. Set your alarm and get up there for sunrise.

Heading through farmland south of Te Araroa, the first town you come to is Tikitiki. If you haven't yet made it into a *marae*, you'll get a fair idea of what you're missing out on by visiting the extraordinary St Mary's Church (☑021 890 645; 1889 SH35, Tikitiki; by donation; ☺9am-5pm), built in 1926.

Beyond Tikitiki, Mt Hikurangi (1752m) juts out of the Raukumara Range – it's the highest nonvolcanic peak on the North Island and the first spot on Earth to see the sun each day. According to local tradition it was the first piece of land dragged up when Māui snagged the North Island. The Ngāti Porou version of the Māui story has his canoe and earthly remains resting here on their sacred mountain. Check out the Ngāti Porou website (www.maungahikurangi.com) for more info.

Continuing south, the road passes Ruatoria (a shop, petrol and general desolation) and Te Puia Springs (ditto). Along this stretch a 14km loop road offers a worthwhile detour to Waipiro Bay.

Eleven kilometres south of Te Puia Springs is Tokomaru Bay, perhaps the most interesting spot on the entire route, its broad beach framed by dramatic cliffs. The town has weathered hard times since the freezing works closed in the 1950s, but it still sports several attractions including easy-breaking surf, swimming and a cheery pub (p354). You'll also find a supermarket, takeaway and post office in the town (and a B&B in the former post office), plus some crumbling surprises at the far end of the bay.

Tracking south from Tokomaru Bay is a bucolic 22km stretch of highway to the turn-off to Anaura Bay, 6km away. It's a definite 'wow' moment when the bay springs into view far below. Captain Cook arrived here in 1769 and commented on the 'profound peace' in which the people were living and their 'truly astonishing' cultivations.

ESSENTIAL EAST COAST

Eat delicious fresh produce from the Hawke's Bay Farmers Market (p379).

Drink a few Gisborne Gold lagers at the Sunshine Brewery (p360).

Read Witi Ihimaera's 1987 novel *Whale Rider;* then watch the powerful 2002 movie adaptation.

Listen to international and NZ DJs at Gisborne's Rhythm & Vines (p358) festival.

Watch *Boy* (2010), Taika Waititi's hilarious film, shot at Waihau Bay.

Go green at Millton Vineyards & Winery (p361) – organic, biodynamic and delicious to boot.

Go online at www.hawkesbaynz.com; www.tairawhitigisborne.co.nz; www.lonelyplanet.com/new-zealand/the-east-coast

Back on the highway it's 14km south to Tolaga Bay, East Cape's largest community (population 830). Just off the main street, the very low-key Tolaga Bay Cashmere Company (☑06-862 6746; www.cashmere.co.nz; 31 Solander St, Tolaga Bay; ☺10am-4pm Mon-Fri) inhabits a 1922 former council building.

Tolaga is defined by its amazing historic wharf. Built in 1929 and commercially functional until 1968, it's one of the longest in the southern hemisphere at 660m, and is now largely restored after dedicated (and expensive) preservation efforts.

From Tolaga Bay it's an easy 60km drive south to Gisborne.

🏃 Activities

Cooks Cove Walkway   HIKING
(☑06-869 0460; www.doc.govt.nz; Wharf Rd, Tolaga Bay; ☺Nov-Jul) Near the amazing old wharf at Tolaga Bay is Cooks Cove Walkway, an easy 5.8km, 2½-hour loop through farmland and native bush to a cove where the captain landed in 1769. At the northern end of the beach is the Tatarahake Cliffs Lookout, a sharp 10-minute jaunt to an excellent vantage point.

Dive Tatapouri   SNORKELLING
(☑06-868 5153; www.divetatapouri.com; 532 Whangara Rd, Tatapouri; ☺8am-5pm) Dive Tatapouri offers an array of watery activities including dive trips (prices on application),

reef-ecology tours (from $55 per person) and snorkelling trips (from $80 per person). The local stingrays put in a regular up-close appearance.

Wet 'n' Wild Rafting   RAFTING

(☑07-348 3191; www.wetnwildrafting.co.nz; 2- to 5-day tours $1095-1695) Based on the outskirts of Rotorua, Wet 'n' Wild Rafting also offers multiday excursions on the wild Motu River east of Ōpōtiki, with trips taking you 100km down the river. The two-day tour requires you to be helicoptered in – exciting!

🛏 Sleeping

★ Stranded in Paradise   HOSTEL $

(☑06-864 5870; www.stranded-in-paradise.net; 21 Potae St, Tokomaru Bay; campsites per person $25, dm/d/f $30/85/135, cabin d/tr $50/85; P 🛜) Up on the hill behind town, the 15-bed Stranded in Paradise scores points for show-stopping views and eco loos. There are two tricky loft dorm rooms, a double (or family) room downstairs and two wave-shaped cabins (double and triple). Tenters have a panoramic knoll with astonishing bay views on which to pitch. Short walk to the pub.

Anaura Bay Motor Camp   CAMPGROUND $

(☑06-862 6380; www.anaurabaymotorcamp.co.nz; 680 Anaura Rd, Anaura Bay; sites per adult/child unpowered $20/11, powered $22/12; P 🛜 ♿) Affable Anaura Bay Motor Camp is all about the location – right on the beachfront by the little stream where Captain Cook once stocked up with water. There's a decent kitchen, showers and toilets.

Tolaga Bay Holiday Park   HOLIDAY PARK $

(☑06-862 6716; www.tolagabayholidaypark.co.nz; 167 Wharf Rd, Tolaga Bay; sites unpowered/powered $40/44, cabins $60-100; P 🛜 ♿) Tolaga Bay Holiday Park is right next to the very long Tolaga Bay wharf. The stiff ocean breeze tousles Norfolk Island pines as open lawns bask in the sunshine. It's a special spot. Cabins are basic but perfectly decent (you'll probably be spending most of your time outside anyway). There's a summertime shop here, too.

Lottin Point Motel   MOTEL $$

(☑06-864 4455; www.lottinpoint.co.nz; 365 Lottin Point Rd, Hicks Bay; d/3-bedroom unit from $160/240, extra person $50; P 🛜) Effervescent new owners have breathed life back into this ol' motel at remote Lottin Point, a wiggly 4km detour off the highway. Two accommodation blocks house 14 contemporary

rooms, all with kitchenettes and the best with knockout ocean views. Land-based fishing is big here, or rent a kayak and go paddling ($50 per day). Helipad for rock-star arrivals.

Nga Puriri   COTTAGE $$

(☑06-864 4035; www.thepuriris.co.nz; 5138 Te Araroa Rd, Hicks Bay; d incl breakfast from $160; P 🛜) Overlooking Hicks Bay, this wee self-contained weatherboard cottage is a delight, with room for two and breakfast eggs from the chooks next door. There's safe sandy swimming at Onepoto Bay nearby.

Hicks Bay Motel Lodge   MOTEL $$

(☑06-864 4880; www.hicksbaymotel.co.nz; 5198 Te Araroa Rd, Hicks Bay; d $107-171, 2-bedroom units $178; P 🛜 ♿) Knockout views distract from the mildly barracks-like ambience at this 50-something-year-old motel, squatting high above Hicks Bay. The clean, old-fashioned rooms are nothing flash, although the restaurant (mains $20 to $35, open for breakfast and dinner), shop, pool and glow-worm grotto compensate. Four-bed bunk room also available (from $60).

🍴 Eating

Cottle's Cafe & Bakery   BAKERY $

(☑06-862 6484; 30 Cook St, Tologa Bay; pies/meals from $4/12; ⏱5am-1pm Mon-Fri) Decent coffee and excellent savoury pies make Cottle's an essential stop on Tologa Bay's main drag. The bacon-and-egg pie is deservedly popular all around East Cape, but we reckon the fish and chips are just as good. Extended hours in summer.

Pacific Coast Macadamias   ICE CREAM $

(☑07-325 2960; www.macanuts.co.nz; 8462 SH35, Whanarua Bay; snacks $5-12; ⏱10am-3pm Sat & Sun Dec, daily Jan-Mar; ♿) Heaven is a tub of homemade macadamia-and-honey ice cream from this blue nut hut, accompanied by views along one of the most spectacular parts of the coast. Toasted sandwiches and nutty sweet treats make this a great lunch stop. Call ahead to check it's open – hours can be very sketchy outside of summer.

Te Puka Tavern   PUB FOOD $$

(☑06-864 5465; www.tepukatavern.co.nz; 135 Beach Rd, Tokomaru Bay; mains $13-29; ⏱11am-late; 🛜) This well-run pub with cracker ocean views is a cornerstone of the community, keeping everyone fed and watered (good burgers), and offering visitors a place to stay. Four natty split-level, self-contained units sleep up to six (doubles $160, extra person $30) and there's room for four campervans (powered sites $15, unpowered sites free).

The pub was for sale when we visited: we hope the new owners keep up the good work.

Waihau Bay Lodge　　PUB FOOD $$
(☑07-325 3805; www.thewaihaubaylodge.co.nz; Orete Point Rd, Waihau Bay; mains $27-37; ⊙11am-late) A rather stately two-storey timber pub by the pier, serving hefty meals such as pork chop with apple sauce and offering accommodation ranging from grassy campsites ($15) to four-bed dorms (from $35 per person), en-suite doubles ($140) and roomy en-suite units sleeping eight (double $195, extra person $30). No lunch during winter.

🔒 Shopping

East Cape Manuka Company　　FOOD
(☑06-864 4824; www.eastcapemanuka.co.nz; 4464 Te Araroa Rd, Te Araroa; ⊙8am-4pm daily Oct-Apr, Mon-Fri May-Sep) The progressive East Cape Manuka Company sells soaps, oils, creams and honey made from potent East Cape manuka. It's also a good stop for a coffee, a slice of cheesecake, a pie or a well-stuffed roll (meals and snacks $6 to $18).

ℹ Getting There & Away

By far the most fun way to experience the Pacific Coast Hwy (SH35) is with your own wheels (motorised or pedal-powered). Otherwise, **Bay Hopper** (www.baybus.co.nz) runs between Ōpōtiki and Potaka/Cape Runaway on Tuesday and Thursday afternoons. **Cooks Couriers** (☑021 371 364) runs between Gisborne and Te Araroa daily Monday to Saturday.

Gisborne

POP 48,020

'Gizzy' to her friends – and Tairāwhiti to Māori – Gisborne (pronounced Gis-born, not Gis-bun) is a pretty place, squeezed between surf beaches and a sea of chardonnay. It proudly claims to be the first city on Earth to see the sun each day, and is a top spot to put your feet up for a few days, hit the beach and sip some wine.

If you're into festivals, make a dance-music-and-DJ date for late December, or experience the best of the local food, wine and beer scene in October. At other times of the year, walking in an arboreal wonderland or exploring one of New Zealand's best regional museums will tempt you to visit the country's most remote city.

History

The Gisborne region has been settled for more than 700 years. A pact between two migratory *waka* (canoe) skippers, Paoa of the *Horouta* and Kiwa of the *Takitimu*, led to the founding of Turanganui a Kiwa (now Gisborne). Kumara (sweet potatoes) flourished in the fertile soil and the settlement blossomed.

In 1769 this was the first part of NZ sighted by Captain Cook's expedition on the *Endeavour*. Eager to replenish supplies and explore, they set ashore, much to the amazement of the locals. Setting an unfortunate benchmark for intercultural relations, the crew opened fire when the Māori men performed their traditional blood-curdling challenge, killing a leader named Te Maro. The following day as tensions escalated, Cook's men shot eight more Māori, before the *Endeavour* set sail without provisions. In dismay, Cook named the area Poverty Bay as 'it did not afford a single item we wanted'.

In October 2019, on the 250th anniversary of Cook's 1769 landing, Laura Clarke, the British High Commissioner to New Zealand, attended a ceremony in Gisborne to mark the event, and expressed regret over the deaths of the nine Māori, though she stopped short of issuing the formal apology that many Māori had hoped for.

European settlement in Gisborne began in 1831 with whaling and farming; missionaries followed. In the 1860s battles between settlers and Māori erupted. Beginning in Taranaki, the Hauhau insurrection spread to the East Coast, culminating in the battle of Waerenga a Hika in 1865, 10km inland from Gisborne.

To discover Gisborne's historical spots from the Māori perspective, pick up the *Tupapa* pamphlet from Gisborne i-SITE (p361).

◉ Sights

⭐**Tairāwhiti Museum**　　MUSEUM
(☑06-867 3832; www.tairawhitimuseum.org.nz; Kelvin Rise, 10 Stout St; adult/child $5/free; ⊙10am-4pm Mon-Sat, 1.30-4pm Sun) The Tairāwhiti Museum, with its fab gallery extension, focuses on East Coast Māori and colonial history. This is Gisborne's arts hub, with rotating exhibits and excellent historic photographic displays. There's also a maritime wing, with displays on *waka*, whaling and Cook's Poverty Bay, although these pale in comparison to the vintage surfboard collection. There's also a shop and a park-view

Gisborne

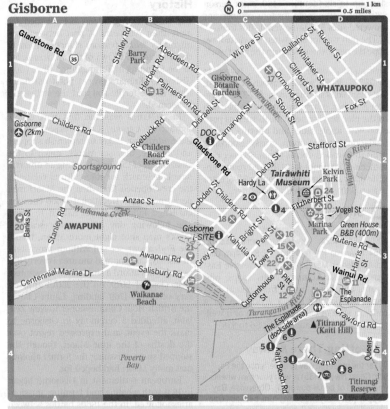

Gisborne

◎ Top Sights

◎ Sights

◎ Activities, Courses & Tours

◎ Sleeping

◎ Eating

◎ Drinking & Nightlife

◎ Entertainment

◎ Shopping

THE EAST COAST GISBORNE

cafe. Outside is the immaculately reconstructed Wyllie Cottage (1872), Gisborne's oldest house – a fascinating window into old-time domestic life.

Footrot Flats Statue
STATUE

(Bright St, outside HB Williams Memorial Library) Gisborne is already well endowed with statues, but this one commemorating the hugely popular Footrot Flats cartoons (p358) by Gisborne local, the late Murray Ball, is one of our faves. Wal, the series' archetypal Kiwi farmer, stands with his devoted canine companion, 'The Dog', looking on. For more on *Footrot Flats*, see www.footrotflats.com, or check out the 1986 movie *Footrot Flats: The Dog's Tale*.

C Company
Memorial House
CULTURAL CENTRE

(☑ 06-868 9035; www.ngatamatoa.co.nz; 10 Stout St; by donation; ⊙ noon-3pm Tue-Fri & Sun, from 10am Sat) This cultural centre commemorates the dedication and commitment of the famed 28th Māori Battalion of the New Zealand Army who fought bravely in the European and North African theatres in WWII. In particular, the role of Māori men from the East Coast who made up the battalion's C Company – many of whom paid the ultimate 'price of citizenship' – is brought to life with poignant photos and stories. Stirring stuff.

Puhi Kai Iti Cook Landing Site
MONUMENT

(www.gdc.govt.nz; Kaiti Beach Rd) At the foot of Titirangi Reserve (p357) is the spot where Captain Cook first landed in NZ in 1769, and where nine Māori were killed by Cook's crew. In 2019, a $5.3-million upgrade of the formerly grim obelisk marked the 250th anniversary of Cook's arrival, and 750 years since the Horouta *waka*, a pioneering Polynesian canoe, landed at the same site. The addition of 112 huge steel *tukutuku* (weaving) panels symbolises the meeting of – and differences between – two cultures.

Titirangi Reserve
PARK

(☑ 06-867 2049; www.gdc.govt.nz; Titirangi Dr, off Queens Dr; ⊙ daylight hours; ⓘ) FREE High on a hill overlooking Gisborne, Titirangi was once a *pā* (fortified village). Reach it via Queens Dr, or on the steep track from the revamped Puhi Kai Iti Cook Landing Site (p357) monument down at the port. Near the lookout (Titirangi Dr; ⊙ daylight hours) at the top is yet another Cook edifice, at Cook's Plaza (Titirangi Dr). Adjacent is a modest pohutukawa tree planted by Princess Diana in 1983.

Also here is a new sculpture of Te Maro (☑ 06-867 2049; www.gdc.govt.nz; off Kaiti Beach Rd; ⊙ daylight hours), the first of nine Māori men killed by Cook's crew when they landed in Gisborne in 1769. The 10m-high, perforated steel sculpture was erected in 2019 to mark 250 years since 'the most disagreeable day' of Cook's life (and certainly Te Maro's).

Eastwoodhill Arboretum
GARDENS

(☑ 06-863 9003; www.eastwoodhill.org.nz; 2392 Wharekopae Rd, Ngatapa; adult/child/family $15/2/28; ⊙ 9am-5pm; ⓘ) An arboreal paradise, Eastwoodhill Arboretum is the largest collection of northern-hemisphere trees and shrubs in the southern hemisphere. It's staggeringly beautiful – you could easily lose a day wandering around the 25km of themed tracks in this pine-scented paradise. It's well signposted, 35km northwest of Gisborne. There's accommodation and an excellent kids' playground, too.

East Coast Museum
of Technology
MUSEUM

(ECMoT; ☑ 06-927 7080; www.ecmot.org.nz; 67 Main Rd, Makaraka; adult/child $10/2; ⊙ 10am-4pm Sun-Fri, from 1pm Sat) Think analogue not digital; old-age not space-age. About 6km west of the town centre, this improbable medley of farm equipment, fire engines and sundry appliances has found an appropriate home in an old milking barn and surrounding outhouses. Dig the millennium welcome sign!

🏃 Activities
On the Water

Surfing is de rigueur in Gisborne, with the teenage population looking appropriately shaggy. Waikanae Beach and Roberts Road are good for learners; experienced surfers get tubed south of town at the Pipe, or east at Sponge Bay and Tuamotu Island. Further east along SH35, Wainui and Makorori also have quality breaks.

There's safe swimming between the flags at Waikanae and Midway Beach.

Rere Rockslide
SWIMMING

(Wharekopae Rd, Ngatapa; ⊙ daylight hours) FREE This natural phenomenon occurs in a section of the Rere River, about 50km northwest of Gisborne along Wharekopae Rd. Grab a tyre tube or boogie board to cushion the bumps (the Gisborne i-SITE (p361) can advise) and slide down the 60m-long rocky run into the pool at the bottom. Three kilometres downriver, the Rere Falls send

FOOTROT FLATS

From 1976 to 1994, the *Footrot Flats* cartoon strip by long-time Gisborne resident Murray Ball (1939–2017) ran in newspapers across New Zealand, and compilation books of the series sold millions throughout NZ and Australia. Oddly, it was also a big hit in Denmark.

At its heart, *Footrot Flats* is the story of the relationship between Wallace 'Wal' Footrot and his loyal Border collie, nicknamed 'The Dog' in a fine example of Kiwi understatement. Life in the country is the ongoing background of the cartoon strip – along with quintessentially NZ locations like the local rugby club in the fictional town of Raupo.

Beyond the gentle humour, cartoonist Ball was a fierce opponent of inequality, and over its lifespan, *Footrot Flats* also incorporated subtle commentary on environmentalism. The series was at its peak in the mid-1980s, spawning a feature-length animated film in 1986, and an Auckland theme park which was open from 1986 to 1991.

a mesmerising, 20m-wide curtain of water over a 5m drop; you can walk behind it if you don't mind getting wet. Great fun!

Walking On Water Surf School SURFING
(WOW; ☎022 313 0213; www.wowsurfschool. com; 90min/3-day/4-day lessons per person from $65/180/220; ☺) Surfing is just like walking on water, right? Wrong. It's even harder than that – but these guys know how to turn the most naive novice into an upstanding surfer in no time. Kids' lessons and gear hire, too.

On Land
There are many miles of walks to tackle around Gisborne, starting with a gentle stroll along the river. The Gisborne i-SITE (p361) can help you out with advice and maps.

Winding its way through farmland and forest with commanding views, the Te Kuri Farm Walkway (two-hour loop, 5.6km, November to July) starts 4km north of town at the end of Shelley Rd.

Haurata High Country Walks HIKING
(☎06-867 8452; www.haurata.co.nz; 1257 Makaretu Rd, Matawai; walks unguided/guided per person from $15/25) Take a hike in the hills with Haurata, which offers guided or unguided short and long day walks through the gorgeous high country behind Gisborne. Meals, farmhouse accommodation (dorms/doubles from $35/50) and hot-tub soaks also available. Haurata's property is around 65km northwest of Gisborne; give yourself 70 minutes for the drive.

Gisborne Railbike Adventure CYCLING
(☎021 525 700; www.railbikes.nz; 500 Awapuni Rd, Gisborne; tours per person per 1hr/day $35/115; ☺8am-6pm) Here's something different: two side-by-side bicycles fixed together by a steel frame and rigged up to ride along old disused rail tracks. Guided tours run from one

hour to a full day, taking you to wineries, beaches, rail tunnels and more. Book at least a day before you want to ride.

Cycle Gisborne CYCLING
(☎06-927 7021; www.cyclegisborne.com; 124 Ormond Rd, Whataupoko; tours from $150, bicycle hire per half-/full day from $35/50) Half-day to multiday guided cycle tours around local sights and further afield, including wineries and Eastwoodhill Arboretum (p357). Bike hire (including tandems) also available with maps and advice on tap.

Festivals & Events

First Light Wine & Food Festival WINE
(www.firstlightwineandfood.co.nz; ☺Oct) Cellar-door spectacular, with local winemakers and foodies pooling talents. Buses leave from the Gisborne i-SITE (p361), transporting revellers between the venues. Live music ahoy.

Te Tairāwhiti Arts Festival ART
(www.tetairawhitiartsfestival.nz; ☺Oct) Two-and-a-half weeks crammed full of singing, dancing, music, installations, film and theatre at various venues around Gisborne. Big on the connections between land, people and culture.

Rhythm & Vines MUSIC
(R&V; www.rhythmandvines.co.nz; ☺Dec) A huge event on Gisborne's music calendar, R&V is a three-day festival leading up to New Year's Eve, featuring big-time local and international bands and DJs and boundless East Coast wine. Local accommodation feels the squeeze.

Sleeping

Gisborne YHA HOSTEL $
(☎06-867 3269; www.yha.co.nz; 32 Harris St; dm/s/d/f from $28/54/70/140; P☺☺) A short wander across the river from town, this rambling, mustard-coloured 1925 charmer

houses a well-kept hostel. The rooms are large and comfy (even the 10-bed dorm in the attic), while a shared outdoor deck and lawns kindle conversation. There's a family en-suite unit (sleeps four), and surfboards and wet-suits for hire if you feel like hitting the beach.

Waikanae Beach
Top 10 Holiday Park HOLIDAY PARK **$**
(☑06-867 5634; www.gisborneholidaypark.co.nz; 280 Grey St; sites per person from $28, cabins & units $95-200; P🛜🏊🐾) Right by the beach and an easy 10-minute walk into town, this grassy holiday park offers basic cabins, better units and grassy lanes for pitching tents and parking vans. There are surfboards and bikes for hire, and there's a swimming pool if it's a bit too blowy down at the beach.

⭐**Ahi Kaa Motel** MOTEL **$$**
(☑06-867 7107; www.ahikaa.co.nz; 61 Salisbury Rd; d $140-190; P🛜) ✎ An uptown motel on a quiet backstreet, Ahi Kaa is just a short, sandy-footed stroll across the road from Waikanae Beach. Fancy linen, tasteful bathrooms, double glazing, outdoor showers, recycled timbers, solar power, supercomfy beds and recycling savvy – nice one!

Green House B&B B&B **$$**
(☑021 301 375; www.the-green-house.co.nz; 9 Hinaki St; d from $120; P🛜) ✎ Beyond lovingly tended lawns and flowerbeds, this good-looking 1920s villa (yes, it's green) offers a bright guest room with a private bathroom adjacent. Breakfast is continental-style, best consumed on the sunny patio. A quiet backstreet location and a mindful approach to recycling, water use, and using local breakfast produce adds further appeal.

Portside Hotel HOTEL **$$**
(☑06-869 1000; www.portsidegisborne.co.nz; 2 Reads Quay; d/apt from $185/215; P🛜🏊) The wandering business traveller's hotel of choice in Gisborne, Portside offers three levels of sassy two-bedroom apartments, right by the river mouth where the big ships come and go. There's a charcoal-and-cream colour scheme, with little glass-fronted balconies overlooking the harbourside pool.

Teal Motor Lodge MOTEL **$$**
(☑06-868 4019; www.teal.co.nz; 479 Gladstone Rd; d from $145, 1-/2-bedroom unit from $220/270; P🛜🏊) With super street appeal on the main drag (500m into town), the vaguely alpine (and just a bit *Mad Men*) Teal boasts a solid offering of tidy, family-friendly units plus a saltwater swimming pool and immaculate lawns to run around on.

🍴 Eating

⭐**Frank & Albie's** CAFE **$**
(☑06-867 7847; www.frankandalbie.co.nz; 24 Gladstone Rd; mains $10-17; ⊙7.30am-2.30pm Mon-Fri; 🅿) ✎ 'We cut lunch, not corners' is the motto at Frank & Albie's, a neat little hipster place on Gisborne's main drag (check out the old art-deco leadlighting above the door). Nifty plywood benches and recycled timber tables set the scene for super sandwiches, bagels, salads, wraps, coffee, teas and smoothies. Free-range produce and compostable containers, all the way.

Neighbourhood Pizzeria PIZZA **$**
(☑06-868 7174; www.facebook.com/neighborhoodpizzeria; 9 Ballance St; pizzas $12-20; ⊙4.30-8.30pm, closed Mon & Tue Jun-Sep) Serving pizzas out of a converted shipping container north of the river, Neighbourhood Pizzeria draws loyal locals for the East Coast's best pizzas. Traditional flavours like margherita segue into pork and jalapeño or chicken and chorizo, with mozzarella from nearby Waimata. There aren't many spots to sit – it's more of a grab-and-go operation.

Muirs Bookshop & Cafe CAFE **$**
(☑06-867 9742; www.muirsbookshop.co.nz; 62 Gladstone Rd; meals $7-16; ⊙9am-3.30pm Mon-Fri, to 3pm Sat) Nooked away above a beloved, age-old independent bookseller (since 1905) in a lovely heritage building, this simple cafe offers a small but sweet selection of counter food and cakes. Fans of fine espresso and literature may need to be forcibly removed. Over-street balcony for balmy days. Show up by 9.30am for the best chance of a freshly baked chocolate brioche.

SUMMER CAMPING

The **Gisborne District Council** (GDC; ☑06-867 2049; www.gdc.govt.nz/summer-camping; 15 Fitzherbert St, Gisborne; campsites $17-73) operates a handful of designated 'summer camping' sites along the East Coast between Te Araroa and Gisborne from the end of September to early April. Apply for a permit in person or online for two, 10 or 28 consecutive nights at a cost of $17, $35 and $73 respectively, for up to six people,or buy one at the Gisborne (p361) or Ōpōtiki (p344) i-SITEs,. Your own gas cooker, chemical toilet and water supply are obligatory. No actual site bookings – just turn up and hope for a spot!

THE EAST COAST GISBORNE

THE EAST COAST GISBORNE

The main *iwi* (tribes) in the region are Te Whānau-ā-Apanui (www.apanui.co.nz; west side of East Cape), Ngāti Porou (www.ngatiporou.com; east side of East Cape), Ngāti Kahungunu (www.kahungunu.iwi.nz; the coast from Hawke's Bay down) and Ngāi Tūhoe (www.ngaituhoe.iwi.nz; inland in Te Urewera).

Ngāti Porou and Ngāti Kahungunu are the country's second- and third-biggest *iwi*, respectively. In the late 19th century they produced the great leaders James Carroll (the first Māori cabinet minister) and Āpirana Ngata (who was briefly acting prime minister). Ngata, whose face adorns New Zealand's $50 note, worked tirelessly in parliament to orchestrate a cultural revival within Māoridom. The region's magnificent carved *marae* are part of his legacy.

Māori life is at the forefront around East Cape, in sleepy villages centred upon the many *marae* that dot the landscape. Living in close communities, drawing much of their livelihoods from the sea and the land, the *tangata whenua* (local people) of the Cape offer a fascinating insight into what life might have been, had they not been so vigorously divested of their land in the 19th century.

You will meet Māori wherever you go. For an intimate introduction to *Māoritanga* (things Māori), take a guided tour with Long Island Guides (p377) in Napier or Waimārama Māori Tours (✆021 057 0935; www.waimaramamaori.co.nz; tours per person from $150, transport from $40) based in Havelock North.

For a more passive brush with the culture, visit Gisborne's Tairāwhiti Museum (p355) and C Company Memorial House (p357), Otatara Pā (Map p366; ✆06-834 3111; www.doc.govt.nz; off Springfield Rd, Taradale; ⊙24hr) **FREE** in Napier and Tikitiki's St Mary's Church (p353).

Surfin' Taco   MEXICAN $$

(www.facebook.com/surfingtaco; 155A Grey St; mains $18-26; ⊙5-9pm Wed-Sat) The long-winded sign above the door reads, 'The World's Farthest East Mexican Restaurant', and this little burgundy box does some of the best Mexican on the East Coast – a simple array of tacos (beef, chicken, fish, shrimp or veg) burritos and quesadillas, washed down with kickin' margaritas.

Crawford Road Kitchen   BISTRO $$

(✆06-867 4085; www.crawfordroadkitchen.co.nz; 3/50 The Esplanade; mains $22-24; ⊙11.30am-9pm Tue-Sat, to 5pm Sun) Alongside the Gisborne Wine Centre (✆06-867 4085; www.gisbornewinecentre.co.nz; 3/50 The Esplanade; ⊙11am-9pm Tue-Sat, to 5pm Sun), this bistro combines culinary smarts and international flavours with an interesting harbourside locale. Good-value sharing plates might include pork belly with peanut slaw and brown rice, or mussels with turmeric, coriander and coconut. The thoughtful wine list features around 15 local drops by the glass and Gisborne-brewed craft beers. Coffee and cake, too.

USSCO Bar & Bistro   MODERN NZ $$$

(✆06-868 3246; www.ussco.co.nz; 16 Childers Rd; mains $32-45; ⊙5pm-late Mon-Sat) Inside the restored Union Steam Ship Company building (hence USSCO), this place is all class. Kitchen skills shine on a highly seasonal menu featuring the likes of confit duck with bok choy and ginger soy, and devilishly good desserts. Look forward to local wines, NZ craft beers, generous portions and multicourse deals.

Drinking & Nightlife

★ Smash Palace   BAR

(✆06-867 7769; www.smashpalacebar.com; 24 Banks St; ⊙3-8pm Tue, Thu & Sun, to 11pm Wed & Fri, noon-11pm Sat) Get juiced at the junkyard: an iconic drinking and live-music den in Gisborne's industrial wastelands (make as much noise as you like!), packed to the rafters with ephemera (old surfboards, bike wheels, Morris Minor car parts) and with its very own DC3 crash-landed in the beer garden. Regular vinyl sessions wind back the clock.

Sunshine Brewery   MICROBREWERY

(✆06-867 7777; www.sunshinebrewery.co.nz; 49 Awapuni Rd; ⊙noon-8pm Mon-Sat, to 6pm Sun) Bottling up a clutch of quality beers since '89, including its flagship Gisborne Gold lager, Gisborne's pioneering craft brewery has a fab tasting room near Waikanae Beach. Quaff a few on the deck out the front, or peer through the windows to the big stainless-steel vats bubbling away out the back. Twenty-plus taps mean there's something for most tastes.

☆ Entertainment

★ Dome Cinema CINEMA, BAR
(☏ 027 590 2117; www.domecinema.co.nz; 38 Childers Rd; tickets $14; ⊗from 5pm Tue-Sun) The excellent, artful Dome is located inside the charming old Poverty Bay Club building (1874): beanbags and art-house flicks now occupy the glass-domed ballroom. There's a cool bar next door serving beer, wine and pizzas amid black-painted floorboards. The very serviceable PBC Cafe (☏06-863 3165; https:// pbc-cafe.business.site; 38 Childers Rd; mains $15-30; ⊗7am-3pm Mon-Fri, from 8am Sat & Sun; 🍴🚲) is also here. Occasional live bands, too.

Lawson Field Theatre THEATRE
(☏06-8672049;www.gisbornetheatres.nz/lawson-field-theatre; 7 Fitzherbert St, Whataupoko; tickets from $45; ⊗box office noon-5pm Mon-Fri) Re-opened in 2019 after earthquake strengthening, the versatile, 250-seat Lawson Field Theatre hosts everything from the New Zealand Symphony Orchestra to stand-up comedy and travelling Bee Gees tribute shows.

🔒 Shopping

Gisborne Farmers Market MARKET
(☏027 251 8608; www.gisbornefarmersmarket. co.nz; cnr Stout & Fitzherbert Sts; ⊗9.30am-12.30pm Sat) Fill your travelling saddlebags with fresh fruit, macadamia nuts (and macadamia nut paste), smallgoods, honey, herbs, coffee, bread, pastries, fish, cheese and Gisborne oranges...all of it locally grown or procured. Oh, and wine!

ℹ Information

Gisborne i-SITE (☏06-868 6139; www. tairawhitigisborne.co.nz; 209 Grey St; ⊗8.30am-5pm; 📶) Beside a doozy of a Canadian totem pole, the local info centre has all and sundry, including a travel desk, history displays, bike hire and a gazillion brochures.
DOC (Department of Conservation; ☏06-869 0460; www.doc.govt.nz; 63 Carnarvon St; ⊗8am-4.30pm Mon-Fri) Great info on the great outdoors.
Gisborne Hospital (☏06-869 0500; www. hauoratairawhiti.org.nz; 421 Ormond Rd, Riverdale; ⊗24hr) Accident and emergency.

ℹ Getting There & Around

AIR
Gisborne Airport (☏06-868 7951; www. eastland.co.nz/gisborne-airport; Aerodrome Rd, Awapuni) is 3km west of the city. Air New Zealand (www.airnewzealand.co.nz) flies to/ from Auckland and Wellington.

BUS
InterCity (www.intercity.co.nz) services depart from Gisborne i-SITE, with daily buses to Auckland ($104, nine hours), Ōpōtiki ($51, two hours), Wairoa ($19, 1½ hours), Napier ($54, four hours), Rotorua ($66, five hours) and beyond.

TAXI
Gisborne Taxis (☏06-867 2222; www. gisbornetaxi.com) Taxis, all sizes.

South of Gisborne

From Gisborne heading south towards Wairoa, you can take the coast road or the inland road. The coastal route is possibly a better choice, being quicker and offering occasional views out to sea. However, SH36 (Tiniroto Rd) is also a decent drive (or bike route) with several interesting points along the way.

THE EAST COAST SOUTH OF GISBORNE

GISBORNE WINERIES

With hot summers and fertile, loamy soils, the Waipaoa River valley to the northwest of Gisborne is one of New Zealand's foremost grape-growing areas. The region is traditionally famous for its chardonnay, and is increasingly noted for gewürztraminer and pinot gris. Check out www.gisbornewine.co.nz for a cellar-door map, or pick one up from the Gisborne i-SITE. Opening hours scale back out of peak season. Four of the best:

Bushmere Estate (☏06-868 9317; www.bushmere.com; 166 Main Rd, Matawhero; ⊗11am-3pm Wed-Sun Oct-Mar, by appointment Apr-Sep)

Matawhero (☏06-867 6140; www.matawhero.co.nz; 189 Riverpoint Rd, Matawhero; ⊗11am-5pm, reduced winter hours)

Millton Vineyards & Winery (☏06-862 8680; www.millton.co.nz; 119 Papatu Rd, Manutuke; ⊗11am-5pm, reduced winter hours) 🌿

Doneraille Park, 49km from Gisborne, is a peaceful bush riverside reserve with freedom camping for self-contained vehicles. Hackfalls Arboretum (06-863 7083; www.hackfalls.org.nz; 187 Berry Rd, Tiniroto; adult/child $10/free; 9am-5pm), with its 3000 rare plants, is a 3km detour from the turn-off at the Tiniroto Tavern. The snow-white cascades of Te Reinga Falls, 12km further south, are well worth a stop.

The busier SH2 route heads inland and soon enters the Wharerata State Forest (beware of logging trucks). Just out of the woods, 55km from Gisborne, Morere Hot Springs (06-837 8856; www.morerehot springs.co.nz; SH2, Morere; adult/child $14/7, private pools $18/12, nonswimmers $3; 10am-6pm) burble up from a fault line in the Morere Springs Scenic Reserve. Take a bushwalk, a swim, or both.

From Gisborne on SH2, keep an eye out for the brightly painted Taane-nui-a-Rangi Marae on the left. You can get a decent view from the road; don't enter unless invited.

Continuing south, SH2 leads to Nuhaka at the northern end of Hawke's Bay. From here it's west to Wairoa or east to the sea-salty Mahia Peninsula (p363). Not far from the Nuhaka roundabout is Kahungunu Marae (06-876 2718; www.kahungunu.iwi.nz/our-marae; cnr Ihaka St & Mataira St, Nuhaka). Check out the carvings from the roadside (it's not open to the public).

Morere Lodge & Holiday Park   LODGE $
(06-837 8824; www.morerelodge.co.nz; SH2, Morere; d $100-120, extra person $50; P) A farmy enclave where the lambs gambol, the dog wags its tail and the chooks roam free. Sleeping options include a classic 1917 farmhouse (sleeps 12) with kitchen and sweet sleep-out, another two-bedroom farmhouse (sleeps four) and two photogenic cabins. Great value. Larger campervans might struggle with the wiggly driveway and creek crossing – call ahead.

Smokey Bros BBQ Cafe   BARBECUE $$
(06-837 8792; www.facebook.com/smokey brosnz; 3983 SH2, Morere; mains $16-20; 8am-8pm, reduced winter hours) Opposite Morere Hot Springs (p362) is this casual, good-time barbecue joint, plating up tangy ribs, beefy burgers and tender brisket, alongside breads, pickles and sauces all made from scratch on-site. The pulled-pork burger will fuel your journey ahead.

TE KOOTI

Māori history is filled with mystics, prophets and warriors, one of whom is the celebrated Te Kooti (rhymes with naughty, not booty).

In 1865 he fought with the government against the Hauhau (adherents of the Pai Mārire faith, founded by another warrior-prophet) but was accused of being a spy and imprisoned on the Chatham Islands without trial.

While there, Te Kooti studied the Bible and claimed to receive visions from the archangel Michael. His charismatic preaching and 'miracles' – including producing flames from his hands (his captors claimed he used phosphorus from the head of matches) – helped win over the Pai Mārire to his distinctly Māori take on Christianity.

In 1867 Te Kooti led an astounding escape from the Chathams, hijacking a supply ship and sailing to Poverty Bay with 200 followers. En route he threw a doubter overboard as a sacrifice. Upon their safe arrival, Te Kooti's disciples raised their right hands in homage to God rather than bowing submissively; Ringatū (meaning 'upraised hand') became the name of his church.

Te Kooti requested a dialogue with the colonial government but was once again rebuffed, with magistrate Reginald Biggs demanding his immediate surrender. Unimpressed by Pākehā (white settler) justice, Te Kooti commenced a particularly effective guerrilla campaign – starting with killing Biggs and around 50 others (including women and children, both Māori and Pākehā) at Matawhero near Gisborne.

A four-year chase ensued. Eventually Te Kooti took refuge in the King Country, the Māori king's vast dominion where government troops feared to tread.

Proving the pointlessness of the government's approach to the whole affair, Te Kooti was officially pardoned in 1883. By this time his reputation as a prophet and healer had spread and his Ringatū Church was firmly established. Today it claims more than 16,000 adherents.

WORTH A TRIP

MAHIA PENINSULA

Between Gisborne and Napier, the Mahia Peninsula's eroded hills, sandy beaches, dramatic cliffs and vivid blue sea look a little like the Coromandel, minus the tourist crowds.

Spend a day or two exploring the scenic reserve and the bird-filled Maungawhio Lagoon, hanging out at the beach (Mahia Beach at sunset can be spectacular), or teeing off with some golf. Mahia has several small settlements offering between them a few guesthouses, a holiday park, a bar-bistro and a couple of stores. Check out www.voyagemahia.co.nz for accommodation listings.

In recent years, the peninsula's eastern edge has become the launch location for New Zealand's very own rocket company. See Rocket Lab's website (www.rocketlabusa.com) for the low-down (up high?) on this innovative Kiwi startup.

Mahia is a short detour east of the road between Gisborne and Wairoa (SH2). Turn off at Nuhaka – the main settlements are about 20km away. No buses run here – you'll need your own vehicle.

ⓘ Getting There & Away

InterCity (www.intercity.co.nz) buses take the SH2, departing daily from Gisborne i-SITE (p361) for Wairoa ($19, 1½ hours) and Napier ($54, four hours).

Te Urewera

Shrouded in mist and mysticism, Te Urewera encompasses 2127 sq km of virgin forest cut with lakes and rivers. The highlight is Lake Waikaremoana (Sea of Rippling Waters), a deep crucible of water encircled by the Lake Waikaremoana Track, one of New Zealand's Great Walks. Rugged bluffs drop away to reedy inlets, the lake's mirror surface disturbed only by mountain zephyrs and the occasional waterbird taking to the skies.

History

The name Te Urewera still has the capacity to make Pākehā (white) New Zealanders feel slightly uneasy – and not just because it translates as 'The Burnt Penis'. There's something primal and untamed about this wild woodland, with its rich history of Māori resistance.

The local Ngāi Tūhoe people – prosaically known as the 'Children of the Mist' – never signed the Treaty of Waitangi and fought with Rewi Maniapoto at Ōrākau during the Waikato Wars. The army of Te Kooti took refuge here during running battles with government troops. The claimant of Te Kooti's spiritual mantle, Rua Kenana, led a thriving community beneath the sacred mountain Maungapohatu (1366m) from 1905 until his politically motivated 1916 arrest. This effectively erased the last bastion of Māori

independence in the country. Maungapohatu never recovered, and only a small settlement remains today. Nearby, Ruatāhuna's extraordinary Mataatua Marae celebrates Te Kooti's exploits.

Tūhoe remain proud of their identity and traditions, with around 40% still speaking *te reo* (the language) on a regular basis.

In 2014, following a settlement under the Treaty of Waitangi, administration of Te Urewera was passed to the Te Urewera Board, comprising both Tūhoe and the NZ government. Tūhoe and this board lead the formulation of annual plans for Te Urewera, and work with the Department of Conservation (DOC) to maintain tracks and visitor facilities in the area.

🏃 Activities

Kicking off at either Onepoto in the south or Hopuruahine Landing in the north, the epic 46km, four-day Lake Waikaremoana Track (p351; map p364) is one of NZ's Great Walks. There are dozens of other hikes within Te Urewera's vast boundaries, including plenty of short walks starting from near the eastern end of Lake Waikaremoana or the Waikaremoana Holiday Park.

With its untouched islands, Lake Waikareiti is an enchanting place. Starting near the far eastern end of Lake Waikaremoana, it's an hour's walk to its shore.

Accessed from the track to Lake Waikareiti, the more challenging Ruapani Circuit Track (a six-hour loop) passes through wetlands and dense, virgin forest. Also from Lake Waikareiti it's a three-hour walk to the Sandy Bay Hut at the northern end of the lake. It's a basic bunkhouse (adult/child $15/7.50) – book through DOC (www.doc.govt.nz).

Lake Waikaremoana Track

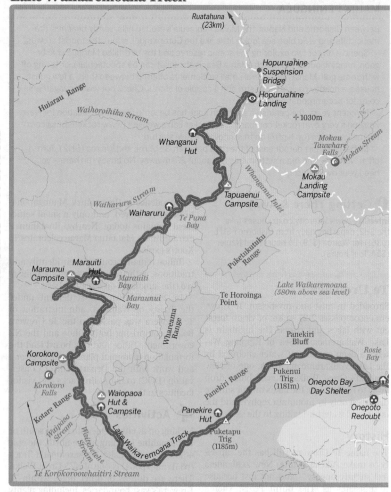

🛏 Sleeping

There are more than 30 huts and camp-sites within Te Urewera, most of which are very basic, plus the Waikaremoana Holiday Park (p364).

Waikaremoana
Holiday Park HOLIDAY PARK **$**
(☑ 06-837 3826; www.doc.govt.nz/waikaremoana -holiday-park; 6249 Lake Rd; campsites unpow-ered/powered from $40/46, cabins/chalets from $80/130; P ℍ) Right on the eastern shore of the lake, this place has Swiss-looking chalets, fishers' cabins and campsites, most with watery views, plus an on-site

shop. It's managed by DOC, so everything is shipshape and well maintained. If you're not staying in Wairoa, it's the pick of the few accommodation options within Te Urewera.

ℹ Information

Te Urewera Visitor Centre (Te Kura Whenua Visitor Experience Centre; ☑ 06-837 3803; www.ngaituhoe.iwi.nz; 6249 Lake Rd; ☉ 8am-4.15pm) Opened by the Ngāi Tūhoe people in 2017, this spectacular lakeside visitor centre includes a cafe, and displays and galleries on the natural and cultural history of Te Urewera. DOC info and bookings for the Lake Waikare-

You can drive to either trailhead of the Lake Waikaremoana Track, but leaving vehicles alone in the wilderness is never a great idea. Instead, park at the Waikaremoana Holiday Park and get a **water taxi** (one-way per adult/child $50/25): book in advance through the Te Urewera Visitor Centre (p364).

HAWKE'S BAY

Hawke Bay, the name given to the body of water that stretches from the Mahia Peninsula to Cape Kidnappers, looks like it's been bitten out of the North Island's eastern flank. Add an apostrophe and an 's' and you've got a region that stretches south and inland to include fertile farmland, surf beaches, mountainous ranges and forests. With food, wine and architecture the prevailing obsessions, it's all smugly comfortable but thoroughly appealing here, best viewed through a rosé-tinted wine glass.

Wairoa & Around

The small river town of Wairoa (population 4260) is trying hard to shake its rough-edged rep. Not scintillating enough to warrant an extended stay, the town does have a couple of points of interest, including an exceptional pie shop called Osler's (☑06-838 8299; 116 Marine Pde, Wairoa; mains $4-15; ⊗8am-4pm Mon-Fri, to 2.30pm Sat & Sun). The arty Eastend Cafe (☑06-838 6070; 250 Marine Pde, Wairoa; mains $11-19; ⊗7am-3pm Tue-Fri, 8am-4pm Sat & Sun; 🛜) is part of the revamped Gaiety Cinema & Theatre (☑06-650 8127; www.gaietytheatre.co.nz; 252 Marine Pde, Wairoa; tickets $10; ⊗1.30-10.30pm Wed-Sun) complex – the town's cultural hub.

◎ Sights

Diversions include the plaque-studded Riverside Walk, extending to Whakamahia Beach, and the impressive little Wairoa Museum (☑06-838 3108; www.facebook.com/pg/wairoamuseum; 142 Marine Pde, Wairoa; ⊗10am-4pm Mon-Fri) FREE inside an old bank. Inside you'll find passionately curated and creative displays on local town, river, political and Māori history – the undisputed highlight of which is the amazing Māori flag from the 1865 Land Wars, recently repatriated from Scotland.

The stretch of highway between Wairoa and Napier traipses through unphotogenic

moana Track (p351) are available (though the track is so popular, you'll most likely be booking months before you get here).

Staff can also help you book water taxis to/from the trailheads.

❶ Getting There & Away

Lake Waikaremoana is about an hour (64km) from Wairoa on SH38, which continues through to Rotorua – the entire SH38 route is named the **Te Urewera Rainforest Route** (look for the brochure of the same name). Around 95km of the entire 195km Wairoa–Rotorua route is unsealed: it's a four-hour, bone-rattling drive, but a great adventure.

Hawke's Bay

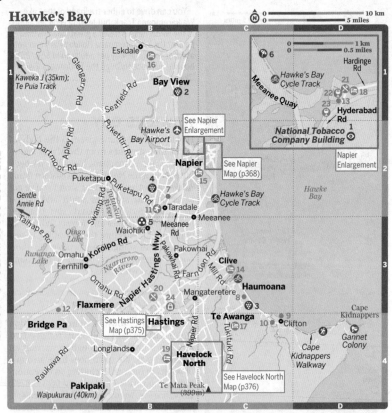

THE EAST COAST WAIROA & AROUND

Hawke's Bay

◎ **Top Sights**
1 National Tobacco
   Company Building.............................D2

◎ **Sights**
2 Crab Farm Winery..B1
3 Elephant Hill...C3
4 Mission Estate Winery................................B2
5 Otatara Pā Historic
   Reserve...B3
6 Westshore Beach...C1

◆ **Activities, Courses & Tours**
7 Bike About Tours..B2
8 Coastal Wine Cycles....................................C3
9 Gannet Beach Adventures.........................C4
10 Gannet Safaris...C4
11 My Ride Taradale..B2
12 On Yer Bike Winery
   Tours..A3
13 Tākaro Trails...D1

▣ **Sleeping**
14 Clive Colonial Cottages............................C3
15 Kennedy Park Resort................................C2
16 Kiwiesque..B1
17 Millar Road..C4
18 Navigate Seaside Hotel............................D1
19 St Andrews Escape....................................B4

✕ **Eating**
20 Bare Knuckle BBQ.....................................B3
21 Milk & Honey...D1

🍷 **Drinking & Nightlife**
22 4th Door Lounge Bar.................................D1
23 Thirsty Whale...D1
   Union Hotel...(see 22)

✦ **Entertainment**
   Globe Theatrette.....................................(see 21)

🛍 **Shopping**
24 Hawke's Bay Farmers Market.................B3

farmland and forestry blocks for much of its 117km. Most of it follows a railway line, currently only used for freight – you'll realise what a travesty this is when you pass under the Mohaka Viaduct (1937), the highest rail viaduct (97m) in Australasia.

Occupied by early Māori, Lake Tutira has walkways and a bird sanctuary. At Tutira village, just north of the lake, Pohokura Rd leads to the wonderful Boundary Stream Scenic Reserve, a major conservation area. Three loop tracks start from the road, ranging in length from 40 minutes to three hours. Also along this road you'll find the Opouahi and Bellbird Bush Scenic Reserves, which both offer rewarding walks. See www.doc.govt.nz for info.

Off Waipatiki Rd, 34km outside Napier, Waipatiki Beach is a beauty spot boasting a low-key campsite and the 64-hectare Waipatiki Scenic Reserve. Further down the line, White Pine Bush Scenic Reserve, 29km from Napier on SH2, bristles with kahikatea and nikau palms. Tangoio Falls Scenic Reserve, 27km north of Napier, has Te Ana Falls, stands of *whekī-ponga* (tree ferns) and native orchids. Again, the DOC website has the low-down. Between White Pine and Tangoio Reserves, the Tangoio Walkway (three hours return) follows Kareaara Stream.

The highway surfs the coast for the last 20km, with broad views towards Napier. Hawke's Bay wine country starts in earnest around the Esk River, about 10km north of Napier.

ℹ Information

Wairoa i-SITE (📞 06-838 7440; www.visitwairoa.co.nz; cnr SH2 & Queen St; ⏱ 8.30am-5pm Mon-Fri, 10am-4pm Sat & Sun; 🛜) The spot for local info, including advice on Lake Waikaremoana and accommodation around town.

ℹ Getting There & Away

The closest sizeable town to Te Urewera, Wairoa is 98km southwest of Gisborne and 117km northeast of Napier. **InterCity** (www.intercity.co.nz) buses trundle in from Gisborne ($19, 1½ hours) and Napier ($32, 2¼ hours).

Napier

POP 63,340

The Napier of today – a charismatic, sunny, composed city with the air of an affluent English seaside resort – is the silver lining of the dark cloud that was the deadly 1931 earthquake. Rebuilt in the prevailing architectural style of the time, the city retains a unique concentration of art-deco buildings. Don't expect the Chrysler Building – Napier is resolutely low-rise – but you will find amazingly intact 1930s facades and streetscapes, which can provoke a *Great Gatsby*–esque swagger in the least romantic soul. Linger a while to discover some of regional New Zealand's best restaurants and also a few excellent wineries less visited than the bigger names around nearby Hastings and Havelock North.

History

The Napier area has been settled since around the 12th century and was known to Māori as Ahuriri (now the name of a Napier suburb). By the time James Cook eyeballed the scene in October 1769, Ngāti Kahungunu was the dominant tribe, controlling the whole coast down to Wellington.

In the 1830s whalers hung around Ahuriri, establishing a trading base in 1839. By the 1850s the Crown had purchased – often by dubious means – 1.4 million acres of Hawke's Bay land, leaving Ngāti Kahungunu with less than 4000 acres. The town of Napier was planned in 1854 and obsequiously named after the British general and colonial administrator Charles Napier.

At 10.46am on 3 February 1931, the city was levelled by a catastrophic earthquake (7.9 on the Richter scale). Fatalities in Napier and nearby Hastings numbered 258. Napier suddenly found itself 40 sq km larger, as the earthquake heaved sections of what was once a lagoon 2m above sea level (Napier airport used to be more 'port', less 'air'). A fevered rebuilding programme ensued, resulting in one of the world's most uniformly art-deco cities.

⊙ Sights

Napier's claim to fame is undoubtedly its architecture: a passionate study of these treasures could take several days (especially if you're stopping to eat). Beyond the edge of town, the Hawke's Bay wineries are a treat.

★ **Daily Telegraph Building** ARCHITECTURE
(Map p368; 📞 06-834 1911; www.heritage.org.nz/the-list/details/1129; 49 Tennyson St; ⏱ 9am-5pm Mon-Fri) The Daily Telegraph is one of the stars of Napier's art-deco show, with superb zigzags, fountain shapes and a

Napier

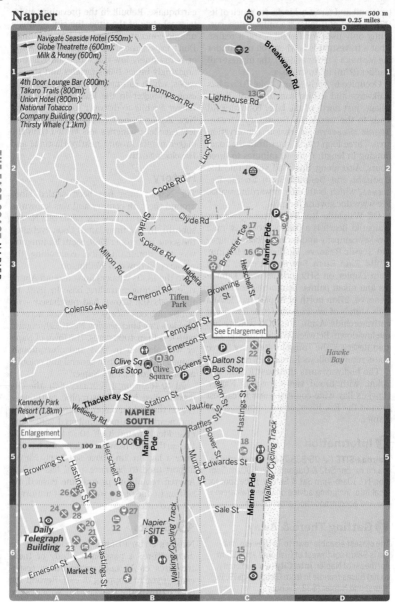

Navigate Seaside Hotel (550m);
Globe Theatrette (600m);
Milk & Honey (600m)

4th Door Lounge Bar (800m);
Tākaro Trails (800m);
Union Hotel (800m);
National Tobacco
Company Building (900m);
Thirsty Whale (1.1km)

symmetrically patterned facade. If the front doors are open, nip inside and ogle the painstakingly restored foyer (it's a resource management office these days). There's a folder of amazing old photos to leaf through on the front counter.

★ National Tobacco
Company Building   ARCHITECTURE
(Map p366; ☎ 06-834 1911; www.heritage.org.
nz/the-list/details/1170; cnr Bridge & Ossian Sts,
Ahuriri; ⊕lobby 9am-5pm Mon-Fri) Around the
shore at Ahuriri, the National Tobacco Company Building (1932) is arguably the region's

Napier

THE EAST COAST NAPIER

deco masterpiece, combining art-deco forms with the natural motifs of art nouveau. Roses, raupo (bulrushes) and grapevines frame the elegantly curved entrance. During business hours, pull on the leaf-shaped brass door handles and enter the first two rooms. There's a wine bar here too, these days.

MTG Hawke's Bay MUSEUM
(Museum Theatre Gallery; Map p368; ☑06-835 7781; www.mtghawkesbay.com; 1 Tennyson St; ⊙9.30am-5pm) **FREE** The beating cultural heart of Napier is the smart-looking MTG – a gleaming-white museum-theatre-gallery space by the water. The MTG showcases live performances, film screenings and regularly changing gallery and museum displays (earthquake gallery, Māori heritage, social history), along with touring and local exhibitions. Napier's rather lovely public library (www.napierlibrary.co.nz) is here too (free wi-fi).

Bluff Hill Lookout VIEWPOINT
(Map p368; Lighthouse Rd) The convoluted route to the top of Bluff Hill (102m) goes up and down like an elevator on speed (best to drive), but rewards intrepid mountaineers with expansive views across the busy port. Bring a picnic or some fish and chips.

National Aquarium of New Zealand AQUARIUM
(Map p368; ☑06-834 1404; www.national aquarium.co.nz; 546 Marine Pde; adult/child/family

$23/11.50/62; ⊙9am-5pm, last entry 4.30pm) Inside this modern complex with its stingray-inspired roof are piranhas, terrapins, eels, kiwi, tuatara and a whole lotta fish. Snorkellers can swim with sharks ($100), or sign up for a 'Little Penguin Close Encounter' ($70). The penguins get a feed at 9.30am, 1.30pm and 3.30pm, the reef fish at 10am and sharks at 2pm.

Napier Prison HISTORIC BUILDING
(Map p368; ☑06-835 9933; www.napierprison. com; 55 Coote Rd; self-guided tours adult/child $20/10; ⊙9am-5pm) On the run from the law? Assuage your guilt with a tour of the grim 1862 Napier Prison (the oldest in NZ) on the hill behind the town. There's a self-guided audio set-up, available in 16 languages, plus occasional guided tours ($25 per person) and spooky adults-only night tours ($25).

🏃 Activities

Napier's pebbly ocean beach isn't safe for swimming. Instead, to cool off, locals head north of the city to Westshore Beach (Map p366; ☑06-834 1918; www.hawkesbaynz.com; off Ferguson Ave, Westshore; ⊙24hr), or to the surf beaches south of Cape Kidnappers.

Ocean Spa SWIMMING
(Map p368; ☑06-835 8553; www.oceanspa napier.co.nz; 42 Marine Pde; adult/child $11/8, private pools 30min $13/10; ⊙6am-10pm Mon-Sat,

from 8am Sun) A spiffy waterfront complex that features a lane pool, hot pools, a beauty spa, gym and cafe. There's been a pool on this site since 1908.

👉 Tours

If you haven't got time for an art deco walking tour, just take to the streets – particularly Tennyson and Emerson. Remember to look up! Wine tours are also a Napier essential.

★ **Art Deco Centre** CULTURAL
(Map p368; ☑ 06-835 0022; www.artdeconapier. com; 7 Tennyson St; ⊙ 9am-5pm) Start your explorations at the Art Deco Centre, which runs a daily 1½-hour guided walk ($24) departing at 10am, plus a 2½-hour walk at 2pm ($26). Additional 11am and 4.30pm tours run between October and March. The 20-minute *Hawke's Bay 1931 Earthquake* movie screens

half-hourly from 9am to 4pm ($5). Pick up some art-deco-style earrings at the shop.

Other options include a 1½-hour minibus tour ($45 per person), and a 45-minute vintage car tour ($125 per four people).

Hawke's Bay Scenic Tours TOURS
(☑ 06-844 5693; www.hbscenictours.co.nz; tours from $55) A grape-coloured bunch of tour options including the 2½-hour 'Napier Whirlwind' ($65), full-day 'Hawke's Bay Scenic' ($185), and a five-hour wine and brewery jaunt ($125). A good all-rounder.

Grape Escape WINE
(☑ 0800 100 489; www.grapeescape.net.nz; tours from $110) Respected half-day winery tours, visiting four or five cellar doors with a cheese board en route to soak up the syrah. The same outfit also runs extremely fancy seven-hour luxury wine tours with lunch, if you're feeling honeymoony ($995 per couple).

CYCLE THE BAY

The 200km network of Hawke's Bay Trails (www.nzcycletrail.com/hawkes-bay-trails) – part of the national Ngā Haerenga, New Zealand Cycle Trails project – offers cycling opportunities from short, city scoots to hilly, single-track shenanigans. Dedicated cycle tracks encircle Napier, Hastings and the coastline, with landscape, water and wine themes. Pick up the *Hawke's Bay Trails* brochure from the Napier i-SITE (p374) or online.

Napier itself is very cycle friendly, particularly along Marine Pde, where you'll find **Fishbike** (Map p368; ☑ 06-835 6979; www.fishbike.co.nz; Pacific Surf Club, 22 Marine Pde; bike hire per half-/full day from $30/40, tandems per hour $40; ⊙ 9am-5.30pm) renting comfortable bikes – including tandems for those willing to risk divorce. **Napier City Bike Hire** (Map p368; ☑ 0800 245 344; www.bikehirenapier.co.nz; 117 Marine Pde; bike hire adult/child half-day from $30/40, full day from $35/50; ⊙ 9am-5pm) is another option. These guys also run self-guided coastal and winery tours, departing from the store with pick-up at the far end (16km to 27km; from $65 per person).

Mountain bikers head to **Pan Pac Mountain Bike Park** (☑ 06-873 8793; www. hawkesbaymtb.co.nz; 1205 SH2, Bay View; 3-week permits $10) for a whole lot of fun in the forest: see the website or call for directions. You can hire mountain bikes from **My Ride Taradale** (Map p366; ☑ 06-844 9771; www.myride.co.nz/taradale; 340 Gloucester St, Taradale; half-/full day from $50/80; ⊙ 8am-5.30pm Mon-Fri, 9am-3pm Sat, 10am-3pm Sun), just out of the city centre, or **Tākaro Trails** (Map p366; ☑ 06-835 9030; www.takarotrails.co.nz; 9 Nelson Quay, Ahuriri; mountain bike hire per half-/full day $75/110; ⊙ 9am-5.30pm).

Given the conducive climate, terrain and multitudinous tracks, it's no surprise that numerous cycle companies pedal fully geared-up tours around Hawke's Bay, with winery visits near-mandatory. Operators include the following:

Bike About Tours (Map p366; ☑ 06-845 4836; www.bikeabouttours.co.nz; 47 Gloucester St, Greenmeadows; tours half-/full day from $45/90; ⊙ 9am-5.30pm Mon-Fri, 10am-4pm Sat, to 3pm Sun)

Coastal Wine Cycles (Map p366; ☑ 06-875 0302; www.winecycles.co.nz; 41 East Rd, Te Awanga; tours per day adult/child $40/20; ⊙ 10am-6pm; 🖢)

On Yer Bike Winery Tours (Map p366; ☑ 021 292 8080; www.onyerbikehb.co.nz; 2543 SH50, Roy's Hill; full-day tours from $55; ⊙ 10am-4pm)

✦✦ Festivals & Events

★ Art Deco Festival
CULTURAL

(www.artdeconapier.com; ⊙Feb) In the third week of February, Napier and Hastings co-host the sensational Art Deco Festival. Around 125 events fill the week (dinners, picnics, dances, balls, bands, Gatsby-esque fancy dress), many of which are free. Expect around 40,000 art deco fans.

🛏 Sleeping

Criterion Art Deco Backpackers
HOSTEL $

(Map p368; ☑06-835 2059; www.criterion artdeco.co.nz; 48 Emerson St; dm/s/d/f without bathroom from $30/50/65/110, d with bathroom from $85; 🛜) The owners have spent a lot of money sprucing up this 1st-floor, ruby-red city-centre hostel – Napier's best Spanish Mission specimen – which has a beaut little balcony over Emerson St and an amazing old fireplace in the lounge area. A character-ful hostel in a top spot.

Kennedy Park Resort
HOLIDAY PARK $

(Map p366; ☑06-843 9126; www.kennedypark. co.nz; 1 Storkey St; sites from $50, cabins & units from $110; 🅿🛜❄🚻) Less a campground and more an entire suburb of holidaymakers, this complex is top dog on the Napier camping scene. It's the closest campsite to town (2.5km out, southwest of the centre) and has every facility imaginable (including a kara-oke machine!), plus a swathe of cabin and unit configurations.

Stables Lodge Backpackers
HOSTEL $

(Map p368; ☑06-835 6242; www.stableslodge. co.nz; 370 Hastings St; dm/d/studios from $29/79/89; 🛜) Formerly an actual stables, this is an atmospheric, laid-back place to get off your horse, with hippie vibes, a barbecue courtyard, murals and saddles festooned around the place. Options include dorms, doubles and a compact self-contained studio. It's more raffish than flashy, but hey, maybe you are too. A block back from the bay.

★ Seaview Lodge B&B
B&B $$

(Map p368; ☑06-835 0202; www.aseaviewlodge. co.nz; 5 Seaview Tce; r $160-210; 🅿🛜) This grand Victorian villa (1890) is queen of all she surveys...which is most of the town and a fair bit of the ocean. Heritage-meets-con-temporary rooms feature either a separate or en-suite bathroom. Don't bother to resist a sunset drink on the veranda, which opens off the airy guest lounge. Chipper host; cooked or continental breakfast included.

Bluff Hill B&B
B&B $$

(Map p368; ☑06-833 7983; www.bluffhill.co.nz; 31 Lighthouse Rd, Bluff Hill; d from $150; 🅿🛜❄) From high on Bluff Hill, make your way down a long driveway past a jasmine-hung fence to this cosy little wooden cabin for two. Dutch owners have infused the cottage with vintage Euro-caravan style: if you must leave, there's a little deck to sit on outside with leafy valley views. Minimum two-night stay. Breakfast is served in the main house.

★ Kiwiesque
B&B $$$

(Map p366; ☑06-836 7216; www.kiwiesque.com; 18 Linden Close, Eskdale; d $295-345; 🅿🛜❄) 🌿 Located in rural Eskdale, around 18km north of Napier, superstylish Kiwiesque overlooks apple trees and expansive vineyards. For freewheeling travellers, the best options are the four suites in the property's modern woolshed-influenced lodge (there's also a luxe private villa, sleeping 10). Breakfast is packed with seasonal produce; bathrooms are oh-so elegant. Eco-aware design includes double glazing and sheep-wool insulation.

Art Deco Masonic Hotel
HOTEL $$$

(Map p368; ☑06-835 8689; www.masonic. co.nz; cnr Tennyson St & Marine Pde; d/ste from $210/340; 🅿🛜) The Art Deco Masonic is the heart of the old town, with its accommoda-tion, restaurants and bars taking up most of a city block. A much-needed refurb has revived the old stager, with stripy carpets and quirky wallpaper adorning the original bones. All 42 rooms and suites have bath-rooms; the best have sea views and access to the roof terrace.Parking is off site ($11).

Navigate Seaside Hotel
HOTEL $$$

(Map p366; ☑06-831 0077; www.navigatenapier. co.nz; 18 Hardinge Rd, Ahuriri; d/f/2-bedroom apt from $255/330/405; 🅿🛜) Navigate your-self towards Navigate for 26 snazzy apart-ment-style units over three levels, with funky furnishings, nifty perforated-metal balconies and sea views from the best rooms. There's a kids' playground across the street for the offspring, and it's close to all of Ahuriri's best eats. The whale mural is part of Napier's Sea Walls (www.napier.govt.nz/napier/community-art/ sea-walls-murals-for-oceans) public art project.

Pebble Beach Motor Inn
MOTEL $$$

(Map p368; ☑06-835 7496; www.pebblebeach. co.nz; 445 Marine Pde; r $249-349; 🛜) Unlike the majority of NZ motels, this one is owner-op-erated (the staff actually own the building) so maintenance and service top the list of priorities. There are 25 immaculate rooms over three levels – from studios to family suites – all with kitchens, spas, balconies and ocean views. It also has a less pricey studio apartment for rent in Ahuriri ($165).

Scenic Hotel Te Pania HOTEL $$$
(Map p368; ☑ 06-833 7733; www.scenichotels. co.nz; 45 Marine Pde; d from $225, 1-/2-bedroom ste from $280/480; P@🛜) Looking like a mini UN HQ by the sea, the refurbished, curvalicious, six-storey Te Pania has instant retro appeal. Rooms are far from retro, however, with designer linen, leather lounges and floor-to-ceiling windows that slide open for lungfuls of sea air.

🍴 Eating

Hapī VEGAN $
(Map p368; ☑ 06-561 0142; www.hapi.nz; 89 Hastings St; mains $10-15; ⊙7am-4pm; 🍴) 🌱 Welcome to Hapī, where virtuous vegan flavours are also damn tasty, and earnest staff make meaningful eye contact. Breakfast bowls packed with açai, chia and quinoa team up with superior snacks like polenta fries or chipotle tofu tacos, and the drinks list of smoothies and cold-pressed organic elixirs is equally beneficial and bargain-priced.

Vinci's PIZZA $
(Map p368; ☑ 06-650 7779; www.vincispizza. co.nz; 29A Hastings St; slices $5-6, pizzas $26-30; ⊙11am-8pm Sun-Thu, to 9pm Fri & Sat) 🌱 Pizza by the slice (or the whole big disc) comes hot and fresh from this great little art-deco nook, with a skinny wedge of a window seat and punky retro mural. Meats, herbs and veggies are all local and/or free-range. A wedge or two of the Capricciosa (tomato, mozzarella, artichokes, olives and honey-smoked ham) will fill any nocturnal void.

⭐ Mister D MODERN NZ $$
(Map p368; ☑ 06-835 5022; www.misterd.co.nz; 47 Tennyson St; mains breakfast $15-24, lunch & dinner $27-38; ⊙7.30am-4pm Sun-Wed, to late Thu-Sat) This long, floorboarded room with its green-tiled bar is the pride and joy of the Napier foodie scene. Hip and slick but not grossly unaffordable, with quick-fire service delivering the likes of chestnut flan with mushrooms or roast-duck risotto. Addictive doughnuts are served with syringes full of chocolate, jam or custard (DIY injecting...adult versions infused with booze). Bookings essential.

⭐ Hunger Monger SEAFOOD $$
(Map p368; ☑ 06-835 9736; www.hungermonger. co.nz; 129 Marine Pde; mains $20-28; ⊙noon-3pm

Thu-Mon, 5-9pm daily) Seemingly always busy when everywhere else is half-full, Hunger Monger is a funky seaside seafood diner with sheepskin-covered seats, quirky tablecloths and a hyperactive open kitchen in one corner. The menu swims from sashimi to chowder, then from fish tacos with lime and jalapeño to smoked-salmon risotto with buttered leeks. It's downright convivial.

Café Tennyson + Bistro CAFE $$
(Map p368; ☑ 06-835 1490; www.facebook.com/ cafetennyson; 28 Tennyson St; mains $11-23; ⊙7am-5pm; 🍴) We mourn the loss of our favourite Napier hippie cafe, but its buzzy and welcoming replacement is a more modern interpretation of East Coast cafe life. Efficient staff plate up big breakfasts and lunches (stuffed croissants, pumpkin and blue-cheese linguine), all-day snacks and of course local wines and craft beers. Kids' menu, too.

Market St PUB FOOD $$
(Map p368; ☑ 06-650 1720; www.marketst.co.nz; 8 Market St; mains $19-28; ⊙11am-late Mon-Fri, 9am-late Sat & Sun) This stylish new bar and eatery below Criterion Art Deco Backpackers (p371) does easy-going bar food (burgers, pastas, beef short ribs and a mean crispy pork belly), sluiced down with a devastatingly good list of craft beers. Hit the courtyard out back, the long communal tables, or slump into a beanbag out on the pedestrian-only street.

Milk & Honey CAFE $$
(Map p366; ☑ 06-833 6099; www.themilk andhoney.co.nz; 19 Hardinge Rd, Ahuriri; mains breakfast $9-21, lunch $14-25, dinner $29-35; ⊙7am-9pm) One of Ahuriri's top options, Milk & Honey combines ocean and boardwalk views with versatile day-to-night menus. Hawke's Bay beers and wines do their thing alongside the likes of a vegan Bircher muesli breakfast bowl, chicken and lemongrass broth for lunch, or tamarind beef cheeks for dinner – all amidst polished concrete, wicker and ambient tunes.

Bistronomy BISTRO $$$
(Map p368; ☑ 06-834 4309; www.bistronomy.co.nz; 40 Hastings St; lunch mains $22-35, dinner 6/9 courses $80/110; ⊙5pm-late Wed & Thu, noon-late Fri & Sat; 🍴) Bistronomy is proof that NZ's regional restaurants can create high-end cuisine just as well as tAuckland, Wellington and Christchurch. Finely judged seasonal menus include lamb loin with sage custard and charred leek, or a blue-cheese omelette with truffle oil and polenta fries. Wines from Argentina to the Esk Valley; interior design from the big-city playbook.

DON'T MISS

HAWKE'S BAY WINERIES

Once upon a time, in a wine-free era long, long ago, this district was famous for its orchards. Today it's vines that have top billing, with Hawke's Bay now New Zealand's second-largest wine-producing region (behind Marlborough). Expect excellent Bordeaux-style reds, shiraz and chardonnay. Pick up the *Hawke's Bay Winery Guide* map or the *Hawke's Bay Trails* cycling map from Hastings (p379) or Napier (p374) i-SITEs, or download them from www.winehawkesbay.co.nz. A few of our faves (most of which also do food):

Black Barn Vineyards (Map p376; ☑06-877 7985; www.blackbarn.com; Black Barn Rd, Havelock North; ☺cellar door 10am-4pm, restaurant 10am-5pm Sun-Wed, to 9pm Thu-Sat, reduced hours Apr-Oct)

Crab Farm Winery (Map p366; ☑06-836 6678; www.crabfarmwinery.co.nz; 511 Main North Rd, Bay View; ☺10am-5pm Thu, Sat & Sun, to 9pm Fri)

Elephant Hill (Map p366; ☑06-872 6073; www.elephanthill.co.nz; 86 Clifton Rd, Te Awanga; ☺11am-5pm Sep-May, to 4pm Jun-Aug) ✿

Mission Estate Winery (Map p366; ☑06-845 9354; www.missionestate.co.nz; 198 Church Rd, Taradale; ☺9am-5pm Mon-Sat, 10am-4.30pm Sun)

Te Mata Estate (Map p376; ☑06-877 4399; www.temata.co.nz; 349 Te Mata Rd, Havelock North; ☺10am-5pm Mon-Sat, 11am-4pm Sun) ✿

Pacifica BISTRO $$$
(Map p368; ☑06-833 6335; www.pacificarestaurant.co.nz; 209 Marine Pde; 5 courses without/with wine pairings $65/115; ☺6-9pm Tue-Sat) Recently judged NZ'S top restaurant by *Cuisine* magazine, Pacifica showcases chef Jeremy Rameka's affinity with *kai moana* (seafood) and traditional meats. The decor is refreshingly un-hip (plastic chairs, office carpet), while the good-value $65 five-course menu could include the likes of spiced creamed paua with gurnard mousse, or warmed venison with kumara butter and shitake foam. Presentation borders on high art.

 Drinking & Nightlife

⭐**Monica Loves** BAR
(Map p368; ☑06-650 0240; www.monicaloves.co.nz; 39 Tennyson St; ☺3pm-late Wed-Sat) Big-city laneway style comes to Napier at this bar tucked away off Tennyson St. Look for the big neon sign proclaiming 'Who shot the barman?' and you're in the right place for cool cocktails, regular surprises in the beer taps and a Hawke's Bay–centric wine list. We love the black wine barrels and Pollock-goes-graffiti mural too, Monica.

Emporium BAR
(Map p368; ☑06-835 0013; www.emporiumbar.co.nz; Art Deco Masonic Hotel, cnr Tennyson St & Marine Pde; ☺7am-late; ☎) Napier's most civilised venue, Emporium is super atmospheric, with its marble-topped bar, fab art-deco details and old-fashioned relics strewn about. Brisk staff, creative cocktails, good coffee,

NZ wines, bistro fare (plates $15 to $39) and a prime location seal the deal. On a warm night the windows fold open to the sea air.

Zeelandt Brewery CRAFT BEER
(☑06-835 1825; www.zeelandt.co.nz; 14 Shaw Rd, Eskdale; ☺9am-5pm Mon-Fri) Take a tootle 19km north of Napier to check out this cool craft brewery in Eskdale – a big lager-coloured shed surrounded by vineyards and sheep paddocks. The emphasis here is on full-flavoured, authentically styled beers, all packaged up with what has to be NZ's most excellent beer-label art. Try the Guv'nor special bitter.

4th Door Lounge Bar COCKTAIL BAR
(Map p366; ☑06-834 0835; www.threedoorsup.co.nz/the-4th-door; 3 Waghorne St, Ahuriri; ☺5pm-late Fri & Sat) The 4th Door offers an alternative to Ahuriri's waterfront bars – a classy, moody little place, perfect for a predinner drink or a nightcap. Occasional live jazz and piano tunes enhance the mood. The deliciously unreformed **Union Hotel** (Map p366; ☑06-835 8914; www.facebook.com/theunionhotelahuriri; 3 Waghorne St, Ahuriri; ☺11am-late) is next door, where anyone who turned 40 before the year 2000 goes for a beer.

Thirsty Whale BAR
(Map p366; ☑06-835 8815; www.thethirstywhale.co.nz; 62 West Quay, Ahuriri; ☺11am-late Mon-Sat, 10am-late Sun; ☎) Does a whale drink? Or just filter krill? Either way, this big dockside bar is a sporty spot to join some fellow mammals for an unashamedly mainstream brew

or bite (mains $12 to $40: steaks, pizzas, fish and chips etc). It's one of four or five similar bars along West Quay.

☆ Entertainment

Globe Theatrette   CINEMA
(Map p366; ☑ 06-833 6011; www.globenapier.co.nz; 15 Hardinge Rd, Ahuriri; tickets adult/child $16/14; ☺1pm-late Tue-Sun, 5pm-late Mon) A vision in purple, this boutique 45-seat cinema screens art-house flicks in a sumptuous lounge, with ready access to pizza and dumpling snacks from a little eatery out the front.

Cabana   LIVE MUSIC
(Map p368; ☑ 06-835 1102; www.cabana.net.nz; 11 Shakespeare Rd; ☺noon-late) This legendary live-music room started in 1958 then died in 1997. But thanks to some forward-thinking rock fans, it's risen from the grave to save the day for Napier's gig lovers. Expect Led Zeppelin tribute acts, NZ original bands, LGBTQI+ afternoons and karaoke nights.

🛍 Shopping

Napier Urban Farmers Market   MARKET
(Map p368; ☑ 027 697 3737; www.hawkesbayfarm ersmarket.co.nz; Clive Sq, Lower Emerson St; ☺9am-1pm Sat) Score some superfresh local produce: fruit, veg, bread, coffee, dairy products, honey, wine... Who needs supermarkets?

❶ Information

Napier i-SITE (Map p368; ☑ 06-834 1911; www.napiernz.com; 100 Marine Pde; ☺9am-5pm, extended hours Dec-Feb; 🛈) Central, brochure-stocked and right by the bay.
DOC (Map p368; ☑ 06-834 3111; www.doc.govt. nz; 59 Marine Pde; ☺9am-4pm Mon-Fri)
City Medical Napier (☑ 06-835 4999; www. citymedicalnapier.co.nz; 76 Wellesley Rd; ☺24hr) Round-the-clock medical assistance.

❶ Getting There & Away

AIR
Hawke's Bay Airport (Map p366; ☑ 06-834 0742; www.hawkesbay-airport.co.nz; cnr SH2 & Watchman Rd) is 8km north of the city.
　Air New Zealand (www.airnewzealand. co.nz) flies direct toAuckland, Wellington and Christchurch. **Jetstar** (www.jetstar.com) also flies to Napier from Auckland, while **Sounds Air** (www.soundsair.com) has direct flights to/from Blenheim a few times a week.

BUS
InterCity (www.intercity.co.nz) buses can be booked online or at the i-SITE (p374), with services departing from **Clive Sq** (Map p368).

Destination	Price	Duration	Frequency
Auckland	$82	7½hr	2 (per day)
Gisborne	$54	4hr	2
Hastings	$23	30min	4
Palmerston North	$35	3hr	2–3
Taupō	$35	2hr	2
Wairoa	$32	2¼hr	1
Wellington	$46	5½hr	2–3

❶ Getting Around

BICYCLE
Bikes (including tandems) can be hired at Fishbike (p370) or Napier City Bike Hire (p370).

BUS
GoBay (www.gobay.co.nz) local buses (with bike racks) run many times daily between Napier, Hastings and Havelock North. Napier to Hastings (adult/child $4.20/3) takes 30 to 55 minutes. Buses depart **Dalton St bus stop** (Map p368).

CAR
Hawke's Bay Airport has desks for most of the big international car-rental outfits, plus local outfits including **RAD Car Hire** (☑ 06-834 0688; www.radcarhire.co.nz; Hawke's Bay Airport, cnr SH2 & Watchman Rd; ☺7.15am-5pm Mon-Fri, 7.45am-1pm Sat, 9am-noon Sun).

TAXI
A city–airport taxi or pre-booked airport shuttle costs around $20 to $25. Try **Hawke's Bay Combined Taxis** (☑ 06-875 7777; www. hawkesbaytaxis.nz) or the door-to-door **Super Shuttle** (☑ 0800 748 885; www.supershuttle. co.nz; one-way $20, extra person $5).

Hastings & Havelock North

POP 80,600

Positioned at the centre of the Hawke's Bay fruit bowl, busy Hastings is the commercial hub of the region, 20km south of Napier. A few kilometres of orchards separate it from Havelock North, with its prosperous village atmosphere and the backdrop of Te Mata Peak.

　Imbibing and dining around the area's restaurants, breweries and vineyards, and trawling farmers markets and seasonal fruit stands are fine foodie-focused ways to explore. Restore a bit of natural balance by hiking around Te Mata's spectacular profile.

◉ Sights

Like Napier, Hastings was devastated by the 1931 earthquake and also boasts some fine

Hastings

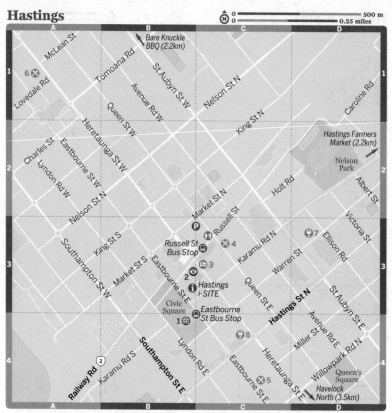

art-deco and Spanish Mission buildings, built in the aftermath. Main-street highlights include the Westerman's Building (Map p375; ☏06-873 5526; www.heritage.org.nz/the-list/details/178; cnr Russell St & Heretaunga St E, Hastings), arguably Hawke's Bay's best example of the Spanish Mission style, although there are myriad architectural gems here. The i-SITE (p379), on the Westerman's corner, stocks the *Art Deco Hastings* brochure ($1), detailing two self-guided walks. There's also the free *Hastings Urban Drive* brochure if you want to see more than art-deco delights.

★ **Te Mata Peak**   MOUNTAIN
(Map p376; ☏027 945 6970; www.tematapark.co.nz; off Te Mata Rd, Havelock North; ☉daylight hours) Rising dramatically from the Heretaunga Plains 16km south of Havelock North, Te Mata Peak (399m) is part of the 1-sq-km Te Mata Trust Park. The summit road passes sheep tracks, rickety fences and vertigo-inducing stone escarpments, cowled in a bleak,

Hastings

◎ Sights
1 Hastings City Art Gallery	B4
2 Westerman's Building	B3

⬤ Sleeping
3 Rotten Apple	C3

⊗ Eating
4 OM Goodness Specialty Breads	C3
5 Opera Kitchen	C4
6 Rush Munro's	A1

⊖ Drinking & Nightlife
7 Brave Brewing Co	D3
8 Common Room	C4

lunar-landscape-meets-Scottish-Highlands atmosphere. On a clear day, views from the lookout fall away to Hawke Bay, the Mahia Peninsula and distant Mt Ruapehu.

The park's 30km of walking trails range from 30 minutes to two hours: ask for a map

Havelock North

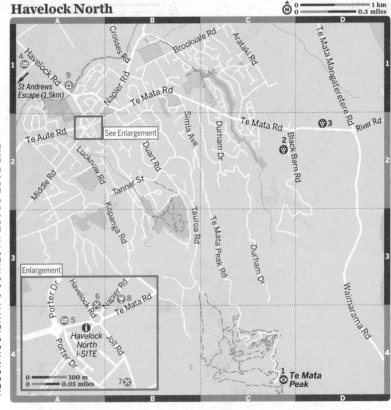

Havelock North

◎ Top Sights
1 Te Mata Peak C4

◎ Sights
2 Black Barn Vineyards C2
3 Te Mata Estate D2

🛏 Sleeping
4 Cottages on St Andrews A1
5 Porters A4

✕ Eating
6 Maina A3
  Malo .... (see 5)
7 Pipi B4

🍷 Drinking & Nightlife
8 Diva B3

🛍 Shopping
9 Strawberry Patch A1

at local i-SITEs. There's also good mountain biking and **paragliding** (📞027 451 2886; www.airplay.co.nz; 1-day course $220) here.

Hastings City Art Gallery   GALLERY
(HCAG; Map p375; 📞06-871 5095; www.hastingscityartgallery.co.nz; 201 Eastbourne St E, Hastings; ⏱10am-4.30pm) **FREE** The city's neat little gallery presents contemporary NZ (including Māori) and international art in a bright, purpose-built space. Expect some wacky

stuff. On the lawns out the front is *Ngā Pou o Heretuanga* – 19 fantastic Māori totems, each carved by reps from a regional *marae*.

Tours

Long Island Guides   CULTURAL
(📞06-561 1214; www.longislandtoursnz.com; half-day tours per person from $250) Customised Hawke's Bay tours across a wide range of interests including Māori culture, hiking,

kayaking, horse riding, fishing and, inevitably, food and wine.

Prinsy's Tours WINE
(☑027 224 0696; www.prinsystours.co.nz; half-/full-day tours from $110/125) Affable half- or full-day wine jaunts, without the wine-speak, at four or five wineries. Door-to-door delivery a bonus.

✺ Festivals & Events

Hawke's Bay Arts Festival PERFORMING ARTS
(www.hbaf.co.nz; ⊙Oct) Barely half-a-dozen years young, this innovative arts fest draws the crowds to venues in Havelock North, Hastings and Napier for two weeks of dance, drama, songs and interactive installations, with lots of free community events.

Hastings Blossom Parade CULTURAL
(www.facebook.com/hastingsblossomparade; ⊙Sep) The Hastings Blossom Parade is an annual spring fling, infamous for its 12-person 'riot' in 1960 when some local teens got a bit testy and were detained for a few hours. The annual flowery celebration happens in the second half of September, featuring parades, arts, crafts and visiting artists.

🛌 Sleeping

Rotten Apple HOSTEL $
(Map p375; ☑06-878 4363; www.rottenapple.co.nz; Upstairs, 114 Heretaunga St E, Hastings; dm/s/d $30/75/80, weekly $140/190/320; ☜) This central-city, 1st-floor option is a fairly fruity affair, with settled-in orchard workers paying weekly rates. There's a little deck, a decent kitchen and a dedicated 'quiet room' if you don't want to par-tay. Staff can help you find work (sorting the rotten apples from the good). There's a 1971 Hastings aerial photo in the stairwell.

Clive Colonial Cottages COTTAGE $$
(Map p366; ☑06-870 1018; www.clivecolonialcottages.co.nz; 198 School Rd, Clive; d from $175; P☜) A two-minute walk to the beach and almost equidistant from Hastings, Napier and Havelock, these three tasteful kitchen cottages encircle a courtyard garden on a 2-acre spread. Communal areas include a barbecue, a giant chess set and a snooker room. Bikes on-site; bike track on the doorstep. Breakfast provisions for your first morning included.

Cottages on St Andrews COTTAGES $$
(Map p376; ☑06-877 1644; www.cottagesonstandrews.nz; 14 St Andrews Rd, Havelock North; units & cottages $150-510; P☜✉✇) Modern

two-bedroom cottages, all with little kitchens, are the mainstays at this versatile spot among the fields, around 1km north of Havelock North. A heated pool, tennis court and a kids' adventure playground maximise the appeal for wandering families – not to mention the lambs, llamas and other farmyard critters. There's also a studio unit at the base of the price tree.

St Andrews Escape B&B $$
(Map p366; ☑06-877 1525; www.standrewsescape.co.nz; 172 St Andrews Rd, Havelock North; d $180-240, cottages from $250, extra person $35; P☜) Four renovated lodge rooms join forces with a stand-alone cottage, fruit trees and a duck-filled lake at this immaculate property, around 3km from Havelock North. The cottage sleeps three, or there's a less fancy four-bedroom house ($400) if you're travelling with a big crew. Don't miss the fab communal lounge room, and a sunset wine by Karamū Stream.

★Millar Road VILLA $$$
(Map p366; ☑06-875 1977; www.millarroad.co.nz; 83 Millar Rd, Hastings; villa/house from $400/650; P☜✉) Set in the Tuki Tuki Hills with vineyard and bay views, Millar Road is architecturally heaven-sent. Two plush villas (each sleeps four) and a stylish house (sleeps eight) are filled with NZ-made furniture and local artworks. Explore the 20-hectare grounds or try to look as cool as the pool. The owners also run Supernatural Wine Co – ask for a sip.

Porters BOUTIQUE HOTEL $$$
(Map p376; ☑06-877 1234; www.portershotel.co.nz; 4 Te Aute Rd, Havelock North; d/ste from $245/310; P☜) Flashy, three-story Porters is all natural timber, marble and glitz, with lifestyle mags scattered about the lobby. It's all very Havelock North (you wouldn't find such indulgences in blue-collar Hastings) – but if you're looking for a stylish, central naughty-weekender, you're in the right place. Modern NZ restaurant Malo (Map p376; ☑06-877 2009; www.malo.co.nz; 4 Te Aute Rd, Havelock North; mains breakfast & lunch $17-28, dinner $36-38; ⊙9am-late Mon-Sat, to 3pm Sun) is here too.

✗ Eating

★OM Goodness
Specialty Breads BAKERY $
(Map p375; ☑06-876 2206; www.omgoodness.co.nz; 106 Queen St E, Hastings; mains $10-13; ⊙9am-4pm Mon-Fri; ☜✪) ✍ OMG! Baked in a 100-year-old oven, the organic, gluten-free, vegan, paleo-friendly, dairy-free loaves produced at this bakery/cafe are seriously high density.

Grab a divinely dense sourdough brick, caked in rosemary and black sesame, or stop by for a slice of pizza or a sandwich for your Friday lunch. Free-range kids underfoot.

Rush Munro's — ICE CREAM $

(Map p375; ☑ 06-878 9634; www.rushmunro.co.nz; 704 Heretaunga St W, Hastings; ice cream $4-12; ⊘ 10.30am-6.30pm Sun-Thu, to 7.30pm Fri & Sat, reduced winter hours) Rush Munro's is a Hastings institution, serving locally made ice cream since 1926. Our favourite is the manuka honey flavour, best licked among the camellia blooms in the shady garden. They also do a pretty decent affogato.

★Maina — CAFE $$

(Map p376; ☑ 06-877 1714; www.maina.co.nz; 11 Havelock Rd, Havelock North; mains breakfast & lunch $10-24, dinner $29-36; ⊘ 7am-11pm Mon-Fri, 8am-11pm Sat, 9am-3pm Sun; 🖊) 🍴 Blur the lines between breakfast, lunch and dinner at Havelock North's best cafe, inside a former post office infused with stylish retro Kiwiana decor. Highlights include creamy Te Mata mushrooms on organic sourdough, and roast pork belly with pumpkin puree. Pizzas and an ever-evolving salad selection are safe bets, while superior homestyle baking includes perfect midmorning coffee and doughnuts.

Pipi — PIZZA $$

(Map p376; ☑ 06-877 8993; www.pipicafe.co.nz; 16 Joll Rd, Havelock North; mains $16-24; ⊘ 4-10pm Tue-Sun) Bright pink with candy stripes, chandeliers and mismatched furniture, cheeky Pipi thumbs its nose at small-town conventionality. The food focus is on simple pasta, thin-crust pizza, craft beer and local wines. Pipi Truck (www.facebook.com/pipitruck) randomly turns up around the bay, taking pizza to the streets.

Pipi Hotel (www.pipihotel.co.nz), a retro two-bedroom house sleeping six (from $250), is across the street.

Opera Kitchen — CAFE $$

(Map p375; ☑ 06-870 6020; www.eatdrinkshareb.co.nz; 306 Eastbourne St E, Hastings; mains $15-26; ⊘ 7.30am-4pm Mon-Fri, 9am-3pm Sat & Sun; 🖊) Occupying a high-ceilinged heritage building – formerly the HB Electric Power Board – our favourite Hastings cafe serves up sophisticated breakfasts and lunches with international accents. Spend a few hours browsing design mags and feasting on all-day omelettes or porcini mushroom risotto with thyme and hazelnuts. Heavenly pastries, great coffee and efficient staff. A 'morning medicine' Bloody Mary will right your rudder.

Bare Knuckle BBQ — BARBECUE $$

(Map p366; ☑ 06-870 4400; www.bareknucklebbq.co.nz; 1024 Pakowhai Rd, Frimley; mains $18-32; ⊘ 4pm-late Wed, 11am-late Thu-Sat, 11am-8pm Sun) This authentic American barbecue joint a couple of kilometres north of Hastings conjures up a Mex-Tex *rancho* vibe with Spanish hacienda architecture, country-and-western tunes and saddles hung from the walls. Pitmaster Jimmy Macken turns out fine brisket, ribs and pulled pork, plus soups, burgers and steaks. Bare Knuckle's own craft beers are always on tap. Head for the courtyard.

🍷 Drinking & Nightlife

★GodsOwn Brewery — CRAFT BEER

(☑ 027 931 1042; www.godsownbrewery.co.nz; 3672 SH50, Maraekakaho; ⊘ noon-10pm Mon & Sat, 3-10pm Fri, noon-8pm Sun) 🍴 This low-key, earthy microbrewery 22km east of Hastings operates out of a safari tent and a 1973 caravan. Bucolic aromas, hop vines, laid-back tunes, outdoor tables, a smouldering fire pit...it's a uniquely NZ scene. Trad European beers like French *biere de garde* and German pilsner emerge from the taps. Spent brewing grains are used in zesty wood-fired flatbreads ($10 to $22).

★Common Room — BAR

(Map p375; ☑ 06-211 2446; www.facebook.com/commonroomhb; 227 Heretaunga St E, Hastings; ⊘ 3pm-late Tue-Thu & Sat, noon-late Fri & Sun) There's pretty much nothing wrong with this hip little bar in central Hastings: cheery staff, bar snacks, craft beer, local wines, zany retro interior, garden bar, Persian rugs, live music and a tune-scape ranging from jazz to alt-country to indie – all the good stuff!

Brave Brewing Co — CRAFT BEER

(Map p375; ☑ 027 460 8414; www.bravebrewing.co.nz; 408 Warren St, Hastings; ⊘ 4-9pm Thu, noon-9pm Fri-Sun) Brave's glass-fronted, industrial tasting room on the edge of the town centre showcases its fine brews – pray that the 6.6% Tigermilk IPA is flowing from one of 10 taps – plus guest beers from brewing mates around NZ. Burgers, tacos, Reuben sandwiches and Vietnamese *bánh mì* (baguettes) emerge from food caravan outside (mains $13 to $16).

Diva — BAR

(Map p376; ☑ 06-877 5149; www.divabar.co.nz; 10 Napier Rd, Havelock North; ⊘ 11.30am-late Tue-Sun) All day and (almost) all night, stylish Diva is all things to all people: wine bar, bistro (mains $15 to $29), craft-beer haven and

DJ venue – it's invariably the busiest spot in Havelock North after the sun goes down. Pavement tables attract glam types, young and old.

Shopping

Hawke's Bay Farmers Market
MARKET

(Map p366; ☑ 027 697 3737; www.hawkesbayfarmers market.co.nz; Showgrounds, off Kenilworth Rd, Hastings; ☺ 8.30am-12.30pm Sun) If you're awake on Sunday morning, the Hawke's Bay market at Hastings is mandatory. Bring an empty stomach, some cash and a roomy shopping bag.

Strawberry Patch
FOOD

(Map p376; ☑ 06-877 1350; www.strawberrypatch. co.nz; 76 Havelock Rd, Havelock North; ☺ 8.30am-5.30pm) Pick your own berries in season (late November to April), or visit year-round for organic produce from local fields, plus coffee and real fruit ice cream ($4; last serve 3pm).

ⓘ Information

Hastings i-SITE (Map p375; ☑ 06-873 5526; www.hawkesbaynz.com; Westermans Bldg, cnr Russell St & Heretaunga St E; ☺ 9am-5pm Mon-Fri, to 3pm Sat, 10am-1.45pm Sun) A bedazzling array of maps, brochures and bookings, in a lovely old art-deco building.

Havelock North i-SITE (Map p376; ☑ 06-877 9600; www.havelocknorthnz.com; 1 Te Aute Rd, Havelock North; ☺ 10am-5pm Mon-Fri, to 3pm Sat, to 1.45pm Sun) Local info in a cute booth.

Hastings Memorial Hospital (☑ 06-878 8109; www.hawkesbay.health.nz; 398 Omahu Rd, Frimley; ☺ 24hr) Accident and emergency.

ⓘ Getting There & Away

Napier's Hawke's Bay Airport (p374) is a 20-minute drive from Hastings. **Air New Zealand** (www. airnewzealand.co.nz) flies direct to Auckland, Wellington and Christchurch. **Jetstar** (www.jetstar.com) also flies to Napier from Auckland, while **Sounds Air** (www.soundsair.com) has direct flights to/from Blenheim a few times a week.

InterCity (www.intercity.co.nz) buses stop at the **Russell St bus stop** (Map p375).

ⓘ Getting Around

GoBay (www.gobay.co.nz) local buses (fitted with bike racks) run many times daily between Hastings, Havelock North and Napier. Hastings to Napier (adult/child $4.20/3) takes 30 minutes (express) or 55 minutes (all stops). Hastings to Havelock North (adult/child $3.60/1.80) takes about 20 minutes. Buses depart from the **Eastbourne St bus stop** (Map p375).

Hawke's Bay Combined Taxis (p374) is the local cab outfit.

Cape Kidnappers

From mid-September to late April, Cape Kidnappers (Te Kauwae-a-Māui to local Māori, who tried to kidnap Captain Cook's Tahitian servant boy here in 1869) erupts with 13,000 squawking Australasian gannets. These large ocean birds usually nest on remote islands but here they settle near the mainland, completely unfazed by human spectators. It's the world's biggest mainland gannet colony.

The birds nest as soon as they arrive, and eggs take around six weeks to hatch, with chicks arriving in early November. In March the gannets start their migration; by May they're gone.

Early November to late February is the best time to visit. Take a tour or the walkway to the colony (Map p366; ☑ 06-834 3111; www.doc.govt.nz; off Clifton Rd, Clifton; ☺ Nov-May) 🆓: it's about a five-hour return walk from Clifton, a beachside enclave 19km east of Hastings. En route are interesting cliff formations, rock pools, a sheltered picnic spot and the gaggling gannets themselves. The walk is tide-dependent: leave no earlier than three hours after high tide; start back no later than 1½ hours after low tide. At the time of writing the track was closed due to rock falls; check the DOC website for updates.

Gannet Beach Adventures
ECOTOUR

(Map p366; ☑ 06-875 0898; www.gannets. com; 475 Clifton Rd, Clifton; adult/child/family $48/26/126; 🖝) Ride along the beach on a tractor-pulled trailer before wandering out onto Cape Kidnappers to see the gannet colony. This four-hour, guided return trip departs from the Clifton waterfront – good fun and great value.

Gannet Safaris
ECOTOUR

(Map p366; ☑ 06-875 0888; www.gannetsafaris. co.nz; 396 Clifton Rd, Te Awanga; adult/child $88/44; 🖝) Overland 4WD trips across farmland into the Cape Kidnappers gannet colony. Three-hour tours depart at 9.30am and 1.30pm September to April. Pick-ups from Napier, Hastings or Havelock North cost extra (adult/child additional $36/18). Bookings essential.

ⓘ Getting There & Away

No regular buses go to Clifton, but it's just a short drive (20km) from Hastings. Alternatively tour operators will transport you for an additional fee, or you could bike it.

Central Hawke's Bay

Grassy farmland stretches south from Hastings, dotted with the grand homesteads of Victorian pastoralists. It's an untouristy area (aka 'Lamb Country'), rich in history and deserted beaches. The main regional town is Waipukurau (or just 'Wai-puk') – not exactly thrilling but a functional hub for petrol, motels, a supermarket and the Central Hawke's Bay Information Centre with adjunct coffee booth. It's also the only town in the world to sit directly *on* the 40°S parallel! Little Waipawa is your best bet for a feed.

There are no fewer than six windswept beaches along the coast here: Kairakau, Mangakuri, Pourerere, Aramoana, Blackhead and Porangahau. The first five are good for swimming, and between the lot they offer a range of sandy, salty activities including surfing, fishing and driftwoody, rock-pooly adventures. Between Aramoana and Blackhead Beach lies the DOC-managed Te Angiangi Marine Reserve – bring your snorkel.

It's a nondescript hill in the middle of nowhere, but the place with the world's longest name is good for a photo op. Believe it or not, Taumatawhakatangihangakoauauotamateaturipukakapikimaungahoronukupokaiwhenuakitanatahu is the abbreviated form of 'The Brow of a Hill where Tamatea, the Man with the Big Knees, Who Slid, Climbed and Swallowed Mountains, Known as Land Eater, Played his Flute to his Brother'. To get there, fuel up in Waipukurau and drive 40km to the Mangaorapa junction on Rte 52. Turn left and go 4km towards Porangahau. At the intersection with the signposts, turn right and continue 4.3km to the sign.

Ongaonga, a historic village 16km west of Waipawa, has interesting Victorian and Edwardian buildings. Pick up a pamphlet for a self-guided walking tour from the info centre in Waipukurau.

Central Hawke's Bay
Settlers Museum MUSEUM
(☎06-857 7288; www.chbsettlersmuseum.co.nz; 23 High St, Waipawa; adult/child $5/1; ◉10am-4pm) This interesting old museum in Waipawa has plenty of pioneer artefacts, old photos and a good specimen of a river *waka*. Look for the anchor of the ill-fated schooner *Maroro* out the front, which hit a reef then washed up on Porangahau Beach in 1927.

★ **Paper Mulberry Café** CAFE $
(☎06-856 8688; www.papermulberrycafe.co.nz; 89 SH2, Pukehou; snacks $5-10, lunch mains $13-22; ◉7am-4pm) Halfway between Waipawa and Hastings, this retro cafe-gallery in a 100-year-old, aquamarine church serves excellent coffee, smoothies and homespun food. A top spot for a chomp, a browse through the local crafts, a takeaway jar of marmalade and to warm your bones by the wood heater in winter.

Central Hawke's Bay
Information Centre TOURIST INFORMATION
(☎06-858 6488; www.lambcountry.co.nz; Railway Esplanade, Waipukurau; ◉9.30am-3.30pm Mon, 10am-3.30pm Tue & Thu, 9.30am-4pm Fri & Sat, closed Wed & Sun) Helpful visitor centre in the old railway station (with coffee booth on one side).

❶ Getting There & Away

InterCity (www.intercity.co.nz) buses pass through Waipawa and Waipukurau on their Wellington–Napier route.

Kaweka & Ruahine Ranges

The remote Kaweka and Ruahine Ranges separate Hawke's Bay from NZ's Central Plateau. These forested wildernesses offer some of the island's best hiking: see www.doc.govt.nz for track, hut and campsite info on Ruahine Forest Park, and the downloadable pamphlet *Kaweka Forest Park & Puketitiri Reserves*.

An ancient 136km Māori track, now known as the Gentle Annie Road, runs inland from Omahu near Hastings to Taihape, via Otamauri and Kuripapango (where there's a basic but endearing DOC campsite, adult/child $6/3). This isolated route takes around three hours to drive (or a couple of days by bike – it's part of the Ngā Haerenga, the New Zealand Cycle Trails project (see www.nzcycletrail.com). On foot, an easygoing hike here is the five-to-six-hour return Sunrise Track (p351), within Ruahine Forest Park.

Kaweka J, the highest point of the Kaweka Range (1724m), can be reached by a three-to five-hour hike from the end of Kaweka Rd; from Napier take Puketitiri Rd then Whittle Rd. The drive is worthwhile in itself; it's partly unsealed and takes three hours return.

Enjoy a soak in Mangatutu Hot Pools (☎06-834 3111; www.doc.govt.nz; off Makahu Rd; ◉daylight hours) FREE before or after the three-hour walk on Te Puia Track, which follows the photogenic Mohaka River. From Napier, take Puketitiri Rd, then Pakaututu Rd, then Makahu Rd. Parts of the road can be dicey – a 4WD is usually a good idea.

The Mohaka River can be rafted with Mohaka Rafting (☎06-839 1808; www.mohaka rafting.com; day trips $115-210).

Wellington Region

Best Places to Eat

➜ Noble Rot (p400)

➜ Logan Brown (p400)

➜ Husk (p398)

➜ Fidel's (p398)

➜ Clareville Bakery (p415)

Best Places to Stay

➜ Ohtel (p397)

➜ City Cottages (p397)

➜ QT Wellington (p397)

➜ YHA Wellington City (p394)

➜ Dwellington (p396)

Why Go?

If your New Zealand travels thus far have been all about sleepy rural towns and the great outdoors, Wellington will deliver a caffeine-charged change of pace. Art-house cinemas, craft-beer bars, live bands and endless cafes await in NZ's cultural capital.

Wellington is the crossing point between the North and South Islands – travellers have been passing through here for centuries. The likes of Te Papa and Zealandia now stop visitors in their tracks, while myriad other urban attractions reveal themselves over the course of a longer sojourn.

Less than an hour away to the north, the Kāpiti Coast has a slower, beachy vibe, with Kāpiti Island nature reserve a highlight. An hour away to the northeast over the Remutaka Range, the Wairarapa plains are dotted with quaint towns and wineries, hemmed in by rugged, wild stretches of coast.

When to Go

➜ Wellington has a bad rep for blustery, cold, grey weather, but this isn't the whole story: 'Windy Welly' breaks into blue skies and T-shirt temperatures at least several days a year, when you'll hear locals exclaim, 'You can't beat Wellington on a good day.'

➜ November to April are the warmer months here, with average maximums hovering around 20°C. From May to August it's colder and wetter – daily temperatures lurk around 12°C.

➜ The Kāpiti Coast and Wairarapa are a different story – both warmer and less windy, with as many blue-sky days as otherwise.

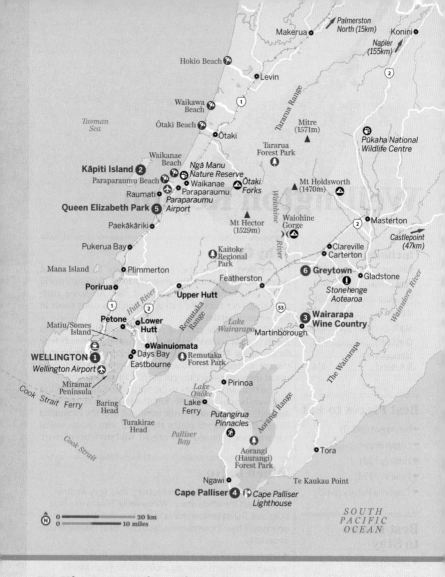

Wellington Region Highlights

1 **Wellington** (p383)
Swimming through a sea of craft beer and top-notch coffee in NZ's artsy, bohemian capital.

2 **Kāpiti Island** (p408)
Hiking through native bush filled with some of the country's rarest bird species, and perhaps even chancing upon a kiwi on a nocturnal walk.

3 **Wairarapa Wine Country** (p412) Struggling to maintain vertical on your bicycle as you tour the wineries around Martinborough.

4 **Cape Palliser** Counting the steps up to the lighthouse on this wild and remote headland.

5 **Queen Elizabeth Park** (p407) Rambling through the dunes near beachy Paekākāriki.

6 **Greytown** (p413) Soaking up the genteel, heritage vibes in this affluent Wairarapa town.

ⓘ Getting There & Away

Wellington is a major transport hub, being the North Island port for the interisland ferries (p405).

If you're flying in, Wellington Airport (p405) is serviced by international and domestic airlines, while Kāpiti Coast Airport (p407) also welcomes a handful of domestic routes.

Back on terra firma, Northern Explorer (p405) trains run between Wellington and Auckland three times a week; there's also a weekday commuter service to/from Palmerston North called the Capital Connection.

InterCity (p405) is the main North Island bus company, travelling from Wellington to just about everywhere.

WELLINGTON

POP 418,500

On a sunny, windless day, Wellington is up there with the best of them. For starters it's lovely to look at, sitting on a hook-shaped harbour ringed with ranges that wear a snowy cloak in winter. Victorian timber architecture laces the bushy hillsides above the harbour, which resonate with native birdsong.

As cities go it's really rather small, but Welly's compact downtown area gives it a bigger-city buzz and, being the NZ capital, it's endowed with museums, theatres, galleries and arts organisations completely disproportionate to its size. Wellingtonians are rightly proud of their kickin' caffeine and craft-beer scene, and there's no shortage of bearded, skateboard-riding, pierced-and-inked types doing arty things in old warehouses across town.

Sadly, windless days are not the norm for Wellington. In New Zealand the city is infamous for two things: its frequent tremors and the umbrella-shredding gales that barrel through with regularity. Wellington: terrible for hairstyles, brilliant for kites.

◉ Sights

★**Mt Victoria Lookout**   VIEWPOINT
(Map p386; Lookout Rd; ⊙24hr) The city's most impressive viewpoint is atop 196m-high Mt Victoria (Matairangi), east of the city centre. You can take bus 20 most of the way up, but the rite of passage is to sweat it out on the walk (ask a local for directions or just follow your nose). If you've got wheels, take Oriental Pde along the waterfront and then

scoot up Carlton Gore Rd. Aside from the views there are some interesting info panels to ogle.

★**Zealandia**   WILDLIFE RESERVE
(Map p386; ☑04-920 9213; www.visitzealandia.com; 53 Waiapu Rd, Karori; admission only adult/child/family $21/10/49, with tour $55/27.50/110; ⊙9am-5pm; 🖪) ⌀ This groundbreaking eco-sanctuary is nooked into a valley in the hills about 2km west of downtown Wellington. Living wild within the fenced, predator-free habitat are more than 30 native bird species, including rare little spotted kiwi, takahe, saddleback, hihi and kaka, as well as NZ's little dinosaur, the tuatara. An excellent exhibition relays NZ's natural history and world-renowned conservation story. Buses 2 and 21 stop nearby, or see the Zealandia website for info on the free shuttle.

★**Te Papa**   MUSEUM
(Map p390; ☑04-381 7000; www.tepapa.govt.nz; 55 Cable St; ⊙10am-6pm; 🖪) ⌀ 𝗙𝗥𝗘𝗘 New Zealand's national museum is hard to miss, taking up a sizeable chunk of the Wellington waterfront. 'Te Papa Tongarewa' loosely translates as 'treasure box': the riches inside include an amazing collection of Māori artefacts and the museum's own colourful *marae* (meeting house); natural history and environment exhibitions; Pacific and NZ history galleries; themed hands-on 'discovery centres' for children; and Toi Art, a revitalised home for the National Art Collection. And don't miss the colossal squid!

Introductory and Māori Highlights tours (adult/child $20/10) depart from the information desk on level two; book ahead.

★**Wellington Botanic Gardens**   GARDENS
(Map p386; ☑04-499 1400; www.wellingtongardens.nz; 101 Glenmore St, Thorndon; ⊙daylight hours) 𝗙𝗥𝗘𝗘 These hilly, 25-hectare botanic gardens can be effortlessly visited via the **Wellington Cable Car** (Map p386; ☑04-472 2199; www.wellingtoncablecar.co.nz; Cable Car Lane, rear 280 Lambton Quay; adult/child one way $5/2.50, return $9/4.50; ⊙departs every 10min, 7am-10pm Mon-Fri, 8.30am-10pm Sat, 8.30am-9pm Sun; 🖪), although there are several other entrances hidden in the hillsides. The gardens boast a tract of original native forest, the beaut Lady Norwood Rose Garden, 25,000 spring tulips and various international plant collections. Add in fountains, a playground, sculptures, a duck pond, cafe, the **Space Place** (Map p386;

WELLINGTON REGION WELLINGTON

HIKING IN
THE WAIRARAPA

TARARUA FOREST PARK

North of Wellington is a place where the wind whips along the sides of mountains and the fog creeps silently in the early morning – a place where gales blow through steep river gorges, snow falls on sharp, greywacke (grey sandstone) peaks and rain trickles down narrow ridges. Welcome to Tararua Forest Park, the largest DOC conservation park on NZ's North Island.

The park centres itself on the Tararua Range, which stretches 80km from the Remutaka Saddle in the south to the Manawatu Gorge, a natural gap that separates the Tararuas from the Ruahine Range, in the north. The highest summit is Mitre (1571m; not to be confused with Mitre Peak at Milford Sound down south), but there are many other peaks close to that height throughout the park. The ridges and spurs above the bushline are narrow, steep and exposed – this really is wild country.

Only 50km from Wellington, the park used to be popular largely with weekend hikers from the windy city. Today, hikers from around the country are attracted to the Tararuas' broken terrain and sheer features, which present a challenge to even the most experienced hikers.

The park has an extensive network of tracks, routes and huts, most accessible from the main gateways of Ōtaki Forks in the west (off SH1), and Holdsworth and Waiohine Gorge on the eastern, Wairarapa side.

These tracks are not as well formed as those in most national parks, so it's easy to lose your way. On the open ridge-tops there are rarely signposts or poles marking the routes – only the occasional cairn. The Mt Holdsworth–Jumbo Circuit is less demanding than most routes through the Tararuas, and thus sees the greatest number of hikers.

☆ Mt Holdsworth–Jumbo Circuit

START/END **HOLDSWORTH LODGE**
DURATION **3 DAYS**
DISTANCE **24KM LOOP**
DIFFICULTY **MODERATE/CHALLENGING**

This classic Tararua hike climbs through beech forest to quickly ascend to the alpine tops of the range. Mt Holdsworth brings wraparound views, while the huts along the route also provide expansive panoramas: there's a serene sense of removal as you look out to the lights of Masterton in the evening.

Although you can cover this hike in two days, it's a better idea to schedule three in order to soak up the above-the-treeline vibes and to allow for the possibility of losing a day to the bad weather, which can easily (almost predictably) force you to sit out a day in one of the alpine huts (Powell and Jumbo adult/child $15/7.50; Atiwhakatu $5/2.50 – book through DOC if you're planning a stay).

CAPE PALLISER

End-of-the-world Cape Palliser is best known for its landmark lighthouse and the North Island's largest and smelliest breeding area for seals, but it also offers a standout half-day hike to a geological oddity that's had more than its 15 minutes of cinematic fame.

☆ Putangirua Pinnacles

START/END **PUTANGIRUA
PINNACLES CAMPSITE**
DURATION **3½ HOURS**
DISTANCE **6.5KM**
DIFFICULTY **EASY/MODERATE**

With their otherworldly appearance, the fragile and fluted cliffs and 'hoodoos' of the Putangirua Pinnacles could easily inspire a

The Wellington region's most rewarding hikes meander across the ranges in the wilds of the Wairarapa. When you've scraped the mud off your boots, the Wairarapa wineries await.

sense of Middle-earth, which is exactly what they did for Sir Peter Jackson, who cast them as the approach to the Paths of the Dead in *The Lord of the Rings: The Return of the King* (he also used them as a location for the opening sequence of his 1992 splatter-horror flick, *Braindead*).

The Pinnacles, as they're usually known, are cut into a wild section of coast near Cape Palliser. They've been formed due to the erosion of the soft earth by rain, creating a series of deep gullies. When boulders are exposed, they shed the rainwater, protecting the ground beneath from erosion and thus creating stone-capped 'hoodoos'.

The Pinnacles present a raft of hiking options, none taking more than half a day, leaving time for a few pinot noirs back in Martinborough, the centrepiece of the Wairarapa wine region, less than 45 minutes' drive away. You can walk to the Pinnacles' base along the stream bed, climb to a high lookout point along a ridge track, combine the two, or make a larger loop that also casts a wide eye along the entire Palliser Bay coast.

You can propel yourself along this hike at any time of year, but skip the stream route after heavy rain or in high wind when rock-fall is common from the loose and fragile gravel cliffs. The stream, which needs to be crossed on the low route, can also rise quickly after a good downpour.

Wellington

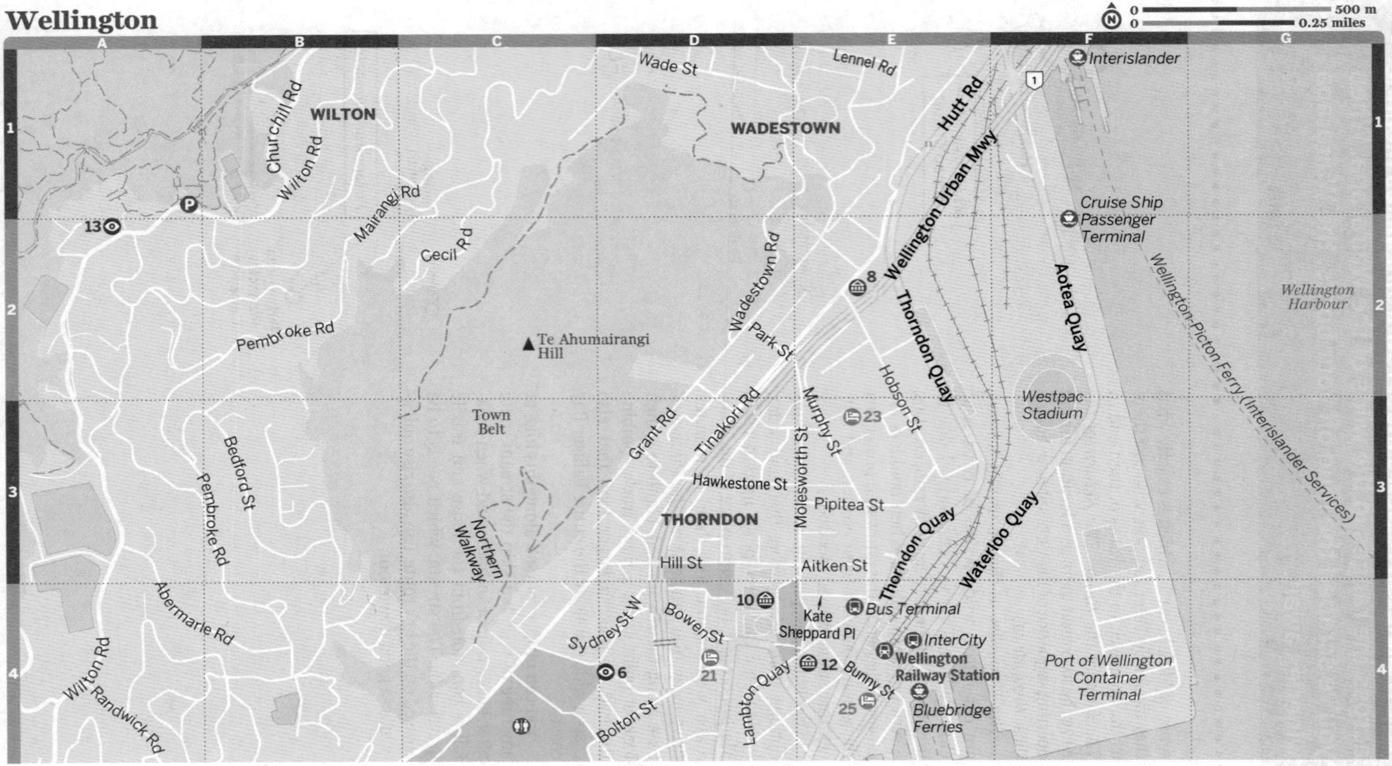

Wellington Harbour

Wellington-Picton Ferry (Interislander Services)

Interislander

Cruise Ship Passenger Terminal

Aotea Quay

Westpac Stadium

Waterloo Quay

Port of Wellington Container Terminal

Hutt Rd

Wellington Urban Mwy

Thorndon Quay

Thorndon Quay

InterCity
Bus Terminal

Wellington Railway Station

Bluebridge Ferries

Lennel Rd

WADESTOWN

Hobson St

Murphy St

Molesworth St

Pipitea St

Aitken St

Burny St

25

Wade St

Park St

Wadestown Rd

Hawkestone St

Kate Sheppard Pl

12

Lambton Quay

Tinakori Rd

Grant Rd

THORNDON

Hill St

Bowen St

10

21

Te Ahumairangi Hill

Town Belt

Northern Walkway

Sydney St W

9

Bolton St

WILTON

Cecil Rd

Mairangi Rd

Wilton Rd

Churchill Rd

Pembroke Rd

Bedford St

Pembroke Rd

Abermarle Rd

Wilton Rd

Randwick Rd

13

500 m
0.25 miles

WELLINGTON REGION

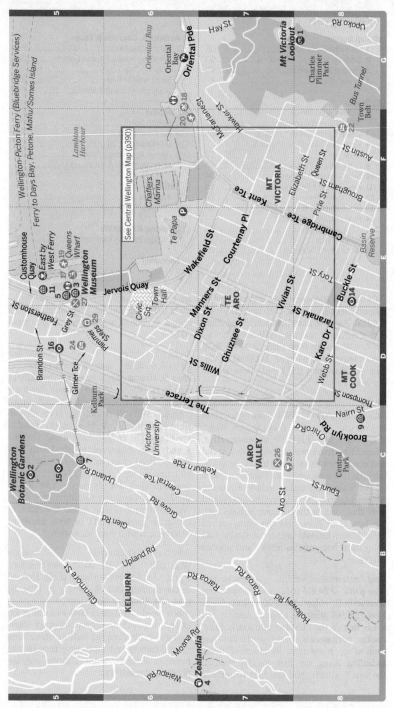

Wellington-Picton Ferry (Bluebridge Services)

Ferry to Days Bay, Petone, Matiu/Somes Island

Oriental Bay

Hay St

Mt Victoria Lookout
1

Upoko Rd

Charles Plimmer Park

Bus Tunnel

Town Belt

Oriental Bay

Oriental Pde

Oriental Pde

McFarlane St

Hawker St

20 18

Austin St

22

Lambton Harbour

Chaffers Marina

See Central Wellington Map (p390)

Elizabeth St

Queen St

Broughham St

MT VICTORIA

Kent Tce

Pirie St

Basin Reserve

Te Papa

Wakefield St

Courtenay Pl

Cambridge Tce

Customhouse Quay

East by West Ferry

19

Queens Wharf

Wellington Museum

17

11
5
3
27

Jervois Quay

Tory St

Vivian St

Buckle St

14

Featherston St

Grey St

Civic Sq

Town Hall

Manners St

Dixon St

TE ARO

Ghuznee St

Taranaki St

Karo Dr

Webb St

MT COOK

Thompson St

Brandon St

16

Gilmer Tce

24

Plimmer Steps

29

Willis St

The Terrace

Nairn St

6

Brooklyn Rd

Ohiro Rd

Kelburn Park

Victoria University

Kelburn Pde

ARO VALLEY

26

28

Aro St

Epuni St

Central Park

Wellington Botanic Gardens
2

15

7

Upland Rd

Grove Rd

Glen Rd

Central Tce

Glenmore St

KELBURN

Upland Rd

Raroa Rd

Raroa Rd

Holloway Rd

Moana Rd

Waiapu Rd

Zealandia
4

Wellington

☑ 04-910 3140; www.museumswellington.org.nz; 40 Salamanca Rd, Kelburn; adult/child/family $14/9/45; ⊙4-11pm Tue & Fri, 10am-11pm Sat, 10am-5.30pm Sun) observatory and the small-but-nifty **Cable Car Museum** (Map p386; ☑04-475 3578; www.museumswellington.org.nz; 1a Upland Rd, Kelburn; ⊙9.30am-5pm) **FREE** and you've a busy day out.

★ **Wellington Museum**   MUSEUM
(Map p386; ☑04-472 8904; www.museumswellington.org.nz; 3 Jervois Quay, Queens Wharf; ⊙10am-5pm; 🎔) **FREE** For an imaginative, interactive experience of Wellington's social and maritime history, head to this bewitching little museum, inside an 1892 bond store on the wharf. Highlights include a moving documentary on the *Wahine,* the interisland ferry that sank in the harbour in 1968 with the loss of 51 lives, and the curio-packed Attic. Māori legends are dramatically told using tiny holographic actors and special effects.

New Zealand Parliament   HISTORIC BUILDING
(Map p386; ☑04-817 9503; www.parliament.nz; Molesworth St; ⊙tours hourly 10am-4pm) **FREE** New Zealand might be a young country but it has one of the oldest continuously functioning parliaments in the world and has chalked up more than its share of firsts, including being the first to give women the vote (in 1893) and the first to include

an openly transgender Member of Parliament (in 1999). You can learn all about NZ's unique version of democracy on a free guided tour.

Weta Workshop   WORKSHOP
(☑04-909 4035; www.wetaworkshop.com; 1 Weka St, Miramar; single tour adult/child $28/13, both tours $48/22; ⊙9am-5.30pm) Academy Award–winning special-effects and props company Weta Workshop has been responsible for bringing the likes of *The Lord of the Rings, The Hobbit, King Kong, District 9* and *Thor: Ragnarok* to life. Learn how they do it on entertaining 45-minute guided tours, starting every half-hour; bookings recommended. There's also a tour to see the *Thunderbirds Are Go* miniatures stage. Weta Workshop is 8km east of the city centre: drive, catch bus 31X or book transport ($40 return) with your admission.

City Gallery Wellington   GALLERY
(Map p390; ☑04-913 9032; www.citygallery.org.nz; Civic Sq; ⊙10am-5pm) **FREE** Housed in the monumental old library in Civic Sq (the new library is next door), Wellington's much-loved City Gallery does a cracking job of securing acclaimed contemporary international exhibitions, as well as unearthing up-and-comers and supporting those at the forefront of the NZ scene. Charges may apply for major exhibits.

Pukeahu National War Memorial Park
MEMORIAL

(Map p386; ☑04-385 2496; www.mch.govt.nz; Buckle St; ⊙hall 10am-5pm) **FREE** It seems strangely fitting that NZ's National War Memorial should be a musical instrument and contain as its centrepiece not a statue of a soldier, but of a grieving mother and her children. The statue is contained within the Hall of Memories at the base of the 51m-high, 74-bell, art-deco Carillon (1932), which you can see from all over Wellington. It's flanked by a sobering and oddly tranquil park with an Australian Memorial consisting of 15 red sandstone columns.

Otari-Wilton's Bush
GARDENS

(Map p386; ☑04-475 3245; www.wellington gardens.nz; 160 Wilton Rd, Wilton; ⊙daylight hours) **FREE** The only botanic gardens in NZ specialising in native flora, Otari features more than 1200 plant species including an extant section of native bush containing the city's oldest trees (such as an 800-year-old rimu). There's also an information centre, an 18m-high canopy walkway, 11km of walking trails and some beaut picnic areas. It's located about 5km northwest of the centre and is well signposted; bus 14 passes the gates.

Bolton Street Cemetery
CEMETERY

(Map p386; ☑04-499 1400; www.wellington gardens.nz; off Bolton St, via Kinross St; ⊙daylight hours) **FREE** Lost beneath a canopy of oak and pohutukawa, between freeway off-ramps and apartment towers, this fabulously dank and atmospheric remnant dates back to the 1840s. Thousands of Wellingtonians were buried here up until 1892. They rested in peace until 1972 when the Wellington Urban Motorway was bulldozed through the middle of the boneyard. The remains of 3693 people were exhumed then reinterred in a common vault at the bottom of the cemetery.

Petone Settlers Museum
MUSEUM

(☑04-568 8373; www.petonesettlers.org.nz; The Esplanade, Petone; ⊙daily Dec-Mar, 10am-4pm Wed-Sun Apr-Nov) **FREE** Built for the centenary of the Treaty of Waitangi in 1940, this gorgeous little art-deco building on the shell-strewn Petone foreshore contains a fun and fascinating wee museum focusing on local history and industry. It's a 15-minute drive from downtown Wellington, or a 23-minute ride on the 83 bus.

Old Government Buildings
HISTORIC BUILDING

(Map p386; ☑04-472 4341; www.heritage.org. nz; 55 Lambton Quay; ⊙9am-5pm Mon-Fri) **FREE** Across the road from Parliament, this grand Italianate structure (1876) is the largest wooden building in the southern hemisphere, although it does a pretty good impersonation of stone. It's now part of Victoria University's law faculty. Check out the magnificent hanging staircase, the former cabinet room and the history displays on the ground and 1st floors.

WELLINGTON IN...

Two Days
To get a feel for the lie of the land, walk (or drive) up to the Mt Victoria Lookout (p383), or ride the cable car up into the Wellington Botanic Gardens (p383). After lunch on boho-hipster Cuba St, catch some Kiwi culture at Te Papa (p383) or the Wellington Museum. Top off the day by doing the rounds of the city's craft-beer bars.

The next day, reconstitute with coffee and an eggy infusion at Fidel's (p398), a real Wellington institution, then head to Zealandia (p383) to be with the birds and learn about New Zealand conservation. Alternatively, walk the halls to see a different species on a tour of the New Zealand Parliament. Grab a meal at one of the central city's excellent restaurants – try classy Logan Brown (p400) on for size – before catching some live tunes, or a movie at the gloriously restored Embassy Theatre (p402).

Four Days
Shake and bake the two-day itinerary, then decorate with the following: hightail it out of Wellington for a seal-spotting safari to wild Cape Palliser (p415), followed by a wine tasting or two around Martinborough (p410) in the heart of Wairarapa Wine Country. The next day, head to Paekākāriki (p407) on the Kāpiti Coast for an ocean swim before stretching out on a hike through the dunes of Queen Elizabeth Park (p407) next door.

Central Wellington

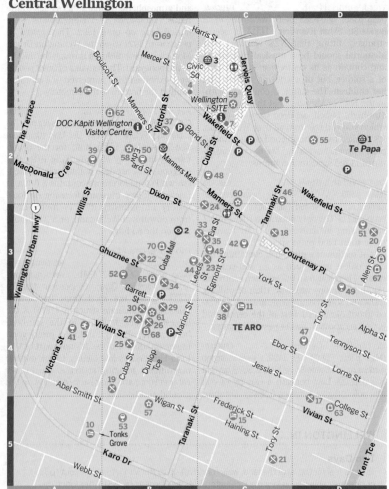

**Katherine Mansfield
House & Garden** HISTORIC BUILDING
(Map p386; ☑04-473 7268; www.katherinemans
field.com; 25 Tinakori Rd, Thorndon; adult/child $10/
free; ☺10am-4pm Tue-Sun) Often compared to
Chekhov and Maupassant, Katherine Mans
field was one of NZ's most distinguished au
thors, who pushed the short-story form to
uncharted heights. Born in 1888, she died of
tuberculosis in 1923 aged 34. This Tinakori
Rd house is where she spent five years of her
childhood. It now contains exhibits in her
honour, including a biographical film. Guid
ed tours by arrangement.

Wellington Zoo ZOO
(☑04-381 6755; www.wellingtonzoo.com; 200
Daniell St, Newtown; adult/child $27/12; ☺9.30am-
5pm; ⏭) ⦿ Committed to conservation,
research and captive breeding, Wellington
Zoo is home to a menagerie of native and
exotic wildlife, including lions and tama-
rins. The nocturnal house has kiwi and
tuatara. 'Close encounters' allow you to
meet the big cats, red pandas, giraffes and
mischievous meerkats (for a fee). The zoo is
4km south of the city centre; catch bus 23.

its own collection, plus frequently changing guest exhibitions. It's New Zealand history as told through the faces of its people – which all sounds a bit serious, but there's plenty of levity here too.

Dowse Art Museum   GALLERY

(☑ 04-570 6500; www.dowse.org.nz; 45 Laings Rd, Lower Hutt; ⊙10am-5pm; 💪) **FREE** A beacon of culture and delight, the excellent Dowse is worth visiting for its jaunty architecture alone. It's a family-friendly, accessible art museum showcasing NZ art, craft and design, with a good cafe to boot. The only permanent showcase is a carved Māori *pataka* (traditional raised storehouse). It's a 20-minute drive, 30-minute ride on bus 83 or 91, or a short train trip from central Wellington.

Academy Galleries   GALLERY

(Map p386; ☑ 04-499 8807; www.nzafa.com; 1 Queens Wharf; ⊙10am-5pm) **FREE** The showcase of the esteemed New Zealand Academy of Fine Arts (founded 1882), the Academy Galleries presents frequently changing exhibitions by NZ artists, from canvases and exquisite drawings to ceramics to photography.

Nairn Street Cottage   MUSEUM

(Map p386; ☑ 04-384 9122; www.museumswellington.org.nz; 68 Nairn St, Mt Cook; adult/child $8/4; ⊙noon-4pm Sat & Sun) Just a five-minute amble from the top of Cuba St, Wellington's oldest cottage (1858) has been carefully restored, complete with an organic garden and wandering chooks. Admission is by tour only (on the hour noon to 3pm), retelling stories of early settlers and life in the mid-19th century.

🏃 Activities

Wellington's harbour offers plenty of opportunities to get active: kayaking, paddle boarding, sailing, windsurfing... (Wellington is windy: might as well make the most of it!) Back on dry land there's rock climbing, cycling and high-wire walking to keep you off the streets. Pick up the *Wellington City Cycle Map* for bike-trail info.

Switched On Bikes   CYCLING

(Map p386; ☑ 0800 386 877; www.switchedonbikes.co.nz; Shed 1, Queens Wharf; city & mountain bike hire 1hr/4hr/day $25/40/60, electric $35/65/75, guided tours from $95; ⊙8.30am-5.30pm) If you're short on puff on those notorious Wellington hills, these guys rent out electric bikes (and regular mountain and city bikes) for cruising the city or taking on guided tours around the

Bucket Fountain   FOUNTAIN

(Map p390; Cuba Mall; 💪) Cuba Mall's landmark (and sneakily splashy) fountain mocks the surrounding commerce with its Zen-like tilt-and-pour processes. The kids (and the wandering Cuba St stoners) will be mesmerised.

New Zealand Portrait Gallery   GALLERY

(Map p386; ☑ 04-472 2298; www.nzportraitgallery.org.nz; Shed 11, Customhouse Quay; ⊙10.30am-4.30pm) **FREE** Housed in a heritage red-brick warehouse on the waterfront, this estimable gallery presents a diverse range of NZ portraiture and caricature from

Central Wellington

harbour. Look for their shipping-container base near the end of the wharf.

Ferg's Kayaks KAYAKING
(Map p386; ☑ 04-499 8898; www.fergskayaks.co.nz; Shed 6, Queens Wharf; ⊙ 10am-9pm Mon-Fri, to 6pm Sat & Sun) Stretch your tendons with indoor rock climbing on an impressive 12m-high wall (adult/child $23/17), cruise the waterfront wearing in-line skates (one/two hours $20/25) or paddle in a kayak (one/two hours $25/35) or on a stand-up paddle board (one/two hours $30/40). Guided kayaking trips and bouldering area also available.

Makara Peak MOUNTAIN BIKING
(www.makarapeak.org; 116 South Karori Rd, Karori; ⊙ daylight hours) In hilly Karori, 7km west of the city centre, this excellent 250-hectare park is laced with 45km of single track, ranging from beginner to extreme. The nearby **Mud Cycles** (☑ 04-476 4961; www.mudcycles.co.nz; 424 Karori Rd, Karori; half-day/full-day/weekend bike hire from $40/70/110; ⊙ 9.30am-6.30pm Mon, Tue, Thu & Fri, to 7pm Wed, 9am-5pm Sat, 10am-5pm Sun) has mountain bikes for hire. To get here by public transport, catch bus 2.

Wellington Ocean Sports   WATER SPORTS

(Map p386; ☑04-939 6702; www.oceansports.
org.nz; 115 Oriental Pde, Oriental Bay; harbour
sails per person $50; ⊘booking office 9am-5pm)
Harness Wellington's infamous wind on a
90-minute harbour sailing trip, departing
most weekends (weather dependent) – no
experience required! Ask about stand-up
paddle boarding, windsurfing and kayaking sessions.

Freyberg Pool
& Fitness Centre   SWIMMING

(Map p386; ☑04-801 4530; www.wellington.govt.
nz; 139 Oriental Pde, Oriental Bay; pool adult/child
$6.30/3.70; ⊘6am-9pm; 🚼) Built in 1963,
modernist Freyberg Pool is the most striking piece of architecture on Oriental Bay. As
well as a big indoor pool there's a gym, spa,
and aerobics, yoga and pilates classes. And
coffee. You're going to need coffee.

Adrenalin Forest   ADVENTURE SPORTS

(☑04-237 8553; www.adrenalin-forest.co.nz; Okowai
Rd, Porirua; adult/child 3hr $45/30; ⊘10am-
2.30pm daily Oct-Apr, Wed-Sun May-Sep) Walk out
on the high wire on this knee-trembling web
of cables, suspension bridges and platforms
strung between high pines. It's located 21km
north of central Wellington; drive or catch
the train to Porirua.

👉 Tours

Walk Wellington   WALKING

(Map p390; ☑04-473 3145; www.walkwellington.
org.nz; departs Wellington i-SITE, 111 Wakefield St;
tour adult/child $20/10; ⊘10am daily year-round,
plus 5pm Mon, Wed & Fri Dec-Mar) Informative
and great-value two-hour walking tours focusing on the city and waterfront, departing from the i-SITE (p404). Book online, by
phone or just turn up.

Flat Earth   DRIVING

(☑04-472 9635; www.flatearth.co.nz; half-day
tours from $95) An array of themed small-
group guided tours: city highlights, *Lord
of the Rings* filming locations and arts and
culture. Pricier full-day Martinborough wine
tours also available.

Kiwi Coastal Tours   DRIVING

(☑021 464 957; www.kiwicoastaltours.co.nz; 3/5hr
tours $150/250) Highly rated 4WD explora-
tion of the rugged coast south of Wellington,
in the company of a local guide with plenty
of stories up his sleeve.

Ship 'N' Chip Tour   CRUISE

(Map p386; ☑04-472 8904; www.museumswel
lington.org.nz/shipnchip; 3 Jervois Quay, Queens
Wharf; adult/child $55/39) Run by the
Wellington Museum (p388), this fishy five-
hour tour kicks off with a tour of the
aforementioned institution, followed by a
fish-and-chip lunch and a ferry ride over
to Matiu/Somes Island (p396) in the middle of Wellington Harbour for a bit of a
look around. Tours begin in the museum at
11am; book ahead.

Wellington Nature Tours   ECOTOUR

(☑04-472 9635; www.wellingtonnaturetours.
co.nz; half-day tour adult/child $125/62.50, full-day
$235/145) Half- and full-day tours dipping
into some key natural realms around Wellington – Zealandia (p383), Otari-Witson's
Bush (p389) and the seal colony south of
town. Also heads to Matiu/Somes Island
(p396) on a four-hour tour (adult/child
$195/115).

Zest Food Tours   FOOD & DRINK

(Map p390; ☑04-801 9198; www.zestfoodtours.
co.nz; departs Wellington i-SITE, 111 Wakefield
St; tours from $205) Runs 3½- to five-hour
small-group foodie tours around the city,
plus day tours over the hills (and not so
far away) into the Wairarapa wine region.
You might want to skip breakfast/lunch
beforehand.

Hop On Hop Off   BUS

(Map p390; ☑0800 246 877; www.hoponhopoff.
co.nz; departs 145 Wakefield St; adult/child $45/30;
⊘departures 9.30am-2.30pm) Flexible 1½-hour
scenic loop of the city with 10 stops en route
(Botanic Gardens, Mt Victoria, Wellington
Zoo, Te Papa etc). Hop on and off as much
as you like; tickets are valid for 24 hours.
Buses trundle past each stop every 30 to 45
minutes.

Te Wharewaka o Pōneke   CULTURAL

(Map p390; ☑04-901 3333; www.wharewaka
oponeke.co.nz; Taranaki Wharf, 2 Taranaki St; tours
walking $30-40, 2hr waka $105, 3hr waka & walk
$140) Get set for (and maybe a little bit wet
on) a two-hour paddle tour in a Māori *waka*
(canoe) around Wellington's waterfront,
with lots of cultural insights along the way.
Call for the latest tour times and bookings –
minimum numbers apply. Cultural walking
tours also available.

WELLINGTON REGION WELLINGTON

ESSENTIAL WELLINGTON

Eat yourself silly: Wellington has a gut-busting number of great cafes and restaurants.

Drink coffee; Wellington is wide awake around the clock.

Read *The Collected Stories of Katherine Mansfield.*

Listen to The Mutton Birds' 'Wellington' (1994) or The Mockers' 'Murder in Manners St' (1980).

Watch *What We Do in the Shadows* (Taika Waititi and Jemaine Clement; 2014), where Wellington's vampires get their moment in the sun.

Go green at Zealandia (p383), a groundbreaking ecosanctuary within the city's confines.

Go online at www.wellingtonnz.com; www.wairarapanz.com; www. kapiticoast.govt.nz; www.lonelyplanet. com/new-zealand/wellington.

Xplor Tours   TOURS
(Map p390; ☑ 021 248 3604; www.xplortours.nz; ⊘ 10.30am & 1.45pm) Three-hour city highlights minivan tours departing the i-SITE (p404), whizzing you around to see the major sights, including Te Papa, the Embassy Theatre, Mt Victoria, the Cable Car, the Beehive and Weta Workshop (drive-by viewing at most; stops with photo ops at some). Book ahead.

✪ Festivals & Events

Check out www.wellingtonnz.com/discover/ events for comprehensive events listings.

Summer City   CULTURAL
(www.wellington.govt.nz; ⊘ Jan-Mar; 🚼) A summertime city-wide events bonanza – many free and outdoor happenings, including the lovely 'Gardens Magic' concerts. The Wellington Pasifika Festival, Chinese New Year and Waitangi Day celebrations also fall under the Summer City umbrella.

Fringe   CULTURAL
(www.fringe.co.nz; ⊘ Feb-Mar) Three weeks of way-out-there experimental visual arts, music, dance and theatre. Although it's held around the same time as the biennial (and much more highbrow) New Zealand Festival, Fringe happens every year.

New Zealand Festival   CULTURAL
(www.festival.co.nz; ⊘ Feb-Mar) A three-week biennial (even years; roughly late February to mid-March) spectacular of theatre, dance, music, visual arts and literature. International acts aplenty. A real 'kick up the arts'!

**NZ International
Comedy Festival**   COMEDY
(www.comedyfestival.co.nz; ⊘ May) Three weeks of hysterics and guffaws. Famous-in-NZ comedians, and some truly world-famous ones, too. Sometimes kicks off in late April.

Wellington Jazz Festival   MUSIC
(www.jazzfestival.co.nz; ⊘ Jun) Five days of finger-snappin', bee-boppin' good times around the capital – an antidote for the winter chills.

**New Zealand
International Film Festival**   FILM
(www.nzff.co.nz; ⊘ Jul-Aug) Roving two-week indie film fest screening the best of NZ and international cinema.

Beervana   BEER
(www.beervana.co.nz; Westpac Stadium, 105 Waterloo Quay, Pipitea; ⊘ Aug) A barrel-load of craft-beer aficionados roll into town (to join the ones that are already here) for a weekend of supping and beard-stroking.

Wellington on a Plate   FOOD & DRINK
(www.wellingtononaplate.com; ⊘ Aug) A lip-smacking roster of gastronomic events held over (roughly) three weeks at restaurants around the city. Bargains aplenty.

★ World of WearableArt   FASHION
(WOW; www.worldofwearableart.com; TSB Arena, 4 Queens Wharf; ⊘ Sep-Oct) A two-week run of spectacular garments (dresses or sculptures – it's a fine line) displayed in a spectacular show. Tickets are hot property; hotel beds anywhere near the city sell out weeks in advance.

🛏 Sleeping

Accommodation in Wellington is more expensive than in regional areas, but there are plenty of options close to the city centre. Free parking spots are a rarity – check before you book. Wellington's budget accommodation largely takes the form of multistorey hostel megaliths. Motels dot the city fringes. Self-contained apartments are popular, and often offer bargain weekend rates. Book well in advance in summer and during major events.

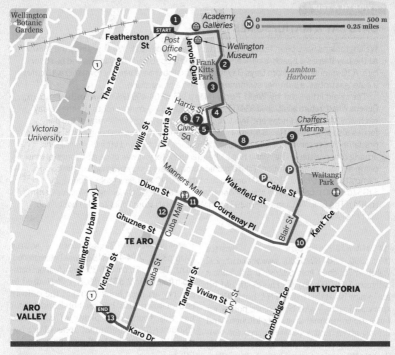

🚶 City Walk
City Sculpture Tour

START POST OFFICE SQ
END KARO DR
LENGTH 3KM; ONE HOUR

Begin in windswept Post Office Sq, where Bill Culbert's **1 SkyBlues** twirls skywards. Cross Jervois Quay and pass between the Academy Galleries and Wellington Museum. At the Queens Wharf waterfront, turn right towards Len Lye's **2 Water Whirler**, a lifeless needle that whirs into life several times daily.

Continue along the promenade below the **3 mast of the Wahine**, which tragically sank in Wellington Harbour in 1968. Around the corner is the white, whale-like **4 Albatross Fountain**. Detour across the flotsamy, sculptural **5 City to Sea Bridge** to Civic Sq to check out Ronnie van Hout's disquieting face/hand **6 Quasi** atop the City Gallery Wellington. Nearby is Weta Workshop's **7 Rugby World Cup statue**, produced for the 2011 RWC, hosted by New Zealand.

Backtrack to the waterfront past the *whare waka* (canoe house) to the **8 Taranaki Wharf Jump Platform** – a sculpture in itself. Take the leap, or continue along the wharf to the naked bronze **9 Solace in the Wind** leaning over the harbour.

Veer right and through Waitangi Park, cross Cable St, cut along Chaffers St, then Blair St with its century-old warehouses.

At Courtenay Pl look left to spy the leggy **10 Tripod**, an industrial-cinematic ode to 'Wellywood', then turn right and continue to wedge-shaped **11 Te Aro Park** with its canoe prow and trip hazards.

Turn left when you hit Cuba St, heading up the pedestrian mall. Watch out for the sly, sloshy **12 Bucket Fountain** (p391) – it exists solely to splash you.

Window-shop to the top of Cuba St, where a remnant heritage precinct is bisected by the controversial inner-city bypass. Regan Gentry's brilliant, ghostly outline of a demolished house, **13 Subject to Change**, sits alongside the curious 7.5m-deep, root-infested Tonks' Well, dating from the 1860s.

WORTH A TRIP

DAYS BAY & MATIU/SOMES ISLAND

Wellingtonians have been taking trips across the harbour to Days Bay since the 1880s. At the bay there's a beach, a park and a cafe, and a boatshed with kayaks and bikes for hire. A 10-minute walk from Days Bay leads to Eastbourne, a beachy township with cafes, a cute 'gastrobar', a summer swimming pool and a playground.

The sweet little East by West Ferry (Map p386; ☑04-499 1282; www.eastbywest.co.nz; Queens Wharf; return adult/child $24/12) plies the 20- to 30-minute route 16 times a day each way Monday to Friday and five to eight times on weekends. Several of the daily ferries also stop at Matiu/Somes Island in the middle of the harbour, a DOC-managed predator-free reserve that is home to weta, tuatara, kakariki and little blue penguins, among other critters. The island has a chequered history: it was once a prisoner-of-war camp and quarantine station. Take a picnic lunch, or even stay overnight in the basic campsite (adult/child $15/7.50) or at one of three DOC cottages (sole-occupancy $105 to $200): book online at www.doc.govt.nz or at the DOC Wellington Visitor Centre (p404). The Ship 'N' Chip Tour (p393) and Wellington Nature Tours (p393) boats also visit the island.

★ **YHA Wellington City** HOSTEL $
(Map p390; ☑04-801 7280; www.yha.co.nz; 292 Wakefield St; dm/s from $32/85, d with/without bathroom $155/100; ☎) ◢ There's an old bit and a new bit at this trusty YHA, but both are spick and span – and both score points for fantastic communal areas, big kitchens and dining areas, and separate spaces for wet-day games, reading and movie-watching. Sustainable initiatives abound (recycling, composting, energy-efficient hot water); espresso machine at reception.

Dwellington HOSTEL $
(Map p386; ☑04-550 9373; www.thedwellington. co.nz; 8 Halswell St, Thorndon; dm/r from $41/115; ℗☎) Two conjoined heritage houses comprise this terrific modern hostel, straddling the political divide between the US and Chinese embassies. There are no en-suite rooms, but everything is clean, bright and comfortable. Handy for ferries, trains, buses and your trade talks with the ambassador, but a fair hike from the nocturnal action on Cuba St.

Cambridge Hotel HOSTEL, HOTEL $
(Map p390; ☑04-385 8829; www.cambridge hotel.co.nz; 28 Cambridge Tce; dm from $28, s with/without bathroom from $99/69, d $119/89; ☎) Built in 1883, the super-central, chocolate-brown Cambridge is a sporty corner pub, with old-fashioned budget rooms above (can you believe that the Queen stayed here in the 1960s?). All of the hotel rooms have fridges and kettles; some have tiny bathrooms. The backpacker wing has a snug kitchen-lounge and dorms with little natural light but sky-high ceilings.

Hotel Waterloo & Backpackers HOSTEL $
(Map p386; ☑04-473 8482; www.hotelwaterloo. co.nz; 1 Bunny St; dm $26-35, s with/without bathroom from $99/72, d $119/89; ☎) ◢ Housed in a curvy art-deco hotel (1937) at the railway end of town, this budget hotel and hostel has tidy rooms and plenty of capacious, character-filled communal areas (don't bypass the bar on the 1st floor). Tasty weekly rates.

Trek Global HOSTEL $
(Map p390; ☑04-471 3480; www.trekglobal.net; 9 O'Reilly Ave; dm/tw/s from $31/40/75, d with/without bathroom $130/96; ℗☎) A highlight of this back-lane hostel is the funky foyer hangout (with pool table) and snug TV lounge. Sleeping quarters and kitchens are squeezed between rabbit-warren corridors; hip Euro wanderers spill out onto the street, smoking. It's relatively quiet with clean rooms, parking ($25 per day) and a women-only dorm with a suntrap terrace.

Wellington Top 10 Holiday Park HOLIDAY PARK $
(☑04-568 5913; www.wellingtontop10.co.nz; 95 Hutt Park Rd, Seaview; sites unpowered/powered per 2 people from $50/55, units with/without bathroom from $135/100; ℗☎⊞) Around 16km northeast of central Wellington, the Top 10 delivers the closest camping to the city. Family-friendly facilities include communal kitchens, a games room and a playground, but the industrial back-block location might leave you feeling a bit culturally barren. Follow the signs off SH2 for Petone and Seaview, or catch bus 83.

★**City Cottages**   RENTAL HOUSE **$$**
(Map p390; ☑021 073 9232; www.wellingtoncity accommodation.co.nz; 5 & 7 Tonks Grove; cottage from $170; P🖙) These two tiny 1880 cottages squat amid a precious historic precinct at the top of Cuba St. These days they're self-contained one-bedroom affairs, comfortable for two but sleeping up to four (thanks to a sofa bed). Not the quietest location, but certainly hip. There's also a modern two-bedroom studio and a historic townhouse (sleeping 10) available.

U Boutique Hotel   BOUTIQUE HOTEL **$$**
(Map p390; ☑04-801 6800; www.uhotelgroup. com; 25 Frederick St; r with/without bathroom from $204/154; P🖙🍴) A bit like a dorm-less hostel for grown-ups, this backstreet hotel has 13 compact rooms, all with different configurations, spread between two neighbouring buildings. Most have en suites and all of them are bright and tastefully designed, with nice linen and natty art. There's a cafe for breakfast, too, at the foot of the copper-clad stairwell.

Booklovers B&B   B&B **$$**
(Map p386; ☑04-384 2714; www.booklovers.co.nz; 123 Pirie St, Mt Victoria; r incl breakfast from $180; 🖙🍴) Author Jane Tolerton's elegant, book-filled B&B has four queen guest rooms (one with an extra single bed). A bus service runs past the front gate to Courtenay Pl and the train station, and the city's 'green belt' begins right next door (including the fab Pirie St Play Area). Free on-street parking.

Apollo Lodge   MOTEL **$$**
(Map p390; ☑04-385 1849; www.apollolodge. co.nz; 49 Majoribanks St, Mt Victoria; d/f/ste from $160/170/200; P🖙) Within staggering distance of Courtenay Pl, Apollo Lodge is a loose collation of a couple of dozen varied units, ranging from studios to family-friendly two-bedroom units with full kitchens, plus a new central block of eight roomy suites with lavishly tiled bathrooms. Great value for a location this close to the city and Majoribanks St eats.

Gilmer Apartment Hotel   HOTEL **$$**
(Map p386; ☑04-978 1400; www.10gilmer.co.nz; 10 Gilmer Tce; d/apt from $145/200; P🖙) There's a sassy, artsy vibe to this natty, 62-unit downtown apartment hotel with its black, mirrored corridors. Sizes range from compact studios to two-bedroom apartments, all with kitchens and laundries. Advance-purchase rates are a steal for this end of town.

Liberty Apartment Hotel   APARTMENT **$$**
(Map p390; ☑04-830 0993; www.libertyhotel. nz; 79 Taranaki St; 1-/2-/3-bedroom apt from $230/340/470; P🖙) About as central as you can get, Liberty opened its doors just a few years ago and has been winning over corporate fans with its tidy, stylish contemporary apartments, all with kitchen and laundry and most with city-rooftop views. Parking is $25 a night; gym passes are free.

★**Ohtel**   BOUTIQUE HOTEL **$$$**
(Map p390; ☑04-803 0600; www.ohtel.nz; 66 Oriental Pde, Oriental Bay; r from $270; 🖙) 🍴 Ever feel like you've walked into a design magazine? This bijou hotel has 10 individually decorated rooms over four levels, with immersive NZ scenes plastered above the bathtubs and original, mid-century Scandi-style furniture and ceramics, avidly collected by the architect owner. The best rooms have decks and harbour views. Cafe/wine bar on-site.

★**QT Wellington**   BOUTIQUE HOTEL **$$$**
(Map p390; ☑04-802 8900; www.qtwellington. com; 90 Cable St; r/apt from $335/360; 🖙🍴) Formerly known as 'Museum Hotel de Wheels' (to make way for Te Papa, it was rolled here from its original location 120m away), this five-storey, art-filled hotel keeps the quirk-factor high. Back lifts open onto darkened corridors leading to flamboyantly decorated rooms with kitchenettes, laundry facilities and pervasive hippopotamus-meets-chandelier style.

Bolton Hotel   HOTEL **$$$**
(Map p386; ☑04-472 9966; www.boltonhotel. co.nz; 12 Bolton St; r from $300; 🖙🍴) Visiting diplomats and corporate types flock to the Bolton (139 rooms, 19 floors), spreading their paperwork across rooms of all shapes and sizes, united by a common theme of muted tones, fine linens and colourful art. Most have full kitchens; some come with park or city views. Independent and just a bit arty.

✕ Eating

Wellington offers a bewildering array of eating options: raffish cafes, upmarket restaurants and oodles of noodles. Stiff competition keeps standards high. Check out www.concreteplayground.com/wellington for new openings.

WELLINGTON REGION WELLINGTON

★ Leeds Street Bakery
BAKERY $

(Map p390; ☑04-802 4278; www.leedsstbakery. co.nz; Unit 6g, 14 Leeds St; mains $9-17; ☺7.30am-3.30pm Mon-Fri, 8.30am-3pm Sat) Watch the top-knotted bakers baking through the big picture window, then head inside to taste some scones, biscuits, cakes and lovely loaves, plus simple mains like halloumi on toast, bacon sandwiches and organic muesli with poached fruit and yoghurt. It's part of the old 1923 Hannah's shoe factory precinct; check out the amazing old employee photo across the laneway.

Little Penang
MALAYSIAN $

(Map p390; ☑04-382 9818; www.facebook.com/littlepenang; 40 Dixon St; mains $9-15; ☺11am-3pm & 5-9pm Mon-Fri, 11am-9pm Sat; ☑) Wellington has a bunch of great Malaysian diners, but Little Penang, in a resolutely scrappy area near the bottom of Cuba St, steals the show with its fresh-flavoured, fiery street food. Order *nasi lemak* (a fragrant rice dish) with the good eggy, nutty, saucy stuff; or go for the bargain $9 roti bread with curry. The lunchtime rush can border on the absurd.

Havana Coffee Works
CAFE $

(Map p390; ☑04-384 7041; www.havana.co.nz; 163 Tory St; snacks $4-8; ☺7am-4pm Mon-Fri) Continuing Wellington's unwavering obsession with all things Cuba, this fantastic retro-imaginative roastery and coffee lounge offers heart-jolting coffee and smiles all round. Nibbles are limited to the likes of scones, bagels, cakes and pies from the warmer. There's also a takeaway counter in the roastery, open till 5pm.

Caffe L'affare
CAFE $

(Map p390; ☑04-385 9748; www.laffare.co.nz; 27 College St; mains $11-20; ☺7am-4pm Mon-Fri, 8am-4pm Sat, 9am-4pm Sun; ☑) One of Wellington's pioneering coffee-roasting cafes (since 1990), L'affare's mod-industrial lines and backstreet vibes feel as fresh as ever. Aside from predictably good bean-brews, expect cooked breakfasts, soups, burgers, steaks, salads and monster-big cheese scones. Look for the patriotic row of NZ flags and the sunny scatter of tables out the front.

Enigma
CAFE $

(Map p390; ☑04-385 2905; www.enigma cafe.co.nz; 128 Courtenay Pl; mains $10-25; ☺7.30am-midnight Mon-Thu, to 2am Fri, to 3am Sat, 8am-midnight Sun) Enigmatic Enigma is the pick of the late-night coffee haunts around Courtenay Pl – a grungy, weathered, lived-in and loved-in cafe serving bagels, lasagne, bacon butties, muffins, pasta salads and all things eggy. Blaring R'n'B, $25 jugs of sangria and a courtyard out the back: what's not to like?

Midnight Espresso
CAFE $

(Map p390; ☑04-384 7014; www.facebook.com/midnightespressowlg; 178 Cuba St; mains $8-17; ☺7.30am-3am Mon-Fri, 8am-3am Sat & Sun; ☑) Let it all hang out after midnight at this devilishly good late opener. Munch on some cheesy lasagne, sticky date pudding, brownies or spinach-and-basil muffins if you must, but caffeine is really why you're here. Dig the little brass repair plates in the old floorboards and the pinball machine.

Phoenician Falafel
LEBANESE $

(Map p390; ☑04-385 9997; 11 Kent Tce, Mt Victoria; mains $9-15; ☺11.30am–9.30pm Mon-Sat) In need of a mid-evening gap-filler? Roll into this long-running, no-frills Lebanese joint for authentic falafel, shish and shawarma (and equally no-frills service). The best kebabs, battered tables and vintage Beirut photos in town.

★ Husk
CAFE $$

(Map p390; ☑04-282 0583; www.huskbar. co.nz; 62 Ghuznee St; mains $14-24; ☺8am-late Mon-Fri, 9am-late Sat & Sun; ☎) Follow the throbbing basslines down the twinkling alley into Husk, where punky leather guys and laptop-wielding students convene for pork-shoulder tacos, chilli eggs and 'dirty' chips with beef brisket, house-smoked cheddar and red chimichurri. In true Wellington form, Husk is a brewery too: the Superunknown APA is appropriately rockin', while the Power of Voodoo white stout is irrefutably magical.

★ Fidel's
CAFE $$

(Map p390; ☑04-801 6868; www.fidelscafe.com; 234 Cuba St; mains $10-20; ☺7.30am-11pm Mon-Fri, 8am-11pm Sat, 9am-11pm Sun; ☑) A Cuba St institution for caffeine-craving rebels, Fidel's cranks out eggs any which way, pizzas, panini and fab salads, along with the city's best milkshakes. Revolutionary memorabilia adorns the walls of the low-lit interior, and there's a weathered outdoor area beneath a huge Cuban flag. The comrades in the kitchen cope with the chaos admirably. Pizzas from noon.

WELLINGTON REGION WELLINGTON

★ **Olive** BISTRO $$

(Map p390; ☑04-802 5266; www.oliverestau
rant.co.nz; 170 Cuba St; mains brunch $10-24, din-
ner $29-40; ☺8am-10pm Tue-Sat, to 3pm Sun &
Mon) Olive boldly attempts to be all things
to all Wellingtonians: breakfast cafe, noc-
turnal bistro, wine bar, craft-beer joint and
live-music venue...and somehow it all hangs
together (the disarmingly familiar '80s font
helps!). Switched-on staff shuffle plates of
Persian guacamole and smoked Kāpiti alba-
core croquettes across two shopfronts, and
into the compact secret-garden courtyard
out the back.

★ **Loretta** CAFE $$

(Map p390; ☑04-384 2213; www.loretta.net.nz;
181 Cuba St; mains $14-34; ☺9am-9.30pm Tue,
7am-9.30pm Wed & Thu, 7am-10pm Fri, 8am-10pm
Sat, 8am-8.30pm Sun; ☞) Italian? Fusion?
Wine bar? Loretta is a hard gal to catego-
rise, but she's won leagues of fans with her
classy, well-proportioned offerings served
in bright, airy surrounds. Split a wood-
fired chicken, sausage and fennel pizza
and a grain-filled salad between two, with
a couple of juniper negronis. Bookings for
lunch only.

Sweet Mother's Kitchen AMERICAN $$

(Map p390; ☑04-385 4444; www.sweetmothers
kitchen.co.nz; 5 Courtenay Pl; mains $8-26; ☺8am-
10pm; ☞) Perpetually brimming with cool
cats, Sweet Mother's serves tasty takes on
the Deep South, such as burritos, gumbo,
pulled-pork po'boys, jambalaya, grilled fish
tacos and Key lime pie. It's cheap and cute,
with a swamp-rock soundtrack, lots of vege-
tarian options and good sun.

Capitol ITALIAN $$

(Map p390; ☑04-384 2855; www.capitolresta
urant.co.nz; 10 Kent Tce, Mt Victoria; mains brunch
$14-29, dinner $28-39; ☺noon-3pm & 5.30-9.30pm
Mon-Fri, 9.30am-3pm & 5.30-9.30pm Sat & Sun)
This consistent culinary star – alongside the
Embassy Theatre (p402) and perfect for a
pre- or post-movie dinner – serves simple,
seasonal fare using premium local ingredients, with a nod to classic Italian cuisine. Try
the homemade *tagliolini* (ribbon pasta) or
the Parmesan-crusted lamb's liver with Gor-
gonzola spinach. The room resonates with
conversation over a black-and-white chequer-
board floor.

Aro Cafe CAFE $$

(Map p386; ☑04-384 4970; www.arocoffee.co.nz;
90 Aro St, Aro Valley; mains brunch $12-24, dinner
$22-33; ☺7.30am-4pm Mon & Tue, 7.30am-4pm
& 5.30-10pm Wed-Fri, 9am-4pm & 5.30-10pm Sat,
9am-5pm Sun; ☞) If this stretch of Aro St –
and this long-running licensed cafe in par-
ticular – were any more photogenic it'd be a
crime. Order from the cabinet or take a seat
and someone will bring you a menu (shoot
for the red vegan curry or the chilli scram-
ble). The coffee's great too. In the evening it
transitions into a neighbourhood bistro.

Shepherd FUSION $$

(Map p390; ☑04-385 7274; www.shepherdres
taurant.co.nz; 1/5 Eva St; mains brunch $16-25, din-
ner $29-36; ☺5.30pm-late Wed-Sat, 10.30am-late
Sun) Shepherd your dining companions up
the pink-and-purple steps into Shepherd for
on-trend fusion cuisine – just three entrées,
three mains and three desserts from which
to choose (hope for the Szechuan Cloudy
Bay clams with pork, kumara and corian-
der). There's a concrete-block bar on one

WELLINGTON REGION WELLINGTON

WELLINGTON FOR CHILDREN

Let's cut to the chase: Welly's biggest hit for kids is Te Papa (p383), with the whole
caboodle looking like it's curated by a team of five-year-old geniuses. It has interactive
activities galore, more creepy, weird and wonderful things than you can shake a squid at,
and heaps of special events for all ages. See the dedicated 'Kids & Families' page on the
website for proof of Te Papa's prowess in this department.

Conveniently located either side of Te Papa are Frank Kitts Park and Waitangi Park,
both with playgrounds and in close proximity to roller skates, ice creams, and life-saving
espresso for the grown-ups.

A ride up the cable car (p383) and a lap around the Wellington Botanic Gardens (p383)
will get the wee ones pumped up. When darkness descends head to Space Place (p383)
to gaze at galaxies far, far away. On a more terrestrial plane, kids can check out some
crazy New Zealand critters at the Wellington Zoo (p390) or Zealandia (p383).

side and open kitchen on the other, beneath a web of globes and cables.

Field & Green
BRITISH $$

(Map p390; ☑04-384 4992; www.fieldandgreen. co.nz; 262 Wakefield St; mains $15-36; ⊗8.30am-2.30pm & 5.30-9.30pm Wed-Fri, 9.30am-9.30pm Sat, 9.30am-2.30pm Sun) 'European soul food' is their slogan, but it's the best of British that dominates here, including Red Leicester scones, Welsh rarebit, kedgeree, fish-finger sarnies, bacon butties with HP sauce and pan-fried pork chops. It's actually way more sophisticated than it sounds, with a Scandi-chic sensibility to the decor and accomplished London-born chef Laura Greenfield at the helm.

Whistling Sisters Fermentery
BISTRO $$

(Map p390; ☑04-381 3208; www.whistlingsisters. co.nz/fermentery; 100 Taranaki St; mains brunch $11-24, dinner $22-29; ⊗3pm-late Tue-Thu, 11.30am-late Fri, 10am-late Sat & Sun) Yes, it's another Wellington craft-beer bar, but this one is just as much about good food as the good stuff in your glass. Roll up for some baked eggs and creamy pesto for brunch, then whistle in the door for some beer-battered fried chicken and a pint of New England IPA later on.

Scopa
ITALIAN $$

(Map p390; ☑04-384 6020; www.scopa.co.nz; cnr Cuba & Ghuznee Sts; pizza $12-31, mains $18-28; ⊗11am-late Mon-Fri, 9am-late Sat & Sun; ☑) Authentic pizza, pasta and gnocchi make dining at this modern *cucina* a pleasure. The *bianche* (white) pizzas change things up a bit, as do Monday-night pork-and-herb meatballs ($15). Weekday lunchtime pasta specials ($12); Peroni on tap.

Mt Vic Chippery
FISH & CHIPS $$

(Map p390; ☑04-382 8713; www.thechippery. co.nz; 5 Majoribanks St, Mt Victoria; meals $14-24; ⊗noon-8.30pm Mon-Thu, to 9pm Fri-Sun; ☑) At this backwater fish shack it's fish and chips by numbers: 1. Choose your fish (at least six varieties). 2. Choose your coating (beer batter, panko crumb, tempura…). 3. Choose your chips (five varieties!). 4. Add aioli, coleslaw, salad, sauce…and maybe a craft beer. 5. Chow-down inside or take away. Burgers, battered sausages and $8 weekday express fish-and-chip lunches, too.

★ Noble Rot
EUROPEAN $$$

(Map p390; ☑04-385 6671; www.noblerot.co.nz; 6 Swan La; mains $29-41; ⊗4pm-late) This warmly lit, atmospheric wine bar serves some of Wellington's best food. Euro influences pervade the menu, featuring the likes of charcuterie plates, duck-liver parfait, ricotta gnocchi and Spanish pork *pastirma* (cured beef). Prop yourself on a tall bentwood stool and survey the wine list: 400 bottles, with 80 by the glass. Cancel your other plans.

★ Logan Brown
BISTRO $$$

(Map p390; ☑04-801 5114; www.loganbrown.co.nz; 192 Cuba St; mains $39-48, 5-/7-course degustation menu $115/145, with wine $165/215; ⊗noon-2pm Wed-Sat & 5pm-late Tue-Sun; ☎) ✈ Deservedly ranked among Wellington's best restaurants, Logan Brown oozes class without being overly formal. Its 1920s banking-chamber dining room is a neoclassical stunner – a fitting complement to the produce-driven modern NZ cuisine. The three-course bistro menu ($50) won't hurt your wallet too badly, but the epic wine list and Saturday-night degustation menu might force a blow-out.

★ Ortega
SEAFOOD $$$

(Map p390; ☑04-382 9559; www.ortega.co.nz; 16 Majoribanks St, Mt Victoria; mains $36-40, set menus from $69; ⊗5.30pm-late) Mounted trout, salty portraits, marine-blue walls and Egyptian floor tiles cast a Mediterranean spell over Ortega – a magical spot for a seafood dinner. Fish comes many ways (including as zingy sashimi), while desserts continue the Mediterranean vibes with Catalan orange crêpes and one of Welly's best cheeseboards.

WBC
FUSION $$$

(Map p390; ☑04-499 9379; www.wbcrestaurant. co.nz; Level 1, 107 Victoria St; small plates $16-22, large $34-46; ⊗11.30am-10pm Tue-Sat) At the one-time Wholesale Boot Company, flavours from Thailand, China and Japan punctuate a menu filled with the best of NZ produce, including freshly shucked oysters and clams (served raw, steamed or tempura-battered) and marvellous meats (lamb neck massaman curry, venison *tataki*). Everything is packed with flavour and designed to be shared.

Charley Noble
MEDITERRANEAN $$$

(Map p386; ☑04-282 0205; www.charleynoble. co.nz; 1 Post Office Sq; mains $28-59; ⊗7am-late Mon-Fri, 5pm-late Sat & Sun) Buzzing to the point of mild chaos once the after-work crowd descends, this cavernous establishment occupies the gloriously renovated Huddart Parker building. Angle for a seat by the large open kitchen for a first-row view of the culinary action. Highlights include shucked-to-order oysters, wood-fired meats and divine natural wines.

🍷 Drinking & Nightlife

Wellingtonians love a boozy night. The inner city is riddled with bars, with high concentrations around raucous Courtenay Pl, bohemian Cuba St and along the waterfront. A creative live-music scene keeps things thrumming, along with great NZ wines and even better craft beer. See www.craftbeer capital.com for beery propaganda. For gig listings see www.undertheradar.co.nz and www.eventfinda.co.nz.

★ Golding's Free Dive   CRAFT BEER
(Map p390; ☑04-381 3616; www.goldingsfree dive.co.nz; 14 Leeds St; ⊙noon-midnight; 🛜) Hidden down a busy little back alley near Cuba St, gloriously garish Golding's is a bijou craft-beer bar with far too many merits to mention. We'll single out ex-casino swivel chairs, a nice wine list, a ravishing Reuben sandwich, and pizza from Pizza Pomodoro (Map p390; ☑04-381 2929; www.pizzapomo doro.co.nz; 13 Leeds St; pizza $15-26; ⊙5-9pm Mon, 11.30am-2pm & 5-9pm Tue-Thu, 11.30am-10pm Fri & Sat, 11.30am-9pm Sun; 🖉) next door. Blues, Zappa and Bowie conspire across the airways.

★ Library   BAR
(Map p390; ☑04-382 8593; www.thelibrary.co.nz; Level 1, 53 Courtenay Pl; ⊙5pm-late Mon-Thu, 4pm-late Fri-Sun) Into books, much? You'll find yourself in the right kind of bind at moody Library, with its velveteen booths, board games and swish cocktails. An excellent all-round drink selection is complemented by a highly shareable menu of sweet and savoury stuff. Killer cocktails, and live music every now and then.

★ El Culo Del Mundo   BAR
(Map p390; ☑04-801 6409; www.elculodelmundo. co.nz; 2 Roxburgh St, Mt Victoria; ⊙4pm-midnight Mon-Thu, 4pm-3am Fri, 11am-3am Sat, 11am-midnight Sun) If Charles Bukowski was gasping for a drink in Wellington, this is where he'd come – an authentic, atmospheric US-style bar serving great cocktails, fried-chicken tacos and cold beer in 16 taps. If you're wondering what the name means, it has something to do with the planet's anatomy (hilarious). Look for the literal red neon 'BAR' sign above the door.

Little Beer Quarter   CRAFT BEER
(Map p390; ☑04-803 3304; www.littlebeerquarter. co.nz; 6 Edward St; ⊙3.30pm-late Mon, noon-late Tue-Sat, 3pm-late Sun) Buried in a back lane, ochre-coloured LBQ is warm, inviting and moodily lit in all the right places. Fourteen well-curated taps (plus two hand-pulls) and a broad selection of bottled beer pack a hoppy punch. There are good cocktails, wines and whiskies, too, plus zesty bar food. Swing by for a $20 pizza and pint on Monday nights.

Hashigo Zake   CRAFT BEER
(Map p390; ☑04-384 7300; www.hashigozake. co.nz; 25 Taranaki St; ⊙noon-late; 🛜) This bricky bunker is the HQ for a zealous beer-import business, splicing big-flavoured international brews into a smartly selected NZ range. Hopheads stand elbow to elbow around the bar, ogling the oft-changing taps and brimming fridges, and squeeze into the sweet little side-lounge on live-music nights (Saturdays, usually).

Garage Project Taproom   CRAFT BEER
(Map p386; ☑04-802 5324; www.garageproject. co.nz; 91 Aro St, Aro Valley; ⊙3-10pm Mon-Fri, noon-10pm Sat & Sun) The actual Garage Project brewery occupies a former petrol station just down the road (68 Aro St), serving beer by the litre, petrol-pump style. If you'd rather consume your brew in less industrial quantities, head to this stylish little bar with 18 taps. Chance your arm on the Snug Juice stout or Fugazi session ale.

Fortune Favours   CRAFT BEER
(Map p390; ☑04-595 4092; www.fortunefavours. beer; 7 Leeds St; ⊙11am-11pm Sun-Thu, to midnight Fri & Sat) The brave? You won't need much courage to enjoy the rusty-panelled rooftop bar atop this old furniture factory, sipping beers brewed in the shiny vats downstairs. Along with its own concoctions, it serves guest brews, wine and cocktails. Head inside if the weather is inclement (Wellington and 'clement' don't coincide too often). Look for the huge hand on the wall.

Dirty Little Secret   ROOFTOP BAR
(Map p390; ☑021 0824 0298; https://dirtylittle secret.co.nz; Level 8, 7-8 Dixon St; ⊙3pm-late Mon-Sun; 🛜) While it's not strictly a secret (it's packed to the gills on balmy evenings) this hip bar atop the historic Hope Gibbons Ltd building plays hard to get, with a nondescript entrance on Taranaki St. Expect some beaut craft beers, slugged-together cocktails, loud indie music and plastic awnings straining to keep the elements at bay.

Black Sparrow   COCKTAIL BAR

(Map p390; ☑04-384 7632; www.theblack sparrow.co.nz; 10a Majoribanks St, Mt Victoria; ⊙10am-midnight Sun-Wed, to 2am Thu-Sat) Tucked into the back-end of the elegant art-deco Embassy Theatre, this little avian bar is a noir, filmic spot for a cocktail or two after the movie. The 'Found Footage' with Strega, yellow chartreuse, lime, mango and mint is delightfully incongruous on a cold Wellington night. Vague whiff of popcorn.

Panhead   CRAFT BEER

(Map p390; ☑04-213 9756; www.facebook.com/ panheadtory; 1 Tory St; ⊙11.30am-11pm Mon-Thu, to midnight Fri & Sat, 9.30am-11pm Sun) Named after a loud Harley-Davidson, the city outlet of this Upper Hutt brewery has a rusted motor built into the bar and beer taps made from exhaust pipes. All sounding a bit macho? Correct. But being Wellington, there are as many kids and glam gals as bearded biker blokes on the sunny terrace. Try the Vandal IPA.

Rogue & Vagabond   CRAFT BEER

(Map p390; ☑04-381 2321; www.rogueandvaga bond.co.nz; 18 Garrett St; ⊙11am-late) Fronting onto a precious pocket park, the Rogue is a scruffy, colourful, kaleidoscopic craft-beer bar with heaps of good beers flowing through 18 taps. Voluminous, chewy-crust pizza, burgers, po'boys, alcoholic milkshakes and regular gigs add further appeal. Swill around on the patio or slouch on the lawn. Oh, and $2 'Taco Tuesdays'!

Hawthorn Lounge   COCKTAIL BAR

(Map p390; ☑04-890 3724; www.hawthorn lounge.co.nz; Level 1, 82 Tory St; ⊙5pm-3am Mon-Sat) This classy cocktail bar has a 1920s speakeasy feel, suited-up in waistcoats and wide-brimmed fedoras. Sip a whisky sour and play poker, or watch the behind-the-bar theatrics from the house mixologists, twisting the classics into modern-day masterpieces. Open till the wee smalls; don't dress lazy.

Counter Culture   BAR

(Map p390; ☑04-891 2345; www.counterculture. co.nz; 211 Victoria St; 3hr of games $5; ⊙noon-10pm Mon-Thu, to 11pm Fri, 11am-11pm Sat, 11am-10pm Sun; 🛜🌐) Who doesn't secretly love a board game? Assume an ironic stance if you must, but here's the chance to embrace your inner games nerd in public. There are almost 600 games to choose from (Battleship!

They have Battleship!) plus Fortune Favours craft beers and cocktails to take the edge off your ugly competitive streak.

Arborist   ROOFTOP BAR

(Map p390; ☑04-931 6161; www.thearborist.co.nz; 166 Willis St; ⊙noon-late) High atop the Trinity Hotel, the Arborist doesn't demonstrate any gardening prowess: aside from the odd cactus, most of the plants here are plastic and the old lawnmower by the entry probably isn't necessary. But the city skyline views are superb, the reggae is chilled and there's endless Tuatara on tap. Happy hour(s) 4pm to 6pm.

Southern Cross   PUB

(Map p390; ☑04-384 9085; www.thecross.co.nz; 39 Abel Smith St; ⊙8am-late Mon-Fri, 9am-late Sat & Sun; 🌐) Welcoming to all – from frenetic five-year-olds unloading boxes of toys to knitting nanas – the democratic Cross rambles around a buzzy bar, dance floor, pool table and the best garden bar in town. There's good beer on tap, food for all wallet widths and regular events (gigs, quiz nights, karaoke, salsa classes).

Ivy   GAY & LESBIAN

(Map p390; ☑04-282 1580; www.ivybar.co.nz; 63 Cuba St; ⊙7pm-late Tue-Sat) Descend the darkened stairs to the clubbiest of Wellington's queer venues. Expect a fun young crowd, including plenty of mic-hoggers on karaoke nights.

☆ Entertainment

Wellington has a simmering theatre scene and is the home of large national companies such as the Royal NZ Ballet and the NZ Symphony Orchestra. Most shows can be booked via Ticketek (www.ticketek.co.nz), Ticketmaster (www.ticketmaster.co.nz) and Ticket Rocket (www.ticketrocket.co.nz). Discounted same-day tickets for productions are sometimes available at the i-SITE (p404).

There are some excellent indie cinemas here, plus the usual mainstream megaplexes. For listings see www.flicks.co.nz.

★ Embassy Theatre   CINEMA

(Map p390; ☑04-384 7657; www.embassytheatre. co.nz; 10 Kent Tce; tickets adult/child $18/12; ⊙10am-late) Wellywood's cinema mother ship is an art-deco darling, built in the 1920s. Today she screens mainly mainstream films with state-of-the-art sound and vision. Be sure to check out the glam Black Sparrow cocktail bar out the back.

Light House Cinema
CINEMA

(Map p390; ☑04-385 3337; www.lighthouse cinema.co.nz; 29 Wigan St; tickets adult/child $17.50/13.50; ⊙10am-late; 🖥) Tucked away near the top end of Cuba St, this small, stylish cinema throws a range of mainstream, art-house and foreign films up onto the screens in three small theatres. High-quality snacks; Tuesday tickets $11.50.

San Fran
LIVE MUSIC

(Map p390; ☑04-801 6797; www.sanfran.co.nz; 171 Cuba St; ⊙3pm-late Tue-Sat) This much-loved, midsize music venue wheels out craft beer and smoky, meaty food to go along with the rock. Dancing is near mandatory, and the balcony gets good afternoon sun.

Meow
LIVE MUSIC

(Map p390; ☑04-385 8883; www.welovemeow. co.nz; 9 Edward St; ⊙4pm-late Tue-Fri, 8pm-late Sat) Truly the cat's pyjamas, Meow goes out on a limb to host a diverse range of gigs and performances: country, ragtime, DJs, acoustic rock, jazz, poetry... At the same time the kitchen plates up good-quality, inexpensive food at any tick of the clock. Mishmashed retro decor; cool craft beers.

Michael Fowler Centre
CONCERT VENUE

(Map p390; ☑04-801 4231; www.venueswelling ton.com; 111 Wakefield St) The city's major concert hall stages regular performances by the NZ Symphony Orchestra (www.nzso.co.nz), Orchestra Wellington (www.orchestrawel lington.co.nz) and assorted pop stars and contemporary musicians.

Opera House
CONCERT VENUE

(Map p390; ☑04-801 4231; www.venueswell ington.com; 113 Manners St; hhours vary with shows) This grand old heritage theatre hosts big-ticket productions such as the Royal NZ Ballet (www.rnzb.org.nz) and NZ Opera (www.nzopera.com), plus the odd rocker and comedian.

Circa Theatre
THEATRE

(Map p390; ☑04-801 7992; www.circa.co.nz; 1 Taranaki St; ⊙box office 10am-2pm Mon, to 7pm Tue-Thu, to 8pm Fri & Sat, 1-4.30pm Sun) This black-and-white waterfront theatre, built onto the side of a historic facade, has two auditoriums in which it shows everything from edgy new works to Christmas panto. Cafe/wine bar on-site.

BATS
THEATRE

(Map p390; ☑04-802 4175; www.bats.co.nz; 1 Kent Tce; ⊙hours vary with shows) Wildly alternative

---

WELCOME TO WELLYWOOD

In recent years Wellington has stamped its name firmly on the world map as the home of New Zealand's dynamic film industry, earning itself the nickname 'Wellywood'. Acclaimed director Sir Peter Jackson still calls Wellington home; the success of his *The Lord of the Rings* films and subsequent productions such as *King Kong*, *The Adventures of Tintin* and *The Hobbit* have made him a powerful Hollywood player, and have bolstered Wellington's reputation.

Canadian director James Cameron is also in on the action; shooting has commenced for his four *Avatar* sequels, the first of which is due for a 2020 release. Cameron and his family are NZ residents, with landholding in rural Wairarapa. They have that in common with Jackson, who also has a property there.

Movie buffs can experience some local movie magic by visiting the Weta Workshop (p388) or one of many film locations around the region – a speciality of local guided-tour companies.

but accessible BATS presents cutting-edge and experimental NZ theatre – varied, cheap and intimate – in its revamped theatre.

🔒 Shopping

Wellington supports a host of independent shops including scores of design stores and clothing boutiques. Despite cheap imports and online shopping, there's still plenty that's Kiwi-made here. Retailers fly their home-grown flags with pride.

★ Unity Books
BOOKS

(Map p390; ☑04-499 4245; www.unitybooks. co.nz; 57 Willis St; ⊙9am-6pm Mon-Thu, to 7pm Fri, 10am-6pm Sat, 10am-5pm Sun) Sets the standard for every bookshop in the land, with dedicated NZ tables piled high, plus regular book launches, author readings and literary events. We could stay all day.

★ Slow Boat Records
MUSIC

(Map p390; ☑04-385 1330; www.slowboat records.co.nz; 183 Cuba St; ⊙9.30am-5.30pm Mon-Thu, to 7.30pm Fri, 10am-5pm Sat & Sun) Country, folk, pop, indie, metal, blues, soul, rock, Hawaiian nose-flute music – it's all here at Slow Boat, Wellington's long-running music shop and Cuba St mainstay.

Goodness
FASHION & ACCESSORIES

(Map p390; ☑ 04-801 6439; www.goodness.co.nz; 19 College St; ⊙ 10am-5pm Mon-Fri, to 4pm Sat, 11am-4pm Sun) There's goodness by the bucketload here, from the charmingly OTT staff through to lovely NZ jewellery, nail polish, belts, shoes, jeans and dresses from Goodness' own label.

Bello
GIFTS & SOUVENIRS

(Map p390; ☑ 04-385 0058; www.bello.co.nz; 140 Willis St; ⊙ 9.30am-6pm Mon-Fri, 10am-4pm Sat & Sun) A sweet little boutique full of gorgeous things – not least of which are the charming staff, who will point you in the direction of designer Euro glassware, ceramics, refined fragrances, floaty scarves and luxurious homewares.

Harbourside Market
MARKET

(Map p390; ☑ 04-495 7895; www.harboursidemarket.co.nz; cnr Cable & Barnett Sts; ⊙ 7.30am-1pm Sun) Around 25,000 locals visit this market every Sunday, shopping for everything from a jar of raspberry jam to an heirloom carrot, paleo sourdough loaf, plate of dumplings or Chilean empanada. Buskers attempting Led Zeppelin, 45-year-old skateboarders...it's all very Wellington.

Hunters & Collectors
CLOTHING

(Map p390; ☑ 04-384 8948; www.facebook.com/huntersandcollectorswellington; 134 Cuba St; ⊙ 10.30am-6pm Mon-Fri, to 5.30pm Sat, 11am-5pm Sun) Beyond the best-dressed window in NZ (since 1985) you'll find off-the-rack and vintage clothing (punk, skate, Western and mod), plus shoes and accessories.

Wellington Night Market
MARKET

(Map p390; ☑ 021 0281 8785; www.wellingtonnightmarket.co.nz; Left Bank, Cuba Mall; ⊙ 5-11pm Fri & Sat) Nocturnal fun and games on Cuba St, with international foods aplenty and more buskers and performers than you have eyes and ears. On Saturdays it moves a block down the road to the corner of Manners St.

Old Bank
SHOPPING CENTRE

(Map p386; ☑ 04-922 0600; www.oldbank.co.nz; 233-237 Lambton Quay; ⊙ 9am-6pm Mon-Fri, to 5.30pm Sat, 9.30am-5pm Sun) This dear old building on a wedge-shaped city site is home to an arcade of indulgent, high-end shops, predominantly jewellers, salons and boutiques, plus a couple of cafes. Check out the fab tiled floors and Corinthian columns.

ℹ Information

EMERGENCY & IMPORTANT NUMBERS

Ambulance, fire service and police	☑ 111
Lifeline Aotearoa	☑ 0800 543 354
Sexual Abuse Help Foundation	☑ 04-801 6655
Wellington Central Police Station	☑ 04-381 2000

INTERNET ACCESS

Free wi-fi is available throughout most of downtown Wellington (www.cbdfree.co.nz).

MEDICAL SERVICES

UFS Pharmacy (☑ 04-384 9499; www.ufs.co.nz; 47 Courtenay Pl; ⊙ 8.30am-6pm Mon, 8am-6pm Tue-Fri, 10am-2pm Sat) Handy city-centre pharmacy.

Wellington Accident & Urgent Medical Centre (☑ 04-384 4944; www.wamc.co.nz; 17 Adelaide Rd, Mt Cook; ⊙ 8am-11pm) No appointment necessary; also home to an after-hours pharmacy.

Wellington Regional Hospital (☑ 04-385 5999; www.ccdhb.org.nz; 49 Riddiford St, Newtown; ⊙ 24hr) Has a 24-hour emergency department; 1km south of the city centre.

MONEY

Major banks with ATMs are clustered along Courtenay Pl, Willis St and Lambton Quay. For currency exchange, try **Travel Money NZ** (☑ 0800 732 304; www.travelmoney.co.nz; 280 Lambton Quay; ⊙ 9am-6pm Mon-Fri, to 5pm Sat, 10am-5pm Sun).

POST

Post Office (Map p390; ☑ 04-472 7510; www.nzpost.co.nz; 49 Manners St; ⊙ 8.30am-5.30pm Mon-Fri, 9am-1pm Sat) Inside the Manners Night 'N Day convenience store.

TOURIST INFORMATION

DOC Kāpiti Wellington Visitor Centre (Map p390; ☑ 04-384 7770; www.doc.govt.nz; 18 Manners St; ⊙ 9.30am-5pm Mon-Fri, 10am-3.30pm Sat) Maps, bookings, passes and information for local and national walks (including Great Walks), parks, huts, camping and Kāpiti Island.

Wellington i-SITE (Map p390; ☑ 04-802 4860; www.wellingtonnz.com; 111 Wakefield St; ⊙ 8.30am-5pm Mon-Fri, 9am-5pm Sat & Sun; 🛜) Staff book almost everything here, and cheerfully distribute Wellington's *Official Visitor Guide*, along with other maps and helpful pamphlets.

ℹ Getting There & Away

AIR

Wellington is an international gateway to NZ. **Wellington Airport** (WLG; ☎ 04-385 5100; www.wellingtonairport.co.nz; Stewart Duff Dr, Rongotai) has the usual slew of airport accoutrements: info kiosks, currency exchange, ATMs, car-rental desks, shops, espresso... If you're in transit or have an early flight, note that you can't linger overnight inside the terminal (it closes between 1.30am and 3.30am).

Domestic services include:

Air New Zealand (www.airnewzealand.co.nz) Flies to/from Auckland, Hamilton, Tauranga, Rotorua, Gisborne, Napier, New Plymouth, Palmerston North, Nelson, Blenheim, Christchurch, Timaru, Queenstown, Dunedin and Invercargill.

Golden Bay Air (www.goldenbayair.co.nz) Flies to/from Takaka.

Jetstar (www.jetstar.com) Services Auckland, Christchurch and Queenstown.

Sounds Air (☎ 0800 505 005; www.soundsair.com) For Taupō, Blenheim, Picton, Nelson and Westport.

BOAT

On a clear day, sailing into Wellington Harbour or into Picton in the Marlborough Sounds is magical. Cook Strait can cut up rough, but the big ferries handle it well, and offer the distractions of sport lounges, cafes, bars, information desks and cinemas.

Car-hire companies allow you to pick up and drop off vehicles at ferry terminals. If you arrive outside business hours, arrangements can be made to collect your vehicle from the terminal car park.

There are two ferry options:

Bluebridge Ferries (Map p386; ☎ 04-471 6188; www.bluebridge.co.nz; 50 Waterloo Quay, Pipitea; adult/child/car/campervan/motorbike from $50/26/120/185/54; 📶) Up to four sailings between Wellington and Picton daily (3½ hours).

Interislander (Map p386; ☎ 04-498 3302; www.interislander.co.nz; Aotea Quay, Pipitea; adult/child/car/campervan/motorbike from $56/28/123/188/56) Up to five sailings between Wellington and Picton daily; crossings take 3¼ to 3½ hours. A free shuttle bus heads from platform 9 at Wellington Railway Station to Aotea Quay, 50 minutes before every daytime sailing, and returns 20 minutes after every arrival.

BUS

Wellington is a major terminus for North Island bus services.

InterCity (Map p386; ☎ 04-385 0520; www.intercity.co.nz) coaches depart several times daily from Platform 9 at Wellington Railway Station. Destinations include Auckland (from $30, 11¼ hours), Rotorua (from $29, 7½ hours), Taupō (from $33, six hours), Napier (from $23, 5¼ hours), Palmerston North (from $18, 2¼ hours) and New Plymouth (from $29, seven hours).

Also departing from Platform 9, **Skip** (☎ 09-394 9180; www.skip.travel) is a budget service running between Wellington and Auckland ($16, 11½ hours) via Taupō ($12, 6¼ hours), Rotorua ($13, 5¾ hours) and Hamilton ($15, 9½ hours). Connections to Tauranga and Whangarei also available.

TRAIN

Regular **Metlink** (☎ 0800 801 700; www.metlink.org.nz) commuter trains head as far as Paekākāriki ($10.50, 46 minutes), Paraparaumu ($12, 55 minutes), Waikanae ($13, one hour) and Masterton ($19, 1¾ hours).

Three days a week the **Northern Explorer** (www.greatjourneysofnz.co.nz) heads to/from Palmerston North (from $69, two hours), Ōhakune (from $109, five hours), National Park Village (from $109, 5¼ hours), Hamilton (from $179, 8½ hours) and Auckland (from $179, 11 hours).

Run by the same folks (Great Journeys), the weekday morning Capital Connection heads to Wellington from Palmerston North ($35, two hours), Waikanae ($14.50, one hour) and Paraparaumu ($13.50, 50 minutes), returning in the evening.

ℹ Getting Around

Metlink is the one-stop shop for Wellington's regional bus, train and harbour ferry networks; there's a handy journey planner on its website. You can pay by cash or use **Snapper** (www.snapper.co.nz), an integrated prepaid smart card. The Snapper fares are cheaper ($1.71 for a one-zone trip as opposed to $2.50) but the card costs $10, so it's probably not worth purchasing for a short stay.

TO/FROM THE AIRPORT

Wellington Airport is 6km southeast of the city. **Wellington Combined Shuttles** (☎ 04-387 8787; www.co-opshuttles.co.nz; 1/2/3 passengers $20/26/32) provides a door-to-door minibus service (15 minutes) between the city and airport. It's cheaper if two or more passengers are travelling to the same destination. Shuttles meet all arriving flights.

The **Airport Flyer** (☎ 04-387 8700; www.airportflyer.co.nz; cash fare to city adult/child $12/9; 📶) bus runs between the airport, Wellington Railway Station and Lower Hutt every 20 minutes (every 10 minutes in peak hours) from around 6am to 8pm.

A taxi between the city centre and the airport takes around 15 minutes and costs $30 to $40.

BICYCLE

If you're fit or keep to the flat, cycling is a viable option. If you'd like some extra help on the hills, consider an electric bike. They're available from Switched On Bikes (p391), along with regular human-powered ones. Also try **My Ride Wellington** (Map p390; 04-384 8480; www.myride. co.nz/wellington; 181 Vivian St; city & mountain bikes per day/week $40/150; 8.30am-5.30pm Mon-Fri, 9am-5pm Sat, 10am-4pm Sun) for bike hire.

BUS

Frequent and efficient Metlink (p405) buses cover the whole Wellington region, running between approximately 6am and 11.30pm. The main **bus terminal** (Map p386; Lambton Quay) is near the Wellington Railway Station; there's another hub on Courtenay Pl near the Cambridge Tce intersection. Pick up route maps and timetables from the i-SITE (p404) and convenience stores, or online.

Metlink also runs **After Midnight** buses, departing from two city stops (Courtenay Pl and Manners St) between midnight and 4.30am Saturday and Sunday, following a number of routes to the outer suburbs. There's a set $7 fare for most trips.

CAR & MOTORCYCLE

There are a lot of one-way streets in Wellington, and parking gets tight (and pricey) during the day. If you've got a car or a caravan, park on the outskirts and walk or take public transport into the city centre. Freedom camping is permitted for self-contained vehicles at Evans Bay marina, 3km southeast of the city centre.

Along with the major international rental companies, Wellington has various lower-cost operators including **Apex Car Rental** (04-388 6581; www.apexrentals.co.nz; 363 Broadway, Miramar; 7am-7pm) and **Omega Rental Cars** (04-388 4337; www.omegarentalcars. com; 5 Tauhinu Rd, Miramar; 7.30am-5pm), all with near-airport locations. Most agencies have offices both at the airport and in the city centre. If you plan on exploring both the North and South Islands, most companies suggest you leave your car in Wellington and pick up another one in Picton after crossing Cook Strait. This is a common (and more affordable) practice, and car-hire companies make it a painless exercise.

There are often cheap deals on car relocation from Wellington to Auckland, as most renters travel in the opposite direction. The catch is that you may have only 24 or 48 hours to make the journey.

SCOOTER

Everywhere you look in central Wellington you'll see seemingly abandoned electric scooters with helmets dangling from their handlebars. **Flamingo Scooters** (04-260 3340; www. flamingoscooters.co.nz) is the main player: download the app and sign up, then it's $1 to unlock a scooter and 30c per minute thereafter. Fun!

TAXI

Packed taxi ranks can be found on Courtenay Pl, at the corner of Dixon St and Victoria St, on Featherston St, and outside the railway station. Major operators include **Green Cabs** (0800 464 7336; www.greencabs.co.nz) and **Wellington Combined Taxis** (04-384 4444; www. taxis.co.nz). There are also plenty of Uber drivers in the city.

TRAIN

Metlink (p405) operates five train routes running through Wellington's suburbs to regional destinations. Trains run frequently from around 6am to 11pm, departing Wellington Railway Station. The lines are as follows:

Johnsonville Via Ngaio and Khandallah.

Kāpiti Via Porirua, Plimmerton, Paekākāriki and Paraparaumu.

Melling Via Petone.

Hutt Valley Via Waterloo to Upper Hutt.

Wairarapa Via Featherston, Carterton and Masterton.

Timetables are available from convenience stores, the train station, Wellington i-SITE (p404) and online. Fares are zone-based; there's a handy calculator on the Metlink site. For visitors, **Metlink Explorer** day tickets give you unlimited bus and train travel after 9am within specified zones: the Zone 1–10 pass ($20) will get you to the Kāpiti Coast and back; the Zone 1–14 pass ($25) will get you to the Wairarapa return.

KĀPITI COAST

With long, driftwood- and pumice-strewn beaches, often with nobody on them, the Kāpiti Coast acts as a summer playground and suburban extension for Wellingtonians. The region takes its name from Kāpiti Island, a wildlife sanctuary 5km offshore from Paraparaumu.

The mountainous Tararua Forest Park forms a dramatic backdrop along the length of the coastline and has some accessible day walks and longer hikes.

The Kāpiti Coast makes an easy day trip from Wellington, though if you're after a chilled-out break there's enough here to keep you out of mischief for a few days.

ℹ️ Information

For online Kāpiti Coast info, see www.kapiticoast.govt.nz.

ℹ️ Getting There & Away

Access to the the Kāpiti Coast is a snap: it's just a short drive north of Wellington, there are good bus and train connections to/from both Auckland and Wellington, and there's an airport in Paraparaumu.

AIR

Kāpiti Coast Airport (☑ 04-298 1013; www.kapiticoastairport.co.nz; 60 Toru Rd, Paraparaumu) is in central Paraparaumu. Sounds Air (p405) flies to/from Blenheim and Nelson; **Air Chathams** (☑ 0800 580 127; www.airchathams.co.nz) flies to/from Auckland.

BUS

InterCity (p405) coaches stop at the major Kāpiti Coast towns, continuing to/from Wellington, Napier, New Plymouth, Taupō and Auckland.

Metlink (p405) runs local bus services around Paraparaumu and Waikanae – handy for getting from the train station to the beach.

CAR & MOTORCYCLE

Getting here from Wellington is a breeze by car: just follow SH1. After Paekākāriki the Kāpiti Expressway takes over, but note that older sat-nav devices might have apoplectic meltdowns over this route, which only opened in 2017.

TRAIN

Metlink (p405) commuter trains between Wellington and the coast are more convenient and more frequent than buses. Services run from Wellington to Waikanae ($13, one hour) departing half-hourly 5am to midnight, stopping in Paekākāriki ($10.50, 45 minutes) and Paraparaumu ($12, 50 minutes) en route.

Paekākāriki

POP 1610

The first stop-worthy Kāpiti Coast town you come to heading north from Wellington is cute little Paekākāriki, 41km north of the capital. It's an arty seaside village stretched along a black-sand beach, serviced by a train station.

Queen Elizabeth Park PARK
(☑ 04-292 8625; www.gw.govt.nz/qep; off Wellington Rd; ⊙ 8am-dusk; 🚗) 🌿 One of the last relatively unchanged areas of dunes and wetlands along the Kāpiti Coast, this undulating 650-hectare park offers swimming, walking, cycling, picnic spots and healthy-looking seagulls, as well as the Wellington Tramway Museum (☑ 04-292 8361; www.wellingtontrams.org.nz; Whareroa Rd, MacKay's Crossing, SH1; admission by donation, tram rides adult/child $12/6; ⊙ 11am-4pm Sat & Sun, daily Jan; 🚗) and a horse riding (☑ 027 355 3046; www.kapitistables.com; Whareroa Rd, MacKay's Crossing, SH1; 20min/40min/1hr/2hr rides $35/60/70/140; ⊙ 10am-4pm Sat & Sun or by appointment; 🚗) outfit. There are three entrances: off Wellington Rd in Paekākāriki, at MacKay's Crossing on SH1, and off the Esplanade in Raumati to the north.

Paekākāriki Escarpment Walkway WALKING
(www.wellingtonregionaltrails.com; SH1; ⊙ daylight hours) Take a hike along this magical 10km track from Paekākāriki south to Pukerua Bay, climbing 220m above the coastline with killer views out to Kāpiti Island. It's a steep, narrow and exposed trail – brilliant if you like a pulse-raising challenge, but not great if you're a vertigo sufferer! Kicks off near the corner of Ames St.

Paekākāriki Holiday Park HOLIDAY PARK $
(☑ 04-292 8292; www.paekakarikiholidaypark.co.nz; 180 Wellington Rd; sites unpowered & powered from $36, unit with/without bathroom from $100/75; 🅿️ 🛜) You couldn't say that this large, leafy park is fully engaged with NZ's contemporary holiday park zeitgeist ('No Visitors Allowed'), but it is well located, 1.5km north of the township at the southern entrance to Queen Elizabeth Park – good for walking and biking. Tidy hedges demarcate sites, and there's a range of cabins and tourist flats.

Finn's HOTEL $$
(☑ 04-292 8081; www.finnshotel.co.nz; 2 Beach Rd; d/2-bedroom unit from $155/295; 🅿️ 🛜) Finn's is a flashy beige suit in this low-key railway village, but redeems itself with spacious, corporate-comfy rooms, big bistro meals (mains $13 to $30) and plenty of craft beer on tap. Double glazing keeps the highway noise at bay.

⭐ **Beach Road Deli** CAFE $
(☑ 04-902 9029; www.beach-road-deli.com; 5 Beach Rd; mains $8-16, pizzas $13-23; ⊙ 7.30am-4pm Tue-Thu, Sat & Sun, to 8.30pm Fri; 🚗)

WORTH A TRIP

KĀPITI ISLAND

Kāpiti Island is the coastline's dominant feature, a rugged 10km by 2km isle that has been a protected reserve since 1897. Predator-free since 1998 (22,500 possums were eradicated here in the 1980s), it's now home to a remarkable range of birds, including many species that are extinct on the mainland.

To visit the island, you must make your arrangements in advance with one of two licensed operators: reconfirm your arrangements on the morning of departure, as sailings are weather-dependent. All boats depart from Paraparaumu Beach, which can be reached by Metlink train/bus from Wellington.

Tours

The island is open to day walkers (there are some fab trails here), limited each day to 100 people at Rangatira, where you can hike up to the 521m high point, Tuteremoana; and 60 visitors at the northern end, which has short, gentle walks to view points and around a lagoon.

Family-run Kāpiti Island Nature Tours (☑ 027 726 7525; www.kapitiislandnaturetours. co.nz; Pier Complex, 12/18 Marine Pde, Paraparaumu Beach) ✐ runs day tours ($184 including boat and lunch) to look at the island's birds (incredible in range and number), seal colony, history and Māori traditions. Overnight stays (from $384, including boat, meals and accommodation) include an after-dark walk in the bush to spot the rare little spotted kiwi. Ferry-only return fares are $82.

Kāpiti Island Eco Experience (☑ 027 271 9818; www.kapitiislandeco.co.nz; Kāpiti Boating Club, Kāpiti Rd, Paraparaumu Beach; return adult/child from $80/40; ☺ Sep-Jun) provides transport to/from Kāpiti Island (to Rangatira), along with guided walks ($20 extra). Fares include the DOC landing permit and a 30-minute presentation at the island's DOC centre. Sea-kayaking jaunts are also available (adult/child $160/80), and trips including transfers to/from Wellington ($185/145).

Information

More information about Kāpiti Island can be found in DOC's *Kāpiti Island Nature Reserve* brochure (downloadable from www.doc.govt.nz), or in person at DOC's Kāpiti Wellington Visitor Centre (p404).

Stocked with home-baked goodies (chubby muffins, bagels, pastrami-stuffed baguettes), this bijou deli and wood-fired pizzeria is heaven-sent for the hungry highway traveller. The coffee's as good as it gets, made by happy staff whistling along to a jazzy soundtrack. Pizzas happen from noon on Fridays: order the slow-roasted pork version with apple, caramelised fennel and chilli.

Paraparaumu

POP 25,270

Busy Paraparaumu is the Kāpiti Coast's major commercial and residential hotspot. It's a tale of two towns: the main hub on the highway, with its deeply unappealing shopping-mall sprawl; and Paraparaumu Beach, with its waterside park and walkway, decent swimming and winning views out to Kāpiti Island (island boat trips set sail from here). And if you're into craft beer and cars, you're in the right town!

The correct pronunciation is 'Pah-ra-pah-ra-*oo*-moo', meaning 'scraps from an oven', which is said to have originated when a Māori war party attacked the settlement and found only scraps of food remaining. It's a bit of a mouthful to pronounce; locals usually just corrupt it into 'Para-pa-ram'.

Southward Car Museum MUSEUM
(☑ 04-297 1221; www.southwardcarmuseum. co.nz; Otaihanga Rd; adult/child/family $20/5/45; ☺ 9am-4.30pm) This huge hangar-like museum looks like a 1960s university but houses one of Australasia's largest collections of antique and unusual cars. Check out the DeLorean, the German-built 1897 Lux and the 1950 gangster Cadillac, complete with bullet holes. Look for the signs off the expressway.

Our Lady of Lourdes Statue
STATUE

(access via 16 Tongariro St) Paraparaumu's oddest claim to fame is surely this 14m-high statue of the Madonna, looming over the town from a 75m-high hill. It was commissioned by the local Catholic priest in 1958 for the 100th anniversary of the Lourdes apparitions. The good lady herself is in good nick, but she's reached by a scrappy path through a dishevelled part of town, and most of the 14 *Stations of the Cross* that line the route are losing their battle to stay vertical.

Marine Parade Eatery
CAFE **$$**

(☑04-892 0098; https://marineparadeeatery.co.nz; 50 Marine Pde; mains $15-25; ⊙7am-4pm; ☜) Conjuring a vaguely Robinson Crusoe–esque look, this chipper cafe offers a sophisticated menu and terrific views of Kāpiti Island out the front window. Roll in for all-day bagels, some spicy chilli lentils with fried kale, tortillas and coconut yoghurt, or maybe just an afternoon glass of wine or cranberry-and-orange whisky sour.

Pram Beach
BISTRO **$$**

(☑04-298 8196; www.prambeach.co.nz; 24 Marine Pde; mains $10-29; ⊙noon-late Mon-Fri, 10am-late Sat & Sun, restaurant 5pm-late Thu-Sat) Covering a lot of bases (cafe, bar, restaurant, takeaway joint), black-painted Pram Beach is a newcomer to the Paraparaumu waterfront, facing off with the skate park, playground and Kāpiti Island across the channel. Budget burgers and dumplings anchor the menu, ascending to Umu restaurant's elevated offerings upstairs (market fish, handmade pastas, confit duck). Love the rooftop bar.

Tuatara Tap Room
CRAFT BEER

(☑04-296 1953; www.tuatarabrewing.co.nz; 7 Sheffield St; ⊙3-8pm Tue-Thu, 11am-8pm Fri-Sun) Visit the oldest and most famous of Wellington's craft breweries at its industrial-estate premises, where you can slurp a pint or two and chew some bar snacks (biersticks, nachos, pizzas). Book in advance for a heady Saturday afternoon tasting experience, matching four beers with beer-friendly edibles ($45, minimum eight people). Regular live bands and DJs.

Waikanae

POP 12,100

Beachy Waikanae has long been a retiree stomping ground, but in recent times has transformed itself into a growing, go-ahead town, bolstered by first-home-buyer flight from unaffordable Wellington. It's a cheery seaside enclave, good for some salt-tinged R&R and natural-realm experiences.

Ngā Manu Nature Reserve
NATURE RESERVE

(☑04-293 4131; www.ngamanu.co.nz; 74 Ngā Manu Reserve Rd; adult/child $18/8; ⊙10am-5pm; ☝) ✎ Waikanae's main visitor lure, Ngā Manu is a 15-hectare bird sanctuary dotted with picnic areas, bushwalks, aviaries and a nocturnal house with kiwi, owls and tuatara. The reserve's endangered long-fin eels get a feed at 2pm daily; guided bird-feeding tours run at 11am daily (adult/child $25/10 including admission). There are also sunset kiwi encounters on Fridays and Saturdays (adult/child $35/25, bookings essential) and accommodation in the simple, self-contained Theo's Cottage (from $140, sleeps four).

Hemi Matenga Memorial Park Scenic Reserve
FOREST

(☑04-384 7770; www.doc.govt.nz; off Tui Cres; ⊙daylight hours) FREE This 330-hectare reserve overlooking Waikanae contains a large remnant of native kohekohe forest. The reserve rises steeply from 150m to its highest point, Te Au (514m), a steep hike of three to four hours on the Te Au Track. The Kohekohe Walk is also here, an easy 30-minute amble on a well-formed path.

Kapiti Gateway Motel
MOTEL **$$**

(☑04-902 5876; www.kapitigateway.co.nz; 114 Main Rd; d/2-bedroom unit from $120/175; ☜☒) This tidy and welcoming motel may look old-fashioned from the outside, but the rooms have been updated, there's a solar-heated pool and, since the new expressway opened in 2017, it's no longer on the truck route into Wellington. All rooms have at least a microwave and a kettle; some have full kitchens.

Long Beach
BISTRO **$$**

(☑04-293 6760; www.facebook.com/longbeach waikanae; 40 Tutere St; mains $10-26; ⊙9am-late; ☜☝) Snare a seat in the large conservatory or garden bar at this uptempo, family-friendly cafe-bar – a sunny spot for an afternoon wine or ale, with live tunes on Sundays. The menu meanders from pizzas to daily soups, salads, big cooked brunches and an amazing fried pork-belly foldover with smoked pineapple chutney. Big, brown Waikanae Beach is just over the dunes.

THE WAIRARAPA

The Wairarapa is the large tract of land east and northeast of Wellington, beyond the Tararua and Remutaka Ranges. It is named after Wairarapa Moana – otherwise known as Lake Wairarapa, translating as 'sea of glistening waters'. This shallow 80-sq-km lake and the surrounding wetland is undergoing much-needed ecological restoration, redressing generations of livestock grazing. Fields of fluffy sheep still abound, as do vineyards and the associated hospitality businesses that have turned the Wairarapa into a decadent naughty-weekender for Wellingtonians.

In recent years this picturesque slice of NZ's rural heartland has gained an unlikely Hollywood connection, with blockbuster movie directors Sir Peter Jackson and James Cameron both putting down roots here.

🏃 Activities

Remutaka Cycle Trail CYCLING
(www.nzcycletrail.com) The 115km, three-day Remutaka Cycle Trail is one of the Ngā Haerenga New Zealand Cycle Trail 'Great Rides'. The trail kicks off at the head of Wellington Harbour before scaling the Remutaka Ranges, then spilling out around the western end of Palliser Bay.

ⓘ Getting There & Away

From Wellington, Metlink (p405) commuter trains run to Masterton ($19, 1¾ hours, five times daily on weekdays, twice daily on weekends), calling at several Wairarapa stations including Featherston and Carterton (though notably not Greytown or Martinborough).

InterCity (p405) has bus services between Masterton and Wellington ($56, 4½ hours) via Palmerston North ($21, two hours) five days a week (no Monday or Saturday buses).

ⓘ Getting Around

Metlink (p405) bus 200 heads from Masterton to Martinborough via Cartertown, Greytown and Featherston at least four times daily ($5.50, 1¼ hours).

Beyond the main towns, you'll need your own wheels. As is often the case in NZ, getting here is half the fun: the drive up over the ranges from Wellington is truly spectacular.

Martinborough

POP 1680

Laid out in the shape of a Union Jack with a leafy square at its heart, Martinborough (Wharekaka) is a photogenic town with endearing old buildings, surrounded by a patchwork of pasture and pinstripe grapevines. It's famed for its wineries, which lure visitors to swill some pinot noir, pair it up with fine food and snooze it off at boutique accommodation.

With most cellar doors arrayed around the edge of the town grid, Martinborough offers a uniquely accessible experience for oenophiles. It's possible to walk between the major wineries, but the classic Martinborough sight is of gaggles of merry pedal-powered punters getting ever more wobbly as the afternoon progresses.

🏃 Activities

If the weather is in agreement, a fun way to explore the Wairarapa wineries is by bicycle, as the flat landscape makes for puff-free cruising. Rental bikes are comfortable cruisers with saddlebags for your booty. We probably don't need to remind you to pay greater attention to your technique as the day progresses.

Rental outfitters include **Green Jersey Cycle Tours** (☑06-306 6027; www.greenjersey.co.nz; 16 Kitchener St; 6hr guided tours incl lunch $175, bike hire per half-/full day $30/40) 🖋, **Indi Bikes** (☑027 306 6090; www.indibikesmartinborough.co.nz; 8 Naples St; 1-6 seater $35-190 per day; ⊙10am-5.30pm), Martinborough Top 10 Holiday Park and Martinborough Wine Merchants (p413).

👉 Tours

Martinborough Wine Walks WINE
(☑06-306 9040; www.martinboroughwinewalks.com; per person $240) 🖋 Martinborough's wine zone is compact enough to experience on foot – and you won't need to nominate some poor sucker to drive! Six-hour walking tours visit three or four close-together cellar doors, and include all tastings and lunch (with a glass of wine). Operated by Martinborough Wine Merchants (p413).

Martinborough Wine Tours WINE
(☑06-306 8032; www.martinboroughwinetours.co.nz; tours half-/full day per person $99/195) Half- and full-day tours around the Martinborough vines (full-day includes lunch), plus longer trips including a detour to Cape Palliser ($310 per person). Ask about 'exclusive' chauffeur-driven tours for couples, if that's more your predisposition.

🎊 Festivals & Events

Toast Martinborough
FOOD & DRINK
(www.toastmartinborough.co.nz; ⊙Nov) A hugely popular wine, food and music event held on the third Sunday in November; book accommodation *waaay* in advance.

🛏 Sleeping

Martinborough Top 10 Holiday Park
HOLIDAY PARK $
(📞06-306 8946; www.mtop10.nz; 10 Vintners Lane, off Dublin St; unpowered/powered sites $44/48, unit with/without bathroom from $162/92; 🅿🛜🏊) Just five minutes' walk from town, this appealing campsite has grapevine views, shady trees and the town pool over the back fence. Cabins are simple but great value, freeing up your dollars for the cellar door. Good-quality bikes for hire, including tandems, will assist your explorations (from $29 per day).

Claremont
MOTEL $$
(📞06-306 9162; www.theclaremont.co.nz; 38 Regent St; 1-/2-bedroom units from $150/205; 🅿🛜) A classy accommodation enclave 15 minutes' walk from town, the Claremont has two-storey, self-contained units in great nick, modern studios with spa baths, and sparkling two-bedroom apartments, all at reasonable rates (even cheaper in winter and/or midweek). It's surrounded by tidy gardens with barbecue areas, and also offers bike hire.

Bonnieux Cottage
RENTAL HOUSE $$
(📞0274 546 959; www.bonnieuxcottage.co.nz; 44 Dublin St; d from $185, extra person $40; 🅿🛜) Behind a lovingly tended garden, this sky-blue weatherboard cottage (with decor best described as 'cottagey') sleeps five in three bedrooms (two doubles, one single). Sit on the porch and ogle the huge oak tree across the street, fronting historic St Andrews Church (1883). Bonnieux is a more recent arrival here: it was ambitiously relocated from Masterton late last century.

Aylstone Retreat
BOUTIQUE HOTEL $$$
(📞06-306 9505; www.aylstone.co.nz; 19 Huangarua Rd; r $290; 🅿🛜) Fronted by quirky sculptures and a white picket fence, this elegant retreat on the edge of town is a winning spot for the romantically inclined. Seven en-suite rooms exude flowery French-provincial charm and share a posh reading room. The whole shebang is surrounded by immaculate lawns, box hedges and chi-chi furniture.

🍴 Eating

Café Medici
CAFE $$
(📞06-306 9965; www.facebook.com/cafe medici1; 9 Kitchener St; mains lunch $12-24, dinner $32-37; ⊙8.30am-4pm daily & 6pm-late Fri & Sat) A perennial local favourite, this airy Italian cafe has a sunny courtyard, great coffee and happy staff (always a good sign). Tasty, home-cooked food includes muffins, Med-flavoured brunches and lunches (try the mushroom and white truffle risotto) and meatier dinner options ranging from fish and chips to steaks and pan-seared duck breast.

MĀORI NZ: WELLINGTON REGION

Referred to in legends as the 'mouth of Maui's fish' and traditionally called Te Whanganui-a-Tara, the Wellington area became known to Māori in the mid-19th century as 'Pōneke' (a transliteration of Port Nick, short for Port Nicholas, its English name at the time).

The major *iwi* (tribes) of the region were Te Āti Awa and Ngāti Toa. Ngāti Toa was the *iwi* of Te Rauparaha, who composed the now famous 'Ka Mate' *haka*. Like most urban areas, the city is now home to Māori from many *iwi*, sometimes collectively known as Ngāti Pōneke.

New Zealand's national museum, Te Papa (p383), has some awesome displays on Māori culture, trad and modern, as well as a colourful *marae* (meeting house). In its gift shop you can see excellent carving and other crafts, as you can in the gorgeous Kura (Map p390; 📞04-802 4934; www.kuragallery.co.nz; 19 Allen St; ⊙10am-6pm Mon-Fri, 11am-5pm Sat & Sun) and Ora (Map p390; 📞04-384 4157; www.oragallery.co.nz; 23 Allen St; ⊙9am-6pm Mon-Sat, 10am-5pm Sat, 10am-4pm Sun) galleries nearby.

Te Wharewaka o Pōneke (p393), Kāpiti Island Nature Tours (p408) and Kiwi Coastal Tours (p393) offer intimate insights into the Māori culture of the rugged coast around Wellington.

DON'T MISS

WAIRARAPA WINE COUNTRY

Wairarapa's world-renowned wine industry was nearly crushed in its infancy. The region's first vines were planted in 1883, but in 1908 the prohibition movement put a cap on that corker of an idea. It wasn't until the late 1970s that winemaking was revived, after Martinborough's terroir was discovered to be similar to that of Burgundy, France. A few vineyards sprang up, the number since ballooning to around 50 across the region. Martinborough is the undisputed hub of the action, but vineyards around Gladstone and Masterton are also on the up. Pinot noir is the region's most acclaimed variety, but sauvignon blanc also does well, as do aromatics and shiraz.

Wairarapa's wineries thrive on visitors: well-oiled cellar doors swing wide open for tastings. Most wineries charge a tasting fee (although many will waive it if you purchase a bottle); others are free. Some have a cafe or restaurant, while others will rustle up a picnic platter to be enjoyed in their gardens. Winter hours wind back to the minimum.

The *Wairarapa Visitor Guide* (available from local i-SITEs) has maps to aid your navigation. Read all about it at www.wairarapanz.com/martinborough-vineyards.

A few of our faves in Martinborough:

Ata Rangi (☑06-306 9570; www.atarangi.co.nz; 14 Puruatanga Rd; tastings $5, waived with purchase; ☉wine shop 10am-4pm, pre-booked tastings 11am & 2pm) 🍸

Coney Wines (☑06-306 8345; www.coneywines.co.nz; 107 Dry River Rd; ☉11am-4pm Fri-Sun Dec-Mar, Sat & Sun only Oct, Nov & Apr-Jul)

Haythornthwaite Wines (☑06-306 9889; www.ht3wines.co.nz; 45 Omarere Rd; tastings from $5; ☉noon-6pm Mon-Fri, 11am-6pm Sat & Sun) 🍸

Martinborough Vineyard (☑06-306 9122; www.martinborough-vineyard.co.nz; 89 Martins Rd, Te Kairanga Cellar Door; tasting $5, waived with purchase; ☉11am-4pm)

Poppies Martinborough (☑06-306 8473; www.poppiesmartinborough.co.nz; 91 Puruatanga Rd; ☉11am-4pm, closed Wed & Thu Jun-Aug)

Martinborough Hotel PUB FOOD $$
(☑06-306 9350; www.martinboroughhotel.co.nz; 10-12 Memorial Sq; mains $19-37; ☉11am-late Mon-Fri, 8.30am-late Sat & Sun) After a hard day's wine tasting, work your way into a quiet beer at this handsome 1882 pub. Most of the space is given over to diners, though, under the banner of the Union Square restaurant. Grab a seat on the sunny terrace and order the prawn linguine. Upstairs is a handful of plush suites (doubles from $250).

🍷 Drinking & Nightlife

Mesita Wine Bar WINE BAR
(☑06-306 8475; www.mesita.net; 14c Ohio St; ☉4pm-late Mon, Thu & Fri, 2pm-late Sat & Sun) Blink and you'll miss little Mesito, a tiny side-street wine bar. But follow the vintage rock and you'll soon find the door. Inside are excellent wines (mostly local with some far-flung stars), craft beers, killer cocktails and Mexican-inspired nibbles. Tasting flights are a good way to sample the vineyards that got away (four pinot noirs $28).

Martinborough Brewery MICROBREWERY
(☑06-306 6249; www.martinboroughbeer.com; 10 Ohio St; ☉2-7pm Mon & Tue, 11am-8pm Thu-Sun) It's hard to go anywhere in NZ these days and not find a craft brewery bubbling away in the corner. Martinborough is no exception. The brewery counters the town's prevailing wine vibe with its range of meaty brews (dark beers a speciality). Sip a tasting paddle or a pint on the sunny terrace out the front. Tours by arrangement.

☆ Entertainment

Circus CINEMA
(☑06-306 9442; www.circus.net.nz; 34 Jellicoe St; adult/child $16/11; ☉3pm-late Wed-Mon) Martinborough has its own stylish art-house cinema – a mod, micro-sized complex with two comfy studio theatres and a cafe opening out on to a sunny, somewhat Zen garden. Food offerings (mains $24 to $34) include pizza, curries, chowder and bar snacks. Take your Wairarapa wine into the movie with you.

🛍 Shopping

Martinborough Wine Merchants   WINE

(☑06-306 9040; www.martinboroughwinemerchants.com; 6 Kitchener St; ⊙9.30am-6pm) Adjoining the busy Village Cafe (☑06-306 8814; www.facebook.com/thevillagecafemartinborough; mains $12-26; ⊙8am-4pm; 🐾), this cavernous store is an excellent place to buy local wine and maybe taste some, too. They also sell divine comestibles (olive oil, relish, jam, coffee, chocolate) and rent out bikes ($30/40 per half/full day) for cellar-door adventures.

ℹ Information

Martinborough i-SITE (☑06-306 5010; www.wairarapanz.com; The Square, cnr Cork & Texas Sts; ⊙9am-4pm Mon-Fri, 9.30am-4pm Sat & Sun) The chipper local info centre stocks wine-region maps and oodles of brochures.

Greytown

POP 2340

The prettiest of several small towns along SH2, Greytown (Te Hupenui) is home to a permanent population of urbane locals and waves of cashed-up Wellington weekenders. It was the country's first planned inland town: intact Victorian buildings line the main street with historic plaques glued to many of them (pick up the *Historic Greytown* brochure for a map). Within the old buildings you'll find accommodation, cafes, restaurants and swanky gift shops. Relief comes in the form of the fabulously brutal 1971 South Wairarapa Working Men's Club building (120 Main St) – what an architectural poke in the eye!

In 1890 Greytown became the first town in NZ to celebrate Arbor Day, bequeathing it a legacy of magnificent mature European trees. Greytown's other historic claim to fame was as the site of a Māori Parliament that held two sessions at nearby Pāpāwai Marae in the 1890s.

⊙ Sights

Cobblestones Museum   MUSEUM

(☑06-304 9687; www.cobblestonesmuseum.org.nz; 169 Main St; adult/child/family $8/3/20; ⊙10am-4pm Oct-May, 10am-4pm Fri-Mon Jun-Sep; 🐾) On the site of an old coach stop, complete with original stables and well-worn cobbled courtyard, this endearing museum features transplanted period buildings and donated old-time objects, dotted around pretty grounds just begging for a snooze on a picnic blanket. There's a blacksmith, a school, a fire station, a church, a wool shed... It's Wairarapa Pākehā history in tangible form.

🛏 Sleeping

Greytown Campground   CAMPGROUND $

(☑06-304 9387; www.greytowncampground.co.nz; Kuratawhiti St, Soldiers Memorial Park; sites unpowered/powered per 2 people $30/38, cabins d/tr from $70/80; 🅿🐾) This lush camping option spreads itself through bird-filled Soldiers Memorial Park, 650m from Greytown's main drag. As well as redwood-shaded sites, sleeping options include a retro gypsy caravan and three handkerchief-sized cabins with bunks. Bush walks, tennis courts and a kids' playground are all on hand.

Greyfriars Motel   MOTEL $$

(☑06-304 9346; www.greyfriars.co.nz; 138 Main St; d & tw from $145; 🅿🐾) Sleepy Friar Tucks should book a bed at this trim little motel complex, right in the middle of town. There are seven free-standing units here, fronted by spiky palms, with double glazing to keep the street hum at bay. Big mirrors, nice linen, interesting art...pretty classy for a motel.

🍴 Eating & Drinking

Food Forest Organics   VEGAN $

(☑06-304 9790; www.foodforestorganics.co.nz; 101 Main St; mains $14-16; ⊙9.30am-4.30pm Wed-Sun; 🐾) The ecofriendly sentiments in *Avatar* weren't an aberration for director James Cameron: the Wairarapa local is a committed vegan, and this health-food store features many organic products from the Cameron Family Farms, such as fresh produce, nuts, honey, candles and moisturisers. Call in at lunchtime for a not-chicken pie, a salad bowl or some borscht. There's also accommodation upstairs (apartments from $160).

Greytown Hotel PUB

(⌨06-304 9138; www.greytownhotel.co.nz; 33 Main St; ⊙10am-late; 🐾) One of New Zealand's oldest hotels (1860), Greytown's 'Top Pub' is looking mighty tidy for its age. There are simple rooms with shared bathrooms upstairs (doubles from $85), while downstairs there's a cosy bar and a restaurant serving pub meals (mains from $15). One of the few places in Greytown with a pulse after 9pm; occasional live music on Saturdays.

ℹ Information

Greytown Visitor Information Centre (www.wairarapanz.com/greytown; 89 Main St; ⊙2-4pm Fri, 11am-3pm Sat & Sun) This volunteer-staffed nook is inside Greytown's historic town hall (1869). Hours can be sketchy.

Masterton & Around

POP 26,300

The Wairarapa's main hub, Masterton (Whakaoriori) is an unremarkable, unselfconscious little city getting on with the business of life. Nobody was more surprised than the Mastertonians themselves when their town was rated New Zealand's most beautiful city in the recent *Keep NZ Beautiful Awards*. Perhaps the judges noticed the town's two rivers, lovely central park and noble 20th-century buildings.

To the southwest is Carterton (population 9340), one of a clutch of small rural towns punctuating SH2. It boasts the best hanging flower baskets of the lot, along with some good secondhand shops and cafe eats.

◉ Sights

**Pūkaha National
Wildlife Centre** WILDLIFE RESERVE

(⌨06-375 8004; www.pukaha.org.nz; 85379 SH2; adult/child $20/6, incl guided walk $45/22.50; ⊙9am-6pm Oct-Apr, to 4.30pm May-Sep; 🐾) 🌿 About 30km north of Masterton, this 10-sq-km centre is one of NZ's most successful wildlife and captive breeding centres. The scenic two-hour Te Arapiki o Tawhiki loop walk gives a good overview. There's also a kiwi house here (with Manukura the white kiwi!) and a series of aviaries for viewing other native birds. You can also spy a tuatara or two, while the eels get a feed daily at 1.30pm. Guided walks kick off at 11am and 2pm daily; book in advance.

Queen Elizabeth Park PARK

(www.wairarapanz.com; Dixon St, Masterton; ⊙daylight hours) Planted in 1877, Queen Elizabeth Park is perfect for stretching your legs. Walk around the lake, assess the blooms in the Hosking Garden, see if the little train is running or practise your slip catches on the cricket oval. If the kids have been cooped-up in the car, make a beeline for the playground.

**Aratoi Wairarapa
Museum of Art & History** MUSEUM

(⌨06-370 0001; www.aratoi.co.nz; 6 Dixon St, Masterton; admission by donation; ⊙10am-4pm) Hushed and refined, with 50 years of art under its belt, this small but splendid gallery hosts an impressive programme of exhibitions and events. Busy cafe and shop on site.

Tararua Forest Park NATURE RESERVE

(www.doc.govt.nz; off Norfolk Rd, Masterton; ⊙24hr) FREE The turn-off to the main eastern entrance of the huge Tararua Forest Park (p384) is just south of Masterton on SH2; follow Norfolk Rd about 15km to the gates. Mountain streams dart through virgin forest in this area, known as Holdsworth, which also features swimming holes, picnic spots and campsites (adult/child $20/10). Another popular section is the Waiohine Gorge, although it's reached by a narrow, unsealed road; look for the turn-off south of Carterton.

Wool Shed MUSEUM

(⌨06-378 8008; www.thewoolshednz.com; 12 Dixon St, Masterton; adult/child $10/3; ⊙10am-4pm) Wake up and smell the lanolin! Occupying two historic woolsheds, this *baaaa*-loody marvellous little museum is dedicated to NZ's famous sheep-shearing and wool-production industries. It's also a good spot to pick up a home-knitted hat.

Stonehenge Aotearoa MONUMENT

(⌨06-377 1600; www.stonehenge-aotearoa.co.nz; 51 Ahiaruhe Rd, Carterton; adult/child $15/5, guided tour $25/5; ⊙10am-4pm) About 11km southeast of Carterton in a farmer's backyard, this to-scale rendering of England's Stonehenge is cosmically orientated for its southern hemisphere location, on a grassy knoll overlooking the Wairarapa Plain. Its mission: to bring the night sky to life (even in daylight). The pre-tour talk and AV presentation are excellent, while the henge itself is a delightfully eccentric sight.

CAPE PALLISER

Rugged and remote, the Wairarapa coast is about as sparsely populated as NZ gets. A trip to climb the 250 steps to the candy-striped 1897 Cape Palliser Lighthouse (www.wairarapanz.com/cape-palliser; Cape Palliser Rd) is a must-do if you can spare the time and have your own wheels. The drive to the Cape takes around 80 minutes from Martinborough, but depending on stops you could give it a full day. There's no public transport.

From Martinborough, the road winds through picturesque farmland before hitting the coast. This section of the drive is impossibly scenic, hugging the coast between wild ocean on one side and sheer cliffs on the other. Look for shadows of the South Island, visible on a clear day. You'll pass the Putangirua Pinnacles (www.doc.govt.nz; off Cape Palliser Rd) en route. Standing like giant organ pipes, these eerie 'hoodoos' were formed by rain washing silt and sand away, exposing the underlying bedrock. The car park is signposted off Cape Palliser Rd: from here it's an easy 1½-hour walk to the lookout, or take the 3½-hour loop track (p384) past hills and coastal viewpoints.

As you approach Cape Palliser (Matakitakiakupe) you'll reach the wind-worn fishing village of Ngawi. The first things you'll notice here are the rusty bulldozers on the beach, used to drag fishing boats ashore.

On the way there or back, take a short detour to the crusty waterside settlement of Lake Ferry, overlooking Lake Onoke. The lake empties directly to the sea through grey, shingled dunes, with big black-backed gulls circling overhead. The Lake Ferry Hotel (06-307 7831; www.lakeferryhotel.co.nz; 2 Lake Ferry Rd, Lake Ferry; 11am-8pm Mon-Fri, to 10pm Sat & Sun, reduced winter hours) is an old-school pub with a beaut outdoor terrace upon which to sit, sip, and snack on some fish and chips. There's basic pub accommodation here too (doubles and twins from $75).

✵ Festivals & Events

Golden Shears   CULTURAL
(www.goldenshears.co.nz; Mar) Masterton's main claim to immortality is this 60-year-old sheep-shearing competition, held over four days in the first week of March. It's billed as the world's premier wool-handling championship – what more could you want?

**Wairarapa Wines
Harvest Festival**   FOOD & DRINK
(www.wairarapaharvestfestival.co.nz; Mar;) Celebrates the beginning of the harvest with an extravaganza of wine, food and family fun. It's held at a remote riverbank setting 10 minutes from Carterton on a Saturday in mid-March (shuttles depart from all the major towns). Tickets go on sale at the end of the preceding November – be quick!

🛏 Sleeping & Eating

U Studios Masterton   MOTEL $$
(06-378 2939; www.uhotelgroup.com; 119 Cornwall St, Masterton; d/tr/2-bedroom apt from $100/130/180;) Hide yourself away on the Masterton backstreets in this tidy, great-value motel. The neat brick units are warm and comfortable (if not unfailingly

stylish), with manicured lawns around a big ol' elm tree. Breakfast is $15 extra.

★ Clareville Bakery   BAKERY $
(06-379 5333; www.theclarevillebakery.co.nz; 3340 SH2, Clareville; mains $7-24; 7.30am-4pm Mon-Sat;) On the highway just north of Carterton, this excellent little bakery-cafe makes famously good sourdough bread, lamb-cutlet pies, steak sandwiches and lavash-style crackers...but everything in the counter is borderline irresistible. There's also garden seating, a kids' play zone, regular live music and an ocean-sized car park (a primary indicator of business brilliance). Try the Basque eggs.

Gladstone Inn   PUB FOOD $$
(06-372 7866; www.gladstoneinn.co.nz; 571 Gladstone Rd, Gladstone; pizzas $17-19, mains $21-36; 11am-late Tue-Sun;) Gladstone, 18km south of Masterton, is less a town, more a state of mind. There's very little here except a handful of vineyards and this classic old timber inn, haven to thirsty locals, bikers, Sunday drivers and lazy afternoon sippers who hog the tables in the glorious garden bar by the river. Plenty of crafty beer on tap.

OFF THE BEATEN TRACK

CASTLEPOINT

On the coast 68km east of Masterton, Castlepoint is a truly awesome, end-of-the-world place, with a reef, the lofty 162m-high Castle Rock, some safe swimming beaches and walking tracks. There's an easy (but sometimes ludicrously windy) 30-minute return walk that goes across the reef to the lighthouse, where 70-plus shell species are fossilised in the cliffs. A one-hour return walk runs to a huge limestone cave (take a torch), or take the 1½-hour return track from Deliverance Cove to Castle Rock. It's a bit of a no-brainer, but keep away from the lower reef when there are heavy seas (fairly often!).

☆ Entertainment

★ **Screening Room**   CINEMA
(☑06-378 6191; www.thescreeningroom.co.nz; 435 Queen St, Masterton; adult/child $16/13; ⊙10am-late) An urbane addition to workaday Masterton's cultural life, the Screening Room is a top spot to catch a movie (two plush 60-seat cinemas) or sip wine on the terrace, along with some top-flight tapas (share plates $8 to $24). Lunch and dinner roam from Balinese sweet soy pork to BBQ-bacon-and-beef burgers (mains $19 to 29).

🛍 Shopping

Wairarapa Farmers Market   MARKET
(☑06-377 1107; www.waifarmersmarket.org.nz; 4 Queen St, Masterton; ⊙9am-1pm Sat) Near the Waipoua River at Masterton's northern end, this buzzy farmers market brings the best local produce from the farms into the town every Saturday morning, rain or shine. Bring your hunger.

❶ Information

Department of Conservation (DOC; ☑06-377 0700; www.doc.govt.nz; 220 South Rd, Masterton; ⊙9am-4.30pm Mon-Fri) A regional office rather than a visitor centre, but you can still call in for Wairarapa-wide DOC information, including advice on tracks.

Masterton i-SITE (☑06-370 0900; www.wairarapanz.com; 6 Dixon St, Masterton; ⊙8.30am-4.30pm Mon-Fri, 10am-4pm Sat & Sun) Can sort you out with local information, including a copy of the map-filled *Wairarapa Visitor Guide*, and advice on accommodation.

Lighthouse at Castle Rock, Wairarapa

Christchurch & Canterbury

Best Places to Eat

Best Places to Stay

Why Go?

Nowhere in New Zealand (NZ) is changing and developing as fast as post-quake Christchurch. The hospitality scene is flourishing and the central city is once again drawing visitors to its pedestrian-friendly streets.

A short drive from the city, Banks Peninsula conceals idyllic hidden bays and beaches that provide the perfect backdrop for wildlife cruises, with a sunset return to the attractions of pretty Akaroa. To the north is whale-watching at Kaikōura, the vineyards of the Waipara Valley and the relaxed ambience of Hanmer Springs, while westwards, the Canterbury Plains morph quickly into the dramatic wilderness of the Southern Alps.

Canterbury's attractions include hiking along alpine valleys and over passes around Arthur's Pass, and mountain biking around the turquoise lakes of Mackenzie Country. During winter (June to September), attention switches to the ski fields. Throughout the seasons, Aoraki/Mt Cook, the country's tallest peak, stands sentinel over this diverse region.

When to Go

➜ Look forward to hot and settled weather in January and March, with plenty of ways to get active amid the region's spectacular landscapes.

➜ From July to September hit the winter slopes at Mt Hutt or on one of Canterbury's smaller club ski fields.

➜ The shoulder season from October to November can be cool and dry, and blissfully uncrowded. Come prepared for all weather; snow is still possible on the mountains. March to May is also less busy.

ℹ Getting There & Away

AIR
Christchurch's international airport is the South Island's main hub with flights from Australia, Singapore, China, Dubai and Fiji. Air New Zealand flies here from 15 domestic destinations.

BUS
Christchurch is the hub for coaches and shuttles heading up the coast as far as Picton, down the coast to Dunedin (and on to Te Anau), over the Alps to Greymouth and inland down to Queenstown.

TRAIN
The year-round *TranzAlpine* service connects Christchurch and Greymouth, and the *Coastal Pacific* chugs north to Picton from late September to late April, with ferry connections across Cook Strait to the North Island.

CHRISTCHURCH

POP 388,000

Welcome to a vibrant city in transition, coping creatively with the aftermath of NZ's second-worst natural disaster. Traditionally the most English of NZ cities, Christchurch's heritage heart was all but hollowed out following the 2010 and 2011 earthquakes that left 186 people dead.

Today Christchurch is in the midst of an epic rebuild that has completely reconstructed the city centre, where over 80% of buildings needed to be demolished after the quake. Scaffolding and road cones will be part of the city's landscape for a while yet, but don't be deterred; exciting new buildings are opening at an astonishing pace, and sights are open for business.

Curious travellers will revel in this chaotic, crazy and colourful mix, full of surprises and inspiring in ways you can't even imagine. And despite all the hard work and heartache, the locals will be only too pleased to see you.

History

The first people to live in what is now Christchurch were moa (bird) hunters, who arrived around 1250. Immediately prior to colonisation, the Ngāi Tahu tribe had a small seasonal village on the banks of the Avon called Ōtautahi.

When British settlers arrived in 1850 it was an orderly Church of England project; the passengers on the 'First Four Ships' were dubbed 'the Canterbury Pilgrims' by the British press. Christchurch was meant to be a model of class-structured England in the South Pacific, not just another scruffy colonial outpost. Churches were built rather than pubs, the fertile farming land was deliberately placed in the hands of the gentry, and wool made the elite of Christchurch wealthy.

In 1856 Christchurch officially became NZ's first city, and a very English one at that. Town planning and architecture assumed a close affinity with the 'mother country' and English-style gardens were planted, earning *Continued on p423*

CHRISTCHURCH IN...

Two Days
After breakfast at C1 Espresso (p440), take some time to walk around the regenerating city centre, visit Quake City (p423) and wander through Cathedral Sq (p424). Make your way to Christchurch Art Gallery (p423) and then visit the nearby Canterbury Museum (p424) and Botanic Gardens (p423). Return across the river for diverse lunch options at the Riverside Market (p440) before checking out the excellent street art (p434) around High St. That evening have a craft beer at the Institution (p443) in New Regent St before dinner at nearby Twenty Seven Steps (p441).

Start day two at Addington Coffee Co-op (p442) and then head up Mt Cavendish on the gondola (p424) for views and a walk at the top. Continue to Lyttelton for lunch at Civil & Naval (p447) before returning through the tunnel and around to Sumner for a late-afternoon swim or stroll. End the day with great pizza at The Brewery (p443) in Woolston followed by a live gig at nearby Blue Smoke (p444).

Four Days
On day three head to Akaroa (p451) to explore its wildlife-rich harbour and walk its pretty streets, enjoying stupendous views on the way there and back again. On day four, visit Orana Wildlife Park (p425) and Riccarton House & Bush (p425) before finishing the day with dinner at Little High Eatery (p441).

Christchurch & Canterbury Highlights

1 Christchurch (p418) Experiencing the dynamic re-emergence of the city post-earthquake and exploring its serene Botanic Gardens.

2 Mt John (p476) Marvelling at the other-worldly views of Mackenzie Country and the surreal azure blue of Lake Tekapo from the top.

3 Hanmer Springs (p460) Soaking in the soothing waters at this famous hot spring.

4 Banks Peninsula (p448) Admiring the surf-bitten edges from Summit Rd before descending to the quaint Gallic ambience of Akaroa.

5 Aoraki/Mt Cook National Park (p481) Gazing at the cloud-piercing silhouette of NZ's highest peak.

Christchurch &...

Lake Ellesmere
(Te Waihora)

Pukeuri

Glenavy

Waitaki River

Dunsandel

Darfield

Glentunnel

Rakaia

Ashburton

Tinwald

Temuka

Pleasant
Point

Timaru

Waimate

83

82

Windwhistle

Methven

Mayfield

Rangitata

Geraldine

79

Albury

8

83

Hunter Hills

Porters
Pass
(945m)

73

Craigieburn
Forest Park

Mt Hutt

72

72

Mt Somers

Peel Forest

Fox Peak
(2331m)

Fairlie

Burkes
Pass

Lake
Benmore

Lake Coleridge

Rakaia River

Rakaia Gorge

Lake
Heron

Rangitata River

Ben McLeod
(1952m)

Two Thumb Range

Lake
Tekapo

Mt John

Lake Tekapo

8

8

Twizel

8

6

Hokitika
Gorge

Mt Bryce
(2188m)

Mt Whitcombe
(2638m)

Mt Arrowsmith
(2795m)

Mesopotamia

The Thumbs
(2545m)

Aoraki/Mt Cook
(3724m)

Mt Cook Village

Lake
Pukaki

80

Ben Ohau Range

Ruataniwha
Conservation
Park

Lake
Ohau

Ross

Harihari

Mt Tyndall
(2524m)

Mt D'Archiac
(2865m)

Southern Alps

Elie de
Beaumont
(3116m)

Westland Tai Poutini
National Park

Mt Tasman
(3498m)

Malte Brun
(3154m)

Aoraki/Mt Cook
National Park

Mt Sefton
(3151m)

Glentanner

Mahinapua

Whataroa

Franz Josef

Fox Glacier

Ōkārito

Lake Ianthe

6

Bruce Bay

Paringa

6

Haast

TASMAN
SEA

2

5

6

7

Christchurch

N 0 _____ 5 km
0 _____ 2.5 miles

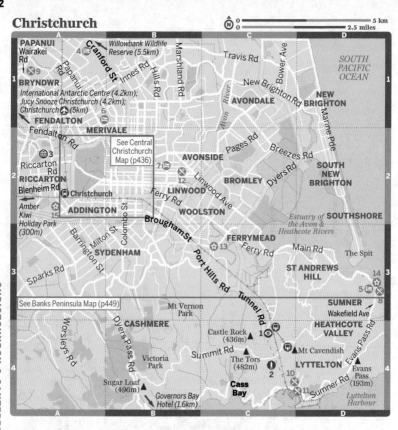

Christchurch

◎ Sights
1 Christchurch Gondola C4
2 Pioneer Women's Memorial C4
3 Riccarton House & Bush A2

🛏 Sleeping
4 Christchurch Top 10 .... A1
5 Le Petit Hotel D3
6 Merivale Manor A1
7 Old Countryhouse B2

🍽 Eating
8 Bohemian Bakery D3
  Christchurch Farmers
    Market .... (see 3)
  Civil & Naval .... (see 10)
9 Kinji A1
  Lyttelton Coffee
    Company .... (see 10)
10 Lyttelton Farmers Market C4
11 Super D4
12 Under the Red Verandah B2

🍷 Drinking & Nightlife
  Eruption Brewing .... (see 10)
  Spooky Boogie .... (see 10)
  The Brewery .... (see 13)
  Village Inn .... (see 8)
  Wunderbar .... (see 10)

☺ Entertainment
13 Blue Smoke C3
14 Hollywood Cinema D3
15 Orangetheory Stadium A2

🛍 Shopping
  Henry Trading .... (see 10)
  London St Bookshop .... (see 10)
  Tannery .... (see 13)

ℹ Information
  Lyttelton Visitor Information
    Centre .... (see 10)

ℹ Transport
  Black Cat .... (see 11)

Continued from p419

it the nickname, 'the Garden City'. To this day, Christchurch in spring is a glorious place to be.

Christchurch is also a city that has known great tragedy in recent years. Following earthquakes in 2010 and 2011, mass shootings at two mosques in the city in March 2019 killed 51 worshippers attending Friday prayers.

◉ Sights

The majority of Christchurch's key sights rebounded soon after the 2011 earthquakes. Today there is more to see than ever. The centre is graced by numerous notable arts institutions and museums, as well as the stunning Botanic Gardens and Hagley Park. Inner-city streets conceal art projects and pocket gardens, dotted among a thinned-out cityscape featuring remnant stone buildings and the sharp, shiny architecture of the new.

◉ City Centre

★ Christchurch Art Gallery GALLERY

(Te Puna o Waiwhetu; Map p436; ✆03-941 7300; www.christchurchartgallery.org.nz; cnr Montreal St & Worcester Blvd; ◷10am-5pm Thu-Tue, to 9pm Wed) FREE Damaged in the earthquakes, Christchurch's fantastic art gallery has re-opened brighter and bolder, presenting a stimulating mix of local and international exhibitions. Collection items range from the traditional to the startlingly contemporary – think light installations and interactive sculptures. Highlights from New Zealand painters capturing the country's bold landscapes include works by Rita Angus and Colin McCahon. Free one-hour guided tours take place at 11am and 2pm daily.

★ Quake City MUSEUM

(Map p436; ✆03-366 5000; www.canterburymuseum.com/quake-city; 299 Durham St N; adult $20, child accompanied/unaccompanied free/$8; ◷10am-5pm) A must-visit for anyone interested in understanding the impact of the Canterbury earthquakes, this compact museum tells stories through photography, video footage and various artefacts, including the remnants of ChristChurch Cathedral's celebrated rose window and other similarly moving debris. There are exhibits aimed at engaging both adults and children. Most affecting of all is the film featuring survivors recounting their own experiences.

★ Botanic Gardens GARDENS

(Map p436; www.ccc.govt.nz; Rolleston Ave; ◷7am-9pm Nov-Feb, to 8.30pm Mar & Oct, to 6.30pm Apr-Sep) FREE Strolling through these 30 blissful riverside hectares of arboreal and floral splendour is a consummate Christchurch experience. Gorgeous at any time of the year, the gardens are particularly impressive in spring when the rhododendrons, azaleas and daffodil woodland are in riotous bloom. There are thematic gardens to explore, lawns to sprawl on, and a playground adjacent to the **Botanic Gardens Visitor Centre** (Map p436; ✆03-941 7590; ◷9am-4pm), which also contains a lovely cafe and gift shop. Guided walks ($10, 1½ hours) depart at 1.30pm (October to May) from the gate near Canterbury Museum (p424), or hop aboard the Caterpillar (p434) electric shuttle.

Arts Centre HISTORIC BUILDING

(Map p436; www.artscentre.org.nz; 2 Worcester Blvd; ◷10am-5pm) FREE Dating from 1877, this enclave of Gothic Revival buildings was originally Canterbury College, the forerunner of Canterbury University. The buildings are now reopening to the public after extensive restoration work due to quake damage. Inside you'll find shops, cafes, museums and galleries. Exhibition spaces play host to regular concerts, rehearsals, markets and events. Of the centre's 23 buildings, 21 are listed by Heritage New Zealand as category 1 Historic Place structures. If there's nothing on during your visit, you can still wander in and check out the North Quad and Great Hall in all their restored heritage splendour.

Canterbury Earthquake National Memorial MEMORIAL

(Oi Manawa; Map p436; www.canterburyearthquakememorial.co.nz; Oxford Tce) Unveiled in 2017, this moving monument comprises a 100m-long memorial wall, curved along the south bank of the Avon and engraved with the names of the 185 people who died as a result of the 22 February 2011 earthquake. On the opposite bank, a shady park provides a space for reflection and remembrance. The memorial's Māori name, Oi Manawa, means 'tremor or quivering of the heart'.

Te Papa Ōtākaro/ Avon River Precinct PUBLIC ART

(Map p436; www.otakaroltd.co.nz) One of the city's key post-earthquake redevelopment projects is reinvigorating the area around

CHRISTCHURCH & CANTERBURY CHRISTCHURCH

the Avon (Ōtākaro) River. Running along the river as a self-guided walk, Ngā Whāriki Manaaki (Woven Mats of Welcome) is a series of 13 paved artworks welcoming visitors to the city. Look for them as you stroll along the riverside from the Canterbury Earthquake National Memorial (p423) to the Margaret Mahy Family Playground (p434).

Hagley Park   PARK
(Map p436; Riccarton Ave) Wrapped around the Botanic Gardens, Hagley Park is Christchurch's biggest green space, stretching for 165 hectares. Riccarton Ave splits it in two, while the Avon River snakes through the northern half. It's a great place to stroll, whether on a foggy autumn morning, or a warm spring day when the cherry trees lining Harper Ave are in flower. Joggers make the most of the tree-lined avenues year-round.

Transitional Cathedral   CHURCH
(Map p436; www.cardboardcathedral.org.nz; 234 Hereford St; entry by donation; ⊙9am-5pm Apr-Oct, to 7pm Nov-Mar) Universally known as the Cardboard Cathedral due to the 98 cardboard tubes used in its construction, this interesting structure serves as both the city's temporary Anglican cathedral and as a concert venue. Designed by Japanese 'disaster architect' Shigeru Ban, the entire building was constructed in 11 months.

Central Art Gallery   GALLERY
(Map p436; ☑03-366 3318; www.thecentral.co.nz; Arts Centre, 2 Worcester Blvd; ⊙10am-4pm Wed-Sun) FREE Housed in the Arts Centre's beautifully restored 1916 Library building, the Central Art Gallery exhibits contemporary works by established and emerging NZ artists.

---

❶ CHRISTCHURCH ATTRACTIONS COMBO TICKETS

Christchurch Attractions (www.christchurchattractions.nz) is the company that runs the punting (p426), tram (p434), gondola and botanic gardens tours (p434), as well as attractions in Hanmer Springs (p462). A baffling array of combo tickets are available, which will save you some money if you're considering doing more than one activity. All four Christchurch attractions are included on the five-hour **Grand Tour** (adult/child $129/69), as well as a stop in Sumner.

Rutherford's Den   MUSEUM
(Map p436; ☑03-363 2836; www.rutherfordsden.org.nz; Arts Centre, 2 Worcester Blvd; adult/child $20/10; ⊙10am-5pm) Canterbury College's most famous alumnus was the father of nuclear physics, Lord Ernest Rutherford, the NZ physicist who first split the atom in 1917 (that's him on the $100 bill). The rooms where Rutherford worked have now been turned into a small interactive science museum, with displays on the scientist's many important discoveries, as well as a room dedicated to renewable energy.

Canterbury Museum   MUSEUM
(Map p436; ☑03-366 5000; www.canterburymuseum.com; Rolleston Ave; ⊙9am-5.30pm Oct-Mar, to 5pm Apr-Sep; 🐾) FREE Yes, there's a mummy and dinosaur bones, but the highlights of this museum are more local and more recent. The Māori galleries contain some beautiful *pounamu* (greenstone) pieces, while Christchurch Street is an atmospheric walk through the colonial past. The reproduction of Fred and Myrtle's gloriously kitsch Paua Shell House embraces Kiwiana at its best, and kids will enjoy the interactive displays in the Discovery Centre (admission $2). Free one-hour guided tours depart from the foyer daily at 2pm.

Christchurch Gondola   CABLE CAR
(Map p422; www.christchurchattractions.nz; 10 Bridle Path Rd; return adult/child $30/15; ⊙10am-5pm) Take a ride to the top of Mt Cavendish (500m) on this 862m cable car for wonderful views over the city, Lyttelton, Banks Peninsula and the Canterbury Plains. At the top there's a cafe and the child-focused Time Tunnel ride, which recounts the history of the area. You can also walk to Cavendish Bluff Lookout (30 minutes return) or the Pioneer Women's Memorial (Map p422; one hour return).

Cathedral Square   SQUARE
(Map p436; www.reinstate.org.nz) Christchurch's city square stands at the heart of the rebuilding efforts, with the remains of ChristChurch Cathedral emblematic of what has been lost. The February 2011 earthquake brought down the 63m-high spire, while subsequent earthquakes in June 2011 and December 2011 destroyed the prized stained-glass rose window. Other heritage buildings around the square were also badly damaged, but one modern landmark left unscathed is the 18m-high metal sculpture *Chalice*, de-

CHRISTCHURCH FOR CHILDREN

There's no shortage of kid-friendly sights and activities in Christchurch. If family fun is a priority, consider planning your travels around NZ's biggest children's festival, KidsFest (p435). It's held every July and is chock-full of shows, workshops and parties. The annual Bread & Circus (p435) buskers festival is also bound to be a hit with young 'uns.

The impressive Margaret Mahy Family Playground (p434) is a must for anyone with small people in tow. For picnics and open-air frolicking, visit the Botanic Gardens (p423); there's a playground beside the cafe, and little kids will love riding on the Caterpillar train. Extend your nature-based experience with a wildlife encounter at Orana Wildlife Park or the Willowbank Wildlife Reserve, or get them burning off excess energy in a rowing boat or kayak from the Antigua Boat Sheds (p426). Fun can be stealthily combined with education at the International Antarctic Centre, the Discovery Centre at Canterbury Museum and Quake City (p423).

If the weather's good, hit the beaches at Sumner or New Brighton.

signed by Neil Dawson. It was erected in 2001 to commemorate the new millennium.

The much-loved Gothic cathedral has been at the centre of a battle between those who seek to preserve what remains of Christchurch's heritage, the fiscal pragmatists, and those ideologically inclined to things new. In 2012 the Anglican Diocese announced that the cathedral was to be demolished, but work was stayed when heritage advocates launched court proceedings. Eventually, in September 2017, the church leadership voted to preserve the building after the government and Christchurch City Council banded together to offer significant financial support. It's thought that the rebuild could take up to 10 years, with an estimated cost of $104 million. Preliminary stabilisation work to make the building safe to enter for restorers began in early 2020. See www.reinstate.org.nz for updates on the project's progress.

◉ Other Suburbs

Riccarton House & Bush HISTORIC BUILDING
(Map p422; www.riccartonhouse.co.nz; 16 Kahu Rd, Riccarton; ◷9am-4pm Sun-Fri, to 1pm Sat) FREE
Historic Riccarton House (1856) sits proudly amid 12 hectares of pretty parkland and forest beside the Avon River. The grounds host the popular Christchurch Farmers Market (p441) on Saturdays; the rest of the week you can visit the lovely restaurant on the ground floor.

The biggest draw, however, is the small patch of bush behind the house. Enclosed by a vermin-proof fence, this is the last stand of kahikatea floodplain forest in Canterbury.

Kahikatea is NZ's tallest native tree, growing to heights of 60m; the tallest trees here are a mere 30m and around 300 to 600

years old. A short loop track heads through the heart of the forest.

The majority of the house is only accessible on a guided tour, departing at 2pm Sunday to Friday (adult/child $18/5, one hour), as well as at 11am on Sundays only.

Orana Wildlife Park ZOO
(✆03-359 7109; www.oranawildlifepark.co.nz; 793 McLeans Island Rd, McLeans Island; adult/child $36.50/9.50; ◷10am-5pm; ▮) Orana is an 'open range' zoo, and you'll know exactly what that means if you opt to jump in the cage on wheels for the lion encounter ($52.50 per person). There's an excellent walk-through native bird aviary, a nocturnal kiwi house, and a reptile exhibit featuring tuatara. Most of the 80-hectare grounds are devoted to Africana, including rhinos, giraffes, zebras, cheetahs and gorillas.

Willowbank Wildlife Reserve ZOO
(✆03-359 6226; www.willowbank.co.nz; 60 Hussey Rd, Northwood; adult/child $32.50/12; ◷9.30am-7pm Oct-Mar, to 5pm Apr-Sep; ▮) ⬧ Willowbank focuses on native NZ critters (including kiwi), heritage farmyard animals and hands-on enclosures with wallabies, deer and lemurs. There's also a re-created Māori village, the setting for the evening Ko Tane (p434). It's 10km north of town, near the airport.

International Antarctic Centre MUSEUM
(✆03-357 0519, 0508 736 4846; www.iceberg.co.nz; Christchurch Airport, 38 Orchard Rd; adult/child $59/29; ◷9am-5.30pm; ▮) As one of only five 'gateway cities' to Antarctica, Christchurch has played a special role in Antarctic exploration since expeditionary ships to the icy continent began departing from Lyttelton in the early 1900s. This huge complex, built for the administration of

CHRISTCHURCH & CANTERBURY CHRISTCHURCH

the NZ, US and Italian Antarctic programs, gives visitors the opportunity to learn about Antarctica in a fun, interactive environment.

Attractions include the Antarctic Storm chamber (where you can get a taste of -18°C wind chill), face-to-face encounters with resident little blue penguins, and a meet-and-greet with rescue huskies. Entry also includes the '4D theatre' (a 3D film with moving seats and a water spray) and a joyride on a Hägglund all-terrain amphibious Antarctic vehicle. An optional extra is the Penguin Backstage Tour (adult/child $25/15), which allows visitors behind the scenes of the Penguin Encounter. A free shuttle to the centre departs from outside Canterbury Museum.

Activities

Boating

Antigua Boat Sheds   BOATING, KAYAKING
(Map p436; 03-366 5885; www.boatsheds.co.nz; 2 Cambridge Tce; ⊙9am-5pm;) Dating from 1882, the photogenic green-and-white Antigua Boat Sheds hires out rowing boats ($40), kayaks ($15), canoes ($40) and bikes (adult/child $10/5); all prices are per hour. There's also a good cafe and discounted combo deals when hiring a bike and a canoe.

Punting on the Avon   BOATING
(Map p436; www.punting.co.nz; 2 Cambridge Tce; adult/child $30/15; ⊙9am-6pm Oct-Mar, 10am-4pm Apr-Sep;) If rowing your own boat down the Avon sounds a bit too much like hard work, why not relax in a flat-bottomed

ESSENTIAL CHRISTCHURCH & CANTERBURY

Eat salmon spawned in the shadow of NZ's tallest mountains.

Drink some of NZ's finest pinot noir and riesling from the Waipara Valley.

Read *Decline and Fall on Savage Street* (2017), a poetic fictionalisation of the 2011 quake by author Fiona Farrell.

Listen to the soulful tones and uplifting beats of Christchurch's Ladi6.

Watch *The Changeover* (Miranda Harcourt and Stuart McKenzie; 2017); set and shot in Christchurch.

Go online www.christchurchnz.com, www.mackenzienz.com, www.midcan terburynz.com, www.visithurunui.co.nz

punt while a strapping lad in Edwardian clobber glides you peaceably through the Botanic Gardens? Tours depart year-round from the Antigua Boat Sheds; during the warmer months alternative trips run from sites at Mona Vale and Worcester Bridge.

Walking

The city offers walking tours as well as self-guided options, including the rewarding **Avon River Walk**, which takes in major city sights, and several excellent trails around the **Port Hills**.

For long-range city views, take the walkway from the **Sign of the Takahe** on Dyers Pass Rd, Cashmere. This walk leads up to the Sign of the Kiwi, through Victoria Park and then along the view-filled Summit Rd to Scotts Reserve. The various 'Sign of the...' places in this area were originally roadhouses built during the Depression as rest stops.

You can walk to Lyttelton on the **Bridle Path** (1½ hours), which starts at Heathcote Valley (take bus 28). The **Godley Head Walkway** (two hours return) begins at Taylors Mistake, crossing and recrossing Summit Rd, and offers beautiful views on a clear day.

Walks in Christchurch and throughout Canterbury are well detailed at www.christchurchnz.com.

Cycling

Being mostly flat and boasting more than 300km of cycle trails, Christchurch is a brilliant place to explore on two wheels. For evidence, look no further than the free *Christchurch City Cycle Map,* available around town or downloadable from www.ccc.govt.nz/transport/cycling. There's some great off-road riding around the Port Hills, while towards Banks Peninsula you'll find the best section of the Little River Trail (p450), one of NZ's Great Rides.

Chill   CYCLING
(Map p436; 03-365 6530; www.chillout.co.nz; 287 Durham St N; per day from $45; ⊙8.30am-5pm Mon-Fri, 9.30am-2.30pm Sat;) Bike hire and guided and self-guided cycling tours of the city. Helmets, locks and local knowledge are all supplied. Options include vintage-style bikes and e-bikes. Mountain-bike hire and advice on where to ride is also on offer.

City Cycle Hire   CYCLING
(0800 343 848; www.cyclehire-tours.co.nz; city bike half/full day from $25/35, touring bike per week from $200;) Offers door-to-door delivery of on- and off-road city bikes and touring bikes. Will also meet you with a

THE CHRISTCHURCH EARTHQUAKES

Christchurch's seismic nightmare began at 4.35am on 4 September 2010. Centred 40km west of the city, a 40-second, 7.1-magnitude earthquake jolted Cantabrians from their sleep, and caused widespread damage to older buildings in the central city. Close to the quake's epicentre in rural Darfield, huge gashes erupted amid grassy pastures, and the South Island's main railway line was bent and buckled. Because the tremor struck in the early hours of the morning when most people were home in bed, there were no fatalities, and many Christchurch residents felt that the city had dodged a bullet.

Fast forward to 12.51pm on 22 February 2011, when central Christchurch was busy with shoppers and workers enjoying their lunch break. This time the 6.3-magnitude quake was much closer, centred just 10km southeast of the city and only 5km deep. The tremor was significantly greater, and many locals report being flung violently and almost vertically into the air. The peak ground acceleration exceeded 1.8, almost twice the acceleration of gravity.

When the dust settled after 24 traumatic seconds, New Zealand's second-largest city had changed forever. The towering spire of the iconic ChristChurch Cathedral lay in ruins; walls and verandas had cascaded down on shopping strips; and two multistorey buildings had pancaked. Of the 185 deaths (across 20 nationalities), 115 occurred in the six-storey Canterbury TV building, where many international students at a language school were killed. Elsewhere, the historic port town of Lyttelton was badly damaged; roads and bridges were crumpled; and residential suburbs in the east were inundated as a process of rapid liquefaction saw tons of oozy silt rise from the ground.

In the months that followed, hundreds of aftershocks rattled the city's traumatised residents (and claimed one more life), but the resilience and bravery of Cantabrians quickly became evident. From the region's rural heartland, the 'Farmy Army' descended on the city, armed with shovels and food hampers. Social media mobilised 10,000 students, and the Student Volunteer Army became a vital force for residential clean-ups in the city's beleaguered eastern suburbs. Heartfelt aid and support arrived from across NZ, and seven other nations sent specialised urban-search-and-rescue teams.

The impact of the events of a warm summer's day in early 2011 will take longer than a generation to resolve. Entire streets and neighbourhoods in the eastern suburbs have had to be abandoned, and Christchurch's heritage architecture is irrevocably damaged. Families in some parts of the city have been forced to live in substandard accommodation, waiting for insurance claims to be settled. Around 80% of the buildings within the city centre's famed four avenues have been demolished, and a few large damaged structures are also still standing due to the machinations of insurance claims. Amid the doomed, the saved, and the shiny new builds are construction sites and a few empty plots still strewn with rubble.

Plans for the next 20 years of the city's rebuild include a compact, low-rise city centre, large green spaces, and parks and cycleways along the Avon River. It's estimated that the total rebuild and repair bill could reach $40 or even $50 billion. See www.otakaroltd.co.nz for details of specific infrastructure projects set to transform the city.

To find out more about the effects of the quakes, and to hear survivors tell their experiences of that time in their own voices, visit the highly recommended Quake City (p423).

bike at the top of the gondola if you fancy a 16km descent ($70 including gondola ride; 1½ hours).

Swimming & Surfing

Despite having separate names for different sections, it's one solid stretch of sandy beach that spreads north from the estuary of the Avon and Heathcote Rivers. Closest to the city centre is New Brighton, with a distinctive pier reaching 300m out to sea. On either side, South New Brighton and North Beach are quieter options. Waimairi, a little further north, is our personal pick.

The superstar is Sumner, 12km from the city centre on the south side of the estuary. Its beachy vibe, eateries and art-house cinema make it a satisfying spot for a day trip.

Further east around the headland, isolated Taylors Mistake has the cleanest water of any Christchurch beach and some good surf breaks. Beginners should stick to Sumner or New Brighton.

CHRISTCHURCH & CANTERBURY CHRISTCHURCH

DAY TRIPS FROM CHRISTCHURCH

LYTTELTON

Christchurch's historic port lies just over the prosaically named Port Hills from the city proper. Although it was badly hit during the earthquakes, it's well worth a trip through the 2km road tunnel during the day to explore its revitalised shopping strip, or at night to have a slap-up meal and catch a band.

☆ Best Things to See/Do/Eat

◉ **Christchurch Gondola** Stop before you reach the tunnel for an 862m ride on the cable car to the top of Mt Cavendish. The views over Christchurch, Lyttelton, Banks Peninsula and the Canterbury Plains are extraordinary. (p424)

🛍 **London St Shopping** Lyttelton has long had a bohemian edge. The best time to visit its compact shopping street is on a Saturday morning, when the farmers market is buzzing. (p447)

✕ **London St Eating & Drinking** Highlights include shared plates at Civil & Naval and craft beer at Eruption Brewing. (p447)

☆ How to Get There

Car From the city centre head southeast on Ferry Rd and veer onto Tunnel Rd (SH74). The journey takes around 20 minutes.
Bus Catch bus 28 or 535, which takes 30 minutes.

BANKS PENINSULA

You only need look at a map of this oddly shaped protuberance to realise what an absolutely unique place this is. Thumb shaped and with enough indents, whorls and contours to give it a fingerprint, this spectacular peninsula offsets rippling hills with sparkling waters. At its heart is an historic anomaly: the sweet little Frenchified village of Akaroa.

☆ Best Things to See/Do/Eat

◉ **Giant's House** Akaroa's most unusual attraction is this artsy garden, jam-packed with sculpture and mosaics made of broken china, mirrors and tiles. The pretty pink 1880 house at its centre is full of yet more of the owner's art. (p451)

🥾 **Walk around Akaroa** Pick up a pamphlet from the i-SITE and meander around Akaroa's heritage houses and churches. If you're after something more challenging, embark on the six-hour Skyline Circuit. (p449)

✕ **Hilltop Tavern** As you crest the hill and begin the descent to Akaroa Harbour, stop for a wood-fired pizza and craft beer at this historic pub. The views are spectacular. (p451)

☆ How to Get There

Car It takes less than 1½ hours to reach Akaroa from central Christchurch. The quickest route is to head southeast on Lincoln Rd and onto SH75. A more scenic route heads due south via Governors Bay. Alternatively, catch a shuttle.

WAIPARA VALLEY

The North Canterbury Wine Region is conveniently spread along either side of SH1, about an hour north of Christchurch. While it's one of New Zealand's smaller wine-producing areas, it's developing a reputation for cool-climate wines such as riesling, gewürztraminer and pinot noir.

☆ Best Things to See/Do/Eat

◉ **Willowbank Wildlife Reserve** As you're leaving the city, take a five-minute detour to the suburb of Northwood. This low-key zoo features a stellar roster of Kiwi critters and a re-created Māori village. (p425)

◉ **Wine Tasting** About a dozen of the region's wineries have public tasting rooms. Our favourite is pretty Pegasus Bay, set in verdant gardens and home to one of Canterbury's best restaurants. (p464)

✗ **Little Vintage Espresso** If you're in the mood for a more low-key lunch – or just a coffee to see you on your way – stop off at this whitewashed cottage as you pass through Amberley. (p464)

☆ How to Get There

Car Head north from the city centre on Sherborne St, Cranford St and Main Rd (SH74). If you're detouring to Willowbank, look for the signs to your left. SH74 joins SH1 at the northern edge of town. Buses aren't a viable option for visiting the wineries.

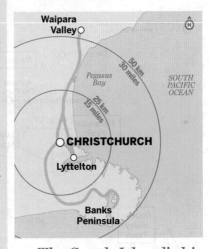

The South Island's big smoke is well positioned for day trips to beaches, mountains and wine regions. In winter you can even head out for a day's skiing on Mt Hutt.

HIKING IN CANTERBURY

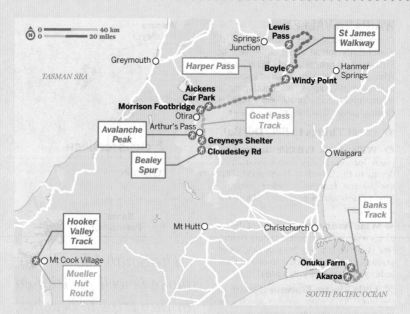

BANKS PENINSULA

☆ Banks Track

START ONUKU FARM
END AKAROA
DURATION 3 DAYS
DISTANCE 29KM
DIFFICULTY EASY TO MODERATE

....

The first private walk established in NZ, the Banks Track takes you across private farmland and forest and along the peninsula's remote outer bays. The route takes in a spectacular volcanic coastline, native bush, waterfalls and sandy beaches, with two crossings of the crater rim high above Akaroa Harbour.

Other than two steep climbs of nearly 700m each, this is a relatively leisurely tramp, which allows plenty of time to take in the marvellous scenery. For the more energetic, cutting the tramp to two days is an option.

Bookings are essential and should be made through **Banks Peninsula Track** (p449).

Tramper numbers are limited to just 16 setting out each day, so book early for peak summer and NZ holiday periods. The three-day package ($330) includes transport from Akaroa to Onuku, three nights of accommodation, landowners' fees, track registration and a copy of *Banks Peninsula Track: A Guide to the Route, Natural Features and Human History*. The two-day package ($195) covers the same route, but just the one night on the track, staying at Stony Bay (plus the night before the tramp at Onuku).

LEWIS PASS

☆ St James Walkway

START LEWIS PASS
END BOYLE
DURATION 5 DAYS
DISTANCE 65KM
DIFFICULTY EASY TO MODERATE

....

Built in 1981, the St James Walkway begins in the Lewis Pass National Reserve, travers-

For heavy-duty hikers, Canterbury is all about the mountains, be it the tightly packed peaks of Arthur's Pass National Park or the valleys and view points that unveil Aoraki/Mt Cook.

• •

es the western side of the St James Conservation Area, and ends in the Lake Sumner Forest Park. Despite taking in two mountain passes – Ada Pass (1008m) and Anne Saddle (1136m) – it's not particularly challenging, though there is one 17km day and some stream crossings. The climbs are not steep, and the rest of the walk is spent hiking through open valleys and beech forests.

The walkway follows historic pack tracks, is well benched and has an excellent series of serviced huts. The heart of the track, from Ada River along Anne River to upper Boyle River, runs through the St James Conservation Area. Vegetation within this area includes red, mountain and silver beech forests, manuka/kanuka and matagouri scrublands, numerous alpine species, at least five species of tussock and a vast expanse of valley-floor native grasslands. It is also home to around 430 indigenous species of flora and 30 native bird species.

ARTHUR'S PASS NATIONAL PARK

☆ Avalanche Peak
START/END ARTHUR'S PASS
DURATION 6–8 HOURS
DISTANCE 7KM
DIFFICULTY MODERATE

In this park of peaks, Avalanche Peak is without question the most popular one to climb and is the only mountain marked with a poled route to the summit. Its location is ideal, looming directly above Arthur's Pass village and just south of Mt Rolleston.

The alpine world experienced during this tramp is stunning on a clear day. Many experienced trampers will claim that this is in fact NZ's best day tramp, outshining the dramatic volcanic peaks and steamy vents of the Tongariro Alpine Crossing.

Unequivocal is the fact that Avalanche Peak is an alpine climb that should only be attempted by the fleet of foot in good conditions. The total climb and descent is 1100m, and although the route is clearly marked

and well trodden, it's still an arduous climb with a climax of 200m of narrow, crumbly ridge. People have died on Avalanche Peak when they failed to heed weather warnings.

Two routes, Avalanche Peak Track and Scotts Track, depart from SH73 and lead towards the peak, merging just before reaching it. Avalanche Peak Track is a much steeper climb, and at times you need to scramble up rock faces. Scotts Track is a more gradual and easier route. It's best to use Avalanche Peak Track to reach the summit and Scotts Track for the return, when your legs will be tired. Of course, the easiest return route to the peak is to simply use Scotts Track both ways, but that's not as much fun or as varied.

☆ Goat Pass Track
START GREYNEYS SHELTER
END MORRISON FOOTBRIDGE
DURATION 2 DAYS
DISTANCE 25KM
DIFFICULTY MODERATE

Goat Pass Track, also referred to as the Mingha-Deception Route (the two rivers the route follows), is an excellent introduction to hiking in Arthur's Pass. It is also one of the least complicated routes in the park, as long as the rivers run in your favour. Typical of the Southern Alps, the Bealey, Mingha and Deception Rivers can be very dangerous when in flood, and the Deception alone requires up to 30 compulsory crossings. This tramp should therefore not be attempted during periods of rain. Should the crossings start to look too difficult, backtrack or stay put – attempting a dicey crossing just isn't worth the risk.

This track forms the running leg of the Coast to Coast (www.coasttocoast.co.nz), NZ's most famous multisport race, which crosses the South Island from the Tasman Sea to the Pacific Ocean by a gruelling combination of cycling, kayaking and running. On your travels, you may come across some competitors training for the event. With luck you'll also encounter whio, the nationally vulnerable and very cute blue duck.

The Goat Pass Track can be tramped in either direction, but the Mingha-Deception direction allows for a shorter day first up.

☆ Harper Pass

START AICKENS CAR PARK
END WINDY POINT
DURATION 5 DAYS
DISTANCE 77KM
DIFFICULTY MODERATE

Māori often travelled over hhh as they crossed to the West Coast in search of *pounamu* (greenstone), and it was that knowledge and experience that would eventually see them lead the first Europeans through the area in 1857. Two guides, Wereta Tainui and Terapuhi, took Leonard Harper across the pass that now bears his name. By 1862, just three years after the first bridle paths were surveyed, the route was serving as the main gateway to the West Coast gold-fields, with stores and liquor shops along the way. When the gold rush ended, however, the track fell into disrepair, until its reinvention as a hiking trail.

Today it is one of NZ's classic tramps, connecting Arthur's Pass to Lewis Pass, and is part of the country-length Te Araroa route (www.teararoa.org.nz), making it a particularly busy tramp during the summer months. The track crosses the Main Divide over Harper Pass, a low saddle at just 963m above sea level. The segment in Arthur's Pass National Park is a valley route along the Taramakau River, but in Lake Sumner Forest Park the track is well cut and marked.

Trampers need to be cautious with the Taramakau. It is a large and unruly river in a high-rainfall area, making it prone to sudden flooding. The track can be walked in either direction, but a west-to-east crossing is recommended as you can be surer of good conditions as you cross the Otira, Otehake and Taramakau Rivers, all of which are prone to flooding during rain. On the eastern side, the track is well defined along the Hurunui and Hope Rivers, and bridged at all major crossings.

☆ Bealey Spur

START/END CLOUDESLEY RD
DURATION 4–6 HOURS
DISTANCE 13.5KM
DIFFICULTY EASY TO MODERATE

To climb almost anything in Arthur's Pass National Park is to submit to steep ground. Bealey Spur is a rare exception, climbing

Hooker Valley Track

steadily but not steeply to a historic hut at around 1230m above sea level. Add to this the fact that the tramp doesn't climb above the bushline, and that it sits east of the Main Divide, making it often drier than other park tracks even when northwesterly winds are bringing rain to Arthur's Pass, and it's a comfort hike of sorts.

It's also a tramp where the rewards far exceed the effort, with expansive views over the national park and the valleys that cut so deeply into it. Though it's not steep, the tramp does climb around 600m from SH73 to Bealey Spur Hut.

AORAKI/MT COOK NATIONAL PARK

☆ Mueller Hut Route

START/END MT COOK VILLAGE
DURATION 2 DAYS
DISTANCE 10KM
DIFFICULTY DEMANDING

This route passes through a dynamic landscape, simultaneously uplifted and eroded in the never-ending battle between powerful natural forces. Rock beds of schist, sandstone, siltstone and greywacke have been

MATTEO COLOMBO/GETTY IMAGES ©

View across Hooker Lake to Aoraki/Mt Cook

carved out by glaciation, dramatically illustrated on the climb to Mueller Hut. Hanging glaciers, moraines and U-shaped valleys are all classic landmarks of icy geological transformation. Populating this inhospitable environment are alpine flowers and herb fields, of which there are many to see during the 1000m climb to the rocky ridge and hut atop it.

Mueller Glacier was named by Julius Haast in 1862, after the Danish explorer and writer Ferdinand von Mueller. A series of Mueller Huts have perched above it since the first one was built between 1914 and 1915.

☆ Hooker Valley Track

START/END WHITE HORSE HILL CAMPSITE
DURATION 3 HOURS
DISTANCE 10KM
DIFFICULTY EASY

Aoraki/Mt Cook National Park's signature tramp, the Hooker Valley Track, is a visual extravaganza to the base of NZ's highest mountain. A journey on foot into a glacial valley where moraines, glacial lakes and the glaciers themselves stand front and centre, it culminates just 10 straight-line kilometres from the summit of Aoraki/Mt Cook, on the shores of iceberg-laden Hooker Lake. And once you're standing beside the lake, the mountain actually looks even closer than that.

The tramp follows a wide and remarkably flat track (given its proximity to a 3724m-high mountain) through the stunning valley, making this a simple wander into mountain magnificence. All of which adds up to one small price to pay – popularity – with more than 80,000 people hiking through the Hooker Valley each year. Beat the crowds by setting out early in the blue light of dawn, or take the chance to spread out along the shore of Hooker Lake, claiming a private audience with the grandest NZ mountain of all.

Other Activities

Margaret Mahy Family Playground
PLAYGROUND

(Map p436; cnr Manchester & Armagh Sts) Named after beloved Kiwi children's author Margaret Mahy, this magical playground has four separate themed zones – peninsula, forest, wetlands and plains. From a splash park to a giant spiral slide, you'll find plenty to keep the kids (and kids at heart) entertained.

☞ Tours

★ Tram
TRAM

(Map p436; ☑03-366 7830; www.christchurchattractions.co.nz; adult/child $25/free; ⊙9am-6pm Oct-Apr, 10am-5pm May-Sep) Excellent driver commentary makes this so much more than just a tram ride. The beautifully restored old dears trundle around a 17-stop loop, departing every 15 minutes, taking in a host of city highlights, including Cathedral Sq and New Regent St. The full circuit takes just under an hour, and you can hop on and off all day.

Also on offer is the evening Tramway Restaurant (four courses with/without wine matches $139/109) taking a leisurely two to three hours.

★ Watch This Space
CULTURAL

(www.watchthisspace.org.nz) With works enlivening post-earthquake derelict spaces and buildings, Christchurch is one of the world's best cities for street art, especially around the High St precinct. Check out this excellent website showcasing Christchurch street art, including a comprehensive map, photos and details of relevant artists. Guided tours of the city's street art scene are available by appointment ($30 per person).

See the website for details. Tours usually leave at 10am from outside the Canterbury Museum. Interviews with urban artists, reviews of new sites and previews of upcoming events are listed under Blogs on the website.

TranzAlpine
RAIL

(Map p436; ☑0800 872 467, 03-341 2588; www.greatjourneysofnz.co.nz; one way from $159) The *TranzAlpine* is one of the world's great train journeys, traversing the Southern Alps between Christchurch and Greymouth, from the Pacific Ocean to the Tasman Sea, passing through Arthur's Pass National Park. En route is a sequence of dramatic landscapes, from the flat, alluvial Canterbury Plains to narrow alpine gorges, an 8.5km tunnel, beech-forested river valleys, and a lake fringed with cabbage trees. The 4½-hour journey is unforgettable, even in bad weather (if it's raining

on one coast, it's probably fine on the other). The train departs Christchurch at 8.15am and Greymouth at 2.05pm.

Amiki Local Tours
FOOD & DRINK

(☑027 532 7248; www.hiddengemsnz.com; per person $65-225) Join passionate and in-the-know locals on walking tours combining the history and culture of the city – including indigenous Māori elements – with the best of eating and drinking around central Christchurch. Options include the one-hour Ōtautahi Hikoi culture walk, the two-hour food-focused City Meander, and a three-hour after-dark Kai Safari (Kai translates to 'food' in Māori).

Guided City Walks
WALKING

(Map p436; ☑0800 423 783; www.walkchristchurch.nz; Rolleston Ave; adult/teen/child $20/10/free; ⊙1pm daily, plus 10am Sep-May) Departing from the red kiosk outside Canterbury Museum, these tours offer a leisurely stroll around the city's main sights in the company of knowledgable guides. See website for booking details.

Hassle Free Tours
BUS

(Soaring Kiwis; Map p436; ☑03-385 5775; www.hasslefree.co.nz; Rolleston Ave) Explore Christchurch in an open-top red double-decker bus on a one-hour Central tour ($35) or two-hour Discover tour ($69). Tours depart outside Canterbury Museum. Regional options include a 4WD alpine safari, Kaikōura whale-watching, and visiting the location of Edoras from the *Lord of the Rings* trilogy.

Caterpillar Botanic Gardens Tour
OUTDOORS

(Map p436; ☑0800 88 22 23; www.christchurchattractions.nz/botanic-gardens-tours; adult/child $20/9; ⊙10am-3.30pm Oct-Mar, 11am-3pm Apr-Sep) Hop aboard the 'Caterpillar' electric shuttle for a tour of Christchurch's stunning Botanic Gardens (p423).

Garden City Helicopters
SCENIC FLIGHTS

(☑03-358 4360; www.helicopters.net.nz; 73-93 Grays Rd; 20min per person $1229) Scenic flights above the city and Lyttelton let you observe the impact of the earthquake and the rebuilding efforts.

Ko Tane
CULTURAL

(☑03-359 6226; www.kotane.co.nz; Willowbank Wildlife Reserve, 60 Hussey Rd, Northwood; adult/child $135/68; ⊙5.15pm) Rousing Māori cultural performance by members of the Ngāi Tahu tribe comprising a *pōwhiri* (welcome), the famous *haka*, a buffet *hāngi* (earth-

435

oven) meal, and plenty of *waiata ā ringa* (singing and dancing). At Willowbank Wildlife Reserve (p425). There's also an option to include a kiwi tour kicking off 45 minutes earlier at 4.30pm.

🎪 Festivals & Events

Check www.ccc.govt.nz/events and www.christchurchnz.com/whats-on for comprehensive festival and event listings.

Bread & Circus
World Buskers Festival PERFORMING ARTS
(World Buskers Festival; www.breadandcircus.co.nz; ⏰ Jan-Feb) National and international talent entertain passers-by for around three weeks from mid-January. Shows span stand-up comedy, burlesque, music and circus arts. Check the website for locations – and don't forget to throw money in the hat.

KidsFest FAIR
(www.kidsfest.org.nz; ⏰ Jul) If family fun is a priority, consider planning your travels around NZ's biggest children's festival. KidsFest offers a smorgasbord of munchkin-friendly shows, workshops and parties, held during the winter school holidays.

Christchurch Arts Festival PERFORMING ARTS
(www.artsfestival.co.nz; ⏰ mid-Aug–mid-Sep) Month-long biennial arts extravaganza celebrating music, theatre and dance; the next festival will be held in 2021.

NZ Cup & Show Week SPORTS
(www.nzcupandshow.co.nz; ⏰ Nov) Various horse races, fashion shows, fireworks and the centrepiece A&P Show, where the country comes to town. Held over a week in mid-November.

🛏 Sleeping

🛏 City Centre

All Stars Inn on Bealey HOSTEL $
(Map p436; ☎ 03-366 6007; www.allstarsinn.com; 263 Bealey Ave; dm $35-39, d with/without bathroom $110/89; P@🖥) Large, well-designed rooms are the hallmark of this purpose-built complex on the city fringe. Dorms have fridges, USB points and individual lights; some have en suites, too. Private rooms are similarly well equipped. It's a 25-minute walk to the centre of town.

YHA Christchurch HOSTEL $
(Map p436; ☎ 03-379 9536; www.yha.co.nz; 36 Hereford St; dm/s/d from $33/95/105; @🖥) Smart, well-run 100-plus-bed hostel conveniently located near Canterbury Museum and the Botanic Gardens. Dorms and doubles include many with en suite bathrooms. If it's full during summer, Christchurch's other YHA, Rolleston House, is one street away (5 Worcester Blvd) and used as an overflow facility from November to April only.

Around the World Backpackers HOSTEL $
(Map p436; ☎ 03-365 4363; www.aroundtheworld.co.nz; 314 Barbadoes St; dm/d $29/79; P@🖥) Friendly, well-run hostel with good facilities, Kiwiana decor and sunny back garden (complete with hammock and barbecue). Rooms are small but clean; doubles have TVs and homey decorative touches.

Dorset House Backpackers HOSTEL $
(Map p436; ☎ 03-366 8268; www.dorset.co.nz; 1 Dorset St; dm $29-37, s $89, d $89-94; P@🖥) Built in 1871, this tranquil wooden villa has a sunny deck, a large regal lounge with a pool table, and great kitchen facilities. Dorms feature beds instead of bunks, and private rooms are small but spotless. It's a short stroll to Hagley Park and the Victoria St restaurant strip.

Chester Street Backpackers HOSTEL $
(Map p436; ☎ 03-377 1897; www.chesterst.co.nz; 148 Chester St E; dm/s $32/67, d $70-96; @🖥) This relaxed wooden villa is painted in bright colours and has a sunny front room for reading. Rooms are cosy and colourful. Pipi the house cat is a regular guest at hostel barbecues in the peaceful wee garden.

Foley Towers HOSTEL $
(Map p436; ☎ 03-366 9720; www.foleytowers.co.nz; 208 Kilmore St; dm $32-36, d with/without bathroom $88/78; P@🖥) Sheltered by well-established trees, Foley Towers provides a range of well-maintained rooms and dorms encircling a quiet, flower-filled garden. Friendly, helpful staff will provide the latest local info.

★Eco Villa GUESTHOUSE $$
(Map p436; ☎ 03-595 1364; www.ecovilla.co.nz; 251 Hereford St; d $145-230; P🖥) There are only eight rooms in this beautifully renovated villa, each individually decorated with luxe fittings and muted colours. The lovely shared lounge, kitchen and dining room all reflect the focus on sustainable, ecofriendly design, as does the lush edible garden (with twin outdoor bathtubs!). Be sure to try the delicious vegan breakfasts ($20 per person).

Central Christchurch

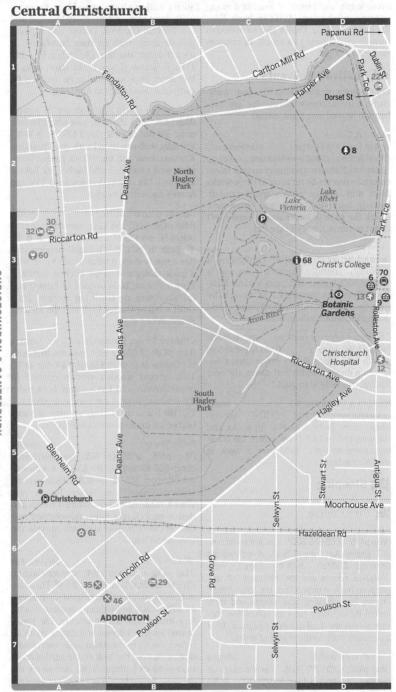

Papanui Rd

Carlton Mill Rd

Fendalton Rd

Harper Ave

Park Tce

Dublin St

Dorset St

North Hagley Park

Lake Albert

Lake Victoria

Deans Ave

Riccarton Rd

Botanic Gardens

Christ's College

Park Tce

Rolleston Ave

Avon River

Christchurch Hospital

South Hagley Park

Riccarton Ave

Hagley Ave

Deans Ave

Stewart St

Antigua St

Blenheim Rd

Christchurch

Moorhouse Ave

Hazeldean Rd

Selwyn St

Lincoln Rd

Grove Rd

Poulson St

ADDINGTON

Poulson St

Selwyn St

Central Christchurch

BreakFree on Cashel   HOTEL $$
(Map p436; ☑ 03-360 1064; www.breakfreeoncashel.
co.nz; 165 Cashel St; d $114-194; 🅿 ⛄) 🌿 This
large, modern hotel in the heart of town has
options to suit all budgets. Rooms are com-
pact, with smart TVs and pod bathrooms.

Pomeroy's on Kilmore   B&B $$
(Map p436; ☑ 03-374 3532; www.pomeroysonkil
more.co.nz; 282 Kilmore St; r $155-205; 🅿 ⛄) Even
if this cute wooden house wasn't the sister
and neighbour of the city's best craft-beer
pub, it would still be one of our favourites.

Three of the five elegant, en suite rooms open onto a sunny garden. Rates include breakfast at Little Pom's (p442) cafe next door.

Focus Motel
MOTEL $$
(Map p436; ✆03-943 0800; www.focusmotel.com; 344 Durham St N; studio $160, 1-/2-bedroom ste from $180/250; P🖵) Sleek and centrally located, this friendly-vibe motel offers studio, one- and two-bedroom units with big-screen TVs, iPod docks, kitchenettes and super-modern decor. There's a guest barbecue and laundry, and pillow-top chocolates sweeten the deal.

★George
HOTEL $$$
(Map p436; ✆03-379 4560; www.thegeorge.com; 50 Park Tce; r $490-525, ste $795-1050; P@🖵) ✎ The George has 53 luxe rooms in a defiantly 1970s-looking building on the fringe of Hagley Park. Discreet staff attend to every whim, and ritzy extras include huge TVs, luxury toiletries and two highly rated in-house restaurants – Pescatore and 50 Bistro.

★Hotel Montreal
HOTEL $$$
(Map p436; ✆03-943 8547; www.hotelmontreal. co.nz; 363 Montreal St; d from $470; P🖵) Handy to all the city sights and Victoria St's restaurants, this upmarket hotel occupies a revamped apartment building. Swanky suites are boldly styled in black, grey and gold, with plush lounge areas, kitchenettes and balconies in all rooms. There's also a light-filled in-house restaurant and a gym. Good deals are available in the low season.

Heritage Christchurch
HOTEL $$$
(Map p436; ✆03-983 4800; www.heritagehotels. co.nz; 28-30 Cathedral Sq; ste $385-410; P🖵) ✎ Still standing grandly on Cathedral Sq, the 1909 Old Government Building owes its survival to a thorough strengthening when it was converted to a hotel in the 1990s. After a three-year post-earthquake restoration its spacious suites are more elegant than ever. All have separate bedrooms and full kitchens. Downstairs is the excellent OGB (p443) cafe and cocktail bar.

🛏 Merivale

Merivale Manor
MOTEL $$
(Map p422; ✆03-355 7731; www.merivalemanor. co.nz; 122 Papanui Rd; d $189-249, apt $320; P🖵) A gracious 19th-century Victorian mansion is the hub of this elegant motel, with units both in the main house and in the more typical motel-style blocks lining the drive.

Accommodation ranges from studios to two-bedroom apartments.

🛏 Riccarton

Amber Kiwi Holiday Park
HOLIDAY PARK $
(✆0800 348 308, 03-348 3327; www.amberpark. co.nz; 308 Blenheim Rd, Riccarton; sites $49-55, cabins & units $75-135; P@🖵🚿) Lovely gardens and close proximity to the city centre make this urban holiday park a great option for campervaners and campers. Tidy cabins and more spacious motel units are also available.

Lorenzo Motor Inn
MOTEL $$
(Map p436; ✆03-348 8074; www.lorenzomotor lodge.co.nz; 36 Riccarton Rd, Riccarton; d $160-175, apt $250; P❄🖵) There's a Mediterranean vibe to this trim two-storey motel – the best of many on the busy Riccarton Rd strip. There are a number of options available including studio and two-bedroom apartments; some have spa baths and little balconies, or sweet sitting areas.

Roma on Riccarton
MOTEL $$
(Map p436; ✆03-341 2100; www.romaonriccarton. co.nz; 38 Riccarton Rd, Riccarton; d $146-181, apt $246; P❄🖵) One of the many motels along the Riccarton Rd strip, this modern two-storey block offers clean, well-proportioned units ranging from studios to two-bedroom apartments.

🛏 Addington

★Jailhouse
HOSTEL $
(Map p436; ✆0800 524 546, 03-982 7777; www. jail.co.nz; 338 Lincoln Rd, Addington; dm $30-40, s/d $75/85; @🖵) From 1874 to 1999 this was Addington Prison; it's now one of Christchurch's most appealing and friendly hostels. Private rooms are a bit on the small side – they don't call them cells for nothing – but there are plenty of communal spaces to relax outside of your room. Perks include a TV room, unlimited free wi-fi and bikes for rent.

🛏 Sumner

Le Petit Hotel
B&B $$
(Map p422; ✆03-326 6675; www.lepetithotel. co.nz; 16 Marriner St, Sumner; d $159-179; P@🖵) Relaxed coffee-and-croissant breakfasts, friendly owners, elegant furnishings and close proximity to Sumner Beach make this charming B&B a definite *oui*. Request an upstairs room with a view.

🛏 Other Suburbs

Jucy Snooze Christchurch
HOSTEL $

(📞03-903 0070; www.jucysnooze.co.nz; 5 Peter Leeming Rd; dm/d $36/129; 🅿✳🛜) Only a 10-minute walk from the airport, this flash-packers offers Japanese-style capsule beds in place of traditional dorms. The 'pods' are cosy and private, with nice touches like USB-charge points and individual lights. There are also tiny but spotless double rooms, with surprisingly spacious en suites and flat-screen TVs. It's a 25-minute bus ride to the city centre.

Old Countryhouse
HOSTEL $

(Map p422; 📞03-381 5504; www.oldcountry housenz.com; 437 Gloucester St, Linwood; dm $38-47, d with/without bathroom $124/90; 🅿@🛜🗙) Spread between three separate villas, 2km east of Cathedral Sq, this chilled-out hostel has bright dorms, a reading lounge, and a lovely garden with native ferns and lavender. A spa pool and sauna heat things up.

Christchurch Top 10
HOLIDAY PARK $

(Map p422; 📞03-352 9176; www.christchurch top10.co.nz; 39 Meadow St, Papanui; sites $39-50, cabins & units $78-153; 🅿@🛜🗙) 🍴 Family owned and operated for nearly 50 years, this large holiday park has a wide range of accommodation along with various campervan nooks and grassy tent sites. It has a raft of facilities, including a pool, games room and bike hire. Enthusiastic staff can help with travel advice and bookings.

🍴 Eating

🍴 City Centre

⭐Riverside Market
MARKET $

(Map p436; www.riverside.nz; 96 Oxford Tce; meals $10-20; ⊙9am-6pm Mon-Wed, to 9pm Thu-Sat, 10am-6pm Sun; 🚼) 🍴 Central Christchurch's new essential destination for travelling foodies is this superb multi-level market combining fresh produce stalls with opportunities for eating and drinking. Many of Christchurch's most popular food trucks are represented, making the market a good one-stop option for great coffee, Greek souvlaki, Argentinean barbecue and Japanese ramen noodles. There's also a craft beer filling station and bar.

C1 Espresso
CAFE $

(Map p436; www.c1espresso.co.nz; 185 High St; mains $10-22; ⊙7am-10pm; 🛜) 🍴 C1 sits pretty in a grand former post office that somehow escaped the cataclysm. Recycled materials fill the interior (Victorian oak panelling, bulbous 1970s light fixtures) and tables spill onto a little square. Excellent coffee, eggy brekkies and bagels are available all day, while sliders (delivered via retro pneumatic tubes!) and burgers combine with craft beer later in the day.

Welder
MARKET $

(Map p436; www.thewelder.nz; 22 Welles St; ⊙7am-late; 🚼) 🍴 This health-and-wellbeing complex – occupying the repurposed industrial warehouses of the Welder – combines a yoga studio and plenty of opportunities for healthy eating and drinking. Options include an organic juicery, an artisan bakery and a traditional Japanese-style izakaya restaurant. The Welder had just opened at the time of writing, so check the website for what else is new.

Caffeine Laboratory
CAFE $

(Map p436; www.caffeinelab.co.nz; 1 New Regent St; mains $11-23; ⊙7am-3pm Mon-Fri, from 8am Sat & Sun; 🚼) The small-scale, corner C-lab is hooked on coffee, but also cooks up delicious brunches like brioche French toast, house-smoked salmon or chipotle pulled pork. Around lunch, the menu switches to tasty hipster classics like fried chicken and mac 'n' cheese partnered with craft beer.

Utopia Ice
ICE CREAM $

(Map p436; www.facebook.com/Utopiaice; 153 High St; from $5; ⊙11am-7pm Wed & Sun, to 10pm Thu-Sat; 🚼🚼) 🍴 Expanding into the central city from its farmers market and Sumner Beach roots, Utopia's thoroughly modern take on icy treats includes interesting flavours like walnut, raspberry and rhubarb. Vegan options are available and there's a strong emphasis on local and seasonal ingredients. Good coffee and waffles stuffed with fresh fruit and ice cream are other flavourful distractions.

⭐Earl
BISTRO $$

(Map p436; 📞03-365 1147; www.earl.co.nz; 128 Lichfield St; mains $22-34; ⊙noon-late Tue-Sun; 🚼) 🍴 Mediterranean flavours are presented with flair in Earl's spacious dining room. Combine slow-cooked lamb and smoked yoghurt with a quinoa salad or mix it up from the shared plates menu including charcuterie, grilled octopus or fish crudo. The Eat like an Earl option ($60) presents the chef's favourites, while the concise wine list highlights a few different local producers each week.

Little High Eatery
FOOD HALL $$

(Map p436; www.littlehigh.co.nz; 255 St Asaph St; dishes $10-20; ⊙7.30am-10pm Mon-Wed, to midnight Thu & Fri, 8.30am-late Sat & Sun; 🚲🍴) Can't decide whether you want sushi, pizza or Thai for dinner? At Little High, you won't have to choose – this stylish and energetic food hall is home to eight different gourmet businesses, offering everything from dumplings to burgers. Stop in for your morning coffee or swing by for a late-night mojito in the beautifully outfitted space.

Unknown Chapter
CAFE $$

(Map p436; www.unknownchaptercoffee.co.nz; 254 St Asaph St; mains $14-22; ⊙6.30am-4pm; 🚲) Polished concrete, reclaimed timber tables, hanging plants and floor-to-ceiling windows give this cafe in the upcoming St Asaph/Welles St precinct an urban hipster vibe. Drop in for your morning caffeine hit, or visit at lunchtime for gourmet sandwiches, tasty salads and an irresistible cake cabinet.

Black Betty
CAFE $$

(Map p436; ☑03-365 8522; www.blackbetty.co.nz; 165 Madras St; mains $13-23; ⊙7.30am-4pm Mon-Fri, from 8am Sat & Sun; 🛜) Black Betty's industrial-chic warehouse is a popular destination for students from the nearby college. Friendly service, great food and a laid-back atmosphere are all pluses, but the biggest attraction is the coffee from specialty roaster Switch Espresso – try pour-over, syphon, aeropress or traditional espresso brews.

Rangoon Ruby
BURMESE $$

(Map p436; ☑022 028 0920; www.facebook.com/RangoonRubyChch; 819 Colombo St; dishes $13-22; ⊙5.30-9.30pm Mon-Sat; 🚲) Rangoon Ruby is the latest iteration of longtime Christchurch fave Bodhi Tree, which has been wowing locals with the nuanced flavours of Burmese cuisine for more than a decade. Feel-good food comes in sharing-sized dishes and sings with zing. Standouts include *le pet thoke* (pickled tea-leaf salad) and *ameyda nut* (slow-cooked beef curry).

Lotus Heart
VEGETARIAN $$

(Map p436; ☑03-377 2727; www.thelotusheart.co.nz; 363 St Asaph St; mains $11-28; ⊙7.30am-3pm Tue-Sun, 5-9pm Fri & Sat; 🚲) 🌱 Run by students of Indian spiritual leader Sri Chinmoy, this colourful vegetarian eatery serves a range of cuisines, from tasty curries and dosas to pizzas, nachos and burgers. Organic, vegan and gluten-free options abound, and you can quench your thirst with freshly squeezed juices, smoothies and a wide tea selection.

★ Inati
BISTRO $$$

(Map p436; ☑03-390 1580; www.inati.nz; 48 Hereford St; shared plates $16-22, 4/6/8-course tasting menus $59/79/99; ⊙noon-2pm & 5pm-late Tue-Fri, from 5.30pm Sat; 🚲) 🌱 Shared plates enjoyed around an elegantly curved bar are divided into Earth, Land and Sea and include innovative and playful dishes harnessing ingredients like smoked mutton tartare, citrus-cured fish with fennel, and kiwifruit sorbet. Four- to eight-course tasting menus are a good way to explore the Inati ethos, and one of Christchurch's best wine lists featuring many South Island varietals.

★ Twenty Seven Steps
MODERN NZ $$$

(Map p436; ☑03-366 2727; www.twentysevensteps.co.nz; 16 New Regent St; mains $33-42; ⊙5pm-late) 🌱 Overlooking the pastel-coloured New Regent St strip, this elegant restaurant showcases locally sourced seasonal ingredients. Mainstays include modern renditions of lamb, beef, venison and seafood, as well as outstanding risotto. Delectable desserts and friendly waitstaff seal the deal; reservations are advised.

King of Snake
ASIAN $$$

(Map p436; ☑03-365 7363; www.kingofsnake.co.nz; 145 Victoria St; mains $27-43; ⊙4pm-late) Dark wood, gold tiles and purple skull-patterned wallpaper fill this hip restaurant and cocktail bar with just the right amount of sinister opulence. The interesting fusion menu gainfully plunders the cuisines of Asia – from India to Korea – to delicious, if pricey, effect.

🍴 Merivale

Gatherings
MODERN NZ $$$

(Map p436; ☑021 0293 5641; www.gatherings.co.nz; 2 Papanui Rd, Merivale; dinner 5-course tasting menu $65-80, with matched wines $120-135; ⊙6-11pm Wed-Sat; 🚲) 🌱 Thoughtful, seasonal vegetarian dishes are the focus at this petite restaurant on the edge of the Papanui Rd dining strip. The set five-course tasting menu changes regularly, with a focus on sustainable, local produce and unique flavour combinations.

🍴 Riccarton

Christchurch Farmers Market
MARKET $

(Map p422; www.christchurchfarmersmarket.co.nz; 16 Kahu Rd, Riccarton; ⊙9am-1pm Sat; 🚲) 🌱 Held in the pretty grounds of Riccarton

House (p425), this excellent farmers market offers a tasty array of organic fruit and veg, South Island cheeses and salmon, local craft beer and ethnic treats.

✖ Addington

Addington Coffee Co-op CAFE $
(Map p436; ☑ 03-943 1662; www.addingtoncoffee. org.nz; 297 Lincoln Rd, Addington; mains $9-29; ☺7.30am-4pm Mon-Fri, from 9am Sat & Sun; 🛜✍) You will find one of Christchurch's biggest and best cafes packed to the rafters most days. A compact shop selling fair-trade gifts jostles for attention with delicious cakes, gourmet pies, legendary breakfasts (until 2pm) and, of course, excellent coffee. An on-site laundry completes the deal for busy travellers.

Mosaic by Simo MOROCCAN $
(Map p436; ☑ 03-338 2882; www.mosaicbysimo. co.nz; 300 Lincoln Rd, Addington; tapas & mains $8-19; ☺9am-9pm; ✍) This deli-cafe is popular for its takeaway *bocadillos* (toasted wraps filled with a huge selection of Middle Eastern– and African-inspired fillings, sauces and toppings). Other tasty offerings include super-generous platters, *merguez* sausages and tagines.

✖ Sumner

Bohemian Bakery BAKERY $
(Map p422; ☑ 021 070 6271; www.bohemianbakery. co.nz; 43 Nayland St, Sumner; pastries $4-6; ☺7.30am-4pm Wed-Sun) The kitchen at this petite bakery is entirely open, so you can see the bakers at work crafting delicious yeasty treats all day long. Grab one of the famed cinnamon rolls and head to the beach.

✖ Other Suburbs

★5th Street BISTRO $$
(Map p436; ☑ 03-365 9667; www.5thstreet.co.nz; 5 Elgin St, Sydenham; shared plates $18-24; ☺4.30-11pm; ✍) Global influences punctuate the shared plates menu at his bespoke restuarant. The honey- and chipotle-fired chicken goes well with beers from Christchurch's Three Boys Brewery, while the pomegranate-glazed lamb shoulder partners with vegetables enlivened by hummus, garlic and feta. A serious approach to cocktails also makes 5th Street ideal for a drink and snacks.

Hello Sunday CAFE $$
(Map p436; ☑ 03-260 1566; www.hellosunday-cafe.co.nz; 6 Elgin St, Sydenham; mains $13-24;

☺7.30am-4.30pm Mon-Fri, from 8.30am Sat & Sun; 🛜✍) Spread across two rooms of a restored old post office building, this popular cafe is a great spot for all-day brunches, spectacular salads and excellent coffee. The beef-cheek hash with poached eggs and the zing of kimchi and sriracha hot sauce is a good way to ease into another day.

Kinji JAPANESE $$
(Map p422; ☑ 03-359 4697; www.kinjirestaurant. com; 279b Greers Rd, Bishopdale; mains $16-26; ☺5.30-10pm Mon-Sat) Despite being hidden away in suburbia, this acclaimed Japanese restaurant has a loyal following, so it's wise to book. Tuck into the likes of sashimi, grilled ginger squid and venison *tataki,* but save room for the green-tea tiramisu, a surprising highlight.

Under the Red Verandah CAFE $$
(Map p422; www.utrv.co.nz; 29 Tancred St, Linwood; mains $15-25; ☺7.30am-3pm Mon-Fri, 8.30am-3pm Sat & Sun; ✍) This lucky suburban backstreet boasts a lovely sunny cafe, beloved by locals and travellers alike. Take a seat under the namesake veranda and tuck into baked goodies, oaty pancakes, homemade pies and eggs multiple ways.

🍷 Drinking & Nightlife

🍺 City Centre

★Smash Palace BAR
(Map p436; ☑ 03-366 5369; www.thesmash palace.co.nz; 172 High St; ☺3pm-late Mon-Thu, from noon Fri-Sun) Epitomising the spirit of transience, tenacity and resourcefulness that Christchurch is now known for, this deliberately downcycled and ramshackle beer garden is an intoxicating mix of grease-monkey garage, trailer-trash park and proto-hipster hang-out, complete with a psychedelic school bus, edible garden and blooming roses. There's craft beer, chips, Cheerios, and burgers made from scratch ($11 to $15).

★Pomeroy's Old Brewery Inn PUB
(Map p436; ☑ 03-365 1523; www.pomspub.co.nz; 292 Kilmore St; ☺3pm-late Tue-Thu, from noon Fri-Sun) With more than 30 taps featuring the best of NZ craft beers, Pomeroy's is an essential Christchurch destination. Among this cosy British-style pub's other endearing features are regular live music, a snug and

sunny courtyard and Victoria's Kitchen, serving comforting pub food (mains $25 to $34). Also onsite, pretty Little Pom's cafe serves excellent brunch fare ($11 to $25) until mid-afternoon.

The Last Word
COCKTAIL BAR

(Map p436; ☑022 094 7445; www.lastword.co.nz; 31 New Regent St; ⊙4pm-late Mon-Fri, 2pm-late Sat & Sun) This cosy spot amid the heritage Spanish Mission facades of New Regent St is a fine option any time of the evening. One of the city's best selections of whisky partners with good cocktails and a well-curated beer menu. Moreish bar snacks include platters and grilled-cheese sandwiches, and also on offer are special whisky and chocolate pairing menus.

Institution
CRAFT BEER

(Map p436; www.theinstitution.co.nz; 28 New Regent St; ⊙4-11pm Tue-Fri, from 2pm Sat & Sun) The Institution may well be Christchurch's smallest bar – there's only room for around 20 punters upstairs – but there's no trade-off in the range of beers on offer. The taps often feature beers from smaller Canterbury breweries and there's a well-priced selection of interesting cans and bottles in the fridge. Service from the barstaff is chatty and friendly.

OGB
COCKTAIL BAR

(Map p436; ☑03-377 4336; www.ogb.co.nz; Heritage Christchurch, 28 Cathedral Sq; ⊙11am-1am) Old-school speakeasy charm reigns at this versatile spot that's equally fine for a cocktail, craft beer or more substantial offering of a shared platter of cheese and charcuterie. In cooler weather sit in the supremely cosy interior, or on the hotel patio with views of Cathedral Sq during summer. If you're wondering, OGB stands for Old Government Building.

Dux Central
BAR

(Map p436; ☑03-943 7830; www.duxcentral. co.nz; 6 Poplar St; ⊙11am-late) Pumping a whole lot of heart back into the flattened High St precinct, the epic Dux complex comprises a brew bar serving its own and other crafty drops, the Emerald Room wine bar, Upper Dux restaurant and the Poplar Social Club cocktail bar, all housed within the confines of a lovingly restored old building.

Boo Radley's
BAR

(Map p436; ☑03-366 9906; www.booradleys. co.nz; 98 Victoria St; ⊙4pm-late) An intimate, speakeasy vibe makes Boo's an alluring late-night hang-out. Southern-style decor meshes with bourbons galore and American comfort food like sliders, fried chicken and curly fries (snacks $7 to $24). There's regular live music, too.

 Merivale

Vesuvio
WINE BAR

(Map p436; ☑03-355 8530; www.vesuvio.co.nz; 4 Papanui Rd, Merivale; ⊙3pm-late) Half-hidden at the back of a busy cluster of eateries, this European-style wine bar is the perfect spot for a pre-dinner *aperitivo* – though the thoughtful selection of local and imported wines, excellent antipasti boards (from $19) and regular live jazz might mean you end up settling in for the night.

 Riccarton

Volstead Trading Company
BAR

(Map p436; www.volstead.co.nz; 55 Riccarton Rd, Riccarton; ⊙4-11pm Mon-Thu, from noon Fri-Sun) Concealed inside a suburban shopping strip, this cosy bar combines comfy old sofas from your last student flat with quirky murals and a wide range of craft beers on tap. The complementary beer-food menu features sliders, burritos and fried chicken. Volstead also makes its own craft brews in the onsite microbrewery. Try the American Amber Ale or hoppy US IPA.

Sumner

Village Inn
PUB

(Map p422; ☑03-326 6973; www.thevillageinnsumner.co.nz; 41b Nayland St, Sumner; ⊙11am-late Tue-Sun) This convivial spot on Sumner's main shopping strip has a sunny courtyard, good meals (mains $20 to $30) including pork souvlaki and rib eye steak, and live music on Sunday afternoons from 4pm. It's also popular for a lazy weekend brunch.

Other Suburbs

The Brewery
CRAFT BEER

(Map p422; www.casselsbrewery.co.nz; 3 Garlands Rd, Woolston; ⊙8am-late) This is an essential destination for beer-loving travellers.

The Cassels & Sons' brewery crafts beers using a wood-fired brew kettle, resulting in well-balanced ales and lagers. Tasting trays are available for the curious and the indecisive, live bands perform regularly, and the food – including wood-fired pizzas ($20 to $26) – is top-notch, too. Cassels' Milk Stout has deservedly won awards internationally.

Allpress Espresso COFFEE
(Map p436; 110 Montreal St, Sydenham; ☺7.30am-3.30pm Mon-Fri) Hidden behind a nondescript facade down the industrial end of Montreal St, the Christchurch branch of this famous Kiwi coffee roastery does a mean espresso – just as you'd expect. If you're feeling peckish, there are also fresh light lunch options and smoothies on offer.

⭐ Entertainment

For live music and club listings, see www.undertheradar.co.nz and www.rdu.org.nz.

Isaac Theatre Royal THEATRE
(Map p436; ☑03-366 6326; www.isaactheatreroyal.co.nz; 145 Gloucester St; ☺box office 10am-5pm Mon-Fri) This century-old dear survived the quakes and emerged restored to full glory in 2014. Its heritage features are enjoyed by patrons venturing inside for everything from opera and ballet to contemporary theatre and rock concerts.

Blue Smoke LIVE MUSIC
(Map p422; ☑03-288 0543; www.bluesmoke.co.nz; The Tannery, 3 Garlands Rd; variable; ☺hours vary by event) Adjacent to the Brewery (p443) in Woolston, Blue Smoke is Christchurch's best small live-music venue. There's often a folk, roots music or Americana vibe to the acts, but rock, rap and spoken word also sometimes feature. Top local musicians to look out for include the Eastern, and Lyttelton's finest, Marlon Williams and Delaney Davidson.

Alice Cinema CINEMA
(Map p436; ☑03-365 0615; www.alice.co.nz; 209 Tuam St; adult/child $17/12) This delightful two-screen art-house cinema can be found within the long-standing and excellent Alice In Videoland DVD library.

Court Theatre THEATRE
(Map p436; ☑03-963 0870; www.courttheatre.org.nz; Bernard St, Addington; ☺box office 9am-8.15pm Mon-Thu, to 10.15pm Fri, 10am-10.15pm Sat) Christchurch's original Court Theatre was an integral part of the city's Arts Centre, but it was forced to relocate to this warehouse after the earthquakes. The new premises are much more spacious; it's a great venue to see popular international plays and works by NZ playwrights.

Darkroom LIVE MUSIC
(Map p436; www.darkroom.bar; 336 St Asaph St; ☺7pm-late Thu-Sat) A hip combination of live-music venue and bar, Darkroom has lots of Kiwi beers and great cocktails. Live gigs are frequent – and frequently free.

Hollywood Cinema CINEMA
(Map p422; www.hollywoodcinema.co.nz; 28 Marriner St, Sumner; adult/child $16/12) Screens art-house and blockbuster flicks in the seaside suburb of Sumner. Cheaper prices on Tuesdays.

Orangetheory Stadium STADIUM
(Map p422; www.crfu.co.nz; 95 Jack Hinton Dr, Addington) After Lancaster Park was irreparably damaged during the 2011 earthquake, Canterbury Rugby Union shifted its home games to this smaller ground in Addington. The Crusaders play here from late February to July in the Super Rugby tournament, while from July to September, Canterbury plays in NZ's domestic rugby championship.

🛍 Shopping

⭐Tannery SHOPPING CENTRE
(Map p422; www.thetannery.co.nz; 3 Garlands Rd, Woolston; ☺10am-5pm) In a city mourning the loss of its heritage, this post-earthquake conversion of a 19th-century tannery couldn't be more welcome. The Victorian buildings have been beautifully restored, and are crammed with all manner of delightful boutiques selling everything from surfboards to vintage clothing to exquisite homewares.

When you're tired of shopping, stop by the Brewery (p443) for an afternoon pick-me-up. There are also several cafes, an art-house cinema and live music at Blue Smoke.

Scorpio Books BOOKS
(Map p436; ☑03-379 2882; www.scorpiobooks.co.nz; BNZ Centre, 120 Hereford St; ☺9am-6pm Mon-Fri, 10am-5pm Sat & Sun) A well-established Christchurch independent bookstore, Scorpio Books relocated after the earthquake to this modern central city loca-

tion after several years in Riccarton. There's in-store seating and relaxed browsing is definitely encouraged.

New Regent St MALL
(Map p436; www.newregentstreet.co.nz) This pretty little stretch of pastel Spanish Mission–style shops was described as NZ's most beautiful street when it was completed in 1932. Fully restored post-earthquake, it's once again a delightful place to stroll, and has become something of a hub for quality cafes, bars and restaurants.

Ballantynes DEPARTMENT STORE
(Map p436; www.ballantynes.com; cnr Colombo & Cashel Sts; ⊙9am-5.30pm Mon-Fri, to 5pm Sat, 10am-5pm Sun) A venerable Christchurch department store selling men's and women's fashions, cosmetics, travel goods, stationery and speciality NZ gifts.

The Crossing SHOPPING CENTRE
(Map p436; ☑027 506 8149; www.thecrossing.co.nz; 166 Cashel St; ⊙9am-6pm Mon-Wed, to 8pm Thu, 10am-5pm Sat & Sun) Opened in 2017, this shiny complex fronting the Cashel St pedestrian mall is home to all manner of local and international retailers. There's also a good range of cafes and food outlets scattered through the Crossing's several floors.

Colombo Mall MALL
(Map p436; www.thecolombo.co.nz; 363 Colombo St, Sydenham; ⊙9am-5.30pm Mon-Sat, 10am-5pm Sun) Within walking distance of the CBD, this hip little mall is home to a few interesting, independent shops, an arthouse cinema and a range of culinary delights – here you'll find macarons, crêpes, dumplings, sushi, salads, craft beer and good coffee.

ℹ Information

EMERGENCY & IMPORTANT NUMBERS

Emergency (police, fire, ambulance)	☑111
Country code	☑64
International access code	☑00

MEDICAL SERVICES
24-Hour Surgery (☑03-365 7777; www.24hoursurgery.co.nz; 401 Madras St) No appointment necessary.

Christchurch Hospital (☑03-364 0640, emergency dept 03-364 0270; www.cdhb.govt.nz; 2 Riccarton Ave) Has a 24-hour emergency department.

TOURIST INFORMATION
ChristchurchNZ (www.christchurchnz.com) Official tourism website for the city and region.

ℹ Getting There & Away

AIR
Christchurch Airport (CHC; ☑03-358 5029; www.christchurchairport.co.nz; 30 Durey Rd) The South Island's main international gateway, with regular flights to Australia, China, Dubai, Fiji, the USA and Singapore. Facilities include baggage storage, car-rental counters, ATMs and foreign-exchange offices.

Air New Zealand (p716) Direct flights to/from Auckland, Wellington, Dunedin and Queenstown. Code-share flights with smaller regional airlines head to/from Blenheim, Hamilton, Hokitika, Invercargill, Napier, Nelson, New Plymouth, Palmerston North, Paraparaumu, Rotorua and Tauranga.

Jetstar (p716) Flies to/from Auckland and Wellington.

BUS
Tourist-oriented services generally stop outside the Canterbury Museum on Rolleston Ave; local and some long-distance services depart from the inner-city **Bus Interchange** (Map p436; cnr Lichfield & Colombo Sts).

Akaroa French Connection (Map p436; ☑0800 800 575; www.akaroabus.co.nz; Rolleston Ave; adult/child return $50/30) Daily service to Akaroa.

Akaroa Shuttle (Map p436; ☑0800 500 929; www.akaroashuttle.co.nz; Rolleston Ave; adult/child one way $36/31, return $6/41) Daily service to Akaroa.

Atomic Shuttles (Map p436; ☑03-349 0697; www.atomictravel.co.nz; Lichfield St) Destinations include Greymouth ($55, 3¾ hours), Timaru ($30, 2½ hours) and Dunedin ($40, 5¾ hours).

Budget Buses & Shuttles (Map p436; ☑03-615 5119; www.budgetshuttles.co.nz; Rolleston Ave; ⊙Mon-Sat) Offers a door-to-door shuttle to Geraldine ($65) and Timaru ($55).

East West Coaches Run between Christchurch and Westport via the Lewis Pass daily except Saturday (adult/child $60/45, five hours).

Hanmer Connection (Map p436; ☑0800 242 663; www.hanmerconnection.co.nz; Rolleston Ave; adult/child one way $30/20, return $50/30) Daily coach to/from Hanmer Springs via Amberley and Waipara.

InterCity (Map p436; ☑ 03-365 1113; www. intercity.co.nz; Lichfield St) New Zealand's widest and most reliable coach network. Coaches head to Timaru (from $31, 2½ hours), Dunedin (from $44, six hours), Queenstown (from $62, eight to 11 hours) and Picton (from $69, 5¼ hours) at least daily.

TRAIN

Christchurch Railway Station (www.greatjour neysofnz.co.nz; Troup Dr, Addington; ☺ ticket office 6.30am-3pm) is the terminus for two highly scenic train journeys, the hero of which is the TranzAlpine (p434). The other, the **Coastal Pacific** (☑ 03-341 2588, 0800 872 467; www. greatjourneysofnz.co.nz; from $59; ☺ Oct-Apr), runs seasonally along the east coast from Christchurch to Picton, stopping at Waipara, Kaikōura and Blenheim.

ⓘ Getting Around

TO/FROM THE AIRPORT

Christchurch Airport is located 10km from the city centre. A taxi into town costs $50 to $65. Alternatively, the airport is well served by public buses (www.metroinfo.co.nz). The Purple Line bus heads through Riccarton (20 minutes) to the central Bus Interchange (30 minutes) and on to Sumner (1¼ hours). Bus 29 heads through Fendalton (10 minutes) to the Bus Interchange (30 minutes). Both services cost $8.50 (pay the driver) and run every 30 minutes from approximately 7am to 11pm. Shuttle services are available for around $25 per person.

Ride-share services Uber, Ola and Zoomy all leave from the airport's Rideshare Pick-up Zone located outside of the main terminal behind the purple Express Car Park.

CAR & MOTORCYCLE

Most major car- and campervan-rental companies have offices in Christchurch, as do numerous smaller local companies. Operators with national networks often want cars from Christchurch to be returned to Auckland because most renters travel in the opposite direction, so you may find a cheaper price on a northbound route.

Local options include the following:

Ace Rental Cars (☑ 03-360 3270; www.ace rentalcars.co.nz; 166 Orchard Rd, Harewood)

Hitch Car Rental (☑ 03-974 4670; www.hitch carrentals.co.nz; 232 Roydvale Ave, Burnside; ☺ 8am-6pm)

New Zealand Motorcycle Rentals & Tours (☑ 09-486 2472; www.nzbike.com)

New Zealand Rent a Car (☑ 03-961 5880; www.nzrentacar.co.nz; 26b Sheffield Cres, Burnside)

Omega Rental Cars (☑ 03-377 4558; www. omegarentalcars.com; 158 Orchard Rd, Harewood; ☺ 7.30am-6pm)

Pegasus Rental Cars (☑ 03-358 5890; www. rentalcars.co.nz; 154 Orchard Rd, Harewood; ☺ 8am-5pm)

E-SCOOTERS

Accessed via a smartphone app, e-scooters from Lime and Flamingo are both available in central Christchurch.

PUBLIC TRANSPORT

Christchurch's **Metro bus network** (☑ 03-366 8855; www.metroinfo.co.nz) is inexpensive, efficient and comprehensive. Most buses run from the inner-city Bus Interchange (p445).

Pick up timetables from the Interchange. Tickets (adult/child $4.20/2.40) can be purchased on board and include one free transfer within two hours. Alternatively, Metrocards allow unlimited zone one travel for two hours/

MĀORI NZ: CHRISTCHURCH & CANTERBURY
....

Only 14% of New Zealand's Māori live on the South Island, and of those, half live in Canterbury. The first major tribe to become established here were Waitaha, who were subsequently conquered and assimilated into the Ngāti Māmoe tribe in the 16th century. In the following century, they in turn were conquered and subsumed by Ngāi Tahu (www. ngaitahu.iwi.nz), a tribe that has its origins in the East Coast of the North Island. Today, Ngāi Tahu is considered to be one of Māoridom's great success stories, with a reputation for good financial management, sound cultural advice and a portfolio including property, forestry, fisheries and many high-profile tourism operations.

There are many ways to engage in Māori culture in Canterbury. Artefacts can be seen at Canterbury Museum (p424), Akaroa Museum (p451), Okains Bay Māori & Colonial Museum (p449) and South Canterbury Museum (p471). Willowbank Wildlife Reserve (p425) in Christchurch has a replica Māori village and an evening cultural show. Further south in Timaru, the Te Ana Māori Rock Art Centre (p471) has interactive displays and arranges tours to see centuries-old work in situ.

one day/one week for $2.65/5.30/26.50. Cards are available from the Interchange; they cost $10 and must be loaded with a minimum of $10 additional credit.

TAXI

Ride-share apps including Uber, Ola and Zoomy all operate in Christchurch.

Blue Star ([☑]03-379 9799; www.bluestartaxis.org.nz)

First Direct ([☑]03-377 5555; www.firstdirect.net.nz)

Gold Band ([☑]03-379 5795; www.goldband taxis.co.nz)

AROUND CHRISTCHURCH

Lyttelton

POP 3100

Southeast of Christchurch, the prominent Port Hills slope down to the city's port on Lyttelton Harbour. Christchurch's first European settlers landed here in 1850 to embark on their historic trek over the hills. Nowadays a 2km road tunnel makes the journey considerably quicker.

Lyttelton was badly damaged during the 2010 and 2011 earthquakes, and many of the town's heritage buildings along London St were subsequently demolished. Today, however, Lyttelton has re-emerged as one of Christchurch's most interesting communities. The town's arty, independent and bohemian vibe is stronger than ever, and it is once again a hub for great bars, cafes and shops. It's well worth catching the bus from Christchurch and getting immersed in the local scene, especially on a sunny Saturday morning when the farmers market is buzzing.

Lyttelton's new passenger terminal will be completed by late 2020; the port should again be a favourite anchorage for cruise ships.

✗ Eating

Lyttelton Farmers Market MARKET $
(Map p422; www.lyttelton.net.nz; London St; ⊙10am-1pm Sat; [☑][♿]) ☞ Every Saturday morning food stalls take the place of cars on Lyttelton's main street. Stock up alongside locals on fresh bread, baked goods, flowers, cheeses, local produce and good coffee.

Super ASIAN $$
(Map p422; [☑]021 0862 2632; www.super.restaurant; 5 Norwich Quay; mains $22-28; ⊙9am-late

Mon-Sat; [☑]) Pan-Asian flavours with a strong Japanese influence are the focus at Super, with the fun ambience further enhanced by bright and colourful *anime*-influenced decor. Standout small plates include the steamed bao buns with ginger beef and sriracha mayonnaise, and its take on ramen noodles is packed full of flavour. A concise drinks list showcases sake, wine and craft beer.

Civil & Naval TAPAS $$
(Map p422; [☑]03-328 7206; www.civilandnaval.co.nz; 16 London St; shared plates $6-18; ⊙10am-11pm Sun-Thu, to 1am Fri & Sat) Steadfast staff at this compact, bijou bar serve a quality selection of cocktails, fine wines and craft beers, while the kitchen keeps patrons civil with an eclectic range of tapas. Try the tasty polenta-crumbed squid.

Lyttelton Coffee Company CAFE $$
(Map p422; [☑]03-328 8096; www.facebook.com/lytteltoncoffeecompany; 29 London St; mains $13-20; ⊙7am-4pm Mon-Fri, 8am-4pm Sat & Sun; [☑][♿]) ☞ Local institution Lyttelton Coffee Company has risen from the rubble and continues its role as a stalwart of the London St foodie scene, serving consistently great coffee and wholesome food in its cavernous, exposed-brick warehouse space.

🍷 Drinking & Nightlife

Eruption Brewing MICROBREWERY
(Map p422; [☑]03-355 5632; www.eruptionbrewing.com; 26 London St; ⊙4-9pm Wed-Thu, to 11pm Fri, 10am-11pm Sat, to 8pm Sun) Every heritage port town needs a decent craft brewery and Eruption Brewing doesn't disappoint. It's a firm local favourite, especially on Friday and Saturday nights when the vintage 1970s furniture hosts punters enjoying decent brews like the Eruption IPA packed with citrusy NZ hops. Dining options include pizza, platters and gourmet burgers. Ask what other interesting seasonal beers are on offer.

Spooky Boogie COFFEE
(Map p422; www.facebook.com/spookyboogies; 54 London St; ⊙7am-4pm Mon-Fri, from 8.30am Sat & 9am Sun) More sweet than spooky, this hip coffee shop cum record store at the top end of London St does a roaring trade in silky coffee and smooth beats alike. There's lots of cool art and retro movie posters to check out too.

Governors Bay Hotel PUB
([☑]03-329 9433; www.governorsbayhotel.co.nz; 52 Main Rd, Governors Bay; ⊙11am-late; [☎]) A scenic

9km drive southwest from Lyttelton is one of NZ's oldest operational pubs (1870). You couldn't ask for a more inviting deck and garden in which to quaff an afternoon tipple. The food is good, too, covering all the classic pub-grub bases (mains $22 to $36) with burgers, bangers and mash, and seafood. Upstairs are chicly renovated rooms with shared bathrooms (doubles $95 to $150).

Wunderbar BAR
(Map p422; ☑ 03-328 8818; www.wunderbar.co.nz; 19 London St; ☺ 5pm-late Mon-Fri, 1pm-3am Sat & Sun) Wunderbar is a top spot to get down, with regular live music covering all spectra, and clientele to match. The kooky decor and decapitated dolls' heads alone are worth the trip. Enter via the stairs in the rear car park.

🛍 Shopping

London St Bookshop BOOKS
(Map p422; 48 London St; ☺ 10am-4pm Tue-Sun) Dimly lit and crammed full of intriguing volumes, this charming secondhand bookshop is a bibliophile's dream.

Henry Trading HOMEWARES
(Map p422; ☑ 03-328 8088; www.henrytrading.co. nz; 33 London St; ☺ 10am-4pm Tue-Sun) This tiny but perfectly curated store stocks a range of lovely homewares and gifts, many made by local producers, as well as a sweet line in artisanal Lyttelton souvenirs.

ℹ Information

Lyttelton Visitor Information Centre (Map p422; ☑ 03-328 9093; www.lytteltoninfocen tre.nz; 20 Oxford St; ☺ 10am-4pm Oct-Apr, 10.30am-2.30pm May-Sep) Friendly staff can provide information on accommodation, local walks and ferry departures.

ℹ Getting There & Away

Lyttelton is 15km from Christchurch CBD via the Lyttelton Tunnel. An alternative, more scenic road links Sumner Beach to Lyttelton (around 8km), which only reopened in mid-2019 after being closed following severe rock falls in the 2011 earthquake.
Bus No 28 runs from Christchurch to Lyttelton (adult/child $4.70/2.60, 30 minutes).
Ferry From Lyttelton, **Black Cat** (Map p422; ☑ 03-328 9078; www.blackcat.co.nz; 5 Norwich Quay) provides ferries to sheltered Quail Island (adult/child return $30/15, 10 minutes, once daily October to April only), as well as to sleepy Diamond Harbour (adult/child one way $6.50/3.20, 10 minutes, hourly).

Banks Peninsula

POP 4750

Gorgeous Banks Peninsula (Horomaka) was formed by two giant volcanic eruptions about eight million years ago. Harbours and bays radiate out from the peninsula's centre, giving it an unusual cogwheel shape. The historic town of Akaroa, 80km from Christchurch, is a highlight, as is the absurdly beautiful drive along Summit Rd around the edge of one of the original craters. It's also worth exploring the little bays that dot the peninsula's perimeter.

The waters around Banks Peninsula are home to the smallest and one of the rarest dolphin species, the Hector's dolphin, found only in NZ waters. A range of tours depart from Akaroa to spot these and other sealife, including white-flippered penguins, orcas and seals.

History

James Cook sighted the peninsula in 1770, believing it to be an island. He named it after the naturalist Sir Joseph Banks.

In 1831, Onawe *pā* (fortified village) was attacked by the Ngāti Toa chief Te Rauparaha and in the massacres that followed, the local Ngāi Tahu population was dramatically reduced. Seven years later, whaling captain Jean Langlois negotiated the purchase of Banks Peninsula from the survivors and returned to France to form a trading company. With French-government backing, 63 settlers headed for the peninsula in 1840, but only days before they arrived, panicked British officials sent their own ship to raise the flag at Akaroa, claiming British sovereignty under the Treaty of Waitangi. Had the settlers arrived two years earlier, the entire South Island could have become a French colony, and NZ's future might have been quite different.

The French did settle at Akaroa, but in 1849 their land claim was sold to the New Zealand Company, and in 1850 a large group of British settlers arrived. The heavily forested land was cleared and soon farming became the peninsula's main industry.

◉ Sights

Hinewai Reserve FOREST
(www.hinewai.org.nz; 632 Long Bay Rd) 🏄 Get a glimpse of what the peninsula once looked like with a stroll through this privately owned 1250-hectare nature reserve, which has been replanted with native forest. Pick up a map

Banks Peninsula

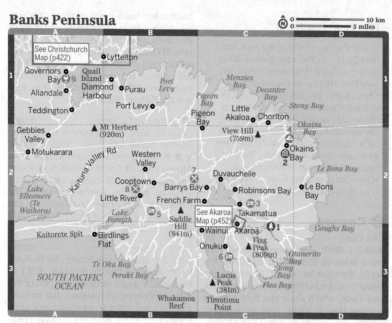

outlining the walking tracks at the visitor centre, a short walk from the main entrance.

Okains Bay Māori & Colonial Museum
MUSEUM

(www.okainsbaymuseum.co.nz; 1146 Okains Bay Rd, Okains Bay; adult/child $10/2; ⏰10am-5pm) Northeast of Akaroa, this museum has a respectable array of European pioneer artefacts, but it is the nationally significant Māori collection, featuring a replica *wharenui* (meeting house), *waka* (canoes), stone tools and personal adornments, that make this a worthwhile detour. Note the cute shop down the road.

🏃 Activities

Akaroa i-SITE (p454) stocks pamphlets on walks around Akaroa township, taking in the old cottages, churches and gardens that lend Akaroa its character. The six-hour Skyline Circuit also starts from town, and there are many more rewarding walks throughout the peninsula.

Banks Peninsula Track
HIKING

(☎03-304 7612; www.bankstrack.co.nz; 2-/3-days from $195/330; ⏰Oct-Apr) This privately owned and maintained 29km three-day tramp traverses farmland and forest along the dramatic coast east of Akaroa. Fees include transport

Banks Peninsula

from Akaroa and hut accommodation. The two-day option covers the same ground only faster, for experienced hikers.

Crater Rim Walks
WALKING

(www.craterrimwalks.co.nz; per person from $175; 🖳) 🌿 Stunning coastal scenery abounds during half- and full-day guided walks around the extinct volcanic landscapes of Banks Peninsula. Owner-guide Nicole Ellwood is a Christchurch local and very experienced in exploring the area.

LITTLE RIVER TRAIL

One of the Great Rides of the New Zealand Cycle Trail, this easy-graded, 49km cycle trail (www.littleriverrailtrail.co.nz) runs from Hornby, on the outskirts of Christchurch, to Little River at the base of Banks Peninsula. It rolls across rural plains, past weathered peaks and along the shores of Lake Ellesmere – home to NZ's most diverse bird population – and its smaller twin, Lake Forsyth. The best section of track can be enjoyed as a return ride from Little River, where there is a cafe (p451) and bike hire.

Courses

Bone Dude   ART
(☑️03-329 0947; www.thebonedude.co.nz; 111 Poranui Beach Rd, Birdlings Flat; from $60; ⏰1-4pm Fri, 10am-1pm Sat; 👪) Creative types should consider booking a session with the Bone Dude, who'll show you how to carve your own bone pendant (allow three hours). Sessions are limited to seven participants, so book ahead. Friendly owner John's always up for a good chat.

Tours

Pohatu Plunge   WILDLIFE
(☑️03-304 8542; www.pohatu.co.nz; adult/child tours $80/55, self-drive $50/30) 🏃 Runs three-hour evening tours from Akaroa to the Pohatu white-flippered penguin colony (a self-drive option is also available). The best time to see the penguins is during the breeding season from August to January, but it is possible throughout the year. Sea kayaking and 4WD nature tours are also available, as is the option of staying overnight in a secluded cottage.

Tuatara Tours   HIKING
(☑️03-962 3280; www.tuataratours.co.nz; per person $1795; ⏰Nov-Apr) 🏃 You'll only need to carry your day pack on the guided Akaroa Walk, a leisurely 39km, three-day guided tramp from Christchurch to Akaroa via the gorgeous Summit Ridge. Good accommodation and gourmet food are included.

Sleeping

⭐Onuku Farm Hostel   HOSTEL $
(☑️03-304 7066; www.onuku.co.nz; Hamiltons Rd, Onuku; sites per person from $15, dm/d from $20/70; ⏰Oct-Apr; 🅿️@🛜) 🏃 Set on a working farm 6km south of Akaroa, this blissfully isolated backpackers has a grassy camping area, simple, tidy rooms in a farmhouse and 'stargazer' cabins with translucent roofing ($50 for two, BYO bedding). Tonga Hut affords more privacy and breathtaking sea views ($80). Ask about the swimming-with-dolphins tours (from $130), kayaking trips (from $40) and the Skytrack walk.

⭐Halfmoon Cottage   HOSTEL $
(☑️03-304 5050; www.halfmoon.co.nz; SH75, Barrys Bay; dm/s/d $35/75/93; ⏰closed Jun-Aug; 🅿️@🛜) This pretty 1896 cottage, 12km from Akaroa and right on the water, is a blissful place to spend a few days lazing on the big verandas or in the hammocks dotting the gardens. It offers proper home comforts and style, with the bonus of bicycles and kayaks to take exploring.

Okuti Garden   HOSTEL $
(☑️03-325 1913; www.okuti.co.nz; 216 Okuti Valley Rd; adult/child $50/25; ⏰Oct-Apr; 🅿️🛜) 🏃 Ecologically sound creds are just part of this delightfully eccentric package that includes a house truck and a series of romantic yurts dotted throughout colourful gardens. Freshly picked herbs, a pizza oven, a fire-warmed bath, hammocks and free-roaming chickens give this place some serious *Good Life* vibes.

Okains Bay Camping Ground   CAMPGROUND $
(☑️03-304 8789; www.okainsbaycamp.co.nz; 1357 Okains Bay Rd, Okains Bay; sites per adult/child $13/7; 🅿️👪) This tidy camp sits on a pine-tree-peppered swathe of land right by a lovely beach and estuary. Facilities include kitchens, toilets and coin-operated hot showers, and the location is unbeatable. Laundry facilities are also available.

Coombe Farm   B&B $$
(☑️03-304 7239; www.coombefarm.co.nz; 18 Old Le Bons Track, Takamatua Valley; d $180-220; 🅿️🛜) Choose between the private and romantic Shepherd's Hut – complete with outdoor bath – or the historic farmhouse lovingly restored in shades of Laura Ashley. After a luxe breakfast you can take a walk to the nearby waterfall, or drive the five minutes into Akaroa.

Eating

Barrys Bay Cheese   CHEESE $
(☑️03-304 5809; www.barrysbaycheese.co.nz; 5807 Christchurch-Akaroa Rd; cheese $7-11; ⏰9am-5pm; ☑️) 🏃 This award-winning cheese factory has a small store attached where you can taste its cheesy goodness and

pick up supplies for seaside picnics. Large windows give you a sneak peek into where the magic happens. It's 12km from Akaroa.

Little River Cafe & Gallery CAFE $$
(☑03-325 1944; www.littlerivergallery.com; SH75, Little River; mains $13-22; ⊘7.30am-4pm Mon-Fri, to 4.30pm Sat & Sun) On SH75 between Christchurch and Akaroa, the flourishing settlement of Little River is home to this fantastic combo of contemporary art gallery, shop and cafe. It's top-notch in all departments, with some particularly delectable home baking on offer as well as yummy deli goods to go.

Hilltop Tavern PUB FOOD $$
(☑03-325 1005; www.thehilltop.co.nz; 5207 Christchurch-Akaroa Rd; pizzas $26, mains $25-30; ⊘10am-late, reduced hours May-Sep) Craft beer, wood-fired pizzas, a pool table and occasional live bands seal the deal for locals and visitors alike at this historic pub. Enjoy stunning views of Akaroa harbour and the peninsula – especially at sunset.

❶ Getting There & Away

The daily Akaroa Shuttle (p454) runs from Christchurch to Akaroa, departing at 8.30am (hotel pick-ups available), returning to Christchurch at 3.45pm (late October to April). From May to late October, shuttles depart Christchurch at 9am and return at 4pm. Check the website for Christchurch pick-up options. Scenic tours from Christchurch exploring Banks Peninsula are also available.

French Connection (p454) has a year-round daily departure from Christchurch at 9am, returning from Akaroa at 4pm.

Akaroa
POP 625

Akaroa (Long Harbour) was the site of the country's first French settlement and descendants of the original French pioneers still reside here. It's a charming town that strives to recreate the feel of a French provincial village, down to the names of its streets and houses. Generally it's a sleepy place, but the peace is periodically shattered by hordes descending from gargantuan cruise ships. The ships used to dock in Lyttelton but since the earthquakes Akaroa has been a popular substitute. At the time of writing, Lyttelton's new cruise terminal was scheduled to open late 2020, but it is expected Akaroa's expansive and spectacular harbour will also remain a popular anchorage.

◉ Sights

★ Giant's House GARDENS
(www.thegiantshouse.co.nz; 68 Rue Balguerie; adult/child $20/10; ⊘11am-4pm Oct-Apr, to 2pm May-Sep) An ongoing labour of love by local artist Josie Martin, this whimsical garden is really one giant artwork, a combination of sculpture and mosaics that cascades down a hillside above Akaroa. Echoes of Gaudí and Miró can be found in the intricate collages of mirrors, tiles and broken china, and there are many surprising nooks and crannies to discover. Martin also exhibits her paintings and sculptures in the lovely 1880 house, the former residence of Akaroa's first bank manager.

★ Akaroa Museum MUSEUM
(www.akaroamuseum.org.nz; cnr Rues Lavaud & Balguerie; ⊘10.30am-4pm) FREE An arduous post-quake revamp has rewarded Akaroa with a smart, contemporary regional museum. Learn about the various phases of the peninsula's settlement, from the Māori to the French, and view interesting temporary exhibitions. The 20-minute historical film screening in the adjacent restored courthouse is worth a look, too. Note the donation box.

Old French Cemetery CEMETERY
The first consecrated burial ground in Canterbury, this hillside monument makes for a poignant wander. Follow the trail (up the hill) off Rue Brittan.

St Patrick's Catholic Church CHURCH
(www.akaroacatholicparish.co.nz; 29 Rue Lavaud; ⊘8am-7pm) Akaroa's Catholic church (1863) is a cute, frilly edged old dear, featuring richly coloured stained glass imported from Stuttgart.

St Peter's Anglican Church CHURCH
(46 Rue Balguerie) Graciously restored in 2015, this 1864 Anglican gem features extensive exposed timbers, stained glass and a historic organ. Well worth a peek whether you're godly or not.

🏃 Activities

Akaroa Adventure Centre OUTDOORS
(☑03-304 7784; www.akaroaadventurecentre.co.nz; 74a Rue Lavaud; ⊘9am-5pm; ⊕) Rents sea kayaks and stand-up paddleboards (per hour/day $25/70), paddle boats (per hour $25) and bikes (per hour/day $15/60). Based at the i-SITE (p454); open later in summer (December through March).

CHRISTCHURCH & CANTERBURY AKAROA

Akaroa

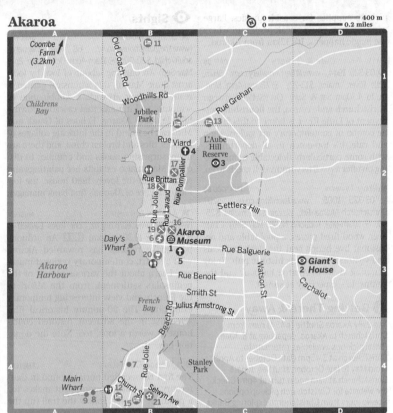

🕝 Tours

Akaroa Guided
Sea Kayaking Safari   KAYAKING
(📞021 156 4591; www.akaroakayaks.com; per person from $130; 🚼) 🏄 Paddle serenely around the harbour on these guided kayaking tours, which cater for beginners and experienced paddlers alike. Slip into the water at 7.30am for a three-hour sunrise safari, or if early starts aren't your thing, try the 11.30am highlights tour.

Eastern Bays
Scenic Mail Run   DRIVING
(📞03-304 7784; tours $80; ⏰departs 9am Mon-Fri) Travel along with the ex-conservation-ranger postie to visit isolated communities and bays on this 120km, five-hour mail delivery service. Departs from the i-SITE (p454); bookings are essential as there are only eight seats available.

Black Cat Cruises   BOATING
(📞03-304 7641; www.blackcat.co.nz; Main Wharf; nature cruises adult/child $90/35, dolphin swims $185/155; 🚼) As well as a two-hour nature cruise, Black Cat offers a three-hour 'swimming with dolphins' experience. Wetsuits and snorkelling gear are provided, plus hot showers back on dry land. Observers can tag along (adult/child $95/55) but only 12 people can swim per trip, so book ahead. Cruises have a 98% success rate in seeing Akaroa's compact Hector's dolphins, and an 83% success rate in actually swimming with them (there's a 25% refund if there's no swim). Note that while concerns over the impact of swimming tours on the bottlenose dolphins in the Bay of Islands have caused such tours to be banned there, they are still allowed here in Akaroa.

Akaroa Dolphins   BOATING
(📞03-304 7866; www.akaroadolphins.co.nz; 65 Beach Rd; adult/child $92/50; ⏰12.45pm year-

Akaroa

round, plus 10.15am & 3.15pm Oct-Apr; 🚲) Two-hour wildlife cruises on a comfortable 50ft catamaran, complete with a complimentary drink, home baking and, most important-ly, the company of an extraordinary wild-life-spotting dog.

Fox II Sailing   BOATING
(🖉 0800 369 7245; www.akaroafoxsail.co.nz; Daly's Wharf; adult/child $90/45; ☺ departs 10.30am & 1.30pm Jan-May) 🧭 Enjoy the scenery, ob-serve the marine wildlife, learn some history and try your hand at sailing on *Fox II,* a gaff-rigged ketch built in 1922.

🎎 Festivals & Events

French Fest   FOOD & DRINK
(www.akaroa.com/akaroa-frenchfest; ☺ Oct) This Gallic-inspired, two-day celebration features historical re-enactments, markets, activities and – *bien sûr* – plenty of food and wine. It's held biennially in odd-numbered years.

🛏 Sleeping

**Akaroa Top 10
Holiday Park**   HOLIDAY PARK $
(🖉 03-304 7471, 0800 727 525; www.akaroa-holiday park.co.nz; 96 Morgans Rd; sites $44-47, cabins & units $72-125; 🅿 @ 🛜 🚲) Grandstand views of the harbour and peninsula hills are the main drawcard at this basic holiday park. Cabins and motel units are dated but tidy, while the facilities blocks are due for an overhaul.

La Rochelle   MOTEL $$
(🖉 0800 452 762, 03-304 8762; www.larochelle motel.co.nz; 1 Rue Grehan; d/q $170/260; 🅿 🛜) Tidy, modern and reasonably priced, La Ro-chelle has a range of excellent motel units within walking distance of the main village. Each room has a kitchenette and opens onto a small private patio or balcony. The friendly family owners have lots of local advice on what to do and where to eat.

Akaroa Village Inn   APARTMENTS $$
(🖉 03-304 1111; www.akaroavillageinn.co.nz; 81 Beach Rd; units $139-299; 🅿 🛜) Right on the harbour front, this sprawling complex of-fers one- and two-bedroom units of varying levels of luxury. The water-view apartments are obviously the pick of the bunch, but ask to see a few, as they are individually owned, and furnishings vary widely.

Tresori Motor Lodge   MOTEL $$
(🖉 03-304 7500; www.tresori.co.nz; cnr Rue Jolie & Church St; d $135-205; 🛜) There are 12 tidy, modern units at this friendly motel set one block back from the esplanade. All have kitchenettes, but given the proximity to Akaroa's cafe and restaurant strip, you needn't worry about using them.

★**Beaufort House**   B&B $$$
(🖉 03-304 7517; www.beauforthouse.co.nz; 42 Rue Grehan; r $395; ☺ closed Jun-Aug; 🅿 🛜) Tucked away on a quiet street behind gorgeous gardens, this lovely 1878 house is adorned with covetable artwork and antiques. Of the

five individually decorated rooms only one is without an en suite, compensated by a large private bathroom with a claw-foot tub just across the hall. A lovely breakfast is included.

✗ Eating

Peninsula General Store   CAFE, DELI **$**
(☑03-3048800; www.peninsulageneralstore.co.nz; 40 Rue Lavaud; ⊙9am-4pm Wed-Sat, to 2pm Sun) 🍴 Not only does this darling little corner shop sell fresh bread, organic local produce and groceries, it also does the best espresso in the village.

Akaroa Boucherie & Deli   DELI **$**
(67 Rue Lavaud; ⊙10am-5.30pm Mon-Fri, 9am-4pm Sat) 🍴 A dream scenario for picnickers and self-caterers, this sharp butcher's shop and deli peddles all manner of local produce from bread, salmon, cheese and pickles, to delicious pies, smallgoods and, of course, meat.

★ Rona's   CAFE **$$**
(☑03-304 8533; www.ronas.co.nz; 74 Rue Lavaud; mains $18-22; ⊙7am-3.30pm Thu-Tue; 🄿) 🍴 Rona's menu is divided neatly into 'On Toast' and 'In a Bowl'. The Turkish poached eggs on ciabatta with chilli and yoghurt is a hearty favourite, while açai and poke bowls hint at healthy Hawaiian influences. Good-value snack options include damn fine grilled cheese sandwiches ($11 to $14).

Little Bistro   FRENCH **$$$**
(☑03-304 7314; www.thelittlebistro.co.nz; 33 Rue Lavaud; mains $28-42; ⊙5.30-11pm Tue-Sat) A decent bet for refined food, this place serves a classic bistro-style menu featuring local seafood, South Island wines and New Zealand craft beers. The menu changes seasonally, but usually includes favourites such as crusted lamb or local salmon. Across the seasonal menu there's a strong commitment to harnessing ingredients from around Banks Peninsula.

🍷 Drinking & Nightlife

Harbar   BAR
(www.facebook.com/harbarakaroa; 83 Rue Jolie; ⊙5-9.30pm) Sporadic opening hours, sometimes dictated by the seasons, weather and demand, should not stop you from trying for a sundowner at Akaroa's favourite waterside bar. There's no better location for a harbour-front tipple. Gourmet burgers, fish tacos and local Canterbury craft beers are other essential attractions. Check the Facebook page for notice of occasional live music.

☆ Entertainment

Akaroa Cinema & Café   CINEMA
(☑03-304 8898; www.cinecafe.co.nz; cnr Rue Jolie & Selwyn Ave; adult/child $17/12) Grab a beer and settle in to watch an art-house, classic or foreign flick with high-quality sound and projection.

ℹ Information

Akaroa i-SITE & Adventure Centre (☑03-304 7784; www.akaroa.com; 74a Rue Lavaud; ⊙9am-5pm) A helpful hub offering free maps, info and bookings for activities, transport etc. Doubles as the post office.

ℹ Getting There & Away

Daily shuttles with **Akaroa Shuttle** (☑0800 500 929; www.akaroashuttle.co.nz; adult/child one way $36/31, return $46/41) from Christchurch to Akaroa depart at 8.30am (hotel pick-ups available), returning to Christchurch at 3.45pm (late October to April). From May to late October, shuttles depart Christchurch at 9am and return at 4pm.

French Connection (☑0800 800 575; www.akaroabus.co.nz; adult/child return $50/30) has a year-round daily departure from Christchurch at 9am, returning from Akaroa at 4pm.

NORTH CANTERBURY

South of Kaikōura, a popular destination for wildlife watching, SH1 crosses the Hundalee Hills and heads into Hurunui District, an area known for its wine and for the thermal resort of Hanmer Springs. It's also the start of the Canterbury Plains, a vast, flat, richly agricultural area partitioned by distinctive braided rivers. The region is bounded to the west by the Southern Alps. If you're crossing into Canterbury from either Westport or Nelson, the most direct route cuts through the Alps on the beautiful Lewis Pass Hwy (SH7).

Kaikōura

POP 1970

Kaikōura is a pretty peninsula town backed by the snow-capped Seaward Kaikōura Range, 180km north from Christchurch. Few places in the world are home to such a variety of easily spottable wildlife: whales, dolphins, NZ fur seals, penguins, shearwaters, petrels and several species of albatross live in or pass by the area.

Marine animals are abundant here due to ocean-current and continental-shelf conditions: the seabed gradually slopes away from the land before plunging to depths of 1200m where the southerly current hits the continental shelf. This creates an upwelling of nutrients from the ocean floor into the feeding zone.

In 2016, the Kaikōura region was struck by a severe magnitude 7.8 earthquake, but following the re-establishment of badly damaged transport links, the town is once again easily reached and an essential destination for anyone with an interest in wildlife.

History

The Kaikōura region was heavily settled by Māori, with excavations showing that the area was a moa-hunter settlement about 800 to 1000 years ago. The name Kaikōura comes from 'kai' (food/eat) and 'kōura' (crayfish).

James Cook sailed past the peninsula in 1770, but didn't land. His journal states that 57 Māori in four double-hulled canoes came towards the *Endeavour,* but 'would not be prevail'd upon to put along side'.

In 1828 Kaikōura's beachfront was the scene of a tremendous battle. A northern Ngāti Toa war party, led by chief Te Rauparaha, bore down on Kaikōura, killing or capturing several hundred of the local Ngāi Tahu tribe.

Europeans established a whaling station here in 1842 and in 1859 a dodgy land deal swindled local Māori out of most of their land. The town remained a whaling centre until 1922, after which time farming and fishing sustained the community. It was in the 1980s that wildlife tours began to transform Kaikōura into a lively tourist town.

The 7.8 magnitude earthquake that struck the Kaikōura region just after midnight on 14 November 2016 was one of the largest and longest quakes to strike the country since European settlement. Fatalities were mercifully limited to two deaths, but the damage done to the landscape was staggering. Huge gashes were torn through farmland, new lakes were formed overnight when rivers were dammed, sections of the coastline were lifted by 8m, and parts of NZ's South Island moved more than 5m closer to the North Island.

⊙ Sights

Kaikoura Museum   MUSEUM
(☑03-319 7440; www.kaikoura-museum.co.nz; 96 West End; adult/child $12/6; ⊙10am-5pm) Housed

in a modern building designed to resemble a crayfishing pot, this whizz-bang museum illuminates the region's geology and natural and social histories with well-curated exhibitions. Highlights include the fossilised remains of a plesiosaur and a mosasaur, a holographic prisoner in a padded cell, and poignant displays on the 2016 earthquake.

Fyffe House   HISTORIC BUILDING
(☑03-319 5835; www.fyffehouse.co.nz; 62 Avoca St; adult/child $10/free; ⊙10am-5pm Oct-Apr, to 4pm Thu-Mon May-Sep) Kaikōura's oldest surviving building and the last remaining part of the Waiopuka whaling station, Fyffe House's whale-bone foundations were laid in 1844. Fronted with a colourful garden, the little two-storey cottage offers a fascinating insight into the lives of early British settlers. Interpretive displays are complemented by historic objects (including the biggest moa egg ever found), while peeling wallpaper and the odd cobweb lend authenticity. There's a cute heritage-themed shop, too.

Point Kean Seal Colony   WILDLIFE RESERVE
New Zealand fur seals can usually be spotted lazing around on the rocks at the end of the peninsula. Give them a wide berth (10m), and never get between them and the sea – they will attack if they feel cornered and can move surprisingly fast. Since the uplift of the coastline during the 2016 earthquake, the seals have moved further from the road and car park, so keep a close eye on tides.

Emporium Brewing   BREWERY
(☑03-319 5897; www.emporiumbrewing.co.nz; 57a Beach Rd; ⊙10am-7pm daily Dec-Apr, Wed-Mon May-Nov) Fill up a takeaway rigger or buy bottles of Emporium's tasty brews at this simple taproom. There are also escape rooms (two players $70; book ahead) and an on-site minigolf course (adult/child $10/5). Check out the hole featuring the 'earthquake cows', three bovine locals that were stranded on a tiny 'island' of farmland for three days following the 2016 earthquake.

⚐ Activities

There's a safe swimming beach on the Esplanade. Decent surfing can be found around the area, particularly at Mangamaunu Beach (15km north of town), where there's a 500m point break. Fishing is a common obsession in Kaikōura, with local boaties offering trips starting from around $70; the i-SITE (p459) has a full list of operators.

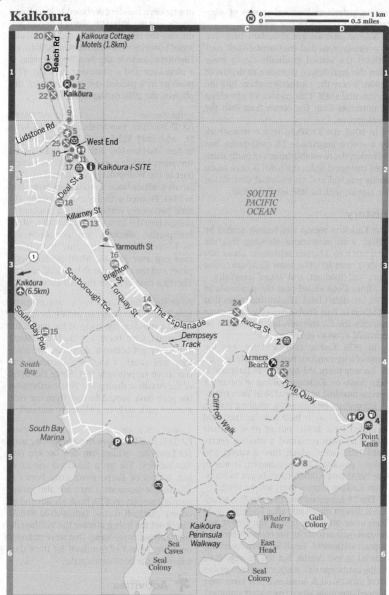

Kaikōura Cottage Motels (1.8km)

20
1
Beach Rd
7
19
12
22
Kaikōura
9
Ludstone Rd
5
25
West End
10
11
17
3 Kaikōura i-SITE
18
Deal St
Killarney St
13
6
Yarmouth St
16
Brighton St
Scarborough Tce
Torquay St
14
The Esplanade
24
21
Avoca St
Dempseys Track
2
Kaikōura
(6.5km)
South Bay Pde
15
Armers Beach
23
Fyffe Quay
South Bay
Clifftop Walk
South Bay Marina
P
4
Point Kean
P
8
Kaikōura Peninsula Walkway
Whalers Bay
Gull Colony
Sea Caves
East Head
Seal Colony
Seal Colony

SOUTH PACIFIC OCEAN

CHRISTCHURCH & CANTERBURY KAIKŌURA

In 2019 the government announced funding of a 200km cycle route between Picton and Kaikōura to be known as the **Whale Trail** (www.thewhaletrail.nz); check the website for the most recent developments.

Kaikōura Peninsula Walkway WALKING
Starting from town, this must-do three- to four-hour loop heads out to Point Kean, along the cliffs to South Bay, then back to town over the isthmus (or in reverse, of course). En route you'll see fur seals and

Kaikōura

red-billed seagull and shearwater colonies. Lookouts and interesting interpretive panels abound. Collect a map at the i-SITE (p459) or follow your nose.

Kaikoura Coast Track HIKING
(📱03-319 2715; www.kaikouratrack.co.nz; 356 Conway Flat Rd, Ngaroma; adult/child $200/190) This easy two-day, 26km, self-guided hike across private farmland combines coastal and alpine views. The price includes two nights' cottage accommodation, including one night before actually beginning the walk, and pack transport; BYO sleeping bag and food, or pay extra for linen ($20), breakfast ($20), lunch ($20) and dinner ($50). It starts 45km south of Kaikōura.

Coastal Sports OUTDOORS
(📱03-319 5028; www.coastalsports.co.nz; 24 West End; ⊙9am-5.30pm Mon-Sat, 10am-4pm Sun, extended hours Oct–Easter) The friendly folk at this sports shop can hook you up with hire bikes (half/full day $30/40), surf gear (board and wetsuit $40 per day) and lots of local intel. There's also a good selection of hiking and outdoor gear to purchase.

👉 Tours

Wildlife tours are Kaikōura's speciality, particularly those involving whales (including sperm, pilot, killer, humpback and southern right), dolphins (Hector's, bottlenose and dusky – a particularly social species sometimes seen in the hundreds) and New Zealand fur seals. There's also plenty of birdlife, including albatrosses and blue penguins.

Your choices are boat, plane or helicopter. Aerial options are shorter and pricier, but allow you to see the whole whale, as opposed to just a tail, flipper or spout. During sum-

mer, book your tour a few weeks ahead, and allow some leeway for lousy weather.

Air Kaikoura WHALE WATCHING
(📱03 319 6579; www.airkaikoura.co.nz; Kaikoura Airport, 627 Kaikoura South Rd, Peketa; 30/40min flights $150/180) The local aero club offers professional and highly successful whale-watching tours plus scenic and charter flights. If you want to cross 'piloting a two-seater plane' off your bucketlist, it offers that too (20 minutes, $120).

Wings over Whales WHALE WATCHING
(📱03-319 6580; www.whales.co.nz; Kaikoura South Rd, Peketa; 30min flights adult/child $195/100; ⊙8am-5pm) Light-plane flights departing from Kaikōura Airport, 8km south of town on SH1. Whale-spotting success rate: 95%.

South Pacific Helicopters WHALE WATCHING
(📱03-319 5548; www.southpacifichelicopters.co.nz; 72 West End; per person $275-950) Offers a wide range of whale-watching and flightseeing trips by helicopter.

Kaikōura Helicopters WHALE WATCHING
(📱03-319 6609; www.worldofwhales.co.nz; Whaleway Station Rd) Reliable whale-spotting flights plus jaunts around the peninsula, Mt Fyffe and peaks beyond. Ask about flights taking in the area's spectacular post-earthquake landscapes from above.

Whale Watch Kaikoura WHALE WATCHING
(📱03-319 6767; www.whalewatch.co.nz; Whaleway Station Rd; tours adult/child $150/60) 🖊 With knowledgable guides and fascinating on-board animation, Kaikōura's biggest operator heads out on boat trips (with admirable frequency) in search of some of the big fellas. It'll refund 80% of your fare if no whales

CHRISTCHURCH & CANTERBURY KAIKŌURA

are sighted (success rate: 95%). If this trip is a must for you, allow a few days' flexibility in case the weather turns to custard.

Albatross Encounter
BIRDWATCHING

(📞 03-319 6777; www.albatrossencounter.co.nz; 96 Esplanade; adult/child $130/65; ⊙tours 9am & 1pm year-round, plus 6am Nov-Apr) 🏆 Even if you don't consider yourself a bird-nerd, you'll love this boat trip providing close encounters with pelagic species such as shearwaters, shags, mollymawks and petrels. It's the various albatross species, however, that steal the show.

Seal Swim Kaikōura
WILDLIFE

(📞 03-319 6182; www.sealswimkaikoura.co.nz; 58 West End; adult/child $120/80, viewing $60/40; ⊙Nov-Apr) 🏆 Take a warmly wet-suited swim with Kaikōura's healthy population of playful seals – including very cute pups – on guided snorkelling tours (by boat).

Dolphin Encounter
WILDLIFE

(📞 03-319 6777; www.encounterkaikoura.co.nz; 96 Esplanade; adult/child swim $180/165, observation $95/55; ⊙tours 8.30am & 12.30pm year-round, plus 5.30am Nov-Apr) 🏆 Claiming NZ's highest success rate (over 90%) for locating dolphins, this operator runs DOC-permitted three-hour tours, which often encounter sizeable pods of sociable duskies. Note that while concerns over the impact of swimming tours on the bottlenose dolphins in the Bay of Islands have caused such tours to be banned, they are currently still allowed here.

Clarence River Rafting
RAFTING

(📞 03-319 6993; www.clarenceriverrafting.co.nz; 1/3802 SH1, Clarence; half-day trips adult/child $140/80) Raft the rapids of the Clarence/Waiau-Toa River and experience the spectacular uplift and changes to the landscape following the 2016 Kaikōura earthquake. Half-day trips incorporate 2½ hours on the water, while longer journeys include a three-to five-day adventure with wilderness camping. Based on SH1, 35km north of Kaikōura near the Clarence Bridge. Grade II; all gear provided.

Kaikoura Kayaks
KAYAKING

(📞 03-319 7118; www.kaikourakayaks.nz; 19 Killarney St; 3hr tours adult/child $110/70; ♿) Excellent, family-friendly, guided sea-kayak tours to view fur seals and explore the peninsula's coastline. Kayak fishing and other on-demand trips available, plus freedom kayak

and paddleboard hire. Ask about visiting Hope Springs, a sulphurous, bubbling section of the ocean that was discovered following the 2016 earthquake.

Seal Kayak Kaikoura
KAYAKING

(📞 027 261 0124; www.sealkayakkaikoura.com; 18 Beach Rd; adult/child $95/69) Sightseeing, seal encounters, sunset tours and fishing trips using pedal kayaks, which provide the option of propelling the craft either with your arms or legs.

🛏 Sleeping

Albatross Backpacker Inn
HOSTEL $

(📞 03-319 6090; www.albatross-kaikoura.co.nz; 1 Torquay St; dm/tw/d without bathroom from $32/79/84; 🅿🛜) 🏆 This arty backpackers resides in three sweet buildings, one a former post office. It's colourful and close to the beach but sheltered from the breeze. As well as a laid-back lounge with musical instruments for jamming, there are decks and verandas to spread out on.

Kaikoura Cottage Motels
MOTEL $$

(📞 03-319 5599; www.kaikouracottagemotels.co .nz; 7 Old Beach Rd; units $150-180; ⊙Sep-May; 🅿🛜) This enclave of eight modern freestanding units looks mighty fine, surrounded by attractive native plantings. Oriented for mountain views, the spick-and-span self-contained units sleep four between an open-plan studio-style living room and one private bedroom. Lovely hosts seal the deal.

Anchor Inn
MOTEL $$

(📞 03-319 5426; www.anchorinn.co.nz; 208 Esplanade; units from $175; 🅿❄🛜) These sharp and spacious units are a pleasant 15-minute walk from town and about 10 seconds from the ocean. Choose between studios with either sea or garden views, or a one- or two-bedroom apartment, sleeping up to five people.

Bay Cottages
MOTEL $$

(📞 03-319 7165; www.baycottages.co.nz; 29a South Bay Pde; cottages $150-170; 🅿🛜) Here's a great-value option in South Bay, a few kilometres south of town, close to Kaikōura's new harbour. Five cottages sleeping up to four all feature a kitchen, lounge area and free Netflix. The surrounding area is private and quiet, and there's even a barbecue to grill your fish on.

Kaikoura

Boutique Hotel
BOUTIQUE HOTEL **$$$**

(☑ 03-319 5748; www.kaikouraboutiquehotel.co.nz; 146 Esplanade; r $188-399; P ☎) Occupying a gorgeous heritage building halfway along the Esplanade, this chic hotel has plush rooms in the main building and a brace of smaller rooms edging the back garden. Quirky art, excellent bathrooms, balconies with sea views and chandeliers like disco balls elevate the waterfront rooms out of the ordinary.

Lemon Tree Lodge
B&B **$$$**

(☑ 03-319 7464; www.lemontree.co.nz; 31 Adelphi Tce; r $320-380; ☺ Nov-Mar; ☎) Enjoying superb ocean and mountain views, Lemon Tree Lodge combines four charming and stylish rooms in the main house with two quiet and secluded garden units. Our favourites are the Ocean View Suites with expansive windows and private balconies showcasing brilliant Pacific vistas. The well-travelled and friendly owners have plenty of great advice on how best to enjoy the region.

Nikau Lodge
B&B **$$$**

(☑ 03-319 6973; www.nikaulodge.com; 53 Deal St; d $220-280; ☺ Oct-Mar; P ☎) Expect high standards and grand-scale vistas at this beautiful B&B high on the hill. The five ensuite rooms are plush and comfy, with additional satisfaction arriving in the form of cafe-quality breakfasts accompanied by fresh local coffee. Good humour, home baking, free wi-fi, complimentary drinks, a hot tub and blooming gardens: you may want to move in.

✕ Eating

Beach House Cafe
CAFE **$**

(☑ 03-319 6035; 39 Beach Rd; mains $7-19; ☺ 7am-3.30pm; ☎) Beachy artwork fills the walls of this cosy cottage cafe but, despite the name, it's on the highway with no water in sight. Choose between tasty muffins and an excellent eggs Benedict for breakfast, and return at lunchtime for seafood chowder, souvlaki or burgers.

Kaikoura Seafood BBQ
SEAFOOD **$**

(☑ 027 376 3619; www.facebook.com/kkseafood bbq; Fyffe Quay; items $10-12; ☺ 9.30am-5pm Sun-Fri, 11am-3pm Sat, extended hours in summer) Conveniently located on the way to the Point Kean Seal Colony, this long-standing road-side barbecue is a great spot to sample local seafood, including crayfish (half from $45), chowder and whitebait fritters.

Cods & Crayfish
SEAFOOD **$**

(☑ 03-319 7899; www.codsncray.co.nz; 81 Beach Rd; mains $8-12; ☺ 8am-6pm; ☎) This combo fish shop and fast-food joint serves fish and chips, fish burgers and half crays grilled to order. Scoff them on the outdoor tables or at the nearby beach.

Pier Hotel
PUB FOOD **$$**

(☑ 03-319 5037; www.thepierhotel.co.nz; 1 Avoca St; lunch $15-36, dinner $24-36; ☺ 11am-late) Situated in a primo seaside spot, with panoramic views over the water to the Inland Kaikōura Range, this venerable pub (built in 1885) is a friendly place for a drink and respectable food, including crayfish and paua (abalone). You'll find beers here from Kaikōura's two craft breweries: Emporium Brewing and the Kaikōura Brewing Company.

Green Dolphin
EUROPEAN **$$**

(☑ 03-319 6666; www.greendolphin.co.nz; 12 Avoca St; mains $28-39; ☺ 5pm-late Tue-Sat) Under new ownership, this upmarket place continues to deliver French-style fare using top-quality local produce including crayfish, paua, beef, lamb and venison. There are also lovely homemade pasta dishes. Ask for a window table to enjoy the ocean and mountain views.

Zephyr
BISTRO **$$$**

(☑ 03-319 6999; www.zephyrrestaurant.co.nz; 40 West End; mains $34-37; ☺ 5.30pm-late Mon-Sat) Focusing on a concise and seasonal menu, Zephyr's modern dining room is a good place to enjoy seafood chowder, mushroom-crusted venison or local fish with a gourmet spin. The wine and beer list is equally focused and well curated.

❶ Information

Kaikoura i-SITE (☑ 03-319 5641; www.kaik oura.co.nz; West End; ☺ 9am-5pm, extended hours Dec-Mar) Helpful staff make tour, accommodation and transport bookings, and help with DOC-related matters.

❶ Getting There & Away

The 2016 earthquake resulted in 85 landslides on SH1 on either side of Kaikoura. Roadworks are still continuing, with lots of stop/go, one-way sections; expect delays.

BUS

InterCity (p717) buses stop outside the i-SITE, with two buses a day heading to/from Christchurch (from $22, three hours), Waipara (from $20, 1¾ hours), Blenheim (from $19, 1¾ hours) and Picton (from $25, 2½ hours).

TRAIN

KiwiRail's scenic Coastal Pacific (p446) service operates daily from October to April, heading to/from Picton (three hours), Blenheim (2½ hours) and Christchurch (3¼ hours); fares start from $59.

ℹ Getting Around

Kaikoura Shuttles (✆ 03-319 6166; www.kaikourashuttles.co.nz) will run you around the local sights as well as to and from the airport. For local car hire, contact **Kaikoura Rentals** (✆ 03-319 3311; www.kaikourarentals.co.nz; 94 Churchill St).

Lewis Pass

The northernmost of the three main mountain passes connecting the West Coast to the east, 864m-high Lewis Pass is not as steep as the others (Arthur's and Haast), but the drive is arguably just as scenic. Vegetation comprises mainly beech (red and silver) and kowhai trees growing along river terraces. From Lewis Pass the highway wiggles east for 62km before reaching the turn-off to Hanmer Springs. Heading northeast to Kaikōura, the road travels through Waiau before reaching SH1.

◉ Sights

Marble Hill   FOREST

(www.doc.govt.nz; SH7) Located within Lewis Pass Scenic Reserve, Marble Hill is home to one of NZ's most beautiful DOC camping grounds – a row of sites tucked into beech forest, overlooking a grassy meadow and encircled by snow-capped mountains.

This special place represents a landmark victory for NZ's conservation movement. Back in the 1970s, this significant forest was saved from the chop by a 341,159-signature petition known as the 'Maruia Declaration', which played a part in the Department of Conservation's establishment in 1987.

🏃 Activities

The area has some interesting hikes, passing through beech forest backed by snow-capped mountains, lakes and alpine tarns. Popular tracks include the St James Walkway (66km; four to five days) and those through Lake Sumner Forest Park; see the DOC pamphlet *Lake Sumner & Lewis Pass* ($2). Subalpine conditions apply; make sure you sign the intentions books at the huts.

Maruia Springs   HOT SPRINGS

(✆ 03-523 8840; www.maruiahotsprings.nz; SH7; adult/child $40/18; ⊙ 8am-9pm) Maruia Springs is a small hot-spring resort on the banks of the Maruia River. The water temperature varies between 36°C and 42°C across a variety of pools, including outdoor rock pools, indoor baths, a sauna and a cold plunge pool. It's a magical setting during winter (June to September) but mind the sandflies in summer (December to March).

New owners have recently invested in the resort with renovations and improvements including new outdoor bathing pools and private spas. Accommodation is available in simple but cosy rooms (doubles from $249); guests have 24-hour access to the pools. There's also an overnight campground and a cafe with a sunny deck overlooking the river. It's 6km west of Lewis Pass.

ℹ Getting There & Away

East West Coaches (✆ 03-789 6251; www.eastwestcoaches.co.nz) runs between Christchurch and Westport via the Lewis Pass daily except Saturday stopping at Maruia Springs and the St James Walkway.

Hanmer Springs

POP 840

Ringed by mountains, pretty Hanmer Springs has a slightly European feel, enhanced by the fact that many of the streets are named after English spa towns (Bath, Harrogate, Leamington). The town is the main thermal resort on the South Island, and it's a pleasantly low-key spot to indulge yourself, whether by soaking in hot pools, dining out, or being pampered in the spa complex. If that all sounds too soporific, fear not; there are plenty of family-friendly outdoor activities on offer, including a few to get the adrenaline pumping.

🏃 Activities

★ **Hanmer Springs**
Thermal Pools   HOT SPRINGS

(✆ 03-315 0000; www.hanmersprings.co.nz; 42 Amuri Ave; adult/child $35/20, locker per 2hr $3; ⊙ 10am-9pm; 👶) 🍴 Māori legend has it that these hot springs are the result of embers from Mt Ngauruhoe on the North Island falling from the sky. Whatever their origin, visitors flock to Hanmer Springs year-round to soak in the warming waters. The main complex consists of a series of large pools of various temperatures.

There are also smaller, adult-only landscaped rock pools, a freshwater 25m lap pool, private thermal pools, a cafe and an adjacent spa. Kids of all ages will love the water slides – including the biggest in NZ, Conical Hill – and the whirl-down-the-plughole-thrill of the Superbowl ($10).

Hanmer Horse Trekking HORSE RIDING
(☑ 022 462 1435; www.hanmerhorsetrekking.com; 1/2hr $80/120, half/full day $160/350; 👪) 🌿 Treks exploring the forest and mountain scenery around Hanmer. Riders of all levels of experience are catered for and longer excursions venture into the rugged and remote St James Station area.

Hanmer Forest Park HIKING, MOUNTAIN BIKING
(www.visithurunui.co.nz; 👪) 🌿 Trampers and mountain bikers will find plenty of room to move within the 130 sq km expanse of forest abutting Hanmer Springs. The easy Woodland Walk starts 1km up Jollies Pass Rd and goes through Douglas fir, poplar and redwood stands before joining Majuba Walk, which leads to Conical Hill Lookout and then back towards town (1½ hours).

The Waterfall Track is an excellent half-day tramp starting at the end of McIntyre Rd. The i-SITE (p464) stocks a *Forest Park Walks* booklet and a mountain-biking map (both $3).

Hanmer Springs Spa SPA
(☑ 03-315 0000, 0800 873 529; www.thespa hanmersprings.nz; 42 Amuri Ave; ⊙ 10am-9pm) If you're looking to be pampered, you've come to the right place. Hanmer Springs Spa offers every kind of treatment you would expect from an international-standard spa, including facials (from $110), hot-stone massages ($180) and full-body treatments ($320).

Mt Lyford Alpine Resort SKIING
(☑ 03-366 1220, 027 471 0717; www.mtlyford.co.nz; day passes adult/child $83/40; ⊙ lifts 9am-4pm) Around 60km from both Hanmer Springs and Kaikōura, this is more of a 'resort' than most NZ ski fields, with accommodation and eating options. There's a good mix of runs and a terrain park.

A shuttle service runs from Mt Lyford village (a 45-minute drive from Hanmer

Hanmer Springs ⓝ

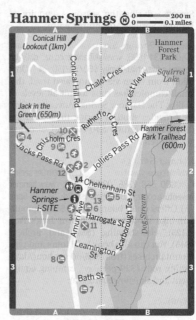

Hanmer Springs

Springs) during the season – enquire at Hanmer Springs Adventure Centre.

Hanmer Springs Ski Area · SKIING

(📞027 434 1806; www.skihanmer.co.nz; daily lift passes adult/child/family $60/30/130; 🚗) Only 17km from town via an unsealed road, this small complex has runs to suit all levels of ability. The Hamner Springs Adventure Centre provides shuttles during the ski season (adult/child return $40/32) and also has gear for rent.

Hanmer Springs Adventure Centre · ADVENTURE SPORTS

(📞0800 368 7386, 03-315 7233; www.hanmeradventure.co.nz; 20 Conical Hill Rd; ⏱9am-5pm; 🚗) Offers quad biking (from $139), mountain-bike shuttles to the top of Jack's Pass ($125), clay-shooting ($59) and archery ($45). You can also book local tours and rent mountain bikes (from $25/60 per hour/day), fishing rods ($29 per day), camping equipment and ski/snowboard gear.

Hanmer Springs Attractions · ADVENTURE SPORTS

(📞03-315 7046, 0800 661 538; www.hanmerspringsattractions.nz; 839 Hanmer Springs Rd; ⏱9am-5.30pm) Bungy off a 35m-high bridge ($169), jetboat the Waiau Gorge (one hour, adult/child $125/70), explore the Waiau River by raft (two hours, adult/child $169/99), get dirty on a quad bike (two hours, adult/child $169/99), or self-drive an off-road buggy (two hours, $249). The activities base is next to the bridge near the turn-off from SH7, but there's also a booking office (📞0800 661 538, 03-315 7346; www.hanmerspringsattractions.nz; 12 Conical Hill Rd; ⏱9am-5pm) in town.

A free shuttle bus is available from your accommodation to the activities base.

🛏 Sleeping

Hanmer Springs has a wide range of accommodation options, from basic camping through to luxury B&Bs and swanky apartments. If you're planning on staying awhile, check out websites like www.alpineholidayhomes.co.nz and www.hanmerholidayhomes.co.nz for local rentals.

Kakapo Lodge · HOSTEL $

(📞03-315 7472; www.kakapolodge.co.nz; 14 Amuri Ave; dm $33, d with/without bathroom from $100/80; 🅿🛜) The YHA-affiliated Kakapo has a cheery owner, a roomy kitchen and lounge, chill-busting underfloor heating and a 1st-floor sundeck. Bunk-free dorms (some with bathrooms) and spotless double rooms are available.

Jack in the Green · HOSTEL $

(📞03-315 5111; www.jackinthegreen.co.nz; 3 Devon St; sites per person $20, dm $32, d with/without bathroom $92/76; 🅿🛜) This charming converted old home is a 10-minute walk from the town centre. Large rooms (no bunks), relaxing gardens and a cosy lounge area are the main drawcards. For extra privacy, book an en suite garden 'chalet'. Excellent mountain bikes can be rented ($35 per day).

Hanmer Springs Top 10 · HOLIDAY PARK $

(📞0800 904 545, 03-315 7113; www.hanmerspringstop10.co.nz; 5 Hanmer Springs Rd; sites $44-54, units with/without bathroom from $154/99; 🅿@🛜🚗) This family-friendly park is just a few minutes' walk from the town's eponymous pools. Kids will love the playground and jumping pillow. Take your pick from basic cabins (BYO everything) to attractive motel units with everything supplied. Extremely comfortable new two-bedroom apartments were opened in late 2019.

★ Woodbank Park Cottages · COTTAGE $$

(📞03-315 5075; www.woodbankcottages.co.nz; 381 Woodbank Rd; d $190-225; 🅿❄) Nestled among the trees, these two plush cottages are a six-minute drive from Hanmer but feel a million miles away. Decor is crisp and modern, with wrap-around wooden decks that come equipped with gas barbecues and rural views. Log-burning fireplaces and well-stocked kitchens seal the deal.

Drifters Inn · LODGE $$

(📞03-315 7554; www.driftersinn.co.nz; 2 Harrogate St; d from $120; 🅿🛜) Compact and spotless rooms combine with spacious shared facilities, including a modern and well-equipped kitchen and comfortable lounge, providing guests at Drifters Inn with the advantages of both a motel and a lodge. Save money by cooking up a storm and you'll have more holiday funds for Hanmer's attractions and activities. Book online for good discounts.

Chalets Motel · MOTEL $$

(📞03-315 7097; www.chaletsmotel.co.nz; 56 Jacks Pass Rd; d $170-210; 🅿🛜) Soak up the mountain views from these tidy, reasonably priced, free-standing wooden chalets, set on the slopes behind the town centre. All chalets have full kitchens; the larger spa unit is the pick of the bunch.

MOLESWORTH STATION

Filling up 1807 mountainous sq km between Hanmer Springs and Blenheim, Molesworth Station is NZ's largest farm, with the country's largest cattle herd (up to 10,000). It's also an area of national ecological significance and the entire farm is now administered by DOC (☑03-572 9100; www.doc.govt.nz; Gee St, Renwick).

Visits are usually only possible when the Acheron Rd through the station is open from November to early April, weather permitting; check with DOC or at the Hanmer Springs i-SITE (p464). Note that the gates are only open from 7am to 7pm. Pick up DOC's *Molesworth Station* brochure from the i-SITE or download it from the website.

Highlights of a visit include wild and spectacular scenery, scree-covered mountains, expansive river valleys and windswept tussocky slopes.

Overnight camping (adult/child $6/3) is permitted in certain areas (no open fires allowed). There are also a couple of basic DOC huts (adult/child $5/2.50).

Molesworth Heritage Tours (☑027 201 4536, 03-315 7401; www.molesworth.co.nz; tours $235-770; ☺Oct-May) leads 4WD coach trips to the station from Hanmer Springs. Day tours include a picnic lunch, but there's also a five-hour 'no frills' option. From the Blenheim side, Molesworth Tours (☑03-572 8025; www.molesworthtours.co.nz) offers one- to four-day all-inclusive heritage and 4WD trips ($220 to $1487), as well as four-day fully supported (and catered) mountain-bike adventures (from $1460).

Cheltenham House
B&B $$$
(☑03-315 7545; www.cheltenham.co.nz; 13 Cheltenham St; r $255-295; P☎) This large 1930s house has room for both a billiard table and a grand piano. There are four art-filled suites in the main house and two in cosy garden cottages. Cooked gourmet breakfasts are delivered to the rooms and wine is served in the evening.

St James
APARTMENT $$$
(☑03-315 5225, 0508 785 2637; www.thestjames.co.nz; 20 Chisholm Cres; d $245-295, apt from $320; P✳☎) Luxuriate in a stylish modern apartment with all the mod cons, including an iPod dock and fully equipped kitchen. Sizes range from studios to two-bedroom apartments; most have mountain views.

✕ Eating

Hanmer Springs Bakery
BAKERY $
(☑03-315 7714; 24 Conical Hill Rd; pies $5-6, rolls from $6; ☺6am-4pm) In peak season queues stretch out the door for this humble bakery's meat pies and filled rolls.

Coriander Leaf
INDIAN $$
(☑03-315 7616; www.corianderleaf.co.nz; Chisholm Cres; mains $16-22; ☺noon-2pm & 5-10pm Tue-Sun; ✓) Spice up your life at this brightly painted North Indian restaurant complete with *bhangra*-beats soundtrack. There are plenty of tasty lamb, chicken and seafood dishes to choose from, plus a fine vegetarian selection.

Takeaways are especially popular and we can recommend the vegetable samosas.

Powerhouse Cafe
CAFE $$
(☑03-315 5252; www.powerhousecafe.co.nz; 8 Jacks Pass Rd; mains $16-28; ☺7.30am-2pm; ✓) Delicious cakes and good-quality coffee are on the menu at this local favourite, tucked away off the main street. Power up with a huge High Country breakfast or try the Highland Fling – caramelised, whisky-infused porridge topped with banana. Lunch offerings are equally palatable.

No. 31
MODERN NZ $$$
(☑03-315 7031; www.restaurant-no31.nz; 31 Amuri Ave; mains $37-40; ☺5-11pm) Substantial servings of good-quality, albeit conservative, cuisine are on offer in this pretty wooden cottage. The upmarket ambience befits the prices, though you're also paying for the location, directly opposite the hot springs. Canterbury lamb and venison feature along with craft beer and wine from the nearby Waipara region. Book ahead on weekends.

☕ Drinking & Nightlife

Monteith's Brewery Bar
PUB
(☑03-315 5133; www.mbbh.co.nz; 47 Amuri Ave; ☺9am-11pm) This large, slightly worn pub is the town's busiest watering hole. The kitchen serves decent pub-style meals all day (mains $22 to $35). Live musicians kick off from 4pm Sundays.

❶ Information

Hanmer Springs i-SITE (☑ 03-315 0020, 0800 442 663; www.visithanmersprings.co.nz; 40 Amuri Ave; ⊙10am-5pm) Books transport, accommodation and activities.

❶ Getting There & Away

The **main bus stop** is near the corner of Amuri Ave and Jacks Pass Rd.

Hanmer Connection (☑ 0800 242 663, 03-382 2952; www.hanmerconnection.co.nz; adult/child one way $30/20, return $50/30) Runs a daily bus to/from Christchurch via Waipara and Amberley, departing Christchurch at 9am and Hanmer Springs at 4.30pm.

Hanmer Tours & Shuttle (☑ 03-315 7418; www.hanmertours.co.nz) Runs daily buses to/from Culverden ($15, 30 minutes), Waikari ($15, 45 minutes), Waipara ($20, one hour), Amberley ($20, one hour), Christchurch city centre ($35, two hours) and Christchurch Airport ($45, two hours).

Waipara Valley

POP 5200

Conveniently stretched along SH1 60km north of Christchurch, this resolutely rural area makes for a tasty pit stop. The valley's warm dry summers followed by cool autumn nights have proved a winning formula for growing grapes, olives, hazelnuts and lavender. While Waipara accounts for less than 3% of NZ's vines, it nonetheless produces some of the country's finest cool-climate wines, including riesling, pinot noir and gewürztraminer.

Of the region's 30 or so wineries, around a dozen have cellar doors to visit, four with restaurants. To explore the valley's bounty fully, pick up a copy of the *North Canterbury Wine Region* map (www.northcanterburywines.co.nz). Otherwise, you'll spot several of the big players from the highway. The area's main towns are tiny Waipara and slightly larger Amberley, but you're likely to spend most of your time in the countryside between the two.

❂ Sights

★**Pegasus Bay**   WINERY
(☑ 03-314 6869; www.pegasusbay.com; Stockgrove Rd; ⊙restaurant noon-4pm Thu-Mon, tastings 10am-5pm daily) It's fitting that Waipara Valley's premier winery should have the loveliest setting and one of Canterbury's best restaurants (mains $36 to $43). Verdant

manicured gardens set the scene, but it's the contemporary NZ menu and luscious paired wines that steal the show.

Black Estate   WINERY
(☑ 03-314 6085; www.blackestate.co.nz; 614 Omihi Rd, SH1; ⊙10am-5pm, shorter hours Jun-Oct) ◢ Perched on a hillside overlooking the valley, this striking black barn is home to some excellent drops – try the pinot noirs from the winery's three nearby vineyards, each of which have a distinctive terroir of their own. The attached light-filled restaurant offers stunning views and food that champions local producers (mains $32 to $38).

Brew Moon   BREWERY
(☑ 03-314 8036; www.brewmoon.co.nz; 12 Markham St, Amberley; ⊙3pm-late Wed-Fri, from noon Sat & Sun) The variety of craft beers available to taste at this wee brewery never wanes. Stop in to fill a rigger (flagon) to take away, or sup an ale alongside a tasty woodfired pizza in the cosy bar (pizzas $16 to $22). Our favourite brew is the Wolf of Washington American Pale Ale and there's always interesting seasonal beers on offer.

▦ Sleeping & Eating

Old Glenmark Vicarage   B&B $$$
(☑ 03-314 6775; www.glenmarkvicarage.co.nz; 161 Church Rd, Waipara; d $230, barn d $250; P ☎ 🖰) There are two divine options in this beautifully restored vicarage: cosy up with bed and breakfast in the main house, or lounge around in the character-filled, converted barn that sleeps up to six (perfect for families or groups). The lovely gardens and swimming pool are a blessed bonus.

Little Vintage Espresso   CAFE $
(20 Markham St, Amberley; breakfast $10-21; ⊙7am-4pm Mon-Fri, to 2pm Sat) This petite whitewashed cottage just off SH1 has the best coffee in town, with food to match. All-day breakfasts, gourmet sandwiches and delectable homemade cakes are all on offer.

Pukeko Junction   CAFE, DELI $$
(☑ 03-314 8834; www.pukekojunction.co.nz; 458 Ashworths Rd, SH1, Leithfield; mains $7.50-20; ⊙9am-4.30pm Tue-Sun; ◢) A deservedly popular roadside stop, this bright, friendly cafe in Leithfield (south of Amberley) serves delicious bakery fare, like gourmet sausage rolls and tarts filled with goat's cheese, leek and walnut. The attached shop stocks an excellent selection of local wines.

ℹ Getting There & Away

Hanmer Connection (📱0800 242 663; www.hanmerconnection.co.nz) One daily bus stops in Waipara on request on the road between Hanmer Springs ($20, 50 minutes) and Christchurch ($20, 1¼ hours).

Hanmer Tours & Shuttle (📱03-315 7418; www.hanmertours.co.nz) Runs a daily shuttle to/from Hanmer Springs ($20), Christchurch city centre ($15) and Christchurch Airport ($25).

InterCity (📱03-365 1113; www.intercity.co.nz) Coaches head to/from Picton (from $34, five hours), Kaikōura (from $18, 1¾ hours) and Christchurch (from $15, one hour) at least daily.

CENTRAL CANTERBURY

While the dead-flat agricultural heartland of the Canterbury Plains blankets the majority of the region, there's plenty of interest for travellers in the west, where the Southern Alps soar to snowy peaks. Here you'll find numerous ski fields and some brilliant wilderness walks.

Unusually for NZ, the most scenic routes avoid the coast, with most places of interest accessed from one of two spectacular roads: the Great Alpine Highway (SH73), which wends from the Canterbury Plains deep into the mountains and over to the West Coast, and the Inland Scenic Route (SH72), which skirts the mountain foothills on its way south towards Tekapo.

Selwyn District

POP 56,400

Named after NZ's first Anglican bishop, this largely rural district has swallowed an English map book and regurgitated place names such as Lincoln, Darfield and Sheffield. Yet any illusions of Britain are quickly dispelled by the looming presence of the snow-capped Southern Alps, providing a rugged retort to 'England's mountains green'.

The highly scenic Great Alpine Hwy pierces the heart of the district on its journey between Christchurch and the West Coast. On the Canterbury Plains, it passes through the small settlement of Springfield, notable for a monument to local Rewi Alley (1897–1987), who became a great hero of the Chinese Communist Party.

Selwyn's numerous ski fields may not be the country's most glamorous, but they provide plenty of thrills for ski bunnies. **Porters** (📱03-318 4731; www.skiporters.co.nz; daily

lift passes adult/child weekend $99/69, midweek $79/49; ☉lifts 9am-4pm) is the main commercial field; club fields include **Mt Olympus** (📱03-318 5840; www.mtolympus.co.nz; daily lift passes adult/child $75/35), **Cheeseman** (📱03-344 3247, snow phone 03-318 8794; www.mtcheeseman.co.nz; daily lift passes adult/child $79/39; ☉lifts 9am-4.30pm, shorter hours midweek), **Broken River** (📱03-318 8713; www.brokenriver.co.nz; daily lift passes adult/child $75/35; ☉lifts 9am-4pm), **Craigieburn Valley** (📱03-318 8711; www.craigieburn.co.nz; daily lift passes adult/child $75/35) and **Temple Basin** (📱03-377 7788; www.templebasin.co.nz; daily lift passes adult/child $69/35).

🏃 Activities

Rubicon Valley Horse Treks   HORSE RIDING
(📱03-318 8886; www.rubiconvalley.co.nz; 534 Rubicon Rd, Springfield; ♿) Operating from a sheep farm 6km from Springfield, Rubicon offers a variety of horse treks to suit both beginner and advanced riders, including hourlong farm rides ($55), two-hour river or valley rides ($98), two-hour sunset rides ($120) and six-hour mountain trail rides ($285).

🛏 Sleeping & Eating

Smylies Accommodation   HOSTEL $
(📱03-318 4740; www.smylies.co.nz; 5653 West Coast Rd, Springfield; dm/s/d $38/60/90; 🅿🛜) 🏊 This well-seasoned, welcoming, YHA-associated hostel has a piano, manga comics galore, a DVD library and a wood-burning fire in the large communal kitchen. As well as traditional dorms, there are also self-contained motel units ($105) and a three-bedroom cottage ($280). Winter packages (June to September), including ski-equipment rental and ski-field transport, are available.

Famous Sheffield Pie Shop   BAKERY $
(📱03-318 3876; www.sheffieldpieshop.co.nz; 51 Main West Rd, Sheffield; pies $5-7; ☉6.30am-4pm Mon-Fri, from 7am Sat & Sun) Blink and you'll miss this stellar roadside bakery, a purveyor of more than 20 varieties of pies, from traditional beef to more experimental flavour combinations – think whisky and venison, or chicken, camembert and apricot. While you're here, snaffle a bag of the exemplary Afghan biscuits – such cornflakey, chocolatey goodness!

ℹ Getting There & Away

Public transport is limited in Selwyn District, so it's best to have your own transport.

CHRISTCHURCH & CANTERBURY SELWYN DISTRICT

Arthur's Pass

POP 30

Having left the Canterbury Plains at Springfield, the Great Alpine Hwy heads over Porter's Pass through the mountainous folds of the Torlesse and Craigieburn Ranges and into Arthur's Pass.

Māori used this pass to cross the Southern Alps long before its 'discovery' by Arthur Dobson in 1864. The Westland gold rush created the need for a dependable crossing over the Alps from Christchurch, and the coach road was completed within a year. Later, the coal and timber trade demanded a railway, duly completed in 1923.

Today it's an amazing journey. Successive valleys display their own character, not least the spectacular braided Waimakariri River Valley, encountered as you enter the national park proper.

Arthur's Pass village is 4km from the actual pass. At 900m, it's NZ's highest-altitude settlement and a handy base for tramps, climbs and skiing. The weather, however, is a bit of a shocker. Come prepared for rain.

⊙ Sights

★ Arthur's Pass

National Park   NATIONAL PARK

(www.doc.govt.nz) Straddling the Southern Alps, known to Māori as Ka Tiritiri o Te Moana (Steep Peak of Glistening White), this vast alpine wilderness became the South Island's first national park in 1929. Of its 1144 sq km, two-thirds lies on the Canterbury side of the main divide; the rest is in Westland. It is a rugged, mountainous area, cut by deep valleys, and ranging in altitude from 245m at the Taramakau River to 2408m at Mt Murchison.

There are plenty of well-marked day tramps throughout the park, especially around Arthur's Pass village. Pick up a copy of DOC's *Discover Arthur's Pass* booklet to read about popular tramps, including: the Arthur's Pass Walkway, a reasonably easy track from the village to the Dobson Memorial at the summit of the pass (2½ hours return); the one-hour return walk to Devils Punchbowl falls; and the steep walk to beautiful views at Temple Basin (three hours return). More challenging, full-day options include the Bealey Spur track and the classic summit hike to Avalanche Peak.

The park's many multiday trails are mostly valley routes with saddle climbs in between, such as Goat Pass and Cass-Lagoon Saddles Tracks, both two-day options. These and the park's longer tracks require previous hiking experience as flooding can make the rivers dangerous and the weather is extremely changeable. Always seek advice from DOC before setting out.

Cave Stream Scenic Reserve   CAVE

(www.doc.govt.nz) Near Broken River Bridge, 2km northeast of Castle Hill, you'll find this 594m-long cave. As indicated by the information panels in the car park, the walk through the cave is an achievable adventure, but only with a foolproof torch and warm clothing, and definitely only if the water level is less than waist deep where indicated. Heed all notices, take necessary precautions and revel in the spookiness.

Failing that, just wander around the 15-minute loop track for a gander at the surrounds, including limestone formations that featured in the *Chronicles of Narnia* movie.

Castle Hill/Kura Tawhiti   LANDMARK

Scattered across lush paddocks around 33km from Springfield, these limestone formations reach up to 30m high, and look so other-worldly they were named 'treasure from a distant land' by early Māori. A car park (with toilets) provides easy access to a short walk into the strange rock garden (10 minutes), favoured by rock climbers and photographers.

🛏 Sleeping

Camping is possible near the basic Avalanche Creek Shelter (www.doc.govt.nz; SH73; adult/child $8/4; P), opposite the DOC, where there's running water, tables, a sink and toilets. You can also camp for free at Klondyke Corner (www.doc.govt.nz; SH73; adult/child $8/4) or Hawdon Shelter (www.doc.govt.nz; Mount White Rd, off SH37), 8km and 24km south of Arthur's Pass respectively, where facilities are limited to toilets and stream water for boiling. If you're not camping, there are plenty of accommodation options in Arthur's Pass village and surrounds.

Mountain House YHA   HOSTEL $

(☏ 03-318 9258; www.trampers.co.nz; 83 Main Rd; dm/s/d/tr/q $34/94/94/120/144; P🖢) This well-kept hostel has cosy dorms and private rooms and the efficient and enthusiastic manager can provide extensive local hiking information. Note all rooms share bathroom facilities. The family room set-up ($238) sleeping up to seven people is a good option for groups.

Arthur's Pass Village B&B
B&B $$

(☑ 021 394 776; www.arthurspass.org.nz; 72 School Tce; d $160-180; P🐕) This lovingly restored former railway cottage is now a cosy B&B, with two well-appointed guest rooms. Breakfast on free-range bacon and eggs, pancakes and freshly baked bread, while enjoying the company of the friendly owners. Delicious home-cooked dinners ($40) and afternoon snacks and nibbles ($10) are also available.

Arthur's Pass Motel & Lodge
MOTEL $$

(☑ 03-3189099;www.arthurspass-accommodation. com; 107 Main Rd; d/apt $169/226; P🐕) Stylishly decorated options at this diverse complex include modern bedrooms sharing a fully equipped kitchen, lounge and dining area – a good way to meet other travellers – and an apartment with a separate bedroom and en suite bathroom. Note the property is not available to families with children. Check online for good discounts.

Arthur's Pass Alpine Motel
MOTEL $$

(☑ 03-318 9233; www.apam.co.nz; 52 Main Rd; d $130; P🐕) On the southern approach to the village, this cabin-style motel complex combines the homey charms of yesteryear with the beauty of double-glazing and the advice of active, enthusiastic hosts.

Flock Hill Lodge
MOTEL, HOSTEL $$

(☑ 03-318 8196; www.flockhill.co.nz; Great Alpine Hwy, Craigieburn Valley; dm/d $35/100, cottages $170-300; P@🐕) Near Craigieburn Forest Park and Lake Pearson, this historic high-country sheep station offers a genuine taste of rural life in its Shearers' Quarters bunkhouse, set in a picturesque farmyard. Tidy cottage units enjoy a more manicured garden setting.

Wilderness Lodge
LODGE $$$

(☑ 03-318 9246; www.wildernesslodge.co.nz; Cora Lynn Rd, Bealey; half board s $595-810, d $980-1300; P🐕) 🌱 For tranquillity and natural grandeur, this midsize alpine lodge tucked into beech forest just off the highway takes some beating. It's a class act, with a focus on immersive, nature-based experiences. Two daily guided activities (such as hiking and kayaking) are included in the tariff, along with gourmet breakfast and dinner.

✗ Eating

There are only two mediocre dining options in the village – stock up on self-catering supplies before you leave the plains.

Arthur's Pass Store & Cafe
CAFE $

(85 Main Rd; breakfast & lunch $7-24; ☺8am-5pm; 🐕) If you want to stock up on supplies, this is your best chance, with odds-on for egg sandwiches, hot chips, decent coffee, basic groceries and petrol.

Wobbly Kea
CAFE $$

(www.wobblykea.co.nz; 108 Main Rd; mains $25-27; ☺11am-7pm Mon-Thu, to 8pm Fri & Sat) Don your big-eatin' pants for brunch, lunch or dinner at the Wobbly Kea, which offers a short menu of simple but tasty home-cooked meals, such as meaty stew and curry. Pricey pizza ($33) is available to take away.

ℹ Information

DOC Arthur's Pass Visitor Centre (☑ 03-318 9211; www.doc.govt.nz; Main Rd; ☺8.30am-4.30pm) Helpful staff can provide advice on suitable tramps and the all-important weather forecast. Detailed route guides and topographical maps are also available, as are locator beacons for hire. Before you leave, log your trip details on AdventureSmart (www.adventuresmart.org.nz) via the on-site computer.

ℹ Getting There & Away

Fill your fuel tank before you leave Springfield (or Hokitika or Greymouth, if you're coming from the west). There's a pump at Arthur's Pass Store but it's expensive and only operates from 8am until 5pm.

Buses depart from various stops all a stone's throw from the store – check with the bus company for the latest information.

Atomic Shuttles (☑ 03-349 0697; www.atomic travel.co.nz) From Arthur's Pass buses head to/from Christchurch ($40, 2¼ hours), Springfield ($40, one hour), Lake Brunner ($30, 50 minutes) and Greymouth ($40, 1¼ hours).

East West Coaches (☑ 0800 142 622; www. eastwestcoaches.co.nz) Buses stopping at Arthur's Pass head to/from Christchurch ($45, 2¾ hours) and Greymouth ($35, 1¾ hours).

TranzAlpine (☑ 0800 872 467, 04-495 0775; www.greatjourneysofnz.co.nz/tranzalpine; fares from $89) One train daily in each direction stops in Arthur's Pass, heading to/from Springfield (1½ hours) and Christchurch (2½ hours), or Lake Brunner (one hour) and Greymouth (two hours).

Methven

POP 1700

Methven is busiest in winter (June to September), when it fills up with snow bunnies heading to nearby Mt Hutt. At other times tumbleweeds don't quite blow down the main street – much to the disappointment of the wannabe gunslingers arriving for the raucous October rodeo. Over summer (December to March) it's a low-key and affordable base for trampers and mountain bikers heading into the spectacular mountain foothills.

🏃 Activities

Most people come to Methven for the nearby ski slopes, but there are plenty of other activities nearby. Ask at the i-SITE about local walks (including the town heritage trail and Methven Walk/Cycleway) and longer tramps, horse riding, mountain biking, fishing, clay-shooting, archery, golfing, scenic helicopter flights, and jetboating through the nearby Rakaia Gorge.

Rakaia Gorge Walkway   WALKING
(www.doc.govt.nz; Rakaia Gorge Bridge, SH72) Following river terraces into the upper gorge, this well-graded tramp passes through forest and past the historic ferryman's cottage and coal mines, with plenty of pretty picnic spots. The highlight is the lookout at the end with epic alpine views. The walk is four hours return, but a shorter tramp to the lower lookout (one hour return) is also worthwhile.

Black Diamond Safaris   SKIING
(☑ 027 450 8283; www.blackdiamondsafaris.co.nz) Provides access to uncrowded club ski fields by 4WD. Prices start from $150 for transport, safety equipment and familiarisation, while $295 includes a lift pass, lunch and a guide.

Methven Heliski   SKIING
(☑ 03-302 8108; www.methvenheli.co.nz; Main St; 5-run day trips $1110) Epic guided, all-inclusive backcountry heliski trips, featuring five runs averaging drops of 750 to 1000 vertical metres.

Discovery Jet   BOATING
(☑ 0800 538 2628, 021 538 386; www.discoveryjet.co.nz; Rakaia Gorge Bridge, SH72; adult/child $99/75; 🚻) A speedy, exhilarating way to explore the Rakaia Gorge is via jetboat. Discovery Jet, based downstream of the bridge, offers a 45-minute blood-pumping ride with twists, turns and 360-degree spins, all with a backdrop of majestic mountain scenery. Shorter joyrides are also available.

Skydiving Kiwis   SKYDIVING
(☑ 0800 359 549; www.skydivingkiwis.com; Ashburton Airport, Seafield Rd) Offers tandem jumps from 6000ft ($249), 9000ft ($299) and 13,000ft ($360) departing Ashburton Airport.

Shuttles leave from central Christchurch if you don't have your own transport.

🛏 Sleeping

Methven is a hub for skiers headed to nearby Mt Hutt, and there is a wide range of accommodation available in town for all budgets. Book ahead during the ski season, especially for budget accommodation. Prices can rise significantly in winter (June to September); some places close in the summer months from December through February

Alpenhorn Chalet   HOSTEL $
(☑ 03-302 8779; www.alpenhorn.co.nz; 44 Allen St; dm $30, d $65-85; 🅿 @ 🕸 🛜) This small, inviting home has a leafy conservatory housing an indoor spa pool, a log fire and complimentary espresso coffee. Bedrooms are spacious and brightly coloured, with lots of warm, natural wood; one double room has an en suite bathroom.

Mt Hutt Bunkhouse   HOSTEL $
(☑ 03-302 8894; www.mthuttbunkhouse.co.nz; 8 Lampard St; dm $32, d $72-80, cottage $280-350; 🅿 🛜) Enthusiastic on-site owners run this basic, well-equipped, bright and breezy hostel. There's a comfy lounge, and a large garden sporting a barbecue and a volleyball court. The cottage (sleeps up to 18) is economical for large groups.

Big Tree Lodge   HOSTEL $
(☑ 03-302 9575; www.bigtreelodge.co.nz; 25 South Belt; dm $30-40, d $75-90, apt $110-130; 🅿 🛜) Once a vicarage, this relaxed hostel has bunk-free dorms and wood-trimmed bathrooms. Tucked just behind is Little Tree Studio, a self-contained unit sleeping up to four people.

Rakaia Gorge Camping Ground   CAMPGROUND $
(☑ 03-302 9353; 6686 Arundel-Rakaia Gorge Rd; sites per adult/child under 12yr $10/free) There are no powered sites here, only toilets, showers and a small kitchen shelter, but don't let that put you off. This is the best camping ground for miles, perched picturesquely above the ultra-blue Rakaia River, and a good base for exploring the area. Amenities closed May to September.

Redwood Lodge   HOSTEL, LODGE $$
(☑ 03-302 8964; www.redwoodlodge.co.nz; 3 Wayne Pl; s $65-75, d $115-129; 🅿 @ 🕸 🛜 🚻) Expect a warm welcome and no dorms at this charming and peaceful family-friendly lodge. Most rooms are en suite, and bigger rooms can be reconfigured to accommodate

families. The large shared lounge is ideal for resting ski-weary limbs.

Whitestone Cottages RENTAL HOUSE $$$
(📞 03-928 8050; www.whitestonecottages.co.nz; 3016 Methven Hwy; cottages $275; P🐕) When you just want to spread out, cook a meal, do your laundry and have your own space, these four large free-standing cottages in leafy grounds are just the ticket. Each sleeps six in two en suite bedrooms. Rates are for two people; each extra person is $35.

✕ Eating & Drinking

⭐ Dubliner BISTRO $$
(📞 03-302 8259; www.dubliner.co.nz; 116 Main St; meals $19-34; ⊙5pm-late daily mid-Jun–Mar, Wed-Sat only Apr–mid-Jun) This atmospheric Irish bar and restaurant is housed in Methven's lovingly restored old post office. Great food includes pizza, Irish stew and other hearty fare suitable for washing down with a pint of beer. It's very popular and booking for dinner on Friday and Saturday nights is recommended.

Topp Country Cafe CAFE $$
(📞 03-302 9393; 45 Forest Dr; mains $15-25; ⊙8am-3pm Mon-Fri, from 9am Sat & Sun) The Topp Twins are NZ entertainment legends and this cafe owned by Dame Lynda Topp and her wife Donna is a fine addition to Methven's dining scene. Check out the cosy rural vibe and ease into the day with a stonking cooked breakfast or come back for a burger for lunch. A mid-afternoon coffee and caramel slice is also recommended.

Aqua JAPANESE $$
(📞 03-302 8335; 112 Main St; mains $9-23; ⊙11.30am-2pm & 5.30-9pm Thu-Sun) A ski-season stalwart with unpredictable hours at other times (ring ahead), this tiny restaurant sports kimono-clad waitresses and traditional Japanese cuisine, including *yakisoba* (fried noodles), ramen (noodle soup) and izakaya-style small plates to share, with ice-cold beer or warming sake. Booking ahead for dinner is recommended and note credit cards are not accepted.

Blue Pub PUB
(📞 03-302 8046; www.thebluepub.co.nz; 2 Barkers Rd; ⊙11am-late; 🐕) Have a drink at the bar, crafted from a huge slab of native timber, or tuck into robust meals in the quieter cafe (mains $28 to $36). Afterwards, challenge the locals to a game of pool or listen to regular live music. Check the website for what's on.

MT HUTT

One of the highest ski areas in the southern hemisphere **Mt Hutt** (📞 0800 697 547; www.mthutt.co.nz; daily lift passes adult/child $119/59; ⊙9am-4pm) has one of the largest skiable areas of any of NZ's commercial fields (365 hectares). The ski field is only 26km from Methven but in wintry conditions the drive takes about 40 minutes; allow two hours from Christchurch. Road access is steep: be extremely cautious in lousy weather.

Methven Travel runs shuttle buses from Methven during the ski season ($25). Return bus transport from Christchurch ($60) is also available when the mountain is open for skiing. Check the website for departure details. Half of the terrain is suitable for intermediate skiers, with a quarter each for beginning and advanced skiers. The longest run stretches for 2km. Other attractions include chairlifts, heliskiing and wide-open faces that are good for learning to snowboard. The season usually runs from mid-June to mid-October.

☆ Entertainment

Cinema Paradiso CINEMA
(📞 03-302 1975; www.cinemaparadiso.co.nz; 112 Main St; adult/child $17/12; ⊙Wed-Sun) Quirky 35-seat cinema with an art-house slant.

ℹ Information

Medical Centre (📞 03-302 8105; The Square, Main St; ⊙8.30am-5.30pm)

Methven i-SITE (📞 03-302 8955; www.methvenmthutt.co.nz; 160 Main St; ⊙8.30am-5.30pm Mon-Fri Jun-Sep, 9am-5pm Mon-Fri Oct-May, 11am-3pm Sat & Sun year round; 🐕) Ask staff here about local walks and other activities. Methven Travel are also based here for transport needs and there's a convenient guest services desk for Mt Hutt during winter.

ℹ Getting There & Away

Methven Travel (📞 03-302 8106, 0800 684 888; www.methventravel.co.nz; 160 Main St) Runs shuttles between Methven and Christchurch Airport (adult/child $47/30) three times a week from October to June, increasing to three times daily during the ski season. Also runs shuttles up to Mt Hutt ski field from June to September (adult return $25, kids free with paying adult). Also return transport from Christchurch to Mt Hutt ($60) in winter when the mountain is open for skiing.

Mt Somers

POP 2650

The small settlement of Mt Somers sits on the edge of the Southern Alps, beneath the mountain of the same name. The biggest drawcard to the area is the Mt Somers track (26km), a two-day tramp circling the mountain, linking the popular picnic spots of Sharplin Falls and Woolshed Creek. Trail highlights include volcanic formations, Māori rock drawings, deep river canyons and botanical diversity. The route is subject to sudden weather changes, so precautions should be taken.

There are two DOC huts on the track: Pinnacles Hut and Woolshed Creek Hut (adult/child $15/7.50). Hut tickets and information are available at Mt Somers General Store and Staveley Store.

🛏 Sleeping & Eating

Mt Somers Holiday Park   HOLIDAY PARK $
(☑ 03-303 9719; www.mountsomers.co.nz; 87 Hoods Rd; sites $20-32, cabins with/without bathroom $90/60; ℗) This small, friendly-vibe park offers pleasant sites in leafy grounds along with standard (bring your own linen) and en suite cabins. All guests have access to basic shared kitchen and lounge areas.

Staveley Store & Cafe   CAFE $
(☑ 03-303 0859; www.staveleystore.co.nz; 2 Burgess Rd, Staveley; mains $6-13; ⊘ 9am-4.30pm) Call into this cute little country store for the best coffee for miles around, as well as tasty lunch rolls, delectable cakes, gourmet ice cream and locally sourced groceries. Also sells hut tickets for the Mt Somers track.

Stronechrubie   BISTRO $$
(☑ 03-303 9814; www.stronechrubie.co.nz; cnr Hoods Rd & SH72; mains bistro $18-30, restaurant $39-41; ⊘ bistro 5.30pm-late Thu-Sat, restaurant 6.30pm-late Wed-Sat, Sun lunch by appointment; ☜) This motel complex offers comfortable chalets overlooking bird-filled gardens (doubles $140 to $160), but it's the up-and-coming culinary hub that's the main draw here. Enjoy a more formal meal in the lauded, long-standing restaurant, or head to the flash bar and bistro for modern, tapas-style fare alongside lovely wines and craft beer. Reservations recommended.

ℹ Information

Mt Somers General Store (☑ 03-303 9831; 61 Pattons Rd; ⊘ 7am-5.30pm Mon-Fri, 8am-5.30pm Sat, 9am-5pm Sun) Hut tickets for the Mt Somers track, plus information, petrol and basic groceries.

ℹ Getting There & Away

There are no public buses to/from Mt Somers village, so you will need your own transport.

SOUTH CANTERBURY

After crossing the Rangitata River into South Canterbury, SH1 and the Inland Scenic Route (SH72) narrow to within 8km of each other at the quaint town of Geraldine. Here you can choose to take the busy coastal highway through the port city of Timaru, or continue inland on SH79 into Mackenzie Country, where NZ's tallest peaks rise above powder-blue lakes.

The Mackenzie Basin is a wild, tussock-strewn bowl at the foot of the Southern Alps, carved out by ancient glaciers. It takes its name from the legendary James 'Jock' McKenzie, who ran his stolen flocks in this then-uninhabited region in the 1840s.

Director Sir Peter Jackson made the most of this rugged and untamed landscape while filming the *Lord of the Rings,* choosing Mt Cook Village as the setting for Minas Tirith and a sheep station near Twizel as Gondor's Pelennor Fields.

Timaru

POP 29,000

Trucking on along the SH1 through Timaru, travellers could be forgiven for thinking that this small port city is merely a handy place for food and fuel halfway between Christchurch and Dunedin. Drop the anchors, people! Straying into the CBD reveals a remarkably intact Edwardian precinct boasting some good dining and interesting shopping, not to mention a clutch of cultural attractions and lovely parks, all of which sustain at least a day's stopover.

The town's name comes from the Māori name Te Maru, meaning 'place of shelter'. No permanent settlement existed here until 1839, when the Weller brothers set up a whaling station. The *Caroline,* a sailing ship that transported whale oil, gave the picturesque bay its name.

⊙ Sights

★ Aigantighe Art Gallery   GALLERY
(www.aigantighe.co.nz; 49 Wai-iti Rd; ⊙10am-4pm Tue-Fri, from noon Sat & Sun) **FREE** One of the South Island's largest public galleries, this 1908 mansion houses a notable collection of NZ and European art across various eras, alongside temporary exhibitions staged by the gallery's ardent supporters. The Gaelic name means 'at home' and is pronounced 'egg-and-tie'.

Sacred Heart Basilica   CHURCH
(7 Craigie Ave, Parkside) Roman Catholic with a definite emphasis on the Roman, this beautiful neoclassical church (1911) impresses with multiple domes, Ionian columns and richly coloured stained glass. Its architect, Francis Petre, also designed the large basilicas in Christchurch (now in ruins) and Ōamaru. Inside, there's an art-nouveau feel to the plasterwork, which includes intertwined floral and sacred-heart motifs. There are no set opening hours; try the side door.

Caroline Bay Park   PARK, BEACH
(Marine Pde) Fronting the town, this expansive park ranges over an Edwardian-style garden under the Bay Hill cliff, then across broad lawns to low sand dunes and the beach itself. It has something for everyone between the playground, skate park, soundshell, ice-cream kiosk, minigolf, splash park and myriad other attractions. Don't miss the Trevor Griffiths Rose Garden (Caroline Bay Park, Marine Pde), a triumphant collection of heritage varieties, and consider an evening picnic making the most of the late sun. If you're lucky enough to spot a seal or penguin on the beach, do keep your distance.

Te Ana Māori Rock Art Centre   MUSEUM
(☑03-684 9141; www.teana.co.nz; 2 George St; adult/child $22/11, tours $130/52; ⊙10am-3pm) Passionate Ngāi Tahu guides bring this innovative multimedia exhibition about Māori rock paintings to life. You can also take a three-hour excursion (departing at 2pm, November to April) to see isolated rock art in situ; prior booking is essential.

Timaru Botanic Gardens   GARDENS
(cnr King & Queen Sts; ⊙8am-dusk) Established in 1864, these gardens are a restful place to while away an hour or two, with a pond, lush lawns, shady trees, a playground and vibrant floral displays. With luck you'll arrive during rhododendron or rose bloom time. Enter from Queen St, south of the city centre.

South Canterbury Museum   MUSEUM
(http://museum.timaru.govt.nz; Perth St; admission by donation; ⊙10am-4.30pm Tue-Fri, 1-4.30pm Sat & Sun) Historic and natural artefacts of the region are displayed here. Highlights include the Māori section, a full-scale model of a ship's cabin from 1859, and a replica of the aeroplane designed and flown by local pioneer aviator and inventor Richard Pearse. It's speculated that his mildly successful attempts at flight came before the Wright brothers' famous achievement in 1903.

✨ Festivals & Events

Timaru Festival of Roses   CULTURAL
(www.festivalofroses.co.nz; ⊙Nov/Dec) Featuring a market day, concerts and family fun, this week-long celebration capitalises on Timaru's obsession with all things rosy. The festival is held annually for one week at the end of November or early December.

⌂ Sleeping

Timaru Top 10 Holiday Park   HOLIDAY PARK $
(☑03-684 7690; www.timaruholidaypark.co.nz; 154a Selwyn St, Marwiel; sites $40-45, cabins & units $70-140; P🞵👶) ⚑ Tucked away in the suburbs, this excellent holiday park has clean, colourful amenities and a host of accommodation options throughout mature, leafy grounds. Helpful staff go out of their way to assist with local advice and bookings.

Grosvenor   HOTEL $
(☑03-687 9190; www.thegrosvenor.co.nz; 26 Cains Tce; s/d from $95/125; P🞵) In a heritage building right in the centre of town, this good-value budget hotel offers clean, no-frills rooms with comfy beds, fridge and TV. The quirky Mondrian-styled corridors give the place a hip vibe. Try and book ahead as it's popular.

Glendeer Lodge   B&B $$$
(☑03-686 9274; www.glendeer.co.nz; 51 Scarborough Rd, Scarborough; d $210-260; P🞵) ⚑ Set on 5 acres 4km south of Timaru, this purpose-built lodge is a peaceful option away from busy SH1. Walk to the lighthouse, relax in the garden watching fallow deer nibbling the paddock, then retire to the plush, self-contained lodge offering three en suite rooms. The owners' fly-fishing guiding business lends a wilderness vibe.

Timaru

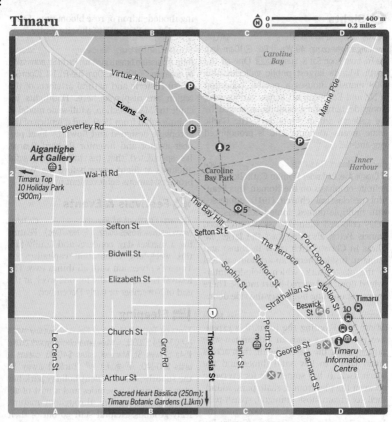

Timaru

◎ Top Sights
1 Aigantighe Art Gallery A2

◎ Sights
2 Caroline Bay Park.................................. C2
3 South Canterbury Museum C4
4 Te Ana Māori Rock Art Centre D4
5 Trevor Griffiths Rose Garden C2

🛏 Sleeping
6 Grosvenor D3

✕ Eating
7 Arthur Street Kitchen........................... C4
8 Oxford D4
   Street Food Kitchen .... (see 4)

◎ Drinking & Nightlife
   Speight's Ale House .... (see 4)

ⓘ Transport
9 Atomic Shuttles D4
   Budget Buses & Shuttles............... (see 9)
10 InterCity D3

✕ Eating & Drinking

Arthur Street Kitchen CAFE $
(www.arthurstkitchen.co.nz; 8 Arthur St; mains $11-21; ☉7am-5pm Mon-Fri, 9am-3pm Sat;) Timaru's hippest coffee house follows the recipe for success: namely great coffee, contemporary cafe fare, good tunes and a mix of arty inside and sunny outside seating. Made with flair and care, the food offering includes grainy salads, refined sandwiches and pastry treats, plus an à la carte breakfast and lunch menu.

★ Oxford MODERN NZ $$
(☎03-688 3297; www.theoxford.co.nz; 152 Stafford St; mains $31-34; ☉10am-late Mon & Wed-Fri, 9.30am-late Sat & Sun) This sophisticated corner restaurant honours its 1925 building

with stylish monochrome decor and a feature wall commemorating the day Timaru went bust. The menu offers high-class comfort food, starring local produce like venison, beef and salmon, while an alluring drinks list encourages you to pop in for pinot and cheese, or a glass of sticky wine alongside golden syrup pudding.

Street Food Kitchen   STREET FOOD $$
(📞 03-686 6036; www.streetfoodkitchen.co.nz; 2 George St; shared plates $14-17; ⊙ 11.30am-late Tue-Sun) Asian and Mediterranean flavours underpin the concise menu of shared plates at Street Food Kitchen. Highlights include the steamed bao buns with crispy pork belly and the pumpkin and Parmesan arancini. Good cocktails and Timaru's best selection of NZ craft beers also make it a fine spot for an end-of-the-day drink.

Speight's Ale House   PUB
(📞 03-686 6030; www.timarualehouse.co.nz; 2 George St; ⊙ 11.30am-late; 🛜) The pub most likely to be registering a pulse of an evening, this enterprise – housed in an interesting 1870s stone warehouse – redeems its overly ostentatious branding with friendly staff and a sunny courtyard, including bean bags for slumping in.

ℹ️ Information

Timaru Information Centre (📞 03-687 9997; www.southcanterbury.org.nz; 2 George St; ⊙ 10am-4pm Mon-Fri, to 3pm Sat & Sun; 🛜) Across from the train station (trains in this area only carry freight, not passengers), the visitor centre shares its building with the Te Ana Māori Rock Art Centre (p471). There's free wi-fi throughout Timaru's CBD and Caroline Bay Park.

ℹ️ Getting There & Away

AIR

Air New Zealand (📞 0800 737 000; www. airnewzealand.co.nz) Flies from Timaru's Richard Pearse Airport to/from Wellington at least once daily.

BUS

Atomic Shuttles (📞 03-349 0697; www.atomic travel.co.nz) Stops by the Timaru Information Centre twice daily, en route to Christchurch ($30, 2½ hours), Ōamaru ($25,1¼ hours) and Dunedin ($30, 2¾ hours).

Budget Buses & Shuttles (📞 03-615 5119; www.budgetshuttles.co.nz; ⊙ Mon-Sat) Offers door-to-door shuttles to Christchurch ($55).

InterCity (📞 03-365 1113; www.intercity.co.nz) Stops outside the train station.

DESTINATION	FARES ($) FROM	DURATION (HR)
Christchurch	20	2½
Dunedin	34	3
Gore	51	6
Ōamaru	23	1

Inland & Mackenzie Country

Heading to Queenstown and the southern lakes from Christchurch means a turn off SH1 onto SH79, a scenic route towards the high country and the Aoraki/Mt Cook National Park's eastern foothills. The road passes through Geraldine and Fairlie before joining SH8, which heads over Burkes Pass to the sparkling blue Lake Tekapo.

The expansive high ground from which the scenic peaks of Aoraki/Mt Cook National Park escalate is known as Mackenzie Country, after the legendary James 'Jock' McKenzie, who ran his stolen flocks in this then-uninhabited region in the 1840s. When he was finally caught, other settlers realised the potential of the land and followed in his footsteps. The first people to traverse the Mackenzie were the Māori, trekking from Banks Peninsula to Otago hundreds of years ago.

Peel Forest

POP 180

Tucked away between the foothills of the Southern Alps and the Rangitata River, Peel Forest is a small but important remnant of indigenous podocarp (conifer) forest. Many of the totara, kahikatea and matai trees here are hundreds of years old and are home to an abundance of birdlife, including riflemen, kereru (wood pigeons), bellbirds, fantails and grey warblers. There's a small settlement, mostly to serve the visitors who come to tramp, ride and raft the beautiful surrounds.

A road from nearby Mt Peel sheep station leads to Mesopotamia, the run of English writer Samuel Butler in the 1860s. His experiences here partly inspired his famous satire *Erewhon* ('nowhere' backwards, almost).

👁️ Sights

St Stephen's Church   CHURCH
(1200 Peel Forest Rd) Sitting in a pretty glade right next to the general store, this gorgeous little Anglican church (1885) has a warm wooden interior and some interesting

stained glass. Look for St Francis of Assisi surrounded by NZ flora and fauna (get the kids to play spot the tuatara).

🏃 Activities

Big Tree Walk (30 minutes return) is a gentle stroll through the forest to a particularly fine example of a totara, which is 31m tall, has a circumference of 9m and is over 1000 years old. There are also trails to **Emily Falls** (1½ hours return), **Rata Falls** (two hours return) and **Acland Falls** (one hour return). Pick up the *Peel Forest Area* brochure from the Green Man at Peel Forest cafe or download it from the DOC website (www.doc.govt.nz).

★ Rangitata Rafts   RAFTING
(☑ 0800 251 251; www.rafts.co.nz; Rangitata Gorge Rd; ⊙ Oct-May; 🕸) Begin your adventure in the stupendously beautiful braided Rangitata River valley before heading on an exhilarating two-hour ride through the gorge's Grade V rapids ($219, minimum age 15). A gentler alternative route encounters only Grade II rapids ($179, minimum age six).

Peel Forest Horse Trekking   HORSE RIDING
(☑ 03-696 3703; www.peelforesthorsetrekking.
co.nz; 105 Dennistoun Rd; 1hr/2hr/half day/full day $65/120/220/320, multiday $800-1450; 🕸) Ride through lush forest on short rides or multiday treks with experienced guides. Accommodation packages are available in conjunction with Peel Forest Lodge.

Hidden Valleys   RAFTING
(☑ 03-696 3560; www.hiddenvalleys.co.nz; ⊙ Sep-May) They may be based in Peel Forest but this crew doesn't limit itself to rafting the Rangitata. Multiday expeditions head to the Waimakariri, Waiau, Landsborough, and Grey and Waiatoto Rivers, peaking with a five-day trip ($1750) down the Clarence near Kaikōura. Shorter, child-friendly trips on the Rangitata River are also available (adult $120 to $200, child $80 to $160).

🛏 Sleeping & Eating

★ Peel Forest DOC Campsite   CAMPGROUND $
(☑ 03-696 3567; www.thegreenmanpeelforest.co.
nz; sites per adult/child powered $23/11.50, un-
powered $20/10, cabins $50-80) Near the Ran-
gitata River, around 3km north of Green Man at Peel Forest store, this lovely camp-ing ground is equipped with basic two- to four-berth cabins (bring your own sleeping bag), hot showers and a kitchen. Check in at the store. The campsite is only open from mid-September to April.

Peel Forest Lodge   LODGE $$$
(☑ 03-696 3703; www.peelforestlodge.co.nz; 96 Brake Rd; d $400, additional adult/child $45/25; 🅿🤙) This delightful log cabin hidden in the forest has four rooms and sleeps eight people. It only takes one booking at a time, so you and your posse will have the place to yourself. The cabin is fully self-contained, but meals can be arranged, as can horse treks, rafting trips and other explorations of the beautiful surrounds.

Green Man at Peel Forest   CAFE $$
(☑ 03-696 3567; www.thegreenmanpeelforest.co.nz; 1202 Peel Forest Rd; mains lunch $6-19, dinner $21-30; ⊙ cafe 9.30am-4.30pm daily, bar 6pm-late Wed-Sat; 🤙) Your one-stop shop for basic groceries, hut tickets, internet access and DOC campsite bookings. The attached cafe has good espresso coffee and does a roaring trade in toasties and burgers come lunchtime. There's occasionally live music in the evenings; check the website for dates. Make a night of it with decent craft beer.

❶ Getting There & Away

InterCity (p476) buses will get you as close as Geraldine, but you'll need your own transport or a lift to get to Peel Forest itself.

Geraldine

POP 2300

Consummately Canterbury in its dedication to English-style gardening, pretty Geraldine has a village vibe and an active arts scene. In spring (September to November), duck behind the war memorial on Talbot St to the River Garden Walk, where green-fingered locals have gone completely bonkers plant-ing azaleas and rhododendrons. If you've still got energy to burn, try the well-marked trails in Talbot Forest on the town fringe.

◎ Sights & Activities

Geraldine Historical Museum   MUSEUM
(☑ 03-693 7028; 5 Cox St; ⊙ 10am-3pm Mon-Sat, from 12.30pm Sun) FREE Occupying the photo-genic Town Board Office building (1885), this cute little museum tells the town's story with an eclectic mix of exhibits, including an extensive collection of photographs.

Geraldine Vintage Car &
Machinery Museum   MUSEUM
(☑ 03-693 8756; 178 Talbot St; adult/child $15/free; ⊙ 9.30am-4pm Oct-May, 10am-4pm Sat & Sun Jun-Sep) Rev-heads will enjoy this lovingly

maintained vintage car collection, featuring a 1907 De Dion-Bouton and a gleaming 1926 Bentley. There's also a purpose-built Daimler used for the 1954 royal tour, plus some very nice Jags, 1970s muscle cars and all sorts of farm machinery.

Big Rock Canyons ADVENTURE SPORTS
(☎0800 244 762; www.bigrockcanyons.co.nz; tours from $219; ☺Oct-Apr) Offers slippy, slidey day-long adventures in the Kaumira Canyon near Geraldine, as well as in five other canyons with varying degrees of difficulty. Pickup is available in Geraldine or Christchurch.

🛏 Sleeping

Geraldine Top 10 Holiday Park HOLIDAY PARK $
(☎03-693 8147; www.geraldinetop10.co.nz; 39 Hislop St; sites $39-46, d $60-142; P@🛜🏊) 🏖 This top-notch holiday park is set amid well-established parkland right in the centre of town. Tidy accommodation ranges from budget cabins to plusher motel units, plus there's a TV room and playground.

Rawhiti Backpackers HOSTEL $
(☎03-693 8252; www.rawhitibackpackers.co.nz; 27 Hewlings St; dm/s/tw/d $38/54/84/84; P🛜) On a hillside on the edge of town, this former maternity hospital is now a sunny and spacious hostel with well-maintained communal areas, bright rooms with colourful bed linen, a lemon tree and three cute cats. The guests' kitchen is spacious and modern, and the hosts have plenty of ideas for exploring the region.

★Vicarage BOUTIQUE HOTEL $$$
(www.thevicaragegeraldine.co.nz; 69 Talbot St; r/ste $250/395; P🛜) Housed in a restored Anglican vicarage, this charming boutique hotel is a very relaxing place to stay. Named for former vicars of Geraldine, the seven rooms and suites are stylish and modern, with heritage design features blending with contemporary decor. In-room facilities include Nespresso coffee machines, and it's just metres to good eating at the associated Barker's Foodstore & Eatery.

🍴 Eating

Long overdue to be lauded 'Cheese & Pickle Capital of NZ', Geraldine is paradise for self-caterers. Numerous artisan producers line the Four Peaks Plaza; seek out a bag of Heartland potato chips, made just down the road. There's an excellent **farmers market** (Talbot St, St Mary's Church car park; ☺9am-

12.30pm Sat Oct-Apr) 🏖, and, if you're not in the mood to DIY, there are also a few good cafes in town.

Talbot Forest Cheese DELI $
(www.talbotforestcheese.co.nz; Four Peaks Plaza, Talbot St; cheeses $5-10; ☺9am-5pm; 🏖) This little shop not only showcases the plethora of cheeses made on-site (including delicious Parmesan- and Gruyère-style ones), it doubles as a deli with all you need for a tasty picnic. Fans of funky cheeses should check out the Mt Talbot Blue.

Verde CAFE $
(☎03-693 9616; 45 Talbot St; mains $9-18; ☺9am-4pm; 🏖) Down the lane beside the old post office and set in beautiful gardens, this excellent cafe is one of Geraldine's best eateries. Drop in for coffee and cake, or linger over a lazy lunch of salads, soup, sandwiches and the like.

Barker's Foodstore & Eatery DELI $$
(☎03-693 9727; www.barkersfoodstore.nz; 71 Talbot St; mains $15-25; ☺8.30am-4.30pm; 🏖) Relocated in late 2019 to include an excellent cafe and boutique accommodation, Barker's is a long-standing producer of favourite fruity preserves, including raspberry jam, tamarillo chutney and cherry juice. It's the perfect spot to stock up on picnic essentials or enjoy excellent cafe fare. Try the lamb burger or a tasting platter ($25 to $45) with a selection of Barker's products.

Running Duck BURGERS $$
(☎03-693 8320; www.therunningduck.co.nz; 1 Peel St; burgers $8-19; ☺8am-4pm Mon, Wed & Thu, to 8pm Fri, 9am-4pm Sat & Sun; 🏊) This hip burger joint is the perfect setting to feast on tasty gourmet burgers and crispy fries, topped with chef Al's special spicy sauce. There's a fridge full of NZ craft beers and an adjacent food truck open on summer evenings serving fish and chips.

☆ Entertainment

Geraldine Cinema CINEMA
(☎03-693 8118; www.geraldinecinema.co.nz; 78 Talbot St; adult/child $12/8) Snuggle into an old sofa to watch a Hollywood favourite or an art-house surprise at this ageing dame, built in 1924. There's also occasional live music, usually with a folk, blues or country spin.

ℹ Information

Geraldine Visitor Information Centre (☎03-693 1101; www.southcanterbury.org.nz; 38 Waihi Tce; ☺8am-5.30pm) Located inside the Kiwi Country visitor complex. Don't miss the world's biggest woollen jumper (sweater) hanging on the wall.

ℹ️ Getting There & Away

Budget Buses & Shuttles (📞 03-615 5119; www.budgetshuttles.co.nz; ⊘ Mon-Sat) Offers a door-to-door shuttle to Christchurch ($65).

InterCity (📞 03-365 1113; www.intercity.co.nz) Runs daily services to the following:

DESTINATION	FARES ($) FROM	DURATION (HR)
Christchurch	37	2¼
Cromwell	47	4¾
Lake Tekapo	25	1¼
Mt Cook Village	111	3
Queenstown	49	5¾

Fairlie

POP 720

Leafy Fairlie describes itself as 'the gateway to the Mackenzie', but in reality this wee, rural town feels a world away from tussocky Mackenzie Country over Burkes Pass, to the west. The bakery and picnic area make it a good lunchtime stop.

👁 Sights & Activities

The information centre can provide details on nearby hiking and mountain-biking tracks. The main ski resort, Mt Dobson (📞 03-281 5509; www.mtdobson.co.nz; daily lift passes adult/child $88/43), lies in a 3km-wide treeless basin 26km northwest of Fairlie. There's also a club ski field 29km northwest at Fox Peak (📞 03-685 8539, snow phone 03-688 0044; www.foxpeak.co.nz; daily lift passes adult/child $70/20) in the Two Thumb Range.

Fairlie Heritage Museum MUSEUM (www.fairlieheritagemuseum.co.nz; 49 Mt Cook Rd; adult/child $10/free; ⊘ 9.30am-5pm; 🚗) A somewhat dusty window on to rural NZ of old, this museum endears with its farm machinery, model aeroplanes, dodgy dioramas and eclectic ephemera. Highlights include the homespun gyrocopter, historic cottage and new automotive wing featuring tractors. The attached Swiss-owned cafe has superb cakes and delicious hot chocolate.

🛏 Sleeping & Eating

Musterer's MOTEL $$ (📞 03-685 8284; www.musterers.co.nz; 9 Gordon St; units $95-205; P 🖨) On the western edge of Fairlie, these stylish self-contained cottages afford all mod cons with the bonus of a shared barbecue area and woolshed 'lounge' – complete with donkeys, goats and a pony to pet. Units are plush and spacious; the larger ones come complete with their own wood-fired hot tub ($45 extra) for a stargazing soak.

⭐ **Fairlie Bakehouse** BAKERY $ (📞 03-685 6063; www.liebers.co.nz; 74 Main St; pies $5-8.50; ⊘ 7.30am-4.30pm Mon-Sat, to 4pm Sun; 🚗 🖨) Famous for miles around and the top-ranking reason to stop in Fairlie, this superb bakery turns out exceptional pies, including the legendary salmon and bacon. The ultimate steak pie with cheese and mushroom is also a winner. On the sweet side, American doughnuts and raspberry cheesecake feature alongside Kiwi classics such as custard squares and cream buns. An essential stop.

ℹ️ Information

Fairlie Heartland Resource & Information Centre (📞 03-685 8496; www.fairlienz.com; 67 Main St; ⊘ 10am-4pm Mon-Fri) Has maps and brochures, and can advise on nearby activities.

ℹ️ Getting There & Away

InterCity (📞 03-365 1113; www.intercity.co.nz) runs daily services to the following:

DESTINATION	FARES ($) FROM	DURATION (HR)
Christchurch	41	3¼
Cromwell	43	4
Lake Tekapo	19	¾
Mt Cook Village	87	2½
Queenstown	47	5

Lake Tekapo

POP 370

Born of a hydropower scheme completed in 1953, today Tekapo is booming off the back of a tourism explosion, although it has long been a popular tour-bus stop on the route between Christchurch and Queenstown. Its popularity is well deserved: the town faces out across the turquoise lake to a backdrop of snow-capped mountains.

Such splendid Mackenzie Country and Southern Alps views are reason enough to linger, but there's infinitely more to see if you wait till dark. In 2012 the Aoraki Mackenzie area was declared an International Dark Sky Reserve, one of only 12 in the world, and Tekapo's Mt John – under light-pollution-free

AORAKI MACKENZIE INTERNATIONAL DARK SKY RESERVE

The stars really do seem brighter in Mackenzie Country. A unique combination of clear skies and next to no light pollution makes this region one of the best stargazing sites in the world – a fact that led to 4367 sq km of Aoraki/Mt Cook National Park and the Mackenzie Basin being declared the southern hemisphere's first International Dark Sky Reserve in 2012.

If you're up for some amateur stargazing, all you'll need are a cloud-free night and some warm clothes. For best results, time your visit to coincide with a new moon, when the skies will be at their darkest. For those who'd like a bit more guidance, join one of the nightly tours of the Mt John Observatory run by the Dark Sky Project. Ask at the information centre (p479) about other smaller local companies also offering stargazing.

skies – is the ultimate place to experience the region's glorious night sky.

⊙ Sights

Church of the Good Shepherd CHURCH
(Pioneer Dr; ⊙9am-5pm) The picture window behind the altar of this pretty stone church (built in 1935) gives worshippers a distractingly divine view of the lake and mountains; needless to say, it's a firm favourite for weddings. Come early in the morning or late afternoon to avoid the peace-shattering crowds – this is the prime disembarkation point for tour buses. Nearby is a statue of a collie, a tribute to the sheepdogs that helped develop Mackenzie Country.

🏃 Activities

Lake Tekapo is a great base for outdoor activities enthusiasts. In winter (June to September), snow bunnies can go downhill skiing at Mt Dobson and Roundhill (📞021 680 694, snow phone 03-680 6977; www.roundhill.co.nz; daily lift passes adult/child $84/36), and cross-country skiing on the Two Thumb Range.

When the Mackenzie Basin was scoured out by glaciers, Mt John (1029m) remained as an island of tough bedrock in the centre of a vast river of ice. Nowadays, a road leads to the summit, or you can tramp via a circuit track (2½ hours return) for rewarding views. To extend it to an all-day tramp, continue on to Alexandrina and McGregor Lakes.

The free town map details this and other walks in the area, along with cycling tracks, including Cowan's Hill and those in Lake Tekapo Regional Park.

Dark Sky Project STARGAZING
(📞0800 327 5759; www.darkskyproject.co.nz; SH8; 🚻) 🏃 A recognised International Dark Sky Reserve, the Mackenzie region is one of the world's best places for stargazing. Night-

ly tours head up to the University of Canterbury's observatory on Mt John (adult/child $175/99), where you'll get a guided tour of the sky from qualified astronomers. Other options include a multi-media presentation blending science and Māori astronomy at Dark Sky Project's new lakefront Rehua base, stargazing at the Church of the Good Shepherd, and viewing the night sky from Cowan's Observatory.

Dark Sky Project's spectacular lakefront base includes a good cafe and gift shop, and is also home to the Brashear Telescope, an 1894 telescope recently restored after being in storage at the University of Canterbury. It's hoped the telescope, crafted of brass, iron, steel and wood, will once again be used for surveying the Southern Hemisphere night sky in the future.

**Mackenzie Alpine
Horse Trekking** HORSE RIDING
(📞0800 628 269; www.maht.co.nz; Godley Peaks Rd; 30min/1hr/2hr $50/90/140; ⊙Oct-May; 🚻) Located on the road to Mt John, this place runs various treks taking in the area's amazing scenery, catering for everyone from novice to experienced riders.

Tekapo Springs SPA
(📞03-680 6550; www.tekaposprings.co.nz; 6 Lakeside Dr; adult/child pools $27/15, ice skating $19/14; ⊙10am-9pm; 🚻) There's nothing nicer on a chilly day than soaking in the thermal waters of these landscaped outdoor pools, with views over the lake to the snow-capped mountains beyond. Pools range in temperature from 28°C to 40°C, and include an artificial beach and aqua play area. There's also a steam room and sauna ($6 extra), along with a day spa. During the colder months (May to September) the attached ice-skating rink and snow-tubing slide are available, while in summer (December to March) there's the

DON'T MISS

LAKE PUKAKI LOOKOUT

The largest of the Mackenzie's three alpine lakes, Pukaki is a vast jewel of totally surreal colour. On its shore, just off SH8 between Twizel and Lake Tekapo, is a well-signed and perennially popular lookout affording picture-perfect views across the water all the way up to snow-capped Aoraki/Mt Cook and its surrounding peaks. Opened in 2019, the Ngāi Tahu Lake Pukaki Centre (SH8, Lake Pukaki; ⏰24hr) FREE presents the historical, geological and Māori cultural background of the lake and the region. Don't miss the superb lake and mountain views from the centre's windows.

Near the centre and the lookout, there's a retail outlet for Mt Cook Alpine Salmon (www.mtcookalpinesalmon. com; SH8; ⏰8.30am-5.30pm Oct-Jun, 9am-5pm Jul-Sep), the highest salmon farm on the planet, which operates in a hydroelectric canal system some distance away. Pick up some sashimi (from $10) and snack with stellar views.

world's largest inflatable slide and slippery-slope tubing.

Air Safaris SCENIC FLIGHTS
(☎03-680 6880; www.airsafaris.co.nz; SH8) Awe-inspiring views of Aoraki/Mt Cook National Park's peaks and glaciers are offered on the 'Grand Traverse' fixed-wing flight (adult/child $395/295); there are also various other flights available, including similar trips in a helicopter.

🛏 Sleeping

Lake Tekapo Motels & Holiday Park HOLIDAY PARK $
(☎03-680 6825; www.laketekapo-accommodation. co.nz; 2 Lakeside Dr; sites $50-60, dm $38, d $110-180; P🅿🛜🐕) With a prime position right on the lakefront, this sprawling complex has something for everyone. Backpackers get the cosy, log-cabin lodge, while others can enjoy cute Kiwi bachs, basic cabins, glamping tents or smart en suite units with particularly good views. Campervaners and campers are spoilt for choice, and share the sparkling amenities block.

YHA Lake Tekapo HOSTEL $
(☎03-680 6857; www.yha.co.nz; 5 Motuariki Lane; dm $37-42, s/d from $125/140; 🛜) New Zealand's newest YHA is also one of the country's best with colourful dorms and private rooms, excellent shared spaces including an upstairs lounge with lake and mountain views, and a modern and spacious kitchen. Downstairs, check out Our Dog Friday for burgers and craft beer.

Tailor Made Tekapo Backpackers HOSTEL $
(☎03-680 6700; www.tekapohostelnz.com; 11 Aorangi Cres; dm $30-40, d $100-120, d without bathroom $80-100; 🛜) Spread over three well-tended houses on a peaceful street five minutes' walk from town, this sociable hostel offers bright dorms (with no bunks) and cosy doubles. There's also a large garden complete with barbecue, hammock, chickens and bunnies, plus tennis and basketball courts next door for the energetic.

Chalet Boutique Motel APARTMENT $$$
(☎03-680 6774; www.thechalet.co.nz; 14 Pioneer Dr; units from $235; P🛜) The 'boutique motel' tag doesn't do justice to this collection of attractive accommodation options in three adjacent properties beside the lake. The wonderfully private 'Henkel hut' is a stylish option for lovebirds. Charming hosts will happily provide all the local information you need.

🍴 Eating & Drinking

Astro Café CAFE $
(Mt John University Observatory; mains $8-18; ⏰9am-6pm Oct-Apr, 10am-5pm May-Sep, weather dependent; 🚲) This glass-walled pavilion atop Mt John has spectacular 360-degree views across the entire Mackenzie Basin – just maybe one of the planet's best locations for a cafe. Tuck into bagels with salmon or a stonking slice of bacon and egg pie. There is a charge of $8 per car to access Mt John, but it's worth it for the views.

Blue Lake Eatery & Bar BISTRO $$
(☎03-680 6677; www.facebook.com/bluelaketeka po; SH8; mains $29, pizza $26, platters $26-59; ⏰3-9pm Mon & Tue, to 10pm Wed, Thu & Sun, to 11pm Fri & Sat) Craft beers from the Mackenzie Country's Burkes Brewing Co partner a seasonal menu including platters and pizza at this cosmopolitan spot in Lake Tekapo's commercial hub. Smaller plates could include porcini mushroom croquettes, and there's always interesting dishes with local South Island lamb and Mt Cook alpine salmon. Ask if any

Belgian-style beers from Ōamaru's tiny Craftwork Brewery are available.

Kohan JAPANESE **$$**
(📞03-680 6688; www.kohannz.com; SH8; dishes $6-20, bento $28-39; ⏱11am-2pm daily, plus 6-9pm Mon-Sat; 🐾) Despite its basic decor, this is one of Tekapo's best dining options, both for its distracting lake views and its authentic Japanese food, including fresh-off-the-boat sashimi. Leave room for the handmade green-tea ice cream.

Greedy Cow CAFE **$$**
(📞027 434 4445; www.greedycowtekapo.com; 16 Rapuwai Lane; mains $13-22; ⏱7.30am-4pm; 🐾🍴) Classic breakfast dishes (until 2.30pm), a cabinet full of cakes, pies and sandwiches, good espresso and free wi-fi are all reasons to visit this petite cafe. Gourmet deli items – including freshly baked ciabatta – will tempt the self-catering crew.

ℹ Information

Kiwi Treasures & Information Centre (📞03-680 6686; SH8; ⏱8am-5.30pm Mon-Fri, to 6pm Sat & Sun) This little gift shop doubles as the post office and info centre with local maps and advice, plus bookings for nearby activities and national bus services.

Tekapo Springs Sales & Information Centre
(📞03-680 6579; SH8; ⏱10am-6pm) The folks from Tekapo Springs dispense brochures and advice, as well as take bookings for their own complex down the road. See also www.tekapotourism.co.nz.

ℹ Getting There & Away

Cook Connection (📞0800 266 526; www.cookconnect.co.nz) Has a shuttle service to Mt Cook Village ($42, 2¼ hours).

InterCity (📞03-365 1113; www.intercity.co.nz) Runs daily services to the following:

DESTINATION	FARES ($) FROM	DURATION (HR)
Christchurch	41	3¾
Cromwell	41	2¾
Geraldine	24	1
Mt Cook Village	87	2½
Queenstown	40	4

Twizel

POP 1200

Pronounced 'twy-zel' but teased with 'Twizzel' and even 'Twizzelsticks' by outsiders, Twizel gets the last laugh. The town was

CHRISTCHURCH & CANTERBURY INLAND & MACKENZIE COUNTRY

DON'T MISS

ALPS 2 OCEAN CYCLE TRAIL

One of the best Great Rides within the New Zealand Cycle Trail (www.nzcycletrail.com), the 'A2O' serves up epic vistas on its way from the foot of the Southern Alps all the way to the Pacific Ocean at Ōamaru.

New Zealand's highest mountain – Aoraki/Mt Cook – is just one of many stunning sights. Others include braided rivers, glacier-carved valleys, turquoise hydro-lakes, tussock-covered highlands and lush farmland. Off-the-bike activities include wine tasting, penguin spotting, glider flights and soaking in alfresco hot tubs. Country hospitality, including food and accommodation, along with shuttles and other services, make the whole trip easy to organise and enjoy.

The trail is divided into nine easy-to-intermediate sections across terrain varying from canal paths, quiet country roads, old railway lines and expertly cut cross-country track, to some rougher, hilly stuff for the eager. The whole journey takes around four to six days, but it can easily be sliced into short sections.

Twizel is an excellent base for day rides. Options include taking a shuttle to Lake Tekapo (p476) for a five- to six-hour, big-sky ride back to Twizel, or riding from Twizel out to Lake Ohau Lodge (p480) for lunch or dinner. Both rides serve up the sublime lake and mountain scenery for which the Mackenzie is famous.

The trail is well supported by tour companies offering bike hire, shuttles, luggage transfers and accommodation. These include Twizel-based Cycle Journeys (📞0800 224 475, 03-435 0578; www.cyclejourneys.co.nz; 3 Benmore Pl; all-inclusive packages from $1389) and Jollie Biker (📞03-435 0517, 027 223 1761; www.thejolliebiker.co.nz; 193 Glen Lyon Rd; bike hire per day from $50). The Alps 2 Ocean website (www.alps2ocean.com) has comprehensive details.

OFF THE BEATEN TRACK

RUATANIWHA CONSERVATION PARK

Stretched between Lake Pukaki and Lake Ohau, the 368-sq-km protected area of **Ruataniwha Conservation Park** (www.doc.govt.nz) includes the rugged Ben Ohau Range along with the Dobson, Hopkins, Huxley, Temple and Maitland Valleys. It offers plenty of hiking and mountain-biking opportunities, as detailed in DOC's *Ruataniwha Conservation Park* pamphlet (available online), with several day trails close to Twizel.

DOC huts and camping areas are scattered throughout the park, and a more comfortable stay is available at Lake Ohau Lodge (p480). Passing through these parts is the Alps 2 Ocean Cycle Trail (p479), a great way to survey the majestic surroundings.

built in 1968 to service construction of the nearby hydroelectric power station, and was due for obliteration in 1984 when the project was completed. But there was no way the locals were upping their twizzlesticks and relinquishing their relaxed, mountain country lifestyle.

Today the town is thriving with a modest boom in holiday-home subdivisions and recognition from travellers that – as everyday as it may be – Twizel is actually in the middle of everything and has almost everything one might need (within reason).

🏃 Activities

Twizel sits amid some spectacular country offering all sorts of adventure opportunities. **Lake Ruataniwha** is popular for rowing, boating and windsurfing. Nearby hiking and cycling trails are illustrated on the excellent town map, available from the information centre (p481), including a nice river ramble. Twizel is also the best hub for rides on the Alps 2 Ocean Cycle Trail (p479).

Fishing in local rivers, canals and lakes is big business; enquire at the information centre about local guides, and ask them about swimming in **Loch Cameron** while you're at it (but don't tell them we tipped you off!).

👉 Tours

OneRing Tours   TOURS
(☏03-435 0073, 0800 213 868; www.lordofthe ringstour.com; cnr Ostler & Wairepo Sts; 🚐) How

often do you get the opportunity to charge around like a mad thing wielding replica *LOTR* gear? Not often enough! A range of tours is available – head to the sheep station used for the location of the Battle of the Pelennor Fields (adult/child $89/59), or take a lunchtime visit to Laketown (adult/child $119/89), as seen in the *Hobbit* films.

There's also a breakfast tour (adult/child $109/89) or an adults-only twilight tour ($139); enjoy beer, wine and nibbles as the sun sets over Gondor.

Helicopter Line   SCENIC FLIGHTS
(☏03-435 0370; www.helicopter.co.nz; Pukaki Airport, Harry Wigley Dr) Flights range from the hour-long Tasman Glacier Experience ($750) to the 20-minute Alpine Experience ($280), with several options in between. All but the shortest guarantee snow landings.

🛏 Sleeping

Twizel Holiday Park   HOLIDAY PARK $
(☏03-435 0507; www.twizelholidaypark.co.nz; 122 Mackenzie Dr; sites from $44, cabins & units $85-180; 🅿🛜🚼) Offers green, flower-filled grounds, with grassed sites and tidy communal facilities. Basic rooms are available in an old converted maternity hospital. The modern, self-contained cottages are particularly good value. Bike hire is also available.

Lake Ohau Lodge   LODGE $$
(☏03-438 9885; www.ohau.co.nz; Lake Ohau Rd; s $114-225, d $123-246; 🅿🛜) Idyllically sited on the western shore of remote Lake Ohau, 42km west of Twizel, accommodation includes everything from budget rooms with shared facilities to upmarket rooms with decks and mountain views. The lodge is the buzzy wintertime hub of the **Ohau Ski Field** (☏03-438 9885; www.ohau.co.nz; daily lift passes adult/child $100/40), which runs from June to September. In summer (December to February) it's a quieter retreat. Half-board packages are available (the nearest dining options are in Twizel).

Omahau Downs   LODGE, COTTAGE $$
(☏03-435 0199; www.omahau.co.nz; SH8; d $165-170, cottages from $180; ⊗closed Jun-Aug; 🅿🛜) This farmstead, 2km north of Twizel, has three cosy, self-contained cottages (one sleeping up to 15), and a lodge with sparkling, modern rooms and a deck looking out at the Ben Ohau Range.

★Lakestone Lodge   LODGE $$$
(☏03-971 1871; www.lakestonelodge.co.nz; 4589 Tekapo-Twizel Hwy, Lake Pukaki; r/ste $595/655;

P ⊗) 🍴 Daytime views from Lakestone Lodge's spectacular hilltop location include Lake Pukaki and alpine peaks, and there's a guests-only opportunity to survey the region's night sky after dark. Rooms are modern and exceedingly comfortable, and the lodge is well situated for day adventures on the nearby Alps 2 Ocean Cycle Trail. Breakfast is provided and dinners are also available ($90 per person).

Heartland Lodge
B&B, APARTMENT $$$

(📞03-435 0008; www.heartland-lodge.co.nz; 19 North West Arch; d $310-370, apt $145; P ⊗) On the leafy outskirts of town, this elegant modern house offers spacious, en suite rooms and a comfortable, convivial communal space. Friendly hosts prepare a cooked breakfast using organic, local produce where possible. The adjacent 'retreat' apartment sleeps up to six and has its own kitchenette (breakfast is not provided).

🍴 Eating & Drinking

Shawty's
CAFE $$

(📞03-435 3155; www.shawtys.co.nz; 4 Market Pl; mains $17-24; ⊗7.30am-3.30pm) The town centre's best cafe serves up big breakfasts including waffles with bacon and maple syrup, and Middle Eastern-inspired shakshuka baked eggs. For lunch the global menu includes a great Korean chicken burger and Thai-style Massaman lamb curry. Local flavours and ingredients include beer-battered blue cod and a warm smoked salmon salad. Look forward to good beers and wine too.

Poppies Cafe
CAFE $$

(📞03-435 0848; www.poppiescafe.com; 1 Benmore Pl; mains brunch $10-21, dinner $27-38; ⊗9am-9pm; ⊗) A favourite with locals, this well-run cafe serves up classic brunch faves and good coffee in the mornings, while come evening you'll find tasty curries, fresh fish and pasta dishes on the menu. Craft beer encourages a wee sup and snack, if you're not going the whole hog. It's south of town just off SH8.

High Country Salmon
SEAFOOD $$

(📞0800 400 385; www.highcountrysalmonfarm.co.nz; SH8; salmon per kg from $38; ⊗8am-6pm) The glacial waters of this floating fish farm, 3km from Twizel, produce mighty delicious fish, available to buy as fresh whole fillets and smoked portions. Our pick is the hot-smoked salmon, flaked into hot pasta, perhaps with a dash of cream. There's also a small cafe selling sashimi and other salmon-inspired dishes. Try the delicious Hawaiian-style poke.

MoW Bar & Eatery
BAR

(📞03-435 3257; www.facebook.com/MinistryofWorksBarandEatery; 2 Market Pl; ⊗4.30-9pm Sun-Thu, 3-10pm Fri & Sat) A decent selection of NZ craft beers and ciders partners with good pizza ($20 to $26) and bar snacks at this convivial hybrid of bar and restaurant. Score an outdoor table on a warm summer's evening or cosy up inside on cooler nights. The industrial decor references NZ's Ministry of Works, the government agency responsible for Twizel's development in the 1960s.

🛍 Shopping

Twizel Bookshop
BOOKS

(📞027 464 5062; www.twizelbookshop.co.nz; 12b Market Pl; ⊗9am-5pm Mon-Fri, shorter hours Sat & Sun) A sweet, well-curated bookshop offering both new and secondhand titles.

❶ Information

Twizel Information Centre (📞03-435 3124; www.twizel.info; Market Pl; ⊗8.30am-5pm Mon-Fri, 10am-3pm Sat) Can advise on hiking and cycling paths in the area, as well as book accommodation. Also offers bike hire (one hour/three hours/full day $25/35/45).

❶ Getting There & Away

Cook Connection (📞0800 266 526; www.cookconnect.co.nz) Runs daily shuttle services to Mt Cook Village (one way/return $30/55, one hour).

InterCity (📞03-365 1113; www.intercity.co.nz) Runs daily services to the following:

DESTINATION	FARES ($) FROM	DURATION
Christchurch	47	5¼hr
Cromwell	32	2hr
Lake Tekapo	19	50min
Mt Cook Village	78	1hr
Queenstown	39	3hr

Naked Bus (www.nakedbus.com) Services Christchurch and Queenstown/Wānaka.

Aoraki/Mt Cook National Park

POP 200

The spectacular 700-sq-km Aoraki/Mt Cook National Park is part of the Southwest New Zealand (Te Wāhipounamu) World Heritage

Aoraki/Mt Cook National Park

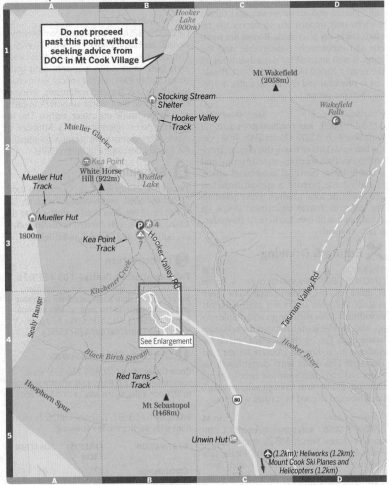

Area, which extends from Westland's Cook River down to Fiordland. More than one-third of the park has a blanket of permanent snow and glacial ice; of the 23 NZ mountains over 3000m, 19 are in this park. The highest is mighty Aoraki/Mt Cook – at 3724m, the tallest peak in Australasia. Among the region's other great peaks are Sefton, Tasman, Silberhorn, Malte Brun, La Perouse, Hicks, De la Beche, Douglas and the Minarets.

Aoraki/Mt Cook is a wonderful sight, assuming there's no cloud in the way. Most visitors arrive on tour buses, stop at the Hermitage hotel for photos, and then zoom off back down SH80. Hang around to soak up this awesome peak and the surrounding landscape, and to try the excellent short walks in the area, including to the Tasman Glacier.

History

Known to Māori as Aoraki (Cloud Piercer), after an ancestral deity in Māori mythology, the mountain was given its English name in 1851, in honour of explorer Captain James Cook.

This region has always been the focus of climbing in NZ. On 2 March 1882 William Spotswood Green and two Swiss alpinists failed to reach the summit after an epic 62-hour ascent. Two years later a trio of local climbers – Tom Fyfe, George Graham and

Aoraki/Mt Cook National Park

◎ Top Sights

◎ Sights

◎ Activities, Courses & Tours

◎ Sleeping

◎ Eating

◎ Drinking & Nightlife

◎ Transport

◉ Sights

★ Aoraki/Mt Cook National Park Visitor Centre
MUSEUM

(☏ 03-435 1186; www.doc.govt.nz; 1 Larch Grove; ⊙ 8.30am-5pm Oct-Apr, to 4.30pm May-Sep) **FREE** Arguably the best DOC visitor centre in NZ. It not only dispatches all necessary information and advice on hiking routes and weather conditions, it also houses excellent displays on the park's natural and human history. It's a fabulous place to commune with the wilderness, even on a rainy day. Most activities can be booked here.

Tasman Glacier
GLACIER

(www.doc.govt.nz) At 27km long and up to 4km wide, the Tasman is the largest of NZ's glaciers, but it's melting fast, losing hundreds of metres of length each year. It is also melting from the surface, shrinking around 150m in depth since it was first surveyed in 1891. Despite this considerable shrinkage, at its thickest point the ice is still estimated to be over 600m deep.

Jack Clarke – were spurred into action by the news that two well-known European alpinists were coming to attempt the peak, and set off to climb it before the visitors. On Christmas Day 1894 they ascended the Hooker Glacier and north ridge to stand on the summit.

In 1913 Australian climber Freda du Faur became the first woman to reach the summit. New Zealander Edmund Hillary first climbed the south ridge in 1948; Hillary went on to become one of the first two people to reach the summit of Mt Everest. Since then, most of the daunting face routes have been climbed.

In its lower section the melts have exposed rocks, stones and boulders, which form a solid unsightly mass on top of the ice.

Tasman Lake, at the foot of the glacier, started to form only in the early 1970s and now stretches to 7km. The ongoing effects of climate change are expected to extend it much further in the next decade. The lake is covered by a maze of huge icebergs, which are continuously being sheared off the glacier's terminal face. On 22 February 2011 the Christchurch earthquake caused a 1.3km-long, 300m-high, 30-million-tonne chunk of ice to break off, causing 3.5m waves to roll into the tourist boats on the lake at the time (no one was injured). You can kayak on Tasman Lake with Glacier Kayaking.

In the glacier's last major advance (17,000 years ago), the glacier crept south far enough to carve out Lake Pukaki. A later advance did not reach out to the valley sides, so there's a gap between the outer valley walls and the lateral moraines of this later advance. The unsealed Tasman Valley Rd, which branches off Mt Cook Rd 800m south of Mt Cook Village, travels through this gap. From the Blue Lakes shelter, 8km along the road, the Tasman Glacier View Track (30 minutes return) climbs interminable steps to an aptly rewarding viewpoint on the moraine wall, with a side trip to Blue Lakes on the way. Now only replenished by rainfall, the Blue Lakes have reduced in size and are now a muddy green colour.

Sir Edmund Hillary Alpine Centre MUSEUM (www.hermitage.co.nz; Hermitage, Terrace Rd; adult/child $20/10; ⏰ 7.30am-9.30pm Oct-Mar, 8am-7pm Apr-Sep) This multimedia museum opened just three weeks before the 2008 death of the man regarded by many as the greatest New Zealander of all time, explorer and mountain climber Sir Edmund Hillary. The main attraction is a cinema and domed digital planetarium that screens films all day, including the *Mt Cook Magic* 3D movie and a fascinating 75-minute documentary about Sir Ed's conquest of Everest. The foyer houses memorabilia both from St Ed's various expeditions and from the 1884-built Hermitage (p486) hotel itself.

🏃 Activities

Hiking & Climbing

Various easy tramps from the village are outlined in the (multilingual) *Walking & Cycling Tracks* pamphlet available from the Aoraki/Mt Cook National Park Visitor Centre (p483) and online. On the trails, look for the thar, a Himalayan goat; the chamois, smaller and of lighter build than the thar, and originally hailing from Europe; and red deer, also European. Summertime (December through March) brings into bloom the Mt Cook lily, a large mountain buttercup, and mountain daisies, gentians and edelweiss.

Longer tramps are only recommended for those with mountaineering experience, as tracks and conditions at higher altitudes can become dangerous. Highly changeable weather is typical: Aoraki/Mt Cook is only 44km from the coast and weather conditions rolling in from the Tasman Sea can mean sudden storms.

As for climbing, there's unlimited scope for the experienced, but those without experience must go with a guide. Regardless of your skills, take every precaution – more than 200 people have died in climbing accidents in the park. The bleak *In Memoriam* book in the visitor centre begins with the first death on Aoraki/Mt Cook in 1907; since then more than 80 climbers have died on the peak.

Check with the park rangers before attempting any climb and always heed their advice. If you're climbing, or even going on a longer tramp, fill out an intentions card before starting out so rangers can check on you if you're overdue coming back. Sign out again when you return. The visitor centre also hires locator beacons ($30/40 per three/ seven days).

If you intend to stay at any of the park's huts, it's essential to register your intentions at the visitor centre and pay the hut fees. Walkers can use the public shelter in Mt Cook Village, which has running water, toilets and coin-operated showers. Note that this shelter cannot be used for overnight stays.

Hooker Valley Track HIKING
Perhaps the best of the area's day walks, this track (three hours return from the DOC White Horse Hill Campground; p486) heads up the Hooker Valley and crosses three swing bridges to the Stocking Stream and the terminus of the Hooker Glacier. After the second swing bridge, Aoraki/Mt Cook totally dominates the valley, and you may see icebergs floating in Hooker Lake.

Kea Point Track HIKING
The trail to Kea Point (two hours return from the visitor centre) is lined with native plants and ends with excellent views of Aoraki/Mt Cook, the Hooker Valley, and the ice faces of Mt Sefton and the Footstool. De-

spite the name, you're no more likely to see a kea (bird) here than anywhere else. If you do, don't feed it.

Sealy Tarns Track   HIKING

The walk to Sealy Tarns (three to four hours return) branches off the Kea Point Track (p484) and continues up the ridge to Mueller Hut (dorm $36), a comfortable 28-bunk hut with gas, cooking facilities and long-drop toilets.

Southern Alps Guiding   CLIMBING

(☑ 03-435 1890; www.mtcook.com; Old Mountaineers' Cafe, Bowen Dr) Offers mountaineering instruction and guiding, plus three- to four-hour helihiking trips on Tasman Glacier year-round ($599). From June to October heliskiers can head up the Tasman, Murchison and Mannering Glaciers for a series of 5km to 15km runs (four runs, from $1250; extra runs per person from $125).

Alpine Guides   CLIMBING

(☑ 03-435 1834; www.alpineguides.co.nz; 81 Bowen Dr; beginners climbing course from $2350) Offers guided climbs and mountaineering courses for all skill levels, along with ski-touring, including heli options. It also stocks outdoor clothing and mountaineering gear, and rents ice axes, crampons, day packs and sleeping bags.

Alpine Recreation   TRAMPING

(☑ 03-680 6736, 0800 006 096; www.alpinerecreation.com; guided tramps 2/4/6 days from $810/1750/2590) Based in Lake Tekapo, these folks organise high-altitude guided tramps, as well as mountaineering courses and ski touring. Also on offer are guided ascents of Aoraki/Mt Cook, Mt Tasman and other peaks.

Other Activities

Glacier Kayaking   KAYAKING

(☑ 03-435 1890; www.mtcook.com; Old Mountaineers' Cafe, Bowen Dr; per person $250; ⊙ Oct-Apr) Suitable for paddlers with just an ounce of experience, these guided kayaking trips head out on the terminal lake of the Tasman or Mueller Glaciers. With luck there will be icebergs to negotiate, but regardless there will be spectacular scenery, with a fascinating geology lesson thrown in. Trips last four to six hours, depending on conditions; book at the Old Mountaineers' Cafe (p486).

Big Sky Stargazing   STARGAZING

(☑ 03-435 1809, 0800 686 800; www.hermitage. co.nz; Hermitage, Terrace Rd; adult/child $80/45; ⊕)

New Zealand's southern sky is introduced with a 45-minute presentation in the Alpine Centre's digital planetarium. Afterwards participants venture outside to study the real deal with telescopes, binoculars and an astronomy guide.

☞ Tours

Mount Cook Ski Planes & Helicopters   SCENIC FLIGHTS

(☑ 03-430 8026; www.mtcookskiplanes.com; Mt Cook Airport) Get an aerial view of Mt Cook and surrounding glaciers via ski plane or helicopter with this outfit, based at Mt Cook Airport. Most flights include a snow or glacier landing; options include the 45-minute Grand Circle (adult/child $599/479) and the 35-minute Tasman Experience (adult/child $359/295).

Glacier Explorers   BOATING

(☑ 03-435 1641; www.glacierexplorers.com; Hermitage, Terrace Rd; adult/child $170/87; ⊙ Sep-May; ⊕) Head out on the terminal lake of the Tasman Glacier for this small-boat tour, which gets up close and personal with old icebergs and crazy moraines. Includes a 30-minute walk. Book at the activities desk at the Hermitage (p486).

Helicopter Line   SCENIC FLIGHTS

(☑ 03-435 1801; www.helicopter.co.nz; Glentanner Park, Mt Cook Rd, Glentanner) Departing from Glentanner Park, the Helicopter Line offers 20-minute Alpine Vista flights ($270), an exhilarating 35-minute flight over the Ben Ohau Range ($415), and a 40-minute Mountains High flight over the Tasman Glacier and alongside Aoraki/Mt Cook ($480). All feature snow landings.

Heliworks   SCENIC FLIGHTS

(☑ 0800 666 668, 03-435 1460; www.queenstown helicopters.nz; Mt Cook Airport; flights per person $380-605) Offers a range of scenic helicopter flights over some of NZ's most majestic scenery, all with a glacier landing. The 55-minute Aoraki/Mt Cook Ultimate flight ($605) circumnavigates the country's highest peak.

Tasman Valley 4WD Tours   TOURS

(☑ 0800 686 800; www.hermitage.co.nz/en/activities/tasman-valley-tour; adult/child $68/48; ⊕) Offers two-hour 4WD tours to the Tasman Glacier and its terminal lake, with alpine flora and interesting commentary along the way. Book online or at the Hermitage (p486) activities desk.

🛏 Sleeping

YHA Aoraki Mt Cook HOSTEL $
(📞 03-435 1820; www.yha.co.nz; 1 Bowen Dr; dm/d $41/145; 🅿 🛜) 🏊 Handsomely decked out in pine, this excellent hostel has a free sauna, a drying room, log fires, a large kitchen and friendly, helpful staff. Rooms are clean and warm, although some are a tight squeeze (particularly the twin bunk rooms).

DOC White Horse Hill Campground CAMPGROUND $
(📞 03-435 1186; www.doc.govt.nz; Hooker Valley Rd; sites per adult/child $15/7.50; 🅿) Located 2km up the Hooker Valley from Mt Cook Village, this self-registration camping ground has a basic shelter with (cold water) sinks, tables and toilets, along with blissful views and close proximity to various walking tracks.

Glentanner Park Centre HOLIDAY PARK $
(📞 03-435 1855; www.glentanner.co.nz; SH80, Glentanner; sites $22-25, dm $40, units $125-240; 🅿 @ 🛜) 🏊 On the northern shore of Lake Pukaki, 22km south of Mt Cook village, this is the nearest fully equipped camping ground to the national park. Features include cabins and motel units, a bunk room, a cafe and free-roaming rabbits.

★Aoraki/Mt Cook Alpine Lodge LODGE $$
(📞 03-435 1860; www.aorakialpinelodge.co.nz; Bowen Dr; d $185-260; 🅿 🛜) This lovely family-run lodge has en suite rooms, including some suitable for families and two with kitchenettes; most have views. The huge lounge and kitchen area also has a superb mountain outlook, as does the barbecue area – a rather inspiring spot to sizzle your dinner.

Aoraki Court Motel MOTEL $$$
(📞 03-435 1111; www.aorakicourt.co.nz; 26 Bowen Dr; d $325-455; 🅿 🛜) While they wouldn't command these prices elsewhere, this clump of modern motel units offers classy decor, all the requisite mod cons and good views. Some units have spa baths, and there are bikes for hire.

Hermitage HOTEL $$$
(📞 03-435 1809; www.hermitage.co.nz; Terrace Rd; r $184-429; 🅿 @ 🛜) Completely dominating Mt Cook Village, this famous hotel offers awesome views. While the corridors in some of the older wings can seem a little hospital-like, all of the rooms have been renovated to a reasonable standard (the cheapest do not have mountain views). In addition to the on-site shop and Alpine Centre, there are three dining options of reasonable standard.

🍴 Eating & Drinking

Old Mountaineers' Cafe CAFE $$
(www.mtcook.com; Bowen Dr; mains breakfast $10-18, lunch $18-30, dinner $26-40; ⏱ 10am-9pm; 🛜) 🏊 Encouraging lingering with books, memorabilia and mountain views through picture windows, the village's best eatery also supports local and organic suppliers via an all-day menu offering salmon and bacon pies, cooked breakfasts, burgers and pizza.

Chamois Bar & Grill PUB
(Bowen Dr; ⏱ 4pm-late; 🛜) This large bar offers basic pub meals, a pool table, a big-screen TV and the occasional live gig, but the views are its best feature. Come at sunset and watch the mountains change colour.

ℹ Information

The Aoraki/Mt Cook National Park Visitor Centre (p483) is the best source of local information. The nearest ATM and supermarket are in Twizel.

ℹ Getting There & Away

Mt Cook Village's small airport only serves aerial sightseeing companies. Some of these may be willing to combine transport to the West Coast (ie Franz Josef) with a scenic flight, but flights are heavily dependent on weather.

If you're driving, fill up at Lake Tekapo or Twizel. There is a self-service pump at Mt Cook, but it's expensive.

Cook Connection (📞 0800 266 526; www.cookconnect.co.nz) runs shuttle services to Lake Tekapo ($42, 2¼ hours) and Twizel ($30, 45 minutes).

InterCity (📞 03-365 1113; www.intercity.co.nz) coaches stop at the Hermitage; however, they are operated as part of a 'tour' and can be pricey – you might be better off catching a shuttle back to Twizel and picking up an InterCity connection from there.

DESTINATION	FARES ($) FROM	DURATION (HR)
Christchurch	162	5¼
Lake Tekapo	78	2½
Queenstown	186	4

Dunedin & Otago

Best Places to Eat

➜ Riverstone Kitchen (p497)
➜ Fleur's Place (p497)
➜ Good Good (p506)
➜ Cucina (p496)
➜ Bracken (p506)

Best Places to Stay

➜ Pen-y-bryn Lodge (p495)
➜ Oliver's (p521)
➜ Oamaru Backpackers (p495)
➜ Terminus Hotel (p504)
➜ Hogwartz (p504)

Why Go?

Wine, wildlife, the weird and the wonderful – travellers who take the time to explore this quirky corner of the country are in for a treat.

Cruising down the coast from Christchurch you come to seaside Ōamaru, a town that has let its gracious Victorian buildings weave a steampunk fantasy of costume and creativity around its residents. The coastal road also sweeps past the sweet Moeraki Boulders and two of New Zealand's most acclaimed restaurants (both of which are sprinkled with eccentricity in keeping with the region) on the way to Dunedin. This city is full of hidden treasures, from the world-class street art down every alley to the stunning coastline providing sanctuary to royal albatross, fur seals and penguins.

Heading inland you soon find yourself on deserted roads stretching to mountains on the far horizon and dotted with isolated gold-rush villages. It's perfect cycling country, and there are plenty of chances to do just that, including the famous Otago Central Rail Trail. Nearby in Cromwell and Bannockburn, charming wineries are busy producing the best pinot noir in NZ.

When to Go

➜ February and March have sunny, settled weather (usually...), and the juicy appeal of fresh apricots, peaches and cherries.

➜ At Easter, hook yourself a 'Southern Man' at the biennial Middlemarch Singles Ball, or drown your sorrows at the Clyde Wine & Food Festival.

➜ Take to two wheels on the Otago Central Rail Trail during the quieter months of September and October.

➜ In November, watch the pros battle it out at the Highlands Motorsport Park, then ride graciously into the past on a penny-farthing bicycle at Ōamaru's Victorian Heritage Celebrations.

Dunedin & Otago Highlights

1 Dunedin (p498) Hunting for street-art Easter eggs down Dunedin's alleyways.

2 Ōamaru (p491) Going bonkers for steampunk in this town of vintage costumery and warehouses of offbeat art.

3 Otago Peninsula (p509) Peering at penguins, admiring albatross and staring at seals.

4 Otago Central Rail Trail (p514) Cycling through breathtaking vistas and frontier towns.

5 Naseby (p517) Relishing the wintry delights of curling, luging, skating and stargazing.

6 Taieri Gorge Railway (p502) Winding through gorges, along canyons and across viaducts on this snaking heritage railway.

7 Cromwell (p521) Taste-testing some of the planet's best pinot noir in the wineries scattered around the fruit bowl of the south.

ℹ️ Getting There & Away

From Dunedin, **Air New Zealand** (📞 0800 737 000; www.airnewzealand.co.nz) flies to Christchurch, Wellington and Auckland, **Jetstar** (📞 0800 800 995; www.jetstar.com) flies to Auckland and **Virgin** (📞 0800 670 000; www.virginaustralia.com) flies direct to Brisbane (Australia).

The only train services are heritage trips (p502) from Dunedin to Pukerangi or Waitati.

The main bus routes follow SH1 or SH8.

WAITAKI DISTRICT

The broad, braided Waitaki River provides a clear dividing line between Otago and Canterbury to the region's north. The Waitaki Valley is a direct but less-travelled route from the Southern Alps to the sea, featuring freaky limestone formations, Māori rock paintings and ancient fossils, spotlighted in the Waitaki Whitestone Geopark (p491). The area is also one of New Zealand's newest winemaking regions, and is a major component of the Alps 2 Ocean Cycle Trail (p479), which links Aoraki/Mt Cook National Park to the coast. The district's main town, Ōamaru, is a place of penguins, steampunk and glorious heritage architecture.

Ōmarama

POP 270

At the head of the Waitaki Valley, sleepy Ōmarama is surrounded by mountain ranges and fabulous landscapes. Busy times include the rodeo (28 December) and the sheepdog trials (March).

◉ Sights & Activities

Clay Cliffs Paritea LANDMARK
(Henburn Rd; cars $5) About as 'hidden gem' as you can get in an area rife with nosy tourists, these eerie and kinda creepy pinnacles, ravines and ridges have been shaped by around two million years of erosion along the active Ostler fault. Short trails lead around and between the forms to make you feel like an ant crawling in a sandcastle. Be careful – some look like they could crumble at any moment.

ESSENTIAL DUNEDIN & OTAGO

Eat nectarines, apricots, peaches, plums and cherries from Central Otago.

Drink pinot noir from Central Otago and the Waitaki Valley.

Read *To the Is-land* (1982), the first volume of Otago author Janet Frame's lyrical autobiography.

Listen to the Dunnerstunners playlist on Spotify curating a list of Dunedin greats from Kane Strang to the Chills.

Gaze at the paintings of Grahame Sydney, capturing the melancholy magic of Central Otago.

Celebrate at Ōamaru's Victorian Heritage Celebrations (p495) in late November.

Go green and tiptoe down to Otago Peninsula beaches in search of rare yellow-eyed penguins.

Go online www.dunedinnz.com, www.centralotagonz.com

⭐ Omarama Hot Tubs SPA
(📞 03-438 9703; www.hottubsomarama.co.nz; 29 Omarama Ave, SH8; 1-/2-/3-/4-person tub $56/98/123/148, pod $85/160/210/240; ⊙ 11am-late) 🌿 If your legs are weary after mountain biking or hiking, or you just want to cosy up with your significant other, these private, wood-fired hot tubs could be just the ticket. Choose between a 90-minute soak in a tub (each has its own dressing room) or a two-hour session in a 'wellness pod', which includes a sauna.

These tubs are popular – book ahead online (last booking 8.30pm). Clothing is optional and the chemical-free glacier and snow-melt water is changed after each booking; the used water is recycled for irrigation. The concept is Japanese, but with the surrounding mountain ranges, the lakeside setting and a pristine night sky, you could only be on the South Island of NZ. Therapeutic massages (30/60/90 minutes $65/120/170) and other treatments are also available.

DUNEDIN & OTAGO ŌMARAMA

📖 Sleeping & Eating

Buscot Station
FARMSTAY $

(📱027 222 1754; www.bbh.co.nz; 912 SH8; sites/dm/s/d from $10/25/40/60; 🅿) For a completely different and uniquely Kiwi experience, grab a room in the home-style farmhouse attached to a huge sheep and cattle station, or a bed in the large dormitory out the back. The sunset views are terrific and there's plenty of acreage for quiet explorations. Look for it on SH8, 10km north of Ōmarama.

Omarama Top 10 Holiday Park
HOLIDAY PARK $

(📱03-438 9875; www.omaramatop10.co.nz; 1 Omarama Ave, SH8; sites from $45, units with/without bathroom $150/80; 🅿🛜♿) 🖉 Facilities are good at this holiday park, squeezed between the highway and a stream. Standard cabins are on the cosy side, but larger ensuite cabins and self-contained motel units are also available.

Wrinkly Rams
CAFE $$

(📱03-438 9751; www.thewrinklyrams.co.nz; 24-30 Omarama Ave, SH8; mains $12-30; ⊘6.30am-4.30pm; 🕿) Restaurants attached to tourist attractions can be dodgy, but the meals here are perfectly fine (the coffee is hit and miss, though). Big glass windows and outside tables give a nice view of the mountains while you eat. If a group has booked, you can tag along to see a sheepdog or shearing show (adult/child $25/12.50).

ℹ Information

Omarama Information Centre (📱021 195 5572; www.facebook.com/omaramainfo; 4 Omarama Ave; ⊘10am-4pm) This friendly centre can assist with accommodation and help you organise an Alps 2 Ocean Cycle Trail (p479) trip.

ℹ Getting There & Away

The road from Ōmarama to Cromwell heads over the striking Lindis Pass.

Cycle Journeys (📱03-377 2060; www.cyclejourneys.co.nz; ⊘Oct-Apr) Runs seasonal shuttles for cyclists on the Alps 2 Ocean Cycle Trail between Ōmarama and Ōamaru ($50), stopping at Kurow and Duntroon – call ahead to see if you can book a seat.

InterCity (📱03-471 7143; www.intercity.co.nz) Has two coaches a day heading to/from Christchurch (from $49, six hours), Twizel (from $19, 25 minutes), Cromwell (from $27, 1½ hours) and Queenstown (from $37, 2½ hours), and one heading to/from Mt Cook Village ($78, 3½ hours).

Waitaki Valley

Wine, waterskiing and salmon-fishing are just some of the treats on offer along this little-travelled route. Coming from Ōmarama, the winding SH83 passes a series of glassy blue lakes. For a scenic detour along the north bank (with basic lakeside camping in summer for $10), leave the highway at Otematata and cross over Benmore Dam, then cross back over Aviemore Dam to rejoin the route.

A succession of sleepy little towns line the highway. One of the most appealing is tiny Kurow, the home town of World Cup–winning retired All Blacks captain Richie McCaw, with a handful of lovely cafes. At almost-as-cute Duntroon, a couple of heritage buildings, including an evocative blacksmiths shop, have been restored.

Although they've got a way to go to attain the global reputation of Central Otago, a few winemaking pioneers in Waitaki Valley are producing wine of which international experts are taking notice.

◉ Sights

◉ Kurow

Kurow Heritage & Information Centre
MUSEUM

(📱03-436 0950; www.kurow.org.nz; 57 Bledisloe St, Kurow; ⊘9am-5pm Mon-Fri, 10am-4pm Sat & Sun Oct-Mar, 9am-4pm Mon-Fri Apr-Sep) FREE Local hero Richie McCaw rates a mention at this very sweet community-run museum, filled with lovingly preserved curios. Staff are knowledgeable and friendly, and can give excellent advice on local activities and routes. It's celebrating 50 years in operation in 2020.

Vintner's Drop
WINERY

(📱03-436 0545; www.ostlerwine.co.nz; 45 Bledisloe St, Kurow; tastings 3/5 wines $10/15; ⊘noon-5pm Nov-Mar, to 3.30pm Mon-Fri Apr-Oct) Housed in Kurow's old post office, Vintner's Drop acts as a tasting room for Ostler Vineyards, along with other small local producers. Try the signature Caroline's pinot noir.

River T Estate
WINERY

(📱021 190 8875; www.rivertestate.co.nz; SH83; lunch $13-16; ⊘9am-6pm Oct-Mar, from 11am Apr-Sep) Offering over 40 local wines by the glass, including River T's own well-regarded pinot gris and chardonnay, this new cellar door is gaining a reputation for its platters featuring local Waitaki Valley produce ($20 per person). Dine overlooking the vines –

you're encouraged to stroll around and sample the grapes when they're in season.

◉ Duntroon & Around

Takiroa Māori
Rock Painting Site   ARCHAEOLOGICAL SITE

(SH83) FREE Hidden within the honeycomb cliffs lining the highway, this well-signposted site, 3km west of Duntroon, is of special significance to the Ngāi Tahu. It features mainly 19th-century drawings, including people riding horses and European sailing ships.

Maerewhenua Māori
Rock Painting Site   ARCHAEOLOGICAL SITE

(Livingstone-Duntroon Rd, cnr Settlement Rd) FREE Sheltered by an impressive limestone overhang with amazing views over the valley, this site contains charcoal-and-ochre paintings dating to before the arrival of Europeans. Moa bones have been found here, indicating hundreds of years of occupation. Head east from Duntroon and take the first right after crossing the Maerewhenua River; the site is on the left after about 400m down the road to Elephant Rocks.

Elephant Rocks   LANDMARK
Sculpted by wind, rain and rivers, the huge limestone boulders of this bizarre landscape were used as Aslan's Camp in the NZ-filmed *Narnia* movies (2005-10). They're located on farmland about 5.5km south of the highway; follow the signs after crossing the Maerewhenua River. To climb them, contact Cycle Ventures (p495) in Ōamaru.

Vanished World Centre   MUSEUM
(☑ 03-431 2024; www.vanishedworld.co.nz; 7 Campbell St, Duntroon; adult/child $10/free; ☺ 10am-4.30pm; ☝) Stop into this volunteer-run centre to dig out your own real limestone fossils (to keep!) or check out the frightening 25-million-year-old shark-toothed dolphin and giant penguin. There are lots of activities for kids, and you can pick up a copy of the Vanished World Trail map ($6.50) outlining 20 different interesting geological locations around the Waitaki Valley and North Otago coast.

🛏 Sleeping

Valley Views Glamping   TENTED CAMP $$$
(☑ 021 192 8282; www.valleyviews.co.nz; 161 Domett Rd, Otiake; dome for 2 incl breakfast $280-350) 🏕 Camp in luxury in this scattering of spacious geodesic domes on a working cattle farm 13km from Kurow. Each has a private deck

---

WAITAKI WHITESTONE GEOPARK

Earth scientists and fossil fans should check out this geopark (www.white stonegeopark.nz), a collection of sites linking coastal geology and culture, from 60 million years ago to the present. It includes the Moeraki Boulders (p497), Clay Cliffs Paritea (p489), Takiroa, Maerewhenua, Elephant Rocks and more, and is currently shortlisted to become the first Unesco Global Geopark in Australasia (to be decided in early 2021). Download the free app to check it out.

---

and a huge window overlooking the valley. Bathrooms are shared – including standard facilities in the lodge and four outdoor baths in the forest. Running on solar power and good vibes, this is a great romantic getaway.

Three-course meals are available Wednesday to Sunday for $50 per person.

❶ Getting There & Away

Cycle Journeys runs seasonal shuttles for cyclists on the Alps 2 Ocean Cycle Trail between Ōamaru and Ōmarama ($50), stopping at Kurow ($35) and Duntroon ($25) – call ahead to see if you can book a seat. Otherwise you'll need your own car or bike along this route.

Ōamaru

POP 13,670

Ōamaru is offbeat small-town New Zealand at its very best. Rattling around inside its enormous and ramshackle Victorian warehouses are oddballs, antiquarians and bohemians of all stripes who make art, age fruity whisky and dress up at the drop of a top hat. Most visible are the steampunks, boldly celebrating the past and the future with an ethos of 'tomorrow as it used to be'. Plus there's the penguins. The nightly beach waddle of adorable blue penguins draws plenty of visitors to Ōamaru, but many find they are just as charmed by the creative community of humans. Put simply, Ōamaru is *cool*.

Away from the docks, the town's gracious whitestone buildings harbour an increasing array of restaurants and bars, and some excellent accommodation options are available. You may find find yourself lingering in this laid-back coastal town.

Ōamaru

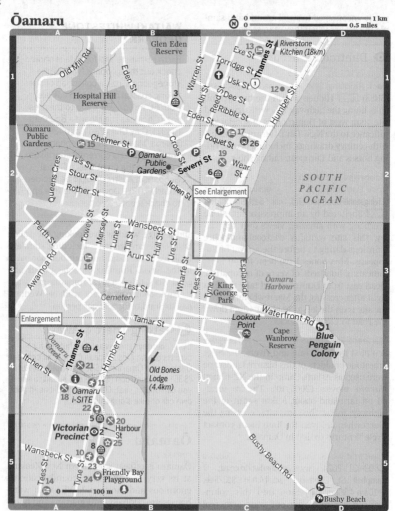

History

Ōamaru used to be rich and ambitious. In its 1880s heyday, it was about the same size as Los Angeles was at the time. Refrigerated meat-shipping had its origins nearby and the town became wealthy enough to erect the imposing buildings that grace Thames St today.

These buildings are all the more striking as they were constructed from the milky local limestone (known as Ōamaru stone or whitestone), with their forms reflecting the fashion of the times; there's a particular emphasis on the neoclassical. Impressive examples include the 1883 Forrester Gal-

lery (p494), the 1882 North Otago Museum (p494), the 1873 **St Patrick's Basilica** (☎03-434 8543; www.cdd.org.nz/st-patrick-oamaru; 68 Reed St) and the 1907 Opera House (p496). Many heritage buildings along Thames St are lit with coloured lights at night.

However, after the building boom, the town overreached itself and spent the end of the 19th century teetering on the verge of bankruptcy. Economic decline in the 20th century meant that there wasn't the impetus to swing the wrecking ball here with the same reckless abandon that wiped out much of the built heritage of NZ's main centres. It's

Ōamaru

only in recent decades that canny creative types have cottoned on to the uniqueness of Ōamaru's surviving Victorian streetscapes and have started to unlock this otherwise unremarkable town's potential for extreme kookiness.

◉ Sights

★ **Victorian Precinct**   AREA
Consisting of only a couple of blocks centred on Harbour and Tyne Sts, this atmospheric enclave has some of NZ's best-preserved Victorian commercial buildings. Descend on a dark and foggy night and it's downright Dickensian. It's also ground zero for all that is hip, cool and freaky in Ōamaru, and one of the best places to window shop on the entire South Island.

Wander around during the day and you'll discover antiquarian bookshops, antique stores, galleries, vintage clothing shops, artist studios and artisan bookbinders.

The precinct is at its liveliest on Sunday when the excellent Ōamaru farmers market is in full swing, the steam train (www.oamaru-steam.org.nz; adult/child/family return $10/4/24; ⊙11am-3pm Sun; 🚂) is running, and artisans are busy in their studios.

★ **Blue Penguin Colony**   BIRD SANCTUARY
(📞03-433 1195; www.penguins.co.nz; 2 Waterfront Rd; adult/child evening visit from $40/25, day $25/15; ⊙10am-2hr after sunset) 🐧 Every

evening the tykes from the Ōamaru blue penguin colony surf in and wade ashore, heading to their nests in an old stone quarry near the waterfront. Stands are set up on either side of the waddle route. General admission will give you a good view of the action but the premium stand (adult/child $55/32), accessed by a boardwalk through the nesting area, will get you closer.

You'll see the most penguins (up to 250) in November and December. From March to August there may be only 10 to 50 birds. They arrive in groups called rafts just before dark (around 5.30pm in midwinter and 9.30pm midsummer), and it takes about an hour for them all to come ashore; nightly viewing times are posted at the i-SITE (p496). Use of cameras is prohibited and you're advised to dress warmly.

To understand the centre's conservation work and its success in increasing the penguin population, take the daytime behind-the-scenes tour, when you can (usually) peer into the underground world of nesting penguins in residence; packages that combine night viewing and the daytime tour are also available.

Do not under any circumstances wander around the rocks beside the sea here at night looking for penguins. It's damaging to their environment and spoils studies into the human effects on the birds.

DUNEDIN & OTAGO ŌAMARU

MĀORI NZ: DUNEDIN & OTAGO

The early Māori history of Otago echoes that of Canterbury (p419), with Ngāi Tahu the dominant tribe at the time the British arrived. One of the first parcels of land that Ngāi Tahu sold was called the Otago block, a 1618-sq-km parcel of land that changed hands in 1844 for £2400. The name Otago reflects the Ngāi Tahu pronunciation of Ōtākou, a small village on the far reaches of the Otago Peninsula, where there's still a *marae* (meeting place).

Dunedin's Otago Museum (p499) has the finest Māori exhibition on the South Island, including an ornately carved *waka taua* (war canoe) and a finely crafted *pounamu* (greenstone); there's wonderful exhibits at Toitū Otago Settlers Museum (p498) too. One of the most important collections of first settlement Māori artefacts in the country can be viewed at Ōamaru's North Otago Museum. Māori rock art can be seen in situ in the Waitaki Valley (p491), which was an important *ara tawhito* (travel route).

Steampunk HQ   GALLERY

(🗐 027 778 6547; www.steampunkoamaru.co.nz; 1 Humber St; adult/child $10/2; ⊙10am-5pm) Discover an alternative past – or maybe a quirky version of the future – at this fascinating art project celebrating steampunk culture. Ancient machines wheeze and splutter, and the industrial detritus of the last century or so is repurposed and reimagined to creepy effect. Bring a $2 coin to fire up the sparking, space-age locomotive out the front.

The brainchild of artists Don Patterson, Jac Grenfell and Brian de Geest in 2011, at this whimsical workshop you can play the Metagalactic Pipe Organ of extraterrestrial sounds, and visit the Portal, an infinity light chamber. You are allowed to touch everything and photography is encouraged.

Grainstore Gallery   GALLERY

(🗐 027 366 6201; 9 Harbour St; ⊙10.30am-2.30pm) Crammed with weird theatrical sculpture, papier-mâché masks and vintage curiosities, this former Victorian grain store houses an ever-changing cornucopia of creativity. Owner Donna Dementé shows her evocative portraits here, as well as the work of other local talents, and hosts occasional live music and other delightful distractions.

Whitestone City   MUSEUM

(🗐 0508 978 663; www.whitestonecity.com; 12 Harbour St; adult/child $15/10; ⊙10am-6pm, to 4.30pm winter) Ōamaru's heyday is brought to life by costumed guides inside this 1882 grain store – and you too can don vintage costumes (adult/child $20/10) and get some shots of yourself dining at a Victorian table. Stroll through the replica Victorian streetscape, visit the schoolroom complete with slates, play old-fashioned games in the dimly lit saloon, and take a ride on the pièce de résistance – a penny-farthing carousel.

Art-house movies are shown in the theatre – check the website for details.

Yellow-Eyed Penguin Colony   BIRD SANCTUARY

(Bushy Beach Rd) 𝗙𝗥𝗘𝗘 Larger and much rarer than their little blue cousins, yellow-eyed penguins waddle ashore at Bushy Beach in the late afternoon from a day of fishing. In order to protect these endangered birds, the beach is closed to people from 3pm onwards, but there are hides set up on the cliffs (you'll need binoculars for a decent view). The best time to see them is two hours before sunset.

**Childhood Home of
Janet Frame**   HISTORIC BUILDING

(🗐 03-434 1656; www.jfestrust.org.nz; 56 Eden St; $5; ⊙2-4pm Nov-Apr, or by appointment) Nobel Prize–nominated writer Janet Frame (1924–2004) grew up in this simple suburban home and drew on her time here to write her three acclaimed autobiographies, *To the Is-Land* (1982), *An Angel at My Table* (1984) and *The Envoy from Mirror City* (1984). Frame's typewriter is here, as is her writing desk.

Forrester Gallery   GALLERY

(🗐 03-433 0853; www.culturewaitaki.org.nz/forrester-gallery; 9 Thames St; ⊙10.30am-4.30pm Mon-Fri, from 1pm Sat & Sun; ♿) 𝗙𝗥𝗘𝗘 Housed in an elegant, temple-like former bank building, the Forrester Gallery was closed for renovations at the time of research but reopening in 2020. It stages excellent temporary exhibitions of local and NZ art, and the 2nd floor hosts interactive exhibitions especially designed for children.

North Otago Museum   MUSEUM

(🗐 03-433 0852; www.culturewaitaki.org.nz; 58-60 Thames St; ⊙10am-4.30pm Mon-Fri, from 1pm Sat & Sun) 𝗙𝗥𝗘𝗘 This weighty museum was renovated in early 2020. The new space houses Waitaki Taonga (the Willetts Collection), one of the most important collections of first settlement Māori artefacts in NZ, as well as exhibitions linked to the Waitaki Whitestone Geopark (p491) and European heritage, including the Victorian era.

Activities

Whitestone Cheese Factory FOOD & DRINK
(☎03-434 0182; www.whitestonecheese.com; 3 Torridge St; adult/child $30/free, with wine $45; ⌚shop 9am-5pm Mon-Fri, 10am-4pm Sat & Sun) The home of award-winning artisanal cheeses, Whitestone is a local culinary institution. Tours run at 10am and 11.45am (45 to 60 minutes), and you get a goodie bag at the end. Pick up some cheesy souvenirs in its shop, or try the NZ 'Deep South' classic – the mighty cheese roll. They're a bargain here at three for $6. Book tours online.

Cycle Ventures CYCLING
(☎03-434 5010; www.verticalventures.co.nz; 4 Wansbeck St; ⌚10am-5pm Mon-Fri, to 12.30pm Sat summer, 10am-5.30pm Thu & Fri, 10am-1pm Sat winter) Hire a mountain bike (from $45 per day), or join guided mountain-biking trips, including the Alps 2 Ocean Cycle Trail (seven days including transport, food and accommodation from $3095). You can also arrange rock-climbing day trips (from $150 per person).

Festivals & Events

Victorian Heritage Celebrations CULTURAL
(www.vhc.co.nz; ⌚mid-Nov) Five days of costumed capers and historical hi jinks, culminating in a grand fete.

Steampunk Festival ART
(www.steampunk.org.nz; ⌚late May-early Jun) Celebrating the Queen's Birthday holiday (Queen Victoria that is), Ōamaru dusts off her bonnet and kicks up her heels at a gala ball, monster teapot races and tea-duelling championships.

Sleeping

★**Oamaru Backpackers** HOSTEL $
(☎021 190 0069; www.oamarubackpackers.co.nz; 47 Tees St; dm/s/d/tr from $32/52/90/95; P 📶) A stone's throw from the Victorian quarter, this snug hostel has lovely, individually decorated rooms and a great dorm with privacy curtains and individual outlets. Best of all is the view of the harbour from the giant windows (with telescope) in the airy, light-filled lounge.

Old Bones Lodge LODGE $
(☎03-434 8115; www.oldbones.co.nz; Beach Rd; r $100; P 📶) Five kilometres south of Ōamaru on the coast road, this top-notch lodge has tidy rooms off a huge, sunny, central space. Great for groups. Listen to the surf crashing over the road while relaxing by the wood-burning fire, or book one of the hot tubs (from $90 for two people) and drift into ecstasy while gazing at the stars.

Oamaru Top 10 Holiday Park HOLIDAY PARK $
(☎03-434 7666; www.oamarutop10.co.nz; 30 Chelmer St; sites $40, units with/without bathroom from $99/75; P 📶) Grassy and well maintained, this Top 10 has trees out the back and is right next door to the lush public gardens. Standard cabins are basic, but the other units (with varying levels of self-contained comfort) are much nicer. There's a spa pool and a jumping pillow for kids.

Highfield Mews MOTEL $$
(☎03-434 3437; www.highfieldmews.co.nz; 244 Thames St; units from $175; P 📶) The units at this motel are basically smart apartments, with kitchens, desks, stereos and tiled bathrooms, most with spa baths.

★**Poshtel** BOUTIQUE HOTEL $$$
(☎03-434 8888; www.poshtelnz.com; 126 Thames St; d from $259; P 📶) Anyone for polo? Crammed with sporty vintage collectables in themed rooms (like the Steeplechase room or the Antarctic Explorer Suite), this plush new hotel is the perfect balance of quirk and luxury. Thick whitestone walls, deep carpets and comfy beds keep you snug and the odd steampunk firearm keeps you interested. Great location on the main street.

Check out the excellent on-site art gallery specialising in NZ and Pacific art.

★**Pen-y-bryn Lodge** B&B $$$
(☎03-434 7939; www.penybryn.co.nz; 41 Towey St; r May-Sep $495-750, Oct-Apr $525-825; P 📶) Well-travelled foodie owners have thoroughly revitalised this beautiful 1889 residence and continue to upgrade. There are two rooms in the main house but the three recently and luxuriously refurbished ones in the rear annexe are nicer. Complimentary predinner drinks and canapés are served in the antique-studded drawing room; arrange a four-course dinner in the fabulous dining room (from $135 per person).

Eating

Harbour St Bakery BAKERY $
(☎021 0248 5351; 4 Harbour St; pies $5.50; ⌚8am-4pm Tue-Sat, to 2pm Sun & Mon) Artisan sourdough bread and simply enormous pies,

croissants and pastries – all baked using German, Dutch and Kiwi traditions. Try a Kiwi favourite: the custard square.

Steam CAFE **$**
(www.facebook.com/steamoamaru; 7 Thames St; mains $10-13; ⊙7am-4pm Mon-Sat, 8am-3pm Sun; 🛜) This popular little cafe near the Victorian quarter roasts its own coffee in-house – it's a good spot to stock up on freshly ground beans for your own travels. Check the counter cabinet for the day's culinary choices, including freshly baked muffins, croissants and the like.

Fat Sally's PUB FOOD **$$**
(📞03-434 8368; www.fatsallys.co.nz; 84 Thames St; mains $22-30; ⊙11.30am-late Tue-Sun) Cosy pub in a heritage building with sports on the telly and Speights on the taps. There's a nice open fire, and friendly staff will adapt the meat-heavy menu for vegos. Quiz night is Wednesday from 7pm. There's often live music on Saturday night.

★Cucina ITALIAN **$$$**
(📞03-434 5696; www.cucinaoamaru.co.nz; 1 Tees St; mains $24-38; ⊙5pm-late Mon-Sat) The most sophisticated kitchen in Ōamaru serves superb seasonal food in a heritage dining room painted black and filled with plants. Try dishes like 55-day-aged rib-eye with smoked pommes Anna, broccolini and caramelised baby onion, or beetroot rigatoni with salt-baked beetroot, mint pesto and marinated feta. The chef's menu is $115/65 with/without wine.

🍷 Drinking & Nightlife

Scott's Brewing Co. BREWERY
(📞03-434 2244; www.scottsbrewing.co.nz; 1 Wansbeck St; ⊙11am-9.30pm Mon-Thu, to 11pm Fri, 10am-11pm Sat, 10am-9.30pm Sun) Drop into this old waterfront warehouse to sample the output of Ōamaru's popular craft brewers. Slouch against the counter for a tasting or head out onto the sunny deck for a pint (including many gluten-free options) and an excellent pizza.

New Zealand Whisky Collection DISTILLERY
(📞027 942 5739; www.thenzwhisky.com; Harbour St; per glass $18-25, 4-whisky flight $30; ⊙10.30am-4.30pm) Actually a maturation house rather than a distillery, where the whiskies are uniquely aged in red-wine barrels, giving them spicy, cherry-plum, Christmas-

cake flavours. There are six whiskies to taste and the selection changes regularly, or try a hot toddy ($10).

Criterion Hotel PUB
(📞03-434 6247; www.criterionhotel.co.nz; 3 Tyne St; ⊙11am-late Mon-Fri, from 10am Sat & Sun) The most Victorian of the Victorian Precinct's watering holes, this corner beauty has a good beer selection and plenty of local wines. There's usually live music on Fridays, and a couple of nice rooms upstairs (single/double from $75/100).

☆ Entertainment

Oamaru Opera House THEATRE
(📞03-433 0770; www.oamaruoperahouse.co.nz; 94 Thames St; ⊙ticket office 10am-4pm Mon-Fri, to 1pm Sat) First opened in 1907 and now beautifully restored to its original glory, Ōamaru's opera house hosts a variety of shows, including music, dance, theatre and comedy. The main auditorium seats 500-plus patrons under the stunning 1900s cupola and chandelier, while the smaller Inkbox theatre is home to more intimate performances.

Penguin Club LIVE MUSIC
(www.thepenguinclub.co.nz; Emulsion Lane, off Harbour St; cover charge varies) Tucked down an atmospheric alley off a 19th-century street, the Penguin's unusual location matches its acts: everything from touring Kiwi bands to punky/grungy/rocky/country locals. It's a members club (you can join at the door) and shows are intermittent (check www.facebook.com/thepenguinclub).

ℹ Information

Ōamaru i-SITE (📞03-434 1656; www.waitakinz.com; 1 Thames St; ⊙9am-5pm; 🛜) Friendly staff here can offer mountains of information including details on local walking trips and wildlife, plus daily penguin-viewing times. There's an interesting 10-minute film on the history of the town.

ℹ Getting There & Away

Ōamaru sits on the main SH1 coastal route between Christchurch (3¼ hours) and Dunedin (1½ hours).

Most buses and shuttles depart from the **Lagonda Tearooms** (📞03-434 8716; www.facebook.com/lagondatearooms.oamaru; 191 Thames St; ⊙9am-4.30pm; 🛜). Both the tearooms and the i-SITE take bookings.

DUNEDIN & OTAGO ŌAMARU

WORTH A TRIP

RIVERSTONE

This idiosyncratic complex, 14km north of Ōamaru, is the home of **Riverstone Kitchen** (☑03-431 3505; www.riverstonekitchen.co.nz; 1431 SH1, Waitaki Bridge; mains $25-36, feasting menu $70; ☺9am-late Thu-Sat, to 5pm Sun & Mon), a sophisticated destination restaurant headed by award-winning chef Bevan Smith. Much of the produce comes from the extensive on-site kitchen gardens (go for a stroll, they're impressive), plus locally sourced venison, pork, salmon, beef and wine. It's a smashing brunch option, with excellent coffee and legendary truffled scrambled eggs. Save room for dessert, too.

Next door, behind a set of fake heritage shopfronts, **Riverstone Country** (☑03-431 3872; 1431 SH1, Waitaki Bridge; ☺9am-5.30pm) is literally packed to the rafters with gifts, crafts, homewares, fake flowers, garden ornaments and Christmas decorations, like the cast-offs of an overstocked kingdom of cute. And what's that looming over the complex? A moated **castle** of course. It's all the brainchild of Bevan's mum Dot Smith, one of the owners of Riverstone and queen of the castle.

Atomic Shuttles (☑210 867 6001; www.atomictravel.co.nz) Buses once daily to/from Christchurch ($35, four hours), Timaru ($25, 1¼ hours), Moeraki Boulders ($20, 30 minutes) and Dunedin ($25, 1¼ hours).

InterCity (☑03-471 7143; www.intercity.co.nz) Three or four daily coaches to/from Christchurch (from $24, four hours), Timaru (from $16, one hour), the Moeraki turn-off (from $12, 28 minutes) and Dunedin (from $16, 1½ hours), and one to Te Anau (from $48, 6½ hours).

Moeraki

POP 60

The name Moeraki means 'a place to sleep by day', which should give you some clue as to the pace of life in this little fishing village. You might be surprised to learn that this was one of the first European settlements in New Zealand, with a whaling station established here in 1836. Since then, Moeraki has nurtured the creation of several national treasures, from Frances Hodgkins' paintings to author Keri Hulme's *The Bone People*, and Fleur Sullivan's cooking. Apart from Fleur's eponymous restaurant, the main reason travellers stop in town is the **Moeraki Boulders** (Te Kaihinaki; off SH1), beloved of photographers and children alike.

**Riverside Haven Lodge
& Holiday Park** CAMPGROUND $
(☑03-439 5830; www.riversidehaven.nz; 2328 Herbert Hampden Rd/SH1, Waianakarua; unpowered/powered sites from $29/32, d with/without bathroom from $110/90; ☺) ♪ Nestled in a loop of the Waianakarua River, 12km

north of the Moeraki turn-off, this certified-organic riverside property offers both bucolic camping sites and colourful lodge rooms, some with en suites. Kids will love the playground and farm animals; parents will love the spa and peaceful vibe.

Moeraki Haven Motel COTTAGE $$
(☑03-439 4859; www.moerakihavenmotel.co.nz; 28 Haven St; 1-/3-bed units from $150/165, studio from $125; Ⓟ☺) Commanding jaw-dropping views over the shoreline, these spic-and-span, self-contained units perched high above the ocean are a great choice for families or groups. The owners have a range of accommodation in the area.

★**Fleur's Place** SEAFOOD $$$
(☑03-439 4480; www.fleursplace.com; Old Jetty, 169 Haven St; mains $22-45; ☺10.30am-late Wed-Sun) There's a rumble-tumble look about it, but this tin-and-timber fishing hut houses one of the South Island's best – and most popular – seafood restaurants. The straightforward, scribble-covered decor mirrors the simple, clean handling of the food. Tuck into fresh shellfish, tender blue cod and other recently landed ocean bounty. There's a smokehouse on-site and you can try mutton bird here too. Book ahead.

ⓘ Getting There & Away

Moeraki is on SH1, a 30-minute drive from Ōamaru and one hour from Dunedin. Buses travelling between the two stop on SH1 by the Moeraki turn-off, if you ask in advance. From here it's about a 2km walk to both the centre of the village and to the boulders.

DUNEDIN

POP 130,700

Dunedin is full of hidden surprises. Firmly on the international street-art map since A-list Belgian aerosol artist ROA put up his beautiful tuatara at 7 Bath St in 2014, it now has artists from around the world vying for the best wall space in town. Many of them are drawn to the city's blossoming warehouse precinct, south of The Octagon, home to funky burger joints and vegan cafes. Dunedin also boasts a vibrant live-music scene, supported by the students of New Zealand's oldest university, and the wildlife-rich Otago Peninsula, which officially lies within the city limits.

And Dunedin has not forgotten its roots. The 'Edinburgh of the South' is immensely proud of its Scottish heritage, never missing an opportunity to break out the haggis and bagpipes on civic occasions. In fact, the very name Dunedin is derived from the Scottish Gaelic name for Edinburgh – Dùn Èideann – and the city even has its own tartan.

History

The first permanent European settlers, two shiploads of pious, hard-working Scots, arrived at Port Chalmers in 1848, including the nephew of Scotland's favourite son, Robbie Burns. A statue of the poet dominates The Octagon, the city's civic heart.

In the 1980s Dunedin spawned its own internationally influential indie music scene, with Flying Nun Records and the 'Dunedin sound'. And not to be left out of this creative profusion, Dunedin's literary heritage and culture was recognised in 2014 when the city became NZ's first Unesco City of Literature.

◉ Sights

◉ City Centre

★ **Toitū Otago Settlers Museum**   MUSEUM
(Map p500; ☑03-477 5052; www.toituosm.com; 31 Queens Gardens; ☺10am-5pm; 🅿) FREE Storytelling is the focus of this excellent interactive museum, which traces the history of human settlement on the South Island. Pass through the new albatross *waharoa* (entranceway) by master carver James York to enter the engrossing Māori section, followed by a large gallery where floor-to-ceiling portraits of Victorian-era settlers stare out from behind their whiskers and lace. Walk through a re-created passenger-ship cabin (you can try out a bunk) and check out the fascinating array of obsolete technology.

Dunedin Railway Station   HISTORIC BUILDING
(Map p500; 22 Anzac Ave; ☺8am-5pm Mon-Fri, 8.30am-3pm Sat & Sun) Featuring mosaic-tile floors and glorious stained-glass windows, Dunedin's striking bluestone railway station (built between 1903 and 1906) claims to be NZ's most photographed building. Head upstairs for the **New Zealand Sports Hall of Fame** (Map p500; ☑03-477 7775; www.nzhalloffame.co.nz; Dunedin Railway Station, 22 Anzac Ave; adult/child $6/2; ☺10am-4pm), a small museum devoted to the nation's obsession, and the **Art Station** (Map p500; ☑03-477 9465; www.otagoartsociety.co.nz; Dunedin Railway Station, 22 Anzac Ave; ☺10am-4pm) FREE, the local Art Society's gallery and shop. The station is the departure point for several popular scenic rail journeys (p502).

Dunedin Public Art Gallery   GALLERY
(Map p500; ☑03-474 3240; www.dunedin.art.museum; 30 The Octagon; ☺10am-5pm; 🅿) FREE Gaze upon local and international art – including a small collection of Impressionists – at this expansive and airy gallery. Only a fraction of the collection is displayed at any given time, with most of the space given over to often-edgy temporary exhibitions with a focus on interactive art. A new playspace (open 10am to 4.30pm) encourages kids to get crafty and hands-on.

St Paul's Cathedral   CHURCH
(Map p500; www.stpauls.net.nz; Moray Pl; ☺10am-4pm Oct-Apr, to 3pm May-Sep) Even in Presbyterian Dunedin, the 'established church' (aka the Church of England) gets the prime spot on The Octagon. A Romanesque portal leads into the Gothic interior of this beautiful Anglican cathedral, where soaring white Ōamaru-stone pillars spread into a vaulted ceiling. The main part of the church dates from 1919, although the sanctuary was left unfinished until 1971, hence the slightly jarring modern extension. The massive organ (3500 pipes) is said to be one of the finest in the southern hemisphere.

Dunedin Chinese Garden   GARDENS
(Map p500; ☑03-477 3248; www.dunedinchinesegarden.com; cnr Rattray & Cumberland Sts; adult/child $9.50/free; ☺10am-5pm) Built to recognise the contribution of Dunedin's Chinese community, this walled garden was constructed in Shanghai before being dismantled and reassembled in its current location. The tranquil confines contain all of the elements of a classical Chinese garden, including ponds, pavilions, rockeries, stone bridges and a tea

house. There's also a small display on the history of the local Chinese community.

Speight's Brewery BREWERY
(Map p500; ☑03-477 7697; www.speights.co.nz; 200 Rattray St; adult/child $30/14; ⊙tours noon, 2pm, 4pm Apr-Sep, plus 5pm, 6pm & 7pm Oct-Mar) Speight's has been churning out beer on this site since the late 19th century and is the oldest operating brewery in NZ. The 60-minute tour gives an insight into the history of the building, the company and the brewing process, and finishes up in the tasting room for a guided 30-minute, six-beer sampling session. On the street outside, a tap delivers the chemical-free spring water that feeds the brewery to passers-by. Donations go to local wetland rehabilitation. Tours can be combined with a meal at Speight's Ale House (Map p500; ☑03-471-9050; www.thealehouse. co.nz; 200 Rattray St; ⊙11.30am-2pm & 5-9pm).

⊙ North Dunedin

★ **Olveston** HOUSE
(Map p500; ☑03-477 3320; www.olveston.co.nz; 42 Royal Tce, Roslyn; adult/child $23/13; ⊙tours 9.30am, 10.45am, noon, 1.30pm, 2.45pm & 4pm) Although it's a youngster by European standards, this spectacular 1906 mansion provides a wonderful window into Dunedin's past. Entry is via fascinating one-hour guided tours; it pays to book ahead. There's also a pretty little garden to explore (entry free) with a beautifully preserved 1921 Fiat 510 on display.

Until 1966 Olveston was the family home of the wealthy Theomin family, notable patrons of the arts who were heavily involved with endowing the Public Art Gallery. This artistic bent is evident in Olveston's grand

interiors, which include works by Charles Goldie and Frances Hodgkins (a family friend). A particular passion was Japanese art, and the home is liberally peppered with exquisite examples. The family was Jewish, and the grand dining table is set up as if for Shabbat dinner.

Otago Museum MUSEUM
(Map p500; ☑03-474 7474; www.otagomuseum. nz; 419 Great King St, North Dunedin; ⊙10am-5pm) ☑FREE The centrepiece of this august institution is Southern Land, Southern People, showcasing Otago's cultural and physical past and present, from geology and dinosaurs to the modern day. The Tāngata Whenua Māori gallery houses an impressive *waka taua* (war canoe), wonderfully worn old carvings, and some lovely *pounamu* (greenstone) weapons, tools and jewellery. Other major galleries include Pacific Cultures, People of the World (including the requisite mummy), Nature, Maritime and the Animal Attic. The Tūhura Otago Community Trust Science Centre (adult/child $15/10) boasts 45 hands-on interactive science displays, a Tropical Forest butterfly enclosure and a 7.5m-high double helix slide. There's also a planetarium ($12/7), which screens films on its 360-degree dome.

Guided tours depart from the information desk at 11am, 1pm, 2pm and 3pm daily ($15 per person).

Dunedin Museum of Natural Mystery MUSEUM
(Map p500; ☑021 032 9906; www.royaldunedin museum.com; 61 Royal Tce; adult/child $5/free; ⊙noon-5pm Fri, from 10am Sat & Sun) This oddball collection of skulls, body bits, ethnographic art and beautiful bone sculptures

Central Dunedin

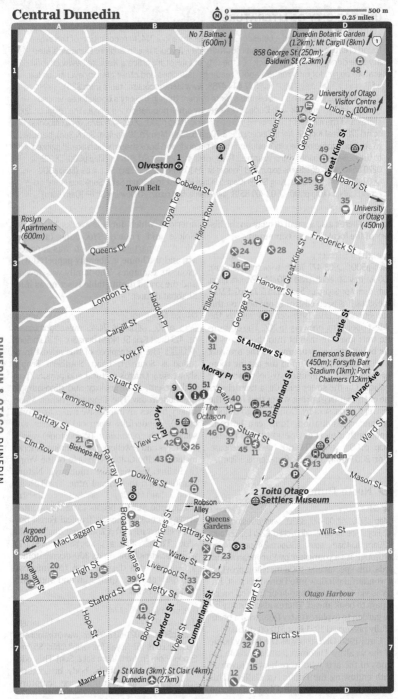

0   500 m
0   0.25 miles

No 7 Balmac
(600m)

Dunedin Botanic Garden
(1.2km); Mt Cargill (8km)

858 George St (250m);
Baldwin St (2.3km)

University of Otago
Visitor Centre
(100m)

48

22

17

49   7

25
36

Olveston   1

4

Cobden St

Town Belt

35

University
of Otago
(450m)

Roslyn
Apartments
(600m)

Queens Dr

London St

34
24   28

16

Frederick St

Cargill St

31

St Andrew St

York Pl

Stuart St

Moray Pl

53

Emerson's Brewery
(450m); Forsyth Barr
Stadium (1km); Port
Chalmers (12km)

Tennyson St

9   50   51
The
Octagon

40
54
52

30

Rattray St

Elm Row

21

5
41
42   26
43

46
37
45   11

6
Dunedin
13

Bishops Rd

Dowling St

47

14

8

2 Toitū Otago
Settlers Museum

Argoed
(800m)

38

Robson
Alley

Queens
Gardens

Wills St

MacLaggan St

27   23
3

20

High St
19

Water St

18

39   33
29

Jetty St

Stafford St

44

Otago Harbour

St Kilda (3km); St Clair (4km);
Dunedin (27km)

32   10

15

12

Birch St

Manor Pl

Central Dunedin

DUNEDIN & OTAGO DUNEDIN

has been assembled by local mural artist and sculptor Bruce Mahalski. If you feel at home with a few skeletons in the closet, you can stay here too (double from $120).

Emerson's Brewery   BREWERY
(Map p510; ☑ 03-477 1812; www.emersons.co.nz; 70 Anzac Ave; tours per person $28; ⊙ tours 10am, noon, 2pm, 4pm & 6pm Oct-Mar, 11am, 2pm & 6pm Apr-Sep, restaurant 10am-late, cellar door 10am-8pm) This impressive brick-and-glass structure is the flash home of Emerson's, the microbrewery founded by local-boy-made-good Richard Emerson in 1992. Forty-five-minute tours take you behind the scenes of the brewing process, ending with the all-important tasting. There's also a cellar door where you can fill a rigger with your favourite drop – or, if you'd like to linger longer, drop into the

lively, cavernous restaurant for hearty meals (mains $17 to $35).

Baldwin Street   LANDMARK
(Map p510; North East Valley) This street proudly held the title of steepest street in the world until July 2019, when Ffordd Pen Llech in the Welsh town of Harlech was officially recognised as steeper by Guinness World Records. Dunedin went into shock and at the time of writing local surveyor Toby Stoff was mounting a challenge to the controversial decision. Stay tuned... However, not even the Welsh can deny that Baldwin St is pretty bloody steep, with a gradient of 1 in 2.86 (19 degrees).

To reach the street from the city centre, head 2km north up Great King St and stay in the right-hand lane to continue on when the left lane branches off towards Timaru. Baldwin St is signposted after 1km.

University of Otago
HISTORIC BUILDING

(Map p510; www.otago.ac.nz; 362 Leith St) Founded in 1869, the University of Otago is NZ's oldest. Today the university is home to some 21,000 students, and is well worth a wander, with many magnificent bluestone buildings to admire. The historic heart – bounded by Leith, St David and Castle Sts – is the most photogenic part of the campus. Check the university website for a self-guided tour map. You can buy uni merch from the visitor centre (Map p510; www.otago.ac.nz; cnr Cumberland & David Sts; ⊙9am-4.30pm Mon-Fri, 10.30am-3pm Sat).

Activities

Swimming, Surfing & Diving

St Clair and St Kilda are both popular swimming beaches (though you need to watch for rips at St Clair). Both have consistently good left-hand breaks, and you'll also find good surfing further south at Blackhead, and at Aramoana on Otago Harbour's North Shore.

Esplanade Surf School
SURFING

(Map p510; ☑0800 484 141; www.espsurfschool. co.nz; 1 Esplanade, St Clair; 90min group lesson $60, private instruction $120) Operating from a van parked at St Clair Beach in summer whenever the surf is up (call at other times), this experienced crew provides board hire ($40 for two hours including wetsuit) and lessons to suit all levels.

St Clair Hot Salt Water Pool
SWIMMING

(Map p510; www.dunedin.govt.nz; Esplanade, St Clair; adult/child $6.70/3; ⊙6am-7pm Mon-Fri, from 7am Sat & Sun Oct-Mar) This heated outdoor pool, averaging 28°C, sits on the western headland of St Clair Beach.

Dive Otago
DIVING

(Map p500; ☑03-466 4370; www.diveotago.co.nz; 2 Wharf St; full-day guided dive from $150; ⊙8.30am-5.30pm Mon-Sat) Guided shore dives to see the likes of inquisitive blue cod and sea lions. You can also hire gear ($100) and tanks ($20).

Walking

Tunnel Beach Walkway
WALKING

(Tunnel Beach Rd, Blackhead) This short but extremely steep pathway (20 minutes down, 40 back up) brings you to a dramatic stretch of coast where the wild Pacific has carved sea stacks, arches and unusual formations

out of the limestone. The tunnel is cut off at high tide so check tide times online or with the i-SITE (p508) before you set off. Strong currents make swimming here dangerous, but the views are spectacular.

Mt Cargill-Bethunes
Gully Walkway
WALKING

(Map p510; www.doc.govt.nz; Norwood St, Normanby) Yes, it's possible to drive up 676m Mt Cargill, but that's not the point. The track (four hours, 8.5km return) starts from Norwood St, which is accessed from North Rd. From Mt Cargill, a trail continues to the 10-million-year-old, lava-formed Organ Pipes and, after another half hour, to Mt Cargill Rd on the other side of the mountain.

Other Activities

★ Dunedin Railways
RAIL

(Map p500; ☑03-477 4449; www.dunedinrailways. co.nz; Dunedin Railway Station, 22 Anzac Ave; ⊙office 8am-5pm Mon-Fri, 8.30am-3pm Sat & Sun) Two scenic heritage train journeys set off from Dunedin's railway station (p498). The best is the Taieri Gorge Railway, with narrow tunnels, deep gorges, winding tracks, rugged canyons and viaduct crossings. The four-hour return trip aboard 1920s heritage coaches travels to Pukerangi (one way/return adult $72/115, child $19/29), 58km away, leaving at 9.30am and 3pm daily.

On Sundays Taieri Gorge trains carry on for another 20km from Pukerangi to Middlemarch (adult/child one way from Dunedin $81/21) – the start of the Otago Central Rail Trail (p514).

The Seasider heads north along the coast as far as Waitati (adult/child return $70/25, two hours) once or twice daily, depending on the season. Aim for a seat on the right-hand side of the train for better sea views.

Check the website for precise schedules.

Ocho
FOOD & DRINK

(Map p500; ☑03-425 7819; www.ocho.co.nz; 10 Roberts St; adult/child $25/15; ⊙tours 11am & 2pm Mon-Sat) Dunedin chocaholics shed a tear when Cadbury World shut down its much-loved chocolate factory tours in 2018. But filling the gap is indie choccy maker Ocho, with single-origin chocolate sourced from PNG, the Solomons and further afield that is far less processed than its big competitor. Drop into the Bay Road Peanut Butter (Map p500; ☑022 679 6420; www.bayroad.nz; 8 Roberts St; ⊙7.30am-1.30pm Mon-Fri) roastery next door too.

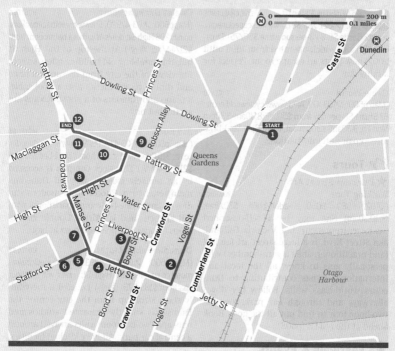

Walking Tour
Street Art Stroll

START TOITŪ OTAGO SETTLERS MUSEUM
END SPEIGHT'S BREWERY
LENGTH 2KM; THREE HOURS

Wander through the excellent ❶ **Toitū Otago Settlers Museum** (p498) to emerge just outside street-art central. Cross Cumberland St and head a block west then left down Vogel St. You'll spot a number of pieces as you make your way to ❷ **Vogel St Kitchen** (p506), which sports UK artist Phlegm's stunning artwork of a fish swallowing an armada of *waka* and other boats. Swing up Jetty St and up to Bond St to see Polish artist Natalia Rak's ❸ **Love is in the Air** featuring portraits of herself and her husband, fellow street-artist Bezt, as children – she's stealing a kiss. Back on Jetty St, check out Italian Pixel Poncho's floral/robot ❹ **Riding Dreams**. Cross Princes St and duck around the corner to see the ❺ **collaboration piece** by Pixel Poncho and Phlegm. Each started at a diagonal corner of the wall and their unique styles intertwined as they met in the middle. Contin-

ue along Stafford for Chinese artist DALeast's portrayal of NZ's extinct ❻ **Haast eagle**, a creation of shining steel ribbons. Duck back up Manse St, past another Phlegm wall, ❼ **Song Pipe Organ**, then right down High St to Polish artist Bezt's enormous painting of a dying woman ❽ **The Hunter has Been Hunted**, featuring a fantail (*pīwakawaka*), a Māori symbol of death.

Head east down High St, north on Princes and right onto Rattray and through the car park on your left to see the stunning 3D chrome-style ❾ **bull** by Puerto Rico's Bik-Ismo. Head back west on Rattray to see Australian artist Fintan Magee's ❿ **Chasing the Thin White Cloud** featuring three local kids netting the famous symbol of Aotearoa. Round the corner of the ⓫ **Crown Hotel** (p507) to the Broadway-facing wall where Dunedin's Aroha Novak and Guy Howard Smith pay tribute to Chi Fooi, an early citizen whose four grandsons still run the pub. Have a drink here or cross the road to ⓬ **Speight's** (p499), where they brew with water from the natural spring below.

Escape Dunedin Prison
LIVE CHALLENGE

(Map p500; ☑027 783 8811; www.escapedunedin.
com; 2 Castle St; 2-/3-person game $50/75) Dun-
edin Prison (which operated from 1896 until
2007) now hosts an escape room. Perfect for
a rainy day.

Cycle World
CYCLING

(Map p500; ☑03-477 7473; www.cycleworld.co.nz;
67 Stuart St; per day from $50; ⊘8.30am-5.30pm
Mon-Fri, 9.30am-3.30pm Sat, 10am-3pm Sun) Bike
hire, repair and information.

🖝 Tours

★Dunedin Street Art
Walking Tour
WALKING

(☑027 389 9060; adult/child $30/free;
⊘10.30am) She may be a self-described
'senior entrepreneur' but Victoria Gilliand,
aka Street Kiwi, is a huge street-art fan girl
(and practitioner: she's a yarn-bomber) who
personally gets to know all the local and
international artists contributing to Dunedin's world-class walls. Follow her down
alleyways and through car parks on this
two-hour tour to find out all the goss. Book
ahead at the i-SITE (p508).

🎊 Festivals & Events

Dunedin Fringe Festival
PERFORMING ARTS

(www.dunedinfringe.nz; ⊘Mar) The world's
southernmost fringe festival puts arty events
in venues across town.

🛏 Sleeping

Rates in Dunedin skyrocket when big events
are in town and at the start of the academic
year (mid to late February). Also take into
account the calf-burning climb if you choose
a place uphill.

🛏 City Centre

★Hogwartz
HOSTEL $

(Map p500; ☑03-474 1487; www.hogwartz.co.nz;
277 Rattray St; dm/s/d from $28/60/80, d with
bathroom $95, studio $120; ⊘Oct-Jun; 🅿@🛜)
The Catholic bishop's residence from 1872
to 1999, this beautiful building is now a fascinating warren of comfortable and sunny
rooms, many with harbour views. Shared
bathrooms include welcome touches like
waterfall showers and underfloor heating. The old coach house and stables have
swankier en suite rooms and apartments.

Chalet Backpackers
HOSTEL $

(Mapp500;☑03-4792075;www.chaletbackpackers.
co.nz; 296 High St; dm/s/d without bathrooom from
$21/44/72; @🛜) At the top of the High St
hill, this rambling old building offers sweeping views of the city from its sunny lounge
and dining room; there's also a pool table,
a piano and rumours of a ghost. Rooms are
ageing but tidy.

315 Euro
MOTEL $$

(Map p500; ☑03-477 9929; www.eurodunedin.
co.nz; 315 George St; studio from $178, 1-bed apt from
$210; 🅿@🛜) This sleek complex is accessed
by an unlikely looking alley off Dunedin's
main retail strip. Choose from modern stu-
dios or larger one-bedroom apartments with
full kitchens and laundries. Double glazing
keeps George St's incessant buzz at bay.

Dunedin Palms Motel
MOTEL $$

(Map p500; ☑03-477 8293; www.dunedinpalms
motel.co.nz; 185-195 High St; units with/without
spa from $189/179; 🅿🛜) Located a merciful-
ly short stroll up from the city centre, the
Palms has smartly renovated studios and
one- and two-bedroom units arrayed around
a central car park. All have kitchen facilities.

★Terminus Hotel
APARTMENT $$$

(Map p500; ☑021 762 667; www.warehousepre
cinct.co.nz/terminus-apartments; 42 Queens Gar-
dens; 1-/2-bedroom apt from $225/330; 🛜) This
late-Victorian building always had great
bones, with its high ceilings and arched
windows, but owners Steve and Antonia
have worked makeover magic turning the
once dilapidated hotel into chic apartments.
Some have balconies and loft spaces; all
have beautiful exposed red-brick walls, a
modern kitchen, a laundry and everything
else you need for a comfy stay – even a pop-
corn machine.

Fletcher Lodge
B&B $$$

(Map p500; ☑03-474 5552; www.fletcherlodge.
co.nz; 276 High St; s/d incl breakfast from
$310/355; 🅿🛜) 🍃 Originally home to one of
NZ's wealthiest industrialists, this gorgeous
red-brick mansion is just minutes from the
city, but the secluded gardens feel wonderfully remote. Rooms are elegantly trimmed
with antique furniture and ornate plaster
ceilings and are snug on cold nights with
underfloor bathroom heating.

📍 North Dunedin

★ Kiwi's Nest   HOSTEL $

(Map p500; 📞 03-471 9540; www.kiwisnest.co.nz; 597 George St, North Dunedin; dm $28, s with/without bathroom $80/55, d $100/80, apt $120; 🅿@🛜) This wonderfully homey two-storey house has a range of tidy centrally heated rooms, some with en suite, fridge and kettle. Plus it's a flat walk to The Octagon – something few Dunedin hostels can boast.

858 George St   MOTEL $$$

(Map p510; 📞 03-474 0047; www.858georgestreet motel.co.nz; 858 George St, North Dunedin; units $180-325; 🅿🛜) 🧭 Recently refreshed with new furniture and a paint job, this top-quality motel complex has modern units ranging in size from studios to two bedrooms. Studios are fitted with a microwave, fridge, toaster and a kettle, while the larger units also have a stove top or a full oven.

Bluestone on George   APARTMENT $$$

(Map p500; 📞 03-477 9201; www.bluestonedune din.co.nz; 571 George St, North Dunedin; apt from $225; 🅿@🛜) If you're expecting an imposing old bluestone building, think again: this four-storey block couldn't be more contemporary. The elegant studio units are decked out in muted tones, with kitchenettes, laundry facilities and decks or tiny balconies – some with harbour views. There's also a small gym and a guest lounge.

📍 St Clair

★ Majestic Mansions –
Apartments at St Clair   APARTMENT $$

(Map p510; 📞 03-456 5000; www.apartmentsatst clair.co.nz; 15 Bedford St, St Clair; 1-/2-bedroom apt from $179/250; 🅿🛜) One street back from St Clair Beach, this venerable art-deco apartment block has been thoroughly renovated and restyled by its new owners, sprucing it up with feature wallpaper and smart furnishings. Each has a kitchen and laundry facilities and some have sea views. Prices drop in low season.

Hotel St Clair   HOTEL $$$

(Map p510; 📞 03-456 0555; www.hotelstclair.com; 24 Esplanade, St Clair; r $234-394; 🅿🛜) Soak up St Clair's surfy vibe from the balcony of your chic room in this contemporary medium-rise hotel. All but the cheapest rooms have ocean views, and the beach is only metres from the front door.

📍 Other Suburbs

Dunedin Top 10
Holiday Park   HOLIDAY PARK $

(Map p510; www.aaronlodgetop10.co.nz; 162 Kaikorai Valley Rd, Kaikorai; sites from $28, d cabins from $78, motel r $142-169; 🅿🛜🏊) About 2.5km from the city centre, this spic-and-span park has great facilities and some fun extras like a trampoline, a petanque court, a spa and a heated pool. There's a range of accommodation packed in quite tight.

Leah & the Llama   B&B $$

(Map p510; 📞 03-476 2113; 76 Dalziel Rd, Mt Grand; s/d $140/150; 🅿🛜) Spacious home high up on the hill with comfortable rooms sharing a bathroom. There are sheep and horses in the paddocks all around, but it's still just a short run into town. An enormous breakfast spread, a beautiful garden and lovely warm hosts make you feel right at home.

Argoed   B&B $$$

(Map p510; 📞 03-474 1639; www.argoed.co.nz; 504 Queens Dr, Belleknowes; r from $175-250; 🅿🛜) Roses and rhododendrons encircle this gracious two-storey wooden villa, built in the 1880s. Each of the three charmingly old-fashioned bedrooms has its own bathroom, though only one is en suite. Guests can relax in the conservatory or tinkle the ivories of the grand piano in the lounge.

🍽 Eating

Forage for cheap eats from around the world, from Khmer to Mexican, along George St, or hit the hip nosh spots in the converted warehouses along Vogel St. There's a cluster of relaxed bars and cafes in North East Valley, on the way to Baldwin St, while the beachy ambience of St Clair is great for a lazy brunch or sunset drinks.

🍽 City Centre

★ Otago Farmers Market   MARKET $

(Map p500; www.otagofarmersmarket.org.nz; Dunedin Railway Station; ⏰8am-12.30pm Sat) This thriving market is all local, all edible (or drinkable) and mostly organic. Grab a freshly baked pastry and a flat white to sustain you while you browse, and stock up on fresh meat, seafood, veggies and cheese for your journey. Sorted.

JUST GIVE ME THE COFFEE & NO ONE WILL GET HURT

Dunedin has loads of excellent coffee bars in which you can refuel and re-charge. Try these:

Mazagran Espresso Bar (Map p500; 36 Moray Pl; ⊙8am-4.30pm Mon-Fri, to 2pm Sat)

Insomnia by Strictly Coffee (Map p500; ☑03-479 0017; www.strictlycoffee.co.nz; 23 Bath St; ⊙7.30am-4pm Mon-Fri)

Allpress (Map p500; ☑03-477 7162; www.allpressespresso.com; 12 Emily Siede-berg Pl; ⊙8am-4pm Mon-Fri)

Daily Coffee Co (Map p500; ☑021 054 0736; 366a Princes St; ⊙7.30am-2.30pm Mon-Sat; 🎅) 🍴

★ **Good Good** BURGERS $
(Map p500; www.goodgood.co.nz; 22 Vogel St; burgers $15; ⊙11.30am-2.30pm & 5-8pm) The crafty cooks here sizzle up famously good burgers from a kitchen in a retro caravan parked inside a cool warehouse space. There's tags on the walls, couches on the floor, electronica on the speakers and occasionally someone playing live. Nice place for a drink, too.

Kind Grocer VEGAN $
(Map p500; ☑021 217 4910; www.facebook.com/kindgrocernz; 49 Vogel St; lunch $9-13; ⊙10am-5pm Tue-Fri, to 3pm Sat & Sun; 🎅☑) Fully vegan and fully delicious, you can dig into the likes of loaded jackfruit with nasturtium and delectable cakes such as raw salted caramel snickers cheesecake or gluten-free chocolate fudge. Then pick up some fresh veg and treats for your travels, including plant pastrami, vegan jerky or marshmallows.

Harry's Kitchen JAPANESE $
(Map p500; ☑03-477 0123; 358 George St; noodles $14; ⊙11am-8pm) Student favourite with authentic Japanese and Korean dishes at a great price. Get your ramen fix here.

Vogel St Kitchen CAFE $$
(Map p500; ☑03-477 3623; www.vogelstkitchen.co.nz; 76 Vogel St; sandwiches $16, pizzas $25; ⊙7.30am-3pm Mon-Fri, 8.30am-4pm Sat & Sun; 🎅) In the heart of Dunedin's warehouse precinct, Vogel St Kitchen offers smashing breakfasts and wood-fired pizzas in a cavernous two-storey red-brick building. It gets especially busy on weekends, when local res-idents make the most of large shared tables for long lazy brunches.

Etrusco at the Savoy ITALIAN $$
(Map p500; ☑03-477 3737; www.etrusco.co.nz; 8a Moray Pl; mains $18-27; ⊙5.30pm-late) This boisterous pizza-and-pasta joint resides in the elegant Edwardian dining room of the Savoy, with its moulded ceilings, stained-glass crests and green Ionian columns. It's a slightly strange fit but it works, with hearty food and chandeliers setting just the right tone for big birthday celebrations and stu-dents taking out-of-town parents to dinner.

Paasha TURKISH $$
(Map p500; ☑03-477 7181; www.paasha.co.nz; 31 St Andrew St; mains lunch $13-20, dinner $19-36; ⊙11.30am-3pm & 5-9pm Mon-Wed, from 11am Thu-Sun; 🍴) Authentic kebabs, dips and salads are on the menu at this long-running Dune-din favourite. It's a top place for takeaways, and most nights the spacious and warm interior is filled with groups drinking Efes beer and sharing heaving platters of tasty Turkish goodness.

★ **Bracken** MODERN NZ $$$
(Map p500; ☑03-477 9779; www.brackenrestaurant.co.nz; 95 Filleul St; menus from $55; ⊙11.30am-2pm & 5pm-late Tue-Sat) 🍴 Bracken's seasonal tasting menus offer a succession of pretty little plates bursting with flavour. While the dishes are intricate, nothing's overly gim-micky, and the setting, in an old wooden house, is classy without being too formal. Meals can be paired with wine (from $45) or whisky (from $35).

Plato MODERN NZ $$$
(Map p500; ☑03-477 4235; www.platocafe.co.nz; 2 Birch St; mains lunch $20-25, dinner $36; ⊙noon-2pm Wed-Sun, 6pm-late daily) The unpromising locale and kooky decor (including collec-tions of toys and beer tankards) gives little indication of the seriously good food on offer at this relaxed eatery. Fresh fish and shell-fish, including oysters in season, feature prominently. Try the house-brewed beer.

✕ North Dunedin

Buster Greens CAFE $$
(Map p500; ☑03-470 1233; 466 George St, North Dunedin; mains $22-25; ⊙6.30am-3.30pm Mon-Fri, from 7.30am Sat, from 8.30am Sun; 🍴) Bright and bustling cafe with top-notch brunches, healthy raw sweet treats and colourful sal-ads. Great vegan selection. There's more

seating downstairs and blankets to ward off the chill at the tables outside.

 St Clair

Starfish
CAFE $$
(Map p510; ☑ 03-455 5940; www.starfishcafe.co.nz; 7/240 Forbury Rd, St Clair; mains $15-24; ⊙ 6.30am-late Tue-Sat, to 5pm Sun, to 4.30pm Mon) Part of the growing restaurant scene at St Clair Beach, Starfish is a popular all-day eatery offering decadent brunch dishes, good coffee and a great buzz. Pop in for a quick lunch on the balcony overlooking the beach, or drop by in the evening for a hearty dinner accompanied by a glass of wine or a wide selection of craft beer.

Esplanade
ITALIAN $$
(Map p510; ☑ 03-456 2544; www.esplanade.co; 2 Esplanade, St Clair; mains $21-26; ⊙ 8am-late; 🛜) A prime position overlooking St Clair Beach is only the beginning at this relaxed Italian cafe-restaurant from the same team as No 7 Balmac. Drop in during the morning for an espresso and a panino, or come by in the evening for authentic thin-crust pizzas. At sunset the windows offer the perfect frame as lavender twilight descends over the beach.

Other Suburbs

No 7 Balmac
CAFE $$$
(Map p510; ☑ 03-464 0064; www.no7balmac.co.nz; 7 Balmacewen Rd, Maori Hill; mains brunch $14-26, dinner $35-40; ⊙ 7am-late Mon-Fri, from 8am Sat, 8am-5pm Sun; 🛜) We wouldn't recommend walking to this sophisticated cafe at the top of Maori Hill, but luckily it's well worth the price of a cab. The fancy cafe fare stretches from smashing brunches to the likes of confit duck and applewood-grilled pork and fennel. Take a stroll through the organic garden where many of the greens are sourced.

🍷 Drinking & Nightlife

⭐ Dog with Two Tails
BAR
(Map p500; ☑ 03-477 4188; www.dogwithtwotails.co.nz; 25 Moray Pl; ⊙ 11am-late Tue-Fri, from 10am Sat, 10am-4pm Sun) Nightly events here range from jazz jams and soulful singer-songwriters, to indie rock and literary readings with a peppering of quiz nights and open mics. Tuck into its signature crêpes ($6.50 to $12) in the red-painted room under a beautiful stained-glass entranceway.

⭐ Pequeno
COCKTAIL BAR
(Map p500; ☑ 03-477 7830; www.pequeno.co.nz; behind 12 Moray Pl; ⊙ 5pm-late Mon-Fri, from 7pm Sat) Head down the alley opposite the Rialto Cinema, with the black-and-white *kākāpō* street-art piece by Phlegm, to discover this intimate and sophisticated lounge bar. Music is generally laid-back, with regular live acts. The leather couches, fireplace, tapas menu and excellent wine and cocktail list make this backstreet bar perfect for a chilled night out.

Inch Bar
BAR
(Map p510; ☑ 03-473 6496; 8 Bank St, North East Valley; ⊙ 3pm-late) Make the short trek from town to this cosy bar for its selection of Kiwi craft beers and tasty nibbles, and the cute indoor/outdoor beer garden. Despite its diminutive dimensions, it hosts live music on Friday and Saturday nights, plus there's Vinyl Revival on Monday, open-mic music on Wednesday (free drink if you play) and open-mic comedy Thursday.

Carousel
COCKTAIL BAR
(Map p500; ☑ 03-477 4141; 141 Stuart St; ⊙ 5pm-midnight Wed, to 2am Thu, to 3am Fri & Sat) Monochrome tartan wallpaper, a roof deck and great cocktails leave the classy clientele looking pleased to be seen somewhere

---

DUNEDIN'S LIVE-MUSIC SCENE

Don't miss the chance to check out Dunedin's live-music scene. Consult Under the Radar (www.undertheradar.co.nz/utr/gig_guide/otago) for upcoming gigs, or try your luck at one of these venues:

The Cook (Map p500; ☑ 03-777 3603; www.thecook.nz; 354 Great King St; ⊙ 10am-late Sat, to 3.30pm Sun) Raucous rock driven by nearby uni students.

Dog with Two Tails Indie folk, singer-songwriters, and spoken word.

Pequeno Underground bar with stylish loungers tapping toes to jazz and fusion.

The Crown (Map p500; ☑ 03-477 0132; 179 Rattray St; ⊙ 11am-2.30am Fri & Sat, to 11pm Mon-Thu) Anything from punk to funk with posters from Dunedin's dirty '90s on the walls.

Inch Bar Blues, country and local musos.

so deadly cool. It gets going around 10pm and DJs spin deep house until late. Find it upstairs.

Aika + Co
BAR

(Map p500; 357 George St; ⊙7.30am-5pm Mon-Thu, to 7pm Fri, 9am-7pm Sat, 9am-3pm Sun) 'Dunedin's littlest bar' might only be 1.8m wide, but this bolthole on George St is still full of punters. There's sometimes even live musicians squeezed in here in summer. By day, it's a handy caffeine-refuelling spot.

☆ Entertainment

Forsyth Barr Stadium
STADIUM

(Map p510; www.forsythbarrstadium.co.nz; 130 Anzac Ave) Constructed for the 2011 Rugby World Cup, this is the only major stadium in NZ with a fully covered roof, and it holds 30,000 spectators. It's the home ground of the Highlanders Super 15 rugby team (www. thehighlanders.co.nz) and the Otago rugby team (www.orfu.co.nz), and also plays regular host to the All Blacks, international sporting matches, concerts and shows.

Rialto Cinemas
CINEMA

(Map p500; ☑03-474 2200; www.rialto.co.nz; 11 Moray Pl; adult/child $16/10) Screens blockbusters and art-house flicks. Tickets are cheaper ($9) on Tuesdays.

🛍 Shopping

Gallery De Novo
ART

(Map p500; ☑03-474 9200; www.gallerydenovo. co.nz; 101 Stuart St; ⊙9.30am-5.30pm Mon-Fri, 10am-3pm Sat & Sun) This interesting, contemporary, fine-art gallery is worth a peek whether you're likely to invest in a substantial piece of Kiwi art or not.

Guild
FASHION & ACCESSORIES

(Map p500; www.guilddunedin.co.nz; 145 Stuart St; ⊙10am-5pm Mon-Sat) This cooperative of Dunedin designers sells high-end fashion, jewellery and homewares made by its 12 members and special guests. You'll find bright and beautiful fabrics, artful clothing cuts and very wearable designs. Pop in for a chat with a local maker – it's always staffed by a member of the co-op.

ℹ Information

The **Dunedin i-SITE** (Map p500; ☑03-474 3300; www.isitedunedin.co.nz; 50 The Octagon; ⊙8.30am-5.30pm Mon-Fri, from 8.45am Sat & Sun) incorporates the **DOC Visitor Centre** (Department of Conservation; Map p500; ☑03-474 3300; www.doc.govt.nz; 50 The Octagon; ⊙8.30am-5.30pm Mon-Fri), providing a one-stop shop for all of your information needs, including Great Walks and hut bookings.

Dunedin Hospital (☑03-474 0999; 201 Great King St)

Urgent Doctors (☑03-479 2900; www. dunedinurgentdoctors.co.nz; 18 Filleul St; ⊙8am-10pm) There's also a late-night pharmacy next door.

ℹ Getting There & Away

AIR

Air New Zealand (☑0800 737 000; www. airnewzealand.co.nz) flies to/from Auckland, Wellington and Christchurch.

Jetstar (☑0800 800 995; www.jetstar.com) flies to/from Auckland.

Virgin Australia (p489) flies to/from Brisbane, Australia.

BUS

Regional buses leave from Moray Pl, just around the corner from the Bus Hub.

Atomic Shuttles (Map p500; ☑210 867 6001; www.atomictravel.co.nz; 331 Moray Pl) Buses to/from Christchurch ($40, 5¾ hours), Timaru ($30, three hours) and Ōamaru ($25, 1¾ hours), once daily.

InterCity (Map p500; ☑03-471 7143; www. intercity.co.nz; 331 Moray Pl) Coaches run to/from Christchurch (from $29, 5½ hours), Ōamaru (from $23, 1½ hours), Cromwell (from $23, 3¼ hours) and Queenstown (from $24, 4¼ hours) around four times daily, and once daily to Gore (from $15, 2¾ hours) and Te Anau (from $19, 4½ hours). There's also a direct service once weekly to Invercargill (from $23, 3¼ hours).

ℹ Getting Around

TO/FROM THE AIRPORT

Dunedin Airport (DUD; ☑03-486 2879; www. dunedinairport.co.nz; 25 Miller Rd, Momona; 📶) is 27km southwest of the city. There is no public transport to the airport. A standard taxi ride to/from the city costs around $100. For door-to-door shuttles, try **Kiwi Shuttles** (☑03-487 9790; www.kiwishuttles.co.nz; per 1/2/3/4 passengers $20/36/48/60) or **Super Shuttle** (☑0800 748 885; www.supershuttle.co.nz; per 1/2/3/4 passengers $20/30/40/50) – book in advance.

BUS

Dunedin's **Orbus** (☎ 0800 672 8736; www.orc.govt.nz/public-transport/dunedin-buses; adult $1.92-11.41) network extends across the city. It's particularly handy for getting to St Clair, St Kilda and Port Chalmers, and as far afield as Palmerston or the Otago Peninsula. Buses run regularly from the **Bus Hub** (Map p500; ☎ 0800 672 8736; www.orc.govt.nz/public-transport/dunedin-buses; Great King St) in the city Monday to Friday, with reduced services on weekends.

Individual tickets are available from the bus driver; for longer stays, invest in a GoCard – purchase from bus drivers, from the council offices in The Octagon, or from the University Book Shop (p499) – which offers reduced fares.

CAR

The big international car-hire companies all have offices in Dunedin; local outfits include **Hanson Rental Vehicles** (☎ 03-453 6576; www.hanson.net.nz; 313 Kaikorai Valley Rd; ⊙7.30am-5.30pm) and **Ezi Car Rental** (☎ 03-486 1245; www.ezicarrental.co.nz; Dunedin Airport; ⊙7.30am-2pm).

SCOOTER

Lime electric scooters (www.li.me; $1, plus per minute 38¢) have arrived in Dunedin. You're allowed to ride them on the footpath if you're considerate of pedestrians.

TAXI

There are several taxi companies in Dunedin. Options include:

Dunedin Taxis (☎ 03-477 7777; www.dunedintaxis.co.nz)

Southern Taxis (☎ 03-476 6300; www.southerntaxis.co.nz)

Green Cabs (☎ 0800 46 47 336; www.greencabs.co.nz).

AROUND DUNEDIN

Port Chalmers

POP 1365

Little Port Chalmers is only 13km from central Dunedin but it feels a world away. Somewhere between working class and bohemian, Port Chalmers is dominated by its huge container terminal, but the coastal landscapes surrounding it are beautiful and the town has long attracted Dunedin's arty types. The main drag, George St, is home to a handful of cafes, design stores and galleries, perfect for a half-day's worth of wandering, browsing and sipping away from the city crush.

Orokonui Ecosanctuary WILDLIFE RESERVE
(Map p510; ☎ 03-482 1755; www.orokonui.nz; 600 Blueskin Rd; adult/child $20/10; ⊙9.30am-4.30pm) 🌿 From the impressive visitor centre there are great views over this 307-hectare predator-free nature reserve, which encloses cloud forest on the mountainous ridge above Port Chalmers and stretches to the estuary on the opposite side. Its mission is to provide a mainland refuge for species usually exiled to offshore islands for their own protection. Visiting options include self-guided explorations, hour-long 'highlights' tours (adult/child $35/17.50; 11am and 1.30pm daily) and two-hour 'forest explorer' tours (adult/child $50/25; 11am daily).

Hare Hill HORSE RIDING
(Map p510; ☎ 03-472 8496; www.horseriding-dunedin.co.nz; 207 Aramoana Rd, Deborah Bay; treks $110-220) Horse treks include thrilling beach rides and harbour views.

Carey's Bay Hotel PUB FOOD $$
(Map p510; ☎ 03-472 8022; www.careysbayhotel.co.nz; 17 Macandrew Rd, Carey's Bay; mains $22-35; ⊙10am-late) Just around the corner from Port Chalmers you'll find this cosy historic pub, popular with locals for its hearty meals and unbeatable location – on sunny days grab a table out the front.

❶ Getting There & Away

On weekdays bus 14 (adult/child $6/3.60, 30 minutes, half-hourly) travels between Dunedin's Bus Hub and Port Chalmers between 6.30am and 9.30pm (11.30pm on Friday). On Saturday buses run hourly between 8.30am and 11.30pm, and between 9.30am and 5.30pm on Sunday. The Port to Port (p513) private ferry operates from Port Chalmers' Back Beach to Portobello on the Otago Peninsula up to three times daily.

Otago Peninsula

POP 5000

It's hard to believe that the Otago Peninsula – a picturesque haven of rolling hills, secluded bays, sandy beaches and clifftop vistas – is only half an hour's drive from downtown Dunedin. As well as interesting historical sites and wild walking trails, this small sliver of land is home to the South Island's most accessible diversity of wildlife, including albatross, penguins, fur seals and sea lions. The peninsula's only town is the petite Portobello and, despite a host of tours exploring the region, it maintains its quiet rural air.

Dunedin & the Otago Peninsula

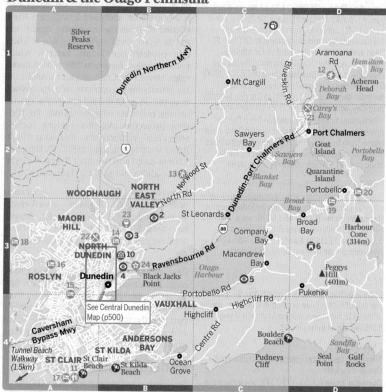

◉ Sights

★ Nature's Wonders
Naturally

WILDLIFE RESERVE

(Map p510; ☑ 03-478 1150; www.natureswonders. co.nz; Taiaroa Head; adult/child Argo $99/45, coach $45/22.50, boat $55/22.50; ⓢ tours 10.15am-sunset) What makes the improbably beautiful beaches of this coastal sheep farm different from other important wildlife habitats is that (apart from pest eradication and the like) they're left completely alone. Many of the multiple private beaches haven't suffered a human footprint in years. The result is that yellow-eyed penguins can often be spotted (through binoculars) at any time of the day, and NZ fur seals laze around rocky swimming holes, blissfully unfazed by tour groups passing by.

Depending on the time of year, you might also see whales and little penguin chicks. The tour is conducted in 'go-anywhere' Argo vehicles by enthusiastic guides, at least some of whom double as true-blue Kiwi farmers. A less bumpy coach option is also available, and there's also the *Albatross Express* boat tour, departing 3km south from Wellers Rock Wharf (p513), devoted to spotting albatross and sea birds. Combo tours are available.

Royal Albatross Centre
& Fort Taiaroa

BIRD SANCTUARY

(Map p510; ☑ 03-478 0499; www.albatross.org.nz; Taiaroa Head; adult/child albatross $52/15, fort $26/10, combined $62/20; ⓢ 10.15am-sunset) Taiaroa Head (Pukekura), at the peninsula's northern tip, has the world's only mainland royal albatross colony, along with a late 19th-century military fort. The only public access to the area is by guided tour. There's an hour-long albatross tour and a 30-minute fort tour available, or the two can also be combined. Otherwise you can just call into the centre to look at the displays and have a bite in the cafe.

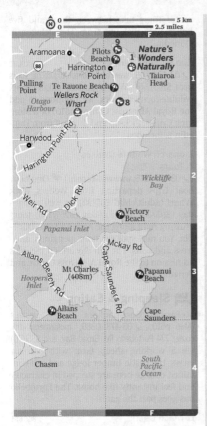

Albatross are present on Taiaroa Head throughout the year, but the best time to see them is from December to March, when one parent is constantly guarding the young while the other delivers food throughout the day. Sightings are most common in the afternoon when the winds pick up; calm days don't see as many birds in flight.

Little penguins swim ashore at Pilots Beach (just below the car park) around dusk to head to their nests in the dunes. For their protection, the beach is closed to the public every evening one hour before sunset, but viewing is possible from a specially constructed wooden platform (adult/child $35/10). Depending on the time of year, 50 to 200 penguins might waddle past. Photos are allowed, but no flashes.

Fort Taiaroa was built in 1885 in response to a perceived threat of Russian invasion. Its **Armstrong Disappearing Gun** was designed to be loaded and aimed underground, then popped up like the world's slowest jack-in-the-box to be fired.

Larnach Castle   CASTLE
(Map p510; ☑03-476 1616; www.larnachcastle.
co.nz; 145 Camp Rd; adult/child castle & grounds

$34/12, grounds only $17/5; 8am-7pm Oct-Apr, 9am-5pm May-Sep) Standing proudly on top of a hill overlooking the peninsula, this gorgeous Gothic Revival mansion was built in 1871 by Dunedin banker, merchant and Member of Parliament William Larnach. The castle fell into disrepair after Lanarch's death, until it was purchased by the Barker family in 1967, and a long period of restoration began. The four floors are now filled with intricate woodwork and exquisite antique furnishings, and the crenellated tower offers expansive views.

Penguin Place   BIRD SANCTUARY
(Map p510; 03-478 0286; www.penguinplace. co.nz; 45 Pakihau Rd, Harington Point; adult/child $55/16; tours from 10.15am Oct-Mar, 3.45pm Apr-Sep) On private farmland, this reserve protects nesting sites of the rare yellow-eyed penguin (hoiho). The 90-minute tours cover 2km and focus on penguin conservation and close-up viewing from a system of hides. Bookings are recommended.

🏃 Activities

A popular walking destination is beautiful Sandfly Bay, reached from Seal Point Rd (one hour return). You can also follow a track from the end of Sandymount Rd to the Sandymount summit and on to the impressive Chasm and Lovers Leap (one hour return). Note that this track is closed from September to mid-October for lambing. Download the helpful DOC *Dunedin Walks* brochure to plan your hike.

🧭 Tours

Back to Nature Tours   BUS
(0800 286 000; www.backtonaturetours.co. nz) The full-day Royal Peninsula tour (adult/child $205/130) heads to points of interest around Dunedin before hitting the Otago Peninsula. Stops include Larnach Castle's (p511) gardens (castle entry is extra), Penguin Place and the Royal Albatross Centre (p510). There's also a half-day option that visits various beaches ($85/55) and another tackling the Lovers Leap walking track ($99/55). Will pick up from your accommodation.

Wild Earth Adventures   KAYAKING
(03-489 1951; www.wildearth.co.nz; per person $115) Offers guided tours in double sea kayaks, with wildlife often sighted en route. Tours take between three and five hours, with pick-ups from The Octagon in Dunedin.

Elm Wildlife Tours   WILDLIFE
(03-454 4121; www.elmwildlifetours.co.nz; tours from $103) Well-regarded, small-group, wildlife-focused tours, with options to add the Royal Albatross Centre (p510) or a Monarch Cruise. Pick-up and drop-off from Dunedin is included.

Monarch Wildlife Cruises & Tours   BOATING
(03-477 4276; www.wildlife.co.nz) One-hour boat trips departing from Wellers Rock Wharf (adult/child $57/22), as well as half-day ($95/35) and full-day ($257/125) tours cruising right along the harbour from Dunedin. You may spot sea lions, penguins, albatross and seals. The full-day option includes admission to the Royal Albatross Centre and Penguin Place.

🍴 Sleeping & Eating

McFarmers Backpackers   HOSTEL $
(Map p510; 03-478 0389; mcfarmers@xtra. co.nz; 774 Portobello Rd, Broad Bay; s/d $35/70) On a working sheep farm with harbour views, the rustic timber lodge and self-contained cottage here are steeped in character and feel instantly like home. The Portobello bus goes past the gate.

Larnach Castle   B&B $$$
(Map p510; 03-476 1616; www.larnachcastle. co.nz; 145 Camp Rd; d stable/lodge/estate $170/330/540;) Larnach Castle's pricey back-garden lodge has 12 unique, whimsically decorated rooms with views. Less frivolous are the atmospheric rooms in the 140-year-old stables (bathrooms are shared). A few hundred metres from the castle, Camp Estate has luxury suites worthy of a romantic splurge. Each option includes breakfast and castle entry; dinner in the castle is extra ($70).

Portobello Hotel & Bistro   PUB FOOD $$
(Map p510; 03-478 0759; www.portobellohotel andbistro.com; 2 Harington Point Rd, Portobello; mains lunch $18-23, dinner $23-36; 11.30am-9pm, to late Fri & Sat) Refreshing thirsty travellers since 1874, the Portobello pub is still a popular pit stop. Grab a table in the sun and tuck into the chef's special seafood chowder,

a burger or a fillet of freshly caught blue cod. On Wednesday the kitchen closes after lunch.

1908 Cafe   CAFE, BISTRO **$$**
(Map p510; ✆ 03-478 0801; www.1908cafe.co.nz; 7 Harington Point Rd, Portobello; mains lunch $12-28, dinner $14-34; ⊘ noon-2pm & 5-8.30pm, closed Mon & Tue Apr-Oct) Salmon, venison and steak are joined by fresh fish and blackboard specials at this casual eatery. Cafe fare, such as soup and toasted sandwiches, is served at lunch. As the name suggests, the building originally opened as a tearoom in 1908, and many of the original features are still in place.

❶ Getting There & Away

Portobello is a scenic 20km drive from Dunedin along the harbour. A $64 million upgrade to the road was underway at the time of research, with a cycleway/walkway to Portobello along the stunning coastline expected to be completed in 2020.

On weekdays, buses make the journey from Dunedin's Bus Hub to Portobello Village from 7.30am to 10.30pm (adult/child $6/3.60, one hour, half-hourly), with four services continuing to Harington Point ($10.20/6.10) at the tip of the peninsula. On weekends the service reduces to hourly from 8.30am.

The **Port to Port** (✆ 020 4162 4250; www.porttoport.co.nz; adult/child $12/6) private ferry operates from Port Chalmers' Back Beach to Portobello up to three times daily. This 10-minute trip is an economical way to get out on the water with the possibility of seeing wildlife. The company also runs two-hour wildlife cruises (adult/child $90/46) from **Wellers Rock Wharf** (Map p510; Harrington Point Rd).

Once on the peninsula, it's tough to get around without your own transport. Most tours will pick you up from your Dunedin accommodation.

CENTRAL OTAGO

Central Otago is a remote region of far horizons, rolling hills and distant mountains that turn from green to gold in the relentless summer sun and are blanketed in snow in winter and spring. These lonely landscapes provide a backdrop to a succession of tiny, charming gold-rush towns where farmers mingle with Lycra-clad cyclists in lost-in-time pubs. As well as being one of the country's top wine regions, the area provides fantastic opportunities for those

on two wheels, whether mountain biking along old gold-mining trails or traversing the district on the Otago Central Rail Trail (p514).

Middlemarch

POP 156

With the Rock and Pillar Range as an impressive backdrop, the small town of Middlemarch is the terminus of both the Taieri Gorge Railway and the Otago Central Rail Trail. It's famous in New Zealand for the **Middlemarch Singles Ball** (www.facebook.com/middlemarchsinglesdance; held over Easter in odd-numbered years), where southern men gather to entice city gals to the country life.

🏃 Activities

There are a number of reliable companies offering bike hire and logistical support to riders on the Otago Central Rail Trail. (p514) This includes shuttles, bag transfers and an accommodation booking service.

Trail Journeys   CYCLING
(✆ 03-464 3213; www.trailjourneys.co.nz; 20 Swansea St; per day from $50, e-bikes from $100; ⊘ 8.30am-4.30pm Sep-May) Provides bike hire and logistical support to riders on the Otago Central Rail Trail. Also has a depot in Clyde (p520), at the other end of the trail.

Cycle Surgery   CYCLING
(✆ 03-464 3630, 0800 292 534; www.cyclesurgery.co.nz; cnr Swansea & Aberafon Sts; per day from $45; ⊘ depot 8.30am-5pm mid-Sep–mid-May) Bikes and logistics for Rail Trailers. At the time of writing the company was renovating the historic Dunstan Hotel on Clyde's main street (33 Sunderland St) to be its new depot at the other end of the trail. Until then you can organise for pick-up/drop off by shuttle in Clyde.

🛏 Sleeping & Eating

Otago Central Hotel   B&B **$$**
(✆ 027 544 4800; www.otagocentralhotelhyde.com; SH87, Hyde; d with/without bathroom from $170/130; ⊘ Oct-Apr) Most of the tidy rooms in this cool old hotel, 27km along the trail from Middlemarch, have private bathrooms, but not en suite.

There's a very sweet pop-up 'honesty cafe' on the veranda for passing Rail Trailers.

CYCLING IN OTAGO

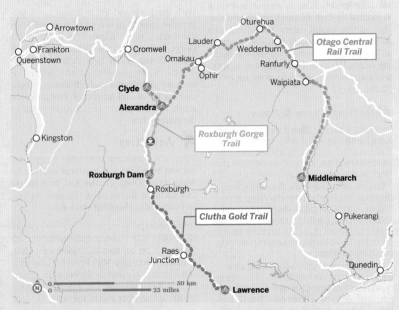

OTAGO CENTRAL RAIL TRAIL

START CLYDE OR MIDDLEMARCH
END MIDDLEMARCH OR CLYDE
DURATION 3 TO 4 DAYS
DISTANCE 152KM
DIFFICULTY EASY

From the early 20th century through to the 1990s, the Central Otago rail line linked small, inland goldfield towns between Dunedin and Clyde. After the 150km stretch from Middlemarch to Clyde was permanently closed, the rails were ripped up and the trail resurfaced. The result is a year-round, mainly gravel cycling and walking trail. Culverts, beautiful old rail bridges, viaducts, dramatic rock cuttings and spooky tunnels remove most of the ups and downs, making this a very accessible trail popular with families, older folks and weekend cyclists.

With excellent trailside facilities (toilets, shelters and information), gob-smacking scenery and profound remoteness, the trail attracts over 80,000 users annually. March

is the busiest time, when there are so many city slickers on the track that you might have to wait 30 minutes at cafes en route for a panini. Consider September/October for a quieter ride.

The trail can be followed in either direction – Clyde (p520) to Middlemarch (p513) is the most popular. The whole thing takes three to four days to complete by bike (or a week on foot), but you can obviously choose to do as short or as long a stretch as suits your plans. There are also easy detours to towns such as Naseby (p517) and St Bathans (p516).

Due to the popularity of the trail, a whole raft of sleeping and eating options have sprung up in remote locales en route, like Alexandra (p518), Ophir (p518), Oturehua (p519), Ranfurly (p516) and Waipiata (p516).

However, some sections are less well served than others, particularly the 52km between Waipiata and Middlemarch. This, combined with the fact that much of the accommodation is closed in low season (June

Otago is the most popular destination for cycle touring in the whole of New Zealand. These three trails can easily be linked together to make one mega ride.

to August) and in high demand during peak season (November to April), means it's well worth getting one of the outfitters to book accommodation for you – they don't charge extra for this service. Any of the area's i-SITEs can also provide detailed information and bookings. See www.otagocentralrailtrail.co.nz and www.otagorailtrail.co.nz for track information, recommended timings, accommodation options and tour companies.

One-way bike hire, secure parking and transport back to the start is easily arranged with bike operators. They also offer shuttle transport to the trailheads at Clyde and Middlemarch from Queenstown and Dunedin.

The gorgeous heritage tourist trains operated by **Dunedin Railways** (p502) can be used as a transport connection between Middlemarch and Dunedin. The Taieri Gorge Railway travels between Dunedin and Pukerangi twice daily – Rail Trail operators can shuttle you between Pukerangi and the trailhead at Middlemarch, 20km away (around $30). On Sunday trains go all the way to Middlemarch.

ROXBURGH GORGE TRAIL

START **ALEXANDRA**
END **ROXBURGH DAM**
DURATION **4 TO 5 HOURS**
DISTANCE **21KM CYCLE, 13KM BOAT RIDE**
DIFFICULTY **MODERATE**

Opened to considerable fanfare in 2013, this well-constructed mountain-biking and walking track was intended to connect Alexandra to Roxburgh Dam. As access through some of the farmland in the middle section wasn't successfully negotiated, however, riding the 'full trail' requires prearranging a scenic 13km jet-boat ride (adult/child $110/65, October to May) via the local information centres or directly with **Clutha River Cruises** (p519).

An alternative is to make a return trip from each end: Alexandra–Doctors Point (20km return) or Roxburgh Dam–Shingle Creek (22km return).

It's requested that you purchase a $10 day tag to assist with the maintenance of the track, although this is not compulsory. They can be bought at i-SITEs, cycle shops and tour operators. For more information see www.centralotagonz.com/roxburgh-gorge-trail.

CLUTHA GOLD TRAIL

START **ROXBURGH DAM**
END **LAWRENCE**
DURATION **2 TO 4 DAYS**
DISTANCE **73KM**
DIFFICULTY **EASY**

From Roxburgh Dam you can continue on this far easier trail that follows the turquoise Clutha (Mata-au) River through Roxburgh to Beaumont and then on to Lawrence. The same voluntary maintenance fee tag system covers both tracks.

Look out for evidence of the area's gold-mining past during the 10km ride from the dam to the Roxburgh (p520) township. The following 20km stretch to Millers Flat is flanked by unusual rock formations and native kanuka (tea tree); stop for a cooling dip at Pinders Pond. From Millers Flat it's 25km to Beaumont, passing through farmland and beneath the Horseshoe Bend suspension bridge. The trail climbs from Beaumont to the highest point of the track and then heads through 434m Big Hill Tunnel on its way to Lawrence.

InterCity has direct buses from Lawrence to Dunedin (from $16, 1½ hours). Bikes are allowed as checked luggage if you pre-book and collapse them down (both wheels removed, the handlebars turned sideways and the chain covered).

BIKE HIRE & LOGISTICS

Bikes and equipment can be hired in **Dunedin** (p504), Middlemarch (p513), **Alexandra** (p519), Clyde (p520) and **Roxburgh** (p520). Bike-hire companies, especially those located on the relevant route, offer detailed information and logistical support to get you out on the trails.

WORTH A TRIP

ST BATHANS

A 17km detour north from SH85 heads into the foothills of the imposing Dunstan Mountains and on to diminutive St Bathans. This once thriving gold-mining town of 2000 people is now home to only half a dozen permanent residents living amid a cluster of cutesy 19th-century buildings. There's not much in town but the historic Vulcan Hotel (☑ 03-447 3629; mj.kavanagh@xtra.co.nz; Main St; r per person $70, dinner $28-35) – an atmospheric (and famously haunted) spot to drink, eat or stay.

The Blue Lake is an accidental attraction: a large hollow filled with blue water that has run off abandoned gold workings. Walk along the sculpted cliffs to the lookout for a better view of the alien landscape (one hour return).

Kissing Gate Cafe   CAFE $
(☑ 03-464 3224; 2 Swansea St; mains $7-15; ⊙ 7.30am-3.30pm; 🛜) Sit out under the fruit trees in the pretty garden of this lovely little wooden cottage and tuck into a cooked breakfast, a meat pie, a zingy salad or some home baking. Nana-chic at its best.

❶ Getting There & Away

Middlemarch is an hour's scenic drive from Dunedin.

Both of the main cycle companies offer shuttles to Dunedin, Pukerangi and the Rail Trail towns. The scenic Taieri Gorge Railway (☑ 03-477 4449; www.dunedinrailways.co.nz) runs between Dunedin and Pukerangi (adult/child $72/19), leaving Dunedin at 9.30am and 3pm daily. On Sunday trains run all the way to Middlemarch ($81/21).

Ranfurly & Waipiata

POP 663

After a series of fires in the 1930s, Ranfurly was rebuilt in the architectural style of the day, and a few attractive art-deco buildings still line its sleepy main drag.

Most travellers come through Ranfurly as part of a journey on the Otago Central Rail Trail (p514), which passes right through town. Much smaller Waipiata, 10km closer to Middlemarch along the Rail Trail, with a lovely pub and accommodation, is also a handy stop.

🏃 Activities

Real Dog Adventures   DOG SLEDDING
(☑ 03-444 9952; www.realdog.co.nz; 2 Bypass Rd, Ranfurly; sled dog team ride $150; ⊙ Apr-Oct) Six to eight Alaskan malamutes or Siberian huskies are harnessed to a snow sled when there's enough snow (otherwise a dog rig with bike-style wheels) and off you go for a 4km run through the forest. In summer (November to March) you can still do a kennel tour ($40). Book ahead.

🛏 Sleeping

Old Post Office Backpackers   HOSTEL $
(☑ 03-444 9588; www.oldpobackpackers.co.nz; 11 Pery St, Ranfurly; dm $35, s/d with shared bathroom $55/80; ⊙ closed Jun-Sep; 🅿🛜) Tidy rooms with bright paint and a cheery lounge-room fire make this backpackers a welcome sight for Rail Trailers. Discounts on laundry and loads of DVDs to borrow.

Behind the Bike Sheds   B&B $$
(☑ 022 352 3147; www.behindthebikesheds.co.nz; 32 Waipiata Domain Rd, Waipiata; per person with shared bathroom $70) 🅿 Two sweet handmade cabins (a double and a four-bed bunkhouse) in the garden comprise this lovely B&B on the Rail Trail. There's a composting loo and an outdoor bath for stargazing, heated by a gas-fired burner underneath – watch your toes! Breakfast includes homemade jams and jellies. It's across the trail from the Waipiata pub.

Hawkdun Lodge   MOTEL $$
(☑ 03-444 9750; www.hawkdunlodge.co.nz; 1 Bute St, Ranfurly; s/d from $125/150; 🛜) 🅿 This smart boutique motel is the best option in Ranfurly's town centre by far, with a spa pool and free laundry facilities. Even studio units are spacious, with kitchenettes, sitting areas and en suites. Travelling chefs can flex their skills in the smart guest kitchen and dining area. Breakfast costs $15.

Kokonga Lodge   B&B $$$
(☑ 03-444 9774; www.kokongalodge.co.nz; 33 Kokonga-Waipiata Rd; s/d $265/295; @🛜) Just off SH87 between Waipiata and Hyde, this upmarket rural property offers six contem-

porary en suite rooms, newly refurbished in neutral tones. One was occupied by Sir Peter Jackson when he was filming *The Hobbit* in the area. It's right on the Rail Trail.

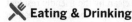 Eating & Drinking

Maniototo Cafe CAFE $
(☑03-444 9023; www.maniototocafe.co.nz; 1 Pery St, Ranfurly; mains $8; ⊙7am-4.30pm Mon-Fri, 8am-5pm Sat & Sun) Attached to the Four Square supermarket, this sunny cafe is a good lunch option, with a tempting array of sandwiches, sausage rolls and cakes, like spiced apricot, Brie and chicken pretzel rolls.

Waipiata Country Hotel PUB
(☑03-444 9470; www.waipiatahotel.co.nz; 29 Main St, Waipiata; ⊙10am-late; ☎) Around 10km from Ranfurly, this friendly country pub right on the Rail Trail is a great spot to quench your post-ride thirst. It also offers good pub meals – like slow-cooked beef and smokey cheese pies or grilled haloumi salad. It also has rooms available (doubles with/without bathroom $150/140) and a comfortable lodge (doubles $160) down the road.

❶ Information

Ranfurly i-SITE (☑03-262 7999; www.central otagonz.com; 3 Charlemont St, Ranfurly; ⊙9am-5pm; ☎) Call into the Ranfurly i-SITE in the old train station. While you're there, check out the short film about the Rail Trail and interesting local history displays.

❶ Getting There & Away

Both on the Rail Trail, Ranfurly sits on route SH85, 1¾ hours' drive from Dunedin, while Waipiata is 10km off SH85. Seasonal local shuttles can take you to Naseby and other locales; enquire at the i-SITE.

Naseby
POP 100

Cute as a button, surrounded by forest and dotted with 19th-century stone buildings and heritage shopfronts, Naseby (*naze-bee*) is the kind of small settlement where life moves slowly. That the town is pleasantly obsessed with the fairly insignificant world of New Zealand curling (a Winter Olympic sport resembling lawn bowls on ice) indicates the pace of life here. It's that lazy small-town vibe, along with summer swimming dams and good mountain-biking and walking trails through the surrounding forest, that makes Naseby a delightful stopover.

✈ Activities

Maniototo Curling International ICE SKATING
(☑03-444 9878; www.curling.co.nz; 1057 Channel Rd; adult/child per 90min $40/15; ⊙10am-5.30pm May-Oct, 9am-6pm Nov-Apr) All year round you can shimmy after curling stones at this indoor ice rink; tuition and grippy shoes included. Upstairs you can watch the games from the bar.

Naseby Ice Luge SNOW SPORTS
(☑03-444 9270; www.lugenz.com; 1057 Channel Rd; adult/child $35/25; ⊙10am-4pm Jun-Aug) In winter, hurtle 360m down a hillside on a wooden sled on the southern hemisphere's only ice luge. Weather dependent; call ahead, bookings recommended. There's also an outdoor ice rink to skate around.

Naseby Night Sky Tours OUTDOORS
(☑03-444-9908; https://nasebynightskytours. wixsite.com/home; 17 Leven St; per person $35) Astrophysicist Paul Bishop leads fascinating tours to see planets, star clusters and constellations with the aid of two telescopes, binoculars and Naseby's low-light-pollution skies.

🛏 Sleeping & Eating

Naseby Lodge APARTMENT $$
(☑03-444 8222; www.nasebylodge.co.nz; cnr Derwent & Oughter Sts; 1-/2-bedroom apt $170/260) These free-standing modern apartments are smart and spacious, with fully equipped kitchens and underfloor heating in the bathrooms. There's also a good restaurant, constructed of straw-bale walls sheathed in rustic corrugated iron, and a bike-repair workshop.

Old Doctor's Residence B&B $$$
(☑03-444 9775; www.olddoctorsresidence.co.nz; 58 Derwent St; r/ste $295/350; ☎) ✿ Old doctors take note: this is how to reside! Sitting behind a pretty garden, this gorgeous 1870s house offers two luxurious guest rooms and a lounge where wine and nibbles are served in the evening. The suite has a sitting room and an en suite bathroom, while the smaller room's bathroom is accessed from the corridor.

Black Forest Cafe
CAFE $

(☑ 03-444 9820; 7 Derwent St; mains $8-19; ⊙ 9am-3pm Wed-Mon; ☎) Inside this cute old building with a skylight, a sunny deck and an undulating wooden floor, you'll find hearty soups, cakes and toasties. Plus great coffee.

ⓘ Information

Naseby Information Centre (☑ 03-444 9961; www.nasebyinfo.org.nz; Old Post Office, Derwent St; ⊙ 11am-2pm Fri, Sun & Mon, to 4pm Sat, extended hours summer) Gold pans ($20) sold.

ⓘ Getting There & Away

The Ranfurly–Naseby Rd leaves SH85, 4km north of Ranfurly. There's no public transport and cyclists should factor in a 12km detour from the Rail Trail. Many accommodation providers will collect you, or you can arrange seasonal shuttles with local operators – ask at the information centre or at Ranfurly i-SITE (p517).

From Naseby, you can wind your way on unsealed roads northeast through spectacular scenery to Danseys Pass and through to Duntroon in the Waitaki Valley.

Lauder, Omakau & Ophir

Separated by 8km of SH85, tiny Lauder (population 18) and larger Omakau (population 260) are good stops if you're a hungry cyclist in need of a feed and a bed. However, the area's real gem is Ophir (population 50), 2km from Omakau across the Manuherikia River.

Ophir was bypassed by the railway in 1904, leaving its main street trapped in time. The most photogenic of its heritage buildings is the 1886 post office (www.historic.org. nz; 53 Swindon St, Ophir; ⊙ 9am-noon Mon-Fri). At the far end of town, the road heads over the heritage-listed 1870s Dan O'Connell Bridge, a bumpy but scenic crossing that loops back to SH85.

Ophir lays claim to the country's widest range of recorded temperatures: from -21.6°C to 35°C.

🛏 Sleeping & Eating

Blacks Hotel
PUB $$

(☑ 03-447 3826; www.blackshotel.co.nz; 170 Swindon St, Ophir; r $155; ⊙ 4pm-late Mon, from 11am Tue-Sat, from noon Sun; P ☎) Decorated like an OTT wedding in a Scots hunting lodge, this popular local watering hole is a great spot to enjoy a pint or a pub-style meal (mains $23 to $30). Sit under the wall of pink roses and be licked clean by the friendly resident dogs. Out the back is a row of basic, clean en suite rooms.

Chatto Creek Tavern
HERITAGE HOTEL $$

(☑ 03-447 3710; www.chattocreektavern.co.nz; 1544 SH85, Chatto Creek; dm/s/d without bathroom $60/100/130; ⊙ 10am-late; P ☎) Dating from 1886, this attractive stone hotel sits right beside the Rail Trail and highway, 10km southwest of Omakau. Pop in for hearty pub meals (mains $17 to $30), or rest your weary calf muscles in a dorm bed or a double room. Rates include breakfast. Informal camping is also possible.

Stationside Cafe
CAFE $

(☑ 03-447 3580; Lauder-Matakanui Rd, Lauder; mains $9-18; ⊙ 8am-4pm Oct-Apr) Country hospitality is on show at this great little trailside place with wonderfully charming hosts. Options include tasty breakfasts, healthy salads and soups, as well as a mouthwatering selection of just-baked scones, cakes and muffins.

Pitches Store
RESTAURANT $$$

(☑ 03-447 3240; www.pitches-store.co.nz; 45 Swindon St, Ophir; lunch $19-28, dinner $26-40; ⊙ 10am-8.30pm daily Nov-Apr, to 4pm Thu & Mon, to 8.30pm Fri-Sun May & Sep-Oct, closed Jun-Aug) Formerly a general store and butcher, this heritage building has been sensitively transformed into a humdinger of a cafe-restaurant. Exposed stone walls may speak of the past but the menu offers contemporary gourmet fare. There are also six elegant guest rooms ($296) here.

ⓘ Getting There & Away

There's no public transport to these parts but many of the bike crews servicing the Otago Central Rail Trail provide shuttles, and many accommodation providers can pick you up from the trail if you enquire in advance.

Alexandra

POP 5510

Unless you've come especially for the Easter Bunny Hunt or the springtime Blossom Festival (www.blossom.co.nz) and NZ Merino Shearing Championships, the main reason

OTUREHUA

Well worth a stop on the Rail Trail, Oturehua boasts New Zealand's oldest continually operating store, the lost-in-time Gilchrist Store (☑03-444 5808; www.gilchriststore.co.nz; 3353 Ida Valley-Omakau Rd; ⊙7.30am-5pm Mon-Fri, 8am-4pm Sat & Sun), established in 1902, where floor-to-ceiling wooden shelves are still stocked with old boxes of soap powder, rolling tobacco and laxative tablets.

Also here is Hayes Engineering Works (☑03-444 5801; www.hayesengineering.co.nz; 39 Hayes Rd; adult/child \$12/free; ⊙10am-5pm Sep-May), where you can wander about the workshop where inventor and engineer Ernest Hayes manufactured all manner of useful farm devices, including his famous fencing wire strainer (1924). Also visit the homestead (1920), fitted with mod cons from piped radio to electricity.

Stay overnight at Marchburn Country Lodge (☑021 253 1941; www.marchburn.co.nz; 16 Reef Rd; r \$295; 🗑) to enjoy amazing views of the snow-covered peaks right from your bed through the big windows. A crackling fire, big leather lounges and a fine collection of vintage books make for a cosy evening.

to visit unassuming Alexandra is mountain biking. It's the biggest Otago Central Rail Trail (p514) settlement by far, offering more eating and sleeping options than the rest of the one-horse (or fewer) towns on the route. It's also the start of the Roxburgh Gorge Trail (p515).

Alex, as it's known to the locals, marks the southeastern corner of the acclaimed Central Otago wine region. Of the 25 wineries in the Alexandra Basin (www.alexandra basinwines.co.nz), only 10 are seasonally open for tastings.

◉ Sights

Central Stories MUSEUM
(☑03-448 6230; www.centralstories.co.nz; 21 Centennial Ave; by donation; ⊙10am-4pm) Central Otago's history of gold mining, winemaking, fruit growing and sheep farming is covered in this excellent regional museum and gallery,.

☆ Activities

As well as the obvious – the Otago Central Rail Trail and Roxburgh Gorge Trail – walkers and mountain bikers will love the old gold trails weaving through the hills; contact Altitude Bikes, or download the Trailforks app (www.trailforks.com).

Altitude Bikes CYCLING
(☑021 456 918; www.altitudebikes.co.nz; 88 Centennial Ave; adult/child per day \$50/35; ⊙8.30am-5.30pm Mon-Fri, 9am-1pm Sat) Hires bikes in conjunction with Henderson Cycles and organises logistics for riders on the Otago

Central, Clutha Gold and Roxburgh Gorge Trails. Also get in touch for info on local mountain-biking trails.

Clutha River Cruises BOATING
(☑022 068 3302; www.clutharivercruises.co.nz; boat ramp, Dunorling St; adult/child \$95/55; ⊙2.30pm Oct-Apr) Explore the scenery and history of the region on a 2½-hour heritage cruise. The same company runs the jetboat transfer for cyclists on the Roxburgh Gorge Trail (adult/child \$110/65, October to May).

🛏 Sleeping & Eating

Marj's Place HOSTEL \$
(☑03-448 7098; www.marjsplace.co.nz; 5 Theyers St; dm/s/d without bathroom \$30/45/90; 🅿🗑) The standard varies widely between the three neighbouring houses that comprise this sprawling hostel. The 'homestay' has private rooms, a Finnish sauna and a spa bath. It's much nicer than the 'backpackers' across the road, which is let mainly to seasonal workers. Grandmotherly Marj can hook you up with work if you're looking for it.

Asure Avenue Motel MOTEL \$\$
(☑03-448 6919; www.avenue-motel.co.nz; 117 Centennial Ave; units \$145-170; 🅿🗑) The pick of the motels on the main drag, these clean, modern units have all the mod cons, and full kitchens, too. Studio, one- and two-bedroom apartments are available.

Courthouse Cafe & Larder CAFE \$\$
(☑03-448 7818; www.packingshedcompany.com; 8 Centennial Ave; mains \$11-24; ⊙6.15am-4pm Mon-Fri, from 9am Sat) Bounteous botanical

WORTH A TRIP

ALEXANDRA TO MILTON ON SH8

Heading south from Alexandra, SH8 winds along rugged, rock-strewn hills above the Clutha River as it passes Central Otago's famous orchards. In season (roughly December to March) roadside fruit stalls sell just-picked stone fruit, cherries and berries. En route there's a scattering of small towns, many dating from gold-rush days.

Further south, the Clutha broadens into Lake Roxburgh, with a large hydroelectric power station at its terminus, before rushing past Roxburgh itself. Call into the friendly i-SITE (☑03-262 7999; www.centralotagonz.com; 120 Scotland St; ⊙9am-5pm daily Oct-Apr, Mon-Fri May-Sep) for information on cycling and seasonal fruit picking (December to April) in the surrounding apple and stone-fruit orchards. You can hire bikes and get all the information you need for the Clutha Gold and Roxburgh Gorge Trails from Highland Bike Hire (☑03-446 8009; www.highlandbikehire.co.nz; 107 Scotland St; adult/child per day from $40/25; ⊙9am-5.30pm Mon-Thu, to 7pm Fri, plus 10am-2pm Sat Sep-May).

Before you leave Roxburgh, drop into Jimmy's Pies (☑03-446 9012; www.jimmyspies. co.nz; 143 Scotland St; pies from $3.50; ⊙7.30am-5pm Mon-Fri), renowned across the South Island since 1959. If you're at a loss to which of the 20 different varieties of pies to choose, try the apricot chicken – you're in orchard country, after all.

Continuing south from Roxburgh, the road passes through Lawrence and the Manuka Gorge Scenic Reserve, a picturesque route through wooded hills and gullies. SH8 joins SH1 near Milton.

displays dispel any lingering austerity in this stone courthouse building, dating from 1878. The counter groans under the weight of an extraordinary array of baked goods (cakes, doughnuts, croissants and more), which compete with gourmet brunch and lunch options.

❶ Getting There & Away

Alexandra lies on SH8, around 2½ hours' drive from Dunedin and 1¼ hours from Queenstown.

InterCity (☑03-442 4922; www.intercity. co.nz) coaches head to/from Dunedin (from $23, three hours), Roxburgh (from $14, 34 minutes), Clyde (from $10, nine minutes), Cromwell (from $11, 24 minutes) and Queenstown (from $15, 1½ hours).

Clyde

POP 1010

More charming than his buddy Alex, 8km down the road, Clyde looks more like a 19th-century gold-rush film set than a real town. Set on the banks of the emerald-green Clutha River, Clyde retains a friendly, small-town feel, even when holidaymakers arrive in numbers over summer. It's also the trailhead of the Otago Central Rail Trail (p514).

🏃 Activities

The Alexandra–Clyde 150th Anniversary Walk (12.8km, three hours one way) is a riverside walking and cycling trail that's fairly flat, with ample resting spots and shade. This makes a nicer riverside cycle than the official Rail Trail route between the towns. A new cycle trail from Clyde to Cromwell, through the Cromwell Gorge, is also in development, aiming to open in 2021.

Trail Journeys   CYCLING
(☑03-449 2150; www.trailjourneys.co.nz; 16 Springvale Rd; rental per day from $50, e-bikes from $100; ⊙9am-5pm Mon-Fri May-Oct, from 8am daily Nov-Apr) 🚲 Right by the Otago Central Rail trailhead (1.7km from the town centre), Trail Journeys rents bikes and arranges cycling tours, baggage transfers and shuttles. It also has a depot in Middlemarch (p513).

🎉 Festivals & Events

Clyde Wine & Food Festival   WINE, FOOD
(www.promotedunstan.org.nz; adult/child $15/ free; ⊙10.30am-4.30pm Easter Sun) Held in the main street on Easter Sunday each year, this local festival showcasing the region's produce and wines brings folks from across the South Island.

🛏 Sleeping & Eating

Postmaster's House BOUTIQUE HOTEL **$$**
(📞 03-449 2488; www.postofficecafeclyde.co.nz; 4
Blyth St; d with/without bathroom $140/105; 🅿)
Antique furnishings are dotted around the
large and lovely rooms in this pretty 1865
stone cottage. Two of the three rooms share
a bathroom; the third has its own. Wi-fi is
available in the attached restaurant.

Dunstan House B&B **$$$**
(📞 03-449 2295; www.dunstanhouse.co.nz; 29
Sunderland St; s/d without bathroom from
$110/130, d/ste with bathroom from $220/265; 🛜)
This restored late-Victorian balconied inn
has cosy lounge areas, a magnificent kauri
staircase and stylish rooms decorated with
William Morris wallpaper. The less expensive rooms share bathrooms but are just as
comfortable and atmospheric. Breakfast is
served in the lovely licensed cafe (open 7am
to 4pm), which specialises in gluten-free, vegan and keto dishes.

★ **Oliver's** B&B **$$$**
(📞 03-449 2600; www.oliverscentralotago.co.nz;
Holloway Rd; d $255-465; 🅿🛜) 🍴 Oliver's
fills an 1860s merchant's house and stone
stables with luxurious rooms decked out
with old maps, heritage furniture and
claw-foot baths. Most of the rooms open
onto a secluded garden courtyard. The
attached **restaurant** (📞 03-449 2805; www.
oliverscentralotago.co.nz; 34 Sunderland St;
mains lunch $21-26, dinner $34-43; ⊙restaurant
noon-2pm & 6-8pm, bar noon-late, shorter hours
Jun-Aug), housed in a gold-rush-era general
store, incorporates a bar, cafe-deli and bis-
tro showcasing the best local produce with
dishes like braised hare leg and apricot-
frangipani pie.

**Paulina's Restaurant
& Bar** MULTICUISINE **$$**
(📞 03-449 3236; www.paulinasrestaurant.co.nz;
6 Naylor St; lunch $22, dinner $30-36; ⊙noon-
2.30pm & 5.30pm-late) International dishes are
whipped up here, including in the traditional wood-fire oven, but Paulina particularly
showcases her South American heritage
with treats such as *gambas al ajillo* (garlic
prawns) and Peruvian-style blue cod on the
menu, and pisco sours behind the bar.

ℹ Getting There & Away

InterCity (📞 03-471 7143; www.intercity.co.nz)
Coaches head to/from Dunedin (from $23,

three hours), Roxburgh (from $14, 44 minutes),
Alexandra (from $10, nine minutes), Cromwell
(from $10, 14 minutes) and Queenstown (from
$14, 1½ hours).

Cromwell
POP 4143
Cromwell has a charming lakeside historic precinct, a great weekly farmers market
and perhaps the South Island's most OTT
'big thing' – a selection of giant fruit by the
highway, representing the area's extensive
fruit-growing industry.

During the cherry season (mid-December
to February) local growers sell fruit on the
roadsides and put out 'PYO' ('pick your own')
signs. You can pick up seasonal work here
too – contact Seasonal Solutions Cooperative
(www.ssco.co.nz).

It's also at the very heart of the prestigious Central Otago wine region (www.cowa.
org.nz), known for its extraordinarily good
pinot noir and, to a lesser extent, riesling,
pinot gris and chardonnay. The Cromwell
Basin – which stretches from Bannockburn,
7km southwest of Cromwell, to north of
Lake Dunstan – accounts for over 70% of
Central Otago's total wine production. Pick
up the *Central Otago Wine Map* for details
of upwards of 50 local wineries.

◎ Sights & Activities

**Cromwell
Heritage Precinct** HISTORIC SITE
(www.cromwellheritageprecinct.co.nz; Melmore Tce;
⊙10am-4pm) **FREE** When the Clyde Dam
was completed in 1992 it flooded Cromwell's
historic town centre – 280 homes, six farms
and 17 orchards. Many historic buildings
were disassembled before the flooding and
have since been rebuilt in a pedestrianised
precinct beside Lake Dunstan. While some
have been set up as period museum pieces
(stables, newspaper presses and the like),
others house good cafes, galleries and some
interesting shops – look for the shop selling
a rainbow of hand-spun yarn.

In summer the area plays host to an excellent weekly farmers market (p523).

**Bendigo
Historic Reserve** HISTORIC SITE
(www.doc.govt.nz; Bendigo) **FREE** Gold was
discovered in Bendigo in 1862; relics from
the rush can be seen at this historic reserve,

accessible off SH8, near the north of Lake Dunstan. Sights include mine shafts and tunnels, ruined buildings and water races. Reaching the site is part of the adventure – it's up an extremely steep dirt road, accessible by 2WD, but only just. Don't attempt this in wet weather or if your car's a bit dodgy. Signposted walking trails thread through the ruins and offer great views.

Highlands
Motorsport Park
ADVENTURE SPORTS

(☑ 03-445 4052; www.highlands.co.nz; cnr SH6 & Sandflat Rd; ⊙ 10am-4pm winter, to 5pm summer) Transformed from a paddock into a top-notch 4km racing circuit in just 18 months, this revheads' paradise hosted its first major event in 2013. The action isn't reserved just for the professionals, with various high-octane experiences on offer, along with an excellent museum.

Budding speed freaks can start out on the go-karts ($49 per 10 minutes) before taking a 200km/h ride in the Highlands Taxi ($129 for up to four people), completing a lap in a Ferrari 488 at 230km/h ($179), or having a go at the wheel of a V8 muscle car ($395).

If you'd prefer a less racy experience, the National Motorsport Museum (adult/child $25/10) showcases racing cars and displays about Kiwi legends such as Bruce McLaren, Possum Bourne, Emma Gilmour and Scott Dixon. There's minigolf (free with museum entry) and a good cafe.

Also check out the New Zealand Endurance Championship in November, a weekend-long motor-sports festival, and the Highlands Festival of Speed, classic motor racing in early April.

Tours

Goldfields Jet
ADVENTURE

(☑ 03-445 1038; www.goldfieldsjet.co.nz; SH6; adult/child 40min $125/65, 20min $89/59; ⊙ 9am-5pm) Zip through the Kawarau Gorge on a jetboat ride.

Central Otago
Motorcycle Hire
TOURS

(☑ 03-445 4487; www.comotorcyclehire.co.nz; 271 Bannockburn Rd; per day from $185) The sinuous and hilly roads of Central Otago are perfect for negotiating on two wheels. This crew hires out motorbikes and advises on improbably scenic routes. It also offers guided trailbike tours (from $195 per person for two people) and extended road tours (from $575).

Goldfields Mining Tours
WALKING

(☑ 0800 111 038; www.goldfieldsmining.co.nz; SH6; adult/child $25/10; ⊙ 9am-5pm) Take a tour of the goldfields, including the Chinese Village, or wander around with a self-guided map. Either way, you'll be taught how to pan for gold – and you get to keep your finds. It's 8km from Cromwell.

Sleeping

Cromwell Backpackers
HOSTEL $

(☑ 03-445 1378, 028 406 4088; www.cromwell backpackers.co.nz; 33 The Mall; dm per night/week from $35/170; ℗ 🛜) This small, popular and somewhat ramshackle hostel is right in the centre of town, with bunk beds packed quite tight. There's a no-shoes policy, instruments to play in the lounge, a decent coffee machine and a share-house vibe. It's the sort of place where long-stayers keep their toothbrushes in the bathroom.

There's one women-only dorm. This backpackers is a good place to hook up fruit-picking work June to September.

Firewood Creek House
B&B $$

(☑ 021 209 1705; www.firewoodcreekhouse. com; 10 Roberts Dr; d incl breakfast from $160; ℗ 🛜 ♨) A roomy retreat just outside the town centre. You can take in the mountains from the outdoor pool or spa in summer. Spotless rooms, fantastic cooked brekkie, private balconies, electric blankets and a beautiful garden make for a comfortable stay.

Burn Cottage Retreat
B&B, COTTAGE $$$

(☑ 027 208 8565; www.burncottageretreat.co.nz; 168 Burn Cottage Rd; cottage $235-265; ℗ 🛜) Set among walnut trees and gardens 3km northwest of Cromwell, this peaceful retreat has three luxurious, self-contained cottages with classy decor, spacious kitchens and modern bathrooms. Enjoy the gorgeous garden with a game of petanque.

Eating

For a small town, Cromwell's dining scene encompasses a wide range of international flavours, including Italian, Japanese, Mexican, Turkish, Indian and Thai.

Black Rabbit Kitchen & Bar
CAFE $

(☑ 03-445 1553; www.blackrabbit.nz; 430a Bannockburn Rd, Bannockburn; baked items $8-10; ⊙ 9am-2pm Tue & Wed, to 3pm Thu, to 8.30pm Fri, Sat & Sun) It's much cheaper to get a take-

CELLAR-DOOR DINING

A fantastic way to sample some local wine is to dine at one of the local wineries.

As well as making the region's most prestigious pinot noir, **Mt Difficulty** (☑03-445 3445; www.mtdifficulty.co.nz; 73 Felton Rd, Bannockburn; mains $34-39, tastings from $5; ⊗tastings 10.30am-4.30pm, restaurant noon-4pm) is a lovely spot for a leisurely lunch looking down over the valley. There are large, wine-friendly platters to share, but save room for the decadent desserts. Book ahead.

The winery dates back to the early 1990s, when five growers collaborated to produce wine from the promising but unproven Central Otago region. Not only does it offer the chance to taste various wines at its welcoming cellar door, its spectacular perch overlooking the Cromwell Basin encourages a very long lunch. Sharp and modern, with scrumptious fare and alfresco dining on the terrace, it pays to book a table and sort out well in advance who's responsible for driving onward.

The stylish restaurant at **Carrick** (☑03-445 3480; www.carrick.co.nz; Cairnmuir Rd, Bannockburn; tastings from $15, mains $35; ⊗tastings 10am-5pm, restaurant 11am-4pm) opens out on to a terrace and lush lawns. The seasonal menu features excellent share platters and is a pleasurable complement to the wine range. The flagship drop is the intense, spicy pinot noir, as well as a rich, toasty chardonnay and citrusy aromatic varietals.

Round the back of a fruit-and-veg shed, the outdoor kitchen **Stoaker Room** (☑03-445 4841; www.thestoakerroom.co.nz; 180 SH8B, Cromwell; mains $20-25; ⊗10am-10pm) will smoke your meal in an old French-oak pinot-noir wine barrel and serve it with a tasty Wild Earth wine. Sit in the outdoor space beside the orchard and after lunch taste some more wine from the two other cellar doors in the complex.

away from this hip cafe in Bannockburn, like a spinach and feta roll with homemade chutney ($8). But you can also sit down for an excellent meal – try the famous seafood chowder, or a gourmet pizza with venison, capsicum, blueberry, red onion, blue cheese and mozzarella ($30); pizzas are half price on Sunday night.

Amigos MEXICAN $$
(☑03-445 8263; www.amigosmexicangrill.co.nz; 50 The Mall; mains $29; ⊗11am-9.30pm; ☑) A local favourite with a creative menu of Mexican-inspired fare from rattlesnake wings to tacos with sweet potato, beetroot and mint puree. Don't miss the house-made chipotle and jalapeño sauces. If you find the place is packed, step across the mall to Bargarita, a great little cocktail bar run by Amigos' owners where you can order off the same menu.

Shopping

Cromwell Farmers Market MARKET
(www.cromwellheritageprecinct.co.nz; ⊗9am-1pm Sun late-Oct–Easter) In summer the Cromwell Heritage Precinct plays host to an excellent farmers market, running every Sunday from Labour weekend (late October) to Easter.

❶ Getting There & Away

InterCity (☑03-471 7143; www.intercity.co.nz) Coaches to Queenstown (from $11, one hour, frequent), Fox Glacier (from $52, 6½ hours, one daily), Christchurch (from $54, 7½ hours, three daily), Alexandra (from $11, 24 minutes, four daily) and Dunedin (from $22, 3½ hours, four daily).

Ritchies (☑0800 405 066; www.ritchies.co.nz/queenstown) Scheduled shuttles to/from Wānaka ($20, 45 minutes), Queenstown Airport ($20, one hour) and Queenstown CBD ($20, 1¼ hours).

Fiordland & Southland

Best Places to Eat

➡ Niagara Falls (p534)

➡ Orepuki Beach Cafe (p539)

➡ Redcliff Cafe (p551)

➡ Church Hill (p544)

➡ Louie's (p536)

Best Places to Stay

➡ Te Anau Lodge (p550)

➡ Newhaven Holiday Park (p531)

➡ Southern Comfort Backpackers (p535)

➡ Slope Point Accommodation (p533)

➡ Manapōuri Motels & Holiday Park (p546)

Why Go?

Brace yourself for sublime scenery on a breathtaking scale. Fiordland National Park's mountains, forests and mirror-smooth waters hold visitors in thrall. Framed by kilometre-high cliffs, Milford Sound was carved by epic battles between rock and ice over millennia. Leading here is the Milford Hwy, which reveals a magnificent alpine view at every bend. Shying away from attention is Doubtful Sound, the pristine 'place of silence' (which leaves many admiring visitors speechless, too).

From here, a chain of towns characterised by friendliness and fresh seafood is strung along the Southern Scenic Route. The road snakes through Southland to the Catlins, where meadows roll to golden bays and sawtooth cliffs are speckled with dozing seals.

Then there's the end of the line – Stewart Island/Rakiura, an isolated isle seemingly lost in time, and home to New Zealand's beloved icon, the kiwi.

When to Go

➡ Late October to late April is the Great Walks season for the Milford, Kepler and Routeburn Tracks – book in advance if you want to hike these popular routes.

➡ Visit from December to April for the best chance of settled weather in Fiordland's notoriously fickle climate (although chances are, you'll still see rain!).

➡ Stewart Island/Rakiura's changeable weather can bring four seasons in a day, at any time of year. Tackle the island's walks in summer (December to February), or come in winter for the stargazing.

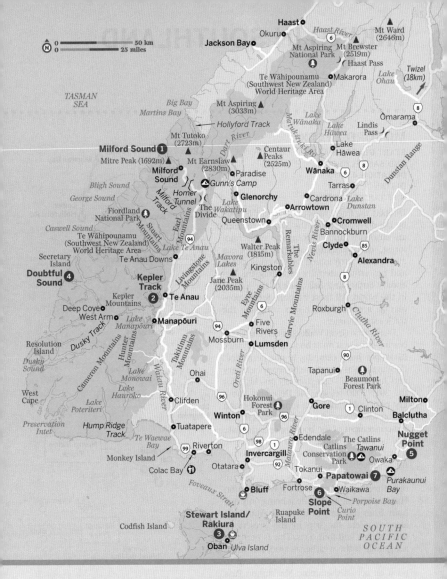

Fiordland & Southland Highlights

❶ **Milford Sound** (p553)
Being overwhelmed by your first glimpse of Mitre Peak rising from the fiord's inky waters.

❷ **Kepler Track** (p527)
Feeling on top of the world traversing a sharp ridgeline among Fiordland peaks.

❸ **Stewart Island/Rakiura** (p540) Savouring solitude on NZ's 'third island', a haven for bird life.

❹ **Doubtful Sound** (p546)
Embracing silence when the boat engine snaps off on this remote cruise.

❺ **Nugget Point** (p530)
Watching waves crash against stepping-stone islands extending into the ocean.

❻ **Slope Point** (p533)
Trudging through a cow paddock to the sea-ravaged cliffs at the South Island's southernmost point.

❼ **Papatowai** (p532)
Discovering forest waterfalls, acoustic sea caves and an organic mechanic.

HIKING IN SOUTHLAND

MILFORD TRACK

START GLADE WHARF
END SANDFLY POINT
DURATION 4 DAYS
DISTANCE 53.5KM
DIFFICULTY MODERATE

Dubbed 'the finest walk in the world' in 1908 by London's *Spectator,* the Milford remains an absolute stunner, complete with rainforest, deep glaciated valleys, a glorious alpine pass surrounded by towering peaks and powerful waterfalls, including the legendary Sutherland Falls, one of the loftiest in the world. All these account for its popularity: around 8000 hikers complete the track each summer.

During the Great Walks season (late October to April), you must book huts in advance ($140 per hut); camping is not permitted. Bookings open sometime between February and June and fill up extremely quickly – for the 2019/2020 season, the December/January peak sold out in six minutes. Keep an eye on www.doc.govt.nz/milfordtrack for the announcement of the booking opening date and be ready to move fast. If you miss out, it's worth checking back as there are sometimes cancellations.

During the season, you can only walk in one direction and you must stay at Clinton Hut the first night, despite it being only one hour from the start of the track. You must also complete the trip in the prescribed three nights and four days. This is perfectly acceptable if the weather is kind, but when the weather turns sour you'll still have to push on across the alpine Mackinnon Pass and may miss some rather spectacular views. It's all down to the luck of the draw.

The track starts at Glade Wharf, at the head of Lake Te Anau, accessible by a 1¼-hour boat trip from Te Anau Downs, itself 29km from Te Anau on the road to Milford Sound. It finishes at Sandfly Point, a 15-minute boat trip from Milford Sound village, from where you can return by road to Te Anau, around two hours away. You must book these connecting transfers in advance

and you'll be given options to do this online when you book your hut tickets.

DOC advises against tackling the Milford Track between early May and late October because of the significant risk of avalanches and floods, and the fact that bridges at risk of avalanche are removed. It's wet, very cold, and snow conceals trail markers. If

The deep-green deep south, a still-untamed outdoor treasure, is home to some of New Zealand's most famous tracks including four of its Great Walks.

you're a well-equipped hiking pro considering the Milford Track out of season, get DOC advice on weather conditions. During this low season, huts revert to the basic 'serviced' category ($15).

Tracknet (p552) offers transport from Queenstown and Te Anau to connect with boats at Te Anau Downs and Milford Sound. There are other options for transport to and from the track; **Fiordland i-SITE** (p551) and the **Fiordland National Park Visitor Centre** (p551) can advise on options to best suit you.

An alternative is to book a guided hike package through **Ultimate Hikes** (p550), which includes transfers and private en-suite rooms in comfortable lodges with all meals included.

HOLLYFORD TRACK

START LOWER HOLLYFORD RD
END MARTINS BAY
DURATION 4-5 DAYS (ONE WAY)
DISTANCE 56.8KM
DIFFICULTY ADVANCED

The four- to five-day (each way), 56km Hollyford Track is a backcountry hike requiring navigation and river-crossing skills. It passes through the lower Hollyford – the longest valley in Fiordland National Park – to remote Martins Bay. Expect splendid mountain and lake vistas, forest, extensive bird life and magical coast, as well as fewer crowds than the Great Walks in the region.

The majority of hikers start at Lower Hollyford Rd then turn tail at Martins Bay and retrace their steps back to the start; however, you can also connect by air to/from Martins Bay so you only have to walk one way. Advanced hikers can take the super challenging Pyke–Big Bay Route back from Martins Bay to create a round trip of around 10 days.

Hikers have the use of six DOC huts on the track; most are serviced huts ($15). Camping ($5) is permitted next to the huts, although sandflies will prevent this from being remotely enjoyable. Tickets should be obtained in advance.

Tracknet (p552) runs one daily shuttle to/from the Lower Hollyford Rd trailhead ($62 from Te Anau). **Trips & Tramps** (p549) offers return services from Te Anau – flying you into Martins Bay and picking you up from Lower Hollyford Rd after the hike ($410). Nine kilometres (two hours' walk) shy of the trailhead is **Gunn's Camp** (p554), a good bolthole before or after the feat, with car storage available.

For a less rugged experience in this wilderness, Ngāi Tahu–owned **Hollyford Track** (p550) leads three-day guided trips for small groups on the Hollyford, staying at luxurious private huts or lodges. A jetboat trip and a scenic flight to Milford Sound shorten the journey.

KEPLER TRACK

START/END LAKE TE ANAU CONTROL GATES
DURATION 3-4 DAYS
DISTANCE 60.1KM
DIFFICULTY MODERATE

Opened in 1988, the Kepler is one of NZ's best-planned tracks and now one of its most popular. This Great Walk takes the form of a moderately strenuous 60km loop beginning and ending at the Waiau River control gates at the southern end of Lake Te Anau. It features an all-day hike above the bushline, traversing the sharp edge of a ridge with incredible panoramas to either side, including the lake, the Jackson Peaks and the Kepler Mountains. Along the way it passes tussock lands, waterfalls, peaceful beech forest, lakeside beaches and cheeky kea.

The route is usually covered in four days, staying in all three huts ($130 per hut), although some people skip a hut or two. For example you can skip Moturau Hut and combine two mostly flat days and even cut 10km from this section by starting or leaving the track at the Rainbow Reach swing bridge. However, spending a night at Moturau Hut on the shore of Lake Manapōuri (maybe with a dip in the lake) is beautiful. The track can be walked in either direction, although the most popular (and safest in high winds) is Luxmore–Iris Burn–Moturau.

This is a heavily weather-dependent track at any time of year and the alpine sections require a good level of fitness. Parts of the track may be hazardous or impassible in winter.

You must book in advance during the Great Walk Season (late October to April). In the low season (highly inadvisable for all but the most experienced NZ hikers) the huts revert to the 'serviced' category ($15). There are campsites (in/out of season $40/5) at Brod Bay and Iris Burn.

Conveniently, the track begins under an hour's walk from the **Fiordland National Park Visitor Centre** (p551), via the lakeside track alongside the Manapōuri–Te Anau Rd (SH95). There's a car park and a shelter near the control gates. **Tracknet** (p552) and **Topline Tours** (p552) both run shuttles to and from both the control gates and Rainbow Reach trailheads. **Kepler Water Taxi** (p549) offers morning boat services across Lake Te Anau to Brod Bay, slicing 1½ hours off the first day's hike.

DUSKY TRACK

START LAKE HAUROKO
END WEST ARM
DURATION 8-10 DAYS
DISTANCE 84KM
DIFFICULTY ADVANCED

This challenging track begins (or ends) on the northern shores of dark, brooding Lake Hauroko, the deepest lake in NZ (462m). An epic journey, it only suits hikers at the top of their game: you'll wobble across 21 three-wire bridges, wade through rivers and trudge through knee-deep mud. Book a boat with Clifden-based **Lake Hauroko Tours** (☑03-225 5677, 0800 376 174; www.wjet.co.nz; track transport $99; ☺8.30am Thu Nov–mid-Dec & Feb-Apr, Mon & Thu mid-Dec–Jan) to access the southern trailhead. **Trips & Tramps** (p549) offers transport ($55 per head) from Te Anau to Clifden Suspension Bridge, 12km north of Tuatapere, timed to meet boats near their launching point for the Dusky Track trailhead.

As there's only one or two boats per week accessing the southern trailhead, it's far better to embark on the walk from the south. The northern trailhead at Manapōuri is well served with four boats per day. This is useful, because the walk can take longer than expected – delays due to weather and conditions are common. Take extra food for

this reason. It's also a good idea to pack a tent – the standard DOC huts ($5, pit toilets, no cooking facilities) cannot be booked and are sometimes filled with multiday stayers or people visiting by helicopter.

HUMP RIDGE TRACK

START/END RARAKAU CAR PARK
DURATION 3-4 DAYS
DISTANCE 62KM
DIFFICULTY MODERATE

This track is rich in natural and cultural history, from coastal and alpine scenery to the relics of a historic timber town. The hiking days are long (up to nine hours on the first two days, ascending 890m on the first) and the terrain suits intermediate-level hikers. There's bird life aplenty, and the chance to see Hector's dolphins on the lonely windswept coast. En route the path crosses a number of towering historic wooden viaducts, including NZ's highest. At the time of writing the Hump Ridge Track was being upgraded to a Great Walk, with improvements to the coastal section and the construction of a third hut, expected to be launched in February 2020.

However, unlike the other Great Walks, the Hump Ridge Track will continue to be operated privately, with upmarket lodges featuring extras like chefs in the kitchen, shops selling food and well-stocked bars. There are options ranging from Freedom Walks ($245 per person sleeping in a dorm, including a hot breakfast) through to Guided Walks ($1695) that include three-course meals, motel-style rooms, a helicopter connection and pack transfer. Any walker can upgrade to a private room for $100 per night or take a hot shower ($20).

To hike the track you need to book through the **Hump Ridge Track Office** (p540). Transport connections to the trailhead (19km from Tuatapere) are available to/from Queenstown, Invercargill, Te Anau and Tuatapere. For hardy walkers, limited backcountry accommodation is available in winter ($50). Advance bookings are essential. Camping is not permitted.

RAKIURA TRACK

START/END OBAN, STEWART ISLAND/ RAKIURA
DURATION 2-3 DAYS
DISTANCE 39KM
DIFFICULTY MODERATE

Waterfall on Milford Track (p526)

One of NZ's Great Walks, the 32km, two-to-three-day Rakiura Track is a peaceful loop that sidles around beautiful beaches before climbing over a 250m-high forested ridge and traversing the sheltered shores of **Paterson Inlet/Whaka ā Te Wera**. It passes sites of historical interest, including Māori sites and sawmilling relics, and introduces many common sea and forest birds.

Rakiura Track is 32km long, but adding in the road sections at either end bumps it up to 39km, conveniently forming a circuit from Oban. It's a well-defined loop requiring a moderate level of fitness, suitable for hiking year-round. Being a Great Walk, it has been gravelled to eliminate much of the mud for which the island is infamous, though some boot-deep sections remain.

There are two Great Walk huts ($22 to $24; kids free) en route at Port William and North Arm, which need to be booked in advance via the DOC website (www.greatwalks.co.nz). They have toilets, water and a fireplace for heating, but no cooking facilities. Camping (adult/child $6/free) can be booked at the 'standard' campsites near (but not adjacent to) the huts, and also at Māori Beach.

NORTH WEST CIRCUIT TRACK

START/END OBAN, STEWART ISLAND/RAKIURA
DURATION 9-11 DAYS
DISTANCE 125KM
DIFFICULTY ADVANCED

The North West Circuit Track is Stewart Island/Rakiura's legendary hike, a demanding coastal epic around a remote coastline featuring isolated beaches, sand dunes, birds galore and miles of mud. It's 125km, and takes nine to 11 days, although there are several options for shortening it involving boats and planes.

There are well-spaced huts along the way, all of which are 'standard' ($5) except for two Great Walk Huts ($22 to $24), which must be booked in advance. A North West Circuit Pass ($35), available only at the **Rakiura National Park visitor centre** (p545), provides for a night in each of the 'standard' huts.

Locator beacons are advised and be sure to call into the visitor centre for up-to-date information and to purchase the essential topographical maps. You should also register your intentions with a friend (see www.adventuresmart.org.nz) as this is no easy walk in the park.

❶ Getting There & Away

Invercargill is the main transport hub, with flights to/from Wellington, Christchurch, Auckland and Stewart Island/Rakiura, and buses from as far afield as Queenstown and Dunedin. Te Anau has direct bus connections with Queenstown, Dunedin and Christchurch.

THE CATLINS

The Catlins' meandering roads thread together a medley of pretty-as-a-picture landscapes. Bypassed entirely by SH1, this southeasterly swathe of the South Island is a road-tripper's dream. Narrow winding roads weave past golden-sand bays, zip through bucolic meadows and trace boulder-studded coast, while gravelly detours expose you to startled sheep and even more startled farmers.

❶ Information

Get maps and local tips at the small Owaka Museum & Catlins Information Centre and the even smaller **Waikawa Museum & Information Centre** (❷03-246 8464; waikawamuseum@hyper. net.nz; 604 Niagara–Waikawa Rd; ◷10am-5pm). En route to the Catlins, you can also grab lots of info from the i-SITEs in Invercargill (p536) and **Balclutha** (❷03-418 0388; www.cluthaz. com; 4 Clyde St, Balclutha; ◷8.30am-5pm Mon-Fri year-round, 9.30am-3.30pm Sat & Sun Nov-Apr, 10am-2pm Sat & Sun May-Oct).

For further information, see www.catlins.org. nz, www.cluthanz.com and www.catlins-nz.com.

There are no banks in the Catlins but there's an ATM at the **Four Square** (❷03-415 8201; 3 Ovenden St; ◷7.30am-7pm) supermarket in Owaka. Most businesses accept credit cards but we recommend bringing some cash.

❶ Getting There & Away

There is no public transport in the Catlins area so you'll need your own vehicle or you can take a tour – try Catch-a-Bus South (p537) or Headfirst Travel (https://headfirsttravel.com).

Kaka Point

The township might be sedate but the views at Kaka Point, 23km east of Owaka, are among the most mesmerising in the Catlins. The primary draws of this small coastal community of holiday homes are Nugget Point, a remarkable rock-studded peninsular shoreline, and Roaring Bay, where (with good timing) you can spot yellow-eyed penguins (hoiho). A much more common sight are sea lions and fur seals, which you'll see basking on beaches and camouflaging themselves among the rocks.

★ **Nugget Point**   NATURAL FEATURE
(off Nugget Point Rd) Reach one of the South Island's most jaw-dropping coastal lookouts via the 900m Nugget Point (Tokatā) walkway. Wave-thrashed cliffs give way abruptly to sapphire waters dotted with toothy islets known as the Nuggets. The track to the lighthouse is dotted with poetic placards, and you can spot seals and sea lions lolling below. Look out for bird life, such as soaring tītī (muttonbird) and spoonbills huddling in the lee of the breeze.

Roaring Bay   VIEWPOINT
(Nugget Point Rd) Your best chance of spotting rare yellow-eyed penguins (hoiho) is from a hide at Roaring Bay, 8km south of Kaka Point's main drag. The hide is accessible throughout daylight hours but suggested viewing times are posted on a noticeboard at the car park. Penguin behaviour changes seasonally but times are usually before 7am or after 3pm or 4pm; ask locally or at your guesthouse.

Kaka Point Motels   MOTEL $$
(❷03-412 8602; www.catlins.co.nz; 24 Rata St; d units $145-165; 🅿🛜) Recently upgraded, these modern units all have beautiful views over the ocean. Some have kitchenettes, double-glazed windows and heat pumps to keep out the chill, and a couple have two bedrooms so you can spread out. Free use of surf and body boards.

Point Cafe & Bar   PUB
(❷03-412 8800; 58 Esplanade; ◷restaurant noon-3pm & 5.30-7.30pm Jun-Aug, longer hours Sep-May, shop 11am-6pm, bar noon-late) A one-stop shop for souvenirs, takeaway fried everything or decent full-blown meals of blue cod or lamb shank (mains $19.50 to $29), the Point is best for a beer at a window seat facing the sea – try the locally brewed Catlins Yellow Eyed Pilsner. You can also hire bikes here for $50/40 per day per adult/child.

❶ Getting There & Away

Kaka Point is 20km south of Balclutha on the Southern Scenic Route. You'll need your own vehicle – there is no public transport in the Catlins area.

The Catlins

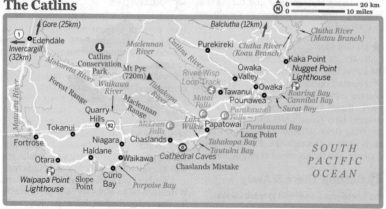

Owaka

Languid Owaka township may be tiny but it has a top-quality museum, a few eating options and a supermarket and petrol station (no vain boast in these parts).

It makes a good base for exploring the Catlins, but most people prefer to stay close to the beach. There's good options 4km southeast of Owaka town at Pounawea, a beautiful hamlet on the edge of the Catlins River Estuary and just across the inlet at Surat Bay, notable for the sea lions that lie around the beach between here and Cannibal Bay, an hour's beach-walk away.

★Purakaunui Falls   WATERFALL
(Purakaunui Falls Rd) If you only see one waterfall in the Catlins, make it this magnificent cascade down three tiers of jet-black rock. It's an easy 10-minute clamber to reach the falls from the small parking area. Purakaunui Falls are almost equidistant between Owaka and Papatowai (respectively 15km and 12km by road).

Owaka Museum &
Catlins Information Centre   MUSEUM
(🖉info centre 03-415 8371, museum 03-415 8323; www.owakamuseum.org.nz; 10 Campbell St; museum adult/child $6/free; ⊙ 9.30am-4.30pm Mon-Fri, 10am-4pm Sat & Sun) Vaguely canoe-shaped in honour of the town name (Owaka means 'place of the canoe'), this modern museum is a pleasant surprise. Salty tales of shipwrecks are well explained in short video presentations, Māori and frontier stories grippingly displayed, and an interesting array of artefacts exhibited. It doubles as the main in-

formation centre for the Catlins; ask about the 24km Catlins River–Wisp Loop Track (www.doc.govt.nz).

Teapotland   LANDMARK
(21 Main Rd) Get a selfie in this wacky collections of teapots and statuettes arranged in Graham Renwick's garden.

Catlins Horse Riding   HORSE RIDING
(🖉027 629 2904; www.catlinshorseriding.co.nz; 41 Newhaven Rd, Owaka; 1/2/3hr rides from $70/110/150) Learners' treks and the full-gallop available, and trips are tailored to your level of experience. Full safety briefing (and glorious coastal views) included. Book ahead. Full-day treks also available (per person from $230).

★Newhaven Holiday Park   HOLIDAY PARK $
(🖉03-415 8834; www.catlinsnewhavenholiday park.com; 324 Newhaven Rd, Surat Bay; unpowered/powered sites from $35/40, units from $85, with bathroom from $120; ⊙Aug-May; 🛜) This exemplary holiday park is on an incredible beach at the entrance to Surat Bay, 5km from Owaka, where sea lion pups can be spotted in December and January. It has a choice of cabins and self-contained units and bags of camping space. The best site is steps from the sand. There's a merry village atmosphere throughout. Showers are $2.

Pounawea Grove Motel   MOTEL $$
(🖉03-415 8339; www.pounaweagrove.co.nz; 5 Ocean Grove, Pounawea; d & tw $150; 🛜) More sophisticated than the average motel, Pounawea Grove has a boutique feel thanks to its roomy units with sharp, modern bathrooms, kitchenettes and plush textiles.

Throw in a warm welcome and the bucolic estuary setting, and a relaxing stay is almost guaranteed.

★ **Mohua Park** COTTAGE $$$
(☑03-415 8613; www.catlinsmohuapark.co.nz; 744 Catlins Valley Rd, Tawanui; cottages $250; ☜) ✦ Situated on the edge of a peaceful 14-hectare nature reserve (7km off the highway), these four spacious self-contained cottages offer peace, quiet and privacy with stunning views. Instead of TV, you'll watch birds flitting through the forest on your doorstep and sigh at views of rolling hills.

❶ Getting There & Away
You'll need your own wheels to reach Owaka.

Papatowai
Nature shows off some of her best angles at Papatowai, which is perched at a meeting of forest, sea and the Tahakopa River. The leafy village has barely 40 inhabitants but swells with holidaymakers in summer, drawn by a languid vibe and glittering views of waterfalls and golden bays.

◉ Sights

Cathedral Caves CAVE
(www.cathedralcaves.co.nz; 1069 Chaslands Hwy; adult/child $5/1; ⊘Nov-May) Cutting back into cliffs right on the beach, the huge, arched Cathedral Caves were carved out of the limestone by 160 million years of waves. Named for their acoustic properties, they are only accessible for two hours at either side of low tide (tide timetables are posted on the website, at the highway turn-off and at visitor information centres) – and even then they can be closed at short notice if the conditions are deemed dangerous. Cash only.

★ **Lost Gypsy Gallery** GALLERY
(☑021 122 8102; www.thelostgypsy.com; 2532 Papatowai Hwy; gallery $8; ⊘10am-5pm Thu-Tue Nov–Apr) Fashioned from remaindered bits and bobs, artist and 'organic mechanic' Blair Somerville's intricately crafted automata are wonderfully irreverent. The bamboozling collection inside a converted bus (free entry) is a teaser for the carnival of creations through the gate (kids under 13 years not allowed, sorry...). The buzz, bong and bright lights of the organ are bound to tickle your ribs. Food truck and wi-fi on-site.

☈ Activities
Eight kilometres north of Papatowai a short walk through verdant forest takes you to **Matai & Horseshoe Falls** (Papatowai Hwy, Caberfeidh) (30 minutes return); from here you can also access the 2km **Matai Rail Trail** following a former rail line through deep cuttings and over high embankments.

Four kilometres west of town, an easy walk along moss-scented pathways and boardwalks takes you out onto the waters of pretty **Lake Wilkie** (Chaslands Hwy) (30 minutes return). If you're pressed for time but want a photo of this Ice Age mirror lake, it's a 10-minute return walk to a lookout point.

A further 7km west, at the Whistling Frog, is the turn-off to **McLean Falls** (off Rewcastle Rd, Chaslands), reached by a thrilling walk along fern-fringed trails. Allow 40 minutes to walk to the falls and back; the car park is 4km from the main highway along a rough road.

Papatowai Freedom Kayak Hire KAYAKING
(☑021 024 12925; www.catlinskayakhirepapatowai.com; 2519 Papatowai Hwy, Papatowai; single/double 2hr rental $45/59, 4hr $55/69) With over 25km of paddle-able waterways, this river-filled region is a great place to kayak. Explore native forest filled with birdsong, fertile estuaries and farmland on a self-guided paddle. Safety briefing, route advice, maps and transport to the river included, no experience necessary.

🛏 Sleeping & Eating

Hilltop LODGE $
(☑03-415 8028; 77 Tahakopa Valley Rd, Papatowai; s/d $100/110) High on a hill 1.5km out of town, with native forest at the back door and surrounded by a sheep farm, these two ship-shape cottages command spectacular views of the Tahakopa Valley and coast. Rent by the room or the whole house ($340 for nine people); the en-suite double is the pick of a very nice bunch.

★ **Whistling Frog** CAFE $$
(☑03-415 8338; www.whistlingfrogresort.com; 9 Rewcastle Rd, Chaslands; mains $17-42.50; ⊘8.30am-8pm Nov-Mar, 10am-6pm Apr, May & Oct, closed Jun-Sep; ☜) Colourful and fun, the Frog is the best dining option in the Catlins, offering craft beer on tap and crowd-pleasing meals, often garnished with flowers from the garden. We're talking seafood chowder, wood-fired pizza, gourmet burgers, craft-beer-battered blue cod, and veggie feeds like risotto and big salads. Excellent coffee and breakfast spreads, too. Ribbit!

There's a holiday park here also with powered/unpowered sites from $55/45, cabins without bathrooms from $110 and motel units from $165.

ℹ Getting There & Away

There is no public transport in the Catlins. Papatowai is a pleasant 36km drive east from Waikawa, or 25km west of Owaka.

Curio Bay

Chasing sun and surf, droves of holiday-makers descend on Curio Bay in summer. For beach lovers the focal point is Porpoise Bay, a reliably wave-lashed arc of sand and arguably the best swimming beach in the Catlins. Hector's dolphins come here to rear their young.

Nearby, other natural curiosities merit a visit: a Jurassic-age forest lies just south in Curio Bay while 15km west is the trailhead for a short walk to Slope Point, South Island's most southerly point.

Curio Bay is whisper-quiet in winter (June to August). Regardless of the season, it's handy to bring food provisions and a full tank of fuel along this sparse stretch of coast.

◉ Sights & Activities

★**Slope Point**   LANDMARK
(Slope Point Rd, Haldane) South Island's true southerly point lies not in Bluff, as many mistakenly believe, but at the end of a 20-minute trudge through a cliff-side cow paddock. From the car park, walk towards the sea and veer left along the fencing; a humble signpost marks this spectacular spot where blackened rocks tumble into turquoise sea while waves smash and swirl below.

Curioscape   MUSEUM
(☑03-246 8897; www.curioscape.co.nz; 590 Waikawa Curio Bay Rd, Curio Bay; museum adult/child $15/2; ⊙10am-10pm Tue-Sun, to 7pm Mon Nov-Apr, shorter hours May-Oct) Incorporated in this new centre is a pleasant cafe (lunch mains $10 to $22, dinner $26 to $38), visitor centre and the Gateway, a modern museum with a multiscreen film experience describing the evolution of the area, and a touchwall to learn about the petrified forest, penguins and local history.

To the side of the centre is the start of the walk to the petrified forest, via a penguin boardwalk that takes you over nest-ing grounds for endangered yellow-eyed penguin (hoiho). They waddle ashore from the beach at dusk and you might see them through the peep flaps, but do the right thing and keep your distance (at least 50m).

Petrified Forest   NATURAL FEATURE
(Curio Bay) FREE Marvel at the rare phenomenon of fossilised forest, extending south of Curio Bay. Preserved by silica in the ashy floodwaters that submerged these Jurassic-era trees, craggy stumps and entire logs create a dramatic contrast with the frothing waves. The wood grain is still clearly visible. The petrified forest is revealed for around four hours either side of low tide.

Waipapā Lighthouse   LIGHTHOUSE
(Waipapā Lighthouse Rd, Otara) FREE Standing on a desolate but beautiful point surrounded by farmland, this 13.4m-high lighthouse was built after the SS *Tararua* disaster, an 1881 shipwreck that claimed 131 lives.

Catlins Surf   SURFING
(☑021 208 0501; www.catlins-surf.co.nz; 601 Curio Bay Rd; 2hr lesson $60, 3hr board & suit hire $50; ⊙Oct-Apr) Based at the Curioscape Campground (☑03-246 8897; www.curioscape.co.nz; 601 Curio Bay Rd; unpowered/powered sites for 2 from $35/40), this surf school offers lessons on Porpoise Bay, much to the amusement of any passing dolphins.

🍽 Sleeping & Eating

★**Slope Point Accommodation**   FARMSTAY $
(☑03-246 8420; www.slopepoint.co.nz; 164 Slope Point Rd, Slope Point; dm $27, d with/without bathroom $90/60, 3-bed cottage for 2 $100; 🐾) In the midst of a working farm 4km north of Slope Point, this family-run accommodation plunges you into the rhythms of rural life: calf-feeding time, scampering pets, and kids eager to introduce you to their favourite lamb. Double rooms and self-contained units are cosy and modern, or there's a whole cottage up the road with amazing views of the estuary.

Lazy Dolphin Lodge   HOSTEL $
(☑03-246 8579; www.lazydolphinlodge.co.nz; 529 Curio Bay Rd; dm/r without bathroom $40/90; @🐾) This perfect hybrid of seaside holiday home and hostel has light-filled bedrooms sporting cheerful linen. There are two kitchens and lounges, but you'll want to hang out upstairs on the deck overlooking Porpoise Bay. A path at the rear of the property leads directly to the beach.

★ **Curio Bay**

Accommodation APARTMENT **$$**

(☑ 03-246 8797; www.curiobay.co.nz; 521a Curio Bay Rd; apt $190-260; 🛜) Three plush units are on offer here – one apartment attached to the hosts' house, and two similar units down the road. All are self-contained, decorated in rustic, beachy style, with big windows and sun-drenched decks right next to the beach. There's also an old-fashioned Kiwi bach, sleeping up to six people. No TV, but plenty of books and games to occupy you instead.

★ **Niagara Falls** CAFE **$$**

(☑ 03-246 8577; www.niagarafallscafe.co.nz; 256 Niagara–Waikawa Rd, Niagara; mains $15-25; ☺ 10am-3pm & 9pm-late daily Dec-Feb, 11am-4pm Thu-Mon Mar-May & Jul-Nov, closed Jun; 🛜 ♿) ✔ Located in a former Victorian schoolhouse, this excellent 'old-school' cafe puts the emphasis on local produce – free-range eggs, veggies from the garden, house-smoked salmon and spring water (fill your bottle). Chef Laura Thompson moonlights as coach of the NZ Paralympic cycling team – her gold, silver and bronze medals for riding as tandem bicycle pilot at London and Rio are casually displayed in the corner.

❶ Getting There & Away

There is no public transport to Curio Bay. Curio and Porpoise Bays are 4km south of Waikawa.

ESSENTIAL FIORDLAND & SOUTHLAND
·····································

Eat Bluff oysters, a New Zealand gourmet obsession, followed by Stewart Island salmon, whitebait and blue cod.

Drink Hokonui Moonshine Whisky in Gore.

Read poems by Hone Tuwhare (1922–2008), who drew inspiration from the landscapes of the Catlins.

Listen to roaring surf in Te Waewae, the crackle of static on road trips (radio signal is patchy), and dead silence in Doubtful Sound.

Watch *The World's Fastest Indian* (director: Roger Donaldson, 2005), to understand Invercargill's devotion to the legacy of Burt Munro.

Go online www.fiordland.org.nz, https://southlandnz.com

CENTRAL SOUTHLAND

Sandwiched between world-famous Fiordland National Park and the scene-stealing Catlins, Central Southland is often forgotten about by travellers. But its peaceful farmland and savage coast form a memorable contrast, while its seam of small-town quirk is heaps of fun.

There's Gore, with a proud history of moonshine distilling; oyster-mad Bluff; and Tuatapere, famous for its challenging hiking trails. Invercargill, the closest thing to a city slicker in Central Southland, has a long-standing revhead culture and a slew of impressive museums dedicated to classic cars, fast bikes and big diggers.

Gore

POP 12,033

Gore struts to its own beat. The town declares itself New Zealand's 'home of country music', and 'brown trout capital of the world'. If that wasn't enough to boast about, it also had a proud history of illegal distilleries and creative collectors, all of which it celebrates through the Gold Guitar Awards (www.goldguitars.co.nz; ☺ May/Jun), the Hokonui Moonshine Festival (☑ 03-208 9907; www.moonshinefest.co.nz) and its excellent set of distinctive museums.

Hokonui Moonshine Museum MUSEUM

(☑ 03-203 9288; www.gorenz.com/visit/things-to-see-do/hokonui-moonshine-museum; 16 Hokonui Dr; adult/child $5/free; ☺ 9am-4.30pm Mon-Fri, to 3pm Sat & Sun) In the early 20th century, Gore's enterprising Scottish immigrants responded to 50 years of prohibition by distilling their own moonshine. This museum shines a tongue-in-cheek light on some colourful characters and whisky-drenched escapades of the era. On display is fascinating homemade distilling apparatus hidden for decades in the back of local sheds.

Admission includes three tastes of the local tipple ranging from rough to polished – 'fast and furious', 'whisky wannabe' and 'dessert'; also available for purchase.

Located in the Hokonui Heritage Centre at the time of research, the museum will expand into its own building in late 2020, and launch an on-site distillery.

Eastern Southland Gallery GALLERY

(☑ 03-208 9907; www.facebook.com/easternsouthlandgallery; 14 Hokonui Dr; ☺ 10am-4.30pm Mon-Fri, 1-4pm Sat & Sun) FREE Nicknamed the

'Goreggenheim', this gallery has a truly impressive treasury of contemporary New Zealand art, including a large Ralph Hotere collection and works by esteemed NZ artist Rita Angus. There's also a fascinating indigenous folk art collection from West Africa and Australia. It's worth breaking up a road trip in Gore purely to step inside this attractive brick building; allow an hour to sidle between hefty Congolese statues, Ivory Coast masks and temporary exhibitions of thought-provoking modern art.

Croydon Aviation Heritage Centre　　　SCENIC FLIGHTS
(☑ 03-208 6046; www.croydonaviation.co.nz; 1558 Waimea Hwy, SH94; adult/child $12/free; ☺ 9.30am-4.30pm Mon-Fri Oct-Apr, 10am-4pm May-Sep) Aircraft from the 1930s and '40s are lovingly restored and showcased within Croydon Aviation's hangar, 16km northwest of Gore on SH94 (towards Queenstown). But that's just a taster of life in the air: you can also book a flight in a two-seater 1930s Tiger Moth biplane or other wee aircraft (from $150 for 15 minutes). A restored steam railway runs once a month on open days (adult/child $5/2.50). There's a stylish cafe (☑ 03-208 9662; www.misscocoa.co.nz; 1558 Waimea Hwy, SH94; mains $20; ☺ 7am-4pm Mon-Fri, 10am-4pm Sat & Sun) and gift store attached to the aviation centre.

❶ Information

Gore Visitor Centre (www.gorevisitorcentre.co.nz; 16 Hokonui Dr; ☺ 9am-5pm Mon-Fri, to 3pm Sat & Sun) Sharing the premises is the **Gore Historical Museum** (☑ 03-203 9288; www.gorenz.com/visit/things-to-see-do/gore-museum; 16 Hokonui Dr; admission free; ☺ 9am-4.30pm Mon-Fri, to 3pm Sat & Sun), which celebrates the town's history.

❶ Getting There & Away

Gore is a 66km drive northeast of Invercargill. Most buses on the Te Anau–Dunedin, Invercargill–Queenstown and Invercargill–Dunedin routes stop in Gore, including **Intercity** (☑ 03-471 7143; www.intercity.co.nz), which runs to Invercargill (from $13, one hour), Dunedin (from $22, two hours), Te Anau (from $33, 1½ hours) and Queenstown (from $71, 9½ hours).

Invercargill

POP 51,700

Poor old Invercargill has lost much of its mojo lately with the closure of both its Anderson Park gallery and Southland Museum

due to earthquake risks and the transformation of its inner city into a construction site as a new mall is built.

Thank goodness for its trio of motoring attractions, which keep alive the legacy of Burt Munro. The local legend still holds the world land-speed record for an under-1000cc motorcycle, which he set in 1967 at the age of 68 riding a 47-year-old bike that he modified himself in Invercargill.

◎ Sights

★ Transport World　　　MUSEUM
(☑ 0800 151 252; www.transportworld.co.nz; 491 Tay St; adult/child $30/20; ☺ 10am-5pm; ♿) A kingdom of shiny chrome lies beyond the doors of Transport World, touted as the largest private automotive museum on the planet. Across 15,000 sq metres of warehouse space you'll find classic cars, hulking tractors and vintage petrol pumps (even the bathrooms are on theme). Kids' play areas, a miniature movie theatre, displays of fashions of yesteryear and a great cafe round out Transport World as a crowd-pleaser, rather than just one for the petrolheads.

Revved up for more? Smaller museum **Classic Motorcycle Mecca** (☑ 0800 151 252; www.transportworld.co.nz; 25 Tay St; adult/child $25/15; ☺ 10am-5pm) holds a collection of bikes, while **Dig This** (☑ 0800 151 252; www.transportworld.co.nz; 84 Otepuni Ave; ☺ 9am-5pm; ♿) puts you behind the controls of a bulldozer to dig ditches, stack tyres and smash cars. A 'Turbo Pass' (adult/child $48/28) grants access to both Transport World and Classic Motorcycle Mecca.

E Hayes & Sons　　　MUSEUM
(☑ 03-218 2059; www.ehayes.co.nz; 168 Dee St; ☺ 7.30am-5.30pm Mon-Fri, 9am-4pm Sat & Sun) FREE Hardware shops aren't usually a mustsee, but this one holds a piece of motoring history. In among the aisles of bolts, barbecues and brooms in this classic art-deco building are more than 100 items of motoring memorabilia, including the actual motorbike on which the late Burt Munro broke the world speed record (as immortalised in the 2005 film *The World's Fastest Indian*, starring Sir Anthony Hopkins).

⊨ Sleeping

★ Southern Comfort Backpackers　　　HOSTEL $
(☑ 03-218 3838; www.southerncomfortbackpackers.com; 30 Thomson St, Avenal; dm/d without bathroom from $32/75; @ 🛜) A mix of snug and swish, this large Victorian house has

a lounge with a fireplace, a fully equipped kitchen and peaceful gardens. Adding to the perks are the use of two free bikes, a laundry and a herb garden where you can pluck your own garnish. A restful package, just five minutes' walk from town.

Invercargill Top 10   HOLIDAY PARK $
(✆03-215 9032, 0800 486 873; www.invercargill top10.co.nz; 77 McIvor Rd, Waikiwi; campervan sites per person from $22, units $115, d without bathroom $85; 🏕 🛜) 🚲 Continually upgrading and adding facilities, this well-kept park has backpacker dorms, modern motels and plenty of lush grass to camp upon, along with well-tended communal kitchens, laundry facilities and lounges. It's 6.5km north of town. Consider the new shingled hobbit pod ($100) near the outdoor pizza oven.

Victoria Railway Hotel   HOTEL $$
(✆0800777557,03-2181281;www.hotelinvercargill. com; cnr Leven & Esk Sts; r $155-185; P🛜) This beautifully restored 1896 building is awash with nostalgia and is a little worn, but comfy, like a favourite armchair. With old portraits and an old-fashioned bar, the dining area feels like a snapshot of more genteel times, amplified by kind, personalised service.

Quest Apartments   APARTMENT $$$
(✆03-211 3966; www.questapartments.co.nz; 10 Dee St; studio $124-204; 🛜) The vibe is business more than pleasure, but serviced apartments from this accommodation chain have perfectly kitted-out studios and apartments (good cotton bedsheets, trim kitchens, modern bathrooms, in-room laundry, solid wi-fi) within easy walking distance of Dee St's food and drink scene. Good value.

🍴 Eating & Drinking

Seriously Good Chocolate Company   CAFE $
(✆03-218 8060; www.seriouslygoodchocolate.nz; 147 Spey St; bakery items $6.90-8.40; ⊙8am-4pm Mon-Fri, 8.30am-1.30pm Sat) The fantastic smell hits you as soon as you walk in the door: house-made chocolates. This is a great place to pick up tasty Kiwi gifts, like chocolate-covered Allpress coffee beans, hokey pokey, and suspicious but delicious 'sheep poo'. If you don't have a sweet tooth, it also does great lunch and coffee.

★ Batch   CAFE $$
(✆03-214 6357; 173 Spey St; mains $13.50-20; ⊙7am-4.30pm Mon-Fri, 8am-4pm Sat & Sun;

🛜📵) Large shared tables, a relaxed beachy ambience, and top-notch coffee and smoothies give this cafe its reputation as Southland's best. Delicious counter food includes bagels, generously crammed rolls, cheese scones and great salads, along with full-blown brunches and cakes that are little works of art.

★ Louie's   MODERN NZ $$
(✆03-214 2913; www.facebook.com/pg/Louies Restaurant; 142 Dee St; tapas $13-16, mains $32-35; ⊙5.30pm-late Tue-Sat) Part tapas and cocktail bar, part chic fusion eatery, Louie's is a great place to while away an evening snuggled into a sofa or a fireside nook. The seasonally changing menu veers from creative tapas (venison tacos, muttonbird, mussels with lime and chilli) to more substantial mains. Slow-cooked pork, locally sourced blue cod, magnificent steaks...you can't go wrong.

Elegance at 148 on Elles   FRENCH, BRITISH $$$
(✆03-216 1000; 148 Elles Rd, Georgetown; mains $37-40; ⊙6-11pm Mon-Sat; 📵) Welcome to 1984, and we mean that in a completely affectionate way. Where else can you still get a shrimp cocktail? Elegance is the sort of old-fashioned, upmarket, regional restaurant where the menu is vaguely French, vaguely British, and the venison is perfectly cooked atop a bed of creamy mash. Vegos: ask for the special menu.

Tillermans Music Lounge   BAR, CLUB
(✆027 482 2677; www.facebook.com/tillermans; 16 Don St; ⊙10pm-3.30am Thu-Sat) The saviour of Southland's live-music scene, Tillerman's hosts everything from thrash to flash, with a battered old dance floor to show for it. Visit the fun downstairs Vinyl Bar, which is open from 8pm Friday and Saturday, to find out what's coming up. It's behind Devil Burger.

❶ Information

Invercargill i-SITE (✆03-211 0895; www. southlandnz.com; Wachner Pl; ⊙8.30am-5pm Mon-Fri, to 4pm Sat & Sun) The i-SITE can help with general enquiries, including about Stewart Island/Rakiura and the Catlins.

❶ Getting There & Away

AIR
Air New Zealand (www.airnewzealand.com) Flights link Invercargill Airport to Christchurch and Wellington daily and Auckland around four times weekly.

Invercargill

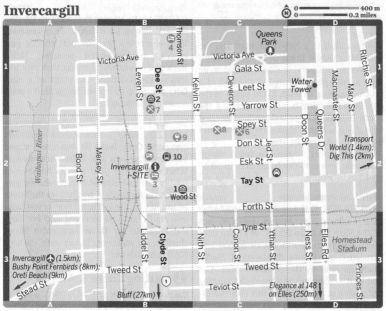

Invercargill

◎ Sights
1 Classic Motorcycle Mecca B2
2 E Hayes & Sons B1

⌂ Sleeping
3 Quest Apartments B2
4 Southern Comfort
   Backpackers B1
5 Victoria Railway Hotel B2

✕ Eating
6 Batch C2
7 Louie's B1
8 Seriously Good Chocolate Company ... C2

◐ Drinking & Nightlife
9 Tillermans Music Lounge B2

✦ Transport
10 InterCity B2
   Tracknet...(see 10)

Stewart Island Flights (☏ 03-218 9129; www. stewartislandflights.co.nz; Airport Ave; adult/ child return $220/135) Connects Invercargill to Stewart Island/Rakiura three times a day year-round.

BUS

Buses leave from Dee St outside the Invercargill i-SITE (p536), where you can also book your tickets.

Catch-a-Bus South (☏ 24hr 027 449 7994; www.catchabussouth.com) Offers scheduled shuttle services at least daily to Bluff ($25, 35 minutes), Queenstown ($60, three to 3¼ hours), Queenstown Airport ($65, three hours), Gore ($30, 1½ hours) and Dunedin ($60, 3½ hours). Book ahead.

InterCity (☏ 03-471 7143; www.intercity.co.nz) Direct coaches to and from Gore ($14, one

hour, two or three daily), Queenstown ($49, 3½ hours, daily) and Queenstown Airport (from $49, 3½ hours, daily).

Tracknet (☏ 03-249 7777; https://tracknet. net) Runs to Te Anau ($51) and Queenstown ($51) once daily.

✦ Getting Around

Invercargill Airport (☏ 03-218 6920; www. invercargillairport.co.nz; 106 Airport Ave) is 3km west of central Invercargill. The door-to-door **Executive Car Service** (☏ 03-214 3434; https://executivecarservice.co.nz) costs around $20 from the city centre; more for residential pickup. By taxi it's around $20; try **Blue Star Taxis** (☏ 03-217 7777; www.bluestar taxis.co.nz).

Bluff

POP 1794

Mention Bluff to a New Zealander and the first thing they'll think of is oysters. Bluff is Invercargill's port, windswept and more than a little bleak, located at the end of a protruding strip of land, 27km south of the city. Bluff's bulging bivalves are among the South Island's most prized produce, guzzled with gusto between March and August, and feted with a festival in May.

Outside oyster season, the main reason folk come here is to catch the ferry to Stewart Island/Rakiura.

Bluff Maritime Museum MUSEUM

(☑03-212 7534; 241 Foreshore Rd; adult/child $3/1; ⊙10am-4.30pm Mon-Fri year-round, plus 12.30-4.30pm Sat & Sun Oct-Apr; ⛫) Salty tales whisper from the portholes, driftwood and barnacle-clung planks displayed at Bluff's small museum by the container port. The best part is clambering aboard the *Monica* and posing at the control of this 1909 oystering boat, though steam and pump engines (which clank to action at the touch of a button) come a close second.

BLUFF OYSTERS

Bluff oysters are in huge demand from the minute they come into season (late March to late August). Top restaurants as far away as Auckland compete to be the first to add them to their menus. As oysters go, they're whoppers. Don't expect to be able to slurp one down in a dainty gulp – these beasts take some chewing. If you want to know what all the fuss is about, you can buy fresh or battered Bluff oysters when they're in season from Fowlers Oysters, on the left-hand side as you head into town.

Up by the signpost for **Stirling Point** (off SH1) is **Oyster Cove** (☑03-212 8855; www.oystercove.co.nz; 8 Ward Pde; half-dozen oysters from $27, mains $25-32; ⊙11am-7.30pm Sep-Mar, to 4pm Apr-Aug; 🛜), where you can guzzle oysters while admiring sea views through epic, wraparound windows. Or time your visit for the annual **Bluff Oyster & Food Festival** (www.bluffoysterfest. co.nz; ⊙May).

Jimi Rabbitz Gallery ART STUDIO

(☑03-212 7611; https://helenback.com; 158 Gore St; ⊙11am-4pm Sat & Sun, or by appointment) With characters that are part cheeky, part creepy, award-winning sculptor Helen Back makes whimsical works that look like they've stepped from the pages of a dark fairy tale. Stop by her studio on Bluff's main street to take a peek.

Fowlers Oysters SEAFOOD $$

(☑03-212 8792; www.facebook.com/fowlers oysters; 99 Ocean Beach Rd; half-dozen battered $12, dozen raw from $24; ⊙9am-7pm Mar-Aug) Whether you like your oysters battered or freshly shucked, stop at Fowlers during oyster season for the best bivalves on the South Island. It's on the left-hand side as you head into Bluff. Battered blue cod and hot dogs are available for those squeamish about slurping on molluscs. Hours vary, cash or NZ bank cards only.

❶ Getting There & Away

Catch-a-Bus South (☑03-479 9960; www. catchabussouth.com) Offers scheduled shuttle services to Invercargill ($25, 30 minutes, two daily), Gore ($47, two hours, two daily) and Dunedin ($85, four hours, two daily). With prior notice, daily buses reach Queenstown Airport ($90, 3½ hours) and Queenstown ($85, 3¾ hours).

Stewart Island Experience (☑03-212 7660; www.stewartislandexperience.co.nz) Runs a shuttle (adult/child $28/14) between Bluff and Invercargill connecting with its Stewart Island/Rakiura ferry. Transfers from Te Anau and Queenstown to Bluff are available from late November to April.

Riverton

POP 1430

Quiet and friendly little Riverton (in Māori, Aparima) is worth a detour for its dreamy bay views and gripping museum of local history. If near-Antarctic swimming takes your fancy, the long, broad sands of **Taramea Bay** are good for a dip; otherwise take a stroll along **Palmerston St**, studded with cafes and 19th-century buildings.

⭐ **Te Hikoi Southern Journey** MUSEUM

(☑03-234 8260; www.tehikoi.co.nz; 172 Palmerston St; adult/child $9/free; ⊙10am-4pm Apr-Sep, to 5pm Oct-Mar) Oh, that all small-town museums could be this good! The riveting Riverton museum starts with a 16-minute film about Pākehā sealer Jack Price and his

Māori wife Hinewhitia who were stranded on the Solander Islands, far south of Fiordland. Legends behind the landscape are entertainingly told, as are anecdotes about characters including cabbage-tree rum distillers, heroic castaways and the first recorded Pākehā (white European) Māori, James Caddell.

Southland Surf School SURFING
(☑ 027 864 7230; www.facebook.com/www.surfing nz.co.nz; 1½hr group lessons incl gear from $50, private lessons from $120; ⊘ Nov-Apr) Despite the chill, Riverton is an excellent place to learn to surf, with a very reliable, gentle break at Riverton Rocks on Taramea Beach. Former NZ champion surfer Jess Terrill runs this surf school and rents gear ($50 per day for suit and surfboard or paddleboard). She also has studio accommodation (doubles with en suite and kitchenette $150) right opposite the beach.

★ Beach House MODERN NZ **$$**
(☑ 03-234 8274; www.rivertonbeachhouse.co.nz; 126 Rocks Hwy; mains lunch $18-32, dinner $34-44; ⊘ 10am-4pm Mon & Tue, until late Wed-Sun Nov-Mar, 10am-4pm Wed, until late Thu-Sun Apr-Oct; 🛜) Looking over Taramea Bay, Beach House is a stylish, comfortable cafe famous for seafood, especially its creamy chowder studded with juicy mussels and hunks of salmon. On a sunny day with a warm breeze wafting off Foveaux Strait you can admire the distant snow-capped peaks from the outside tables. The other 90% of the time, retire inside to admire them through the windows.

❶ Getting There & Away

Riverton is on SH99, on the Southern Scenic Route. **Riverton Freight** (☑ 027 433 9678; $8.50) runs twice daily on weekdays to/from Invercargill.

Te Waewae & Colac Bays

Between Riverton and Tuatapere on SH99, a section of the Southern Scenic Route, long, moody bays set a steely glare towards Antarctica. If you're travelling from the east, driving this stretch of SH99 provides a first glimpse of the snow-capped Southern Alps descending into the sea, framing the western end of the bay.

Colac Bay has a small but dedicated following among hardy surfers, but most travellers simply stop for a brisk dip or a beach stroll before continuing the drive. Further west, Monkey Island (off SH99, Orepuki) is a former Māori whaling lookout accessible at low tide. And just beyond, what's this? A beacon of gastronomic hope, beaming out good vibes along a desolate stretch of highway? The chipper, award-winning Orepuki Beach Cafe (☑ 03-234 5211; www.facebook. com/pg/orepukibeachcafe; cnr Dudley & Stafford Sts, SH99, Orepuki; mains $19-29; ⊘ 9am-5pm Sun-Thu, to 11pm Fri & Sat; ☑) 🍃 grows its own salad veg, bakes its own bread, grinds its own beef and rears its own lamb right there on the paddock between the cafe and the ocean. Pure seaside charm.

One kilometre further is Orepuki Beach, nicknamed 'Gemstone Beach' for the lovely stones that occasionally wash up here, including quartz, jasper and even sapphire. Seven kilometres further, pause at McCracken's Rest (SH99), a lovely lookout point with views of wind-lashed Te Waewae Bay (and, if you're lucky, Hector's dolphins and southern right whales).

Tuatapere

POP 558
Formerly a timber-milling town, sleepy Tuatapere is gently shaken awake by hikers who pass through before embarking on the Hump Ridge (p528) or Dusky (p528) Tracks. The town's early woodcutters were very efficient, so only a remnant of a once-large tract of native podocarp (conifer) forest remains.

Wairaurahiri Wilderness Jet BOATING
(☑ 0800 270 556; www.river-jet.co.nz; 17 Main St, Otautau; day tours incl lunch from $270) Offers jetboat rides on the Wairaurahiri River, packaged together with a guided forest walk (total six hours). Other options include a jetboat-helicopter combo or overnighting at the remote Waitutu Lodge.

Clifden Caves CAVING
(www.doc.govt.nz; Clifden Gorge Rd) **FREE**
Around 16km north of Tuatapere (1km north of Clifden), this 22-million-year-old natural limestone cave is a strange find in a sheep paddock. You can travel the 300m underground route marked by orange triangles (allow 1½ to two hours) to see stalactites, stalagmites and glow worms (titiwai). It requires some ladder-climbing, squeezing, crawling and a sidle along a narrow ledge.

Bring two torches (flashlights) per person in case one fails, tell someone your plans and don't take any unmarked corridors. It's signposted from the highway – download the DOC brochure for more information.

Last Light Lodge
CAFE $$

(☑03-226 6667; www.lastlightlodge.com; 2 Clifden Hwy; mains $19-37; ⊗8.30am-late; 🐾) 🍴 This friendly cafe, surrounded by food gardens, bees and a chook run, stands out for its homemade cookies, pies and truffles, and smoothies thick enough to hold up a straw. There's a good all-day selection of food: fish and chips, panini, chicken curry and plenty more. The deck is a fine place to tackle a beer in fair weather.

It also has fairly ordinary rooms in a former forestry workers' bunkhouse (single/double $60/90), though its campsites (from $16), edged with edible plants, are lovely. Dorm beds in a yurt are $22, though they get hot in summer.

ℹ Information

Hump Ridge Track Office (☑03-226 6739, 0800 486 774; www.humpridgetrack.co.nz; 31 Orawia Rd; ⊗7.30am-5.30pm Nov-Apr) Assists with local information, accommodation, Hump Ridge hut passes and transport.

ℹ Getting There & Away

Buses must be booked through the Hump Ridge Track Office; with demand, services go to/from Queenstown ($95, 2½ to 3¾ hours), Te Anau ($50, 1¾ hours) and Invercargill ($60, 1½ hours), and also to the Rarakau car park at the trailhead ($45 return).

STEWART ISLAND/ RAKIURA

POP 380

Visitors to Stewart Island often imagine they've been transported to a primordial wilderness, dominated by birds and filled with ferny gullies that spill down to pristine beaches – the kind where a moa might step into view at any moment. Time travel aside, this is a great place to spot the moa's more compact cousin, the kiwi, in the wild. The island is a bird sanctuary of international repute, and even amateur spotters will be distracted by the glorious squawking, singing and flitting of feathery flocks.

It's also famous for its amazing walks, from 10-minute strolls to 10-day treks, including a Great Walk. Some people even get lucky and see the aurora australis (the Southern Lights). Stewart Island is the world's southernmost International Dark Sky Sanctuary (for an aurora forecast check www.aurora-service.net/aurora-forecast).

The main community of Oban is a welcoming town with everything you need for a comfortable stay. But don't get stuck here or you'll miss the best the island has to offer. Get out on the trails!

History

Stewart Island's Māori name is Rakiura (Glowing Skies). According to myth, New Zealand was hauled up from the ocean by Māui, who said, 'Let us go out of sight of land, far out in the open sea, and when we have quite lost sight of land, then let the anchor be dropped'. The North Island was the

---

SPOTTING A KIWI

Stewart Island/Rakiura is one of the few places on earth where you can spot a kiwi in the wild. As big as a barnyard chicken, with a population estimated to number around 13,000 birds, the Stewart Island/Rakiura brown kiwi (*Apteryx australis lawryi*, also known as the tokoeka) is larger in size, longer in the beak and thicker in the legs than its northern cousins.

The birds are most easily spotted in grassed areas where they are less camouflaged, and sometimes even on beaches where they mine sandhoppers under washed-up kelp. Use a red torch (or put red cellophane over your usual torch) to increase your chances. If you spot one, keep silent, and stay still and well away. The birds' poor eyesight and single-mindedness in searching for food will sometimes lead them to bump right into you.

Organised tours are your best bet for a sighting, as locals know where kiwi families have most recently been spotted. Given the island's fickle weather – with tours sometimes cancelled – allow a few nights here if you're desperate for an encounter. Otherwise, some people get lucky and spot the birds in and around Oban itself. Try the bushy fringes of Traill Park or the path to Bathing Beach after sundown.

fish that Māui caught, the South Island his canoe and Rakiura was the anchor – Te Punga o te Waka o Māui. The sculpture of the giant chain at the start of the Rakiura Track, which (symbolically) runs beneath the Foveaux Strait to reemerge at Stirling Point (p538) in Bluff, is a reference to this story.

There is evidence that parts of Rakiura were occupied by moa (bird) hunters as early as the 13th century. The tītī (muttonbird) on adjacent islands were an important seasonal food source for the southern Māori.

The first European visitor was Captain Cook. Sailing around the eastern, southern and western coasts in 1770 he mistook it for the bottom end of the South Island and promptly named it South Cape. In 1809 the sealing vessel *Pegasus* circumnavigated Rakiura and named it after its first officer, William Stewart.

Flora & Fauna

With an absence of mustelids (ferrets, stoats and weasels) and large areas of intact forest, Stewart Island/Rakiura has one of the largest and most diverse bird populations of anywhere in NZ. Even in the streets of Oban the air resonates with birds such as tui, bellbirds and kaka, which share their island home with weka, kakariki, fernbirds, robins and Rakiura tokoeka/kiwi. There are also plenty of shore- and seabirds, including dotterels, shags, mollymawks (albatross), prions and petrels, as well as the tītī (muttonbirds), which are seen in large numbers during breeding season. Ask locals about the evening parade of penguins on cliffs near the wharf; and *please* – don't feed the birds. It's bad for them.

Exotic animals include two species of deer, the red and the Virginia (whitetail), introduced in the early 20th century, as were brushtail possums, which are now numerous throughout the island and destructive to the native bush. Stewart Island/Rakiura also has NZ fur seals, NZ sea lions and (rare) elephant seals dawdling on its beaches and rocky shores.

Beech, the tree that dominates much of NZ, is absent from Stewart Island/Rakiura. The predominant lowland bush is podocarp (conifer) forest, with exceptionally tall rimu, miro and totara forming the canopy. Because of mild winters, frequent rainfall and porous soil, most of the island is a lush forest, thick with vines and carpeted in deep green ferns and mosses.

DON'T MISS

WALKING RAKIURA

Rakiura National Park protects 85% of the island, making it a paradise for hikers and birdwatchers. There are plenty of trails to explore the wilderness, including short, easy tracks from Oban – pick up the *Stewart Island/Rakiura Short Walks* brochure ($2) from DOC's visitor centre (p545) or download it for free. Popular day-hike destinations include Māori Beach and nearby Port William (p529), Ackers Point or Observation Rock (Map p544).

For multiday hikers who have booked ahead there's the stunning Rakiura Track Great Walk (p529), the advanced 71.5km Southern Circuit Track and the epic North West Circuit (p529), one of New Zealand's most isolated backcountry hikes.

Longer hikes can also be shortened via water taxis (p545) or an air hop with Stewart Island Flights (p545). The latter offers the fulfilling day-long Coast to Coast cross-island hike with air and water transfers ($235).

⊙ Sights & Activities

★ Ulva Island   WILDLIFE RESERVE

(Te Wharawhara) A tiny paradise covering only 269 hectares, Ulva Island / Te Wharawhara is a great place to see lots of native birds. Established as a bird sanctuary in 1922, it remains one of Stewart Island/Rakiura's wildest corners. The island was declared rat-free in 1997 and three years later was chosen as the site to release endangered South Island saddlebacks. Any water-taxi company will run you to the island (around $25 return) from Stewart Island's Golden Bay wharf, with scheduled services offered by Ulva Island Ferry (☑03-219 1013; return adult/child $20/10; ⊙departs 9am, 10am, noon, 2pm, 4pm, returns 12.15pm, 2.15pm, 4.15pm Sep-May, also returns 6pm Dec-Feb).

Rakiura Museum   MUSEUM

(Map p544; ☑03-219 1221; www.rakiuramuseum.co.nz; 9 Ayr St, Halfmoon Bay; adult/child $2/50c; ⊙10am-1.30pm Mon-Sat, noon-2pm Sun) Historic photographs are the stars of this small museum focused on local natural and human history, and featuring Māori artefacts, whaling gear and household items. Cash only.

Stewart Island/Rakiura (North)

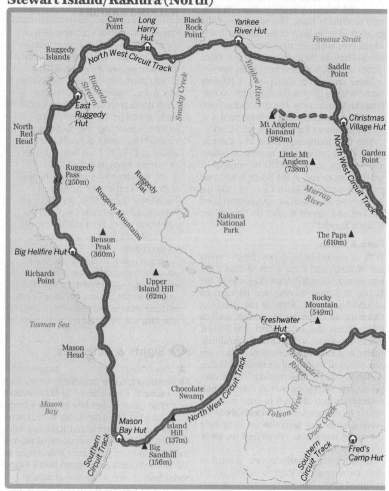

Big plans are in the works for a revamped, state-of-the-art Rakiura Museum to open on Main Rd, next to the DOC office, in mid-2020.

Rakiura Jade ARTS & CRAFTS
(Map p544; ☎ 021 025 93958; www.rakiurajade.co.
nz; 45 Elgin Tce; $180; ⊗ 10.30am-3pm Oct-Apr, reduced hours May, Aug & Sep) Step into Dave Goodin's atmospheric workshop suspended right over the water to learn the skills of carving *pounamu* (greenstone). Over 4½ hours Dave will guide you through selecting the right piece of stone, carving and polishing it, and even braiding the twine to hang it around your neck.

👉 Tours

Beaks & Feathers WALKING
(Map p544; ☎ 027 316 3077; www.beaksandfeathers.
co.nz; 12 Main Rd, Oban; ⊗ 9am-5pm Oct-Jun) 🌱
Small-group tours with Ange, a passionate local guide, including half-day tours of Ulva Island (from $220), kiwi spotting on the airstrip (from $100), as well as tours with a holistic healing slant, such as a mindful meditation walk (from $140) and a walk focused on medicinal and healing native plants (from $140).

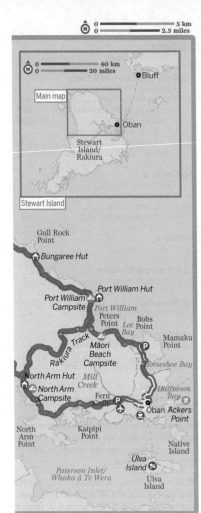

Ruggedy Range Wilderness Experience   ECOTOUR

(Map p544; ☑ 027 478 4433, 03-219 1066; www.ruggedyrange.com; 14 Main Rd, Oban) ✦ Highly customisable tours with a nature focus offered on land and water (through co-owned Aihe Eco Charters & Water Taxi, www.aihe.co.nz). Options include walking, cruising, flying, bus touring, wildlife viewing (including kiwi), photography and combo packages featuring any of these, tailored to your interests. See the websites for a wide range of offerings.

Rakiura Charters & Water Taxi   BOATING

(Map p544; ☑ 03-219 1487, 0800 725 487; www.rakiuracharters.co.nz; 10 Main Rd, Oban; adult/child from $130/90) Pelagic birding tours and water-taxi services. A popular trip is to Port William (adult/child $50/25), the first hut on the Rakiura Track, from where you can walk back to Oban along the track (12km, three to five hours). Trips can be tailored to suit timing and interests, such as wildlife-spotting and hiking.

Phil's Sea Kayak   KAYAKING

(☑ 027 444 2323; www.seakayakstewartisland.nz; 2½-/4½-hour trips $90/145; ☉ Oct–May) Stewart Island/Rakiura's only kayaking guide, Phil runs trips on Paterson Inlet tailored for all abilities, with sightings of wildlife along the way.

Stewart Island Experience   TOURS

(Map p544; ☑ 03-219 0056, 0800 000 511; www.stewartislandexperience.co.nz; 12 Elgin Tce) ✦ This large operator runs 2½-hour Ulva Island Explorer cruises (adult/child $99/30), including a 1¼-hour guided walk; and 1½-hour minibus tours of Oban and the surrounding bays ($49/30). There's also a Wild Kiwi Encounter between September and May ($199).

Ulva's Guided Walks   WALKING

(☑ 027 688 1332; www.ulva.co.nz) ✦ Focused firmly on birding and guided by expert naturalists, these excellent half-day tours (adult/child $145/70; transport included) explore Ulva Island in small groups, developed by Ulva Goodwillie who is named after the island. Book at the Stewart Island Gift Shop (Map p544; ☑ 03-219 1453; www.facebook.com/StewartIslandGiftShop; 20 Main Rd, Oban; ☉ 10.30am-5pm Sep-Apr, by appointment May-Aug). There are also kiwi-spotting tours to Mamaku Point (from $130 per person including transport).

🛌 Sleeping

Finding accommodation can be difficult, especially in the low season when many places shut down – book ahead. The island has many holiday rentals, which are often good value and offer the benefit of self-catering, which is especially handy if you do a spot of fishing. (Note that many impose a two-night minimum stay or charge a surcharge for one night.) For holiday listings, see www.stewartisland.co.nz.

Oban

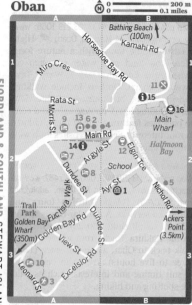

N 0 ——— 200 m
0 ——— 0.1 miles

Jo & Andy's B&B
B&B $

(Map p544; ☑ 027 455 2191, 03-219 1230; jriksem @gmail.com; 22 Main Rd, Oban; s $70, d & tw $100; P 🛜) A great option for budget travellers, this cosy blue home offers rooms with shared-bathroom facilities. A big breakfast of muesli, fruit and eggs prepares you for the most active of days and free transfers are available. Jo is splendid company and there are hundreds of books if the weather packs up. Bookings essential; two-night minimum stay.

Bunkers Backpackers
HOSTEL $

(Map p544; ☑ 027 738 1796; www.bunkersback packers.co.nz; 14 Argyle St, Oban; dm/d $35/85; ⊙ closed May-Sep; 🛜) A converted wooden villa houses Stewart Island/Rakiura's smaller, but better, hostel option. It's somewhat squeezed but offers the benefits of a cosy lounge, a sunny garden, an inner-village location and a friendly, shoes-off vibe. Perks include a barbecue area, hammock chairs and board games.

Bay Motel
MOTEL $$

(Map p544; ☑ 03-219 1119; www.baymotel.co.nz; 9 Dundee St, Oban; units from $180, with spa from $205; P 🛜) This hillside motel offers spacious, comfortable units with lots of light, views over the harbour and a shared balcony. Some rooms have spa baths, all have

kitchens, and two are wheelchair-accessible; kids under 12 years are not allowed. Complimentary pickup from the wharf or airport with advance notice.

★ Observation Rock Lodge
B&B $$$

(Map p544; ☑ 027 444 1802, 03-219 1444; www. observationrocklodge.co.nz; 7 Leonard St, Oban; r with/without bathroom $395/195; 🛜) Secluded in bird-filled bush, and angled for sea, sunset and aurora views, are three stylish, luxurious rooms with private decks and a shared lounge. Guided activities, a sauna, a hot tub and Annett's gourmet dinners are included in the deluxe package ($780) or by arrangement as additions to the standard B&B rate.

✕ Eating & Drinking

★ Church Hill
MODERN NZ $$$

(Map p544; ☑ 03-219 1123; www.churchhill.co.nz; 36 Kamahi Rd, Oban; mains $38-41; ⊙ 6pm-late daily Sep-May) ✔ Top-notch nosh is prepared at this friendly restaurant, making use of home-grown veggies, house-made pasta and Stewart Island/Rakiara seafood, such as mussels, crayfish and salmon. Dishes like paua ravioli, muttonbird and watercress dumplings and *hāngi*-baked kumara bring local flavours together in refined modern style. During summer the heritage villa's sunny deck provides hilltop views, in cooler months there's an open fire. Bookings advisable.

South Sea Hotel   PUB
(☑ 03-219 1059; www.stewart-island.co.nz; 26 Elgin Tce, Oban; ⊙ 7am-9pm; ☎) Welcome to one of NZ's classic pubs, complete with stellar cod and chips, beer by the quart, a reliable restaurant (mains $16 to $33) and plenty of friendly banter in the public bar. Great at any time of day (or night), and the Sunday-night quiz offers an unforgettable slice of island life. Basic rooms (single/double from $75/95) are available, too.

❶ Information

Rakiura National Park Visitor Centre (Map p544; ☑ 03-219 0009; www.doc.govt.nz; 15 Main Rd, Oban; ⊙ 8am-5pm Dec-Mar, 8.30am-4.30pm Mon-Fri, 8am-4pm Sat & Sun Apr, May, Oct & Nov, 8.30am-4.30pm Mon-Fri, 10am-2pm Sat & Sun Jun-Sep) Stop in to obtain information on walking tracks, as well as hut bookings and passes, topographical maps, locator beacons, books and a few hiking essentials, such as insect repellent and wool socks. Information displays introduce Stewart Island/Rakiura's flora and fauna, while a video library provides entertainment and education (a good rainy-day Plan B).

Red Shed Oban Visitor Centre (Map p544; ☑ 03-219 0056, 0800 000 511; www.stewart islandexperience.co.nz; 12 Elgin Tce, Oban; ⊙ 8am-6.30pm Oct-Apr, to 5pm May-Sep) Conveniently located next to the wharf, this Stewart Island Experience (p543) booking office can hook you up with nearly everything on and around the island, including guided tours, boat trips, bikes, scooters and hire cars.

Stewart Island/Rakiura has no banks. In the Four Square supermarket there's an ATM, which has a mind of its own; credit cards are accepted for most activities except water taxis.

❶ Getting There & Away

AIR

Stewart Island Flights (☑ 03-218 9129; www. stewartislandflights.co.nz; Elgin Tce, Oban; adult/child one way $130/85, return $220/135; ⊙ 7.30am-5pm Mon-Fri, 8.30am-4pm Sat & Sun, reduced hours Jun-Aug) Flies between the island and Invercargill at least three times daily, with good standby discounts. The price includes transfers between the island airport

and its office on the Oban waterfront. It also offers charter flights and tours.

BOAT

The passenger-only ferry **Stewart Island Experience** (Map p544; ☑ 03-219 0034, 0800 000 511; www.stewartislandexperience.co.nz; Main Wharf, Oban; adult/child one way $79/40, return $139/80) runs between Bluff and Oban up to four times daily (reduced to twice daily June to August). Book a few days ahead in summer (December to February). The crossing takes one hour and can be a rough ride. The company also runs a shuttle between Bluff and Invercargill (adult/child $28/14), with pickups and drop-offs in Invercargill at the i-SITE, inner-city hotels and Invercargill Airport.

Vehicles can be stored in a secure car park at Bluff for an additional cost (one/two/three/four/five days $21/31/41/52/62); there's also free unsecured parking opposite the wharf.

❶ Getting Around

Roads on the island are limited to Oban and the bays surrounding it. Stewart Island Experience offers car and scooter hire from the Red Shed. E-bikes can be hired from the **Electric Bike Depot** (☑ 020 4023 8155; www.landsea.co.nz; 4 Main Rd; 1hr $35, half-/full day $55/84; ⊙ 9-11am, 1-2pm & 4-5pm or by appointment).

Water taxis offer pickups and drop-offs for trips to Ulva Island and to remote parts of the main island – a handy service for hikers. Operators include Aihe Eco Charters & Water Taxi (p543), Ulva Island Ferry (p541) and Rakiura Charters & Water Taxi (p543).

FIORDLAND

If you picture New Zealand, it might just be Fiordland National Park that flashes into your mind's eye. Part of the Te Wāhipounamu (Southwest New Zealand) World Heritage Area, this formidable tract of mountains and forest spanning 26,000 sq km has deeply recessed sounds (technically fiords) that spider inland from the Tasman Sea.

Some of the South Island's most iconic destinations are here. Along the world-famous Milford Hwy, views of mountains and mirror lakes are only surpassed in beauty by the road's end point, Milford Sound. Here, granite giants cast their reflection in waters where dolphins and penguins frolic. Even more secluded is Doubtful Sound: the Māori-named 'place of silence' is teeming with wildlife; it's larger than Milford Sound, but much less visited.

Cruises enter the watery wilderness but walkers can delve deepest into Fiordland either on the multiday Milford, Kepler and Hollyford Tracks or shorter walks, easily reached from the highway.

Before embarking on a multiday hike, register your intentions with a friend – see AdventureSmart (www.adventuresmart.org. nz) for details.

Manapōuri

POP 228

Manapōuri, 20km south of Te Anau, is the jumping-off point for cruises to Doubtful Sound. Most visitors head straight to Pearl Harbour for the ferry to West Arm across Lake Manapōuri, known to early Māori as Roto Ua or 'Rainy Lake', and later as Moturau, the 'Many Island Lake'.

But little Manapōuri has a few tricks up its sleeve. The town can't compete with Te Anau's abundance of restaurants and motels but even the locals admit its mountain-backed lake views are more impressive. At 440m, Lake Manapōuri is the second-deepest lake in New Zealand. And with far fewer overnight visitors than Te Anau, you can enjoy the spectacular sunsets all to yourself.

🏃 Activities

Manapōuri is a staging point for the remote and challenging Dusky Track (p528).

By crossing the Waiau River at Pearl Harbour (p547) you can embark on day walks as detailed in DOC's *Fiordland Day Walks* brochure ($3 from the DOC office or download for free). A classic circuit with glimmering lake views (and occasional steep parts) is the Circle Track (3½ hours), or you can take the branch to Hope Arm (five to six hours return). Cross the Waiau River aboard a water taxi operated by Adventure Manapouri (☑021 925 577, 03-249 8070; www.adventurem-anapouri.co.nz; water taxi per person return $20; ⊙Oct-May), departing Pearl Harbour at 11am daily and returning at 3pm (also available on demand by arrangement).

Running between the northern entrance to Manapōuri township and Pearl Harbour, the 30-minute Frasers Beach walk offers picnic and swimming spots as well as fantastic views across the lake.

🛏 Sleeping & Eating

Possum Lodge   HOLIDAY PARK $
(☑03-249 6623; www.possumlodge.co.nz; 13 Murrell Ave; campervan sites $38-42, dm $25, units with/without bathroom $129/69; ☞) Nestled into forest near the lake, Possum Lodge is old-fashioned in the best kind of way. There's basic cabins, time-worn motel units, enviably green campervan sites, laundry facilities and a fully equipped kitchen.

★Manapouri Motels &
Holiday Park   HOLIDAY PARK $
(☑03-249 6624; www.manapourimotels.co.nz; 86 Cathedral Dr; unpowered/powered sites from $20/50, s/d from $100/120, without bathroom from $75; ☞) Ramshackle and eccentric, Manapouri Motels is not everyone's cup of tea, but if you like the sound of staying in a little wooden cabin that's part Swiss Alpine chalet, part hobbit house, you may find yourself at home. There's also a lovely green camping area, a fleet of Morris Minors and a games room full of old pinball machines.

The Church   PUB FOOD $$
(☑03-249 6001; www.facebook.com/pg/manap ouri.co.nz; 23 Waiau St; mains $10-30; ⊙4-8pm Tue, to 9pm Wed, noon-10pm Thu, to midnight Fri & Sat, to 9pm Sun; ☞) No need to head up to Te Anau for a satisfying feed and a few beers, hurrah! Plates heavy with steaks, burgers and butter chicken are hauled to tables in the mezzanine of this converted church building, now a merry pub with exceptionally welcoming staff.

❶ Getting There & Away

Topline Tours (p552) Offers year-round shuttles between Te Anau and Manapōuri (from $25). Shuttles must be booked in advance.

Tracknet (p552) One to two daily buses to/from Te Anau ($25, 20 minutes) from November to April, and on demand at other times of the year.

Doubtful Sound

Remote Doubtful Sound is humbling in size and beauty. Carved by glaciers, it's one of New Zealand's largest fiords – at least three times the length of more popular Milford. Boats gliding through this maze of forested valleys have good chances of encountering fur seals, bottlenose dolphins and Fiordland penguins. Aside from haunting birdsong, Doubtful Sound deserves its Māori name, Patea, the 'Place of Silence'.

Until relatively recently, Doubtful Sound was isolated from all but intrepid explorers. Even Captain Cook only observed it from off the coast in 1770, because he was 'doubtful' whether winds would be sufficient to blow the ship back to sea. Access improved when the road over Wilmot Pass opened in 1959 to facilitate construction of the underground West Arm power station, NZ's second-largest power generator.

Boat and coach transfers from Manapōuri to Deep Cove are easily organised through tour operators, but time-consuming enough to deter some travellers...ideal for those who want to enjoy the silence.

⭐**Real Journeys** CRUISE
(☎0800 656 501; www.realjourneys.co.nz) 🖉 A family-run tourism trailblazer, Real Journeys is ecofriendly, and just plain friendly. One-day 'wilderness cruises' (adult/child from $265/80) include a 2¾-hour journey aboard a modern catamaran with a specialist nature guide. The overnight cruise, which runs from September to May, is aboard the *Fiordland Navigator*, which sleeps 72 in en-suite cabins (quad share $503, single/double from $785/1570).

Deep Cove Charters CRUISE
(☎03-249 6828; https://doubtfulsoundcruise.nz; s $650, cabin tw/d $1450/1550; ⊙mid-Nov–mid-Mar) Overnight cruises onboard the *Seafinn* (maximum 12 passengers) run by home-grown crew who nimbly tailor the cruise to the day's weather and wildlife-spotting conditions. There are options to kayak and fish, but they had us at 'crayfish lunch and venison supper included'.

Doubtful Sound Kayak KAYAKING
(☎0800 452 9257, 03-249 7777; www.fiordland adventure.co.nz; day tours $359; ⊙Oct–Apr) Runs day trips to Doubtful Sound, including four hours of paddling time, suitable for beginners or seasoned kayakers. Tours depart Te Anau at 6.30am.

Go Orange CRUISE
(☎0800 505 504, 03-442 7340; www.goorange. co.nz) Real Journeys' low-cost sister operation runs kayak tours (from $259) and cruises in a 45-seater vessel (from $199) on Doubtful.

ℹ Getting There & Away

Getting to Doubtful Sound is only possible by guided tour. This involves boarding a boat at **Pearl Harbour** (Waiau St, Manapōuri) for a one-

---

OFF THE BEATEN TRACK

SOUTHERN SCENIC ROUTE

The Southern Scenic Route (www. southernscenicroute.co.nz) skirts lonesome beaches, forest-clad lakes and awe-inspiring lookout points, cutting a lazy arc from Queenstown to Te Anau, Manapōuri, Tuatapere, Riverton and Invercargill. From Invercargill it continues east and then north through the Catlins to Dunedin. Yes, there are more direct routes than this 610km meander, but these roads were custom-made for relaxed motoring with scenic stops sprinkled liberally along the way. See Lonely Planet's *New Zealand's Best Trips* or pick up the free *Southern Scenic Route* map to join all the dots.

---

hour trip to West Arm power station, followed by a 22km (40-minute) drive over Wilmot Pass to Deep Cove (permanent population: two), where you hop aboard a boat for your cruise or kayak on the sound. Tour operators will arrange all your transfers. Manapōuri is the closest place to base yourself, although Te Anau (20km) and Queenstown (170km) pickups are standard offerings (for an extra fee).

Te Anau

POP 1911

Picturesque Te Anau is the main gateway to Milford Sound and three Great Walks: the Milford, Kepler and Routeburn Tracks. Firmly focused on servicing travellers and holidaymakers, there's a sizeable accommodation scene, an array of places to eat, and the chance to stock up on dehydrated food and hiking gear. And while Te Anau doesn't party nearly as hard as effervescent Queenstown, there are a few places to sink a beer – which will taste all the better after a long day of hiking, kayaking or driving the unforgettable Milford Hwy.

Te Anau stretches along Lake Te Anau, New Zealand's second-largest lake, whose glacier-gouged fiords spider into secluded forest on its western shore. To the east are the pastoral areas of central Southland, while west across Lake Te Anau lie the rugged mountains of Fiordland. A day or two in town is more than enough before you'll be itching to get out into the wilderness.

Te Anau

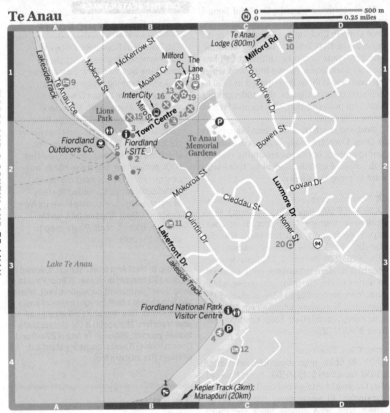

◉ Sights

Te Anau Glowworm Caves   CAVE
(☑ 0800 656 501; www.realjourneys.co.nz; adult/
child $103/30) Stare up at constellations
of glowworms on an underground boat
ride. First described in Māori stories, this
200m-long cave system was lost in time until it was 'rediscovered' in 1948. Its sculpted
rocks, waterfalls and whirlpools are impressive by themselves, but the bluish sparkle
of glowworms, peculiar territorial larvae
who lure prey with their come-hither lights,
is the main draw. The caves can only be
reached by a 2¼-hour guided tour with Real
Journeys (p549), departing from its office on
Lakefront Dr.

🏃 Activities

Lake2Lake   CYCLING
(www.trailstrust.co.nz) A local-community initiative, this easy cycle trail along the Waiau
River will eventually link Te Anau with Man-

apōuri, starting from the DOC visitor centre
(p551). At the time of research the section
between Balloon Loop, 19km from Te Anau,
and Supply Bay Rd, 4.7km from Manapōuri,
was not yet complete (though a detour along
the highway is possible for this section).

Bike Fiordland (☑ 03-280 0116, 0800 960
096; www.wildridesfiordland.co.nz; 68 Town Centre;
bike hire 2/4hr $30/39, full day $50, ebikes 2/4hr
$55/75; ⊙ 9am-6pm daily Nov-Apr, 10am-4pm Tue-
Fri, to 3pm Sat May-Oct) offers regular shuttles
to or from Balloon Loop ($78 including bike
hire).

Day Hikes

Te Anau's **Lakeside Track** makes for a very
pleasant stroll or cycle in either direction –
north to the marina and around to the
Upukerora River (about an hour return),
or south past the Fiordland National Park
Visitor Centre and **Punanga Manu o Te
Anau** (Te Anau Bird Sanctuary; www.doc.govt.
nz/teanaubirdsanctuary; Te Anau–Manapōuri Rd;

Te Anau

⊘dawn-dusk) **FREE** bird sanctuary to the Waiau River control gates and the start of the Kepler Track (50 minutes).

Day hikes in the national park are readily accessible from Te Anau. Kepler Water Taxi (☑0800 004 191, 021 197 4555; www.fiordlandout-doors.co.nz; one way $25; ⊘Oct-Apr) can scoot you over to Brod Bay, from where you can walk back along the Kepler and Lakeside Tracks to Te Anau (two to three hours).

Or take a cab or twice-daily Tracknet (p552) shuttle to Rainbow Reach, from where you can cross the swing bridge and walk 15km along the Kepler and Lakeside Tracks back to Te Anau.

During summer, Trips & Tramps (☑0800 305 807, 03-249 7081; www.tripsandtramps.com) offers small-group, guided day hikes on the Milford, Kepler and Routeburn Tracks with the aid of helicopter and boat transfers. Real Journeys (p547) runs guided day hikes (adult/child $195/99, November to mid-April) along an 11km stretch of the Milford Track. Southern Lakes Helicopters (p550) offers a heli-hike ($270) on the Kepler flying into Luxmore Hut for the downhill walk to Brod Bay, with a boat pickup from there.

For self-guided adventures, pick up DOC's *Fiordland Day Walks* brochure ($3) from the Fiordland i-SITE (p551) or Fiordland National Park Visitor Centre (p551), or download it for free at www.doc.govt.nz.

Multiday Hikes

Te Anau is the gateway to three Great Walks – the Kepler (p527), Milford (p526) and Routeburn (www.doc.govt.nz; huts/camping $65/20, outside of Great Walks season $15/5) – and the less visited but equally worthy Hol-

lyford (p527). The Kepler trailhead is walking distance from Te Anau, the other walks are accessed from the Milford Hwy. Detailed information can be found in Lonely Planet's *Hiking & Tramping New Zealand* guide, and from the helpful folk at the Fiordland National Park Visitor Centre (p551). If you need gear, you can hire everything from Bev's Tramping Gear Hire (☑03-249 7389, 027 249 7389; www.bevs-hire.co.nz; 16 Homer St; ⊘9am-noon & 6-7pm Mon-Fri Oct-Apr, or by arrangement). The Great Walks special ($160) includes warm clothing, a quality sleeping bag, a pack, cooking gear and other bits and pieces.

🎫 Tours

★Real Journeys   TOURS
(☑0800 656 501; www.realjourneys.co.nz; 85 Lakefront Dr; ⊘7am-8.30pm Mar-Oct, 6.45am-9.30pm Nov-Apr) 🐾 You can count on sharp service and well-organised tours from this major player, which offers cruises on Doubtful and Milford Sounds on its big menu of tours, walks and outdoor activities – always with sensitivity to local wildlife.

To see the highlights, take the Fiordland Inside and Out tour (adult/child including lunch $211/99), combining a cruise on Milford with a tour of the glowworm caves (p548) and a guided walk at Lake Gunn.

Fiordland Jet   ADVENTURE SPORTS
(☑0800 253 826; www.fjet.nz; 84 Lakefront Dr; adult/child $159/79) Thrilling two-hour jet-boating trips on the Upper Waiau River (in *Lord of the Rings*, the River Anduin), zipping between mountain-backed beech

forest, with commentary on the area's natural (and fictional) highlights.

Hollyford Track
HIKING

(☑️03-442 3000; www.hollyfordtrack.com; adult/child from $2050/1625; ⏱️late Oct-Apr) 🥾 Brimming with insight into Māori history and Fiordland wildlife, this Ngāi Tahu–owned operator leads small-group (less than 16 people) three-day guided trips on the Hollyford staying at private huts or lodges. The journey is shortened with a jetboat trip down the river and Lake McKerrow on day two, and ends with a scenic flight to Milford Sound.

A two-day helicopter and jetboating experience with short walks (7km) around Martins Bay is also available ($1890).

Ultimate Hikes
HIKING

(☑️03-450 1940, 0800 659 255; www.ultimatehikes.co.nz; 5-day hikes incl food dm/s/d $2295/3330/5590; ⏱️Nov–mid-Apr) 🥾 Booking yourself onto a guided hike of the Milford Track with Queenstown-based Ultimate Hikes puts route planning and logistics in the capable hands of an experienced operator. The guides' expert knowledge of fauna and flora enhances the journey, and walkers will overnight in lodges with hot showers and proper food.

Southern Lakes Helicopters
SCENIC FLIGHTS

(☑️03-249 7167; www.southernlakeshelicopters.co.nz; Lakefront Dr) Offering flights over Te Anau for 30 minutes ($240), half-day heli-hike options to Luxmore Hut on the Kepler Track ($270), and longer trips with landings over Doubtful, Dusky and Milford Sounds (from $685), this operator's three decades of experience in Fiordland will reassure nervous flyers.

🛏️ Sleeping

⭐ Te Anau Lakefront Backpackers
HOSTEL $

(☑️03-249 7713, 0800 200 074; www.teanaubackpackers.co.nz; 48-50 Lakefront Dr; tent sites $25, dm $37, d with/without bathroom from $135/88; P🌐) Tidy dorm and private rooms with a lakefront location hoist this backpackers to the top spot among Te Anau's budget beds. There's a range of options, including garden cabins ($120) and glamping tented dorms in summer ($32). Ask for a room with a view. The place has a cosy, lived-in feel, plus two lounges, two kitchens and a barbecue area.

Te Anau Lakeview Kiwi Holiday Park & Motels
HOLIDAY PARK $

(☑️03-249 7457, 0800 483 262; www.teanauholidaypark.co.nz; 77 Manapōuri–Te Anau Hwy; unpowered/powered sites $25/26, dm/s/d without bathroom from $36/59/80, d units from $379; P@🌐) This 9-hectare grassy lakeside holiday park has plenty of space to pitch your tent or park your van. It also has a wide range of accommodation from basic dorms through to tidy cabins and the rather swanky Marakura two-bedroom motel units with enviable lake and mountain views. Friendly staff will hook you up with local activities and transport.

Getaway Te Anau
HOLIDAY PARK $$

(☑️0800 249 746, 03-249 7462; www.getawayteanau.co.nz; 128 Te Anau Tce; 2-person powered sites from $68, cabins without bathroom from $119, units with bathroom $199-700; @🌐🛏️) Accommodation at this holiday park covers all budgets: motel units have slate-grey decor and compact kitchens, while private tent sites and cabins share modern kitchen facilities and bathrooms. A playground, bike hire, a games room and a sauna provide distractions for kids and parents alike, but the best feature is the private lake-facing hot tubs, perfect for soaking away your hiking pains.

Keiko's Cottages
B&B $$

(☑️03-249 9248; www.keikos.co.nz; 228 Milford Rd; d $145-190; ⏱️closed Jun-Aug; 🌐) Surrounded by Japanese-style flower gardens, complete with babbling water features and a fish pond, Keiko's self-contained cottages are private, comfortable and decorated with feminine flair. The welcome is ebullient and breakfast ($25 per person) poses a difficult choice: Kiwi-style or a full Japanese banquet? The spa and sauna are worthy extras.

⭐ Te Anau Lodge
B&B $$$

(☑️03-249 7477; www.teanaulodge.com; 52 Howden St; s $225-325, d $250-350, tr $300-375, all incl breakfast; 🌐) In a sea of functional but fusty motels, Te Anau's former Sisters of Mercy Convent distinguishes itself with unique history. The place oozes comfort and historic character from the elaborate confession box in reception to the complimentary fireside wine and ample continental breakfast. For a real treat, book into the heritage train carriage in the garden, complete with claw-foot bath.

Eating

Bao Now FOOD TRUCK $
(www.facebook.com/baonowbyhabitfoods; cnr Wong Way & Milford Cres; baos $13; ⊙9am-7.30pm Mar-Oct, to 9pm Nov-Apr) Fantastic food truck delivering Kiwi-Asian fusion baos, rice burgers and salads to hungry travellers and locals alike. Try the Bambi Bao, with wild Fiordland venison, or the Vega, with crispy tofu, shiitake and chilli mayo. Good luck getting your mouth around one of these bulging baos – grab extra napkins. Cash only.

Next door another truck, Fumi, makes sushi fresh to order.

Sandfly Cafe CAFE $
(☑03-249 9529; 9 The Lane; mains $11.50-21; ⊙7am-4.30pm; 🛜) As popular with locals as travellers, Sandfly serves the town's best espresso alongside breakfasts, light meals of pasta or club sandwiches, and an impressive rack of sweet treats from caramel slices to berry friands. Sun yourself on the lawn, or try to get maximum mileage out of the free 15 minutes of wi-fi.

Ristorante Paradiso ITALIAN $$
(Pizzeria da Toni; ☑03-249 4305; www.paradiso pizzeria.co.nz; 1 Milford Cres; mains $23-35; ⊙11am-10pm; 🍴) Simple wood-fired pizzas and homemade pastas are the stars of the show at this surprisingly authentic Italian restaurant, which scoops gelato from its streetside trolley and flies its *fiocchi* in from Italy. Vespa decorations and the odd splash of Italian art don't quite transport you to Rome but the marinara sauce comes close.

Redcliff Cafe MODERN NZ $$$
(☑03-249 7431; www.theredcliff.co.nz; 12 Mokonui St; mains $32-40; ⊙restaurant 11am-2pm & 5-9.30pm, bar 11am-late Sep-May) Housed in a replica settler's cottage, candlelit and cosy Redcliff offers well-executed, locally sourced food amid nostalgic decor (including old photos and antique sewing machines). Hearty meals include succulent slow-roasted pork belly with pear chutney or NZ prime beef with chimichurri. But Redcliff is just as good for a drink in the antique bar or on the sunny outdoor terrace.

Kepler's SOUTH AMERICAN $$$
(☑03-249 7909; 90 Town Centre; mains $29-45; ⊙5-9.30pm) Mountains of crayfish, mouthwatering ceviche and perfectly seared steaks are whisked to tables at this efficient but friendly family-run place. South American flair permeates the menu (quinoa salads, empanadas, Argentine *carménère*); but for Kiwi flare try the lamb – roasted whole over coals in the centre of the restaurant – with a generous pour of merlot.

Drinking & Entertainment

Ranch Bar & Grill PUB
(☑03-249 8801; www.theranchbar.co.nz; 111 Town Centre; ⊙8am-late) An open fire and chalet-style eaves heighten the appeal of this popular local pub, most loved for its hefty Sunday roast dinners ($17.50), Thursday jam nights and sports matches on big screens. Show up for big pancake breakfasts (until 11.30am) or generous schnitzels and mostly meaty mains like surf 'n' turf and BBQ pork ribs ($28 to $45).

Fiordland Cinema CINEMA
(☑03 249 8844; www.fiordlandcinema.co.nz; 7 The Lane; adult/child $16/10; 🛜) In between regular showings of the excellent *Ata Whenua/Fiordland on Film* (adult/child $12/6), essentially a 32-minute advertisement for Fiordland scenery, Fiordland Cinema serves as the local movie house.

The **Black Dog Bar** (☑03-249 9089; www.blackdogbar.co.nz; 7 The Lane; ⊙10am-late Oct-Apr, 2.30pm-late May-Sep; 🛜), next to the cinema, is the town's most sophisticated watering hole.

ℹ Information

Fiordland i-SITE (☑03-249 8900; www.fiordland.org.nz; 19 Town Centre; ⊙9am-5pm May-Sep, 8.30am-7pm Oct-Apr) The official information centre, offering activity, accommodation and transport bookings.

Fiordland Medical Practice (☑03-249 7007; 25 Luxmore Dr; ⊙8.15am-5pm Mon-Fri, 9am-noon Sat, 10-10.30am & 5-5.30pm Sun) If you need medical help after hours, the centre's number will give the details of an on-call GP.

Fiordland National Park Visitor Centre (DOC; ☑03-249 7924; www.doc.govt.nz; cnr Lakefront Dr & Te Anau–Manapōuri Rd; ⊙8am-5pm daily Nov-Apr, 8.30am-4.30pm Mon-Fri, to 4pm Sat & Sun May-Oct) Can assist with Great Walks bookings, general hut tickets and information, with the bonus of a natural-history display and a shop stocking hiking supplies and essential topographical maps for backcountry trips.

ℹ Getting There & Away

InterCity (☑03-442 4922; www.intercity.co.nz; Miro St) Services to Milford Sound (from $33, three hours, two to three daily) and Queenstown (from $33, 2¼ hours, four daily), and daily 8am buses to Gore (from $33,

1¾ hours), Dunedin (from $26, 4¾ hours) and Christchurch (from $42, 11¼ hours). Buses depart from a stop on Miro St outside Kiwi Country, at the Town Centre end.

Topline Tours (☑03-249 8059; www.topline tours.co.nz; 32 Caswell Rd) Offers year-round shuttles between Te Anau and Manapōuri (from $25), and transfers from Te Anau to the Kepler Track trailheads at the control gates (from $5) and Rainbow Reach (from $10). Shuttles must be booked in advance.

Tracknet (☑0800 483 262; www.tracknet. net) From November to April Te Anau–based Tracknet has at least three daily scheduled buses to/from Te Anau Downs ($29, 30 minutes), the Divide ($43, 1¼ hours) and Milford Sound ($55, 2¼ hours), two buses to/from Manapōuri ($25, 20 minutes), one to Invercargill ($51) and four daily to Queenstown ($49, 2¾ hours). In winter, services are by demand. Buses depart from near the Te Anau Lakeview Kiwi Holiday Park (p550).

Milford Hwy

Expert travellers know it's all about the journey, and that's certainly true of the 119km road stretching north of Te Anau – though in this case the destination is not bad either. The Milford Hwy offers the most easily accessible experience of Fiordland in all its diversity, taking in expanses of beautiful beech forest, gentle river valleys, mirror-like lakes, exquisite alpine scenery and ending at arguably New Zealand's most breathtaking vista, Milford Sound.

The journey should take 2½ hours each way, but expect to spend time dawdling along walking trails and maxing out your camera's memory card. Most travellers embark on the Milford Hwy as a day trip from Te Anau, with a cruise on Milford Sound to break up the return journey. But the prospect of longer hikes or camping beneath jagged mountains might entice you to stay.

◉ Sights & Activities

Leaving Te Anau north along the Milford Hwy (SH94), the road meanders through rolling farmland atop the lateral moraine of the glacier that once gouged out Lake Te Anau. At the 29km mark it passes Te Anau Downs, where boats for the Milford Track depart. From here, an easy 45-minute return walk leads through forest to Lake Mistletoe (Te Anau Downs), a small glacier-formed lake.

The road then heads into the Eglinton Valley, at first pocketed with sheepy pasture, then reaching deeper wilderness immersion as it crosses the boundary into Fiordland National Park: knobby peaks, thick beech forest, lupin-lined riverbanks and grassy meadows.

Just past the Mackay Creek Campsite (at 51km) are the Eglinton Flats, a wide-open space exposing truly epic views of Pyramid Peak (2295m) and Ngatimamoe Peak (2164m). The most popular roadside stop is Mirror Lakes (SH94; at 58km). A short boardwalk (five minutes' walk) overlooks glassy waters, their surface interrupted by occasional mallards. If you're lucky enough to stop by on a calm, clear day, the lakes perfectly reflect the mountains across the valley.

At the 77km mark, after an enchanting stretch of forest-framed road, is Cascade Creek and Lake Gunn. This area was known to Māori as O Tapara, and a stopover for parties heading to Anita Bay in search of *pounamu* (greenstone). The bewitching Lake Gunn Nature Walk (SH94; 45 minutes return) loops through tall red beech forest. Moss-clung logs and a chorus of birdsong create a fairy-tale atmosphere, and side tracks lead to quiet lakeside beaches.

At 84km you pass across the Divide, the lowest east–west pass in the Southern Alps; from here the highway narrows and weaves. This is a trailhead for the Routeburn and Greenstone and Caples Tracks; those with less time can embark on a marvellous three-hour return walk along the start of the Routeburn, climbing up through beech forest to the alpine tussockland of Key Summit. On a good day the views of the Humboldt and Darran Mountains are sure to knock your socks off, and there's a nature walk around the boggy summit through stands of twisted beech.

From the Divide, the road falls into the beech forest of the Hollyford Valley – stop at Pop's View (SH94) for a great outlook...if you can get a parking space. The road climbs through a cascade-tastic valley to the Homer Tunnel, 101km from Te Anau and framed by a high-walled, ice-carved amphitheatre. Begun as a relief project in the 1930s and completed in 1953, the tunnel is one way (traffic lights direct vehicle flow – patience required). Kea (alpine parrots) hang around the tunnel entrance looking for food from tourists, but don't feed them as it's bad for their health. Dark, rough-hewn and dripping with water, the 1270m-long tunnel delivers you to the head of the spectacular Cleddau Valley. Any spare 'wows' might pop out about now.

About 10km before Milford Sound, the wheelchair- and pram-friendly Chasm Walk (SH94; 20 minutes return) affords staggering views over the churning Cleddau River. Pebbles caught in its frenetic currents have hollowed boulders into shapes reminiscent of a Salvador Dalí scene. An espresso van parks here November to April. Along the final 9km to Milford Sound, watch for glimpses of Mt Tutoko (2723m), Fiordland's highest peak, above the beech forest.

🛏 Sleeping

There are eight basic first-come, first-served DOC campsites (per adult/child $15/7.50) along the highway; the closest to Milford Sound is Cascade Creek, 43km away. Be warned they are popular with sandflies. There's no freedom camping on the Milford Hwy, the closest is at Lumsden, 78km east of Te Anau.

If you prefer four walls to canvas or campervans, find more robust accommodation at Te Anau Downs at Fiordland National Park Lodge (☑03-249 7811; www.fiordlandnational parklodge.com; 2681 Milford Hwy, Te Anau Downs; d/ste from $175/290; ☎) or the attached Lone Moose Backpackers (dorms/doubles from $35/110); Knob's Flat (☑03-249 9122; www. knobsflat.co.nz; 6178 SH94; unpowered sites per adult/child $20/10, d $150-180); or reserve a frontier-feel cabin at Gunn's Camp (p554). Otherwise, you're better off returning to the abundant accommodation choices in Te Anau, 119km south.

❶ Getting There & Away

Check when you book bus tickets whether the operator is purely A-to-B or incorporates scenic lookouts.

➡ InterCity (p551) runs three daily bus services to Milford Sound from Te Anau (from $33, three hours) and Queenstown (from $66, six hours).

➡ Tracknet (p552) is handy for hikers. From November to April Te Anau–based Tracknet has at least three daily scheduled buses between Te Anau and Te Anau Downs ($29, 30 minutes), the Divide ($43, 1¼ hours) and Milford Sound ($55, 2¼ hours). Two of these connect all the way to Queenstown (from Milford Sound $95, five hours). One service runs to the Hollyford Rd end (from Te Anau/Queenstown $62/95) for the Hollyford Track. In winter (June to August), services are by demand.

Milford Sound

POP 200

The pot of gold at the end of Milford Hwy (SH94) is sublime Milford Sound (Piopiotahi). Rising above the fiord's indigo water is Mitre Peak (Rahotu), the deserved focal point of millions of photographs. Tapering to a cloud-piercing summit, the 1692m-high mountain appears sculpted by a divine hand.

In truth, it's the action of glaciers that carved these razor-edge cliffs. Scoured into the bare rock are pathways from tree avalanches, where entangled roots dragged whole forests down into darkly glittering water. When rain comes (and that's often), dozens of temporary waterfalls curtain the cliffs. Stirling and Lady Bowen Falls gush on in fine weather, with rainbows bouncing from their mists when sunlight strikes just right.

Milford Sound receives an estimated one million annual visitors which is an almighty challenge to keep its beauty pristine. But out on the water, all human activity – cruise ships, divers, kayakers – seems dwarfed into insignificance.

---

❶ MILFORD MOTORING

The Milford Hwy is notorious throughout New Zealand for terrible driving. The majority of drivers along its 119km length are sightseers. Be on the lookout for cars decelerating suddenly, drifting across the centre line or parking dangerously. Fill up with fuel before you set out, allow plenty of time for your journey and leave adequate space between cars to avoid annoyance at fellow drivers (or worse).

In an effort to keep traffic under control, a parking fee of $10 per hour has been introduced in the main car park at Milford Sound. If you're heading up the highway on a day trip, consider taking a coach. These services stop for photos in key spots, and some have glass ceilings, through which you'll see a lot more scenery than if your eyes are glued to that winding road.

HUMBOLDT FALLS & GUNN'S CAMP

Three kilometres north of the Divide, look out for a northeasterly detour off SH94. Follow the unsealed road (leading to the Hollyford Track) for 8km to reach Gunn's Camp. Blow dust off antique agricultural implements in the museum (Hollyford Rd; adult/child $2/free; ⊙ hours vary), or consider an overnight stay (www.gunnscamp.org.nz; Hollyford Rd; unpowered sites per person from $20, dm $30, d cabins $80) in an unvarnished cabin, heated by a wood fire. A further 9km northeast is the trailhead for the Hollyford Track, where you will find the track to Humboldt Falls (off Hollyford Rd; 30 mins return). It's an easy 1.2km hike through rainforest to a viewing platform where you can spy this distant 275m-high cascade.

◉ Sights & Activities

Milford Underwater Observatory
AQUARIUM

(www.southerndiscoveries.co.nz; Harrison Cove; ⊙8am-5pm) Run by Southern Discoveries, this small observatory is NZ's only floating underwater observatory, with displays on the unique natural environment of the fiord. The centre offers a chance to view corals, tube anemones and bottom-dwelling sea perch from 10m below the waterline. It's only accessible on a cruise by any of the operators – some include a visit (such as Southern Discoveries' Scenic Cruise, from $90/55 per adult/child), others offer it as an add-on; check when you book.

Rosco's Milford Kayaks
KAYAKING

(⊋03-249 8500, 0800 476 726; www.roscosmilford kayaks.com; 72 Town Centre, Te Anau; trips $115-225) Offers guided tandem-kayak trips such as the 'Morning Glory' ($225), a challenging paddle the full length of the fiord to Dale Point, and the 'Stirling Sunriser' ($219), which ventures beneath the 151m-high Stirling Falls for a 'glacial facial'. Beginners can take it easy on a two-hour paddle on the sound ($115) assisted by water taxi transfers.

Descend Scubadiving
DIVING

(⊋027 337 2363; www.descend.co.nz; dives incl gear from $345) Black coral, more than 150 species of fish, the possibility of dolphins...

Milford Sound is as beautiful underwater as it is above. Descend's six-hour trips offer a sampler of both realms: cruising on Milford Sound in a 10m boat and one or two dives along the way. There are excursions for experienced divers and novices. Transport, equipment, hot drinks and snacks included.

High rainfall at Milford Sound ensures a near-permanent layer of fresh water floats on the sea water. This blocks the light and tricks species that are usually only found at depths of up to 100m into shallow waters. You can expect to see black and red coral at just 8m, along with deepwater sea dragons.

⏻ Tours

Fiordland's most accessible experience is a cruise on Milford Sound, usually lasting 90 minutes or more. Numerous companies have booking desks in the flash cruise terminal, a 10-minute walk from the main car park, but it's always wiser to book ahead.

Each cruise company claims to be quieter, smaller, bigger, cheaper or in some way preferable to the rest. What really makes a difference is timing. Buses coming all the way from Queenstown aim for sailings between around noon and 2pm, so if you avoid that time of day there will be fewer people on the boat, fewer boats on the water and fewer buses on the road. Cruises outside this window are also around 30% cheaper.

Most companies offer coach transfers from Te Anau for an additional cost. Day trips from Queenstown are common, but they make for a very long 13-hour day, about eight hours of which is spent sitting on a bus. Air transfers are also available.

★ Real Journeys
BOATING

(⊋0800 656 501, 03-249 7416; www.realjourneys. co.nz; adult/child from $81/30) ⬦ Milford's biggest and most venerable operator runs a popular 1¾-hour scenic cruise. More specialised is the 2¼-hour nature cruise (adult/child from $89/30), which homes in on wildlife with commentary from a nature guide. Overnight cruises (from $363) are also available, from which you can take nature tours in small boats en route.

Southern Discoveries
BOATING

(⊋0800 264 536, 03-441 1137; www.southerndis coveries.co.nz; adult/child from $55/30) A major operator with a range of Milford Sound trips, from standard scenic tours on large boats (1½ hours) to wildlife-focused cruises on smaller, 75-passenger vessels (2¼ hours; adult/child from $99/30), always with engaging commentary and complimentary hot drinks. Add-ons include kayaking or visits to the Underwater Observatory. There's a booking office in Te Anau (☑0800 264 536; www.southerndiscoveries.co.nz; 80 Lakefront Dr; ☺9am-6pm).

Cruise Milford BOATING
(☑0800 645 367; www.cruisemilfordnz.com; adult/child from $99/18; ☺10.45am, 12.45pm & 2.45pm) Offering a more personal touch than some of the big-boat tours, Cruise Milford's smaller vessels head out at least three times a day on 1¾-hour cruises, divulging great info from tectonics to wildlife. It never books more than half the seats so there's plenty of room.

Go Orange BOATING
(☑0800 505 504, 03-442 7340; www.goorange.co.nz; adult/child from $57/25; ☺9am, 12.30pm & 3pm) These low-cost two-hour cruises along the full length of Milford Sound have a cafe and a bar on board serving own-brewed beer. There's also kayaking trips (from $159, four to five hours on the water). You can book at Milford Sound or Te Anau (☑03-442 7340, 0800 505 504; www.goorange.co.nz; 21 Town Centre; ☺8am-8pm Nov-Mar, 9am-4pm Apr-Oct), with transfers available for an extra fee.

Mitre Peak Cruises BOATING
(☑0800 744 633, 03-249 8110; www.mitrepeak.com; adult/child from $95/30) Two-hour cruises in smallish boats (maximum capacity 75), allowing closer views of waterfalls and wildlife than larger vessels. The 4.30pm cruise is the last of the day, and a good choice because many larger boats are heading back at this time.

Milford Helicopters SCENIC FLIGHTS
(☑03-249 8384; www.milfordhelicopters.com; Milford Airport; scenic flights from $265; ☺8.30am-5.30pm Nov-Apr, 10am-4pm May-Oct) Swing past Mitre Peak, follow the Milford Track from above or land on a glacier on a scenic flight. Also offers air transfers to Te Anau and Queenstown ($800).

🛏 Sleeping

Milford Sound Lodge LODGE $$$
(☑03-249 8071; www.milfordlodge.com; SH94; powered campervan sites per person $35, chalets $615-849; ☎) Alongside the Cleddau River, 1.5km from the Milford hub (there's a free shuttle), this modern lodge is the only accommodation at the sound. It offers luxurious self-contained chalets with a lovely riverside setting. The forest-clad campervan area (no tents please) suits smaller budgets. There's a chic restaurant (mains $28 to $41) here, open to nonguests. Book far in advance for November to April.

ⓘ Information

Although it's run by Southern Discoveries, the **Discover Milford Sound Information Centre** (☑03-249 7931; www.southerndiscoveries.co.nz; SH94; ☺8am-4pm Nov-Apr, from 9am May-Oct) near Milford's main car park sells tickets for most of the operators. There's a cafe attached.

ⓘ Getting There & Away

BUS
➡ InterCity (p551) runs two to three daily buses to Milford Sound from Te Anau (from $33, three hours) and Queenstown (from $66, six hours); you can also include a cruise (from $115/125 from Te Anau/Queenstown).
➡ Tracknet (p552) has three daily scheduled buses to/from the Divide ($42), Te Anau Downs ($54) and Te Anau ($55), and two to Queenstown ($95) from November to April. In winter (June to August) services are by demand.

CAR & MOTORCYCLE
A parking fee of $10 per hour ($20 overnight) applies in the main car park. There's also a free car park on Deepwater Basin Rd about 1.5km before the cruise terminal (a free shuttle runs from here to the terminal every 15 to 20 minutes).

If you decide to drive, fill up with petrol in Te Anau before setting off. There are no petrol stations on the road to Milford Sound, and you'll want to avoid the high prices at Milford's self-serve petrol pump – the next closest, near Gunn's Camp (p554), is also costly and only accepts cash. Snow chains must be carried on ice- and avalanche-risk days from May to November (there will be signs on the road), and can be hired from petrol stations in Te Anau.

Queenstown & Wānaka

Best Places to Eat

➡ Amisfield Bistro & Cellar Door (p584)

➡ Aosta (p585)

➡ Akarua Wines & Kitchen by Artisan (p584)

➡ Fergbaker (p574)

➡ Yonder (p574)

Best Places to Stay

➡ Camp Glenorchy (p581)

➡ Adventure Queenstown (p572)

➡ Wanaka Haven (p592)

➡ Criffel Peak View (p591)

➡ Millbrook Resort (p584)

Why Go?

Few people come to Queenstown to wind down. The self-styled 'adventure capital of the world' is a place where visitors come to throw their inhibitions out the window...and throw themselves out of planes and off mountain tops and bridges.

The region has a cinematic backdrop of mountains and lakes and a smattering of valley towns just as enticing as Queenstown itself. Wānaka may resemble Queenstown – a lakeside setting, a fringe of mountains, a lengthy menu of adventures – but it runs at a less frenetic pace. Glenorchy is even more sedate, and yet it's the final stop for many on their way into arguably the finest alpine hiking terrain in New Zealand.

History makes its home in gold-rush Arrowtown, where the main-street facades still hint at past glory. Settle in for dinner and a drink after the crowds disperse – the following day there'll be plenty more opportunities to dive back into Queenstown's action-packed whirlwind.

When to Go

➡ The fine and settled summer weather from January to March is the perfect backdrop to Queenstown's active menu of adventure sports and outdoor exploration.

➡ Gold returns to Arrowtown in autumn (March to May) with a vivid display of colour in the turning of the leaves.

➡ In late June the Queenstown Winter Festival celebrates the coming of the ski season. From June to August, the slopes of the four ski fields surrounding Queenstown and Wānaka are flush with skiers and snowboarders.

➡ The winter play season ends with a flourish in August with Queenstown's Winter Pride and the Remarkables Ice & Mixed Festival.

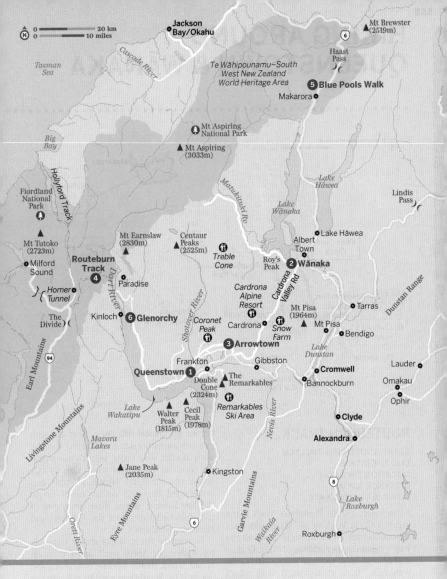

Queenstown & Wānaka Highlights

1 **Queenstown** (p562)
Taking the literal leap into any number of once-in-a-lifetime activities in this paradise for thrill seekers.

2 **Wānaka** (p586) Scaling a waterfall via ferrata before dining at one of the lakeside town's bevy of interesting restaurants and cafes.

3 **Arrowtown** (p582)
Spending a day in a lower gear strolling this historic gold-rush town before discovering some very chic restaurants and bars.

4 **Routeburn Track** (p558)
Hiking high into the mountains on arguably the greatest of NZ's Great Walks.

5 **Blue Pools Walk** (p595)
Taking a short stroll to a luminous bloom of river colour just outside Makarora.

6 **Glenorchy** (p580)
Discovering that Paradise really is just around the corner at one of NZ's most enticing hiking bases.

HIKING AROUND QUEENSTOWN & WĀNAKA

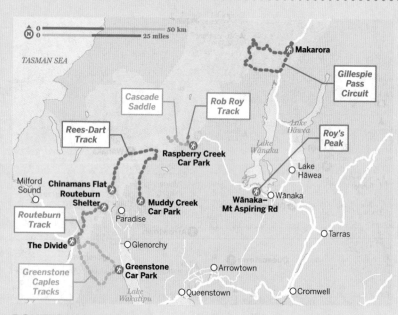

ROUTEBURN TRACK

START ROUTEBURN SHELTER
END THE DIVIDE
DURATION 2-4 DAYS
DISTANCE 32KM
DIFFICULTY MODERATE

Some hikers say the Routeburn Track is the greatest Great Walk of all. It's a high-level mountain route with fantastic views all the way – expansive panoramas of other ranges, and near-at-hand views of mirror-like tarns, waterfalls, fairy glades lined with plush moss, and gnarled trees with long, straggly, lichen beards.

The track can be started from either end. From the Routeburn Flats end, you'll walk along the top of **Routeburn Gorge** and then ascend past the impressive **Routeburn Falls**. Arriving at alpine **Lake Harris** is an awe-inspiring mountain moment, as is the moment you rise onto **Harris Saddle** with its vast view. From here, if you have any energy left, you can make a steep 1½- to two-hour

detour up **Conical Hill**. On a clear day you can see waves breaking at Martins Bay, far away on the west coast, but it's not worth the climb on a cloudy or windy day. Shortly before you reach the Divide, a highly recommended one-hour detour heads up to the **Key Summit**, where there are views of the Hollyford Valley and the Eglinton and Greenstone Valleys.

During the Great Walks season (late October through April) you'll need to book ahead, which should be done online at www.doc.govt.nz. You'll then need to call into the DOC visitor centre in either **Queenstown** (p578) or **Te Anau** (p547) to collect actual tickets, either the day before or on the day of departure. Outside of the season, bookings aren't required, but you'll still need to visit one of the DOC centres to purchase your hut and campsite tickets. There are four basic huts along the track: Routeburn Flats, Routeburn Falls, Lake Mackenzie and Lake Howden. Both the Routeburn Flats and Lake Mackenzie huts have campsites near-

At the quiet end of Lake Wakatipu some of New Zealand's finest mountain country awaits, but you barely need to leave Wānaka for a memorable hike.

by. The other option is to take a guided walk, staying at private lodges along the way, operated by **Ultimate Hikes** (p565).

The Routeburn Track remains open in winter, though traversing the alpine section after the snow falls is not recommended for casual hikers, as winter mountaineering skills are required. There are 32 avalanche paths across the section between Routeburn Falls and Lake Howden, and the avalanche risk continues through to spring. Always check conditions with DOC.

There are car parks at both ends of the track, but they're unattended, so don't leave any valuables in your vehicle. Track shuttles are plentiful, and many people arrange to get dropped at the Divide to start their walk after a Milford Sound tour or, alternatively, time the end of their walk to catch one of the Milford Sound buses. This needs to be arranged in advance as there's no mobile phone reception on the track.

GREENSTONE CAPLES TRACKS

START/END **GREENSTONE CAR PARK**
DURATION **4 DAYS**
DISTANCE **61KM**
DIFFICULTY **MODERATE**

From the shores of Lake Wakatipu, this scenic route circuits through the Caples and Greenstone Valleys, crossing the subalpine McKellar Saddle, where it almost intersects with the Routeburn Track.

The name of the Greenstone Valley hints at its ancient use as a route for Māori to access the Dart Valley to collect highly prized *pounamu* (greenstone/jade), though no Māori archaeological sites have been found in the Greenstone and Caples Valleys themselves. Europeans would later traverse the valleys in search of grazing sites, with farming commencing in the Caples in 1880. The Greenstone and Pass Burn were utilised as stock routes.

The Greenstone Valley is wide and open with tussock flats and beech forest. The Caples is narrower and more heavily forested, interspersed with grassy clearings. Many hikers consider the Caples, with its parklike appearance, to be the more beautiful of the two.

The two tracks link at McKellar Saddle and again near Greenstone car park, where the road links to Glenorchy and on to Queenstown. Hikers can choose to walk just one track in one direction (joining the end of the Routeburn Track down to the Divide), or traverse both as a there-and-back journey of four days. Routeburn hikers planning to continue on the Greenstone can easily walk from Lake Mackenzie Hut to McKellar Hut, which takes around five to seven hours.

REES-DART TRACK

START **MUDDY CREEK CAR PARK**
END **CHINAMANS FLAT**
DURATION **4 DAYS**
DISTANCE **63KM**
DIFFICULTY **DEMANDING**

The Rees-Dart Track connects two splendid schist-lined valleys shaped by glaciation. The relatively small **Dart Glacier** was once part of an enormous system that terminated at Kingston, 135km away at the southern end of Lake Wakatipu.

As this hike winds up one valley and back down the other, it takes in a variety of scenery, such as meadows of flowering herbs and mighty bluffs and moraine walls.

Pinched between the Routeburn Track and Cascade Saddle, the Rees-Dart has become a popular hike, but it is longer and definitely more challenging than either the Routeburn or Greenstone Caples, and has several stream crossings, which can be hazardous in heavy rain or snowmelt.

The most common approach to the hike is to head up the Rees Valley and return down the Dart; this is the easiest direction in which to climb **Rees Saddle**. Plan an extra night at Dart Hut if you want to include a day trip to Dart Glacier or even on to Cascade Saddle.

CASCADE SADDLE

START/END RASPBERRY CREEK
CAR PARK
DURATION 3 DAYS
DISTANCE 30KM
DIFFICULTY DEMANDING

Cascade Saddle is one of the most beautiful and dramatic of all the passes that hikers can reach in New Zealand. Pinched between the West Matukituki and Dart Valleys, it's a very steep and demanding climb. On a fine day, the rewards are as numerous as the mountains you can see from atop the alpine pass, including an eyeball-to-eyeball view of Tititea/Mt Aspiring.

Cascade Saddle can also be reached from Dart Hut on the Rees-Dart Track, providing an enticing opportunity for a four-day hike, crossing the pass from the West Matukituki Valley and exiting along the Dart Valley. The recommended approach is from the West Matukituki.

The West Matukituki is hiking royalty in the South Island, and it's worth building in a couple of extra days to explore upstream to Liverpool Hut, and take a detour out to **Rob Roy Glacier**. You could easily while away a decent week based at Aspiring Hut, branching out on day walks and soaking up the spectacular mountain scenes.

Be warned: Cascade Saddle is a difficult climb, partially smothered in super-slippery snow grass, and hikers have fallen to their deaths here. It should not be attempted by inexperienced hikers, or in adverse conditions. If you have any doubts, seek advice from the warden in Aspiring Hut (staffed only in summer), who will have current weather forecasts on hand, or from the **DOC Visitor Centre** (p593) in Wānaka.

ROB ROY TRACK

START/END RASPBERRY CREEK
CAR PARK
DURATION 3–4 HOURS
DISTANCE 10KM
DIFFICULTY EASY TO MODERATE

It's not uncommon to hear this short hike, into a side pocket of the Matukituki Valley, described as the finest day walk in the South Island, and it's not difficult to understand why. Few tracks provide such large-scale mountain scenery in such a short time

TTONY/SHUTTERSTOCK ©

Lake Harris, Routeburn Track (p558)

frame, with the walk beginning along the Matukituki Valley before climbing 400m through beech forest into a high and dramatic enclosure of mountains, providing a spectacular view of the **Rob Roy Glacier**.

The mix of beech forest and the clear blue water of Rob Roy Stream creates a bit of a fantasy land, before it all peels back to reveal the sort of mountain scene you might normally expect to find only after days of wilderness hiking.

Pay careful heed to the avalanche advisories if you're hiking in winter or spring, as the track beyond the lower lookout is susceptible to avalanches from the sheer-sided walls of the valley.

GILLESPIE PASS CIRCUIT

START/END MAKARORA
DURATION 3 DAYS
DISTANCE 58KM
DIFFICULTY MODERATE TO DEMANDING

Located in the northern reaches of Mt Aspiring National Park, this popular hike offers outstanding mountain scenery – some

ONFOKUS/GETTY IMAGES ©

Rob Roy Track

would say it rivals both the Matukituki and Glenorchy area hikes.

There is plenty to see and enjoy along this route, including valleys filled with silver beech (tawhai), and alpine tussock fields alive with grasshoppers, black butterflies, buttercups and mountain daisies. The bird life you might encounter includes the fantail, tomtit and rifleman, as well as the mōhua (yellowhead) and the parakeet known as the kākāriki.

The hike, which should only be undertaken by experienced parties, is best approached from the Young Valley to the Wilkin Valley, the easiest way to cross Gillespie Pass. This also makes for a thrilling finish if you choose, as many do, to eschew the final four to five hours' walking in favour of a jetboat ride (and thus avoiding a river crossing).

It is recommended that you carry a tent, as huts are often overcrowded in summer.

ROY'S PEAK

START/END WĀNAKA–MT ASPIRING RD
DURATION 5–6 HOURS
DISTANCE 16KM
DIFFICULTY MODERATE

If you've seen any one photo of Lake Wānaka (other than of *that* tree), it's likely to have been taken from the Roy's Peak Track, which provides a particularly photogenic vantage point. In the kindest of descriptions, the climb to Roy's Peak is a grind, ascending 1220m from near the lakeshore to the antenna-tipped summit, but oh, those views... It truly is a spectacular vista.

Those very views have made this an extremely popular track, though many hikers aspire only to reach the ridge, about three-quarters of the way up, from where the famous 'selfie with Lake Wānaka' moment bombards Instagram. If you'd prefer to escape the narcissists and experience a little more solitude, there are plenty of alternative viewpoints in the vicinity (p587).

ℹ️ Getting There & Away

Domestic flights head to Queenstown from Auckland, Wellington and Christchurch. There are also direct international flights from Australia (Melbourne, Sydney, the Gold Coast and Brisbane). Queenstown is the main bus hub for the region, with services radiating out to the West Coast (via Wānaka and Haast Pass), Christchurch, Dunedin (via Central Otago) and Invercargill.

QUEENSTOWN

POP 15,800

Queenstown is as much a verb as a noun, a place of doing that likes to spruik itself as the 'adventure capital of the world'. It's famously the birthplace of bungy jumping, and the list of adventures you can throw yourself into here is encyclopedic – from alpine heliskiing to ziplining. It's rare that a visitor leaves without having tried something that ups their heart rate, but to pigeonhole Queenstown as just a playground is to overlook its cosmopolitan dining and arts scene, its fine vineyards, and the diverse range of bars that can make evenings as fun-filled as the days.

Leap, lunge or luge here, but also find time to simply sit at the lakeside and watch the ever-dynamic play of light on the Remarkables and Lake Wakatipu, creating one of the most beautiful and dramatic natural scenes in NZ.

Expect big crowds, especially in summer and winter, but also big experiences.

History

The Queenstown region was deserted when the first British people arrived in the mid-1850s, although there is evidence of previous Māori settlement. Sheep farmers came first, but after two shearers discovered gold on the banks of the Shotover River in 1862, a deluge of prospectors followed.

Within a year the settlement was a mining town with streets, permanent buildings and a population of several thousand. It was declared 'fit for a queen' by the NZ government; hence Queenstown was born. Lake Wakatipu was the principal means of transport, and at the height of the boom there were four paddle steamers and 30 other craft plying the waters.

By 1900 the gold had petered out and the population was a mere 190. It wasn't until the 1950s that Queenstown became a popular holiday destination.

👁️ Sights

★ Lake Wakatipu   LAKE

(Map p566) Shaped like a cartoon lightning bolt, Lake Wakatipu is NZ's third-largest lake. It reaches a depth of 372m, meaning the lake bed actually sits below sea level. Five rivers flow into it but only one (the Kawarau) flows out, making it prone to sometimes dramatic floods. The lake can be experienced at any number of speeds: the classic TSS Earnslaw (p572) steamboat trip, a spin with KJet (p568), below decks in the Time Tripper (p564), or a shark's-eye view with Hydro Attack (p568).

If the water looks clean, that's because it is. Scientists have rated it as 99.9% pure – you're better off dipping your glass in the lake than buying bottled water. It's also very cold. That beach by Marine Pde may look tempting on a scorching day, but trust us – you won't want to splash about for long in water that hovers around 11.5°C year-round. Because cold water increases the risk of drowning, local by-laws require the wearing of life jackets in all boats under 6m, including kayaks, on the lake (and all of the district's lakes).

Māori tradition sees the lake's shape as the burnt outline of the evil giant Matau sleeping with his knees drawn up. Local lad Matakauri set fire to the bed of bracken on which the giant slept in order to rescue his beloved Manata, a chief's daughter who was kidnapped by the giant. The fat from Matau's body created a fire so intense that it burnt a hole deep into the ground.

Queenstown Gardens   PARK

(Map p566; Park St) Set on its own tongue of land framing Queenstown Bay, this pretty park is the perfect city escape right within the city. Laid out in 1876, it features an 18-'hole' frisbee golf course (Map p566; www.queenstowndiscgolf.co.nz; Queenstown Gardens) FREE, a skate park, lawn-bowls club, tennis courts, Queenstown Ice Arena (Map p566; 🕿 03-441 8000; www.queenstownicearena.co.nz; 29 Park St; entry incl skate hire $19; ⊗ hours vary), mature exotic trees (including large sequoias and some fab monkey puzzles by the rotunda) and a rose garden.

Near the tip of the gardens there's a memorial to Captain Robert Scott (1868–1912), leader of the doomed South Pole expedition, which includes an engraving of his moving final message.

Queenstown Region

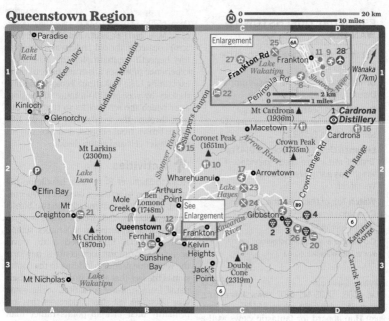

Queenstown Region

St Peter's on Church St   CHURCH
(Map p570; ☎ 03-442 8391; www.stpeters.co.nz; 2 Church St) This pretty Anglican church, built in 1932 from local greywacke stone, has colour-ful stained glass and an impressive gilded and painted organ. Take a look at the eagle-shaped cedar lectern, carved and donated in 1874 by John Ah Tong, a Chinese immigrant.

ESSENTIAL QUEENSTOWN & WĀNAKA

Eat at a winery by Lake Hayes or in the Gibbston Valley.

Drink vodka or gin from the Cardrona Distillery (p594).

Read Robert Scott's final message, displayed on his memorial in Queenstown Gardens (p562).

Listen to *Out of the Woods* (2014) by Taylor Swift and re-enact the video, which was partly shot around Lake Wakatipu.

Watch *Top of the Lake*, the Jane Campion–directed TV series set around Glenorchy.

Go online www.queenstownnz.co.nz, www.lakewanaka.co.nz

Skyline Gondola   CABLE CAR

(Map p566; ☑03-441 0101; www.skyline.co.nz; Brecon St; adult/child return $44/26; ☺9am-9pm) Hop aboard for fantastic views as the gondola squeezes through pine forest to its grandstand location 400m above Queenstown. At the top there's the inevitable cafe, restaurant, souvenir shop and observation deck, as well as the Queenstown Bike Park (p567), Skyline Luge (p569), Ledge Bungy (p567), Ledge Swing (p567), GForce Paragliding (p569) and Ziptrek Ecotours (p568). At night there are stargazing tours (including gondola, adult/child $99/54).

Walking trails include the Skyline Loop track through the Douglas firs (30 minutes return). The energetic (or frugal) can forgo the gondola and hike to the top on the Tiki Trail (Map p566), while the popular Ben Lomond Track (p565) climbs on another 940m.

Kiwi Birdlife Park   BIRD SANCTUARY

(Map p566; ☑03-442 8059; www.kiwibird.co.nz; Brecon St; adult/child $55/25; ☺9am-5pm) These 2 hectares are home to 10,000 native plants, geckos, skinks, tuatara (an endemic reptile) and scores of birds, including kiwi, kea (alpine parrots), kārearea (NZ falcons), kākāriki (parakeets) and the endangered whio (blue ducks). Stroll around the aviaries, watch the conservation show and tiptoe quietly into the darkened kiwi houses. Kiwi feedings take place five times a day.

Time Tripper   VIEWPOINT

(Map p570; ☑03-409 0000; www.timetripper. co.nz; Main Town Pier; adult/child $25/12; ☺9am-5pm) Located in the old underwater observatory beneath the main pier, this 30-minute experience promises a journey back in time, explaining Lake Wakatipu's geology and mythology by way of a 30-minute animation, after which the screen lifts so that you can peer through the windows at the lake life. Large brown trout abound, and look out for freshwater eels and scaup ducks.

🏃 Activities

Head to Shotover St to get a handle on the baffling array of activities on offer in Queenstown. This street, particularly the two blocks between Stanley and Brecon Sts, is wall-to-wall with adventure-tour operators selling their products, interspersed with travel agencies and 'information centres' hawking the very same products. Adding to the confusion is the fact that some stores change their name from summer to winter, while some tour operators list street addresses that are primarily their pick-up points rather than distinct shopfronts for the business.

Several operators are based at The Station, a large hub on the corner of Shotover St and Camp St; various tours and shuttle buses depart from here.

If you're planning on tackling several activities, various combination tickets are available, including those offered by Queenstown Combos (Map p570; ☑03-442 7318; www.combos.co.nz; The Station, cnr Shotover St & Camp St).

Skiing & Snowboarding

Queenstown has two excellent ski fields: The Remarkables (Map p563; ☑03-441 1456; www.theremarkables.co.nz; Remarkables Ski Field Access Rd; daily lift pass adult/child $129/69) and Coronet Peak (Map p563; ☑03-441 1516; www. coronetpeak.co.nz; Coronet Peak Rd; daily lift pass adult/child $129/69), both of which can be booked from the Queenstown Snow Centre (Map p570; ☑03-442 4615; www.nzski.co.nz; 9 Duke St). You can hire gear here too, and the NZSki Snowline Express Ski Bus (p579) leaves from out the front. Coronet Peak is the only field to offer night skiing (staying open until 9pm on Wednesdays, Fridays and Saturdays at the peak of the season), which is an experience not to be missed if you strike a starry night. If you fancy a change of scenery, there's also Cardrona Alpine Resort (p594) and Treble Cone (p587) near Wānaka.

The ski season generally lasts from around June to early October. In winter, shops throughout Queenstown are full of ski gear for purchase and hire; Outside Sports (p567) and Small Planet Outdoors (Map p570; ☑ 03-442 5397; www.smallplanetsports.com; 15-17 Shotover St; ☺ 8am-8pm) are reliable options.

Heliskiing is an option for serious, cashed-up skiers; try Over the Top (p570), Harris Mountains Heli-Ski (Map p570; ☑ 03-442 6722; www.heliski.co.nz; 19 Shotover St; from $995; ☺ Jul-Sep), Southern Lakes Heliski (Map p570; ☑ 03-442 6222; www.southernlakes heliski.com; Torpedo 7, 20 Athol St; from $975) or Alpine Heliski (Map p570; ☑ 03-441 2300; www.alpineheliski.com; Info & Snow, 37 Shotover St; from $975; ☺ Jul-Sep).

Hiking

DOC publishes a dedicated *Wakatipu Walks* brochure, as well as the *Head of Lake Wakatipu* brochure, which covers trails closer to Glenorchy. Between them, they outline more than 60 day walks in the area. They can be picked up from the DOC Visitor Centre (p578) or downloaded from its website.

★ **Ben Lomond Track**   HIKING
(Map p566; www.doc.govt.nz) The popular, six-to eight-hour (return) track to Ben Lomond (1748m) culminates in probably the best accessible view in the area. From the top gondola station, the track climbs almost 1000m, and past Ben Lomond Saddle it gets pretty steep and rocky, but the views are incredible, stretching over Lake Wakatipu and as far as Tititea/Mt Aspiring.

Snow and ice can make it even more difficult, so in winter, check at the DOC Visitor Centre (p578) before setting out.

★ **Queenstown Hill/ Te Tapunui Time Walk**   HIKING
(Map p566) Ascend 500m to the summit of Queenstown Hill/Te Tapunui for a 360-degree view over the lake and along the Remarkables. The walk takes around three hours return. Access is from Belfast Tce.

Ultimate Hikes   HIKING
(Map p570; ☑ 03-450 1940; www.ultimatehikes. co.nz; The Station, Duke St; ☺ Nov-Apr) ✐ If you like your adventure with a little comfort, Ultimate Hikes offers three-day guided hikes on the Routeburn (from $1375) and Milford (from $2130) Tracks, staying in its own well-appointed private lodges. It also runs day walks on both tracks (from $179) and a couple of combinations of tracks. Prices include transfers from Queenstown, meals and accommodation.

In winter the office is rebranded as Snowbiz and rents skis and snowboards.

Guided Walks New Zealand   HIKING
(Map p563; ☑ 03-442 3000; www.nzwalks. com; unit 29, 159 Gorge Rd) Guided walks ranging from half-day nature walks near Queenstown (adult/child $119/79) to a day on the Routeburn Track ($199/140) and the full three-day Hollyford Track (from $2050/1625). It also offers snowshoeing in winter.

QUEENSTOWN & WĀNAKA QUEENSTOWN

QUEENSTOWN WITH CHILDREN

While Queenstown is brimming with activities, some of them have age restrictions that may exclude the youngest in your group. Nevertheless, you shouldn't have any trouble keeping the littlies busy.

All-age attractions include the Kiwi Birdlife Park (p564) and lake cruises on the TSS Earnslaw (p572). There's a good beachside playground (Map p566) off Marine Pde, near the entrance to the Queenstown Gardens (p562). Also in the gardens, Queenstown Ice Arena (p562) is great for a rainy day, and a round of frisbee golf (p562) will easily fill in a couple of hours. The Skyline Gondola (p564) offers a slow-moving activity with a dizzying view. Even small children can ride the luge (p569) with an adult, but need to be at least 110cm in height to go it alone.

Family Adventures (p569) runs gentle rafting trips suitable for three-year-olds. Under-fives can ride on the Shotover Jet (p568) for free, provided they're over 1m in height, and six-year-olds can tackle the ziplines with Ziptrek Ecotours (p568). Children as young as eight can tackle the Kawarau Zipride (p567), though eight- and nine-year-olds must ride tandem with an adult.

For more ideas and information, including details of local babysitters, visit the i-SITE (p579) or www.kidzgo.co.nz.

Queenstown

QUEENSTOWN & WĀNAKA

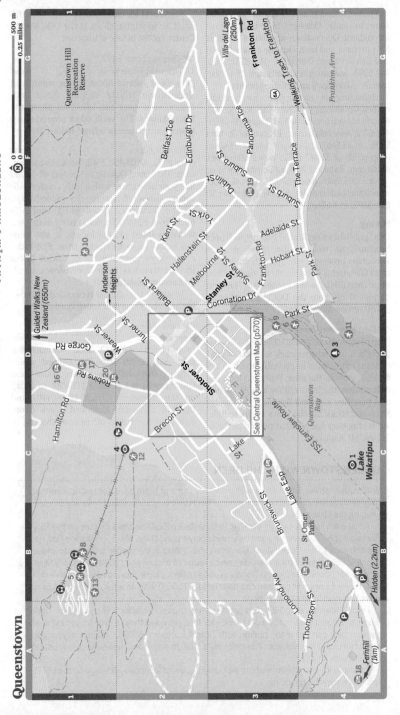

0 — 500 m
0 — 0.25 miles

Queenstown Hill
Recreation
Reserve

Villa del Lago (250m)

Frankton Rd

Walking Track to Frankton

Frankton Arm

Belfast Tce

Edinburgh Dr

Panorama Tce

Suburb St

Dublin St

The Terrace

19

Suburb St

Kent St

York St

Adelaide St

Hallenstein St

Melbourne St

Hobart St

Sydney St

Frankton Rd

Park St

Guided Walks New
Zealand (650m)

Anderson
Heights

Ballarat St

Stanley St

Coronation Dr

Park St

9
6

3

11

Gorge Rd

Weaver St

Turner St

16

17

20

Robins Rd

Shotover St

See Central Queenstown Map (p570)

Hamilton Rd

2

4

12

Brecon St

Lake St

Queenstown
Bay

TSS Earnslaw Route

1
Lake
Wakatipu

14

Lake Esp

Brunswick St

Queenstown Earnslaw Route

St Omer
Park

15

21

Lomond Ave

Thompson St

Hidden (2.2km)

Fernhill
(1km)

18

5

8

7

13

Cycling

Since the opening of the Queenstown Bike Park in 2011, the town has become entrenched as an international destination for mountain bikers. Coronet Peak (p564) also opens from December to March, with cross-country and downhill trails (day pass adult/child $55/35) and a shuttle from Queenstown ($25 return).

One of NZ's 22 Great Rides, the Queenstown Trail (www.queenstowntrail.co.nz) links various scenic cycling routes that radiate out like spokes to Arrowtown, Gibbston, Jack's Point, Lake Hayes and along the shores of Lake Wakatipu – 130km of off-road trails in total. The trail is suitable for cyclists of all levels. Bike-hire places such as Charge-About (Map p563; 03-442 6376; www.charge-about.co.nz; Hilton Hotel, 79 Peninsula Rd, Kelvin Heights; e-bike half/full day from $79/119; 10am-5pm) and Arrowtown Bike Hire (p584) typically offer packages that include shuttle-bus pick-ups from Gibbston – ride one way, sip a few wines and get a designated driver for the return trip.

Your best bets for hiring serious wheels in central Queenstown are Vertigo Bikes (Map p570; 03-442 8378; www.vertigobikes.co.nz; 4 Brecon St; rental half/full day from $39/59; 8am-7pm Oct-May) and Outside Sports (Map p570; 03-441 0074; www.outsidesports.co.nz; 9 Shotover St; 8am-9pm).

Queenstown Bike Park   MOUNTAIN BIKING
(Map p566; 03-441 0101; www.skyline.co.nz; Skyline Gondola; day pass incl gondola adult/child $110/75; 9am-7pm mid-Sep–mid-May) More than 30 different trails – from easy (green) to extreme (double black) – radiate out from the top of the Skyline Gondola. Once you've descended the 400m of vertical, simply jump on the gondola and do it all over again. The best trail for novice riders is the 6km-long Hammy's Track, which is studded with lake views and picnic spots.

Bungy & Swings

AJ Hackett Bungy   BUNGY JUMPING
(Map p570; 03-450 1300; www.bungy.co.nz; The Station, cnr Camp St & Shotover St) The bungy originator now offers jumps from three sites in the Queenstown area, with giant swings available at two of them. It all started at the historic 1880 Kawarau Bridge (Map p563; 03-450 1300; www.bungy.co.nz; Gibbston Hwy; adult/child $205/155), 23km from Queenstown, which became the world's first commercial bungy site in 1988. The 43m river leap is the only bungy site in the region to offer tandem jumps.

The Kawarau Bridge site also features the Kawarau Zipride (Map p563; 03-450 1300; www.bungy.co.nz; Gibbston Hwy; adult/child $50/40, 3-/5-ride pack $105/150), a flying fox zooming above the riverbank that reaches speeds of 60km/h. Multiride packs can be split between groups, making it a far cheaper alternative to the bungy.

The closest options to Queenstown are the Ledge Bungy (Map p566; 0800 286 4958; www.bungy.co.nz; Skyline Gondola; adult/child $205/155) and Ledge Swing (Map p566; www.bungy.co.nz; Skyline Gondola; adult/child $165/115), set just beneath the top station of the Skyline Gondola. The drop is 47m, but it's 400m above town. From July to September you can even leap into the dark.

QUEENSTOWN & WĀNAKA QUEENSTOWN

Queenstown

FIXING THE KNOTS

After days of adventure and activity, your body might well be craving a break in the pace. Here's our pick of the best ways to slow down and recharge in Queenstown.

➡ **Onsen Hot Pools** (☎ 03-442 5707; www.onsen.co.nz; 160 Arthurs Point Rd, Arthurs Point; 1/2/3/4 people from $88/126/175/212; ⊙ 9am-11pm) has private Japanese-style hot tubs with mountain views. Book ahead and one will be warmed up for you.

➡ Make the short trek to Millbrook Resort near Arrowtown, where the **Spa at Millbrook** (Map p563; ☎ 03-441 7017; www.millbrook.co.nz/spa; treatments from $79) is regularly rated as one of NZ's best spas.

➡ Catch a water taxi across the lake to **Eforea Spa at Hilton** (Map p563; ☎ 03-450 9416; www.queenstownhilton.com; 79 Peninsula Rd, Kelvin Heights; treatments from $85; ⊙ 9am-8pm).

Last but most airy is the **Nevis Bungy** (☎ 03-450 1300; www.bungy.co.nz; bungy $275), the highest leap in New Zealand. From Queenstown, 4WD buses will transport you onto private farmland where you can jump from a specially constructed pod, 134m above the Nevis River. The **Nevis Swing** (☎ 03-450 1300; www.bungy.co.nz; adult/child $225/175, tandem $440) starts 160m above the river and cuts a 300m arc across the canyon on a rope longer than a rugby field – yes, it's the world's biggest swing.

If you're keen to try more than one AJ Hackett experience, enquire about the range of combo tickets.

Shotover Canyon
Swing & Fox   ADVENTURE SPORTS
(Map p570; ☎ 03-442 9186; www.canyonswing.co.nz; 34 Shotover St; swing $249, fox $169, swing & fox combo $299) 🎋 Pick from any number of jump styles – backwards, in a chair, upside down – and then leap from a 109m cliff above the **Shotover River**, with 60m of free fall and a wild swing across the canyon at 150km/h. The Canyon Fox zipline can have you whizzing across the Shotover Canyon, more than 180m above the river. The price includes transfer from the Queenstown booking office, and if you liked the swing the first time, you can go again for $45.

Ziptrek Ecotours   ADVENTURE SPORTS
(Map p566; ☎ 03-441 2102; www.ziptrek.co.nz; Sky-line Gondola; 🖐) 🎋 Incorporating a series of flying foxes, this thrill-ride takes you whirring through the forest canopy, from treetop platform to treetop platform, high above Queenstown. Choose from the two-hour, four-line Moa (adult/child $145/99); the gnarlier and faster three-hour, six-line Kea ($195/149); and the one-hour, two-line Keruru ($99), which evens with a 21m controlled drop.

Jetboating
Skippers Canyon Jet   BOATING
(Map p563; ☎ 03-442 9434; www.skipperscanyon jet.co.nz; Skippers Rd; adult/child $159/85) 🎋 A 30-minute jetboat blast through the remote and hard-to-access Skippers Canyon, among the narrowest gorges on the **Shotover River**. Trips pick up from The Station in Queenstown, taking around three hours in total. It also offers a scenic bus tour of the canyon (adult/child $155/95), which can be combined with the jetboat ($195/115).

Shotover Jet   BOATING
(☎ 03-442 8570; www.shotoverjet.com; 3 Arthurs Point Rd, Arthurs Point; adult/child $159/89) 🎋 Half-hour jetboat trips through the narrow Shotover Canyon, with lots of thrilling 360-degree spins and reaching speeds of 90km/h.

KJet   BOATING
(Map p570; ☎ 03-409 0000; www.kjet.co.nz; Main Town Pier; adult/child/family $135/69/307; ⊙ 9am-6pm) Skim, skid and spin around Lake Wakatipu and the Kawarau and Lower Shotover Rivers on these one-hour trips, leaving every hour on the hour.

Hydro Attack   BOATING
(Map p570; ☎ 0508 493 762; www.hydroattack. co.nz; Lapsley Butson Wharf; 25min ride $154; ⊙ 9am-6pm Nov-Mar, 10am-4.30pm Apr-Oct) That shark you see buzzing about Lake Wakatipu is the Hydro Attack – jump inside, strap yourself in and take a ride. This 'Seabreacher X' watercraft can travel at 80km/h on the water, dive 2m underneath and then launch itself nearly 6m into the air. It's mesmerising to watch, let alone travel inside.

Riverboarding & Rafting
Serious Fun Riverboarding ADVENTURE SPORTS
(Map p570; ☎ 03-442 5262; www.riverboarding. co.nz; Info & Track, 37 Shotover St; from $225) Steer buoyant sledges or bodyboards on the rapids and whirlpools of the Kawarau River.

The gentlest option is bodyboard drifting ($255, January and February only), followed by sledging ($235, November to March) and full-on riversurfing ($235, September to May).

Family Adventures
RAFTING
(Map p570; ☑ 03-442 8836; www.familyadventures.co.nz; 39 Shotover St; adult/child $189/120; ⊙ Oct-Apr; ⊞) These gentle (Grades I to II) and good-humoured rafting trips on the Shotover River are much loved by families as they're suitable for even three-year-olds. Trips depart from Browns Ski Shop and include a 45-minute scenic drive to the Skippers Canyon launch site, which *Lord of the Rings* nuts will recognise as the Ford of Bruinen.

Go Orange Rafting
RAFTING
(Map p570; ☑ 03-442 7340; www.goorange.co.nz; 35 Shotover St; rafting/helirafting from $189/299; ⊙ 7.30am-7pm) 🌿 Rafts year-round on the churning Shotover River (Grades III to V) and calmer Kawarau River (Grades II to III). The Kawarau trips include a thrilling 30-minute jetboat ride from town to the launch site, then two hours on the water. Accessing the Shotover site involves a scenic coach trip along Skippers Canyon, but in snow a helicopter is required.

Paragliding, Parasailing & Skydiving

GForce Paragliding
PARAGLIDING
(Map p566; ☑ 03-441 8581; www.nzgforce.com; Skyline Gondola; flight $239) Tandem paragliding from the top of the gondola (early departures are $20 cheaper).

Queenstown Paraflights
PARASAILING
(Map p570; ☑ 03-441 2242; www.paraflights.co.nz; Main Town Pier; solo/tandem/triple per person $199/129/99) Take a solo, tandem or triple paraflight, zipping along 180m above the lake, pulled behind a boat.

NZone
SKYDIVING
(Map p570; ☑ 03-442 5867; www.nzoneskydive.co.nz; 35 Shotover St; from $299) Jump out of a perfectly good airplane from 9000, 12,000 or 15,000ft...in tandem with someone who actually knows what they're doing.

Other Activities
If you've heard it can be done, it's likely that it can be done in Queenstown. To save us writing an activities encyclopedia, check in at the i-SITE (p579) if you're interested in the likes of golf, minigolf, sailing or diving.

Climbing Queenstown
CLIMBING
(Map p563; · ☑ 027 477 9393; www.climbingqueenstown.com; Basecamp Adventures Climbing Centre, 3/15 Red Oaks Dr, Frankton; half-/full day $179/299) Rock-climbing, mountaineering and guided hiking and snowshoeing trips in the Remarkables. Trips depart from Outside Sports (p567).

Canyoning Queenstown
CLIMBING
(Map p570; ☑ 03-441 3003; www.canyonexplorers.nz; 39 Camp St; ⊙ Oct-Apr) Jump, slide, zip line and abseil your way through Queenstown Canyon (half day $219), 10 minutes' drive from town, or the remote Routeburn Canyon (full day $319) out past Glenorchy. It also operates via ferrata trips on Queenstown Hill ($189), climbing cliffs that overlook Queenstown using metal rungs and safety cables.

Skyline Luge
ADVENTURE SPORTS
(Map p566; ☑ 03-441 0101; www.skyline.co.nz; Skyline Gondola; 2/3/5 rides incl gondola adult $61/63/67, child $43/45/49; ⊙ 10am-8pm) 🌿 Ride the gondola to the top, then hop on a three-wheeled cart to ride 800m of track. Your first run must be on the easy Blue Track then you're allowed to advance to the Red Track, with its banked corners and tunnel. Children must be over 110cm in height to ride the Blue Track and over 135cm for the Red.

👉 Tours

Winery Tours
Most winery tours include cellar-door stops in the Lake Hayes, Gibbston, Bannockburn and Cromwell Basin subregions.

New Zealand Wine Tours
WINE
(☑ 0800 666 778; www.nzwinetours.co.nz; from $235) Small-group (maximum seven people) or private winery tours, including lunch – platter, degustation or à la carte, depending on the tour.

Appellation Wine Tours
WINE
(☑ 03-442 0246; www.appellationcentral.co.nz; from $169) Take a tipple at wineries in Gibbston, Bannockburn and Cromwell, including cheese platters (on half-day tours) or a platter or degustation lunch. It also offers general sightseeing tours and combinations of the two.

Hop on Hop off Wine Tours
WINE
(☑ 0800 6937 2273; www.hoponhopoffwinetours.com; half-/full day $60/80) Jump on outside

Central Queenstown

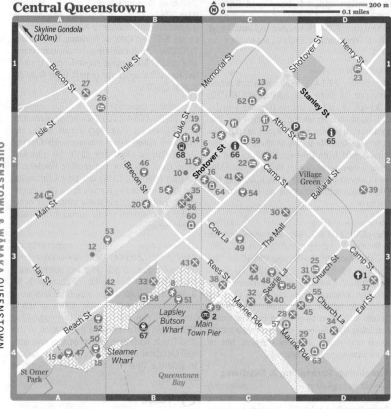

The Station for a 17-stop loop around Lake Hayes and Gibbston wineries, breweries and notable sites such as the Shotover Jet, Arrowtown and the original AJ Hackett bungy site.

Scenic Flights

Air Milford   SCENIC FLIGHTS
(Map p563; ☎03-442 2351; www.airmilford.co.nz; 3 Tex Smith Lane, Frankton) Options include a Milford Sound & Big Five Glaciers flyover (adult/child $420/260), a fly-cruise-fly combo (from $565/340), and longer flights to Doubtful Sound (summer only) and Aoraki/Mt Cook.

Glenorchy Air   SCENIC FLIGHTS
(Map p563; ☎03-442 2207; www.glenorchyair.co.nz; Queenstown Airport, Frankton) Scenic trips include a Milford Sound fly-cruise-fly option (adult/child $535/360), an Aoraki/Mt Cook glacier flight with a landing ($685/415), and various kayaking and hiking combos.

Over The Top   SCENIC FLIGHTS
(Map p563; ☎03-442 2233; www.flynz.co.nz; 10 Tex Smith Lane, Frankton) Offers a range of helicopter flights, from a picnic on a peak near town (per person $995) to an Ultimate Milford flight with four landings (from $7950). From July to October it offers heliskiing.

Milford Sound Tours

Day trips from Queenstown to Milford Sound via Te Anau take 12 to 13 hours, including a cruise on the sound. Bus-cruise-flight options are also available, as is pick-up from the Routeburn Track (p558) trailhead at the Divide. It's a long day in the saddle, so you might consider visiting Milford from Te Anau. Another way to speed things up are plane or helicopter sightseeing flights to Milford.

BBQ Bus by Altitude Tours   TOURS
(☎03-441 4788; www.bbqbus.co.nz; adult/child $250/125) Small-group bus tours to Milford Sound (maximum 19 people), including a

Central Queenstown

barbecue lunch followed by a cruise. Te Anau drop-offs and pick-ups are $40 cheaper.

Real Journeys   TOURS
(Map p570; ☑0800 656 501; www.realjourneys.co.nz; Steamer Wharf) ⊘ Runs a host of trips, including day and overnight tours to Milford (from $210) and Doubtful (from $285) Sounds.

Other Tours
Off Road Adventure Centre   DRIVING
(Map p570; ☑03-442 7858; www.offroad.co.nz; 61a Shotover St) Exciting off-road trips by quad

bike (from $219), dirt bike (from $309) or buggy (two-seater $368), with exclusive access to a 4500-hectare property along the Kawarau River and Nevis Range. Also on offer are 4WD sightseeing tours (from $189) to Glenorchy or Skippers Canyon.

Private Discovery Tours   DRIVING
(☑03-442 2299; www.privatediscoverytours.co.nz) Offers a range of small-group 4WD tours, including the half-day High Country Discovery (adult/child $195/98) offering exclusive access to Mt Earnslaw Station, a sheep farm in a remote valley past Glenorchy, complete

with Middle-earth movie locations. The station is also included on the full-day Paradise Discovery ($395/205), which visits the Dart River, Paradise, Diamond Lake and further Hobbit-infested sites.

Nomad Safaris
DRIVING

(Map p570; ☑03-442 6699; www.nomadsafaris.co.nz; 37 Shotover St; adult/child from $195/95) Runs 4WD tours into hard-to-get-to back-country destinations such as Skippers Canyon and Macetown, as well as a trip through Middle-earth locations around Glenorchy and the Wakatipu Basin. You can also quad-bike through a sheep station on Queenstown Hill ($275).

TSS Earnslaw
CRUISE

(Map p570; ☑03-249 6000; www.realjourneys.co.nz; Steamer Wharf) The stately, steam-powered TSS *Earnslaw* was built in the same year as the *Titanic* (1912) but has fared somewhat better. The ship was once the lake's major means of transport, though now its ever-present cloud of black soot (it burns a tonne of coal an hour) seems a little incongruous in such a pristine setting.

🎉 Festivals & Events

Queenstown

Winter Festival
CARNIVAL

(www.winterfestival.co.nz; ☉ Jun) Four days of wacky ski and snowboard activities, live music, comedy, fireworks, a community carnival, parade, ball and plenty of frigid frivolity in late June.

Winter Pride
LGBT

(www.winterpride.co.nz; ☉ Aug/Sep) The South Island's biggest and best gay-and-lesbian event, held over 10 party-packed days in late August/early September.

🛏 Sleeping

🛏 Central Queenstown

Flaming Kiwi Backpackers
HOSTEL $

(Map p566; ☑03-442 5494; www.flamingkiwi.co.nz; 39 Robins Rd; dm/r without bathroom from $35/90; P☎) Close to the town centre but still quietly removed, this friendly hostel offers tidy dorms with a locker for every bed, three kitchens, unlimited wi-fi and a bottle of sunblock at reception. The lounge is like being back at home, and there are free bikes, frisbees and international phone calls to 21 countries.

Haka Lodge
HOSTEL $

(Map p570; ☑03-442 4970; www.hakalodges.com; 6 Henry St; dm/apt from $33/216, r with/without bathroom $103/94; P❄☎) Part of a small Kiwi chain of higher-brow hostels, the warren-like Haka has cosy dorms with solid bunks that include large lockable storage chests, privacy curtains, personal lights and electrical sockets. There's a one-bedroom apartment attached, with its own kitchen, spacious lounge, laundry facilities and private deck where you can watch paragliders swirl down from the gondola.

Butterfli Lodge
HOSTEL $

(Map p566; ☑03-442 6367; www.butterfli.co.nz; 62 Thompson St; dm/r from $35/95; P☎) This little hostel sits on a quiet hillside west of the town centre. There are no bunks but no en suites either. The views from the deck are like a sightseeing tour in themselves.

★ Adventure Queenstown
HOSTEL $$

(Map p570; ☑03-409 0862; www.aqhostel.co.nz; 36 Camp St; dm $38-44, r $140; ❄☎) Run by experienced travellers (as the photos displayed throughout testify), this central hostel has spotless dorms, a modern kitchen and balconies that are like a window onto the city. The private room has an en suite, as do some of the dorms. There are activities every night, from an in-house quiz to a Saturday pub crawl.

Adventure Q2 Hostel
HOSTEL $$

(Map p570; ☑03-927 4625; www.adventureq2.co.nz; 5 Athol St; dm $37-39, r $135; ☎) Opened in 2016, this sister hostel to Adventure Queenstown is pretty much its twin (complete with the nightly activities etc), but with sturdier bunks, disabled-access bathrooms and an elevator.

Creeksyde Queenstown Holiday Park & Motels
HOLIDAY PARK $$

(Map p566; ☑03-442 9447; www.camp.co.nz; 54 Robins Rd; sites $65, r with/without bathroom $139/95, apt $159-329; P☎) 🍃 In a pretty garden setting, this extremely well-kept holiday park has accommodation ranging from powered sites to fully self-contained two-bedroom apartments. There are quirky sculptures throughout and an ablutions block disguised as a medieval oast house (hop kiln). In 2018 it became the first holiday park in the world to be environmentally certified by EarthCheck.

Queenstown Motel Apartments
MOTEL $$

(Map p566; ☑03-442 6095; www.qma.co.nz; 62 Frankton Rd; unit from $170; P☎) This well-run, sunlit spot is like two distinct properties in one – smallish but comfortable newer units at the front and cheaper 1970s-style units (with renovated bathrooms) lined along the back. It has good views across the lake to Cecil and Walter Peaks. No children under 18.

YHA Queenstown Lakefront   HOSTEL $$

(Map p566; 03-442 8413; www.yha.co.nz; 88-90 Lake Esplanade; dm/s/tw/d without bathroom from $34/90/110/115, r with bathroom $150-160; P 🛱) 🏄 This large lakefront hostel, fully renovated in 2017, has basic but neat-as-a-pin bunkrooms and an industrial-sized kitchen with window benches to absorb the view. The TV room is filled with beanbags and there are even a couple of massage chairs in the lounge. Lakeview rooms get a shared balcony (and some traffic noise).

Nomads   HOSTEL $$

(Map p570; 03-441 3922; www.nomadsworld. com; 5-11 Church St; dm/r from $32/154; 🛱) With a prime location in the heart of Queenstown's nightlife, this massive hostel has facilities galore, including its own mini-cinema, private en-suite rooms, a large lounge with a pool table, a free sauna and an on-site travel agency. Dorms range from three to 12 beds, and some have en suites, too.

Queenstown Park   BOUTIQUE HOTEL $$$

(Map p566; 03-441 8441; www.queenstownpark hotel.co.nz; 21 Robins Rd; r from $405; P ❄ 🛱) White curtains billow over beds decked out in luxurious linen at this very chic 19-room hotel. The 'Remarkables' rooms overlook a park, to the namesake mountain range (there aren't any lake views), while the 'Gondola' rooms are smaller but have courtyards or balconies. All have kitchenettes, and there's free wine and nibbles during 'canapé hour' (6pm to 7pm).

The Dairy   BOUTIQUE HOTEL $$$

(Map p570; 03-442 5164; www.thedairy. co.nz; cnr Brecon & Isle Sts; r/ste from $337/480; P ❄ 🛱) Its dining room was once a corner store, but the Dairy is now a luxury B&B with 13 rooms packed with classy touches such as designer bed linen, silk cushions and luxurious mohair rugs. Rates include cooked breakfasts and complimentary NZ bubbly on arrival.

Lomond Lodge   MOTEL $$$

(Map p570; 03-442 8235; www.lomondlodge. com; 33 Man St; r from $255; P 🛱) This lodge on the fringe of the town centre has smartly designed rooms with indulgent bathrooms and USB sockets, and a landscaped, sunny terrace and barbecue area out back. It's worth splurging on one of the upstairs Lake View rooms, which come with lookout-worthy balconies.

🛏 Surrounds

Queenstown Top 10   HOLIDAY PARK $$

(03-442 9306; www.qtowntop10.co.nz; 70 Arthurs Point Rd, Arthurs Point; sites from $60, r with bathroom $121, units with/without bathroom from $155/95; P 🛱 🐕) 🏄 High above the Shotover River, this relatively small and extremely neat park with better-than-the-norm motel units is 10 minutes' drive from the hustle and bustle of Queenstown. There's bike storage, a ski drying room and a complimentary shuttle bus into town. Fall out of your campervan straight onto the famous Shotover Jet.

Villa del Lago   APARTMENT $$$

(Map p563; 03-442 5727; www.villadellago.co.nz; 249 Frankton Rd, Queenstown East; apt from $333; P 🛱) Clinging to the slopes between the highway and the lake, these spacious one- to three-bedroom apartments have lake-facing terraces, incredible views and all the mod cons, including full kitchens, laundries and gas fires. The water taxi can stop at the private jetty, or you can walk along the lake to Queenstown in 25 minutes.

Hidden   B&B $$$

(Map p563; 03-442 6636; www.hiddenlodge queenstown.co.nz; 28 Evergreen Pl, Sunshine Bay; r from $595-695; P @ 🛱) The well-named Hidden is literally the last place west in Queenstown. Tucked away in Sunshine Bay, it has enormous rooms, unfettered lake and mountain views, complimentary beer and wine, and an outdoor hot tub.

Platinum Villas   RENTAL HOUSE $$$

(Map p566; 03-746 7700; www.platinumqueens town.co.nz; 96 Fernhill Rd, Fernhill; house from $485; P 🛱) Nab one of these 36 identical, luxurious, three-bedroom townhouses and make yourself at home. Each has a large open-plan living area with a big stone fireplace, bespoke furniture, laundry facilities and most have a garage. 'Lakeview' vil-

ⓘ QUEENSTOWN ON A BUDGET

Queenstown is a notoriously expensive destination, especially if you're planning on undertaking the thrill-seeking adventures it's famous for. However, not everything costs a small fortune.

➡ Play frisbee golf (p562) for free in Queenstown Gardens.

➡ Shun the gondola and hike to a view on Queenstown Hill (p565) or the Tiki Trail (p564); for a free and full day out to Queenstown's finest view, continue along the Ben Lomond Track (p565).

➡ Fuel up at Fergbaker, Taco Medic, Empanada Kitchen or Caribe Latin Kitchen.

➡ Skip an organised lake tour and ride the ferry (p580) across to Kelvin Heights.

las get the better outlook, but 'Alpine' villas get the melodic burble of the creek below.

Groups aged under 25 not accepted.

🍴 Eating

🍴 Central Queenstown

⭐**Fergbaker**   BAKERY $
(Map p570; 📞03-441 1206; 40 Shotover St; items $3-7.50; ⏲6.30am-4.30pm) The sweeter sister of Fergburger bakes all manner of tempting treats – and though most things look tasty with 3am beer goggles on, it withstands the daylight test admirably. Goodies include inventive pies (such as venison and portobello mushroom) and breads, filled rolls and a sugary wealth of sweet treats. If you're after gelato, call into Mrs Ferg next door.

Caribe Latin Kitchen   LATIN AMERICAN $
(Map p570; 📞03-442 6658; www.caribelatin kitchen.com; 36 The Mall; mains $8-16; ⏲10.30am-11pm; 🍴) One of the Mall's more characterful and colourful restaurants, Caribe is a small nook dishing out quality tacos, quesadillas and burritos stuffed fuller than a piñata. The tiled decor plays to a Day of the Dead theme, and the few tables are brighter than a Mexican sun. Excellent value.

Empanada Kitchen   EMPANADAS $
(Map p570; 📞021 0279 2109; www.theempanada kitchen.com; 60 Beach St; empanadas $5.50; ⏲10am-5.30pm) Yes, this little hole-in-the-wall kiosk is built into a public toilet, but that's far from a statement about its food. The empanadas are absolutely delicious, with flavours that change daily and include savoury and sweet options.

Taco Medic   TACOS $
(Map p570; 📞03-442 8174; www.tacomedic.co.nz; 3 Searle Lane; tacos $8; ⏲11am-10pm) Taco Medic began life as a food truck, but has put on the handbrake to become a stylishly simple bolthole eatery. Cosy up to the bar and choose from eight tacos made with local free-farmed meats and a changing fish-of-the-day taco.

Erik's Fish & Chips   FISH & CHIPS $
(Map p570; 📞03-441 3474; www.eriksfishand chips.co.nz; 13 Earl St; fish $6.50-12; ⏲noon-9pm) A pair of food trucks squeezed into a lane between buildings – order your hoki, monkfish or blue cod from one, and eat inside the other. Ever fancied a deep-fried kiwifruit to finish your meal? You've come to the right place.

Patagonia   SWEETS $
(Map p570; 📞03-409 2465; www.patagoniachoc olates.co.nz; 2 Rees St; ice cream $6-9, breakfast $9-14; ⏲9am-9pm; 🛜) Its popularity is its only detraction, but fight your way in and you'll find 24 superb ice-cream flavours, a host of chocolate and the truly Patagonian touch of churros and *dulce de leche* ice cream.

⭐**Yonder**   CAFE $$
(Map p570; 📞03-409 0994; www.yonderqt.co.nz; 14 Church St; mains $12-24; ⏲8am-late; 🛜) With a menu inspired by 'the things we've loved around our travels', this cafe brings to the table a cosmopolitan assortment of dishes: bacon butties, kimchi bowls, salmon poké bowls. There are power points and USB ports by many of the indoor tables, but when the sun's out you'll want to be on the outdoor patio.

Bespoke Kitchen   CAFE $$
(Map p570; 📞03-409 0552; www.bespokekitchen. co.nz; 9 Isle St; mains $20-25; ⏲8am-5pm; 🛜🍴) Occupying a light-filled corner site near the gondola, Bespoke delivers everything you'd expect of a smart Kiwi cafe. It has a mouth-watering selection of counter food, beautifully presented cooked options, outside seating in sight of the mountains and, of course, great coffee. Vegans will find plenty of choice, too.

Blue Kanu
FUSION $$

(Map p570; ☑ 03-442 6060; www.bluekanu.co.nz; 16 Church St; mains $29-36; ⊙ 4pm-late) Disproving the rule that all tiki houses are inherently tacky, Blue Kanu serves up a food style it calls 'Polynasian' – Fijian *kokoda* (raw fish with coconut and lime) in one hand, XO pork dumplings in the other. It's relaxed and personable, and although the marriage of the Polynesian decor and chopsticks sounds impossible to pull off, it works.

Vudu Cafe & Larder
CAFE $$

(Map p570; ☑ 03-441 8370; www.vudu.co.nz; 16 Rees St; mains $9-25; ⊙ 7.30am-6pm) At this ever-popular cafe, excellent home-style baking combines with great coffee and the sort of breakfasts that make bacon and eggs seem very passé – try the French-toast pudding. Admire the huge photo of a far less populated Queenstown from an inside table, or head outside to graze by the lake. Service can be slow, but that's the weight of numbers.

The Taj
INDIAN $$

(Map p570; ☑ 03-442 5270; www.thetajqueenstown.co.nz; 75 Beach St; mains $27-36; ⊙ noon-10pm) For a tiny place (only seven tables) this upmarket Indian restaurant sure has a long menu. Try the *maacher jhol*, a delicious Bengali-style fish curry served with pickled vegetables.

Eichardt's Bar
TAPAS $$

(Map p570; ☑ 03-441 0450; www.eichardtsdining.com; Marine Pde; breakfast $16-20, tapas $8-13; ⊙ 7.30am-late) Elegant without being stuffy, the small bar attached to Eichardt's Private Hotel is a wonderful refuge from the buzz of the streets. The breakfast menu is full of interesting options (smashed edamame, chorizo hash). From lunchtime, the focus shifts to tapas, and though the selection isn't particularly Spanish (steamed buns or grilled bruschetta, for example), it is particularly delicious.

Fergburger
BURGERS $$

(Map p570; ☑ 03-441 1232; www.fergburger.com; 42 Shotover St; burgers $13-20; ⊙ 8am-5am) Who knew a burger joint could ever be a destination restaurant? Such are the queues at Fergburger that it often looks like an All Blacks scrum out the front. The burgers are as tasty and satisfying as ever, but the wait can be horrendous and the menu has more choices than the place has seats.

Devil Burger
BURGERS $$

(Map p570; ☑ 03-442 4666; www.devilburger.com; 5/11 Church St; burgers $11-20; ⊙ 10am-midnight Sun-Wed, to 3am Thu-Sat; ☑ ⦿) If gluttony is a sin, this Devil is doing its job, with 18 burgers coming in sizes regular and large. Wraps include the hangover-busting 'Walk of Shame', which is basically a rolled-up full cooked breakfast. It gives Fergburger a run for its bun, even if purely for the lack of queues.

Winnie's
PIZZA $$

(Map p570; ☑ 03-442 8635; www.winnies.co.nz; 1st fl, 7-9 The Mall; mains $18-37; ⊙ noon-late; ⦿ ⦿) It's a Tardis-like journey leaving the mall and finding Winnie's – part pizza joint and part bar, looking a little like a '50s diner with a drinking habit. Pizzas come in various accents – Moroccan, Mexican, Chinese – along with burgers, nachos, chicken wings and salads. On balmy nights the roof opens up and the party continues into the wee smalls.

Halo Forbidden Bite
CAFE $$

(Map p570; ☑ 03-441 1411; www.haloforbiddenbite.co.nz; 1 Earl St; brunch $18-25, dinner $25-29; ⊙ 6am-9pm; ⦿) Pitching itself as both heavenly and devilish, Halo is a stylish, sunny place that effortlessly blurs the line between breakfast, lunch and dinner. The breakfast burrito will set you up for a day's adventuring. There's almost as much seating outside as in.

Tatsumi
JAPANESE $$$

(Map p570; ☑ 03-442 5888; www.tatsumi.co.nz; 9 Beach St; dishes $15-35, lunch/dinner set menu from $50/75; ⊙ 4pm-late) Since losing its original business in the Christchurch earthquakes, Tatsumi has brought its blend of traditional and modern Japanese 'tapas' to central Queenstown. The service is exemplary and the food consistently excellent, including gorgeous sashimi platters, delicate squid-ink-tempura calamari and crispy *kara-age* chicken. Set menus of signature dishes, and indulgent dégustation dining, are also offered.

Rātā
INTERNATIONAL $$$

(Map p570; ☑ 03-442 9393; www.ratadining.co.nz; 43 Ballarat St; mains $42-48, 2-/3-course lunch $38/45; ⊙ noon-late) After gaining Michelin stars for restaurants in London, New York and LA, chef-owner Josh Emett now wields his exceptional but surprisingly unflashy cooking back home in this upmarket yet informal back-lane eatery. Native bush, edging the windows and in a large-scale photographic mural, sets the scene for a short menu showcasing the best seasonal NZ produce.

Botswana Butchery
INTERNATIONAL $$$

(Map p570; ☑ 03-442 6994; www.botswanabutchery.co.nz; 17 Marine Pde; lunch mains $23-34, dinner $40-48; ⊙noon-11pm) This swish lakefront restaurant is one of the flag-bearers of Queenstown high-end dining. Despite that, it doesn't come across as sniffy, especially at lunch when prices drop and a casual air pervades. The menu bounces from a decadent French onion soup to curries and game meats. Evenings are predominantly but not exclusively meaty – a 1.4kg cut of Cardrona lamb, anyone?

✗ Frankton & Kelvin Heights

Boat Shed   CAFE $$
(Map p563; ✆03-441 4146; www.boatshedqueens town.com; Frankton Marina, 847 Frankton Rd, Frankton; mains $17-26; ⊙8am-5pm; ☎) Occupying a historic NZ Railways shipping office right by the lake, this great little cafe serves excellent, artfully arranged breakfasts and the likes of beef cheeks and *cioppino* (seafood stew) for lunch. It's the perfect pit stop if you're cycling or walking the lakeside trail. Service can be slow at busy times.

Wakatipu Grill   EUROPEAN $$$
(Map p563; ✆03-450 9402; www.queenstownhilton. com; Hilton Queenstown, Peninsula Rd, Kelvin Heights; mains $30-49; ⊙6-10.30am & 4-10pm) The Hilton sprawls along the lakeside by the Kawarau River outlet, and part of the fun of visiting its signature restaurant is the ferry ride. As the name implies, there's always a decent selection of steak on the menu, but much more besides, including locally sourced fish and lamb.

⚑ Drinking & Entertainment

Pick up a copy of *Source* (www.sourcemaga zine.co.nz), a free monthly publication with articles and details of goings-on around the Southern Lakes.

Perky's   BAR
(Map p570; ✆021 664 043; www.facebook.com/ perkysqueenstown; Lapsley Butson Wharf; ⊙noon-11pm) That hint of wobbliness you feel isn't the alcohol (yet), it's the fact that you're drinking on an old tour boat that's now permanently moored at the lakeshore. If you're feeling peckish, you're welcome to bring your own food aboard.

Atlas Beer Cafe   CRAFT BEER
(Map p570; ✆03-442 5995; www.atlasbeercafe. com; Steamer Wharf; ⊙10am-late) There are usually 23 craft beers on tap at this pint-sized lakefront bar, headlined by brews from Dunedin's Emerson's Brewery and Queenstown's Altitude; pick four to sample on a tasting paddle. It also serves excellent cooked breakfasts ($17 to $22), and simple substantial fare such as steaks and burgers.

Smiths Craft Beer House   CRAFT BEER
(Map p570; ✆03-409 2337; www.smithscraftbeer. co.nz; 1st floor, 53 Shotover St; ⊙noon-late; ☎) It's back to basics in everything but the taps, with bare concrete floors and industrial tables and chairs, but 36 creative NZ craft beers to sample. The folks behind the bar will chat brews as long as you'll listen, and there's a menu (mains $17 to $20) of burgers and po'boys (Louisiana-style sandwiches) to mop up the suds.

Zephyr   BAR
(Map p570; ✆03-409 0852; www.facebook.com/ zephyrqt; 1 Searle Lane; ⊙7pm-4am) Queenstown's hippest rock bar is located – as all such places should be – in a dark, grungy, concrete-floored space off a back lane. There's a popular pool table and live bands on Wednesday nights. Beer comes only in bottles, and there's a permanently raucous soundtrack.

1789   BAR
(Map p570; ✆03-450 0045; www.sofitel-queens town.com; entry on Brecon St; ⊙4pm-late) Tucked into a corner of the Sofitel, this velvet-smooth jazz lounge is named for the French Revolution, with a bloody colour scheme to suit. There are around 350 wines by the bottle and 50 by the glass, and live jazz sessions on Friday and Saturday evenings.

Bunker   COCKTAIL BAR
(Map p570; ✆03-441 8030; www.thebunker.co.nz; 14 Cow Lane; ⊙4pm-4am) Bunkered upstairs rather than down, this chi-chi little bar clearly fancies itself as the kind of place Sean Connery's James Bond might frequent, if the decor is anything to go by. Best of all is the outside terrace, with couches, a fire in winter and a projector screening classic movies onto the wall of a neighbouring building.

World Bar   BAR
(Map p570; ✆03-450 0008; www.theworldbar. co.nz; 12 Church St; ⊙11.30am-late) Queenstown's legendary party hub before it was destroyed by fire in 2013, the World is once again spinning. Decor swings between degrees of eclectic, from the mounted moose head with halo, to the cocktails that come in teapots. The food's good, there are regular DJs and the outdoor area is prime real estate on balmy afternoons and evenings.

EXPLORING THE GIBBSTON VALLEY

Queenstown's adrenaline junkies might be happiest dangling off a giant rubber band, but as they're plunging towards the Kawarau River, they might not realise they're in the heart of Gibbston, one of Central Otago's main wine subregions, accounting for around 20% of plantings.

Strung along Gibbston Hwy (SH6) is an interesting and beautiful selection of vineyards. Almost opposite the Kawarau Bridge, a precipitous 2km gravel road leads to Chard Farm (Map p563; 03-442 8452; www.chardfarm.co.nz; 205 Chard Rd; ⊙10am-5pm) FREE, the most picturesque of the wineries. A further 1km along SH6 is Gibbston Valley (Map p563; 03-442 6910; www.gibbstonvalley.com; 1820 Gibbston Hwy; ⊙10am-5pm), the area's oldest commercial winery. As well as tastings ($5 to $15), it has a restaurant, cheesery, tours of the winery ($35) and NZ's largest wine cave ($20), as well as bike hire. It also operates its own bus from Queenstown ($35 return) – you could always take the bus and then hire a bike to get between cellar doors.

Another 3km along SH6, Peregrine (Map p563; 03-442 4000; www.peregrinewines. co.nz; 2127 Gibbston Hwy/SH6; ⊙11am-5pm) FREE has an impressive, award-winning cellar door – a bunker-like building with a roof reminiscent of a falcon's wing in flight. As well as tastings, you can take a stroll through the adjoining barrel room.

The Gibbston River Trail, part of the Queenstown Trail, is a walking and cycling track that follows the Kawarau River for 11km from the Kawarau Bridge, passing all of the wineries. From Peregrine, walkers (but not cyclists) can swing onto the Peregrine Loop (one hour, 2.7km), which crosses over old mining works on 11 timber and two steel bridges, one of which passes through the branches of a willow tree.

While you're in the area, be sure to call into the rustic Gibbston Tavern (Map p563; 03-409 0508; www.gibbstontavern.co.nz; 8 Coalpit Rd; ⊙11am-8pm), just off the highway past Peregrine. It stocks Gibbston wines, fires up good pizzas and has the cellar door for Rockburn (Map p563; 03-445 0555; www.rockburn.co.nz; 8 Coalpit Rd; tastings $10, free if you buy two bottles; ⊙noon-4pm) in the front yard, producers of one of the region's most acclaimed pinot noirs.

If you're keen to explore the valley's wineries without needing to contemplate a drive afterwards, consider staying among the vines at Kinross (Map p563; 03-746 7269; www. kinrosscottages.co.nz; 2300 Gibbston Hwy; r from $266; P ♠), where the heritage-looking cottages are a front for modern, luxurious studio rooms. It has its own cellar door, representing six Central Otago vineyards (tastings $15, free with purchases over $50), plus a bistro and bike-hire outlet.

Ask at the Queenstown i-SITE (p579) for maps and information about touring the area.

Vinyl Underground   CLUB
(Map p570; www.facebook.com/Vinylundergroundqt; 12b Church St; ⊙10pm-4am Tue-Sat) Enter the underworld, or at least the space under the World Bar, to find the heartbeat of Queenstown's late-night life. It's a proper, sweaty, industrial-style bunker club – the bar alone must weigh several tonnes.

Bardeaux   WINE BAR
(Map p570; 03-442 8284; www.goodgroup.co. nz; Eureka Arcade, off The Mall; ⊙4pm-4am) This small, cavelike wine bar is all class. Under a low ceiling are plush leather armchairs and a fireplace made from Central Otago schist. Whisky is king here, but the wine list is extraordinary, especially if you're keen to drop $4500 on a bottle once in your life. It's surprisingly relaxed for a place with such lofty tastes.

Pub on Wharf   PUB
(Map p570; 03-441 2155; www.pubonwharf.co.nz; 88 Beach St; ⊙10am-late) Schmick interior design combines with handsome woodwork at this popular pub, with fake sheep heads to remind you that you're still in NZ. Mac's beers on tap, scrummy nibbles and a decent wine list make this a great place to settle in for the evening. There's live music every night and comedy occasionally.

Little Blackwood   COCKTAIL BAR
(Map p570; 03-441 8066; www.littleblackwood. com; Steamer Wharf; ⊙2pm-2am) Slink into the darkened interior of this slick bar for a sneaky afternoon cocktail, or perch yourself on the waterfront terrace for views over the lake.

The Winery
WINE BAR

(Map p570; ☑03-409 2226; www.thewinery.co.nz; 14 Beach St; ☺10.30am-late) Ignore the uninspiring location and settle in for a journey around NZ wine. Load up cash on a smart card and then help yourself to tasting pours or glasses of more than 80 NZ wines dispensed through an automated gas-closure system. There's also a whisky corner, and cheese and salami platters are available. Wines are arranged by varietals along the walls.

Sherwood
LIVE MUSIC

(Map p563; ☑03-450 1090; www.sherwoodqueenstown.nz; 554 Frankton Rd) The faux-Tudor motel architecture might have you expecting lutes and folk ballads, but the Sherwood is Queenstown's go-to spot for visiting musos. Many of NZ's bigger names have performed here; check the website for coming gigs. The food's great, too.

🛍 Shopping

Vesta
ARTS & CRAFTS

(Map p570; ☑03-442 5687; www.vestadesign.co.nz; 19 Marine Pde; ☺9am-5pm Mon-Sat) Arguably Queenstown's most interesting store, inside inarguably the town's oldest building; Vesta sells a collection of prints, jewellery and homeware as fascinating as the original wallpaper and warped-by-time floorboards of the 1864 wooden cottage.

Artbay Gallery
ART

(Map p570; ☑03-442 9090; www.artbay.co.nz; 13 Marine Pde; ☺10am-5pm) Occupying an attractive 1863-built Freemason's Hall on the lakefront, Artbay is always an interesting place to peruse, even if you don't have $10,000 to drop on a painting. It showcases the work

---

MĀORI NZ: QUEENSTOWN & WĀNAKA

Like in other parts of the South Island, this region was first settled by moa hunters before being ruled by Waitaha, Ngāti Māmoe and then Ngāi Tahu. Lake Wakatipu is shrouded in legend, and sites to its north were highly valued sources of *pounamu* (greenstone/jade).

The Ngāi Tahu *iwi* (tribe) owns Shotover Jet (p568), Guided Walks New Zealand (p565) and Dart River Adventures (p580), the last of which offers a cultural component with its jetboat excursions.

---

of contemporary NZ artists, most of whom have a connection to the region.

Romer Gallery
PHOTOGRAPHY

(Map p570; ☑021 171 1771; www.romer-gallery.com; 15 Earl St; ☺11am-5.30pm) Call in to ogle large-format, perspex-finished NZ landscapes from Queenstown-based photographer Stephan Romer. You may want to leave your credit card in the hotel safe, though; images are up to $12,500 a pop.

Ivan Clarke Gallery
ART

(Map p570; ☑03-442 5232; www.ivanclarkeartist.com; 39 Camp St; ☺10am-6pm) Be prepared for industrial-strength levels of whimsy in this gallery devoted to the work of pooch-loving local artist, Ivan Clarke. Hanging alongside his large-scale landscapes are his *Lonely Dog* series (dogs skiing, dogs playing guitar, dogs riding motorbikes etc), which have also been published as part of an illustrated novel. There are even dog-shaped suits of armour.

Walk in Wardrobe
CLOTHING

(Map p570; ☑03-409 0190; www.thewalkinwardrobe.co.nz; Beech Tree Arcade, 34 Shotover St; ☺10am-6pm Tue & Wed, to 8.30pm Thu-Mon) Benefitting from travellers lightening their suitcases before jetting out, this 'preloved fashion boutique' is a great place to hunt for bargain designer duds. Womenswear fills most of the racks.

Creative Queenstown Arts 'n Crafts Market
MARKET

(Map p570; www.queenstownmarket.com; Earnslaw Park; ☺9.30am-3.30pm Sat) Gifts and souvenirs crafted from around the South Island; on the lakefront beside Steamer Wharf.

Remarkable Sweet Shop
FOOD

(Map p570; ☑03-409 2630; www.rss.co.nz; 39 Beach St; ☺9am-11pm) Stock up on local and imported confectionery (fudge, chocolate truffles, boiled lollies – you name it!) at this Wonka-esque pantry. There's another branch in Arrowtown (☑03-442 1374; 27 Buckingham St; ☺8.30am-6pm).

ℹ Information

Queenstown has free wi-fi in four town-centre locations: the Village Green, Earnslaw Park, Beach St and the Mall.

DOC Whakatipu-wai-Māori/Queenstown Visitor Centre (Map p570; ☑03-442 7935; www.doc.govt.nz; 50 Stanley St; ☺8.30am-4.30pm) Head here for advice about hiking tracks, as well as maps, backcountry hut passes, locator beacons, weather alerts and to check in for your Routeburn Track booking.

Queenstown i-SITE (Map p570; ☑ 03-442 4100; www.queenstownisite.com; cnr Shotover & Camp Sts; ☺ 8.30am-8pm) Friendly and informative despite being perpetually frantic, the saintly staff here can help with bookings and information on the Southern Lakes region and further afield.

❶ Getting There & Away

AIR

Air New Zealand (☑ 0800 737 000; www.air newzealand.co.nz) flies directly to Queenstown from Auckland, Wellington and Christchurch, as well as Melbourne, Sydney and Brisbane.

Jetstar (☑ 0800 800 995; www.jetstar.com) also flies the Auckland and Wellington routes, along with Melbourne, Sydney and the Gold Coast.

Qantas (www.qantas.com) and **Virgin Australia** (www.virginaustralia.com) fly directly from Australia (Melbourne, Sydney and Brisbane).

BUS

Most buses and shuttles stop on Athol St or Camp St; check when you book.

InterCity (☑ 03-442 4922; www.intercity.co.nz) The main operator; destinations include Wānaka (from $24, 1¾ hours, two daily), Franz Josef ($73, 8½ hours, daily), Dunedin (from $27, 4¼ hours, two daily), Invercargill ($51, three hours, daily) and Christchurch (from $62, 8¾ to 11¾ hours, two daily).

Ritchies (☑ 03-441 4471; www.ritchies.co.nz; ☎) Operates the Expresslink shuttle to/from Wānaka four times daily ($30, 1¾ hours), with three stopping in Cromwell ($20, one hour). For Arrowtown services, see Orbus (p580).

Catch-a-Bus South (☑ 03-214 4014; www.catchabussouth.co.nz) Door-to-door daily bus from Invercargill ($60, 3¼ hours) and Bluff ($75, 3¾ hours), heading via Gore ($61, 2½ hours) three times a week.

HIKERS' & SKIERS' TRANSPORT

All of the following services are seasonal, heading either to the snowfields during the ski season or to the tracks in the warmer months.

Buckley Track Transport (☑ 03-442 8215; www.buckleytracktransport.nz) Has scheduled shuttles between Queenstown and the Routeburn trailheads – Routeburn Shelter ($50), The Divide ($85), into one and out of the other ($125) – Te Anau ($50), Te Anau Downs for the Milford Track ($75) and the Greenstone trailhead ($60).

EasyHike (☑ 021 445 341; www.easyhike.co.nz) Offers a car-relocation service for the Milford ($299), Routeburn ($299) and Kepler

($99) Tracks, dropping you at the start and shifting your car to the end. It can also kit you out entirely for the hike, offering a range of packages up to a 'Premium' service that includes booking your hut tickets, track transport, food and all the gear you'll need.

Info & Track (Map p570; ☑ 03-442 9708; www.infotrack.co.nz; 37 Shotover St; ☺ 7.30am-9pm) During the Great Walks season, this agency provides scheduled transfers to Glenorchy ($25), the Routeburn Shelter ($47), The Divide ($84) and the Rees, Dart and Greenstone trailheads (all $60). In winter it morphs into **Info & Snow** and heads to the Coronet Peak ($35), Remarkables ($35), Cardrona ($55) and Treble Cone ($60) ski fields instead.

Ski Bus (Map p570; ☑ 0800 697 547; www.nzski.com) During the ski season shuttles depart from outside the Snow Centre on Duke St every 20 minutes from 8am until 11.30am (noon for Coronet Peak), heading to both Coronet Peak and the Remarkables (return $25). Buses return as they fill up, from 1.30pm onwards. They also depart on the hour from 3pm to 6pm for night skiing at Coronet Peak, returning on the half-hour (last bus 9pm). From December to March it also runs a summer bus service to Coronet.

Trackhopper (☑ 021 187 7732; www.trackhopper.co.nz) Offers a handy car-relocation service for the Routeburn (from $285), Milford ($260), Greenstone Caples ($180) and Rees-Dart ($180) Tracks, driving you to one end of the track and leaving your car for you at the other.

Tracknet (☑ 03-249 7777; www.tracknet.net) This Te Anau–based outfit offers Queenstown connections to the Routeburn, Kepler, Hollyford and Milford Tracks throughout the Great Walks season. Its Invercargill bus service can connect with transport to the Rakiura Track on Stewart Island. It continues to operate on a restricted timetable in winter.

❶ Getting Around

TO/FROM THE AIRPORT

Queenstown Airport (ZQN; Map p563; ☑ 03-450 9031; www.queenstownairport.co.nz; Sir Henry Wrigley Dr, Frankton) is 7km east of the town centre.

Blue Bubble Taxis (☑ 0800 228 294; www.queenstown.bluebubbletaxi.co.nz) and **Green Cabs** (☑ 0800 464 7336; www.greencabs.co.nz) charge around $45 to $50 for trips between the airport and town.

Orbus (p580) buses run every 15 minutes on route 1 between Queenstown and the airport ($10).

Super Shuttle (☑ 0800 748 885; www.supershuttle.co.nz) runs a door-to-door service (shared shuttle from $15).

QUEENSTOWN & WĀNAKA QUEENSTOWN

BOAT

Queenstown Ferries (Map p570; ☑ 03-441 1124; www.queenstownferries.co.nz; Steamer Wharf; single/return $9/15; ☺ departs Queenstown 7.45am-9.45pm Sun-Thu, to 10.45pm Fri & Sat) zip across the lake from the town centre to the Hilton Hotel on the Kelvin Peninsula (and four stops in between). Pay the driver on the boat either in cash or electronically.

PUBLIC TRANSPORT

Orbus (☑ 0800 672 8778; www.orc.govt.nz/ orbusqt; cash/GoCard trip $5/2) has four main routes, reaching Sunshine Bay, Fernhill, Arthurs Point, Frankton, Lake Hayes and Arrowtown. Cash fares are a standard $5 per trip, regardless of distance ($10 for the airport). If you're staying in Queenstown for a while, consider buying a GoCard ($5, minimum top-up $10), which drops the fare to $2. Pick up a route map and timetable from the i-SITE (p579); buses leave from directly outside, on Camp St.

AROUND QUEENSTOWN

Glenorchy

POP 363

Perhaps best known as the gateway to the Routeburn Track (p558), Glenorchy sits on a rare shelf of flat land at the head of Lake Wakatipu. The small town is a great option if you want to be beside the lake and the mountains but prefer to stay once removed from the bustle and bluster of Queenstown. The hiking around Glenorchy is sensational, and the town is also a base for horse treks, jetboat rides, helicopter flights and skydives. It's Queenstown on sedatives.

There's often a sense of déjà vu when you arrive in Glenorchy, with areas around the town featuring heavily in the *Lord of the Rings* trilogy, as well as being the setting for Jane Campion's *Top of the Lake* BBC series.

The town centre sits slightly back from the lake, so be sure to wander down to the picturesque wharf.

⚐ Activities

Shuttles from Queenstown to the Routeburn (p558), Rees-Dart (p559) and Greenstone Caples Tracks (p559) pass through Glenorchy; you can be picked up here along the way. Other activities on offer include farm tours, fly-fishing and guided photography tours; enquire at the Queenstown i-SITE (p579) or the Glenorchy Information Centre & Store.

Hiking

DOC's *Head of Lake Wakatipu* and *Wakatipu Walks* brochures detail more than 60 day walks in the area. Both brochures can be downloaded from the DOC website (www.doc.govt.nz). Two of the best short tracks are the Routeburn Flats (four hours return), which follows the first section of the Routeburn Track (p558), and Lake Sylvan (1½ hours return).

Another good wander, especially if you like birds, is the Glenorchy Walkway, which starts in the town centre and loops around Glenorchy lagoon, switching to boardwalks for the swampy bits. It's split into the Southern Circuit (30 minutes) and the Northern Circuit (one hour) and there are plenty of seats along the way, well positioned for views over the water to the Humboldt Mountains.

Before setting out on any longer hikes, call into DOC's Queenstown Visitor Centre (p578) for the latest track conditions and to purchase detailed maps. Another good resource is Lonely Planet's *Hiking & Tramping in New Zealand*.

For track snacks or meals, stock up on groceries in Queenstown, though you'll also find a small selection of trail-perfect fodder at Mrs Woolly's General Store (☑ 03-409 0051; www.theheadwaters.co.nz; 64 Oban St; ☺ 8am-7pm). Track transport is at a premium during the Great Walks season (late October to April), so try to book in advance.

Other Activities

Heli Glenorchy   SCENIC FLIGHTS
(☑ 03-442 9971; www.heliglenorchy.co.nz; 35 Mull St) It takes the best part of a day to drive from Glenorchy to Milford Sound, but it's only 15 minutes by helicopter. Options include a three-hour Milford Sound heli-cruise-heli package ($1025) and a wilderness drop-off so that you can walk the last few kilometres of the Milford Track before being whisked back over the mountains ($1725 for two people).

Dart River Adventures   ADVENTURE
(☑ 03-442 9992; www.dartriver.co.nz; 45 Mull St, Glenorchy; adult/child from $279/169) The only jetboat operator on the Dart River, with trips including a 30-minute walk through the rainforest. It also offers horse riding, guided wilderness walks, kayaking and jetboat rides combined with a river descent in an inflatable three-seater 'funyak' (adult/child from $399/305). Prices include Queenstown pickups, which depart an hour before each trip.

High Country Horses   HORSE RIDING
(Map p563; ☑ 03-442 9915; www.highcountryhorses.
nz; 243 Priory Rd) Offers more equine options than the Auckland Cup, from the easy
90-minute 'Isengard *Lord of the Rings*' trek
(with/without Queenstown transfer $195/175)
to an overnight 'Around the Mountain' trek
($850 including Queenstown transfer).

🛏 Sleeping

Little Paradise Lodge   LODGE $$
(Map p563; ☑ 03-442 6196; www.littleparadise.co.
nz; Glenorchy–Queenstown Rd, Mt Creighton; s/d
without bathroom from $110/160, r with bathroom
$195; P) This isolated and peaceful lodge,
almost midway between Queenstown and
Glenorchy, is a whimsical gem. From the
toilet-cistern aquariums to the huge garden
with 3000 roses, monkey puzzle trees and
the Swiss owner's own sculptural work, you
won't have seen a place like it.

Glenorchy Motel   MOTEL $$
(☑ 03-442 6993; www.glenorchymotels.co.nz; 87
Oban St; unit $180; P ❄ 🛜) Given the full nip
and tuck by new owners in 2017, the seven
units here have some design savvy: an outdoor hot tub has been added, and there's a
wood sauna out the back if you need to thaw
some limbs after a day on the trails.

★**Camp Glenorchy**   HOLIDAY PARK $$$
(☑ 03-409 0401; www.campglenorchy.co.nz; 42
Oban St; dm/site/cabin from $68/75/315; P 🛜) ♿
As much a statement about sustainability as
it is a fabulous place to stay, this main street
'eco retreat' offers luxurious designer-rus-
tic cottages showcasing recycled materials,
odourless composting toilets, and digital
controls that allow you to adjust the ambient
temperature and see how much electricity
you're drawing from or adding to the grid.
There's a big communal kitchen, too.

Glenorchy Lake House   B&B $$$
(☑ 03-442 4900; www.glenorchylakehouse.co.nz;
13 Mull St; r/house $340/565; 🛜) ♿ The suit-
ably-named Lake House (it's the closest
place in town to the lake) is a boutique
B&B attached to the excellent Trading Post
store and cafe. The two guest bedrooms are
decked out with Egyptian cotton sheets and
TVs and there's an outdoor spa in which to
soak away the rigours of a day's hiking.

🍴 Eating

Glenorchy Cafe   CAFE $$
(GYC; ☑ 03-442 9978; www.facebook.com/glen
orchycafe; 25 Mull St; mains $12-20; ⊙10am-

OFF THE BEATEN TRACK

THE ROAD TO PARADISE

Road signs in Glenorchy promote the
town as the 'Gateway to Paradise' and it
is...literally. Paradise lies around 15km
north of Glenorchy, near the start of the
Dart Track.

The road from Glenorchy to Paradise,
which is unsealed from the Kinloch
turn-off, heads up the broad Rees Val-
ley, edging along the foot of the Rich-
ardson Range. Approaching Paradise
it cuts through a beautiful section of
beech forest on the shores of Diamond
Lake before fording the River Jordan –
how's that for a biblical entrance! – and
arriving at Paradise. There's not much
here (OK, there's pretty much nothing
here); it's just paddocks. But it sure is
pretty!

4.30pm Sun-Fri, to 1.30am Sat) Grab a sunny
table out the back of this cute little cottage
and tuck into cooked breakfasts, sandwich-
es and soup. Head inside on Saturday night
to partake in pizza and beer underneath the
oddball light fixtures.

Queenie's Dumplings   DUMPLINGS $$
(☑ 03-442 6070; www.queeniesdumplings.wixsite.
com/queeniesdumplings; 19 Mull St; mains $14-19;
⊙11am-4pm) Where else would you expect to
find an authentic little dumpling joint than
far-flung, rural Glenorchy? Choose from
seven types of dumplings, or a handful of
noodle soups.

ℹ Information

Glenorchy Information Centre & Store (☑ 03-
409 2049; www.glenorchyinfocentre.co.nz;
42-50 Mull St; ⊙ 8.30am-9pm) Attached to the
Glenorchy Hotel, this little shop is a good source
of weather and track information. Fishing rods
and mountain bikes can be hired, and it sells
hiking supplies, including gas canisters and a
good selection of maps. It also has a bottle shop,
bless it.

ℹ Getting There & Away

Glenorchy is a scenic 45-minute (46km) drive
northwest from Queenstown, winding around
bluffs and coves with sweeping views over the
lake and its frame of mountains. There are no
bus services, but there are hikers' shuttles
(p579) during the Great Walks season (late
October to April).

KINLOCH

Just 3km from Glenorchy, but 26km by road Kinloch Lodge (☑03-442 4900; www.kin lochlodge.co.nz; 862 Kinloch Rd; dm $45, r with/without bathroom from $195/120, cabin $435; 🛜) is the perfect escape if getting away from it all to Glenorchy isn't getting away from it all enough. This wonderfully remote 1868 lodge has small heritage rooms with shared bathrooms, while rooms in the YHA-associated hostel next door are comfy and colourful. The open-air hot tub has cracking views.

By way of complete contrast, it's also rents two 'EcoScapes' cabins. Built using passive design, they feature ultra-modern furnishings, en-suite bathrooms and feel almost like a city apartment plonked into the wilderness. The view from the bed across the lake is better than TV, but if you really must watch something else, the electronic blinds whirr down to become a screen for a data projector with Apple TV and Netflix.

The lodge also has mountain bikes and fishing rods for hire, offers guided kayaking (one/two hours $60/110) and provides transfers to the Routeburn ($27) and Greenstone Caples ($22) trailheads.

It's worth driving here just to gaze across the lake from the terrace of its restaurant (mains $27 to $37). It's open year-round for drinks and simple meals (the venison stew is a great winter warmer), although you'll need to pre-order dinner in the off-season.

Arrowtown

POP 2450

Beloved by day-trippers from Queenstown, exceedingly quaint Arrowtown sprang up in the 1860s following the discovery of gold in the Arrow River. Today its pretty, tree-lined avenues retain more than 60 of their original gold-rush buildings, and history is so ingrained here that even the golf course wraps around the ruined cottages and relics of the town's gold-mining heyday. But don't be fooled by the rustic facades; Arrowtown has a thriving contemporary scene, with chic modern dining, a cool cinema and a couple of drinking dens to rival the finest in Queenstown.

The pace in Arrowtown is very different to that of Queenstown, just 20km away. Strolling Buckingham St, with its gold-era facades, is the major activity here; when you need something more, there are gentle bike rides along the valleys, or an expanding network of walks along the Arrow River and Bush Creek.

◉ Sights

Arrowtown Chinese Settlement
HISTORIC SITE

(Buckingham St; ⊙24hr) **FREE** Strung along the creek, near the site of Arrowtown's first gold find, is NZ's best example of an early Chinese settlement. Interpretive signs explain the lives of Chinese miners during and after the gold rush (the last resident died in 1932), while restored huts and the only remaining Chinese store in the southern goldfields make the story more tangible. Subjected to significant racism, the Chinese often had little choice but to rework old tailings rather than seek new claims.

Lakes District Museum & Gallery
MUSEUM

(☑03-442 1824; www.museumqueenstown.com; 49 Buckingham St; adult/child $10/3; ⊙8.30am-5pm) Exhibits cover the gold-rush era and the early days of Chinese settlement around Arrowtown. Kids are kept engaged by the likes of an 'Odd One Out' game that they can play as you wander the exhibits. You can also hire pans ($3) to try your luck panning for gold on the Arrow River; you're more likely to find some traces if you head away from the town centre. There's a good gift shop, too.

Arrowtown Gaol
HISTORIC BUILDING

(Cardigan St) **FREE** With gold rushes came lawlessness. Arrowtown's prisoners were originally manacled to logs, but in 1876 this schist jail, now surrounded by homes, was constructed. The building was used as a jail as recently as 1987 when two men were held here for drunkenness. The jail is kept locked, but you can grab the key ($10 deposit) from the Lakes District Museum.

St Patrick's Catholic Church
CHURCH

(www.stjosephsqueenstown.co.nz; 7 Hertford St) Apart from its impressive Star of David–shaped rose window, this 1874 stone Gothic Revival church, built from local schist rock, wouldn't be worth noting if it weren't for its connection to Australasia's only Catholic

Arrowtown

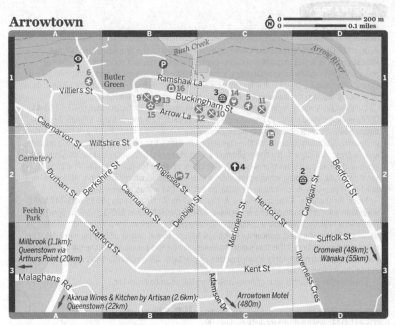

QUEENSTOWN & WĀNAKA ARROWTOWN

Arrowtown

saint. Acclaimed educator St Mary of the Cross, aka Mary MacKillop (1842–1909), founded a convent in the tiny 1870s miners cottage next door. There are interesting displays about the saint in the church and in the restored cottage. The church and cottage are usually unlocked – go to the back door of the cottage.

🏃 Activities

The information centre stocks a *Cycling & Walking Trail* brochure ($1) outlining some excellent tracks in the area. One particularly good cycling route is the **Arrow River Bridges Ride** (12km) from Arrowtown to the Kawarau Bridge, which traverses various purpose-built suspension bridges and a tunnel cut under the highway. If you have more time and energy, you can connect onto the Gibbston River Trail at the Kawarau Bridge to cycle past a string of cellar doors. Local walks include hour-long strolls along Bush Creek and the Arrow River, and the enjoyable, well-marked **Sawpit Gully Trail** (two-to-three-hour loop).

LAKE HAYES

Around 14,000 years ago, little Lake Hayes was joined to the Frankton Arm of Lake Wakatipu. Now it sits in quiet isolation, its often-mirror-perfect reflections of the surrounding hills and mountains leading some to claim it as the most photographed lake in New Zealand. It's a great place for an easy stroll, with the 8km, bike-friendly **Lake Hayes Walkway** looping right around it. Allow two to three hours to walk it.

On the lake's eastern flank is **Amisfield Bistro & Cellar Door** (Map p563; ☑03-442 0556; www.amisfield.co.nz; 10 Arrowtown–Lake Hayes Rd; 3-/5-course lunch $75/95, 7-course dinner $140; ⊙cellar door 10am-6pm, restaurant noon-8pm), a match for any of the wineries in nearby Gibbston, though it's the stylish bistro that's the real showstopper. It's an exercise in trust: simply inform the waiters of any dietary restrictions or aversions you might have and strap yourself in for whatever the chefs choose for you that day. The focus is on local produce, including foraged ingredients, presented in whimsical ways. Wine tastings are free if you dine or purchase a bottle, or $10 for five wines otherwise.

North of the lake, **Akarua Wines & Kitchen by Artisan** (Map p563; ☑03-442 1090; www.akaruaandartisan.co.nz; 265 Arrowtown–Lake Hayes Rd; mains $25-32; ⊙9am-5pm) features a restaurant inside a cottage originally built as offices for a flour mill, and a cellar door in a shipping container (tastings $10, or free if dining or buying a bottle). The most enticing option if the sun's out, however, will be the beanbags in the garden. Lunch comes in the form of hearty shared plates or platters; we wholeheartedly endorse the confit duck ($58 for two).

Lake Hayes is 4km south of Arrowtown, on the road to Frankton.

Arrowtown Bike Hire CYCLING
(☑03-441 1144; www.arrowtownbikehire.co.nz; 59 Buckingham St; half-/full-day hire $42/55, e-bikes $85/120; ⊙8.30am-5.30pm daily Sep-Apr, Tue-Sat May-Aug) Hires out bikes and provides great advice about local trails. If you fancy tackling the 16km Arrow River Bridges ride through to the Gibbston wineries, a pick-up service (from $10 per person, minimum $50) is offered. Multiday hires are also available, and bikes can be delivered to your Arrowtown accommodation.

Better by Bike CYCLING
(☑03-442 0339; www.betterbybike.co.nz; Dudley's Cottage, 4 Buckingham St; half-/full-day hire $45/55) Offers straightforward bike hire (including e-bikes) along with packages including hire and return transport from Queenstown, Gibbston or Lake Hayes (adult/child $95/55, minimum two people). It operates on a bookings-only basis through winter, so call ahead to secure your wheels.

Arrowtown Time Walks WALKING
(☑021 782 278; www.arrowtowntimewalks.com; adult/child $20/12) Guided walks (1½ hours) depart from the Lakes District Museum on demand, tracing a path through Arrowtown's golden past, pointing out places of interest along the way and delving into gold-rush history. Book through the website, or in person at the museum (p582).

🛏 Sleeping

Arrowtown Motel MOTEL $$
(☑03-442 1833; www.arrowtownmotel.co.nz; 48 Adamson Dr; units $164-229; 🅿🛜♿) This child of the 1980s is better on the inside than the outside, with spacious units with colourful feature walls, soft furnishings and interesting art. It's on a suburban road, facing onto a reserve, so peace and quiet is all but assured.

Shades of Arrowtown MOTEL $$
(☑03-442 1613; www.shadesofarrowtown.co.nz; 9 Merioneth St; units from $155; 🅿🛜) Tall shady trees and a garden setting give these bungalow-type cottages a relaxed air. Some have full kitchens and spa baths. The two-bedroom, self-contained cottage is good value if you're travelling with the whole clan.

★Millbrook Resort RESORT $$$
(☑03-441 7000; www.millbrook.co.nz; 1124 Malaghans Rd; r from $355; 🅿🛜🏊) 🌱 Further from Arrowtown in aesthetics than kilometres, this massive manicured resort is a town unto itself. Rooms range from studios to luxury homes overlooking the fairways of the resort's golf course, which has been rated among the top 10 courses in NZ. At the end of the day, take your pick from five restaurants, or relax at the spa (p568).

Arrowtown Lodge B&B $$$
(☑03-442 1101; www.arrowtownlodge.co.nz; 7 Anglesea St; r/cottage from $232/395; 🅿🛜) From the outside, the guest rooms look like her-

MACETOWN

Macetown, 15km north of Arrowtown, is a gold-rush ghost town, built in the 1860s but abandoned by the 1930s. Many of its buildings have been restored, creating an isolated and evocative destination. It's reached along a rugged, flood-prone road (the original miners' wagon track) that crosses the Arrow River more than 25 times.

Don't even think about taking your hire car here. A much more sensible option is the 4WD tour offered by Nomad Safaris (p572), which also includes gold panning in the Arrow River. Or you can hike from Arrowtown (15km each way, three to four hours one way), but it's particularly tricky in winter and spring; check with the information centre (p586) about conditions before heading out. An alternative route (four to five hours each way) climbs over Big Hill, avoiding many of the river crossings. This track climbs above 1000m, however, so shouldn't be attempted if the weather forecast isn't looking good.

The road to Macetown can also be tackled on a mountain bike (two to three hours each way), but it's not for beginners. You'll need a good bike and there are some steep drop-offs, and almost no mobile-phone coverage if you do get into trouble.

itage cottages, but inside they're cosy and modern, with en-suite bathrooms. There are three rooms, including a large cottage with its own outdoor living space and spa. Continental breakfast is provided, and Buckingham St is a two-minute walk away.

✗ Eating

Slow Cuts GRILL $$
(☑03-441 0066; www.slowcuts.co.nz; 46-50 Buckingham St; mains $12-38; ☺noon-9pm; 🛜🍴)
From the *amigas* at La Rumbla comes Slow Cuts, dishing up fast food in slow motion. There are rotisserie chickens, burgers, ribs, smashed fries, a delicious smoked beef sandwich, craft beers and a good wine list.

Provisions CAFE $$
(☑03-442 0714; www.provisionsofarrowtown.co.nz; 65 Buckingham St; mains $15-24; ☺8am-5pm; 🛜🗾🍴) In a strip of old miners' cottages, this cute cafe serves up inventive creations – the likes of black rice ginger porridge, vegan Bombay bowls and dukkah poached eggs. Everything is baked on-site, including bread, bagels and the deservedly famous sticky buns.

La Rumbla TAPAS $$
(☑03-442 0509; www.larumbla.co.nz; 54 Buckingham St; tapas $17-34; ☺4pm-late Tue-Sun) Tucked behind the post office, this little gem does a brilliant job of bringing the bold flavours and late-dining habits of Spain to sleepy little Arrowtown. Local produce is showcased in tasty bites on an ever-changing menu, and the cocktail list goes long and strong in the evening.

★Aosta ITALIAN $$$
(☑03-442 0131; www.aosta.nz; 18 Buckingham St; mains $26-42; ☺5pm-late Mon-Thu, noon-3pm

& 5pm-late Fri-Sun) Everything at this elegant restaurant is designed to be shared, from the *cicchetti* (Venetian-style bar snacks) to the pasta and substantial *secondi* (mains). Highlights include crayfish dumplings, wild thar *polpette* (meatballs), goats' cheese tortellini and inventive salads. We're also fond of the big, bubbly light fixtures over the bar and the white flying saucers illuminating the tables.

Kobe Cuisine JAPANESE $$$
(Map p563; ☑03-441 7070; www.millbrook.co.nz; Millbrook Resort, 1124 Malaghans Rd; dishes $24-42; ☺5.30-9pm daily Jul-Apr, Tue-Sat May & Jun) An open kitchen occupies an entire wall of this relaxed Japanese restaurant in the heart of Millbrook Resort. Alongside the greatest hits of Japanese cuisine (sashimi, sushi, gyoza, ramen, teppanyaki... all deftly executed) are some more unusual choices, such as sushi tacos and (our favourite) Cardrona merino *kohitsuji* – perfectly barbecued lamb ribs served with black-garlic custard. Charming service, too.

🍷 Drinking & Entertainment

★Blue Door BAR
(☑03-442 0415; www.facebook.com/TheBlueDoor Bar; 18 Buckingham St; ☺4.30pm-12.30am; 🛜) The only indications that you've arrived are the unmarked blue doors – push them open and it's like stepping into a prohibition-era speakeasy. The low-lit little bar has a formidable wine list and enough rustic ambience to keep you mellow for the evening. Low ceilings, an open fire and abundant candles create an intimate setting.

Fork & Tap PUB
(☑03-442 1860; www.theforkandtap.co.nz; 51 Buckingham St; ☺11am-11pm; 🍴) Built as a bank in

1870, Fork and Tap's currency is now craft beer, with up to 19 suds on tap. Add in good food, including shared meat and cheese platters, and a large, sunny, kid-friendly back garden, and you have the pick of Arrowtown's pubs. Grab a tasting paddle of four 150mL beers of your choice ($16). There's Irish music every Wednesday night, and live music in the garden on summer Sunday evenings.

Dorothy Browns CINEMA
(☑ 03-442 1964; www.dorothybrowns.com; 18 Buckingham St; adult/child $18.50/15) This is what a cinema should be like: wide, ultra-comfortable seating with fine local wine, cheese boards and olives available to accompany the mostly art-house films on offer. Most screenings in the main theatre have an intermission – the perfect opportunity to tuck into a tub of gourmet ice cream. The cinema doubles as a neat little bookstore.

ℹ Information

Arrowtown Visitor Information Centre (☑ 03-442 1824; www.arrowtown.com; 49 Buckingham St; ⊙ 8.30am-5pm) Shares premises with the Lakes District Museum & Gallery. Sells maps and a selection of NZ books.

ℹ Getting There & Away

Orbus (p580) buses (line 2) run hourly from 6am to 10pm between Arrowtown and Arthurs Point (49 minutes), via Frankton (25 minutes) and Queenstown (36 minutes). The terminus is on Ranshaw Lane, directly behind the Lakes District Museum.

WĀNAKA

POP 6480

So long described as Queenstown's smaller and more demure sibling, Wānaka now feels grown up enough to have moved out of home and asserted its own identity.

What it does share with Queenstown is the fact that they're both lake and mountain towns bristling with outdoors and adventure opportunities. Wānaka's list of adventure options is impressive by almost any measure, except against the Queenstown ruler. The breadth and selection of adventures here might not be as comprehensive, but the lakefront is more natural and less developed – complete with a day-at-the-beach feel on sunny days – and the town centre has a more soulful atmosphere.

Despite constant growth – in both size and costs – Wānaka retains a fairly laid-back, small-town atmosphere. Days are invariably active here, but evenings are an invitation into a wave of new eateries and some truly quirky bars.

◉ Sights

Rippon WINERY
(☑ 03-443 8084; www.rippon.co.nz; 246 Mt Aspiring Rd; ⊙ 11am-5pm) It's worth raising a glass to the view alone at Rippon since the Tuscan-styled cellar door has surely the finest winery view in NZ. In a bid to contain numbers, the popular free tastings must now be booked in advance online. Tasting sessions are limited to 12 people and commence promptly on the hour, sampling four to six wines over 30 to 45 minutes.

Wānaka Station Park PARK
(Homestead Cl; 🚼) Wānaka Station Park is a piece of Wānaka that existed before Wānaka did. This remnant of the sheep station that once covered the entire south side of the lake is a beautiful, secluded space with a playground and plenty of mature trees. These include giant sequoias, three immense Douglas firs, Himalayan cedars, a large walnut tree, an enormous rhododendron hedge and the station's surviving orchard, with pears and apples that are free for picking.

The park extends to the lake's edge, where you'll find one of the true stars of the Instagram age: **That Wānaka Tree**. Sprouted from a fence post but now almost as famous as the town itself, this water-bound willow provides a classically photogenic prop to the mountains and Ruby Island behind. If you are here for the Instagram moment, come at dawn, when reflections are typically at their best.

If you think it's a bit strange that there's now a constant stream of tourists queuing to get a shot of this particular tree, you're not alone. Arguably the scrum of would-be influencers is more of a spectacle than the tree itself.

Puzzling World AMUSEMENT PARK
(☑ 03-443 7489; www.puzzlingworld.co.nz; 188 Wānaka–Luggate Hwy; adult/child $23/16, maze or illusions only $18/14; ⊙ 8.30am-5.30pm; 🚼) A 3D Great Maze and lots of fascinating brain-bending visual illusions serve to keep people of all ages bemused, bothered and bewildered at this entertaining little attraction. Even the cafe tables come equipped with puzzles. It's 2km from town, en route to Cromwell.

National Transport & Toy Museum MUSEUM
(☑ 03-443 8765; www.nttmuseumwanaka.co.nz; 891 Wānaka–Luggate Hwy; adult/child $19/5;

⊚ 8.30am-5pm; 📶) Mixing Smurfs with Studebakers and skidoos (and an authentic MiG jet fighter flown by the Polish Air Force), this completely eclectic and absorbing collection of more than 60,000 items fills four huge hangars (one mostly filled with vintage fire engines). Suitably, it's as jumbled as a toy box, making it all a bit of a treasure hunt, but it's a nostalgic journey even if you're only young enough to remember as far back as the Sylvanian Families.

Warbirds & Wheels   MUSEUM
(📞 03-443 7010; www.warbirdsandwheels.com; 11 Lloyd Dunn Ave, Wānaka Airport; adult/child $20/5; ⊚ 8am-4pm) Dedicated to NZ combat pilots, the aircraft they flew and the sacrifices they made, this museum features a replica of a Hawker Hurricane, a de Havilland FB5 Vampire and twin rows of gleaming classic cars – pride of place goes to the 1934 Duesenberg Model J, described as the finest car ever made in the USA. There's a retro diner attached.

🏃 Activities

Wānaka might not have bridges to leap off, but you could still bottle the adrenaline here. For powder monkeys it's the gateway to the Treble Cone, Cardrona (p594) and Snow Farm (p594) ski areas, and it's the last stop before Mt Aspiring National Park for those in hiking boots.

Skiing

Like Queenstown, the ski season lasts from roughly June to September. From Wānaka the Cardrona (p594) and Treble Cone ski fields are roughly equidistant (about 24km). At the time of writing, Cardrona was seeking Commerce Commission approval to purchase Treble Cone; watch this space.

During the season, Treble Cone offers free shuttles from outside its office (📞 03-443 1406; 24 Dungarvon St; ⊚ 7am-6pm Jun-Oct, 8.30am-5pm Mon-Fri Nov-May), departing at 8am and 8.45am and returning from the mountain at 4pm and 4.30pm; book your spot online. There are also free shuttles from the base of the mountain to the ski field, departing every 20 to 30 minutes.

Cardrona's Wānaka base of operations is **Cardrona Corner** (📞 03-443 4512; www.cardrona.com; 20 Helwick St; ⊚ 7am-7pm Jun-Oct, 9am-5pm Nov-May). You can book your ski packages, purchase outdoorsy clothing and hire gear here, and mountain shuttles depart nearby (adult/child $35/30 return). In summer, its focus shifts to mountain biking.

Treble Cone   SKIING
(📞 03-443 7443; www.treblecone.com; Treble Cone Access Rd; daily lift pass adult/child $149/75) 🏂
The highest and largest of the region's ski areas, spectacular Treble Cone delivers powder with panoramas. Its steep slopes are suitable for intermediate to advanced skiers, with a beginners' area that includes free lift access. There's around 700m of vertical, as well as numerous half-pipes.

Hiking

For walks close to town, including various lakeside wanders, download DOC's *Wānaka Outdoor Pursuits* brochure or pick it up from the visitor centre ($3.50). For something low-level, the **Glendhu Bay Track** bobbles along the southern shore of Lake Wānaka, passing That Wānaka Tree and Rippon before rolling into Glendhu Bay after three to four hours. It's also a good track for a gentle mountain-bike ride.

Roy's Peak (p561) is Wānaka's hike *du jour* for the Instagram mob, though you can get lofty views with far less effort atop **Mt Iron** (527m, 1½ hours return) – although it's a rather grandiose name for what's really just a hill. Other excellent (many would say far superior) alternatives to Roy's Peak include **Diamond Lake** (circuit: 45 minutes; Lake Wānaka lookout: two hours return) and **Isthmus Peak** (1385m, five to seven hours return); both reward your efforts with views of an additional lake.

Two highly scenic Mt Aspiring National Park tracks start from Raspberry Creek at the end of Mt Aspiring Rd, 50km from Wānaka: the excellent half-day Rob Roy Track (p560) and the challenging, multiday Cascade Saddle (p560). The road to Raspberry Creek is unsealed for 30km and involves eight creek fords. It's usually fine in a 2WD, except in very wet conditions; check at the visitor centre, which can also provide you with contacts and/or bookings for the three main shuttle operators ($40 to $50 per person).

Cycling

Hundreds of kilometres of tracks in the region are open to mountain bikers; see **Bike Wanaka** (www.bikewanaka.org.nz) for interactive maps. DOC's *Wānaka Outdoor Pursuits* brochure also describes a range of rides, including the popular **Deans Bank Track** (12km).

One particularly scenic route is the **Newcastle Track** (12km), which follows the raging blue waters of the Clutha River from Albert Town to the Red Bridge on Kane Rd.

You can make it a 30km loop by joining the Upper Clutha River Track at Luggate.

The Glendhu Bay Track provides easy riding along the shore of Lake Wānaka. Sticky Forest is a local favourite, with around 30km of purpose-built trails through pine forest on the edge of town, complete with jumps, drops and berms.

Bike hire is easy to find in town – try Outside Sports (☑ 03-443 7966; www.outside sports.co.nz; 17/23 Dunmore St; half/full day from $35/55; ☺ bike hire 9am-6pm) for a quality dual-suspension, downhill mountain bike or e-bike. Good Rotations (☑ 03-443 4349; www.goodrotations.co; 34 Anderson Rd; half/full day from $59/89; ☺ 10am-5pm Tue-Fri, extended summer) specialises in e-bikes.

Wanaka Bike Tours   CYCLING
(☑ 03-443 6363; www.wanakabiketours.co.nz; from $199) Offers bike rentals (from $65 per day), bike and shuttle packages for self-guided one-way spins (adult/child from $85/55), Clutha River jetboat/bike combos ($199/112), guided e-bike tours (from $299) and helibiking (from $650).

Climbing, Canyoning & Mountaineering

Excellent rock climbing can be found at Hospital Flat, around 20km from Wānaka towards Mt Aspiring National Park, and the adjoining Diamond Lake Conservation Area.

★ **Wild Wire**   CLIMBING
(☑ 0800 9453 9473; www.wildwire.co.nz; 1 Umbers St) The Italian world of *via ferrata* – climbing using the likes of iron rungs, plank bridges and cables – arrives in Wānaka, scaling the cliffs beside (and sometimes across) Twin Falls. Make the half-day climb partway up the falls (from $199), or go the whole hog on 'Lord of the Rungs' ($599), the world's highest waterfall *via ferrata,* with a helicopter flight back down.

Wanaka Rock Climbing   CLIMBING
(☑ 022 015 4458; www.wanakarock.co.nz; 99 Ardmore St; ☺ 8.30am-12.30pm, by apt winter) ✆ This long-standing and highly respected operator offers introductory rock-climbing courses (half/full day $203/293), a half-day abseiling intro on 40m-high rock walls ($203) and guided climbs around the region.

Basecamp Adventures   CLIMBING
(☑ 03-443 1110; www.basecampadventures.co.nz; 50 Cardrona Valley Rd; day pass adult/child $20/17; ☺ noon-7pm Mon-Fri, 10am-5pm Sat & Sun) At this indoor climbing centre at the town's edge, even fearless three-year-olds can have

a go on the Clip 'n Climb automatic belay system (from $11, booking recommended). It also offers outdoor climbs, including intro sessions (half-/full day $189/299), family adventures (from $299) and more advanced ascents. Plus there's snowshoeing (half-/full day $189/299), guided alpine hikes and mountaineering, too.

Deep Canyon   ADVENTURE SPORTS
(☑ 03-443 7922; www.deepcanyon.co.nz; Log Cabin, 100 Ardmore St; from $290; ☺ Oct-Apr) Climb, walk, leap, zip-line and abseil your way through narrow, wild gorges on a canyoning expedition. There are 10 options on offer, rated either 'Get Into It' (easy), 'Step It Up' (intermediate) or 'Go Big' (advanced).

Adventure Consultants   ADVENTURE SPORTS
(☑ 03-443 8711; www.adventureconsultants.com; 20 Brownston St) This highly respected mountain guiding outfit (it's been leading climbs on Everest for decades) offers treks to Brewster Glacier (two days, from $890) and Gillespie Pass (four days, from $1450). It runs mountaineering and ice-climbing courses, too.

Other Activities

Paddle Wanaka   KAYAKING
(☑ 0800 926 925; www.paddlewanaka.co.nz; lakefront, Ardmore St; ☺ 9am-6pm Oct-Apr, 10am-4pm May & Jul-Sep) Offers kayaks (one/two hours $20/30) and stand-up paddle boards (SUP, $20 per hour) for hire, and guided paddle-powered tours of the lake (half/full day $179/349) and the rapids of the Clutha River (half day $199). It also offers jetboat pickups if you'd prefer a one-way lake paddle. For something unique, how about a heli-SUP trip to a remote mountain lake?

Wanaka River Journeys   ADVENTURE SPORTS
(☑ 03-443 4416; www.wanakariverjourneys.co.nz; adult/child $249/149) ✆ Combination walk (50 minutes) and jetboat ride in the gorgeous Matukituki Valley. Also offers packrafting and heli-jetboating.

Skydive Wanaka   SKYDIVING
(☑ 03-443 7207; www.skydivewanaka.com; 14 Mustang Lane, Wānaka Airport) Grab some airtime, jumping from 9000ft ($299), 12,000ft ($369), or going the whole banana with a 15,000ft leap ($469) and 60 seconds of free fall.

☞ Tours

Scenic Flights

Classic Flights   SCENIC FLIGHTS
(☑ 03-443 4043; www.classicflights.co.nz; 6 Spitfire Lane, Wānaka Airport; from $299) Sightseeing flights in a vintage Tiger Moth biplane.

Wānaka

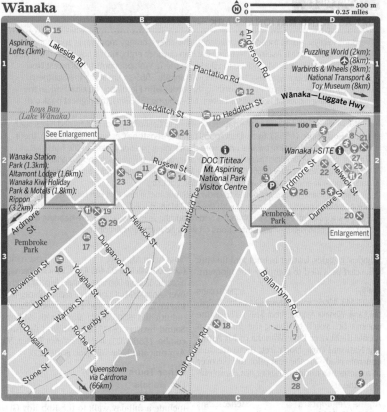

Wānaka

⊕ Activities, Courses & Tours
1	Adventure Consultants	B2
2	Cardrona Corner	D2
3	Deep Canyon	D2
4	Good Rotations	C1
5	Outside Sports	D2
6	Paddle Wanaka	C2
7	Treble Cone office	A3
8	Wanaka Rock Climbing	D2
9	Wild Wire	D4

⊜ Sleeping
10	Archway	C2
11	Asure Brookvale Motel	B2
12	Criffel Peak View	C1
13	Lakeside	B2
14	Mountain View Backpackers	B2
15	Wanaka Bakpaka	A1
16	Wanaka View Motel	A3
17	YHA Wanaka Purple Cow	A3

⊗ Eating
18	Bistro Gentil	C4
19	Charlie Brown	B3
20	Federal Diner	D3
21	Francesca's Italian Kitchen	D2
22	Kai Whaka Pai	D2
23	Kika	B2
24	Red Star	B2
	Relishescafé	(see 8)
25	Ritual	D2

⊖ Drinking & Nightlife
26	Gin & Raspberry	D2
27	Lalaland	D2
28	Rhyme x Reason	D4

⊕ Entertainment
| 29 | Paradiso | B3 |

DON'T MISS

MT ASPIRING NATIONAL PARK

Verdant valleys, alpine meadows, braided glacial rivers, craggy mountains and more than 100 glaciers make Mt Aspiring National Park an outdoor enthusiast's paradise. Protected as a national park in 1964, and later included in the Te Wāhipounamu (Southwest New Zealand) World Heritage Area, the park now blankets 3555 sq km along the Southern Alps, from the Haast River in the north to its border with Fiordland National Park in the south. Lording it over all is colossal Tititea/Mt Aspiring (3033m), the highest peak outside the Aoraki/Mt Cook area.

While the southern end of the national park near Glenorchy includes famed hikes such as the Routeburn (p558), Rees-Dart (p559) and Greenstone Caples Tracks (p559), there are plenty of blissful short walks and more demanding multiday hikes in the Matukituki Valley, close to Wānaka. These include the dramatic Rob Roy Track (p560) and challenging Cascade Saddle (p560); see DOC's *Matukituki Valley Tracks* brochure, which can be downloaded from its website (www.doc.govt.nz).

Many of these tracks are prone to snow and avalanche risk and can be treacherous. It is extremely important to consult with the DOC staff at the Tititea/Mt Aspiring National Park Visitors Centre (p593) in Wānaka and to purchase hut tickets before heading off. You should also register your intentions on www.adventuresmart.org.nz.

'Biggles' goggles, leather helmet and flowing silk scarf provided to complete the moment.

U-Fly SCENIC FLIGHTS
(☑03-443 4005; www.u-flywanaka.co.nz; 8 Spitfire Lane, Wānaka Airport; from $199) The name doesn't lie...you'll be flying the plane on a scenic flight over Lake Wānaka or Mt Aspiring National Park. Don't fret; there are dual controls ready for the real pilot to take over at a moment's notice – they're not completely insane.

Alpine Helicopters SCENIC FLIGHTS
(☑03-443 4000; www.alpineheli.co.nz; 10 Lloyd Dunn Ave, Wānaka Airport) Options range from a 20-minute flight over Wānaka with a hilltop landing ($295), to the half-day Fiordland Heli Traverse ($2865), which includes multiple landings, checking crayfish pots on the fiords and scoffing the bounty during a remote alpine picnic.

Aspiring Helicopters SCENIC FLIGHTS
(☑03-443 7152; www.aspiringhelicopters.co.nz; Cattle Flat Station, 2211 Mt Aspiring Rd) Offers a range of flight options, from a 20-minute buzz over Lake Wānaka ($225) to a three-hour flight to Milford Sound ($1460), choppering along the sound's length and making four landings.

Wanaka Helicopters SCENIC FLIGHTS
(☑03-443 1085; www.wanakahelicopters.co.nz; 6 Lloyd Dunn Ave, Wānaka Airport) Options range from a 25-minute 'Wanaka Experience' ($250, one landing) to a three-hour trip to Aoraki/Mt Cook ($1595, two landings).

Southern Alps Air SCENIC FLIGHTS
(☑0800 345 666, 03-443 4385; www.southernalpsair.co.nz; 12 Lloyd Dunn Ave, Wānaka Airport) Flights over Aoraki/Mt Cook in a small plane, taking in Tasman, Fox and Franz Josef Glaciers (adult/child $505/340), along with Milford Sound flyovers ($475/320), Milford fly-cruise combos ($560/375) and whirls over Tititea/Mt Aspiring and Lake Wānaka ($310/225).

Other Tours

Eco Wanaka OUTDOORS
(☑03-443 2869; www.ecowanaka.co.nz) 🏳 Trips include a full-day walk to the Rob Roy Glacier (adult/child $315/215), a four-hour cruise and walk on Mou Waho Island to find a lake within a lake ($245/165), and a full-day cruise-4WD combo ($494/295). Also offers helihikes.

Ridgeline Adventures DRIVING
(☑0800 234 000; www.ridgelinenz.com) 🏳 Choose from a range of 4WD explorations ranging from a 'safari' through a high-country farm (adult/child $249/130) to a 4WD/jetboat/helicopter combo ($939/584).

Funny French Cars DRIVING
(☑027 386 6932; www.funnyfrenchcars.co.nz) Ride in a classic Citroën around local wineries and/or craft breweries ($199), or tour scenic highlights of Wānaka ($159).

🎉 Festivals & Events

TUKI MUSIC
(www.tukifestival.nz; tickets from $140; ⊙Feb) One-day music festival featuring big-name

Kiwi artists, held in even-numbered years in Glendhu Bay.

Warbirds Over Wanaka   AIR SHOW
(🗘03-443 8619; www.warbirdsoverwanaka.com; Wānaka Airport; 1-/3-day pass from $60/189) Held every second Easter (in even-numbered years), this incredibly popular international airshow attracts upwards of 50,000 people.

🛏 Sleeping

🛏 Central Wānaka

Wanaka Bakpaka   HOSTEL $
(🗘03-443 7837; www.wanakabakpaka.co.nz; 117 Lakeside Rd; dm $32-33, r with/without bathroom from $94/66; P@🛜) The only lakeside hostel in town delivers million-dollar views at backpacker prices. Amenities are top-shelf and it's worth paying a bit extra for the en-suite double with the gorgeous views, though you can also just lap it all up from the wide lounge windows. There are bikes for hire and the hot-water bottles come free.

Altamont Lodge   LODGE $
(🗘03-443 8864; www.altamontlodge.co.nz; 121 Mt Aspiring Rd; s/d $89/109; 🛜) At the quiet end of town, Altamont is like a hostel for grown-ups. There are no dorms but the 12 tidy little rooms share spotless bathrooms and a spacious, well-equipped kitchen. Pine-lined walls give it a ski-lodge ambience, while the spa pool and roaring fire in the lounge with its views of Roy's Peak will warm you up post-slopes.

Mountain View Backpackers   HOSTEL $
(🗘03-443 9010; www.mtnview.co.nz; 7 Russell St; dm/r without bathroom from $34/84; P🛜) Set beneath Monument Lookout, the Mountain View is effectively a hostel within a house, complete with a back lawn and clothesline. Rooms are simple but warm and comfortable, and there's a drying room for ski gear.

★Criffel Peak View   B&B $$
(🗘03-443 5511; www.criffelpeakview.co.nz; 98 Hedditch St; r from $180; P🛜) Situated in a quiet cul-de-sac, this excellent B&B has three rooms sharing a large lounge with a log fire and a sunny wisteria-draped deck. The charming hostesses live in a separate house behind, which also has a self-contained two-bedroom apartment attached.

YHA Wanaka Purple Cow   HOSTEL $$
(🗘03-443 1880; www.yha.co.nz; 94 Brownston St; dm $39-48, r with/without bathroom from

$160/115; P🛜) 🖋 This Wānaka stalwart is older than many of its guests, and it has mellowed comfortably with age. It has a mix of dorms and private rooms, but best of all are the large lounge, with commanding lake and mountain views, and the quiet reading room. The giant topo map in the lounge is great for planning hikes.

Wanaka Kiwi Holiday Park & Motels   HOLIDAY PARK $$
(🗘03-443 7766; www.wanakakiwiholidaypark.nz; 263 Studholme Rd North; sites $45-61, units with/without bathroom from $149/84; P✳🛜🐾) This charming and relaxing campground has grassy terraced sites for tents and campervans, lots of trees and pretty views. Facilities include a barbecue area with heaters, a spa pool and a sauna. Older-style motel units have been renovated, and the newest budget cabins are warm and cosy. There's a courtesy van for runs into (but not back from) town.

Wanaka View Motel   MOTEL $$
(🗘03-443 7480; www.wanakaviewmotel.co.nz; 122 Brownston St; units from $195; P🛜) The refurbished Wanaka View has five apartments with spa baths and full kitchens squeezed tightly into a standard section. The largest has three bedrooms and most have lake views. There's also a comfortable studio unit tucked around the back, which is cheaper but doesn't have a kitchen or view.

Archway   MOTEL $$
(🗘03-443 7698; www.archwaymotels.co.nz; 64 Hedditch St; unit from $165; P🛜) A short uphill walk from the town centre, this older-style motel has spacious units and pine-clad 'chalets' with kitchenettes. The cedar hot tubs with mountain views are an appealing perk.

Asure Brookvale Motel   MOTEL $$
(🗘03-443 8333; www.brookvale.co.nz; 35 Brownston St; unit from $166; P🛜🏊) The patios at this old-fashioned concrete-block motel open onto a grassy lawn edged by a gently flowing creek. It also has a barbecue, hot tub and plunge pool.

Lakeside   APARTMENT $$$
(🗘03-443 0188; www.lakesidewanaka.co.nz; 9 Lakeside Rd; apt from $349; P🛜🏊) Luxuriate in a modern apartment in a prime position overlooking the lake, right by the town centre. All 23 apartments have three bedrooms, but can be rented with only one or two bedrooms open. The swimming pool is a relative rarity in these parts, and if you hire ski gear through the website it can be delivered to your door.

🛏 Surrounds

★ Wanaka Haven
B&B $$$

(☑ 03-443 4995; www.wanakahaven.co.nz; 42 Halliday Rd; r from $425; 🅿🅢🏊) Luxurious B&Bs seem to be constantly sprouting in the Wānaka countryside. This one has the advantage of gorgeous views over manicured lawns to the mountains, and a heated outdoor swimming pool. There's also a large guest lounge where you can help yourself to tea and coffee from the machine.

Alpine View Lodge
B&B $$$

(☑ 03-443 7111; www.alpineviewlodge.co.nz; 23 Studholme Rd Sth; r/cottage from $245/360; 🅿🅢) In a peaceful rural setting on the edge of town, this excellent lodge has three B&B rooms, one of which has its own private deck with mountain views. Little extras include homemade shortbread in the rooms and a hot tub. Alternatively, you can opt for one of the fully self-contained one-, two- or three-bedroom cottages.

Lime Tree Lodge
B&B $$$

(☑ 03-443 7305; www.limetreelodge.co.nz; 672 Ballantyne Rd; r $395-495; 🅿🅢🏊) 🍃 Quietly removed from town, this intimate lodge has four luxury rooms and two suites. Outside there's a pool, spa, pétanque court and croquet lawn, while the lodge is centred on an inviting living area with open kitchen where the in-house chef prepares meals. The owners – former sheep farmers – host canapés and aperitifs every evening.

Wanaka Alpine Lodge
B&B $$$

(☑ 03-443 5355; www.wanakaalpinelodge.co.nz; 4 Monteith Rd, Albert Town; r $269-299; 🅿🅢) Guests in the four spacious, modern bedrooms are pampered with home baking and a cedar hot tub. It's 4km from town, tucked in behind Mt Iron, but there are bikes onsite for guests.

🍴 Eating

Red Star
BURGERS $

(☑ 03-443 9322; www.redstarburgers.co.nz; 26 Ardmore St; burgers $12-16; ⊘ 11.30am-9pm) The burger menu is exhaustive and inventive – beef, chicken, venison, fish and vegie burgers on crunchy toasted buns. Grab a seat on the terrace and sip on a craft beer with your craft burger.

Charlie Brown
CRÊPES $

(www.charliebrowncrepes.co.nz; 77-79 Brownston St; crêpes $6-17; ⊘ 8am-9.30pm) Both the retro green 1975 caravan and its owners hail from France, so you can be sure that the sweet crêpes and savoury galettes whisked up within are *très français*, even if the name isn't. Seasonal specials are chalked up on a board, or you can order from the permanent menu of perennial favourites.

Kai Whaka Pai
CAFE $$

(☑ 03-443 7795; 121 Ardmore St; mains $14-25; ⊘ 7am-11pm; 🖉) As Wānaka as *that* tree, this local institution is where the town seems to congregate on a sunny evening for a liquid sundowner over excellent pizza. Locally brewed craft beers are on tap and there are Central Otago wines as well. There are plenty of vegetarian options, including some suitable for vegans.

Federal Diner
CAFE $$

(☑ 03-443 5152; www.federaldiner.co.nz; Pembroke Lane; brunch $14-22, dinner $15-30; ⊘ 7am-3pm Sun & Mon, to 9.30pm Tue-Sat; 🖉🖉🖕) When it's this hidden away and still this popular, you know to expect good things. This cosmopolitan cafe delivers robust breakfasts, excellent coffee, legendary scones, croissants and salads. In the evenings the menu shifts to substantial dishes such as pork belly and slow-roasted lamb shoulder. There are vegan options, too.

Relishescafé
CAFE $$

(☑ 03-443 9018; www.relishescafe.co.nz; 99 Ardmore St; brunch $17-24, dinner $32-36; ⊘ 7am-10pm) A cafe by day with good breakfast and lunch options, this place transforms into a sophisticated restaurant with a fine wine list at night. Central Otago wines take centre stage.

Francesca's
Italian Kitchen
ITALIAN $$

(☑ 03-443 5599; www.fransitalian.co.nz; 93 Ardmore St; mains $23-29; ⊘ noon-3pm & 5pm-late) Pretty much the matriarch of Wānaka eateries, perennially busy Francesca's has the big flavours and easy conviviality of an authentic Italian family *trattoria*. Even simple things such as pizza, pasta and polenta chips are exceptional.

Ritual
CAFE $$

(☑ 03-443 6662; 18 Helwick St; mains $12-21; ⊘ 9am-5pm) A classic 21st-century Kiwi cafe, Ritual is smart but not too trendy, and filled to the gills with delicious food. The counter positively groans under the weight of tasty salads, slices and scones.

Kika

TAPAS $$$

(☑03-443 6536; www.kika.nz; 2 Dunmore St; plates $14-48; ⊙5.30pm-late) One of Otago's best restaurants, Kika's menu is underpinned by modern Italian cuisine, served tapas-style in a casual dining space and enlivened by some Asian flavours. Unsure what to choose? Let the chefs decide with the 'Just Feed Me' menu.

Bistro Gentil

FRENCH $$$

(☑03-443 2299; www.bistrogentil.co.nz; 76a Golf Course Rd; mains $36-40; ⊙6pm-late Tue-Sat) Far removed from the madding crowd, Gentil ticks plenty of boxes for a memorable night out. Expect a short, focused menu of delicious modern French cuisine, featuring the likes of confit duck and venison shortloin. On a balmy night, request an outside table. By day, the space transforms into the tasting room for Maude Wines (tastings $10).

🍸 Drinking & Nightlife

Rhyme x Reason

BREWERY

(☑03-265 1101; www.rhymeandreason.beer; 17 Gordon Rd; tasting paddles $18-22; ⊙noon-10.30pm) Beer-loving locals head to this inconspicuous tin shed – situated in a light-industrial strip on the edge of town – to escape the tourists down at the lakefront and to sip on quality crafts brewed by one of their own, Jess Wolfgang. Her regular range (including an award-winning *kölsch*) is joined on tap by seasonal and guest brews. Bring your own food.

Lalaland

COCKTAIL BAR

(☑03-443 4911; www.facebook.com/Lalalandwanaka; L1, 99 Ardmore St; ⊙5pm-2.30am) Before the Ryan Gosling and Emma Stone flick, there was already this Lalaland in Wānaka. Sink into a comfy chair at the little, low-lit palace/bordello, where bar staff concoct elixirs to suit every mood. The lake view might be better at other upstairs Ardmore St bars, but can they top this playlist or cocktail list? Enter via the rear stairs.

Gin & Raspberry

COCKTAIL BAR

(☑03-443 4216; www.ginandraspberry.co.nz; L1, 155 Ardmore St; ⊙3pm-late) If you're in the swing for bling, this lush bar is like stepping into a Baz Luhrmann film set. Gilded mirrors, a grand piano (yes, you can ask to play it) and mood lighting provide a backdrop to classic cocktails (including various martinis). The gin collection is impressive and the deck is the perfect sunset perch.

☆ Entertainment

Paradiso

CINEMA

(☑03-443 1505; www.paradiso.net.nz; 72 Brownston St; adult/child $15/9.50) Sprawl on a comfy couch, or recline in a dentist's chair or an old Morris Minor at this Wānaka institution, screening the best Hollywood and art-house flicks. At intermission head to the lobby for freshly baked cookies (simply follow your nose), though the homemade ice cream is just as enticing.

Ruby's

CINEMA

(☑03-443 6901; www.rubyscinema.co.nz; 50 Cardrona Valley Rd; adult/child $19/13) How very Wānaka that an art-house cinema should adjoin an indoor climbing wall. Channelling a lush New York or Shanghai vibe, Ruby's has a whiff of cinema's glory days. Watch a movie from a reclining leather chair with a warming blanket over your knees, or just chill in the red-velvet lounge with local craft beers and wine or classic cocktails.

Ruby's is in the Basecamp Wānaka (p588) building on the outskirts of town.

ℹ Information

DOC Tititea/Mt Aspiring National Park Visitor Centre (☑03-443 7660; www.doc.govt. nz; 1 Ballantyne Rd; ⊙8am-5pm daily Dec-Apr, 8.30am-5pm Mon-Sat May-Nov) In an A-framed building on the edge of the town centre, this DOC office takes hut bookings and offers advice on tracks and conditions. Be sure to call in before undertaking any wilderness hikes.

Wanaka i-SITE (☑03-443 1233; www.lake wanaka.co.nz; 103 Ardmore St; ⊙8am-7pm Nov-Mar, 9am-5.30pm Apr-Oct) Lakefront office that's ever helpful, but always busy.

Wanaka Lakes Health (☑03-443 0710; www. wanakamedical.co.nz; 23 Cardrona Valley Rd; ⊙8am-6pm Mon-Fri, 9am-noon & 3-6pm Sat & Sun) The place to go if you need to patch up any adventure mishaps.

ℹ Getting There & Away

Buses depart from outside the Log Cabin on the lakefront.

➡ **InterCity** (p579) Destinations include Queenstown (from $24, 1¾ hours, two daily), Cromwell (from $24, 40 minutes, two daily), Lake Hāwea ($28, nine minutes, daily), Makarora ($28, 1½ hours, daily) and Franz Josef ($55, daily).

➡ **Ritchies** (p579) Operates the Expresslink shuttle to/from Queenstown four times daily ($30, 1¾ hours), with three stopping in Cromwell ($20, 40 minutes).

ℹ️ Getting Around

Adventure Car Rentals (📞 03-443 6050; www.adventurerentals.co.nz; 51 Brownston St) Hires cars and 4WDs (the latter is the best option if you're heading to Mt Aspiring National Park).

Yello! (📞 03-443 5555; www.yello.co.nz) Operates taxis and scheduled winter shuttles to the Snow Farm near Cardrona ($35 return).

AROUND WĀNAKA

Cardrona

Gouged between the Crown and Criffel Ranges, the cute settlement of Cardrona reached its zenith in the 1870s at the height of the gold rush, when its population numbered more than 1000. Today it's effectively a ski field balanced atop a pub, albeit perhaps the most recognisable and evocative pub in New Zealand.

Cardrona wakes with a jolt for the ski season, but even if you're not here for powder, it's well worth a visit. Drink in the views and the beer, take a horse ride through the open tussock country, be slightly bemused at the bra fence and understand that a distillery rightly belongs here since the landscape is so reminiscent of the Scottish Highlands.

🔴 Sights & Activities

★ **Cardrona Distillery**   DISTILLERY
(Map p563; 📞 03-443 1393; www.cardronadistillery.com; 2125 Cardrona Valley Rd; tours $25; ⏱️ 9.30am-5pm) Enter past the fence of bras (Bra-drona!) and you'll find the beautiful cellar door of this fledgling single-malt distillery inside a building made of local schist. Have a complimentary sip of the liqueurs, gin and unusual single-malt vodka, or take the 75-minute distillery tour, which leaves on the hour from 10am to 3pm. Its first whisky won't be completely ready until 2025, but it released a three-year-old teaser in 2018 and plans to follow up with a six-year-old in 2021.

Cardrona Alpine Resort   SKIING
(Map p563; 📞 03-443 9284; www.cardrona.com; Cardrona Skifield Rd; daily lift passes adult/child $120/62; ⏱️ 8.30am-4pm) Well organised and professional, this 345-hectare ski field offers runs to suit all abilities (25% beginners, 25% intermediate, 30% advanced, 20% expert) at

elevations ranging from 1670m to 1860m. Cardrona has several high-capacity chairlifts (including a gondola cable car), beginners' tows and extreme snowboard terrain.

Buses run from Wānaka ($35) and Queenstown ($55) during ski season, and you can shuttle up from the base ($10 return) if you don't want to drive to the top; cheaper deals are available with lift passes.

In summer, the mountain bikers take over. The Cardrona Peak to Pub, from the ski fields to the Cardrona Hotel, is a classic NZ ride with 1270m of descent – the resort runs shuttles back up the mountain.

Snow Farm   SKIING
(Map p563; 📞 03-443 7542; www.snowfarmnz.com; Snow Farm Access Rd; ski day pass adult/child $45/25, snowshoe day pass $20/10; ♿) In winter this is home to fantastic cross-country skiing and snowshoeing, with 55km of groomed ski trails and 24km of snowshoe trails. Lessons and ski hire are available.

The Cardrona   HORSE RIDING
(Map p563; 📞 03-443 1228; www.thecardrona.co.nz; 2125 Cardrona Valley Rd) Guided horse rides through the Cardrona Valley, including a 'High Country Pub' ride (from $159) that'll have you tying up at the Cardrona Hotel hitching rail for a beer. Also runs quad-bike tours and 4WD buggy rides.

Backcountry
Saddle Expeditions   HORSE RIDING
(Map p563; 📞 03-443 8151; www.backcountrysaddles.co.nz; 2130 Cardrona Valley Rd; adult/child $100/80) Two-hour horse treks across Mt Cardrona Station on Appaloosa horses.

🛌 Sleeping

Waiorau Homestead   B&B $$$
(Map p563; 📞 03-443 2225; www.waiorauhomestead.co.nz; 2127 Cardrona Valley Rd; r $280; 🅿️ 🛜 ♨️) Tucked away in a private bucolic nook near the distillery, this lovely stone house, fringed by an old stand of conifers, has deep verandas and three luxurious guest bedrooms, each with their own bathroom. Rates include a full cooked breakfast.

🍷 Drinking & Nightlife

Cardrona Hotel   PUB
(📞 03-443 8153; www.cardronahotel.co.nz; 2312 Cardrona Valley Rd; ⏱️ 9am-11pm; 🛜) The wood-panelled facade looks like a film set, but it's the real deal – NZ's most photographed pub is a gold-rush relic from 1863.

The sense of history is palpable and things get busy in the après-ski thawing hours. Meals are delicious (bao buns, burgers, beef stew; mains $24 to $36), and there are 14 lovingly restored rooms (from $150) if you don't want to leave.

ℹ Getting There & Away

There are no scheduled bus services to Cardrona, but the Cardrona Alpine Resort runs buses from Wānaka ($35) and Queenstown ($55) during the ski season, and from Queenstown during the mountain biking season. Winter ski shuttles are also offered by Yello! (p594) in Wānaka, and Info & Snow (p579) in Queenstown.

The 45km drive from Queenstown to Cardrona along the Crown Range Rd is one of the South Island's most scenic drives. Topping out at 1076m, it's the highest sealed road in NZ. There are some great places to stop and ogle the view, particularly at the Queenstown end of the road. However, the road is narrow and winding, and needs to be tackled with care in poor weather. In winter it's sometimes closed after heavy snows, and you'll often need snow chains for your tyres.

Makarora

POP 40

Just 20km from Haast Pass, where the West Coast begins its wild ways, remote Makarora is very much a last frontier – and it certainly feels like it. Traffic to and from the West Coast rolls through, but then Makarora settles back to silence.

🏃 Activities

Haast Pass Lookout Track (one hour return, 3.5km) offers great views from above the bush line. If you really want the upstairs view, the Mt Shrimpton Track climbs high onto the McKerrow Range (five hours return to the bush line, 6km); the track begins just a few hundred metres north of the Wonderland Makarora Lodge (☏03-443 8372; www.makarora.co.nz; 5944 Haast Pass-Makarora Rd/SH6; ⊙7am-8pm; ☎).

Longer hikes including the Gillespie Pass Circuit (p560) go deep into the valleys that radiate through the mountains around Makarora, but shouldn't be undertaken lightly. Changeable alpine and river conditions mean you must be well prepared; call into the DOC Tititea/Mt Aspiring National Park Visitor Centre (p593) in Wānaka to

WORTH A TRIP

LAKE HĀWEA

People looking to escape the bright lights of Queenstown typically gravitate to Wānaka; those looking to escape the slightly less bright lights of Wānaka come to Lake Hāwea.

This small town, 15km north of Wānaka, is strung along the southern shore of its 141-sq-km namesake. Separated from Lake Wānaka by a narrow strip of land called the Neck, the blue-grey Lake Hāwea (with an average water temperature of just 9°C) is 35km long and 410m deep. It's particularly popular with fisherfolk looking to do battle with its trout and landlocked salmon. The lake was raised 20m in 1958 when it was dammed to facilitate the power stations downriver. There's little here, but that's the town's appeal.

check conditions and routes before undertaking any wilderness hikes.

⭐ **Blue Pools Walk**   WALKING
(Haast Pass–Makarora Rd) Far and away the most popular walk in the Makarora area is the 750m (30-minute return) track to the luminously blue pools at the point where the Makarora and Blue Rivers converge. The water is so clear you can see the trout seemingly suspended in it. The trailhead is around 8km north of the Wonderland Makarora Lodge.

If you want to stride out a bit further, you can continue along the track to the mouth of the Young River (three to four hours return).

Siberia Experience   ADVENTURE
(☏03-443 4385; www.siberiaexperience.co.nz; Wonderland Makarora Lodge, 5944 Haast Pass–Makarora Rd; adult/child $415/340) 🏞 This thrill-seeking extravaganza combines a 25-minute scenic flight, a three-hour hike through a remote valley and a half-hour jetboat trip down the Wilkin and Makarora Rivers in Tititea/Mt Aspiring National Park.

ℹ Getting There & Away

InterCity (p579) has a daily coach to/from Queenstown ($33, 3¾ hours), Cromwell ($28, 2½ hours), Wānaka ($28, 1½ hours), Lake Hāwea ($28, 1¼ hours) and Franz Josef (from $46, 4¾ hours).

The South Island's Birds

New Zealand may lack for mammals, but that's conversely created a unique population of birds – a number of species are flightless, having had no need to take to the air to avoid predators. Check out the excellent Digital Encyclopedia of New Zealand Birds (www.nzbirdsonline.org.nz), the Department of Conservation website (www.doc.govt.nz/nature/native-animals/birds).

1. Kiwi
The national icon with an onomatopoeic name (OK only for the male, which cries 'kiwi!'; females make a sound more like someone with a sore throat). There are five different species, but the small population is endangered by habitat loss and predators.

2. Tui/Tūī
Common throughout town and country, up close the 'parson bird' is metallic bluey-green with white throat tufts. Sometimes tuneful, and sometimes cacophonous, it is always an aerobatic flapper.

3. Fantail/Pīwakawaka
This restless little charmer will entrance you up close, but in truth it cares not a jot about you, merely the insects you displace.

4. Pukeko/Pūkeko
Often seen pecking about in paddocks or crossing the road in front of high-speed traffic. Territorial, highly social and easily recognised, it looks like a smooth blue chicken with a red forehead.

5. Kererū
If you can hear heavy wingbeats overhead, it'll be the kererū, often spotted on powerlines and tree branches. This handsome native pigeon won Bird of the Year in 2019.

6. Silvereye/Tauhou
One of NZ's most prevalent birds, though originally a migrant from Australia, it's easily recognised by a green and grey plumage and silver-white eyes; listen for its sing-song call.

7. Bellbird/Korimako
More like a laser gun than a church bell, this enchanting songbird sounds big but is a small, olive-green slip of a thing, with a curved bill for eating nectar.

8. Grey Warbler/Riroriro
New Zealand's most widely distributed endemic bird species is also one of its smallest. It tends to hide in dense vegetation; you're more likely to hear one warbling its lungs out, than see one.

9. Woodhen/Weka
Often mistaken for a kiwi by visitors to NZ, this large flightless bird (similar in size to a chicken) has a keen nose for lunch crumbs and will often appear at well-frequented picnic spots.

10. Rifleman/Tititi Pounamu
New Zealand's smallest bird, this hyperactive forest-dweller produces a characteristic 'wing-flicking' while moving through the canopy and foraging up and down tree trunks.

11. Kea
Resident only in the mountainous region of South Island, this alpine parrot likes to play. Kea appear innately curious, but this is simply a pretence to peck destructively at your possessions.

The West Coast

Best Places to Eat

→ Hokitika Sandwich Company (p615)

→ Matheson Cafe (p606)

→ Stations Inn (p615)

→ SnakeBite Brewery (p610)

→ Monsoon (p610)

Best Places to Stay

→ Theatre Royal Hotel (p617)

→ Omau Settlers Lodge (p627)

→ Code Time Lodge (p611)

→ Bazil's Hostel & Surf School (p627)

→ Ross Beach Top 10 (p612)

Why Go?

Nowhere is solitude sweeter than on the West Coast (in Māori, Te Tai o Poutini). A few marvels pull big crowds – like Franz Josef and Fox Glaciers, and the magnificent Pancake Rocks – but you'll need jetboats, helicopter rides and hiking trails to explore its inner realms. Hemmed in by the Southern Alps and the savage Tasman Sea, the West Coast forms almost 9% of the land area of New Zealand (NZ) but contains less than 1% of its population.

Nineteenth-century European settlers in this region faced great hardships as fortunes built on gold, coal and timber wavered. A chain of ghost towns and forlorn pioneer cemeteries was left in their wake, and only the hardiest remained. Present-day Coasters exhibit the same grit, softened with ironic humour and unquestioning hospitality. Time spent in these indomitable communities will have you spinning yarns of the wild West Coast long into the future.

When to Go

→ December through February is peak season, so book accommodation a couple of months ahead during this period.

→ The shoulder months of October/November and March/April are increasingly busy, particularly around Punakaiki, Hokitika and the Glaciers.

→ The West Coast gets serious rainfall – in places, up to 5m annually.

→ May to September has fewer crowds and cheaper accommodation; though mild (for the South Island), it's reliably rainy.

→ All year round, backcountry hikers should check conditions with local DOC (Department of Conservation) office staff. Rivers are treacherous and snow hangs around longer than you think.

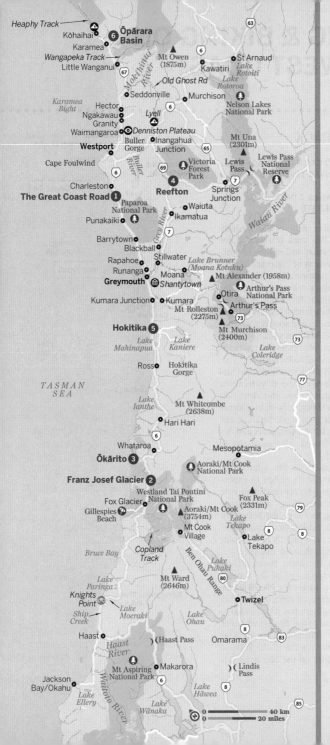

The West Coast Highlights

1 The Great Coast Road (p624) Admiring salt-sprayed beaches, dramatic sea cliffs and the unusual Pancake Rocks along an unforgettable 100km drive.

2 Franz Josef Glacier (p606) Pondering the glacier's swift retreat from a distance or taking a guided helihike on the glistening ice.

3 Ōkārito (p610) Kayaking through rainforest channels and watching the sun set over the pounding surf before joining a kiwi-spotting walk.

4 Reefton (p630) Delving into the gold-mining past of the coast's quaintest town, and taking a tipple at its excellent distillery.

5 Hokitika (p612) Hunting out authentic local *pounamu* (greenstone/jade) in working studios.

6 Ōpārara Basin (p629) Craning your neck at limestone formations girded by dense forest.

HIKING & BIKING ON THE WEST COAST

PAPAROA TRACK

START SMOKE-HO CAR PARK, BLACKBALL
END PORORARI RIVER TRACK CAR PARK, PUNAKAIKI
DURATION/DISTANCE 3 DAYS/55KM
DIFFICULTY MODERATE

Opened in December 2019 as NZ's 10th official Great Walk, this track traverses alpine terrain, limestone karst and rainforest within the dense wilderness of Paparoa National Park. It starts by following the old Croesus mining track, passing relics of the mining glory days, and climbs to 1000m above sea level before exiting through a lush river valley lined with nikau palms and spectacular limestone formations. Hikers can walk it in either direction, but mountain bikers are restricted to riding from Blackball to Punakaiki.

Being a Great Walk, it's well marked and signposted, with huts equipped with bunks, toilets, heating, gas stoves and drinkable water (no showers though); book in advance and bring all your own food, bedding and utensils. However, it's steep in parts and can be muddy, so you'll need to be reasonably fit and well equipped.

For mountain bikers it's a two-day, Grade 4 ride – meaning that it's suited to experienced, hardy riders who are confident with traversing the various swing and suspension bridges along the way. Just before the Punakaiki end the track splits, with mountain bikers exiting via a slightly longer route (to Waikori car park) than the hikers.

Alternatives to the main route include exiting via the western end of the **Croesus Track** to Barrytown, or via the **Pike29 Memorial Track**. At the time of writing this track was still being finalised, but it's planned as an official memorial to the 29 men who died in the Pike River mining disaster in 2010. It connects near the middle of the Paparoa Track and terminates on the access road to the mine.

Take a walk on the wild side, literally. The West Coast is one of the most dynamic hiking and mountain biking regions in New Zealand, with an emerging network of tracks.

OLD GHOST ROAD

START LYELL CAMPSITE
END MOKIHINUI RD, SEDDONVILLE
DURATION/DISTANCE 5 DAYS/85KM
DIFFICULTY MODERATE

One of the gnarliest of NZ's mountain biking and hiking trails, the **Old Ghost Road** (☑ 0800 244 678; www.oldghostroad.org.nz) follows a historic miners' track that was started in the 1870s but never finished, as the gold rush petered out. Following a painstaking, volunteer-led build, the gruelling track now traverses native forests, tussock tops, river flats and valleys.

The southern trailhead is at Lyell, 50 minutes' drive (62km) east of Westport along the scenic Buller Gorge (SH6). The DOC campsite and day walks here have long been popular, with visitors drawn in by readily accessible historic sites, including a graveyard secreted in the bush. The northern trailhead is at Seddonville, 45 minutes' drive (50km) north of Westport off SH67, from where the track sidles along the steep-sided Mokihinui River. Joining the two ends is an alpine section, with entrancing views from sunrise to sunset.

The track is dual use, but favours walkers (allow five days). For advanced mountain bikers who can handle narrow trails and plenty of jolts, it is pretty much the Holy Grail, completed in two to four days, preferably from Lyell to Seddonville. The four huts along the way need to be booked in advance on the Old Ghost Road website, which also details a range of other ways to experience the track other than an end-to-end ride or hike. Day trips from either end are a rewarding, flexible way in, particularly from the Seddonville end, via the inimitable **Rough & Tumble Lodge** (p627).

Being a long and remote track through wild terrain, conditions can change quickly, so check the trail website for its status.

COPLAND TRACK

START/END KARANGARUA RIVER BRIDGE
DURATION/DISTANCE 2 DAYS/36KM
DIFFICULTY MODERATE

This hike up the Copland Valley to Welcome Flat Hut is a popular overnight return trip for visitors to the Glacier Region. It offers a window into Westland Tai Poutini National Park's spectacular forest, river and mountain scenery, while natural hot pools at Welcome Flat are an added attraction for foot-weary adventurers.

The forests of the Copland Valley have a healthy canopy of southern rata, and their bright red blooms make for a spectacular sight during the summer flowering season. The forest gives way at higher altitudes to the upper montane vegetation of tree daisies and *Dracophyllums*, which in turn give way to the truly alpine habitats of tussock grasslands and native herbs.

Regular possum control has been undertaken since the mid-1980s and as a result the forest damage is significantly less than in the neighbouring Karangarua Valley, which has extensive canopy dieback. The only real drawback of this hike is that you must eventually turn around and backtrack to SH6.

Note, there's a river and about a dozen streams to cross (keep your boots on), hence the track is closed in heavy rain; check in with the National Park Visitor Centre before setting out. Book the hut online and be aware that there are no cooking facilities; you'll need to carry all of your equipment with you.

ⓘ Getting There & Away

Most travellers arrive by road from elsewhere in NZ. Buses head here from major South Island destinations, including Nelson, Christchurch and Queenstown. The TranzAlpine (p618) train between Christchurch and Greymouth is the most scenic mode of transport. There are flights between Hokitika and Christchurch, and between Westport and Wellington.

WESTLAND

Long, thin Westland is one of New Zealand's most sparsely populated districts, stretching from Mt Aspiring National Park in the south to the Taramakau River, north of Hokitika. Its sweeping beaches are lined with swamp forests, twisted rata trees aflutter with birdlife, and squabbling colonies of seals and penguins.

Amid this tapestry of farmland and rainforest, the most famous features are Fox and Franz Josef Glaciers. Though in retreat, these frosty monoliths hook thousands of admirers, many of whom stick around for pulse-thudding pursuits like mountain biking the West Coast Wilderness Trail, hiking the Copland Track, soaring above national parks by helicopter, or tiptoeing through the bush on kiwi-spotting walks.

There's culture, too, if you like it quaint and low-key: gold-rush sights in Ross and greenstone-carving classes in Hokitika provide a respite on days when you want to hang up your hiking boots.

Haast & Around

POP 240

A small settlement near the yawning mouth of the Haast River, Haast acts as a springboard to forests, sand dunes, craggy coast and tree-knotted lakes. Only in 1965 was Haast linked to the rest of the West Coast Hwy and the remote feeling endures. It's a handy stop for filling the tank and tummy if you're travelling between Central Otago and the West Coast glaciers. Note: check your fuel gauge as Haast has the last petrol station before Fox Glacier (120km north) and Makarora (78km southeast).

⊙ Sights & Activities

Haast's main selling point is its frontier location, but plenty of hikes hereabouts are easy, hour-long affairs. Explore with the help of the free *Haast Visitor Map* or DOC's brochure *Walks and Activities in the Haast Area* ($2 from the visitor centre (p604), or downloadable online). Some are easily accessible from the highway heading to Fox Glacier, so build in extra travelling time for your journey north.

Knights Point   VIEWPOINT
(Haast Hwy) Admire expansive views of boulder-studded sea from this roadside lookout. A granite column commemorates the opening of this section of coastal highway in 1965. It's an easy pull-over off the highway, 25km northeast of Haast Junction.

HAAST PASS HIGHWAY

The 145km road careening between the West Coast and Central Otago is a spectacular drive. It takes roughly two hours from Haast to Wānaka, but allow more time to drive this Southern Alpine saddle if you want to stop at lookouts and waterfall trails.

Heading inland from Haast, the highway (SH6) snakes alongside the Haast River, crossing the boundary into Mt Aspiring National Park. The further you go, the narrower the river valley becomes, until the road clambers around sheer-sided valley walls streaked with waterfalls and scarred by rock slips. Princely sums are involved in keeping this highway clear, and even so it sets plenty of traps for unwary drivers. Stop at signposted lookouts and short walkways to admire the scenery, such as small, graceful Fantail Falls (10 minutes return) and aptly named Thunder Creek Falls (one hour return). These are detailed in DOC's booklet *Walks along the Haast Highway* ($2), but sufficient detail is provided at the trailheads. The highway tops out at the 563m mark, shortly after which you will reach food and fuel at Makarora. Hello Otago!

Early Māori travelled this route in their quest for *pounamu* (greenstone/jade), naming it Tioripātea, meaning 'Clear Path'. Northern chief Te Puoho led troops across the pass in 1836 to raid southern tribes. German geologist Julius von Haast led a party of Europeans across in 1863 – hence the name of the pass, river and town – but evidence suggests that Scottish prospector Charles Cameron may have pipped Haast to the post. It was clearly no mean feat: the terrain is such that the Haast Pass Hwy wasn't opened until 1965.

THE ROAD TO JACKSON BAY/OKAHU

Most travellers drive northeast from Haast Junction towards Fox and Franz Josef Glaciers, but the road less travelled makes an interesting detour. Steering southwest for 45km from Haast you'll find the pocket-sized outpost of Jackson Bay/Okahu, towered over by the Southern Alps. There's no through road: this fishing hamlet is truly the end of the line. Farms here stand testament to some of the hardiest souls who ever attempted settlement in New Zealand. Migrants arrived in 1875 under a doomed settlement scheme, their farming and timber-milling aspirations shattered by never-ending rain and the lack of a wharf, not built until 1938. Until the 1950s, the only way to reach Haast overland was via bush tracks from Hokitika and Wānaka. Supplies came by an infrequent coastal shipping service.

Unless you're in the market for whitebait, present-day Jackson Bay has few attractions other than some lovely walking tracks spread along the road leading to it.

Near Okuru, 10km west of Haast, is the Hapuka Estuary Walk (20 minutes), a winding boardwalk that loops through a sleepy wildlife sanctuary with good interpretation panels en route.

The road continues west to Arawhata Bridge, where a turn-off leads to the Lake Ellery Track, 3.5km south along unsealed Jackson River Rd. A one-hour round trip takes you through mossy beech forest to a lookout over peaceful Lake Ellery. There's not much besides a picnic bench when you arrive, but you'll likely have it to yourself.

From the end of Jackson Bay Rd the 40-minute return Wharekai-Te Kou Walk leads through bird-filled bush to Ocean Beach, a tiny boulder-strewn bay where penguins are known to nest. The muddy three- to four-hour Smoothwater Track, following an old pioneers' track, also begins nearby.

Lake Moeraki
LAKE

(Haast Hwy) Alongside the highway, 32km northeast of Haast Junction, and within the bounds of the World Heritage wilderness, Lake Moeraki is an undeveloped and tranquil spot to contemplate the forested, mountainous surroundings. There's no trail all the way around, but there are lake beaches where you can park and ponder.

Wayne's Waiatoto River Safari
CRUISE

(☑ 03-750 0780; www.riversafaris.co.nz; 1975 Haast-Jackson Bay Rd, Hannahs Clearing; adult/child $199/139; ☺ trips 10am, 1pm & 4pm Nov-Mar, 11am Apr-Oct) ✿ These two-hour river cruises offer an exhilarating taste of World Heritage wilderness. Knowledgeable operators point out bird life and features of the landscape as the jetboat buzzes past areas otherwise only accessible by helicopter. Birds chatter, ducks race alongside the boat, and there's the occasional white-knuckle rapid on this generally gentle-paced journey. The base is 20km southwest of Haast Junction.

Ship Creek Tauparikākā
WALKING

(www.doc.govt.nz; Haast Hwy) Two contrasting walks begin at Ship Creek, 15km north of Haast, each with interesting interpretive panels. Stroll sand dunes, stunted forest and driftwood-strewn beaches on the Dune Lake Walk (30 minutes return), before embarking on the enchanting Kahikatea Swamp Forest Walk (20 minutes return), along boardwalks that hover above glistening marshland (the bird-watching is superb).

🛏 Sleeping & Eating

Haast River Motels & Holiday Park
HOLIDAY PARK $$

(☑ 03-750 0020; www.haastrivermotels.co.nz; 52 Haast Pass Hwy, Haast Junction; sites/units from $44/139; 🅿 @ 🛜 🐾) A large red hangar serves as the communal facilities for campervan and tenting guests, while a horseshoe of two-storey buildings contains a variety of roomy and well-furnished motel units. On-site facilities include a laundry, a games room, a playground, and a book- and DVD-filled lounge surveyed by mounted deer heads.

Wilderness Lodge Lake Moeraki
LODGE $$$

(☑ 03-750 0881; www.wildernesslodge.co.nz; Haast Hwy; s/d incl breakfast & dinner from $595/980; 🅿 🛜) ✿ Positioned in a verdant setting on the edge of the Moeraki River near Lake Moeraki, 30km north of Haast Junction, this is one of NZ's best nature lodges. It offers comfortable rooms and three-course dinners, but the real delights are the free guided outdoor activities such as kayak trips and coastal walks.

Hard Antler
PUB FOOD $$

(📱03-750 0034; www.facebook.com/HardAntler BarHaast; Marks Rd; mains $15-32; ⊙11am-late) Antlers and a fishing and shooting wall of fame establish the hunting-lodge vibe of Haast's best boozer. Mainly meaty main courses (venison nachos, burgers, toasties and tasty grilled blue cod) are served all day.

❶ Information

With outdoor water features, a hiker-friendly toilet block and a brimming museum, the **DOC Awarua/Haast Visitor Centre** (📱03-750 0809; www.doc.govt.nz; cnr Haast Pass Hwy & Haast-Jackson Bay Rd, Haast Junction; ⊙9am-6pm Nov-Mar, to 4.30pm Apr-Oct) is more than the average info centre. Displays cover local Māori history, whitebaiting and Te Wāhipounamu World Heritage Area. It also sells insect repellent (essential).

General regional information and visitor services listings can be found on www.haastnz.com.

❶ Getting There & Away

Intercity (📱03-365 1113; www.intercity. co.nz) buses stop on Marks Rd on their daily runs between Queenstown ($43, 5¼ hours) and Franz Josef ($29, 3¼ hours) via Cromwell, ($33, four hours), Wānaka ($30, 3¼ hours) and Fox Glacier ($28, 2¾ hours).

Fox Glacier
POP 306

Descending from the brooding Southern Alps, Fox Glacier (in Māori, Te Moeka o Tuawe) seems to flow steadily, ominously towards the township below. But in this fragile landscape it's the glacier that's at risk: despite slight advances in the early years of the millennia, this 13km glacier (named for former New Zealand PM Sir William Fox) has been steadily retreating over the past century. And, sadly, enormous landslides in 2019 have permanently closed the roads and tracks leading towards its terminus. Now, unless you fork out for a pricey helicopter trip, you'll have content yourself with admiring it from a considerable distance.

Compared with the glacier, the eponymous township isn't nearly so dramatic; its cafes, motels and tour operators occupy a very short strip of SH6. However, there are some interesting sights and walks to pursue in the surrounding farmland.

◉ Sights

Lake Matheson
LAKE

(Lake Matheson Rd) On a good day, the famous 'mirror lake' reflects extraordinary views of

---

WESTLAND TAI POUTINI NATIONAL PARK

With colossal mountains, forests, glaciers and surf-pounded beaches, Westland Tai Poutini National Park (www.doc.govt.nz) clobbers visitors with its mind-bending proportions. Reaching from the coast to the razor peaks of the Southern Alps, the park's supreme attractions are twin glaciers Fox and Franz Josef, served by townships 23km apart. The official National Park Visitor Centre (p610) is in Franz Josef.

Diverse and often unique habitats are huddled into the national park's 1280 sq km. Endangered bird species include kākāriki (parakeets), kākā and kea (parrots) and rowi (Ōkārito kiwi). Also scampering through these forests are introduced ungulates such as red deer, chamois and Himalayan tahr.

Out of more than 60 glaciers in the park, only Fox and Franz Josef are easy to view. The glaciers are as fragile as they are amazing to behold. Rising temperatures have beaten the glaciers into retreat, reducing opportunities to view them on foot and clanging a death knell for their long-term future if climate change continues unchecked. The glaciers are the most majestic handiwork of the West Coast's ample precipitation. Snowfall in the glaciers' broad accumulation zones fuses into clear ice at 20m depth, and then creeps down the steep valleys. Nowhere else at this latitude do glaciers descend so close to the ocean. During the last ice age (around 15,000 to 20,000 years ago) Westland's twin glaciers reached the sea. In the ensuing thaw they may have crawled back even further than their current positions, but around the 14th century a mini ice age caused them to advance to their greatest modern-era extent around 1750, and the terminal moraines from this time are still visible. The only way to get onto the ice safely is with a guided tour. Both glacier terminal faces are roped off to prevent people being caught in icefalls and river surges, which can flood the valleys in a matter of minutes. Obey warning signs and stay out of roped-off areas.

distant Aoraki/Mt Cook and Mt Tasman in its forest-shaded waters. The best time to visit is early morning or when the sun is low in the late afternoon, although the presence of an excellent cafe (p606) means that any time is a good time. It's extraordinary to think that this lake was carved out by the now distant Fox Glacier before it started its long retreat.

The shady, moss-lined 2.6km Lake Matheson Track circumnavigates the lake; allow 90 minutes walking at a slow pace. At the far end of the circuit you may, weather permitting, get the money shot, but failing that you can buy a postcard at the excellent gift store by the car park.

Branching off from the eastern side of the main track is the 8km-return Lake Gault Track, which gradually climbs 200m through virgin podocarp forest to another mirror lake. Allow three to five hours and expect to get wet and muddy feet.

Peak Viewpoint VIEWPOINT
(Gillespies Beach Rd) It's a very long way from the actual glacier, but this parking area provides a surprisingly good view over fields to Fox Glacier (weather permitting). There's not much here except a picnic table and a marker pointing out the various peaks. However, it's a good alternative to the two-hour (6km return) Fox Glacier South Side Walk along the slip-damaged old Glacier View Rd to a viewpoint that, while considerably closer, still won't give you a view of the terminus.

Gillespies Beach BEACH
(www.doc.govt.nz; Gillespies Beach Rd) Follow Cook Flat Rd for its full 21km (the final 12km is narrow, winding and unsealed) to this remote beach, a ruggedly beautiful, wind-blasted length of slate-grey sand and shingle near an old mining settlement. Interesting walks from here include a 30-minute, partly sheltered circuit to a rusting gold dredge from 1932, and a 3½-hour return walk to Galway Beach, a seal hang-out; don't disturb them.

Five-hundred metres shy of the beach, signposted from the road, is a well-kept miners' cemetery, reached by a five-minute walk. There's a basic, eight-site DOC campground by the beach.

🗡 Activities
Short helicopter flights (10 to 20 minutes) offer a spectacular vantage point over Fox Glacier with a snow landing up top. On a longer flight (30 to 50 minutes) you can also enjoy sky-high sightseeing over Franz Josef Glacier and Aoraki/Mt Cook. Children are admitted, though age restrictions vary; expect to pay around 70% of the adult price. Shop around: most operators are situated on the main road in Fox Glacier village.

Fox Glacier Guiding ADVENTURE SPORTS
(☑03-751 0825; www.foxguides.co.nz; 44 Main Rd) The only way to get on the actual glacier, this friendly crew offers small-group helihikes. A five-minute helicopter ride whooshes you onto the ice for a three-hour hike (adult/child $499/475), or a more demanding seven-hour hike (adult $750). Scrambling through ice caves, peering into crevasses and sipping glacial meltwater is included with the animated commentary. Age restrictions vary by trip.

Helicopter Line SCENIC FLIGHTS
(☑03-751 0767; www.helicopter.co.nz; cnr Main & Cook Flat Rds; 20-40min flights $280-490) Whisking travellers to giddy heights since 1986, this well-established operator has a big menu of scenic flights. It also operates from Franz Josef, where it offers a three-hour helihike option ($485) in conjunction with Franz Josef Glacier Guides (p608).

HeliServicesNZ SCENIC FLIGHTS
(☑03-751 0866; www.scenic-flights.co.nz; 44 Main Rd; flights from $280; ☺7am-9pm Nov-Mar, 8am-6pm Apr-Oct) Locally run operator zipping sightseers up and down the glaciers, always with a snow landing. A two-glacier flight ($325) is over all too quickly, but longer flights also soar around Aoraki/Mt Cook and Mt Tasman. It also has an office in Franz Josef.

Mountain Helicopters SCENIC FLIGHTS
(☑03-751 0045; www.mountainhelicopters.co.nz; 43 Main Rd; flights from $129) Offers flights over Fox and Franz Josef Glaciers, ranging from a 10-minute taster to a 40-minute all-rounder with a snow landing and views of Aoraki/Mt Cook. It also has an office at Franz Josef.

🍴 Sleeping & Eating

Fox Glacier Top 10 HOLIDAY PARK $$
(☑03-751 0821; www.fghp.co.nz; Kerr Rd; sites $55-58, r with/without bathroom from $165/85; 🅿🛜♨) Inspiring mountain views and ample amenities lift this reliable holiday park above its competition. Trim cabins, basic lodge rooms, and grassy tent and hard campervan sites make use of a quality communal kitchen and dining room. The upmarket self-contained units offer extra comfort and

style. A playground and tandem bikes pile on the family-fun factor.

★ Matheson Cafe
CAFE $$

(☑03-751 0878; www.lakematheson.com; Lake Matheson Rd; breakfast & lunch $13-22, dinner $25-39; ☺8am-late Nov-Mar, to 3pm Apr-Oct; ☎) At the start of the Lake Matheson Track, this cafe does everything right: sharp architecture that maximises mountain views, strong coffee, craft beers and upmarket fare. Bratwurst breakfasts are a good prelude to rambling round the lake, while beef ramen and merino lamb burgers are a delicious way to refuel afterwards. Check out the ReflectioNZ gift shop next door.

ℹ Information

The main national park visitor centre and i-SITE is in Franz Josef (p610). Pick up a copy of DOC's excellent *Glacier Region Walks* booklet ($2), which provides maps and illuminating background reading. You can also find info online at www.glaciercountry.co.nz.

Fox Glacier Clinic (☑03-751 0836; www.wcdhb.health.nz; 3 Main Rd) is open from 9am-4pm Monday to Friday.

ℹ Getting There & Away

InterCity (p604) services trundle through Fox Glacier daily, heading south to Queenstown ($69, eight hours) via Haast ($28, 2¾ hours), and north to Greymouth ($47, 4¾ hours) via Franz Josef ($28, 40 minutes) and Hokitika ($40, 3¼ hours). Buses stop outside the Fox Glacier Guiding building.

Glacier Shuttles & Charters (p610) runs scheduled shuttles to Fox Glacier village and Lake Matheson from Franz Josef ($30 return, three to four daily).

If you're heading south along the coast, be aware that Fox is your last chance for fuel before Haast, 120km away.

Franz Josef/Waiau

POP 444

Franz Josef Glacier's cloak of ice once flowed from the mountains to the sea. Following millennia of gradual retreat, the glacier is now 19km inland. In the last 10 years alone the glacier has receded by nearly a kilometre, and the dismal forecast of a rainier, warmer future is sure to bring further shrinkage.

Swarms of small aircraft from tourist-focused Franz Josef / Waiau village, 5km north, lift visitors to views of sparkling ice and toothy mountains. Some land on the glacier to lead groups to blue-tinged caves and crevasses. A glacier experience is the crowning moment for thousands of annual visitors, but walking trails, hot pools and adventure sports provide a reason to linger.

Geologist Julius von Haast led the first European expedition here in 1865, and named the glacier after the Austrian emperor. Its Māori name is much more evocative: Kā Roimata o Hine Hukatere (Tears of the Avalanche Maiden).

◉ Sights & Activities

The **Franz Josef Glacier/Kā Roimata o Hine Hukatere Walk** (1½ hours return) starts from the glacier car park, 5km from the village. It heads through native bush and then along the broad, stony glacier valley to the best permissible view of the terminal face, an elusive 750m away. A series of information panels are positioned at the previous extents of the glacier at different dates in history, comparing the global temperatures, world population and atmospheric carbon dioxide concentration then to now – a sobering reminder of the effects of climate change.

Branching off from the beginning of the main walk is the steep, 20-minute return track to the top of **Sentinel Rock**. The lookout reveals either impressive views of the glacier valley, flanked by Mt Roon (2233m) and Bismarck Peak (2545m), or a mysterious panorama obscured by mist and cloud.

Other walks include the **Douglas Walk** (one hour return), off the Glacier Access Rd, which passes moraine piled up by the glacier's advance in 1750, and **Peters Pool**, a small kettle lake reflecting mountain views. The **Terrace Track** (15 minutes return) is an easy amble over bushy terraces behind the village, illuminated by glowworms at night. Two good rainforest walks, **Callery Gorge Walk** and **Tatare Tunnels** (both around 1½ hours return), start from Cowan St – bring a torch for the latter and boots that can deal with ankle-deep water.

Much more challenging walks, such as the five-hour **Roberts Point Track** and eight-hour **Alex Knob Track**, are suited to experienced hikers only. Get advice from DOC before setting out as they can be treacherous; people have died at Roberts Point. All of the main walks in the area are detailed in DOC's *Glacier Region Walks* booklet.

West Coast Wildlife Centre
NATURE CENTRE

(☑03-752 0600; www.wildkiwi.co.nz; cnr Cron & Cowan Sts; adult/child $39/20, incl backstage pass $59/35; ⊙8am-5.30pm) 🏻 The purpose of this feel-good attraction is breeding two of the world's rarest kiwi – the rowi and the Haast tokoeka. As well as a chance to hang out with kiwi in their darkened ferny enclosure, there are tuatara (native reptiles) and conservation, glacier and heritage displays. The backstage pass into the incubating and rearing area is a rare opportunity to learn how a species can be brought back from the brink of extinction.

Glacier Hot Pools   HOT SPRINGS
(☑03-752 0099; www.glacierhotpools.co.nz; 63 Cron St; adult/child $29/25; ⊙11am-9pm) Cleverly set into a pretty rainforest on the edge of town, this stylish and well-maintained outdoor hot-pool complex is perfect après-hike or on a rainy day. These aren't thermal springs but they do make use of glacial melt water and the three main pools are heated to 36°, 38° and 40°C. Private pools and massages are also available.

Skydive Franz Josef & Fox Glacier   SKYDIVING
(☑03-752 0714; www.skydivefranz.co.nz; Main Rd; 20,000/16,500/13,000/9000ft jump $649/429/339/289) This company claims to offer NZ's highest jump (20,000ft, 85+ seconds freefall) and, with the glaciers and Aoraki/Mt Cook in your sights, it's certainly one of the most scenic.

Air Safaris   SCENIC FLIGHTS
(☑03-752 0716; www.airsafaris.co.nz; Main Rd) Franz's only fixed-wing flyer offers 50-minute 'grand traverse' ($395) flights that expose breathtaking views of the glaciers, Aoraki/Mt Cook, and far-flung valleys, lakes and waterways en route. Alternatively, take a 30-minute Twin Glacier flight ($305). Either way, charge your camera.

Glacier Helicopters   SCENIC FLIGHTS
(☑03-752 0755; www.glacierhelicopters.co.nz; Main Rd; 20-40min flights $280-490) This reliable operator has been running scenic flights since 1970. Shorter flights take you to one of the glaciers, while the 40-minute option reaches both, as well as soaring to spectacular views of Aoraki/Mt Cook. There's a brief snow landing on each trip.

Glacier Country Helicopters   SCENIC FLIGHTS
(☑03-752 0203; www.glaciercountryhelicopters.co.nz; 10 Main Rd; flights from $280) This family-owned and operated company offers the choice of scenic flights surveying one, two or three glaciers, including a snow landing.

Franz Josef
Clay Target Shooting   OUTDOORS
(☑027 772 6590; www.franzjosefclayshooting.co.nz; 20/30 targets $110/130; ⊙by arrangement) Lock your sights onto clay discs hurtling through the air, before obliterating them... sound like fun? This operator offers exhilarating two-hour shoot-'em-ups. Sessions include transfers to and from the range, on a farm 6km south of Franz Josef township. Book ahead, by phone or through the i-SITE. It's perfect for rainy days: shooters stay undercover in a purpose-built hut.

👉 Tours

★Glacier Country Kayaks   KAYAKING
(☑03-752 0230; www.glacierkayaks.com; 64 Cron St; 3hr kayak adult/child $120/70) 🏻 Enjoy a change of pace on a guided kayak trip on Lake Mapourika (10km north of Franz). The 'kayak classic' is three hours of bird-spotting and mountain views. Alternatively, take the summer-only 'sunset classic' ($130/80) or a four-hour 'kayak & walk' (adult/child $145/85). It also offers SUP tours, rainforest walks, lake cruises, fishing charters and various combos.

Glacier Valley Eco Tours   ECOTOUR
(☑0800 925 586; www.glaciervalley.co.nz; 20 Main Rd; adult/child $80/40) 🏻 These conservation-focused walking tours unlock the geological and wildlife secrets of Glacier Country. Three- to four-hour tours explore either Franz Josef, Fox Glacier, Ōkārito or Lake Matheson, with the Franz Josef tour getting closer to the terminal face than is otherwise

608

Franz Josef Glacier & Village

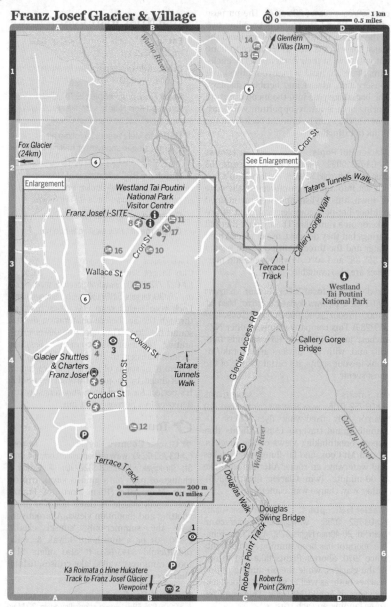

THE WEST COAST FRANZ JOSEF/WAIAU

permitted. Full-day tours immerse you in local flora and fauna over seven hours of hiking (adult/child $180/90).

Franz Josef Glacier Guides ADVENTURE
(☎ 03-752 0763; www.franzjosefglacier.com; 63 Cron St) Take a helicopter ride to the ice and then experience two hours on the glacier exploring dazzling blue ice caves ($485). The daring can seize an ice pick for a four-hour ice climb ($609) or even camp on the glacier overnight ($999). Three-hour guided valley walks are also available (adult/child $82/67).

Franz Josef Glacier & Village

🛏 Sleeping

Rainforest Retreat HOLIDAY PARK $
(📞 03-752 0220; www.rainforest.nz; 46 Cron St; sites $48, dm/r/units from $37/100/195; P 🌐 🚰) Options abound in these forested grounds: dorm rooms that sleep between four and six (four-bed 'flashpacker' en-suite rooms are worth the higher rate), en-suite doubles and luxurious free-standing cottages set among the trees, with underfloor heating, rain showers and private decks. Campervan sites are nestled in native bush. There's also a gigantic hot tub and an excellent on-site pub/restaurant, Monsoon (p610).

58 on Cron MOTEL $$
(📞 03-752 0627; www.58oncron.co.nz; 58 Cron St; units from $170; P 🌐) Guests staying in these 16 comfortable motel units, from petite studios to two-bedroom apartments, enjoy sweet service and a barbecue area. Bonus: you won't forget the motel's address.

Franz Josef Glacier YHA HOSTEL $$
(📞 03-752 0754; www.yha.co.nz; 2-4 Cron St; dm $33, s/d without bathroom $115/125, r with bathroom $145; P 🌐) ⚡ Functional and friendly, the YHA has warm, spacious communal areas, family rooms, a large free sauna, and a booking desk for transport and activities. It can accommodate 115 people, but you'll still need to book ahead.

Franz Josef Top 10 HOLIDAY PARK $$
(📞 03-752 0735; www.franzjoseftop10.co.nz; 2902 Franz Josef Hwy; sites $55, units with/without bathroom from $150/99; P 🌐 🚰) ⚡ Tents and motorhomes are afforded free-draining grassy sites away from the road at this spacious holiday park, 1.5km north of the township. Travellers who prefer four walls can

choose cabins (sharing the well-maintained bathroom and kitchen areas) or trim self-contained units. A playground, games room and TV lounge provide distractions during rainy days.

Holly Homestead B&B $$$
(📞 03-752 0299; www.hollyhomestead.co.nz; 2900 Franz Josef Hwy; r $295-395; 🌐) This two-storey wisteria-draped B&B stays true to its 1926 beginnings with an old-fashioned welcome and freshly baked bread for breakfast. Choose between three characterful en-suite rooms or a suite, all of which share a classy lounge and a deck that's perfect for a sundowner. It's positioned on the highway, 1.5km to the north of the village.

Glenfern Villas APARTMENT $$$
(📞 03-752 0054; www.glenfern.co.nz; Franz Josef Hwy; villas $279-315; P 🌐) ⚡ Forming something of a tiny, elite village 3km north of town, Glernfern's one- and two-bedroom houses are equipped with every comfort from quality beds to plump couches, gleaming kitchenettes and private decks where you can listen to birdsong. Book well ahead.

Te Waonui Forest Retreat HOTEL $$$
(📞 03-752 0555; www.tewaonui.co.nz; 3 Wallace St; s/d $679/809; 🕙 Sep-Apr; P 🌐) ⚡ Luxurious Te Waonui is filled with design flourishes that evoke the land: twinkly lights suggest glowworms, coal-black walls nod to the mining past, and local stone provides an earthy backdrop. Beyond the gorgeous, greenery-facing rooms, the prime draw is the five-course degustation dinner (included in some packages). Top-notch green credentials include building materials that are either recycled or sustainably sourced.

Aspen Court
MOTEL $$$

(☑ 03-752 0210; www.aspencourtfranzjosef.co.nz; 76 Cron St; units $280-335; P 🐾 🛜) It couldn't be accused of being reasonably priced, but this motel near the visitor centre offers a brace of smart brick units grouped around a central car park. All have kitchens and some have spa baths. There's a communal barbecue, too.

✕ Eating

★ SnakeBite Brewery
ASIAN $$

(☑ 03-752 0234; www.snakebite.co.nz; 28 Main Rd; mains $16-29; ⊙ 7.30am-10.30pm) SnakeBite's flavour-packed meals awaken taste buds after their long slumber through the West Coast's lamb-and-whitebait menus. Indonesian, Malaysian, Thai, Chinese and Japanese dishes all feature, along with burgers and pies. Try the mussel fritters with wasabi mayo and, the speciality, the beef-cheek rendang. Between courses, glug craft beers on tap or a 'snakebite' (cider with beer).

★ Monsoon
PUB FOOD $$

(☑ 03-752 0101; www.monsoonbar.co.nz; 46 Cron St; mains $16-39; ⊙ 4.30pm-late) Sip drinks in the sunshine or within the cosy, chalet-style bar of the Rainforest Retreat (p609) which usually buzzes with a sociable crowd of travellers. Bar snacks, burgers, curries, roasts, steaks and posh pizzas ensure you needn't move from your comfy spot by the fire.

King Tiger
ASIAN $$

(☑ 03-752 0060; www.kingtiger.co.nz; 70 Cron St; mains $21-30; ⊙ 11.30am-9.30pm; 🛜 ☑ 🍴) Voyaging from India to China via Thailand, this atmospheric restaurant matches piquant dishes with Asian-inspired cocktails, red-and-black decor, Chinese lanterns, Buddha statues and a big gilded birdcage shaped like a maharaja's palace. There's a long menu but we're particularly partial to the lamb *saag-wala* (spinach curry).

❶ Information

Franz Josef Clinic (☑ 03-752 0700; www.wcdhb.health.nz; 97 Cron St; ⊙ 8.30am-5pm Mon-Fri) South Westland's main medical centre. After hours, calls connect to a local nurse.

Franz Josef i-SITE (☑ 0800 354 748; www.glaciercountry.co.nz; 69 Cron St; ⊙ 8.30am-5pm) Helpful local centre offering advice and booking service for activities, accommodation and transport in the local area and beyond.

Westland Tai Poutini National Park Visitor Centre (☑ 03-752 0360; www.doc.govt.nz; 69 Cron St; ⊙ 8.30am-5pm) Insightful exhibits, weather information, maps, locator beacons, and all-important track updates and weather forecasts.

❶ Getting There & Away

➜ InterCity (p604) buses stop outside the Four Square supermarket on Main St. Daily services head south to Queenstown ($73, 8½ hours) via Fox Glacier ($28, 40 minutes) and Haast ($29, three hours), and north to Greymouth ($44, four hours) via Hokitika ($38, 2½ hours). Book online, or at the i-SITE or YHA.

➜ **Glacier Shuttles & Charters** (☑ 027 205 5922; www.glaciershuttlescharters.co.nz; 20 Main Rd) runs scheduled shuttles to the glacier car park ($12.50 return, five to six daily), Fox Glacier village and Lake Matheson ($30 return, three to four daily), Lake Mapourika ($15 return, two daily) and Ōkārito ($30 return, two daily).

Ōkārito
POP 30

The seaside hamlet of Ōkārito has a magnificent setting, with a pounding surf beach at its doorstep, the snow-capped Southern Alps as a backdrop, forest-clad hills on one flank and an expansive lagoon on the other.

Barely 10km from SH6, Ōkārito Lagoon is the largest unmodified wetland in NZ. More than 76 bird species preen and glide among its waterways, including the kōtuku (white heron). Hiding out in the forest are rowi kiwi, the rarest species of NZ's iconic land-bird – for a great chance of seeing one in the wild, hook up with the South Island's only licensed kiwi-tour operator, based in the village.

Ōkārito has no shops, limited visitor facilities and patchy phone reception, so stock up and book before you arrive. It's hard to believe that during the height of the gold rush, 4000 people lived here.

🏃 Activities & Tours

From a car park on the Strand you can begin the easy Wetland Walk (20 minutes), which leads into the 10km-long Three Mile Pack Track (3½ hours; the coastal return route is tide dependent, so check in with the locals for tide times). Otherwise, branch off on the Ōkārito Trig Walk (1½ hours return), where a jolly good puff to the top is rewarded with spectacular Southern Alps and Ōkārito Lagoon views (weather contingent).

★ **Okarito Kiwi Tours** BIRDWATCHING

(☑ 03-753 4330; www.okaritokiwitours.co.nz; 53 The Strand; 3-5hr tour $75) ✎ Spotting the rare kiwi in Ōkārito's tangle of native forest isn't easy, but bird-whisperer Ian has a 98% success rate for his small-group evening tours. Patience, tiptoeing and fine weather are essential. If you have your heart set on a kiwi encounter, book ahead and be within reach of Ōkārito for a couple of nights, in case of poor weather.

Okarito Kayaks KAYAKING

(☑ 0800 652 748; www.okarito.co.nz; 1 The Strand; 2hr/3hr tour $110/130, half-/full-day rental $70/80; ☺ hours vary) This hands-on operator hires out kayaks for paddles across Ōkārito's shallow lagoon in the company of strutting waterfowl and beneath a breathtaking mountainscape. Honest advice is offered on weather, tides and paddling routes. Personalised guided kayaking trips are ideal for getting to know the landscape. It also serves homemade ice cream and cake, and surprisingly good coffee.

Okarito Boat Eco Tours BIRDWATCHING

(☑ 03-753 4223; www.okaritoboattours.co.nz; 31 Wharf St; ☺ late Oct–May) Runs bird-spotting lagoon tours, the most fruitful of which is the 80-minute 'early bird' (adult/child $85/40, 7.30am). The popular two-hour 'eco tour' offers deeper insights into this remarkable natural area ($95/45, 9am and 11.30am), or there's a 90-minute afternoon 'wetlands tour' ($75/35, 2.30pm) if you aren't a morning person. Book at least 24 hours in advance.

🛏 **Sleeping**

★ **Code Time Lodge** APARTMENT $$$

(☑ 021 037 2031; www.codetimelodge.co.nz; 8 Albert St; units $230; ☎) Driftwood decorations and soft colour schemes impart a dreamy air to the Code Time Lodge, whose two roomy, self-contained apartments (kitchen included) are kept toasty by log-burning stoves. Essentials are provided for a do-it-yourself breakfast (eggs, bread, homemade jams).

🛈 **Getting There & Away**

Ōkārito is 10km northwest off SH6 between Franz Josef and Whataroa. There are no buses but Glacier Shuttles & Charters (p610) runs scheduled shuttles to and from Franz Josef ($30 return, two daily).

Whataroa

POP 288

Although it's not much to look at, Whataroa (www.whataroa.org) is a gateway to rare natural wonders. Strung out along the SH6, 30km northwest of Franz Josef, this nondescript village is the departure point for tours of NZ's only nesting site for the kōtuku (white heron). With wings as delicately pretty as a bridal veil, these rare birds hold a special significance for Māori, who treasure their feathers and use 'kōtuku' as a compliment describing seldom-seen guests.

White Heron Sanctuary Tours BIRDWATCHING

(☑ 03-753 4120; www.whiteherontours.co.nz; 64 Main Rd; adult/child $150/75; ☺ tours 9am, 11am, 1pm & 3pm Oct-Feb) ✎ The sight of scores of rare kōtuku nesting, nuzzling and soaring over the water is sheer delight, whether you're a bird-watcher or along for the ride. The 2½-hour tour involves a gentle jetboat ride to Waitangiroto Nature Reserve and a short boardwalk to the viewing hide, where you're also likely to see royal spoonbills and little shags. Book ahead.

Alpine Fault Tours OUTDOORS

(☑ 03-753 4236; www.alpinefaulttours.co.nz; 70 Main Rd; adult/child $60/25; ☺ tours 1pm, or by arrangement) Stand astride two tectonic plates, marvelling at Mother Nature's might, on a two-hour fault-line tour. The experience is geared towards casual tourists as much as geology buffs: small groups take a 20-minute 4WD bus to an area 10km from Whataroa where the Australian and Zealandia plates meet. Engaging commentary discuses the forces that created the Southern Alps. Book ahead.

Glacier Country Scenic Flights SCENIC FLIGHTS

(☑ 0800 423 463; www.glacieradventures.co.nz; off Whataroa Hwy; 20-50min flights $235-535) Offers a range of scenic flights and helihikes, lifting off from near the Whataroa River bridge. These guys give you more mountain-gawping for your buck than many of the operators flying from the glacier townships, with optional snow landings.

🛈 **Getting There & Away**

This stretch of SH6 is serviced once daily by InterCity (p604) buses heading to/from Fox Glacier ($28, 1¼ hours), Franz Josef ($28, 44 minutes), Ross ($28, 1½ hours), Hokitika ($30, two hours) and Greymouth ($38, 3½ hours).

DON'T MISS

THE WEST COAST'S GREAT RIDE

One of the 22 Great Rides that together form the Ngā Haerenga NZ Cycle Trail, the easy (Grade 2) 133km West Coast Wilderness Trail (www.westcoastwildernesstrail.co.nz) stretches from Ross to Greymouth via Hokitika and Kumara, following gold-rush tracks, reservoirs, old tramways and railway lines. The trail reveals dense rainforest, glacial rivers, lakes and wetlands, and views to the Southern Alps and wild Tasman Sea.

The trail can be ridden in either direction and is gently graded most of the way. Although the full shebang takes a good four days by bike, it can easily be sliced up into sections of various lengths, catering to every ability and area of interest. Novice riders can tackle the relatively flat *Ross Railway* section between Ross and Hokitika (33km, three to five hours). Another goodie is the 49km *Majestic Forests & Lake Ride* from the Kawhaka Intake to Hokitika via Lake Kaniere, which takes in major highlights over seven hours, or a 45km ride following Kumara's gold trails (four hours).

Bike hire, transport and advice are available from the major setting-off points. In Hokitika, contact Cycle Journeys (☑ 021 263 3299; www.cyclejourneys.co.nz; 23 Hamilton St; bike hire per day from $55, shuttles $20-55) or Hokitika Cycles & Sports World (p614), and in Greymouth, Trail Transport (p621).

Ross

POP 297

When folks sensed gold in these hills in the 1860s, the township of Ross was hurriedly established. From 1865 to 1914 it was the most productive alluvial goldfield in NZ, reaching giddy heights of fame in 1909 with the discovery of the 'Honourable Roddy' gold nugget, weighing in at nearly 3kg (check out the replica in the Goldfields Heritage Centre). At its peak it was home to 3000 people, 10 times the current population.

It's the start or finish point of the West Coast Wilderness Trail, but its gold-rush history also makes Ross an interesting diversion on drives between the glacier towns and Hokitika. A cluster of gold-rush-era buildings on St James St are open to the public, free of charge, including St Patrick's Catholic Church from 1866, an 1885 cottage and a 1915 gaol. A Chinese-style garden and picnic area by the lake acknowledges the contribution of Chinese miners.

The Ross Water Race Walkway (one hour return) starts near the mildly interesting Goldfields Heritage Centre (☑ 03-755 4077; 4 Aylmer St; $2; ⊙ 10am-3pm), passing old gold diggings, caves, tunnels and a cemetery. Hire a gold pan ($10) from the centre and head to Jones Creek to look for Roddy's great, great grandnuggets. Gold is still found here; there are three active mines in the area.

★ Ross Beach Top 10   HOLIDAY PARK $
(☑ 03-429 8277; www.rossbeachtop10.co.nz; 145 Ross Beach Rd; sites $45-55, dm $35, pods with/ without bathroom from $110/101; P 🛜 🐾) 🐾
Perched on a ruggedly beautiful stretch of windswept beach, 2km northwest of Ross, this holiday park has plenty of space for tents and motorhomes, as well as a neat amenities block with a kitchen and laundry. We adore the converted shipping containers, upcycled into chic, self-contained 'pods'.

Historic Empire Hotel   PUB
(☑ 03-755 4005; 19 Aylmer St; ⊙ 10am-late) Nostalgia wafts from every brightly painted beam of the Empire. Since 1866, West Coasters have huddled inside the pub, amid yellowing photographs and dusty antiques, to spin yarns and swap gossip about whitebaiting locations. Breathe in the authenticity, along with a whiff of woodsmoke, over a pint and a bowl of chowder.

❶ Getting There & Away

One daily InterCity (p604) bus heads to/from Fox Glacier ($34, 2¼ hours), Franz Josef ($30, 1¾ hours), Whataroa ($28, 1½ hours), Hokitika ($28, 25 minutes) and Greymouth ($28, two hours).

Hokitika & Around

POP 2970

Hokitika is the archetypal West Coast town, positioned between a surf-battered beach and the snow-capped Southern Alps. Of the coast's three major towns (the others being Greymouth and Westport), Hokitika is by far the most appealing. There are some good places to eat, and a thriving community of local artisans selling their wares in shops scattered around the compact town centre. The town's artsy credentials have been buoyed further by its starring role in Eleanor Catton's 2013 book *The Luminaries*. There are just enough grand buildings from Hokitika's golden days dotted about to capture the imagination of fans of the Man Booker–winning novel, set during the 1860s gold rush.

Radiant sunsets and a glowworm dell add extra sparkle to this coastal idyll, though many visitors prefer to work up a sweat on the West Coast Wilderness Trail and the scenic tracks at lakes Kaniere and Māhinapua.

◉ Sights

Hokitika Gorge　　　　　　　　GORGE
(www.doc.govt.nz; Whitcombe Valley Rd) Water this turquoise doesn't come easily. Half a million years of glacial movement sculpted Hokitika's ravine; the rock 'flour' ground over millennia intensifies the water's hue. The gorge is a scenic 32km drive south of Hokitika, well signposted from Stafford St (past the dairy factory). From the car park it's a 150m walk to a viewing platform, then a further 300m to a swing bridge and 200m to a point where you can access the river.

En route, you will pass a poignant monument in Kōwhitirangi, the site of one of NZ's deadliest mass murders (immortalised in the 1982 classic film *Bad Blood*). Visitors can peer towards the farmstead site through a shaft bored through the stone.

Lake Māhinapua　　　　　　　　LAKE
(www.doc.govt.nz; Shanghai Rd, Ruatapu) Serene Lake Māhinapua lies 10km southwest of Hokitika, screened from SH6 by its surrounding forest. The scenic reserve, gazetted in 1907, has a picnic area and DOC campsite that bask in mountain views, and the shallow water is warm enough for a paddle. There are several short walks (an hour return or less) signposted along the shore.

The starting point of the Mahinapua Walkway is on SH6, 8km south of Hokitika. It's an easy four- to five-hour return walk (6km each way) following an old logging tramway to Woodstock Rimu Rd, with a short spur track connecting to the lake.

Lake Kaniere　　　　　　　　　LAKE
(www.doc.govt.nz; Lake Kaniere Rd) Lying at the heart of a 7000-hectare scenic reserve, 18km southeast of Hokitika, beautiful Lake

Kaniere is 8km long, 2km wide, up to 195m deep, and freezing cold (as you'll discover if you swim). You can camp or picnic at Hans Bay, peer at Dorothy Falls (4km south of the campground), or undertake one of numerous walks, ranging from the 15-minute Canoe Cove Walk to the seven-hour return gut-buster up Mt Tuhua.

The historic Kaniere Water Race Walkway (3½ hours one-way) forms part of the West Coast Wilderness Trail.

Note: the road from Hans Bay to Dorothy Falls is narrow and unsealed, and hence not suitable for motorhomes.

Glowworm Dell　　　　NATURAL FEATURE
(Kumara Junction Hwy) At nightfall, bring a torch (or grope your way) into this grotto on the northern edge of town, signposted off SH6. The dell is an easy opportunity to glimpse legions of glowworms (aka fungus gnat larvae), which emit an other-worldly blue light. An information panel at the entrance will further illuminate your way.

Sunset Point　　　　　　　VIEWPOINT
(Gibson Quay) A visit to Sunset Point is a quintessential Hokitika experience: watch the day's light fade away, observe whitebaiters casting nets, munch fish and chips, or stroll around the quayside shipwreck memorial.

Hokitika Museum　　　　　　　MUSEUM
(☑ 03-755 6898; www.hokitikamuseum.co.nz; 17 Hamilton St; ☺ 10am-5pm Nov-Mar, to 2pm Apr-Oct) FREE Housed in the gorgeous, recently strengthened Carnegie Building (1908), this museum has displays on greenstone, gold mining, history and whitebait fishing.

National Kiwi Centre　　　NATURE CENTRE
(☑ 03-755 5251; www.thenationalkiwicentre.co.nz; 64 Tancred St; adult/child $26/15; ☺ 9am-5pm; ⊕) Tiptoe through the darkened kiwi house to watch the birds rummage for tasty insects, or stare a tuatara – a reptile unchanged for 150 million years – in its beady eyes. There's also a pond where you can catch-and-return crayfish and a large tank full of giant eels, the oldest of which is thought to be over 120 years old.

Time your visit for eel feeding time (10am, noon and 3pm) when you can hold out scraps of meat for these slithery critters to grab from a pair of tongs (or your bare hands, if you dare).

Hokitika

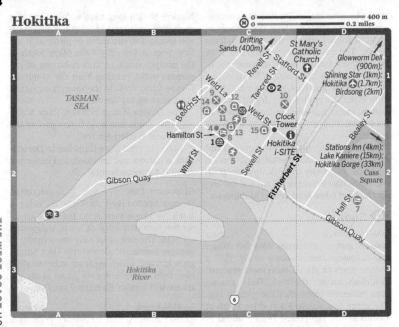

Hokitika

⊙ Sights

1 Hokitika Museum	C2
2 National Kiwi Centre	C1
3 Sunset Point	A2

⊙ Activities, Courses & Tours

4 Bonz 'N' Stonz	C2
5 Cycle Journeys	C2
6 Hokitika Cycles & Sports World	C1

⊜ Sleeping

| 7 Stopforths | D2 |
| 8 Teichelmann's B&B | C2 |

⊗ Eating

9 Hokitika Sandwich Company	C1
10 Ramble + Ritual	C1
11 Stella Cafe & Cheesery	C1

⊙ Shopping

12 Hokitika Glass Studio	C1
13 Sweet Alice's Fudge Kitchen	C2
14 Tectonic Jade	C1
15 Waewae Pounamu	C2
Wilderness Gallery	(see 13)

🏃 Activities

Hokitika is a great base for walking and cycling. Download DOC's *Walks in the Hokitika Area,* and visit **Hokitika Cycles & Sports World** (☑03-755 8662; www.hokitikasportsworld.co.nz; 33 Tancred St; bike rental per day $55; ⊙9am-5pm Mon-Sat Oct-Mar, 9am-5pm Mon-Fri, to 1pm Sat Apr-Sep) for bike rental, repairs and advice on tracks, including the West Coast Wilderness Trail (p612).

Bonz 'N' Stonz   ARTS & CRAFTS
(☑03-755 6504; www.bonz-n-stonz.co.nz; 16 Hamilton St; carving per hour $35) Design, carve and polish your own *pounamu* (green-

stone/jade, $190), bone ($100) or paua-shell ($100) masterpiece, with tutelage from Steve Gwaliasi. Bookings recommended, and 'laughter therapy' included in the price. There's also a good range of Steve's accomplished carvings to purchase.

West Coast Treetop Walk   OUTDOORS
(☑03-755 5052; www.treetopsnz.com; 1128 Woodstock-Rimu Rd, Ruatapu; adult/child $32/16; ⊙9am-3.15pm) Visitors strolling along this wobbly but wheelchair-friendly steel walkway, 450m long and 20m off the ground, can enjoy an unusual perspective on the canopy of native trees (allow 45 minutes).

The highlight is the 47m-high tower, from which views extend to the Southern Alps and the Tasman Sea. It's 17km south of Hokitika, near the southern shore of Lake Māhinapua.

⚘ Festivals & Events

Driftwood & Sand ART
(www.driftwoodandsand.co.nz; Hokitika Beach; ☻Jan) Free spirits and budding artists transform flotsam and jetsam into sculptures on Hokitika Beach during this five-day, volunteer-led festival. Participants range from beginners to pros, and accordingly their creations span the full spectrum from enigmatic to delightfully daft.

Wildfoods Festival FOOD & DRINK
(www.wildfoods.co.nz; Cass Sq; entry $35; ☻Mar) Give your taste buds the equivalent of a defibrillator shock at this one-day festival of daredevil eating in early March. Fish eyes, pigs' ears, lamb testicles and huhu grubs usually grace the menu. Don't worry, there are other food stands to expunge the lingering taste of blood casserole.

🛏 Sleeping

Shining Star HOLIDAY PARK $$
(☎03-755 8921; www.accommodationwestcoast.co.nz; 16 Richards Dr; sites/units from $30/140; ▣☎⊕) This attractive and versatile beachfront spot has everything from camping to log-lined cabins facing the sea. Kids will love the menagerie, including pigs and alpacas straight from Dr Doolittle's appointment book. Parents might prefer the spa or sauna.

Drifting Sands B&B $$
(☎021 0266 5154; www.driftingsands.nz; 197 Revell St; r from $133; ☎) Natural tones and textures, upcycled furniture and hip vibes make this boutique beachside guesthouse a winner on style and location. Heightening the feel-good factor, there's a lounge warmed by a log burner and fresh bread every morning, plus bikes to borrow. Bathrooms are shared.

Birdsong HOSTEL $$
(☎03-755 7179; www.birdsong.co.nz; 124 Kumara Junction Hwy, Seaview; dm $37, s/d without bathroom $83/98, r with bathroom $134; ▣☎) Sigh at sea views from the shared lounge

and kitchen of this adorable YHA-affiliated hostel, 2.5km northeast of the town centre. Rooms are themed around native bird life. Our only gripe is that bathrooms could be bigger (and with better privacy than saloon-style doors).

Teichelmann's B&B B&B $$$
(☎03-755 8232; www.teichelmanns.nz; 20 Hamilton St; s/d/cottages $200/280/300; ☎) Once home to surgeon, mountaineer and professional beard-cultivator Ebenezer Teichelmann, this B&B holds on to its venerable history but adds first-rate hospitality and complimentary port. Its six rooms each have an airy, restorative ambience, replete with great beds, quality cotton sheets and private bathrooms; the best enjoy fern-filled garden views. For added privacy, request self-contained Teichy's Garden Cottage.

Stopforths MOTEL $$$
(☎03-755 7625; www.stopforths.co.nz; 30 Hall St; units $180-340; ▣☎) Several steps up from your average motel, friendly well-run Stopforths offers spacious, modern units with kitchenettes and king-sized beds, ranging from studios to two-bedroom apartments. Some have spa baths and desks.

🍴 Eating

★**Hokitika**
Sandwich Company SANDWICHES $
(☎03-429 2019; www.facebook.com/TheHokitika SandwichCompany; 83a Revell St; half/full sandwiches $9/18; ☻10am-2pm Tue-Sat) To say this hip place is serious about sandwiches is an understatement. Everything's made to order and served on chunky slices of freshly baked bread, generously loaded with the best locally sourced goodies: free-range meat, organic vegetables, South Island cheeses and its own in-house condiments. Grab a seat on one of the communal tables and tuck in. Smoothies, too.

★**Stations Inn** BISTRO $$
(☎03-755 5499; www.stationsinnhokitika.co.nz; 11 Blue Spur Rd; mains $29-39; ☻6-10pm Tue-Sat) Attached to an out-of-the-way but upmarket motel-style complex 4km southeast of the town centre, this restaurant delivers the best bistro-style fare in Hokitika. Expect hearty serves of pork, lamb, salmon, vegetarian

pasta and a delicious Middle Eastern–style chicken on couscous.

Stella Cafe & Cheesery CAFE $$
(☑03-755 5432; www.facebook.com/StellaCafe Hokitika; 84 Revell St; mains $10-24; ☺8am-4pm; ☜) Kids will love peering through the glass at the beehive in this large deli-style cafe, while their parents occupy themselves in the separate cheese room. Breakfasts of tasty omelettes and strong coffee are followed with burgers and pasta at lunch, along with a good range of counter food.

🛍 Shopping

Hokitika has a buzzing arts and crafts scene centred on carving and polishing *pounamu* (greenstone/jade) into ornaments and jewellery. Be aware that some galleries sell jade imported from Europe and Asia, so ask before you buy. Along for the ride are woodworkers, textile weavers and glass-blowers, all represented at classy boutiques in the centre of town.

★**Waewae Pounamu** ARTS & CRAFTS
(☑03-755 8304; www.waewaepounamu.co.nz; 39 Weld St; ☺8.30am-6.30pm Nov-Mar, 8.30am-5pm Mon-Fri, 10am-4pm Sat & Sun Apr-Oct) Linked to Ngāti Waewae, a local *hapū* (subtribe) of the broader Ngāi Tahu tribe, this stronghold of *pounamu* carving displays traditional and contemporary designs in its main-road gallery-boutique. Watch the carvers at work before deciding on a piece to purchase.

Wilderness Gallery ARTS & CRAFTS
(☑03-755 7575; www.wildernessgallery.co.nz; 29 Tancred St; ☺10.30am-1.30pm Tue-Sun, extended summer) Juergen Schacke's large-scale nature photography takes centre stage at this gallery/gift shop, which also sells an excellent range of NZ-made craft: woodwork, pottery and carved *pounamu*, in particular.

Hokitika Glass Studio ARTS & CRAFTS
(☑03-755 7775; www.hokitikaglass.co.nz; 9 Weld St; ☺8.30am-4.30pm Mon-Fri, 10am-3pm Sat & Sun) Call in on weekdays to watch the blowers at work at the furnace producing glistening glass birds, multicoloured bowls and stemware. And yes, these fragile objects are secured in oodles of protective wrapping.

Tectonic Jade ARTS & CRAFTS
(☑03-755 6644; www.tectonicjade.com; 67 Revell St; ☺9am-5pm Oct-Apr) If you like your greenstone art and jewellery with a side-

order of spirituality, the lustrous *pounamu* carved by local artist Rex Scott will leave you entranced.

Sweet Alice's Fudge Kitchen FOOD
(☑027 858 0802; 27 Tancred St; ☺11.30am-4.30pm Wed-Mon) Treat yourself to a slice of Alice's handmade fudge, real fruit ice cream or a bag of boiled lollies – or maybe all three. A slice of fudge costs around $7.

ℹ Information

Hokitika i-SITE (☑03-755 6166; www.hokiti kainfo.co.nz; 36 Weld St; ☺9am-5pm) Information and bookings, including buses and DOC passes. It also rents locator beacons.
Westland Medical Centre (☑03-755 8180; www.westlandmedical.co.nz; 54a Sewell St; ☺8am-4.45pm Mon-Fri) Call ahead for appointments, or use the after-hours phone service (24 hours). For urgent cases on weekends, use the walk-in service at 10am and 5pm.

ℹ Getting There & Away

AIR
Hokitika Airport (HKK; ☑03-756 8050; www. hokitikaairport.co.nz; Airport Dr) is on the town's eastern fringe and has the usual collection of rental-car counters. **Air New Zealand** (www.airnewzealand.com) has two flights most days to/from Christchurch.

BUS
InterCity (p604) has a daily service between Greymouth ($28, 55 minutes) and Fox Glacier ($40, 3¼ hours) via Ross ($28, 25 minutes), Whataroa ($30, two hours) and Franz Josef ($38, 2½ hours). All buses stop outside both the National Kiwi Centre and the i-SITE.

ℹ Getting Around

Hokitika Taxis (☑03-755 5075; www.face book.com/hokitikataxis) Expect to pay $10 to $15 for a cab to/from the airport.

Kumara
POP 309

Once upon a time, folks piled into Kumara's two theatres, waltzing until dawn and roaring with delight at travelling circus acts that passed through this gold-rush town. But with the glittering 1880s long faded into memory, only a scattering of well-preserved historic buildings remains, spread along the road to Arthur's Pass. Thanks to local enthusiasm for Kumara's boom time, display pan-

THE POWER OF POUNAMU

Pounamu (greenstone, NZ jade) was the most treasured natural resource in traditional Māori society, valued for its strength, durability and beauty. With no metal tools or weapons it was one of the hardest materials available, and it could be honed to a fine edge. It is believed that the stone can absorb spiritual energy from the people handling it and can accumulate *mana* (prestige) over time. For this reason, always ask permission before touching anyone's personal *pounamu.*

Only found on the South Island (in Māori, Te Waipounamu, meaning Waters of Greenstone), the ownership of all naturally occurring *pounamu* resides with the Ngāi Tahu *iwi* (tribe). It is, however, legal to rummage around beaches and rivers for stones, limited to what an individual can carry on their person. The exception is Westland's Arahura River, which is owned in its entirety by Ngāi Tahu.

The West Coast has a thriving community of artists sourcing the stone and carving it into sculptures and jewellery, particularly in Hokitika and Greymouth. It's considered luckier to buy greenstone for others, rather than yourself, and a few recurring shapes carry distinctive meanings.

Koru Unfurling spiral reminiscent of a fern shoot, signifying creation and growth.

Toki A wedge shape harking to traditional Māori tools; a symbol of strength.

Pikorua Contemporary 'twist' design symbolising bonds between people.

Hei matau Stylised fish hook with various meanings: health, safe travel and prosperity.

For authentic products by Māori artisans, try Garth Wilson Jade (p620) or Waewae Pounamu (p616), a studio linked to the Ngāti Waewae subtribe of Poutini Ngāi Tahu.

Ngāi Tahu also own and operate Franz Josef Glacier Guides (p608) and Glacier Hot Pools (p607).

els around town tell stories of feisty figures from yesteryear.

In recent times Kumara's main claim to fame is as the starting point of the multisport **Coast to Coast race** (www.coasttocoast.co.nz). Held each February, the strong, the brave and the totally knackered run, cycle and kayak a total of 243km all the way from Kumara Beach across the mountains to Christchurch, with top competitors dusting it off in around 11 hours. Kumara's also a stop on the West Coast Wilderness Trail (p612) and a good base for day cycles.

Don't expect big-ticket attractions, but Kumara has a couple of ramble-worthy sights where you can stretch your legs. There's a **glowworm dell** in the bush behind the Theatre Royal's miners' cottages. Some 800m south of town, off the highway, you'll find a **historic swimming pool** from the 1930s; at 46m by 30m it was once New Zealand's largest, though little but overgrown walls remain today.

Keep an eye out for the **Kumara Chinese Miner Memorial Reserve**, an attractive new garden that was in the process of being laid out alongside the main road when we last visited.

★ **Theatre Royal Hotel** PUB $$
(☎03-736 9277; www.theatreroyalhotel.co.nz; 81 Seddon St; r/cottages from $144/200; P 📶) Themed around colourful figures from Kumara's past, rooms at this beautifully restored 1876 pub are reason enough to stay in town. We especially loved the feminine flourishes of Barbara Weldon's room, honouring a former lady of the night. Motel-style miners' cottages (sleeping up to four) are new but have vintage finishes such as clawfoot tubs.

The opulence continues with two suites in the picturesque Bank of New Zealand building across the road. The Theatre Royal's downstairs bar is a good spot for a hearty meal and a yarn with the locals; with a bit of encouragement, one of them might thump out a tune on the piano.

ℹ Getting There & Away

East West Coaches (p628) stop outside the Theatre Royal Hotel daily, en route between Westport ($40, 1¾ hours) and Christchurch ($55, 3¼ hours) via Punakaiki ($25, 1¼ hours), Greymouth ($20, 10 minutes) and Arthur's Pass ($50, 1¼ hours).

GREY DISTRICT

The smallest of the three districts that make up the West Coast, Grey struggles to shrug off the lacklustre promise of its name. Its largest town, Greymouth, is big on services but light on attractions, although it is the northern trailhead of the West Coast Wilderness Trail (p612). Inland, Lake Brunner is a soothing spot for fishing or bird-watching, and remote Blackball is firmly in hikers' and mountain bikers' sights as a gateway to new Great Walk, the Paparoa Track (p600).

Even by NZ's standards, the Grey District is a standout for friendliness; its down-to-earth folk might be reason enough to dawdle here before you travel on.

Greymouth

POP 9660

Greymouth (in Māori, Māwhera) is the largest town on the West Coast and what passes for the Big Smoke in these parts. For locals it's an administrative and shopping pit stop; for travellers it's a noteworthy portal to hiking and biking trails, and the somewhat anticlimactic terminus of one of the world's most scenic rail journeys.

Arriving on a dreary day, it's no mystery why Greymouth, crouched at the mouth of the Grey River, is sometimes the butt of jokes. But with gold-mining history, a scattering of *pounamu* (greenstone/jade) studios, and worthy walks in its surrounds, it pays to look beyond the grey.

Sights

Left Bank Art Gallery   GALLERY
(📌03-768 0038; www.bankarts.com; 1 Tainui St; ⊙10am-4pm Tue-Fri, 11am-2pm Sat) FREE A wide community of West Coast artists is represented in this former bank, which displays contemporary NZ prints, paintings, photographs, jewellery and ceramics; much of it is for sale.

Monteith's Brewing Co   BREWERY
(📌03-768 4149; www.thebrewery.co.nz; 60 Herbert St; tour $28; ⊙11am-9pm) The original Monteith's brewhouse is the HQ for this nationally famous beer brand: glossy and a wee bit corporate, but it delivers a high-quality experience. Book ahead for a guided tour (45 minutes, including generous samples) or DIY in the industrial-chic tasting room and bar, complete with a roaring fire, outdoor seating and a kitchen serving pizza, burgers and steaks.

Shantytown   MUSEUM
(📌03-762 6634; www.shantytown.co.nz; Rutherglen Rd, Paroa; adult/child $34/17; ⊙8.30am-5pm; 🚼) Good fun for kids and young-at-heart travellers, Shantytown is a recreated 1860s gold-mining town, 10km south of Greymouth. Peer inside a church, a tavern, a hospital and a Chinese encampment, all painstakingly crafted to evoke the spirit of the era. Take cheesy souvenir pics in period costume and try gold-panning ($7), but the highlight is a steam train ride into the bush (five to seven daily, last departure 4pm).

 Activities

TranzAlpine   RAIL
(📌04-4950775; www.greatjourneysofnz.co.nz; one-way adult/child from $119/83) The *TranzAlpine* is one of the world's great train journeys. It traverses the Southern Alps between Christchurch and Greymouth, through Arthur's Pass National Park, from the Pacific Ocean to the Tasman Sea. Dramatic landscapes span its 223km length, from the flat, alluvial Canterbury Plains, through alpine gorges, an 8.5km tunnel, beech-forested valleys and a lake fringed with cabbage trees.

Floodwall Walk   WALKING
(Mawhera Quay) Once subject to serious flooding, Greymouth hasn't experienced a deluge since the building of this floodwall, masterminded after a flood in 1988. Take a 10-minute riverside stroll along Mawhera Quay, the start of the West Coast Wilderness Trail (p612), or stretch your legs by pressing on for the full 50-minute route.

The walk takes in the fishing boat harbour, Blaketown Beach and the breakwater at the mouth of the Grey River – a great place to experience the power of the ocean and savour a West Coast sunset. On Mawhera Quay, look out for the memorial to those lost in coal-mining incidents, including the 29 men killed at Pike River Mine in 2010.

Sleeping

Global Village   HOSTEL $
(📌03-768 7272; www.globalvillagebackpackers.co.nz; 42 Cowper St; dm/r without bathroom from $32/78; P@🛜) This colourful hostel has African, Asian and Pacific art on its walls, and a passionate traveller vibe at its core. Borrow a kayak to explore the adjacent wetlands or a bike to pedal around town. Relaxation comes easily with a spa, a sauna, a barbecue and a firepit.

Greymouth

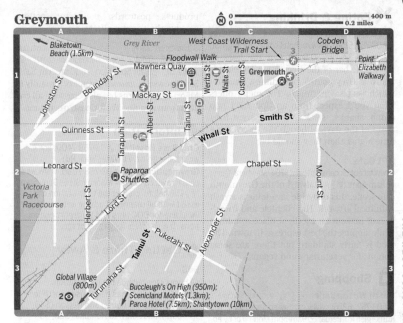

Greymouth

◎ Sights
1 Left Bank Art Gallery B1
2 Monteith's Brewing Co A3

✪ Activities, Courses & Tours
3 Floodwall Walk......................................C1
4 Trail Transport.......................................B1
5 TranzAlpine...C1

🛏 Sleeping
6 Duke..B2

🍷 Drinking & Nightlife
7 DP1 Cafe..C1

🛍 Shopping
8 Nimmo Gallery & Store B1
9 Shades of Jade......................................B1

ⓘ Information
Greymouth i-SITE...........................(see 5)

Duke   HOSTEL $
(☑ 03-768 9988; www.duke.co.nz; 27 Guinness St;
dm $26, s/d without bathroom from $50/61, r with
bathroom $85; 🛜) The former Duke of Ed-
inburgh Hotel dates to at least the 1870s,
although we strongly suspect it wasn't painted purple and green then. New owners have
been busily renovating the rooms, which
circle a central light well upstairs. The best
have sharp contemporary decor and en-suite
bathrooms. Downstairs there's a huge kitch-
en and a guest lounge with a roaring fire.

Scenicland Motels   MOTEL $$
(☑ 03-768 5100; www.sceniclandmotel.co.nz; 108-
110 High St; units from $125; P ❄ 🛜) The decor
is simple-bordering-on-spartan but the units
at this friendly motel are comfortable and

well-kept. Opt for a studio with a kitchen-
ette or a one- or two-bedroom unit with a
full kitchen. Town's only a 20-minute walk
away (or you can hire a bike if you'd prefer)
and there's a very convenient supermarket
next door.

Paroa Hotel   MOTEL $$
(☑ 03-762 6860; www.paroa.co.nz; 508 Main
South Rd, Paroa; units from $180; P 🛜) A family
affair since 1954, the venerable Paroa has
benefitted from a slick makeover. The sizeable motel-style units have kitchenettes and
great beds, and share a garden. The warm
service continues inside the noteworthy
bar and restaurant. It's opposite the Shantytown turn-off, 8km south of Greymouth
town centre.

Eating & Drinking

Buccleugh's On High   BISTRO $$
(☎03-768 5154; www.rechotel.co.nz; 68 High St; mains $25-37; ⏱5.30-9pm) Out the back of the public bar of the Recreation Hotel, this bistro is Greymouth's best dining option – which isn't saying much. The menu offers what you'd expect from an upmarket pub (lamb shanks, steak, venison, roast/fish/pasta of the day), although the prices are a little higher than they should be.

DP1 Cafe   CAFE
(www.facebook.com/dp1cafe; 104 Mawhera Quay; ⏱8am-5pm; 🛜) A stalwart of the Greymouth cafe scene, this quayside java joint is awash with local artwork. Hip clientele and friendly staff make it an excellent place to mingle while sipping the best espresso in town. The food is fairly standard but there are some options for vegetarians and vegans.

Shopping

Garth Wilson Jade   ARTS & CRAFTS
(☎03-762 6226; www.garthwilsonjade.co.nz; 63 Rutherglen Rd, Paroa; ⏱9am-5pm Mon-Fri or by appointment) *Whakapapa* (genealogy) links to two West Coast *hapū* (subtribes) give Garth the right to collect *pounamu* all along the coast, which he then carves in his home studio near Shantytown. Call in to watch him at work and to buy a truly authentic piece; he also takes commissions. Garth's an avid mountain biker,too; ask about local tracks.

Nimmo Gallery & Store   ARTS & CRAFTS
(☎03-768 6499; www.nimmophoto.co.nz; 102 Mackay St; ⏱9am-5pm Mon-Fri, 10am-2pm Sat & Sun) Ostensibly the gallery of local landscape photographer Stewart Nimmo, this stylish space overflows with cracking souvenirs (with more handicrafts and clothing sold in the courtyard out back). Honeyed beauty products, postcards, *pounamu*, pottery, woodwork: it's got it all.

Shades of Jade   JEWELLERY
(☎03-768 0794; www.shadesofjade.co.nz; 22 Tainui St; ⏱9am-5pm Mon-Fri, 10am-2pm Sat & Sun) Browse *pounamu* jewellery – mainly in Māori-style designs but also crosses – all created from genuine West Coast greenstone.

ⓘ Information

Grey Base Hospital (☎03-769 7400; www.wcdhb.health.nz; 71 Water Walk Rd)

Greymouth i-SITE (☎03-768 7080; www.westcoasttravel.co.nz; 164 Mackay St; ⏱9am-5pm; 🛜) The helpful crew at the train station can assist with all manner of advice and bookings, including for DOC huts and transport connections. It also offers luggage storage.

ⓘ Getting There & Away

BUS
All buses stop outside the train station.

➡ InterCity (p604) has daily buses north to Westport ($21, 2¼ hours) and Nelson ($48, six hours), and south to Hokitika ($28, 55 minutes), Franz Josef ($44, four hours) and Fox Glacier ($47, 4¾ hours).

➡ East West Coaches (p628) stop daily en route between Westport ($25, 1¼ hours) and Christchurch ($60, 3½ hours) via Punakaiki ($20, 45 minutes), Kumara ($20, 10 minutes) and Arthur's Pass ($40, 1½ hours).

➡ **Atomic Travel** (☎021 0867 6001; www.atomictravel.co.nz) runs daily shuttle buses to/from Christchurch ($55, 3¾ hours) via Moana ($40, 25 minutes), Arthur's Pass ($40, 1½ hours) and Springfield ($50, 2½ hours).

➡ **Paparoa Shuttles** (☎021 286 2233; www.paparoashuttles.co.nz; cnr Tarapuhi St & Sheilds Ln) offers timetabled transfers to Blackball ($20, 30 minutes, three daily), Paparoa Track's Smoke-ho trailhead ($30, 1½ hours, daily), Barrytown ($40, 40 minutes,

---

WHITEBAIT FEVER
....

If you visit the West Coast between September and mid-November, you're sure to catch a whiff of whitebait fever. The West Coast is gripped by an annual craze for tiny, transparent fish, and netting buckets of whitebait is an all-consuming, highly competitive passion.

In season you'll see whitebait sold from back doors and served in cafes and restaurants. They mostly surface in a pattie, made best with just an egg, and accompanied by a wedge of lemon or perhaps mint sauce. We've seen them topping pizzas and salads, too.

Whitebait are the young of native fish, including inanga, kokopu, smelt and eels. Conservationists say they shouldn't be eaten at all, with some species threatened or in decline. DOC applies stiff penalties for anyone breaching their rules on whitebaiting season and the size of nets, and they urge locals to keep their catch small.

two daily) and Punakaiki ($50, one hour, two daily); bikes cost $10 extra. **Trail Transport** (☑03-768 4060; www.trailtransport.co.nz; 53 Mackay St; bike hire per day from $50, shuttle transport $28-65) covers the same route, but on demand.

TRAIN

The TranzAlpine (p618) train takes a highly scenic route to/from Christchurch (from $119, 4½ hours) daily, via Moana (from $79, one hour), Arthur's Pass (from $139, 2¼ hours) and Springfield (from $119, 3½ hours).

ⓘ Getting Around

Greymouth Taxis (☑03-768 7078) A taxi to Shantytown will cost you around $35 (one-way).

Lake Brunner

Expect your pulse to slow almost as soon as you arrive at Lake Brunner. Named for England-born explorer Thomas Brunner (not the German footballer), this 40 sq km expanse of sapphire water lies 35km southeast of Greymouth. The lake is large but its main settlement Moana (population 270), on the northern shore, is minuscule. Nonetheless it brims with accommodation options to suit the families and trout-fishing enthusiasts drawn to this sedate spot.

Brunner is a scenic place to idle away a day or two strolling lakeside tracks, fishing or bird-watching. Book ahead in summer (and note that it's whisper-quiet in winter).

Brunner is a tranquil spot for bush walks, bird-spotting and water sports, including boating and fishing. Indeed, the local boast is that the lake and Arnold River are 'where the trout die of old age', which suggests that this is a good spot to dangle a line. Greymouth i-SITE can hook you up with a guide.

Lake Brunner
Country Motel   HOLIDAY PARK $$
(☑03-738 0144; www.lakebrunnermotel.co.nz; 2014 Arnold Valley Rd; sites $20-45, units with/without bathroom from $148/77; ⓟ@⬚) Birdsong, flower beds and 2.4 hectares of greenery... feeling relaxed yet? At this motel and campground, 2km from Lake Brunner, choose from powered and unpowered tent sites, and simple cabins, all of which share bathrooms and kitchen facilities. More plush are the self-contained cottages, complete with floral trimmings and nice bathrooms.

Stationhouse Cafe   CAFE $$
(☑03-738 0158; www.lakebrunner.net; 40 Koe St, Moana; mains $17-23; ⊙10.30am-8.30pm Mon-Sat, 9am-10pm Sun) It's one of the only shows in town, but luckily the Stationhouse (built 1901) is a winner. The cafe serves fruit smoothies, good coffee, excellent eggs Benedict, savoury muffins and indulgent baked goods, along with a sizeable menu of main courses. In good weather, grab a spot on the deck for views of the water and Mt Alexander.

ⓘ Getting There & Away

Atomic Travel shuttle buses stop in Moana daily, en route between Greymouth ($40, 25 minutes) and Christchurch ($55, 3¼ hours) via Arthur's Pass ($40, one hour) and Springfield ($50, 2¼ hours).

The TranzAlpine (p618) train pulls into Moana train station daily on its journey from Christchurch (from $119, 3½ hours) to Greymouth (from $79, one hour) and back, via Arthur's Pass (from $139, 1½ hours) and Springfield (from $119, 2½ hours).

Blackball

POP 291

Ramshackle Blackball is a shadow of its mining glory days, but this spirited town offers more than meets the eye. Around 23km upriver of Greymouth, Blackball was established in 1866 to service gold diggers, before coal mining kicked off in 1890. The town is often trumpeted as the birthplace of the NZ Labour movement, after a successful miners' strike in 1908 led to the formation of a national Federation of Labour. It's been something of a low-key pilgrimage site for Labour supporters and politicians ever since.

When its coal mine closed in 1964, Blackball had a population of 1580 people. With most mining families forced out, the town was kept alive by the arrival of a small community of hippies, attracted by the cheap housing and lush natural setting.

The Paparoa Track (p600) – newly inscribed as a Great Walk – is a 55km hiking and mountain-biking trail through Paparoa National Park that starts at the Smoke-ho car park, 6km north of town.

At the time of research Blackball was gearing up for the opening of the Paparoa Track and the influx of hikers and mountain bikers expected to follow, but accommodation remained limited. Blackball Salami Co (p622) was in the process of installing modern shipping-container sized en-suite units in a field out the back. Formerly the Blackball Hilton offers simple, shared-bathroom pub rooms.

Formerly the Blackball Hilton
HISTORIC BUILDING

(✐03-732 4705; www.blackballhilton.co.nz; 26 Hart St; ⊙midday-late, from 2.30pm Mon & Tue outside summer) Blackball's major talking point is this century-old pub, once known as the Dominion. When it was renamed in the 1990s, a certain global hotel chain got antsy – hence the addition of 'formerly' to its name. These days it's something of a shrine to the Labour movement, proudly bedecked in old trade-union banners, posters and portraits of significant politicians. Call in for a beer or pub meal and take some time to peruse the walls.

Blackball Museum of Working Class History (Mahi Tūpuna)
MUSEUM

(✐03-732 4010; www.blackballmuseum.org.nz; 26 Hart St; ⊙24hr) FREE Consisting of outdoor displays and a couple of shipping containers, this appropriately humble 'museum' tells the fascinating story of how Blackball came to be so important to the story of workers' rights in NZ. Look out for the Workers' Memorial Wheel dedicated to people killed in their workplaces since 1990, with a special focus on the 29 men who died at nearby Pike River Mine in 2010.

Blackball Salami Company Ltd
FOOD

(✐03-732 4111; www.blackballsalami.co.nz; 11 Hilton St; ⊙8am-4pm Mon-Fri, 9am-2pm Sat) Take time to sample Blackball's namesake salami, beloved up and down the West Coast. The garlic and peppercorn varieties have a kick, the venison version is rich and distinctive, but we like the fattier 'Italian-style' cut. Also available from this humble shop are bacon, black pudding, cheeses and sausages.

❶ Getting There & Away

There's no bus service, but Paparoa Shuttles (p620) runs two or three timetabled transfers per day to Blackball from Greymouth ($20, 30 minutes), Barrytown ($50, 1¼ hours) and Punakaiki ($60, 1½ hours), which continue on to the Paparoa Track trailhead (add $10); bikes cost $10 extra.

Trail Transport (p621) offers on-demand shuttles to the trailhead from Greymouth (per person $60, minimum $140) and Punakaiki (per person $70, minimum $200); prices include bikes.

Runanga, Rapahoe & Barrytown
POP 1480

The southernmost stretch of the Great Coast Road, between Greymouth and Punakaiki, carves a path between rocky bays and the steep, bushy Paparoa Ranges. First you'll pass through tiny Runanga before hitting the coast at blink-and-you'll-miss-it Rapahoe, with its friendly local pub. Aside from some excellent walks, there's not much to do except to pull up along the coast and take in the expansive views.

Craggy islets strike dramatic poses off each headland as you head towards sleepy, sparsely populated Barrytown, where the mountains take a half step back from the sea allowing for a thin stretch of farmland. Barrytown is the western trailhead of the Croesus Track, an old mining trail that connects to the Paparoa Track (p600).

🏃 Activities

Coal Creek Track
WALKING

(www.doc.govt.nz; Ballance St, Runanga) This 30-minute (each way) walk through mixed beech-podocarp forest leads to a broad waterfall tumbling into a swimmable basin.

Point Elizabeth Walkway
WALKING

(www.doc.govt.nz; North Beach Rd, Cobden) Starting in Cobden, 6km north of Greymouth, this enjoyable coastal track (three hours return) skirts around a richly forested headland in the shadow of the Rapahoe Range to an impressive ocean lookout, before continuing on to the northern trailhead at Rapahoe. If you want a shorter walk, it's 45 minutes to the ocean lookout (one-way).

Barrytown Knifemaking
ARTS & CRAFTS

(✐03-731 1053; www.barrytownknifemaking.com; 2662 Coast Rd, Barrytown; classes $170) Fashion your own knife on a day-long course under the expert tutelage of Steve and Robyn. You'll hand-forge the steel blade and craft its handle from native rimu timber. Bonuses include axe-throwing, a big swing, and a stream of entertainingly bad jokes from Steve. Courses begin with an enthusiastic greeting from the dog and include a sandwich lunch. Bookings essential.

🛏 Sleeping

Breakers   B&B $$$
(📞 03-762 7743; www.breakers.co.nz; 1367 Coast Rd, Nine Mile Creek; r $285-405; 🅿️ 📶) 🏄 Crafted to tug at the heart strings of surfers, every room at Breakers has a view and easy access to the shore. Tucked into a hillside nook 3km north of Rapahoe, all four units are tasteful and modern, with decks for sighing over the sunset. Knowledgeable hosts are on hand for surf tips.

ℹ️ Getting There & Away

➡ InterCity (p604) services ply this leg of the Great Coast Road once a day on their way between Greymouth ($10, 30 minutes) and Nelson ($45, 5¼ hours), via Punakaiki ($10, 20 minutes), Westport ($17, two hours) and Murchison ($29, 3½ hours).

➡ East West Coaches (p628) stop daily en route between Westport ($20, 40 minutes) and Christchurch ($70, 4¼ hours), via Greymouth ($20, 20 minutes).

➡ Paparoa Shuttles (p620) offers two daily time-tabled transfers to Barrytown from Punakaiki ($30, 20 minutes), Greymouth ($40, 40 minutes), Blackball ($50, 1½ hours) and the Paparoa Track's Smoke-ho trailhead ($70, two hours).

BULLER REGION

Forest and coast unite in dramatic form in the Buller Region. This northwesterly expanse of the South Island is a promised land for hikers. Riverside trails wend their way through primeval forest, accessing geological marvels like the Ōpārara Arch and Punakaiki's Pancake Rocks.

Gold was found in the Buller River in the mid-19th century, and coal mining scorched the landscape soon after. Mining history is carefully conserved in main towns Westport and Reefton, though agriculture and tourism are the Buller Region's prime moneymakers today. Mining history makes a pleasant diversion if you need a breather from muddy trails, white-water rafting and kayaking tannin-stained waterways.

Punakaiki & Paparoa National Park

Located midway between Westport and Greymouth is Punakaiki, a small settlement on the edge of rugged 430-sq-km Paparoa National Park. Most visitors come for a quick squiz at the Pancake Rocks, layers of limestone that resemble stacked crepes. But these are just one feature of the impressive, boulder-sprinkled shoreline. Pebble beaches (keep an eye out for greenstone/jade) are kissed by spectacular sunsets, and there are some riveting walking and mountain-biking trails into the national park, most notably the Paparoa Track, which became an official Great Walk in December 2019.

Paparoa National Park is blessed with high cliffs and empty beaches, a dramatic mountain range, crazy limestone river valleys, diverse flora and a profusion of bird life, including weka (native woodhens) and the Westland petrel, a rare sea bird that nests only here.

◎ Sights & Activities

The Paparoa National Park Visitor Centre (p624) has free maps detailing hikes in the area, including the Paparoa Track (p600). Note that many of Paparoa's inland walks are susceptible to river flooding, so it is vital that you obtain updates from the centre before you depart, and always heed warning signs and roped-off trails.

Shorter walks include the wonderful **Truman Track** (1.4km, 30 minutes return), which leads through native bush to an isolated beach. It's well signposted from the highway, 1.5km north of the township.

For a taste of the Great Walk, take the **Punakaiki–Pororari Loop** (11km, three hours), which follows the **Pororari River Track** (a section of the Paparoa Track) along a spectacular Jurassic-looking limestone gorge lined with nikau palms. It then joins the **Inland Pack Track**, pops over a hill and heads back down the bouldery Punakaiki River; the last section is along the highway.

★ **Pancake Rocks**   NATURAL FEATURE
(www.doc.govt.nz; SH6) Punakaiki's claim to fame is Dolomite Point, where a layering-weathering process called stylobedding has carved the limestone into what looks like piles of thick pancakes. Aim for high tide (tide timetables are posted at the visitor centre) when, if the swell and wind are cooperating, the sea surges into caverns and booms menacingly through blowholes. See it on a wild day and be reminded that nature really is the boss.

Allow 20 minutes for the straightforward walk, which loops from the highway out to the rocks and blowholes (or 40 minutes if

THE WEST COAST PUNAKAIKI & PAPAROA NATIONAL PARK

DON'T MISS

THE GREAT COAST ROAD

One hundred kilometres of salty vistas line the road between Westport and Greymouth. One of New Zealand's most beautiful drives, the Great Coast Road meanders past foaming surf and shingle beaches on one side, and forbidding, overhanging cliffs on the other. The best-known stop along this inspiring stretch of SH6 is Punakaiki's geologically fascinating Pancake Rocks (p623). But there are numerous wind-whipped lookouts where you can pull over to gaze at waves smashing against haggard turrets of stone. Fill up in Westport or Greymouth if you're low on petrol or cash.

you want to take photos). Parts of the trail are suitable for wheelchairs.

Punakaiki Horse Treks HORSE RIDING
(📋 03-731 1839; www.pancake-rocks.co.nz; 4224 SH6; 2½hr ride $200; ⊘mid-Oct–early May) Trek through the beautiful Punakaiki Valley right onto the beach on these guided tours, suitable for all experience levels. Private rides start at $250 (minimum two people).

🛌 Sleeping

Te Nikau Retreat HOSTEL $
(📋 03-731 1111; www.tenikauretreat.co.nz; 19 Hartmount Pl; dm $32, s/d without bathroom from $50/85, r with bathroom $110, cottages $65-220; P🐾🛜) 🍃 Checking in to Te Nikau feels instantly restorative. Kindly staff establish a relaxing tone, and there are charming wooden cottages tucked into the rainforest, a short walk from the beach. Our favourite is tiny Stargazer: it's little more than a double bed in a low hut, but glass roof panels allow you to count constellations on clear nights.

Punakaiki Beach Hostel HOSTEL $
(📋 03-731 1852; www.punakaikibeachhostel.co.nz; 4 Webb St; sites/dm/d without bathroom $22/34/89; 🛜) The ambience is laid-back but Punakaiki Beach is efficiently run. This spick-and-span hostel has all the amenities a traveller could need, from laundry and a shared kitchen to staff who smile because they mean it. Comfy dorm rooms aside, the en-suite house truck is the most novel stay, but cutesy Sunset Cottage is also worth a splurge (both $150).

Punakaiki Beachfront Motels MOTEL $$
(📋 03-731 1008; www.punakaikibeachfrontmotels.co.nz; Mabel St; units from $180; 🛜) Six basic motel units are sandwiched between cliff and sea, with private access to a wind-blown pebble beach. Larger groups (up to nine) can rent a two-storey, four-bedroom house, or a two-bedroom 'kiwi bach' (old-fashioned holiday home). The setting feels pleasingly remote, but it's only 900m north of the visitor centre.

Hydrangea Cottages COTTAGE $$$
(📋 03-731 1839; www.pancake-rocks.co.nz; 4224 SH6; cottages $145-485; P🛜) On a hillside overlooking the Tasman Sea, this set of stand-alone and mostly self-contained cottages is built from salvaged timber and stone. At the top of the price range is a chic self-contained cottage that sleeps up to 12 people; at the other end, the rustic Stables Hut is aimed at budget travellers. Occasional quirks like outdoor bathtubs add to the charm.

ℹ Information

Paparoa National Park Visitor Centre (📋 03-731 1895; www.doc.govt.nz; 4294 SH6; ⊘9am-5pm) Across the road from the Pancake Rocks walkway, the visitor centre has information on the national park – including track conditions and tide times – and sells hut tickets.

Punakaiki Promotions (www.punakaiki.co.nz) Online directory of accommodation, activities and tide times.

ℹ Getting There & Away

→ InterCity (p604) services stop here for 45 minutes (long enough to admire the Pancake Rocks) en route between Greymouth ($11, 40 minutes) and Nelson ($44, 4¼ hours), via Barrytown ($10, 20 minutes), Westport ($16, 49 minutes) and Murchison ($28, 2¼ hours).

→ East West Coaches (p628) stop daily en route between Westport ($20, 30 minutes) and Christchurch ($70, 4½ hours), via Greymouth ($20, 45 minutes) and Arthur's Pass ($40, 2½ hours).

→ Paparoa Shuttles (p620) offers two daily timetabled transfers to Punakaiki from Barrytown ($30, 20 minutes), Greymouth ($50, one hour), Blackball ($60, 1½ hours) and the Paparoa Track's Smoke-ho trailhead ($80, 2¼ hours); bikes cost $10 extra.

→ Trail Transport (p621) offers on-demand shuttles from Greymouth (per person $70, minimum $180) and the Smoke-ho trailhead (per person $70, minimum $200); prices include bikes.

Charleston & Around

POP 342

Heading north from Punakaiki the Great Coast Road continues to enthral, passing a series of dramatic bays and headlands; stop at one of the designated viewpoints to admire them safely. Just before it leaves the coast to cut across country to Westport, the highway passes through Charleston, an 1860s gold-rush boom town that once boasted 80 hotels, three breweries and thousands of thirsty gold-diggers staking claims along the Nile River. There's not much left now except a motel, a camping ground, a clutch of local houses, and a whole lot of tall tales.

Mitchells Gully Goldmine   MINE

(☑03-789 6257; www.mitchellsgullygoldmine.co.nz; SH6; adult/child $10/free; ⊙9am-4pm) For a true taste of the region's gold-mining past, swing into this former mine, 3km north of Charleston. You'll get a friendly primer on the 1860s mining days and then be left to explore mining tunnels and railway tracks on a short bush walk, goggling at Charleston's last remaining waterwheel and stamping battery along the way. If you're staying in the area, reserve a spot on a night-time glowworm tour (adult/child $25/5).

Underworld Adventures   CAVING

(☑03-788 8168; www.caverafting.com; SH6) Glow with the flow on black-water rafting trips deep into the glowworm-filled Nile River Caves (adult/child $190/150, four hours). This friendly operator also runs cave excursions without rafting (adult/child $125/90). Short on time? Take the rainforest train ride (adult/child $25/20), a 1½-hour return journey departing two or three times daily. The Adventure Caving trip ($375, five hours) includes a 40m abseil into Te Tahi cave system, with rock squeezes, waterfalls, fossils and trippy cave formations.

Kids aged 10 and over can raft, while the cave tours suit anyone who can walk on slippery surfaces for a couple of hours.

Beaconstone Eco Lodge   LODGE $

(☑027 448 9007; www.beaconstoneecolodge.com; 115 Birds Ferry Rd; s/d without bathroom from $70/100; 🛜) 🍃 Set in 42 serene hectares, 10km north of Charleston, this solar-powered, energy-efficient lodge is both eco- and guest-friendly. Fashioned from sustainably sourced native timber and featuring comfy beds and a laid-back communal area, the lodge's style is Americana cool meets West Coast charm. Bush walks start at the doorstep.

ℹ Getting There & Away

➤ InterCity (p604) buses stop here en route between Greymouth ($19, two hours) and Nelson ($35, 3½ hours), via Punakaiki ($16, 30 minutes), Westport ($12, nine minutes) and Murchison ($19, two hours).

➤ East West Coaches (p628) stop daily en route between Westport ($10, 10 minutes) and Christchurch ($70, 4¾ hours), via Punakaiki ($20, 20 minutes), Greymouth ($25, 50 minutes) and Arthur's Pass ($50, 2¾ hours).

Westport & Around

POP 4040

The 'capital' of Buller District, Westport's fortunes have historically waxed and waned with the coal mining industry, but fishing, dairy farming and, increasingly, tourism are rapidly taking its place. Chief among the town's natural attractions are the long, sandy beaches on either side of the Buller River – Carters Beach and North Beach – and the craggy, seal- and seabird-populated headland of Cape Foulwind.

It would be a stretch to accuse Westport of being exciting, but it does have respectable visitor services and makes a good base for exploring the fascinating coast north to Denniston, Charming Creek, Karamea and Kahurangi National Park. It's also an increasingly popular surfing destination, with good breaks south of Cape Foulwind at Tauranga Bay and Nine Mile Beach.

◉ Sights

The most interesting sights are beyond Westport's urban limits, particularly heading north on SH67, which passes Granity, Ngakawau (home to the well-named Charming Creek) and Hector, where there's a monument to Hector's dolphins, NZ's smallest, although you'll be lucky to see them unless your timing is impeccable. It's also worth taking a look at Seddonville, a small bush town on the Mokihinui River that's the northern trailhead for the thrilling Old Ghost Road (p601).

Coaltown Museum   MUSEUM

(☑03-789 6658; www.coaltown.co.nz; 123 Palmerston St; adult/child $10/2; ⊙9am-4.30pm) Westport's 'black gold' is paid homage at this remarkably interesting museum, adjoining the i-SITE. A replica mine, well-scripted

Westport

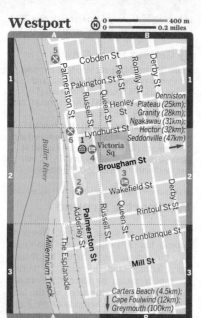

Westport

◉ Sights
1 Coaltown Museum................................A2

✪ Activities, Courses & Tours
2 Habitat Sports.....................................A2

🛏 Sleeping
3 Archer House..B2
4 Bazil's Hostel & Surf School.............A2

🍴 Eating
5 PortSide Bistro & Bar.........................A1
6 PR's Cafe..A2

ℹ Information
Westport i-SITE..............................(see 1)

display panels and an excellent selection of photographs and pioneer ephemera allow for an informative trip into the coal-blackened past. Best of all are the Denniston displays, including a whopping brake drum and panels explaining the daily tribulations of miners.

Denniston Plateau   HISTORIC SITE
(www.doc.govt.nz; Denniston Rd) FREE Six hundred metres above sea level, Denniston was once NZ's largest coal town, with 1500 residents in 1911. By 1981 there were eight. Its claim to fame was the fantastically steep Denniston Incline, which hurtled laden wagons down a 45-degree hillside. Display panels bring the plateau's history to life and trails provide sweeping views and a direct route into the past. The turn-off to Denniston is 16km east of Westport at Waimangaroa; Denniston is a further eight winding kilometres inland.

🏃 Activities

There are some good walking and cycling trails in and around town. The **Millennium Track** (1km, 15 minutes) starts near the Buller Bridge and heads through bush alongside the river to the town centre. This is the first part of the **Kawatiri River Trail**, which continues, partly on road and then via boardwalks, up to North Beach and the mountain-biking trails through **Kawatiri Beach Reserve**.

Cape Foulwind Walkway   WALKING
(www.doc.govt.nz; Lighthouse Rd, Omau) Screaming gulls and crashing waves are the soundtrack to hikes around Cape Foulwind (one hour each way), as wind-battered a walk as its name promises. The trail traverses the coastal cliffs between Omau and Tauranga Bay, passing a **lighthouse**, mounted **astrolabe** (navigational instrument) and, near the southern end, a **seal colony**.

The seal colony is only a 15-minute walk along the cliffs from the southern trailhead at **Tauranga Bay**, a popular surfing beach. Depending on the season, up to 200 fur seals loll on the rocks below the track; binoculars are set up at the designated viewpoint to help you spot them. Nearby, another set of binoculars is trained on craggy **Wall Island**, an important nesting site for sea birds.

Abel Tasman was the first European to sight the Cape, in 1642, naming it Clyppygen Hoeck (Rocky Point). However, his name was supplanted by James Cook in 1770, who clearly found the Cape less than pleasing. From Westport, it's 12km to the parking area for the northern trailhead or 16km for the southern trailhead; both are well signposted.

Charming Creek Walkway   WALKING
(www.doc.govt.nz; Tyler Rd, Ngakawau) Starting from either Ngakawau (30km north of Westport), or near Seddonville, a few kilometres further on, this is one of the best day walks on the coast, taking around three hours each way (9.5km). It's also open to bikes.

Following an old coal line through the Ngakawau Gorge, the walkway passes tunnels, a suspension bridge, a waterfall, rusty relics galore, and lots of interesting plants and geological formations.

Habitat Sports   CYCLING
(📞03-788 8002; www.habitatsports.co.nz; 234 Palmerston St; bike rental from $35; ⊙9am-5pm Mon-Fri, 9am-1pm Sat) As well as bike rental, repairs, maps and plentiful advice, this Westport sports shop offers transport to various track trailheads including Denniston ($35), Ngakawau ($40), Seddonville ($45), Lyell ($50) and Kōhaihai ($90); prices include bikes and are per person, with a minimum of two. It also offers a car relocation service ($200).

🛏 Sleeping

🛏 Westport

★Bazil's Hostel & Surf School   HOSTEL $
(📞03-789 6410; www.bazils.com; 54 Russell St; dm $32, r with/without bathroom $110/78; ℗🛜) Mural-painted Bazil's has well-maintained dorm and private rooms (some with kitchenettes, en-suite bathrooms and mezzanine bedrooms) in a sociable setting. It's managed by worldly types who offer surfing lessons (free if you stay for five nights), stand-up paddleboarding (SUP) trips, and social activities aplenty.

Archer House   B&B $$$
(📞03-789 8778; www.archerhouse.co.nz; 75 Queen St; r $245; 🛜) This beautiful house, built in 1890 and formerly the home of a goldfields trader, has original features galore. There are three individually decorated rooms with private bathrooms, and three tastefully attired lounges in which to swirl a glass of complimentary wine while admiring the stained glass, tiled fireplaces and flourishing garden. A generous continental breakfast rounds out the experience.

🛏 Surrounds

Old Slaughterhouse   HOSTEL $
(📞027 529 7640; www.oldslaughterhouse.co.nz; SH67, Hector; sites/dm/r without bathroom $22/40/95; ⊙Oct-Jun; ℗🛜) ⌀ Perched on a hillside 32km northeast of Westport, this lodge offers epic views over the Tasman Sea. Powered largely by a waterwheel, the central lodge has a roomy lounge, shared kitchen,

reading nooks and a deck; wi fi is limited. A steep, 10-minute walk from the car park bolsters its off-the-grid charm.

Carters Beach Top 10   HOLIDAY PARK $
(📞03-789 8002; www.top10westport.co.nz; 57 Marine Pde, Carters Beach; sites from $40, units with/without bathroom from $119/71; ℗🛜🛁) Right on Carters Beach, 5km from Westport, this tidy complex has pleasant sites as well as comfortable cabins and motel units. It's a good option for tourers seeking a peaceful stop-off with a swim (or on foul-weather days, a games room and playground to distract the kids).

★Omau Settlers Lodge   MOTEL $$
(📞03-789 5200; www.omausettlerslodge.co.nz; 2 Omau Rd, Cape Foulwind; units $175-195; ℗🛜) Relaxation is the mantra at this faultless motel near Cape Foulwind. Beds are plump, bathrooms are glossy and fragrant, plus there's a hot tub surrounded by bush. Chatty hosts Karen and Lee offer superb service, and lay out a satisfying free continental breakfast. Ask nicely and you might get a lift to the end of Cape Foulwind Walkway.

Rough & Tumble Lodge   LODGE $$$
(📞03-782 1337; www.roughandtumble.co.nz; Mokihinui Rd, Seddonville; r $240; 🛜) ⌀ With invigorating views of river and bush, this luxe lodge sits in splendid isolation at the northern end of the Old Ghost Road. Its five split-level quad rooms have silver-birch banisters, posh bathrooms and verdant views. An onsite cafe provides meals and brews in the warmer months. Bonus: profits are poured back into the maintenance of the walking track.

🍴 Eating

PortSide Bistro & Bar   BISTRO $$
(📞03-789 7133; www.portsidebistro.co.nz; 13 Cobden St; brunch $17-28, dinner $25-37; ⊙11am-late Tue-Fri, 9am-late Sat, 9am-3pm Sun; 🛜) Way up at the northern end of the main Palmerston St strip, this smart bistro serves cooked breakfasts on the weekends, along with the usual pubby bistro classics at lunch and dinner (burgers, steaks, market fish, pasta etc). Otherwise, just drop in for a beer on the deck.

PR's Cafe   CAFE $$
(📞03-789 7779; www.facebook.com/PrsCafe; 124 Palmerston St; mains $7-23; ⊙7am-4.30pm Mon-Fri, to 3pm Sat & Sun, closed Mon winter; 🛜) Westport's most popular cafe has a cabinet full

of sandwiches and pastries, and a counter groaning under the weight of cakes and cookies. An all-day menu delivers the likes of salmon omelettes, fish and chips, pies, quiches and burgers.

Star Tavern PUB FOOD $$
(☑ 03-789 6923; www.facebook.com/TheStarTaven; 6 Lighthouse Rd, Cape Foulwind; meals $8-33; ⊙4-8.30pm Mon-Fri, noon-8.30pm Sat & Sun) Refuel after tackling the Cape Foulwind Walkway at this convivial rural pub. Options include lamb shanks, fish and chips, sizeable steaks doused with garlic butter, burgers and, that West Coast speciality, whitebait fritters.

ⓘ Information

Buller Hospital (☑ 03-788 9030; www.wcdhb.health.nz; Cobden St; ⊙24hr)

Westport i-SITE (☑ 03-789 6658; www.coaltown.co.nz; 123 Palmerston St; ⊙9am-4.30pm; ⊛) Information on local tracks, tours, accommodation and transport. Self-help terminal for DOC information, hut and track bookings, and fishing licences.

ⓘ Getting There & Away

AIR

Westport Airport is near the mouth of the Buller River, on the opposite side from town; a **taxi** (☑ 03-789 6900; www.facebook.com/westportshuttles) costs around $25. **Sounds Air** (☑ 03-520 3080; www.soundsair.com; adult/child from $199/179) has one to six flights daily to/from Wellington (50 minutes).

BUS

➡ InterCity (p604) buses stop outside the i-SITE daily en route between Nelson ($36, 3½ hours) and Greymouth ($21, 2¼ hours) via Murchison ($19, 1½ hours), Charleston ($12, nine minutes) and Punakaiki ($16, 49 minutes).

➡ **East West Coaches** (☑ 0800 142 622; www.eastwestcoaches.co.nz) has services to/from Reefton ($25, 50 minutes, most days), Punakaiki ($20, 30 minutes, daily), Greymouth ($25, 1¼ hours, daily), Kumara ($40, 1¾ hours, daily) and Christchurch ($70, 3½ hours, two most days).

➡ Karamea Express (p630) heads to/from Karamea ($35, two hours) on weekdays year-round, and on Saturdays from October to April.

➡ From November to April, the Heaphy Bus (p630) stops here once or twice a week en route between Nelson ($65, 3½ hours) and the Heaphy Track trailhead at Kōhaihai ($60, 2½ hours), via Lyell ($50, 1¼ hours), Seddonville ($40, 40 minutes) and Karamea ($55, 2¼ hours).

From November to March, Golden Bay Coachlines (p644) has a daily service to Kōhaihai ($55, 1¾ hours) via Granity ($15, 20 minutes), Seddonville ($35, 40 minutes) and Karamea ($50, 1½ hours).

Track transport is also offered by Habitat Sports (p627) and **Trek Express** (☑ 03-540 2042; www.trekexpress.co.nz).

Karamea & Around
POP 375

Friendly hiking-hub Karamea is colourful, pint-sized and perched by the enticing wilderness of Kahurangi National Park (p659). As the beginning (or end) point of the Heaphy and Wangapeka Tracks, it's common to see hikers gearing up for adventure (or shuffling wearily to the pub). You can delve into the national park on much shorter walks, in particular around the 35-million-year-old Ōpārara Basin, where rainforest hides limestone caverns and natural rock arches.

Never swim at Karamea's beaches, where currents are wild and waves smash the shore. If you must dip a toe in some water, ask at the information centre about freshwater swimming holes.

Karamea is 98 scenic (and petrol-station-free) kilometres north from Westport along SH67 (fill your tank before you set out). You'll find the main cluster of businesses at Market Cross, just across the bridge at the approach to the village.

◉ Sights & Activities

The outdoor wonderland of nikau palms, moss-clad forests and dramatic coastline is the prime reason to visit Karamea. The West Coast road continues (unsealed) for 14km north to Kōhaihai, the western trailhead (and most commonly, the finish point) of the Heaphy Track (p638), where there's a standard DOC campsite (adult/child $8/4).

The Karamea Information & Resource Centre (p629) distributes the free *Karamea Visitor Guide & Map*, which details walks such as the 800m Karamea Estuary Walk, a very pleasant stroll bordering the estuary and Karamea River; Big Rimu (45 minutes return to a whopping tree); and the South Terrace Zig Zag (one hour return), which accesses lookouts over peaceful farmland. At sunset, take a walk along Karamea Beach, which can be reached via Flagstaff Rd, north of town. Longer walks around Karamea include the Fenian Track and Fenian Caves

Loop Track (5km, three hours return, bring a torch) leading to three open-access caves. The Wangapeka Track (p638) is a four-to-six-day backcountry trip suitable for highly experienced hikers only.

Scotts Beach BEACH
It's almost an hour's walk each way from Kōhaihai along the beginning of the Heaphy Track and over the hill to Scotts Beach – a wild, empty shoreline shrouded in mist, awash in foamy waves, strewn with driftwood and backed by a nikau-palm-punctuated forest. Wander in wonder, but don't even think about dipping a toe in – there are dangerous currents at work. There's a DOC Great Walks campsite here; bookings required (adult/child $14/free).

About 30 minutes into the trail, you can detour to a lookout over the beach if you don't want to walk the whole distance.

★**Ōpārara Basin** HIKING
Lying within Kahurangi National Park, the Ōpārara Basin is a hidden valley concealing limestone arches and caves within a thick forest of massive, moss-covered trees. The valley's signature sight is the 200m-long, 37m-high **Ōpārara Arch**, spanning the picturesque Ōpārara River, tannin-stained a fetching shade of caramel, which wends along the easy walkway (45 minutes return).

The main car park is the trailhead for walks of various lengths, and there are excellent information panels here, too. At the cave mouth of the Ōpārara Arch walk, some hikers continue uphill for lofty views but it's steep and treacherous (especially after rain), so we advise against it.

The smaller but no less impressive **Moria Gate Arch** (43m long, 19m high) is reached via a gorgeous forest loop walk (1½ hours), which also passes the **Mirror Tarn** (itself 15 minutes from the car park). The trail connects to the **Ōpārara Valley Track**, a rewarding five-hour (one-way) route through ancient forest, along the river, popping out at the Fenian Track car park.

Just a 10-minute walk from the second Ōpārara Basin car park are the **Crazy Paving and Box Canyon Caves**. Take your torch to enter a world of weird subterranean shapes and rare, leggy spiders.

Beyond this point are the superb **Honeycomb Hill Caves and Arch**, accessible only by guided tours ($150) run by the Karamea Information & Resource Centre; enquire about other guided tours of the area.

To drive to the basin from Karamea, travel 10km along the main road north and turn off at McCallum's Mill Rd, where signposts will direct you a further 14km up and over into the valley along a road that is winding, gravel, rough in places and sometimes steep. Don't attempt it with a campervan.

Karamea Outdoor Adventures OUTDOORS
(📞03-782 6181; www.karameaadventures.co.nz; Bridge St, Market Cross; kayaking/tubing/mountain-biking/horse-riding tour from $50/65/35/105) Guided and go-it-alone kayaking, tubing and riverbug trips, plus mountain-bike hire, horse treks, caving and a host of other ways to make your pulse race.

🍽 Sleeping & Eating

Last Resort LODGE $
(📞03-782 6617; www.lastresortkaramea.co.nz; 71 Waverley St; dm $37, r with/without bathroom $107/74, cottages $155; 🛜) Enclosed by greenery, this rambling resort suits most budgets, with dorms, a choice of private rooms with and without bathrooms, and self-contained two-bedroom cottages. Bonus points for laundry facilities, a comfy communal lounge with tea-making facilities, and showers for passing hikers ($5). The attached cafe/restaurant is one of the few options for a feed in Karamea.

Vinnie's CAFE $$
(📞027 781 1583; Bridge St, Market Cross; mains $8-22; ⏰9am-3pm) Operating from a hole-in-the-wall counter attached to a barn-like hall, Vinnie's dishes up strong coffee and simple fare such as cooked breakfasts, soup, toasties, omelettes and meat pies.

Karamea Village Hotel PUB FOOD $$
(📞03-782 6800; www.karameahotel.co.nz; 141 Waverley St; meals $25-34; ⏰noon-10pm Oct-Mar, 3-10pm Mon-Thu & noon-10pm Sat & Sun Apr-Sep) Within this 1876-built pub lie simple pleasures and warm hospitality: a game of pool, a pint of ale, and a choice of roast dinners, nachos and beer-battered whitebait, to a soundtrack of local gossip and dinging pokie machines. There are motel-style rooms out the back.

ℹ Information

Karamea Information & Resource Centre
(📞03-782 6652; www.karameainfo.co.nz; 106 Bridge St, Market Cross; ⏰9am-4pm Mon-Fri, to 1pm Sat & Sun) This excellent, community-owned centre has the local low-down, internet

access, maps and DOC hut tickets. It also doubles as the petrol station. Enquire about guided tours to the Honeycomb Hill Caves and Arch ($150).

ⓘ Getting There & Away

AIR

Golden Bay Air (☑03-525 8725; www.golden bayair.co.nz; flights $99-209) has scheduled flights between Karamea and Takaka.

Adventure Flights Golden Bay (☑03-525 6167; www.adventureflightsgoldenbay.co.nz) flies charters to/from the other Heaphy trail-head ($200), Takaka ($200), Motueka ($240) and Nelson ($285).

Helicopter Charter Karamea (☑03-782 6111; www.helicharterkaramea.com; 78 Aerodrome Rd) offers charter flights to all of the main track trailheads.

BUS

Karamea Express (☑03-782 6757; www. karameaexpress.co.nz) heads to/from West-port ($35, two hours) on weekdays year-round, and on Saturdays from October to April. It also offers a daily shuttle between Karamea and the Kōhaihai trailhead ($20); bookings essential. Wangapeka Track transport is also available.

From November to March, Golden Bay Coach-lines (p644) has a daily service to Kōhaihai ($20, 15 minutes), Seddonville ($30, 50 minutes), Granity ($40, 70 minutes) and Westport ($50, 1½ hours).

From November to April, the **Heaphy Bus** (☑03-540 2042; www.theheaphybus.co.nz) stops here once or twice a week en route between Nelson ($115, 5¾ hours) and Kōhaihai ($20, 15 minutes), via Lyell ($100, 3½ hours), Westport ($55, 2¼ hours) and Seddonville ($55, 1½ hours).

Reefton

POP 1030

In picturesque Reefton, the town's golden days are never far from mind, with nostalgia permeating every well-preserved goldrush-era building. Early adoption of hydro-electric power generation (1888) and street lighting (1923) gave Reefton its tag line 'the town of light', but these days it's the great outdoors that shines brightest.

Located on the Inangahua River, at the conjunction of the highways linking West-port and Greymouth to the Lewis Pass, the town is an increasingly appealing base for mountain biking, hiking and rafting. A hip distillery has recently been added to the antique stores, galleries and cafes lining Reefton's unrelentingly quaint main street.

◉ Sights & Activities

Pick up the *Walks and Tracks of Reefton* leaflet detailing the Golden Fleece Walk (15 minutes), Bottled Lightning Power-house Walk (30-minute loop) and other easy strolls. Note, a local charitable trust is working to re-establish the historic hydro-electric power station, with a new turbine in the historic shell and a visitor centre; it should be up and running by 2021.

Surrounding Reefton is the 206,000-hectare Victoria Forest Park (NZ's largest forest park), which hides historic sites, such as the old goldfields around Blacks Point. Starting at Blacks Point, the enjoyable Mur-ray Creek Track is a four-hour return trip. Various walks, from 90 minutes to three hours, begin in or around the ghost town of Waiuta, 23km south of Reefton. Longer hikes in the Forest Park include the two- to three-day Kirwans or two-day Big River Track.

Many of these tracks can also be tack-led on a mountain bike. Pick up the free *Reefton Mountain Biking* leaflet ($1 from the i-SITE) for an outline of 15 local tracks.

★ **Reefton Distilling Co.**   DISTILLERY
(☑03-732 7083; www.reeftondistillingco.com; 10 Smith St; tour & tasting $35; ◷10am-4pm Thu-Tue, from noon Wed) Every gold-rush town needs a still, and Reefton's got a goodie in the form of this operation that makes use of foraged botanicals and spring water sourced from the surrounding mountains. Book an hour-long tour or call in for a free tasting of its signature firewater, including the excellent Little Biddy gin, Wild Rain vodka, and Tay-berry and Blueberry liqueurs. You'll have to wait a few years for the whisky.

Bearded Mining Company   HISTORIC BUILDING
(46 Broadway; admission by donation; ◷9am-2pm) Looking like a ZZ Top tribute band, the straight-talkin', bearded fellas at this recreat-ed high-street mining hut rollick your socks off with tales tall and true about the good ol' mining days. If you're lucky, you'll be served a cuppa from the billy along with local tips.

🛏 Sleeping & Eating

Reef Cottage B&B   B&B $$
(☑03-732 8440; www.reefcottage.co.nz; 51-55 Broadway; s/d from $131/150; P🐾) Enjoy total immersion into old-world Reefton at this converted 1887 solicitor's office. Compact rooms are furnished in period style, with

modern touches like swish bathrooms and a well-equipped guest kitchen. In our favourite room, a vault has been converted into the bathroom. There's extra elbow room in the communal lounge and garden, too. Breakfast is in its cafe, next door.

Lantern Court Motels MOTEL $$
(☑ 03-732 8574; www.lanterncourtmotel.co.nz; 63 Broadway; units $130-220; ⓟ ⓡ) Occupying a heritage building (formerly a draper's shop), this friendly establishment has self-catering options for everyone from singles to family groups. Next door, its newer motel block offers all mod cons with a nod to Victorian architecture.

Future Dough Co. CAFE $
(☑ 03-732 8497; www.thefuturedoughco.co.nz; 31 Broadway; mains $5-20; ⊙ 6.30am-4pm) Also known as the Broadway Tearooms, this wooden-floored bakery cafe gets by far the most daytime traffic in Reefton, whether for a freshly baked loaf, iced slices and shortbread to take away, or a bigger sit-down feed of sausage breakfasts, eggs Benedict, toasties and pies. On a sunny day, the outdoor tables are perfect for people-watching.

ℹ Information

Reefton i-SITE (☑ 03-732 8391; www.reefton.co.nz; 67-69 Broadway; ⊙ 9.30am-5pm Mon-Sat, 10am-2pm Sun Oct-Mar, 9.30am-4.30pm Mon-Sat Apr-Sep) This i-SITE has helpful staff, free maps, and you can visit a compact recreation of a mine inside (gold coin entry) and spark NZ's oldest winding engine into action ($2). Enquire about the mooted new Oceana gold-mining museum.

ℹ Getting There & Away

East West Coaches (p628) stops in Reefton every day except Saturday on the run between Westport ($25, 50 minutes) and Christchurch ($60, four hours) via Waipara ($54, three hours).

Murchison
POP 492

In Murchison, tumbling river rapids add freshness to the air and forested hills beckon bushwalkers. This humble township, 125km southwest of Nelson and 95km east of Westport, lies on the 'Four Rivers Plain'. The mightiest waterway is the Buller (in Māori, Kawatiri, meaning 'deep and swift'), where class II-IV rapids have made it hugely popu-

Remote Waiuta (www.waiuta.org.nz; Waiuta Rd) is one of the West Coast's most famous ghost towns. Spread over a plateau, this once-burgeoning gold town was swiftly abandoned after the mineshaft collapsed in 1951. Waiuta grew quickly after a gold discovery in 1905 but these days the forest-shrouded settlement is reduced to bits of rusting machinery, an overgrown swimming pool, stranded brick chimneys, fenced-off mine shafts and the odd intact building, including the old hospital (now a lodge).

From the signposted turn-off on SH7, 23km south of Reefton, it's another 17km to Waiuta, the last half of which is unsealed, winding and narrow in places but easy enough in a 2WD (keep your headlights on). Ask at Reefton's i-SITE for information and maps or consult the DOC website.

lar with experienced rafters, as well as those testing the waters for the first time (some jetboat operators have trips to suit kids... and risk-averse grown-ups).

Unless you have a passion for small-town history and antiques, Murchison itself won't excite you. But a day spent rafting or hiking here is a satisfying way to break up journeys between Nelson and the West Coast.

⊙ Sights & Activities

Ask at the Murchison Information Centre (p632) about local walks, such as the Skyline Walk, a 90-minute hike through fern-filled beech and podocarp forest, and the Johnson Creek Track, a two-hour circuit through pine forest to the 'big slip', formed during the 1929 earthquake. Staff can also hook you up with mountain-bike hire and trout-fishing guides.

Murchison Museum & Information Service MUSEUM
(☑ 03-523 9392; www.visitmurchison.nz; 60 Fairfax St; ⊙ 10am-3pm) FREE This small volunteer-run museum showcases all sorts of local memorabilia (coins, minerals, telephones, sewing machines, toasters etc), the most interesting of which relate to the 1929 and 1968 earthquakes. In winter it covers as the information centre.

★ **Wild Rivers Rafting** RAFTING
(📱03-789 8953; www.wildriversrafting.co.nz; departs Iron Bridge, SH6; 2hr rafting adult/child $160/85; ⊙trips 10am & 2pm) Head out white-water rafting with Bruce and Marty on the particularly exciting Earthquake Rapids section of the beautiful Buller River (good luck with the 'gunslinger' and 'pop-up toaster'!). Kids aged 10 and up can join rafting tours, but check ahead – when the river's high, the minimum age is 13.

Ultimate Descents RAFTING
(📱03-523 9899; www.rivers.co.nz; 38 Waller St; ⚐) This Murchison-based outfit offers white-water rafting and kayaking trips on the Buller, including the classic grade II-IV gorge trip ($160), and gentler family excursions (adult/child $130/100) suitable for kids aged five or more. You can usually count on departures at 9.30am and 1.30pm between September and April, but you'll need to book ahead in winter. Helirafting trips by arrangement ($500).

Buller Canyon Jet ADVENTURE SPORTS
(📱03-523 9883; www.bullercanyonjet.co.nz; 32 Waller St; adult/child $125/75; ⊙Sep-May) Launching from the whopping 110m Buller Gorge Swingbridge, this is one of NZ's most scenic and best-value jetboat trips – 40 minutes of ripping through the beautiful Buller with a good-humoured captain. Its safety record is unblemished.

Natural Flames Experience TOURS
(📱027 698 7244; www.naturalflames.co.nz; 34 Waller St; adult/child $105/65) This informative half-day 4WD and bushwalking tour through verdant valleys and beech forest arrives at a hot spot where natural gas seeping out of the ground has been burning since 1922. Boil a billy on the flames and cook pancakes before returning to civilisation.

🛏 Sleeping

Lazy Cow HOSTEL $
(📱03-523 9451; www.lazycow.co.nz; 37 Waller St; dm $32-35, r with/without bathroom $110/90; 🖥) It's easy to be a lazy cow here, with all the comforts of home in a stress-free, small-scale package. Dorms and private rooms all have electric blankets, and guests can order

a pizza from the adjoining Cow Shed restaurant and scoff it in the backyard or cosy lounge.

Murchison Lodge B&B $$$
(📱03-523 9196; www.murchisonlodge.co.nz; 15 Grey St; d $240-280; 🖥) This quality B&B surrounded by extensive gardens and paddocks is a short walk from the Buller River. Attractive timber features and charming hosts add to the comfortable feel. A hearty breakfast, home baking and plenty of local information are complimentary.

Eating

Cow Shed PIZZA $$
(📱03-523 9523; www.lazycow.co.nz; 37 Waller St; mains $18-24; ⊙5-9pm Mon-Sat) Attached to the Lazy Cow hostel, the cute Cow Shed is a popular option for its crisp, generously topped pizzas served in intimate surrounds. Gluten-free options available.

🛍 Shopping

Dust & Rust ANTIQUES
(📱03-523 9300; www.dustandrust.nz; 35 Fairfax St; ⊙10am-5pm daily Dec-Feb, Thu-Mon Sep-Nov & Mar-May) Rummage through an ever-changing array of vintage cars, foreign number-plates, hubcaps, 1970s kitchenware and vintage clothing at this impressive archive of curios housed in the historic Commercial Stables building. They're all originals – dust and rust comes included in the price.

ℹ Information

Murchison Information & Booking Centre
(📱03-523 9350; www.murchison.info; 47 Waller St; ⊙9am-6pm Dec-Mar, 10am-4pm Mon-Fri Apr & Sep-Nov) Helpful tourist centre that assists with activity and hotel bookings, and offers bags of local info.

ℹ Getting There & Away

InterCity (p604) buses stop at Beechwoods Cafe on Waller St daily en route between Nelson ($23, 1¾ hours) and Greymouth ($31, four hours) via Westport ($19, 1½ hours), Charleston ($19, two hours) and Punakaiki ($28, 2¼ hours).

Nelson & Marlborough

Best Places to Eat

➡ Scotch Wine Bar (p672)

➡ Harry's Hawker House (p642)

➡ Rock Ferry (p671)

➡ Urban (p643)

➡ Mills Bay Mussels (p663)

Best Places to Stay

➡ Adrift in Golden Bay (p656)

➡ Kaiteri Motels & Apartments (p649)

➡ Tombstone Backpackers (p666)

➡ Eden's Edge Lodge (p650)

➡ Tasman Bay Backpackers (p640)

Why Go?

For sauvignon blanc lovers the world over, the name Marlborough denotes crisp, herbaceous wine that seems to capture the very essence of summer sunshine and green spaces. The minute you set foot in this sun-soaked and verdant region, you'll see exactly how apposite an impression that is.

Consisting of the fertile Tasman and Marlborough districts, with the chilled-out city of Nelson squeezed in between, the 'Top of the South' has renowned coastal holiday spots – particularly Golden Bay, Tasman Bay and the curlicued emerald inlets of the Marlborough Sounds. There are also three national parks (Nelson Lakes, Abel Tasman and Kahurangi) and three of the country's most famous multiday hikes (the Abel Tasman Coast, Heaphy and Queen Charlotte tracks), two of which number among New Zealand's official list of Great Walks.

If you're arriving by ferry from often-blustery Wellington, it's an impressive introduction to what South Islanders refer to as 'the Mainland'.

When to Go

➡ The forecast is good: this area soaks up some of New Zealand's sunniest weather, with January and February being the warmest months.

➡ June and July are the coldest months, averaging highs of 12°C. However, the Top of the South sees some wonderful winter weather, with frosty mornings often giving way to clear skies and T-shirt temperatures.

➡ From around Christmas until the end of January, the whole region teems with Kiwi holidaymakers, so plan ahead during this time and be prepared to jostle for position with bucket-and-spade-wielding families.

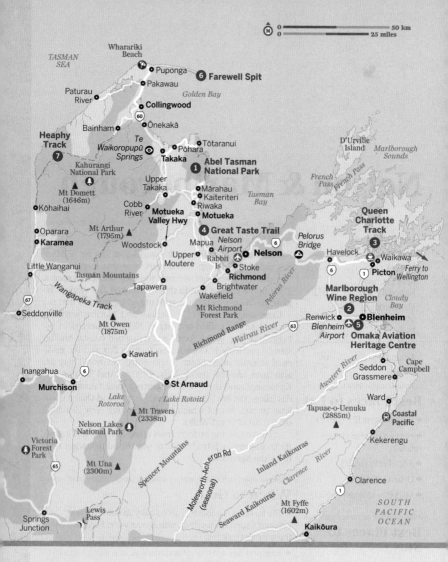

TASMAN
SEA

Wharariki
Beach

Puponga

Pakawau

6 Farewell Spit

Golden Bay

Paturau
River

Collingwood

Bainham

Ōnekakā

60

Te
Waikoropupū
Springs

Tōtaranui

Pōhara

Takaka

**1 Abel Tasman
National Park**

D'Urville
Island

Marlborough
Sounds

**Heaphy
Track**

7

Kahurangi
National Park

Mt Domett
(1646m)

Kōhaihai

Upper
Takaka

Mārahau

Kaiteriteri

French
Pass

French Pass

Cobb
River

Riwaka

**Motueka
Valley Hwy**

Motueka

Tasman
Bay

**Queen
Charlotte
Track**

Oparara

Karamea

Mt Arthur
(1795m)

Woodstock

4 Great Taste Trail

Pelorus
Bridge

Havelock

3

Waikawa

Little Wanganui

Tasman Mountains

Mapua

Upper
Moutere

Nelson
Airport

Rabbit
Is

6

Stoke

Nelson

Pelorus River

6

1 Picton

Ferry to
Wellington

Wangapeka Track

Tapawera

Richmond

Brightwater

Wakefield

Mt Richmond
Forest Park

**Marlborough
Wine Region**

Renwick

2

63

Blenheim
Airport

Cloudy
Bay

Blenheim

5

**Omaka Aviation
Heritage Centre**

67

Seddonville

Mt Owen
(1875m)

Kawatiri

Richmond Range

Wairau River

Awatere River

Seddon

Grassmere

Cape
Campbell

Inangahua

6

Murchison

St Arnaud

Ward

Lake
Rotoroa

Lake Rotoiti

Tapuae-o-Uenuku
(2885m)

**Coastal
Pacific**

Victoria
Forest
Park

Mt Travers
(2338m)

Nelson Lakes
National Park

Kekerengu

65

Mt Una
(2300m)

Spencer Mountains

Molesworth-Acheron Rd
(seasonal)

Inland Kaikouras

Clarence River

Clarence

1

SOUTH
PACIFIC
OCEAN

Springs
Junction

Lewis
Pass

Seaward Kaikouras

Mt Fyffe
(1602m)

Kaikōura

Nelson & Marlborough Highlights

**1 Abel Tasman National
Park** (p651) Kayaking or
hiking to blissful golden-sand
beaches.

**2 Marlborough Wine
Region** (p670) Diving into a
sea of sauvignon blanc in NZ's
most famous wine region.

3 Queen Charlotte Track
(p638) Hiking or biking

through the myriad inlets of
the Marlborough Sounds.

4 Great Taste Trail (p636)
Pausing regularly for food,
drink, art and beach breaks
along this popular cycle trail.

**5 Omaka Aviation
Heritage Centre** (p667)
Immersing yourself in life-

sized tableaux showcasing
original WWI and WWII aircraft.

6 Farewell Spit (p658)
Touring through a dunescape
with gannets and godwits for
company.

7 Heaphy Track (p638)
Reaching the wild West Coast
on foot, crossing through
Kahurangi National Park.

❶ Getting There & Away

Picton is the South Island's main interisland ferry port, with multiple daily sailings to and from Wellington. Nelson has the busiest domestic airport, followed by Blenheim and Picton. Buses link the region to Canterbury and the West Coast. From October to April, KiwiRail's *Coastal Pacific* train takes the scenic journey between Picton and Christchurch.

NELSON

POP 46,400

Dishing up a winning combination of beautiful surroundings, sophisticated art and culinary scenes, and lashings of sunshine, Nelson is hailed as one of New Zealand's most liveable cities. In summer it fills up with local and international visitors, who come to take advantage of its proximity to both the Marlborough Sounds and the diverse natural attractions of the Tasman District.

Known to Māori as Whakatū, it was renamed Nelson after the hero of the Battle of Trafalgar by the canny New Zealand Company in 1841, in a bid to entice British colonists to its dubiously acquired settlement. In 1858 it was declared a city when it was still little more than a muddy village by dint of having acquired for itself a bishop and the promise of a cathedral. It still feels more like a big provincial town than a proper city, but that's part of Nelson's appeal.

◉ Sights

Tahunanui Beach BEACH
(♿) Nelson's primo playground takes the form of a long sandy beach (with lifeguards in summer) backed by dunes and a large grassy park with a playground, an espresso cart, a hydroslide, go-karts, a roller-skating rink and a model railway.

**Christ Church
Cathedral** CATHEDRAL
(Map p641; ☏03-548 1008; www.nelsoncathedral.org; Pikimai; ⊙9am-6pm) FREE The enduring symbol of Nelson, Christ Church lords it over the city from the top of Pikimai/Church Hill. It's an unusual mix of Gothic and art-deco style, with its nave constructed in Takaka marble in 1932 and the sanctuary and tower completed in ferroconcrete in 1972.

ESSENTIAL NELSON & MARLBOROUGH

Eat greenshell mussels from the Marlborough Sounds.

Drink Marlborough sauvignon blanc.

Read *The Voyage*, a short story about a ferry trip to Picton, from Katherine Mansfield's *The Garden Party and Other Stories* (1922).

Listen to OMC's *Land of Plenty* (1997), which namechecks Nelson and the Picton ferry.

Watch *The Hobbit: The Desolation of Smaug* (2013) – the barrel scene was filmed on the Pelorus River.

Celebrate at the Marlborough Wine & Food Festival (p670).

Go green at Motuara Island (p660).

Go online www.marlboroughnz.com, www.nelsonnz.com

**Nelson Provincial
Museum** MUSEUM
(Map p641; ☏03-548 9588; www.nelsonmuseum.co.nz; 270 Trafalgar St; adult/child $5/3; ⊙10am-5pm) This modern museum is filled with a jumble of cultural heritage and natural history exhibits with a strong regional focus, including an almost Easter Island–esque stone statue, beautiful greenstone *hei-tiki* (stylised human figures) pendants, *patu* (warriors' clubs) and even the gown worn by Nobel Prize–winning scientist and Nelson College alumni Ernest Lord Rutherford at his christening. The top floor is given over to regular touring exhibitions (for which admission fees vary), and also features a roof garden.

Suter Art Gallery GALLERY
(Map p641; ☏03-548 4699; www.thesuter.org.nz; 208 Bridge St; ⊙9.30am-4.30pm) FREE Redeveloped in 2016 with a series of contemporary, light-filled exhibition spaces, Nelson's public art gallery presents changing exhibitions from a collection that includes Kiwi big hitters such as Gordon Walters, Ralph Hotere and Don Binney. The complex incorporates an art-house cinema, an excellent gift shop and a riverside cafe.

HIKING & BIKING IN NELSON & MARLBOROUGH

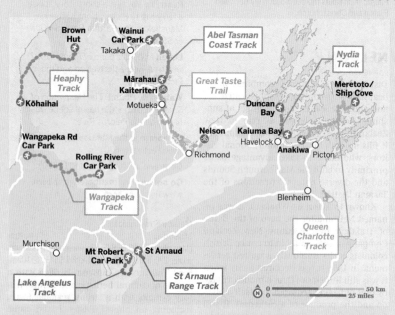

GREAT TASTE TRAIL

ACTIVITY CYCLING
START NELSON
FINISH KAITERITERI
DURATION ONE OF TWO DAYS
DISTANCE 77KM
DIFFCULTY EASY

In a stroke of genius inspired by great weather and easy topography, the Tasman District has developed one of New Zealand's most popular cycle trails. Why is it so popular? Because no other route is so frequently punctuated by stops for food, wine, craft beer and art, as it passes through a range of landscapes from bucolic countryside to estuary boardwalk.

While the **Great Taste Trail** (www.heartof biking.org.nz) can be ridden in full in a few days, stopping at accommodation en route, it is more commonly ridden as day trips of various lengths. The most popular and diversion-filled section stretches from Nelson to Kaiteriteri (77km, six to nine hours), via Stoke, Richmond, Moturoa/Rabbit Island, Māpua, Motueka and Riwaka. To get from **Moturoa/Rabbit Island** (p646) to Māpua requires a trip on the Māpua Ferry; check the schedule before setting out.

The full Great Taste Trail circuit is still being completed but will eventually include a 1325m section of former rail tunnel (you'll need a light). The route doubles back from Kaiteriteri to Riwaka (6km, 30 minutes to one hour) and heads inland to Woodstock (31km, two to three hours). From here, the main circuit will head south to Kohatu, through the Spooners Tunnel and then northeast through Wakefield, Brightwater and Richmond. Until that's completed, an alternative, shorter route heads on road directly from Woodstock to Wakefield (29km, 1½ to three hours) and then back to Nelson (32km, two to 3½ hours).

Kiwi Journeys (Map p641; ☑03-548 0093; www.kiwijourneys.co.nz; 37-39 Halifax St; day tours

Welcome to the sunny side! This end of the South Island has more sunshine hours than any other part, which means long, sun-baked days perfect for getting outdoors.

from $99; ⊙9am-5pm) – which operates the bike-friendly Māpua Ferry and has depots in Nelson, Māpua Wharf and Kaiteriteri – is one of several excellent companies offering bike hire, drop-offs and cycle tours along this and other trails. Others include **Nelson Cycle Hire & Tours** (✉03-539 4193; www.nelson cyclehire.co.nz; Nelson Airport; day tours from $99), **Gentle Cycling Company** (✉03-929 5652; www. gentlecycling.co.nz; 411 Nayland Rd, Stoke; day tours from $75; ⊙Sep-Apr) and **Wheelie Fantastic** (✉03-543 2245; www.wheeliefantastic.co.nz; 151 Aranui Rd, Māpua; bike hire per day from $55).

ABEL TASMAN COAST TRACK

ACTIVITY **HIKING**
START **MĀRAHAU**
END **WAINUI CAR PARK**
DURATION **5 DAYS**
DISTANCE **60KM**
DIFFICULTY **EASY**

Think of this as a beach holiday on foot. Arguably the most beautiful of the Great Walks, the Abel Tasman Coast Track is a seductive combination of reliably pleasant weather, sparkling seas, golden sand, quintessential NZ coastal forest and hidden surprises with intriguing names such as Cleopatra's Pool. Another attraction is the terrain, for this is not a typical, rugged New Zealand track. It is better serviced than any other track in the country: well cut, well graded and well marked. It's difficult to get lost and can be hiked in a pair of running shoes. Leaving the boots behind is a bonus, as you'll probably get your feet wet – indeed, you'll probably want to get your feet wet.

This is a track with long stretches of beach walking and crazy tides to work around. The tidal ranges in the park are among the greatest in the country – up to a staggering 6m. At Awaroa Bay you have no choice but to plan on crossing at low tide. Daylight tide times are published on the DOC website (www.doc.govt.nz), and also displayed at DOC's **Whakatū/Nelson Visitor Centre** (p644) and regional i-SITEs. It's important to consult these at the time of planning your trip, as the times of the tides will affect the huts or campsites that you use and the direction in which you walk the track.

The track is so well trodden that a topographical map isn't essential for navigation. The maps in DOC's trip information sheet and the *Abel Tasman Coast Track Guide* provide sufficient detail, and you can readily buy more illuminating maps at local visitor centres.

The path finishes at a car park near Wainui Bay, though most people extend their hike beyond Wainui by returning to Tōtaranui via the Gibbs Hill Track to pick up the water taxis back to Mārahau or Kaiteriteri. You could always just stop at Tōtaranui the first time you walk through, but by continuing north you will discover the most dramatic viewpoint (Separation Point), the least-crowded hut (Whariwharangi) and some of the best beaches (Anapai and Mutton Cove) in the park.

The entire hike takes only three to five days, although with water-taxi transport you can convert it into an almost endless array of options, particularly if you combine it with a kayak leg. Note, however, that kayaks aren't available from within the park and have to be brought in and out from Mārahau/Kaiteriteri each day. If you plan to combine a hike with kayaking, you should arrange the logistics with a kayak hire company before you book huts or campsites to ensure everything aligns.

Such is the pulling power of this track that it now attracts more than 37,000 hikers and kayakers each year who stay at least one night in the park. By way of comparison, the next most popular Great Walk is the Routeburn Track, which draws around 17,000. Don't expect to just turn up and hike; you'll need to plan and book your Great Walks huts and campsites online, well in advance, especially if you're planning to hike between Christmas and the end of January.

HEAPHY TRACK

ACTIVITY HIKING (ALL YEAR) OR
MOUNTAIN BIKING (MAY TO NOVEMBER)
START BROWN HUT
END KŌHAIHAI
DURATION 5 DAYS
DISTANCE 78.5KM
DIFFICULTY MODERATE

The Heaphy Track is one of the most popular hikes in the country. A Great Walk in every sense, it traverses diverse terrain – dense native forest, the mysterious Gouland Downs, secluded river valleys, and beaches dusted in salt spray and fringed by nikau palms.

Although quite long, the Heaphy is well cut and benched, making it easier than any other extended hike found in Kahurangi National Park. That said, you may still find it arduous, particularly in unfavourable weather.

Walking from east to west, most of the climbing is done on the first day and the scenic beach walk is saved for the end; a fitting and invigorating grand finale.

The track is open to mountain bikers between May and November. Factoring in distance, remoteness and the possibility of bad weather, this epic journey is only suited to well-equipped cyclists with advanced riding skills. A good port of call for more information is the **Quiet Revolution Cycle Shop** (p655) in Takaka.

A strong hiker could walk the Heaphy in three days, but most people take four or five days. For a detailed track description, see DOC's *Heaphy Track* brochure.

The seven designated Great Walk huts ($34) have bunks and kitchen areas, heating, toilets (composting or pit) and washbasins with cold water. Most but not all have gas rings; a couple have lighting. There are also nine Great Walk campsites ($14), plus the beachside **Kōhaihai Campsite** (www.doc. govt.nz; Karamea-Kohaihai Rd; site per adult/child $8/4) at the West Coast trailhead. Like all of the Great Walks, you'll need to book huts and campsites in advance.

WANGAPEKA TRACK

ACTIVITY HIKING
START ROLLING RIVER CAR PARK
END WANGAPEKA RD CAR PARK
DURATION 5 DAYS
DISTANCE 59KM
DIFFICULTY MODERATE TO DIFFICULT

The more challenging Wangapeka Track is not as well known as the Heaphy, but some advanced hikers consider it the more enjoyable Kahurangi National Park hike due to its rugged scenery and isolation. It traverses two saddles over 1000m and passes through beech forest in the Wangapeka, Karamea, Taipo and Little Wanganui River valleys.

There's a chain of DOC huts along the track; purchase your backcountry hut passes in advance and check with DOC before setting out.

QUEEN CHARLOTTE TRACK

ACTIVITY HIKING (ALL YEAR) OR
MOUNTAIN BIKING (MARCH TO NOVEMBER ONLY)
START MERETOTO/SHIP COVE
END ANAKIWA
DURATION 4 DAYS
DISTANCE 71KM
DIFFICULTY MODERATE

The hugely popular, meandering Queen Charlotte Track (www.qctrack.co.nz) offers gorgeous coastal scenery on its way from historic Meretoto/Ship Cove to Anakiwa, passing through a mixture of privately owned land and DOC reserves. The coastal forest is lush, and from the ridges there are regular views into both Queen Charlotte and Kenepuru Sounds.

Queen Charlotte is a well-defined track, suitable for people of most fitness levels. It can be completed in three to five days, and can be walked in either direction, though Meretoto/Ship Cove is the usual (and recommended) starting point. This is mainly because it's easier to arrange a boat from Picton to Meretoto/Ship Cove than the reverse. It can also be walked in sections by hopping aboard numerous boat services. A good two-day hike is from Meretoto/Ship Cove to Punga Cove (27km), while recommended day walks include the sections from Mistletoe Bay to Anakiwa (12.5km), or Meretoto/Ship Cove to Furneaux Lodge (15km).

You can also turn the hike into a multisport outing by combining sections of hiking with kayaking or mountain biking. In 2013 the track was opened to cyclists, though they're forbidden from riding the section between Meretoto/Ship Cove and Kenepuru Saddle from 1 December to the end of February.

There are six DOC camping grounds along the route, while other accommodation ranges from old-fashioned homestays to luxury waterfront lodges. This is one of the enduring draws of the track – the chance to spend the day hiking, then to enjoy a hot shower and a cold beer at the end of it. Boat operators will also happily transport your pack along the track for you. At first it seems decadent...then it just seems welcome.

The district council, DOC and private landowners manage the track as a partnership. The private landowners are members of the Queen Charlotte Track Land Cooperative. They require each track user to purchase and display a pass for the private-land sections between Kenepuru Saddle and Bottle Bay (a one-day pass costs $12, while $25 covers you for up to five consecutive days). Passes can be purchased from various accommodation providers and boat operators near the track, from the Picton and Blenheim i-SITEs, and from the ticket machine at the Anakiwa trailhead.

NYDIA TRACK

ACTIVITY HIKING OR MOUNTAIN BIKING
START KAIUMA BAY
END DUNCAN BAY
DURATION 2 DAYS
DISTANCE 27KM
DIFFICULTY EASY

This track can be tackled as a very long day walk (9½ hours not counting breaks, or five hours on a mountain bike), but most people prefer the two-day option, staying in beautiful Nydia Bay along the way.

Hidden in the inner reaches of Pelorus Sound, the track crosses the Kaiuma Saddle (387m) before descending to Nydia Bay, the site of a long-gone sawmilling settlement. In the early 1900s, steam-powered haulers would drag logs from the saddles down to the bay where there was a large mill and a 300m wharf. Accommodation options here now include a DOC campsite and unhosted 50-bed lodge, and the excellent privately owned **On the Track Lodge** (p660).

The track then continues over the Nydia Saddle (347m) and through a patch of broadleafed coastal forest to Duncan Bay; allow around four to 4½ hours for the 15km walk.

Although rather remote, each trailhead is accessible by both water and road; there's no road to Nydia Bay.

LAKE ANGELUS TRACK

ACTIVITY HIKING
START/END MT ROBERT CAR PARK
DURATION 2 DAYS
DISTANCE 32.2KM
DIFFICULTY MODERATE TO DIFFICULT

Despite its relatively short length, this hike rates as one of the best in the country, showcasing all that's good about Nelson Lakes National Park. In fine weather, the walk along Robert Ridge is spectacular – seldom do hikes afford such an extended stretch across such open tops. The views will blow your socks off, as they will again as you descend into the extraordinary Lake Angelus basin (1650m) and Angelus Hut, which is a good base for short forays to the ridge above the lake and to Mt Angelus. A two-night stay at Angelus Hut is highly desirable, but be aware that bookings are required from December to April and it often books out.

Angelus Hut is an alpine hut and weather conditions can change rapidly. Snow, frost and freezing winds can occur even in midsummer, so hikers should be experienced and well equipped before attempting this route. Don't underestimate it: two people died here in 2019. Talk to the staff at the DOC Nelson Lakes Visitor Centre before setting out; locator beacons are recommended.

ST ARNAUD RANGE TRACK

ACTIVITY HIKING
START/END ST ARNAUD
DURATION 5 HOURS RETURN
DISTANCE 11KM
DIFFICULTY MODERATE

This popular up-and-down day walk provides one of the best viewpoints of Nelson Lakes National Park and beyond, surveyed from the top of the St Arnaud Range. It's around a 1000m ascent (and subsequent descent) from lake to ridge, but achy legs will be soothed by the splendour of beech forest – red, silver and mountain – that gradually changes with altitude.

Equally diverting is the chatter of native birds, the population of which is bolstered by the work of the Rotoiti Nature Recovery Project, through which this track passes.

Above the bushline (1400m) the views are worthy of a sit-down, but don't be content with gawping at the lake and Mt Robert from Parachute Rocks, as many hikers are. Fuel up with some scroggin (trail mix) and conquer the final 30-minute climb through alpine tussock to the ridge (1650m). You won't be disappointed.

Queen's Gardens
GARDENS

(Map p641; Bridge St) Immerse yourself in botanical history in this ornamental garden, founded in 1887 to commemorate the 50th jubilee of Queen Victoria's coronation. It's set around a horseshoe-shaped pond, with a bridge leading to a walled Chinese-style garden.

Botanical Reserve
PARK

(Milton St) Walking tracks through this 12-hectare reserve ascend Botanical Hill, where a spire proclaims the Centre of New Zealand. The actual centre is 55km southwest of here, but the views are great regardless. NZ's first-ever rugby match was played at the foot of the hill on 14 May 1870.

Founders Heritage Park
MUSEUM

(☑03-548 2649; www.founderspark.co.nz; 87 Atawhai Dr; adult/child/family $7/5/15; ⊙10am-4.30pm) A collection of heritage buildings has been relocated to this site, 2km northeast of the city centre, creating a Victorian-era village complete with a church, pub, windmill and model railway (rides adult/child $6/4). Quaint shops now stock artisan products, while larger sheds display stagecoaches and vintage buses. Wet your whistle with a visit to McCashin's Hop Garden.

McCashin's Brewery
BREWERY

(☑03-547 5357; www.mkb.co.nz; 660 Main Rd, Stoke; tour incl tastings $25; ⊙7am-4.30pm Mon-Wed, to 9.30pm Thu-Sat, 9am-4.30pm Sun) McCashin's was a forerunner of the craft brewing craze in NZ, which started way back in the 1980s. Visit the historic Rochdale Cider building in Stoke (8km southwest of central Nelson) for a tasting, bistro meal or tour.

🏃 Activities & Tours

There's plenty of walking and cycling to be enjoyed in and around the town, for which the i-SITE (p644) has maps. Nelson has two of the New Zealand Cycle Trail's 22 Great Rides: the Coppermine Trail (www.heartofbiking.org.nz), an awesome but challenging one-day ride ranging over the hills to the south of the city; and the Great Taste Trail (p636), which offers a blissfully flat meander through beautiful countryside dotted with wine, food and art stops.

Cable Bay Kayaks
KAYAKING

(☑027 223 6594; www.cablebaykayaks.co.nz; Cable Bay Rd, Pepin Island; half-/full-day guided trips $90/160) Twenty minutes' drive from Nelson city, this team offers richly rewarding guided sea-kayaking trips exploring the cave-indented coast around Pepin Island, where you'll likely meet local marine life (snorkelling gear on board helps).

Moana SUP
WATER SPORTS

(☑027 285 0772; www.moananzsup.co.nz; Bizley Walk, Tahunanui Beach; lessons from $70) Learn stand-up paddle boarding with the crew at Moana, or hire a board or kayak if you're already enlightened.

Nelson Tours & Travel
TOURS

(☑027 237 5007; www.nelsontoursandtravel.co.nz) CJ and crew run various small-group, flexible tours honing in on Nelson's wine, craft beer, art and scenic highlights. The five-hour 'Best of Both Worlds' tour ($160) includes beer, wine and lunch at the heritage Moutere Inn. Day tours of Marlborough wineries also available ($295).

🎆 Festivals & Events

For current info on Nelson's active events program, visit www.itson.co.nz.

Nelson Jazz Festival
MUSIC

(www.nelsonjazzclub.co.nz; ⊙Jan) More scoobe-doo-bop events over four days in January than you can shake a leg at. Features local and national acts.

Nelson Arts Festival
PERFORMING ARTS

(www.nelsonartsfestival.co.nz; ⊙Oct) Held over two weeks in October; events include a street carnival, exhibitions, cabaret, writer talks, theatre and music.

🛏 Sleeping

⭐ Tasman Bay Backpackers
HOSTEL $

(☑03-548 7950; www.tasmanbaybackpackers.co.nz; 10 Weka St; dm $28-30, r with/without bathroom $88/76; @🛜) This well-designed, friendly hostel has airy communal spaces with a 100% Kiwi music soundtrack, colourful rooms, a sunny outdoor deck and a well-used hammock. Good freebies: wi-fi, decent bikes, breakfast during winter, and chocolate pudding and ice cream year-round.

Prince Albert
HOSTEL $

(Map p641; ☑03-548 8477; www.theprincealbert.co.nz; 113 Nile St; dm/s/d from $26/55/85; P🛜) A five-minute walk from the city centre, this lively, well-run backpackers has roomy ensuite dorms surrounding a sunny courtyard. Private rooms are upstairs in the historic pub where guests can meet the locals and refuel with a good-value meal. A simple free breakfast is provided.

Central Nelson

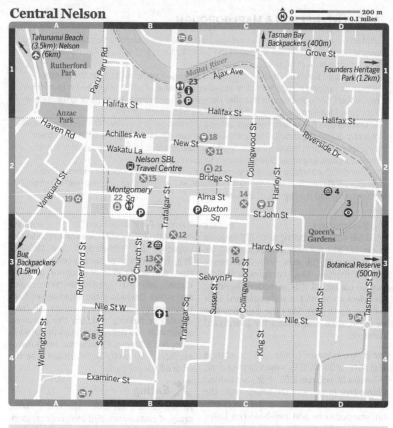

Central Nelson

◎ Sights
1 Christ Church Cathedral B4
2 Nelson Provincial Museum B3
3 Queen's Gardens D2
4 Suter Art Gallery D2

⊕ Activities, Courses & Tours
5 Kiwi Journeys B1

⊜ Sleeping
6 Cedar Grove Motor Lodge B1
7 Century Park Motor Lodge A4
8 Palazzo A4
9 Prince Albert D4

⊗ Eating
10 Cod & Lobster B3
11 DeVille C2
12 Falafel Gourmet B3
13 Harry's Hawker House B3
Hopgood's & Co .... (see 13)

14 Indian Café C2
15 Swedish Bakery & Cafe B2
16 Urban C3

⊜ Drinking & Nightlife
17 Free House C2
18 Rhythm & Brown C2
Sprig & Fern .... (see 16)

⊕ Entertainment
19 Theatre Royal A2

⊜ Shopping
20 Jens Hansen B3
21 Nelson Farmers Market C2
22 Nelson Market B2

ⓘ Information
23 DOC Whakatū/Nelson Visitor
Centre B1
Nelson i-SITE .... (see 23)

MĀORI NZ: NELSON & MARLBOROUGH

In Māori mythology the South Island was the canoe from which the demigod Māui fished up the North Island. Hence the top of the South Island is known as *Te Tau Ihu o te Waka a Māui* – the prow of Māui's canoe.

The Wairau Bar, near Blenheim, is the oldest known settlement site in the country, with finds radiocarbon-dated to the 13th century, some of which originated in East Polynesia. You'll find objects from this site, alongside other *taonga* (treasures), in the Nelson Provincial Museum (p635) and the Marlborough Museum (p668).

Control over the area has shifted between various *iwi* (tribes) over the centuries, most recently during the chaos of the early-19th-century Musket Wars, when it was invaded by displaced North Island tribes. Nowadays the tribal areas overlap substantially, and there's a confusing array of *iwi* with links to the region.

Significant *wāhi tapu* (sacred places) that can be visited include the Riuwaka Resurgence (p650) and Te Waikoropupū Springs (p654). At both sites, you're asked to refrain from eating and to keep out of the water.

Bug Backpackers
HOSTEL $

(☑ 03-539 4227; www.thebug.co.nz; 226 Vanguard St; dm $27-30, r with/without bathroom $82/69; @🛜) About 15 minutes' walk from town, the VW-themed Bug occupies a boldly painted converted villa, a modern building next door to it, and a self-contained unit sleeping up to four. Start the day with free breakfast, then return later for a backyard barbecue.

Cedar Grove Motor Lodge
MOTEL $$

(Map p641; ☑ 03-545 1133; www.cedargrove.co.nz; 59 Trafalgar St; unit from $160; P🛜) Set behind a large tree just across the bridge from the town centre, this modern motel offers studio, one-bedroom and two-bedroom units, each with cooking facilities and either patios or balconies.

Beaches
MOTEL $$

(☑ 03-548 6008; www.beachesnelson.nz; 71 Tahunanui Dr, Tahunanui; unit $159-219; P🛜) These 16 well-equipped units are closer to the highway than the beach but still handy for all of Tahunanui's watery attractions. All have patios or balconies, and free wi-fi.

Palazzo
MOTEL $$$

(Map p641; ☑ 03-545 8171; www.palazzomotor lodge.co.nz; 159 Rutherford St; unit $155-420; P❄🛜) This modern, Italian-tinged motor lodge offers stylish and comfortable studio, one-, two- and three-bedroom apartments within a block from the city centre. All have enviable kitchens with decent cooking equipment, classy glassware and a dishwasher.

Century Park Motor Lodge
MOTEL $$$

(Map p641; ☑ 03-546 6197; www.centuryparkmotor lodge.com; 197 Rutherford St; unit $169-285; P❄🛜) Portraits of golden-era Hollywood stars add a sprinkle of glamour to these highly polished apartment-style studios and suites (including the super-duper two-bedroom 'presidential spa suite'). All have a patio or balcony catching the sunshine, along with pod coffee machines in the well-equipped kitchens. Continental breakfast is available, and pretty floral fringes take the edge off the car park.

✖ Eating

Nelson has a lively cafe scene and a varied array of restaurants. Self-caterers can stock up on locally grown produce at the Nelson Market (p644) on Saturdays and the Nelson Farmers' Market (Map p641; ☑ 022 010 2776; www.nelsonfarmersmarket.org.nz; Kirby Lane, Bridge St; ⏰8.30am-1.30pm Wed) on Wednesdays.

Swedish Bakery & Cafe
BAKERY $

(Map p641; ☑ 03-546 8685; www.facebook.com/ TheSwedishBakeryandCafe; 54 Bridge St; mains $5.80-9; ⏰8am-3pm Tue-Fri, to 1.30pm Sat) Nelson's resident Scandinavian baker serves up delicious breads, pastries, cakes and small chocolate treats in this bijou bakery cafe. The freshly filled baguettes and croissants are excellent, too. Take your goodies away or pray that one of three small tables is free.

★ Harry's Hawker House
ASIAN $$

(Map p641; ☑ 03-539 0905; www.hawkerhouse. co.nz; 296 Trafalgar St; dishes $8-28; ⏰3pm-late Tue-Thu, from noon Fri-Sun) Step into a dimly lit room imbued with the glamour of old Shanghai and order a Singapore-style cocktail before delving into a menu filled with delectable dishes inspired by the street food of China and Southeast Asia, such as beef-cheek rendang roti rolls, pot stickers and curries. Don't miss the chicken laksa dumplings; the master broth they're served in is extraordinarily good.

★ Urban   STREET FOOD $$

(Map p641; ☑ 03-546 7861; www.urbaneatery. co.nz; 278 Hardy St; dishes $18-27; ☺ 4pm-late Mon, 11am-late Tue-Sat) Slurp oysters from the shell, or revitalise with sashimi and ceviche, then sate your cravings with street-food dishes such as *kung pao* Sichuan fried chicken or smoked venison tostadas. Black butchers' tiles, edgy artwork, craft beers and a fine wine list all bolster this metropolitan experience.

DeVille   CAFE $$

(Map p641; ☑ 03-545 6911; www.devillecafe.co.nz; 22 New St; meals $15-22; ☺ 8am-4pm Mon-Sat, 9am-3pm Sun; 🐾🖊) Most of DeVille's tables lie in its sweet walled courtyard, a hidden boho oasis in the inner city and the perfect place for a meal or morning tea. The food's good and local – from fresh baking to a chorizo burrito brunch and proper burgers, washed down with regional wines and beers. It's open late for live music in summer.

Indian Café   INDIAN $$

(Map p641; ☑ 03-548 4089; www.theindiancafe. com; 94 Collingwood St; mains $14-20; ☺ noon-2pm Mon-Fri, 5pm-late daily; 🖊) This saffron-coloured Edwardian bungalow houses a convivial Indian restaurant serving impressive interpretations of standards such as tandoori chicken, rogan josh and beef Madras. Share the mixed platter to start, then mop up your mains with one of 10 different breads.

Falafel Gourmet   MIDDLE EASTERN $$

(Map p641; ☑ 03-545 6220; 195 Hardy St; mains $12-18; ☺ 10am-4pm Mon-Sat; 🖊) This humble joint dishes out healthy pitta pockets, platters and the best kebabs for miles around. Choose between chicken, lamb or tasty falafels.

Hopgood's & Co   BISTRO $$$

(Map p641; ☑ 03-545 7191; www.hopgoods.co.nz; 284 Trafalgar St; mains $40-42; ☺ 5.30pm-late Mon-Sat) Hopgood's relaxed approach to service and gastro-pub feel seem a little at odds with the hefty prices, although the bistro menu (two/three courses $49/59, served Monday to Wednesday) lessens the pain somewhat. The food is deftly prepared but unfussy (roast duck, merino lamb), allowing quality local ingredients to shine. The five-course tasting menu ($95) affords the full Hopgood's experience.

Cod & Lobster   SEAFOOD $$$

(Map p641; ☑ 03-546 4300; www.codandlobster. com; 300 Trafalgar St; mains $36-38; ☺ 11am-11pm Tue-Sun; 🐾) Stellar cocktails and a vast array of gin make the corner bar an essential destination, but this heritage space also serves up excellent food. A concise selection of steak, lamb and vegetarian dishes is available, but it's the briny-fresh catch of the day you're really here for. At lunchtime there's a good-value set menu (two/three courses $35/45).

 ## Drinking & Entertainment

Free House   CRAFT BEER

(Map p641; ☑ 03-548 9391; www.freehouse.co.nz; 95 Collingwood St; ☺ 3-10.30pm Mon-Thu, to midnight Fri, noon-midnight Sat, noon-10.30pm Sun) Tastefully converted from its original, more reverent purpose, this former church is now home to an excellent, oft-changing selection of NZ craft beers. Munch on bar snacks on the outside deck, and visit on a Friday or Saturday afternoon to browse the vinyl at the excellent Family Jewels Records pop-up store.

IN PURSUIT OF HOPPINESS

Nelson and the neighbouring Tasman region lay claim to the title of craft-brewing capital of New Zealand. World-class hops have been grown here since the 1840s. Pick up a copy of the *Nelson Craft Beer Trail* map (available from the i-SITE (p644) and other outlets, and online at www.craftbrewing capital.co.nz) and wind your way between brewers and pubs. Top picks for a tipple include Free House and McCashin's Hop Garden (p640) in Nelson, McCashin's Brewery (p640) in Stoke, Hop Federation (p650) in Riwaka, and the Townshend Brewery at Motueka's T.O.A.D Hall (p647).

NELSON & MARLBOROUGH NELSON

Sprig & Fern CRAFT BEER
(Map p641; ☑03-548 1154; www.sprigandfern.
co.nz; 280 Hardy St; ⊙11am-midnight; ⊛) This
outpost of a Richmond brewery offers 18
brews on tap, including three limited releases. No pokies and no TV; just decent beer, NZ
wines, pizza, $10 lunch specials, occasional
live music and a pleasant outdoor area. Look
for a second Sprig at 143 Milton St.

Theatre Royal THEATRE
(Mapp641;☑03-5483840;www.theatreroyalnelson.
co.nz; 78 Rutherford St; ⊙box office 10am-4pm
Mon-Fri) Built in 1878, this charmingly
restored heritage theatre hosts a full roster
of local and touring drama, dance and musical productions. Check the website for the
current programme or visit the box office.

🛍 Shopping

Nelson Market MARKET
(Map p641; ☑03-546 6454; www.nelsonmarket.
co.nz; Montgomery Sq; ⊙8am-1pm Sat) This big,
busy weekly market has fresh produce, food
stalls, fashion, local arts, crafts and buskers.

Jens Hansen JEWELLERY
(Map p641; ☑03-548 0640; www.jenshansen.com;
320 Trafalgar Sq; ⊙9am-5pm Mon-Fri, to 2pm Sat
year-round, 10am-1pm Sun Nov-Easter) Catapulted to fame after designing the One Ring for
the *Lord of the Rings* movies, this contemporary jeweller now does a brisk trade in
Elvish-inscribed engagement rings for those
unfazed by the prospect of their fiancé or fi-
ancée vanishing or turning into an evil meg-
alomaniac. There are plenty of other elegant
designs available for those with quibbles
about such things.

ℹ Information

MEDICAL SERVICES

Medical & Injury Centre (☑03-546 8881; 98
Waimea Rd; ⊙8am-10pm) Duty doctors working late at a clinic attached to Nelson Hospital.
Nelson Hospital (☑03-546 1800; www.
nmdhb.govt.nz; Tipahi St)

TOURIST INFORMATION

DOC Whakatū/Nelson Visitor Centre (Map
p641; ☑03-546 9339; www.doc.govt.nz; 77
Trafalgar St; ⊙8.30am-5pm) The main DOC
Visitor Centre for the Top of the South, includ-
ing the Kahurangi and Abel Tasman National
Parks. Call in for up-to-date information on
tracks including the Heaphy, Abel Tasman
Coast and Queen Charlotte.
Nelson i-SITE (Map p641; ☑03-548 2304; www.
nelsontasman.nz; 77 Trafalgar St; ⊙8.30am-

5pm Oct-Easter, 10am-4pm Easter-Sep) A slick,
information-packed tourist office, sharing space
with the DOC Visitor Centre. Pick up a copy of the
Nelson Tasman Visitor Guide.

ℹ Getting There & Away

AIR

Nelson Airport is 5km southwest of town, near
Tahunanui Beach. A taxi between the airport
and the town centre will cost around $30, while
Super Shuttle (☑0800 748 885; www.super-
shuttle.co.nz) offers a door-to-door service for
around $18.
  Scheduled flights include:
Air New Zealand (☑0800 737 000; www.
airnewzealand.co.nz) To/from Auckland, Wellington and Christchurch;
Golden Bay Air (p655) To/from Takaka;
Originair (☑0800 380 380; www.originair.
co.nz) To/from Palmerston North, New Plymouth and Napier;
Sounds Air (☑03-520 3080; www.soundsair.
com) To/from Wellington and the Kāpiti Coast.

BUS

Regional buses depart from outside the centrally
located **Nelson SBL Travel Centre** (Map p641;
☑03-548 1539; www.nelsoncoachlines.co.nz;
27 Bridge St; ⊙7am-5.15pm Mon-Fri).

ScenicNZ Abel Tasman (☑03-548 0285;
www.scenicnzabeltasman.co.nz) operates one
or two buses a day to Motueka ($14, one hour),
Kaiteriteri ($21, 1½ hours) and Mārahau ($21,
1¾ hours).

Golden Bay Coachlines (☑03-525 8352;
www.goldenbaycoachlines.co.nz) has a daily
service to Motueka ($14, 45 minutes) and
Takaka ($39, two hours) year-round, with a
second bus from November to March that continues on to Collingwood ($54, 2½ hours) and
the Heaphy Track trailhead ($65, three hours),
or to Pōhara ($49, 2¼ hours) and Tōtaranui
($59, three hours).

InterCity (☑03-365 1113; www.intercity.co.nz)
heads to destinations including Havelock ($15,
1¼ hours), Picton ($23, 2¼ hours), Blenheim
($23, 1¾ hours), Westport ($36, 3½ hours) and
Greymouth ($48, six hours).

ℹ Getting Around

NBus (☑03-548 3290; www.nbus.co.nz)
Nelson Suburban Bus Lines (SBL) operates
services between Nelson and Richmond ($4)
via Tahunanui ($3) and Stoke ($3.50). Buses
run from roughly 7am to 7pm; pay the driver in
cash or buy a 10-trip ticket. On weekends, the
Late Late Bus (flat fare $4) departs from the
Westpac Bank on Trafalgar St at 10pm, 11pm,
1am, 2am and 3.15am.

TASMAN DISTRICT

Named after Dutch explorer Abel Tasman, who landed here in 1642, the Tasman District stretches north to Farewell Spit at the very tip of the South Island and south to the Nelson Lakes. With the twin delights of Tasman Bay (Te Tai-o-Aorere) and Golden Bay (Mohua) along with three highly scenic national parks (Kahurangi, Abel Tasman and Nelson Lakes), it's easy to see why it's such a popular travel destination for international and domestic travellers alike. It's also one of New Zealand's sunniest spots.

Nelson Lakes National Park

Nelson Lakes National Park surrounds two lakes – Rotoiti ('small lake') and Rotoroa ('long lake') – fringed by sweet-smelling beech forest with a backdrop of greywacke mountains. Located at the northern end of the Southern Alps, and with a dramatic glacier-carved landscape, it's an awe-inspiring place to get up on high.

Part of the park, east of Lake Rotoiti, is classed as a 'mainland island' where a conservation scheme aims to eradicate introduced pests (rats, possums and stoats), and regenerate native flora and fauna. It offers excellent hiking, including short walks, lake scenery and one or two sandflies... The park is flush with bird life, and famous for brown-trout fishing. The human hub of the Nelson Lakes region is the small, low-key village of St Arnaud.

🏃 Activities

Many spectacular walks allow you to appreciate this rugged landscape, but before you tackle them, stop by the DOC Nelson Lakes Visitor Centre (p645) for maps, track and weather updates, and to pay your hut or camping fees.

There are two fantastic day hikes to be had: the St Arnaud Range Track (p639) and the five-hour Mt Robert Circuit Track, which starts at Mt Robert car park – a short, rough drive away from St Arnaud – and circumnavigates the mountain. The optional side trip along Robert Ridge offers staggering views into the heart of the national park. Only attempt these hikes in fine weather. At other times they are pointless (no views) and potentially dangerous.

There are also plenty of shorter (and flatter) walks from Lake Rotoiti's Kerr Bay and the road end at Lake Rotoroa. These and the longer day hikes are described in DOC's *Walks in Nelson Lakes National Park* pamphlet ($2). The fit and well equipped can embark upon longer hikes such as the Lake Angelus Track (p639).

🛏 Sleeping

Travers-Sabine Lodge   HOSTEL $
(☑ 03-521 1887; www.nelsonlakes.co.nz; Main Rd, St Arnaud; dm/r without bathroom $35/79; 🅿 🐾 📶) This hostel is a great base for outdoor adventure – it's a short walk to Lake Rotoiti, inexpensive, clean and comfortable. It also has particularly cheerful technicolor linen in the dorms, doubles and family room. The owners are experienced adventurers themselves, so advice comes as standard.

Alpine Lodge   LODGE $$
(☑ 03-521 1869; www.alpinelodge.co.nz; Main Rd, St Arnaud; r from $180; 🅿 📶) Family owned and a consistent performer, this large Swiss chalet–style complex offers a range of accommodation, the pick of which are the split-level studios with mezzanine bedrooms and spa baths. If nothing else, go for the inviting in-house restaurant – a snug affair sporting an open fire, mountain views, good food (mains $20 to $35) and local beer.

ℹ Information

DOC Nelson Lakes Visitor Centre (☑ 03-521 1806; www.doc.govt.nz; View Rd; ⊘ 9am-4pm) Proffers park-wide information (weather, track status, activities) and hut passes, plus displays on park ecology and history.

ℹ Getting There & Away

There's no public transport to this national park. If you don't have a car, your best bet is to book an on-demand hikers' shuttle with the likes of **Nelson Lakes Shuttles** (☑ 03-547 6896; www.nelsonlakesshuttles.co.nz) or **Trek Express** (☑ 03-540 2042; www.trekexpress.co.nz).

ℹ Getting Around

Lake Rotoiti Water Taxis (☑ 021 702 278; www.rotoitiwatertaxis.co.nz; Kerr Bay; up to 3/4 passengers $110/140) Runs to/from Kerr Bay (St Arnaud) to West Bay, Coldwater or Lakehead at the southern end of Rotoiti. It also hires out kayaks (per hour/day $15/75) and canoes ($25/100).

Ruby Coast & Moutere Hills

It's possible to blast between Nelson and Motueka in 40 minutes via SH6 and SH60 but, if you've got the time, there are plenty of interesting diversions to slow you down. This is the heart of Nelson's wine region; pick up the *Nelson Wine Guide* pamphlet (www.winenelson.co.nz), which lists details for 21 wineries.

A short detour leads along the Ruby Coast to little Māpua with its surprisingly hip wharf precinct consisting of cafes, artsy shops, a brewery, wine bar and coffee roastery. Alternatively, take the inland Moutere Hwy, which traverses gently rolling countryside dotted with farms, orchards and lifestyle blocks. It's a scenic and fruitful drive, particularly in high summer when roadside stalls are laden with fresh produce. The main settlement along the way is Upper Moutere, a sleepy hamlet that was first settled by German immigrants.

The whole area can be explored by bicycle on the Great Taste Trail (p636).

◉ Sights

The Nelson and Motueka i-SITEs stock a range of pamphlets – including *Great Taste Trail*, *Nelson Wine Guide*, *Nelson Art Guide*, *Nelson's Creative Pathways* and *Moutere Artisans map* (www.moutereartisans.co.nz) – outlining an eclectic set of stops in the area.

★ **Moturoa/Rabbit Island**   ISLAND
(⊙ dawn-dusk) With a Māori name that translates as 'Long Island', this low-lying expanse forms an 8km-long barrier to the ocean with a gorgeous sandy beach spread along its entire length. A pine plantation forest provides shade for the cyclists on the Great Taste Trail (p636), which passes through. You're likely to see weka, inquisitive flightless birds similar to kiwi but with much shorter beaks, here. Rabbit Island is the largest of a brace of islands at the mouth of the Waimea River with similarly prosaic names such as Best, Rough, Bird and Bell. A signposted turn-off from SH60 leads onto Redwood Rd, which passes by bridge onto Rough Island and then Rabbit Island. The bridge closes at sunset and overnight stays are not allowed. The island can also be reached by the Māpua Ferry ($12 return, 10 minutes), run by Kiwi Journeys (p636), but in winter this only operates on weekends.

Höglund Art Glass   GALLERY
(☑ 03-544 6500; www.hoglundartglass.com; 52 Lansdowne Rd, Appleby; ⊙ 10am-5pm) The Höglunds have had their art glass exhibited internationally and even featured on a jointly issued Swedish and New Zealand postage stamp. Call into their shop to admire the colourful collection and then pop into the next room, which has displays on the process and windows facing onto the furnace and workshop. If you don't fancy weighing down your luggage with a signature vase, the jewellery and penguins make memorable souvenirs.

Neudorf Vineyards   WINERY
(☑ 03-543 2643; www.neudorf.co.nz; 138 Neudorf Rd, Upper Moutere; ⊙ 11am-5pm Oct-Apr, hours vary May-Sep) 🥐 Sitting pretty in Upper Moutere, with views across the grapes to the mountains of Kahurangi National Park, bijou Neudorf produces gorgeous wines including seductive pinot noir and some of NZ's finest chardonnay. A $5 donation to the local rescue helicopter service is requested for tastings. Cheese platters can be purchased, but you're welcome to bring your own picnic to enjoy in the grounds.

Seifried   WINERY
(☑ 03-544 5599; www.seifried.co.nz; 184 Redwood Rd, Appleby; ⊙ 10am-4pm) Situated at the SH60 Moturoa/Rabbit Island turn-off, Seifried is one of the region's biggest wineries. Try its chardonnay and delicious Sweet Agnes riesling.

✖ Eating & Drinking

Smokehouse   FISH & CHIPS $
(☑ 0800 540 2280; www.smokehouse.co.nz; Māpua Wharf, Māpua; fish & chips $9.40-13; ⊙ 11am-7pm) Visit this Māpua institution to order fish and chips and eat them on the wharf while the gulls eye off your crispy bits. Get some wood-smoked fish and pâté to go.

Jester House   CAFE $$
(☑ 03-526 6742; www.jesterhouse.co.nz; 320 Aporo Rd, Tasman; mains $13-22; ⊙ 9am-4.30pm, closed Aug; 🖥) Long-standing Jester House is reason alone to take this coastal detour, as much for its tame eels (friendly critters that like to be hand fed) as for the peaceful sculpture gardens that encourage you to linger over lunch. A short, simple menu includes a few twists (venison goulash; twice-cooked three-cheese soufflé). It's roughly 8km from both Māpua and Motueka.

Moutere Inn   PUB
([☎]03-543 2759; www.moutereinn.co.nz; 1406
Moutere Hwy, Upper Moutere; [☺]noon-9pm) One
of NZ's oldest pubs, the Moutere Inn (built
1850) is a welcoming establishment serving
meals (homemade burgers, fish and chips,
curries) and craft beer, including its own
Moutere Brewing Co range. Sit in the sunshine or settle inside on music nights, which
have a folksy bent.

❶ Getting There & Away

Buses on the Nelson–Motueka route head along
SH60 but there are no buses to the Ruby Coast
or Moutere Hills. Biking the Great Taste Trail
(p636) is a good way of exploring.

Motueka

POP 7600

Motueka (pronounced maw-tu-eh-ka) is a
bustling agricultural hub and the closest
decent-sized town to the Abel Tasman and
Kahurangi National Parks. It has a good selection of accommodation and cafes, a large
supermarket and roadside fruit stalls; stock
up here if you're heading north. If you're cycling the Great Taste Trail (p636), it's a great
place to break up the trip.

While you might not realise it from the
main street, Motueka is just a stone's throw
from the sea. Walk or cycle along the muddy
estuary, with its saltwater baths and exposed
shipwreck, then continue on foot along the
Motueka Sandspit, an important habitat
for birds such as oystercatchers, terns, shags
and godwits. The last of these are known to
migrate between here and Alaska's Yukon
Delta – a distance of 11,500km – in less than
a week, flying nonstop.

◉ Sights & Activities

Motueka District Museum   MUSEUM
(Map p648; [☎]03-528 7660; www.motuekadistrict
museum.org.nz; 140 High St; [☺]10am-3pm Sun-Fri
Dec-Mar, Tue-Fri & Sun Apr-Nov) [FREE] Housed in
an attractive 1913-built school building, this
museum has a tiny but interesting collection
of regional artefacts.

Skydive Abel Tasman   ADVENTURE SPORTS
([☎]03-528 4091; www.skydive.co.nz; Motueka Aerodrome, 16 College St; jumps 9000/13,000/16,500ft
$279/329/419) Move over, Taupō: we've
jumped both and think Motueka takes the
cake. Presumably so do the many sports
jumpers who favour this drop zone, some of

whom you may see rocketing in. Spectators
can spread out on the front lawn.

🛏 Sleeping

Motueka Top 10 Holiday Park   HOLIDAY PARK $
(Map p648; [☎]03-528 7189; www.motuekatop10.
co.nz; 10 Fearon St; sites from $50, unit with/with-
out bathroom from $120/66; [🛜][♿][👶]) Close to
town and the Great Taste Trail, this place is
packed with grassy, green charm – check out
those lofty kahikatea trees! Shipshape communal amenities include a swimming pool,
a spa and a jumping pillow. There are several accommodation options, from tent sites
to smart cabins and a three-bedroom apartment. Staff can hire bikes, dispense advice
and book local activities.

Equestrian Lodge Motel   MOTEL $$
(Map p648; [☎]03-528 9369; www.equestrianlodge.
co.nz; 2 Avalon Ct; unit $150-225; [P][🛜][♿]) No
horses, no lodge, but no matter. This ex-
cellent motel complex is close to town and
features expansive lawns, rose gardens, and
a heated pool and spa alongside a series of
continually refreshed units. Cheerful owners
will hook you up with local activities.

🍴 Eating & Drinking

Motueka Sunday Market   MARKET $
(Map p648; [☎]03-540 2709; https://motueka
sundaymarket.co.nz; Decks Reserve car park, Wal-
lace St; [☺]8am-1pm Sun) On Sunday morn-
ings the car park behind the i-SITE fills
up with trestle tables laden with produce,
jewellery, clothing, secondhand books, art
and crafts. Food trucks and coffee carts
provide sustenance, while buskers provide
entertainment.

T.O.A.D Hall   CAFE $$
(Map p648; [☎]03-528 6456; www.toadhallmotueka.
co.nz; 502 High St; breakfast $17-22, lunch $9-28,
dinner $25-31; [☺]8am-5pm Sun-Thu, to 10pm Fri
& Sat; [✚][👶]) This fantastic cafe serves excellent breakfasts and lunches such as salmon
hashcakes, lamb burgers, pies and some
good vegan options, then stays open late on
weekends for bistro-style meals and, in summer, live music. Also on offer are smoothies,
juices, baked goods and selected groceries.
Beer and cider are brewed on-site by Townshend Brewery and served in an adjacent
taproom.

Smoking Barrel   BARBECUE $$
(Map p648; [☎]03-528 0693; www.facebook.com/
thesmokingbarrelnz; 105 High St; breakfast $16-

NELSON & MARLBOROUGH MOTUEKA

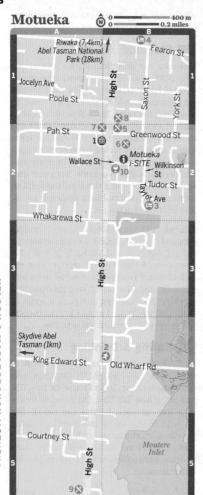

Motueka

Sights

1 Motueka District Museum A2

Activities, Courses & Tours

2 Wilsons B4

Sleeping

3 Equestrian Lodge Motel B2
4 Motueka Top 10 Holiday Park B1

Eating

5 Chokdee B2
6 Motueka Sunday Market B2
7 Precinct Dining Co A2
8 Smoking Barrel B1
9 T.O.A.D Hall A5

Drinking & Nightlife

10 Sprig & Fern B2

11am-2pm & 5pm-late Tue-Sun; 🖉) There's a huge menu to peruse at this highly fragrant restaurant, so cut straight to the house specialties, such as the venison yellow curry and the delicious *phad prik khing pla* (crispy fish red curry). Your next choice is 'mild', 'hot' or 'Thai hot'. Be warned: regular hot is pretty darned hot! There are lots of vegetarian options, too.

Sprig & Fern   CRAFT BEER
(Map p648; 🖉03-528 4684; www.sprigandfern. co.nz; Wallace St; ⊙2pm-late; 🛜🖐) A member of the local Sprig & Fern Brewery family, this back-lane tavern is the pick of Motueka's drinking holes. Small and pleasant, with two courtyards, it offers 20 hand-pulled brews, simple food (pizza, fish and chips, and an awesome burger; meals $16 to $25) and occasional live music.

ℹ Information

Motueka i-SITE (Map p648; 🖉03-528 6543; www.nelsontasman.nz/visit-abel-tasman; 20 Wallace St; ⊙9am-6pm Nov-Mar, to 4pm Apr-Oct) An endlessly busy info centre with helpful staff handling bookings and providing local expertise. DOC information, bookings and passes are also available. There's even an e-bike charging station.

ℹ Getting There & Away

ScenicNZ Abel Tasman (p644) runs daily buses to/from Nelson ($14, one hour), Kaiteriteri ($11, 20 minutes) and Mārahau ($11, 40 minutes). It adds a second bus from November to March.

22, lunch $9-24, dinner $24-40; ⊙8am-10pm Wed-Sun) An old Austin truck serves as the coffee station inside this hip, greenery-filled barbecue joint, where lamb and pork shoulders are grilled for 12 hours and served with flatbread or in Cubano sandwiches. On top of that there are burgers, steaks, bagels, chicken chimichangas and a crazy selection of doughnuts (bacon French toast flavour, anyone?).

Chokdee   THAI $$
(Map p648; 🖉03-528 0318; www.chokdee.co.nz; 109 High St; mains $21-30; ⊙5pm-late Mon,

Golden Bay Coachlines (p644) has a daily service to Nelson ($14, 45 minutes) and Takaka ($28, 1¼ hours) year-round, with a second bus from November to March that continues on to Collingwood ($41, 1¾ hours) and the Heaphy Track trailhead ($52, 2¼ hours), or to Pōhara ($38, 1½ hours) and Tōtaranui ($50, 2¼ hours).

Buses depart from outside the i-SITE.

Kaiteriteri

POP 789

Thanks to its gorgeous golden-sand beach, this seaside hamlet, 13km from Motueka, is the most popular resort town in the area. During the summer holidays there can be more towels than sand, but off-season it's a sleepy place. Kaiteriteri is also a major departure point for Abel Tasman National Park boats, although Mārahau is the main base.

Its other claim to fame is as a cycling destination. It's one of the main hopping-off points of the Great Taste Trail (p636), which passes through a corner of the wonderful Kaiteriteri Mountain Bike Park (☑03-527 8010; www.bikekaiteriteri.co.nz; Martin Farm Rd) FREE on its way into town. This free-to-access, 180-hectare parcel of DOC land has mountain-bike trails to suit all levels of ability. Call into Kiwi Journeys (☑03-548 0093; www.kiwijourneys.co.nz; 3 Kaiteriteri-Sandy Bay Rd), opposite the beach, for bike rental and advice.

★Kaiteri Motels
& Apartments   MOTEL $$
(☑03-527 8063; www.kaiterimotelsandapartments.co.nz; 8 Kotare Pl, Little Kaiteriteri Beach; unit from $190; P🐾) Just 200m from Little Kaiteriteri Beach (around the corner from the main beach) is this congregation of comfortable, stylishly furnished, roomy units with full kitchens and laundry facilities. Guests can also make use of a ferny barbecue area and spa pool.

Bellbird Lodge   B&B $$$
(☑03-527 8555; www.bellbirdlodge.co.nz; 160 Kaiteriteri-Sandy Bay Rd; s/d $350/375; ⊗Oct-Apr; P🐾) This upmarket B&B, 1.5km up the hill from Kaiteriteri Beach, offers two en-suite rooms, bush and sea views, extensive gardens, spectacular breakfasts (featuring homemade muesli and fruit compote), and gracious hosts.

❶ Getting There & Away

ScenicNZ Abel Tasman (p644) runs daily buses to/from Nelson ($21, 1½ hours), Motueka ($11, 20 minutes) and Mārahau ($8, 20 minutes); two daily in summer.

Mārahau

POP 120

Just up the coast from Kaiteriteri and 18km north of Motueka, Mārahau (properly pronounced '*Mah*-rah-ho') is the main gateway to Abel Tasman National Park. It's less of a town, more of a procession of holiday homes and tourist businesses lining a big beach.

🏃 Activities

Abel Tasman Horse Trekking   HORSE RIDING
(☑03-527 8232; www.abeltasmanhorsetrekking.co.nz; Ocean View Chalets, 305 Sandy Bay–Mārahau Rd; 2hr ride $115) Head here for the chance to belt along the beach on horseback; training is available for newbie riders. Younger ones (under 12) can be led around a paddock on a pony for 30 minutes ($40) after helping to brush and saddle up their mount.

🛌 Sleeping

Adventure Inn   HOSTEL $
(☑0800 713 000; www.adventureinn.co.nz; 269 Sandy Bay–Mārahau Rd; dm $35; P❄🐾) With a 20-seat cinema, two pool tables, takeaways served from an old bus, and air-conditioned dorms with personal lights and charging ports, this isn't your run-of-the-mill hostel. Plus there's a barbecue and a firepit – perfect for swapping Coast Track tips over a few beers.

The Barn   HOSTEL $
(☑03-527 8043; www.barn.co.nz; 14 Harvey Rd; sites per person from $22, dm/tw/d without bathroom $30/89/99; P🐾) Part backpackers, part campground, The Barn offers comfortable dorms, private microcabins and a grassy camping field, along with alfresco kitchens and barbecue areas. The barn itself is the hub – the communal kitchen and lounge area are good for socialising, as is the central deck, which has a fireplace. Activity bookings and secure parking are available.

Ocean View Chalets   CHALET $$
(☑03-527 8232; www.accommodationabeltasman.co.nz; 305 Sandy Bay–Mārahau Rd; unit from $145; P🐾) 🍃 On a leafy hillside affording plenty of privacy, these cheerful, cypress-lined chalets

RIWAKA

Just over the river from Motueka, Riwaka is a small settlement at the heart of fertile plains planted with orchards, vineyards and hops. If you're peckish while you're careering along SH60, there is a couple of roadside cafes and, in season, a stall selling cherries.

It's well worth taking a 6km detour to the end of Riwaka Valley Rd where a 10-minute walk through native bush leads to the peaceful **Riuwaka Resurgence** (Te Puna o Riu-waka in Māori, meaning 'The Spring of Riuwaka'). In this pocket of Kahurangi National Park, the Riuwaka River emerges from the base of Takaka Hill in a crystalline pool set within a ferny glade. This *wāhi tapu* (sacred place) was once used by the local Te Ātiawa and Ngāti Rārua people for cleansing and healing rituals. If you're wondering about the different spellings, Riwaka is a historic misspelling of the Māori name Riuwaka. It's been officially corrected for the name of the river but not the town.

Hop Federation (☑ 03-528 0486; www.hopfederation.co.nz; 483 Main Rd; ⊙ 11am-6pm) Pop in for tastings and fill a flagon to go at this teeny-weeny but terrific craft brewery. Pick of the ales is the Red IPA.

Eden's Edge Lodge (☑ 03-528 4242; www.edensedge.co.nz; 137 Lodder Lane; d/tw/tr $120/120/150; [P][🛜]) Surrounded by farmland, this friendly lodge's facilities include attractive, comfy, en-suite rooms and relaxed communal areas. A do-it-yourself breakfast is included – with organic eggs from the owners' hens – and there are fresh herbs aplenty in the garden for cooking up in the spotless kitchen. An arcade machine in the lounge is loaded with every game imaginable.

Resurgence (☑ 03-528 4664; www.resurgence.co.nz; 574 Riwaka Valley Rd; s/d from $725/745; [P][🛜][🏊]) Choose a luxurious en-suite room or a self-contained 'bush suite' chalet at this magical green retreat. At peak times, rates include breakfast as well as aperitifs and a four-course dinner. At other times B&B-only rates are available.

Ginger Dynamite (☑ 021 168 8736; www.gingerdynamite.co.nz; 488 Main Rd; mains $6-8; ⊙ 8am-2.30pm) Operating out of a pair of brightly painted shipping containers, one of them set up to resemble a 1970s Kiwi bach (holiday house), this quirky coffee cart serves tasty meat pies, seafood chowder and scones to passing cyclists and motorists.

are 300m from the Coast Track with views out to Motuareroiti/Fisherman Island. All except the cheapest studios are self-contained; buffet breakfast and packed lunches are available.

Abel Tasman Lodge MOTEL $$$
(☑ 03-527 8250; www.abeltasmanlodge.co.nz; 295 Sandy Bay–Mārahau Rd; unit from $200; [P][❄][🛜])
🍴 Evoke halcyon days in this renovated arc of studios and self-contained apartments with hip styling and cathedral ceilings, opening onto landscaped gardens. There's also a communal kitchen, barbecues and a spa pool. Tui and bellbirds squawk and warble in the bushy surrounds, and some of the interior decor is styled after local bird life.

🍴 Eating

Fat Tui BURGERS $
(☑ 03-527 8420; cnr Sandy Bay–Mārahau & Mārahau Valley Rds; mains $12-17; ⊙ noon-8pm Nov-May) Everyone's heard about this bird, based in a caravan that isn't going anywhere. Thank goodness. It serves superlative burg-

ers, such as the Cowpat (beef), the Ewe Beaut (Morrocan lamb) and Roots, Shoots & Leaves (vegie). Fish and chips, and coffee, too.

Hooked CAFE $$
(☑ 03-527 8576; www.hookedonmarahau.co.nz; 229 Sandy Bay–Mārahau Rd; breakfast $17-20, mains $24-29; ⊙ 8am-10pm Dec-Mar, 8-11am & 4-8pm Mon, Tue, Thu & Fri, 8am-8pm Sat & Sun Oct, Nov & Apr; 🍴)
🍴 The art-bedecked interior of this popular place opens on to an outdoor terrace with distracting views. Seafood is showcased on the menu, including *kokoda/ika mata* (Pasifika-style raw fish in lemon and coconut milk), fish and chips, grilled salmon, banana-leaf snapper and seafood spaghetti, alongside local lamb, burgers and salad bowls. Pop in for happy hour drinks from 4pm to 6pm.

Park Cafe CAFE $$
(☑ 03-527 8270; www.parkcafe.co.nz; 350 Sandy Bay–Mārahau Rd; pizza $18-24; ⊙ 8am-late Wed-Sun Nov-May; 🍴) At the Coast Track trailhead, this breezy cafe is perfect for fuelling up or

replenishing reserves. High-calorie options include the big breakfast, burgers and cakes, but there are also seafood and salad options, plus wood-fired pizza Wednesday through Saturday evenings. Enjoy in the room with a view or the sunny courtyard garden. Check online for occasional live music listings.

❶ Getting There & Away

ScenicNZ Abel Tasman (p644) runs daily buses to/from Nelson ($21, 1¾ hours), Motueka ($11, 40 minutes) and Kaiteriteri ($8, 20 minutes); two daily in summer.

Abel Tasman National Park

Coastal Abel Tasman National Park blankets the northern end of a range of marble and limestone hills that extends from Kahurangi National Park. There are various tracks in the park, although the Coast Track (p637) is what everyone is here for – it's New Zealand's most popular Great Walk.

The main reason for the track's popularity is that it traverses some of New Zealand's (and arguably the world's) finest golden-sand beaches. Only a few can be reached by road, but non–Great Walkers can access others by kayak, water taxi or one of the scheduled boat transfers.

🏃 Activities

Those wanting a quieter alternative to the Coast Track (p637) might like to consider the Inland Track, a tougher and much less frequented path taking three days. It

explores the forested interior and hence doesn't compete with the coast in terms of scenery. It can be combined with the Coast Track to form a five- to six-day loop.

If you can only spare a couple of days, a deservedly popular option is the loop around the northern end of the park, hiking the Coast Track from Tōtaranui, passing Anapai and Mutton Cove, overnighting at Whariwharangi Hut, then returning to Tōtaranui via the Gibbs Hill Track. This will give you a slice of the park's best features (beaches, seals, coastal scenery) and will be far less crowded than any other segment.

Perhaps the best non-coastal walk is the Wainui Falls Track, an easy 25-minute, 2km-each-way path through beautiful native bush. The track leads alongside a boulder-strewn river and across two suspension bridges to the waterfall, which crashes violently into a green-tinged pool. The car park is well signposted from Abel Tasman Drive, 11km east of Pōhara.

🌿 Tours

Tour companies usually offer free Motueka pick-up/drop-off, with Nelson pick-up available at extra cost.

★ Abel Tasman Canyons   ADVENTURE
(📞 03-528 9800; www.abeltasmancanyons.co. nz; full-day trip $289; ☺ Oct-Apr) Few Abel Tasman visitors see the Torrent River, but here's your chance to journey down its staggeringly beautiful granite-lined canyon, via a fun-filled combination of swimming, sliding, abseiling, ziplining and big leaps into jewel-like pools. Other trips explore

---

THE PEOPLE'S BEACH

When an 800m arc of Awaroa Bay in Abel Tasman National Park was offered for sale by a private owner in late 2015, there was concern that overseas buyers could secure the sheltered slice of paradise. But following chats over a few beers on Christmas Day 2015, up stepped two proud South Islanders to rally the public of NZ and instigate the biggest crowd-funding campaign the country has ever seen.

Against the threat of offshore purchasers winning the tender for the 7 hectares of coastal perfection, Duane Major and Adam Gard'ner – both regular summertime visitors to the bays and coves of Abel Tasman National Park – launched a campaign on the NZ crowdfunding website, Givealittle, to secure the beach for all New Zealanders.

By the time the deadline was reached in February 2016, 29,239 private donors had raised $2,259,923, and, along with significant corporate donations and $350,000 from the NZ government, the winning tender of more than $2.8 million was reached.

Less than five months later, Awaroa Bay was officially incorporated into Abel Tasman National Park. With its now-protected status, there are ongoing efforts to restore the beach's sand-dune ecosystem, and native plant species are being replanted to improve the habitat for coastal birds, including oystercatchers, dotterel and godwits.

PADDLING THE ABEL TASMAN

The Abel Tasman Coast Track has long been hiking territory, but its coastal beauty makes it an equally seductive spot for sea kayaking, which can easily be combined with walking and camping.

A variety of professional outfits are able to float you out on the water, and the possibilities and permutations for guided or freedom trips are vast. You can kayak from half a day up to three days, staying in DOC huts or campsites (book in advance online before entering the park), or in any of the other park accommodation. You can kayak one day, camp overnight then walk back, or walk further into the park and catch a water taxi back.

Most operators offer similar trips at similar prices, focusing on the safer southern half of the park (as far as Onetahuti Beach). Mārahau is the main base, but trips also depart from Kaiteriteri. There are numerous day-trip options, including guided trips often departing from Mārahau and taking in bird-filled Motuareronui/Adele Island (around $200). There are also various multiday guided trips, with three days a common option, costing anything from $285 to $900 depending on accommodation and other inclusions.

Freedom rentals (double-kayak and equipment hire) are around $85/130 per person for one/two days; all depart from Mārahau with the exception of Golden Bay Kayaks (p657), which is based at Tata Beach in Golden Bay. Instruction is given to everyone, and most tour companies have a minimum age of either eight or 14 depending on the trip. None allow solo hires. Camping gear is usually provided on overnight trips; if you're disappearing into the park for a few days, most operators provide free car parking.

November to Easter is the busiest time, with December to February the absolute peak. You can, however, paddle all year round, with winter offering its own rewards; the weather is surprisingly amenable, the seals are more playful, and there's more bird life and less haze. Here are the key players in this competitive market (shop around):

Abel Tasman Kayaks (☑ 03-527 8022; www.abeltasmankayaks.co.nz; 273 Sandy Bay–Mārahau Rd, Mārahau; guided tours from $120, full-day rental $45) 🛶

Kahu Kayaks (☑ 03-527 8300; www.kahukayaks.co.nz; 325 Sandy Bay-Mārahau Rd, Mārahau; guided tour from $100, full-day rental $85)

Kaiteriteri Kayaks (☑ 03-527 8383; www.seakayak.co.nz; 3 Kaiteriteri-Sandy Bay Rd, Kaiteriteri; ⊙ half-day tour adult/child from $90/65, 1/2/3/4hr rental $30/45/55/60)

Mārahau Sea Kayaks (☑ 03-527 8176; www.msk.co.nz; 229 Sandy Bay-Mārahau Rd, Mārahau; tours from $130, full-day rental from $85) 🛶

R&R Kayaks (☑ 03-527 8197; www.rrkayaks.co.nz; 279 Sandy Bay-Mārahau Rd, Mārahau; tours from $150, full-day rental $85)

Wilsons (p652)

Kahurangi National Park and Mt Richmond Forest Park, and combo adventures including kayaking or skydiving are also available.

Wilsons OUTDOORS
(Map p648; ☑ 03-528 2027; www.abeltasman.co.nz; 409 High St, Motueka; walks, cruises $38-89, tours $79-185) This long-standing, family-owned operator offers an impressive array of cruises, walking, kayaking and combo tours. Overnight stays are available at Wilsons' lodges in pretty Awaroa and Torrent Bay for guided-tour guests. Offers an Explorer Pass for unlimited boat travel on three days over a seven-day period (adult/child $158/79).

🛏 Sleeping

Along the Abel Tasman Coast Track are four Great Walk huts ($75) with bunks, heating, flush toilets and limited lighting, but no cooking facilities. There are also 18 designated Great Walk campsites ($30). All Great Walks huts and campsites must be booked in advance online year-round (www.doc.govt.nz). Penalty fees apply to those who do not have a valid booking, and you may be required to leave the park if caught.

Tōtaranui Campground CAMPGROUND **$**
(☑ 03-528 8083; www.doc.govt.nz; adult/child $15/7.50) Not to be confused with the adjacent Tōtaranui Great Walk Campsite, this extremely popular facility has a whopping

Abel Tasman National Park

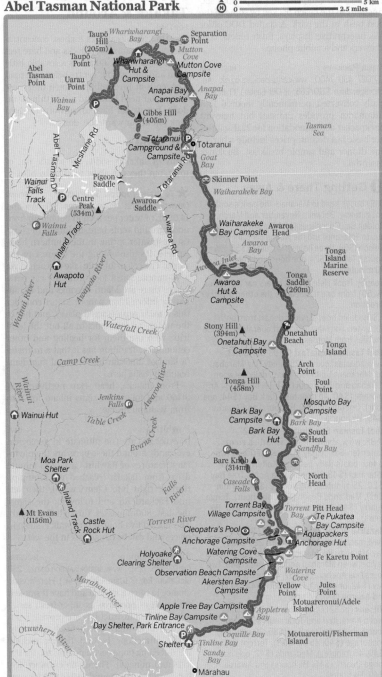

capacity (850 campers) and a splendid setting next to the beach backed by some of the best bush in the park. A staffed DOC office has interpretive displays, flush toilets, cold showers and a public phone.

Aqua Packers   HOSTEL $$$

([phone] 027 430 7400; www.aquapackers.co.nz; Anchorage; dm/r $110/265; ⊙ Oct–Easter) This specially converted, permanently moored 13m catamaran provides unusual but buoyant backpacker accommodation for 22. Facilities are basic but decent; prices include a barbecue dinner and simple breakfast. Bookings essential.

ⓘ Getting There & Away

Daily buses head to Mārahau, the park's southern gateway. Between November and March, Golden Bay Coachlines (p644) also has a daily bus to Tōtaranui and the Wainui car park from Nelson ($59, three hours), Motueka ($50, 2¼ hours), Takaka ($24, one hour) and Pōhara ($20, 50 minutes).

Heaphy Track Help (p659) offers car relocation ($250) from one trailhead to the other, in either direction.

Scheduled boat services depart from both Kaiteriteri and Mārahau. Most operators provide shuttles from Motueka.

Abel Tasman AquaTaxi ([phone] 03-527 8083; www.aquataxi.co.nz; 275 Sandy Bay-Mārahau Rd, Mārahau) Up to four boats daily between Mārahau and Tōtaranui ($51, 1¾ hours) via Anchorage ($40, 45 minutes), Bark Bay ($44, one hour), Onetahuti ($46, 1¼ hours) and Awaroa ($49, 1½ hours).

Abel Tasman Sea Shuttle ([phone] 03-527 8688; www.abeltasmanseashuttles.co.nz; 2 Kaiteriteri-Sandy Bay Road, Kaiteriteri) Two to four boats daily between Kaiteriteri and Tōtaranui ($48, 1½ hours) via Apple Tree Bay ($20, 25 minutes), Anchorage ($34, 50 minutes), Medlands Beach ($38, one hour), Tonga Quarry ($40, 1¼ hours) and Awaroa ($45, 1½ hours).

Marahau Water Taxis ([phone] 03-527 8176; www.marahauwatertaxis.co.nz; 229 Sandy Bay-Mārahau Rd, Mārahau) Two to four boats a day between Mārahau and Tōtaranui ($49, two hours) via Anchorage ($37, 45 minutes), Bark Bay ($42, one hour), Onetahuti ($44, 1¼ hours) and Awaroa ($47, 1½ hours).

Wilsons (p652) One to four boats daily between Kaiteriteri and Tōtaranui ($51, two hours) via Apple Tree Bay ($35, 20 minutes), Anchorage ($40, 45 minutes), Torrent Bay ($40, 45 minutes), Medlands ($42, one hour), Tonga Quarry ($46, 1½ hours) and Awaroa ($49, 1¾ hours).

NELSON & MARLBOROUGH TAKAKA & AROUND

Takaka & Around

POP 1240

Boasting New Zealand's highest concentration of yoga pants, dreadlocks and bare feet in the high street, Takaka is a lovable little town and the last 'big' centre before the road west ends at Farewell Spit. You'll find most things you need here, and a few things you don't, but we all have an unworn tie-dyed tank top in our wardrobe, don't we?

⊙ Sights

Many of Takaka's sights are a little out of town, but they can all be reached by bike.

★ **Te Waikoropupū Springs**   SPRING
(www.doc.govt.nz; Pupu Springs Rd) Around 14,000L of water per second bubble up from underground vents here, making it the largest freshwater spring in the southern hemisphere. It's also among the clearest in the world. The colourful little lake is reached via a 45-minute forest loop from the car park, where there are Māori carvings and illuminating information panels. Māori consider this a *wāhi tapu* (sacred place), and hence the waters are off limits to all but the local tribe who use them for healing and other ceremonies. Tradition has it that a *taniwha* (a kind of dinosaur-like spiritual guardian) regularly visits here.

From Takaka, head 4km northwest on SH60 and follow the signs inland for 3km from Waitapu Bridge.

Rawhiti Cave   CAVE
(www.doc.govt.nz) The ultimate in geological eye-candy around these parts are the phyto-karst features of Rawhiti Cave, a 15-minute drive from Takaka (reached via Motupipi, turning right into Glenview Rd, then left into Packard Rd and following the signs; the last 800m passes through farmland). The rugged two-hour-return walk is steep in places and can be dangerous in the wet.

Anatoki Salmon   HATCHERY
([phone] 03-525 7251; www.anatokisalmon.co.nz; 230 McCallum Rd; ⊙ 10am-4.30pm; [icon]) Here's your chance to catch a salmon and have it smoked for lunch or prepared as super-fresh sashimi. Rods and instructions are provided, but the fish pretty well catch themselves anyway. Other attractions beyond fishing include hand-feeding tame eels, a petting zoo for the kids and minigolf. There's no entrance fee, but expect to pay around $40 to $55 for your

salmon. Salmon snacks and platters (from $21) are available at the Salmon Cafe.

🏃 Activities

Pupu Hydro Walkway   HIKING
(www.doc.govt.nz; Pupu Valley Rd) Part of Kahurangi National Park, this enjoyable two-hour circuit follows an old water race through beech forest, past engineering and gold-mining relics to the restored (and operational) Pupu Hydro Powerhouse, built in 1929. It's 9km from Takaka at the end of the unsealed but well-maintained Pupu Valley Rd; just follow the signs at the Te Waikoropupū Springs junction and be prepared to cross a couple of fords.

Golden Bay Air   SCENIC FLIGHTS
(☏03-525 8725; www.goldenbayair.co.nz; Takaka Aerodrome, 290 Takaka–Collingwood Hwy; scenic flights per person $50-290) As well as their scheduled flights, this crew offers scenic and charter flights around Golden Bay and its surrounds.

Adventure Flights Golden Bay   SCENIC FLIGHTS
(☏03-525 6167; www.adventureflightsgoldenbay.co.nz; Takaka Aerodrome, 290 Takaka-Collingwood Hwy; scenic flights per person $40-320) Offers scenic and charter flights over the national parks, Farewell Spit and the West Coast.

Quiet Revolution Cycle Shop   CYCLING
(☏03-525 9555; 11 Commercial St; bike hire per day from $25; ⊘9am-4.30pm Tue-Fri, to 12.30pm Sat) You'll get personal service at this most proper of bike shops. It offers town-, mountain- and e-bike hire, plus top-notch servicing and sales, local ride maps and a car relocation service for the Heaphy Track in winter, too.

🛏 Sleeping

Some of the area's best accommodation is out of the town centre, with a couple of great options by the beach at Tukurua, 18km to the north.

Golden Bay Holiday Park   HOLIDAY PARK $
(☏03-525 9742; www.goldenbayholidaypark.co.nz; 99 Tukurua Rd, Tukurua; site/cabin/house from $50/105/195; P@⊚) With a quiet beach right out front, this gem of a park has acres of grass, graceful shade trees and hedgerows, atoning for older communal facilities. There are tidy, family-friendly cabins for budget travellers, and luxury beach houses sleeping up to four.

Kiwiana Backpackers   HOSTEL $
(☏03-525 7676; www.kiwianabackpackers.co.nz; 73 Motupipi St; sites/dm/s/d $20/30/55/70; ⊚) Beyond the welcoming garden and rainbow picket fence is a cute cottage where rooms are named after classic Kiwiana (the jandal, Buzzy Bee...). The garage has been converted into a convivial lounge, with wood-fired stove, table tennis, pool table, music, books and games; free bikes for guest use.

Golden Bay Motel   MOTEL $$
(☏03-525 9428; www.goldenbaymotel.co.nz; 132 Commercial St; unit from $145; P⊚⊞) At the

---

TAKAKA HILL

Takaka Hill (791m) butts in between Tasman Bay and Golden Bay, and between the Abel Tasman and Kahurangi National Parks. It looks fairly bushy but closer inspection reveals a remarkable marble landscape formed by millions of years of erosion. Its smooth beauty is revealed on the one-hour drive over the hill road (SH60), a steep, winding route punctuated by spectacular lookout points and a smattering of other interesting stops.

Just before the summit is the turn-off to Canaan Downs Scenic Reserve, reached at the end of a rough 11km gravel road. This area stars in both *The Lord of the Rings* and *The Hobbit* movies, but Harwoods Hole is the most famous feature here. It's one of the largest *tomo* (caves) in the country at 357m deep and 70m wide, with a 176m vertical drop – although you can't really see much from ground level. It's a 30-minute walk from the car park. Allow us to state the obvious: the cave is off limits to all but the most experienced cavers.

It is possible, however, to take a guided tour of the Ngarua Caves (☏03-528 8093; www.ngaruacaves.co.nz; 1242 SH60; adult/child $20/8; ⊘45min tours hourly 10am-4pm Oct-Apr, phone ahead other months), situated on private land just below the summit of Takaka Hill. The myriad subterranean delights on display here include stalagmites, stalactites and moa bones.

Mountain bikers with intermediate-level skills can venture along a couple of loop tracks, or head all the way down to Takaka via the titillating Rameka Track. Also close to the top, the Takaka Hill Walkway is a 2½-hour loop through marble karst rock formations, native forest and farmland. For more walks, see DOC's *Walks in Golden Bay* brochure.

time of research, new owners were in the process of renovating this old motel, which has units in various configurations. Some of the decor's still a bit dated, but units have kitchens and there's a big garden at the rear with a kids' play set.

★ **Adrift in Golden Bay** COTTAGE $$$
(☑ 03-525 8353; www.adrift.co.nz; 53 Tukurua Rd, Tukurua; villa $399-488; ☺ Sep-May; 🅿 🛜) ✿ Adrift on a bed of beachside bliss is what you'll be in one of these five cottages dotted within gardens, right on the beach. Tuck into your breakfast hamper, then self-cater in the fully equipped kitchen, dine on the sunny deck, or soak in the spa bath. A minimum two-night stay usually applies. A stylish studio is also available.

✖ Eating & Drinking

Wholemeal Cafe CAFE $
(☑ 03-525 9426; www.wholemealcafe.co.nz; 56 Commercial St; mains $9-22; ☺ 7.30am-3pm Sun-Thu, to 7.30pm Fri & Sat; 🛜 ☑ 🍴) Within the cavernous, brightly painted interior of this old theatre is a cabinet groaning under the weight of tempting savoury and sweet options. They bake their own bread, which makes its way into cooked breakfasts and sandwiches. Lunch and dinner options include soup, curry and spanakopita; vegetarians and vegans are well catered for.

Curry Leaf FAST FOOD $
(☑ 03-525 8481; www.thecurryleaf.co.nz; 5a Commercial St; mains $10-19; ☺ 11.30am-9pm; ☑) Trust Takaka to have a kooky takeaway joint in a shipping container, painted with a giant squid mural. The menu isn't run-of-the-mill either. Sure, they do burgers, but there are also naan wraps, and various other Indian and Thai dishes. The fish green curry is excellent; enjoy it at one of the tables out the front or take it away.

Choco Loco SWEETS $
(☑ 027 363 6622; www.chocoloco.co.nz; 47b Commercial St; items $2.50-4.50; ☺ 9am-3pm Mon-Fri, 10am-1pm Sat) Sweet-toothed travellers should start their days with a chocolate-and-almond croissant at this cute little shop, where all the chocolate truffles, brownies and cakes are handcrafted on-site. Order a coffee, tea or hot chocolate and choose a dainty receptacle for it from the 'cup library'.

Roots Bar PUB FOOD $$
(☑ 03-525 9592; www.rootsbar.co.nz; 1 Commercial St; mains $19-32; ☺ 11am-late; 🛜) ✿ Aside from being Takaka's best bar, this hip joint also turns out its most interesting food. Wild game meat finds its way into venison burgers, goat meatballs and Jamaican goat curries, served alongside lamb shanks, steaks and a large selection of burgers. There's a range of good local craft beers, too. Check online for details of regular gigs and DJ sets.

Dangerous Kitchen CAFE $$
(☑ 03-525 8686; www.thedangerouskitchen.co.nz; 46a Commercial St; mains $17-22; ☺ 9am-9pm Mon-Sat, closed Aug; ☑ 🍴) ✿ This cafe serves good-value fare such as falafel salads, pizza, burritos, pasta and baked goods, as well as juices and local wines and craft beer. It's mellow and musical, with a sunny courtyard out the back and people-watching out the front. Check out the quirky mural near the entrance, and ask about occasional live music.

Mussel Inn PUB
(☑ 03-525 9241; www.musselinn.co.nz; 1259 Takaka–Collingwood Hwy, Ōnekakā; ☺ 11am-late) You will find one of NZ's most beloved brewery-taverns halfway between Takaka and Collingwood. The Mussel Inn is rustic NZ at its most genuine, complete with creaking timbers, a rambling beer garden with a brazier, regular music and other events, and hearty, homemade food (snacks $6 to $19, dinner $30). Try the signature Captain Cooker, a brown beer brewed naturally with mānuka.

🛍 Shopping

Shopping in Takaka is a highlight if you enjoy homespun art and craft. Galleries along the main street are worthy of attention.

Dancing Sands Distillery DRINKS
(☑ 03-525 9899; www.dancingsands.com; 46a Commercial St; ☺ 10am-4pm Mon-Sat Nov-Easter, Mon-Fri Easter-Oct) ✿ Here's a surprise – an award-winning distillery tucked down a laneway off Takaka's main street. Its gin and vodka is crafted from water from the same aquifer that feeds the pristine waters of the nearby Te Waikoropupū Springs, and variations include NZ's first barrel-aged gin, and gin flavoured with wasabi, chocolate or saffron. Free tastings will help you choose.

❶ Information

Golden Bay Visitor Centre (☑ 03-525 9136; www.goldenbaynz.co.nz; 8 Willow St; ☺ 9am-5.30pm Oct-Easter, 9.30am-2.30pm Mon-Sat Easter-Sep) A friendly little centre with all the necessary information, including a free tourist map, bookings and DOC passes.

ℹ Getting There & Away

Golden Bay Air (p655) flies to/from Wellington, Nelson and Karamea.

Golden Bay Coachlines (p644) has a daily service from Nelson ($39, two hours) and Motueka ($28, 1¼ hours) year-round, with a second bus from November to March that continues on to Collingwood ($15, 25 minutes) and the Heaphy Track trailhead ($35, one hour), or to Pōhara ($12, 10 minutes) and Tōtaranui ($24, one hour).

Pōhara

POP 571

About 8km northeast of Takaka is pint-sized Pōhara, a beachy village with a population that quadruples over summer. It has more flash holiday homes than other parts of Golden Bay, but an agreeable air persists nonetheless, aided by decent food and lodging, and a beach that at low tide is as big as Heathrow's runway.

Pōhara lies close to the northern gateway of Abel Tasman National Park. The largely unsealed road into the park passes Tarakohe Harbour (Pōhara's working port), followed by Ligar Bay and beautiful Tata Beach. It's worth climbing to the Abel Tasman lookout as you pass by.

◉ Sights & Activities

Grove Scenic Reserve VIEWPOINT
(www.doc.govt.nz; Rocklands Rd, Clifton) Between Pōhara and Takaka (signposted down Clifton Rd), you will find this crazy limestone maze punctuated by gnarled old rata trees and tall pencil-thin nikau palms. The walkway takes around 10 minutes and passes an impressive lookout.

Golden Bay Kayaks KAYAKING
(☑03-525 9095; www.goldenbaykayaks.co.nz; 29 Cornwall Pl, Tata Beach; half-day guided tours $100, half/full day rental $60/80; ⊕) Based at Tata Beach, this long-standing operator runs guided trips (including family-friendly options) and rents kayaks for hour-long to multiday paddles in Abel Tasman National Park, as well as stand-up paddle boards and sit-on-tops.

🛏 Sleeping & Eating

The Sandcastle COTTAGE $$
(☑03-525 9087; www.goldenbayaccommodation. co.nz; 32 Haile Lane; cottages $120-150; P🐾) There's more than a hint of hippy to this complex of six colourful, self-contained cottages set in a peaceful garden with views to the ocean. Don't expect anything flash but there is a pizza oven, a tinkling water feature, and massage and yoga on offer.

Sans Souci Inn LODGE $$
(☑03-525 8663; www.sanssouciinn.co.nz; 11 Richmond Rd; s/d $110/130, units from $170; ⊙mid-Sep–Jun; P🐾) 🌿 Sans souci means 'no worries' in French, and this will be your mantra too after staying in one of the seven Mediterranean-flavoured, mud-brick rooms. Guests share a plant-filled, mosaic bathroom with composting toilets, and an airy lounge and kitchen that open onto a semitropical courtyard. Dinner in the restaurant is highly recommended (bookings essential; summer only); breakfast by request.

Pohara Beach Top 10 HOLIDAY PARK $$
(☑03-525 9500; www.poharabeach.com; 809 Abel Tasman Dr; sites $51-57, unit with/without bathroom $121/85; @🐾) Lining grassy parkland between the dunes and the main road, this place is in prime position for some beach time. Some sites are right by the beach and there are some beaut cabins, but be warned – this is a favourite spot for NZ holidaymakers so it goes a bit mental in high summer. There's a general store and takeaway on-site.

Ratanui LODGE $$$
(☑03-525 7998; www.ratanuilodge.com; 818 Abel Tasman Dr; r $425-455; ⊙closed Aug; 🐾🎴) A romantic wisteria- and grapevine-draped haven close to the beach, this boutique lodge is styled with Victorian panache. It features myriad sensual stimulants such as perfumed rose gardens, a swimming pool, a spa, cocktails and a candelabra-lit restaurant showcasing local produce (open to the public; bookings required). Free bikes, too.

ℹ Getting There & Away

Between November and March, Golden Bay Coachlines (p644) has a daily bus to/from Tōtaranui ($20, 50 minutes), Takaka ($12, 10 minutes), Motueka ($38, 1½ hours) and Nelson ($49, 2¼ hours).

Collingwood & Around

POP 244

Far-flung Collingwood is the northernmost town in Golden Bay, and has a real end-of-the-line vibe. It's busy in summer, though for most people it's simply a launch pad for the Heaphy Track (p638) or Farewell Spit (p658).

NELSON & MARLBOROUGH PŌHARA

CAPE FAREWELL & FAREWELL SPIT

Bleak, exposed and positively sci-fi, Farewell Spit is a wetland of international importance and a renowned bird sanctuary. At low tide a large sandy intertidal zone is exposed on the Golden Bay side – the summer home of thousands of migratory waders, notably the godwit, Caspian tern and Australasian gannet. Unfortunately, the shallow waters are also notorious for mass strandings of pilot whales – in one incident in February 2017, over 400 beached themselves simultaneously; despite the best efforts of an army of volunteers, most of them died.

Walkers can explore the first 4km of the spit via a network of tracks (see DOC's *Farewell Spit & Puponga Farm Park* brochure; $2 or download from www.doc.govt.nz). Beyond that point, access is limited to trips with the brilliant Farewell Spit Tours (p658), scheduled according to tides.

The spit's 35km beach features colossal, crescent-shaped dunes, from where panoramic views extend across Golden Bay and a vast low-tide salt marsh. At the foot of the spit is a hilltop visitor-centre-cum-cafe – a convenient spot to write a postcard over a coffee, especially on an inclement day.

Wharariki Beach This remote, dramatically beautiful beach is a magnificent introduction to the West Coast, with a seal colony at its eastern end and otherworldly rock formations scattered about including, just offshore, the extraordinary Archway Islands. As inviting as the water may seem, don't even think about swimming: strong undertows make it incredibly dangerous. From the turn-off at Puponga it's 6km along an unsealed road, then a 1km walk from the car park over farmland (part of the DOC-administered Puponga Farm Park).

Cape Farewell Horse Treks (☑03-524 8031; www.horsetreksnz.com; 36 McGowan St, Puponga; treks from $100) Befitting a frontier, this is the place to saddle up. Treks in this wind-blown country range from 1½ hours along Puponga Beach to five hours, continuing over Old Man's Range to Wharariki Beach.

Like Takaka, it's got its fair share of hippies. Like Nelson, it's named after a British military hero: the admiral who was Nelson's second in charge at the Battle of Trafalgar.

◉ Sights & Activities

Collingwood Museum   MUSEUM
(☑03-524 8131; 2 Tasman St; ⊙9am-6pm) FREE This tiny unstaffed museum fills a corridor of the former council office with a quirky collection of saddlery, moa bones, shells, sewing machines and old typewriters. Next door, the Aorere Centre has historic photographs of the town by pioneer photographer Fred Tyree.

★ Farewell Spit Tours   ECOTOUR
(☑03-524 8257; www.farewellspit.com; 6 Tasman St; tours $135-170) ✐ Operating for more than 70 years and employing expert, knowledgeable guides, this company runs memorable tours of Farewell Spit ranging from two to 6½ hours. Tours take in the lighthouse and plenty of birdwatching. Expect ripping yarns aplenty.

🛏 Sleeping & Eating

The Innlet   HOSTEL $
(☑03-524 8040; www.theinnlet.co.nz; 839 Collingwood-Puponga Rd, Pakawau; dm $40 s/d with bathroom from $75/95, without $70/90; ⊙Oct-May; 🐾) This leafy charmer is 10km from Collingwood on the way to Farewell Spit. The main house has attractive backpacker rooms, and self-contained options including a cottage sleeping six. Enjoy the garden and explore the local area on a bike, in a kayak or on foot.

Station House Motel   MOTEL $$
(☑03-524 8464; www.accommodationcollingwood. co.nz; 7 Elizabeth St; r/unit from $120/135; 🐾) It seems like false modesty to call this charming accommodation a motel. Rather than a row of cookie-cutter units, there are two small cottages in the back garden and two rooms in an attractive century-old wooden villa. All four are self-contained with en-suite bathrooms and kitchenettes, and there's a guest barbecue, too.

Zatori Retreat   LODGE $$$
(☑03-524 8692; www.zatori.co.nz; 2321 Takaka-Collingwood Hwy; s/tw/d without bathroom $55/

60/140, r with bathroom $229-399; (P)(🛰)) 🌙 This former maternity hospital has been transformed into a stylish, relaxing retreat. Chic suites surround a spacious lounge area enlivened with colourful artworks from Asia, and offering brilliant views over the water. A separate wing houses rooms with shared bathrooms for budget travellers. The restaurant and bar are also open to nonguests.

MAD Café   CAFE **$$**
(🖉 03-524 8660; www.facebook.com/madcafegoldenbay; 7 Tasman St; mains $16-28; ⊙8am-8pm Wed-Sun, daily summer; 🖉 🖬) 🌙 With oddball art on the walls and a barista that looks like he's been beamed in from Woodstock, this is the ultimate Golden Bay hippy cafe. The name stands for Make A Difference; don't be surprised if you stumble into an art class or other community event. The menu is succinct but tasty: breakfasts, laksa, slow-cooked venison, burgers and pan-fried fish.

ℹ Getting There & Away

From November to March, Golden Bay Coachlines (p644) has a daily bus to/from the Heaphy Track trailhead ($25, 40 minutes), Takaka ($15, 25 minutes), Motueka ($41, 1¾ hours) and Nelson ($54, 2½ hours).

Kahurangi National Park

Kahurangi – 'blue skies' in one of several translations – is the second largest of New Zealand's national parks, and also one of its most diverse. Its most eye-catching features are geological, ranging from windswept beaches and sea cliffs to earthquake-shattered slopes and moraine-dammed lakes, and the smooth, strange karst forms of the interior tableland.

Around 85% of the 5173 sq km park is forested, and more than 50% of NZ's plant species can be found here, including more than 80% of its alpine plant species. Among the park's 60 bird species are great spotted kiwi, kea, kākā, takahē and whio (blue duck). There are creepy cave weta, weird beetles and a large, leggy spider, but there's also a majestic and ancient snail known as Powelliphanta – something of a flag bearer for the park's animal kingdom. If you like a field trip filled with the new and strange, Kahurangi National Park will certainly satisfy.

🏃 Activities

The Heaphy Track (p638) and Wangapeka Track (p638) are just part of a 650km network of trails that includes excellent full-day and overnight hikes such as those in the Cobb Valley and Mt Arthur/Tablelands. See www.doc.govt.nz for detailed information on all Kahurangi tracks.

ℹ Getting There & Away

The two road ends of the Heaphy Track are an almost unfathomable distance apart: 449km to be precise. **Heaphy Track Help** (🖉 027 446 0128; www.heaphytrackhelp.co.nz) offers car relocation ($375) from one trailhead to the other, in either direction.

From November to March, Golden Bay Coachlines (p644) has a daily service to the Brown Hut (northeastern) trailhead from Collingwood ($25, 40 minutes), Takaka ($35, one hour), Motueka ($52, 2¼ hours) and Nelson ($65, three hours); and to the Kōhaihai (southwestern) trailhead from Westport ($55, 1¾ hours), Granity ($45, 1½ hours) and Karamea ($20, 15 minutes).

Karamea Express (🖉 03-782 6757; www.karameaexpress.co.nz) operates a daily shuttle between Karamea and the Kōhaihai trailhead ($20); booking ahead is essential. Wangapeka Track transport is also available.

From November to April, **Heaphy Bus** (🖉 03-540 2042; www.theheaphybus.co.nz) offers a scheduled round-trip shuttle service from Nelson to each trailhead ($170); on-demand track transport is also available.

Adventure Flights Golden Bay (p655) will fly you to Karamea and the Brown Hut trailhead from Takaka, Motueka or Nelson. Per person prices range from $85 (Takaka–Brown Hut) to $285 (Nelson–Karamea); two people minimum.

Another option is to charter a flight to any of the Heaphy or Wangapeka trailheads with Helicopter Charter Karamea (p630).

MARLBOROUGH DISTRICT

Picton is a major gateway to the South Island and the main launching point for Marlborough Sounds exploration. A cork's pop south of Picton is Blenheim and its world-famous wineries. Highlights of this region include negotiating the famed Queen Charlotte Track, either on foot or by mountain bike, and discovering the many hidden bays and coves of the Marlborough Sounds by boat. At the end of a busy day, relaxing over a glass of local sauvignon blanc and a bowl of greenshell mussels is highly recommended.

History

Abel Tasman sheltered on the east coast of D'Urville Island in 1642, more than 100 years before James Cook blew through in 1770. It was Cook who named Queen Charlotte Sound (in Māori it's Tōtaranui); his reports made the area the best-known sheltered anchorage in the southern hemisphere. In 1827 French navigator Jules Dumont d'Urville discovered the narrow strait now known as French Pass. His officers named the island just to the north in his honour. In the same year a whaling station was established at Te Awaiti in Tory Channel, which brought about the first permanent European settlement in the district.

Marlborough Sounds

The Marlborough Sounds are a maze of peaks, bays, beaches and watery reaches, formed when the sea flooded deep river valleys after the last ice age. They are very convoluted: Pelorus Sound, for example, is 42km long but has 379km of shoreline.

The main gateways are Havelock, at the base of Pelorus Sound (Te Hoiere), and Picton, at the apex of Queen Charlotte Sound. The wiggly 35km route along Queen Charlotte Drive between the two is a great Sounds snapshot but, if you have a spare day, you're best to head out on the water. Better still, put aside four days to tackle the wonderful Queen Charlotte Track (p638).

There are loads of other hiking, kayaking, boating and biking opportunities, and there's diving as well – notably the wreck of the *Mikhail Lermontov*, a Russian cruise ship that sank in Port Gore in 1986.

◉ Sights & Activities

Motuara Island   WILDLIFE RESERVE
(www.doc.govt.nz) 🏃 This DOC-managed, predator-free island reserve at the entrance to Queen Charlotte Sound is chock-full of rare NZ birds including the Ōkārito brown kiwi (rowi), wood pigeon (kererū), saddleback (tīeke) and king shag. You can get here by water taxi and on tours from Picton.

Lochmara   BAY
(☑03-573 4554; www.lochmara.co.nz; Lochmara Bay; day trips from $40) 🏃 As well as offering lodge accommodation, this tourist complex can be visited on a variety of short cruises from Picton. Activities include kayaking; stand-up paddle boarding; bushwalks; a

sculpture walk; hand-feeding stingrays, eels and endangered kākāriki parakeets; and checking out Lochmara's underwater observatory (adult/child $20/10). Lunch and dinner options are also available.

Sea Kayak Adventures   KAYAKING, BIKING
(☑03-574 2765; www.nzseakayaking.com; cnr Queen Charlotte Dr & Anakiwa Rd; half-/full-day guided paddles $99/135) Guided kayaking and bike/hike options around Queen Charlotte, Kenepuru and Pelorus Sounds. It also offers kayak and mountain-bike rental (half-/full day $40/60).

🛏 Sleeping

Some Sounds sleeping options are accessible only by boat and are deliciously isolated, but the most popular are those on (or just off) the Queen Charlotte Track. Some places close over winter; call ahead to check. There are over 30 DOC camping grounds throughout the Sounds (many accessible only by boat), providing water and toilet facilities but not much else.

Smiths Farm Holiday Park   HOLIDAY PARK $
(☑03-574 2806; www.smithsfarm.co.nz; 1419 Queen Charlotte Dr, Linkwater; sites per person $20-22, units with/without bathroom from $120/65; 🅿🛜🐾) 🏃 Located on the aptly named Linkwater flat between Queen Charlotte and Pelorus, friendly Smiths makes a handy base camp for the track and beyond. Well-kept cabins and motel units face out onto the bushy hillside, while livestock nibble around the lush camping lawns. Short walks extend to a waterfall and magical glowworm dell.

On the Track Lodge   LODGE $$
(☑03-579 8411; www.onthetracklodge.nz; Nydia Bay; chalet s/d without bathroom $110/150, train s/d with bathroom $130/190, yurt $300; ☺Nov-Apr) 🏃 Providing an alternative to the DOC accommodation on the Nydia Track, this tranquil, ecofocused lodge offers breakfasts ($15), packed lunches ($20), evening meals (mains $25) and a hot tub. Accommodation options include a yurt, a 1930s railway carriage and cosy wooden chalets. There's no road access but the Pelorus Mail Boat stops in Nydia Bay twice a week.

Hopewell Lodge   LODGE $$
(☑03-573 4341; www.hopewell.co.nz; 7204 Kenepuru Rd, Double Bay; r with/without bathroom $165/125, cottage $265; ☺Sep-May; 🛜) Beloved of travellers, remote Hopewell sits waterside surrounded by native bush. Savour the long,

Marlborough Sounds

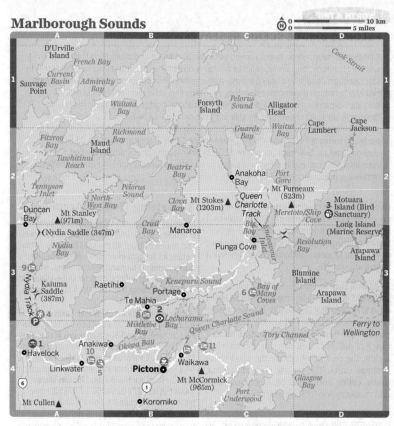

winding drive to get there, or take a water taxi from Te Mahia ($50 return). Stay a couple of days so you can chill out or enjoy the roll-call of activities: mountain biking, kayaking, sailing, fishing, eating pizza, soaking in the outdoor hot tub and more.

Anakiwa 401　　　　　GUESTHOUSE **$$**
(☑ 03-574 1388; www.anakiwa401.co.nz; 401 Anakiwa Rd, Anakiwa; s/tw without bathroom $85/110, r/apt with bathroom $140/160; ⊗ Aug–May; ☜) At the southern end of the track, this former schoolhouse is a soothing spot to rest and reflect. There are two rooms (one en suite) and a beachy self-contained unit. Jocular owners will have you jumping off the jetty for joy and enjoying espresso and ice cream from their green caravan (open afternoons). Free bikes and kayaks.

Mistletoe Bay　　　　HOLIDAY PARK **$$**
(☑ 03-573 4048; www.mistletoebay.co.nz; Onahau Bay; sites per person $18, unit $140-190; ⊗ closed

Marlborough Sounds

⊙ Sights
1 Cullen Point Lookout	A4
2 Lochmara	B3
3 Motuara Island	D2

⊕ Activities, Courses & Tours
4 Nydia Track	A3
5 Sea Kayak Adventures	A4

⊜ Sleeping
6 Bay of Many Coves	C3
7 Bay Vista Waterfront Motel	B4
8 Mistletoe Bay	B3
9 On the Track Lodge	A3
10 Smiths Farm Holiday Park	A4
11 Whatamonga Homestay	C4

Jul; ☜) ◢ Surrounded by bushy hills, Mistletoe Bay offers attractive camping with no-frills facilities. There are also modern en-suite cabins and two self-contained

WORTH A TRIP

PELORUS BRIDGE SCENIC RESERVE

A pocket of deep, green forest tucked between paddocks and plantation forests, 18km west of Havelock, this scenic reserve contains one of the last stands of river-flat forest in Marlborough. It survived only because a town planned in 1865 didn't get off the ground by 1912, by which time obliterative logging made this little remnant look precious. Visitors can explore its many tracks, admire the historic bridge, take a dip in the limpid Pelorus River (alluring enough to star in Peter Jackson's *The Hobbit*), and partake in some home baking at the cafe. The fortunate few can stay overnight in DOC's small but perfectly formed **Pelorus Bridge (Kahikatea Flat) Campground** (☑ 03-571 6019; www.doc.govt.nz; SH6; sites per person $20-23), with its snazzy facilities building. Come sundown, keep an eye out for long-tailed bats – the reserve is home to one of the last remaining populations in Marlborough.

two-bedroom cottages (unusually, linen is an extra $7.50 per person). Environmental sustainability abounds, as does the opportunity to jump off the jetty, kayak in the bay, or hike the Queen Charlotte Track. There's a shop/cafe on-site.

Te Mahia Bay Resort   RESORT $$$
(☑ 03-573 4089; www.temahia.co.nz; 63 Te Mahia Rd; d $170-268; 🛜) This lovely low-key resort is close to the Queen Charlotte Track in a picturesque bay on Kenepuru Sound. It has a range of delightful self-catering rooms-with-a-view, the pick of which are the good-value heritage units. The on-site shop has pizza, cakes, coffee and wine, plus personal chef and massage services are available.

Bay of Many Coves   RESORT $$$
(☑ 03-579 9771; www.bayofmanycoves.co.nz; Arthurs Bay; apt from $1345; 🛜🍽) Not accessible by road, these stylish, secluded apartments feature all mod cons and private balconies overlooking Queen Charlotte Sound. As well as upmarket cuisine, there are various indulgences such as massage, a spa and a hot tub. Kayaking and bush walks are also on the cards, as are adventures in the Sounds organised by the charming, hands-on owners and staff.

Mahana Lodge   LODGE $$$
(☑ 03-579 8373; www.mahanalodge.co.nz; Camp Bay, Endeavour Inlet; r $225-275; ⊙ Oct-Apr) 🌿 This beautiful property features a pretty waterside lawn and purpose-built lodge with four en-suite doubles and a separate studio. Ecofriendly initiatives include bush regeneration, pest trapping and an organic vegetable garden. In fact, feel-good factors abound: free kayaks, home baking and a blooming conservatory where prearranged evening meals are served (three courses $75).

❶ Getting There & Around

Sounds travel is invariably quicker by boat (for example, Punga Cove from Picton by car takes two hours, but just 45 minutes by boat). Fortunately, an armada of vessels offers scheduled cruises and on-demand boat services, with the bulk operating out of Picton for Queen Charlotte Sound, and some from Havelock for Kenepuru and Pelorus Sounds.

Options include **Arrow Water Taxis** (☑ 03-573 8229; www.arrowwatertaxis.co.nz; Town Wharf, Picton; fares from $30), **Kenepuru Water Taxi** (☑ 03-573 4344; www.kenepuru.co.nz; Havelock Marina), **Pelorus Sound Water Taxi** (☑ 027 444 2852; www.pelorussoundwatertaxis.co.nz; Pier C, Havelock Marina) and **Picton Water Taxis** (☑ 027 227 0284, 03-573 7853; www.pictonwatertaxis.co.nz; Town Wharf, Picton).

What roads there are along the ridges are narrow and occasionally unsealed; allow plenty of driving time and keep your wits about you.

Havelock

POP 486

Havelock (not to be confused with Havelock North in Hawkes Bay) sits at the head of Pelorus Sound and is the main hub for the western half of the Marlborough Sounds. It's the self-proclaimed 'Greenshell Mussel Capital of the World' and hence a great place to try this particular New Zealand delicacy. Aside from some well-preserved heritage buildings, there's not a lot to the town itself – but it's a good base from which to explore Pelorus and Kenepuru Sounds.

Māori knew Havelock as Motuweka (there's another town named Motueka in Tasman) and there were three major pā (fortified villages) in the area. The British followed the trend set with Nelson, Collingwood and Picton, and renamed it after one of their military heroes: Sir Henry Havelock, who had recently died during an uprising in India.

◉ Sights

Cullen Point Lookout VIEWPOINT

Cullen Point curves around to the northeast of Havelock, sheltering the marina from the rest of Pelorus Sound. A 10-minute walk loops up and around the headland overlooking the village, the surrounding valleys and the Sound. Another track provides a hour-long loop along the coast. Both start from a car park 3km from Havelock along Queen Charlotte Dr.

Havelock Museum MUSEUM

(www.havelockmuseum.nz; 74 Main Rd; �) 10am-4pm) FREE Inhabiting an old Methodist church, this cute, locally focused museum presents old colonial tales in a contemporary, easily digestible style.

🏃 Activities & Tours

Pelorus Mail Boat CRUISE

(☑ 03-574 1088; www.themailboat.co.nz; Pier B, Havelock Marina; adult/child $132/free; ☺ departs 10am daily Nov-Apr, Mon, Wed & Fri May-Oct) This popular full-day cruise heads through the far reaches of Pelorus Sound on a genuine postal delivery run, taking different routes on different days. Bookings essential; BYO lunch.

Pelorus Eco Adventures KAYAKING

(☑ 021 133 3705; www.kayak-newzealand.com; Bluemoon Lodge, 48 Main Rd; adult/child $185/155) Float in an inflatable kayak on scenic Pelorus River, star of the barrel scene in *The Hobbit*. Wend your way down exhilarating rapids, through crystal-clear pools and past native forest and waterfalls. No experience required; tours last around four hours.

🛌 Sleeping

Bluemoon Lodge HOSTEL $

(☑ 021 133 3705; www.bluemoonhavelock.co.nz; 48 Main Rd; dm/apt $37/132, r with/without bathroom from $102/84; ℗ 🛜) ✿ This pleasant and relaxed backpackers has homely rooms in the main house, a self-contained apartment with a spa bath, and bunk-filled cabins in the yard. Notable features include a sunny barbecue deck, inflatable kayak trips on the Pelorus River, and Nydia Track (www.doc.govt.nz) transport.

Havelock Garden Motel MOTEL $$

(☑ 03-574 2387; www.gardenmotels.com; 71 Main Rd; units $130-160; ℗ 🛜) Set in a large garden with old trees and blooms galore, these 1960s units have been tastefully revamped to offer home comforts. Local activities are happily booked for you.

🍴 Eating

★ Mills Bay Mussels SEAFOOD $

(☑ 03-574 2575; www.millsbaymussels.co.nz; 23a Inglis St; mains $6.50-17; ☺ 11am-3pm Thu, Sat & Sun, to 8pm Fri) How would you like your greenshell mussels? Steamed with white wine and garlic? Grilled in garlic butter? Beer-battered? Crumbed? In a chowder, fritter or Dutch-style croquette? If you can't decide, try a tasting platter ($30 for two). It's a simple set-up, right by the marina, with a shared table inside and more outside.

Slip Inn CAFE $$

(☑ 03-574 2345; www.slipinn.co.nz; Havelock Marina; mains $21-28; ☺ 8am-4pm Mon-Wed, to 7.30pm Thu-Sun) With a deck jutting over the water, this brasserie-style cafe serves plenty of seafood: fish and chips, steamed greenshell mussels, and a particularly delicious *oka* – a Samoan dish of raw fish and mussels cured in a lime, coconut cream and green-chilli broth – served with lots of crusty ciabatta. Burgers, pizza, steaks, lamb and chicken Parmigiana are also offered.

ℹ Information

Havelock i-SITE (☑ 03-574 2161; www.marlboroughnz.com; 61 Main Rd; ☺ 9am-4pm Nov-Apr)

ℹ Getting There & Away

InterCity (p644) has a daily coach to/from Nelson ($15, 1¼ hours), Blenheim ($12, 25 minutes) and Picton ($14, one hour). Buses depart from near the i-SITE.

During the summer school holidays (Christmas through January) the **Link Bus** (☑ 027 314 8569; www.thelinkbus.co.nz) operates three to four timetabled shuttles per day (except Wednesday) between Havelock and Picton ($35, 1¼ hours) via Anakiwa.

Havelock is also linked to Picton by the 42km **Link Pathway** walking and cycling trail.

Picton

POP 2745

Half asleep in winter, but hyperactive in summer (with up to eight fully laden ferry arrivals per day), boaty Picton clusters around a deep and beautiful gulch at the head of Queen Charlotte Sound. It's a major

Picton

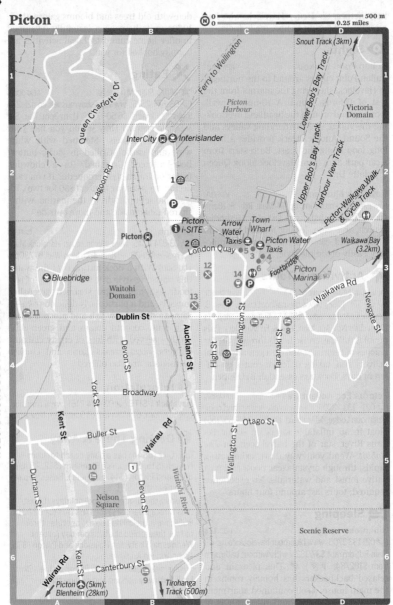

entry point for the South Island, and the best base for tackling the Marlborough Sounds and Queen Charlotte Track. Over the last few years this little town has really bloomed, and offers visitors plenty of reasons to linger even after the obvious attractions are knocked off the list.

Originally called Waitohi, the British renamed it after (surprise, surprise) a military hero, Sir Thomas Picton, who died at the Battle of Waterloo. The local Te Ātiawa people joined their kin a little further up the coast at Waipawa, which still has the area's

Picton

main *marae* (community meeting place) along with a small beach and large marina.

⦿ Sights

Edwin Fox Maritime Museum   MUSEUM
(📱03-573 6868; www.edwinfoxsociety.com; Dunbar Wharf; adult/child $15/5; ⏰9am-3pm) Built near Calcutta and launched in 1853, the *Edwin Fox* is purportedly the world's ninth-oldest surviving ship. During its chequered career it carried troops to the Crimean War, booze to India and immigrants to NZ. Most notably, it's the last remaining ship to have transported convicts to Australia. Displays relate its fascinating story but the real thrill is walking around the ship itself, moored in a dry dock next door.

Heritage & Whaling Museum   MUSEUM
(📱03-573 8283; www.pictonmuseum-newzealand. com; 9 London Quay; adult/child $5/1; ⏰10am-4pm) There's something quite appealing about this style of regional museum: it cheerfully leaps between displays on the local hospital and jail, Māori family portraits, whaling paraphernalia and a collection of old irons. It's well worth a look.

🏃 Activities & Tours

The town has some very pleasant walks. A free i-SITE map details many of these, including an easy 1km track to Bob's Bay. The

Snout Track (three hours return) continues along the ridge offering superb water views. Climbing a hill behind the town, the Tirohanga Track is a two-hour leg-stretching loop offering the best view in the house. The Link Pathway (www.linkpathway.nz) is a 42km walking and cycling track connecting Picton to Havelock, with a spur heading to the Queen Charlotte Track trailhead at Anakiwa. When fully completed in 2020 it will all be off-road.

★**Wilderness Guides**   OUTDOORS
(📱03-573 5432; www.wildernessguidesnz.com; Town Wharf; guided day trips from $130, kayak/bike hire per day $60) Guided kayaking, hiking and mountain-biking trips are offered by this popular crew, including combinations of all three over multiple days.

Marlborough Sounds
Adventure Company   OUTDOORS
(📱03-573 6078; www.marlboroughsounds.co.nz; Town Wharf; half-/full-day tour $105/140, kayak hire per half/full day $40/60, bike hire per 1/2/3 days $60/110/150) Bike-hike-kayak trips, with options to suit every inclination and interest. Trip durations range from half a day to five days, and the popular 'Paddle & Walk' option combines two days of kayaking with two days of hiking.

Cougar Line   CRUISE
(📱03-573 7925; www.cougarline.co.nz; Town Wharf; adult/child from $95/48) Queen Charlotte Track transport, plus various half- and full-day cruise/walk trips, including the rather special (and flexible) ecocruise to Motuara Island (p660).

Beachcomber Cruises   CRUISE
(📱03-573 6175; www.beachcombercruises.co.nz; Town Wharf; cruises from $87, track round trips $105) Various cruise adventures, including the classic 'Magic Mail Run', plus walking, biking and resort lunch options and round-trip track transport.

E-Ko Tours   WILDLIFE
(📱03-573 8040; www.e-ko.nz; 1 Wellington St; adult/child from $75/34) Offers a variety of wildlife-focused tours including trips to Motuara Island (p660).

Escape to Marlborough   BUS
(📱03-573 5573; www.escapetomarlborough.co.nz; day ticket $75; ⏰8am-6pm) Hop-on/hop-off bus services linking Picton and Blenheim, and then stopping at 13 key attractions including vineyards and breweries. Bespoke

wine tours are also offered. Check the website for the service timetables.

🛏 Sleeping

★ Tombstone Backpackers   HOSTEL $
(📞 03-573 7116; www.tombstonebp.co.nz; 16 Gravesend Pl; dm $30-40, r with/without bathroom $95/88, apt $120; 🅿 @ 🖃) Rest in peace in a smart dorm, double room or self-contained apartment at this hillside hostel, opposite the cemetery. Perks include a spa pool overlooking the harbour, free breakfast, a sunny reading room, table tennis, free internet, free bikes and two big fluffy cats.

Jugglers Rest   HOSTEL $
(📞 03-573 5570; www.jugglersrest.com; 8 Canterbury St; dm/s/d/cabin without bathroom $35/75/80/90; ⊙ Oct-May; 🖃) 🌿 A jocular host keeps all her balls in the air at this well-run, ecofriendly, bunk-free backpackers. It's peacefully located a 10-minute walk from town, or even less on one of its free bikes. The attractive gardens are a good place to socialise with fellow travellers, especially during the occasional circus-skills shows.

Sequoia Lodge Backpackers   HOSTEL $
(📞 0800 222 257; www.sequoialodge.co.nz; 3a Nelson Sq; van site $23, dm $28-32, r with/without bathroom from $86/76; 🅿 🖃) This well-managed backpackers in a colourful Victorian house offers bikes, barbecues, a hot tub, free wi-fi and nightly chocolate pudding. A complimentary breakfast is served from May to October. In the special Netflix room, you can fire up your on-demand content of choice. Family rooms sleep up to five people.

Bay Vista Waterfront Motel   MOTEL $$
(📞 03-573 6733; www.bayvistapicton.co.nz; 303 Waikawa Rd, Waikawa; unit from $145; 🖃) This smart motel enjoys an enviable position on the Waikawa foreshore, with views down Queen Charlotte Sound. All units have their own patio and share a large lawn. It's 4km from Picton (courtesy transfer available).

Whatamonga Homestay   B&B $$
(📞 03-573 7192; www.whsl.co.nz; 425 Port Underwood Rd, Whatamango Bay; r with/without bathroom $195/180; 🅿 🖃) Follow Waikawa Rd, which becomes Port Underwood Rd, for 8km and you'll bump into this classy waterside option – two units with king-sized beds, kitchenettes and balconies with magical views. Two other rooms under the main house share a bathroom. Keen fisherfolk can borrow a dinghy and a rod and try their luck. Minimum two-night stay.

Gables B&B   B&B $$
(📞 03-573 6772; www.thegables.co.nz; 20 Waikawa Rd; d $185-208, units $235; 🖃) This historic B&B (once home to Picton's mayor) has three individually styled rooms in the main house and two homely self-contained units out the back. The lovely hosts provide excellent local advice.

Harbour View Motel   MOTEL $$
(📞 03-573 6259; www.harbourviewpicton.co.nz; 30 Waikawa Rd; unit from $153; 🅿 🖃) Its elevated position means this motel commands good views of Picton's mast-filled marina from the timber decks of its smart, self-contained studios and two-bedroom apartments. Luggage storage is offered for guests walking the Queen Charlotte Track.

🍴 Eating & Drinking

Picton Village Bakkerij   BAKERY $
(📞 03-573 7082; www.facebook.com/PictonVillage Bakery; 46 Auckland St; items $3-8.50; ⊙ 6am-4pm Mon-Sat; 🖉) Dutch owners bake trays of European and Kiwi goodies here, including interesting breads, filled rolls, cakes, tarts and savoury pies. It's an excellent place to stock up for a packed lunch.

Gusto   CAFE $$
(📞 03-573 7171; 33 High St; mains $8-22; ⊙ 7am-2.30pm Sun-Fri) With only a handful of tables and a bench by the window, this friendly joint does beaut cooked breakfasts including a warming porridge in winter. Lunch options include homemade savoury pies, local mussels, curry and pasta.

Seumus' Irish Bar   IRISH PUB
(📞 03-573 5050; www.seumusirishbar.co.nz; 25 Wellington St; ⊙ 3-11pm Wed & Thu, noon-1am Fri & Sat, noon-10pm Sun; 🖃) Modelled on a bar in Northern Ireland, Seumus' is a cosy nest of dark wood and leather booths. Of course there's Guinness on tap and regular live music, and it also serves hearty fare such as fish and chips, bangers and mash, burgers, hot pots and Sunday roasts.

ℹ Information

Picton i-SITE (📞 03-520 3113; www.marlbor oughnz.com; Auckland St; ⊙ 8.30am-6pm Dec-Feb, 9am-4pm Mar-Nov; 🖃) All vital tourist guff including maps, Queen Charlotte Track information, lockers and transport bookings.

Picton Library (67 High St; ⊙ 8am-5pm Mon-Fri, 10am-4pm Sat, 1-4pm Sun; 🖃) This flash modern library offers free wi-fi.

❶ Getting There & Away

The main transport hub (with car-rental depots) is at the Interislander ferry terminal, which also has a cafe and internet facilities. Most buses also depart from here or at the nearby i-SITE.

AIR

Sounds Air (☑ 03-520 3080, 0800 505 005; www.soundsair.co.nz; 10 London Quay; ⊙7.30am-5.30pm Mon-Thu & Sat, to 7pm Fri, 9am-7pm Sun) flies between Picton and Wellington; a shuttle bus to/from the airstrip at Koromiko is available ($10).

BOAT

There are two operators crossing Cook Strait between Picton and Wellington, and although all ferries leave from more or less the same place, each has its own terminal. Crossings take around 3½ hours.

Bluebridge (☑ 04-471 6188; www.bluebridge. co.nz; Lagoon Rd; adult/child/motorbike/car/ campervan from $50/26/54/120/150; 🐾) has four sailings in each direction daily.

Interislander (☑ 04-498 3302; www.great-journeysofnz.co.nz; Auckland St; adult/ child/motorbike/car/campervan from $56/26/43/111/132) has five sailings in each direction daily.

Picton is also the hub for water taxis and cruises along Queen Charlotte Sound (p662).

BUS

InterCity (☑ 03-365 1113; www.intercity. co.nz; outside Interislander Ferry Terminal, Auckland St) has two coaches a day to/from Christchurch (from $37, six hours) via Blenheim (from $10, 30 minutes) and Kaikōura (from $25, 2½ hours); and one or two daily to Nelson ($23, 2¼ hours) via Blenheim and Havelock ($14, one hour).

Escape to Marlborough (p665) has three morning departures to Blenheim ($19), with two returning in the afternoon as part of its hop-on/hop-off bus service.

There's also a bus to/from Blenheim ($4, 30 minutes), operated by Ritchies, which runs twice a day on Tuesdays and Thursdays only.

During the summer school holidays (Christmas through January) the Link Bus (p663) operates three or four shuttles per day (except Wednesday) between Picton and Havelock ($35, 1¼ hours) via Anakiwa ($20, 45 minutes).

TRAIN

KiwiRail's scenic **Coastal Pacific** (☑ 04-495 0775; www.greatjourneysofnz.co.nz) service operates daily from October to April, heading to/from Christchurch (from $99, 6¼ hours) via Blenheim (from $39, 26 minutes) and Kaikōura (from $59, three hours).

Blenheim & Around

POP 31,600

Set on the fertile Wairau Plains, a large flat expanse wedged between the Richmond Ranges and the Wither Hills, Blenheim is very much an agricultural hub. While there's not a lot to get excited about in the town itself, wine lovers will find plenty of thrills in the surrounding countryside. This is the heart of the Marlborough Wine Region, the most famous and most productive of the country's viticultural areas. Blenheim is a good base from which to explore it, with a couple of interesting museums and an increasingly lively food scene.

⊙ Sights

★Omaka Aviation Heritage Centre
MUSEUM
(Map p669; ☑ 03-579 1305; www.omaka.org.nz; 79 Aerodrome Rd, Omaka; adult/child WWI $25/12, WWII $20/10, both $39/16; ⊙10am-5pm) When Sir Peter Jackson has a passion for something, there are no half measures. That's abundantly clear in the 'Knights of the Sky' exhibition, which features the movie director's personal collection of WWI aircraft and memorabilia, brought to life in a series of life-sized dioramas that depict dramatic wartime scenes such as the death of the Red Baron. The other half of the centre, WWII-themed 'Dangerous Skies', is the work of local aviation enthusiasts.

The latter may not be as slick as Sir Peter's section – the backgrounds are hand painted and there are fewer of the hyper-realistic mannequins produced by the Oscar-winning Weta Workshop – but all of these aircraft have been restored and are airworthy, and it includes an eight-minute immersive 'Stalingrad Experience'.

Book ahead to take a flight in a US military biplane (10/20 minutes, $250/380 for up to two people) or a Soviet WWII fighter (20/30 minutes, $2300/2599).

Omaka Classic Cars
MUSEUM
(Map p669; ☑ 03-577 9419; www.omakaclassic-cars.co.nz; Aerodrome Rd, Omaka; adult/child $15/free; ⊙noon-4pm daily Oct-May, Fri-Sun Jun-Sep) Opposite the Aviation Heritage Centre is this collection of more than 100 restored cars dating from the 1950s to the '80s.

Pollard Park
PARK
(Map p669; Parker St) Ten minutes' walk from town, this 25-hectare park has beau-

tiful blooming and scented gardens, a playground, tennis courts and a nine-hole golf course. It's pretty as a picture when lit up on summer evenings. Five minutes away, on the way to town, is the extensive Taylor River Floodway Reserve, a lovely place for a stroll.

Marlborough Museum
MUSEUM

(Map p669; ☑ 03-578 1712; www.marlborough museum.org.nz; 26 Arthur Baker Pl; adult/child $10/5; ⊙ 10am-4pm) The history of NZ's wine industry is celebrated here, along with fascinating displays devoted to finds from Wairau Bar, the site of the country's earliest known settlement. Look out for the *kare-tao*, a traditional wooden puppet covered in *moko* (tattoos) and designed to perform a *haka* (ceremonial dance). The museum is situated within the Bradshaw Heritage Park, a collection of transported Victorian buildings that includes a miniature railway and a farm-machinery museum.

🏃 Activities & Tours

Wither Hills Farm Park
WALKING

(Map p669; Rifle Range Pl, Witherlea) In a town as flat as a pancake, this hilly 11-sq-km working sheep and cattle farm provides welcome relief, offering over 60km of walking and mountain-biking trails with grand views across the Wairau Valley and out to Cloudy Bay. Pick up a map from the i-SITE (p672) or check the information panels at the many entrances.

Driftwood Eco-Tours
ECOTOUR

(☑ 03-577 7651; 🌱 www.driftwoodecotours.co.nz; tours from $180) 🌱 Tour through private farmland to the ecologically and historically significant Wairau Lagoon, 10 minutes' drive from Blenheim. Alternatively book one of the specialist-led themed day or multiday tours to learn about the flora and fauna.

🛏 Sleeping

Watson's Way Lodge
HOSTEL $

(Map p669; ☑ 027 800 4664; www.watsonsway lodge.co.nz; 56 High St, Renwick; sites from $15, dm $30, r with/without bathroom $99/88; ⊙ Oct-Jul; 🛜) This traveller-focused lodge has spick-and-span rooms in a sweetly converted bungalow with a full kitchen and a comfy lounge with a pool table. There are also spacious leafy gardens dotted with fruit trees and hammocks, bikes for hire and local information aplenty.

St Leonards
COTTAGE $$

(Map p669; ☑ 03-577 8328; www.stleonards.co.nz; 18 St Leonards Rd, Springlands; cottage from $170; P 🛜 ✈) Tucked into the grounds of an 1886 homestead, these five stylish and rustic cottages offer privacy and a reason to stay put. Each is unique in its layout and perspective on the gardens and vines. Our pick is the capacious and cosy Woolshed, exuding agricultural chic. Resident sheep, chickens and deer await your attention.

Olde Mill House
B&B $$

(Map p669; ☑ 03-572 8458; www.oldemillhouse. co.nz; 9 Wilson St, Renwick; d $180-190; P 🛜) On an elevated section in otherwise flat Renwick, this charming old house is a treat. Home-grown fruit and homemade jams and pickles are offered as part of the continental breakfast. Free bikes, an outdoor spa pool and pretty gardens make this a tip-top choice in the heart of the wine country.

Montana Lodge Motel
MOTEL $$

(Map p669; ☑ 03-578 9259; www.montanalodge motel.co.nz; 71 Main St; units $135-160; P 🛜 ✈) One of the cheaper motels in a pricey town, this angular, 1970s-looking complex offers clean and comfortable units with kitchenettes, and a cute kidney-shaped pool.

Marlborough Vintners Hotel
HOTEL $$$

(Map p669; ☑ 03-572 5094; www.mvh.co.nz; 190 Rapaura Rd, Rapaura; r from $315; P ✳ 🛜) 🌱 The 16 architecturally designed suites here make the most of valley views and are decked out with modern bathrooms and abstract art. The stylish reception building has a bar and restaurant opening out onto a cherry orchard and organic vegetable garden.

🍴 Eating

Ritual
CAFE $

(Map p669; ☑ 03-578 6939; www.ritualcoffee.co.nz; 10 Maxwell Rd; mains $9-20; ⊙ 7am-4pm Mon-Sat) A shopfront for a local fair-trade and organic coffee roaster, this cool little cafe is all leadlights and lampshades. Cooked breakfasts include the usual eggy options alongside more unusual dishes such as huevos rancheros (eggs served with a tortilla and a spicy tomato sauce). There's a good selection of quick-and-easy counter food, along with great coffee, naturally.

The Burleigh
PIES $

(Map p669; ☑ 03-579 2531; www.facebook.com/ theburleighnz; 72 New Renwick Rd, Burleigh; pies

Marlborough Wine Region

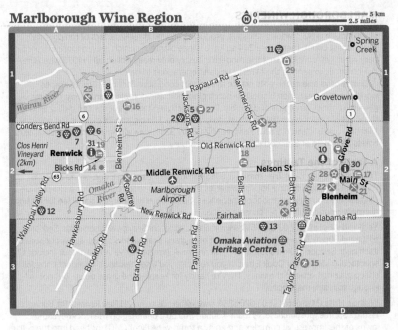

Marlborough Wine Region

◎ Top Sights
1 Omaka Aviation Heritage Centre C3

◎ Sights
2 Allan Scott Family Winemakers B1
3 Bladen A2
4 Brancott Estate B3
5 Cloudy Bay B1
6 Forrest A2
7 Framingham A2
8 Huia B1
9 Marlborough Museum D3
Omaka Classic Cars .... (see 1)
10 Pollard Park D2
11 Saint Clair Estate C1
12 Spy Valley Wines A2
13 Wither Hills C3

◎ Activities, Courses & Tours
14 Bike 2 Wine A2
15 Wither Hills Farm Park D3

◎ Sleeping
16 Marlborough Vintners Hotel B1
17 Montana Lodge Motel D2
Olde Mill House .... (see 14)

18 St Leonards C2
19 Watson's Way Lodge A2

◎ Eating
20 Arbour B2
21 Gramado's D2
22 Ritual D2
23 Rock Ferry C2
Scotch Wine Bar .... (see 22)
24 The Burleigh C2
25 Wairau River A1

◎ Drinking & Nightlife
26 Dodson Street D2
27 Moa Brewing Company C1

◎ Entertainment
28 ASB Theatre Marlborough D2

◎ Shopping
29 Makana Confections C1

◎ Information
30 Blenheim i-SITE D2
31 DOC Marlborough District Office A2

MARLBOROUGH WINERIES

Marlborough is NZ's vinous colossus, producing around three-quarters of the country's wine. At last count, there were 244 sq km of vines planted – which is even more extraordinary when you consider that the modern industry only really kicked off in 1973 when the Yukich family expanded their West Auckland operations to here.

Sunny days and cool nights create the perfect conditions for cool-climate grapes: world-famous sauvignon blanc, top-notch pinot noir, and notable chardonnay, riesling, gewürztraminer, pinot gris and bubbly. Drifting between tasting rooms and dining among the vines is a quintessential South Island experience. The big annual event is the one-day **Marlborough Wine & Food Festival** (☑03-577 9299; www.wine-marlborough-festival.co.nz; tickets $63), held at Brancott Estate in mid-February.

A Taste of the Tastings

The *Marlborough Wine Trail* map – available from Blenheim i-SITE and online at www.wine-marlborough.co.nz – lists 35 wineries that are open to the public. Our picks provide a range of high-quality cellar-door experiences. Some wineries charge a small fee for tasting, normally refunded if you purchase a bottle.

Yealands Estate (☑03-575 7618; www.yealands.co.nz; cnr Seaview & Reserve Rds, Seddon; ⊙10am-4.30pm) Zero-carbon winemaking on a grand scale at this space-age winery out by itself near Seddon, 30km southeast of Blenheim. A 7km self-drive vineyard tour includes spectacular views over Cook Strait. If you're lucky, you'll see Yealands' compact babydoll sheep grazing between the vines. They're handy for keeping the grass down, but not tall enough to reach the grapes.

Wither Hills (Map p669; ☑03-520 8284; www.witherhills.co.nz; 211 New Renwick Rd, Burleigh; tastings $5, free with purchase; ⊙10am-4.30pm) Pull up a beanbag on the Hockneyesque lawns of this impressive complex and enjoy a three-wine flight ($10), or head into the cellar for a more traditional tasting session. It also offers a Wine Blending Experience ($60 for four people). The restaurant is excellent, too.

Brancott Estate (Map p669; ☑03-520 6975; www.brancottestate.com; 180 Brancott Rd, Fairhall; tastings $5-15, free with purchase; ⊙10am-4.30pm) Under its previous name, Montana Wines, this was the trailblazer of the wine region. Now it has Marlborough's most impressive cellar door and restaurant complex, poised atop a hillock overlooking the vines. It offers an hour-long **Vineyard Bike Tour** ($35, 10.30am) and, from December to March, a **Falcon Encounter** (adult/child $30/10, 11am) featuring the kārearea (NZ falcon); bookings essential.

Spy Valley Wines (Map p669; ☑03-572 6207; www.spyvalleywine.co.nz; 37 Lake Timara Rd West, Waihopai Valley; tastings $5-10, free with purchase; ⊙10.30am-4.30pm daily Nov-Apr, Mon-Fri May-Oct) Stylish, edgy architecture features at this espionage-themed winery with drops in the top echelons. Memorable merchandise.

Clos Henri Vineyard (☑03-572 7293; www.clos-henri.com; 639 State Hwy 63, Waihopai Valley; ⊙10am-4pm Mon-Sat Oct-Apr) French winemaking meets Marlborough terroir with *très bon* results. The cellar door is housed in a beautifully restored wooden church.

Bladen (Map p669; ☑03-572 9417; www.bladen.co.nz; 83 Conders Bend Rd, Renwick; ⊙11am-4.30pm Nov-Apr) Bijou family winery that's big on charm.

Framingham (Map p669; ☑03-572 8884; www.framingham.co.nz; 19 Conders Bend Rd, Renwick; tastings $5, free with purchase; ⊙10.30am-4.30pm) Consistent, quality wines including exceptional riesling and stellar dessert wines. Check out the '90s song lyrics on the pavers of the cloister.

Forrest (Map p669; ☑03-572 9084; www.forrest.co.nz; 19 Blicks Rd, Renwick; tastings free-$10; ⊙10am-4.30pm) Doctor-owners produce and prescribe a range of fine vinous medicines, including some mood-altering riesling.

Huia (Map p669; ☎03-572 8326; www.huiavineyards.com; 22 Boyces Rd, Rapaura; ⊙10.30am-4.30pm Nov-Mar) Sustainable, small-scale family winemaking and a personable cellar-door experience. Delectable dry-style gewürztraminer.

Allan Scott Family Winemakers (Map p669; ☎03-572 9054; www.allanscott.com; 229 Jacksons Rd, Rapaura; tastings $3, free with purchase or lunch; ⊙9am-4.30pm) Highlights of this esteemed range include a lovely gewürztraminer and a *méthode traditionnelle* sparkling wine. The attached Twelve Trees restaurant is good, too.

Cloudy Bay (Map p669; ☎03-520 9147; www.cloudybay.co.nz; 230 Jacksons Rd, Rapaura; tastings $10-25; ⊙10am-4pm) The most famous, most upmarket and most expensive tasting experience; private tastings and tours are also offered. Jack's Raw Bar shucks and serves oysters and clams from December to mid-April.

Saint Clair Estate (Map p669; ☎03-570 5280; www.saintclair.co.nz; 13 Selmes Rd, Rapaura; tastings $5-10, free with meal or purchase; ⊙9am-5pm Nov-Apr, 11am-4pm May-Oct) Prepare to be blown away by the Pioneer Block and Reserve range sauvignon blanc and pinot noir at Marlborough's most awarded winery. There's a good restaurant on-site, too.

Wining & Dining

Rock Ferry (Map p669; ☎03-579 6430; www.rockferry.co.nz; 80 Hammerichs Rd; mains $28-30, tastings $5, free with purchase or meal; ⊙cafe 11.30am-3pm, cellar door 10am-4.30pm) Although it calls itself a cafe, that doesn't really cover the sophisticated but concise modern NZ menu on offer here (for example, monkfish, steak and a delicious crusted baked salmon served on pearl barley). A very pleasant environment, inside and out.

Wairau River (Map p669; ☎03-572 9800; www.wairauriverwines.com; 11 Rapaura Rd, Rapaura; mains $27-30, tastings $5, free with purchase or meal; ⊙noon-3pm; 🐾) This modish, mud-brick cellar door and bistro has a wide veranda and beautiful gardens with plenty of shade. The adventurous cuisine-straddling menu may include the likes of *togarashi* (Japanese spice mix) prawns with miso mayo, Marlborough mussel chowder, braised beef cheeks with sambal (Malaysian chilli paste), hot-smoked salmon salad or tandoori chicken burger.

Arbour (Map p669; ☎03-572 7989; www.arbour.co.nz; 36 Godfrey Rd, Renwick; set menu $89-109; ⊙5.30-11pm Tue-Sat Aug-Jun) Located in the thick of Renwick wine country, Marlborough's most lauded restaurant focuses on local produce fashioned into top-notch contemporary dishes. Settle in for a multiple-course degustation, either with or without suggested matches from the mesmerising wine list.

Wine Tours

Wine tours are generally conducted in a minibus, last between four and seven hours, take in four to seven wineries and range in price from $95 to $130 (with a few grand tours costing up to around $250 for the day, including a winery lunch).

Bubbly Grape Wine Tours (☎027 672 2195; www.bubblygrape.co.nz; tours $100-195) Three different tours including a gourmet lunch option.

Highlight Wine Tours (☎03-577 9046; www.highlightwinetours.co.nz; tours $90-130) Tours visit a chocolate factory, too. Custom tours available.

Hop 'n Grape (☎021 157 4094; www.hopngrapetours.co.nz; half/full day $115/150) Winemaker-led, small-group wine tours with an optional side serving of beer.

Sounds Connection (☎03-573 8843; www.soundsconnection.co.nz; tours from $95) Some tour options combine tastings with a Marlborough Sounds cruise.

Bike 2 Wine (Map p669; ☎03-572 8458; www.bike2wine.co.nz; 9 Wilson St, Renwick; standard/tandem per day $30/60, pick-ups within 15km $10; ⊙10am-5.30pm) An alternative to the usual minibus tours, this operator offers self-guided, fully equipped and supported two-wheeled tours. There are more than 20 wineries in a 5km radius of its Renwick base, and it offers a pick-up service from Blenheim and its surrounds for $10 return.

$6-9; ⊙7.30am-3pm Tue-Fri, to 1.30pm Sat) The humble pie rises to stratospheric heights at this fabulous bakery-deli on Blenheim's rural fringes; try the pork-belly or steak and blue cheese, or perhaps both. Freshly filled baguettes, local sausage, French cheeses and great coffee also make tempting appearances. Avoid the lunchtime rush.

★ Scotch Wine Bar
TAPAS $$

(Map p669; ☑03-579 1176; www.scotchbar.co.nz; 24-26 Maxwell Rd; dishes $7-28, tasting menu $45; ⊙4pm-late Mon-Fri) A versatile and sociable spot in central Blenheim, Scotch offers local wines, craft beer on tap and delicious sharing plates in a range of sizes. The southern fried chicken with chilli mayo is a crispy and filling crowd-pleaser but, if you're feeling adventurous, we'd recommend the raw hangar steak with juniper, pine needles and sorrel.

Gramado's
BRAZILIAN $$$

(Map p669; ☑03-579 1192; www.gramadosrestaurant.com; 74 Main St; mains $37-40; ⊙4pm-late Tue-Sat; 🕙🚲) Injecting a little Latin passion into the Blenheim dining scene, Gramado's is a fun place to tuck into unashamedly hearty meals such as lamb *assado*, feijoada (smoky pork and bean stew) and Brazilian-spiced fish. Kick things off with a caipirinha, of course.

🍺 Drinking & Entertainment

Moa Brewing Company
CRAFT BEER

(Map p669; ☑03-572 5146; www.moabeer.com; 258 Jacksons Rd, Rapaura; tastings $10; ⊙11am-6pm) Take a break from wine-tasting at Moa's laid-back beer-tasting room amid Rapaura's vineyards. Food trucks often rock up Thursday to Sunday, and there's always a few seasonal brews on tap. Travelling beer geeks should try Moa's excellent sour beers; the $28 beer flight is the equivalent of 2½ pints.

Dodson Street
CRAFT BEER

(Map p669; ☑03-577 8348; www.dodsonstreet.co.nz; 1 Dodson St; ⊙11am-11pm) This pub and garden has a beer-hall ambience and suitably Teutonic menu featuring pork knuckle, bratwurst and schnitzel (its pizza and burgers are also good). The stars of the show, however, are the 24 taps pouring quality, ever-changing craft beer from around Marlborough and the rest of NZ.

ASB Theatre Marlborough
THEATRE

(Map p669; ☑03-520 8558; www.asbtheatre.com; 2 Hutcheson St) Opened in 2016, this large, modern theatre presents a wide programme of concerts and performances. Check the website to see what's on.

Shopping

Makana Confections
CHOCOLATE

(Map p669; ☑03-570 5370; www.makana.co.nz; cnr Rapaura & O'Dwyers Rds, Rapaura; ⊙9am-5.30pm) Large windows face the factory, allowing you to watch the chocolates being made while you're engulfed in the most mouthwatering fragrances and tempted with free samples. Resistance is futile.

ℹ Information

Blenheim i-SITE (Map p669; ☑03-577 8080; www.marlboroughnz.com; Train Station, 8 Sinclair St; ⊙9am-4pm Mon-Fri, 10am-3pm Sat & Sun) Information on Marlborough and beyond, including wine-trail maps.

Wairau Hospital (☑03-520 9999; www.nmdhb.govt.nz; Hospital Rd, Witherlea)

ℹ Getting There & Away

AIR

Marlborough Airport (Map p669; ☑03-572 8651; www.marlboroughairport.co.nz; 1 Tancred Cres, Woodbourne) is 6km west of town. **Blenheim Shuttles** (☑03-577 5277; www.blenheimshuttles.co.nz) provides door-to-door services between the airport and the town centre, as does **Marlborough Taxis** (☑03-577 5511); expect to pay around $20.

➤ Air New Zealand (p644) has direct flights to/from Wellington and Auckland.

➤ Sounds Air (p667) flies to Wellington, Kāpiti Coast and Christchurch.

BUS

InterCity (p644) buses depart from the Blenheim i-SITE. Destinations include Picton (from $10, 30 minutes), Havelock ($12, 25 minutes), Nelson ($23, 1¾ hours), Kaikōura (from $19, 1¾ hours) and Christchurch (from $37, 5½ hours).

There's also a bus to/from Picton ($4, 30 minutes), operated by Ritchies, which runs twice a day on Tuesdays and Thursdays only.

TRAIN

KiwiRail's scenic Coastal Pacific (p667) service operates daily from October to April, heading to/from Picton (from $39, 26 minutes), Kaikōura (from $59, 2½ hours) and Christchurch (from $99, 5¾ hours).

ℹ Getting Around

The **Blenheim Bus** (☑03-578 5467; www.ritchies.co.nz/blenheim; adult/child $2/1), operated by Ritchies, runs on two loops around central Blenheim.

Understand
New
Zealand

History

Western historians continue to unravel New Zealand's early history, with much of what they have discovered confirming traditional Māori narratives passed on through the generations. In less than 1000 years NZ has hosted two new peoples: the Polynesian Māori and European New Zealanders (or Pākehā). New Zealand shares some of its history with the rest of Polynesia, and with other European colonial nations. This cultural intermingling has created the unique Kiwi spirit you'll experience today.

Māori Settlement

The first settlers of NZ were the Polynesian forebears of today's Māori. Archaeologists and anthropologists continue to search for the details, but the most widely accepted evidence suggests they arrived in the 13th century. The DNA of Polynesian rat bones found in NZ, dated to centuries earlier, has been written off as unreliable (and certainly not conclusive evidence of earlier settlement). Most historians now agree on 1280 as the Māori's likeliest arrival date. Scientists have sequenced the DNA of settlers buried at the Wairau Bar archaeological site on the South Island, and confirmed the settlers as originating from east Polynesia (though work is ongoing to pinpoint their origins more precisely). The genetic diversity of the buried settlers suggests a fairly large-scale settlement – a finding consistent with Māori narratives about numerous vessels reaching the islands.

Prime sites for first settlement were warm coastal gardens for the food plants brought from Polynesia (kumara or sweet potato, gourd, yam and taro); sources of workable stone for knives and adzes; and areas with abundant big game. New Zealand has no native land mammals apart from a few species of bat, but 'big game' is no exaggeration: the islands were home to a dozen species of moa (a large flightless bird) – the largest of which weighed up to 240kg, about twice the size of an ostrich – preyed upon by *Harpagornis moorei*, a whopping 15kg eagle that is now extinct. Other species of flightless birds and large sea mammals, such as fur seals, were easy game for hunters from small Pacific Islands. The first settlers spread far and fast, from the top of the North Island to the bottom of the

The Ministry for Culture & Heritage's history website (www.nzhistory. govt.nz) is an excellent source of information on NZ's history.

TIMELINE	1280 CE	1500–1642	1642
	Based on evidence from archaeological digs, the most likely arrival date of east Polynesians in NZ, now known as Māori.	The 'classic period' of Māori culture, where weapon-making and artistic techniques were refined. Many remain cultural hallmarks to this day.	First European contact: Abel Tasman arrives on an expedition from the Dutch East Indies (Indonesia) but leaves in a hurry after a sea skirmish with Māori.

THE MYTHICAL MORIORI

One of NZ's most persistent legends is that Māori found mainland NZ already occupied by a more peaceful and racially distinct Melanesian people, known as the Moriori, whom they exterminated. This myth has been regularly debunked by scholars since the 1920s, but somehow persists.

To complicate matters, there were real 'Moriori', and Māori did treat them badly. The real Moriori were the people of the Chatham Islands, a windswept group about 900km east of the mainland. They were, however, fully Polynesian, and descended from Māori – 'Moriori' was their version of the same word. Mainland Māori arrived in the Chathams in 1835, as a spin-off of the Musket Wars, killing some Moriori and enslaving the rest, but they did not exterminate them.

South Island within the first 100 years. High-protein diets are likely to have boosted population growth.

By about 1400, however, with big-game supply dwindling, Māori economics turned from big game to small game – forest birds and rats – and from hunting to farming and fishing. A good living could still be made, but it required detailed local knowledge, steady effort and complex communal organisation, hence the rise of the Māori tribes. Competition for resources increased, conflict did likewise, and this led to the building of increasingly sophisticated *pā* (fortified villages), complete with wells and food-storage pits. Vestiges of *pā* earthworks can still be seen around the country (on the hilltops of Auckland, for example).

Around 1500 is considered the dawn of the 'classic period', when Māori developed a social structure and aesthetic that was truly distinct, rather than an offshoot of the parent Polynesian culture. Māori had no metals and no written language (and no alcoholic drinks or drugs). Traditional Māori culture from these times endures, including performance art like *kapa haka* (cultural dance) and unmistakable visual art, notably woodcarving, weaponry and *pounamu* (greenstone) carving.

Spiritual life was similarly distinctive. Below Ranginui (sky father) and Papatūānuku (earth mother) were various gods of land, forest and sea, joined by deified ancestors over time. The mischievous demigod Māui was particularly important. In legend, he vanquished the sun and fished up the North Island before meeting his death between the thighs of the goddess Hine-nui-te-pō in an attempt to bring immortality to humankind.

Similarities in language between Māori and Tahitian indicate close contact in historical times. Māori is as similar to Tahitian as Spanish is to French, despite the 4294km separating these island groups.

Enter Europe

The first authenticated contact between Māori and European explorers took place in 1642. Seafarer Abel Tasman had just claimed Van Diemen's Land (Tasmania) for the Dutch when rough winds steered his ships east,

1769	1772	1790s	1818–36
European contact recommences with visits by James Cook and Jean de Surville. Despite violence, both manage to communicate with Māori. This time NZ's link with the outside world proves permanent.	Marion du Fresne's French expedition arrives; it stays for some weeks at the Bay of Islands. Relations with Māori start well, but a breach of Māori *tapu* (sacred law) leads to violence.	Whaling ships and sealing gangs arrive in the country. Relations are established with Māori, with Europeans depending on the contact for essentials, such as food, water and protection.	Intertribal Māori 'Musket Wars' take place: tribes acquire muskets and win bloody victories against tribes without them. The wars taper off, probably due to the equal distribution of weapons.

where he sighted New Zealand. Tasman's two ships were searching for southern land and anything valuable it might contain. Tasman was instructed to pretend to any natives he might meet 'that you are by no means eager for precious metals, so as to leave them ignorant of the value of the same'.

CAPTAIN JAMES COOK

Countless obelisks, faded plaques and graffiti-covered statues remember the renowned navigator James Cook (1728–79). It's impossible to travel the Pacific without encountering the captain's image and his controversial legacy in the lands he opened to the West.

Cook came from an extremely pinched and provincial background. The son of a day labourer in rural Yorkshire, he was born in a mud cottage, had little schooling and seemed destined for farm work. Instead, Cook went to sea as a teenager, worked his way up from coal-ship servant to naval officer, and attracted notice for his exceptional charts of Canada. But Cook remained a little-known second lieutenant until, in 1768, the Royal Navy chose him to command a daring voyage to the South Seas.

In a converted coal ship called *Endeavour*, Cook sailed to Tahiti and then became the first European to land in NZ and on the east coast of Australia. While he was there, Cook sailed and mapped NZ's coastline in full – with impressive accuracy. The ship almost sank after striking the Great Barrier Reef, and 40% of the crew died from disease and accidents, but somehow the *Endeavour* arrived home in 1771. On a return voyage (1772–75), Cook became the first navigator to pierce the Antarctic Circle and circled the globe near its southernmost latitude, demolishing the ancient myth that a vast, populous and fertile continent surrounded the South Pole.

Cook's travels made an enormous contribution to world thought. During his voyages, Cook and his crew took astronomical measurements. Botanists accompanied him on his voyages, diligently recording and studying the flora they encountered. Cook was also remarkable for completing a round-the-world voyage without any of his crew dying of scurvy – adding 'nutrition' to his impressive roster of specialist subjects.

But these achievements exist beneath a long shadow. Cook's travels spurred colonisation of the Pacific, and within a few decades of his death, missionaries, whalers, traders and settlers began transforming (and often devastating) island cultures. As a result, many indigenous people now revile Cook as an imperialist villain who introduced disease, dispossession and other ills to the region (hence the frequent vandalising of Cook monuments). However, as islanders revive traditional crafts and practices, from tattooing to *tapa* (traditional barkcloth), they have turned to the art and writing of Cook and his men as a resource for cultural renewal. Significant geographical features in NZ bear his name, including Aoraki/Mt Cook, Cook Strait and Cook River, along with countless streets and hotels. For good and ill, a Yorkshire farm boy remains one of the single most significant figures in shaping the modern Pacific.

1837	1840	1844	1858
European settlers introduce possums from Australia to NZ, creating a possum population boom that comes to threaten native flora and birdlife.	Starting at Waitangi in the Bay of Islands on 6 February, around 500 chiefs countrywide sign the Treaty of Waitangi to 'settle' sovereignty once and for all. NZ becomes a nominal British colony.	Young Ngāpuhi chief Hōne Heke challenges British sovereignty, first by cutting down the British flag at Kororāreka (now Russell), then by sacking the town itself. The ensuing Northland Land War continues until 1846.	The Waikato chief Te Wherowhero is installed as the first Māori king.

When Tasman's ships anchored in Wharewharangi Bay, local Māori came out in their canoes to make the traditional challenge: friends or foes? The Dutch blew their trumpets, unwittingly challenging back. When a boat was lowered to take a party between the two ships, it was attacked and four crewmen were killed. Having not even set foot on the land, Tasman sailed away and didn't return; nor did any other European for 127 years. But the Dutch did leave a name: initially 'Statenland', later changed to 'Nova Zeelandia' by cartographers.

Contact between Māori and Europeans was renewed in 1769, when English and French explorers arrived, under James Cook and Jean de Surville – Cook narrowly pipped the latter to the post, naming Doubtless Bay before the French party dropped anchor there. The first French exploration ended sourly, with mistrust between the ailing French seamen and Māori, one of whom they took prisoner (he died at sea). Bloody skirmishes took place during a second French expedition, led by Marc-Joseph Marion du Fresne, when cultural misunderstandings led to violent reprisals; later expeditions were more fruitful. Meanwhile Cook made two more visits between 1773 and 1777. Exploration continued, motivated by science, profit and political rivalry.

Unofficial visits, by whaling ships in the north and seal-hunting gangs in the south, began in the 1790s (though Māori living in New Zealand's interior remained largely unaffected). The first Christian missionaries established themselves in the Bay of Islands in 1814, followed by dozens of others – Anglican, Methodist and Catholic. Europe brought such things as pigs and potatoes, which benefited Māori and were even used as currency. Trade in flax and timber generated small European–Māori settlements by the 1820s. Surprisingly, the most numerous category of 'European' visitor was probably American. New England whaling ships favoured the Bay of Islands for rest and recreation. Their favourite haunt, the little town of Kororāreka (now Russell), was known as 'Gomorrah, the scourge of the Pacific'. As a result, New England visitors today may well have distant relatives among the locals.

One or two dozen bloody clashes dot the history of Māori–European contact before 1840, but given the number of visits, interracial conflict was modest. Europeans needed Māori protection, food and labour, and Māori came to need European articles, especially muskets. Whaling stations and mission stations were linked to local Māori groups by intermarriage, which helped keep the peace. Most warfare was between Māori: the terrible intertribal 'Musket Wars' of 1818–36. Because Northland had the majority of early contact with Europe, its Ngāpuhi tribe acquired muskets first. Under their great general Hika, Ngāpuhi then raided south, winning bloody victories against tribes without muskets. Once they acquired muskets, these tribes then saw off Ngāpuhi, but also

Abel Tasman named NZ 'Statenland', assuming it was connected to Staten Island near Argentina. It was subsequently named after the province of Zeeland in Tasman's native Holland.

One of the first European women to settle in NZ was Charlotte Badger, a convict mutineer/pirate who escaped to the Bay of Islands with her daughter in 1806, integrating into local society, learning Māori fluently and, later in life, Tongan, too.

1860–69	1861	1863–64	1867
The Taranaki wars, starting with the controversial swindling of Māori land by the government at Waitara, and continuing with outrage over the confiscation of more land as a result.	Gold discovered in Otago by Gabriel Read, an Australian prospector. As a result, the population of Otago climbs from less than 13,000 to over 30,000 in six months.	Waikato Land War. Up to 5000 Māori resist an invasion mounted by 20,000 imperial, colonial and 'friendly' Māori troops. Despite surprising successes, Māori are defeated and much land is confiscated.	All Māori men (rather than individual land owners) are granted the right to vote.

raided further south in their turn. The domino effect continued to the far south of the South Island in 1836. The missionaries claimed that the Musket Wars then tapered off through their influence, but the restoration of the balance of power through the equal distribution of muskets was probably more important.

The Māori population for 1769 has been estimated at between 85,000 and 110,000. The Musket Wars killed perhaps 20,000, and new diseases (including typhoid, tuberculosis and venereal disease) did considerable damage, too. Fortunately NZ had the natural quarantine of distance: infected Europeans often recovered or died during the long voyage, and smallpox, for example, which devastated indigenous North Americans, never arrived. By 1840 Māori had been reduced to about 70,000, a decline of at least 20%. Māori bent under the weight of European contact, but they certainly did not break.

Growing Pains

Māori tribes valued the profit and prestige brought by the Pākehā and wanted both, along with protection from foreign powers. Accepting nominal British authority was the way to get them. James Busby was appointed New Zealand's first British Resident in 1833, though his powers were largely symbolic. Busby selected the country's first official flag and established the Declaration of the Independence of New Zealand. But he was too ineffectual to curb rampant colonisation.

By 1840 the British government was overcoming its reluctance to undertake potentially expensive intervention in NZ. The British were eager to secure their commercial interests, and they also believed, wrongly but sincerely, that Māori could not handle the increasing scale of unofficial European contact. In 1840 the two peoples struck a deal, symbolised by the treaty first signed at Waitangi on 6 February that year. The Treaty of Waitangi now has a standing not dissimilar to that of the Constitution in the US, but is even more contested. The original problem was a discrepancy between British and Māori understandings of it. The English version promised Māori full equality as British subjects in return for complete rights of government. The Māori version also promised that Māori would retain their chieftainship, which implied local rights of government. The problem was not great at first, because the Māori version applied outside the small European settlements. But as those settlements grew, conflict brewed.

In 1840 there were only about 2000 Europeans in NZ, with the shanty town of Kororāreka the capital and biggest settlement. By 1850 six new settlements had been formed, with 22,000 settlers between them. About half of these had arrived under the auspices of the New Zealand Company and its associates. The company was the brainchild of Edward Gibbon Wakefield, who also influenced the settlement of South Australia.

'I believe we were all glad to leave New Zealand. It is not a pleasant place. Amongst the natives there is absent that charming simplicity...and the greater part of the English are the very refuse of society.' Charles Darwin, writing about his 1835 visit to Kororāreka (Russell).

'Kaore e mau te rongo – ake, ake!' (Peace never shall be made – never, never!) War chief Rewi Maniapoto in response to government troops at the battle of Ōrākau, 1864.

1868–72	1886–87	1893	1901
East Coast war. Te Kooti, having led an escape from his prison on the Chatham Islands, leads a holy guerrilla war in the Urewera region. He finally retreats to establish the Ringatū Church.	Tūwharetoa tribe gifts the mountains of Ruapehu, Ngāuruhoe and Tongariro to the government to establish NZ's first national park.	NZ becomes the first country in the world to grant the vote to women, following a campaign led by Kate Sheppard, who petitioned the government for years.	NZ politely declines the invitation to join the new Commonwealth of Australia, but thanks for asking.

Wakefield hoped to short-circuit the barbarous frontier phase of settlement with 'instant civilisation', but his success was limited. From the 1850s his settlers, who included a high proportion of upper-middle-class gentlefolk, were swamped by succeeding waves of immigrants, who continued to wash in until the 1880s. These people were part of the great British and Irish diaspora that also populated Australia and much of North America, but the NZ mix was distinctive. Lowland Scots settlers were more prominent in NZ than elsewhere, for example, with the possible exception of parts of Canada. New Zealand's Irish, even the Catholics, tended to come from the north of Ireland. New Zealand's English tended to come from the counties close to London. Small groups of Germans, Scandinavians and Chinese made their way in, though the last faced increasing racial prejudice from the 1880s, when the Pākehā population reached half a million.

Much of the mass immigration from the 1850s to the 1870s was assisted by the provincial and central governments, which also mounted large-scale public-works schemes, especially in the 1870s under Premier Julius Vogel. In 1876 Vogel abolished the provinces on the grounds that they were hampering his development efforts. The last imperial governor with substantial power was the talented but Machiavellian George Grey, who ended his second governorship in 1868. Thereafter, the governors (governors-general from 1917) were largely just nominal heads of state; the head of government, the premier or prime minister, had more power. The central government, originally weaker than the provincial governments, the imperial governor and the Māori tribes, eventually exceeded the power of all three.

The Māori tribes did not go down without a fight. Indeed, their resistance was one of the most formidable ever mounted against European expansion. The first clash took place in 1843 in the Wairau Valley, now a wine-growing district. A posse of settlers set out to enforce the myth of British control, but encountered the reality of Māori control. Twenty-two settlers were killed, including Wakefield's brother, Arthur, along with about six Māori. In 1845 more serious fighting broke out in the Bay of Islands, when Hōne Heke sacked a British settlement. Heke and his ally Kawiti baffled three British punitive expeditions, using a modern variant of the traditional *pā* fortification. Vestiges of these innovative earthworks can still be seen at Ruapekapeka (south of Kawakawa). Governor Grey claimed victory in the north, but few were convinced at the time. Grey had more success in the south, where he arrested the formidable Ngāti Toa chief Te Rauparaha, who until then wielded great influence on both sides of Cook Strait. Pākehā were able to swamp the few Māori living on the South Island, but the fighting of the 1840s confirmed that the North Island at that time comprised a European fringe around an independent Māori heartland.

The Waitangi Treaty Grounds, where the Treaty of Waitangi was first signed in 1840, is now a tourist attraction for Kiwis and non-Kiwis alike. Each year on 6 February, Waitangi hosts treaty commemorations and protests.

Former NZ prime minister Julius Vogel (1835–99) wrote a science-fiction novel *Anno Domini 2000* (1889) in which he imagines a utopian society led by women. Very prescient, considering NZ was the first country to give women the vote... Available on Kindle.

1908	1914–18	1931	1935–49
NZ physicist Ernest Rutherford is awarded the Nobel Prize in chemistry for 'splitting the atom', investigating the disintegration of elements and the chemistry of radioactive substances.	NZ's contribution to WWI is staggering: for a country of just over one million people, about 100,000 NZ men serve overseas. Some 60,000 become casualties, mostly on the Western Front in France.	A massive earthquake in Napier and Hastings kills at least 256 people.	First Labour government in power, under Michael Savage. This government creates NZ's pioneering version of the welfare state, and also takes some independent initiatives in foreign policy.

In the 1850s settler population and aspirations grew, and fighting broke out again in 1860. The wars burned on sporadically until 1872 over much of the North Island. In the early years the King Movement, seeking to establish a monarchy that would allow Māori to assume a more equal footing with the European settlers, was the backbone of resistance. In later years some remarkable prophet-generals, notably Titokowaru and Te Kooti, took over. Most wars were small-scale, but the Waikato Land War of 1863–64 was not. This conflict, fought at the same time as the American Civil War, involved armoured steamships, ultra-modern heavy artillery, and 10 proud British regular regiments. Despite the odds, Māori forces won several battles, such as that at Gate Pā, near Tauranga, in 1864. But in the end they were ground down by European numbers and resources. Māori political, though not cultural, independence ebbed away in the last decades of the 19th century. It finally expired when police invaded the last Māori sanctuary, the Urewera Mountains, in 1916.

From Gold Rush to Welfare State

From the 1850s to the 1880s, despite conflict with Māori, the Pākehā economy boomed. A gold rush on the South Island made Dunedin NZ's biggest town, and a young, mostly male population chased their fortunes along the West Coast. Fretting over the imbalance in this frontier society, the British government tried to entice women to settle in NZ. Huge amounts of wool were exported, and there were unwise levels of overseas borrowing for development of railways and roads. By 1886 the population reached a tipping point: the population of non-Māori people were mostly born in NZ. Many still considered Britain their distant home, but a new identity was taking shape.

Depression hit in 1879, when wool prices slipped and gold production thinned out. Unemployment pushed some of the working population to Australia, and many of those who stayed suffered miserable working conditions. There was still cause for optimism: NZ successfully exported frozen meat in 1882, raising hopes of a new backbone for the economy. Forests were enthusiastically cleared to make way for farmland.

In 1890 the Liberals, NZ's first organised political party, came to power. They stayed there until 1912, helped by a recovering economy. For decades, social-reform movements such as the Woman's Christian Temperance Union (WCTU) had lobbied for women's freedom, and NZ became the first country in the world to give women the vote in 1893. (Another major WCTU push, for countrywide prohibition, didn't take off.) Old-age pensions were introduced in 1898, but these social leaps forward didn't bring universal good news. Pensions only applied to those falling within a very particular definition of 'good character', and the pension reforms deliberately excluded the population of Chinese

1936	1939–45	1953	1974
NZ aviatrix Jean Batten becomes the first aviator to fly solo directly from Britain to NZ.	NZ troops back Britain and the Allied war effort during WWII; from 1942 as many as 45,000 American soldiers camp in NZ to guard against Japanese attack.	New Zealander Edmund Hillary, with Tenzing Norgay, 'knocks the bastard off'; the pair become the first men to reach the summit of Mt Everest.	Pacific Island migrants who have outstayed visas are subjected to crackdowns by immigration police under Robert Muldoon's National government. Raids continue until the early 1980s.

settlers who had arrived to labour in the goldfields. Meanwhile, the Liberals were obtaining more and more Māori land for settlement. By now, the non-Māori population outnumbered the Māori by 17 to one.

Nation-Building

New Zealand had backed Britain in the Boer War (1899–1902) and WWI (1914–18), with dramatic losses in WWI. However, the bravery of Anzac (Australian and New Zealand Army Corps) forces in the failed Gallipoli campaign endures as a nation-building moment for NZ. In the 1930s NZ's experience of the Great Depression was as grim as any. The derelict farmhouses still seen in rural areas often date from this era. In 1935 a second reforming government took office, campaigning on a platform of social justice: the First Labour government, led by Australian-born Michael Joseph Savage. In WWII NZ formally declared war on Germany: 140,000 or so New Zealanders fought in Europe and the Middle East, while at home women took on increasing roles in the labour force.

By the 1930s giant ships were regularly carrying frozen meat, cheese and butter, as well as wool, on regular voyages from NZ to Britain. As the NZ economy adapted to the feeding of London, cultural links were also enhanced. New Zealand children studied British history and literature, not their own. New Zealand's leading scientists and writers, such as Ernest Rutherford and Katherine Mansfield, gravitated to Britain. Average living standards in NZ were normally better than in Britain, as were the welfare and lower-level education systems. New Zealanders had access to British markets and culture, and they contributed their share to the latter as equals. The list of 'British' writers, academics, scientists, military leaders, publishers and the like who were actually New Zealanders is long.

New Zealand prided itself on its affluence, equality and social harmony. But it was also conformist, even puritanical. The 1953 Marlon Brando movie, *The Wild One,* was banned until 1977. Full Sunday trading was not allowed until 1989. Licensed restaurants hardly existed in 1960, nor did supermarkets or TV. Notoriously, from 1917 to 1967, pubs were obliged

Wellington-born Nancy Wake (code-named 'The White Mouse') led a guerrilla attack in France against the Nazis with a 7000-strong army. Her honours included being the Gestapo's most wanted person and a highly decorated Allied servicewoman. Her story has been told via books, a film and a TV miniseries.

LAND WARS

Starting in Northland and moving throughout the North Island, the New Zealand Wars had many complex causes, but *whenua* (land) was the one common factor. In these conflicts, also referred to as the Land Wars or Māori Wars, Māori fought both for and against the NZ government, on whose side stood the Imperial British Army, Australians and NZ's own Armed Constabulary. Land confiscations imposed on the Māori as punishment for involvement in these wars are still the source of conflict today, with the government struggling to finance compensation for what are now acknowledged to have been illegal seizures.

1981	1985	1992	2004
Springbok rugby tour divides the nation. Many Kiwis take an anti-apartheid stance and protest the games. Others feel that sport and politics shouldn't mix, and support the South African tour going ahead.	*Rainbow Warrior* sunk in Auckland Harbour by French government agents to prevent the Greenpeace protest ship from making its intended voyage to Moruroa, where France is conducting nuclear tests.	Government begins reparations for Land Wars confiscations, and confirms Māori fishing rights in the 'Sealord deal'. Major settlements follow, including the 1995 reparations for Waikato land confiscations.	Māori TV begins broadcasting – for the first time, a channel committed to NZ content and the revitalisation of Māori language and culture hits the small screen.

to shut at 6pm (which, ironically, paved the way for a culture of fast, heavy drinking before closing time). Yet puritanism was never the whole story. Opposition to Sunday trading stemmed not so much from belief in the sanctity of the sabbath, but from the belief that workers should have weekends, too. Six o'clock closing was a standing joke in rural areas. There was always something of a Kiwi counterculture, even before imported countercultures took root from the 1960s onward.

In 1973 'Mother England' ran off and joined the budding EU. New Zealand was beginning to develop alternative markets to Britain, and alternative exports to wool, meat and dairy products. Wide-bodied jet aircraft were allowing the world and NZ to visit each other on an increasing scale. Women were beginning to penetrate first the upper reaches of the workforce and then the political sphere. Gay people came out of the closet, despite vigorous efforts by moral conservatives to push them back in. University-educated youths were becoming more numerous and more assertive.

> New Zealand's staunch anti-nuclear stance earned it the nickname 'The Mouse That Roared'.

The Modern Age

From the 1930s, Māori experienced both a population explosion and massive urbanisation. Life expectancy was lengthening, the birth rate was high, and Māori people were moving to cities for occupations formerly filled by Pākehā servicemen. Almost 80% were urban dwellers by the mid-1980s, a staggering reversal of the status quo that brought cultural displacement but simultaneously triggered a movement to strengthen pride in Māori identity. Immigration was broadening, too, first encouraging Pacific Islanders in, for their labour, and then (East) Asians for their capital.

Then, in 1984, NZ's next great reforming government was elected – the fourth Labour government, led by David Lange, though in fact by Roger Douglas, the Minister of Finance. This government adopted a more market-led economic policy (dubbed 'Rogernomics'), delighting the right, and an anti-nuclear foreign policy, delighting the left. New Zealand's numerous economic controls were dismantled with breakneck speed. Revelling in their new freedom, NZ investors engaged in a frenzy of speculation, and suffered even more than the rest of the world from the economic crash of 1987.

> In 2015 there was a public referendum to decide between five proposed designs for a new national flag, and the winner was a black-and-blue-backed silver fern. During a second referendum in 2016, Kiwis decided that, on reflection, they preferred the original flag – if it ain't broke...!

In 1985 French spies sank the Greenpeace anti-nuclear protest ship *Rainbow Warrior* in Auckland Harbour, killing one crewman. The lukewarm American condemnation of the French act brought middle NZ in behind the anti-nuclear policy, which became associated with national independence.

From the 1990s, a change to a points-based immigration policy has woven an increasingly multicultural tapestry in NZ. Numbers of migrat-

2010	2011	2013	2013
A cave-in at Pike River coalmine on the South Island's West Coast kills 29 miners.	A severe earthquake strikes Christchurch, killing 185 people and badly damaging the central business district.	New Zealand becomes one of just 15 countries in the world to legally recognise same-sex marriage.	Auckland teenager Ella Yelich-O'Connor, aka Lorde, hits No 1 in the US music charts with her mesmeric tune 'Royals'.

Māori wood carving, Rotorua (p306)

ing Brits fell, while new arrivals from Pacific Islands, Asia, North Africa, the Middle East and other European countries increased, particularly to NZ's cities.

In 2017 NZ voted in a new face to show the world. Helmed by Jacinda Ardern, a coalition government was formed by Labour and NZ First, with support from the Green Party. New Zealand's third female prime minister has faced challenges satisfying the various elements of her governing coalition while trying to tackle a national housing crisis and effect bigger investment in education and health. Ardern's response to the 2019 Christchurch mosque attacks was widely admired for her compassion and leadership. It's no wonder that her ascendancy has been touted as the dawn of a new period of major reform.

Scottish settler influence is still apparent in NZ, particularly in the south of the South Island. Dunedin is called the 'Edinburgh of the South'.

2015	2017	2017	2019
New Zealand's beloved All Blacks win back-to-back Rugby World Cups in England, defeating arch-rivals Australia 34-17 in the final.	Whanganui River is granted the same legal rights as a human being, a global first.	Jacinda Ardern becomes NZ's youngest PM for 150 years, heralding a new direction for NZ politics.	The Christchurch mosque shootings shocked NZ, but the country's response inspired the world.

Environment

New Zealand's landforms have a diversity that you would expect to find across an entire continent: snow-dusted mountains, drowned glacial valleys, rainforests, dunelands and an otherworldly volcanic plateau. Straddling the boundary of two great colliding slabs of the earth's crust – the Pacific plate and the Indo-Australian plate – NZ is a plaything for nature's powerful forces.

The Land

New Zealand is a young country – its present shape is less than 10,000 years old. Having broken away from the supercontinent of Gondwanaland (which included Africa, Australia, Antarctica and South America) some 85 million years ago, it endured continual uplift and erosion, buckling and tearing, and the slow fall and rise of the sea as ice ages came and went.

Evidence of NZ's tumultuous past is everywhere. The South Island's mountainous spine – the 650km-long ranges of the Southern Alps – grew from the clash between plates at a rate of 20km over three million years; in geological terms, that's a sprint. Despite NZ's highest peak, Aoraki/Mt Cook, losing 10m from its summit overnight in a 1991 landslide (and a couple of dozen more metres to erosion), the Alps are overall believed to be some of the fastest-growing mountains in the world.

Volcanic New Zealand

The North Island's most impressive landscapes have been wrought by volcanoes. Auckland is built on an isthmus peppered by some 48 scoria cones (cinder cones, or volcanic vents). The city's largest, and most recently formed volcano, 600-year-old Rangitoto Island is a short ferry ride from downtown. Another 300km south, the classically shaped cone of snowcapped Mt Taranaki overlooks tranquil dairy pastures.

New Zealand is one of the most spectacular places in the world to see geysers. On the North Island, Rotorua's short-lived Waimangu geyser, formed after the 1886 Mt Tarawera eruption, was once the world's largest, often gushing to a spectacular height of 400m.

But NZ's real volcanic heartland runs through the centre of the North Island, from the restless bulk of Mt Ruapehu in Tongariro National Park, northeast through the Rotorua lake district and out to NZ's most active volcano, White Island, in the Bay of Plenty, which tragically erupted in December 2019. This great 350km-long rift valley – part of a volcano chain known as the 'Pacific Ring of Fire' – has been the seat of massive eruptions that have left their mark on the country physically and culturally. The volcano that created Lake Taupō last erupted 1800 years ago in a display that was the most violent (a VEI-7 score) anywhere on the planet within the past 2000 years.

You can experience the aftermath of volcanic destruction on a smaller scale at Te Wairoa, the Buried Village (p324), near Rotorua on the shores of Lake Tarawera. Here, partly excavated and open to the public, lie the remains of a 19th-century Māori village overwhelmed when nearby Mt Tarawera erupted without warning. The famous Pink and White Terraces, spectacular naturally formed pools (and one of several claimants to the title 'eighth wonder of the world'), were destroyed overnight by the same upheaval.

Born of geothermal violence, Waimangu Volcanic Valley (p323) is the place to go to experience hot earth up close and personal amid geysers, silica pans, bubbling mud pools and the world's biggest hot spring. Alternatively, wander around Rotorua's Whakarewarewa village (p307), where descendants of Māori displaced by the eruption live in the middle of steaming vents and prepare food for visitors in boiling pools.

The South Island also displays evidence of volcanism – if the remains of the old volcanoes of Banks Peninsula weren't there to repel the sea, the vast Canterbury Plains, built from alpine sediment washed down the rivers from the Alps, would have eroded long ago.

NEW ZEALAND'S CHALLENGES

New Zealand's reputation as an Eden, replete with pristine wilderness and ecofriendly practices, has been repeatedly placed under the microscope. The industry most visible to visitors, tourism, appears studded in green accolades, with environmental best practices employed in areas as broad as heating insulation in hotels to minimum-impact wildlife-watching. But mining, offshore oil and gas exploration, pollution, biodiversity loss, funding cuts and questionable urban planning have provided endless hooks for bad-news stories.

Water quality is arguably the most serious environmental issue faced by New Zealanders and one the government started to tackle seriously in 2019. Research from diverse sources suggests that the health of New Zealand's waterways has been in decline, the primary culprit: 'dirty dairying' – cow effluent leaching into freshwater ecosystems, carrying with it high levels of nitrates, as well as bacteria and parasites such as *E. coli* and giardia. A 2017 government push to make 90% of rivers and lakes swimmable by 2040 was met with initial scepticism about the metrics involved, but there's a strong impetus to make NZ's waterways worthy of the country's clean and green reputation.

Another ambitious initiative kicked off in 2016: Predator Free 2050. The aim is to rid NZ of introduced animals that prey on native flora and fauna. The worst offenders are possums, stoats and rats, which eat swathes of forest and kill wildlife, particularly birds. However, controversy rages at the Department of Conservation's (DOC) use of 1080 poison (sodium fluoroacetate) to control these pests, despite it being sanctioned by prominent environmental groups as well as the Parliamentary Commissioner for the Environment. Vehement opposition to 1080 is expressed by such diverse camps as hunters and animal-rights activists, who cite detriments such as by-kill and the potential for poison passing into waterways. Proponents of its use argue that it's biodegradable and that aerial distribution of 1080 is the only cost-effective way to target predators across vast, inaccessible parts of NZ. Still, 'Ban 1080' signs remain common in rural communities and the controversy is unlikely to end until the poison is banned.

As well as its damaging impact on waterways, the $12 billion dairy industry – the country's biggest export earner – generates 48% of NZ's greenhouse gas emissions. Some farmers are cleaning up their act, lowering emissions through improved management of fertilisers and higher-quality feed, and major players DairyNZ and Fonterra have pledged support. But when it comes to contributing to climate change, the dairy industry isn't NZ's only dirty habit. New Zealand might be a nation of avid recyclers and solar-panel enthusiasts, but it also has the world's fourth-highest ratio of motor vehicles to people.

There have been fears about safeguarding the principal legislation governing the NZ environment, the 1991 *Resource Management Act,* in the face of proposed amendments. NGOs and community groups – ever-vigilant and already making major contributions to the welfare of NZ's environment – will find plenty to keep them occupied in coming years. But with an eco-conscious prime minister, Jacinda Ardern, leading a coalition government, New Zealanders are hopeful of a greener future – Ardern has pledged an ambitious goal of reducing net greenhouse gas emissions to zero by 2050.

With more trains, 100% renewable energy sources and planting 100 million trees per year, NZ could take a lead in the global response to our current climate emergency.

Humpback whale off the coast of Kaikōura (p454)

Earthquakes

Earthquakes are common in NZ, but most only rattle the glassware. A few have wrecked major towns. In 1931 an earthquake measuring 7.9 on the Richter scale levelled the Hawke's Bay city of Napier, causing huge damage and loss of life. Napier was rebuilt almost entirely in the then-fashionable art-deco architectural style.

On the South Island in September 2010, Christchurch was rocked by a magnitude 7.1 earthquake. Less than six months later, in February 2011, a magnitude 6.3 quake destroyed much of the city's historic heart and claimed 185 lives, making it the country's second-deadliest natural disaster, and Christchurch is still recovering from it. Then, in November 2016, an earthquake measuring 7.8 on the Richter scale struck Kaikōura – further up the coast – resulting in two deaths and widespread damage to local infrastructure. Roads and rail have since been rebuilt but the landscape stills wears the evidence.

Native Fauna

New Zealand's long isolation has allowed it to become a veritable warehouse of unique and varied plants. Separation of NZ's landmass occurred before mammals appeared on the scene, leaving birds and insects to evolve in spectacular ways. As one of the last places on earth to be colonised by humans, NZ was for millennia a safe laboratory for risky evolutionary strategies. But the arrival of Māori, and later Europeans, brought new threats and sometimes extinction.

The now-extinct flightless moa, the largest of which grew to 3.5m tall and weighed more than 200kg, browsed open grasslands much as cattle do today (skeletons can be seen at Auckland Museum), while the smaller kiwi still ekes out a nocturnal living rummaging among forest leaf lit-

Travellers seeking sustainable tourism operators should look for businesses accredited with Qualmark (www.qualmark.co.nz) or those listed at Organic Explorer (www.organic explorer.co.nz).

ter for insects and worms. One of the country's most ferocious-looking insects, the mouse-sized giant weta, meanwhile, has taken on a scavenging role elsewhere filled by rodents.

Many endemic creatures, including moa and the huia, an exquisite songbird, were driven to extinction, and the vast forests were cleared for timber and to make way for agriculture. Destruction of habitat and the introduction of exotic animals and plants have taken a terrible environmental toll – and New Zealanders are now fighting a rearguard battle to save what remains.

Birds & Bats

Pause in any NZ forest and listen: this country is aflutter with melodious feathered creatures. The country's first Polynesian settlers found little in the way of land mammals – just two species of bat – and most of NZ's present mammals are introduced species. New Zealand's birds generally aren't flashy, but they have an understated beauty that reveals itself in more delicate details: the lacy plumage of a rare white heron (kōtuku), the bespectacled appearance of a silvereye or the golden frowns of Fiordland penguins.

The most beautiful songbird is the tui, a nectar-eater with an inventive repertoire that includes clicks, grunts and chuckles. Notable for the white throat feathers that stand out against its dark plumage, the tui often feeds on flax flowers in suburban gardens but is most at home in densely tangled forest ('bush' to New Zealanders). The bellbird (korimako) is also musical; it's common in both native and exotic forests everywhere except Northland (though it is more likely to be heard than seen). Its call is a series of liquid bell notes, most often sounded at dawn or dusk. Fantails (pīwakawaka) are also common on forest trails, swooping and jinking to catch insects stirred up by passing hikers.

At ground level, the most famous native bird is of course the kiwi, NZ's national emblem, with a rounded body and a long, distinctive bill with nostrils at the tip for sniffing out food. Sightings in the wild require patience and luck, but numerous sanctuaries allow a peep of this iconic bird. Look out for other land birds like pukeko, elegant swamp-hens with blue plumage and bright-red beaks. They're readily seen along wetland margins and even on the sides of roads nearby – be warned, they have little road sense. Far rarer (though not dissimilar in appearance) is the takahe, a flightless bird thought to be extinct until a small colony was discovered in 1948. It's worth seeking them out at Te Anau's bird sanctuary (p548).

If you spend any time in the South Island high country, you are likely to spot the kea (unless it finds you first). A dark-green parrot with red underwings and a sense of mischief, its bold antics are a source of frustration and delight to New Zealanders. Kea are particularly common in car parks along the Milford Hwy, and in the West Coast's glacier country, where they hang out for food scraps or tear rubber from car windscreens (we've also seen them nibbling at ski bindings in winter sports resorts around Queenstown: consider yourself warned). Resist the urge to feed them, as it's hugely damaging to their health.

And what of the native bats? Populations of both short-tailed and long-tailed bats are declining at frightening speed, though Kahurangi National Park and Nelson are believed to be home to small populations. DOC (Department of Conservation) is hard at work protecting bats, including ambitious plans to resettle them on predator-free islands. If you spot a bat, count yourself lucky – and consider telling DOC.

New Zealand's Ancient Lizard

The largest native reptile in NZ is the tuatara, a crested lizard that can grow up to 50cm long. Thought to be unchanged for more than 220

B Heather and H Robertson's *Field Guide to the Birds of New Zealand* (2015) is a comprehensive guide for bird-watchers and a model of helpfulness for anyone even casually interested in the country's remarkable bird life. Another good guide, only available second-hand, is *Birds of New Zealand: Locality Guide* (2000) by Stuart Chambers.

Rumours of late survivals of the giant moa bird abound, but none has been authenticated. In recent years there has been enthusiasm around attempting to 'de-extinct' the moa using DNA samples, although most environmentalists see conserving existing species as the bigger priority.

million years, these endearing creatures can live for up to a century. Meet them at Auckland Zoo (p94) and Hokitika's National Kiwi Centre (p613), and other zoos and sanctuaries around NZ.

Marine-Mammal-Watching

Kaikōura, on the northeast coast of the South Island, is NZ's nexus of marine-mammal-watching. The main attraction here is whale-watching. The sperm whale, a toothed whale that can grow up to 18m long, is pretty much a year-round resident here, although please note it's sometimes shy of whale-spotting cruises. Depending on the season, you may also see migrating humpback whales, pilot whales, blue whales and southern right whales. Other mammals – including fur seals and dusky dolphins – are seen year-round.

However, wildlife tourism remains controversial. Whale populations around the world have declined rapidly over the past 200 years, and the same predictable migration habits that once made the giants easy prey for whalers make them easy targets for whale-watching tourism. As NZ's whale-watching industry has grown, so has concern over its impact.

At the centre of the debate is the practice of swimming with whales and dolphins. While it's undoubtedly one of the more exhilarating experiences you can have on the planet, many observers suggest that human interaction with these marine mammals has a disruptive effect on behaviours and breeding patterns. Taking a longer view, others say that, given humanity's historic propensity for slaughtering whales by the tens of thousands, it's time we gave them a little peace and quiet.

Dolphin swimming was banned on the North Island of NZ in 2019 due to the significant reduction in bottlenose dolphins in the Bay of Islands region. Kaikōura is still a hotspot for swimming with dolphins, with pods of up to 500 dusky dolphins commonly seen there. You can also swim with seals in Kaikōura and in Abel Tasman National Park.

You'll be glad to know that the Department of Conservation's guidelines and protocols ensure that all operators are licensed and monitored, and forbids swimming with dolphin pods that have vulnerable young calves. If it's truly a bucket-list essential for you, give yourself a few days to do it so that there is no pressure on the operator to 'chase' marine mammals to satisfy paying customers. If you feel your whale-, dolphin- or seal-swim operator has 'hassled' the animals or breached the boundaries in any way (like loud noises, feeding them or circling them), report them to DOC immediately. New Zealand does take animal welfare seriously.

National Parks

More than 85,000 sq km of NZ – almost one third of the country – is protected and managed within parks and reserves. Almost every conceivable landscape is found in this diminutive island nation: from mangrove-fringed inlets in the north to the snow-topped volcanoes of the Central Plateau, and from the forested fastness of the Urewera ranges in the east to the Southern Alps' majestic mountains, glaciers and fiords. The 13 national parks and more than 30 marine reserves and parks, along with numerous forest parks, offer huge scope for wilderness experiences, ranging from climbing, skiing and mountain biking to hiking, kayaking and trout fishing.

Three places are World Heritage Areas: NZ's Sub-Antarctic Islands; Tongariro National Park (on the North Island); and Te Wāhipounamu (Southwest New Zealand), an amalgam of several national parks in southwest NZ that boasts the world's finest surviving Gondwanaland plants and animals in their natural habitats.

Access to the country's wild places is relatively straightforward, though huts on walking tracks require passes and may need to be booked in

Nature Guide to the New Zealand Forest (2000) by J Dawson and R Lucas is a beautifully photographed foray into NZ's forests, home to ancient species dating from the time of the dinosaurs.

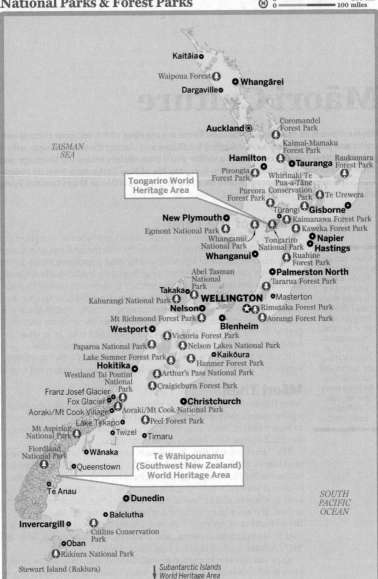

advance. In practical terms, there is little difference for travellers between a national park and a forest park, though pets are generally not allowed in national parks. Disability-assist dogs can be taken into dog-controlled areas without a permit. Camping is possible in all parks, but may be restricted to dedicated camping grounds – always check where camping is allowed via DOC's website and information leaflets before you pitch up.

Māori Culture

Māori culture is as diverse as its people. Some are engaged with traditional cultural networks and pursuits; others are adapting traditions and placing these in dialogue with a globalised New Zealand culture. As a visitor you'll immediately notice the language and cultural understandings imbued in the everyday life of New Zealanders from its indigenous population, though areas where there's a larger proportion of Māori families living today are mainly in the North Island.

People of the Land

The indigenous Māori are New Zealand's *tangata whenua* (people of the land), and the Māori spiritual relationship with the land has grown over hundreds of years. Once a predominantly rural population, many Māori people now live in urban centres, away from their traditional homelands, but it's still the practice in formal settings to introduce oneself by reference to 'home': an ancestral mountain, river, sea or lake, or an ancestor.

Kupe's passage is marked around NZ: he left his sails (Nga Ra o Kupe) near Cape Palliser as triangular landforms; he named the two islands in Wellington Harbour Matiu and Makoro after his daughters; his blood stains the red rocks of Wellington's south coast.

The Māori concept of *whanaungatanga* – family relationships – is central to the culture: families spread out from the *whānau* (extended family) to the *hapū* (subtribe) and *iwi* (tribe) and even, in a sense, beyond the human world and into the natural and spiritual worlds.

If you're looking for a Māori experience in NZ you'll find it – in conversations, galleries, gigs, cultural performances, on an organised tour...

Māori Then

Some three millennia ago people began moving eastward into the Pacific, sailing against the prevailing winds and currents (hard to go out, easier to return safely). Some stopped at Tonga and Samoa, and others settled the small central East Polynesian tropical islands.

The Māori colonisation of Aotearoa began from an original homeland known to Māori as Hawaiki. Skilled navigators and sailors travelled across the Pacific, using many navigational tools – currents, winds, stars, birds and wave patterns – to guide their large, double-hulled ocean-going craft to a new land. The first of many was the great navigator Kupe, who arrived, the story goes, chasing a giant octopus named Muturangi. But the distinction of giving NZ its well-known Māori name – Aotearoa – goes to his wife, Kuramarotini, who cried out, '*He ao, he ao tea, he ao tea roa!*' (A cloud, a white cloud, a long white cloud!).

Kupe and his crew journeyed around the land, and many places around Cook Strait (between the North and South Islands) and the Hokianga in Northland still bear the names that the crew gave them and the marks of their passage. Kupe returned to Hawaiki, leaving from (and naming) Northland's Hokianga. He gave other seafarers valuable navigational information. And then the great *waka* (ocean-going craft) began to arrive.

The *waka* that the first settlers arrived on, and their landing places, are immortalised in tribal histories. Well-known *waka* include *Tākitimu, Kurahaupō, Te Arawa, Mātaatua, Tainui, Aotea* and *Tokomaru*. There are many others. Māori trace their genealogies back to those who arrived on the *waka* (and further back as well).

HOW THE WORLD BEGAN

In the Māori story of creation, first there was the void, then the night, then Ranginui (sky father) and Papatūānuku (earth mother) came into being embracing, with their children nurtured between them. But nurturing became something else. Their children were stifled in the darkness of their embrace. Unable to stretch out to their full dimensions and struggling to see clearly in the darkness, their children tried to separate them. Tāwhirimātea, the god of winds, raged against them; Tūmatauenga, the god of war, assaulted them. Each god child in turn tried to separate them, but still Rangi and Papa pressed against each other. And then Tāne Mahuta, god of the great forests and of humanity, placed his feet against his father and his back against his mother and slowly began to move them apart. Then came the world of light, of demigods and humanity.

In this world of light, Māui, the demigod ancestor, was cast out to sea at birth and was found floating in his mother's topknot. He was a shape-shifter, becoming a pigeon or a dog or an eel if it suited his purposes. He stole fire from the gods. Using his grandmother's jawbone, he bashed the sun so that it could only limp slowly across the sky, allowing people enough time during the day to get things done (if only he would do it again!). Using the South Island as a canoe, he used the jawbone as a hook to fish up Te Ika-a-Māui (the fish of Māui) – the North Island. And, finally, he met his end trying to defeat death itself. The goddess of death, Hine-nui-te-pō, had obsidian teeth in her vagina (obsidian is a volcanic glass that has a razor edge when chipped). Māui attempted to reverse birth (and hence defeat death) by crawling into her birth canal to reach her heart as she slept. A small bird – a fantail – laughed at the absurd sight. Hine-nui-te-pō awoke, and crushed Māui to death between her thighs. Death one, humanity nil.

What would it have been like, making the transition from small tropical islands to a much larger, cooler landmass? Goodbye breadfruit, coconuts, paper mulberry; hello moa, fernroot, flax – and immense space (relatively speaking). New Zealand has more than 15,000km of coastline. Rarotonga, by way of contrast, has a little over 30km. There was land, lots of it, and flora and fauna that had developed more or less separately from the rest of the world for 80 million years. There was an untouched, massive fishery. There were great seaside mammalian convenience stores – seals and sea lions – as well as a fabulous array of birds.

The early settlers went on the move, pulled by love, trade opportunities and greater resources; pushed by disputes and threats to security. When they settled, Māori established *mana whenua* (regional authority), whether by military campaigns or by the peaceful methods of intermarriage and diplomacy. Looking over tribal history it's possible to see the many alliances, absorptions and extinctions that went on.

Histories were carried by the voice, in stories, songs and chants. Great stress was placed on accurate learning – after all, in an oral culture where people are the libraries, the past is always a generation or two away from oblivion.

Māori lived in *kāinga* (small villages), which often had associated gardens. Housing was cosy by modern standards – often it was hard to stand upright while inside. From time to time people would leave their home base and go to harvest seasonal foods. When peaceful life was interrupted by conflict, people would withdraw to *pā* (fortified villages).

And then Europeans began to arrive.

Māori legends are all around you as you tour NZ: Māui's *waka* became today's Southern Alps; a *taniwha* (legendary water being) formed Lake Waikaremoana in its death throes; and a rejected Mt Taranaki walked into exile from the central North Island mountain group, carving the Whanganui River.

Māori Today

Today's culture is marked by new developments in the arts, business, sport and politics. Many historical grievances still stand, but some *iwi* (Ngāi Tahu and Tainui, for example) have settled major historical grievances and are significant forces in the NZ economy. Māori have also addressed the decline in Māori language use by establishing *kōhanga reo*, kura kaupapa and wānanga (Māori-language preschools, schools and universities). There is now a generation of people who speak Māori as a first language. There is a network of Māori radio stations, and Māori TV attracts a committed viewership. A recently revived Māori event is becoming more and more prominent – Matariki (Māori New Year). The constellation Matariki is also known as the Pleiades. It begins to rise above the horizon in late May or early June and its appearance traditionally signals a time for learning, planning and preparing as well as singing, dancing and celebrating. Look out for talks and lectures, concerts, dinners and parties to celebrate and learn more.

The best way to learn about the relationship between the land and the *tangata whenua* (people of the land) is to get out there and start talking with Māori. Learn some language first via apps like Kupu (www.kupu. co.nz).

Religion

Christian churches and denominations are prominent in the Māori world, including televangelists, mainstream churches for regular and occasional worship, and two major Māori churches (Ringatū and Rātana). But in the (non-Judeo-Christian) beginning there were the *atua Māori*, the Māori gods, and for many Māori the gods are a vital and relevant force still. It is common to greet the earth mother and sky father when speaking formally at a *marae* (meeting house). The gods are represented in art and carving, sung of in *waiata* (songs) and invoked through *karakia* (prayer and incantation) when a meeting house is opened, when a *waka* is launched, even (more simply) when a meal is served. They are spoken of in the *marae* and in wider Māori contexts. The traditional Māori creation story is well known and widely celebrated.

The Arts

There are many collections of Māori *taonga* (treasures) around the country. Some of the largest and most comprehensive are at Wellington's Te Papa museum (p383) and the Auckland Museum (p91). Canterbury Museum (p424) in Christchurch also has a good collection, while Te Hikoi Southern Journey (p538) in Riverton has riveting displays on early interactions between Māori and Pākehā.

You can stay up to date with what's happening in the Māori arts by tuning into *iwi* radio stations or Māori TV (www.maoritelevision.com) for regular features. Māori TV first went to air in 2004, an emotional time for many Māori, who could at last see their culture, their concerns and their language in a mass medium.

Over 90% of content is NZ made, and programs are in both Māori and English: they're subtitled and accessible to everyone. If you want to really get a feel for the rhythm and metre of spoken Māori from the comfort of your own chair, switch to Te Reo (www.maoritelevision.com/tv/te-reo-channel), a Māori-language-only channel.

E-Tangata (e-tangata.co.nz) is an online magazine run by the Mana Trust specialising in stories that reflect the experiences of Māori and Pasifika in Aotearoa.

Arriving for the first time in NZ, two crew members of *Tainui* saw the red flowers of the pohutukawa tree, and they cast away their prized red feather ornaments, thinking that there were plenty to be had on shore.

Tā Moko

Tā moko is the Māori art of tattoo, traditionally worn by men on their faces, thighs and buttocks, and by women on their chins and lips. *Moko* were permanent grooves tapped into the skin using pigment (made from burnt caterpillar or kauri gum soot) and bone chisels (fine, sharp combs for broad work, and straight blades for detailed work). Museums in the major centres – Auckland Museum (p91), Te Papa (p383) in Wellington and Canterbury Museum (p424) in Christchurch – all display traditional implements for *tā moko*.

The modern tattoo machine is common now, but bone chisels are coming back into use for Māori who want to reconnect with tradition. Since the general renaissance in Māori culture in the 1960s, many artists

VISITING MARAE

As you travel around NZ, you will see many *marae* complexes. Often *marae* are owned by a descent group. They are also owned by urban Māori groups, schools, universities and church groups, and they should only be visited by arrangement with the owners. Some *marae* that may be visited with an invitation include Koriniti Marae (p266) on the Whanganui River Rd; Mataatua (p338) in Whakatāne; and the *marae* at Te Papa museum (p383) in Wellington.

Marae complexes include a *wharenui* (meeting house), which often embodies an ancestor. Its ridge is the backbone, the rafters are ribs, and it shelters the descendants. There is a clear space in front of the *wharenui*, the *marae ātea*. Sometimes there are other buildings: a *wharekai* (dining hall); a toilet and shower block; perhaps even class-rooms, play equipment and the like.

Hui (gatherings) are held at *marae*. Issues are discussed, classes conducted, mile-stones celebrated and the dead farewelled. Te reo Māori is prominent, and sometimes the only language used.

Visitors sleep in the meeting house if a *hui* goes on for longer than a day. Mattresses are placed on the floor, someone may bring a guitar, and stories and jokes always go down well as the evening stretches out.

The Pōwhiri

If you visit a *marae* as part of an organised group, you'll be welcomed in a *pōwhiri* (wel-coming ceremony).

Outside the *marae*, there may be a *wero* (challenge). Using *taiaha* (quarter-staff) moves, a warrior will approach the visitors and place a baton on the ground for a visitor to pick up, to demonstrate their peaceful intent.

There is a *karanga* (ceremonial call). A woman from the host group calls to the visi-tors and a woman from the visiting group responds. Their long, high, falling calls begin to overlap and interweave and the visiting group walks on to the *marae ātea* (meeting house courtyard). It is then time for *whaikōrero* (speech-making). The hosts welcome the visitors, the visitors respond. Speeches are capped off by a *waiata* (song), and the visitors' speakers present a *koha* (gift, usually an envelope of cash). The hosts then invite the visitors to *harirū* (shake hands) and *hongi*. Visitors and hosts are now united and will share light refreshments or a meal.

The Hongi

To perform the *hongi*, press forehead and nose together gently, shake hands, and per-haps offer a greeting such as *'Kia ora'* or *'Tēnā koe'*. Some prefer one press (for two or three seconds, or longer), others prefer two shorter (press, release, press). Men and women sometimes kiss on one cheek. The *hongi* symbolises the sharing of breath – or life – with the nose touch, followed with a metaphoric exchanging of knowledge by press-ing foreheads together.

Tapu

Tapu (spiritual restrictions) and *mana* (power and prestige) are taken seriously in the Māori world. Sit on chairs or seating provided (never on tables), and walk around people, not over them. The *pōwhiri* has *tapu*, and mixing food and *tapu* is right up there on the offence-o-meter, so only eat and drink when invited to do so by your hosts. You needn't worry about going hungry, though: an important Māori value is *manaakitanga* (hospitality).

Depending on area, the *pōwhiri* has gender roles: women *karanga* (call), men *whaikōre-ro* (orate); women lead the way on to the *marae*, men sit on the *paepae* (the speakers' bench at the front). In a modern context, the debate around traditional roles continues.

have taken up *tā moko* and now many Māori wear *moko* with quiet pride and humility.

Can visitors get some work done? The art of *tā moko* is learned by, and inked upon, Māori people – but the term *kirituhi* (skin inscriptions) has arisen to describe Māori-motif-inspired modern tattoos that non-Māori can wear. *Kirituhi* can be profoundly meaningful and designed to fit the wearer's personal story, but there is an important distinction between *kirituhi* and *tā moko*.

Wikipedia has a good list of *iwi* websites and a map showing *iwi* distribution (www.wikipedia.org/wiki/list_of_iwi).

Carving

Traditional Māori carving, with its intricate detailing and curved lines, can transport the viewer. It's quite amazing to consider that it was done with stone tools, themselves painstakingly made, until the advent of iron (nails suddenly became very popular).

Some major traditional forms are *waka* (canoes), *pātaka* (storage buildings) and *wharenui* (meeting houses). Along the greenstone-rich West Coast, numerous workshop-boutiques double as galleries that showcase fine examples of modern *pounamu* carving (particularly in Hokitika). You can see sublime examples of traditional carving at Te Papa (p383) in Wellington, and at the following:

➡ Auckland Museum (p91) – Māori Court.

➡ Hell's Gate (p324) – Workshop where you can try your hand at woodcarving; near Rotorua.

➡ Otago Museum (p499) – Impressive *waka taua* (war canoe); Dunedin.

➡ Putiki Church (p261) – Interior covered in carvings and *tukutuku* (wall panels); Whanganui.

➡ Taupō Museum (p281) – Carved meeting house.

➡ Te Manawa (p270) – Museum with a Māori focus; Palmerston North.

For information on Māori arts today, check out Toi Māori at www.maoriart.org.nz.

➡ Waikato Museum (p191) – Beautifully carved *waka taua*; Hamilton.

➡ Wairakei Terraces (p284) – Carved meeting house; Taupō.

➡ Waitangi Treaty Grounds (p168) – *Whare Rūnanga* (carved meeting house) and *waka taua*.

➡ Whakarewarewa (p307) – The 'living village' – carving, other arts, meeting house and performance; Rotorua.

➡ Whanganui Regional Museum (p259) – Wonderful carved *waka*.

The apex of carving today is the *whare whakairo* (carved meeting house). A commissioning group relates its history and ancestral stories to a carver, who then draws (sometimes quite loosely) on traditional motifs to interpret or embody the stories and ancestors in wood or composite fibreboard.

Rongomaraeroa Marae at Te Papa in Wellington, carved by pioneering artist Cliff Whiting, is a colourful example of a contemporary reimagining of a traditional art form. The biggest change in carving (as with most traditional arts) has been in the use of new mediums and tools. Rangi Kipa uses a high-density plastic to make his *hei tiki* (traditional pendants).

See Ngahuia Te Awekotuku's book *Mau Moko: The World of Māori Tattoo* (2007) for a close-up of Māori body art, including powerful, beautiful images and incisive commentary.

Weaving

Weaving was an essential art that provided clothing, nets and cordage, footwear for rough country travel, mats to cover earthen floors, and *kete* (bags) to carry stuff in. Many woven items are beautiful as well as practical. Some are major works – *korowai* (cloaks) could take years to finish. Woven predominantly with flax and feathers, they are worn now on ceremonial occasions – a stunning sight.

Today, tradition is greatly respected, but not all traditions are necessarily followed. Flax was (and still is) the preferred medium for weaving. To get a strong fibre from flax leaves, weavers scraped away the leaves'

Top The *hongi* (Māori traditional greeting; p693)

Bottom Māori people celebrating Waitangi Day (p36)

flesh with a mussel shell, pounded it until it was soft, dyed it, then dried it. But contemporary weavers are using everything in their work: raffia, copper wire, rubber – even polar fleece and garden hoses!

The best way to experience weaving is to contact one of the many NZ weavers running workshops where you're visiting (see www.nztextileexperiences.com). By learning the techniques, you'll appreciate the examples of weaving in museums even more. And if you want to take a shortcut and buy something? Woven *kete* and backpacks have become fashion accessories and are on sale in most cities. Weavings are also sold in dealer art galleries around the country.

Read Hirini Moko Mead's *Tikanga Māori* (2006; available on Kindle), Pat and Hiwi Tauroa's *Te Marae* (2009), and Anne Salmond's *Hui* (2009) for detailed insights into Māori knowledge and customs.

Haka

Haka can be adrenaline-pumping, awe-inspiring and uplifting. The *haka* is not only a war dance – it is used to welcome visitors, honour achievement, express identity and to put forth very strong opinions.

Haka involve chanted words, vigorous body movements and *pūkana* (when performers distort their faces, eyes bulging with the whites showing, perhaps with the tongue extended).

The well-known *haka* 'Ka Mate', performed by the All Blacks before rugby test matches, is credited to the cunning fighting chief Te Rauparaha. It celebrates his escape from death. Chased by enemies, he hid himself in a food pit. After they had left, a friendly chief named Te Whareangi (the 'hairy man' referred to in the *haka*) let him out; he climbed out into the sunshine and performed 'Ka Mate'.

You can experience *haka* at various cultural performances, including at the Waitangi Treaty Grounds (p168), Mitai Māori Village (p320), Tamaki Māori Village (p320), Te Puia (p307) and Whakarewarewa (p307) in Rotorua, and Ko Tane (p434) at Willowbank in Christchurch.

But the best displays of *haka* are at the biannual **Te Matatini National Kapa Haka Festival** (www.tematatini.co.nz), when NZ's top groups compete for honours.

Contemporary Theatre

Powered by a wave of political activism, the 1970s saw the emergence of many Māori playwrights and plays, and theatre remains a prominent area of the Māori arts today. Māori theatre drew heavily on the traditions of the *marae*. Instead of dimming the lights and immediately beginning the performance, many Māori theatre groups began with a stylised *pōwhiri*, had space for audience members to respond to the play, and ended with a *karakia* or a farewell.

The best route into culture is through language. Pick up some te reo Māori with apps Kupu (www.kupu.co.nz) and Drops (language drops.com). Another popular language app, Duolingo, plans to include a te reo Māori course for beginners in 2020. You can also fill your messages with EmoTikis (www.tepuia.com/emotiki).

Taki Rua is an independent producer of Māori work for children and adults and has been in existence for more than 30 years. As well as staging shows in the major centres, it tours most of its work – check out www.takirua.co.nz for the current offerings. Māori drama is also showcased at the professional theatres in the main centres as well as the biennial New Zealand Festival (p36). Look out for work by Hone Kouka, Briar Grace-Smith and Mitch Tawhi Thomas.

Contemporary Dance

Contemporary Māori dance often takes its inspiration from *kapa haka* and traditional Māori imagery. The exploration of pre-European life also provides inspiration.

New Zealand's leading specifically Māori dance company is the Atamira Dance Collective (www.atamiradance.co.nz), which has been producing critically acclaimed, beautiful and challenging work since 2000. If that sounds too highbrow, get acquainted with the work of musician and visual artist Mika Haka, who blends *kapa haka*, drag, opera, ballet and disco. Check out clips of his work at www.mikahaka.com.

Māori Film-Making

Although there had already been successful Māori documentaries (*Patu!* and the *Tangata Whenua* series are brilliant), it wasn't until 1987 that NZ had its first fictional feature-length movie by a Māori writer and director, with Barry Barclay's *Ngati*. Merāta Mita was the first Māori woman to direct a fiction feature, with *Mauri* (1988). Both Mita and Barclay had highly political aims and ways of working, which involved a lengthy pre-production phase, during which they would consult with their *kaumātua* (elders). Films with significant Māori participation include the harrowing *Once Were Warriors (1994)* and the uplifting *Whale Rider (2002)*. And of course Oscar winner Taika Waititi, of Te Whānau-ā-Apanui descent, has dominated international screens in recent years after *Boy* (2010).

Ngā Taonga Sound & Vision (www.ngataonga.org.nz) is a great place to experience Māori film, with most showings being either free or relatively inexpensive. It has locations in Auckland and Wellington.

Māori Writing

There are many novels and short stories by Māori writers, and personal taste will govern your choices. Read Patricia Grace *(Potiki, Cousins, Dogside Story, Tu)* around Wellington, and Witi Ihimaera *(Pounamu, Pounamu; The Matriarch; Bulibasha; The Whale Rider)* on the North Island's East Coast.

Keri Hulme *(The Bone People, Stonefish)* and the South Island go together like a mass of whitebait bound in a frying pan by a single egg (ie very well). Read Alan Duff *(Once Were Warriors)* anywhere, but only if you want to be saddened, even shocked. Definitely take James George *(Hummingbird, Ocean Roads)* with you to Auckland's west-coast beaches and Northland's Ninety Mile Beach. Paula Morris *(Queen of Beauty, Hibiscus Coast, Rangatira)* and Kelly Ana Morey *(Bloom, Grace Is Gone)* – hmm, Auckland and beyond? If poetry appeals, you can't go past the giant of Māori poetry in English, the late, lamented Hone Tuwhare *(Deep River Talk: Collected Poems)*. Famously sounding like he's at church and in the pub at the same time, you *can* take him anywhere.

Contemporary Visual Art

A distinctive feature of Māori visual art is the tension between traditional Māori ideas and modern artistic mediums and trends. Shane Cotton produced a series of works that conversed with 19th-century painted meeting houses, which themselves departed from Māori carved houses. Kelcy Taratoa uses sci-fi, superheroes and pop-art imagery.

Of course, Māori motifs aren't necessarily the dominant features of work by Māori artists. Major NZ artist Ralph Hotere was wary about being assigned any cultural, ethnic or genre label and his work confronted a broad range of political and social issues.

Contemporary Māori art is by no means only about painting. Many other artists use installations or digital formats – look out for work by Jacqueline Fraser, Peter Robinson and Lisa Reihana.

There are some great permanent exhibitions of Māori visual arts in the major centres. Both the Auckland Art Gallery (p85) and Christchurch Art Gallery (p423) hold strong collections, as does Wellington's Te Papa (p383).

The first NZ hip-hop song to become a hit was Dalvanius Prime's 'Poi E', which was sung entirely in Māori by the Patea Māori Club. It was the highest-selling single of the mid-'80s in NZ.

MĀORI CULTURE MĀORI TODAY

Could heavy metal be the newest form of expressing Māori identity? Singing (or screaming) in te reo Māori, Waipu guitar trio Alien Weaponry (www.facebook.com/AlienWeaponry) thrash out songs that narrate the battles of their ancestors.

Arts & Music

Music, storytelling, dance and visual arts have been a part of New Zealand's cultural identity since its precolonial days. Then European settlers imported their artistic sensibilities, and mixed with Māori modes and motifs, a distinctive postcolonial artistic identity has developed. Writers and visual artists led the way, but it has been music and cinema that has really catapulted NZ's unique creative worldview on to the world stage.

Literature

The TV show *Popstars* originated in New Zealand, though the resulting group, TrueBliss, was short-lived. The series concept was then picked up in Australia, the UK and the US, inspiring the *Idols* series.

In 2013, 28-year-old Eleanor Catton became only the second NZ writer to win the Man Booker Prize, one of the world's most prestigious literary awards, for her epic historical novel *The Luminaries,* set on the West Coast. *Mister Pip* by Lloyd Jones was shortlisted in 2007, but the only other Kiwi to take the prize to date was Keri Hulme, in 1985, for her gritty magic-realist novel *The Bone People.*

New Zealand has a proud lineage of female authors, beginning in the early 20th century with Katherine Mansfield, who was famous for her short fiction. The tradition was carried forward by Janet Frame, whose dramatic life was depicted in Jane Campion's film *An Angel at My Table (1990)* – which was based on an autobiographical trilogy including the much-loved novella *To the Is-land* (1982). Frame's *The Carpathians* won the Commonwealth Writers' Prize in 1989. Also on New Zealanders' must-read lists is Catherine Chidgey, whose heart-rending novel *The Wish Child* (2016) won the country's top fiction prize at 2017's NZ Book Awards.

Less recognised internationally, Maurice Gee gained the nation's annual top fiction gong six times, most recently with *Blindsight* in 2006. A landmark survey in 2018 voted Gee's *Plumb* (1978) as the best Kiwi book of the past 50 years. His children's novel *Under the Mountain* (1979) was made into a seminal NZ TV series in 1981, and then a motion picture in 2009. In 2004 the adaptation of another of his novels, *In My Father's Den* (1972), won major awards at international film festivals.

The late Maurice Shadbolt also achieved acclaim for his many novels, particularly those set during the New Zealand Wars. Try *Season of the Jew* (1987) or *The House of Strife* (1993).

For children's literature fans, the *Hairy Maclary* series by New Zealand author Lynley Dodd holds a special spot in all our hearts.

MĀORI VOICES IN PRINT

Some of the most interesting and enjoyable NZ fiction voices belong to Māori writers, with Booker-winner Keri Hulme the most well known. Witi Ihimaera's novels give a wonderful insight into small town life on the East Coast – especially *Bulibasha* (1994) and *The Whale Rider* (1987), which was made into the acclaimed film in 2002. Patricia Grace's work is filled with exquisitely told stories of rural life: try *Mutuwhenua* (1978), *Potiki* (1986), *Dogside Story* (2001) or *Tu* (2004). *Chappy* (2015) is Grace's expansive tale of a prodigal son returning to NZ to untangle his cross-cultural heritage.

MIDDLE-EARTH TOURISM

Did the scenery of the epic film trilogy *Lord of the Rings (LOTR)* lure you to Aotearoa? The North Island has most of the big-ticket filming locations, but both islands have knowledgeable operators that can take you set-jetting on foot, horseback or by 4WD. Dedicated enthusiasts can buy a copy of Ian Brodie's *The Lord of the Rings: Location Guidebook* (2004) for detail on filming locations and their GPS coordinates. Online, DOC has a useful primer (www.doc.govt.nz/lordoftherings).

North Island

Matamata, aka Hobbiton Peter Jackson's epic film trilogy *LOTR* put this town on the map, and after the filming of *The Hobbit,* the town wholeheartedly embraced its Middle-earth credentials. Hobbiton Movie Set Tours (p208) allows you to pose by hobbit holes and enjoy a drink at the Green Dragon Inn.

Mt Ngauruhoe, aka Mt Doom Turns out the one ring to rule them all was forged in Tongariro National Park, in the North Island's youngest volcano (p293). Stickler for detail? A few Mt Doom scenes were filmed at Mt Ruapehu (best take a look at both).

Putangirua Pinnacles, aka Paths of the Dead An eerie landscape resembling giant organ pipes, the pinnacles (p384) were an obvious fit to portray the spooky passage through the White Mountains in *Lord of the Rings: Return of the King*.

Rover Rings (☑04-471 0044; www.wellingtonrover.co.nz; adult/child tours from $110/55) and **Wellington Movie Tours** (☑027 419 3077; www.adventuresafari.co.nz; tours from $60) both offer half- to full-day tours of *LOTR* locations in and around Wellington.

South Island

Southern Alps, aka Misty Mountains Peter Jackson made the most of this untamed landscape, choosing Mt Cook Village as the setting for Minas Tirith.

Nomad Safaris (p572) and Private Discovery Tours (p571) offer a range of 4WD tours out of Queenstown, complete with Middle-earth movie locations. Glenorchy-based Dart River Adventures (p580) runs horse treks along a *LOTR* theme.

Cinema & TV

If you first dreamt of visiting NZ when watching *The Lord of the Rings* and *The Hobbit* on the silver screen, you're in good company. Sir Peter Jackson's NZ-made trilogies have been the best thing to happen to NZ tourism since the *Endeavour* sailed past.

Yet NZ cinema is not always easy watching. In his BBC-funded documentary, *Cinema of Unease* (1995), NZ actor Sam Neill examines the often bleak, haunted work of Kiwi filmmakers. One need only watch Lee Tamahori's harrowing *Once Were Warriors* (1994) to see what he means.

The uniting factor on its screens is its wild landscapes, which provide an unnerving backdrop to films such as Jane Campion's *The Piano* (1993); the BBC co-production TV series *Top of the Lake* (2013); Brad McGann's *In My Father's Den* (2004); and Jackson's *Heavenly Creatures* (1994). Each mixes lush scenery with disturbing violence, a land that is mystical and isolating all at once.

Even when Kiwis do humour, it is as resolutely black as their rugby jerseys. Check out Jackson's early splatter-fests, and Taika Waititi's *Boy* (2010) for some early examples. But NZ humour has found an international audience with Waititi and Jemaine Clement's *What We Do in the Shadows* (2014) and Waititi's *Hunt for the Wilderpeople* (2016), propelling the scriptwriter and director to critical acclaim. Then Marvel Studio's *Thor: Ragnarok* (2017) made him a household name, while some argue that the director's role voicing Thor's friend Krog was the film's

Jane Campion was the first Kiwi nominated as Best Director at the Academy Awards and Peter Jackson the first to win. *The Return of the King* won a mighty 11 Oscars in 2004.

accidental highlight. His Hitler comedy *Jojo Rabbit* (2019) was nominated for six Academy Awards, winning for Best Adapted Screenplay.

The HBO-produced TV musical parody *Flight of the Conchords* – featuring a mumbling, bumbling Kiwi folk-singing duo (Jemaine Clement and Bret McKenzie) trying to get a break in New York – also received international renown and a cult following.

Kiwis have won more Oscars for behind-the-scenes work than on camera. Acting awards go to Anna Paquin (for *The Piano*, 1993) and Russell Crowe (for *Gladiator*, 2000). Paquin was born in Canada but moved to NZ when she was four, while Crowe moved from NZ to Australia at the same age.

Visual Arts

The NZ 'can do' attitude extends to the visual arts. If you're visiting a local's home, don't be surprised to find one of the owner's paintings on the wall or one of their mate's sculptures in the back garden, pieced together out of bits of shell, driftwood and a length of the magical 'number 8 wire'.

This is symptomatic of a flourishing local art-and-crafts scene cultivated by lively tertiary courses churning out traditional carvers and weavers, jewellery-makers, and moulders of metal and glass. The larger cities have excellent dealer galleries representing interesting local artists working across all media.

Traditional Māori art has a distinctive visual style with important motifs that have been embraced by NZ artists of every background. In the painting medium, these include the cool modernism of Gordon Walters and the more controversial pop-art approach of Dick Frizzell's *Tiki* series. Likewise, Pacific Island themes are common, particularly in Auckland; look out for the intricate, collage-like paintings of Niuean-born, Auckland-raised John Pule.

Charles Frederick Goldie painted a series of compelling, realist portraits of Māori, who were feared to be a dying race. Debate over the political propriety of Goldie's work raged for years, but its value is widely accepted now: not least because Māori themselves generally acknowledge and value them as ancestral representations. In 2016 Goldie's last work became the first NZ painting to be sold for more than $1 million.

Recalibrating the ways in which Pacific Islander and Māori people are depicted in art, Lisa Reihana wowed the Venice Biennale in 2017 with her multimedia work *In Pursuit of Venus*.

Depicting the Land

It's no surprise that in a nation so defined by its natural environment, landscape painting constituted the first post-European body of art. In the late 19th century, John Gully and Petrus van der Velden were among those to arrive and capture the drama of the land in paintings.

Colin McCahon is widely regarded to have been NZ's most important artist. Even where McCahon lurched into Catholic mysticism, his spirituality was rooted in geography. His brooding landscapes evoke the land's power but also its vulnerability to colonialism. McCahon is widely quoted as describing his work as a depiction of NZ before its seas become cluttered with debris and the sky turns dark with soot.

A wide range of cultural events are listed on www.eventfinda. co.nz. This is a good place to find out about gigs, classical-music recitals and *kapa haka* performances. For more specific information on the NZ classical-music scene, see www. sounz.org.nz.

Landscape photographers also capture the fierceness and fragility of NZ's terrain. It's worth detouring to a few of the country's resident photographers, many of whom have their own gallery (sometimes within or adjoining their own home). Westland is home to the gallery of exceptionally gifted photographer Andris Apse (www.andrisapse.com) and to the Petr Hlavacek Gallery (www.nzicescapes.com), which showcases some of NZ's finest landscape photography.

Music

New Zealand music began with the *waiata* (singing) developed by Māori following their arrival in the country. The main musical instruments were wind instruments made of bone or wood, the most well known of which is the *nguru* (also known as the 'nose flute'), while percussion was provided by chest and thigh slapping. These days, the liveliest place to see Māori music being performed is at *kapa haka* competitions in which groups compete with their own routines of traditional song and dance.

Classical & Opera

Early European immigrants brought their own styles of music that evolved into local variants during the early 1900s. In the 1950s Douglas Lilburn became one of the first internationally recognised NZ classical composers. More recently the country has produced a number of world-renowned musicians in this field, including legendary opera singer Dame Kiri Te Kanawa, million-selling classic-to-pop singer Hayley Westenra, composer John Psathas (who created music for the 2004 Olympic Games) and composer/percussionist Gareth Farr (who also performs in drag under the name Lilith LaCroix).

Tickets for most events can be bought at www.ticketek.co.nz, www.ticketmaster.co.nz or, for smaller gigs, www.undertheradar.co.nz.

Rock & Metal

New Zealand's most acclaimed rock exports are the revered indie label Flying Nun and the music of the Finn Brothers.

Started in 1981 by Christchurch record-store owner Roger Shepherd, many of Flying Nun's early groups came from Dunedin, where local musicians took the DIY attitude of punk, but used it to produce a lo-fi indie-pop that received rave reviews from the likes of *NME* in the UK and *Rolling Stone* in the US. Many of the musicians from the Flying Nun scene still perform live to this day, including David Kilgour (from the Clean) and Shayne Carter (from the Straitjacket Fits, and subsequently Dimmer and the Adults).

Want something heavier? Hamilton heavy-metal act Devilskin's 2014 debut album hit the top spot on NZ's charts, as did their punchy 2016 follow-up *Be Like the River*. Beastwars, a rasping, trance-inducing sludge metal band from Wellington, is another stalwart of NZ's heavy-metal scene. Meanwhile, hitting the big leagues during tours of North America and Europe, technical death metal band Ulcerate have risen to prominence as NZ's best-known extreme metal act.

Reggae, Hip-Hop & Dance

The genres of music that have been adopted most enthusiastically by Māori and Polynesian New Zealanders have been reggae (in the 1970s) and hip-hop (in the 1980s), which has led to distinct local forms. In Wellington, a thriving jazz scene took on a reggae influence to create a host of groups that blended dub, roots and funky jazz – most famously: Fat Freddy's Drop.

THE BROTHERS FINN

There are certain tunes that all Kiwis can sing along to, given a beer and the opportunity. A surprising proportion of these were written by Tim and Neil Finn, many of which have been international hits. Tim Finn first came to prominence in the 1970s group Split Enz, who amassed a solid following in Australia, NZ and Canada before disbanding in 1985. Neil then formed Crowded House with two Australian musicians (Paul Hester and Nick Seymour) and one of their early singles, 'Don't Dream It's Over', hit number two on the US charts. Tim later did a brief spell in the band, during which the brothers wrote 'Weather with You' – a song that reached number seven on the UK charts, pushing their album *Woodface* to gold sales. Neil has also remained busy, organising a set of shows/releases under the name 7 Worlds Collide – a collaboration with well-known musicians. Tim and Neil have both released a number of solo albums, as well as releasing material together as the Finn Brothers. Neil is now playing with rock stalwarts Fleetwood Mac.

GOOD LORDE!

The biggest name in Kiwi music is Lorde, a singer-songwriter from Devonport on Auckland's North Shore. Known less regally to her friends as Ella Yelich-O'Connor, Lorde was 16 years old when she cracked the number-one spot on the US Billboard charts in 2013 with her hit 'Royals' – the first NZ solo artist to top the American charts. 'Royals' went on to win the Song of the Year Grammy in 2014. Her debut album *Pure Heroine* spawned a string of hits and sold millions of copies worldwide, while moody follow-up *Melodrama* instantly topped charts in NZ and the US upon its release in 2017.

New Zealand's Music Scene Deep Dive

Audio Culture
(www.audio culture.co.nz)

NZ Musician
(www.nzmusi cian.co.nz)

13th Floor
(www.13thfloor. co.nz)

Ambient Light
(www.ambient lightblog.com)

The local hip-hop scene has its heart in the suburbs of South Auckland, which have a high concentration of Māori and Pacific Island residents. This area is home to one of New Zealand's foremost hip-hop labels, Dawn Raid, which takes its name from the infamous 1970s early-morning house raids that police performed on Pacific Islanders suspected of outstaying their visas. Dawn Raid's most successful artist is Savage, who sold a million copies of his single 'Swing' after it was featured in the movie *Knocked Up*. Within New Zealand, the most well-known hip-hop acts are Scribe, Che Fu and Smashproof (whose song 'Brother' held number one on the NZ singles charts for 11 weeks).

Dance music gained a foothold in Christchurch in the 1990s, spawning dub/electronica outfit Salmonella Dub and its offshoot act, Tiki Taane. Drum 'n' bass remains popular locally and has spawned internationally renowned acts such as Concord Dawn and Shapeshifter.

Movers & Shakers

Since 2000, the NZ music scene has hit its stride after the government convinced commercial radio stations to adopt a voluntary quota of 20% local music. Since then Kiwi bands have had enough commercial airplay to gain large folllowings, though social media, streaming and YouTube have all played their part in the rising popularity of many NZ artists.

The soul/dance/reggae fusion outfit Six60 are now playing at a level previously only international bands enjoyed in NZ, selling out 50,000-seat venues like Auckland's Western Springs.

Following in the foosteps of soulful Māori songstress Bic Runga, Troy Kingi won best Māori artist at the 2019 NZ Music Awards. Teeks (Te Karehana Gardiner-Toi) sings in te reo and English, and hip-hop artist Kings had the longest-running NZ single with 'Don't Worry 'Bout It' at number one for 33 weeks in 2017.

On the female solo artist front, check out Benee, Bailey Wiley, Tami Neilson and Holly Smith. New Zealand also produced internationally acclaimed pop electronica bands like Drax Project and Broods.

Survival Guide

Directory A–Z

Accessible Travel

Kiwi accommodation generally caters fairly well for travellers with mobility issues, with most hostels, hotels and motels equipped with one or two wheelchair-accessible rooms. (B&Bs aren't required to have accessible rooms.) Many tourist attractions similarly provide wheelchair access, with wheelchairs often available. For advice on local attractions with maximum accessibility ask at i-SITE visitor centres.

Tour operators with accessible vehicles operate from most major centres. Key cities are also serviced by 'kneeling' buses (buses that hydraulically stoop down to kerb level to allow easy access), and many taxi companies offer wheelchair-accessible vans. Large car-hire firms (Avis, Hertz etc) provide cars with hand controls at no extra charge (but advance booking is required, of course). Air New Zealand accommodates travellers in wheelchairs.

Download Lonely Planet's free Accessible Travel guides from https://shop.lonelyplanet.com/products/accessible-travel-online-resources-2019.

Activities

Out and about, the DOC has been hard at work improving access to short walking trails (and some of the longer ones). Tracks that are wheelchair accessible are categorised as 'easy access short walks': the Cape Reinga Lighthouse Walk and Milford Foreshore Walk are two prime examples.

If cold-weather activity is more your thing, see Snow Sports NZ's page on adaptive winter sports: www.snowsports.co.nz/get-involved/adaptive-snow-sports.

Resources

Access4All (www.facebook.com/Access4all.Ltd) Now only a Facebook page, but a travel company with good links to accommodation and other accessible essentials.

Firstport (www.firstport.co.nz) Includes a high-level overview of transport in NZ, including mobility taxis and accessible public transport.

Mobility Parking (www.mobilityparking.org.nz) Apply for an overseas visitor mobility parking permit ($35 for 12 months) and have it posted to you before you even reach NZ (for a further $10).

Accommodation

B&Bs

Bed and breakfast (B&B) accommodation in NZ pops up in the middle of cities, in rural hamlets and on stretches of isolated coastline, with rooms offered in everything from suburban bungalows to stately manors.

Breakfast may be 'continental' (a standard offering of cereal, toast and tea or coffee); a heartier version with yoghurt, fruit, home-baked bread or muffins; or a stomach-loading cooked breakfast (eggs, bacon, sausages; though, with notice, vegetarians are increasingly well catered for). Some B&B hosts may also cook dinner for guests and advertise dinner, bed and breakfast (DB&B) packages.

Midrange B&B tariffs are typically in the $160 to $250 bracket (per double), though upwards of $350 per double is not unusual. Some hosts charge cheeky prices for what is, in essence, a bedroom in their home, though room-sharing websites like Airbnb have impacted this market in NZ too.

BOOK YOUR STAY ONLINE

For more accommodation reviews by Lonely Planet authors, check out www.lonelyplanet.com/new-zealand/hotels. You'll find independent reviews, as well as recommendations on the best places to stay. Best of all, you can book online.

Camping & Holiday Parks

Campers and campervan drivers converge on NZ's hugely popular 'holiday parks', pitching up in powered and unpowered sites, cheap bunk rooms (dorm rooms), cabins (using the shared bathroom facilities) or fully self-contained units (often called motels or tourist flats). Features often include well-equipped communal kitchens, dining areas, games and TV rooms, and playgrounds for kids to run riot. In cities, holiday parks are usually a fair way from the action, but in smaller towns they can be impressively central or near lakes, beaches, rivers and forests.

The nightly cost of holiday-park tent sites is usually $20 to $30 per adult, with children charged half price; powered campervan sites can be anything from $35 to around the $50 mark. Cabin/unit accommodation normally ranges from $90 to $150 per double.

The 'glamping' scene has not really taken hold in NZ as it has in other places, but expect to see more bell tents popping up over the next year or two as rural property owners look to diversify their incomes.

DOC & FREEDOM CAMPING

A fantastic option for those in campervans is the 200-plus vehicle-accessible 'Conservation Campsites' around the country run by the Department of Conservation (DOC; www.doc.govt.nz), with fees ranging from free (basic toilets and fresh water) to $23 per adult (flush toilets, showers and powered sites). DOC publishes free brochures with detailed descriptions and instructions to find every campsite (even GPS coordinates). Pick up copies from its offices before you hit the road, or visit the website.

DOC also looks after hundreds of 'Backcountry Huts'

WWOOFING

If you don't mind some hard work, an economical way of travelling around NZ involves doing some voluntary work as a member of the international **Willing Workers On Organic Farms** (WWOOF; ☑02-2052 6624; www.wwoof.co.nz; ☺9am-3pm Mon-Fri) scheme. Down on the farm, in exchange for a short, hard day's work, owners provide food, accommodation and some hands-on organic farming experience. Contact farm owners a week or two beforehand to arrange your stay, as you would for a hotel or hostel – don't turn up unannounced!

A one-year online membership costs $40 for an individual or a couple. A farm-listing book, which is mailed to you, costs an extra $10 to $30, depending on where in the world your mailbox is. You should have a Working Holiday visa when you visit NZ, as the immigration department considers WWOOFers to be working.

---

and 'Backcountry Campsites', which can only be reached by foot. Nearly 60 'Great Walk' huts and campsites are also managed by DOC, and can be found on all Great Walks.

New Zealand is so photogenic, it's tempting to just pull off the road at a gorgeous viewpoint and camp the night. But never assume it's OK to camp somewhere – always ask a local or check with the local i-SITE visitor centre, DOC office or commercial campsite.

If you are 'freedom camping', treat the area with *kaitiakitanga* (guardianship). If your chosen campsite doesn't have toilet facilities and neither does your campervan, it's illegal for you to sleep there (your campervan must also have an on-board grey-water storage system). Legislation allows for $200 instant fines for camping in prohibited areas or improper disposal of waste (in cases where dumping waste could damage the environment, fees are up to $10,000). See www.camping.org.nz for more freedom-camping tips and consider downloading the free Campermate app (www.campermate.co.nz), which flags freedom-camping spots, drinking-water sources, petrol stations, public toilets and

showers, and locals happy to rent their driveway to campervans.

Farmstays

Farmstays open the door to the agricultural side of NZ life, with visitors encouraged to get some dirt beneath their fingernails at orchards and on dairy, sheep and cattle farms. Costs can vary widely, with bed and breakfast generally costing $90 to $150. Some farms have separate cottages where you can fix your own food; others offer low-cost, shared, backpacker-style accommodation.

Farm Helpers in NZ (www.farmhelpers.co.nz) hosts an online database of hundreds of farms across the country providing lodging in exchange for four to six hours' work per day. Registration costs $40.

Hostels

New Zealand is packed to the rafters with backpacker hostels, both independent and part of large chains, ranging from small, homestay-style affairs with a handful of beds to refurbished hotels and towering modern structures in the big cities. Hostel bed prices listed by Lonely Planet are nonmember rates, usually $30 to $50 per night.

HOSTEL ORGANISATIONS

Budget Backpacker Hostels (www.bbh.co.nz) A network of more than 160 hostels. Membership costs $35 for 12 months and entitles you to stay at member hostels at rates listed in the annual (free) *BBH Backpacker Accommodation* booklet. Nonmembers pay 10% more per night. Pick up a membership card from any member hostel or order one online.

YHA New Zealand (www.yha. co.nz) Over 35 hostels in prime NZ locations. The YHA is part of the Hostelling International network (www.hihostels.com), so if you're already an HI member in your own country, membership entitles you to use NZ hostels. If you don't already have a home membership, you can join at major NZ YHA hostels or online for $25, valid for 12 months (it's free for under-18s). Nonmembers pay 10% more per night. Membership has other perks, such as discounts on some car-hire providers, restaurants and cafes, travel insurers, DOC hut passes and more.

Base Backpackers (www.stayat base.com) Chain with seven hostels around NZ: Auckland, Rotorua, Taupō, Wellington, Wānaka, Queenstown and Paihia. Expect clean dorms, women-only areas and party opportunities aplenty. Offers flexible seven-night 'Bed Hopper'' accommodation passes for A$225 (bookable online).

Passes are valid in five affiliate hostels too, and can be bought for longer periods.

Haka Lodges (www.hakalodges. com) A local chain with five snazzy hostels in Auckland, Queenstown, Christchurch, Taupō and Paihia. Rates are comparable to other hostels around NZ, dorms are no bigger than six beds and quality is high. Private en suites, female-only dorms, and tours are also available.

Pubs, Hotels & Motels

The least expensive form of NZ hotel accommodation is the humble pub. Some are full of character (and characters); others are grotty, ramshackle places that are best avoided (especially if travelling solo). Check whether there's a band playing the night you're staying, or you could be in for a sleepless night. In the cheapest pubs, singles/doubles might cost as little as $50/80 (with a shared bathroom down the hall); $70/90 is more common.

At the top end of the hotel scale are five-star international chains, resort complexes and architecturally splendid boutique hotels, all of which charge a hefty premium for their mod cons, snappy service and/or historic opulence. We quote 'rack rates' (official advertised rates) for such places, but discounts and special deals often apply.

New Zealand's towns have a glut of often nondescript low-rise motels and 'motor lodges', charging $90 to $200 for double rooms. These tend to be squat structures skulking by highways on the edges of towns. The best ones have been thoroughly modernised, but some have been neglected with decor mired in the 1990s (or earlier). Expect basic facilities, namely tea- and coffee-making equipment, fridge and TV. Prices vary with standards.

Rental Accommodation

The basic Kiwi holiday home is called a 'bach' (short for 'bachelor', as they were historically used by single men as hunting and fishing hideouts); in Otago and Southland they're known as 'cribs'. These are simple self-contained cottages that can be rented in rural and coastal areas, often in isolated locations, and sometimes include surf, fishing or other outdoor gear hire in the cost. Prices are typically $150 to $250 per night, which isn't bad for a whole house or self-contained bungalow. For more upmarket holiday houses, expect to pay anything from $250 to $500 per double.

For more on accommodation see p28.

Customs Regulations

For the low-down on what you can and can't bring into NZ, see the New Zealand Customs Service website (www.customs.govt. nz). Per-person duty-free allowances:

→ Three 1125mL (max) bottles of spirits or liqueur

→ 4.5L of wine or beer

→ 50 cigarettes, or 50g of tobacco or cigars

Climate

Auckland

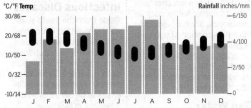

°C/°F Temp — Rainfall inches/mm

Christchurch

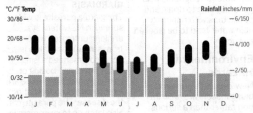

°C/°F Temp — Rainfall inches/mm

Queenstown

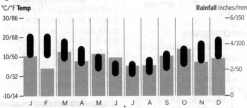

°C/°F Temp — Rainfall inches/mm

➔ Dutiable goods up to the value of $700

It's a good idea to declare any unusual medicines. Hiking gear (boots, tents etc) will be checked and may need to be cleaned before being allowed in. You must declare any plant or animal products (including anything made of wood), and food of any kind. Weapons and firearms are either prohibited or require a permit and safety testing. Don't take these rules lightly – noncompliance penalties will really hurt your wallet.

Discount Cards

The internationally recognised **International Student Identity Card** is produced by the ISIC Association (www.

isic.org), and issued to full-time students aged 12 and over. It provides over 150,000 discounts across more than 130 countries – on accommodation, transport, entertainment and attractions. The same folks also produce the **International Youth Travel Card**, available to travellers aged under 31 who are not full-time students, with equivalent benefits to the ISIC. Similar is the **International Teacher Identity Card**, available to teaching professionals. All three cards are $30 and can be bought online.

The **New Zealand Card** (www.newzealandcard.com) is a $35 discount pass that'll score you between 5% and 50% off a range of accommodation, tours, sights and activities. Browse participating businesses before

you buy. A one-year **Budget Backpacker Hostels** (www. bbh.co.nz) membership card costs $35 and entitles you to discounts at BBH member hostels, usually snipping 10% off the price per night.

Travellers aged over 60 with some form of identification (eg an official seniors card from your home country) are often eligible for concession prices.

Electricity

To plug yourself into the electricity supply (230V AC, 50Hz), use a three-pin adaptor (the same as in Australia; different to British three-pin adaptors).

Type I
230V/50Hz

Health

New Zealand poses minimal health risks to travellers. Diseases such as malaria and typhoid are unheard of, venomous snakes and other dangerous animals are absent, and there are currently no dangerous insect-borne diseases.

Health Insurance

Health insurance is essential for all travellers, even to safe, wealthy countries such as New Zealand. While health care in NZ is of a high quality and not overly expensive by international standards, considerable costs can be built up, and repatriation is pricey.

If you don't have a health insurance plan that covers you for medical expenses incurred overseas, buy a travel insurance policy – see www.lonelyplanet.com/travel-insurance.

Recommended Vaccinations

New Zealand has no vaccination requirements for any traveller, but the World Health Organization recommends that all travellers should be covered for chickenpox, diphtheria, hepatitis B, measles, mumps, pertussis (whooping cough), polio, rubella, seasonal flu, tetanus and tuberculosis, regardless of their destination.

Medications

Bring any prescribed medications for your trip in their original, clearly labelled containers. It is also wise to bring a signed and dated letter from your physician describing your medical conditions and medications (including generic names), and any requisite syringes or needles.

Availability & Cost of Health Care

New Zealand's public hospitals offer a high standard of care (free for residents). All travellers are covered for medical care resulting from accidents that occur while in NZ by the Accident Compensation Corporation (www.acc.co.nz). For more details, see www.health.govt.nz.

The 24-hour **Healthline** (☑0800 611 116; www.healthline.govt.nz) offers health advice throughout NZ (free from local mobile phones or landlines). Interpreters are available.

Pharmaceuticals

Over-the-counter medications are widely available in NZ through private chemists (pharmacies); some, such as antibiotics, are only available via a prescription. If you take regular medications, bring an adequate supply and details of the generic name, as brand names differ from country to country.

Tap Water

Tap water throughout NZ is generally safe to drink, and public taps with nondrinkable water tend to be labelled as such.

Environmental Hazards

New Zealand's numerous biting insects are an irritation rather than a serious health risk, but hypothermia and drowning are genuine threats.

HYPOTHERMIA

Hypothermia, a dangerous drop in body temperature, is a significant risk to travellers in NZ, especially during winter and year-round at altitude. Mountain ranges and/or strong winds produce a high chill factor, which can cause hypothermia even in moderate temperatures. Early signs include the inability to perform fine movements (such as doing up buttons), shivering and a bad case of the 'umbles' (fumbles, mumbles, grumbles, stumbles).

SURF BEACHES

Check with local surf lifesaving organisations before jumping in the sea, always heed warning signs at beaches, and be realistic about your own limitations and expertise.

BITING INSECTS

Wear long, loose clothing and use an insect repellent containing 20% or more DEET to ward off sandflies and mosquitoes, which are particularly common in lake areas and

tree-lined clearings. Bites are intensely itchy, but fortunately don't spread disease.

Infectious Diseases

Aside from the same sexually transmitted infections that are found worldwide (take normal precautions), giardiasis and (following an outbreak in 2019) measles are the main infectious diseases to be aware of when travelling in NZ.

GIARDIASIS

The giardia parasite is widespread in NZ waterways: drinking untreated water from streams and lakes is not recommended. Using water filters and boiling or treating water with iodine are effective ways of preventing the disease. The parasite can also latch on to swimmers in rivers and lakes (try not to swallow water), or through contact with infected animals. Symptoms consist of diarrhoea, vomiting, stomach cramps, abdominal bloating and wind. Effective treatment is available (tinidazole or metronidazole).

Insurance

➡ A watertight travel-insurance policy covering theft, loss and medical problems is essential when travelling. Some policies specifically exclude designated 'dangerous activities', such as scuba diving, bungy jumping, whitewater rafting, skiing and even hiking. If you plan on doing any of these things (a distinct possibility in NZ!), make sure your policy covers you fully.

➡ It's worth mentioning that, under NZ law, you cannot sue for personal injury (other than exemplary damages). Instead, the country's Accident Compensation Corporation (www.acc.co.nz) administers an accident compensation scheme that provides accident insurance for NZ residents and visitors to the country, regardless of fault. This scheme, however, does not negate the necessity for your own comprehensive travel-insurance policy, as it doesn't cover you for such things as income loss, treatment at home or ongoing illness.

➜ Consider a policy that pays doctors or hospitals directly, rather than you paying on the spot and claiming later. If you have to claim later, keep all documentation. Some policies ask you to call a centre in your home country where an immediate assessment of your problem is made. Check that the policy covers ambulances and emergency medical evacuations by air.

➜ Worldwide travel insurance is available at www.lonelyplanet.com/travel-insurance. You can buy, extend and claim online anytime – even if you're already on the road.

Internet Access

Getting online in NZ is easy in all but remote locales. Expect abundant wi-fi in cafes and accommodation in big towns and cities, but thrifty download limits elsewhere.

Wi-Fi Access

Wi-fi You'll be able to find wi-fi access around the country, from hotel rooms and pub beer gardens to hostel dorms. Usually you have to be a guest or customer to log in, and you should be issued with an access code. Sometimes it's free, sometimes there's a charge, and often there's a limit on time or data.

Hotspots The country's main telecommunications company is Spark New Zealand (www.spark.co.nz), which has more than 1000 wireless hotspots around the country, recognisable by the company's pink-and-white phone boxes and wi-fi signs. You can purchase prepaid access cards or a prepaid number from the login page at any wireless hotspot using your credit card, while all Spark mobile and broadband plans come with up to 1GB of free daily data. See the website for hotspot listings.

Equipment and ISPs If you've brought your tablet or laptop, consider buying a prepay USB modem (aka a 'dongle') with a local SIM card: both Spark and Vodafone (www.vodafone.co.nz) sell these from $65.

Legal Matters

If you are questioned or arrested by police, it's your right to ask why, to refrain from making a statement, and to consult a lawyer in private.

A binding referendum on the decriminalisation of marijuana will be held in New Zealand in 2020, but for the time being it remains illegal, with the threshold for presumption of supply standing at 28g, or 100 joints. Anyone caught carrying this or other illicit drugs will have the book thrown at them.

Drink-driving is a serious offence and remains a significant problem in NZ. The legal blood alcohol limit is 0.05% for drivers aged 20 years and over, and zero for those under 20.

LGBTQI+ Travellers

The gay tourism industry in NZ isn't as high profile as it is in some other developed nations, but LGBTQI+ communities are prominent in Auckland and Wellington, with myriad support organisations across both islands. New Zealand has progressive laws protecting human rights: same-sex marriage and adoption by same-sex couples were legalised in 2013 (ahead of anywhere else in the Asia-Pacific region). Generally speaking, Kiwis are fairly relaxed and accepting about same-sex relations and gender fluidity, but that's not to say that homophobia and/or transphobia don't exist. Rural communities tend to be more conservative, and public displays of affection may attract unwelcome attention.

Resources

There are loads of websites dedicated to gay and lesbian travel in NZ. Gay Tourism New Zealand (www.gaytourismnewzealand.com) is a starting point, with links to various sites. Other worthwhile websites include the following:

➜ www.gaynz.net.nz
➜ www.lesbian.net.nz
➜ www.gaystay.co.nz

Check out the nationwide monthly magazine *express* (www.gayexpress.co.nz) for the latest happenings, reviews and listings on the NZ gay scene. RainbowYOUTH (www.ry.org.nz) supports queer and gender-diverse people between 13 and 28, and New Zealand Awaits (www.newzealandawaits.com) is a local operator specialising in tours serving LGBTQI+ travellers.

Festivals & Events

Auckland Pride Festival (www.aucklandpridefestival.org.nz) Two-and-a-bit weeks of rainbow-hued celebrations in February.

Big Gay Out (www.biggayout.co.nz) Part of February's Auckland Pride Festival, this flagship day features live music, DJs, stalls, art and more.

Winter Pride (www.winterpride.co.nz) Ten days and two weekends of inclusive partying in and around Queenstown every August/September.

Maps

New Zealand's **Automobile Association** (AA; ☏0800 500 222; www.aa.co.nz/travel) sells maps. Scan the larger bookshops, or try the nearest Department of Conservation (DOC) office or visitor information centre for topo maps.

Map geeks will also love www.topomap.co.nz.

Online, log onto AA Maps (www.aamaps.co.nz) to pinpoint exact NZ addresses.

Money

Bank cards are used for most purchases, and are accepted in most hotels and restaurants. ATMs are widely available in cities and larger towns.

ATMs & Eftpos

Branches of the country's major banks provide ATMs (cashpoints) across the country, but you may not find them in the very smallest towns. It's generally better to decline the on-the-spot conversion rate ATMs will offer, although this depends on your home bank's rates and market movements.

Many NZ businesses use Eftpos (electronic funds transfer at point of sale), allowing you to use your bank card (credit or debit) to make direct purchases and often withdraw cash as well. With over 52,500 devices connected to its New Zealand network, the system is close to universal. Just like at an ATM, you'll need your PIN unless it's a small purchase where contactless payment is available.

Bank Accounts

You'll need to open a bank account if you want to work in NZ in any capacity (including working holidays) and it's best to arrange this in advance. Some banks, such as ANZ, allow you to apply before you arrive and activate the account at a branch when you get here (armed with the requisite ID, usually a passport, certified translation if applicable, and proof of NZ residence). Proof of address might involve using an identity verification service. All interest earned on accounts is taxed at 33%

(the highest rate) for those without an Inland Revenue (IRD) number.

Credit Cards & Debit Cards

CREDIT CARDS

Credit cards are widely accepted for everything from a hostel bed to a bungy jump, and are pretty much essential for car hire. Credit cards can also be used for over-the-counter cash advances at banks and from ATMs, but be aware that such transactions incur charges. Diners Club and American Express cards are not as widely accepted as Visa and MasterCard.

DEBIT CARDS

Debit cards enable you to draw money directly from your home bank account using ATMs, banks or Eftpos facilities. Any card connected to the international banking network (Cirrus, Maestro, Visa Plus and Eurocard) should work with your PIN. Fees will vary depending on your home bank; check before you leave. Alternatively, companies such as Travelex offer prepaid currency cards with set withdrawal fees and a balance you can top up from your personal bank account while on the road.

Currency

New Zealand's currency is the NZ dollar, comprising 100 cents. There are 10c, 20c, 50c, $1 and $2 coins, and $5, $10, $20, $50 and $100 notes. Prices are often marked in single cents and then rounded to the nearest 10c when you hand over your money.

Money Changers

Changing foreign currency (and to a lesser extent travellers cheques) is usually no problem at NZ banks or at licensed money changers (eg Travelex) in major tourist areas, cities and airports. However, withdrawing di-

rectly from ATMs usually secures the most favourable rates.

Taxes & Refunds

The Goods and Services Tax (GST) is a flat 15% tax on all domestic goods and services. New Zealand prices listed by Lonely Planet include GST. There's no GST refund available when you leave the country.

Tipping

Tipping is completely optional in NZ.

Guides Your kayaking guide or tour-group leader would happily accept tips; $10 is kind.

Restaurants The total on your bill is all you need to pay. If you like, reward good service with 5% to 10%.

Taxis If you round up your fare, don't be surprised if the driver hands back your change.

Travellers Cheques

Amex, Travelex and other international brands of travellers cheques are a bit old hat these days, but they're still easily exchanged at banks and money changers. Present your passport for identification when cashing them, and shop around for the best rates if you can.

Opening Hours

Opening hours vary seasonally depending on where you are. Most places close on Christmas Day and Good Friday.

Banks 9am to 4.30pm Monday to Friday; some also 9am to noon Saturday

Cafes 7am or 8am to 3pm or 4pm

Post offices 8.30am to 5pm Monday to Friday; larger branches also 9.30am to 1pm Saturday

Pubs and bars noon to late ('late' varies by region, and by day)

Restaurants noon to 2.30pm and 6pm to 9pm

Shops and businesses 9am to 5.30pm Monday to Friday and 9am to noon or 5pm Saturday

Supermarkets 7am to 9pm

Public Holidays

New Zealand's main public holidays are as follows:

New Year 1 and 2 January

Waitangi Day 6 February

Easter Good Friday and Easter Monday; March/April

Anzac Day 25 April

Queen's Birthday First Monday in June

Labour Day Fourth Monday in October

Christmas Day 25 December

Boxing Day 26 December

For an up-to-date list of provincial anniversaries, see www.govt.nz/browse/work/public-holidays-and-work/public-holidays-and-anniversary-dates.

School Holidays

The Christmas holiday season, from mid-December to late January, is part of the summer school vacation: expect some transport and accommodation to be booked out in advance and queues at tourist attractions. There are three shorter school-holiday periods during the year: from mid- to late April, early to mid-July, and late September to mid-October. For exact dates, see the Ministry of Education website (www.education.govt.nz).

Safe Travel

New Zealand is no more dangerous than other developed countries, but take normal safety precautions, especially after dark on city streets and in remote areas.

➡ Kiwi roads are often made hazardous by map-distracted tourists, wide-cornering campervans and traffic-ignorant sheep.

➡ Avoid leaving valuables in vehicles: theft is a problem, even in remote areas.

➡ New Zealand's climate is unpredictable: hypothermia is a risk in high-altitude areas.

➡ At the beach, beware of rips and undertows, which can drag swimmers out to sea.

Telephone

New Zealand uses regional two-digit area codes for long-distance calls, which can be made from any landline or mobile. If you're making a local call (ie to someone else in the same town), you don't need to dial the area code. But if you're dialling within a region (even if it's to a nearby town with the same area code), you do.

To make international calls from NZ, the international access code is 00. If dialling NZ from overseas, the country code is 64, followed by the appropriate area code minus the initial '0'.

Mobile Phones

It's simple to buy a local SIM card and prepaid account at outlets in airports and large towns (provided your mobile is unlocked).

Mobile coverage is good in built-up areas and most

of the North Island, but can be patchy in places on the South Island.

Local carriers can set you up with a NZ Travel SIM and phone number from around $20.

Payphones

Local calls from payphones cost $1 for the first 15 minutes, and 20c per minute thereafter, though coin-operated machines are scarce (and if you do find one, chances are the coin slot will be gummed up). You're better off relying on a phonecard. Calls to mobile phones or numbers outside the locality attract higher rates.

Premium-Rate & Toll-Free Calls

➡ Numbers starting with ☑0900 sometimes charge nearly $2 per minute (more from mobiles). These numbers cannot be dialled from payphones, and sometimes not from prepaid mobile phones.

➡ Toll-free numbers in NZ have the prefix ☑0800 or ☑0508, and can be called from anywhere in the country, though they may not be accessible from certain areas or from mobile phones.

➔ Numbers beginning with 0508, 0800 or 0900 cannot be dialled from outside NZ.

Phonecards

New Zealand has a wide range of phonecards available, which can be bought at hostels, newsagents and post offices for a fixed-dollar value (usually $5, $10, $20 and $50). These can be used with any public or private phone by dialling a toll-free access number and then the PIN number on the card. Shop around – rates vary from company to company.

Time

➔ New Zealand is 12 hours ahead of GMT/UTC and two hours ahead of Australian Eastern Standard Time (AEST).

➔ The Chathams are 45 minutes ahead of NZ's main islands.

➔ In summer, NZ observes daylight saving time: clocks are wound forward by one hour on the last Sunday in September; clocks are wound back on the first Sunday of April.

Tourist Information

The website for the official national tourism body, Tourism New Zealand (www. newzealand.com), is an excellent place for pre-trip research. The site has information in several languages, including German, Spanish, French, Chinese and Japanese.

Local Tourist Offices

Almost every Kiwi city or town seems to have a visitor information centre. The bigger centres stand united within the outstanding i-SITE network (www.newzealand. com/travel/i-sites) – more than 80 info centres affiliated with Tourism New Zealand. The i-SITE centres have trained staff, information on local activities, itineraries and attractions, and free brochures and maps. Staff can also book activities, transport and accommodation.

Bear in mind that some information centres only promote accommodation and tour operators who are paying members of the local tourist association, and that staff shouldn't recommend any providers over others.

There's also a network of 19 Department of Conservation (DOC; www.doc.govt.nz) visitor centres to help you plan outdoor activities and make bookings (particularly for hiking tracks and huts). The visitor centres – in national parks, regional centres and major cities – usually also have displays on local flora and fauna.

Visas

Visa application forms are available from NZ diplomatic missions overseas, travel agents and **Immigration New Zealand** (☎ 0508 558 855, 09-914 4100; www.immigration.govt.nz). Immigration New Zealand has more than 25 offices overseas, including the US, UK and Australia – consult the website for exact requirements and the list of nationals entitled to a visa waiver. Such entrants to NZ must still obtain a NZeTA (New Zealand Electronic Travel Authority), unless they're NZ nationals or Australians travelling on Australian passports. NZeTAs take from 10 minutes to three days to come through, and cost $9 through the Immigration Department's app, or $12 through its website.

Visitor Visa

Citizens of Australia don't need a visa to visit NZ and can stay indefinitely (provided they have no criminal convictions). UK citizens don't need a visa either and can stay for up to six months.

Citizens of another 58 countries that have visa-waiver agreements with NZ don't need a visa for stays of up to three months, for no more than six months within any 12-month period, provided they have an onward ticket and sufficient funds to support their stay: see the website for details. Nations in this group include Canada, France, Germany, Ireland, Japan, the Netherlands, South Africa and the USA.

Citizens of other countries must obtain a visa before entering NZ. Visitor visas allow stays of up to nine months within an 18-month period, and cost $170 to $220, depending on where in the world the application is processed.

A visitor's visa can be extended from nine to 12 months, but if you get this extension you'll have to leave NZ after your 12-month stay has expired and wait another 12 months before you can come back. Applications are assessed on a case-by-case basis; you may need to provide proof of adequate funds to sustain you during your visit ($1000 per month) plus an onward ticket establishing your intent to leave. Apply for extensions at any Immigration New Zealand office – see the website (www.immigration.govt.nz) for locations.

Work Visa

It's illegal for foreign nationals to work in NZ on a visitor visa, except for Australian citizens or permanent residents, who can legally gain work without a visa or permit. If you're visiting NZ to find work, or you already have an employment offer, you'll need to apply for a work visa, which can be valid for up to three years, depending on the type in question and your particular circumstances. You can apply for a work permit after you're in NZ, but its validity will be backdated to when you entered the country. The fee for a work visa can be anything upwards of $495, depending on where and how it's processed (paper or online) and the type of application.

Working-Holiday Scheme

Eligible travellers looking for short-term and seasonal employment to supplement their travels can take part in one of NZ's working-holiday schemes (WHS). Under these, citizens aged 18 to 30 (occasionally 35) from 45 countries – including France, Germany, Ireland, Japan, Malaysia, the Netherlands, Scandinavian countries and the USA – can apply for a working-holiday visa. For most nationalities the visa is valid for 12 months, but citizens of Canada and the UK can extend theirs for up to 23 months. It's only issued to those seeking a genuine working holiday, not permanent work, so you're not supposed to work for one employer for more than three months.

Eligible nationals must apply for a WHS visa from within their own country. Applicants must have an onward ticket, a passport valid for at least three months from the date they will leave NZ and evidence of at least $350 in accessible funds for each month of their stay. The application fee is $280 and isn't refunded if your application is declined.

The rules vary for different nationalities, so make sure you read up on the specifics of your country's agreement with NZ at www.immigration.govt.nz.

Volunteering

New Zealand presents an array of active, outdoorsy volunteer opportunities for travellers to get some dirt under their fingernails and participate in conservation and other programs. These can include anything from tree planting and weed removal to track construction, habitat conservation and fencing. Ask about local opportunities at any regional i-SITE visitor information centre, join one of the programs run by DOC (www.doc.govt.nz/get-involved), or check out these online resources:

➜ www.conservation volunteers.org.nz

➜ www.helpx.net

➜ www.nature.org

➜ www.volunteeringnz.org.nz

➜ www.wwf.org.nz

Women Travellers

New Zealand is generally a very safe place for female travellers, although the usual sensible precautions apply (for all genders): avoid walking alone at night; never hitchhike alone; and if you're out on the town, have a plan for how to get back to your accommodation safely. Sexual harassment is not a widely reported problem in NZ, but of course that doesn't mean it doesn't happen. See www.womentravel.co.nz for tours aimed at solo women.

Work

If you have been approved for a working-holiday scheme (WHS) visa, there are a number of possibilities for temporary employment in NZ. Pay rates start at the minimum wage ($17.70 per hour, at the time of writing with $18.90 mooted for 2020 and $20 an hour planned in 2021), but depend on the work. There's plenty of casual work around, mainly in agriculture (fruit picking, farming, wineries), hospitality (bar work, waiting tables) or at ski resorts. Office-based work can be found in IT, banking, finance and telemarketing. Register with a local office-work agency to get started.

Seasonal fruit picking, pruning and harvesting is prime short-term work for visitors. Kiwifruit and other fruit and veg are harvested from December to May (and other farming work is available outside that season). Fruit picking is physically taxing toil – working in the dirt under the hot sun – and turnover of workers is high. You're usually paid by how much you pick (per bin, bucket or kilogram): if you stick with it for a while, you'll get faster and fitter and can actually make some reasonable cash. Prime North Island picking locations include the Bay of Islands (Kerikeri and Paihia), rural Auckland, Tauranga and the Bay of Plenty, Gisborne and Hawke's Bay (Napier and Hastings); on the South Island try Nelson (Golden Bay), Marlborough (around Blenheim) and Central Otago (Alexandra and Roxburgh).

Winter work at ski resorts and their service towns includes bartending, waiting, cleaning, ski-tow operation and, if you're properly qualified, ski or snowboard instructing.

Resources

Backpacker publications, hostel managers and other travellers are often good sources of info on local work possibilities. Base Backpackers (www.stayatbase.com/work) runs an employment service via its website, while the Notice Boards page on the Budget Backpacker Hostels website (www.bbh.co.nz) lists job vacancies in BBH hostels and a few other possibilities.

Kiwi Careers (www.careers.govt.nz) lists professional opportunities in various fields (agriculture, creative, health, teaching, volunteer work and recruitment), while Seek (www.seek.co.nz) is one of the biggest NZ job-search networks, with thousands of jobs listed.

Try the following websites for seasonal work:

➡ www.backpackerboard.co.nz

➡ www.seasonalwork.co.nz

➡ www.seasonaljobs.co.nz

➡ www.picknz.co.nz

➡ www.pickingjobs.com

➡ www.picktheworld.org

Income Tax

For most visitors, Kiwi dollars earned in NZ will be subject to income tax, which is deducted from payments by employers – a process called PAYE (Pay As You Earn).

Income tax rates are 10.5% for annual salaries up to $14,000, then 17.5% up to $48,000, 30% up to $70,000, and 33% for higher incomes. The national Accident Compensation Corporation (ACC) scheme levy (around 1.2%, but fluctuating each year) will also be deducted from your pay packet.

If you visit NZ and work for a short time (eg on a working-holiday scheme), you may qualify for a tax refund when you leave. Lodging a tax return before you leave NZ is the best way of securing a refund. For more info, see the Inland Revenue Department website (www.ird.govt.nz), or call ☑0800 775 247.

IRD Number

Travellers undertaking paid work in NZ (including working holidays) must first open a New Zealand bank account, then obtain an Inland Revenue Department (IRD) number. Download the *IRD number application – non-resident/offshore individual IR742* form from the IRD website (www.ird.govt.nz). IRD numbers normally take eight to 10 working days to be issued.

Transport

GETTING THERE & AWAY

New Zealand is a long way from almost everywhere – most travellers jet in from afar. Flights, cars and tours can be booked online at lonelyplanet.com/bookings.

Entering the Country

Entering NZ is a fairly straightforward affair and customs officials are relatively friendly, provided you have all your paperwork in order and follow the rules around what you need to declare to maintain NZ's biosecurity. Most airlines will not let you check in to your flight to NZ without your 90-day NZeTA (New Zealand Electronic Travel Authority) pre-approved.

Passport

There are no restrictions when it comes to foreign citizens entering NZ. If you have a current passport and visa (or don't require one), you should be fine.

Air

New Zealand's abundance of seasonal activities and attractions means that airports here are busy most of the year. If you want to fly at a particularly popular time (eg over the Christmas period), book well in advance.

The high season for flights into NZ is during summer (December to February), with slightly less of a premium on fares over the shoulder months (October/November and March/April). The low season generally tallies with the winter months (June to August), though this is still a busy time for airlines servicing the ski fields.

Airports & Airlines

A number of NZ airports handle international flights, with Auckland receiving the most traffic:

Auckland Airport (AKL; ☎09-275 0789; www.auckland airport.co.nz; Ray Emery Dr, Māngere)

Christchurch Airport (CHC; ☎03-358 5029; www.christchurchairport.co.nz; 30 Durey Rd)

Dunedin Airport (DUD; ☎03-486 2879; www.dunedin airport.co.nz; 25 Miller Rd, Momona; ☎)

Queenstown Airport (ZQN; ☎03-450 9031; www.queens townairport.co.nz; Sir Henry Wrigley Dr, Frankton)

Wellington Airport (WLG; ☎04-385 5100; www.wellington airport.co.nz; Stewart Duff Dr, Rongotai)

Note that Hamilton, Rotorua and Palmerston North airports are capable of handling direct international arrivals and departures, but are not currently doing so.

CLIMATE CHANGE & TRAVEL

Every form of transport that relies on carbon-based fuel generates CO_2, the main cause of human-induced climate change. Modern travel is dependent on aeroplanes, which might use less fuel per kilometre per person than most cars but travel much greater distances. The altitude at which aircraft emit gases (including CO_2) and particles also contributes to their climate change impact. Many websites offer 'carbon calculators' that allow people to estimate the carbon emissions generated by their journey and, for those who wish to do so, to offset the impact of the greenhouse gases emitted with contributions to portfolios of climate-friendly initiatives throughout the world. Lonely Planet offsets the carbon footprint of all staff and author travel.

AIRLINES FLYING TO & FROM NEW ZEALAND

➡ New Zealand's international carrier is Air New Zealand (www.airnewzealand.co.nz), which flies to runways across Europe, North America, eastern Asia, Australia and the Pacific, and has an extensive network across NZ.

➡ Winging in with direct flights from Australia, Virgin Australia (www.virginaustralia.com), Qantas (www.qantas.com.au), Jetstar (www.jetstar.com) and Air New Zealand are the key players.

➡ Joining Air New Zealand from North America, other operators include Air Canada (www.aircanada.com) and American Airlines (www.aa.com) – the latter has direct flights from Los Angeles to Auckland.

➡ From Europe, the options are a little broader, with Lufthansa (www.lufthansa.com) and Virgin Atlantic (www.virginatlantic.com) entering the fray. Flights go via major Middle Eastern or Asian airports. Several other airlines stop in NZ on broader round-the-world routes.

➡ From Asia and the Pacific there are myriad options, with direct flights from China, Japan, Singapore, Malaysia, Thailand and Pacific Island nations.

Sea

Cruise Ship If you're travelling from Australia and content with a slow pace, try P&O (www.pocruises.com.au) and Princess (www.princess.com) for cruises to New Zealand.

Yacht It is possible (though by no means straightforward) to make your way between NZ, Australia and the Pacific Islands by crewing on a yacht. Try asking around at harbours, marinas, and yacht and sailing clubs. Popular yachting harbours in NZ include the Bay of Islands and Whangārei (both in Northland), Auckland and Wellington. March and April

are the best months to look for boats heading to Australia. From Fiji, October to November is a peak departure season to beat the cyclones that soon follow in that region.

GETTING AROUND

New Zealand is long and skinny, and many roads are two-lane country byways: getting from A to B requires some planning.

Car Travel at your own tempo, explore remote areas and visit regions with no public transport. Hire cars in major towns. Drive on the left; the steering wheel is on the right (...in case you can't find it).

Bus Reliable, frequent services to most destinations around the country (usually cheaper than flying), though services thin out in rural areas. To get further than main cities, you'll need to rely on tours.

Plane Fast-track your visit with affordable, frequent, fast internal flights.

Train Reliable, regular services (if not fast or cheap) along specific routes on both islands.

Air

Those who have limited time to get between NZ's attractions can make the most of a widespread (and very reliable and safe) network of intra- and inter-island flights.

Airlines in New Zealand

The country's major domestic carrier, Air New Zealand, has an aerial network covering most of the country, often operating under the Air New Zealand Link moniker on less-popular routes. Australia-based Jetstar also flies between main urban areas. Between them, these two airlines carry the vast majority of domestic passengers in NZ.

Beyond this, several small-scale regional operators provide essential transport

services to outlying islands, such as Great Barrier Island (in the Hauraki Gulf), Stewart Island and the Chathams. There are also plenty of scenic- and charter-flight operators around NZ, not listed here. Operators include the following:

Air Chathams (☎0800 580 127; www.airchathams.co.nz) Services to the remote Chatham Islands from Wellington, Christchurch and Auckland. Whakatāne–Whakatāne flights also available.

Air New Zealand (☎0800 737 000; www.airnewzealand.co.nz) Offers flights between 20-plus domestic destinations, plus myriad overseas hubs.

Barrier Air (☎0800 900 600; www.barrierair.kiwi) Connects Auckland with Great Barrier Island and Kaitāia.

FlyMySky (☎0800 222 123; www.flymysky.co.nz) At least three flights daily from Auckland to Great Barrier Island.

Golden Bay Air (☎0800 588 885; www.goldenbayair.co.nz) Flies regularly to Takaka in Golden Bay from Wellington and Nelson. Also connects to Karamea for Heaphy Track hikers.

Jetstar (☎0800 800 995; www.jetstar.com) Joins the dots between key tourism centres: Auckland, Wellington, Christchurch, Dunedin, Queenstown, Nelson, Napier, New Plymouth and Palmerston North.

Sounds Air (☎0800 505 005; www.soundsair.co.nz) Numerous flights daily between Picton and Wellington, plus flights from Wellington to Blenheim, Nelson, Westport and Taupō. Also flies Blenheim to Christchurch, Paraparaumu and Napier, and Nelson to Paraparaumu.

Stewart Island Flights (☎03-218 9129; www.stewartislandflights.co.nz) Flies between Invercargill and Stewart Island three times daily.

Sunair (☎0800 786 247; www.sunair.co.nz) Numerous North Island connections between Hamilton, Tauranga, Great Barrier Island, Gisborne, Whangārei and Whitianga.

Bicycle

Touring cyclists proliferate in NZ, particularly over summer. The country is clean, green and relatively uncrowded, and has lots of cheap accommodation (including camping) and abundant fresh water. The roads are generally in good nick, and the climate is typically mild. Road traffic is the biggest danger: trucks overtaking too close to cyclists are a particular threat. Bikes and cycling gear are readily available to hire or buy in the main centres, and bicycle-repair shops are common.

By law all cyclists must wear an approved safety helmet (or risk a $55 fine); it's also vital to have good reflective safety clothing. Cyclists who use public transport will find two- and three-tier exterior racks on all Christchurch buses (and many elsewhere) where bikes can be secured for free. Some of the smaller shuttle-bus companies also have storage space for bikes, but may impose a surcharge.

If importing your own bike or transporting it by plane within NZ, check with the relevant airline for costs and the degree of dismantling and packing required.

See www.nzta.govt.nz/walking-cycling-and-public-transport for more bike safety and legal tips, and check out the New Zealand Cycle Trail (p59) – a network of 22 'Great Rides' across NZ.

Hire

Rates offered by most outfits for hiring road or mountain bikes are usually around $25 for a short hire to $60 per day. Longer-term hire is usually available, at reduced rates. Hire basic bikes from your accommodation (hostels, holiday parks etc), or better machines from bike shops in the larger towns.

Buying a Bike

Bicycles can be readily bought in NZ's larger cities, but prices for newer models are high.

For a decent hybrid bike or rigid mountain bike you'll pay anywhere from $800 to $1800, though you can get a cheap one for around $500 (factor in panniers, helmet, lock etc, and the cost quickly climbs). Other options include the post-Christmas sales and mid-year stocktakes, when newish cycles can be heavily discounted.

Boat

New Zealand may be an island nation, but there's virtually no long-distance water transport around the country. Obvious exceptions include the boat services between Auckland and various islands in the Hauraki Gulf, the inter-island ferries plying the Cook Strait between Wellington and Picton, and the passenger ferry that negotiates Foveaux Strait between Bluff and the town of Oban on Stewart Island.

If you're cashed-up, consider the cruise liners that chug around the NZ coastline as part of broader South Pacific itineraries: P&O Cruises (www.pocruises.com.au) is a major player.

Bus

Bus travel in NZ is easy-going and well organised, with services transporting you to the far reaches of both islands (including the start/end of various walking tracks)...but it can be expensive, tedious and time-consuming.

New Zealand's main bus company is **InterCity** (www.intercity.co.nz), which can drive you to just about anywhere on the North and South Islands and offers fares as low as $1(!). InterCity also has a sightseeing arm called **GreatSights New Zealand** (www.greatsights. co.nz) handling scenic routes such as Queenstown to Mt Cook and Milford Sound.

The low-fare bus company Skip (www.skip.travel) only

operates on the North Island at present.

Privately run shuttle buses can transport travellers to some trailheads or collect them from the end point of a hike; advance booking essential.

Seat Classes & Smoking

There are no allocated economy or luxury classes on NZ buses (very democratic), and smoking on the bus is a definite no-no.

InterCity has a sleeper class on overnight services between Auckland and Wellington, stopping at Hamilton, Palmerston North and three other intervening towns. You'll get a 1.8m-long bed and small pillow; bring a sleeping bag, pillowcase and maybe earplugs. See www. intercity.co.nz for details.

Reservations

Over summer (December to February), school holidays and public holidays, book a week or two ahead for seats on popular routes. At other times, a day or two ahead is usually fine. The best prices are generally available online, and in advance.

Bus Passes

If you're covering a lot of ground, InterCity offers a range of passes, priced according to your proposed itinerary and length of journey. If the itineraries and fare schemes offered suit you, this can be cheaper than paying as you go, but do the maths before buying and note that you'll be locked into using one network. Passes are usually valid for 12 months.

InterCity offers a discount of around 10% on standard fares for students and YHA, ISIC, HI, Nomads, BBH or VIP backpacker card holders, on selected services. Senior discounts only apply to NZ citizens.

NATIONWIDE PASSES

FlexiPass A hop-on/hop-off InterCity pass, allowing travel to pretty much anywhere in NZ, in any direction, including the Inter-islander ferry across Cook Strait. The pass is purchased in blocks of travel time: the minimum is 15 hours ($132) and the maximum 60 ($459). The average cost of each block becomes cheaper the more hours you buy. You can top up the pass if you need more time.

TravelPass Hop-on/hop-off, fixed-itinerary nationwide passes offered by InterCity. With names like Aotearoa Explorer and Island Loop, these passes link tourist hotspots across either or both is-lands, and range from simple re-gional itineraries costing as little as $125 to grand, country-wide circuits worth $1045. See www.intercity.co.nz/bus-pass/travel-pass-overview for details.

NORTH ISLAND PASSES

InterCity offers six hop-on/hop-off, fixed-itinerary North Island TravelPasses, from short $125 runs between Auckland and Paihia, to $405 trips from Auckland to Wel-lington via the big sights in between. See www.intercity.co.nz/bus-pass/travel-pass-overview for details.

SOUTH ISLAND PASSES

On the South Island, Inter-City offers six hop-on/hop-off, fixed-itinerary TravelPasses, from the Picton-to-Queenstown West-coast Passport ($125) to the Scenic South loop ($549). See www.intercity.co.nz/bus-pass/travelpass-over view for details.

Shuttle Buses

As well as InterCity's net-work, regional shuttle buses fill in the gaps between the smaller towns. Operators in-clude the following (see www.tourism.net.nz/transport/bus-and-coach-services for a complete list), offering regu-lar scheduled services and/or bus tours and charters:

Abel Tasman Travel (www.scenicnzabeltasman.co.nz) Trav-erses the road between Nelson and Marahau, on the fringe of Abel Tasman National Park.

Atomic Shuttles (www.atomic travel.co.nz) Has services from Christchurch to Dunedin and Greymouth, stopping at points of interest along the way.

Catch-a-Bus South (www.catchabussouth.co.nz) Inver-cargill and Bluff to Dunedin and Queenstown.

Cook Connection (www.cookconnect.co.nz) Triangulates between Mt Cook, Twizel and Lake Tekapo.

East West Coaches (www.eastwestcoaches.co.nz) Offers a service between Christchurch and Westport via Lewis Pass, and Greymouth via Arthur's Pass.

Go Kiwi Shuttles (www.go-kiwi.co.nz) Links Auckland with Whitianga on the Coromandel Peninsula daily.

Hanmer Connection (www.hanmerconnection.co.nz) Daily services between Hanmer Springs and Christchurch.

Headfirst Travel (www.travel headfirst.com) Does a loop from Rotorua to Waitomo (with an option to finish in Auckland).

Tracknet (www.tracknet.net) Track transport (Milford, Hollyford, Routeburn, Kepler) with Queenstown, Te Anau and Invercargill connections. Services are sparser in winter.

Trek Express (www.trekexpress.co.nz) Shuttle services to all hiking tracks in the top half of the South Island (eg Heaphy, Abel Tasman, the Ghost Trail).

Bus Tours

Clock up some kilometres with like-minded fellow travellers. The following operators run fixed-itiner-ary bus tours, nationwide or on the North or South Islands. Accommodation, meals and hop-on/hop-off flexibility are often included. Styles vary from activity-fo-cused itineraries through to hangover-mandatory back-packer buses.

Flying Kiwi (www.flyingkiwi.com) Good fun, activity-based trips around NZ with camping and cabin accommodation from a few days to a few weeks.

Haka Tours (www.hakatours.com) Three- to 24-day tours with adventure, snow or mountain-biking themes.

Headfirst (www.headfirsttravel.com) Three-day tours of the North and South Island's nether regions: Dunedin, Invercargill, Queenstown, as well as Auck-land, Rotorua and Taupō.

Kirra Tours (www.kirratours.co.nz) Four- to 20-day upmarket coach tours (graded 'Classic' or 'Platinum' by price) from an operator with 50 years in the business.

Kiwi Experience (www.kiwiex perience.com) A major hop-on/hop-off player with ecofriendly credentials. Myriad tours cover the length and breadth of the country.

Stray Travel (www.straytravel.com) A wide range of flexible hop-on/hop-off passes and tours.

Car & Motorcycle

The best way to explore NZ in depth is to have your own wheels. It's easy to hire cars and campervans, though it's worth noting that fuel costs can be eye-watering. Alterna-tively, if you're in NZ for a few months, you might consider buying your own vehicle.

Automobile Association (AA)

New Zealand's **Automobile Association** (AA; ☎0800 500 222; www.aa.co.nz/travel) provides emergency break-down services, distance cal-culators and accommodation guides (from holiday parks to motels and B&Bs).

Members of overseas au-tomobile associations should bring their membership cards – many of these bodies have reciprocal agreements with the AA.

Driving Licences

International visitors to NZ can use their home-country

driving licence – if your licence isn't in English, it's a good idea to carry a certified translation with you. Alternatively, use an International Driving Permit (IDP), which will usually be issued on the spot (valid for 12 months) by your home country's automobile association.

Fuel

Fuel (petrol, aka gasoline) is available from service stations across NZ: unless you're cruising around in something from the 1970s, you'll be filling up with 'unleaded', or LPG (gas). LPG is not always stocked by rural suppliers – if you're on gas, it's safer to have dual-fuel capability. Aside from remote locations like Milford Sound and Mt Cook, petrol prices don't vary much from place to place: per-litre costs at the time of research were hovering around $2.40.

Hire

CAMPERVAN

Check your rear-view mirror on any far-flung NZ road and you'll probably see a shiny white campervan (aka mobile home, motor home, RV), packed with liberated travellers, mountain bikes and portable barbecues, cruising along behind you.

Most towns of any size have a campsite or holiday park with powered pitches (where you can plug your vehicle in) for around $50 per night. There are also 250-plus vehicle-accessible Department of Conservation (DOC; www.doc.govt. nz) campsites around NZ, priced from $20 per adult. Weekly Campsite Passes for hired campervans slice up to 50% off the price of stays in some of these campsites; check the DOC website for info, and make sure your intended site(s) offer the discount.

You can hire campervans from dozens of companies. Prices vary with season, vehicle size and length of hire, and it pays to book months in advance.

A small van for two people typically has a mini kitchen and fold-out dining table, the latter transforming into a double bed when dinner is done and dusted. Larger, 'superior' two-berth vans include shower and toilet. Four- to six-berth campervans are the size of trucks (and similarly sluggish) and, besides the extra space, usually contain a toilet and shower.

Over summer, rates offered by the main firms for two-/four-/six-berth vans booked three months in advance start at around $120/150/230 per day (though they rise much higher, depending on model) for hire for two weeks or more. Rates drop to $60/75/100 per day during winter.

Major operators include the following:

Apollo (📞0800 113 131, 09-889 2976; www.apollocamper.co.nz)

Britz (📞09-255 3910, 0800 081 032; www.britz.co.nz) Also does 'Britz Bikes' (add a mountain or city bike from $16 per day) and electric campervans.

Maui (📞09-255 3910, 0800 688 558; www.maui-rentals.com)

Wilderness Motorhomes (📞09-282 3606; www.wilderness.co.nz)

Budget players in the campervan industry offer slick deals and funky (often gregariously spray-painted), well-kitted-out vehicles for backpackers. Rates are competitive (from $50/90 per day for a two-/four-berth van from May to September; from $120/300 per day from December to February). Operators include the following:

Escape Campervans (📞0800 216 171; www.escaperentals. co.nz)

Hippie Camper (📞0800 113 131; www.hippiecamper.co.nz)

Jucy (📞0800 399 736, 09-374 4360; www.jucy.co.nz)

Mighty Cars & Campers (📞0800 422 505; www.mightycampers.co.nz)

Spaceships (📞0800 772 237, 09-526 2130; www.spaceships rentals.co.nz)

Tui Sleeper Vans (📞03-359 4731; www.sleepervans.co.nz)

CAR

Competition between car-hire companies in NZ is fierce, particularly in the big cities and Picton. Remember that if you want to travel far, you need to specify unlimited kilometres. Some (but not all) companies require drivers to be at least 21 years old – ask around.

International car-hire firms don't generally allow you to take their vehicles between islands on the Cook Strait ferries. Instead, you leave your car at either Wellington or Picton terminal and pick up another car once you've crossed the strait. This saves you paying to transport a vehicle on the ferries, and is a pain-free exercise. However, some local car-hire firms (such as Apex) are fine with you taking your rental vehicle on the ferry and will even book your ferry ticket for you.

INTERNATIONAL RENTAL COMPANIES

The big multinational companies have offices in most major cities, towns and airports. Firms sometimes offer one-way rentals (eg collect a car in Auckland, leave it in Wellington), but there are usually restrictions and fees.

The major companies offer a choice of either unlimited kilometres, or 100km (or so) per day free, plus so many cents per subsequent kilometre. Daily rates in main cities typically start at around $40 per day for a compact, late-model, Japanese car, and from $70 for medium-sized cars (including GST, unlimited kilometres and insurance).

Avis (📞09-526 2847, 0800 655 111; www.avis.co.nz)

Budget (📞09-529 7788, 0800 283 438; www.budget.co.nz)

Europcar (☎0800 800 115; www.europcar.co.nz)

Hertz (☎0800 654 321; www.hertz.co.nz)

Thrifty (☎0800 737 070, 03-359 2721; www.thrifty.co.nz)

LOCAL RENTAL COMPANIES

Local hire firms proliferate. These are almost always cheaper than the big boys – sometimes half the price – but the cheap rates obviously have strings attached: vehicles are often older, depots might be further away from airports/city centres, and with less formality sometimes comes a less-protective legal structure for renters.

Rentals from local firms start at around $30 or $40 per day for the smallest option. It's cheaper if you hire for a week or more, and there are often low-season and weekend discounts.

Affordable, independent operators with national networks include the following:

Ace Rental Cars (☎0800 502 277, 09-303 3112; www.acerentalcars.co.nz)

Apex Rentals (☎03-595 2315, 0800 500 660; www.apexrentals.co.nz)

Ezi Car Rental (☎0800 545 000, 09-254 4397; www.ezicarrental.co.nz)

Go Rentals (☎0800 467 368, 09-974 1598; www.gorentals.co.nz)

Omega Rental Cars (☎09-377 5573, 0800 525 210; www.omegarentalcars.com)

Pegasus Rental Cars (☎0800 803 580; www.rentalcars.co.nz)

Transfercar (☎09-630 7533; www.transfercar.co.nz) Relocation specialists with massive money-saving deals on one-way car hire.

MOTORCYCLE

Born to be wild? New Zealand has great terrain for motorcycle touring, despite the fickle weather in some regions. Most of the country's motorcycle-hire shops are in Auckland and Christchurch, where you can hire anything from a little 50cc moped (aka nifty-fifty) to a throbbing 750cc touring motorcycle and beyond. Recommended operators (who also run guided tours) offer rates beginning around $100 per day:

New Zealand Motorcycle Rentals & Tours (☎09-486 2472; www.nzbike.com)

Te Waipounamu Motorcycle Tours (☎03-372 3537; www.motorcycle-hire.co.nz)

Insurance

Rather than risk paying out wads of cash if you have an accident, you can take out your own comprehensive insurance policy, or (the usual option) pay an additional fee per day to the hire company to reduce your excess. This brings the amount you must pay in the event of an accident down from around $1500 or $2000 to around $200 or $300. Smaller operators offering cheap rates often have a compulsory insurance excess, taken as a credit-card bond, of around $900.

Many insurance agreements won't cover the cost of damage to glass (including the windscreen) or tyres, and insurance coverage is often invalidated on beaches and certain rough (4WD) unsealed roads – read the fine print.

See www.acc.co.nz for info on NZ's Accident Compensation Corporation (ACC) insurance scheme (fault-free personal injury insurance).

Purchase

Planning a long trip? Buying a car then selling it at the end of your travels can be one of the cheapest and best ways to see NZ. Auckland is the easiest place to buy a car, followed by Christchurch: scour the hostel noticeboards. Turners Auctions (www.turners.co.nz) is NZ's biggest car-auction operator, with 31 locations.

LEGALITIES

Make sure your prospective vehicle has a Warrant of Fitness (WoF) and registration valid for a reasonable period: see the New Zealand Transport Agency website (www.nzta.govt.nz) for details.

Buyers should also take out third-party insurance, covering the cost of repairs to another vehicle in an accident that is your fault: try the **Automobile Association** (AA; ☎0800 500 222; www.aa.co.nz/travel). New Zealand's no-fault Accident Compensation Corporation (www.acc.co.nz) scheme covers personal injury, but make sure you have travel insurance, too.

If you're considering buying a car and want someone to check it out for you, various companies inspect cars for around $150; find them at car auctions, or they will come to you. Try Vehicle Inspection New Zealand (☎09-573 3230, ☎0800 468 469; www.vinz.co.nz) or the AA.

Before you buy it's wise to confirm ownership of the vehicle, and find out if there's anything dodgy about it (eg stolen, or outstanding debts). The AA's LemonCheck (☎09-420 3090; www.lemoncheck.co.nz) offers this service.

BUY-BACK DEALS

You can avoid the hassle of buying/selling a vehicle privately by entering into a buy-back arrangement with a dealer. Predictably, dealers often find sneaky ways of knocking down the return-sale price, which may be 50% less than what you paid, so hiring or buying and selling a vehicle yourself (if you have the time) is usually a better bet.

Road Hazards

A higher percentage of international drivers are involved in road accidents in NZ – suggesting something about the challenges its roads pose. Kiwi traffic is usually pretty light, but it's easy to get stuck behind a slow-moving truck or campervan – pack plenty of patience, and know your road rules before you get behind the wheel. There are also lots of slow wiggly roads, one-way bridges and plenty of gravel roads, all of which require a more cautious driving approach. And watch out for sheep!

To check road conditions, call ☎0800 444 449 or see www.nzta.govt.nz/traffic.

Road Rules

➡ Kiwis drive on the left-hand side of the road; cars are right-hand drive. Give way to the right at intersections.

➡ All vehicle occupants must wear a seatbelt or risk a $150 fine. Small children must be belted into approved safety seats.

➡ Always carry your licence when driving.

➡ Drink-driving is a serious offence and remains a significant problem in NZ, despite widespread campaigns and severe penalties. The legal blood-alcohol limit is 0.05% for drivers aged over 20, and zero for those under 20.

➡ At single-lane bridges (of which there are a surprisingly large number), a smaller red arrow pointing in your direction of travel means that you give way.

➡ Speed limits on the open road are generally 100km/h; in built-up areas the limit is usually 50km/h. Speed cameras and radars are used extensively.

➡ Be aware that not all rail crossings have barriers or alarms. Approach slowly and look both ways.

➡ Don't pass other cars when the centre line is yellow.

➡ It's illegal to drive while using a mobile phone.

Hitching

Hitchhiking is never entirely safe, and we don't recommend it. Travellers who hitch should understand that they are taking a small but potentially serious risk. That said, it's not unusual to see hitchhikers along NZ country roads.

For an alternative, check hostel noticeboards for rideshare opportunities.

Local Transport
Bus, Train & Tram

New Zealand's larger cities have extensive bus services but, with a few honourable exceptions, they are mainly daytime, weekday operations; weekend services can be infrequent or nonexistent. Negotiating inner-city Auckland is made easier by Link buses; Hamilton has a free city-centre loop bus; Christchurch has city buses and the historic tramway. Most main cities have late-night buses for boozy Friday and Saturday nights. Don't expect local bus services in more remote areas.

The only cities with decent local train services are Auckland and Wellington, with four and five suburban routes respectively.

Taxi

The main cities have plenty of taxis and even small towns may have a local service. Taxis are licensed, metered, and generally reliable and trustworthy.

Ridesharing

With the global explosion of ride-sharing apps, there are plenty of hungrily circling alternatives to traditional taxis in Kiwi cities. They're still principally a city-based convenience, you can expect surge pricing at busy times, and fares are usually similar across the different providers. Here are a few of the most common:

Uber (www.uber.com) The original, and still easily the biggest. Covers Auckland, Wellington, Christchurch, Hamilton, Tauranga, Dunedin and Queenstown.

Ola (www.ola.co.nz) Trades on more equitable profit-sharing; currently servicing Auckland, Wellington and Christchurch.

Zoomy (www.zoomy.co.nz) Kiwi-owned, serving Auckland, Wellington and Christchurch.

Train

New Zealand train travel is all about the journey, not about getting anywhere in a hurry. **Great Journeys of New Zealand** (☎04-495 0775, 0800 872 467; www.greatjourneysofnz.co.nz) operates the routes listed below. It's best to reserve online or by phone; reservations can be made directly through Great Journeys of New Zealand (operated by KiwiRail), or at most train stations, travel agents and visitor information centres. Cheaper fares appear if you book online within NZ. All services are for day travel (no sleeper services).

Coastal Pacific The scenic Christchurch to Picton route finally reopened to much fanfare in 2019, several years after the track was damaged in the 2016 Kaikōura earthquakes.

Northern Explorer Between Auckland and Wellington: southbound on Mondays, Thursdays and Saturdays; northbound on Tuesdays, Fridays and Sundays.

TranzAlpine Over the Southern Alps between Christchurch and Greymouth – one of the world's most famous train rides.

Train Passes

Great Journeys of New Zealand's **Flexi** and **Flexi Plus** passes allow you to break your journey and change bookings up to 24 hours before departure. Both types of pass require you to book your seats a minimum of 24 hours before you want to travel, and have discounts for early birds and kids.

Behind the Scenes

SEND US YOUR FEEDBACK

We love to hear from travellers – your comments keep us on our toes and help make our books better. Our well-travelled team reads every word on what you loved or loathed about this book. Although we cannot reply individually to your submissions, we always guarantee that your feedback goes straight to the appropriate authors, in time for the next edition. Each person who sends us information is thanked in the next edition – the most useful submissions are rewarded with a selection of digital PDF chapters.

Visit **lonelyplanet.com/contact** to submit your updates and suggestions or to ask for help. Our award-winning website also features inspirational travel stories, news and discussions.

Note: We may edit, reproduce and incorporate your comments in Lonely Planet products such as guidebooks, websites and digital products, so let us know if you don't want your comments reproduced or your name acknowledged. For a copy of our privacy policy visit lonelyplanet.com/privacy.

WRITER THANKS

Brett Atkinson

It's always a privilege to explore my own country. Cheers to Cate and Riwai Grace in Christchurch for tips and friendship, and Mum and Dad provided invaluable support during a busy time. Thanks to my co-authors: Peter, Tasmin and Monique; and to Kat and Angela in Melbourne for answering all my questions.

Andrew Bain

For retaining me in the squad, primary thanks to Tasmin Waby and subsequently to Angela Tinson and Kat Rowan for your calm and considered responses to my queries. A big debt is owed to Nicki Dent and Courtney Harrison for alerting me to a lot of new openings in the centre of the North Island. For the peaceful place in which to set myself up in Rotorua for a while, along with some fine finds, thank you Lisa.

Peter Dragicevich

Many thanks to all the people that make working on the *New Zealand* guidebook such a joy. Special thanks goes to Hamish Blennerhassett for his outstanding hospitality in Wanaka and Queenstown, and to Liam Beattie for making my Glenorchy and Arrowtown stays so pleasurable. Thanks to my fellow authors, too, for tips and advice along the way – particularly Brett Atkinson, my hometown colleague, for being a sensible sounding board on many matters.

THIS BOOK

This 20th edition of Lonely Planet's *New Zealand* guidebook was researched and written by Brett Atkinson, Andrew Bain, Peter Dragicevich, Monique Perrin, Charles Rawlings-Way and Tasmin Waby. The previous edition was curated by Charles Rawlings-Way, and researched and written by Brett Atkinson, Andrew Bain, Peter Dragicevich, Samantha Forge, Anita Isalska and Sofia Levin. This guidebook was produced by the following:

Destination Editor Tasmin Waby

Senior Product Editors Kate Chapman, Kathryn Rowan

Regional Senior Cartographer Diana Von Holdt

Product Editor Kate Kiely

Book Designers Virginia Moreno, Catalina Aragón

Assisting Editors Melanie Dankel, Gemma Graham, Rosie Nicholson, Kristin Odijk, Mani Ramaswamy, Fionnuala Twomey, Anna Tyler, Simon Williamson

Cartographer Mick Garrett

Cover Researcher Brendan Dempsey-Spencer

Thanks to Grace Dobell, Sasha Drew, Martine Power, Angela Tinson

Monique Perrin

Thanks so much to Tasmin Waby for trusting me with this gig. Big kisses to Bob Scott for flying 36 hours to join me on the bike trail and to Matt Drake-Brockman for tramping with me through the snow. Enormous thanks to Peter Dragicevich for the patient pro tips. And a huge bouquet of gratitude to Sonnet Curé, Acey Teasdale and Zyra McAuliffe – without your generosity and flexibility I simply could not have hit the road.

Charles Rawlings-Way

Thanks to the many generous, knowledgeable and quietly self-assured Kiwis I met on the road, who didn't bat an eye when I bombarded them with queries about local beer and bus stops. Huge thanks to Tasmin Waby for signing me up, and the unflappable in-house Lonely Planet crew who have all of the answers to all of the questions. Humongous gratitude to my tireless, witty and professional co-authors, who always bring the humour and the class. Most of all, thanks to Meg, Ione, Remy, Liv and Reuben for sitting tight while I was away.

Tasmin Waby

Thanks to my co-writers, especially Brett and Peter for the mentoring on the road and back at my desk. Cheers, too, to Clare Loudon and Dave Tucker for putting up with me in Auckland. Thanks to my gorgeous family: Hugh, Willa and Maisie, for all the love and support this year. And finally my huge gratitude to ALL the Lonely Planeteers who made this excellent title (you know who you are). Your quest for excellence in publishing, and travel advice, continues to inspire me on every single trip.

ACKNOWLEDGEMENTS

Climate map data adapted from Peel MC, Finlayson BL & McMahon TA (2007) 'Updated World Map of the Köppen-Geiger Climate Classification', *Hydrology and Earth System Sciences*, 11, 1633–44.

Cover photograph: Tasman Glacier, Canterbury, Stefan Damm/4Corners Images ©

Index

Map Pages **000**
Photo Pages **000**

Map Legend

Sights
- Beach
- Bird Sanctuary
- Buddhist
- Castle/Palace
- Christian
- Confucian
- Hindu
- Islamic
- Jain
- Jewish
- Monument
- Museum/Gallery/Historic Building
- Ruin
- Shinto
- Sikh
- Taoist
- Winery/Vineyard
- Zoo/Wildlife Sanctuary
- Other Sight

Activities, Courses & Tours
- Bodysurfing
- Diving
- Canoeing/Kayaking
- Course/Tour
- Sento Hot Baths/Onsen
- Skiing
- Snorkelling
- Surfing
- Swimming/Pool
- Walking
- Windsurfing
- Other Activity

Sleeping
- Sleeping
- Camping
- Hut/Shelter

Eating
- Eating

Drinking & Nightlife
- Drinking & Nightlife
- Cafe

Entertainment
- Entertainment

Shopping
- Shopping

Information
- Bank
- Embassy/Consulate
- Hospital/Medical
- Internet
- Police
- Post Office
- Telephone
- Toilet
- Tourist Information
- Other Information

Geographic
- Beach
- Gate
- Hut/Shelter
- Lighthouse
- Lookout
- Mountain/Volcano
- Oasis
- Park
- Pass
- Picnic Area
- Waterfall

Population
- Capital (National)
- Capital (State/Province)
- City/Large Town
- Town/Village

Transport
- Airport
- Border crossing
- Bus
- Cable car/Funicular
- Cycling
- Ferry
- Metro station
- Monorail
- Parking
- Petrol station
- Subway station
- Taxi
- Train station/Railway
- Tram
- Underground station
- Other Transport

Routes
- Tollway
- Freeway
- Primary
- Secondary
- Tertiary
- Lane
- Unsealed road
- Road under construction
- Plaza/Mall
- Steps
- Tunnel
- Pedestrian overpass
- Walking Tour
- Walking Tour detour
- Path/Walking Trail

Boundaries
- International
- State/Province
- Disputed
- Regional/Suburb
- Marine Park
- Cliff
- Wall

Hydrography
- River, Creek
- Intermittent River
- Canal
- Water
- Dry/Salt/Intermittent Lake
- Reef

Areas
- Airport/Runway
- Beach/Desert
- Cemetery (Christian)
- Cemetery (Other)
- Glacier
- Mudflat
- Park/Forest
- Sight (Building)
- Sportsground
- Swamp/Mangrove

Note: Not all symbols displayed above appear on the maps in this book

OUR STORY

A beat-up old car, a few dollars in the pocket and a sense of adventure. In 1972 that's all Tony and Maureen Wheeler needed for the trip of a lifetime – across Europe and Asia overland to Australia. It took several months, and at the end – broke but inspired – they sat at their kitchen table writing and stapling together their first travel guide, *Across Asia on the Cheap*. Within a week they'd sold 1500 copies. Lonely Planet was born.

Today, Lonely Planet has offices in Tennessee, Dublin, Beijing and Delhi, with a network of over 2000 contributors in every corner of the globe. We share Tony's belief that 'a great guidebook should do three things: inform, educate and amuse'.

OUR WRITERS

Brett Atkinson

Auckland Region, Christchurch & Canterbury, Waikato & the Coromandel Peninsula Brett is based in Auckland, New Zealand, but is frequently on the road for Lonely Planet. He's a full-time travel and food writer specialising in adventure travel, unusual destinations and surprising angles on more well known destinations. Craft beer and street food are Brett's favourite reasons to explore places, and he is featured regularly on the Lonely Planet website, as well as in newspapers, magazines and websites across New Zealand and Australia. Since becoming a Lonely Planet author in 2005, Brett has covered areas as diverse as Vietnam, Sri Lanka, the Czech Republic, New Zealand, Morocco, California and the South Pacific.

Andrew Bain

Taupō & the Ruapehu Region, Rotorua & the Bay of Plenty Andrew is an Australia-based writer, specialising in outdoors and adventure. He's cycled and trekked across every continent bar the icy one, and is the author of *Headwinds*, the story of his 20,000km bike ride around Australia. He's written Lonely Planet titles such as *A Year of Adventures*, *Walking in Australia* and *Cycling Australia*. Find Andrew on Instagram at @bainonbike.

Peter Dragicevich

Queenstown & Wānaka, Marlborough & Nelson, the West Coast After a successful career in niche newspaper and magazine publishing, both in his native New Zealand and in Australia, Peter finally gave in to Kiwi wanderlust, giving up staff jobs to chase his diverse roots around much of Europe. Over the last 15 years he's written over 100 books for Lonely Planet on an oddly disparate collection of countries, all of which he's come to love. He once again calls Auckland, New Zealand his home – although his current nomadic existence means he's often elsewhere.

Monique Perrin

Dunedin & Otago, Fiordland & Southland Monique is a freelance writer, organic gardener, keen bushwalker and wannabe singer-songwriter. She's written on Tibet, the Philippines, Australia, India and travelling with kids for Lonely Planet, and she's worked across the world, including for the United Nations in Sri Lanka and as a journalist in Hong Kong. But her secret love is unearthing the hidden highlights of her awesome home town, Sydney.

OVER PAGE | MORE WRITERS

Published by Lonely Planet Global Limited
CRN 554153
20th edition – April 2021
ISBN 978 1 78701 603 3
© Lonely Planet 2021 Photographs © as indicated 2021
10 9 8 7 6 5 4 3 2 1
Printed in China

Although the authors and Lonely Planet have taken all reasonable care in preparing this book, we make no warranty about the accuracy or completeness of its content and, to the maximum extent permitted, disclaim all liability arising from its use.

Charles Rawlings-Way
Taranaki & Whanganui, the East Coast, Wellington Region Charles is an indefati-
gable travel, walking, food and music writer (all the good things). After dabbling
in the dark arts of architecture, cartography, project management and busking
for some years, Charles hit the road for Lonely Planet in 2005 and hasn't stopped
travelling since. He has penned more than 40 titles for Lonely Planet, including
guides to Singapore, Toronto, Canada, Tonga, New Zealand, the South Pacific,
every state in Australia (including his native terrain of Tasmania and current homeland of South
Australia), as well as countless articles. He's also the author of a best-selling rock biography on
Glasgow band Del Amitri, *These Are Such Perfect Days*, which was published in 2018. Follow
Charles at @crawlingsway.

Tasmin Waby
Bay of Islands & Northland London-born to Kiwi parents, Tasmin was raised in
Australia, for which she is incredibly grateful. As well as travelling, learning and
writing, Tasmin is madly in love with cartography, wild swimming and starry
skies. When not on assignment she lives on a narrowboat in England, raising two
hilarious school-aged children and a fat Russian Blue cat called Millie. Tasmin also
wrote the Plan Your Trip, Understand and Survival Guide chapters of this book.